The Books of Nahum, Habakkuk, and Zephaniah

THE NEW INTERNATIONAL COMMENTARY
ON THE
OLD TESTAMENT

General Editors

E. J. YOUNG
(1965–1968)

R. K. HARRISON
(1968–1993)

ROBERT L. HUBBARD JR.
(1994–   )

The Books of
NAHUM, HABAKKUK, and ZEPHANIAH

Thomas Renz

William B. Eerdmans Publishing Company

Grand Rapids, Michigan

Wm. B. Eerdmans Publishing Co.
4035 Park East Court SE, Grand Rapids, Michigan 49546
www.eerdmans.com

27 26 25 24 23 22 21   1 2 3 4 5 6 7

ISBN 978-0-8028-2626-8

Library of Congress Cataloging-in-Publication Data

Names: Renz, Thomas, 1969– author.
Title: The books of Nahum, Habakkuk, and Zephaniah / Thomas Renz.
Description: Grand Rapids, Michigan : William B. Eerdmans Publishing
    Company, [2021] | Series: The new international commentary on the Old
    Testament | Includes bibliographical references and indexes. | Summary:
    "A commentary for scholars and pastors on the biblical books of Nahum,
    Habakkuk, and Zephaniah, with an emphasis on reading them as authorita-
    tive Christian Scripture"—Provided by publisher.
Identifiers: LCCN 2020042342 | ISBN 9780802826268 (hardcover)
Subjects: LCSH: Bible. Nahum—Commentaries. | Bible. Habakkuk—
    Commentaries. | Bible. Zephaniah—Commentaries.
Classification: LCC BS1625.53 .R46 2021 | DDC 224/.9077—dc23
LC record available at https://lccn.loc.gov/2020042342

Dedicated to the humiliated and the humble
and those who associate with them.

Good is YHWH—as a stronghold—in the day of distress.

Contents

List of Excursuses   xi

General Editor's Preface   xiii

Author's Preface   xv

Abbreviations   xvii

Select Bibliography   xxv

INTRODUCTION TO NAHUM, HABAKKUK, AND ZEPHANIAH

  I. THE NATURE OF PROPHETIC BOOKS   1

  II. THE MINOR PROPHETS IN THE CANON   3

  III. THE UNITY OF THE BOOK OF THE TWELVE   4

  IV. NAHUM, HABAKKUK, AND ZEPHANIAH IN THE BOOK
      OF THE TWELVE   13

  V. NAHUM, HABAKKUK, AND ZEPHANIAH AND
      THEIR CONSTITUENT UNITS   16

  VI. AN OUTLINE OF THE LATE NEO-ASSYRIAN AND
      EARLY NEO-BABYLONIAN PERIOD   18

THE BOOK OF NAHUM

INTRODUCTION   23

  I. THE PROFILE OF THE BOOK   23

    A. The Superscription   23

    B. Macrostructure   27

    C. Language and Style   36

    D. Textual Witnesses   38

II. THE DEVELOPMENT OF THE BOOK 40

   A. General Comments on the Origin of the Book 40

   B. The Individual Units within the Book 42

   C. The Redaction of the Book of the Twelve 46

III. THE RHETORICAL FUNCTION OF THE BOOK 47

   A. The Message of Nahum's Poetry at the Time of Its Origin 47

   B. Nahum's Place in the Book of the Twelve 49

   C. Nahum's Place in the Biblical Canon 53

   D. Nahum in the History of Interpretation 54

   E. Nahum's Place in the Church Today 57

TEXT AND COMMENTARY 59

   I. THE SUPERSCRIPTION TO THE BOOK (1:1) 59

   II. CONTEMPLATING YHWH, THE AVENGING GOD (1:2–10) 63

   III. ACCUSATION AGAINST THE CITY (1:11) 89

   IV. YHWH'S VERDICT (1:12–14) 91

   V. ANNOUNCEMENT OF DELIVERANCE (1:15 [2:1]) 102

   VI. IMAGES OF THE FALL OF NINEVEH (2:1–10[2–11]) 111

   VII. RIDICULE OF THE KING OF NINEVEH (2:11–12[12–13]) 138

   VIII. PROPHECY OF COMPLETE DESTRUCTION (2:13[14]) 148

   IX. DOOM AND HUMILIATION FOR THE BLOODFLOW CITY (3:1–7) 152

   X. DENUNCIATION OF THE CITY'S COMPLACENCY (3:8–12) 163

   XI. EXPOSITION OF THE USELESSNESS OF THE CITY'S DEFENSES (3:13–17) 174

   XII. EXPOSITION OF THE HELPLESSNESS OF THE CITY'S RULER (3:18–19) 188

THE BOOK OF HABAKKUK

INTRODUCTION 195

   I. THE PROFILE OF THE BOOK 195

   A. The Superscriptions 195

   B. Macrostructure 196

C. Language and Style 201

D. Redaction History 203

E. Textual Witnesses 206

II. THE HISTORICAL SETTING OF THE BOOK 207

III. THE RHETORICAL FUNCTION OF THE BOOK 211

   A. Habakkuk's Message in Its Original Context 211

   B. Habakkuk's Place in the Book of the Twelve 215

   C. Habakkuk's Place in the Biblical Canon 216

   D. Habakkuk in the History of Interpretation 216

   E. Habakkuk's Place in the Church Today 218

TEXT AND COMMENTARY 221

   I. THE SUPERSCRIPTION (1:1) 221

   II. THE FIRST PART OF HABAKKUK'S COMPLAINT (1:2–4) 223

   III. THE CITATION OF AN EARLIER ORACLE (1:5–11) 230

   IV. THE FINAL PART OF THE COMPLAINT (1:12–17) 253

   V. THE PROPHET'S RESOLVE TO GET AN ANSWER (2:1) 266

   VI. THE INSTRUCTION TO THE PROPHET (2:2–3) 272

   VII. THE REVELATION (2:4–5) 284

VIII. THE AGREEMENT OF THE OPPRESSED NATIONS, FIRST SAYING (2:6–8) 299

   IX. THE SECOND SAYING (2:9–11) 308

   X. THE THIRD SAYING (2:12–14) 313

   XI. THE FOURTH SAYING (2:15–17) 318

   XII. THE FIFTH SAYING (2:18–20) 325

   XIII. THE HEADING FOR HABAKKUK'S PRAYER (3:1) 331

   XIV. THE OPENING PART OF THE PRAYER (3:2) 343

   XV. A REFLECTION ON YHWH'S APPEARANCE (3:3–7) 351

   XVI. EXPRESSION OF MARVEL AT YHWH'S ATTACK ON HIS ENEMIES (3:8–15) 371

XVII. EXPRESSION OF CONFIDENCE IN THE MIDST OF DISTRESS (3:16–19A) 396

XVIII. THE POSTSCRIPT (3:19B) 413

CONTENTS

THE BOOK OF ZEPHANIAH

INTRODUCTION   423

   I. THE PROFILE OF THE BOOK   423

      A. The Superscription   423

      B. Macrostructure   424

   II. THE HISTORICAL SETTING OF THE BOOK   432

   III. THE RHETORICAL FUNCTION OF THE BOOK   444

      A. Zephaniah's Message in Its Original Context   444

      B. Zephaniah's Place in the Biblical Canon   444

      C. Zephaniah in the History of Interpretation   447

      D. Zephaniah's Place in the Church Today   449

TEXT AND COMMENTARY   451

   I. SUPERSCRIPTION (1:1)   451

   II. DECLARATION OF SWEEPING JUDGMENT (1:2–6)   460

   III. ANNOUNCEMENT OF THE DAY OF YHWH (1:7–18)   480

   IV. CALL TO SUBMIT TO GOD'S JUDGMENT (2:1–4)   517

   V. ANNOUNCEMENTS OF THE FATE OF NATIONS (2:5–15)   537

   VI. JERUSALEM WILL SHARE THE FATE OF NATIONS (3:1–5)   579

   VII. REAFFIRMATION OF COMPREHENSIVE JUDGMENT (3:6–8)   593

   VIII. ANNOUNCEMENT OF A FUTURE BEYOND
      JUDGMENT (3:9–13)   603

   IX. CELEBRATION OF LIFE BEYOND JUDGMENT (3:14–17)   620

   X. PROMISE OF SALVATION (3:18–20)   634

      Index of Authors   647

      Index of Subjects   658

      Index of Scripture and Other Ancient Sources   664

      Index of Hebrew Words   702

List of Excursuses

ANCIENT AND MEDIEVAL MANUSCRIPTS   5

TRADITIONAL PARAGRAPH DIVISIONS   35

THE PLACE OF THE PHRASE "AND WITH/IN A SWEEPING FLOOD"   80

THE RELATIONSHIP BETWEEN NAHUM 1:15 (2:1) AND ISAIAH 52:7   106

THE DESTRUCTION OF NINEVEH   129

DIFFERENT HEBREW TERMS FOR LIONS   141

LION IMAGERY IN ASSYRIA   146

ASSYRIAN CAMPAIGNS AGAINST EGYPT   169

TRADITIONAL PARAGRAPH DIVISIONS   200

"LOOK, YOU SCOFFERS" OR "LOOK AT THE NATIONS"?   239

SIGNIFICANT WORDS IN ZEPHANIAH   431

FINDING THE BOOK OF THE LAW   435

General Editor's Preface

Long ago St. Paul wrote: "I planted, Apollos watered, but God gave the growth" (1 Cor. 3:6 NRSV). He was right: ministry indeed requires a team effort—the collective labors of many skilled hands and minds. Someone digs up the dirt and drops in seed, while others water the ground to nourish seedlings to growth. The same team effort over time has brought this commentary series to its position of prominence today. Professor E. J. Young "planted" it more than fifty years ago, enlisting its first contributors and himself writing its first published volumes. Professor R. K. Harrison "watered" it, signing on other scholars and wisely editing everyone's finished products. As General Editor, I now tend their planting, and, true to Paul's words, through five decades God has indeed graciously "[given] the growth."

Today the New International Commentary on the Old Testament enjoys a wide readership of scholars, priests, pastors, rabbis, and other serious Bible students. Thousands of readers across the religious spectrum and in countless countries consult its volumes in their ongoing preaching, teaching, and research. They warmly welcome the publication of each new volume and eagerly await its eventual transformation from an emerging "series" into a complete commentary "set." But as humanity experiences a new century of history, an era commonly called "postmodern," what kind of commentary series is NICOT? What distinguishes it from other similarly well-established series?

Its volumes aim to publish biblical scholarship of the highest quality. Each contributor writes as an expert, both in the biblical text itself and in the relevant scholarly literature, and each commentary conveys the results of wide reading and careful, mature reflection. Ultimately, its spirit is eclectic, each contributor gleaning interpretive insights from any useful source, whatever its religious or philosophical viewpoint, and integrating them into his or her interpretation of a biblical book. The series draws on recent methodological innovations in biblical scholarship: for example, canon criticism, the so-called new literary criticism, reader-response theories, and sensitivity to gender-based and ethnic readings. NICOT volumes also aim to be irenic in tone, summarizing and critiquing influential views with fairness while defending their own. Its list of contributors includes male and female scholars from a number of Christian faith-groups. The diversity of contributors and their freedom to draw on all relevant methodologies give the entire series an exciting and enriching variety.

What truly distinguishes this series, however, is that it speaks from within that interpretive tradition known as evangelicalism. Evangelicalism is an informal movement within Protestantism that cuts across traditional denominational lines. Its heart and soul is the conviction that the Bible is God's inspired Word, written by gifted human writers, through which God calls humanity to enjoy a loving personal relationship with its Creator and Savior. True to that tradition, NICOT volumes do not treat the Old Testament as just an ancient literary artifact on a par with the *Iliad* or Gilgamesh. They are not literary autopsies of ancient parchment cadavers but rigorous, reverent wrestlings with wonderfully human writings through which the living God speaks his powerful Word. NICOT delicately balances "criticism" (i.e., the use of standard critical methodologies) with humble respect, admiration, and even affection for the biblical text. As an evangelical commentary, it pays particular attention to the text's literary features, theological themes, and implications for the life of faith today.

Ultimately, NICOT aims to serve women and men of faith who desire to hear God's voice afresh through the Old Testament. With gratitude to God for two marvelous gifts—the Scriptures themselves and keen-minded scholars to explain their message—I welcome readers of all kinds to savor the good fruit of this series.

ROBERT L. HUBBARD JR.

Author's Preface

I began working on this commentary before either of my children were born. By the time it sees the light of day, both children will have left their parental home. Both tasks—bringing up children and writing on Nahum, Habakkuk, and Zephaniah—have been a joy, and both have taught me about my shortcomings as well as my strengths. Both have given me more reason to praise God for his faithfulness and goodness.

Just over half this commentary was written in an academic context, preparing men and women for various forms of pastoral ministry at Oak Hill College in North London. Oak Hill also gave me a research leave in 2002, during which I wrote *Colometry and Masoretic Accentuation*, focusing on Nahum, Habakkuk, and Zephaniah. I am grateful for colleagues who took on extra responsibilities back then, especially James Robson. The commentary was completed during my time as incumbent of Monken Hadley Church in the Church of England Diocese of London. I am deeply grateful for the support of my colleague Adele Burgess and of the diocese, which enabled me to take another research leave in 2018, during which I took a major step toward the completion of the commentary. Many friends have been a source of encouragement. They are too numerous to mention by name. I single out David Field and Steffen Jenkins, who, with their families, offered hospitality that gave me uninterrupted writing time, as did my parents-in-law and my father. The librarians Wendy Bell, Evelyn Cornell, and Donald Mitchell were ever helpful. Gabriele Renz and Susanna Baldwin helped with formatting and indexing. I am indebted also to the developers of BibleWorks, a piece of software with which I have worked daily. Finally, I am grateful to Bob Hubbard for the invitation to contribute this volume to the NICOT series; for his persistence, encouragement, and trust even when the project took longer than anticipated; and for his comments on the manuscript.

The requirements of pastors and academics, while overlapping, are different. I have by and large confined myself to matters that, in my judgment, illuminate our understanding of the received Hebrew text. While this involves some discussion of textual criticism and redaction history, the commentary does not include in-depth consideration of text-critical matters or detailed discussion of the various redaction-critical proposals on offer. Nevertheless, the commentary became more technical than anticipated. To help pastors use this commentary without being overwhelmed by the detail, much of the technical discussion has been placed in the translation notes, the footnotes, and the sections immediately following the translation notes, which are titled "Composition."

Each unit of the commentary proper offers, first of all, a translation of the biblical text in its masoretic form, which is very rarely emended. This is not to claim that the Masoretic Text (MT) is the original text, nor is it to disparage attempts to ascertain a "better" text. But in my view, the MT has a good claim to being close to the earliest text form, and my expertise would not lend itself to improving on it consistently. Because emendations tend to smooth the text, making it more straightforward to read, readers whose primary interest is in earlier versions of the text than the MT will likely find a surplus of meaning in my reading of the MT. They are, of course, free to ignore this surplus of meaning. The translation notes indicate alternative renderings and text forms.

Each translation is followed by a discussion (titled "Composition") of the passage's structure and design, not least in its relationship to what precedes or follows. My form-critical analysis is conducted along the lines of the Old Testament Form Criticism Project, whose results are most prominently displayed in the Forms of the Old Testament Literature series, which regularly proved helpful to me—not least Floyd's work on Nahum, Habakkuk, and Zephaniah. I have found little reason to distinguish between redactional layers, mostly because many of the inconsistencies other scholars perceive seem to me nothing of the kind. The argument for coherence is made largely in the "Composition" sections. The verse-by-verse commentary that follows this section focuses on the text as a piece of communication at the time of its composition and gives relevant historical background as well as discussion of the meaning of particular phrases. The final section (titled "Reflection") should be of particular help to those who want to listen to the text within a wider canonical context as a word in which the Creator of the universe reveals something about himself and his purposes.[1]

My prayer is that this commentary will help many to receive the texts of Nahum, Habakkuk, and Zephaniah as truthful and authoritative, carrying divine authority and bringing good news related to *the* good news: the gospel about our Lord and Savior, Jesus Christ.

---

1. My use of the masc. pronoun with reference to God reflects the conviction that we are utterly dependent on the Scriptures for true knowledge of our Creator. The Scriptures only use the masc. pronoun with reference to God, even if they do not thereby imply that God is male.

Abbreviations

ÄAT	Ägypten und Altes Testament
AB	Anchor Bible
ABD	*Anchor Bible Dictionary*. Edited by David Noel Freedman. 6 vols. New York: Doubleday, 1992
ACCS NT	Ancient Christian Commentary on Scripture, New Testament
ACCS OT	Ancient Christian Commentary on Scripture, Old Testament
AfO	*Archiv für Orientforschung*
AJSL	*American Journal of Semitic Languages and Literatures*
ANEP	*The Ancient Near East in Pictures Relating to the Old Testament*. Edited by James B. Pritchard. 2nd ed. Princeton: Princeton University Press, 1969
ANET	*Ancient Near Eastern Texts Relating to the Old Testament*. Edited by James B. Pritchard. 3rd ed. Princeton: Princeton University Press, 1969
AnOr	Analecta Orientalia
AOAT	Alter Orient und Altes Testament
AP	*Aramaic Papyri of the Fifth Century B.C.* Edited with translation and notes by Arthur E. Cowley. Oxford: Clarendon, 1923
ARAB	*Ancient Records of Assyria and Babylonia*. Edited by Daniel David Luckenbill. 2 vols. Chicago: University of Chicago Press, 1926–1927. Repr., New York: Greenwood, 1968
ArBib 14	The Aramaic Bible 14. Kevin J. Cathcart and Robert P. Gordon, eds. *The Targum of the Minor Prophets: Translated, with a Critical Introduction, Apparatus, and Notes*. Edinburgh: T&T Clark, 1989
ATD	Das Alte Testament Deutsch
ATSAT	Arbeiten zu Text und Sprache im Alten Testament
BA 23.4–9	*La Bible d'Alexandrie*. Vol. 23: *Les Douze Prophètes*. Parts 4–9: *Joël, Abdiou, Jonas, Naoum, Ambakoum, Sophonie*. Edited by Marguerite Harl, Cécile Dogniez, Laurence Brottier, Michel Casevitz, and Pierre Sandevoir. Paris: Cerf, 1999

BASOR	*Bulletin of the American Schools of Oriental Research*
BBB	Bonner Biblische Beiträge
BBR	*Bulletin for Biblical Research*
BDB	Francis Brown, S. R. Driver, and Charles A. Briggs. *A Hebrew and English Lexicon of the Old Testament*. Oxford: Clarendon, 1907
BET	Beiträge zur biblischen Exegese und Theologie
BETL	Bibliotheca Ephemeridum Theologicarum Lovaniensium
BHK	*Biblia Hebraica*. Edited by Rudolph Kittel. Leipzig: Hinrichs, 1905–1906
BHQ	*Biblia Hebraica Quinta*. Edited by Adrian Schenker et al. Stuttgart: Deutsche Bibelgesellschaft, 2004–
BHRG	*A Biblical Hebrew Reference Grammar*. Christo H. J. Van der Merwe, Jackie A. Naudé, and Jan H. Kroeze. Biblical Languages: Hebrew 3. Sheffield: Sheffield Academic, 1999
BHS	*Biblia Hebraica Stuttgartensia*. Edited by Karl Elliger and Wilhelm Rudolph. Stuttgart: Deutsche Bibelgesellschaft, 1983
Bib	*Biblica*
BibInt	Biblical Interpretation Series
BibOr	Biblica et Orientalia
BibSem	The Biblical Seminar
BKAT	Biblischer Kommentar Altes Testament
BLS	Bible and Literature Series
BM	British Museum
BN	*Biblische Notizen*
BSac	*Bibliotheca Sacra*
BT	*The Bible Translator*
BWANT	Beiträge zur Wissenschaft vom Alten und Neuen Testament
BWM	Bibelwissenschaftliche Monographien
BZAW	Beihefte zur Zeitschrift für die alttestamentliche Wissenschaft
CAD	*The Assyrian Dictionary of the Oriental Institute of the University of Chicago*. Edited by Martha T. Roth et al. Chicago: The Oriental Institute of the University of Chicago, 1956–2006
CANE	*Civilizations of the Ancient Near East*. Edited by Jack M. Sasson. 4 vols. New York, 1995. Repr. in 2 vols. Peabody, MA: Hendrickson, 2006
CBQ	*Catholic Biblical Quarterly*
CBQMS	Catholic Biblical Quarterly Monograph Series
CHANE	Culture and History of the Ancient Near East
CHP	*Classical Hebrew Poetry: A Guide to Its Techniques*. Wilfred G. E. Watson. 2nd ed. Sheffield: Sheffield Academic, 1986
CJB	Complete Jewish Bible
ConBOT	Coniectanea Biblica: Old Testament Series

COS	*The Context of Scripture*. 3 vols. Ed. William W. Hallo. Leiden: Brill, 1997–2002
CTAT	*Critique textuelle de l'Ancien Testament*. Edited by Dominique Barthélemy et al. 4 vols. Fribourg: Academic Press; Göttingen: Vandenhoeck & Ruprecht, 1982–2005
CurBR	*Currents in Biblical Research*
CurBS	*Currents in Research: Biblical Studies*
DCH	*Dictionary of Classical Hebrew*. Edited by David J. A. Clines. 9 vols. Sheffield: Sheffield Phoenix, 1993–2014
DDD	*Dictionary of Deities and Demons in the Bible*. Edited by Karel van der Toorn, Bob Becking, and Pieter W. van der Horst. 2nd ed. Leiden: Brill; Grand Rapids: Eerdmans, 1999
DJD	Discoveries in the Judean Desert
DOTP	*Dictionary of the Old Testament Prophets*. Edited by Mark J. Boda and J. Gordon McConville. Downers Grove: IVP Academic; Nottingham: Inter-Varsity Press, 2012
DSD	*Dead Sea Discoveries*
ESV	English Standard Version
EvQ	*Evangelical Quarterly*
FAT	Forschungen zum Alten Testament
FOTL	Forms of the Old Testament Literature
FRLANT	Forschungen zur Religion und Literatur des Alten und Neuen Testaments
Ges[18]	Wilhelm Gesenius, *Hebräisches und Aramäisches Handwörterbuch über das Alte Testament*. 18th ed. Edited by Donner, Herbert et al. Berlin and Heidelberg: Springer, 2013
GKC	*Gesenius' Hebrew Grammar*. Edited by Emil Kautzsch. Translated by Arther E. Cowley. 2nd ed. Oxford: Clarendon, 1910
HALOT	*The Hebrew and Aramaic Lexicon of the Old Testament*. Ludwig Koehler, Walter Baumgartner, and Johann Jakob Stamm. Translated and edited under the supervision of Mervyn E. J. Richardson. 5 vols. Leiden: Brill, 1994–1999
HANE	History of the Ancient Near East
HBAI	*Hebrew Bible and Ancient Israel*
HBM	Hebrew Bible Monographs
HBS	Herders Biblische Studien
HBT	*Horizons in Biblical Theology*
HCOT	Historical Commentary on the Old Testament
HCSB	Holman Christian Standard Bible
HGHS	*Historische Grammatik der hebräischen Sprache des Alten Testaments*. Hans Bauer and Pontus Leander. Vol. 1: *Einleitung—*

	Schriftlehre—Laut- und Formenlehre. Halle: Max Niemeyer, 1922. Repr., Hildesheim: Olms Verlag, 1991
HS	*Hebrew Studies*
HSM	Harvard Semitic Monographs
HThKAT	Herders Theologischer Kommentar zum Alten Testament
HTR	*Harvard Theological Review*
HUC	Hebrew Union College
IBHS	*An Introduction to Biblical Hebrew Syntax*. Bruce K. Waltke and Michael O'Connor. Winona Lake, IN: Eisenbrauns, 1990
ICC	International Critical Commentary
IDBSup	*The Interpreter's Dictionary of the Bible, Supplementary Volume*. Edited by Keith Crim. Nashville: Abingdon, 1976
IECOT	International Exegetical Commentary on the Old Testament
Int	*Interpretation*
Iraq	*Iraq: Journal of the British Institute for the Study of Iraq*
ISBE	*International Standard Bible Encyclopedia*. Edited by Geoffrey W. Bromiley. 4 vols. Grand Rapids: Eerdmans, 1979–1988
ITC	International Theological Commentary
JANES	*Journal of the Ancient Near Eastern Society of Columbia University*
JAOS	*Journal of the American Oriental Society*
JBL	*Journal of Biblical Literature*
JBQ	*Jewish Bible Quarterly*
JESOT	*Journal for the Evangelical Study of the Old Testament*
JETS	*Journal of the Evangelical Theological Society*
JHebS	*Journal of Hebrew Scriptures*
JM	Paul Joüon. *A Grammer of Biblical Hebrew.* Translated and revised by Takamitsu Muraoka. 2 vols. Rome: Pontifical Biblical Institute, 1991
JNES	*Journal of Near Eastern Studies*
JNSL	*Journal of Northwest Semitic Languages*
JOTT	*Journal of Translation and Textlinguistics*
JPOS	*Journal of the Palestine Oriental Society*
JPS	Jewish Publication Society
JSCS	*Journal of Septuagint and Cognate Studies*
JSem	*Journal of Semitics*
JSNTSup	Journal for the Study of the New Testament Supplement Series
JSOT	*Journal for the Study of the Old Testament*
JSOTSup	Journal for the Study of the Old Testament Supplement Series
JSPSup	Journal for the Study of the Pseudepigrapha Supplement Series
JSS	*Journal of Semitic Studies*
JTS	*Journal of Theological Studies*
KAT	Kommentar zum Alten Testament

KBW	Katholisches Bibelwerk
KJV	King James Version
KTU	*Die keilalphabetischen Texte aus Ugarit.* Edited by Manfried Dietrich, Oswald Loretz, and Joaquín Sanmartín. 2nd ed. Münster: Ugarit-Verlag, 1995
KUSATU	*Kleine Untersuchungen zur Sprache des Alten Testaments und seiner Umwelt*
KUSATU	Kleine Untersuchungen zur Sprache des Alten Testaments und seiner Umwelt [monograph series]
LEH	Johan Lust, Erik Eynikel, and Katrin Hauspie, eds. *Greek-English Lexicon of the Septuagint.* Rev. ed. Stuttgart: Deutsche Bibelgesellschaft, 2003
LHBOTS	Library of Hebrew Bible / Old Testament Studies
LNTS	Library of New Testament Studies
LSJ	Henry George Liddell, Robert Scott, and Henry Stuart Jones. *A Greek-English Lexicon.* 9th ed. with revised supplement. Oxford: Clarendon, 1996
LW	*Luther's Works.* Edited by Jaroslav Pelikan and Helmut T. Lehmann. 55 vols. Minneapolis: Fortress; St. Louis: Concordia, 1957–1986
LXX	Septuagint
MT	Masoretic Text
MurXII	The Twelve Minor Prophets scroll found in the Wadi Murabbaʻat
NAB	New American Bible
NAC	New American Commentary
NASB	New American Standard Bible
NEB	New English Bible
NET	New English Translation
NETS	*A New English Translation of the Septuagint.* Edited by Albert Pietersma and Benjamin G. Wright. New York: Oxford University Press, 2007
NIBCOT	New International Biblical Commentary on the Old Testament
NICNT	New International Commentary on the New Testament
NICOT	New International Commentary on the Old Testament
NIDOTTE	*New International Dictionary of Old Testament Theology and Exegesis.* Edited by Willem A.VanGemeren. 5 vols. Grand Rapids: Zondervan, 1997
NIV	New International Version
NJB	New Jerusalem Bible
NJPS	New Jewish Publication Society Translation
NKJV	New King James Version
NLT	New Living Translation

NovTSup	Supplements to Novum Testamentum
NRSV	New Revised Standard Version
NSKAT	Neuer Stuttgarter Kommentar, Altes Testament
OBO	Orbis Biblicus et Orientalis
OLA	Orientalia Lovaniensia Analecta
ORA	Orientalische Religionen in der Antike / Oriental Religions in Antiquity
OTE	*Old Testament Essays*
OTG	Old Testament Guides
OTL	Old Testament Library
OTS	*Oudtestamentische Studiën*
PEQ	*Palestine Exploration Quarterly*
Pericope	Pericope: Scripture as Written and Read in Antiquity
PNTC	Pillar New Testament Commentary
RA	*Revue d'assyriologie et d'archéologie orientale*
REB	Revised English Bible
RevQ	*Revue de Qumran*
RPP	*Religion Past and Present: Encyclopedia of Theology and Religion.* Edited by Hans Dieter Betz et al. 14 vols. Leiden: Brill, 2007–2013
RST	Regensburger Studien zur Theologie
RSV	Revised Standard Version
SAAS	State Archives of Assyria Studies
SATB	Soprano, Alto, Tenor, and Bass voice types
SBAB	Stuttgarter Biblische Aufsatzbände
SBLAIL	Society of Biblical Literature Ancient Israel and Its Literature
SBLANEM	Society of Biblical Literature Ancient Near Eastern Monographs
SBLDS	Society of Biblical Literature Dissertation Series
SBLMS	Society of Biblical Literature Monograph Series
SBLSCS	Society of Biblical Literature Septuagint and Cognate Studies
SBLSP	Society of Biblical Literature Seminar Papers
SBL SymS	Society of Biblical Literature Symposium Series
SBS	Stuttgarter Bibelstudien
SBT	Studies in Biblical Theology
SHBC	Smyth & Helwys Bible Commentary
SHCANE	Studies in the History and Culture of the Ancient Near East
SJOT	*Scandinavian Journal of the Old Testament*
SSN	Studia Semitica Neerlandica
StBibLit	Studies in Biblical Literature (Lang)
SubBib	Subsidia Biblica
Syr.	Syriac, Peshitta
TBN	Themes in Biblical Narrative

TDOT	*Theological Dictionary of the Old Testament.* Edited by G. Johannes Botterweck and Helmer Ringgren. Translated by John T. Willis et al. 16 vols. Grand Rapids: Eerdmans, 1974–2006
Textus	*Textus: A Journal on Textual Criticism of the Hebrew Bible*
Tg.	Targum
TNK	JPS Tanakh (1985)
TNTC	Tyndale New Testament Commentary
TOTC	Tyndale Old Testament Commentary
TRu	*Theologische Rundschau*
TUAT	*Texte aus der Umwelt des Alten Testaments.* Edited by Otto Kaiser et al. Gütersloh: Mohn, 1984–
TynBul	*Tyndale Bulletin*
UF	*Ugarit-Forschungen*
UUA	Uppsala Universitetsårskrift
VT	*Vetus Testamentum*
VTSup	Supplements to *Vetus Testamentum*
Vulg.	Vulgate
WAW	Writings from the Ancient World
WBC	Word Biblical Commentary
WMANT	Wissenschaftliche Monographien zum Alten und Neuen Testament
WStB	Wuppertaler Studienbibel
WTJ	*Westminster Theological Journal*
WUNT	Wissenschaftliche Untersuchungen zum Neuen Testament
ZAW	*Zeitschrift für die alttestamentliche Wissenschaft*
ZBK AT	Zürcher Bibelkommentare, Altes Testament
ZDPV	*Zeitschrift des deutschen Palästina-Vereins*
ZNW	*Zeitschrift für die neutestamentliche Wissenschaft*

Select Bibliography

Achtemeier, Elizabeth. *Nahum–Malachi*. Atlanta: John Knox, 1986.

Ahlström, Gösta W. *The History of Ancient Palestine from the Palaeolithic Period to Alexander's Conquest*. JSOTSup 146. Sheffield: Sheffield Academic, 1993.

Albertz, Rainer, James D. Nogalski, and Jakob Wöhrle. *Perspectives on the Formation of the Book of the Twelve: Methodological Foundations—Redactional Processes—Historical Insights*. BZAW 433. Berlin: de Gruyter, 2012.

Allis, Oswald T. "Nahum, Nineveh, Elkosh." *EvQ* 27 (1955): 67–80.

Alonso Schökel, Luis. *A Manual of Hebrew Poetics*. SubBib 11. Rome: Pontifical Biblical Institute, 1988.

Andersen, Francis I. *Habakkuk: A New Translation with Introduction and Commentary*. AB 25. New York: Doubleday, 2001.

Armerding, Carl E. "Obadiah, Nahum, Habakkuk." Pages 333–534 in *Daniel and the Minor Prophets*. Vol. 7 of *The Expositor's Bible Commentary*. Edited by Frank E. Gaebelein. Grand Rapids: Zondervan, 1985.

Avishur, Yitzhak. *Studies in Hebrew and Ugaritic Psalms*. Jerusalem: Magnes Press, 1994.

Ball, Edward. " 'When the Towers Fall': Interpreting Nahum as Christian Scripture." Pages 211–30 in *In Search of True Wisdom: Essays in Old Testament Interpretation in Honour of Ronald E. Clements*. Edited by Edward Ball. JSOTSup 300. Sheffield: Sheffield Academic, 1999.

Ball, Ivan J. "The Rhetorical Shape of Zephaniah." Pages 155–65 in *Perspectives on Language and Text: Essays and Poems in Honor of Francis I. Andersen on His Sixtieth Birthday*. Edited by Edgar Conrad and Edward Newing. Winona Lake, IN: Eisenbrauns, 1987.

———. *A Rhetorical Study of Zephaniah*. Berkeley: BIBAL, 1988.

Banister, Jamie Aislinn. "Theophanies in the Minor Prophets: A Cross-Analysis of Theophonic Texts in Micah, Habakkuk, and Zechariah." PhD diss., Catholic University of America, 2013.

Barré, Michael L. "Newly Discovered Literary Devices in the Prayer of Habakkuk." *CBQ* 75 (2013): 446–62.

Barthélemy, Dominique. *Ézéchiel, Daniel et les 12 Prophètes.* Vol. 3 of *Critique textuelle de l'Ancien Testament.* OBO 50/3. Fribourg: Presses Universitaires; Göttingen: Vandenhoeck & Ruprecht, 1992.

Bauer, Hans, and Pontus Leander. *Einleitung—Schriftlehre—Laut- und Formenlehre.* Vol. 1 of *Historische Grammatik der hebräischen Sprache des Alten Testaments.* Halle: Max Niemeyer, 1922. Repr., Hildesheim: Olms Verlag, 1991. = *HGHS*.

Baumann, Gerlinde. "Connected by Marriage, Adultery, and Violence: The Prophetic Marriage Metaphor in the Book of the Twelve and in the Major Prophets." Pages 552–69 in *Society of Biblical Literature 1999 Seminar Papers.* SBLSP 38. Atlanta: Society of Biblical Literature, 1999.

———. "Das Buch Nahum: Der gerechte Gott als sexueller Gewalttäter." Pages 347–53 in *Kompendium Feministische Bibelauslegung.* Edited by Louise Schottroff and Michael T. Wacker. Gütersloh: Kaiser, 1998.

———. *Gottes Gewalt im Wandel: Traditionsgeschichtliche und intertextuelle Studien zu Nahum 1,2–8.* WMANT 108. Neukirchen-Vluyn: Neukirchener Verlag, 2005.

Beck, Martin. "Das Dodekapropheton als Anthologie." *ZAW* 118 (2006): 558–81.

Becking, Bob. "Divine Wrath and the Conceptual Coherence of the Book of Nahum." *SJOT* 9 (1995): 277–96.

Beentjes, Pancratius C. *The Book of Ben Sira in Hebrew: A Text Edition of All Extant Hebrew Manuscripts and a Synopsis of All Parallel Hebrew Ben Sira Texts.* VTSup 68. Leiden: Brill, 1997.

Ben Zvi, Ehud. *A Historical-Critical Study of the Book of Zephaniah.* BZAW 198. Berlin: de Gruyter, 1991.

———. "Remembering Twelve Prophetic Characters from the Past." Pages 6–36 in *The Book of the Twelve—One Book or Many? Metz Conference Proceedings, 5–7 November 2015.* Edited by Elena di Pede and Danatella Scaiola. FAT 2/91. Tübingen: Mohr Siebeck, 2016.

Ben Zvi, Ehud, and Michael H. Floyd, eds. *Writings and Speech in Israelite and Ancient Near Eastern Prophecy.* SBL SymS 10. Atlanta: Society of Biblical Literature, 2000.

Ben Zvi, Ehud, and James D. Nogalski, eds. *Two Sides of a Coin: Juxtaposing Views on Interpreting the Book of the Twelve/the Twelve Prophetic Books.* Analecta Gorgiana 201. Piscataway, NJ: Gorgias, 2009.

Berlejung, Angelika. "Erinnerungen an Assyrien in Nahum 2,4–3,19." Pages 325–56 in *Die unwiderstehliche Wahrheit: Studien zur alttestamentlichen Prophetie, Festschrift für Arndt Meinhold.* Edited by Rüdiger Lux and Ernst-Joachim Waschke. Arbeiten zur Bibel und ihrer Geschichte 23. Leipzig: Evangelische Verlagsanstalt, 2006.

Berlin, Adele. *Zephaniah: A New Translation with Introduction and Commentary*. AB 25A. New York: Doubleday, 1994.

Berrin, Shani L. *The Pesher Nahum Scroll from Qumran: An Exegetical Study of 4Q169*. Studies on the Texts of the Desert of Judah 53. Leiden: Brill, 2004.

Boda, Mark J. "Freeing the Burden of Prophecy: *Maśśā'* and the Legitimacy of Prophecy in Zech 9–14." *Bib* 87 (2006): 338–57.

Boda, Mark J., Carol Dempsey, and LeAnn Snow Flesher, eds. *Daughter Zion: Her Portrait, Her Response*. SBLAIL 13. Atlanta: Society of Biblical Literature, 2012.

Boda, Mark J., and J. Gordon McConville. *Dictionary of the Old Testament Prophets: A Compendium of Contemporary Biblical Scholarship*. Downers Grove: IVP Academic; Nottingham: Inter-Varsity Press, 2012. = *DOTP*.

Bosman, Jan P. "The Paradoxical Presence of Exodus 34:6–7 in the Book of the Twelve." *Scriptura* 87 (2004): 233–43.

Bosshard-Nepustil, Erich. *Rezeptionen von Jesaia 1–39 im Zwölfprophetenbuch: Untersuchungen zur literarischen Verbindung von Prophetenbüchern in babylonischer und persischer Zeit*. OBO 154. Göttingen: Vandenhoeck & Ruprecht; Fribourg: Presses Universitaires, 1997.

Brownlee, William H. *The Midrash Pesher of Habakkuk*. SBLMS 24. Missoula: Scholars Press, 1979.

———. "The Placarded Revelation of Habakkuk." *VT* 82 (1963): 319–25.

Cathcart, Kevin J. " 'Law Is Paralysed' (Habakkuk 1.4): Habakkuk's Dialogue with God and the Language of Legal Disputation." Pages 339–53 in *Prophecy and the Prophets in Ancient Israel: Proceedings of the Oxford Old Testament Seminar*. Edited by John Day. LHBOTS 531. London: T&T Clark, 2010.

———. *Nahum in the Light of Northwest Semitic*. BibOr 26. Rome: Pontifical Biblical Institute, 1973.

———. "Treaty-Curses and the Book of Nahum." *CBQ* 35 (1973): 179–87.

Cathcart, Kevin J., and Robert P. Gordon. *The Targum of the Minor Prophets: Translated, with a Critical Introduction, Apparatus, and Notes*. The Aramaic Bible 14. Edinburgh: T&T Clark, 1989. = ArBib 14.

Chapman, Cynthia R. *The Gendered Language of Warfare in the Israelite-Assyrian Encounter*. HSM 62. Winona Lake, IN: Eisenbrauns, 2004.

Christensen, Duane L. "The Book of Nahum: A History of Interpretation." Pages 187–94 in *Forming Prophetic Literature: Essays on Isaiah and the Twelve in Honor of John D. W. Watts*. Edited by James W. Watts and Paul R. House. JSOTSup 235. Sheffield: Sheffield Academic, 1996.

———. "The Book of Nahum as a Liturgical Composition: A Prosodic Analysis." *JETS* 32 (1989): 159–69.

———. *Nahum: A New Translation with Introduction and Commentary*. AB 24F. New Haven: Yale University Press, 2009.

Cleaver-Bartholomew, David. "An Alternative Approach to Hab 1,2–2,20." *SJOT* 17 (2003): 206–25.

Clendenen, E. Ray. "Salvation by Faith or by Faithfulness in the Book of Habakkuk?" *BBR* 24 (2014): 505–13.

Coggins, Richard J., and Jin H. Han. *Six Minor Prophets through the Centuries: Nahum, Habakkuk, Zephaniah, Haggai, Zechariah, and Malachi.* Blackwell Bible Commentaries 29. Chichester: Wiley-Blackwell, 2011.

Cook, Gregory D. "Ashurbanipal's Peace and the Date of Nahum." *WTJ* 79 (2017): 137–45.

———. "Human Trafficking in Nahum." *HBT* 37 (2015): 142–57.

———. "Nahum's Prophetic Name." *TynBul* 67 (2016): 37–40.

———. "Naqia and Nineveh in Nahum: Ambiguity and the Prostitute Queen." *JBL* 136 (2017): 895–904.

———. "Power, Mercy, and Vengeance: The Thirteen Attributes in Nahum." *JESOT* 5 (2016): 27–37.

Dangl, Oskar. *Das Buch Habakuk.* NSKAT 25. Stuttgart: KBW, 2014.

———. "Habakkuk in Recent Research." *CurBS* 9 (2001): 131–68.

Davidson, Andrew Bruce. *The Books of Nahum, Habakkuk, and Zephaniah.* Cambridge Bible for Schools and Colleges 28. Cambridge: Cambridge University Press, 1899.

Davis, Ellen F. *Scripture, Culture, and Agriculture: An Agrarian Reading of the Bible.* Cambridge: Cambridge University Press, 2009.

Dearman, Andrew. "Daughter Zion and Her Place in God's Household." *HBT* 31 (2009): 144–59.

Delitzsch, Franz. *Der Prophet Habakuk.* Exegetisches Handbuch zu den Propheten des Alten Bundes. Leipzig: Tauchnitz, 1843.

———. "Wann weissagte Obadja?" *Zeitschrift für die gesamte lutherische Theologie und Kirche* 12 (1851): 91–102.

DeRouchie, Jason S. "YHWH's Future Ingathering in Zephaniah 1:2: Interpreting אָסֹף אָסֵף." *HS* 59 (2018): 173–91.

Dietrich, Walter. *Nahum, Habakkuk, Zephaniah.* IECOT. Stuttgart: Kohlhammer, 2016.

Dietrich, Walter, and Milton Schwantes, eds. *Der Tag wird kommen: Ein interkontextuelles Gespräch über das Buch des Propheten Zefanja.* SBS 170. Stuttgart: KBW, 1996.

Driver, Samuel R. *The Minor Prophets: Nahum, Habakkuk, Zephaniah, Haggai, Zechariah, Malachi.* The Century Bible. London: Nelson and Sons, 1906.

Eaton, John H. "The Origin and Meaning of Habakkuk 3." *ZAW* 76 (1964): 144–71.

Edler, Rainer. *Das Kerygma des Propheten Zefanja.* Freiburger Theologische Studien 126. Freiburg: Herder, 1984.

Ego, Beate, Armin Lange, Hermann Lichtenberger, and Kristin de Troyer, eds. *Biblica Qumranica*. Vol. 3. Leiden: Brill, 2005.

Ehrlich, Arnold B. *Ezechiel und die Kleinen Propheten*. Vol. 5 of *Randglossen zur Hebräischen Bibel: Textkritisches, Sprachliches und Sachliches*. Leipzig: Hinrichs'sche Buchhandlung, 1912.

Elliger, Karl. *Die Propheten Nahum, Habakuk, Zephanja, Haggai, Sacharja, Maleachi*. 6th ed. ATD 25. Göttingen: Vandenhoeck & Ruprecht, 1967.

Emerton, John A. "The Textual and Linguistic Problems of Habakkuk II.4–5." *JTS* 28 (1977): 1–18.

Fabry, Heinz-Josef. "Ambakuk/Habakuk." Pages 2413–28 in *Septuaginta Deutsch: Erläuterungen und Kommentare*. Edited by Martin Karrer and Wolfgang Kraus. Vol. 2. Stuttgart: Deutsche Bibelgesellschaft, 2011.

———. *Habakuk/Obadja*. HThKAT. Freiburg: Herder, 2018.

———. *Nahum*. HThKAT. Freiburg: Herder, 2006.

———. "Naum/Nahum." Pages 2405–12 in *Septuaginta Deutsch: Erläuterungen und Kommentare*. Edited by Martin Karrer and Wolfgang Kraus. Vol. 2. Stuttgart: Deutsche Bibelgesellschaft, 2011.

Faust, Avraham, and Ehud Weiss. "Judah, Philistia, and the Mediterranean World: Reconstructing the Economic System of the Seventh Century B.C.E." *BASOR* 338 (2005): 71–92.

Ferreiro, Alberto, ed. *The Twelve Prophets*. ACCS OT 14. Downers Grove: InterVarsity, 2003.

Fishbane, Michael A. *Biblical Interpretation in Ancient Israel*. Oxford: Clarendon Press, 1985.

———. "Torah and Tradition." Pages 275–300 in *Tradition and Theology in the Old Testament*. Edited by Douglas A. Knight. BibSem. Philadelphia: Fortress, 1977. Repr., Sheffield: JSOT Press, 1990.

Floyd, Michael H. "The Chimerical Acrostic of Nahum 1:2–10." *JBL* 113 (1994): 421–37.

———. "The Daughter of Zion Goes Fishing in Heaven." Pages 177–200 in *Daughter Zion: Her Portrait, Her Response*. Edited by Mark J. Boda, Carol J. Dempsey, and LeAnn Snow Flesher. SBLAIL 13. Atlanta: Society of Biblical Literature, 2012.

———. "The מַשָּׂא (*MAŚŚĀʾ*) as a Type of Prophetic Book." *JBL* 121 (2002): 401–22.

———. "The Meaning of *Maśśāʾ* as a Prophetic Term in Isaiah." *JHebS* 18 (2018): art. 9. doi:10.5508/jhs.2018.v18.a9

———. *Minor Prophets: Part 2*. FOTL 22. Grand Rapids: Eerdmans, 2000.

———. "Prophecy and Writing in Habakkuk 2,1–5." *ZAW* 105 (1993): 462–81.

———. "Prophetic Complaints about the Fulfillment of Oracles in Habakkuk 1:12–17 and Jeremiah 15:10–18." *JBL* 110 (1991): 397–418.

———. "Welcome Back, Daughter of Zion." *CBQ* 70 (2008): 484–506.

Fuller, Russell E. "The Form and Formation of the Book of the Twelve." Pages 86–101 in *Forming Prophetic Literature: Essays on Isaiah and the Twelve in Honor of John D. W. Watts.* Edited by James W. Watts and Paul R. House. JSOTSup 235. Sheffield: Sheffield Academic, 1996.

Gesenius, Wilhelm, and Herbert Donner, eds. *Hebräisches und Aramäisches Handwörterbuch über das Alte Testament.* 18th ed. Heidelberg: Springer, 2013. = Ges[18].

Geva, Hillel. "Jerusalem's Population in Antiquity: A Minimalist View." *Tel Aviv* 41 (2014): 131–60.

Ginsburg, Christian D. *Introduction to the Massoretico-Critical Edition of the Hebrew Bible.* London: Trinitarian Bible Society, 1897. Repr., Jerusalem: Ktav, 1966.

Grabbe, Lester L., ed. *Good Kings and Bad Kings: The Kingdom of Judah in the Seventh Century BCE.* LHBOTS 393. London: T&T Clark, 2005.

Gruber, Mayer I. "Fear, Anxiety and Reverence in Akkadian, Biblical Hebrew and Other North-West Semitic Languages." *VT* 40 (1990): 411–22.

Grütter, Nesina. *Das Buch Nahum: Eine vergleichende Untersuchung des masoretischen Texts und der Septuagintaübersetzung.* WMANT 148. Neukirchen-Vluyn: Neukirchener Verlag, 2016.

Guillaume, Philippe. "A Reconsideration of Manuscripts Classified as Scrolls of the Twelve Minor Prophets (XII)." *JHebS* 7 (2007): art. 16. doi:10.5508/jhs.2007.v7.a16.

———. "The Unlikely Malachi-Jonah Sequence (4QXIIa)." *JHebS* 6 (2006): art. 15. doi:10.5508/jhs.2006.v6.a15.

Haak, Robert D. *Habakkuk.* VTSup 44. Leiden: Brill, 1992.

Hadjiev, Tchavdar S. "Survival, Conversion and Restoration: Reflections on the Redaction History of the Book of Zephaniah." *VT* 61 (2011): 570–81.

———. "Zephaniah and the 'Book of the Twelve' Hypothesis." Pages 325–38 in *Prophecy and the Prophets in Ancient Israel: Proceedings of the Oxford Old Testament Seminar.* Edited by John Day. LHBOTS 531. London: T&T Clark, 2010.

Hagedorn, Anselm C. "When Did Zephaniah Become a Supporter of Josiah's Reform?" *JTS* 62 (2011): 453–75.

Haring, James W. " 'He Will Certainly Not Hesitate, Wait for Him!': Evidence for an Unrecognized Oath in Habakkuk 2,3b, and Its Implications for Interpreting Habakkuk 2,2–4." *ZAW* 126 (2014): 372–82.

Harl, Marguerite, Cécile Dogniez, Laurence Brottier, Michel Casevitz, and Pierre Sandevoir, eds. *La Bible d'Alexandrie.* Vol. 23. Parts 4–9: *Joël, Abdiou, Jonas, Naoum, Ambakoum, Sophonie.* Paris: Cerf, 1999. = BA 23.

Harper, Joshua L. *Responding to a Puzzled Scribe: The Barberini Version of Habakkuk 3 Analysed in the Light of the Other Greek Versions.* LHBOTS 608. London: Bloomsbury T&T Clark, 2014.

Henige, David. "Found but Not Lost: A Skeptical Note on the Document Discovered in the Temple Under Josiah." *JHebS* 7 (2007): art. 1. doi:10.5508/jhs.2007.v7.a1.

Hiebert, Theodore. *God of My Victory: The Ancient Hymn in Habakkuk 3*. HSM 38. Atlanta: Scholars Press, 1986.

Holladay, William L. "Plausible Circumstances for the Prophecy of Habakkuk." *JBL* 120 (2001): 123–42.

Holt, John Marshall. "So He May Run Who Reads It." *JBL* 83 (1964): 298–302.

Hope, Edward R. "Problems of Interpretation in Amos 3.4." *BT* 42 (1991): 201–5.

House, Paul R. *The Unity of the Twelve*. JSOTSup 77. Sheffield: Sheffield Academic, 1990.

———. *Zephaniah: A Prophetic Drama*. BLS 16. Sheffield: Almond Press, 1988.

Irsigler, Hubert. *Zefanja*. HThKAT. Freiburg: Herder, 2002.

Janzen, J. Gerald. "Eschatological Symbol and Existence in Habakkuk." *CBQ* 44 (1982): 394–414.

———. "Habakkuk 2:2–4 in the Light of Recent Philological Advances." *HTR* 73 (1980): 58–78.

Jastrow, Marcus. *A Dictionary of the Targumim, the Talmud Babli and Yerushalmi, and the Midrashic Literature*. London: Luzak; New York: Putnam, 1903.

Jeremias, Jörg. *Kultprophetie und Gerichtsverkündigung in der späten Königszeit Israels*. WMANT 35. Neukirchen-Vluyn: Neukirchener Verlag, 1970.

———. *Nahum*. BKAT XIV/5,1. Göttingen: Vandenhoeck & Ruprecht, 2019.

———. "Neuere Tendenzen der Forschung an den Kleinen Propheten." Pages 122–136 in *Perspectives in the Study of the Old Testament and Early Judaism: A Symposium in Honour of Adam S. van der Woude on the Occasion of His 70th Birthday*. Edited by Florentino García Martínez and Edward Noort. VTSup 73. Leiden: Brill, 1998.

Jerome. *Commentaries on the Twelve Prophets*. Edited by Thomas P. Scheck. Vol. 1. Ancient Christian Texts. Downers Grove: IVP Academic, 2016.

Jöcken, Peter. *Das Buch Habakuk: Darstellung der Geschichte seiner kritischen Erforschung mit einer eigenen Beurteilung*. BBB 58. Cologne-Bonn: Hanstein, 1977.

Johnson, Marshall D. "The Paralysis of Torah in Habakkuk I 4." *VT* 35 (1985): 257–66.

Johnston, Gordon H. "Nahum's Rhetorical Allusions to the Neo-Assyrian Lion Motif." *BibSac* 158 (2001): 287–307.

———. "Rhetorical Allusions to Neo-Assyrian Treaty Curses." *BibSac* 158 (2001): 415–36.

Jones, Barry A. *The Formation of the Book of the Twelve: A Study in Text and Canon*. SBLDS 149. Atlanta: Scholars Press, 1995.

Jong, John Hans de. "Sanctified or Dedicated? הקדיש in Zephaniah 1:7." *VT* 68 (2018): 94–101.

Kahn, Dan'el. "The Historical Setting of Zephaniah's Oracles Against the Nations (Zeph 2:4–15)." Pages 439–53 in *Homeland and Exile: Biblical and Ancient Near Eastern Studies in Honour of Bustenay Oded*. Edited by Gershon Galil, Markham J Geller, and Alan R. Millard. VTSup 130. Leiden: Brill, 2009.

———. "Why Did Necho II Kill Josiah?" Pages 511–28 in *There and Back Again— the Crossroads II: Proceedings of an International Conference Held in Prague, September 15–18, 2014*. Edited by Jana Mynářová, Pavel Onderka, and Peter Pavúk. Prague: Charles University in Prague, 2015.

Kapelrud, Arvid S. *The Message of the Prophet Zephaniah: Morphology and Ideas*. Oslo: Universitetsforlaget, 1975.

Kartveit, Magnar. *Rejoice, Dear Zion! Hebrew Construct Phrases with "Daughter" and "Virgin" as Nomen Regens*. BZAW 447. Berlin: de Gruyter, 2013.

Keel, Othmar. *The Symbolism of the Biblical World: Ancient Near Eastern Iconography and the Book of Psalms*. Translated by Timothy J. Hallett. Winona Lake, IN: Eisenbrauns, 1997.

Keil, Carl Friedrich. *Minor Prophets: Two Volumes in One*. Commentary on the Old Testament 10. Edinburgh: T&T Clark, 1871. Repr., Peabody: Hendrickson, 1989.

Kelle, Brad E. "Judah in the Seventh Century: From the Aftermath of Sennacherib's Invasion to the Beginning of Jehoiakim's Rebellion." Pages 350–82 in *Ancient Israel's History: An Introduction to Issues and Sources*. Edited by Bill T. Arnold and Richard S. Hess. Grand Rapids: Baker Academic, 2014.

Kennedy, James M. "The Root G^{C}R in the Light of Semantic Analysis." *JBL* 106 (1987): 47–64.

Kessler, Rainer. "Nahum-Habakuk als Zweiprophetenschrift: Eine Skizze." Pages 149–58 in *"Wort JHWHs, das geschah . . ." (Hos 1,1): Studien zum Zwölfprophetenbuch*. Edited by Erich Zenger. HBS 35. Freiburg: Herder, 2002.

Kline, J. Bergman. "The Day of the Lord in the Death and Resurrection of Christ." *JETS* 48 (2005): 757–70.

Kolyada, Yelena. *A Compendium of Musical Instruments and Instrumental Terminology in the Bible*. London: Equinox, 2009.

Kotzé, Zacharias. "Metaphors and Metonymies for Anger in the Old Testament: A Cognitive Linguistic Approach." *Scriptura* 88 (2005): 118–25.

Kuhrt, Amélie. *The Ancient Near East c. 3000–330 BC*. London: Routledge, 1995.

Laato, Antti. *Josiah and David Redivivus: The Historical Josiah and the Messianic Expectations of Exilic and Postexilic Times*. ConBOT 33. Stockholm: Almqvist & Wiksell, 1992.

Lakoff, George, and Mark Johnson. *Metaphors We Live By*. Chicago: The University of Chicago Press, 1980.

Lane, Nathan C. *The Compassionate, But Punishing God: A Canonical Analysis of Exodus 34:6–7*. Eugene, OR: Pickwick, 2010.

Lange, Armin. "Die Wurzel *PHZ* und ihre Konnotationen." *VT* 51 (2001): 497–510.

Lanner, Laurel. *"Who Will Lament Her?": The Feminine and the Fantastic in the Book of Nahum.* LHBOTS 434 / Playing the Texts 11. New York: T&T Clark, 2006.

Lévi, Israel, ed. *The Hebrew Text of the Book of Ecclesiasticus: Edited with Brief Notes and a Selected Glossary.* Semitic Study Series 3. Leiden: Brill, 1951.

Levin, Christoph. "Zephaniah: How This Book Became Prophecy." Pages 117–39 in *Constructs of Prophecy in the Former and Latter Prophets and Other Texts.* Edited by Lester L. Grabbe and Martti Nissinen. SBLANEM 4. Atlanta: Society of Biblical Literature, 2011.

Lindström, Fredrik. " 'I Am Rousing the Chaldaeans'—Regrettably? Habakkuk 1.5–11 and the End of the Prophetic Theology of History." Pages 39–60 in *The Centre and the Periphery: A European Tribute to Walter Brueggemann.* Edited by Jill Middlemas, David J. A. Clines, and Else Holt. HBM 27. Sheffield: Sheffield Phoenix, 2010.

Longman, Tremper, III. "Nahum." Pages 765–829 in *The Minor Prophets: An Exegetical and Expository Commentary.* Edited by Thomas Edward McComiskey. Vol. 2. Grand Rapids: Baker, 1993.

Maier, Walter A. *The Book of Nahum: A Commentary.* Saint Louis: Concordia, 1959.

Markl, Dominik. "Hab 3 in intertextueller und kontextueller Sicht." *Bib* 85 (2004): 99–108.

Mazar, Amihai. *Archaeology of the Land of the Bible: 10,000–586 B.C.E.* New York: Doubleday, 1990.

Mech, L. David, Douglas W. Smith, and Daniel R. MacNulty. *Wolves on the Hunt: The Behavior of Wolves Hunting Wild Prey.* Chicago: University of Chicago Press, 2015.

Meier, Samuel A. *Speaking of Speaking: Marking Direct Discourse in the Hebrew Bible.* VTSup 46. Leiden: Brill, 1992.

Meyer, Rudolf. *Hebräische Grammatik.* 4 vols. Berlin: de Gruyter, 1992.

Mulroney, James A. E. *The Translation Style of Old Greek Habakkuk: Methodological Advancement in Interpretive Studies of the Septuagint.* FAT 2/86. Tübingen: Mohr Siebeck, 2016.

Muraoka, Takamitsu. *A Greek-English Lexicon of the Septuagint.* Louvain: Peeters, 2009.

Myers-O'Brien, Julia. *Nahum.* Readings: A New Biblical Commentary. Sheffield: Sheffield Academic, 2002.

Na'aman, Nadav. "Josiah and the Kingdom of Judah." Pages 189–247 in *Good Kings and Bad Kings: The Kingdom of Judah in the Seventh Century BCE.* Edited by Lester L. Grabbe. LHBOTS 393. London: T&T Clark, 2005.

———. "The Kingdom of Judah under Josiah." *Tel Aviv* 18 (1991): 3–71.

Nogalski, James D. *The Book of the Twelve: Micah–Malachi*. SHBC 18b. Macon: Smyth & Helwys, 2011.

———. *Literary Precursors to the Book of the Twelve*. BZAW 217. Berlin: de Gruyter, 1993.

———. "Recurring Themes in the Book of the Twelve: Creating Points of Contact for a Theological Reading." *Int* 61 (2007): 125–36.

———. *Redactional Processes in the Book of the Twelve*. BZAW 218. Berlin: de Gruyter, 1993.

———. "Zephaniah 3: A Redactional Text for a Developing Corpus." Pages 207–18 in *Schriftauslegung in der Schrift: Festschrift für Odil Hannes Steck zu seinem 65. Geburtstag*. Edited by Reinhard G. Kratz, Thomas Krüger, and Konrad Schmid. BZAW 300. Berlin: de Gruyter, 2000.

Nogalski, James D., and Marvin A. Sweeney, eds. *Reading and Hearing the Book of the Twelve*. SBL SymS 15. Atlanta: Society of Biblical Literature, 2000.

O'Connor, Michael. *Hebrew Verse Structure*. Winona Lake, IN: Eisenbrauns, 1997.

O'Neal, G. Michael. *Interpreting Habakkuk as Scripture: An Application of the Canonical Approach of Brevard S. Childs*. StBibLit 9. New York: Lang, 2007.

Oesch, Josef M. *Petucha und Setuma: Untersuchungen zu einer überlieferten Gliederung im hebräischen Text des Alten Testament*. OBO 27. Fribourg: Presses Universitaires; Göttingen: Vandenhoeck & Ruprecht, 1979.

Pardee, Dennis. "*YPḤ* 'Witness' in Hebrew and Ugaritic." *VT* 28 (1978): 204–13.

Parpola, Simo K. A., and Robert M. Whiting, eds. *Assyria 1995: Proceedings of the 10th Anniversary Symposium of the Neo-Assyrian Text Corpus Project, Helsinki, 1995*. Helsinki: University of Helsinki Press, 1997.

Patterson, Richard D. *Nahum, Habakkuk, Zephaniah*. The Wycliffe Exegetical Commentary. Chicago: Moody Bible Institute, 1991.

Peckham, Brian. "The Vision of Habakkuk." *CBQ* 48 (1986): 617–36.

Perlitt, Lothar. *Die Propheten Nahum, Habakuk, Zephanja*. ATD 25/1. Göttingen: Vandenhoeck & Ruprecht, 2004.

Petit, Lucas P., and Daniele Morandi Bonacossi, eds. *Nineveh, the Great City: Symbol of Beauty and Power*. Papers on Archaeology of the Leiden Museum of Antiquities 13. Leiden: Sidestone Press, 2017.

Pinker, Aron. "Infertile Quartet of Flora." *ZAW* 115 (2003): 617–23.

———. "Nahum 2,4 Revisited." *ZAW* 117 (2005): 411–19.

———. "Nineveh's Defensive Strategy and Nahum 2–3." *ZAW* 118 (2006): 618–25.

Price, James D. *The Syntax of Masoretic Accents in the Hebrew Bible*. Studies in the Bible and Early Christianity 27. Lewiston: Mellen, 1990.

Prinsloo, Gert T. M. "Life for the Righteous, Doom for the Wicked: Reading Habakkuk from a Wisdom Perspective," *Skrif en Kerk* 21 (2000): 621–40.

———. "Petuhot/Setumot and the Structure of Habakkuk: Evaluating the Evidence." Pages 196–227 in *The Impact of Unit Delimitation on Exegesis*.

Edited by Raymond de Hoop, Marjo C. A. Korpel, and Stanley E. Porter. Pericope 7. Leiden: Brill, 2009.

———. "Reading Habakkuk as a Literary Unit: Exploring the Possibilities." *OTE* 12 (1999): 515–35.

———. "Reading Habakkuk 3 in Its Literary Context: A Worthwhile Exercise or Futile Attempt?" *JSem* 11 (2002): 83–111.

Redditt, Paul L. "Recent Research on the Book of the Twelve as One Book." *CurBR* 9 (2001): 47–80.

Redditt, Paul L., and Aaron Schart, eds. *Thematic Threads in the Book of the Twelve*. BZAW 325. Berlin: de Gruyter, 2003.

Renz, Thomas. *Colometry and Accentuation in Hebrew Prophetic Poetry*. KUSATU 4. Waltrop: Spenner, 2003.

———. "The Colour Red and the Lion King: Two Studies in Nahum." Pages 163–77 in *Sprache lieben—Gottes Wort verstehen: Beiträge zur biblischen Exegese; Festschrift für Heinrich von Siebenthal*. Edited by Walter Hilbrands. BWM 17. Gießen: Brunnen, 2011.

———. "An Emendation of Hab 2:4a in the light of Hab 1:5." *JHebS* 13 (2013): art. 11. doi:10.5508/jhs.2013.v13.a11.

———. "Habakkuk and Its Co-Texts." Pages 13–36 in *The Book of the Twelve: An Anthology of Prophetic Books or the Result of Complex Redactional Processes?* Edited by Heiko Wenzel. Osnabrücker Studien zur Jüdischen und Christlichen Bibel 4. Göttingen: Vandenhoeck & Ruprecht, 2018.

———. "Martin Luther as an Example of Participatory Exegesis." Forthcoming in *The Book of the Minor Prophets* [provisional title]. Edited by David G. Firth and Brittany N. Melton. Bellingham: Lexham Press.

———. "A Perfectly Broken Acrostic in Nahum 1?" *JHebS* 9 (2009): art. 23. doi:10.5508/jhs.2009.v9.a23.

———. "Proclaiming the Future: History and Theology in Prophecies against Tyre." *TynBul* 51 (2000): 17–58.

———. "Reading and Running: Notes on the History of Translating the Final Clause of Hab 2:2." *VT* 69 (2019): 435–46.

———. *The Rhetorical Function of the Book of Ezekiel*. VTSup 76. Leiden: Brill, 1999.

———. "Torah in the Minor Prophets." Pages 73–94 in *Reading the Law: Studies in Honour of Gordon J. Wenham*. Edited by J. Gordon McConville and Karl Möller. LHBOTS 461. London: T&T Clark, 2007.

Roberts, J. J. M. *Nahum, Habakkuk, and Zephaniah*. OTL. Louisville: Westminster John Knox, 1991.

Robertson, O. Palmer. *The Books of Nahum, Habakkuk, and Zephaniah*. NICOT. Grand Rapids: Eerdmans, 1990.

Rosenberg, Abraham J. *The Book of the Twelve Prophets: A New English Trans-*

lation of the Text, Rashi, and a Commentary Digest. Vol. 2. Judaica Book of the Prophets. New York: Judaica Press, 1988.

Roth, Martin. *Israel und die Völker im Zwölfprophetenbuch: Eine Untersuchung zu den Büchern Joel, Jona, Micha und Nahum.* FRLANT 210. Göttingen: Vandenhoeck & Ruprecht, 2005.

Rudolph, Wilhelm. *Micha-Nahum-Habakuk-Zephanja.* KAT 13. Gütersloh: Mohn, 1975.

Ryou, Daniel H. *Zephaniah's Oracles against the Nations: A Synchronic and Diachronic Study of Zephaniah 2:1–3:8.* BibInt 13. Leiden: Brill, 1995.

Sabottka, Liudger. *Zephanja: Versuch einer Neuübersetzung mit philologischem Kommentar.* BibOr 25. Rome: Biblical Institute Press, 1972.

Schart, Aaron. *Die Entstehung des Zwölfprophetenbuchs: Neubearbeitungen von Amos im Rahmen schriftenübergreifender Redaktionsprozesse.* BZAW 260. Berlin: de Gruyter, 1998.

———. "Redactional Models: Comparisons, Contrasts, Agreements, Disagreements." Pages 893–908 in *SBL Seminar Papers 1998, Part Two.* Atlanta: Society of Biblical Literature, 1998.

Schipper, Bernd U. "Egypt and the Kingdom of Judah under Josiah and Jehoiakim." *Tel Aviv* 37 (2010): 200–226.

Schneider, Thomas. "Nahum und Theben: Zum Topographisch-Historischen Hintergrund von Nahum 3,8f." *BN* 44 (1988): 63–73.

Scoralick, Ruth. *Gottes Güte und Gottes Zorn: Die Gottesprädikationen in Exodus 34,6f und ihre intertextuellen Beziehungen zum Zwölfprophetenbuch.* HBS 33. Freiburg im Breisgau: Herder, 2002.

Seitz, Christopher R. *Joel.* ITC. London: Bloomsbury, 2016.

Sellin, Ernst. *Das Zwölfprophetenbuch.* 3rd ed. KAT 12. Leipzig: Deichert, 1930.

Seybold, Klaus. *Nahum, Habakuk, Zephanja.* ZBK AT 24. Zürich: Theologischer Verlag, 1991.

———. *Profane Prophetie: Studien zum Buch Nahum.* SBS 135. Stuttgart: KBW, 1989.

———. *Satirische Prophetie: Studien zum Buch Zefanja.* SBS 120. Stuttgart: KBW, 1985.

Shepherd, Michael B. *The Twelve Prophets in the New Testament.* StBibLit 140. New York: Lang, 2007.

Sinker, Robert. *The Psalm of Habakkuk.* Cambridge: Deighton, Bell and Co., 1890.

Smith, Ralph L. *Micah–Malachi.* WBC 32. Waco: Word, 1984.

Soll, Will M. "Babylonian and Biblical Acrostics." *Bib* 69 (1988): 305–23.

Sperber, Alexander. *The Latter Prophets according to Targum Jonathan.* Vol. 3 of *The Bible in Aramaic: Based on Old Manuscripts and Printed Texts.* Leiden: Brill, 1992.

Spronk, Klaas. "Acrostics in the Book of Nahum." *ZAW* 110 (1998): 209–22.

———. *Nahum.* HCOT. Kampen: Kok Pharos, 1997.

———. "Synchronic and Diachronic Approaches to the Book of Nahum." Pages 159–86 in *Synchronic or Diachronic? A Debate on Method in Old Testament Exegesis.* Edited by Johannes C. Moor. Leiden: Brill, 1995.

Steck, Odil Hannes. "Zur Abfolge Maleachi–Jona in 4Q76 (4QXIIa)." *ZAW* 108 (1996): 249–53.

Stern, Ephraim. *The Assyrian, Babylonian, and Persian Periods (732-332 B.C.E.).* Vol. 2 of *Archaeology of the Land of the Bible.* New York: Doubleday, 2001.

Strobel, August. *Untersuchungen zum eschatologischen Verzögerungsproblem auf Grund der spätjüdisch-urchristlichen Geschichte von Habakuk 2,2ff.* NovTSup 2. Leiden: Brill, 1961.

Sweeney, Marvin A. "Concerning the Structure and Generic Character of the Book of Nahum." *ZAW* 104 (1992): 364–77.

———. "A Form-Critical Reassessment of the Book of Zephaniah." *CBQ* 53 (1991): 388–408.

———. *Isaiah 1–39 with an Introduction to Prophetic Literature.* FOTL 16. Grand Rapids: Eerdmans, 1996.

———. "The Place and Function of Joel in the Book of the Twelve." Pages 570–95 in *Society of Biblical Literature 1999 Seminar Papers.* SBLSP 38. Atlanta: Society of Biblical Literature, 1999.

———. "Structure, Genre, and Intent in the Book of Habakkuk." *VT* 41 (1991): 63–83.

———. *The Twelve Prophets.* Vol. 2. Berit Olam. Collegeville, MN: Liturgical Press.

———. *Zephaniah: A Commentary.* Philadelphia: Fortress, 2003.

———. "Zephaniah: A Paradigm for the Study of the Prophetic Books." *CurBS* 7 (1999): 119–45.

Tachik, Christopher S. *"King of Israel" and "Do Not Fear, Daughter of Zion": The Use of Zephaniah 3 in John 12.* Phillipsburg: P&R Publishing, 2018.

Theodoret of Cyrus. *Commentary on the Twelve Prophets.* Vol. 3 of *Commentaries on the Prophets.* Translated by Robert Charles Hill. Brookline, MA: Holy Cross Orthodox Press, 2006.

Thirtle, James W. *The Titles of the Psalms: Their Nature and Meaning Explained.* London: Henry Frowde, 1904.

Timmer, Daniel C. "Nahum's Representation of and Response to Neo-Assyria: Imperialism as a Multifaceted Point of Contact in Nahum." *BBR* 24 (2014): 349–62.

———. *The Non-Israelite Nations in the Book of the Twelve: Thematic Coherence and the Diachronic-Synchronic Relationship in the Minor Prophets.* Biblical Interpretation Series 135. Leiden: Brill, 2015.

Tov, Emanuel. *The Greek Minor Prophets Scroll from Naḥal Ḥever (8ḤevXIIgr).* DJD 8. Oxford: Clarendon, 1990.

———. *Textual Criticism of the Hebrew Bible*. 3rd ed. Minneapolis: Fortress, 2011.

Tsumura, David Toshio. *Creation and Destruction: A Reappraisal of the Chaoskampf Theory in the Old Testament*. Winona Lake, IN: Eisenbrauns, 2006.

———. "Hab 2:2 in the Light of Akkadian Legal Practice." *ZAW* 94 (1984): 294–95.

———. "Ugaritic Poetry and Habakkuk 3." *TynBul* 40 (1988): 24–48.

Uehlinger, Christoph. "Astralkultpriester und Fremdgekleidete, Kanaanvolk und Silberwäger—Zur Verknüpfung von Kult- und Sozialkritik in Zef 1." Pages 49–83 in *Der Tag wird kommen: Ein interkontextuelles Gespräch über das Buch des Propheten Zefanja*. Edited by Walter Dietrich and Milton Schwantes. SBS 170. Stuttgart: KBW, 1996.

Van der Merwe, Christo H. J., Jackie A. Naudé, and Jan H. Kroeze. *A Biblical Hebrew Reference Grammar*. Biblical Languages: Hebrew 3. Sheffield: Sheffield Academic, 1999. = BHRG.

Vanderhooft, David Stephen. *The Neo-Babylonian Empire and Babylon in the Latter Prophets*. HSM 59. Atlanta: Scholars Press, 1999.

Vlaardingerbroek, Johannes. *Zephaniah*. HCOT. Leuven: Peeters, 1999.

Wakeling, Simon. "The Minor Prophets as a Unity Developing Theodicy." *Ecclesia Reformanda* 2 (2010): 124–53.

Watson, Wilfred G. E. *Classical Hebrew Poetry: A Guide to Its Techniques*. 2nd ed. Sheffield: Sheffield Academic, 1986. = CHP.

Weigl, Michael. "Current Research on the Book of Nahum: Exegetical Methodologies in Turmoil?" *CurBR* 9 (2001): 81–130.

———. *Zefanja und das "Israel der Armen"*. Österreichische Biblische Studien 13. Klosterneuburg: Österreichisches KBW, 1994.

Weinfeld, Moshe. *Deuteronomy and the Deuteronomic School*. Oxford: Clarendon, 1972. Repr., Winona Lake, IN: Eisenbrauns, 1992.

———. "The Protest against Imperialism in Ancient Israelite Prophecy." Pages 169–82 in *The Origins and Diversity of Axial Age Civilizations*. Edited by Shmuel N. Eisenstadt. Albany: State University of New York Press, 1986.

Weis, Richard D. "A Definition of the Genre *Maśśā'* in the Hebrew Bible." PhD diss., The Claremont Graduate School, 1986.

———. "Oracle (Old Testament)." *ABD* 5:28–29.

Wellhausen, Julius. *Skizzen und Vorarbeiten—Fünftes Heft: Die kleinen Propheten übersetzt, mit Noten*. Berlin: Reimer, 1892.

Wendland, Ernst R. *The Discourse Analysis of Hebrew Prophetic Literature: Determining the Larger Textual Units of Hosea and Joel*. Mellen Biblical Press Series 40. Lewiston: Mellen, 1995.

Wenzel, Heiko, ed. *The Book of the Twelve: An Anthology of Prophetic Books or the Result of Complex Redactional Processes?* Osnabrücker Studien zur Jüdischen und Christlichen Bibel 4. Göttingen: Vandenhoeck & Ruprecht, 2018.

Werse, Nicholas R. *Reconsidering the Book of the Four: The Shaping of Hosea, Amos, Micah, and Zephaniah as an Early Prophetic Collection.* BZAW 517. Berlin: de Gruyter, 2019.

Willi-Plein, Ida. "Wort, Last oder Auftrag? Zur Bedeutung von מַשָּׂא in Überschriften prophetischer Texteinheiten." Pages 431–38 in *Die unwiderstehliche Wahrheit: Studien zur alttestamentlichen Prophetie, Festschrift für Arndt Meinhold.* Edited by Rüdiger Lux and Ernst-Joachim Waschke. Arbeiten zur Bibel und ihrer Geschichte 23. Leipzig: Evangelische Verlagsanstalt, 2006.

Willi-Plein, Ina. "Das Zwölfprophetenbuch." *Theologische Rundschau* 64 (1999): 351–95.

Witte, Markus. "Orakel und Gebete im Buch Habakuk." Pages 67–91 in *Orakel und Gebete: Interdisziplinäre Studien zur Sprache der Religion in Ägypten, Vorderasien und Griechenland in hellenistischer Zeit.* Edited by Markus Witte and Johannes F. Diehl. FAT 2/38. Tübingen: Mohr Siebeck, 2009.

Woude, Adam S. van der. "The Book of Nahum: A Letter Written in Exile." *OTS* 20 (1977): 108–26.

Yeivin, Israel. *Introduction to the Tiberian Masorah.* Edited and translated by E. John Revell. Masoretic Studies 5. Missoula: Scholars Press, 1980.

Ziegler, Joseph. *Duodecim Prophetae.* Vol. 13 of *Septuaginta: Vetus Testamentum Graecum.* 3rd. ed. Göttingen: Vandenhoeck & Ruprecht, 2012.

Introduction to Nahum, Habakkuk, and Zephaniah

I. THE NATURE OF PROPHETIC BOOKS

The question of the nature of prophetic books is still contested. Roberts claims that "if one were looking for a modern analogy to the ancient prophetic book, a collection of relatively short sermons by a particular minister would be a good analogy. When reading such a modern collection, one cannot assume that the sermons will be arranged in a particular, logical order." Consequently, "sometimes . . . too much attention to the book as a whole may lead to misinterpretation of a particular sermon."[1] Yet my previous research led me to conclude that at least the book of Ezekiel had been carefully arranged to communicate a message.[2] Because many prophetic books are plausibly thought to go back to the oral ministry of a prophet, the genre of anthology is a distinct option, but the possibility that there is a coherent rationale behind the arrangement of a prophetic book and that the book *itself* functions as a piece of communication cannot be excluded. The question needs to be asked for each book afresh. There is, in my view, no one genre "prophetic book"—not in the narrow sense anyway.

In the light of ancient Near Eastern evidence, it is probable that many prophecies were written down soon after being uttered. Collections of prophetic oracles are found elsewhere, but there is nothing known to us that is comparable to prophetic books of the kind we have in the Bible.[3] Therefore,

1. J. J. M. Roberts, *Nahum, Habakkuk, and Zephaniah*, OTL (Louisville: Westminster John Knox, 1991), 9.

2. See Thomas Renz, *The Rhetorical Function of the Book of Ezekiel*, VTSup 76 (Leiden: Brill, 1999).

3. According to William R. Osborne's review in *JETS* 2 (2013): 252–55, R. Russell Mack

based on the observation that in the ancient world oracles were transcribed with a concern for accuracy and then transmitted unchanged from one generation to another, we cannot conclude that within ancient Israel and Judah prophetic words could not have been recast to speak into new contexts. Even the larger prophetic books in the Bible reflect a literary shape suggesting a process that involved more than anthologizing individual oracles. The prophetic books seem to be the product of careful theological reflection.

As indicated in the preface to this commentary, I am skeptical about a number of redaction-critical proposals made in relation to Nahum, Habakkuk, and Zephaniah. But this does not mean that I rule out a process of redaction on principle. Bearing in mind that much of biblical literature is anonymous, there is no reason to believe that every word within a book associated with a particular prophet must have been said or written down by that prophet. Nonetheless, it seems to me a fair assumption that the people who collected prophecies and arranged them in rhetorically shaped books were respectful of the original prophecies and that any redactional expansions sought to develop the text itself—sometimes even in an unexpected direction—rather than to merely add words that would speak to their generation.[4] To put it differently, redactors were first of all close readers. A passage like Isa 16:13–14 clearly indicates its origin at a later time than the preceding verses, but there is no reason to think that later elaborations, whether by the prophet or by someone else, were always marked in this way.

The distinction between prophetic discourse speaking about God in the third person and oracles consisting of first-person divine speech has been more or less emphasized by different commentators. My own view is that the distinction is often blurred in prophetic literature, which frequently uses third-person references to God in first-person divine speech (enallage), a feature that will be discussed further in relation to Zephaniah.[5] Rhetorically, we

---

(*Neo-Assyrian Prophecy and the Hebrew Bible: Nahum, Habakkuk, and Zephaniah*, Perspectives on Hebrew Scripture and Its Contexts 14 [Piscataway, NJ: Gorgias, 2011]) assumes that prophecy looked alike all across the region during the seventh century. The dissimilarity between Neo-Assyrian literature and the books of Nahum, Habakkuk, and Zephaniah leads him to conclude that the latter must be later compositions that developed earlier genres. I have no access to Mack's work.

4. The German word *Fortschreibung* is often used in this context. It has no ready equivalent in English. Attempts to identify and then resolve contradictions within the text by attributing different parts of the text to different layers, as if prophetic books were proceedings of conferences, seem to me less plausible.

5. Paul R. House (*Zephaniah: A Prophetic Drama*, BLS 16 [Sheffield: Almond Press, 1988]) relies on a firm distinction between the speeches of Zephaniah and YHWH and yet allows that YHWH refers to himself in both the first and third person. Marvin A. Sweeney (*Zephaniah: A Commentary*, Hermeneia [Philadelphia: Fortress, 2003]) does not allow for enallage in divine speech. He uses quotation marks in his translation to delimit divine speech

may distinguish three main types of communication that feature prophetic and divine speech:[6] (1) prophetic discourse, like a sermon, which cites divine speech; (2) divine oracles, or instances in which someone impersonates God in order to bring a revelation from him, to which prophetic commentary is appended; and (3) prophetic-divine speech, in which the speakers are not clearly distinguished. To suggest these *three* types is to claim that a distinction between prophetic and divine speech is sometimes warranted rhetorically but that there are also cases in which it will not be helpful to claim a hard-and-fast distinction between the two.[7]

II. THE MINOR PROPHETS IN THE CANON

The traditional Jewish understanding of the prophetic literature is that it expounds the Torah; the traditional Christian understanding is that it points forward to Christ. Both are true in my view. Once it is part of the canon of Scripture, no part of prophetic literature is understood as competing with or substituting for the fundamental revelation that is Torah. The Minor Prophets are only a small part of the prophetic literature, if one follows the traditional Jewish understanding that includes Joshua to Kings in the prophetic canon. While obvious links with the Former Prophets are few and far between, the basic theological outlook and even some of the characteristic vocabulary is similar. This has often been explained with the thesis that the prophetic books underwent a redaction by those responsible for or familiar with the Former Prophets. Yet it is hard to distinguish between the common phraseology due to similar social and ideological background and that due to actual identity of authorship (redaction), and some books are closer to the "Deuteronomistic" style than others (see below). All in all, considering that (1) the prophets build on tradition in their condemnation of the sins of their people, (2) the redactors of the prophetic books were likely to increase the links with other parts of the tradition rather than decrease them, and (3) the injunction toward the end of the Book of the Twelve to "remember the law of Moses my servant, which I commanded him in Horeb for all Israel,

---

but cannot altogether avoid gray areas. Cf. the marking of divine speech in Zeph 2:5–7 on p. 124 with his commentary on p. 129, and note the identification of 2:12 as prophetic speech on p. 145.

6. There is of course also a sense in which everything we find in prophetic literature is human speech and a sense in which it is all to be received as the word of God, but my concern here is with the literary features of the text.

7. Cf. Michael H. Floyd, *Minor Prophets: Part 2*, FOTL 22 (Grand Rapids: Eerdmans, 2000), 166–67, on the fine line between prophets speaking for YHWH and speaking for themselves.

statutes and ordinances," we have strong encouragement to pay attention to links with the Torah.[8]

But the links are not all backward. The Christian interpreter will want to ask in what sense the prophets proclaim Christ, and the answer will most often be in a typological sense. The forward links relate to God's history with his people, to the exposition of his design for creation, and to the reality of guilt and reconciliation. These issues are embodied in God's central self-revelation in Jesus Christ, and the full significance of the prophetic word is therefore discerned in the light of Jesus Christ. For those like myself who accept the truth of the New Testament, the link to the second part of the Christian two-part canon is not one among many one could make but is as firm and important a link (forward) as the (backward) link to Torah.

Is there a specific contribution made by the Minor Prophets to the canon? Many of the same motifs and themes are found in Isaiah, Jeremiah, and Ezekiel. But none of these gives us the idea of a succession of prophets like the Book of the Twelve. The prophets in the narrative corpus of the Bible fulfill such a variety of functions that one does not get the same sense from them of a prophetic tradition exhorting and encouraging the people of God across the centuries. The similarities of themes dealt with in the Minor Prophets create a sense of unity across the ages, but the particularities of each of the books testify to a dynamic vitality and the fact that the prophetic word is spoken into specific situations.

III. THE UNITY OF THE BOOK OF THE TWELVE

Many scholars have come to believe that the Minor Prophets constitute in some sense a single literary entity. They claim that such a unity is suggested by the traditional designation "the Book of the Twelve" and by the scribal tradition of copying the Twelve on a single scroll. These conventions indeed indicate that the writings of the Minor Prophets were thought to belong together. Certainly, each writing associated with a minor prophet is on its own too short to count as a book in the full sense.[9] It is no surprise, therefore, that these writings were collected together and that early counts of

8. It seems to me reasonable to assume that the Torah contains a substantial amount of early material to which the prophets could refer back. In particular, I am persuaded of the largely preexilic origin of the priestly material and accept the existence of an early Deuteronomic core. Were these sources dated later, the relationship would take on a more typological nature. In other words, as portrayed in the prophetic books, the prophets based their proclamation on a tradition of the type now contained in the Torah.

9. By way of illustration, the Minor Prophets comprise 180 cols. in the Cairo Codex (see "Excursus: Ancient and Medieval Manuscripts" immediately below). Even if they are taken

the books in the Hebrew canon were given as twenty-two (the number of letters of the Hebrew alphabet) or twenty-four (the number of letters of the Greek alphabet).[10] In a sense, it is uncontroversial to speak of the Book of the Twelve as a unit that comprises all the Minor Prophets. What is debatable is whether the individual writings therein belong together as chapters of a carefully constructed book that develops an argument or whether they form an anthology—a more or less loose collection of writings that share similar themes and motifs.[11] The canonical text does not include a separate superscription for the Book of the Twelve, and while the headings used for the different collections are sufficiently similar to invite comparison, they are not in my view similar enough to suggest a single origin.

EXCURSUS: ANCIENT AND MEDIEVAL MANUSCRIPTS

The Minor Prophets have been transmitted as a unit for a long time (e.g., in 8ḤevXIIgr), but the manuscript evidence does not tell us in which sense the Twelve formed a canon of shorter prophetic writings. A unified composition would be put on one scroll for literary reasons; an anthology could be put on one scroll for pragmatic reasons, and maybe also to suggest a historical succession of prophets.[12] Philippe Guillaume argues that there are substantially fewer manuscripts of the Twelve at Qumran than usually assumed and that none of the manuscripts transmitting the complete collection of the Twelve is earlier than the first century BC, the date of 8ḤevXIIgr.[13] He concludes:

---

together, the only other book in the codex to be shorter is Judges (110 cols.). Zechariah, the most substantial minor prophet, fits into 39 cols.; the rest average at fewer than 13 cols.

10. 1–2 Samuel, 1–2 Kings, 1–2 Chronicles, and Ezra-Nehemiah are counted one book each. The lower count also associates Ruth with Judges and Lamentations with Jeremiah.

11. Cf. David Willgren, *The Formation of the "Book" of Psalms: Reconsidering the Transmission and Canonization of Psalmody in Light of Material Culture and the Poetics of Anthologies*, FAT 2/88 (Tübingen: Mohr Siebeck, 2016), for a study that raises similar questions about the book of Psalms, concluding that the book is an anthology. Willgren's comments on the Book of the Twelve are cautious (see pp. 46–47, 51–52, 54, 75, 77, 79) but point in the same direction.

12. For discussion, see Barry A. Jones, *The Formation of the Book of the Twelve: A Study in Text and Canon*, SBLDS 149 (Atlanta: Scholars Press, 1995); Odil Hannes Steck, "Zur Abfolge Maleachi–Jona in 4Q76 (4QXIIa)," *ZAW* 108 (1996): 249–53; Russell Earl Fuller, "The Form and Formation of the Book of the Twelve," in *Forming Prophetic Literature: Essays on Isaiah and the Twelve in Honor of John D. W. Watts*, ed. James W. Watts and Paul R. House, JSOTSup 235 (Sheffield: Sheffield Academic, 1996), 86–101; and the essays listed below in n. 14.

13. Note that, e.g., in MurXII, three empty lines (five before and after Obadiah because the change of book coincides with a change of column) separate the individual writings.

"Nothing supports claims that the XII formed a collection before their translation in Greek."[14] In fact, the twelve writings are still treated as separate books in Codex Sinaiticus (fourth century AD), with the individual minor prophets being given book titles and having the column in which each book ends left blank, just like the major prophets.

The Leningrad Codex (AD 1008), the oldest complete manuscript of the Hebrew Bible in Hebrew, concludes biblical books with the record of a verse count. It does so for each of the Minor Prophets, albeit usually in a slightly abbreviated form.[15] The Aleppo Codex (AD tenth century), even older but no longer preserved in full,[16] also offers a verse count for each of the Minor Prophets, but only in short form, the number being signified by Hebrew letters. Medieval codices give verse counts sometimes for individual books within the Twelve but sometimes only for the Book of the Twelve. The St. Petersburg Codex of the Latter Prophets (AD 916) offers a verse count for the Book of the Twelve only.[17] It does, however, leave three empty lines between the individual writings.[18]

According to the production notes at the end of the book, the Cairo Codex of the Prophets was created "at the end of the year 827, after the destruction of the second temple" (= AD 895), although carbon dating indicates that it is

---

See Josef M. Oesch, *Petucha und Setuma: Untersuchungen zu einer überlieferten Gliederung im hebräischen Text des Alten Testament*, OBO 27 (Göttingen: Vandenhoeck & Ruprecht; Fribourg: Presses Universitaires, 1979), 286.

14. Philippe Guillaume, "A Reconsideration of Manuscripts Classified as Scrolls of the Twelve Minor Prophets (XII)," *JHebS* 7 (2007): art. 16, doi:10.5508/jhs.2007.v7.a16. See also his article "The Unlikely Malachi-Jonah Sequence (4QXIIa)," *JHebS* 6 (2006): art. 15, doi:10.5508/jhs.2006.v6.a15, which counters Jones's proposal (n. 12). Cf. Mika S. Pajunen and Hanne von Weissenberg, "The Book of Malachi, Manuscript 4Q76 (4QXIIa), and the Formation of the 'Book of the Twelve'," *JBL* 135 (2015): 731–51, who conclude that in its present state "4Q76 attests only to the books of Malachi and Jonah" (738). Christophe L. Nihan ("Remarques sur la question de l'«unité» des XII," in *The Book of the Twelve—One Book or Many? Metz Conference Proceedings, 5–7 November 2015*, ed. Elena di Pede and Danatella Scaiola, FAT 2/91 [Tübingen: Mohr Siebeck, 2016], 145–65) highlights the fluidity of textual traditions and of the sequencing of books (147–56).

15. Elsewhere, the phrase "the count of the verses" usually precedes the number in Hebrew words and is found in the Twelve with Obadiah and Nahum. Hosea, Amos, and Zechariah only have the actual verse count. Joel, Jonah, Micah, Habakkuk, Zephaniah, Haggai, and Malachi each conclude with the number followed by "verses."

16. Of the original 491 pages of the Aleppo Codex, 196 have been lost, including three pages from Amos 8:13 to Mic 5:1 (including the books of Obadiah and Jonah) and four pages from the end of Zephaniah to Zech 9:17 (including Haggai).

17. Cf. Christian D. Ginsburg, *Introduction to the Massoretico-Critical Edition of the Hebrew Bible* (London: Trinitarian Bible Society, 1897; repr., Jerusalem: Ktav, 1966), 95.

18. An image of the Hosea-Joel transition in the St. Petersburg Codex of the Latter Prophets is at https://www.alamy.com/ (Image ID: EAJXRY); see https://bit.ly/2DanOOS.

not earlier than the eleventh century.[19] While not the oldest known surviving Hebrew manuscript that contains the entire text of the Nevi'im (Former and Latter Prophets), it belongs to roughly the same period as the Aleppo and Leningrad Codices. One of its interesting features is the use of *bqšw 't-yhwh kl* ("seek YHWH everyone," from Zeph 2:3) or *dršw yhwh bhmṣ'w* ("seek YHWH while he may be found," from Isa 55:6) at the end of each book.[20] In between Joshua and Judges (text damaged), Judges and Samuel, Samuel and Kings, and so on, this inscription is part of a whole column that marks the break between books. The individual minor prophets, except for Habakkuk, are separated by the inscription but by no additional space or artwork. So again, the individual minor prophets are treated as distinct entities but not as full-scale books. A verse count is offered for the Book of the Twelve and not for individual parts thereof. Whether the lack of an inscription between Nahum and Habakkuk is an oversight or meant as an invitation to read them together as one is difficult to determine. Nahum-Habakkuk form a good unit, but it seems unlikely that the scribes of this codex thought of eleven rather than twelve minor prophetic books.

Apart from such questions of designation, there are two main lines of argument to support the idea that this collection of prophetic writings is designed to be read as a complete literary work. One focuses on interconnections within the Book of the Twelve and the other on discerning an overarching plot or global structure. Some connections between neighboring books are impressive and may indicate an attempt to stitch consecutive books together.[21] But others are less persuasive and suggest that no such attempt of stitching books together was carried through the whole corpus.[22] Indeed, Franz Delitzsch, who appears to have been the first to observe these keyword connections, thought that they were the reason for the sequence in which the already completed books were arranged rather than the product of redactional work specifically designed to stitch the books together.[23] In

19. Cf. Emanuel Tov, *Textual Criticism of the Hebrew Bible*, 3rd ed. (Minneapolis: Fortress, 2011), 45–46.

20. The line from Isaiah concludes Jeremiah, Ezekiel, Hosea, Micah, and Malachi; the other books conclude with the line from Zephaniah. Only Habakkuk is not given a concluding inscription.

21. Hos 14:1(2) // Joel 2:12; Joel 3:16 (4:16) // Amos 1:2; Amos 9:12 // Obad 19; Obad 1 // Jonah (a messenger sent to the nations); Jonah 4:2 // Mic 7:18–19 // Nah 1:2–3; Nah 1:1 // Hab 1:1 (same genre designation); Hab 2:20 // Zeph 1:7.

22. E.g., the link between Obad 1 and Jonah is not, strictly speaking, of a literary nature. Jonah 4:2; Mic 7:18–19; and Nah 1:2–3 all reflect Exod 34:6–7, a tradition that is often alluded to in other parts of Scripture. The *maśśā'* designation in Nah 1:1 and Hab 1:1 is of course also found in Zech 9:1; 12:1; Mal 1:1 and outside the Book of the Twelve.

23. Franz Delitzsch, "Wann weissagte Obadja?" *Zeitschrift für die gesamte lutherische*

the light of the varying quality of these links, this view has something to be said for it. But even if the links were redactional, this is not sufficient evidence for substantial editorial work with the aim of creating a larger literary unit. As regards additional literary and thematic connections between the books, similar links can be seen with books outside the Twelve, especially to the book of Isaiah.[24] Such links could be either the unintentional result of a common tradition or the product of an intentional cross-referencing that invites reading the canonical books as a theologically coherent whole, rather than editorial work seeking to establish a strong literary-rhetorical unit.

The search for keyword connections as well as the attempt to trace a storyline through the collection are at first sight hampered by the fact that the sequence of the Minor Prophets varies in different traditions. But a case has been made for purposeful ordering of each major tradition.[25] Indeed, it has been suggested that the different sequences of LXX and MT reflect the fact that "the Book of the Twelve as a whole might address two very different hermeneutical agendas that originated ultimately in different historical periods."[26] Alas, we do not have evidence from antiquity to confirm that readers perceived these differing agendas. Nogalski examines two examples that he believes demonstrate that in some instances the Book of the Twelve was read as a corpus in its own right even in antiquity: Sirach and Jerome.[27] (He explicitly disclaims that this was necessarily the dominant reading.) But the first example cannot serve to substantiate the presence of a specific hermeneutical agenda that relates to the order in which the prophetic writings appear in the corpus, while the second only attests to a belief that the order of the writings was determined by chronology.

Nogalski observes that Sirach's summary in 49:10 picks up the significant

---

Theologie und Kirche 12 (1851): 91–102. Delitzsch did not consider the second option in this essay, which is really concerned with the dating of the ministry of the prophet Obadiah.

24. See, e.g., Erich Bosshard-Nepustil, *Rezeptionen von Jesaia 1–39 im Zwölfprophetenbuch: Untersuchungen zur literarischen Verbindung von Prophetenbüchern in babylonischer und persischer Zeit*, OBO 154 (Göttingen: Vandenhoeck & Ruprecht; Fribourg: Presses Universitaires, 1997); Gerlinde Baumann, "Connected by Marriage, Adultery, and Violence: The Prophetic Marriage Metaphor in the Book of the Twelve and in the Major Prophets," in *Society of Biblical Literature 1999 Seminar Papers*, SBLSP 38 (Atlanta: Society of Biblical Literature, 1999), 552–69.

25. For the MT, see Paul R. House, *The Unity of the Twelve*, JSOTSup 77 (Sheffield: Sheffield Academic, 1990). For LXX and MT, see Marvin A. Sweeney, "The Place and Function of Joel in the Book of the Twelve," in *Society of Biblical Literature 1999 Seminar Papers*, 570–95. Jones (*Formation*) argues that the original order of books within the collection is that of 4QXIIa, of which the LXX is a close variation.

26. Sweeney, "Place and Function," 595.

27. James D. Nogalski, "The Book of the Twelve Is Not a Hypothesis," in di Pede and Scaiola, *Book of the Twelve*, 37–59.

role hope plays in this corpus, even if more passages are devoted to judgment, and argues that Sirach's commitment to throne and altar influenced the specific example cited from the collection in 49:11–12 (referencing Zerubbabel and Jeshua son of Jozadak). This means that we are not able to deduce from Sirach 49:10–12 what sequence the prophetic writings followed in the Book of the Twelve accessible to Sirach and his readers or whether the sequence mattered to him. The longer prophetic books offer Sirach the opportunity to identify some of the experiences of the prophets Isaiah (Sir 48:20–25), Jeremiah (Sir 49:6–7), and Ezekiel (Sir 49:8), alongside key features of the writings attributed to them, but the same cannot be said for his summary of the Book of the Twelve. The summary of the Twelve is serviceable, but it could equally describe the major prophetic books, which also offer hope for the temple and Zion, especially to readers who are looking for it. Thus, the summary would not need to be changed if Hosea, Joel, or Malachi were missing—or indeed Nahum, Habakkuk, or Zephaniah. In other words, the reference in Sirach demonstrates the existence of the corpus, but it does not prove that Sirach considered this corpus a literary unit with a specific argument rather than an anthology of smaller writings attributed to individual prophets whose message was similar to that of the prophets who left behind more substantial works.

As for Nogalski's comments on Jerome, which focus on Jerome's treatment of Jonah, Nogalski is right to note that in his preface to the Vulgate, Jerome says that the Book of the Twelve is one book and establishes the principle that those writings that are undated should be placed in the same period as the last one mentioned, following the order in the Hebrew text. (Jerome does not offer an explanation for the different order in the Christian tradition of which he was a part.) But Nogalski fails to take into account that Jerome wrote commentaries on the individual prophetic writings and did not do so in their presumed chronological or any canonical order. Nahum was the first book on which Jerome commented (AD 392–393), once he apparently decided to offer commentaries on each of the twelve,[28] followed by Micah, Zephaniah, Haggai, and Habakkuk in short order, and then, having been interrupted by the Origenist controversy, Jonah and Obadiah (AD 396) and a decade later Zechariah, Malachi, Hosea, Joel, and Amos (AD 406). Jerome's exegesis of the historical sense is based on the presumed historical setting of each individual prophet. He does not ask what the historical sense of Jonah (or Nahum, Habakkuk, or Zephaniah) was in a Persian period

---

28. In his commentary on Obadiah, Jerome makes reference to an earlier allegorical reading of the book offered in his youth of which he is now ashamed; see *Commentaries on the Twelve Prophets*, ed. Thomas P. Scheck, vol. 1, Ancient Christian Texts (Downers Grove: IVP Academic, 2016), 276–77.

"Book of the Twelve." Nogalski believes that "Jerome's placement of Jonah as contemporary with Hosea, Amos, and Isaiah reflects his application of the reading strategy of the Twelve in the MT sequence."[29] This may well be so, in line with the principle expressed in the preface to the Vulgate of the Twelve. But the eighth-century setting can be inferred from 2 Kgs 14:23-25, which Jerome cites, without reference to the preceding date in the Book of the Twelve (Amos 1:1), and Jerome makes no reference to the presumed "reading strategy" in his introduction to Jonah, nor even in his introduction to Obadiah, the also-undated book preceding Jonah in the Hebrew text. In fact, as is typical for Jerome, he appeals to "the Hebrews" who "say that this is the man who, under Ahab, the king of Samaria and the very wicked Jezebel, fed in caves the one hundred prophets who did not bend their knees to Baal."[30] Not only is there no appeal to Amos 1:1, but the implied setting is in fact *earlier* than Amos's by some seven decades. What this demonstrates is that there was considerable interest at the time in dating these prophetic figures and that people were clutching at any "evidence" that might help with this. Using the last-mentioned date within the anthology to date an otherwise undated prophet seems to have been one of the strategies adopted, possibly as a last resort (as it was overridden in the case of Obadiah by the link with a figure named Obadiah in Ahab's time). This seems to have happened with dates given for Nahum.

Nahum, whose announcement of the fall of Nineveh sounds definitive, must obviously have prophesied later than Jonah, whose announcement of Nineveh's destruction was either postponed or annulled by repentance. But how much later? Nogalski observes that both the author or emender of Tob 14:3-4 (some texts read "Jonah," others "Nahum")[31] and Josephus (*Jewish Antiquities* 9.239-42) place Nahum in the eighth century. He links this with the principle that an undated prophet is to be dated with reference to the last dated prophet mentioned in the (Hebrew) Book of the Twelve, in this case Mic 1:1.[32] This may have been the reasoning, but it is less clear that the specific dating played a significant role in the theological reflection around Nineveh. Jonah's chronological priority was a given, as noted above, and specific attempts to correlate Jonah and Nahum were surely prompted by historical and theological interests that would have been present even if the two writings had not been transmitted within the same scroll. It is notewor-

29. Nogalski, "Not a Hypothesis," 51.

30. Jerome, *Twelve*, 277-78. Cf. 1 Kgs 18:3-4.

31. Tobit, who had been deported by the Assyrians, assembles his sons to instruct them with words that include, "I believe the word of God that Jonah/Nahum spoke about Nineveh, that all these things will take place and overtake Assyria and Nineveh."

32. Nogalski, "Not a Hypothesis," 52.

thy that Josephus places Nahum in the reign of Jotham (*Ant.* 9.236–38),[33] the first mentioned king in Mic 1:1, rather than that of Hezekiah, the last mentioned, thus bringing Nahum as close to Jonah as possible. This was perhaps to suggest that Nineveh's repentance was very short-lived. Other than using the sequence of writings to help determine a prophet's chronology, there is little evidence that anyone in antiquity read the Book of the Twelve as a single literary unit in a way that noticeably influenced the interpretation of the individual prophetic writings therein.

It is to be expected that the debate around how to read the Book of the Twelve will continue for a little while longer. Useful presentations with opposing views can be found in the compilations of essays edited by James D. Nogalski and Marvin A. Sweeney;[34] by Ehud Ben Zvi and James D. Nogalski;[35] by Rainer Albertz, James D. Nogalski, and Jakob Wöhrle;[36] by Elena di Pede and Danatella Scaiola;[37] and by Heiko Wenzel.[38] In my view, the Book of the Twelve is not the result of extensive reshaping of the individual writings, although it seems that some thought went into arranging them in a certain order. Thus, the order Micah-Nahum-Habakkuk-Zephaniah in MT highlights similarities between Micah and Nahum and between Nahum and Habakkuk,[39] encouraging readers to read these prophetic writings alongside

33. See *Ant.* 9.239, although later Nahum is said to have prophesied 115 years before the fall of Nineveh (9.242), which would place him firmly in the reign of Ahaz according to modern reconstructions of the chronology.

34. James D. Nogalski and Marvin A. Sweeney, eds., *Reading and Hearing the Book of the Twelve*, SBL SymS 15 (Atlanta: Society of Biblical Literature, 2000).

35. Ehud Ben Zvi and James D. Nogalski, eds., *Two Sides of a Coin: Juxtaposing Views on Interpreting the Book of the Twelve/the Twelve Prophetic Books*, Analecta Gorgiana 201 (Piscataway, NJ: Gorgias, 2009).

36. Rainer Albertz, James D. Nogalski, and Jakob Wöhrle, eds., *Perspectives on the Formation of the Book of the Twelve: Methodological Foundations—Redactional Processes—Historical Insights*, BZAW 433 (Berlin: de Gruyter, 2012).

37. Di Pede and Scaiola, *Book of the Twelve*.

38. Heiko Wenzel, ed., *The Book of the Twelve: An Anthology of Prophetic Books or the Result of Complex Redactional Processes?*, Osnabrücker Studien zur Jüdischen und Christlichen Bibel 4 (Göttingen: Vandenhoeck & Ruprecht, 2018). See also two literature reviews: Ida Willi-Plein, "Das Zwölfprophetenbuch," *TRu* 64 (1999): 351–95; Paul L. Redditt, "Recent Research on the Book of the Twelve as One Book," *CurBR* 9 (2001): 47–80. Some issues for interpretation with special reference to Hosea and Amos are outlined in Jörg Jeremias, "Neuere Tendenzen der Forschung an den Kleinen Propheten," in *Perspectives in the Study of the Old Testament and Early Judaism: A Symposium in Honour of Adam S. van der Woude on the Occasion of His 70th Birthday*, ed. Florentino García Martínez and Edward Noort, VTSup 73 (Leiden: Brill, 1998), 122–36.

39. Cf. Klaas Spronk, "Synchronic and Diachronic Approaches to the Book of Nahum," in *Synchronic or Diachronic? A Debate on Method in Old Testament Exegesis*, ed. Johannes C. Moor (Leiden: Brill, 1995), 185.

each other. (The LXX sequence ensures that Jonah and Nahum are read together.) Such similarities could easily have arisen as a result of prophets being influenced by each other and by a common liturgical tradition (esp. Exod
34:6–7).[40] This view has been shaped by basic methodological preferences
(on which I side with Ben Zvi more often than Nogalski) and was confirmed
by my examination of specific issues, such as references to Torah within the
Book of the Twelve and the relationship of Habakkuk to its co-texts,[41] as well
as my supervision of an MTh in which my student Simon Wakeling made a
strong, but in my view not ultimately persuasive, case for reading the Book
of the Twelve as a cohesive, single entity.[42]

I do not exclude the possibility that the book of Malachi was written specifically to conclude the Book of the Twelve, nor that significant redactional
work reshaped the book of Hosea to serve as an introduction to the collection, nor that either of these things are true for the book of Joel. It need
not be denied that we can learn things by studying the Book of the Twelve
as a whole, and it may well be profitable to notice connections within this
prophetic collection especially—and perhaps not just because a theological
interpretation needs to consider individual biblical books in the context of
the canon as a whole (including the New Testament). But I see no evidence
for significant editorial work in Nahum, Habakkuk, or Zephaniah to encourage reading them as chapters of a larger whole, and I want to affirm the
individual integrity of these prophetic books as means of communication.[43]
The collection that we designate the Book of the Twelve is neither the small-

40. Developing a proposal by Raymond C. VanLeeuwen ("Scribal Wisdom and Theodicy
in the Book of the Twelve," in *In Search of Wisdom: Essays in Memory of John G. Gammie*,
ed. Leo G. Perdue, Bernard Brandon Scott, and William Johnston Wiseman [Philadelphia:
Westminster John Knox Press, 1993], 31–34), Wakeling ("The Minor Prophets as a Unity
Developing Theodicy," *Ecclesia Reformanda* 2 [2010]: 124–53) argues that citations of and
allusions to Exod 34:6–7 give coherence to the Book of the Twelve. Cf. Jakob Wöhrle, "A
Prophetic Reflection on Divine Forgiveness: The Integration of the Book of Jonah into
the Book of the Twelve," *JHebS* 9 (2009): art. 7, doi:10.5508/jhs.2009.v9.a7; "So Many
Cross-References! Methodological Reflections on the Problem of Intertextual Relationships
and Their Significance for Redaction Critical Analysis," in Albertz, Nogalski, and Wöhrle,
Perspectives on the Formation, 3–20; Donatella Scaiola, "The Twelve, One or Many Books?
A Theological Proposal," in di Pede and Scaiola, *Book of the Twelve*, 180–93, esp. 190–93.

41. Thomas Renz, "Torah in the Minor Prophets," in *Reading the Law: Studies in Honour
of Gordon J. Wenham*, ed. J. Gordon McConville and Karl Möller, LHBOTS 461 (London:
T&T Clark, 2007), 73–94; "Habakkuk and Its Co-Texts," in Wenzel, *Book of the Twelve*,
13–36.

42. An essay based on the thesis was later published as Wakeling, "Minor Prophets"
(see n. 40).

43. Note the illuminating research into the nature of anthologies in antiquity by Martin
Beck, "Das Dodekapropheton als Anthologie," *ZAW* 118 (2006): 558–81.

est defensible literary unit within which to study Nahum, Habakkuk, and Zephaniah nor the largest within which we need to study these writings. If the individual writings originated largely independent of a larger *literary* context,[44] the context of the Book of the Twelve may be best discussed when offering further reflections than in the actual exegesis.

IV. NAHUM, HABAKKUK, AND ZEPHANIAH IN THE BOOK OF THE TWELVE

The question of the place of Nahum, Habakkuk, and Zephaniah within the Book of the Twelve relates to the issue of the redaction and literary unity of the Book of the Twelve (see above). The three books are usually seen as belonging closely together; they are in the same sequence in all manuscripts. In his two-volume work on the origin of the Book of the Twelve, Nogalski proposed that (an earlier form of) Zephaniah originally formed a "Deuteronomistic corpus" with versions of Hosea, Amos, and Micah.[45] But he argues that in the formation of a "Book of the Nine," a predecessor to the Book of the Twelve, three sub-groupings were formed, the middle one comprising Nahum, Habakkuk, and Zephaniah. What do these three books have in common that marks them as a group? If we consider literary style, subject matter, and manner of narration, there is nothing to distinguish these three as a group from other prophetic books in the Twelve and beyond. In House's view, Micah summarizes the first half of the Book of the Twelve before Nahum announces the "crisis," which is brought to a climax and turning point in Habakkuk. Zephaniah embodies both the climax and the "falling action" prior to the resolution offered in the last three prophetic writings.[46] He suggests that Nahum, Habakkuk, and Zephaniah focus on the punishment, while the previous six prophetic volumes focused on sin and the final three will focus on restoration. House recognizes that most prophetic collections

---

44. I believe this to be the case for Nahum, Habakkuk, and Zephaniah. Joel and Malachi—and maybe Obadiah and Jonah—are the most likely candidates for having been composed with the larger collection in mind.

45. James D. Nogalski, *Literary Precursors to the Book of the Twelve*, BZAW 217 (Berlin: de Gruyter, 1993); *Redactional Processes in the Book of the Twelve*, BZAW 218 (Berlin: de Gruyter, 1993). Nogalski was followed by Aaron Schart, "Redactional Models: Comparisons, Contrasts, Agreements, Disagreements," in *SBL Seminar Papers 1998, Part Two* (Atlanta: Society of Biblical Literature, 1998), 893–908. Nogalski's PhD student Nicholas R. Werse recently offered a careful modification in *Reconsidering the Book of the Four: The Shaping of Hosea, Amos, Micah, and Zephaniah as an Early Prophetic Collection*, BZAW 517 (Berlin: de Gruyter, 2019).

46. House, *Unity*, 139–51.

contain all three elements, so how much one of these elements is in the foreground is a matter of degree. In his view, Zephaniah "completes the bottom of the U-shaped [storyline of the Book of the Twelve] and begins the journey upwards."[47] To my mind, the broad brush with which House paints fails to do justice to the individual writings. In a sense there is a "journey upwards" with YHWH's answer in Hab 2 and the prophet's response in Hab 3, while the bulk of Zephaniah could very much represent the bottom of the U-shape. The end of Zephaniah takes us vigorously on "the journey upwards" but so does, for example, the end of Amos.[48]

This leaves me with what was essentially the position advocated by Delitzsch:[49] the traditional arrangement of the collection is broadly in the order of chronological setting so that the prophets of the Assyrian period (including Nahum) precede the material that relates to the Babylonian period (Habakkuk, but especially Zephaniah) and the books of the Persian period prophets (Haggai, Malachi). But chronological considerations have sometimes been discarded in favor of thematic considerations and keyword connections. Within the MT sequence, Hosea opens the Book of the Twelve as the largest of the Minor Prophets, followed by Joel, which (a) opens with a lament over the destruction of the crop, continuing, by way of reversal, the nature theme with which Hosea ended; (b) includes a call to repentance in 2:12 that is reminiscent of Hos 14:1(2); and (c) more or less closes with the depiction of YHWH roaring from Zion in 3:16 (4:16), with which Amos begins (1:2). The phrase about inheriting the remnant of Edom in Amos 9:12 may well have encouraged the positioning of Obadiah straight after Amos, and Jonah is indeed in some sense "an envoy sent among the nations" (Obad. 1). Jonah, Micah, and Nahum share the use of Exod 34:6–7 (see also Joel 2:13).[50]

47. House, *Unity*, 151.

48. Grace Ko ("The Ordering of the Twelve as Israel's Historiography," in *Prophets, Prophecy and Ancient Israelite Historiography*, ed. Mark J. Boda and Lissa M. Wray Beal [Winona Lake, IN: Eisenbrauns, 2013], 315–32) seeks to revive House's proposal with particular attention to Habakkuk's location "at the lowest point of the *U*" (326), but she fails to explain how the U-shape would have been compromised if the positions of Habakkuk and Zephaniah had been reversed.

49. Delitzsch, "Wann weissagte Obadja?"

50. See Ruth Scoralick, *Gottes Güte und Gottes Zorn: Die Gottesprädikationen in Exodus 34,6f und ihre intertextuellen Beziehungen zum Zwölfprophetenbuch*, HBS 33 (Freiburg im Breisgau: Herder, 2002) for the view that this is a key text holding the Book of the Twelve together. Jan P. Bosman ("The Paradoxical Presence of Exodus 34:6–7 in the Book of the Twelve," *Scriptura* 87 [2004]: 233–43) stresses the very diverse use made of the text. Martin Roth (*Israel und die Völker im Zwölfprophetenbuch: Eine Untersuchung zu den Büchern Joel, Jona, Micha und Nahum*, FRLANT 210 [Göttingen: Vandenhoeck & Ruprecht, 2005], 150–52, 247–48, 253–57) is explicit in rejecting the view that the various uses of Exod 34:6–7 belong to the same literary layer, as is Ehud Ben Zvi ("Remembering Twelve Prophetic

Micah separates Nahum from Jonah (not so in much of the Greek tradition, in which Nahum follows straight from Jonah). The reason may have been a desire to bring the two allusions to the Exod 34:6–7 tradition in Micah (toward the end of the book) and Nahum (at the beginning of the book) closer together. But this has the effect of creating a greater gap between the allusions in Jonah and those in Micah and Nahum. The sequence Micah-Jonah-Nahum would have been no less effective for bringing allusions to Exod 34 into closer proximity. It appears to me, therefore, that the juxtaposition of Nahum and Habakkuk created by the order Micah-Nahum is the more important reason. Here chronological and thematic considerations coalesce. Nahum concerns the end of the Assyrian empire and Habakkuk the rise of the Babylonian one not only by way of being set in that period but also by actually addressing the significance of these empires. Zephaniah is the only minor prophet explicitly set in the (preexilic) Babylonian period.[51] No exilic prophet is among the Minor Prophets. The exilic period, as far as explicit setting is concerned anyway, is the domain of the Major Prophets and their editors.

Thus, the main reason for grouping Nahum, Habakkuk, and Zephaniah together in the Book of the Twelve and for discussing them in one commentary is their setting at the point of changing empires, which had a huge impact on the life of the nation of Judah. The thematic links between these books are explained by their historical context. A few scholars have argued that Nahum and Habakkuk form a literary unit, arranged in a palistrophe:[52]

A	Hymn reflecting a theophany	Nah 1
B	Threatening speech against Nineveh	Nah 2–3
X	The problem of theodicy	Hab 1 (or Hab 1:1–2:5)
B'	Threatening speech against evildoers	Hab 2 (or Hab 2:6–20)
A'	Hymn reflecting a theophany	Hab 3

Characters from the Past," in di Pede and Scaiola, *Book of the Twelve*, 6–36), who raises methodological questions about the steps that lead scholars like Wöhrle to conclude that all passages citing Exod 34:6–7 are later additions (9–12).

51. In fact, I suspect that the core of Zephaniah is older than the core of Habakkuk. Habakkuk, while it includes a prophecy of the rise of the Babylonians, focuses on their destructive impact. Zephaniah takes a chronological step back, announcing a disaster yet to come, but its final thrust is the restoration after the destruction, and this makes its position after Habakkuk defensible in terms of the grand chronological movement implied in the collection.

52. See Rainer Kessler, "Nahum-Habakuk als Zweiprophetenschrift: Eine Skizze," in *"Wort JHWHs, das geschah . . ." (Hos 1,1): Studien zum Zwölfprophetenbuch*, ed. Erich Zenger, HBS 35 (Freiburg im Breisgau: Herder, 2002), 149–58. Cf. Duane A. Christensen, "The Book of Nahum: A History of Interpretation," in Watts and House, *Forming Prophetic Literature*, 187–94, 193.

But the generic differences between the two "hymns" are significant, as are those between the two instances of "threatening speech," and there are no clear verbal signals or connections to suggest such an arrangement was in the mind of any of the authors or editors involved in the process.[53] Fabry notes the absence of Habakkuk's key term *ḥāmās* ("violence," 1:2–3, 9; 2:8, 17 [2×]) from Nahum.[54]

V. NAHUM, HABAKKUK, AND ZEPHANIAH AND THEIR CONSTITUENT UNITS

The macrostructure of a biblical book is rarely, if ever, uncontroversial. Proposals for the literary structure of a book are reading strategies. In modern books, some sort of structure is often provided by the author in the form of headings and a table of contents.[55] Readers usually feel the need to divide biblical texts in units smaller than those provided by titles or headings. The use of conventional introductory formulae is sometimes used as a cue for such subdivisions. It is worth bearing in mind that proposals for the literary structure of a book are often not right or wrong but rather more or less appropriate or successful. Criteria for appropriateness and successfulness vary depending on the purpose of the structure, but most readers will probably agree that structures that account for a greater number of the characteristic features of a text are to be considered more successful.

Instead of merely providing a structural outline for each of the three books, the following offers a discussion of noteworthy features which ought to be considered in deciding on a structure.[56] Such a consideration of features of the text gives a sense of the texture of the piece of writing, whether one agrees with the literary structure on which this commentary will settle or not. Indeed, with regard to all three of the writings explored in this commentary, it is unlikely that we will ever come to an agreement on a structure that fulfills all purposes—especially not one that operates on several levels. But it

53. I discuss this in more detail in Thomas Renz, "Habakkuk and Its Co-Texts." I find myself also in substantial agreement with Tchavdar S. Hadjiev, "Zephaniah and the 'Book of the Twelve' Hypothesis," in *Prophecy and the Prophets in Ancient Israel: Proceedings of the Oxford Old Testament Seminar*, ed. John Day, LHBOTS 531 (London: T&T Clark, 2010), 325–38.

54. Heinz-Josef Fabry, *Habakuk/Obadja*, HThKAT (Freiburg: Herder, 2018), 129. Fabry makes this observation in connection with a list of parallels between Nahum and Habakkuk.

55. Even then, readers can conceptualize a different arrangement and may gain new insights into the text in this way.

56. Cf. *CHP*, esp. ch. 7; Ernst R. Wendland, *The Discourse Analysis of Hebrew Prophetic Literature: Determining the Larger Textual Units of Hosea and Joel*, Mellen Biblical Press Series 40 (Lewiston: Mellen, 1995).

is evident that some parts of the text hang more closely together than others, and by paying attention to such things as alterations of speaker, addressee, topic or setting, transitional expressions such as "therefore," exclamatory utterances, rhetorical questions, and repetitions both in successive lines and of earlier material, we gain a greater intimacy with the text. It is debatable how far the ancients thought of literary structures. I am skeptical about the importance of complex structures of divisions and subdivisions in a context in which even what we would call literature was mostly oral. I want to avoid superimposing a carefully worked out structure that corresponds to my own aesthetic sense. But it need not be questioned that ancient readers felt a difference between more and less pronounced breaks, and my aim will be to get the right feel for the text in that respect.

As for the smallest units, there is still little agreement concerning the issue of rhythm in the Hebrew text. I use a twofold method to determine the rhythm of a passage and count "feet" and "stresses" on the basis of the masoretic accentuation.[57] The number of feet (word units) corresponds to the number of masoretic accents (conjunctive and disjunctive) and the number of stresses to the number of disjunctive accents.[58] The masoretic accentuation is designed to fulfill a variety of functions. Its main purpose appears to be "to regulate the musical modulation or recitation."[59] This suggests that the Masoretes were interested in the length of units and in rhythm, even if for a different purpose than modern commentators. I have dealt with the relationship between colometry and masoretic accentuation in more detail in a separate monograph.[60] This commentary largely refrains from technical

57. The use of *maqqep* may not be consistent enough for this method to warrant full confidence. But insofar as word combinations can be drawn together to an accentual unit or pronounced more distinctly as separate units, ignoring the *maqqep* does not automatically lead to more reliable results. In cases of doubt, words combined with *maqqep* need careful (re)examination.

58. In rare cases such as Exod 20:2, there is double accentuation, indicating two different ways of reading (or chanting) the text, and the number of feet and stresses cannot be ascertained simply by counting accents.

59. JM 15e. Cf. Israel Yeivin, *Introduction to the Tiberian Masorah*, ed. and trans. E. John Revell, Masoretic Studies 5 (Missoula: Scholars Press, 1980), 158.

60. Thomas Renz, *Colometry and Accentuation in Hebrew Prophetic Poetry*, KUSATU 4 (Waltrop: Spenner, 2003). The book includes a colography of Nahum, Habakkuk, and Zephaniah in line with my understanding of the masoretic colometry on pp. 106–21. Two mistakes need to be corrected: Nah 3:19a and Hab 1:12a are only one colon each in the masoretic scheme. Sung Jin Park, "Application of the Tiberian Accentuation System for Colometry of Biblical Hebrew Poetry," *JNSL* 39 (2013): 113–27, while supportive, considers my application of the rules too strict, because it occasionally creates unbalanced poetic lines like these. My intention in *Colometry and Accentuation* was to propose a strictly objective procedure for moving from the accentuation to its implied colometry. I accept that the resulting colometry

discussions of the poetry and uses "line" and "lines" interchangeably with "colon" and "cola." Hence, a bicolon can be spoken of here as consisting of two and a tricolon of three lines. Others use "line" for a bicolon and "half-line" for a colon. The usage in this commentary was influenced by the way I have chosen to present the translation of these prophetic texts, with each colon being on a separate line.

VI. AN OUTLINE OF THE LATE NEO-ASSYRIAN AND EARLY NEO-BABYLONIAN PERIOD

In this section, we will briefly consider the implied historical setting of the three books interpreted in this commentary. On my reading, and broadly speaking, Nahum is set in the period before the fall of Nineveh in 612 BC, which brought the Neo-Assyrian Empire to an end, but after 664/663, because it looks back to the fall of Thebes (see below). Habakkuk is set in the period around the rise of the Neo-Babylonian Empire; I will argue below that the setting is in fact after the rise of the Babylonians rather than shortly before, as many others believe. Zephaniah is placed in the days of Josiah in the second half of the seventh century, around the decline and end of the Neo-Assyrian Empire. The question whether Zephaniah should be dated early or late in Josiah's three-decade reign is discussed in the introduction to Zephaniah. For this general overview, it is sufficient to note that the three books are set in the period between 660 and 600 BC. This alone makes it interesting to deal with them in one volume. None of the other prophetic books are set in this period of transition from the Neo-Assyrian to the Neo-Babylonian Empire. The setting need not imply that the three books were written at that time, but it is my best guess that in the case of Nahum, Habakkuk, and Zephaniah, the implied setting is also the time at which (most of) the material originated and was put together.

The beginning of the Neo-Assyrian Empire is usually dated from the reign of Ashur-dan II (934–912), under whom a long period of Assyrian decline was reversed. Its climax came with Tiglath-pileser III (744–727), who seems to have come to the throne as a usurper. In several western campaigns, he consolidated Assyrian control over Syria and the eastern Mediterranean, turning local rulers into Assyrian vassals obliged to pay annual tributes. Failure to pay was punished, usually by the appointment of a new ruler, territorial reductions, deportations of members of the upper class, and increased

---

is occasionally unsatisfactory. My own colometry, therefore, is not always in agreement with that of the MT. Accepting such divergence seems to me preferable to bending the rules to make the alleged masoretic colometry fit my own.

tribute payments. Further anti-Assyrian activity could lead to destruction and annexation. Notably, Damascus fell in 732. The Assyrian preference was for keeping profitable commercial centers such as Tyre and Gaza intact without annexing them. In this way, they tried to extract maximum benefit from these cities at minimum cost.

Tiglath-pileser III was succeeded by his son Shalmaneser V (727–722), who destroyed Shechem and besieged Tyre, bringing Sidon, Akko, and the inland territories of Tyre under Assyrian control. Samaria fell in 722, ending the Northern Kingdom of Israel. Sargon II (721–705) had to quell a series of rebellions triggered by the instability that preceded his reign but proved largely successful doing so both in the west, where he collected tribute from Hezekiah among others and stationed a garrison at the Egyptian border, and in the east, where he ultimately ousted Merodach-baladan, the king of Babylon, who for a while had succeeded in uniting his country in opposition to Assyrian domination. After Sargon's death, Merodach-baladan briefly regained the throne of Babylon, but Sargon's successor, Sennacherib (704–681), who concentrated much of his military effort on Babylonia, proved too strong for him. Sennacherib also campaigned in the west, bringing much destruction to Judah in 701, including, famously, the sacking of the Judean fortresses Lachish and Azekah, but without conquering Jerusalem itself. It seems that Assyrian culture and religion were not forced upon subject nations, but its dominance could not but shape even those who sought to resist Assyria, let alone any who wanted to ingratiate themselves with the empire.

Esarhaddon (681–669) strengthened Assyrian domination in the east, pursuing a policy of appeasement and rebuilding Babylon. Egyptian attempts to shake off the Assyrian yoke were met by the invasion of Egypt; Esarhaddon took Memphis and gained control of the Nile delta.[61] Assyria seemed at the height of its power, but Esarhaddon's successor Assurbanipal (668–627 [?]) was required to recapture Memphis twice, the second time penetrating far enough into Egypt to take the city of Thebes (ca. 664/663). The latter event, which ended Nubian rule over Egypt, is remembered in Nah 3:8. To Judeans, Assyrian power might have seemed irresistible at that time. But Assurbanipal faced serious problems in the east. Esarhaddon had laid careful plans for his succession, appointing one of his sons, Assurbanipal, heir to the throne in Assyria but another, Shamash-shuma-ukin, heir to the throne in Babylonia. If his idea was to thereby strengthen the union of Assyria and Babylonia, it proved a major error of judgment. Shamash-shuma-ukin gained the support of the Babylonians against his brother and, allied with Elamites and Arabs, sought to gain independence from Assyria.

---

61. For more details see the excursus "Assyrian Campaigns against Egypt" in the commentary on Nahum 3:8.

The resulting civil war lasted four years (652–648). It was ultimately won by Assurbanipal, who then conducted raids into Elam, capturing and destroying Susa. Assurbanipal was also keenly interested in cultural pursuits and undertook extensive building projects. With Assurbanipal's attention focused on the east, Egypt apparently transitioned from being an Assyrian vassal to being an ally on a more equal footing, able to exercise influence on the eastern Mediterranean coast.

Either toward the end of Assurbanipal's reign or upon his death, the Babylonians tried again to be free of Assyrian control. Under Nabopolassar's leadership, this fight for freedom was ultimately won. Nabopolassar was crowned king of Babylon (625–605), marking the beginning of the Neo-Babylonian Empire. Elam was very weak at the time, but the Medes allied themselves with the Babylonians as well, and together they managed to inflict one defeat after another on Assyria. In 614, Assur was captured. Nineveh fell in 612. The retreating Assyrian troops, now supported by the Egyptian army, were defeated at Harran in 610. In 605, Nabopolassar's son Nebuchadnezzar II led a surprise attack against the Egyptian army at Carchemish, forcing them to flee south. The news of his father's death prompted Nebuchadnezzar to return to Babylon to be crowned king (604–562) before returning to the west to take control of cities and territories formerly under Assyrian (and Egyptian) vassalage.

Assyria, which had exercised such a strong hold on the eastern Mediterranean shores for some three centuries, had brought the Kingdom of Israel to an end and inflicted oppression and devastation on Judah. But it was finished in a comparatively short period of time. Egypt was humiliated. And Babylonia under Nebuchadnezzar II became the new superpower to be feared. Nebuchadnezzar's relentless campaigning ensured that his empire included more or less the same territory as the former Assyrian Empire. His attempt in 601 to conquer Egypt was not successful, however. This prompted Jerusalem's king, Jehoiakim, to renounce the allegiance to Babylon that he had sworn after the Babylonian victory at Carchemish. The Babylonian response was the beginning of the end of the Kingdom of Judah, a tragedy that the Bible well documents elsewhere.

Nahum speaks to a people for whom Assyria seemed invincible, predicting the fall of Nineveh and the end of its empire. Zephaniah speaks into the period when Assyrian domination began to be less keenly felt but the Neo-Babylonian Empire was not yet on the horizon. Habakkuk addresses the problem that the divinely promised rise of the Neo-Babylonian Empire merely substituted one evil for another.

The Book of
NAHUM

Introduction

I. THE PROFILE OF THE BOOK

A. THE SUPERSCRIPTION

The heading in Nah 1:1 consists of two titles: *maśśā'* ("a pronouncement") *concerning Nineveh* (A) and *the document of a revelation to Nahum the Elkoshite* (B). Three unusual features deserve comment. First, the use of two titles is unique and may suggest that they did not originate together, as many commentators believe.[1] The headings to Amos, Micah, and Isaiah's pronouncement concerning Babylon (13:1), with which some commentators have compared Nah 1:1,[2] are constructed differently; these other headings do not truly constitute two titles, as the relative particle *'ăšer* combines the different parts of the titles in one syntactical unit.

Second, the (A) title is a heading of a form used frequently in the book of Isaiah (13:1; 15:1; 17:1; 19:1; 21:1, 11, 13 [unusually with preposition]; 22:1; 23:1; 30:6), which in one instance is further qualified with the phrase "which the prophet Isaiah saw" (13:1; cf. Hab 1:1). This is what we might have expected here as well: "*Maśśā'* concerning Nineveh that the prophet Nahum saw." Its absolute position at the beginning of a book is unique, and it is striking that readers are told that this is a *maśśā' concerning Nineveh* separately from (and prior to) being told that it is the *document of a revelation to Nahum the*

---

1. So, e.g., Karl Elliger, *Die Propheten Nahum, Habakuk, Zephanja, Haggai, Sacharja, Maleachi*, 6th ed., ATD 25 (Göttingen: Vandenhoeck & Ruprecht, 1967), 3; Klaus Seybold, *Nahum, Habakuk, Zephanja*, ZBK AT 24 (Zürich: Theologischer Verlag, 1991), 17; Jörg Jeremias, *Nahum*, BKAT 14 (Göttingen: Vandenhoeck & Ruprecht, 2019), 43–44.

2. Richard D. Patterson, *Nahum, Habakkuk, Zephaniah*, The Wycliffe Exegetical Commentary (Chicago: Moody Bible Institute, 1991), 20, with reference to Walter A. Maier, *The Book of Nahum: A Commentary* (Saint Louis: Concordia, 1959).

Elkoshite.[3] Only Mal 1:1 employs a strictly nonnarrative superscription that includes the designation *maśśāʾ*, but its use of the designation is different, as it apparently governs the phrase "word of YHWH." Thus, Mal 1:1 more closely resembles titles that use the prophetic word formula. The meaning of *maśśāʾ* has been much discussed. I side with those who believe that *maśśāʾ* designates a genre. This could be either an indirect form of prophetic communication or the prophetic interpretation of an earlier revelation (see commentary on 1:1). Nahum is an indirect prophetic communication in that the implied audience of the message and its main target are different from each other. It can also be read as a prophetic interpretation of an earlier revelation.[4]

Third, the use of *sēper* ("document") in the (B) title is unique among titles or superscriptions to prophetic books in the Bible. It has suggested to some that "Nahum is self-consciously a piece of literature."[5] This may well be true, although it is hard to substantiate.[6] It needs to be borne in mind that the boundary between oral and literary culture is fluid, and it is debatable what a self-conscious "piece of literature" would have looked like in the ancient world, in which probably most written literature was designed to be read out in public.[7] The use of *sēper* in the title is therefore not a reliable indicator that the message was not used orally. Nevertheless, the general scarcity of introductory formulae and of common prophetic speech forms supports the hypothesis that the book did not originate in oral proclamation. Regardless of its origin, the *sēper* designation may encourage readers (performers) to watch out for characteristics that are best perceived by an eye studying the written page.

All in all, the superscription provides us with three designations of the content of the book. The designation *ḥāzôn* is commonly translated "vision,"

---

3. Some believe that the heading originally belonged with chs. 2–3 only (e.g., Jeremias, *Nahum*, 44) but its present location remains unexplained by those who like Jeremias argue that the final composition is not concerned with Nineveh.

4. Floyd, *Minor Prophets 2*, 14–18; cf. Michael H. Floyd, "The Meaning of *Maśśāʾ* as a Prophetic Term in Isaiah," *JHebS* 18 (2018): art. 9, doi:10.5508/jhs.2018.v18.a9.

5. Ralph L. Smith, *Micah–Malachi*, WBC 32 (Waco: Word, 1984), 71; Adam S. van der Woude, "The Book of Nahum: A Letter Written in Exile," *OTS* 20 (1977): 108–26; cf. Carl Friedrich Keil, *Minor Prophets: Two Volumes in One*, Commentary on the Old Testament 10 (Edinburgh: T&T Clark, 1871; repr., Peabody: Hendrickson, 1989), 2:9. Wilhelm Rudolph (*Micha-Nahum-Habakuk-Zephanja*, KAT 13 [Gütersloh: Mohn, 1975], 150) notes Edelkoort's contention that Nahum published a pamphlet in Manasseh's reign, in which oral ministry was impossible; see A. H. Edelkoort, *Nahum, Habakuk, Zefanja: Drie profeten voor onzen tijd* (Amsterdam: H. J. Paris, 1937).

6. But see further below on the use of acrostic features as a sign of literariness.

7. For discussion, see Ehud Ben Zvi and Michael H. Floyd, eds., *Writings and Speech in Israelite and Ancient Near Eastern Prophecy*, SBL SymS 10 (Atlanta: Society of Biblical Literature, 2000), esp. the contributions by Robert C. Culley, John Van Seters, and Michael Floyd.

but the term does not necessarily imply a visionary experience in the common sense of the word. The root is also used in headings in Amos and Isaiah (cf. 2 Chr 32:32), both of which contain nonvisionary alongside visionary material, and in Obadiah, which does not contain any material explicitly derived from visionary experience.[8] The designation makes a claim about divine perception of a situation, not about the means by which this perception was received. This is also evident in occurrences outside titles in which *ḥāzôn* evidently does not refer to a visionary experience (e.g., Hab 2:2–3; 1 Chr 17:15; Prov 29:18). It is in fact only in Dan 8–11 that the term *ḥāzôn* is clearly used in connection with a supernatural visionary experience,[9] although there are other passages where such a reference is possible.[10] The term is therefore translated more generally here as *revelation*. Nahum is understood to be the recipient of the revelation (*revelation to Nahum*), not its originator, as "revelation of Nahum" might suggest. This designation invites us to read the book as divine communication.

Yet readers have access to this divine communication only through its documentation in a written "document." The additional designation alerts readers to the fact that revelation and documentation (and, implicitly, proclamation) are different communicative events. The question why this obvious truth was spelled out cannot be answered with confidence, but it may be simply to acknowledge that the fall of Nineveh is not present to the readers in the same way as to the author who received the initial divine communication. It is possible (but see my decision against this below) that the author received a divine perception of the fall of Nineveh prior to the event and that the book was composed after the event. Alternatively, the book may have been

8. The noun is used only in the headings to Nahum and Isaiah. John E. Goldingay (*Isaiah*, NIBCOT 13 [Peabody: Hendrickson; Carlisle: Paternoster, 2001]) proposed that the heading in Isaiah only covers ch. 1 (to which 2:1 serves as a conclusion) on the basis that *ḥāzôn* "always denotes a particular revelation" (33). But 2 Chr 32:32 suggests otherwise.

9. The expression *ḥāzôn laylâ* ("vision of the night") in Isa 29:7, where it is parallel to "dream," may also imply a supernatural experience. But there it is used as an image of something unsubstantial or unreal.

10. Note that descriptions of visionary experience always employ the root *rʾh*. While *ḥzh* is used with reference to prophetic activity in Isa 30:10 in parallel to *rʾh*, even there it is quite possible that *ḥzh* does not refer to visionary experience. In a similar vein, the references in Ezek 12:27–13:23; 21:29(34); 22:28 are not necessarily to supernatural experiences; they could just as well refer to divine communication more generally. Maybe other derivatives of *ḥzh* (e.g., *ḥizzāywôn*, *maḥăze*) were used to make more specific reference to a visionary experience, but these are rare and not exclusively used in this sense (see 2 Sam 7:17). The term *marʾê* = *marʾâ* was probably the most regular to refer definitely to a visionary experience (with reference to a specific visionary experience, e.g., Ezek 1:1; 11:24; 40:2; 43:3; Dan 8:16, 26–27; 9:23; 10:1, 7–8, 16; more generally, probably also in Num 12:6 where *marʾâ* is parallel to "dream" [*ḥălôm*]).

designed to be read (long) after the event as well as before. Given the use of acrostic features (see below), which seem to me qualities of written more than oral communication,[11] it is also possible that the designation is meant to alert readers to specifically *literary* qualities. As noted above, this would not exclude the possibility of oral performance. It seems to me likely that the biblical prophetic literature from its inception was designed for a larger audience than the small group of highly literate readers available at the time. There are ways in which a public reader could communicate the presence of an acrostic.[12] Sadly, we lack the relevant information about public performances that would allow us to move from speculation to hypothesis.

This *document of a revelation* is now encompassed in or published as *a pronouncement concerning Nineveh*. At first, this designation seems obvious from the contents of the book and easily substitutes for a reference to the historical setting of the prophecy. But the Hebrew text refers to Nineveh only twice in the body of the prophecy (2:9 [Eng. 8]; 3:7), less often and later in the book than we might have expected. In fact, some English translations supply further references to Nineveh (e.g., NIV at 1:8, 11, 14; 2:1[2]; REB at 1:11, 14). It stands to reason that the author deliberately held back on referring to Nineveh in order to stress the universal applicability of the hymn in ch. 1. The title to some extent undoes this, maybe with a view to link Nahum more firmly to its literary context in the Book of the Twelve. But if the title has been provided by a later editor, it is noteworthy that no other references were added in the first chapter. The universality of the hymn is not denied. This is discussed further under "The Rhetorical Function of the Book" (see pp. 47–58).

The person referred to in the title as *Nahum the Elkoshite* is otherwise unknown to us. "Elkosh" could conceivably refer to either a clan or a location, but only the latter has clear parallels elsewhere in the Bible;[13] neither a clan nor a location "Elkosh" is familiar from other sources. The citation of

---

11. Cf. Will M. Soll, "Babylonian and Biblical Acrostics," *Bib* 69 (1988): 305–23.

12. The speaker could announce the letters, use intonation or emphasis, or even display a placard (since many who were unable to read literature might nevertheless have been able to read letters). Nahum's acrostic, however, is especially complex.

13. So "Micah the Morashite" (Mic 1:1; Jer 26:18; cf. "Moresheth Gath" in Mic 1:14), "Jeremiah the Anathothite" (Jer 29:27; cf. 1:1; "the Anathothite" is also used as an appellative in 2 Sam 23:27; 1 Chr 11:28; 12:3; 27:12), and most likely also "Elijah the Tishbite" (1 Kgs 17:1; 21:17, 28; 2 Kgs 1:3, 8; 9:36). Cf. the appellations in the list of "David's mighty men" in 2 Sam 23:8–39 // 1 Chr 11:10–47, some of which refer to known and others to now unknown locations. Even "Eleazar, the son of Dodo, the son of Ahohi" in 2 Sam 23:9, for which 1 Chr 11:12 has "Eleazar, the son of Dodo, the Ahohite" (cf. without final *yod* in 1 Chr 8:4), could refer to a location, although this is less likely, given that other such references are always with the pl. "sons" ("sons/children of" = "inhabitants of").

this name, therefore, does not provide additional clues as to how the book is meant to be read, unless "Nahum the Elkoshite" is a pen name (see the commentary on 1:1).

B. MACROSTRUCTURE

A number of competing proposals for the structure of the book are on offer. This is because there are no unambiguous markers in the text to signal the beginning or end of a unit. Even 3:1, which is taken by most commentators as the beginning of a new unit, is not universally accepted as marking a significant caesura in the text.[14] There are stylistic features in Hebrew poetry that are generally acknowledged as potential boundary markers, but few if any of them are unambiguous. Wendland has correctly pointed out the importance of the principle of convergence: namely, that the more numerous the indications for a caesura are, the firmer the identification of boundaries.[15] But even then, one must bear in mind that a poet may utilize "a convergence of special stylistic features" not only to mark a poem's external boundaries but "also to mark peak passages in hortatory-admonitory discourse."[16] To give one example, a poem whose main body consists of two-line units (bicola) may be opened or concluded by a three-line unit (tricolon).[17] Thus three-line units (tricola) are sometimes used to demarcate segments of poetry.[18] But to decide whether they do so requires readers to take other factors into account, such as the use of an *inclusio*, where the end of a unit takes up motifs or words from its opening lines.

The book of Nahum is in fact a fairly cohesive unit that allows for different ways of segmentation. I advise against putting too much weight on any

14. See Marvin A. Sweeney, "Concerning the Structure and Generic Character of the Book of Nahum," *ZAW* 104 (1992): 364–77; Floyd, *Minor Prophets 2*, 59–62.

15. Wendland, *Discourse Analysis*, 27.

16. Wendland, *Discourse Analysis*, 68.

17. A colon (pl. cola) is a segment of text that, in poetry, is pictured as either a line or a half-line. My translation will treat each colon as a separate line. To avoid confusion for readers who are unfamiliar with the Hebrew text, I have equated "line" with "colon" in this commentary. We think of prose as written in paragraphs and poetry as written in lines, but when Hebrew poetry was first written, people could rarely afford to use up blank space in this way. To speak of the colometric arrangement of a text (its division into lines) is, strictly speaking, to say something about the rhythm of the text, not necessarily its arrangement on the page.

18. See, e.g., *CHP*, 65. But Watson also notes that tricola "often occur quite randomly in sections of poetry where couplets are the norm" (*CHP*, 183). An additional problem is that there is often disagreement about the colometry of the text—the way it should be "lined up."

specific way of subdividing the text. It is more important to get a feel for the overall texture of the book than to identify the one, true structure underlying it. This section, therefore, offers guidance on the various shifts and smaller units of the book. The discussion is fairly technical and will benefit those who have already familiarized themselves with the book of Nahum. Readers who are unfamiliar with the book of Nahum may prefer to read through it a number of times first and read my remarks on the rhetorical function of the book below before returning to this section.

The end of the poem beginning with 1:2 is much disputed. The rhythm in vv. 7–8 is markedly different from that in the immediately preceding verses. Commentators usually scan vv. 7–8 either as two tricola, thus identifying a change from two-line units to three-line units at this point,[19] or as three bicola, in which case some of them are particularly short compared with the preceding verses.[20] The masoretic accentuation, by contrast, suggests two bicola with very long cola in the first halves, not unlike the two bicola in v. 3. Regardless of the specific interpretation of the poetry of 1:7–8, a change of rhythm at this point can easily be observed.[21] This indicates either the end of the poem or a climax. There is a change of content as well, since these two verses spell out the consequences first for people who seek shelter with YHWH (v. 7) and then for people who oppose him (v. 8). If an alphabetic acrostic underlies the poem, its likely end point is in v. 7 or 8.[22]

In its present form, the poem interacts with the superscription in v. 1. The reference of the feminine suffix in the second colon of v. 8 is commonly read with reference to Nineveh, which is not mentioned in the poem itself.[23] This need not mean that v. 1 belongs to the poem itself, but it may suggest reading the poem as part of a literary unit that includes the superscription. The rhetorical question in v. 9 switches to direct address and opens a new subunit. Verses 9–10 are best identified as two tricola, which on my analysis sets them apart from their context. But the testimony to YHWH making *a full*

---

19. The thorny issue of differentiating between pivot-patterned bicola and chiastic tricola is fortunately not relevant for our discussion here because the two fulfill similar functions. See *CHP*, 218–19, for pivot-patterned bicola demarcating segments of poetry, and the remarks above on tricola.

20. In the latter case, *ûbəšeṭep ʿōbēr* (*and with a sweeping flood*) at the beginning of v. 8 is sometimes thought to form a bicolon with the last colon of v. 7.

21. The present interpretation follows the masoretic accentuation here, which for each of the two verses has one bicolon with 3+2 stresses. The preceding poem consisted of bicola with 2+2 stresses. For details, see Renz, *Colometry*.

22. The question of an alphabetic acrostic in Nah 1 will be taken up in the section on the composition of 1:2–10.

23. When v. 8 is read apart from the superscription, other possibilities present themselves; see the commentary on 1:8.

end in v. 8 is repeated in v. 9.[24] This suggests that the subunit belongs closely to the poem, offering an exposition or application of the poem.

The change of person to a feminine singular addressee in 1:11 separates this verse from the preceding. Whether there is a close link to the following verses depends on the identification of the addressee. If Nineveh is addressed here (my view),[25] but Judah or Jerusalem in the following verses, v. 11 does not closely belong with vv. 12–14. The reuse of the root *ḥšb* ("scheming"; cf. "ponder" in v. 9; the root is not used elsewhere in the book) creates a link with the challenge that follows the hymn. Thus, while v. 11 is in some ways situated between two units, it may be better included in what precedes (vv. 2–10) than what follows (vv. 12–14). This would also give due weight to the fact that 1:12 introduces first-person divine speech for the first time in the book. The material up to v. 12 can thus be interpreted as the background for the divine discourse. This background consists of a hymn summarizing theological tradition about YHWH's character and the consequent fates of two groups of people (vv. 2–8), a prophetic challenge based on this hymn (vv. 9–10), and a brief accusation against Nineveh (v. 11).

Verses 12–13 clearly belong together as a divine speech promising a feminine singular addressee (Judah or Jerusalem) a change from oppression to liberation. The short speech in 1:14, ostensibly directed to a masculine singular addressee (the king of Assyria) who had been referred to in the third person in vv. 12–13, forms the basis for the reassurance in vv. 12–13. It can therefore be considered closely related to these verses. Indeed, the introductory "and" may suggest that it is the third item under the heading *thus YHWH said* (v. 12a).[26]

Nahum 1:15 (2:1) brings another change of perspective, returning to a feminine singular addressee, now explicitly identified as Judah. The colometric arrangement is irregular and the parallelism weak. It is therefore hard to be confident that we are dealing with poetry. It is noteworthy that the other reference to *bɘliyyaʿal* ("wicked, wickedness") in the book is also within a verse that, in all likelihood, should be considered prose (1:11). Just as 1:11 portrays an event to which the (preceding) poetic material is going to be applied, so 1:15 (2:1) introduces a scene on which the (subsequent) poetic material elaborates. The phrase *he is completely cut off* could be seen as a summary of the scenario described in the following verses. While the two differ in that 1:11 is more likely a conclusion while 1:15 (2:1) is more likely an introduction,

---

24. Heb. *kālâ*, in both verses, is not found elsewhere in the book.

25. For this interpretation of v. 11, see the commentary. Others think that Jerusalem is addressed, in which case a closer link with the following verses can be argued.

26. The opening of v. 14 is nowhere else used as an introductory formula. For a 3rd per. reference to YHWH commanding within a 1st per. speech of YHWH, see maybe Amos 6:11.

both could be seen as prose hinges between poetic material—that is, verses that provide a link between the poetic material on either side.

The poem in 2:1–10(2–11) is introduced either with an introductory monocolon in 2:1(2), which again features Nineveh as the feminine singular addressee (see the commentary on 2:1),[27] or with a tricolon, if *guard the guardpost* is taken together with *a scatterer has come up against you* as suggested by the masoretic accentuation.[28] The next verse (v. 2[3]) presents an expository aside, increasing the dramatic tension by creating delay.[29] The second half of v. 3(4) opens with an extra-long colon due to the phrase *on the day when he makes ready*, which is thereby stressed, highlighting the single will behind the attacking force.[30] The phrase could be considered pivotal, going with both cola, if it were not for the *and* introducing the last colon.[31] Either way, the change of rhythm may indicate a shift to a different subunit. The reading of the text presented in the commentary supports this. It has to be granted, however, that the argument is not decisive.[32] From v. 5(6) onward, the parallelism is often weak or altogether absent, which speeds up the action. The shift from fight to defeat is nearly seamless,[33] but the action comes to a preliminary halt in v. 7(8), the analysis of whose lines is debatable.[34] If we follow the masoretic accentuation, a tricolon opens the section of the poem that focuses on the aftermath. This section could be analyzed as an alternation of three-line units in vv. 7(8) and 9(10) with four-line units (quatrains) in vv. 8(9) and 10(11), unless v. 8(9) is taken with the masoretic accentuation as two long cola that imitate Nineveh draining away.[35] The qua-

27. See *CHP*, 171, which cites both this verse and 1:12 as examples for an introductory monocolon (one-line unit) introducing a segment. Interestingly, Watson does not add the first colon of 1:14, which could also be considered a monocolon but marks a less pronounced break.

28. Most commentators prefer the arrangement of the text as laid out in *BHS*: an introductory monocolon followed by two bicola.

29. If the effect is deliberate, the "interruption" may well be original to the composition.

30. This reflects the common assumption that the pronoun in v. 3(4) refers back to the *scatterer* of v. 1(2), which is, however, not universally agreed upon. See the commentary on 2:3.

31. The *waw* here could be the result of dittography, but we lack any evidence for this.

32. For cola of extra length as a possible sign of stanza closure, see *CHP*, 165.

33. Counting feet (word-units), there is a 2+2 rhythm from v. 4b(5b) onward before v. 6(7) reverts to 3+2; cf. v. 4a(5a). Counting stress (disjunctive accents), there is a 2+2 rhythm throughout.

34. *BHS*, e.g., suggests 3+2 feet followed by 2+2 feet. The masoretic accentuation groups 3-4-2 feet in a 2-3-2 stress pattern. The significance of these differences can be overstated, but such divergences usually indicate irregular rhythm.

35. The use of a pausal form with the second imperative could be interpreted either as an alternative tradition of colon division or as an attempt to slow down the reading (on the assumption that the simple repetition of the contextual form would have been quicker to

train in v. 10(11) offers thematic closure, reinforcing the end of a subunit or the end of the poem.

The rhetorical question in 2:11–12(12–13) ties these two verses closely together and sets them apart from their context. The verses present two bicola pairs that could be identified as quatrains.[36] The poetically formulated rhetorical question certainly goes together well with the poem and could be considered an extension of it. But its use of the lion metaphor also serves to set it apart. The use of both lion metaphor and chariot motif in 2:13(14) suggests that the verse is meant to integrate vv. 11–12(12–13) with the earlier part of the chapter. It is also noteworthy that this verse reintroduces the verbs "to cut off" (*krt*) and "to hear" (*šmʿ*), which had been used in 1:15 (2:1),[37] as well as the messenger motif, albeit with different vocabulary. Thus, the last colon not only offers thematic closure but also rounds off the larger unit that opened in 1:15.

By way of contrast, Floyd has argued for a major subdivision of the book at 2:11(12) on the grounds that what follows recapitulates 2:1–10(2–11).[38] I agree with the smaller units Floyd identifies in ch. 3 (vv. 1–7, 8–12, 13–17, 18–19)[39] but consider the division between chs. 2 and 3 more significant. Floyd finds a narrative sequence in the second half of the book. It progresses from the prophetic prediction, focused first on the royal house (2:11–13[12–14]) and then on the city (3:1–7), to the fulfillment (3:13–19), focused first on the city (3:13–17) and then on the king (3:18–19). En route, it passes through "a pivotal section (3:8–12) that emphasizes that there is historical precedent for the overthrow of the seemingly permanent status quo."[40] But while there may be a sense of progression, the contrast Floyd proposes between prophecy and fulfillment is overdrawn. There is already stumbling over piles of dead in 3:3, while there are still attempts to strengthen the city's capability to withstand the siege in 3:14. Floyd's argument that 3:1–7 belongs more closely to the preceding section than the following is not persuasive.

---

enunciate). In any case, I suggest a possible heightening of the contrast between the slow (but steady) drain away from the pool that is Nineveh and the excited imperatives trying to avert the movement.

36. Both a quatrain and a bicola pair tie together four lines, but it is possible to distinguish a set of four lines in which the first two and last two lines are closely tied together by parallelism (a bicola pair) from a quatrain, which is not so easily separated or is more easily analyzed as a set of one plus three lines.

37. The verb "to hear" will make a reappearance in the very last verse of the book, where it is employed twice; "cut off" was used in 1:14 already and is employed again in 3:15.

38. Floyd, *Minor Prophets 2*, 59–62.

39. Furthermore, Floyd groups 3:13–17 and 3:18–19 together, which is defensible, and 2:11–13(12–14) with 3:1–7, which is doubtful, to produce a threefold structure for the second half of the book (2:11–3:7 [2:12–3:7]; 3:8–12; 3:18–19).

40. Floyd, *Minor Prophets 2*, 61–62. Note that it is in fact the city that is addressed in 2:13(14), which spoils the thematic chiasm somewhat.

In my view, the interjection *hôy* should be considered the opening of a new section in 3:1, as one might expect after the clear signs of closure at the end of ch. 2. List-type material is followed by the rationale for the disaster in v. 4, which prepares for the divine speech that follows. Rhythmically, v. 4 seems to me different both from vv. 2–3 and from v. 5, which may indicate its function as a hinge between vv. 1–3 and vv. 5–7, but there is no agreement on the rhythm of these verses, and the argument therefore remains tentative.[41] The formula in v. 5, with its shift to second-person address from third-person description, suggests at least a minor break between vv. 4 and 5. The situation is comparable to 2:13(14), which introduced a (new) prophetic unit that closely belonged to the preceding poem. Indeed, vv. 5–7 depend on the imagery of v. 4. It is thus probably best to keep 3:1–7 together. The accentuation may support this, in that it invites reading vv. 2–6 as bicola while setting off vv. 1 and 7.[42] The second rhetorical question in v. 7 provides suitable closure, either to this stanza of the poem or to the poem as a whole.[43] An additional indicator for a break at this point is the change of rhetorical perspective from experienced defeat in v. 7 back to the challenge of complacency prior to the defeat in v. 8.

The comparison with Thebes, introduced in 3:8, extends at least to v. 11, where the consequence for Nineveh is drawn. A tricolon, followed by either a monocolon (with the accentuation) or a bicolon (see the layout in *BHS*) opens the comparison. I propose that a series of paired lines in vv. 9–12 is interrupted in v. 13.[44] The accentuation appears to suggest tricola for the remaining verses of the book,[45] except for the insertion of a bicolon in v. 17

---

41. The *BHS* layout suggests a rhythm for vv. 4–5 different from that in vv. 2–3. The masoretic accentuation offers a more irregular rhythm for the whole section. If v. 5 is analyzed as introductory monocolon followed by a tricolon (contra, e.g., *BHS*), we have the first tricolon since v. 1 on my reading of the text, or the first tricolon in the chapter if v. 1 is treated as two bicola, as is done by the majority of readers.

42. The Masoretes divide 3:1 into three segments, either as an introductory monocolon followed by a bicolon or as a tricolon, and for v. 7 suggest a tricolon followed by a monocolon (note the position of the *atnach*). Another tricolon plus monocolon (bicolon in *BHS*) combination follows in v. 8, introducing another series of bicola in vv. 9–12.

43. Some argue that there is a larger rhetorical structure to the book for which the question whether the units in ch. 3 constitute stanzas of one poem or different poems is decisive, but I am not persuaded. See, e.g., Klaas Spronk, *Nahum*, HCOT (Kampen: Kok Pharos, 1997); Duane L. Christensen, *Nahum: A New Translation with Introduction and Commentary*, AB 24F (New Haven: Yale University Press, 2009).

44. The masoretic accentuation suggests a series of consistently long cola for 3:9–12, while *BHS* offers shorter lines. But there is agreement on cola coming in pairs up to v. 13. Others disagree. Spronk, e.g., scans v. 11 as a tricolon (*Nahum*, 132).

45. Contra my presentation of the text in *Colometry*, 110, which mistakenly adds a colon division at the first *zaqep parvum* in v. 19.

and the addition of a monocolon at the very end of the book. One need not follow this analysis to recognize that v. 17 may mark a small caesura.[46] The short rhetorical question at the end of v. 17 (*Where are they?*) provides a sense of closure. Attention to themes and motifs supports taking vv. 13–17 as a subunit. In this case, a pivot pattern in the first two lines opens both this (vv. 13–17) and the last section (vv. 18–19).[47] The unity of vv. 18–19 is established by the use of the second-person *masculine* address to the king of Assyria in place of the feminine address to the city of Nineveh, although if the "shepherds" and "noblemen" of v. 18 are to be identified with the "guards" and "officials" in v. 17, there is a close link between the two verses and thus between the last two subunits.

While offering further subdivisions, the structural analysis presented here is in agreement with the tradition reflected in masoretic manuscripts (see the excursus below). Most noteworthy is the decision to take the phrase *he is completely cut off* in 1:15 (2:1) as a summary statement of the scenario described in the following verses rather than a concluding summary of the preceding section as the chapter division adopted in English Bibles would suggest.

The commentary will employ the simple division of the text given below. The superscription to the book has already been discussed above and will be treated separately in the commentary as well. The poem about YHWH's character and the consequent fates of two groups of people (1:2–8) is taken together with its exposition in the prophetic challenge based on this hymn (1:9–10). The hinge verse in prose, which establishes the situation to which the following prophecy (in effect) applies the truth of the opening poem, is considered separately (1:11). YHWH's verdict on Nineveh, which is a promise of liberation from oppression and defeat of the enemy, forms the next unit (1:12–14). This verdict seems to combine the truths of 1:2–10 with the situation described in 1:11. There is a sense of thematic closure, with references to cutting off and preparing a grave.[48]

Nahum 1:15 (2:1) can be seen as another hinge verse. On the one hand, the message of good news looks back to the announcement in 1:12–14, whose fulfillment it assumes. On the other hand, the verse serves as a summary statement that introduces the more detailed description of Nineveh's fall in the verses that follow. This picture of the announcement of victory, which is probably in prose, deserves separate treatment. One of the few things on

---

46. The tricolon structure is uncontroversial for 3:16 as it stands but seems forced for 3:14–15.

47. For the relationship between pivot patterns and accentuation, see Renz, *Colometry*, 20–22.

48. The verse is cited as an example of thematic closure through reference to destruction in Watson, *CHP*, 65, along with Isa 28:22; Jer 51:58.

which one may find widespread agreement is that the images of the fall of Nineveh in 2:1–10(2–11) belong together, although commentators disagree on whether any of the preceding or following material should be added to this poem. The rhetorical question in 2:11–12(12–13), which stresses Nineveh's defeat, does indeed belong to the poem. This commentary's separate treatment of 2:11–12(12–13) seeks to give due weight to the lion metaphor without denying that the two verses are tightly integrated with their context. In some ways, they function as an exposition to the poem not unlike 1:9–10 in relation to the opening poem. The prophecy of complete destruction in 2:13(14) follows the poem and exposition not unlike the divine declaration in 1:12–14 that follows a poem and its exposition, except that now no statement of the historical situation is required (as in 1:11).

Nahum 3:1 opens a new section of the book. I have identified v. 4 as a hinge verse, linking vv. 1–3 and 5–7. It therefore seems appropriate to treat the announcement of doom for a murderous city and the prophecy of complete humiliation for a prostitute city together. The exposition of Nineveh's situation in terms of its complacency (vv. 8–12), the uselessness of its defenses (vv. 13–17), and the helplessness of its ruler (3:18–19) will be treated in separate sections.

The above analysis of the structure could be presented like this:

A. The Superscription to the Book (1:1)
B. YHWH, the Avenging God (1:2–10)
   1. A Poem (1:2–8)
   2. Its Exposition (1:9–10)
C. Accusation against the City (1:11)
D. YHWH's Verdict (1:12–14)
   1. The Decision Concerning Judah (1:12–13)
   2. The Command Concerning the King of Nineveh (1:14)
E. Announcement of Deliverance (1:15 [2:1])
F. Description of the End of Nineveh (2:1–13[2–14])
   1. Images of the Fall of Nineveh (2:1–10[2–11])
   2. Ridicule of the King of Nineveh (2:11–12[12–13])
   3. Prophecy of Complete Destruction (2:13[14])
G. Announcement of the End of an Evil City (3:1–7)
H. Ridicule of the City's Complacency and Resources (3:8–19)
   1. Denunciation of the City's Complacency (3:8–12)
   2. Exposition of the Uselessness of the City's Defenses (3:13–17)
   3. Exposition of the Helplessness of the City's Ruler (3:18–19)

However, since I am not convinced that the author or redactor clearly had such a structure in mind, and because it does not seem useful to discuss the text precisely along these lines, the commentary will follow this simpler outline:

A. The Superscription to the Book (1:1)
B. Contemplating YHWH, the Avenging God (1:2–10)
C. Accusation against the City (1:11)
D. YHWH's Verdict (1:12–14)
E. Announcement of Deliverance (1:15 [2:1])
F. Images of the Fall of Nineveh (2:1–10[2–11])
G. Ridicule of the King of Nineveh (2:11–12[12–13])
H. Prophecy of Complete Destruction (2:13[14])
I. Doom and Humiliation for the Bloodflow City (3:1–7)
J. Denunciation of the City's Complacency (3:8–12)
K. Exposition of the Uselessness of the City's Defenses (3:13–17)
L. Exposition of the Helplessness of the City's Ruler (3:18–19)

EXCURSUS: TRADITIONAL PARAGRAPH DIVISIONS

Biblical manuscripts typically divide the text into paragraphs or sections, but the caesurae are not always in the same place. Most Hebrew manuscripts indicate one of two types of paragraphs depending on whether a new paragraph starts at the beginning of a new line (following a *petucha*—an "open" space toward the end of the preceding line) or within a line (following a *setumah*—a space enclosed within text). In Lamentations, a start at the beginning of a new line clearly indicates a stronger break than one in the middle of the line, but elsewhere the difference between the two is often hard to discern.[49] It also needs to be asked whether these spaces were meant as objective markers that clearly identify individual paragraphs. It is evident that spaces were sometimes used to highlight individual verses. They were possibly used rhetorically in some cases to stress a minor caesura. But in other places, paragraph divisions were played down by not marking them.[50]

49. Josef M. Oesch (*Petucha und Setuma: Untersuchungen zu einer überlieferten Gliederung im hebräischen Text des Alten Testament*, OBO 27 [Fribourg: Presses Universitaires; Göttingen: Vandenhoeck & Ruprecht, 1979], 80–81) notes that graphically, especially within a scroll rather than a codex, the *petucha* suggests a more significant division. Note that Oesch uses *petucha* and *setuma(h)* for the relevant sections of text, while I use the terms here to characterize the spaces themselves.

50. Cf., e.g., David J. Clark, "Delimitation Markers in the Book of Numbers," in *Layout*

The Masoretes may have taken for granted that readers would recognize the boundaries between smaller units. If they did, they may have wanted to stress some paragraph divisions (e.g., to mark the end of a poem rather than just a stanza) while ignoring others (e.g., to prevent readers from separating two paragraphs that closely belong together). We must be cautious about simply identifying the use of spaces in individual manuscripts with a presumed division of the text into paragraphs. Even if the spaces were meant to strictly indicate all paragraph divisions, the variation between *petucha* and *setumah* rarely enables us to identify the presumed structure of the book in terms of major sections and subsections.

Emanuel Tov observes that Nahum and Jonah stand out among the Minor Prophets "as having very few section units—one division after an average of 15.66 and 16.0 verses respectively—in both cases only 3 instances, matched by the Judean Desert scroll MurXII."[51] The Leningrad Codex B19a (AD 1008), which forms the basis of *BHS* and *Biblia Hebraica Leningradensis*, opens new paragraphs in Nahum 1:12 following a *setumah* space, in 1:15 (2:1) following a *petucha* space, and in 3:1 again following a *setumah* space. The Aleppo Codex (925), the Cairo Codex (895), the Babylonian Codex of Petrograd (916), the Reuchlin Codex (1105), and a manuscript of the Minor Prophets found in the Wadi Murabbaʿat about twelve miles south of Qumran (2nd century) all agree with these three paragraph divisions in principle. There is disagreement, however, about the nature of the paragraph divisions,[52] and the Cairo Codex has another subsection that begins at 2:2(3), unless the space there is to highlight the verse or indicate its parenthetical nature.

C. LANGUAGE AND STYLE

Words are carefully chosen in the book of Nahum. They are often repeated within short range: for example, *nōqēm* ("avenging") in 1:2; *ʾumlal* ("withered") in 1:4; *wəkēn* ("and likewise") and *ʿnh* ("afflict") in 1:12; and *gəʾôn* ("pride") and *bqq* ("devastate") in 2:2(3).[53] Some roots are repeated to stitch

Markers in Biblical Manuscripts and Ugaritic Tablets, ed. Marjo C. A. Korpel and Josef M. Oesch, Pericope 5 (Assen: Van Gorcum, 2005), 1–20.

51. Emanuel Tov, "Key Characteristics of (Proto-) MT," *TheTorah.com*, 2017, http://the torah.com/proto-masoretic-text/key-characteristics-of-proto-mt/.

52. The Wadi Murabbaʿat manuscript and the Petrograd Codex appear to give the same weight to all three divisions, suggesting a stronger break at 1:12 and 3:1 than the Leningrad Codex. The Aleppo and Cairo codices agree with this in 3:1. The Cairo Codex has a stronger break in 1:12 and a weaker one in 1:15 (2:1). In other words, it might link 1:12–14 more closely with ch. 2 than ch. 1. The Reuchlin Codex has a *petucha* space before 1:12 and 1:15 (2:1) and a *setumah* space before 3:1.

53. Cf. Oswald T. Allis, "Nahum, Nineveh, Elkosh," *EvQ* 27 (1955): 73; Spronk, "Syn-

together separate units: *ḥšb* in 1:9 ("ponder") and 1:11 ("scheming") and *bəliy-yāʿal* ("villain, villainy") in 1:11 and 1:15 (2:1). Allis observes the book's "decided fondness for words which have two adjacent consonants the same" and "a liking for words which are quite similar in sound and sometimes in meaning."[54] Indeed, sound effects seem to have played a significant role in the author's choice of vocabulary. They are, however, more difficult to identify objectively. The deliberate use of *s* sounds in 1:10 and of *m* sounds in 2:8(9) is hardly controversial. In my view, *k*/*q* sounds are also used to good effect in 2:4(5), reinforcing the rumbling of the chariots (see *merkābâ məraqqēdâ*, "chariotry jolting," in 3:2). There is also alliteration in the second half of 2:5(6) that imitates the flow of soldiers toward the wall and its sudden stop.[55] The opening of 2:10(11) is another celebrated case (*bûqâ ûməbûqâ ûməbullāqâ*—"desolation, destruction, and devastation"), a sound play that translators often seek to imitate. The commentary will briefly refer to some of these examples. Those who read or hear Nahum in Hebrew should listen for sound effects that imitate the action described.

The many instances of alliteration, assonance, and wordplay or paronomasia might lead us to expect that the author or redactor also had a feeling for rhythm. It seems likely that rhythmic changes are deliberate, as in 1:7, 9, 11, 12.[56] The best example may be the list-type material in 3:2–3, which features short cola that are followed by a slower, more deliberate exposition in 3:4.[57] Such deliberate discontinuity can also be observed at the level of the meaning of words. Allis notes instances of "sudden transition and rather startling antithesis," for example, in the occurrence of *slow to anger* in 1:3 and *good* in 1:7.[58] Rhetorical questions can have a similar effect, and Nahum has a great number of these (in 1:6, 9; 2:11[12]; 3:7, 8, 17, 19).

The book is full of striking images, irony, and satire—features that are eas-

---

chronic and Diachronic," 183. The repetition in 1:4 may be due to a textual mistake. The repetition of *wəkēn* in 1:12 is lost in my translation. There is also the double use of a root in idiomatic expressions in 1:3 and 1:15 (2:1). Other examples can be found in 2:8(9), 9(10), 12(13); 3:2, 10, 11, 14, 15–16.

54. Allis, "Nahum," 73, listing examples for the former from 1:3, 4, 5; 2:2(3), 4(5), 5(6), 7(8), 8(9), 13(14); 3:3, 15; and for the latter from 1:6b, 8, 9, 11; 2:1(2); 3:2, 7, 10, 17 plus the remarkable case of alliteration in 2:10(11).

55. Louis Alonso Schökel (*A Manual of Hebrew Poetics*, SubBib 11 [Rome: Pontifical Biblical Institute, 1988], 27) also notes onomatopoeia in 2:4–7(5–8).

56. There are also a few possible instances of *anacrusis* (words placed outside the rhythmical structure), a stylistic trait according to *CHP*, 110 (e.g., *wəʿattâ*, "so now," in 1:13).

57. This is not clearly discernible in the masoretic accentuation; for discussion, see my comments on the composition of 3:1–7.

58. Allis, "Nahum," 74–75. He adds the shift of pronouns in 1:8–2:2 (1:8–2:3), the shift of temporal perspective in 1:14–2:1 (1:14–2:2), and the contrasting way in which the metaphor of locusts is used in 3:15–17. I disagree with this last example; see the commentary on these verses.

ily discernible in translation. A noteworthy repetition not so easily spotted in translation is the sixfold use of *wə'ên* (lit. "and [there is] not") in 2:8–9(9–10), 11(12); 3:3, 9, 18,[59] to which may be added two occurrences of *'ên* without *waw* (3:7, 19). Another popular word is *kōl* ("all, whole"), used twelve times in the book.[60] The four occurrences of the particle *'ôd* ("again, still, more") in 1:12, 14; 1:15 (2:1); 2:13(14) constitute a high number in such a small book,[61] but the sample is too small to permit our putting too much weight on this.

D. TEXTUAL WITNESSES

The MT, as reflected in Leningradensis B19A, is the basis text for this commentary. The oldest extant Hebrew texts are close to the later MT. The Wadi Murabba'at scroll (Mur 88) is the most important of these older Hebrew witnesses. It was probably written early in the second century AD and contains major parts of these books in twenty-one columns.[62] It confirms that there was a text very much like the one transmitted in the MT nearly a millennium before the oldest masoretic manuscripts known to us were written. The Greek Scroll of the Minor Prophets from Naḥal Ḥever, which was probably hidden during the Bar Kokhba revolt, is also close to the MT.[63] A useful comparison of these documents, along with the LXX tradition, is available in the Biblia Qumranica series.[64] The Targum Jonathan on the Prophets was also consulted.[65] The Pesher Nahum (4Q169 = 4QpNah) contains the text (with

59. The presence of *waw* in 3:9 is odd. See Tremper Longman III, "Nahum," in *The Minor Prophets: An Exegetical & Expository Commentary*, ed. Thomas Edward McComiskey, vol. 2 (Grand Rapids: Baker, 1993), 819. Longman considers the *waw* in 2:8(9) also problematic and suspects another "peculiarity of Nahum's style" in this use of the *waw*.

60. Twice in 2:10(11) and 3:10, once each in 1:4, 5; 1:15 [2:1]; 2:9[10]; 3:1, 7, 12, 19.

61. The ratio of occurrences of *'ôd* to the total number of words in the book is roughly 0.53%, more than in any other biblical writing; cf. Zechariah (0.35% with 16 occurrences), Hosea (0.32% with 10), Zephaniah (0.29% with 3), Amos (0.28% with 8). All other books have less than half the ratio of Nahum.

62. See Mur 88 in the Leon Levy Dead Sea Scrolls Digital Library, http://www.deadsea scrolls.org.il/explore-the-archive/manuscript/MUR88-1.

63. For further discussion of the date, see Emanuel Tov, *The Greek Minor Prophets Scroll from Naḥal Ḥever (8ḤevXIIgr)*, DJD 8 (Oxford: Clarendon Press, 1990), 22–26.

64. Beate Ego et al., eds., *Minor Prophets*, vol. 3B of *Biblia Qumranica* (Leiden: Brill, 2005). For the LXX with reference to other Greek versions (Aquila, Theodotion, Symmachus), see Joseph Ziegler, ed., *Duodecim Prophetae*, vol. 13 of *Septuaginta: Vetus Testamentum Graecum*, 3rd ed. (Göttingen: Vandenhoeck & Ruprecht, 2012).

65. See ArBib 14. For an introduction, see also Paul V. M. Fletcher and Bruce Chilton, *The Targums: A Critical Introduction* (Waco: Baylor University Press, 2011), 199–228.

commentary) of 1:3–6; 2:11–13(12–14); 3:1–5, 6–9, 10–12.[66] Cave 4 also revealed a few fragments that are consistent with the MT, with the noteworthy exception of a fragment of Nah 2:8(9) that agrees with the Greek and Latin translations against the MT (see the commentary).

The LXX (or Old Greek text) takes us further back in time, maybe to the second century BC. The translator of Nahum may have been responsible for the Book of the Twelve as a whole and maybe for parts of Jeremiah and Ezekiel.[67] It appears to be a fairly literal translation with some hard transitions and sudden changes in tense forms in the LXX of Nahum. Marguerite Harl suggests that for a native speaker "the Greek text would no doubt appear rude, obscure, often incoherent."[68] Heinz-Josef Fabry, however, gives examples where the translator made the text more readily understandable (2:1[2], 10[11]; 3:1, 8, 17) or improved it aesthetically (1:7; 3:12).[69] He classifies its disagreements with the traditional Hebrew text in the following categories:

(1) Different word divisions (e.g., 1:12)
(2) Different vocalization (e.g., 1:13, 14; 2:7[8])
(3) Exchange of similar consonants (e.g., 1:6; 2:3[4])
(4) Different interpretation of homophonic roots (e.g., 1:12; 1:15 [2:1])

In a few instances, the LXX may well preserve an older and better text. A value judgment is appropriate when there are accidents in the transmission of the text, the better text being the one that has not been accidentally changed. I am more reluctant to make value judgments in cases in which differences between textual traditions are deliberate. For example, the fact that the Hebrew text characterizes God in human terms with greater frequency than the Greek translation surely reflects editorial/translational policy on one side or the other. For the period in question, it seems more likely that a later text would avoid instances of anthropomorphism and anthropopathism rather than introducing them, but we cannot be certain about this. Confronted with editorial differences, the earlier text will be considered the

66. See Gregory L. Doudna, *4Q Pesher Nahum: A Critical Edition*, JSPSup 35 / Copenhagen International Series 8 (Sheffield: Sheffield Academic, 2001); Shani L. Berrin, *The Pesher Nahum Scroll from Qumran: An Exegetical Study of 4Q169*, Studies on the Texts of the Desert of Judah 53 (Leiden: Brill, 2004).

67. Cf. Takamitsu Muraoka, "Introduction aux Douze Petits Prophètes" in *Les Douze Prophètes: Osée*, vol. 23.1 of *La Bible d'Alexandrie*, ed. Jan Joosten et al. (Paris: Cerf, 2002), ix–xiii.

68. *BA* 23.4–9, 174.

69. Heinz-Josef Fabry, "Naum/Nahum," in *Septuaginta Deutsch: Erläuterungen und Kommentare*, ed. Martin Karrer and Wolfgang Kraus, vol. 2 (Stuttgart: Deutsche Bibelgesellschaft, 2011), 2406.

better by those who seek to establish the earliest version of the prophetic book.[70] For the purposes of interpreting the Scriptures in and for the church, it is the canonical text that is the better—regardless of its relative age.[71] In my own community, the traditional Hebrew text carries greater canonical weight than the LXX. In cases where the differences appear to be a matter of editorial policy, this has led to a preference for the Hebrew text as the basis of the interpretation offered in this commentary.[72] Fabry believes that the translator has a stronger focus on God and gives the text a more eschatological outlook with addition of apocalyptic metaphors (e.g., "ruler over mighty waters" in 1:12, which he considers a messianic title) alongside a stress on the liberation and restoration of Judah (e.g., 1:12; 2:1–2[2–3]).[73] Grütter, by contrast, argues that the LXX reflects an earlier edition than the MT and seeks to demonstrate this with reference to differences in 3:8, 15.[74]

Other textual witnesses are secondary to those already mentioned. The Old Syriac text is close to the LXX, while the Aramaic Targum is closer to the MT. Jerome worked from a Hebrew text but allowed himself to be guided by the Greek translation when he produced the Latin translation that became the Vulgate.

II. THE DEVELOPMENT OF THE BOOK

A. GENERAL COMMENTS ON THE ORIGIN OF THE BOOK

The historical setting of most of the book of Nahum is dated to the second half of the seventh century by the majority of scholars. Nahum 3:8 looks

---

70. The preference among contemporary biblical scholars is, again, stressing rather than avoiding anthropomorphisms.

71. There is more than one "canonical text," but with the possible exception of some branches of Protestantism, the "canonical text" is not the earliest form of the text but the final, editorially shaped version(s).

72. This does not minimize the importance of historical research but puts such research in the service of theological interpretation. It is arguable that anthropomorphisms and anthropopathisms should be given greater weight in interpretation if they prove to be later editorial changes, as the fact that such a change was thought necessary would signal its importance. But the situation is made more complicated by the fact that the traditional Hebrew text is not the only one valued by the Christian church.

73. Fabry, "Naum/Nahum," 2406.

74. Nesina Grütter, *Das Buch Nahum: Eine vergleichende Untersuchung des masoretischen Texts und der Septuagintaübersetzung*, WMANT 148 (Neukirchen-Vluyn: Neukirchener Theologie, 2016). But see Jeremias, *Nahum*, 40–42.

back to the fall of Thebes (No-Amon) in 664 or 663 (or, less likely, 667) BC and must therefore be later. There is general agreement that no other part of the book originated earlier than 663 BC. The fall of Nineveh in 612 BC is the focus of much of the book and appears to lie in the future.[75] Some have argued that this appearance of looking forward to the fall of Nineveh is deceptive and that (most of) the material in the book does in fact stem from after 612 as a *vaticinium ex eventu* (e.g., E. Sellin; J. Jeremias) or as a liturgy to celebrate the destruction of the oppressor (e.g., P. Humbert).[76] This view is now rarely contemplated in English language research.[77] There seems to be no good reason for thinking that the prophetic challenges (2:13[14]; 3:5–7; cf. 1:12–14) were composed after the event. It is possible that the proclamation only existed in oral form prior to 612, but in that case it would be noteworthy that nothing is made of the success of the prediction in the written version. On balance, the more likely assumption is that a *sēper* ("document") already existed prior to the decisive event. Nahum 1:12 pictures Assyria at ease. This suggests a date for this part of the book either before news about the wars against Babylon and Elam (652–648) came to Judah or well afterward. Gregory D. Cook argues for the latter. He points out that the Akkadian root *šlm* was used prominently in Assurbanipal's inscriptions, noting safe return after successful campaigns, and suggests that *šəlēmîm* in 1:12 mimics this and alludes to Assurbanipal's withdrawal in the final twelve years of his life, after 639 BC.[78] Either way, the prophet speaks of Nineveh's end at a time when to many it must have seemed that the Assyrians were in control of events in the region.

It has sometimes been argued that the bulk of the book was originally unrelated to the prophetic challenge, and in particular unrelated to its more universal-sounding opening section (usually identified as 1:2–8). Thus Seybold considers "Nahum" a poet of secular soldiers' songs and suggests that

75. A useful orientation to Nineveh is Lucas P. Petit and Daniele Morandi Bonacossi, eds., *Nineveh, the Great City: Symbol of Beauty and Power*, Papers on Archaeology of the Leiden Museum of Antiquities 13 (Leiden: Sidestone Press, 2017). This volume can be read online for free at https://www.sidestone.com/books/nineveh-the-great-city. It includes an essay "The Sack of Nineveh in 612 BC" by Marc Van De Mieroop (243–47).

76. Ernst Sellin, *Das Zwölfprophetenbuch*, 3rd ed., KAT 12 (Leipzig: Deichert, 1930), 354–55; Jörg Jeremias, *Kultprophetie und Gerichtsverkündigung in der späten Königszeit Israels*, WMANT 35 (Neukirchen-Vluyn: Neukirchener Verlag, 1970); Paul Humbert, "La Vision de Nahoum 2,4–11," *AfO* 5 (1928–1929): 14–19.

77. See Michael Weigl, "Current Research on the Book of Nahum: Exegetical Methodologies in Turmoil?" *CurBR* 9 (2001): 81–130. For the situation within German scholarship see Jeremias, *Nahum*, esp. pp. 12–15.

78. Gregory D. Cook, "Ashurbanipal's Peace and the Date of Nahum," *WTJ* 79 (2017): 137–45.

the poetic battle depictions existed at one time without the theological perspective now found in the book.[79] If so, the name "Nahum" is maybe better given to the author responsible for the theological perspective found in the *document of the revelation to Nahum the Elkoshite*, because the only occurrence of the name *Nahum the Elkoshite* is in Nah 1:1 in connection with the claim to revelation.[80] (For the relationship between the different types of material in the book, see the next section.) There is in truth little we can know for certain about the authorship and setting of the book. Its development can only be deduced hypothetically from the nature and shape of the book itself. Any putative original performance context (oral communication) is largely eclipsed in the written book,[81] which in turn, however, was probably conceived for popular—that is oral—communication, as noted above.

In its final form, the hymn with which the book opens both provides a foundation for the case against Nineveh and declares the fall of Nineveh to be an instance of a general pattern. What is said about Nineveh is based on what is known about YHWH. The opening poem offers no new revelation but reaffirms basic claims already known about YHWH. The poem provides an exposition of Exod 34:6–7 in particular and is then itself exposited with regard to Nineveh.

B. THE INDIVIDUAL UNITS WITHIN THE BOOK

While attempts to describe the development of the book must remain speculative, they can throw light on how the different parts of the book work together. The discussion above ("Macrostructure," pp. 27–36) focused on the unity of the book (how to read the different parts together); now the discussion will focus on discontinuities as potential signs of redaction. Scholars often identify the following aspects of the text as indicative of joints in the book: generic differences, change of pronouns, redundancies, and different rhetorical situations.[82] The feature that often causes the greatest sense of disjointedness in the modern reader, grammatical discord in gender and number, may be the least certain indicator of literary growth. Such discord is found so frequently in the Hebrew Bible that it may well have been accept-

79. Klaus Seybold, *Profane Prophetie: Studien zum Buch Nahum*, SBS 135 (Stuttgart: KBW, 1989).

80. "Nahum" would then be a person who used preexisting poetic material to convey the divine message. Spronk (*Nahum*, 13, 31–33) suggests that *Nahum the Elkoshite* is a pseudonym, and this seems to me quite possible. See the commentary on Nah 1:1.

81. Some scholars have questioned whether there is any oral prehistory to the book at all; e.g., van der Woude, "Nahum."

82. See Heinz-Josef Fabry, *Nahum*, HThKAT (Freiburg im Breisgau: Herder, 2006), 32.

able Hebrew style.[83] But in Nahum, changes of pronouns seem to go together with generic differences. Thus, taking our cue from the structure presented above, one may want to distinguish between (3rd per.) poems, expository material with an implied (2nd per.) addressee, and (1st per.) divine declarations.[84] Then, taking a cue from the double superscription (*pronouncement* and *document of a revelation*), one might want to distinguish between the (original?) revelation and its (expository?) pronouncement. But such a move runs quickly into problems. The divine declarations are in 1:12–14; 2:13[14]; and 3:5–7.

> **1:12–14** Thus YHWH said: Even though they are completely at ease and likewise many, they are shorn, and he is gone. And: Though I have afflicted you [fem.], I will afflict you no more. So now, I will break his staff from upon you, and your shackles I will tear away. And: YHWH has given a command concerning you [masc.]: No more shall be sown from your name. From the house of your gods I will entirely cut off idol and image; I will prepare your grave, because you are lightweight.

> **2:13(14)** Look, I am against you [fem.]—utterance of YHWH of Hosts, and I will burn up [your] chariotry in the smoke, and a sword will devour your young lions, and I will entirely cut off from the earth your prey, and no more shall be heard the voice of your messenger.

> **3:5–7** Look, I am against you [fem.]—utterance of YHWH of Hosts, and I will strip your skirt over your face, and I will show nations your nudity and kingdoms your shame. I will throw filth at you and declare you contemptuous and make you just like a spectacle. And it shall happen that whoever sees you will run away from you and say "Nineveh is ruined." Where can I find comforters for you?[85]

---

83. See Bruce K. Waltke, *A Commentary on Micah* (Grand Rapids: Eerdmans, 2007), 74, with appeal to Ida Willi-Plein, *Vorformen der Schriftexegese innerhalb des Alten Testaments*, BZAW 123 (Berlin: de Gruyter, 1971), 79. Waltke adds that similar phenomena have been observed in ancient Semitic inscriptions for which an extended period of scribal transmission is implausible. He only cites one inscription, however, and Willi-Plein explicitly considers this a feature of later texts that are produced like a mosaic from citations and allusions to earlier texts ("Musivstil"; i.e., musive style).

84. These formal distinctions have to do with rhetorical standpoint and not with the presence or absence of poetic form or divine inspiration. In fact, the expository material is poetic as well and in the final (canonical) analysis is as much "word of God" as the material here classified as divine revelation.

85. Even if the divine speech continues into v. 7, it is not entirely clear whether the last

There are three oddities to ponder. First, the first oracle addresses two different entities, neither of which is identified. The second oracle appears to address yet another entity, again not identified. Only the third oracle, and only if we include v. 7 in the divine speech, includes an identification of the one to whom punishment is announced, and this identification is made only in passing toward the end of the declaration. (Of course, if we interpret v. 7 as prophetic comment rather than divine speech, there is no identification of the addressees in any of the divine oracles.) Second, the announcement in 2:13(14) uses a mix of metaphors, which is odd if the verse is considered on its own but makes sense as a conclusion to ch. 2. The verse thus appears to be dependent on the preceding material. Third, while the divine oracles are mostly to do with punishment, the reason for the punishment is only alluded to and never explicitly stated. Maybe it was thought to be self-evident, but its omission removes the possibility of expressing the appropriateness of the punishment, usually a great concern in the prophetic writings. The challenge formula (2:13[14]; 3:5) is elsewhere part of a divine speech that includes a number of other elements (see Jer 21:13; 50:31; 51:25; Ezek 21:3[8]; 29:10; 35:3; 38:3; 39:1). The identification of the material presented as divine speech with a *revelation* that forms a distinct part of the *pronouncement* is therefore problematic. Given that the battle scene descriptions can stand on their own without any cultic or theological context, it is easier to imagine that the challenge formula marks later insertions.[86] As noted above, some scholars have indeed considered (imitation of) soldiers' songs the original kernel of the book.[87] But these songs on their own should hardly be identified with either *revelation* or *pronouncement*, and the language of the divine sayings suggests an earlier rather than a later date for them.[88] The differences between much

---

sentence is to be read as a divine exclamation or a comment by the prophet. But this will not make much difference to our analysis.

86. The formula *hinnî 'ēlayik* with which *nə'ūm yhwh ṣəbā'ôt* is always connected in Nahum (2:13[14]; 3:5) is found elsewhere only in Jeremiah (21:13; 50:31; 51:25) and Ezekiel (21:8; 29:10; 35:3; 38:3; 39:1); the formula *nə'ūm yhwh ṣəbā'ôt* is found in Isa 14:22–23; 17:3; 22:25; Jer 8:3; 25:29; 30:8; 49:26; Zeph 2:9; Hag 1:9; 2:4, 8–9, 23; Zech 1:3, 16; 3:9–10; 5:4; 8:6, 11; 13:2, 7 as well as Nah 2:13(14) and 3:5 (Amos 6:8, 14 has *nə'um-yhwh 'ĕlōhê ṣəbā'ôt*, with the article in the latter case).

87. Seybold (*Profane Prophetie*, 22–23, 26–27, 29–30, 41–44, 51–53, 63–64) uses the German "profan" in the sense of (consciously) noncultic. If the battle songs were originally independent, their author was nevertheless not "secular" in the modern sense of the word and, for all we know, may well have shared all the convictions expressed in the more explicitly theological material of the book.

88. Maier (*Nahum*, 209) argues from 1:13 that a date during Manasseh's reign is more plausible than a date during Josiah's reign, as Judah suffered under the Assyrian yoke more at the earlier time. This is probably true, even if the pertinent question is not simply when Judah faced the most Assyrian demands but when it felt the Assyrian yoke most keenly. It is

of chs. 2 and 3 on the one hand and ch. 1 on the other are easily observed. But additional arguments are required, and have been offered, to suggest a different author as well as different context. These arguments relate to views about the growth of the Book of the Twelve, on which more will be said below.

Redundancies may be a sign that different sources have been combined, and they can thus help to identify literary joints,[89] but it needs to be borne in mind that repetition is also part and parcel of effective communication. If observed redundancies can be linked to a difference in the presumed historical situation, however, one has a much firmer indicator of different rhetorical contexts and thus a signal of literary growth.[90] If the book was not written in one setting, the material may well address different contexts and situations. But such different settings are not always discernible. Nothing in the book of Nahum explicitly addresses a situation after 612, and there are no pointers that allow us to more precisely assign different parts of the book to specific settings. It is noteworthy that ch. 2 and 3:1–7 already describe the fall of the city in vivid language, while the rest of ch. 3 seems to be (comparatively!) less urgent, as if the city is not yet under direct attack. Thus ch. 3 may contain material that is older than the material in ch. 2, but this is by no means conclusive, as we are dealing with imaginative poetry, not war reportage.[91]

The most significant question is the date of 1:2–8. Many scholars date this poem later than the bulk of the book, but not all agree (e.g., R. D. Patterson and K. Spronk).[92] A. Schart argues that it was written by a late redactor of the Book of the Twelve.[93] If so, it is compatible with the rest of the book of Nahum but not necessarily written specifically for it. J. Jeremias thinks that it was written too late to have influenced the editorial history of the Book of

---

possible that the reformer Josiah, keen on Judah's independence as he was, suffered under the looser Assyrian bonds more than Manasseh had under a heavier load. But I agree with Maier that, overall, the language used in Nahum suggests that Assyria is still at or near the height of its power.

89. This must be distinguished from redactional layering—that is (creative) redactional work that adds material that had not existed previously. A redactor would hardly add newly written "redundant" material.

90. The traditional view of prophetic books as files of prophetic oracles and sermons is well able to explain such redundancies without appeal to different authors, and this is the most economical explanation, unless additional considerations suggest multiple authorship.

91. Fabry (*Nahum*, 88–89) thinks that Nahum's rhetoric grew in intensity over time and suggests that the reverse ordering indicates a lessening of the conviction that the fall of Nineveh was imminent, but he leaves unexamined why this order was retained when the theological rationale for the fall of Nineveh was supplied.

92. Patterson, *Nahum*; Spronk, *Nahum*.

93. Aaron Schart, *Die Entstehung des Zwölfprophetenbuchs: Neubearbeitungen von Amos im Rahmen schriftenübergreifender Redaktionsprozesse*, BZAW 260 (Berlin: de Gruyter, 1998), 234–51.

the Twelve.[94] The commentary below will suggest that the poem is carefully integrated into Nahum 1:1–11. While it is possible that it represents comparatively later material, it seems to me just as possible that such a poem existed prior to its inclusion in the book of Nahum and even prior to the poems later in the book. In any case, it is clear that the poem is of prime importance for the function of the only edition of the book attested in manuscripts.

C. THE REDACTION OF THE BOOK OF THE TWELVE

Recent scholarship has explored the relationship between individual minor prophets and the collection called the Book of the Twelve. While there are some converging lines in the various redactional models on offer, there is at present no consensus even on the general development of the Book of the Twelve.[95] There are certainly interesting connections between the different minor prophets, and there is of course intertextuality beyond this corpus, but not all instances of parallel phrasing are best explained by assuming different redactional attempts to tie the Minor Prophets more closely. In some instances of similarities, older traditions may have inspired each of the respective works, or one prophet may have had a more direct influence on another. One need not rule out redactional links between individual prophetic writings, but I am not convinced that the Book of the Twelve in its present form reveals itself as a strongly cohesive literary unit.

The book of Nahum has close connections to the end of Micah, to Jonah, and to Habakkuk. Exodus 34:6–7 is the main bridge between Jonah, Micah, and Nahum.[96] The creedal formula in Exod 34 is the biblical text most often cited elsewhere in the Bible. It is likely that the formula featured in the Jerusalemite cult, from which it was taken up by several prophets.[97] These prophets may well have been aware of previous uses of the formula, and thus

94. Jeremias, *Nahum*, 35.

95. Cf. my fuller remarks above under "The Unity of the Book of the Twelve" (pp. 4–13); for Nahum specifically, see Fabry, *Nahum*, 96–104.

96. See the comments under "Nahum, Habakkuk, and Zephaniah in the Book of the Twelve" (pp. 13–16).

97. See also the discussions in Michael A. Fishbane, *Biblical Interpretation in Ancient Israel* (Oxford: Clarendon Press, 1985), 347; "Torah and Tradition," in *Tradition and Theology in the Old Testament*, ed. Douglas A. Knight, BibSem (Sheffield: JSOT Press, 1990, repr.; Philadelphia: Fortress, 1977), 280–81; Josef Scharbert, "Formgeschichte und Exegese von Ex 34,6f und seiner Parallelen," *Bib* 38 (1957): 130–50; Hermann Spieckermann, "Barmherzig und gnädig ist der Herr . . . ," *ZAW* 102 (1990): 1–18; John D. W. Watts, "A Frame for the Book of the Twelve: Hosea 1–3 and Malachi," in Nogalski and Sweeney, *Reading and Hearing*, 209–17, esp. 214–15; Nathan C. Lane, *The Compassionate, But Punishing God: A Canonical*

there is no need to assert complete independence of these passages from one another. But the view that all such references belong to one redactional layer seems neither necessary nor productive.[98]

III. THE RHETORICAL FUNCTION OF THE BOOK

A. THE MESSAGE OF NAHUM'S POETRY AT THE TIME OF ITS ORIGIN

The rhetoric of the book suggests that Assyria was still strong at the time the poems of the book were first uttered. It is possible that an author put himself in the shoes of someone still living under the shadow of Assyria, but the rise of the Babylonian and Persian Empires raised issues in their own right that are not reflected here, and so there is no reason not to take the rhetoric at face value. This, then, suggests that the bulk of the material now collected in the book of Nahum originated before the fall of Nineveh in 612. Its function was to announce the imminent destruction of that mighty city. Israel and Judah had been under the grip of Assyria for about two centuries. The Northern Kingdom had come to an end at the hand of the Assyrians. The Assyrians still have a reputation for having been more brutal than the Babylonians and Persians. The relative cruelty of different empires is not easy to measure at our historical distance, but Assyria's military-imperial ethos did not lend itself to diplomacy and compromise.[99] Assyria's land was agriculturally fruitful but otherwise poor in resources, and its economic potential was continually developed and secured by military conquest. Decentralized garrisons did not have the manpower to micromanage conquered territories, so they relied on deterrence, using heavy force against insurgents. Assyria's policy of moving ethnic groups to different territories aimed to minimize the strength of group ("national") loyalties. The lack of a common culture and identity in different territories also led to more anarchic conditions, which again had to be kept in check by force. It seems that Judeans and others encountered Assyria first of all not as a culture or religion or strong political influence but as sheer force.

Analysis of Exodus 34:6-7 (Eugene, OR: Pickwick, 2010). See also the works cited under "Nahum, Habakkuk, and Zephaniah in the Book of the Twelve" (pp. 13–16).

98. For the proposal that Nahum-Habakkuk form one literary unit, see the comments above under "The Unity of the Book of the Twelve" (pp. 4–5) and my essay "Habakkuk and Its Co-Texts."

99. See Fabry, *Nahum*, 56–59, on which the following few sentences are also dependent.

Nahum challenges the fear and terror that the Assyrians spread and counters it with the claim that YHWH is a far superior force to the might of Assyria. Nahum announces that YHWH will now act to liberate the peoples from Assyria, making Nineveh suffer a fate reminiscent of the curses found in the treaties that Assyria imposed on its vassals.[100] Nahum does not present a call to arms—there is no need for Judah to take matters into their own hands—but a challenge to trust in the superiority and sovereignty of YHWH. The book gives no hint of a conflict between deities; YHWH's enemy is Nineveh, embodied in the king of Nineveh, not the chief Assyrian god Assur or the long-standing patron deity of Nineveh, Ishtar,[101] or any other of the Assyrian deities. Such sidelining of Assyrian deities underlines the incomparability of YHWH, the God of Israel.

In my view, there is no reason to think that the book was composed specifically for liturgical celebration. God is never addressed, and nothing indicates that different speakers would have to be involved in reading the book. It is possible that the congregation was expected to speak some of the passages, but nothing in the book of Nahum demands or even strongly invites being read as a congregational response. Thus, it seems likely that the book was most often dramatically presented by one person. This may have happened as part of a liturgical gathering but not necessarily so. The message was to fear YHWH rather than Nineveh. This message would still be relevant after the fall of the Assyrian empire, when other forces claimed the loyalty of the Judeans and instilled fear in them.[102]

The confusion of referents appears to be a deliberate rhetorical strategy. A recent reader reports:

> On reading Nahum, I was imbued with a sense of uncertainty, a deep feeling of unease. I found myself constantly checking back and forth through

---

100. See Kevin J. Cathcart, "Treaty-Curses and the Book of Nahum," *CBQ* 35 (1973): 179–87; Bob Becking, "A Judge in History: Notes on Nahum 3,7 and Esarhaddon's Succession Treaty § 47:452," *Zeitschrift für Altorientalische und Biblische Rechtsgeschichte* 1 (1995): 111–16; Gordon H. Johnston, "Rhetorical Allusions to Neo-Assyrian Treaty Curses," *BSac* 158 (2001): 415–36.

101. Nah 2:7(8) may allude to Ishtar; see the commentary *ad loc*. Gregory D. Cook ("Of Gods and Kings: Ashur Imagery in Nahum," *BBR* 29 [2019]: 19–31) argues that 3:18 refers to the god Assur. This is unlikely, given that the Hebrew phrase used in Nahum elsewhere means "king of Assyria," not "king Assur," and the Akkadian parallels he cites are imprecise (e.g., "Assur, king of the gods," never "king Assur").

102. As noted above, if the material had been *composed* later, one might expect that a later situation would be explicitly in view, with the fall of Nineveh being cited as an example of YHWH's superiority in the way that the fall of Thebes is referenced in 3:8.

the text, trying to establish identities and events. It was as if the smoke of the battle still lingered and I was struggling to clear my vision.[103]

There is no settled us-against-them in the book. The battle between YHWH and evil still rages, and those listening and watching must take sides by putting their trust in YHWH. In this connection, the contrast between the book of Nahum and Assyrian propaganda is worth noting: "Over against the Assyrian literature's monarch-led march toward world domination stands the complete silence of Nahum with respect to any Judean king, past, present, or future."[104]

It cannot be decided with confidence which, if any, parts of the book were first communicated in oral form only (see also commentary on 1:1). In any case, the author of the written version may well have anticipated that the book would be read beyond the fall of Nineveh; any later compiler or editor certainly did. This does not mean that the prophecy then functioned very differently, say as a prooftext for the fulfillment of prophecy. Rather, the programmatic nature of the opening poem and the minimal references to Nineveh in the main text help to read the text as a token for God's effective opposition to all evil, which will be enacted again and again. Perhaps the decision to put the heading "a pronouncement concerning Nineveh" first was made to encourage such a future-oriented reading in which "Nineveh" is (also) a chiffre for any evil empire or opposition to YHWH. If so, the ordering of the two headings seems to have fulfilled its purpose, judged by the history of interpretation (see below). It would certainly be a mistake to read Nahum merely as "the document of a revelation to Nahum the Elkoshite" concerning Nineveh that has now been fulfilled, as if readers were invited merely to look back to fulfilled prophecy rather than also forward to YHWH's intervention against evil in the future.

B. NAHUM'S PLACE IN THE BOOK OF THE TWELVE

The general introduction above casts doubts on the claims of extensive redactional activity tying the Minor Prophets together. Nevertheless, it is useful to ask what happens if one reads Nahum as part of the Book of the Twelve. Key

---

103. Laurel Lanner, *"Who Will Lament Her?": The Feminine and the Fantastic in the Book of Nahum*, LHBOTS 434 / Playing the Texts 11 (New York: T&T Clark, 2006), 2.

104. Daniel C. Timmer, "Nahum's Representation of and Response to Neo-Assyria: Imperialism as a Multifaceted Point of Contact in Nahum," *BBR* 24 (2014): 359. The whole essay (349–62) is relevant here.

issues here are the use of Exod 34:6-7 in the Book of the Twelve (to which we can attach a discussion of the relationship between Jonah and Nahum, as both apply Exod 34:6-7 to Nineveh) and the view of the nations in the Book of the Twelve (to which we can attach the question of the relationship between Nahum and Habakkuk).

The appeal to God's character echoing the creedal language of Exod 34:6-7 functions in Joel 2:13-14 as a motivation for repentance. We are thus prepared for the move from the characterization of YHWH in Nah 1:2-8 to the challenge offered in vv. 9-10. While the use of traditional phrasing underlines YHWH's reliability and unaltered character, Joel also stresses that YHWH's response is not fully knowable. YHWH is and is not predictable. A similar tension is found in Nahum. YHWH is portrayed as constantly acting in character, but the point at which patient restraint gives way to powerful intervention is unknown. In this way, Nahum contributes to the general portrayal of YHWH in the Book of the Twelve. Through the changing periods of history, with empires coming and going from the Neo-Assyrian to the Persian period, YHWH is portrayed as acting consistently even while responding to different situations and initiating new events.

The claim that the portrayal of YHWH in the Book of the Twelve is coherent can be challenged most forcefully by juxtaposing Jonah and Nahum. In Jonah 3:9-4:4, the characterization of YHWH in terms of Exod 34:6-7 provides the basis for a change of course regarding Nineveh. Like the recipients of Joel's message, the inhabitants of Nineveh could not presume on YHWH relenting from punishment (3:9), but Jonah did not seem to consider such relenting entirely unpredictable (4:2). The move from divine anger to mercy is described using the very root to which the name Nahum is related (Jonah 3:9-10; 4:2), and so the book of Jonah is often considered to have been written in response to Nahum. Its message is then interpreted as "an outright contradiction of Nahum's prophecy."[105] But Nahum, too, knows of YHWH being "long-suffering" (1:3), and Jonah does not imply that YHWH tolerates evil indefinitely. Nahum could indeed be read in nationalistic ways, although it does not lend itself to such a reading quite as readily as some claim,[106] and thus Jonah's stress on the universality of YHWH's compassion can rightly be seen as a follow-up if not a response.[107] But it is not actually difficult to read Jonah and Nahum as chapters of the same book. Jonah as-

105. See Weigl, "Current Research," 105.

106. Daniel C. Timmer (*The Non-Israelite Nations in the Book of the Twelve: Thematic Coherence and the Diachronic-Synchronic Relationship in the Minor Prophets*, Biblical Interpretation Series 135 [Leiden: Brill, 2015], 116-35) reveals that Nahum is more nuanced than sometimes thought.

107. I am inclined to the view that Jonah was written after the demise of the Neo-Assyrian Empire, in which case it is about Israel's vocation more than the fate of Nineveh. It reminds

sumes YHWH's opposition to evil and injustice, and with it, the need for repentance to experience YHWH's compassion. Because Nahum knows of a time of affliction (1:12) followed by a time of peace (1:15 [2:1]), there is no suggestion that YHWH would always bless Judah and curse other nations. In addition, the rhetorical question on which Nahum ends affirms that God's concern includes nations other than Judah. Together, the two writings affirm that God can and will put an end to evil, either by repentance or destruction. Neither of the two writings allows for the view that YHWH might tolerate evil forever or that he distributes compassion and punishment along ethnic lines. The prior position of Jonah within the Book of the Twelve makes sense in terms of the implied storyline, which has Nineveh's repentance postpone its judgment rather than prevent it indefinitely.[108] Israel's own response to calls to repentance may be compared to Nineveh's if the stress falls on it being short-lived (Hos 6:4)[109] or contrasted with it if Israel's failure to repent is highlighted (e.g., Hos 11:2). As far as the storyline of God's dealings with Israel is concerned, Nahum offers hope for renewed blessing beyond judgment.

In the MT, Nahum is immediately preceded by Micah, which uses the descriptors of Exod 34:6-7 to praise God for his readiness to forgive and relent from evil. This is more similar to Jonah than to Nahum, except that God's relenting from evil is applied to his own people. Read contextually, the end of Micah "anticipates the theme of Nineveh in Nah 1 through the humiliation of 'the (female) enemy' of Zion."[110] Micah can encourage us to consider the liberation of which Nahum speaks not only as an expression of God's anger against his enemies but also as evidence of his compassion for his people. The climactic statement about YHWH's goodness in Nah 1:7 arguably makes a similar point (see the commentary). The promise of salvation beyond judgment from Hos 1 onward finds a preliminary resting point in Nahum. Micah

---

us that the reason for the judgment on Nineveh is not the benefit that Nineveh's fall brings to Judah.

108. If Jonah was indeed written later than Nahum, the fact of Nineveh's destruction makes the point that Nineveh's repentance did not secure YHWH's eternal compassion, even without the book of Nahum.

109. As far as Judah is concerned, Hezekiah's repentance in response to Micah's message (Jer 26:19) may be a subject of this comparison, but it is not reported in the Book of the Twelve.

110. Burkard M. Zapff, "The Perspective of the Nations in the Book of Micah as a 'Systematization' of the Nations' Role in Joel, Jonah and Nahum? Reflections on a Context-Oriented Exegesis in the Book of the Twelve," *Society of Biblical Literature Seminar Papers 1999*, SBLSP 38 (Atlanta: Scholars Press, 1999), 609. This essay was reprinted in *Thematic Threads in the Book of the Twelve*, ed. Paul L. Redditt and Aaron Schart, BZAW 325 (Berlin: de Gruyter, 2003), 293-312, and originally published in German in *BN* 98 (1999): 86-99. Following Nogalski, Zapff finds further "catchword-connections" between Mic 7:12-13 and Nah 1:2, 4-5 ("sea," "rivers," "mountains," "earth," "God"), which seem to me rather tenuous.

underlines the need for patient waiting before YHWH's intervention (7:9), which is implied in the characterization of God as slow to anger.

Habakkuk raises questions about the effects of the raising of the Neo-Babylonian Empire, through which Assyria's empire had been brought to an end. Other nations come clearly in view in the Book of the Twelve for the first time in Hos 7:11–16 in a passage condemning Israel's reliance on Egypt and Assyria (cf. Hos 8:9–10; 12:1[2]). The destruction of Nineveh in Nahum puts an end to reliance on Assyria, and Habakkuk affirms that Babylon cannot be relied upon to promote a just state of affairs. One could have also hoped that the end of Assyria would put an end to the exile of the northern Israelites first hinted at in Hos 9:3 (cf. 11:11). The resumption of festivals in Nah 1:15 [2:1] echoes the cessation of acceptable sacrifices and festivals in Hos 9:4–6, which resulted from foreign invasion. This may also be hinted at in Joel (1:16), which otherwise portrays the devastation and desolation brought about by invasion more generally. It is an invasion either of human soldiers represented as grasshoppers or grasshoppers depicted as human soldiers but, in any case, instigated by YHWH as a call to repentance (Joel 2:12–14). Afterward, Joel also describes the blessing that results from the removal of "the northern one" (2:20), thus providing us with images both for the suffering that is brought to an end and the new life that becomes possible with the removal of the wicked one. It is noteworthy that the judgment on "all the nations" in the final chapter (3:2 [4:2]) brings with it the restoration of Judah and Jerusalem (3:1 [4:1]; cf. Nah 2:2[3]) and sees God deal with specific accusations as he avenges blood not previously avenged (3:21 [4:21]; cf. Nah 1:3). As heavens and earth "shake," YHWH is a "stronghold" for his people (3:16 [4:16]; cf. Nah 1:5, 7). Thus, some of the motifs in the opening poem of the book of Nahum are anticipated in Joel.

Joel 3:16 (4:16) finds an echo at the beginning of Amos in a verse (1:2) whose second half anticipates Nahum's depiction of drought-ridden Carmel (Nah 1:4). This may encourage us to interpret the desolation in Nahum's opening poem as the result of God's judgment, not least on the Northern Kingdom of Israel (cf. Mic 1:4–5). In Amos, God's judgment on Israel is the climax of punitive actions against several nations; in Nahum, it is a reminder of God's power, which will now turn against Assyria. While prophets like Amos stress that God's decisive intervention on "the day of YHWH" is not necessarily in Israel's favor, Nahum indicates that the affliction of God's people does not have the last word, as God's forceful intervention punishes those who profited from Israel's affliction. In Amos, the restoration is tied up with the house of David (9:11–15); in Obadiah, Zion is the place of refuge (v. 17). Similarly, in Nahum, Judah is the recipient of the good news and the site of the celebratory festival (1:15 [2:1]) rather than, say, languished Carmel. In this way, Nahum participates in the motif of salvation beyond judgment centered on Jerusalem.

C. NAHUM'S PLACE IN THE BIBLICAL CANON

Nahum's announcement of the end of imperialism and injustice is not unique in the Bible. By way of example, judgment is pronounced on Assyria in Isa 10:5–15, on Edom in Isa 34, on Babylon in Jer 50–51, and on Tyre and Egypt in Ezek 26–32. The New Testament develops the theme in Rev 17–18. Nahum, however, spells out the link between God's character and the end of empire more fully than any of these. Its vivid and detailed language serves to engage the emotions and thus to press home the truth that no force can stand against YHWH. The good news of victory (Nah 1:15 [2:1]) is not limited to the downfall of the Neo-Assyrian Empire. Good news is proclaimed again in the return from the Babylonian exile, a return marking another instance of God asserting his reign over evil (Isa 52:7).[111] These historical events find their climax in God's victory over evil won in the death and resurrection of Christ. This is why Nah 1:15 (2:1) is again fulfilled in the proclamation of the gospel (cf. Rom 10:15; Eph 6:15).

Nahum reminds us that liberation and life in peace entail the destruction of God's enemies. The lifting up of the lowly goes hand in hand with the deposition of the powerful (Luke 1:52). The apostle Paul's affirmation that no powers can separate God's people from God's love can be fleshed out with Nahum's invitation to imagine the most powerful human force defeated, unable to harm God's people without God's permission. The universal and permanent authority given to Christ (e.g., Matt 28:18; 1 Pet 3:22) contrasts with the limited and temporary authority given to governments and empires, just as Christ's exercise of authority contrasts with theirs (e.g., Mark 10:42–45). Habakkuk offers a stark reminder of the fact that the subjugation of Assyria was only one episode in history's cycle of violence. Christ's triumph over rulers and authorities (Col 2:15) did not come about through the violent exercise of superior force but through Jesus's submission to violence. Given that the authorities who put Jesus to death were executing the will of God no less than the Assyrian armies who put an end to the Northern Kingdom (see, e.g., Acts 2:32; 3:18; 4:28), God must be considered both perpetrator and victim in the death of Christ.[112] The resurrection is again, more unambiguously, a demonstration of superior power, but maybe the stress should be on the weakness of death in failing to prevent the inevitable (see

---

111. See the excursus on Nah 1:15 (2:1) and Isa 52:7 below (pp. 106–9). For other links between Nahum and the book of Isaiah, see, e.g., Fabry, *Nahum*, 113.

112. When we who believe in the divinity of Christ affirm that God's wrath was borne on the cross, we affirm both the agency of God ("God's wrath") and his passion as victim ("borne"). It is essential for Christian theology that Christ, while innocent, bore God's wrath willingly. In this sense, his was an active passion.

Acts 2:24). Similarly, the universal submission to God in the final judgment (e.g., Rom 14:11, using Isa 45:23) is not won by superior force. There will be recognition not only of the *futility* of rebelling against a supremely *powerful* God but also of the *evil* and *shamefulness* of rebelling against a supremely *good* God.[113] Universal submission to Christ relates to the name given to him, which expresses his true nature (Phil 2:9–10). The claim made here is not that the Old Testament warrior YHWH has turned into a pacifist God in the New Testament (if by "pacifist" we mean that God is no longer linked with any violence). In the light of Matt 24, the fall of Jerusalem in AD 70 could be cited as a further instance of the divine use of human military force within history. Nevertheless, the decisive victory has been won by God becoming a victim himself, and this fact qualifies all use of force. There is a firm limit to what can be achieved by military force; the end of all violence (to say nothing of sin and death) being one of the things that cannot be won in this way. Nahum's task within the canon is to unmask the pretensions of military power as well as to depict the awful consequences of God's wrath.[114]

D. NAHUM IN THE HISTORY OF INTERPRETATION

The remarks made above about the Septuagint, the Book of the Twelve, and the biblical canon already belong to the history of interpretation. The tendency to read Nahum with specific reference to events later than the fall of Nineveh, which seems already evident in LXX, is clearly manifest in the reception of Nahum in the Qumran community. The Pesher Nahum (4Q169) interprets Nahum as a coded message for later times.[115] Assyrian brutality is a code for the brutality of the Hasmonean ruler Alexander Jannaeus. No-Amon (Thebes), the temple city, stands for the Sadducees,[116] and the fall of Nineveh is a metaphor for the end of all those whom the members of the Qumran community considered their enemies, including the Pharisees. Thus, the interpretation of Nahum in 4Q169 offers comfort to a marginalized group, not least by suggesting that the events through which the community

113. Rom 16:20 may belong in this eschatological context and captures the paradox by speaking of the crushing of Satan under our feet by "the God of peace."

114. See, e.g., John 3:36 and Rom 1:18 for the ongoing canonical significance of speaking of God's wrath beyond the cross of Christ.

115. Berrin (*Pesher Nahum Scroll*, 12–18) argues that the pesher application was understood to supersede the earlier historical reference without invalidating it. Unlike Berrin, I think this is in parallel with rather than in contrast to New Testament usage.

116. Fabry (*Nahum*, 114–16), who offers a fuller discussion of the reception of Nahum in Qumran, points out that in 4Q385a (which makes free use of Nah 3:8–10), No-Amon may be understood as a code for Alexandria, as in the Targum, for which see ArBib 14, 140.

lives have been pre-written a long time ago and thus are fully known and controlled by God.

The Targum Jonathan mentions Jonah's preaching and Nineveh's repentance in an additional note to Nah 1:1 but remarks that Nineveh sinned again subsequently.[117] In v. 2, the Targum equates YHWH's adversaries with "the enemies of his people," a phrase also found in v. 6. In v. 7, YHWH is specifically said to be good to Israel, and 1:9 is read as an address to other nations. Nineveh prefigures the judgment on all nations that plunder and oppress Israel.[118] God's enemies and Israel's seem to be invariably equated. As the Targum writes from a perspective of victimization, such an equation is easy to comprehend. But the comparison with the actual text of Nahum puts into relief the fact that the equation is not made explicit in Nahum.

In ancient Christian interpretation, 1:14–15 (1:15–2:1) is perhaps the most popular section.[119] Fabry reports that Didymus the Blind used these two verses to speak about Christian baptism. The pre-Christian self with all its idols is buried (1:14), and the baptized believer is called to celebrate the festivals of good deeds (1:15). Because in Christ's death God is both the agent of wrath and its recipient, Christians are former enemies of God who are now reconciled. They are recipients of God's wrath in Christ and are those who benefit from the exercise of God's wrath. The book of Nahum can thus speak of death as well as resurrection. The traditional fourfold interpretation of the book is neatly summarized in an exposition (wrongly) attributed to Julian of Toledo:

> The prophet Nahum is set in the kingdom of the Assyrians. According to the historical sense, he speaks of the destruction of Nineveh, its capital; in the allegorical sense, of the world's being laid waste; in the mystical sense, of the restoration of the human race through Christ; in the moral sense, of the restoring of his first dignified state, or to yet greater glory, of the sinner fallen into wickedness.[120]

---

117. See ArBib 14, 131. For some Jewish interpreters, this seems to have raised the question whether Nineveh's repentance was genuine and, if not, to what extent God was willing to accept insincere repentance. See Fabry, *Nahum*, 116–18.

118. Verse 8 likely refers to the destruction of the temple in AD 70; cf. Robert P. Gordon, *Studies in the Targum to the Twelve Prophets: From Nahum to Malachi*, VTSup 51 (Leiden: Brill, 1993), 41–45; Fabry, *Nahum*, 118.

119. Seán P. Kealy (*An Interpretation of the Twelve Minor Prophets of the Hebrew Bible: The Emergence of Eschatology as a Theological Theme* [Lewiston: Mellen, 2009], 122) notes, however, that all six references to Nahum in the *Summa Theologiae* by Thomas Aquinas are to 1:9.

120. Cited in Edward Ball, " 'When the Towers Fall': Interpreting Nahum as Christian Scripture," in *In Search of True Wisdom: Essays in Old Testament Interpretation in Honour*

Eschewing this fourfold approach, a broadly historical approach emerged during the Renaissance and Reformation periods that led to different emphases. The summary of Nahum's message given by Martin Luther in his 1525 lectures on the book is often cited:

> He [Nahum] teaches us to trust God and to believe, especially when we despair of all human help, human powers, and counsel, that the Lord stands by those who are His, shields His own against all attacks of the enemy, be they ever so powerful.[121]

Modern historical-critical research has been largely concerned with distinguishing between the words of the prophet and those of later editors and with establishing the setting of the prophet. Particularly, the denial of the opening hymn to Nahum would make the original prophet's message appear in a very different light from that of the book. While this is still a widely held view,[122] the views that Nahum was one of the false prophets condemned by Jeremiah (J. P. M. Smith) or that he was a cult prophet who wrote a liturgy for the celebration of the fall of Nineveh after the event (Humbert, Sellin) are no longer upheld in contemporary scholarship.[123] Recently, Baumann has read the text as condoning sexual violence against women who are unduly self-confident.[124] If, however, we distinguish between, on the one hand, the cultural-historical context in which the book originates (a context that is deserving of critique, but not as part of a commentary on Nahum) and, on the other hand, the use that texts such as Nah 3:5-6 make of these given cultural conventions, a more nuanced picture is possible.[125] The personification of cities as feminine and the depiction of YHWH in masculine terms (king, warrior, husband) are cultural givens. The depiction of feeble warriors as women and of the stripping of victims was part of Assyrian war propaganda, which

---

of Ronald E. Clements, ed. Edward Ball, JSOTSup 300 (Sheffield: Sheffield Academic, 1999), 212.

121. This is the version usually cited. It is Maier's (*Nahum*, 85–86) translation from the German Walch edition ("St. Louis ed. XIV: 1355" should be corrected to col. 1335). Cf. *Minor Prophets I: Hosea–Malachi*, vol. 18 of *Luther's Works* (Saint Louis: Concordia, 1975), 282.

122. It is characteristic of German scholarship; see Jeremias, *Nahum*, 12–15.

123. See, e.g., Weigl, "Current Research."

124. Gerlinde Baumann, "Das Buch Nahum: Der gerechte Gott als sexueller Gewalttäter," in *Kompendium Feministische Bibelauslegung*, ed. Louise Schottroff and Michael T. Wacker (Gütersloh: Kaiser, 1998), 347–53; Baumann, *Gottes Gewalt im Wandel: Traditionsgeschichtliche und intertextuelle Studien zu Nahum 1,2–8*, WMANT 108 (Neukirchen-Vluyn: Neukirchener Verlag, 2005). Cf. Julia Myers-O'Brien, *Nahum*, Readings: A New Biblical Commentary (Sheffield: Sheffield Academic, 2002).

125. Cf. Fabry, *Nahum*, 110.

Nahum inverts. Nineveh is not depicted as a (married) woman whose honor is violated but as a shameless prostitute with no honor to lose.[126] But we are not to think of a woman driven to prostitution to make a living. Nineveh is not the victim of a system that forces her to sell her body to make ends meet. She is a source of ensnarement and ready to sell peoples for her pleasure; it is not self-confidence that is at issue here.[127] She pays out rather than receives money (cf. Ezek 16). This distances the metaphor from "ordinary" prostitution and suggests that the text is not intended to be read as saying something about prostitutes or women in general.

E. NAHUM'S PLACE IN THE CHURCH TODAY

Much of what could be said here can be gleaned from previous sections. Nahum celebrates YHWH's sovereignty and justice and invites us to join in that celebration. God's retributive anger is good news because it deals with oppression, violence, and wickedness. With Christian interpreters throughout the centuries, the church reads Nahum as a token of the final judgment that ends all oppression and evil: "Everything said to Nineveh is going to happen in the judgment on the devil and his associates" (Haimo of Auxerre).[128] This judgment is anticipated in historical events such as the demise of empires and the deconstruction of injustice, but supremely in the proclamation of the gospel through which enemies of God become his children. Nahum challenges us to trust and submit to YHWH, not a God of violence but a God who ends violence, and to make sure that we are not counted among his adversaries. Sadly, history affords many examples of people who bear the name of Christ blindly supporting militaristic solutions for nationalistic purposes in Germany, Britain, Rwanda, Serbia, and elsewhere. The church in different times and places therefore cannot assume that it will find itself on the right side of God's judgment, which vindicates the oppressed. Where Christians lean toward violent solutions, they must be called to repentance. The encouragement Nahum offers is for those who, under attack, trust in God's vindication rather than their own power.

126. *Pace* Jeremias, *Nahum*, 34, who believes that the punishment in 3:5 demands that specifically an adulteress is in view. See my exegesis of Nah 3:4–5 below.

127. Even if readers wanted to draw a comparison to sexually liberated and self-confident women today, such a comparison is surely anachronistic from the point of view of historical exegesis, which should be taken into account in evaluating Nahum.

128. Quoted in Edward Ball, "Towers," 214. Jeremias, *Nahum*, 27, suggests that interpreters who do not believe, as he does, that 1:2–8 was composed centuries later than chs. 2–3 do not read Nahum primarily as a forward-looking prophecy. This is not borne out by the history of interpretation.

While reflecting on the theology of Nahum, I received an email from Zimbabwe describing some of the horrors that happened there in 2008. It included the following two sentences: "Millions of people in this country are going to die of easily preventable disease while the devil at the top struts around the world stage trying to convince people that he is the legitimate ruler. I have no problem with the imprecatory psalms anymore!" This not merely indicates that there are contexts in which Nahum's fierce language is understandable but also suggests that there are situations in which nothing less than the fierce opposition to evil expressed in Nahum will do. Nahum is first of all a book of comfort in the face of evil and fear. Where people feel helpless and abandoned, the message of God's anger can be a message of hope. At the same time, there is a bit of Nineveh in all of us, and Nahum can serve as a reminder of the wickedness of asserting ourselves over against the Creator. While God's determination to end all wickedness is good news, its execution is not pleasant, and the horror of the fall of Nineveh may speak to us about the horrors of the cross endured by Christ. God's intolerance of evil is not without costs. What is lacking in Nahum itself is an indication that God will ultimately bear this cost himself, but the fact that the book of Nahum does not tell the whole story does not take away from the fact that it tells one part of the story very well. Christian readers must tell the fuller story and cannot speak of God's persistent resistance to evil apart from the cross of Christ.

Text and Commentary

I. THE SUPERSCRIPTION TO THE BOOK (1:1)

¹*A pronouncement concerning Nineveh.*
The document of a revelation to Nahum the Elkoshite.

1 Whether or not the first verse of the book should be included in the poetic structure is disputed. It is scanned more easily as a bicolon than most
headings, the division between the two cola being indicated by an *atnach*.
Spronk observed that if this bicolon is considered the first poetic "line," the
final letters of the first four lines (bicola) form (the consonants of) the divine
name in a telestic.[1] Given that the initial letters of the first three bicola following this bicolon spell the first-person pronoun, this is a noteworthy feature
of the text. The feature may be coincidental, but the order of the two clauses
in v. 1 is unusual, the first one being more specific than the second, which
suggests that the acrostic-telestic combination may be the result of authorial
design rather than mere coincidence, although, as suggested above, there
may be a rhetorical reason for the order. Together, the acrostic and telestic
spell "I am YHWH," which certainly forms a fitting heading for the opening
hymn. In my view, this feature of the text can be acknowledged without
incorporating the verse fully into the first poem. While the double heading
might allow reading v. 1 as a bicolon, the second colon would be twice the
length of the first, which would set it apart from the following, much more
evenly balanced, lines. The reference to Nineveh suggests that the verse is a
title for the book as a whole rather than being merely the introductory line of
the first poem, in spite of the, perhaps secondary, reference back to Nineveh
in 1:8 ("her place").

---

1. See Spronk, "Synchronic and Diachronic," 177–78; *Nahum*, 25, 28.

The precise nuance of the term rendered *pronouncement* (*maśśā'*) has been much debated. The word means "burden" in a number of places,[2] most interestingly in Jer 23:33–34, 36, 38, where we find a play on two different meanings of the word. There are other places where the word refers to some sort of (divine) pronouncement,[3] often associated with the name of a foreign nation.[4] Most commentators have abandoned the practice of translating "burden" in those instances and instead assume that the word refers to a prophetic utterance. Richard D. Weis argues that the term here designates a distinctive genre, the *exposition* of an oracle.[5] Following him, Marvin A. Sweeney offers this definition:

> A prophetic discourse in which the prophet attempts to explain how YHWH's actions are manifested in the realm of human affairs.... The prophetic pronouncement is spoken in response to a particular situation in human events; it is analytical in character in that it examines past and present events in an attempt to draw conclusions about YHWH's activity and intentions. The pronouncement appears to be based on a revelatory experience or vision.[6]

On this understanding, the verse does not introduce a revelation about Nineveh but a revelation that is exposited with regard to Nineveh,[7] or it interprets earlier prophetic words about Assyria.[8] The characterization "prophetic exposition" fits the book of Nahum and would be appropriate for

---

2. Cf. Exod 23:5; Num 4:15, 19, 24, 27, 31, 32, 47, 49; 11:11, 17; Deut 1:12; 2 Sam 15:33; 19:36; 2 Kgs 5:17; 8:9; Job 7:20; 2 Chr 17:11; 20:25; 35:3; Neh 13:15, 19; and in prophetic literature: Isa 22:25; 46:1–2; Jer 17:21, 22, 24, 27; Ezek 24:25 (metaphorically, "the burden of their souls").

3. See Isa 13:1; 14:28; 15:1; 17:1; 19:1; 21:1, 11, 13; 22:1; 23:1; 30:6; Ezek 12:10; Hab 1:1; Zech 9:1; 12:1; Mal 1:1; cf. 2 Kgs 9:25; Lam 2:14; Prov 30:1; 31:1.

4. See Isa 13:1; 15:1; 17:1; 19:1; 21:11; 23:1; cf. Jer 23:33–34, 36, 38 with the divine name.

5. Richard D. Weis, "A Definition of the Genre *Maśśā'* in the Hebrew Bible" (PhD diss., The Claremont Graduate School, 1986); cf. Richard D. Weis, "Oracle (Old Testament)," *ABD*, 5:28–29.

6. Marvin A. Sweeney, *Isaiah 1–39 with an Introduction to Prophetic Literature*, FOTL 16 (Grand Rapids: Eerdmans, 1996), 534–35; cf. Sweeney "Concerning the Structure," 364–77. See also Michael H. Floyd, "The מַשָּׂא (*MAŚŚĀ'*) as a Type of Prophetic Book," *JBL* 121 (2002): 401–22. Floyd ("Meaning," 8) suggests that Sweeney makes too little of "Weis's most important innovative insight, namely that the *maśśā'* reinterprets previous revelation."

7. Admittedly, the Heb. term used for "revelation" (*ḥāzôn*) never stands in a construct relationship with a name ("revelation about Nineveh"), although there are phrases with *ḥāzôn* in which the content or mode is designated rather than the addressee of the revelation (e.g., *ḥăzôn laylâ*, "a nocturnal vision," in Isa 29:7; *ḥăzôn šālōm*, "visions of peace," in Ezek 13:16.

8. E.g., Isa 10:5–19; 14:24–27. See Spronk, *Nahum*, 7–8, who also thinks of Isa 5:24–30 and 30:27–33.

Habakkuk as well, but Boda is not persuaded that this definition works with regard to, for example, the instances in Zechariah.[9]

Another proposal has been offered by Ina Willi-Plein. She argues convincingly against the derivation of the noun from an assumed phrase ("lifting up one's voice") and suggests that in incipits, *maśśāʾ* does not refer to an "utterance" as such but to an assignment or commission that is only indirectly relayed—in other words, an oracle that the prophet does not address directly to the ostensible addressees.[10] This, too, is a plausible meaning for Nahum and Habakkuk. It would seem to fit the many occurrences in headings to oracles concerning foreign nations in Isaiah,[11] oracles that not everyone agrees are best described as expositions in the specific sense Weis proposed.[12] If understood in this way, there is maybe a natural link between *maśśāʾ* and an emphasis on literariness more than oral ministry (see below), although this is not essential.

The use of *sēper* (*document*) is unique in the superscription to a prophetic book and turns attention to the literariness of the scroll. The contrast between the oral and the written in ancient literature is easily overstated,[13] but the use of *sēper* in the superscription can prepare us for traits that are more discernible by the eye of the reader than the ear of the listener—namely, acrostic features. Heb. *ḥăzôn* has been translated *revelation* rather than "vision" because it does not necessarily relate to a visionary experience or even a specific mental image. The term can just as well refer more broadly to a perspective that has been grasped, maybe like a flash of insight that appears to have come without deliberate effort rather than a logical conclusion that has been carefully worked out.[14] In any case, the term seems to locate the source of insight outside the person who receives a *ḥăzôn*.

9. See Mark J. Boda, "Freeing the Burden of Prophecy: *Maśśāʾ* and the Legitimacy of Prophecy in Zech 9–14," *Bib* 87 (2006): 338–57.

10. Ida Willi-Plein, "Wort, Last oder Auftrag? Zur Bedeutung von מַשָּׂא in Überschriften prophetischer Texteinheiten," in *Die unwiderstehliche Wahrheit: Studien zur alttestamentlichen Prophetie, Festschrift für Arndt Meinhold*, ed. Rüdiger Lux and Ernst-Joachim Waschke, Arbeiten zur Bibel und ihrer Geschichte 23 (Leipzig: Evangelische Verlagsanstalt, 2006), 431–38.

11. Floyd ("Meaning," 3) objects to Willi-Plein's proposal, believing that her definition of *maśśāʾ* means that these oracles were specifically "written" and "portable," but she does not make this claim.

12. But see the detailed argument in Floyd, "Meaning."

13. See David M. Carr, *Writing on the Tablet of the Heart: Origins of Scripture and Literature* (New York: Oxford University Press, 2005); Paul J. Griffiths, *Religious Reading: The Place of Reading in the Practice of Religion* (New York: Oxford University Press, 1999).

14. The usage in Isaiah and Obadiah in particular counsels against a narrow understanding as visionary experience. Carl E. Armerding ("Obadiah, Nahum, Habakkuk," in *Daniel and the Minor Prophets*, vol. 7 of *The Expositor's Bible Commentary*, ed. Frank E. Gaebelein

The recipient of this revelation, *Nahum the Elkoshite*, is unknown to us. Indeed, we do not know of any place or clan called Elkosh.[15] In an interesting but speculative line of argument, one scholar has suggested that *Elkoshite* designates a military rank.[16] More plausibly, *Nahum the Elkoshite* may be a pen name.[17] The name "Nahum" is frequently attested in Northwest Semitic inscriptions and relates to "comfort," while Elkosh, which has traditionally been understood as a place name, is suggestive of "severe God."[18] The name of the prophet thus hints at the message of the book: comfort that comes from a severe God. Gregory Cook speaks of "Nahum's prophetic name" and argues that the opening two verses of Nahum allude to Isa 1:24. On this basis, he believes that the one who receives "comfort" (satisfaction) from the act of vengeance is YHWH himself.[19] While this is possible, the use of the root *nḥm* for gaining satisfaction in Isa 1:24 is unusual and likely prompted by a desire for alliteration.[20] In my view, the parallels between the two texts are not strong enough to signal a specific allusion. In the light of v. 7, the comfort seems primarily directed toward those who seek refuge in YHWH rather than YHWH himself, even if this need not prevent seeing a further allusion to the satisfaction that YHWH gains in preserving his honor as he executes vengeance. In any case, whether *Nahum the Elkoshite* was the author's real name or a literary pseudonym, it can be a fertile source of theological reflection.[21]

[Grand Rapids, Zondervan, 1985], 511) suggests that such "revelation" is "almost invariably supersensory in nature" (cited approvingly by Patterson, *Nahum*, 173). I am not convinced that this is a helpful term. One or another of the prophet's senses, even if maybe not physical sight, must have been involved. (Earlier, Patterson stresses the active involvement of the prophet; see 137.) An "exposition" (*maśśāʾ*) is also "seen" (*ḥzh*) in Isa 13:1; Hab 1:1; Lam 2:14.

15. Traditionally, Elkosh is understood as a location with a wide range of speculative identifications; cf. "Elijah the Tishbite" (1 Kgs 17:1; 21:17, 28; 2 Kgs 1:3, 8; 9:36); "Micah the Morashite" (Mic 1:1; Jer 26:18); "Jeremiah the Anathothite" (Jer 29:27). Tg. saw a reference to a clan, as did probably the LXX translator; cf. "Joash the Abiezrite" (Judg 6:11).

16. Thomas Schneider, "Nahum und Theben: Zum Topographisch-Historischen Hintergrund von Nahum 3,8f," *BN* 44 (1988): 73. This presumes a connection with *qešet* ("bow"). Schneider wonders whether Nahum may have been drafted into the Assyrian campaign against Thebes.

17. Spronk, *Nahum*, 31–33; note also the observations made by Allis, "Nahum," 76–77.

18. Spronk, *Nahum*, 31, comparing Song 8:6.

19. Gregory D. Cook, "Nahum's Prophetic Name," *TynBul* 67 (2016): 37–40. Cook does not discuss the second part of the name.

20. See Hugh G. M. Williamson, *A Critical and Exegetical Commentary on Isaiah 1–27*, vol. 1, ICC (London: T&T Clark, 2006), 123, 142–43. Williamson offers the use of the *hitpaʿel* in Gen 27:42 and Ezek 5:13 for comparison. With YHWH as subject, the root is more often used to refer to being sorry (e.g., Gen 6:6–7; 1 Sam 15:11), including relenting from evil (e.g., Exod 32:14; Amos 7:3).

21. On the view that the earliest part of the book was secular songs about the (coming) destruction of Nineveh that were incorporated into a theological vision and then later re-

The double title enables the creation of a sentence acrostic and telestic and so integrates the title with the poem. As I have observed in the introduction (p. 23), the double title may but need not point to two different stages in the redaction of the book. Certainly, 1:1b could have functioned as a superscription to the book in its own right. (This is less clear for 1:1a. Without 1:1b, the superscription would have been very short, arguably better suited to a single oracle than a prophetic book of various poems.) In any case, in the present form of the book, it is not advisable to allocate different parts of the book to the *pronouncement concerning Nineveh* and the *document of a revelation to Nahum* respectively. The whole is to be understood as the document of a revelation given to Nahum and all of it is a pronouncement concerning Nineveh, whereby Nineveh is to be understood both in historical terms and as an example of the opposition to YHWH of which the opening poem speaks more generally.

As the book unfolds it becomes clear that the fall of Nineveh is to be seen as an instantiation of decisive, divine action against evil that flows from the nature of YHWH. The use of the term *revelation* and the inclusion of 1:1a right at the beginning of the book, rather than before 2:1(2) or perhaps even in second position within 1:1, arguably seeks to guard against reading the images of destruction merely as the result of a logical application (exposition) of truths about YHWH. The doctrine of YHWH spelled out in 1:2–8 does not lead by a process of simple reasoning to the announcement of the fall of Nineveh; *revelation* was required for that.

II. CONTEMPLATING YHWH, THE AVENGING GOD (1:2–10)

[2]*A zealous*[a] *and avenging God is YHWH;*
  avenging is YHWH and Master of rage.
Avenging is YHWH toward his foes,
  one who remains agitated against[b] *his enemies.*
[3]*YHWH, he is slow to anger but abounding in power,*
  and he will certainly not absolve.
YHWH—in gale and storm[c] *is his way;*
  clouds are the dust of his feet.
[4]*He blasts*[d] *the sea and dries it up*[e]
  and all the streams he makes dry.

---

dacted, "Nahum" may be most appropriately used to indicate the crucial middle stage for which "author" seems the most appropriate term. The "author" would have used material by one or more poets, and his composition might have been annotated or expounded by one or more redactors. I am inclined to the view that the book essentially goes back to one person—that is, the poet is the author.

Withered are Bashan and Carmel,
the bud of Lebanon is withered.[f]
[5]*Mountains shake because of him;*[g]
the hills go to pieces;
the earth rears[h] *before him,*
the world and all who inhabit it.[i]
[6]*Before his scorn who can stand?*
Who can rise in the heat of his anger?
His rage is poured out like fire;
the rocks are torn asunder[j] *because of him.*
[7]*Good is YHWH—as a stronghold—in the day of distress,*
and he knows those who seek refuge in him.
[8]*And with a sweeping flood, a full end he makes of her place;*
his enemies he pursues into darkness.
[9]*What do you ponder*[k] *concerning YHWH?*
He is making a full end;
distress will not arise a second time.
[10]*For they are akin to thorns entangled*
and like their drink drunk;
they are consumed like fully dry stubble.[l]

a. The particular form of the adj. used here (*qannô'*) is also found in Josh 24:19 and may have been chosen in both instances for euphonic reasons. A note in *BHS* at Exod 20:5 indicates that the form is also found there in the Nash Papyrus.

b. See the commentary for a discussion of the translation.

c. The phrase could be translated "in stormy gale" (cf. "tempestuous whirlwind" in *CHP*, 196), as the two nouns obviously refer to one rather than two events. But such a translation would be rather prosaic, and *gale and storm* works well in English.

d. For this translation, see James M. Kennedy, "The Root GꞋR in the Light of Semantic Analysis," *JBL* 106 (1987): 47–64; see the commentary below.

e. For the form *wayyabbašēhû*, cf. GKC 69u, which offers other examples of elision of the first radical in *piel yiqtol* forms; the full form is found in 1 Kgs 17:7 and Jonah 4:7. The *wayyiqtol* (and *qatal* in the next colon) describes the (present) effect of the (characteristic) action introduced by the participle, but cf. JM 118r. The two verbs for parching or causing to go dry are also found together in Job 14:11; Isa 19:5; 42:15; 44:27; 50:2; Jer 51:36.

f. This translates the MT. It is very well possible that the last word of the verse was different in an earlier form of the text; see the commentary.

g. Most contemporary English translations gloss *mimmennû* "before him," which is possible. But the use of two different phrases in the same verse suggests to me a differentiation, unless the variety is for poetic reasons. The causal meaning is well established; see *HALOT* or *DCH* for examples. It is also accepted in NASB and the JPS Tanakh. Admittedly, the relationship could be precisely the opposite, with *mimmennû* being understood as *before him* and *mippānāyw* as *because of him*. My translation moves from cause to effect, which seems to me most satisfying in the context of a description of divine approach.

h. See Hab 1:3; Ps 89:9(10); Hos 13:1 for other instances in which MT allows *nś'* to function intransitively or reflexively (all of these are queried in *BHS*). Elliger's suggestion in *BHS* to read *ś'h niphal* ("to be devastated") in Nah 1:5 is followed in the entry to *nś'* in *HALOT* but rejected in the entry to *ś'h*. In BDB, these instances are considered dubious; *DCH* allows for the intransitive use of the *qal* but offers as an alternative the possibility of an ellipsis ("lift up one's voice"). For fuller discussion, see the commentary.

i. For the use of the construct with a preposition, see GKC 130a. See Ps 107:34; Isa 24:6; Jer 12:4; Hab 2:8, 17 for further occurrences of the phrase *yōšbê bāh* (*who inhabit it*, "inhabitants of it").

j. The emendation of *niṭṭəšû* (*torn asunder*) to *niṣṣətû* ("burned"), which is sometimes proposed (see *BHS*), is discussed in the commentary.

k. For the paragogic *nun*, see JM 44e–f and the discussion in *IBHS* 31.7, especially for Hoftijzer's notion of contrastivity. W. Randall Garr ("The Paragogic *nun* in Rhetorical Perspective," in *Biblical Hebrew in Its Northwest Semitic Setting: Typological and Historical Perspectives*, ed. Steven E. Fassberg and Avi Hurvitz [Winona Lake, IN: Eisenbrauns; Jerusalem: Magnes Press, 2006], 65–74) argues that paragogic *nun* identifies clauses as rhetorically subordinate within a discourse.

l. The LXX reads, "Because he shall be left dry down to their foundation, and he shall be consumed like a twisted yew tree and like straw fully dried" (NETS). This, in my view, does not reflect a better text.

Composition

The opening letters of the first three bicola spell the first-person pronoun in Hebrew. If the superscript (v. 1) is included, the final letters of the first four bicola spell the divine name. Together, the acrostic (first letters) and telestic (final letters) spell "I am YHWH" (see the commentary on 1:1). At the beginning of the line, the sentence acrostic ends on the *yod* of the divine name in v. 3a, which is followed by two words beginning with the first letter of the alphabet (*aleph*). The next occurrence of the divine name also opens a line (v. 3b) and is followed by two words beginning with the second letter of the alphabet (*bet*). These two bicola form the beginning of an alphabetic acrostic that covers half the alphabet. An increasing number of scholars doubt the existence of an acrostic, but in my view this doubt asks for too much coincidence.[22] Most scholars agree that the hymn in ch. 1 is based on an acrostic—maybe one that only ever covered half the alphabet—even though the acrostic is disturbed in some places.[23] While the disappearance of the *dalet*

---

22. Maier, *Nahum*, 60; Michael H. Floyd, "The Chimerical Acrostic of Nahum 1:2–10," *JBL* 113 (1994): 421–37; Bob Becking, "Divine Wrath and the Conceptual Coherence of the Book of Nahum," *SJOT* 9 (1995): 277–96; Baumann, *Gottes Gewalt*; Fabry, *Nahum*, 132.

23. A few attempts have been made in the past to recover a complete acrostic, but these have now been abandoned. If a complete acrostic was the source behind Nahum, the latter half remained unused.

(v. 4b) may be the result of an accident of textual transmission (see below), it is unlikely that the book of Nahum ever opened with a perfect alphabetic acrostic, as some of the other disturbances cannot be easily explained in this way (see the commentary on vv. 6–7). More likely, the "imperfection" goes back to the author. Whether the poet used an already existing acrostic that he saw no need to preserve[24] or deliberately disordered a known or previously unknown acrostic (i.e., one that only existed as a first draft or as a possibility in his mind) is impossible to tell. It is possible to make rhetorical sense of all the disturbances, even the disappearance of the *dalet*, which suggests that they are not entirely accidental. The dissolution of creation at the appearance of God is in any case well mirrored in the dissolution of the acrostic (as Longman notes[25]).

The hymn puts emphasis on the vengefulness of YHWH and in its present form takes up the language of Exod 34:6–7 to characterize YHWH.[26] The use of participles underlines that the hymn does not focus on a specific historical event but characterizes YHWH more generally. While stress is laid on YHWH's great power and his rage against his enemies, a first climax is reached in v. 7 with *Good is YHWH—as a stronghold—in the day of distress*, to which is added, *he knows those who seek refuge in him*. Thus, God's vengeance is described in the context of protection for his people. This also prepares for the later shaming of the Assyrian king as unable to protect his people.[27] The implied opposition between YHWH and the Assyrian king is perhaps also noteworthy for the lack of reference to a (human) king of Judah here. In the ancient world, more typically, a national god would offer strength and protection to the king tasked with protecting his people. YHWH is portrayed as a refuge for all God's people, not just the king. Verse 8 for the first time alludes to Assyria (see the discussion below) and assures a full end to the foreign power. The first direct address of the book comes in v. 9 and is probably directed to a Judean audience in the first instance. The audience is challenged in vv. 9–10 to trust that YHWH will make a complete end to those who cause their distress.

The divine name is used seven times in this unit. Given the significance of the number seven in the Bible and the focus on God's name with the use of Exod 34:6–7, whose purpose seems to be to spell out what the divine

24. Spronk, "Synchronic and Diachronic," 183–84.

25. Longman, "Nahum," 775.

26. If the author (or editor) used an existing acrostic, it is possible that the original acrostic consisted of vv. 2a, 3b*–8 (and perhaps material not used in Nahum). In this case, vv. 2b–3a, which precede the allusions to Exod 34 and the divine name at the beginning of verse 3b, are the author's additions, with which he created the sentence acrostic-telestic.

27. Noted by William Briggs, "Fluid Dynamics: The Interplay of Water and Gender in Nahum," *JBL* 137 (2018): 859–60.

name entails (note Exod 34:5), this fact adds weight to the delineation of the unit suggested here (vv. 2–10, or maybe vv. 1–10). The focus on the divine name perhaps also adds weight to the view that the sentence acrostic "I am YHWH" mentioned above is not accidental.

Commentary

2 In the Hebrew Bible, the adjective "jealous" (the translation uses *zealous* to avoid contemporary associations of the word "jealous" with loss of control) is always used to characterize *'ēl* (God).[28] In its common form (*qannā'*), the adjective is found in the Ten Commandments (Exod 20:5; Deut 5:9) and in Exod 34:14 (twice) as well as Deut 4:24 and 6:15. All of these passages include injunctions against idol worship.[29] It is noteworthy that *'ēl qannô'* (*A jealous . . . God*) immediately follows *hā'elqōšî* (*the Elkoshite*, which sounds like "severe God"; see the commentary on 1:1).

In the context of covenant renewal, Joshua affirms that Israel cannot serve God because he will not tolerate the worship of other deities or forgive disloyalty (Josh 24:19–20).[30] The covenant context of YHWH's jealousy is noteworthy. Indeed, apart from jealousy or zeal for God (Num 25:11–13),[31] jealousy seems to be acceptable only in the context of marriage among humans (Num 5:14, 30; cf. Prov 6:34; Song 8:6).[32] As R. L. Smith observed, "Jealousy in essence is an intolerance of rivals. It can be a virtue or a sin depending on the legitimacy of the rival."[33] Rivals are illegitimate when the relationship in question is exclusive; such exclusiveness is usually expressed in a covenant.[34] YHWH is not characterized here as jealous for Israel (Jerusalem, Zion, his

28. Interestingly, the divine name YHWH is used where the verb "to be jealous" has God as its agent. YHWH is jealous for his holy name (Ezek 39:25), for his land (Joel 2:18), and for Zion (Zech 1:14; 8:2). All of these passages are later than Nahum. The noun is used with reference to YHWH in the two references from Zechariah and in Num 25:11; Deut 29:20(19); 2 Kgs 19:31 // Isa 37:32; Ps 79:5; Isa 9:7(6); 26:11; 37:32; 42:13; 59:17; Ezek 5:13; 16:38, 42; 23:25 (in these three verses YHWH is implicitly depicted as a jilted husband); 36:5–6; 38:19; Zeph 1:18; 3:8. Cf. Isa 63:15 (in a prayer); Ezek 8:3, 5 (an image provokes jealousy).

29. The verb is used to indicate that Israel has done precisely that: making God jealous with their loyalty to other deities. See Deut 32:16, 21; Ps 78:58 (both *hiphil*); cf. more generally "with their sins," 1 Kgs 14:22 (*piel*).

30. A similar refusal of forgiveness is found here in Nahum in the last line of this verse and the first bicolon of the next verse.

31. Cf. 1 Kgs 19:10, 14; 2 Kgs 10:18; Pss 69:9(10); 119:139.

32. Num 5 describes an ordeal that a woman may have to go through if her husband suspects her of conjugal infidelity.

33. Ralph L. Smith, *Micah–Malachi*, 73.

34. For marriage in the Old Testament, see Gordon Hugenberger, *Marriage as a Cove-*

people), however. The general formulation suggests that God is jealous with regard to all of his exclusive relationships. While there is only one covenant people, YHWH has an exclusive relationship as the creator God to all creatures (cf. the use of nature imagery in vv. 4–5).[35] To say that he is "jealous" is to say that he zealously guards his exclusive privileges. The addition of *avenging* (or "vengeful") stresses the punitive side of this jealousy.

The threefold repetition of *avenging* obviously gives it prominence. While Spronk may be right to suggest that "the primary accent should not be on the violence, but on vengeance making an end to evil,"[36] the evil that is being avenged is a wrong committed against a person, and the retribution may well be harsh.[37] The phrases *Master of rage* (cf. Gen 37:19, "master of dreams") and *toward his foes* bring these aspects to the foreground. *Master of rage* characterizes someone who has made *rage* his own and is consequently an "expert in rage." The use of *ba'al* ("husband," "owner," "master," "Baal") here (*ba'al ḥēmâ*) may well be part of an implicit polemic against Canaanite religion (cf. *'ēl*, "El" at the beginning of the verse), even if *ba'al* was also used in nonreligious contexts.

The durative aspect, implied in the use of adjectives and participles, may be underscored with the last phrase, translated (uncertainly) as *one who remains agitated against his enemies*. The verb *nṭr* is rare in Hebrew and seems to have the same semantic range as *nṣr* (watch over, protect, preserve) used in Nah 2:1(2). Some suggest that a second meaning has evolved from "to preserve one's anger," namely "to rage" as in Akkadian *nadāru*.[38] A dialectical pun seems likely,[39] but the verb is elsewhere used elliptically for preserving anger or bearing a grudge.[40] Thus, it is possible that the elliptical nature of the expression ("one who maintains, namely hostility, against his enemies") was understood by readers and hearers, in which case they may have heard

---

nant: *A Study of Biblical Law and Ethics Governing Marriage, Developed from the Perspective of Malachi*, VTSup 52 (Leiden: Brill, 1994).

35. God could therefore be "jealous" not only with regard to Judah whose "husband" he is, but also with regard to Nineveh, meaning that no one must play the role of creator (owner, master) of Nineveh. Cf. the reflections in Myers-O'Brien, *Nahum*, 68–69, from an angle that is more suspicious of the character of YHWH

36. Spronk, *Nahum*, 34.

37. Cf. Roberts, *Nahum*, 49. But here also there is no hint of loss of control; see above on the preference of *zealous* over "jealous."

38. Cf. Ralph L. Smith, *Micah–Malachi*, 72; Roberts, *Nahum*, 43. Alternatively, we are dealing with homonyms, as suggested by Wolfram von Soden, "Hebräisch NĀṬAR I und II," *UF* 17 (1986): 412–14. See also the discussion in Patterson, *Nahum*, 26–27.

39. So Spronk, *Nahum*, 35–36.

40. Lev 19:18; Ps 103:9; Jer 3:5. In the last instance, the verb is in parallel with *šmr* (keep), which has "anger" as its object in Amos 1:11.

an echo of "preserving steadfast love for a thousand generations" (Exod 34:7, with *nṣr*) in anticipation of the citation of Exod 34:6–7 in the next verse.

3 The divine name is, in a way, the topic of this verse and arguably for that reason carries a heavy stress in the masoretic accentuation. The first half of the verse cites words from Exod 34:6–7, which is an exposition of what is implied in YHWH being YHWH (see its introduction in Exod 34:5):

> YHWH passed by before him and proclaimed, "<u>YHWH, YHWH</u> is a compassionate and gracious God, <u>slow to anger and abounding in</u> steadfast love and faithfulness, *who keeps* steadfast love for a thousand generations, who forgives iniquity, transgression and sin; yet <u>he will certainly not absolve</u>, visiting the iniquity of fathers on the children and on the grandchildren to the third and fourth generations."

Italics mark the allusion to this passage in the previous verse ("who keeps" = *who remains*), while the phrases that are picked up in v. 3 are underlined. It is likely that (some version of) Exod 34:6–7 formed part of the temple liturgy, as allusions to it are found in many other places.[41]

The statement in Exodus is often considered more balanced than its version in Nahum, but the language of balance is not the most appropriate in this context, as if various aspects of God's character were in ultimate conflict with each other. God's compassionate and gracious nature is evident in his being slow to anger, but his compassion is not suspended in his anger. God's forgiveness and his refusal to absolve are not the two extreme poles of the range of divine actions. Indeed, it may be the main contribution of this passage in the context of Exod 32–34 to affirm that God both forgives and certainly does not absolve. His relationship to Israel is restored by forgiveness, but the rebellion does not go unpunished. In Nahum, the accent falls on the latter. While *he will certainly not absolve* may be the key phrase in both contexts, the "opposite" against which it is affirmed in Nahum is not the forgiveness of iniquity as in Exodus but the idea that God might leave something unpunished. This colors the phrase *slow to anger* differently. In Exodus, "slow to anger" is directly related to God's compassionate and gracious nature and his abundance in steadfast love and faithfulness. It is good news that God is not easily angered.[42]

---

41. Exod 34:6–7 and parallels have been explored in a number of essays (see n. 40 and n. 50 in the introduction). Relevant passages are Exod 20:5–6; Num 14:18; Deut 5:9–10; 7:9–10; Pss 86:14–17; 103:6–18; 109:9–12; 145:8–16; Prov 16:4–7; 19:9, 11, 16–17; Jer 32:18–19 (cf. 31:28–30); Joel 2:13–17; Jonah 4:1–4 (cf. 3:9); Micah 7:18; Hab 3:1–2; Zeph 2:3; 3:6–7; Neh 9:17; 2 Chr 33:18–19 LXX (Prayer of Manasseh).

42. Combined with the description of God as angry (Exod 32:10–12), "slow to anger" does, however, indirectly express the enormity of Israel's rebellion.

In Nahum, "abounding in steadfast love" is changed to *abounding in power*, which maybe answers the unspoken thought that God may lack the power to express his anger.[43] God's patience, not powerlessness, is responsible for the impression of divine inactivity in the face of evil. But it is noteworthy that in Num 14, when Israel is threatened with annihilation, Moses petitions God to make his power great "just as you have spoken" (v. 17), appealing to the divine attributes expressed in Exod 34 (v. 18) and asking God to forgive "according to the greatness of his steadfast love" (v. 19).[44] Thus, God's strength can be expressed both in his forgiveness and in his refusal to tolerate evil forever.[45] The slowness with which God gets angry is experienced as painful in some contexts: for example, when one suffers under a brutal regime. In this context, *he will certainly not absolve* is good news, and the absence of "who forgives iniquity, transgression and sin" is significant. His readiness to forgive notwithstanding, YHWH is never indifferent to evil, and it is this latter truth that Nahum highlights.[46]

The second half of the verse also opens with the divine name.[47] *Gale* and *storm* occur in a single phrase also in Isa 29:6 (*sûpâ ûsə'ārâ*) in the context of divine punishment (preceded by thunder and earthquake, followed by

43. Gregory Cook ("Power, Mercy, and Vengeance: The Thirteen Attributes in Nahum," *JESOT* 5 [2016]: 27–37) points out that YHWH's *ḥesed* ("steadfast love") regularly finds expression in vengeance against the enemies of his people (33). An affirmation that YHWH is "abounding in steadfast love" would therefore not be inappropriate in Nahum. But the focus from the beginning is on God's attitude toward his enemies (see 1:2).

44. See Aron Pinker, "On the Genesis of Nahum 1:3a," *Hiphil* 4 (2007), for an argument that the phrasing in Nah 1 is influenced by Num 14. Cf. Cook, "Power," who argues that Nahum primarily quotes Num 14. Given the role of Exod 34:6–7 within the Bible, the fact that Num 14 is explicitly marked as a citation, and the different function of the phrase "abounding in power" in the two places (motivating the formula in Num 14; incorporated into the formula in Nah 1), Cook's is an overstatement, even though Nahum was likely influenced by the use of Exod 34 in Num 14.

45. Already Joseph Ibn Kaspi (1297–1340) made reference to Num 14 in his commentary; see *Adne Kesef*, ed. Isaac Last, vol. 2 (London: Naroditski, 1912), 113. He also refers to Prov 16:32: "Better one who is slow to anger than a mighty warrior, and one who controls his spirit is better than one who captures a city."

46. While Cook ("Power") is right to observe that "God's great power is not at odds with his mercy but enables it" (34), it is not clear that this is suggested here as it is in Num 14 (cf. Exod 32:11). The immediate literary context in Nahum suggests otherwise, as the focus at this point is entirely on the claim that God will now act in vengeance rather than mercy toward his enemies (cf. the use of Exod 34 in relation to Nineveh in Jonah 4:2). The fact that the poem begins in Nah 1:2 (cf. Exod 34:14) rather than 1:3 is given insufficient attention by Cook.

47. The syntax of the two bicola is not identical, however, as the divine name is "dislocated" in this second instance but not in the first; see Robert D. Holmstedt, "Critical at the Margins: Edge Constituents in Biblical Hebrew," *KUSATU* 17 (2014): 109–56.

fire).[48] The use of two nouns allows for the double use of the preposition *beth*, the second letter of the alphabet required for the acrostic (see above). The reference is likely to a violent dry windstorm, a sirocco,[49] in which case vv. 3–6 do not describe a series of disasters but one phenomenon. The reference to *clouds* as *the dust of his feet* stresses the majesty and transcendence of YHWH because it situates YHWH well above the clouds. We could think of the clouds in the sky as the mere footstool of YHWH's throne.[50] But this image may be too stationary. The word used here for *dust* (*'ăbaq*) is not very common in the Bible and may have been particularly suitable for *dust* that is swirled up by the movement of feet. This would be in contrast to, for example, loose topsoil that one might pick up or into which something is thrown or rolled, for which *'āpār* might be better suited.[51] In this case, clouds indicate movement not unlike the sirocco earlier in the verse.

4 The verb *g'r*, with which v. 4 opens, "has connotations of Yahweh's breath as a forceful, irresistible wind accompanied by a frighteningly loud and disconcerting noise."[52] Loud and sharp speech is implied with humans as the subject (Gen 37:10; Ruth 2:16; Jer 29:27). Speech is in all likelihood also implied where humans are the object of *g'r* (e.g., Pss 9:5[6]; 119:21). This explains the traditional rendering "rebuke," which, however, empties the action of its explosive nature and for some readers may add connotations of moral

---

48. Cf. Sirach 43:16, which uses the same phrase but without the focus on divine punishment. The Heb. terms are also used in Amos 1:14; Ps 83:15(16) in the context of divine intervention against enemies. There does not seem to be any significance to the use of *ś* (*ś'ārâ*) in Nah 1:3 and Job 9:17 in place of the more common *s* (*s'ārâ*; also masc. *sa'ar*, again with no obvious change in meaning).

49. See, e.g., the *sûpâ* in the Negev in Isa 21:1 and the storm winds of the south (*sa'ărôt têmān*) in Zech 9:14. Similarly, *sûpâ* in Job 37:9 stands in contrast to the north wind, which brings cold, although in Sir 43:17 it seems identical with it (cf. v. 20). While the storm may cause waves in the sea (Ps 107:25, 29), there is no passage in which *sûpâ* or *s'ārâ* is explicitly said to bring rain. High winds (*rûaḥ s'ārôt*) are mentioned in connection with flooding rains and hailstones in Ezek 13:11, 13, but the reference may well be to disasters following each other. The passages that mention fire in the same context suggest instead that heavy gales are more often thought of as bringing destructive heat (or extreme cold with snow in Sir 43). To designate the wind that brings rain, *rûaḥ* is used (e.g., 1 Kgs 18:45; 2 Kgs 3:17; Ps 147:18), and specifically *rûaḥ ṣāpôn* ("the north wind" in Prov 25:23). A wet storm is a *zerem; śa'ar* is used in parallel to it in Isa 28:2 to stress the destructiveness.

50. See Fabry, *Nahum*, 135.

51. See the other occurrences of *'ăbaq* in Exod 9:9; Deut 28:24; Isa 5:24; 29:5; Ezek 26:10. By contrast, *dakkā'* would refer to something crushed or pulverised; *'āpār* is the most commonly used word for "dust."

52. Kennedy, "Root G'R," 58. He immediately qualifies the significance of the accompanying noise and later identifies "irresistible, powerful breath" as the "basic sense" of the verb (59).

reprimand not inherent in the verb. With impersonal objects, the notion of a noisy "forceful, irresistible wind" without words is likely in the foreground. Thus, when YHWH's threatening rebuke blasts away the water by force and dries up the sea, we should probably not imagine words being spoken. The idea of YHWH rebuking the sea is found in other places with specific reference to God's leading of his people through the Red Sea (or Sea of Reeds, *yam-sûp*, Ps 106:9).[53] As so often, the appearance of God is described in language reminiscent of the Exodus-Sinai narrative. The biblical idea that God's appearance leads to the drying up of watercourses (cf. Ps 74:15; Isa 42:15; 51:10, with these last two in connection with a new exodus; see also Rev 21:1) is related to the connotations of sea with chaos in the ancient Near East.[54] There is thus a hint of restoration of order in such references, but the notion of judgment is probably more prominent, especially where the withering of whole landscapes is in view (Isa 33:9; Amos 1:2). The life-sustaining characteristics of water are there in the foreground. Hence, we find the threat of drying up streams also in the curses of Assyrian treaty texts.[55]

The second bicolon turns our attention to the flush and fertile north of the country, now under Assyrian control. Bashan was known for its oaks (Isa 2:13; Ezek 27:6; Zech 11:2) and its rich pastures (Jer 50:19; cf. Mic 7:14) that sustained well-fed, strong cattle (Ezek 39:18; Amos 4:1; Ps 22:12[13]) and rams (Deut 32:14). Mount Carmel ("orchard," e.g., in Mic 7:14) was also rich (and majestic; see Song 7:5[6]; Isa 35:2) with forests and plantations. Lebanon was renowned for its timber (2 Kgs 19:23; 2 Chr 2:8; Isa 10:34; 37:24; cf. 1 Kgs 7:2) and especially for its cedars.[56] Lebanon's glory was proverbial (Isa 35:2),[57] not least with regard to the fragrance its wood exuded (Hos 14:5–6[6–7]; Song 4:11).[58] If even Bashan and Carmel are withered, if even Lebanon is not allowed to flower, the whole country languishes. A similar picture is painted in Isa 33:9. The double use of the *pul'al* perfect '*umlal*

53. Cf. Exod 14:21. Note also Pss 18:15(16) (cf. 2 Sam 22:16); 104:7; Isa 50:2.

54. See Thomas Podella, "Der 'Chaoskampfmythos' im Alten Testament: Eine Problemanzeige," in *Mesopotamica—Ugaritica—Biblica*, ed. Manfred Dietrich and Oswald Loretz, AOAT 232 (Kevelaer: Butzon & Bercker; Neukirchen-Vluyn: Neukirchener Verlag, 1993), 283–329.

55. See Johnston, "Treaty Curses," 431–32.

56. See Judg 9:15; 1 Kgs 4:33 (5:13); 5:6(20); 2 Kgs 14:9 // 2 Chr 25:18; Ezra 3:7; Pss 29:5; 72:16; 92:12(13); 104:16; Song 5:15; Isa 2:13; 14:8; Jer 22:23; Ezek 17:3; 27:5; 31:3; Zech 11:1. Particularly noteworthy here is Ezek 31:3 because it offers a mocking lament over "Assyria, a cedar of Lebanon, with beautiful branches and forest shade."

57. The exact phrase *peraḥ ləbānôn* (*bud of Lebanon*) is also attested in Sir 50:8.

58. Interestingly, the frankincense-tree is called *libanos* in Greek, a word also used for (frank)incense itself (cf. *libanōtos*). To my knowledge, the kinds of tree from which frankincense is obtained did not grow in Lebanon but in Arabia.

(*withered*)[59] as the first and last word of the bicolon creates pleasant poetry, but it also spoils the acrostic, which requires the bicolon to start with a *dalet*. The *dalet* line can easily be restored by substituting *dāləlû* ("thinned out"; cf. Isa 19:6) for *'umlal*. It is possible that a manuscript that originally read *dllw* (or maybe *dll*) was damaged at this point so that only the presence of two *lameds* could be discerned, and a scribe guessed (wrongly) that the word must be *'mll* (*'umlal*), as found at the end of the verse, thus giving rise to the reading now found in all known Hebrew manuscripts.[60] The LXX provides evidence for a form of the text that reads two different verbs. Repetition of a verb is found quite regularly in the book of Nahum (see 1:2, 3, 12; 2:2[3], 8[9], 9[10]; 3:13, 14, 15), and in none of those cases does the LXX use two different Greek verbs to render identical Hebrew verbs. The use of two different Greek verbs here (*oligoō* aorist passive and *ekleipō* aorist active) suggests that the translator read two different Hebrew verbs.[61] These verbs may well have been *dll* and *'ml*, although it is surprising that *oligoō* is used in the first and *ekleipō* in the second position. (The verb *oligoō* is used in Joel 1:10, 12 to render a form of *'ml* and elsewhere renders other verbs but never *dll*. The verb *ekleipō* is used to translate the root *dll* in Isa 38:14, and the noun *ekleipsis* in Isa 17:4 renders *dll niphal*; the verb is also used in Isa 19:6 in parallel with *xērainō*, the verb that apparently translates *dll*.)[62] All in all, it is perfectly possible that the loss (the "withering away") of the *dalet* is the result of an accident in the early transmission of the text rather than a clever move by the author. But if so, the accident ironically reinforces the semantic content of the line.[63] It is also noteworthy that in this rhythmically harmonious section of the poem

59. In the second instance, a pausal form is used: *'umlāl*. According to Rudolf Meyer (*Hebräische Grammatik*, 4 vols. [Berlin: de Gruyter, 1992], 2:126), the duplication of the third radical of a root with three radicals is found only in the perfect and indicates that the verb is used to identify an attribute.

60. The end of the long strokes of the lamed may have remained visible even with most of the letters in that place being damaged.

61. In 3:15, the repetition of *'kl* is reflected in the repetition of *katesthiō*, while the repetition of *kbd hithpael* is not reflected in standard editions of LXX; see further the note on the translation of 3:15. A fuller examination would need to consider the rest of the Minor Prophets, and maybe other parts of LXX that are often thought to go back to the same translator (Jer 1–28; Ezek 1–27, 40–48).

62. William A. Ross ("Text-Critical Question Begging in Nahum 1:2–8: Re-evaluating the Evidence and Arguments," *ZAW* 127 [2015]: 459–74) offers further support against attempts to restore a better acrostic based on the LXX.

63. A. S. van der Woude ("The Book of Nahum: A Letter Written in Exile," *OTS* 20 [1977]: 108–26) and Duane L. Christensen ("The Book of Nahum as a Liturgical Composition: A Prosodic Analysis," *JETS* 32 [1989]: 159–69, correcting his earlier view expressed in "The Acrostic of Nahum Reconsidered," *ZAW* 87 [1975]: 17–30) consider the absence of the *dalet* line intentional.

(vv. 4–6), it is the second (*dalet*) and the penultimate (*zayin*) bicola that are the odd ones out. Even the disturbance of the acrostic is symmetrical.

5 A gale mighty enough to dry up the sea might at the same time move mountains and result in big earth movements, but the prepositional phrases *because of him* and *before him* turn our attention to YHWH, rather than the storm as such, as the origin and cause of such terror.[64] The first verb (*shake*, or quake) suggests convulsions, the second (*go to pieces*) a falling apart. Some think of a volcanic outburst (Rudolph) or heavy rain (Goslinga) as the implied cause of this falling apart or melting away.[65] A movement of liquid dissolving is indeed implied in Ps 65:10(11) and Amos 9:13, both in positive contexts, but the root does not clearly require that the falling to pieces is by way of melting or dissolving. The falling apart may be as if by a rain-less hurricane in line with the imagery of the preceding verse. This fits better with the second half of the verse as well. Baumann has pointed out that it is usually the earth that quakes at the appearing of YHWH, and more rarely mountains and hills.[66] The reference to mountains and hills is not motivated by the geographical situation of Nineveh. Fabry wonders whether the author wanted to exploit the possibility of using the verb *mwg* with hills in a positive sense (cf. Amos 9:13) to give ambivalence to the theophany, combining the motif of hills flowing with goodness with the motif of landscapes trembling in war.[67] But it is much more likely that the specific reference to mountains and hills in the first half of the verse is meant to stress YHWH's strength and prepares for *the rocks are torn asunder* in verse 6 (see below).

The verb used in the second bicolon has often been considered suspect on the assumption that *nś'* cannot be used without an object, but this assumption is ill-founded.[68] The expression may be elliptical, implying as the object either "its voice" or "its hands," but the lack of any indication in the context as to which object is to be supplied makes this unlikely.[69] Another possibility

---

64. The use of "and" at the beginning of the second colon of each bicolon suggests to me that the bicola are not, strictly speaking, pivot patterned; but see, e.g., *CHP*, 220.

65. Rudolph, *Micha*, 156. For the reference to Goslinga, see Spronk, *Nahum*, 42.

66. Baumann, *Gewalt*, 127; cf. Fabry, *Nahum*, 137. Baumann points to Jer 4:24 as the only parallel. But the motif of mountains becoming unstable is more prominent; with different verbs, we may add 1 Kgs 19:11; Isa 64:3(2); Hab 3:6; and probably Judg 5:5 (reading the root *zll* for *nzl*).

67. Fabry, *Nahum*, 137.

68. See the note on the translation.

69. The situation is different in Gen 4:7, which arguably leaves out the object to allow for the double meaning of raising the face (looking up in confidence) and raising the guilt (experiencing forgiveness), and in Gen 18:24, 26, where the expression is unambiguously elliptical, meaning forgiveness. As regards Nah 1:5, head and face would be unsuitable in context, but we have no means to decide between voice and hands.

is to relate the root to Akkadian *nâšu(m)*, which offers a parallel to the first verb of the verse.[70] The fact that the MT attests apparently intransitive usage of *nś'* elsewhere suggests that an intransitive use of *nś'* is possible here, and the appeal to an Akkadian root is therefore not strictly necessary.[71] But given that the verb is only rarely intransitive, a dialectical pun with *nâšu(m)* may well have motivated the use of *nś'*. In spite of the implied personification of the earth, the movement seems involuntary (a startled jump), as is the quaking of the mountains. The inhabitants of the world presumably do not rise actively either but are carried up with the earth. The preposition *mippānāyw*, rendered *before him*, could alternatively be rendered "away from him." The first bicolon focuses on YHWH as the cause of this terror; the second bicolon stresses that nothing can stand in the way of his approach.

6 This verse presents us with another—indeed, probably a deliberate—disruption of the acrostic. For the sake of the acrostic, one would expect *scorn* to stand prominently at the beginning of the sentence. However, removing it from there makes for a better poetic bicolon with a chiastic structure, whereby the twofold question *Who can stand/rise?* is surrounded by the prepositional phrases referring to God's anger. It may also help to ensure that YHWH's scorn does not become a new topic, separate from YHWH himself.[72] While anger is the theme of the verse, with four different Hebrew words used to refer to God's anger, YHWH remains the theme of the whole poem. The four words that in different contexts could each be translated "anger" appear in this translation as *scorn*, *heat*, *anger*, and *rage*. *Scorn* refers to indignation that finds verbal expression. *Heat* can be used as a word for anger in its own right (always divine anger), but this happens only rarely (e.g., Exod 15:7; Ezek 7:12, 14). It appears most often in construct with *'ap* (nose) as *ḥărôn 'ap-yhwh*, "the blazing nose [= burning anger] of YHWH." The word for nose (*'ap*) is also used on its own to refer to *anger* (e.g., Gen 27:45; Ps 138:7), which is how it is translated here. The final word, *ḥēmā'* (*rage*), could also be related to heat, but this is uncertain.[73] Some scholars suggest that *ḥēmā'*

70. Spronk, *Nahum*, 43.

71. Apart from the occurrences of the verb listed above, note that the noun *śə'ēt* (dignity, majesty) may be based on an intransitive understanding of *nś'*. This may also be true for the hapax legomenon *śî'* (arrogance) in Job 20:6, which, however, could be derived from an internally transitive (reflexive) use of the verb.

72. In an alphabetic acrostic, the colon would have to read something like *his scorn—who can stand before it?* The syntax would be comparable to the syntax of the second half of v. 3 as interpreted by the Masoretes. Such dislocation of *his scorn* could have changed the topic from *YHWH* to *his scorn*. The fronting in the text as it stands, whose syntax is comparable to that of the first half of v. 3, is less pronounced.

73. *HALOT* glosses *ḥēmā'* in Ezek 3:14 with "heat," related to the similar word *ḥammâ*,

denotes "poisonous slaver at the mouth of angry individuals,"[74] but this may make too much of etymological connections, although both a focus on heat and on YHWH's mouth fit the context.

The expression *poured out like fire* fits with the metaphor of anger as "the heat of a fluid in a container," which is known in English and for which Kruger has identified several expressions in Classical Hebrew.[75] Other than in expressions describing anger, fire is never described as being "poured out." This suggests that it is not the comparison with fire that gives rise to the liquid imagery; the rage is at the same time liquid and *like fire*.[76] Fire scorches (cf. Prov 16:27) and devours (cf. Exod 24:17; Isa 9:18[17]; 30:27), quickly and uncontrollably taking over (cf. Ps 118:12; Jer 4:4; 20:9; 21:12; 23:29; Hos 7:6; Amos 5:6; Mal 3:2). Its destructiveness is all-consuming (cf. Ps 83:14[15]; Lam 2:3). The "pouring out" metaphor underscores the comprehensiveness of the destruction. Nothing can withstand, rise up against, or even endure the heat of such rage, not even *the rocks* that *are torn asunder because of him*. Sometimes an emendation of *niṭṭəṣû* (*torn asunder*) to *niṣṣətû* ("burned") is suggested.[77] If "burned," the implication is "completely burned out" rather

which usually refers to the sun (Isa 24:23; 30:26; Song 6:10; cf. Ps 19:6[7]). Cf. *ḥămat miyyāyin* in Hos 7:5: the glow or heat produced by wine consumption.

74. Zacharias Kotzé ("Metaphors and Metonymies for Anger in the Old Testament: A Cognitive Linguistic Approach," *Scriptura* 88 [2005]: 121) identifies two proponents of this view: Harold R. Cohen, *Biblical Hapax Legomena in the Light of Akkadian and Ugaritic*, SBLDS 37 (Missoula: Scholars Press, 1979); Mayer I. Gruber, *Aspects of Nonverbal Communication in the Ancient Near East* (Rome: Biblical Institute Press, 1980). It is not clear in what sense the slaver is poisonous. It seems more intuitive to see drooling as a sign of lack of control.

75. Paul A. Kruger, "A Cognitive Interpretation of the Emotion of Anger in the Hebrew Bible," *JNSL* 26 (2000): 181–91. See Kotzé, "Metaphors," 122. Cf. 2 Chr 12:7; 34:21, 25; Jer 7:20; 42:18; 44:6 for the same object and verb. I am not sure that the fluid in question would necessarily be liquid in the absence of heat. The verb is used in Ezekiel for the melting process (22:20–22; 24:11), in which it is obviously only the heat of the fire that turns the material into a fluid. (As in English, the pouring out need not be of a liquid, whether in metaphor or for real. Pieces of silver are "poured out" in 2 Kgs 22:9 // 2 Chr 34:17.) *Ḥēmā'* is the object of the more common verb for pouring out (*špk*) in Ps 79:6; Isa 42:25; Jer 6:11; 10:25; Lam 2:4 ("like fire"); 4:11; Ezek 7:8; 9:8; 14:19; 16:38; 20:8, 13, 21, 33–34; 22:22; 30:15; 36:18. See further Ellen van Wolde, "Sentiments as Culturally Constructed Emotions: Anger and Love in the Hebrew Bible," *Biblical Interpretation* 16 (2008): 1–24.

76. In other words, the pouring out of fire is metaphorical as well. The expression is thus unlike the references to groanings, which are poured out like water (Job 3:24), or Job feeling poured out like milk (Job 10:10).

77. See *HALOT*, s.v. *ntṣ*. There are no other instances in which rocks are said to be torn asunder or burned with which one could compare this verse. The closest parallels are in the book of Job, in which extraordinary happenings are described as movement of rocks (*'tq*; 14:18; 18:4).

than "singed," as the verb elsewhere appears only to have the former sense. But *nittaṣû* (*torn asunder*) is just as fitting: as metal alloys lose their stability and coherence in the heat of fire, so does the heat of YHWH's fury make rocks disintegrate.[78] Whether burned or *broken asunder*, the rocks cannot provide protection.[79] The use of *ṣûr* rather than *selaʿ* (cf. 1 Kgs 19:11; Jer 23:29) may underline this.[80] While nature apart from humanity has been in the foreground of this poem up to now, the questions *Who can stand?* and *Who can rise?* surely have humanity in particular in mind. No one can withstand YHWH because there is no longer any safe place to stand. The only strong-hold is YHWH himself, as the next verse brings out.

7 The Masoretes scan v. 7 as a bicolon, as do I. This effectively eliminates from the acrostic the *yod* line (*he knows . . .*), which is already obscured by the addition of the *waw* (*and*) in v. 7b. We can produce the *yod* line by scanning the first half of the verse as a bicolon: either "Good is YHWH—as a stronghold— / in the day of distress," or less likely in my view, "Good is YHWH; / indeed, a stronghold in the day of distress." The *lamed* is understood differently in the two cases. The former division could also be rendered "Better is YHWH than a stronghold / in the day of distress" (cf. NJB).[81] The bicolon can be read as a pivot pattern, which means that the middle part (*as a stronghold*) should be read with both parts.[82] The simplest solution in interpreting the present text is to assume that the *lamed* indicates in what respect YHWH is good, namely *as a stronghold*. But it is conceivable that there is a play on the different functions of the preposition *lamed*, inviting us to read, in effect, "Good is YHWH as a stronghold—indeed, a stronghold in the day of distress." A number of possible emendations in response to a number of perceived problems further multiply the options.[83] The best

---

78. The LXX reads *diathryptō* ("break into pieces") and thus supports the received Heb. text. Given the likely allusion to the crossing of the sea in v. 4, vv. 5–6 may allude to the quaking of Mount Sinai (*ḥrd*; see Exod 19:18; cf. Judg 5:5; Ps 68:8[9]) and the striking and splitting of the rock to give water (Exod 17:6; cf. Deut 8:15; Pss 78:15, 20; 105:41; 114:8; Isa 48:21).

79. The prepositional phrase is the same as the first in v. 5 and has therefore been translated identically *because of him*. Alternatively, one could translate "by him" (indicating instrumentality; cf., e.g., Lev 21:7). If any such close distinction is useful here, the preposition is maybe best understood as indicating source rather than reason or instrument, but "from him" (cf., e.g., 1 Kgs 2:15) would make for an awkward English sentence.

80. While a *selaʿ* can be a hiding place (1 Sam 23:25, 28) and is applied metaphorically to mean God's protection, namely in 2 Sam 22:2 // Ps 18:2(3); Pss 31:3(4); 42:9(10); 71:3, *ṣûr* is far more common as a place of protection, safety, and refuge. See *HALOT*, s.v. *ṣûr*, §§1b and 4 for numerous references.

81. While *ṭôb* + noun + *lə* + noun is found elsewhere (1 Sam 20:7; Pss 35:12; 100:5; cf. Song 7:9[10], which has a participle following *ṭôb*), no passage provides a real parallel.

82. See *CHP*, 214–21, for a discussion of the phenomenon.

83. The perceived problems are the shortness of the first colon, the lack of an object for

emendation results in reading the first colon as identical to the first colon of Lam 3:25 ("YHWH is good to those who wait for him"), which would make a good parallel to "a stronghold in the day of distress," assuming an original *waw* instead of the *lamed*. But one would need to assume that the received Greek and Hebrew texts are the result of two different textual mistakes. It is more likely, instead, that one gave rise to the other. If so, the unique Hebrew text should probably be given preference to the Greek text, which may have been an attempt to read a broken text with the help of Lam 3:25.

If the text is left unchanged, there is a change of rhythm in this verse. That such a change is deliberate rather than the result of a textual accident gains plausibility from the observation that the present rhythm is similar to the one in the following verse. The two verses are thus counterparts in terms of rhythm and content. It is also noteworthy that v. 7 provides the first occurrence of the divine name since the beginning of the poem and that the *waw* preceding (and thus obscuring) the *yod* line can hardly be anything but deliberate. This is not the case with the *waw* at the beginning of v. 8, which could be the result of an accident in the transmission of the text (see below). The reuse of the divine name and the pivot pattern suggest that we have reached the climax of the poem. The goodness of YHWH, so regularly celebrated in the liturgy,[84] is affirmed here not over against his wrath but because of it. YHWH's anger ensures that evil does not retain the upper hand, and thus he proves a reliable refuge for those who entrust themselves to him.

The *waw* at the beginning of the *yod* colon thus asks us to read the verse as a single unit: YHWH is a secure *stronghold* only for *those who seek refuge in him*. But this could have been said while maintaining a proper *yod* line. As it is, greater prominence seems to be given to the *tet* line (*Good . . .*, v. 7a). While Nahum makes use of the (ideal or real) *yod* and *kaph* lines, and maybe even *lamed* and *mem* lines albeit in the wrong order, the acrostic in the book in a sense comes to a premature end with this differently structured

---

whom YHWH is good, the form *ləmā'ôz*, and the different reading in the LXX. See Aron Pinker, "Shelter or Strength in Nahum 1,7?" *ZAW* 116 (2004): 610–13, for discussion and a new suggestion. Lawrence Zalcman's modification of Pinker's proposal ("Intertextuality at Nahum 1,7," *ZAW* 116 [2004]: 614–15) is a significant improvement; it leads to "Good is YHWH to his people, / a stronghold [or strength] in the day of distress." But Bob Becking ("Is God Good for His People? Critical Remarks on a Recently Proposed Emendation of Nahum 1,7," *ZAW* 117 [2005]: 621–23) rightly raises two pertinent issues: the lack of genuine support from the versions and the rhetorical significance of the lack of an object in the development of the book of Nahum, suggesting that a reference to God's people would be premature in 1:7.

84. "Give thanks to YHWH, for he is good, for his steadfast love endures forever!" (Pss 106:1; 107:1; 118:1, 29; 136:1; cf. 1 Chr 16:34; 2 Chr 5:13; 7:3). See also Pss 25:8; 100:5; 135:3; 145:9.

tet line. What is being said in this verse echoes the *tet* lines in other acrostics, especially Ps 34:8(9): "Taste and see that YHWH is good; how blessed is the man who seeks refuge in Him."[85] The masoretic pointing invites us to read *he knows* (the *yod* line) as a participial form, suggesting that YHWH's "knowledge" of those who seek refuge in him, in the sense of taking care of them (e.g., Pss 1:6; 37:18; cf. 144:3 with 8:4[5]), is continuous, while the judgment on wickedness in the following verse is something that happens from time to time (cf. Ps 1:6, with the same shift from participle to *yiqtol*).[86]

Daniel Timmer rightly points out that "the goodness of YHWH is not automatically in Judah's favour" and that "it is surely significant that the book's first mention of Yahweh's [*sic*] deliverance is not promised to Judah, but to those who 'take refuge in him' [1:7]."[87] Nahum is not "blindly pro-Judah."[88] The contrast within Nahum between aggressively exploitative Assyria and YHWH-faithful, oppressed Judah paints with broad strokes and implies that any within Judah who opt for violence instead of seeking refuge in YHWH would also fall under divine judgment.

8 As mentioned above, the rhythm of this verse in the masoretic interpretation is similar to the rhythm of the preceding verse, with *kālâ* as the pivot. Again, *kālâ* can be read with both halves: "and with a sweeping flood: a full end" as well as "a full end he makes of her place." It is possible to read *kālâ* in the first instance as a verb (the form would be the same): "And with a sweeping flood it comes to an end." But the change of subject would be harsh.[89] Alternatively, the subject of *sweeping* could be YHWH, continuing the participle from the previous verse: *He knows . . . with a flood he passes through.* But the expression would be unique, and its connection with the *yiqtol* form *yaʿăśê* (*he makes*) awkward.[90] Reading the phrase *ûbəšeṭep ʿōbēr*

---

85. See also Pss 25:8; 145:9; Lam 3:25 for *ṭôb yhwh* ("good is YHWH"); *ṭôb* is also used in Pss 37:16; 112:5; 119:65–66, 68, 71–72; and Lam 4:9 (*ṭôbîm*) for the *tet* line.

86. The participle in v. 9 seems to indicate the immediate future.

87. Daniel C. Timmer, "Boundaries without Judah, Boundaries within Judah: Hybridity and Identity in Nahum," *HBT* 34 (2012): 186.

88. Timmer, "Boundaries," 179, noting that the stereotypes of ideal Judah ("victim, not aggressor," "fair and non-violent," "YHWHistic, aniconic") do not work only in Judah's favor.

89. Read with the second half, it becomes clear that *kālâ* is the object of *ʿśh*, as in the following verse and in Neh 9:31; Isa 10:23; Jer 4:27; 5:10, 18; 30:11; 46:28 (with "I will certainly not absolve"); Ezek 11:13; 20:17; Zeph 1:18. "To make an end" is most commonly expressed with the *piel* of *klh*. The use of the noun with *ʿśh* seems to be more emphatic: "to make a complete end."

90. The verb need not imply a passing through in judgment as in Exod 12:12, 23; cf. Amos 5:17. The verb is also used for YHWH passing by Moses in Exod 34:6 (cf. 1 Kgs 19:11 in the Elijah narrative, which alludes to this event). YHWH is also the subject of the verb in Deut 9:3; 31:3 ("crossing over"; cf. Josh 4 for the ark crossing over before Israel) and Amos 7:8; 8:2 ("pass by" = spare!), as well as implicitly in Mic 2:13, again in a positive context. The

with v. 7 would avoid the second problem, but it would still leave the meaning of the phrase unclear. It is therefore best to interpret the participle as characterizing *šeṭep* (*flood*). The two roots are used together in a few other places, maybe most notably in Isa 8:8, where Assyria is said to overflow and pass through (= flood) Judah.[91]

EXCURSUS: THE PLACE OF THE PHRASE "AND WITH/IN A SWEEPING FLOOD"

Should the phrase *ûbəšeṭep 'ōbēr* be taken with the preceding verse? The key arguments in favor seem to be better preservation of the acrostic and rhythm. As regards the acrostic, the *waw* before the *yod* line remains problematic (see above). The *waw* that introduces the sweeping flood could be an instance of dittography of the last letter of the preceding word. Considered on its own, the result has a good rhythm: "Good is YHWH as a stronghold / in the day of distress. // And he knows those who seek refuge in him, / [even] in an overflowing flood." But the two cola in second position are still noticeably shorter than any of the preceding cola in the poem or the following lines. One may rightly question whether the result presents an improvement of the rhythm in the context of the poem. If the phrase *ûbəšeṭep 'ōbēr* is kept with v. 8, the verse is well balanced with v. 7.

To decide with which verse the phrase should go, we must also consider which of two possible shifts of metaphor is more likely or appropriate in context. Taking *ûbəšeṭep 'ōbēr* with v. 7, the image of YHWH approaching in a devastating sirocco turns into one of him providing a stronghold that the flood (which is not, it seems, dried up) cannot reach before reverting to the idea of YHWH as a pursuer.[92] Taking *ûbəšeṭep 'ōbēr* with v. 8, the image of YHWH approaching in a devastating sirocco turns into one of him bringing a destructive flood, anticipating imagery found later in the book, with a reference to YHWH being a stronghold thrown in between the two. The former

---

LXX interprets YHWH as the subject in Isa 40:27, and the spirit of YHWH (*rûaḥ-yhwh*) is the subject of the verb in 1 Kgs 22:24 // 2 Chr 18:23.

91. See also Ps 124:4; Dan 11:10, 40; cf. Isa 28:15, 18. All of these use the verb *šṭp* rather than the noun *šeṭep,* which occurs only here and in Job 38:25; Ps 32:6; Prov 27:4; Dan 9:26; 11:22. Jon D. Levenson ("Textual and Semantic Notes on Nah. I 7–8," *VT* 25 [1975]: 792–95) proposes the reading *'br* II, which is known only in the *hithpael* ("to show oneself angry") and translated "raging torrent," but this requires an emendation that is difficult to accept as an improvement; *'br* II elsewhere has only humans (Prov 14:16; 20:2; 26:17) or God (Deut 3:26; Pss 78:21, 59, 62; 89:38[39]) as its subject.

92. It is unlikely, in my view, that darkness is the agent pursuing. See the discussion below.

introduces active enemies (*sweeping flood*) into the picture and seems, in my view, to shift the emphasis too much toward YHWH's "passive" provision of a refuge. The *stronghold* of v. 7 can be understood as a contrast to *her place*, which is completely destroyed in v. 8. All in all, it seems best to read *ûbašeṭep ʿōbēr* with v. 8 in agreement with the LXX and the masoretic tradition.[93]

Following the division of the text suggested in the translation, the poem, which up to this point has focused on the natural world, leads to evenly balanced statements contrasting the fate of two categories of people. The *full end* that YHWH prepares for his enemies echoes Isa 10:23, also in the context of judgment on Assyria (cf. Jer 30:11; 46:28 in the context of the end of exile).

The phrase *her place* has caught many by surprise, because it is not clear from the acrostic poem itself to whom *her* might refer. Some scholars suggest reading *mqwmh* with different vowels to render "opposition"; others emend the text to conform with the LXX *tous epegeiromenous* ("those who rise up"; see ESV, NRSV). It is quite possible that *mqwmh* was originally understood differently from what is now reflected in the MT (*maqōmāh*, with fem. sing. suffix), but none of the suggestions is without problems. The forms *maqōmâ* (e.g., Driver, Haldar, Rudolph) or *maqûmâ* (Roberts) are nowhere else attested.[94] The Greek translator, whose *Vorlage* would have been without vowels, may well have had *mqwmh* in front of him, seeking to make sense of it without reading a feminine suffix, for which the translator presumably saw no plausible referent.[95] Another acrostic says that the place (*māqômô*, with masc. sing. suffix) of the wicked one (*rāšāʿ*) will be no more (Ps 37:10). But the poem in Nahum has no (grammatically fem., or indeed masc.) equivalent of "the wicked one" to which the suffix could refer. The only feminine noun in context is *distress* (*ṣārâ*) in the preceding verse. While maybe not impos-

---

93. Another small advantage in my opinion is that the first letter of v. 7 and the first two letters of v. 8 read *ṭûb* ("goodness"; cf. Pss 25:7; 27:13; 31:19[20]; 145:7; Neh 9:35) or, vocalized differently, *ṭôb* ("good"). If the *waw* at the beginning of v. 8 were to be deleted as dittography, the first letter of the first three cola would produce the same consonants. The *waw* of the final colon could be added as a pronominal suffix ("his goodness"). While this is likely to be an accidental aspect of the text, it is poetically satisfying.

94. Godfrey Rolles Driver, "Studies in the Vocabulary of the Old Testament VIII," *JTS* 36 (1935): 300–301; Alfred O. Haldar, *Studies in the Book of Nahum*, UUA 7 (Uppsala: Uppsala Universitet, 1947), 27; Rudolph, *Micha*, 152; Roberts, *Nahum*, 45. The meaning "opposition" is one of those that have been suggested for the hapax legomenon *qîm* in Job 22:20 (see *HALOT*, s.v. *qîm*).

95. It is not clear what other Hebrew text may have been in front of the Greek translator: the *piel* participle (*maqîmîm* without or *maqîmêhû* with suffix) is not really suitable for semantic reasons; the *qal* participle would require the prefixed preposition *min* to come orthographically close enough to suggest a mistake in the history of transmission (*miqqāmāyw*). The preposition is, however, neither suitable nor translated in the Greek.

sible, *distress* seems an unlikely antecedent for the pronoun.[96] There does not seem to be any other place in which *māqôm* is used in this way with an abstract noun such as *distress*. The best connection in the text as it stands is to Nineveh in the heading, on the grounds that the distance from the suffix can be overcome by the fact that the heading suggests reading the poem in a particular context. If Nahum made use of an existing acrostic, the acrostic may have read *mqwrh* ("source," "fountain"), referring to distress, if the combination of *sweeping flood* and *fountain* (of distress) is not too harsh.[97] In sum, the MT *her place* ties the book more strongly together with the focus on Nineveh taken from the superscription; the reading "opposition" (those who oppose him), without reference to the city, facilitates reading the poem apart from the book. If the poem had a life of its own prior to its inclusion in the book, this makes sense, but within the book *her place* does not offer any real problems, and an application beyond the fall of Nineveh remains possible given that the fall of Nineveh is clearly paradigmatic for the failure of opposition to YHWH.

There is no agreement on the syntactical function of *darkness*. A directive accusative or accusative of motion (cf. Gen 27:3; 45:25; Josh 6:19; 1 Kgs 2:9, 41) fits the reference to a complete end in the preceding colon.[98] Darkness is the result of pursuit also in Job 18:18; Ps 35:6; Lam 3:2.[99] Alternatively, one might interpret the word as an accusative of means[100] or take *darkness* as the subject of the verb.[101] The LXX *tous echthrous autou diōxetai skotos* reflects the latter, and a similar construction can be found in Prov 13:21 (*ḥaṭṭāʾîm*

---

96. Contra Floyd, "Chimerical Acrostic," 428. Ibn Kaspi, *Adne Kesef*, 2:113, goes as far back as v. 5 and sees a reference to the earth.

97. In this case, the bicolon would spell "complete end," as from beginning ("source," regularly used in the expression "source of life") to end (*darkness* = death). Obviously, as with other proposed emendations, the contrast between stronghold in v. 7 and place in v. 8 would be lost.

98. On darkness as a symbol for death, see Nicholas J. Tromp, *Primitive Conceptions of Death and the Nether World in the Old Testament*, BibOr 21 (Rome: Pontifical Biblical Institute, 1969), 142–44, cf. 95–98.

99. Cf. Pss 88:6(7) and 143:3, both of which use *maḥšak*, as well as Jer 23:12 (*ʾăpēlâ*).

100. So Maier, *Nahum*, 179–81. Cf. *məraddēp ʾămārîm* ("He pursues them with words") in Prov 19:7. JM 126l considers "the existence of an accusative of instrument . . . doubtful," but see also Mic 7:2; Mal 3:24; Pss 45:7(8); 64:7(8) (examples from *IBHS* 10.2.3d; cf. *BHRG* 33.3). In Ps 119:86 ("With deception they pursue me"), the accusative may be either instrumental or circumstantial.

101. The object or person pursued is regularly introduced with the preposition *ʾaḥar*, but sometimes other prepositions are used, or none are used, like here (see also, e.g., Deut 16:20). A further possibility is that *darkness* is the direct object with *his enemies* as the subject, which would require us to interpret *pursue* as a collective singular, which has little to commend itself.

təraddēp rāʿâ, "harm pursues sinners"). But given the poem's focus on the character and activities of YHWH, it is maybe more fitting to read YHWH as the subject. Conceptually, YHWH is of course the ultimate agent, even if one interprets darkness as the subject of the verb.[102]

9 This verse brings the first direct address in the book but raises questions. Who is the implied addressee? And does the pronoun *ma* introduce a relative sentence ("He is making a full end of what you ponder against YHWH"), as the text is understood in NIV and NASB, or a question, as in the majority of English Bibles and in my translation? Most English Bibles imply that the Assyrians are addressed,[103] an understanding that is nearly inevitable when *ma* is read as a relative pronoun and is also possible when the first colon is understood as a question. The rendering of *ḥšb* as "plot" (NRSV, ESV, NJPS, NIV) or "devise" (NASB) or "plan" (CJB) adopts the same understanding, as apparently does the LXX (*logizesthe epi*, elsewhere nearly always a "devising against").[104] The verb is also used in v. 11 but in a different stem (*qal* instead of *piel*) and with a different preposition (*ʿal* instead of *ʾel*).[105] In the *piel*, which is found here, *ḥšb* can also be rendered as "ponder" or "think of someone" (cf. Pss 73:16; 77:5[6]; 119:59; 144:3), a nuance found only once with the *qal* (Ps 40:17[18]).[106] Indeed, *ḥšb* rarely means to "plan" or "devise" without

102. Johnston ("Treaty Curses," 423–24) notes parallels to darkness curses in Assyrian treaties.

103. NIV changes to the third person: "Whatever they plot against the Lord / he will bring to an end." A footnote offers "What do you foes plot against the Lord? / He" as an alternative (cf. TNIV). Note that in v. 8 *her place* is rendered "Nineveh" (cf. TNIV).

104. See LXX 2 Sam 14:13; Mic 2:3; Jer 11:19; 18:11, 18; 27:45 (MT 50:45); 30:14, 25 (MT 49:20, 30); 31:2 (MT 48:2). Jer 36:11 (MT 29:11) is the exception, but the preposition may have been chosen there precisely because of its hostile connotations elsewhere, thus stressing the reversal.

105. Of the two prepositions, *ʿal* is the one more commonly used with *ḥšb* (14×); *ʾel* is used with the *piel* of *ḥšb* once more, namely in Hos 7:15 with *rāʿ* ("evil," "harm") as direct object, and twice with the *qal* (Jer 49:20; 50:45). The different prepositions do not provide clear indications to any difference in meaning between vv. 9 and 11, although Jeremias (*Nahum*, 101) suggests that Nah 1:9 specifically alludes to Hos 7:15. This is possible, but perhaps two different prepositions have been used to alert us to the use of the verb with two slightly different meanings, for which the shift from *piel* to *qal* is significant. The LXX also varies the preposition, using *kata* in v. 11.

106. The *piel* of *ḥšb* is found sixteen times in the MT. In Leviticus, it always denotes a calculation of value (5×). In 2 Kgs 12:16, it denotes giving thought (paying attention) to someone. The four Psalms references are given above. The two occurrences in Proverbs refer to planning (*darkô*, "his way," 16:9; *ləhārēaʿ*, "to do evil," 24:8); cf. Jonah 1:4 ("The ship was thinking of breaking down"). Evil schemes are denoted in Dan 11:24 (with *maḥšəbōt* as direct object) and Hos 7:14 (*rāʿ*). The *qal* is found seventy-seven times in the MT, including the technical use of the *qal* participle to denote a cloth worker (13× in Exodus) or technician

either a direct object signifying a "plan" (or "harm" or "his way," etc.) or an infinitive construct with *lamed*. Second Samuel 14:13 ("Why, then, do you think of this same kind of thing against the people of God?") seems the only instance in which the devising is not done deliberately.[107] In the light of this, and taking into account the use of the third-person plural with reference to the evildoers in the following verse, it seems more likely that a Judean audience is the implied addressee and that *ḥšb* (*piel*) *'el* refers to "thinking with regard to" YHWH. The root suggests a weighing up of possibilities. The implied audience is probably thought to question YHWH's willingness or ability to end the distress, and so the question is not a neutral one. It challenges the audience: *What do you ponder concerning YHWH?* Against any unworthy thoughts about YHWH, the following two cola stress that he will indeed make a complete end for distress; it will not rise again.[108] The participle envisages the end in the near future; *a second time* means as much as "again" following the anticipated defeat. There is no need to specify a "first time." Rhetorically, the "first time" of experiencing distress is now.[109] Jeremias does not allow for this to be a forceful, poetic statement of decisive divine action against evil. He reads it instead as a literal statement that must be understood eschatologically in the sense of indicating the final defeat of evil and thus an irreversible change of affairs. This becomes a cornerstone for his reading of the book.[110]

10 This verse is difficult to translate with confidence. Patterson observes that "the point of the comparison in all three seemingly unrelated cases is that of total consumption: the bush by its thorns, the drunkard by his drink, the stubble by fire."[111] The images depict the inevitability and irreversibility of the full end YHWH makes of his enemies (*they* in v. 10 = *his enemies* in v. 8), those who are causing the *distress* to which the previous verse refers.

(2 Chr 26:15). It is used in the sense of reckoning someone to be something (e.g., Gen 38:15; 1 Sam 1:13), of imputing righteousness (Gen 15:6) or guilt (2 Sam 19:19[20]; Ps 32:2; cf. Job 35:2) and of valuing something (Isa 13:17) or having regard for someone (Isa 33:8; 53:3; cf. Mal 3:16). But most commonly it denotes devising or planning (e.g., 1 Sam 18:25; 2 Sam 14:13–14).

107. Isa 10:7 is not really an exception, as *kēn* picks up on a number of infinitives in the preceding verse and is contrasted with two other infinitives later in the verse.

108. The A/B/B' structure of the tricolon, "where strong parallelism occurs over the last two lines," is common, as Watson observes (*CHP*, 181).

109. So John Calvin: "For I thus simply interpret the words of the Prophet,—that God can with one onset, when it seems good to him, so destroy his enemies, that there will be no need of striving with them the second time: *Il n'y faudra plus retourner*, as we say in our language" (*Jonah, Micah, Nahum*, vol. 3 of *Commentaries on the Twelve Minor Prophets*, trans. John Owen [1847; repr. Grand Rapids: Christian Classics Ethereal Library]).

110. Jeremias, *Nahum*, 28–32. At least in part this is influenced by his understanding of *baliyyā'al* (*villainy, villain*) in 1:11 and 1:15(2:1) as a term specifically for YHWH's archenemy.

111. Patterson, *Nahum*, 42.

The translation of the first colon assumes a very rare use of the preposition *'ad*.[112] Alternatively, the first colon could be read together with the last: "As far as [= to the extent of] entangled thorns . . . they are consumed." This would fit the standard use of the preposition, but the double metaphor (entangled thorns, fully dry stubble) would be awkward. A more suitable alternative to this commentary's translation might be to render the colon "for even thorns entangled [are they]."[113] The LXX has *hoti heōs themeliou autōn chersōthēsetai* ("For even to their foundation it will be made barren"), maybe reflecting *ysdwm* (read as *yəsôdām*, "their foundation") instead of *syrym* (read as *sîrîm*, "thorns"), that is, with a reversal of the first two letters and reading the orthographically similar *dalet* for *resh*. The noun fits well with the preposition but less well with the verb *sbk* ("entangle," "twist"). The verb is used only once more in the Hebrew Bible, in Job 8:17, where LXX renders it with a form of *koimaō* ("falling asleep"). It is possible that the meaning of the verb *sbk* was not known to the translator.[114]

The expression *like their drink drunk* is also awkward. The LXX has *kai hōs smilax periplekomenē brōthēsetai* ("and like woven bindweed [?] they are consumed"), reflecting not only a different division of the text[115] but possibly a different *Vorlage*.[116] The rendering "like those who are drunken with their drink" (NASB; cf. NJPS and CJB) is smoother but suggests *ûkəsəbû'îm sob'ām* rather than the MT reading *ûkəsob'ām səbû'îm* (cf. NIV, "drunk from their wine").[117] These English translations assume that the passive participle *drunk* can be used both for "inebriated" and "imbibed" in Hebrew as much

---

112. Cf. 1 Chr 4:27 and maybe 2 Sam 23:19; see BDB, 724.

113. Patterson (*Nahum*, 42) appeals to *'ad-'eḥād* ("not even one") in Exod 9:7 and 14:28 for an emphatic use of the preposition (cf. Judg 4:16; 2 Sam 17:22). This use is not restricted to the phrase *'ad-'eḥād*. The prep. *'ad* is used on its own in, e.g., 1 Sam 2:5; Job 25:5; Hag 2:19; cf. the expression *'ad-mə'ōd* in Gen 27:33–34; 1 Sam 11:15; 25:36; 2 Sam 2:17; 1 Kgs 1:4; Pss 38:6, 8(7, 9); 119:8, 43, 51, 107; Isa 64:8, 11; Lam 5:22; Dan 8:8; 11:25. Longman ("Nahum," 796) adopts a locative sense of *'ad* and translates "by."

114. Note that the related noun *səbak* ("thicket") is in effect transliterated in Gen 22:13. The translator knows from the context that it must be a plant but apparently does not know the root *sbk* and renders "plant of Sabek." The only instance in which there is a precise correspondence between *səbak* and the LXX is in Isa 9:18(17), where *dasos* is used. *Mandra* ("lair") in Jer 4:7 may be a free rendering.

115. LXX takes the verb *'kl* of the next line (*consumed*) with this colon and interprets the final *waw* of the verb as the first word of the third colon ("and").

116. It is likely that the LXX relates *sbw'ym* (*səbû'îm*) to another meaning of the verb ("to weave"), but *kai hōs smilax* seems to represent a different text, unless the translator guessed that the noun must refer to something "woven" or "entangled" and so came up with a word for a plant that could be thus characterized.

117. Ambrogio Spreafico ("Nahum I 10 and Isaiah I 12–23: Double-Duty Modifier," *VT* 48 [1998]: 104–10) recommends reading *ûkəsôbā'îm səbû'îm* ("as drunkards inebriated by

as in English,[118] as in the exchange from *The Hitchhiker's Guide to the Galaxy* by Douglas Adams:

> "You'd better be prepared for the jump into hyperspace. It's unpleasantly like being drunk."
> "What's so unpleasant about being drunk?"
> "You ask a glass of water."[119]

The present translation assumes a similar play on the double meaning of *drunk*, interpreting *sobʾām* (*their drink*) as a noun with a pronominal suffix (cf. Isa 1:22).[120] Just as their drink is fully imbibed, so they are fully inebriated. In other words, they are saturated with alcoholic beverage—completely drunk. And so, *they are consumed like fully dry stubble.* Again, as with the overflowing flood after the sirocco, we have a mix of "wet" and "dry" metaphors in the Hebrew text.

Even if the first colon is not syntactically connected to the last, the metaphor of fire consuming stubble may retrospectively remind readers of the use of thorns as fuel for a fire (cf. Eccl 7:6, with wordplay involving *sîrîm*, "thorns," and *sîr*, "cook-pot"). The piling up of the *s* sound in this verse may be heard as imitating the sizzle of the fire.

Reflection

The opening poem was either created or adapted (e.g., *her place*) and prefaced (v. 2) for the book of Nahum. It should be read in this context, but also in the context of the whole of Scripture. The poem offers a powerful description of YHWH—a meditation that focuses on God as avenger. Proverbs 27:4 may

---

wine"), takes *ʾukkəlû* ("they will be devoured") with this as the following phrase, and suggests that the motif of divine judgment unites the two metaphors (106–7).

118. German distinguishes between "drunk" as "imbibed" (*getrunken*) and "drunk" as "inebriated" (*betrunken*). The Hebrew is not the regular word for drinking but one that may suggest heavy drinking. In German, the distinction would still hold (*gesoffen, besoffen*), while in English the passive of "to booze" would not be used with a drink as its subject.

119. Douglas Adams, *The Hitchhiker's Guide to the Galaxy: A Trilogy in Five Parts* (London: Heinemann, 1995), 51.

120. This is also Spronk's view, but he suggests that the participle refers to making beer (*Nahum*, 55): "and like the beer that they brew" (18). An alternative is to read an infinitive construct with a pronominal suffix: "their drinking" (the same ambiguity is found in Hos 4:18). This may underlie ESV, which suffers from similar problems as NASB. James Barr (*Comparative Philology and the Text of the Old Testament* [London: SCM Press, 1983], 33) adopts Reider's suggestion to treat the final *mem* as enclitic, translating "and as the drunken are getting drunk" (cf. NRSV?). I do not understand how he gets to "the drunken."

come to mind: "Rage is cruelty and anger a flood but who can stand before jealousy?" God's anger is not an uncontrollable rage that comes upon people suddenly and unexpectedly. God's anger is his deliberate and consistent hostility toward evil. It is born of his jealousy. YHWH guards his exclusive role as creator and redeemer by executing vengeance on all that opposes him. Evil is thus implicitly defined as whatever seeks to take God's place or does not "render to God the things that are God's" (Matt 22:21 and parallels).

If we accept that God is the only one who can fill the role of God well, then it is good news to hear that God is jealous for his prerogatives. If we are persuaded that God is good and just and true, then it is good to know that he opposes his enemies, because those who oppose this God of goodness, justice, and truth will, wittingly or unwittingly, promote evil, injustice, and falsehood. God's intolerance of such opposition is thus an expression of his goodness and offers genuine hope that victims of evil, injustice, and falsehood may receive relief in the end. The opening of the poem stresses that God's anger is a constant disposition against his enemies, but it becomes quickly clear that God acts on his anger only at specific times. It is therefore possible to call him "slow to anger"—that is, slow to act on his constant hostility toward evil.[121] This is one reason why God's wrath against his enemies (as regards their enmity) need not preclude his love for sinners, to which other parts of Scripture testify (e.g., Rom 5:8). Readers of the book of Jonah have heard a witness to God's love for his enemies applied to Nineveh. This witness is not invalidated by the destruction of the city. Similarly, Nahum's witness to the execution of God's anger against Nineveh does not entail a denial of God's love for his enemies. Those who seek to read Nahum as a witness to an unloving, bloodthirsty God must read the book apart from its Scriptural setting, for which there is no warrant, and even then are forced to minimize Nahum's witness to God being *slow to anger* (v. 3), a *good* and secure *stronghold* (v. 7), one who makes an *end* to *distress* (v. 9).[122]

Our experience of God may be tension-filled, but we need not conclude from this that God is himself full of tensions. Just as God's steadfast love and compassion do not come to an end, as someone calls to mind in the midst of distress (Lam 3:22), so God's hostility to evil remains. Indeed, one demands the other. It is necessary that one who loves truth and goodness must hate falsehood and evil. Only the one who is able and willing to contain those who threaten can offer a sure refuge. But in the context of the whole Bible,

---

121. Cf., e.g., Ps 79:5: "How long, YHWH? Will you be angry forever? Will your jealousy burn like fire?" Here both "anger" and "jealousy" are descriptive of God's *enacted* hostility.

122. It is true that Scripture only rarely characterizes a group of people as "enemies" and "beloved" at the same time (but see Rom 11:28). This is due to the storylike rather than systematic nature of the Bible.

the reverse is also true. The God who is consistently *avenging toward his foes* must be a God who is loving and good because the enemies of the God to whom the Bible testifies are enemies of love and goodness.[123]

The witness to God's love and wrath are combined in the gospel. The proclamation that Jesus is Lord challenges other pretensions to lordship. The cross is the supreme expression of God's love and a triumph over disarmed rulers and authorities (Col 2:15). The very name of Jesus testifies that he is the one who saves (Matt 1:21; cf., e.g., Acts 13:23). Jealousy for the prerogative in this name is expressed in Acts 4:12: "And there is salvation in no one else, for there is no other name under heaven given among people by which we must be saved." If it is indeed true, as I believe, that there is salvation only in one name (cf. Acts 2:21 and Rom 10:13, both applying Joel 2:32 [3:5]), tolerance of other pretenders to that claim is injurious to the welfare of those who need saving. While human jealousy is often mean-spirited, the one who is a *stronghold* (v. 7), indeed the only stronghold, as the poem clearly implies, would be mean-spirited if he allowed false offers of security to remain unchallenged. Assyria was not only an oppressive power but also a force that offered such false security, which must be shown to be without foundation.

The Bible commonly uses motifs from nature to refer to an "earth-shattering" intervention on God's part. The theme here as elsewhere is of things no longer being solid and no longer functioning normally. This is a reminder that, as much as God's attitude toward evil does not change, the enactment of his anger is the exception rather than the rule. A more systematic theologian would rightly point out that the normal functioning of the universe is the result of God constantly upholding what he has created. Our poet does not make this assumption explicit, but the fact that things fall apart when God acts on his anger implies at the least that they only hold together when and because God does not act on his anger. The regularity of the natural world is thus a witness to the fact that God is *slow to anger* as well as *abounding in power* (cf. Rom 1:20).

The tricola in the last two verses provide the prophetic challenge, which is based on the poem. The challenge is expressed in the first line of v. 9: *What do you ponder concerning YHWH?* Reflecting on this poem should lead us to ask what we make of YHWH, whether we need to revise our view of God in conformity to this revelation or whether we resist the witness offered here. The strong language in Nahum 1 mocks any "I like to think of God as . . ." type of thinking. The decisiveness of divine intervention (no second blow is needed)

---

123. Readers who do not accept the truth of Scripture may well apply a hermeneutic of suspicion here, seeing the claims to love, goodness, and justice as a mere front to justify discrimination and violence. I am writing as someone who has come to accept the claims of Scripture as truthful.

does not imply that the text envisages the end of history or even of all opposition against YHWH. What is applied here to the situation in the seventh century BC has found and will find further applications in history, as societies drunken with violence are overcome by violence. But the fuller revelation of Scripture does testify to a time when YHWH will be finally vindicated and all opposition to his good and just rule overcome (e.g., Rev 21–22).

III. ACCUSATION AGAINST THE CITY (1:11)

[11]From you has come forth someone scheming evil against YHWH,
  someone advising villainy.

11 Verse 11 forms a bridge between the opening poem (vv. 2–8) with its poetic exposition (vv. 9–10) on the one hand and the divine declaration (vv. 12–14) on the other hand. It does not seem to belong to the poem itself, which has come to an apt conclusion in the preceding verse, nor with the following, as the citation formula of v. 12 in this case seems to open a new subunit that features first-person divine speech.[124] The key problem is to decide who the implied addressee is. Many believe that Jerusalem is addressed.[125] This has the advantage of agreeing with the use of the second-person feminine singular for Judah or Jerusalem in the following oracle. But a change of rhetorical perspective between v. 11 and the following subunit cannot be excluded. If Jerusalem is addressed, *yāṣā'* (*come forth*) is best interpreted as "departed," and this verse is taken together with the following as a historical reminiscence. The reference would be to the departure of the Assyrian king Sennacherib from Jerusalem in 701 BC after having been unable to conquer the city.[126] While Isa 49:17 demonstrates that *yṣ' min* can be used in such a context,[127] other expressions may be more suitable to express the idea of (unsuccessful) departure.[128] The present text would seem an obscure way

---

124. The citation formula *Thus YHWH said* (v. 12) is often, but by no means exclusively, used at the beginning of a unit.

125. E.g., Rudolph, *Micha*, 161; Roberts, *Nahum*, 53; Sweeney, "Concerning the Structure," 367–68, 371, 374, cf. *The Twelve Prophets*, vol. 2, Berit Olam (Collegeville, MN: Liturgical Press), 431–32; Floyd, "Chimerical Acrostic," 432, cf. *Minor Prophets 2*, 27–29, 44–49; Ball, "Towers," 223. Jeremias (*Nahum*, 99) believes that v. 11 originally had Nineveh in view but with the addition of vv. 12–13 was transformed into a promise of salvation for Judah.

126. Cf. Rudolph, *Micha*, 161; Fabry, *Nahum*, 149–50; see the discussion in Floyd, *Minor Prophets 2*, 45–48.

127. This is also the only reference given by Ibn Kaspi (*Adne Kesef*, 2:114), who understands the verse to refer to Assyria's departure from the earth—presumably its eradication.

128. For other possibilities, see, e.g., 2 Kgs 19:36 and Isa 37:37: "So Sennacherib king of

of presenting Sennacherib's unsuccessful departure from Jerusalem.[129] If v. 11 were a statement referring to this event, it would also remain unclear why *from you* is put emphatically at the beginning of the sentence, as the emphasis should be on the departure rather than the point of departure. But if v. 11 presents, in effect, the accusation against Nineveh, which implies that the introductory poem will find application against Nineveh, the emphatic *from you* makes sense. Thus, it seems best to interpret the addressee to be Nineveh, an interpretation already found in the Targum.[130] But the absence of the name facilitates application of the text beyond Nineveh to any entity from which *someone scheming evil against YHWH* comes forth.

The one *scheming evil against YHWH* is a *yōʿēṣ bəliyyāʿal* (*someone advising villainy*). NJB renders it as "one of Belial's counsellors" (cf. its rendering of 2 Sam 23:6), but other translations rightly interpret *bəliyyāʿal* as attributive, denoting evil, disorder, or destructiveness, as in Prov 6:12: *ʾādām bəliyyaʿal ʾîš ʾāwen* (NJB: "a scoundrel, a vicious man").[131] The use of "Belial" as a personal name (cf. 2 Cor 6:15, "Beliar") seems to be a later development. By way of contrast to *yōʿēṣ bəliyyāʿal*, we read *peleʾ yôʿēṣ* ("someone who counsels wonderfully") in Isa 9:6(5) and *yôʿēṣ baśekel* ("a counsellor with insight" in 1 Chr 26:14. No specific advice need be in view here any more than in these two passages. The verbs *ḥšb* ("plan, scheme"; see the commentary on v. 9) and *yʿṣ* ("counsel, advise") are used in parallel also in Ezek 11:2, where they characterize twenty-five leaders in Jerusalem in general terms, and in Jer

---

Assyria set out (*nsʿ*), departed (*hlk*), and returned (*šûb*), and lived at Nineveh" (cf. the use of šûb elsewhere in this chapter). The use of *sûr* and *pnh* (cf. *HALOT*, s.v. *pnh*, 4.a) would also have been possible, and maybe *mûš* (used in 3:1). Alternatively, a double preposition could remove the ambiguity (see *hlk mēʿāl* in Jer 37:9).

129. Fabry (*Nahum*, 150) suggests that the obscurity is the effect of our historical distance from the events. While he is undoubtedly right to observe that the events surrounding 701 BC must have featured prominently in Judah's historical consciousness at the time, the verse does not provide any specific link to these events. It should also be borne in mind that Judah was devastated in 701, even if Jerusalem itself was spared, so that the emphatic *from you* would introduce a contrast between Jerusalem and Judah, which is ill suited in the context.

130. "From you, Nineveh, there has gone forth a king who plotted evil against the people of the Lord; he gave evil counsel" (ArBib 14, 133). As noted above, NIV and TNIV also add "Nineveh" to the text.

131. The KJV renders *bəliyyāʿal* as "wicked" or similarly eleven times but as a personal name fifteen times in the Old Testament (cf. 2 Cor 6:15). Contrast the Geneva Bible, which never translated "Belial" as a personal name in the Old Testament. In current English translations of the Hebrew Bible, "Belial" is found only in JPS translations of Ps 18:4(5) // 2 Sam 22:5 and in the NJB translation of these verses and the two occurrences in Nahum. J. A. Emerton ("Sheol and the Sons of Belial," *VT* 37 [1987]: 214–18) rejects the identification of Belial with Sheol, which seems to be the basis of translating "torrents of Belial" in David's psalm.

49:20, 30; 50:45, where the reference is always to a specific course of action. Here in Nahum the use of participles indicates general characterization, as in Ezek 11:2. Thus, YHWH, whom the opening poem portrays as characteristically *avenging* and *agitated against his enemies,* finds himself opposed by someone whose scheming is characteristically worthless and wicked. The rest of the book elaborates on their inevitable confrontation.

IV. YHWH'S VERDICT (1:12–14)

¹²*Thus YHWH said:*
*Even though they are completely at ease*ᵃ *and likewise many,*ᵇ
  *they are shorn,*ᶜ *and he is gone.*ᵈ
      *And:*ᵉ *Though*ᶠ *I have afflicted you,*ᵍ *I will afflict you no more.*
¹³*So now, I will break his staff*ʰ *from upon you,*
  and your shackles I will tear away.
¹⁴*And: YHWH has given a command concerning you:*
  *no more shall be sown from your name.*ⁱ
*From the house of your gods*ʲ *I will entirely cut off*ᵏ *idol and image;*
  *I will prepare*ˡ *your grave because you are lightweight.*ᵐ

a. This translates *šəlēmîm,* which could also be translated "at full strength" (e.g., NRSV, NASB). The NIV translation "have allies" (cf. NLT) may go back to Donald J. Wiseman, " 'Is it Peace?'—Covenant and Diplomacy," *VT* 32 (1982): 311–26, and is followed by Patterson, *Nahum,* 48. But see Spronk, *Nahum,* 71.

b. The double use of *wəkēn* ("and so," "and thus") is unusual. It is sometimes interpreted "As they are many, so also the many shall be destroyed" (e.g., Calvin) but this is regularly expressed by *kə . . . kēn* (e.g., Lev 27:13; Deut 8:20) or *ka'ăšer . . . kēn* (e.g., Gen 41:13; Exod 1:12). In my reading, the first *wəkēn* continues the protasis ("if" clause), the second introduces the apodosis ("then" clause) and thus remains invisible in translation. The LXX does not reflect the first *wəkēn* and divides the words differently, producing *tade legei kyrios katarchōn hydatōn pollōn* ("Thus says the Lord who rules over many waters"; the *aleph* may have been interpreted as an abbreviated *'ăšer*), followed by *kai houtōs* ("and thus," corresponding to the second *wəkēn*) *diastalēsontai* ("they shall have been sent away" [?]), which is not easily related to the Hebrew text; maybe the translator saw a *zhr niphal* ("to be warned"; cf. Ezek 3:18–21).

c. The translation assumes the common meaning of the traditional Hebrew text (*nāgōzzû,* *niphal* from *gzz*). The consonantal text could also be read as a *niphal* from the rare *gûz* (*nāgōzû,* "they have passed away"; so already Calvin; cf. the reference to the crossing of the Tigris in Tg.; the root is found in Num 11:31 and Ps 90:10) or from *gzh* (*nigzû,* "they have been cut off"; elsewhere attested only in Ps 71:6 for cutting off the navel string). The *niphal* is not found elsewhere with any of these roots. Maier (*Nahum,* 203) speculates that the *niphal* of *gzz* means "protected" based on a suggested equivalence to the (hypothetical) root *qśś* (in older dictionaries thought to be the root of *qaśqeśet,* which refers to the scale of a fish, e.g., in Lev 11:9, and is now considered a primary noun; see *HALOT*). No emendation of the consonantal text has won widespread support. One possibility is a derivation from *zûz* in the sense of "abundantly overflowing" (the root is not directly attested in Biblical Hebrew, but see BDB and *HALOT*), but this root would likely have been used in the *qal* and thus not look similar enough to suggest a copying mistake.

d. Or "he has passed away." Elliger (*BHS*) and Rudolph (*Micha*, 159), among others, suggest taking the *waw* of the first word of the next line with the last word of this line, thus producing a plural ("they have passed away") and losing the conjunction. The verb is missing in the LXX; *kai hē akoē sou* ("and your report") apparently interprets *w'ntk* (*wə'innītîk*: *I have afflicted you*) differently but reflects the conjunction.

e. In my view, the conjunctions here and at the beginning of v. 14 introduce further instances of *Thus YHWH said*. In contemporary English usage, we would probably number those rather than use *And:*, but numbering would give my (hypothetical) division of the text even greater prominence.

f. Maybe the *'im-* . . . *wə(kēn)* construction in the preceding line carries over, but this is not necessary. The concessive nuance is implied by the logical contrast of the two parts of the sentence; see JM 171f for further examples. Ibn Kaspi (*Adne Kesef*, 2:114) repeats *'im*, but this seems to be by way of explanation.

g. As noted above, the LXX seems to derive *w'ntk* from *'nh* ("to answer"). Elsewhere, Greek *akoē* reflects the Hebrew root *šm'* ("hear").

h. The first vowel of *mōṭēhû* suggests that the root is *môṭ* ("carrying frame," "pole"; cf. *môṭâ*, "yoke"), but the suffix belongs more regularly to the root *maṭṭê* ("staff," "rod"; also "tribe"). Both *maṭṭê* (Exod 7:17 [cf. v. 19]; 8:1; 9:23; 10:13; 14:16; Isa 10:24, 26; 30:32) and *môṭâ* (Jer 27:2 [implicit]; 28:10, 12) can be used with the preposition *'āl* ("upon"), but the masculine *môṭ* is only attested elsewhere in Numbers (4:10, 12; 13:23). Tg. and Syr. interpret it as "yoke" (cf. a number of medieval Hebrew MSS listed by Benjamin Kennicott, *Vetus Testamentum hebraicum cum variis lectionibus* [Oxford: Clarendon, 1776], 280, that have a plene text with *waw*), LXX and Vulg. as "rod" (cf. a number of medieval Hebrew MSS listed by de Rossi that have a *patakh* under the first consonant; so according to Spronk, *Nahum*, 73). See the commentary.

i. The unusual *from your name* is also found in the LXX: *ek tou onomatos sou*. Alternatively, the *mem* may belong to the preceding word as an enclitic, in which case one would translate, "Your name shall not be sown again"; cf. Kevin J. Cathcart, *Nahum in the Light of Northwest Semitic*, BibOr 26 (Rome: Pontifical Biblical Institute, 1973), 65.

j. Or: "your house of gods." Cf. *bêt 'ĕlōhêhem* ("their house of gods" or "the house of their god[s]") in Judg 9:27; see also 2 Chr 32:21; Ezra 1:7; Dan 1:2 and with reference to the God of Israel, e.g., Josh 9:23; 1 Chr 29:2–3; 2 Chr 24:5; Pss 84:10(11), 135:2; and numerous references in Ezra–Nehemiah. A pronominal suffix in a construct phrase may belong to the governing noun or the governed noun. For the former note, e.g., *har qādšî* ("my holy mountain," Isa 11:9 et al.); for the latter see, e.g., *tēpillat 'abdēkā* ("the prayer of your servant," 1 Kgs 8:28 et al.), *nēbî'ê 'ābîkā* ("the prophets of your father," 2 Kgs 3:13), *bērît 'ābōtêkā* ("the covenant with your fathers," Deut 4:31). The latter seems more likely here; cf. *bêt 'abdēkem* ("your servant's house," Gen 19:2), *bêt mišmarkem* ("the house of your custody," Gen 42:19), contra Jeremias, *Nahum*, 108, who believes that only "your house of god(s)" is possible and on this basis had previously argued that the prophecy was originally directed against Manasseh (*Kultprophetie*, 20–25).

k. Heb. *'akrît*. The *hiphil* invites a stronger translation than "cut off" (*qal*), such as "annihilate" or "destroy" (see *HALOT*). Adding *entirely* helps to express this; cf. 2:13(14).

l. Many interpreters (e.g., Cathcart, *Nahum*, 67) prefer a slightly different vocalization (*'aššîm* for *'āśîm*) and find the *hiphil* of *šmm*, which is used elsewhere for causing a land (e.g., Lev 26:32), a city (e.g., Ezek 30:14), or sanctuaries (Lev 26:31) to become desolate.

m. Unusual accentuation suggests reading the second half of the verse as one long colon consisting of nine feet (word units). See the commentary.

Composition

Thus YHWH said is used to open the sayings addressed to individual nations and cities in Amos,[132] but in many other instances the clause appears to continue a speech, even where the Masoretes opened a new paragraph.[133] Thus, the use of the formula itself does not tell us that the following is a new unit, although it can be difficult within the prophetic literature to decide whether a unit should be considered an independent oracle or part of a longer speech.[134] But given that v. 11 referred to YHWH in the third person and given the lack of any indication of divine speech earlier in the book, the citation formula here probably introduces an oracle that may be considered a self-contained unit.[135] At the same time, this oracle is a response to the situation outlined in v. 11. Given the depiction of YHWH in the opening poem, and given that Nineveh is the source of villainy, this is what YHWH has to say to Judah and to Assyria.[136] While Assyria has been YHWH's instrument to afflict Judah, Assyria is now under divine judgment, and thus Judah will be liberated from them (vv. 12–13). YHWH's command is for the complete destruction of Assyrian power (v. 14).

132. Amos 1:3, 6, 9, 11, 13; 2:1, 4, 6. The phrase occurs 293 times in the Hebrew Bible. A common variation of the phrase with *'ădōnāy yhwh*, which occurs 134 times, opens the revelation to Obadiah (v. 1).

133. This is most obvious in narrative texts, such as 1 Sam 15:2; 2 Sam 12:11; 1 Chr 17:7; 2 Chr 34:24, 26. Note that in 1 Chr 17:7 and 2 Chr 34:26, the paragraph break is within the verse.

134. A link to the preceding is regularly marked with *kî* (e.g., Isa 8:11; 18:4; 31:4; Amos 5:4), *lākēn* (e.g., Isa 29:22; 37:33; Amos 5:16; 7:17; Mic 2:3), or *wə'attâ* (Isa 43:1; Jer 44:7; Hag 1:5). But even without an explicit link, it cannot be assumed that the formula introduces an independent speech. See Samuel A. Meier, *Speaking of Speaking: Marking Direct Discourse in the Hebrew Bible*, VTSup 46 (Leiden: Brill, 1992), 273–98.

135. The mixture of first and third person is not decisive, because YHWH refers to himself in the third person in divine speech elsewhere in the Bible. The point is that up to 1:12 no part of Nahum has been marked as divine speech.

136. The addressees are not specified, but there can be no doubt that Judah or Jerusalem is addressed in vv. 12–13 (NIV adds "Judah"), and the oppressor (referenced in the third person in vv. 12–13) in v. 14 (NIV adds "Nineveh" although the masc. suffix indicates that the king of Nineveh is in view). See further below.

The assurance given in v. 9 that *distress will not arise a second time* when God makes a full end of his enemies is picked up in the *no more* of vv. 12 and 14 (cf. the exact same Hebrew phrase for *never again* in 1:15 [2:1]). There are a number of tensions in these three verses. Verse 12a talks as if it is all over already (which is why some have taken this verse with the preceding), while v. 13 indicates a liberation *now*. Verses 12–13 also address a feminine singular (Judah or Jerusalem) with regard to entities referred to in masculine plural (v. 12, the Assyrians) and masculine singular (v. 13, the king of Assyria) forms. Verse 14 addresses a masculine singular (the king of Assyria, maybe as embodying the empire). Thus, each verse brings with it a shift in time or addressee. It may well be that this section collects three originally independent oracles. Indeed, v. 14 has its own introduction, although in its literary context this should probably be seen as subordinate to the heading *thus YHWH said* (see the commentary below on the use of the verb). I interpret line-initial *waw* in vv. 12b and 14a as introducing further YHWH sayings. The initial *waw* of v. 13a could be interpreted similarly but probably flows more naturally as a continuation of v. 12b. The result is a two-line saying (v. 12a) followed by a three-line saying (vv. 12b–13) followed by a four-line saying (v. 14). This lengthening of units may be heard as imitating the effects of an overwhelming flood.[137] What unites these three verses is that they are all formulated as first-person divine speech. (The next such first-person speech in the mouth of YHWH will only occur in 2:13[14]; cf. 3:5.) Another feature that subtly unites the three sayings is judgment on the king of Assyria, who was already featured in v. 11. The king features again briefly and obscurely in v. 12 (*he is gone*) and indirectly in v. 13 (*his staff*) before being directly addressed in the last and longest saying (v. 14). This development of judgment on the king of Assyria is significant for the order of the sayings. It would have been possible alternatively to lead from the judgment on Assyria to the consequent liberation of Judah. As it is, the (divine) burial of the Assyrian king is the point to which this section is heading, not the liberation of Judah.[138] The latter is of course foregrounded in the immediately following verse.

Parallels between 1:12 and 1:15 (2:1) could be interpreted as an *inclusio*, suggesting that the unit should include the next verse. The Masoretes may have tried to prevent this reading by reading an extra-long colon at the end of 1:14 to unambiguously mark the end of this unit,[139] alongside the *petucha* (most MSS, *setumah* in Cairo Codex) following this verse.

---

137. The Masoretes reinforced this effect by taking the last two lines together as one very long line, even if this may have served a different purpose, on which see below.

138. While Judah's liberation stands at the center, the center is not structurally marked. There are other places in the book that highlight the fact that the fall of Nineveh is good news for the oppressed, but the focus of attention here remains on Nineveh and the Assyrian king.

139. For extra-long cola as a sign of stanza closure, see *CHP*, 165.

Commentary

12 The speaking voice remains elusive throughout much of the book of Nahum. The book's opening poem portrays YHWH in the third person (vv. 2–8); the challenge arising from it (vv. 9–10) and the description of the situation at hand (v. 11) continue in that mode. Verses 12–14, however, introduce first-person speech, and it is therefore appropriate that the speaking voice of this section should be explicitly identified.[140] Contrary to popular understanding, *thus YHWH said* is a citation formula, not a messenger formula, and best rendered as past tense.[141] The distribution of the formula across the prophets is uneven.[142] Only here does it occur in Nahum, and it is presumably designed not only to clarify but also to stress the identity of the speaker. The destruction of Nineveh could be considered inevitable in the long run by all those who believe the characterization of YHWH (1:2–8) and Nineveh (1:11) offered previously. The verdict is, however, not simply presented as a logical conclusion. Both the *qatal* forms in v. 12 (looking at the judgment as completed: *shorn . . . gone*) and the *now* in v. 13 call for the assurance offered by *thus YHWH said*.

From all that has been said previously in this chapter, it follows that the end of Nineveh will be YHWH's doing. But just as the king comes slowly into ever greater focus, so does YHWH's action against him. In the first saying (v. 12a), YHWH's involvement is not mentioned at all. In the second saying (vv. 12b–13), YHWH's intervention is focused on the liberation of his oppressed people. In the last saying (v. 14), there is a specific command against the king as well as action specifically targeted at him.

The description of the impressive state in which Assyria finds itself occupies only four words in the Hebrew, counting *'im* (*Even though*) and *šəlēmîm* (*they are completely at ease*) as two words.[143] Taken together, the first letter of each of these words spells "Assyria" (*'šwr*, pronounced *'aššûr*).[144] This

---

140. Other instances of first-person speech in the book are similarly identified; see *nə'um yhwh ṣəbā'ôt* in 2:13(14) and 3:5. The extent of the divine speech in the last instance is not unambiguous. Thus, the ironical *where can I find comforters for you* in 3:7 could be the first-person voice of Nahum.

141. See Meier, *Speaking of Speaking*, 272–98.

142. About two-thirds of all occurrences of the formula are found in the books of Jeremiah and Ezekiel. Jeremiah accounts for 153 instances of the shorter and Ezekiel for 122 instances of the longer phrase. Among the Minor Prophets, Amos and Zechariah account for most occurrences (34 altogether; Haggai employs the shorter form 5 times).

143. They are joined by a *maqqep* in the traditional Hebrew text. Some scholars count units joined by a *maqqep* as one word. The conjunction *wə* is not normally considered a word, as it always attaches itself to the following word (the same goes for inseparable prepositions).

144. This was first pointed out by Joseph Reider, "The Name Ashur in the Initials of a

kind of (sentence) acrostic, which relies on individual words rather than the beginnings of lines or half-lines, is not securely attested elsewhere in the Hebrew Bible. So, in Nahum this phenomenon may be a happy coincidence rather than part of the author's design,[145] but it would explain the choice of a slightly unusual word *šəlēmîm* (*completely at ease*). This adjective refers to something that is intact and in excellent, unimpaired condition.[146] Assurbanipal used the related Akkadian root to describe the safe and victorious return of his troops.[147] The Assyrians seem to be in full strength. Ironically, the related verb is used in the *hiphil* for "making peace" (e.g., Deut 20:12; Prov 16:7; cf. the noun *šālôm*), and the adjective means "peaceful" in Gen 34:21. The size of the Assyrian army must have been impressive given the extent of their military operations. Not only the actual warfare but also the logistics of transporting booty and moving captive populations required the involvement of significant numbers of people. In warfare, there is a certain safety in numbers. It is therefore no surprise that *completely at ease* is paired with *and likewise many*.

But the divine saying states that *they are* already *shorn*. Its verb (*gzz*) is used elsewhere eleven times for shearing sheep (e.g., Gen 31:19) and three times for (completely) cutting off human hair as a sign of distress (Jer 7:29; Mic 1:16; Job 1:20). Its use here is therefore unexpected. If the text is not corrupt,[148] it may be that the idea of Assyria's multitude suggested the picture of the heaps of fleece produced during the sheep shearing season.[149] Assyria will be stripped of its multitude by an event that can be likened to shearing, a time in the calendar that seems to have been of some importance in ancient Israel.[150] We may compare this to the end of the book, where Nineveh's numerous merchants and officials flee like locust swarms (3:16–17), leaving the king with slumbering shepherds and a people scattered across the mountains (3:18).

Difficult Phrase in the Bible," *JAOS* 58 (1938): 153–55; cf. Spronk, *Nahum*, 69. Note that the deity Assur, the city Assur, and Assyria are spelled identically in the Hebrew.

145. Similar acrostics have been suggested for Jer 31:8–9 and Nah 3:18 (see Spronk, *Nahum*, 70), but these are not generally recognized either.

146. It is also used negatively of a "complete deportation" (the deportation of an entire community, Amos 1:6, 9) or "complete guilt" (guilt that has reached its full extent, Gen 15:16).

147. Cook, "Ashurbanipal's Peace." As pointed out in the introduction, Cook thinks that this provides a clue to dating Nahum to 639 BC or shortly thereafter.

148. As noted above, no emendation has won the day.

149. Note that the three instances of cutting human hair do not refer to the trimming of hair but result in baldness.

150. Cf. Gen 31:19; 38:13; 1 Sam 25:2–8, 11; 2 Sam 13:23–28. There may be connotations of joy that we are meant to hear, as sheep shearing was evidently linked with a feast (see especially the examples from 1–2 Samuel; cf. Tob 1:6).

If the following verb (*'br*) is rightly understood to refer to a single person and not read collectively,[151] or more generally,[152] the idea is not so much that the Assyrians "will be cut off and pass away" (NRSV et al.) but that the Assyrians *are shorn* like sheep while their shepherd *is gone*. The verb rendered *is gone* is also used for contravening the covenant (e.g., Josh 7:11, 15) or transgressing commands (e.g., Num 14:41; Deut 26:13) but hardly ever without the object being specified (Ps 17:3 appears to be the sole exception). Thus, it would be inappropriate to render it "has transgressed," but the rendering "has invaded" is defensible (cf., e.g., Isa 8:8). This would be to say that, while the Assyrian shepherd-king has gone away[153] invading other countries, his own sheep were shorn. More likely, the verb is used in the sense of "to perish" (cf., e.g., Job 34:20; 36:12). My translation (*is gone*) allows for either reading because it seems noteworthy that neither of the two verbs in this first saying unambiguously expresses *a full end* (vv. 8–9). Just as shearing is not killing, the one who passed away from his country into other countries is not necessarily gone forever. This may account for the use of *qatal* (perfect) forms. The Assyrians may look impressive, but something has already happened that spells their end.[154]

Some of the older commentators have taken the next saying (*Though I have afflicted you, I will afflict you no more*) as addressed to Nineveh, in which case it should be considered an announcement of a future event in similar terms to v. 9. That is, YHWH will afflict Assyria so decisively that he will not need to afflict her again ("When I will afflict you, I will afflict you no more").[155]

---

151. There is legitimate doubt about this, as noted above. Both Syr. and Tg. render with the plural, and this is also how many commentators take it (see already Ibn Kaspi, *Adne Kesef*, 2:114). But the fact that a prominent individual (sg.) has been introduced in 1:11 and features again in vv. 13–14 leads me to find this individual here as well.

152. That is, "it has passed" either in the sense of "it is over" or with the shearing knife as the implied subject (cf. Num 6:5; 8:7; Ezek 5:1). But I am not convinced that the former can be justified (I am not aware of any parallel use of the verb), and the latter seems to me too obscure. Yet another reading is offered in early English translations: "When he shall pass through" (KJV; cf. Geneva Bible). But this, too, seems to me too obscure.

153. Cf. also Mic 1:11 for the use of the verb to denote leaving one's home.

154. More commonly, the *qatal* forms are considered a rhetorical device, whereby future events are described as if already accomplished; see, e.g., JM 112fh. For a fuller, albeit controversial, discussion, see Max F. Roglund, *Alleged Non-Past Uses of* Qatal *in Classical Hebrew*, Studia Semitica Neerlandica 44 (Assen: Van Gorcum, 2003).

155. Cf. the margin of the Revised Version. See Samuel R. Driver, *The Minor Prophets: Nahum, Habakkuk, Zephaniah, Haggai, Zechariah, Malachi*, The Century Bible (London: Nelson and Sons, 1906), 23, with reference to H. Ewald, F. Hitzig, Julius Wellhausen, Andrew Bruce Davidson, and G. A. Smith. Spronk (*Nahum*, 72) adds J. P. M. Smith and John H. Eaton.

Several commentators insist that a future reference is the more natural rendering of the Hebrew,[156] but their arguments don't convince me.[157] It seems altogether more likely that Judah is addressed here, as in the following verse, which indicates that Assyria has been the instrument of the divine affliction of Judah. Assyrian propaganda would have agreed. The Assyrian kings saw themselves as executors of divine intentions. Their treaties with Israel and Judah most likely included appeal to YHWH as one of the witnesses. Thus, any disloyalty on the part of their covenant partners would obligate even YHWH to act against Israel or Judah.[158] The Assyrian king saw YHWH at his service (cf. Isa 36:18–20). But the truth is the reverse, and this becomes obvious as soon as YHWH declares that he will no longer afflict his people.

13 *So now* introduces the consequence of YHWH's decision to afflict Judah no longer. The rule of the Assyrian king, *his staff*, will be broken. The threat of breaking someone's staff (or scepter) is also found among ancient treaty curses.[159] There may be an allusion here to Isa 10:5, which addresses Assyria as *šēbeṭ 'appî* ("rod of my anger") and *maṭṭê-hû' bəyādām za'mî* ("the staff that is in their hand, my scorn"). This in itself does not demand that we interpret *mōṭēhû* as *maṭṭēhû* ("his staff"; cf. Isa 10:24, 26), but several converging considerations lead to the conclusion that *mōṭēhû* (*mōṭ* with suffix) is unlikely to mean "his yoke" here.[160] The expected Hebrew form for "his yoke" is *môṭāṭô* (plene) or *mōṭāṭô* (defective spelling), since only the feminine form *môṭâ* is used for a yoke.[161] The masculine *mōṭ* is found elsewhere only in Numbers and with more positive connotations (4:10, 12; 13:23).[162] It

156. Andrew Bruce Davidson (*The Books of Nahum, Habakkuk and Zephaniah*, Cambridge Bible for Schools and Colleges 28 [Cambridge: Cambridge University Press, 1899], 29) compares Exod 4:14 (where a *wə-qatal . . . wə-qatal* construction continues a participle, which refers to the immediate future) and Num 23:20 (which is not necessarily future). Here, the *wə-qatal* follows *wə-qatal*, which in turn follows simple *qatal*. Thus, everything depends on how the first *qatal* (*nāgōzzû: they are shorn*) is rendered.

157. The Masoretes supplied *wə'innîtîk* (*And I have afflicted you*) with two accents, which probably mitigates against reading a *waw* consecutive ("and I will afflict you") and thus resolves an ambiguity.

158. Fabry (*Nahum*, 150) makes the same observation.

159. See Delbert R. Hillers, *Treaty-Curses and the Old Testament Prophets*, BibOr 16 (Rome: Pontifical Biblical Institute, 1964), 61; Cathcart, "Treaty-Curses," 179–87, 180; Spronk, *Nahum*, 73. Cf. Isa 14:5.

160. Maier (*Nahum*, 209–10) suggests that *mōṭ* can refer to a "rod," in effect eliminating any difference between *mōṭēhû* and *maṭṭēhû*. But the Hebrew words in question appear to distinguish between implements of different sizes ("pole" and "bar" versus "rod" or "staff").

161. Strictly speaking, the word refers to the "bar" of the yoke, but it stands for the yoke as a whole.

162. BDB adds references to "shaking" in Pss 55:23; 66:9; 121:3; but these belong to the verb (so, correctly, *HALOT*).

is always written in full (plene) and so we would expect *môṭô* or, allowing an irregular suffix form, *môṭēhû*. While we may tolerate an irregular suffix,[163] a defective spelling in the first syllable, and maybe even the use of the masculine form, which elsewhere refers to a pole rather than (the bar of) a yoke, the combination of all three factors suggests that *môṭēhû* reflects a secondary reading tradition—one that may have been inspired by the combination of "yoke" and "shackles" in Jeremiah (27:2 with *môṭôt* and 2:20; 5:5; 30:8 with *'ōl* for "yoke"). The Assyrian rule was perceived as a yoke. Thus, to break the Assyrian *staff* is to break the Assyrian yoke. The *shackles* reinforce the concept of a political dependence, which leaves little room for maneuver (cf. Ps 2:3).

14 The final saying in this short collection turns to the king of Assyria. Meier observed that commands are much less frequently marked as such in the Bible than one might expect and that the root *ṣwh* (*command*) is relatively rare in the prophetic literature, with the exception of Jeremiah.[164] It must be significant, therefore, that the actual command is prefaced here by *YHWH has given a command concerning you*. Spronk seems entirely on the right track when he observes both that its use may have been inspired by Isa 10:6 and that "it emphasizes the contrast between YHWH and the king in Nineveh."[165] When YHWH sought to afflict Judah, he commanded Assyria, the rod of his anger, to attack the people with whom he was angry (Isa 10:5–6). Now that he no longer wants to afflict Judah, *YHWH has given a* different *command* whose execution will prove who is ultimately in charge.[166] The assertion *no more shall be sown from your name* finds its counterpart in the promise given to Israel in Isa 66:22: " 'For just as the new heavens and the new earth, which I will make, will endure before me,' speech of YHWH, 'so will your seed and your name endure.' " The Assyrian king's reputation shall come to an end with no posterity to carry on his name. Such a threat, making reference to "name" and "seed," is also found in treaty curses, sometimes together with the threat of a desecrated grave. Cathcart notes that "tombs, especially royal

---

163. JM 94h offers further examples of rare suffix forms, among them *'ôrēhû* for *'ôrô* (Job 25:3). See also *gibbōrêhû* in Nah 2:3(4). If our poet had a particular liking for this ending, *mar'êhen* in Nah 2:4(5), which some consider improper (*BHS* proposes *mar'êhem*), might be a misreading of an original *mar'êhû*, but a change is in fact unnecessary.

164. Meier, *Speaking*, 197–201. Along with five occurrences in Amos, the root is used in the Minor Prophets only here and in Zech 1:6 and Mal 3:22.

165. Spronk, *Nahum*, 74.

166. This implied polemic, as well as the specifics of the command, argue strongly against seeing a reference to "the personified Assyrian people" (Samuel R. Driver, *Minor Prophets*, 24; cf. Davidson, *Nahum*, 29; Maier, *Nahum*, 211, 214) in the use of the masculine singular here. Hubert Junker (*Die Zwölf Kleinen Propheten, II. Hälfte* [Bonn: Hanstein, 1938], 18) suggests that the Assyrian king is addressed as embodying people and land.

tombs, were often protected by curses directed against persons who might violate and desecrate them, and the very curse kings used to have inscribed on their tombs was precisely the curse of no progeny and no resting-place."[167]

Assurbanipal, grandson of Sennacherib, threatened anyone who would desecrate his grave with the wrath of the most powerful deities in the Assyrian pantheon.[168] But these are no match for YHWH, who announces that he *will entirely cut off idol and image* from the temples of the Assyrian king[169] before taking care of his grave. The word pair *pesel ûmassēkâ* (*idol and image*) denotes all kinds of idols;[170] it should be understood collectively here. A distinction is often made between wooden-carved *idol* and metal-cast *image*, in which case the phrase may be a hendiadys for wooden images with an overlay of metal, but the distinction is not certain.[171]

The curses on royal tombs form an interesting background to the announcement *I will prepare your grave because you are lightweight*, even if we do not interpret the verb as a reference to desecration.[172] The stress on YHWH as the one to prepare the grave is sometimes thought to indicate "the lack of anyone else to perform this task. There is no family left, and the dead ruler is too despised for anyone else to bother with his burial."[173] This reads too much into a phrase that does not claim that YHWH will act without employing human agents. But a *grave* that YHWH *prepares*, even if it were by human hands, will certainly not be a monument singing the Assyrian king's

---

167. Cathcart, "Treaty-Curses," 181. He compares Nah 3:18, which he interprets as a reference to corpses being left unburied. See also Spronk, *Nahum*, 74–77; Hillers, *Treaty-Curses*, 68–69; Timmer, *Non-Israelite Nations*, 127.

168. Arthur Carl Piepkorn, *Historical Prism Inscriptions of Ashurbanipal*, Assyriological Studies 5 (Chicago: University of Chicago Press, 1933), 86–89. See Spronk, *Nahum*, 75; cf. Maier, *Nahum*, 211 (without indication of source).

169. Spronk (*Nahum*, 76–77) notes Assurbanipal's boasts about beautifying the temples of his gods, for which see Piepkorn, *Inscriptions*, 28–29. Spronk rightly argues against the claim of some commentators that the verse has Manasseh in view.

170. The word pair is also found in Deut 27:15; Judg 17:3–4; 18:14; cf. Judg 18:17–18; Isa 42:17; Hab 2:18. 2 Chr 34:3–4 and Isa 30:22 use *pəsîlîm* (always plural) instead.

171. Cathcart points out that in Isa 40:19 and 44:10, the *pesel* is cast rather than carved and that the Ugaritic equivalent has a broader meaning than sculpting (*Nahum*, 66–67). In Isa 30:22, the *pəsîlîm* are overlaid with silver and the *massēkâ* with gold.

172. As noted in the translation, many scholars prefer to read *'aššîm* in favor of the traditional derivation from *śym*. It is true that *śym*, which is used for arranging things or setting them in place, does not have *qeber* (*grave*) as its object anywhere else. But the ancient traditions universally read *śym*, and we cannot even be confident that *śmm* is more idiomatic, as *qeber* is nowhere else the object of *śmm*. A verb used for depopulating a city or country is not *necessarily* suitable for emptying a grave. Sellin, *Zwölfprophetenbuch*, 364, suggests "making lonesome" and compares 2 Sam 13:20 and Isa 54:1; this is hardly more likely.

173. Roberts, *Nahum*, 54.

praises and cursing its desecrators. It may even be a truly shameful "grave" in the open countryside.[174] In God's eyes, the Assyrian king is *lightweight*: insignificant and contemptible.[175] He deserves no "royal treatment."

Reflection

Verse 11 introduced the double reference to city and ruler in a clever way. The syntax emphasized the city (*From you*), but the twofold designation emphasized the ruler (*someone scheming evil against YHWH, someone advising villainy*). Verse 12 opens with a plural reference, as befits the motif, but then focuses on the Assyrian king and reports that *he is gone*. The first saying stresses that the Assyrian king is no match for YHWH in spite of his multitudinous army. The second saying spells out the implications for Judah. Once YHWH has decided no longer to afflict, the Assyrian king loses his power and his shackles break open. Together these two sayings encourage fear of YHWH over fear of the Assyrian king. There are an objective and a subjective side to this, as we consider how this encouragement might speak to us today. The objective side is that all powers are subordinate to YHWH and that those whom he transferred from the domain of darkness into the kingdom of the Son (Col 1:13; cf. 1 Pet 2:9) are no longer subject to the terror of law, sin, and death (cf. Rom 6). The subjective side is that our fears reveal which persons or objects exercise the greatest power over us. We pay homage to what we fear through our obedience, and such obedience enslaves us, ultimately either to sin or to obedience to YHWH (Rom 6:16). While there are many competing powers, Nahum's focus on a single one encourages continuing reflection on the basic opposition of good and evil, life and death. *I will break his staff from upon you* is not only a narrow prediction of the end of the Assyrian king's rule but flows canonically into a larger promise of the end of YHWH's ultimate opposition, death itself (e.g., Rom 5:12–21). This must not be read as a simple dualism, however. Just as Assyria had been an instrument in the hands of YHWH to afflict Judah, so death is not only YHWH's enemy but also his instrument.

The final and longest saying concentrates on the fate of the Assyrian king

---

174. There is a tradition of interpreting the verse to say that the king's grave will be in the house of his idols (Tg., Syr., Rashi, Ibn Ezra, Kimchi); see ArBib 14, 134.

175. Cf. Gen 16:4–5; 1 Sam 2:30; Job 40:4 for this use of the verb. The verb is also used for being swift, and this is how, implausibly, the LXX took it (*tacheis*), presumably rendering it with a masculine plural adjective to link with the feet of the messenger in the next verse (cf. Spronk, *Nahum*, 77–78). Other possibilities for interpreting this phrase, or an emended version of it, are discussed in Cathcart, *Nahum*, 67; Rudolph, *Micha*, 159–160; Spronk, *Nahum*, 77.

himself, now the object of *a command* rather than its executor. A complete end is announced. No posterity to continue the line, no remembrance in the future. The *idol and image* he served will themselves be *entirely cut off* so that both palace and temple (*the house of your gods*) are empty and in ruins with no further exercise of rule from either. YHWH commits himself to prepare the final resting place for one who no longer has any significance in the land of the living precisely because he is *lightweight*, not great in the eyes of God. This invites us to see people, powers, and objects with new eyes. What is *lightweight* in God's eyes is destined to reside not in the houses of power and influence but in the grave. It no longer need be feared; only YHWH is worthy of worship and obedience.

V. ANNOUNCEMENT OF DELIVERANCE (1:15 [2:1])

^{1:15 (2:1)} *Look on the mountains: the feet of a herald who brings news of peace!*
Celebrate, Judah, your festivals; fulfill your vows;
for never again shall the villain pass through you; he is completely cut off.

Composition

This verse has been identified as a hinge in our discussion of the structure of the book. It follows naturally from 1:14 (and *bəliyyāʿal* links it with v. 11). After the Assyrian king has found his end, the messenger brings the good news to Judah. But while 1:12–14 collect divine *announcements* of future events, 1:15 (2:1) sees the *fulfillments* of those threats against the Assyrian king. The verse is in fact just as suitable as an introduction to the images of the fall of Nineveh that flesh out the content of the good news. From 2:1(2) onward, however, the feminine singular again addresses Nineveh (cf. 1:11), not Judah as here (cf. 1:12–13). This indicates at least a minor break, even if not necessarily a new discourse. The second *hinnê* (*Look!*) of the book introduces the verse that concludes ch. 2. These two verses (1:15 [2:1]; 2:13[14]) could in fact be considered suitable bookends to a larger unit consisting of a poem (2:1–10[2–11]) and an exposition (2:11–12[12–13]), relating specifically to the fall of Nineveh.[176] Rhetorically, this verse is later than the following verses: *the villain* is already *completely cut off*. But this could help us to decide on its date, only were we confident that the verse is an independent (self-sufficient)

---

176. Note that 2:13(14) also makes reference to messengers but it uses a different root.

discourse.[177] Read as a hinge between the collection in 1:12–14 and the material in ch. 2, this verse presents us a picture in words that could have been painted before, after, or during the event that it portrays. A case could be made for a date prior to the revival of Passover celebrations under Josiah, as the verse may presume a situation in which such festivities were severely hampered, but this is not certain.[178]

Commentary

1:15 (2:1) A messenger is first seen *on the mountains*. Attention is drawn to *the feet*, suggesting that the herald is running, thus indicating the urgency of the message. While the root used to describe the herald (*bśr*) most often relates to good news, this is not necessarily the case.[179] But this herald brings news of *šālôm* (*peace*) in a reversal of the situation in view at the beginning of 1:12. While Assyria was intact, in full strength, *completely at ease* (*šəlēmîm*), Judah could not have *peace*. The word *šālôm* rarely means *peace* in the narrow sense of absence of war but includes notions of prosperity and well-being.[180] The disintegration of the Neo-Assyrian Empire makes Judah whole again, and consequently she is called to *celebrate* her regular *festivals*—festivals to honor YHWH and to remind the people of YHWH's mighty deeds. Some argue that this encouragement only makes sense after the hiatus of festivals brought about by the destruction of Jerusalem in the sixth century. But Fabry rightly points out that the heavy tribute payments to Sennacherib would have rendered normal festivities impossible already in Hezekiah's time.[181] Indeed, the call to *celebrate . . . your festivals* need not imply a complete hiatus of the cult. It merely suggests that nothing will now hinder full, joyful, and abundant festivities. Note the way the Passover celebrations in Josiah's eighteenth year, about a decade before the fall of Nineveh, are characterized in 2 Kgs 23:22–23 and 2 Chr 35:18–19. Assyrian weakness allowed Josiah to anticipate

177. Cf. Fabry, *Nahum*, 153, who concludes that the verse originated in the immediate context of the fall of Nineveh in 612 BC on the basis that the verse fits best with this event.

178. Such a date would imply that there was already material for which this verse served as a hinge but this seems to me quite possible. As an independent discourse, the verse would have to be dated later; see above. But on this view, its position here in the book remains unexplained.

179. The news is not so good in 1 Sam 4:17. The typical usage of the root in Akkadian and Ugaritic also seems to be positive, but not exclusively so. See Cathcart, *Nahum*, 68.

180. For a fuller discussion, see F. J. Stendebach, "שָׁלוֹם, *šālôm*," *TDOT* 15:13–49.

181. Fabry, *Nahum*, 151–52. See 2 Kgs 18:14–16.

the kind of festivities envisaged here,[182] whether or not he knew this verse as a prophetic word.

Judah is also called to *fulfill* her *vows*. This is likely not a reference to making and fulfilling vows generally but to vows that had been made while Judah suffered under Assyrian rule. In biblical usage, vows are made in the context of prayer. They are conditional promises to God, to be fulfilled if and when God answers the prayer.[183] The use of the plural may indicate that the vows of individuals are in view rather than any corporate vow,[184] but it is possible that, initiated by the king, the nation made (several) public vows, albeit at the risk of raising Assyrian suspicions of sedition. The plural *nədārā-yik* (*your vows*) rhymes with *ḥaggayik* (*your festivals*), an effect that has been produced by a slightly unusual word order at the beginning of the address[185] and would have been lost if the singular had been used. It would therefore be unwise to read too much into the plural. If there was a corporate vow by the nation, this could well be conceived as consisting of individual vows, as several parties (the king, tribal leaders, maybe other representatives) would have to contribute to its fulfillment.

We are not told what items had been promised to God.[186] The *festivals* would provide a natural context for sacrifices, and sacrifices are the most frequent item vowed to YHWH. Pleas for divine deliverance were often underlined with the promise of providing a thanksgiving sacrifice or freewill offering upon deliverance.[187] Such sacrifices fall in the category of *šəlāmîm* ("fellowship") offerings, sacrifices that involve a meal for the worshippers. There is a specific requirement for the thanksgiving sacrifice to be eaten up

---

182. According to 2 Chr 30, Hezekiah was the first to reinitiate all-Israel Passover celebrations. But while a huge Judean crowd gathered, the response from the northern tribes had been disappointing (vv. 10–11). The celebrations came in the context of recent Assyrian devastations (vv. 6–7) and were still in the shadow of God's anger (v. 8).

183. Cf. Tony W. Cartledge, *Vows in the Hebrew Bible and the Ancient Near East*, JSOTSup 147 (Sheffield: JSOT Press, 1992). Distinguishing between oath-taking and vow-making, Cartledge argues that in biblical usage "one may swear to another person, but may vow only to God" (12).

184. This is suggested by Jacques Berlinerblau, *The Vow and the "Popular Religious Groups" of Ancient Israel: A Philological and Sociological Inquiry*, JSOTSup 210 (Sheffield: Sheffield Academic, 1996), 56–57.

185. Cf. *CHP*, 232. One might have expected *yəhûdâ* (*Judah*) to follow *ḥaggayik*, in which case it would have formed a pivot. But *Judah* is quite literally not at the center of the celebrations.

186. See the table in Berlinerblau, *Vow*, 96–97, for various possibilities.

187. In the Psalms, the sacrifice promised to God is a thanksgiving sacrifice (*tôdâ*, cf. Lev 7:12–15) in 50:14; 56:12(13); 116:17–18; and a free-will offering (*nədābâ*, cf. Lev 7:16–17, linked with *neder* [votive offering] both here and in Lev 22) in 54:6(8). Ps 66 apparently, and unusually, speaks of burnt offerings ('*ôlôt*) being sacrificed in fulfilment of a vow (v. 13; cf. v. 15).

on the same day (Lev 7:15), maybe to encourage the participation of a larger group of people. Those who sponsor a thanksgiving sacrifice would invite friends to their party to tell them of the deliverance they have experienced and that has occasioned the celebration.[188] Fulfilling vows made at the time of distress thus becomes a typical way of publicly acknowledging that "deliverance belongs to YHWH" (Ps 3:8; cf. Jonah 2:9[10]). Such acknowledgement is part and parcel of a festival like Passover, and so the fulfillment of *nədārāyik* (*your vows*) and the celebration of *ḥaggayik* (*your festivals*) may combine thanksgiving for the deliverance from Egypt long ago with thanksgiving for the more recent deliverance from the Assyrians. Similar things could be said for other festivals, on which see more below in the reflection.

The motivation is given in the words *for never again shall the villain pass through you,* because *he is completely cut off* (*kî lō' yôsîp 'ôd la'ăbār*[189]*-bāk bəliyya'al kullô nikrāt*). This can be compared to Joel 4:17 ("Strangers shall no longer pass through you": *wəzārîm lō'-ya'abrû-bāh 'ôd*) and Isa 52:1 ("For never again shall the uncircumcised and unclean enter you": *kî lō' yôsîp yābō'-bāk 'ôd 'ārēl wəṭāmē'*), with which it shares five words. The position of *'ôd* (the "ever" in "never") is flexible in sentences with *lō'-'ōsîp* ("not again") and *lə* plus an infinitive.[190] Its position straight after *lō'-'ōsîp* is more suitable here in Nahum than its alternative, after the infinitive, because *la'ăbār-bāk bəliyya'al* arguably runs better off the tongue without intervening *'ôd*. This also keeps *lō'* and *'ôd* closely together, thus maybe alluding more clearly to their prior use in 1:12, 14. But a more important difference to Isa 52:1, which uses the singular "the uncircumcised and unclean" collectively, as well as Joel 4:17 with its plural "strangers," is the use of *bəliyya'al* for an individual who embodies wickedness or villainy.[191] This is again the Assyrian king, who shall be completely cut off. The phraseology establishes further links to previous verses, which may help both in identifying the villain as the Assyrian king, depending on one's interpretation of 1:11–12, and in stressing how inevitable

---

188. This is evident in the references in the Psalms to proclaiming God's praises in the congregation (e.g., 35:18; 111:1). A meal (sacrifice) provides the natural context for such praise.

189. Following the masoretic *qere*, ignoring the written *waw*.

190. Note that Gen 8:21 has the combination twice and uses *'ôd* once before the infinitive construction, as in Nahum (cf. Deut 28:68; Isa 10:20; 23:12; Amos 7:13; and, without *lə* before the infinitive, Exod 10:29; Hos 1:6; Amos 7:8; 8:2), and once after the infinitive, as in Isa 52 (cf. Isa 51:22, by which it may have been influenced, as well as Exod 14:13; Deut 17:16). The difference, if there is one, should not be confused with the difference in English between "it will never happen again" and the emphatic "it will not happen again, ever."

191. It would be theoretically possible to interpret *bəliyya'al* as an abstract noun, signifying the concept "wickedness," but the context, the verb used, and the continuation with *kullô nikrāt* argue strongly against this.

the outcome described here ultimately is.[192] It is precisely because the Assyrian king is the incarnation of villainy that he must be swept away by the one who makes a complete end of those who oppose him (but see further below). Neither the call to celebrate nor its motivation is marked as the words of the herald.[193] We should think of the poet-prophet as the speaker here, as in the verses that follow.

EXCURSUS: THE RELATIONSHIP BETWEEN
NAHUM 1:15 (2:1) AND ISAIAH 52:7

Nah 1:15 (2:1) and Isa 52:7 share six consecutive words with each other in precise agreement ('al-hehārîm raglê məbaśśēr maśmîaʿ šālôm, translated, *on the mountains: the feet of a herald who brings news of peace*). This is hardly coincidental. The two verses may be dependent on a common source[194] (e.g., the liturgy of the New Year festival[195]). But the fact that Nah 2:1 also links with Isa 52:1 and that there are a number of other links between Nahum and Isaiah 40–55 makes it more likely that one is directly dependent on the other.[196] The question of priority is relevant for interpretation. If, on the one hand, Nahum borrowed from Isa 52, we need to ask what the significance of this recourse to Isa 52 is and whether readers were expected to recognize the allusion. If, on the other hand, Nahum is a source for Isa 52, the latter is part of the biblical-theological development of Nah 1:15.

Unfortunately, there is no agreement about the relationship between these two verses. Some have argued that Nah 1:15 was taken from Isa 52 in the (late) exilic period to reapply the message of Nahum to the (late) Babylonian

---

192. For ʿbr, cf. 1:8, 12; for bəliyyaʿal, cf. 1:11; for kullô, cf. klh in 1:8–9 (and kôl in 1:4, 5); for krt, cf. 1:14.

193. In Isa 52:7, the message of the herald is introduced by 'ōmēr ("who says").

194. Coggins (in Richard J. Coggins and S. Paul Re'emi, *Israel among the Nations: Nahum, Obadiah, Esther*, ITC [Grand Rapids: Eerdmans; Edinburgh: Handsel, 1985], 33) thinks of "a stock of oracular material which might be used as appropriate in the particular circumstances of each collection"; cf. Richard J. Coggins, "An Alternative Prophetic Tradition?" in *Israel's Prophetic Tradition*, ed. Richard J. Coggins (Cambridge: Cambridge University Press, 1982), 77–94; John N. Oswalt, *The Book of Isaiah: Chapters 40–66*, NICOT (Grand Rapids: Eerdmans, 1998), 368–69; Rudolph, *Micha*, 163.

195. Cf. Klaus Baltzer, *Deutero-Isaiah: A Commentary on Isaiah 40–55*, trans. Margaret Kohl, Hermeneia (Minneapolis: Fortress, 2001), 378. John Gray ("Kingship of God in the Prophets and Psalms," *VT* 11 [1961]: 1–29) proposes that Nahum wrote the verse for the New Year festival in 612 BC (17) and that Isa 52 drew on this liturgy (21).

196. See, e.g., Spronk, *Nahum*, 80; and already Umberto Cassuto, *Biblical and Oriental Studies*, vol. 1 (Jerusalem: Magnes Press, 1973), 168–71.

period,[197] but while this has been accepted by a number of scholars,[198] few commentaries on Nahum have followed this reading.[199] Others have assumed the priority of Isa 52 on the basis of attributing Isa 52 to the eighth-century prophet Isaiah and Nah 1:15 to a seventh-century prophet.[200] A number of commentators on either passage remain uncommitted about the relationship between Nah 1:15 and Isa 52:7.

Isaiah 52 is more expansive, with *ma-nnā'wû* ("how lovely") instead of simple *hinnê* (*look*) and with the extra *məbaśśēr ṭôb mašmîaʿ yəšûʿâ* ("a herald of good things who brings news of salvation"), echoing *məbaśśēr mašmîaʿ šālôm* (*a herald who brings news of peace*).[201] All else being equal, one expects the more expansive version to be the later one. Thus Spronk concludes that "the easiest way to explain these differences is that the poet of Isa 52 rewrote Nah 1:15, qualifying and clarifying it."[202] While *ma-nnā'wû* could have been changed to *hinnê* in order to increase alliteration within the verse and to establish a link with 2:13(14),[203] the absence of *məbaśśēr ṭôb mašmîaʿ yəšûʿâ* is more difficult to explain. The same applies to *'ōmēr ləṣiyyôn mālak 'ĕlōhāyik*

197. Most notably, Jeremias, *Kultprophetie*, 13–15, cf. *Nahum*, 111–13. In the commentary Jeremias dates Nah 1:15 (2:1) to the Hellenistic period, later than in *Kultprophetie*.

198. E.g., Bernard Renaud, "La composition du livre Nahum: Une proposition," *ZAW* 99 (1987): 198–218; cf. James D. Nogalski, "The Redactional Shaping of Nahum 1 for the Book of the Twelve," in *Among the Prophets: Language, Image, and Structure in the Prophetic Writings*, ed. Philip R. Davies and David J. A. Clines (Sheffield: JSOT Press, 1993), 193–202; Theodor Lescow, "Die Komposition der Bücher Nahum und Habakuk," *BN* 77 (1995): 59–85.

199. But see Seybold, *Nahum*, 25.

200. E.g., Maier, *Nahum*, 219; O. Palmer Robertson, *The Books of Nahum, Habakkuk, and Zephaniah*, NICOT (Grand Rapids: Eerdmans, 1990), 81; Patterson, *Nahum*, 46; Longman, "Nahum," 799–800.

201. Jeremias (*Kultprophetie*, 14) observes that asyndetic juxtaposition (*məbaśśēr [herald]* ... *mašmîaʿ [one who brings news]*) is typical for Second Isaiah and sees this as the decisive observation in favor of the priority of Isa 52 (cf. *Nahum*, 112). This would carry more weight if the construction were also found in Nahum. As it is, one might just as well imagine that Second Isaiah found the tighter phrasing in Nahum and expanded it to conform to his own style.

202. Spronk, "Synchronic and Diachronic," 184; cf. *Nahum*, 79–80. Patricia Tull Willey's study *Remember the Former Things: The Recollection of Previous Texts in Second Isaiah*, SBLDS 16 (Atlanta: Scholars Press, 1997), 116–20, makes good sense of the view that Nahum is the source of Isa 52 but without truly considering whether the reverse might be true; cf. Benjamin D. Sommer, "Allusions and Illusions: The Unity of the Book of Isaiah in Light of Deutero-Isaiah's Use of Prophetic Tradition," in *New Visions of Isaiah*, ed. R. F. Melugin and M. A. Sweeney, JSOTSup 214 (Sheffield: Sheffield Academic, 1996), 156–86; and Benjamin D. Sommer, *A Prophet Reads Scripture: Allusion in Isaiah 40–66* (Stanford: Stanford University Press, 1998).

203. For the proposal that 1:15 (2:1) and 2:13(14) form bookends, see above. In addition, the more urgent *hinnê* seems to me superior in Nahum to *ma-nnā'wû*, which in turn fits better in Isaiah.

("who says to Zion, 'Your God reigns!' "), which is easier to explain as an addition in Isaiah by way of combining motifs from Nahum and the Psalms[204] than a subtraction in Nahum. In my view, the observation that the shared expressions have semantic parallels in Isa 40–55 but not in Nahum does not seem decisive. While it is true that *šālôm* is found nowhere else in Nahum (although we noted its interaction with *šəlēmîm, completely at ease* in 1:12) but in Isa 41:3; 45:7; 48:18, 22 and 53:5; 54:10, 13; 55:12,[205] the context in Isaiah is regularly quite different, and it would be hazardous to argue from this that the notion of *šālôm* resulting from the defeat of an oppressive political and military force is more at home in Isa 40–55 than in Nahum. Similar things could be said about other common words.[206] The only noteworthy semantic feature more at home in Isaiah than Nahum is *məbaśśēr* (*herald*) in Isa 41:27 (cf. 40:9).[207] But if the prophecy of Nahum was a source for this part of the book of Isaiah, it is not surprising that the idea of a herald is found in more than one place.[208] Nahum's influence on Isa 52 may be discerned further in v. 8 ("your watchmen," *ṣōpayik*; cf. *sph in* Nah 2:1[2]; *šûb* for YHWH's return in Nah 2:2[3]), and in v. 9 (the root *nḥm*, "comfort"; cf. the name Nahum; the joyful shouting in Isa 52:9 is perhaps related to the reference to festivals in Nahum). The reference to "the Assyrian" in Isa 52:4 may also reflect Nahum's influence. All in all, while the case can be argued either way, it seems more likely that the language of Isa 52 was inspired by Nahum than the other way around.

In sum, my exegesis of Nahum does not reckon with an allusion to Isa 52. This result would be the same if Nahum used conventional, formulaic language. For a biblical-theological interpretation, the link to Isa 52 is not irrelevant, however. If the book of Nahum is a *pronouncement concerning Nineveh*, its applicability is far wider. Nineveh is also Babylon. It would be wrong to

204. On Isa 52 as a reworking of earlier passages from prophecy and psalmody, cf. John Goldingay and David Payne, *Isaiah 40–55*, 2 vols., ICC (London: T&T Clark International, 2006), 2:262–63.

205. Cf. Isa 9:5–6; 26:3, 12; 27:5; 32:17–18; 33:7; 34:8; 38:17; 39:8 and 57:2, 19, 21; 59:8; 60:17; 66:12.

206. Jeremias, *Kultprophetie*, 13–15, points to the use of *feet* in Isa 41:2–3; 58:13; 59:7 (also 49:23), but the context for all of these occurrences is completely different. Similarly, *šm' hiphil* ("let hear") is used fourteen times in Isaiah 40–55 (to which may be added 30:30; 58:4; 62:11) but in quite varied contexts.

207. Jeremias (*Kultprophetie*, 13–15) also discerns syntactical features that in his view favor the priority of Isa 52, but only one is valid. Nah 1:15 (2:1) indeed has the more common use of an infinitive after *yôsîp* vis-à-vis Isa 52:1 (which is unusual in other respects as well). His assertion that *'ôd* is in a normalized position in Nahum is wrong (see above), and his claim that asyndesis is more typical in Isa 40–55 than Nahum is questionable.

208. The verb *bśr* is found elsewhere in the prophetic literature only in Isa 60:6; 61:1 (!) and Jer 20:15, which is completely unrelated.

conclude that the (newly redacted) book is primarily about the end of the Babylonian oppression, even if Nah 1:15 (2:1) were inspired by Isa 52. The links to the end of the Babylonian exile are far too obscure for that. If Isa 52 came first, we are invited to see the fall of Nineveh as a first installment of the end of exile. If Nahum came first, as argued here, the end of the Babylonian exile is a further instance of *I have afflicted you, I will afflict you no more.*

Reflection

It is theologically significant that the call that ushers from the announcement of deliverance is not simply a call for victory celebrations. The deliverance is celebrated in the context of previous dependence on YHWH as expressed in vows and in the context of previous salvation history as expressed in the festivals. The Passover, which celebrates deliverance from Egypt, now also celebrates that the Assyrian villain has been cut off. Festivals that celebrate the giving of YHWH's Torah now also celebrate that the Assyrian king's word no longer needs to be heeded. Festivals that celebrate God's provision for his people now also celebrate the fact that no part of the harvest ends up as tribute payments to the Assyrians, and each Sabbath also celebrates the rest from the Assyrians. Even the fast days may remind the people that humbling oneself before God is better than being humbled by God (cf. 1:12).

The liturgical rhythm of the year is a gift. It brings out different emphases and motifs with which to celebrate what the people of God have in their God. Nahum 1:15 (2:1) may be an encouragement to the church as well to celebrate her festivals and to do so in a spirit that links the deliverance or provision or guidance experienced at different times.

While there is an inevitable logic to the downfall of the villain, the prediction of a specific event cannot be based on such logic. There is no suggestion that the last Assyrian king was worse than his predecessors and the reuse of *no longer* in the form *never again* hints at the Judean fear that evil may not have been defeated once for all. While Sennacherib had left Jerusalem intact in 701 BC, the Assyrians retained a heavy presence in Judah for a little while longer. How can the people of God know that the Assyrian armies are indeed gone, never to return? The eschatological defeat of evil is certain in the light of the truths expressed in the poem in Nah 1. The historical downfall of evil empires is also certain, whether the villainy is embodied in the Assyrian or Babylonian empire, in Hitler or Stalin. But the announcement of historical turning points needs prophetic insight.[209] Nahum may have been the first

209. The downfall of contemporary evil empires is certain, but the timing cannot be deduced from Scripture. The fall of fascism in Germany came speedily after intense evil, the

prophet among the people of God to announce the imminent demise of an empire.[210] (And, indeed, *never again* was there another Assyrian king to oppress Judah.) The portrayal of *a herald who brings news of peace* is visionary. It is therefore not necessarily a response to a specific past event. The fall of Nineveh and of the Assyrian king may have been still future when these words were first uttered, but the exuberance of the verse suggests as much as the preceding verses that the decisive event is just around the corner. YHWH's command has been given (v. 14).

The same exuberance and urgency are found in Isa 52, the place where Nahum's message of comfort reaches the people of God in the late Neo-Babylonian period. Zion has come through another experience of God's anger (cf. 51:17, 22). The imminent downfall of the Neo-Babylonian Empire, which heralds peace and deliverance to the people of God, calls for joy rather than mourning, as Zion's God is again proven to be in charge. The return from exile (52:11–12) is, however, also linked to the exaltation of the one "wounded for our transgressions" (53:5). The kingdom of God is ultimately established not by superior force but through suffering. It is evident already in the book of Nahum that the response to the Assyrian force does not consist in armament; ascribing vengeance to YHWH means desisting from exercising vengeance oneself. But YHWH's vengeance still uses force to *make an end* of Nineveh, the force of superior human armies, which will in turn lead to further evil, as Habakkuk observed.

It is only in the gospel, the good news about the kingdom of God in Christ, that we hear a message of evil truly defeated for good. Any deliverance from evil political or military forces can only bring temporary relief if the root of evil is not tackled. The gospel is good news because it announces a king whose innocent suffering for his people ends their alienation from God and whose resurrection brings a deliverance from the bondage of sin and death. Christ's refusal to call on superior (heavenly) forces breaks the cycle of violence but also embodies trust in God and thus keeps the human-divine relationship intact. Because God is the source of life, those who are in an intact relationship with God cannot but be alive. Just as death had no hold on Christ, so it cannot hold anyone who belongs to Christ. When the apostle Paul used Isa 52:7, and thus indirectly Nahum, in Rom 10:15, he did so in the context of announcing the one who is "Lord of all" (v. 12) in a letter written

---

fall of communism in Eastern Europe took longer, and the stranglehold that Islamist regimes have on some parts of the world waxes and wanes. But the persistence of such oppressive regimes (e.g., also in North Korea) must not discourage those who take refuge in YHWH.

210. While we are not able to identify precisely which verses in the book of Isaiah derive from the eighth century, I am confident that already the prophet Isaiah had visions of empires being brought low. But Isaiah encouraged Hezekiah to put his trust in YHWH without promising the imminent demise of the Assyrians.

to the congregation in the city that at that time claimed to be the center of all political power. Yet the villain whose hold has been broken is not only the Roman emperor but death itself. This draws Nahum and Isaiah to their logical conclusion, "declaring the good news of the universal rule of God in the world with concomitant peace, good, and salvation."[211]

VI. IMAGES OF THE FALL OF NINEVEH (2:1–10[2–11])

[1(2)]*A scatterer[a] has come up against you: guard[b] the guardpost![c]*
  Watch[d] the road! Brace yourselves![e]
    Marshal all your strength!
[2(3)]*For YHWH is about to turn[f] the pride[g] of Jacob*
  as[h] the pride of Israel;
    for devastators have devastated them[i]
      and ruined their shoots.[j]
[3(4)]*The shields[k] of his heroes[l] are colored red;[m]*
  his mighty warriors[n] are dressed in crimson.[o]
Flaming-red[p] are the coverings[q] of the chariots[r]
  on the day when he makes ready[s]
    and the cypress trunks[t] are being shaken.[u]
[4(5)]*Through the streets the chariots rush madly;[v]*
  they race each other[w] through the plazas.
Its appearance[x] is like torches;
  like lightning they dash around.
[5(6)]*He remembers[y] his officers;[z]*
  they stumble in their going.[aa]
They hasten to her wall;[bb]
  the siege towers[cc] have been set up.
[6(7)]*The gates of the rivers[dd] are opened,*
  and the palace collapses.
[7(8)]*And he is positioned;[ee] she is exposed,[ff] she is offered up[gg]*
  with[hh] her maids sobbing[ii] like the sound of doves,
    beating on their breasts.[jj]
[8(9)]*And Nineveh, like a pool of waters[kk] since her days,[ll]*
  but they are running away.[mm]
    "Stop! Stop!"[nn] but no one turns[oo] around.[pp]
[9(10)]*"Plunder silver! Plunder gold!*
  There is no end to the stockpile,[qq]
    wealth[rr] more than[ss] all precious objects."[tt]

211. Oswalt, *Isaiah 40–66*, 368.

10(11)*Desolation, destruction, and devastation:*[uu]
  fainting hearts[vv] *and knees that totter;*[ww]
    there is trembling[xx] *in all loins,*
      and all their faces are flushed with fear.[yy]

  a. Hebrew *mēpîṣ* is a *hiphil* participle of the root *pûṣ* (cf. Jer 23:1). BDB analyzes the form here and in Prov 25:18 as a noun but suggests reading *mappēṣ* ("war club," related to the root *pṣṣ*, "to shatter" in the *pilpel*; cf. Jer 51:20; Ezek 9:2). A number of commentators prefer *mappēṣ* or *mappîṣ* (*hiphil* participle of *npṣ*, "to smash" in the *qal* and *piel*), but "war club" does not seem to me as suitable and neither *pṣṣ* nor *npṣ* are attested in the *hiphil*. LXX (*emphysōn*) derived the verb from *nph* or *pûḥ* (both could be used for "to blow upon"). For a fuller discussion of the LXX of this verse, see Roberts, *Nahum*, 56–57; Edward Ball, "Interpreting the Septuagint: Nahum 2.2 as a Case-Study," *JSOT* 75 (1997): 59–75.

  b. An infinitive absolute form is used here as equivalent to an imperative. This usage is often found with military commanders or God as subject (JM 123u; cf. *IBHS* 35.5.1).

  c. Reading *maṣṣārâ* (from the root *nṣr*, "to guard") for MT *maṣûrâ* ("fortification," related to *ṣûr*, "to besiege"); cf. Roberts, *Nahum*, 57 (also adopted, e.g., in *BHS* and *HALOT*). The noun *mṣrh* is found elsewhere in 2 Chronicles, often in the phrase *'ārê maṣûrôt* ("fortified cities"; e.g., 11:10) and in Isa 29:3, where it refers to siegeworks, if the text is correct (alternatively "strongholds," following 1QIsa[a] *maṣûdôt* or *HALOT māṣōrôt*). The consonantal text can be related to *nṣr* in all these places, except 2 Chr 14:5 (MT *maṣûrâ*). Those medieval MSS which read the plene form also in Nahum (cf. Spronk, *Nahum*, 84) obviously reflect the masoretic tradition.

  d. The verbal form *ṣappê* is either a masculine singular imperative or an infinitive. If *pnyk* (*against you*) is vocalized as feminine with the Masoretes (*pānayik*), the identification of *ṣappê* as an infinitive recommends itself. The *piel* infinitive absolute is rare, so infinitive construct forms, such as *ṣappê*, are used for either form of the infinitive (cf. JM 52c). See translation note b for the use of infinitives as a substitute for imperatives.

  e. Hebrew *ḥazzēq motnayim* is literally "make firm" (or "gird"; cf. Prov 31:17) "(your) loins." Like the preceding *ṣappê* (*watch*) and the following *'ammēṣ* (*marshal*), *ḥazzēq* is either an infinitive or an imperative form. See the comments above.

  f. Hebrew *šāb* can be the *qal* perfect or participle of *šûb*, transitive or intransitive, and semantically positive ("return, restore") as in modern English translations or negative ("turn aside/away") as in LXX and early English versions (KJV, Geneva Bible; cf. Calvin). Alternatively, one can point the verb *šab* and derive it from *šbb* ("to cut down"; cf. *šəbābîm*, "splinters," in Hos 8:6), as does Maier, *Nahum*, 230–33; cf. *HALOT*, s.v. *šbb*. The translation reads the form here as a participle and assumes that *šûb* can be transitive in the *qal* (cf. *HALOT*, s.v. *šûb*, §6; *DCH*, §§33–34; Ges[18], §2). It is noteworthy that there does not seem to be an instance of such transitive use of the *qal* in which the action is negative ("turn aside/away"). The *hiphil* of *šûb* is used in both positive and negative senses, and the *qal* form may have been chosen to favor positive connotations.

  g. Hebrew *gə'ôn* often has negative connotations and was thus understood by LXX (*hybris*) and Vulg. (*superbia*). Unlike *gə'ôn yiśrā'ēl* in the following line, *gə'ôn ya'āqōb* (*pride of Jacob*) is elsewhere positive (Ps 47:4[5]; Amos 8:7), or at least neutral (Amos 6:8, designating the capital city; the context is negative but not the phrase itself). Inspired by *their shoots* later in the verse, an emendation to *gepen* ("vine") is frequently proposed; cf. *BHS*, *HALOT*, *DCH*. This is creative but, in all likelihood, a modern invention; cf. Cathcart, *Nahum*, 83–84.

h. Spronk (*Nahum*, 86) interprets the *kaph* as emphatic "because this indicates that Jacob and Israel are meant here as names for one and the same people"; cf. Kevin J. Cathcart, "More Philological Studies in Nahum," *JNSL* 7 (1979): 1–12. This would yield the translation "indeed"; see GKC 118x; JM 133g; *IBHS* 11.2.9c.

i. Spronk (*Nahum*, 83) interprets *'ālâ* (*has come up*) in v. 1(2) as a "prophetic perfect" and argues for the same use of the perfect here for consistency's sake. He therefore translates this half-verse, "For destroyers shall destroy them and they shall ruin their branches" and applies it to the Assyrians (87).

j. Hebrew *zəmōrêhem* (*their shoots*) may be *pars pro toto* for vine and branches. Cathcart (*Nahum*, 85–86) suggests a derivation from a cognate of Ugaritic *drm* ("soldier") observing that the verb *šḥt* ("ruin," "annihilate") is also used with personal objects and often found in military contexts.

k. Hebrew *māgēn* is singular, but English usage requires the plural. The reference is probably to a small shield made of (wood covered with?) leather; see *HALOT*; Athalya Brenner, *Colour Terms in the Old Testament*, JSOTSup 21 (Sheffield: JSOT Press, 1982), 110–11.

l. The suffix refers back to the *scatterer*. For the rare form of the suffix see the comment on *mōṭēhû* in 1:13. Cathcart (*Nahum*, 86) compares Hab 3:10 (*yādêhû*) and Job 24:23 (*'ênêhû*).

m. Hebrew *mə'oddām* is a *pual* participle of *'dm* ("to dye red"; cf. the adjective *'ādôm* for reddish-brown; see GKC 52q for the vowel *o*; cf. *šoddədâ* in 3:7). The verb may have indicated the tanning process without reference to color; cf. Brenner, *Colour Terms*, 110–11.

n. Hebrew *'anšê-ḥayil* ("men of might") often designates outstanding men; hence, some think of officers (e.g., Maier, *Nahum*, 236–37). But *ḥayil* is also a term for "army" (see *HALOT*, s.v. *ḥayil*), and *anšê-ḥayil* can refer to soldiers generally, as in, e.g., Judg 20:44, 46. Even then, it is an honorific designation (*mighty warriors*) that contrasts with the more neutral *'anšê haṣṣābā'* ("soldiers," Num 31:21, 53). In English, it reads more smoothly with the possessive pronoun (*his*), which is merely implied in the Hebrew text.

o. Hebrew *məṭullā'îm* is a *pual* participle of *tl'*. The verb occurs only here and is related to *tôlā'*, a term that has been associated with a pea-sized scale insect of the genus kermes, from which red color was extracted. Cf. *šānî*, which apparently refers to the same insect (Brenner, *Colour Terms*, 144).

p. Hebrew *bə'ēš* ("in fire" or "fiery"), interpreting the prep. as a *beth essentiae* (cf. JM 133c). So also Spronk, *Nahum*, 89–90; cf. Cathcart, *Nahum*, 87.

q. *Pəlādôt* is not otherwise attested in Hebrew and its meaning is uncertain. LXX and Vulg. ("bridles," "reins") probably guess from the context. A transposition of the first two consonants produces *lappîdôt* ("torches"; cf. Syr., Symm., *BHS*). Rabbinic commentators note this possibility but without necessarily committing themselves to it (e.g., Rashi). This standard solution (see Geneva Bible, KJV) is problematic because "torches" is elsewhere *lappîdîm*, as in the next verse. The meaning "metal, steel" (found in most modern English translations) derives from Persian *pūlād*, which is also found in Arabic and Syr. (cf. BDB and *HALOT*, s.v. *pəlādâ*). *Coverings* derives from Ugaritic *pld* and is also adopted by Cathcart, *Nahum*, 85–86; Patterson, *Nahum*, 65–66; Spronk, *Nahum*, 89–90. Cf., in a nonmilitary context, the horses covered with red or purple (*phoinikis*) trappings in Xenophon, *Cyropaedia*, 8.3.12. Other possibilities for understanding this as well as the following phrases in the verse can be found in Aron Pinker, "Nahum 2,4 Revisited," *ZAW* 117 (2005): 411–19.

r. Hebrew *hārekeb* is probably a collective singular (the plural is only found in Song 1:9), as it certainly is in the next verse, where *hārekeb* is used with plural verbs. It may be a train of chariots. Unlike *merkābâ* ("chariot"), *rekeb* occasionally refers to the horses (2 Sam 8:4) or to the riders only (Ps 76:6[7]), maybe by metonymy. A reference to the horses (or maybe charioteers; cf. Xenophon, *Cyropaedia* 6.4.2 for a splendidly dressed charioteer) is therefore possible; cf. Cathcart, *Nahum*, 88. For chariot coverings, see Spronk, *Nahum*, 90. See the commentary for the possibility that the verse refers to a single chariot.

s. Or "on the day that he determines." Maybe cf., e.g., Exod 23:20 for a place being determined; see *HALOT*, s.v. *kwn hiphil* 2.a, for further references.

t. Hebrew *habbərōšîm* only has the definite article here. A reference to (a forest of wooden) spears is often favored by commentators; cf., e.g., Cathcart, *Nahum*, 89–90; Jeremias, *Nahum*, 121–22. But the noun regularly refers to cypress or other conifer *trees*, and only once (possibly) to cypress *wood* (Ezek 27:5); the reference here is therefore more likely to living trees or to trunks used as poles or lances rather than wood that has been worked upon; see below. LXX, Vulg., and Syr. read *happārāšîm* ("the horses," "the horsemen"), which often parallels *rekeb* elsewhere. Tg. appears to confirm MT (see ArBib 14, 135).

u. Hebrew *hor'ālû* is the *hophal* of *r'l*, a verb that could relate to the noun *ra'al* ("reeling," only in Zech 12:2; cf. the commentary on Hab 2:4) or to *rə'ālâ* (prob. "veil," only in Isa 3:19; so Tg.; see ArBib 14, 135–36). The translation must remain tentative, given the paucity of evidence and questions about the identity of the subject.

v. Hebrew *yithôlələû* is *hithpolel* of *hll* III (*qal*, "to be infatuated"); cf. 1 Sam 21:13(14); Jer 25:16; 46:9 (!); 50:38; 51:7. The *yiqtol* (imperfect) forms may have an iterative nuance.

w. Hebrew *yištaqšəqûn* is *hithpalpel* of *šqq*, a form not attested elsewhere. The rare conjugation is a reduplicated version of the *hithpael* for geminate roots and most often found with *mhh* (e.g., Hab 2:4). A reciprocal interpretation is also given by Roberts, *Nahum*, 58; cf. LXX ("entangled in each other"); Maier, *Nahum*, 245 ("overrun one another"); Fabry, *Nahum*, 158 ("ram each other"). *HALOT* glosses "rush around" (cf. BDB).

x. Hebrew *mar'êhen*. The feminine suffix refers back to the statement as a whole, as in Gen 15:6; Exod 10:11; Job 38:18; cf. GKC 122q, 135p (cf. JM 152b). See JM 96Ce or GKC 93ss for the singular value of the apparent plural form of the suffix.

y. Hebrew *yizkōr*, maybe iterative: "keeps remembering." Some link the verb with Akkadian *zakāru*, "to command, assign, summon" (Roberts, *Nahum*, 59; Patterson, *Nahum*, 67); cf. already Tg. (using the root *mnh*); see, e.g., RSV, NIV. Further proposals are discussed in Cathcart, *Nahum*, 92–94. The versions attest a plural, but 8ḤevXIIgr confirms MT; cf. Sebastian P. Brock, "To Revise or Not to Revise: Attitudes to Jewish Biblical Translation," in *Septuagint, Scrolls and Cognate Writings*, ed. George J. Brooke and Barnabas Lindars, SBLSCS 33 (Atlanta: Scholars Press, 1992), 314–15; Spronk, *Nahum*, 93; Fabry, *Nahum*, 161.

z. Hebrew *'addîrāyw*, "majestic, powerful ones." This is likely a reference to officers (cf. 3:18), contra Patterson (*Nahum*, 68), who thinks of the whole army of magnificently dressed soldiers in v. 3(4).

aa. The *ketiv* is plural (cf. 8ḤevXIIgr, Syr., Vulg.). The Masoretes read the singular ("on their course"), perhaps to avoid a misunderstanding as "caravans" or "columns" (see Spronk, *Nahum*, 93), but see translation note n on Hab 3:6 for the grammatically plural form. *HALOT*, s.v. *hălîkâ*, wonder whether we may be dealing with a technical term from the military, referring to trenches or columns; cf. Assyrian *aliktu* for a "detachment of soldiers" (*CAD* 1.1.346).

bb. Hebrew *ḥômātāh* with *mappîq*, indicating the suffix. The suffix is missing in Syr. and Tg. but not in Vulg. The suggestion to drop the *mappîq* and read instead a directive *he*, "to the wall" (e.g., *BHS*), is adopted in many English translations.

cc. Hebrew *sōkēk*. The noun, interpreted as a collective singular, is attested only here, but the root is known. The reference is usually understood to be mobile siege towers that were employed to protect attacking forces; see *ANEP* 368, 369, 373 for pictures; cf. Austen Henry Layard, *Nineveh and Its Remains*, vol. 2 (London: J. Murray, 1849), 281–86; see also Jeremias, *Nahum*, 136–37. Isa 23:13 apparently offers a synonym (*baḥûn* or *baḥîn*). LXX interpreted this word as defenses inside the city; so also Fabry, *Nahum*, 171, who argues it is a sheltered observation point for officers. The opening conjunction is left untranslated so as to allow reading either "and" or "but" (see further below).

dd. Heb. *nəhārôt* ("rivers") is plural and rendered thus, e.g., in LXX and Vulg. but less often in English translations. See the discussion below.

ee. MT *huṣṣab*. The text has given rise to well over a dozen interpretations; see Maier, *Nahum*, 259–62; Cathcart, *Nahum*, 96–98; Roberts, *Nahum*, 60; Spronk, *Nahum*, 96–98; Fabry, *Nahum*, 161–62; Aron Pinker, "Descent of the Goddess Ishtar to the Netherworld and Nahum II 8," *VT* 55 (2005): 89–100. *BHS* emends to the fem. hophal perfect of *yṣʾ* ("she is led out"); cf. Jeremias, *Nahum*, 122. MT can be interpreted as a masc. *hophal* perfect of *nṣb*; cf. the *hophal* participle in Gen 28:12 for a ladder ("set up") and in Judg 9:6 for a tree ("located"). The *hiphil* ("to place, set up") is also used in the sense of defining or securing boundaries (Deut 32:8; Ps 74:17; cf. Prov 15:25) but not for fixing a decree. The rendering "it is decreed" (e.g., NRSV, NIV) must therefore remain doubtful. Some postulate a different root *nṣb* for Zech 11:16 (*niphal*), meaning "to be miserable, weak, ill" (e.g., *HALOT*, *DCH*). If this is accepted for the *hophal* here, *wəhuṣṣab* may continue the preceding verse ("the palace . . . is miserable"); maybe cf. Akkadian *naṣābu* ("to suck out"; so, e.g., Patterson, *Nahum*, 69–70, following H. W. F. Saggs, "Nahum and the Fall of Nineveh," *JTS* 20 [1969]: 221–22). A similar result is gained if a third root *nṣb* ("to vanish, die") is accepted, as proposed in *DCH* for the *niphal* in Ps 39:5(6), or if a root *ṣbb* ("to pour out") is postulated, as in *Gesenius' Hebrew and Chaldee Lexicon*, trans. Samuel Prideaux Tregelles (Grand Rapids: Baker, 1979), 561, 700. The versions indicate that there was no more agreement in antiquity. The medieval understanding of *huṣṣab* as a proper name (e.g., Samuel ha-Nagid; Ibn Ezra) is reflected in early English translations but has now been abandoned as historically and linguistically improbable. The most attractive emendation is to *haṣṣəbî* ("the Beauty" or "the gazelle"), which will be discussed below.

ff. Hebrew *gullətâ* is a *pual* form of *glh*. The rendering "carried away into exile" (e.g., NRSV, NIV) is not justified for the *pual*. It reflects a vocalization as a *qal* or maybe as a nominal form with directional *hê* or a change to the *hophal* (see also the difference between *hiphil* and *piel*). Among others, Jeremias, *Nahum*, 122, opts for the emendation. See also the following note.

gg. Hebrew *hōʿălātâ*. The *hophal* is used elsewhere only in Judg 6:28 and 2 Chr 20:34, but the *hiphil* is very common. The regular meaning of the *hophal* would seem to be "made to climb up" or "presented as a sacrifice" (cf. Judg 6:28) or "led up" (into battle or out of exile). It is doubtful that it can be used for "carried away" (e.g., NIV) in the sense of "exiled" (NRSV), although Vulg. and Tg. already take it in this way, perhaps by way of interpretation. For full discussion see *CTAT*, 3:805–8.

hh. This renders the coordinating conjunction *waw* here.

ii. Hebrew *mənahăgôt* is a *piel* participle of *nhg*, which in the sense "to moan, sob" occurs only here; see BDB and *HALOT*, s.v. *nhg* II; Cathcart, *Nahum*, 98–99. *BHS* suggests pointing as a *pual* participle, deriving from the better-attested *nhg* I (*piel*, "to remove forcibly," etc.) and adding *hōgôt* ("cooing," from *hgh*). LXX derives from *nhg* I, Syr. from *nhg* II, and Tg.

may represent both (see ArBib 14, 137). Vulg. seems to represent both (*minabantur gementes*, "led away mourning") as well as *hgh* (*murmurantes*, "murmuring").

jj. Hebrew *'al-libəbēhen* more literally refers to "their hearts"; cf. "on (their) breasts" (*'al-šādayim*, with *spd* for beating) in Isa 32:12. The masculine plural form is only found here.

kk. Hebrew *mayim* is taken up in the next line by *hēmmâ* ("they"). Translating with the plural "waters" here instead of using the more idiomatic "water pool" allows the use of "they" in the next line, which in turn facilitates the recognition of the simile "waters" for people.

ll. Hebrew *mîmê hî'* is literally "from the days of her," using the independent personal pronoun in a way that is not clearly attested in Biblical Hebrew, though it is in Ugaritic (Cathcart, *Nahum*, 101); maybe cf. 1QpHab *pny hm* (*pənê hēm*) in Hab 1:9 (MT *pənêhem*) and *rûaḥ-hî'* in Job 32:8, which offers a parallel if *hî'* refers back to *ḥokmâ* in v. 7 (cf. the phrase *rûaḥ ḥokmâ* in Exod 28:3; Deut 34:9; Isa 11:2), but there are other ways of reading the phrase. Cf. the occasional use of independent personal pronouns with prepositions, e.g., in Hab 1:16 (*bāhēmmâ*), and to reinforce a nominal suffix (see JM 146d; cf. GKC 135 d–h). It is not impossible that a *he* has dropped out (*mîmêhā hî'*). Most of the versions suggest *mêmê hî'* ("the waters of her" = "her waters") or *mêmêhā* ("her waters," *BHS*), which is adopted in many English translations (e.g., NRSV, NIV, ESV), but Tg. interprets as "days of old" (cf. NASB, HCSB).

mm. This ungrammatical rendering in my view best reflects the drama of the verse. Alternatively, one may insert "was" between "Nineveh" and "like" in the first line.

nn. The second imperative is a pausal form. RSV and NIV add "they cry" but thus reduce the drama.

oo. Or "there is no turning." The subject of the verb "turn (around)" is regularly people. In addition, "evening" (e.g., Gen 24:63), "morning" (e.g., Exod 14:27), and "day" (e.g., Jer 6:4) are said to turn in the sense of coming to an end, and various impersonal subjects are said to "face" in a certain direction (e.g., 1 Kgs 7:25). The water imagery may still inform our reading, but it is more likely that people are the implied subject of the verb.

pp. The verb *pnh* probably refers to looking back here. It is also used for "turning around" in order to go away. The translation "turns back" (e.g., NRSV, NIV) would better represent the verb *šûb*. Note that 8ḤevXIIgr has *epistrephō* ("to turn") for LXX *epiblepō* ("to look upon").

qq. Hebrew *təkûnâ* is found elsewhere only in Job 23:3; Ezek 43:11. The root is probably not *tkn*, as in some older dictionaries, but *kûn* (so also BDB, *HALOT*) and echoes the use of the verb "make ready, set up" in vv. 3(4) and 5(6); see below. Reading a *mappîq* ("her stockpile") may be attractive here; cf. LXX and 8ḤevXIIgr.

rr. MT *kābōd* probably interprets this correctly as a defective form (used only here) for the more common *kābôd* ("burden, riches, glory"). LXX interprets it as the verb but struggles to make good sense of the verse. In colloquial English, "loaded" (used attributively) may be suitable.

ss. Interpreting the preposition as comparative. An alternative interpretation of the preposition as "(consisting) of" could have been served by a simple construct phrase.

tt. Hebrew *kəlî* can refer to a broad range of things; *ḥemdâ* qualifies these as desirable or precious.

uu. Hebrew *bûqâ ûməbûqâ ûməbullāqâ*. The three nouns are not attested elsewhere and may have been created by the author. The first two relate to *bûq* (// *bqq*, used above in v. 2[3]), and the last derives from *blq* (only in Isa 24:1, parallel to *bqq*). Preformative *mem*, as in *məbûqâ* and *məbullāqâ*, is common for nouns; cf. JM 88Ld–n and Meyer, *Grammatik*, 2:33–35. Many translators try to imitate the assonance and alliteration; so already LXX: *ektinagmos kai anatinagmos kai ekbrasmos*. The increasing word length is harder to reproduce.

vv. Hebrew *wəlēb nāmēs* is singular ("[the] heart melts"), but English idiom requires the plural.

ww. Hebrew *ûpîq birkayim* is again singular ("shaking of knees"). The noun *pîq* is attested only here; the related verb is also found in Isa 28:7 (*qal*) and Jer 10:4 (*hiphil*); cf. *pûqâ* in 1 Sam 25:31.

xx. Hebrew *ḥalḥālâ* ("trembling" with *HALOT*; BDB glosses "anguish") is also used in Isa 21:3; Ezek 30:4, 9; cf. the verb *ḥîl*, which is often used for being in labor.

yy. Hebrew *qibbəṣû pā'rûr* ("gather a glow [?]") is difficult; cf. the same phrase in Joel 2:6. Comparing Isa 13:8, Jeremias (*Nahum*, 147) opts for a reference to blushing (perhaps with shame, or in feverish panic). Most English translations render "grow pale," which presumably assumes a "gathering" of the face's natural glow somewhere inside to make it disappear from the face itself on the view that "gathering a glow" in the sense of blushing seems physiologically less plausible here. The versions refer to blackness, assuming a relationship to *pārûr* ("cooking-pot"); cf. Cécile Dogniez, "Fautes de traduction, ou bonnes traductions? Quelques exemples pris dans la LXX des Douze Petits Prophètes," in *10th Congress of the International Organization for Septuagint and Cognate Studies, Oslo 1998*, ed. Bernard Taylor, SBLSCS 51 (Atlanta: Society of Biblical Literature, 2001), 241–61; BA 23.4–9, 59. This may refer to covering with soot rather than involuntary physiological response (literally "ashen-faced").

Composition

Nah 1:15 (2:1) has already presented us with the picture of a messenger who brings news about the fall of Nineveh. This picture transports readers in their imagination to the time just after 612 BC, whether it was painted at that time or not. The images of the fall of Nineveh are, in a sense, images conveyed to readers by this messenger who is presented as an eyewitness. These images spell out the *news of peace*, but they do so not by way of a report after the event but as if Nineveh were being conquered at the time of speaking. The images are roughly chronological, moving from witnessing the approach of the attacker in 2:1(2) to a summary of effects in 2:10(11), which gives rise to the rhetorical questions to follow in vv. 2:11–12(12–13). But the chronology or location of events is confused in some places—in my judgment deliberately so, for greater dramatic effect.

The opening verse (2:1[2]) addresses Nineveh and sarcastically encourages the Assyrians to redouble their efforts. The next verse is parenthetical and dramatically delays the report of the attack. The report is further delayed in v. 3(4) by a depiction of the hectic preparations inside the city (as some think) or (more likely) of the attacking force as ready for action. The next verse is generally thought to picture the attackers as already in the city, but it may in fact describe the defenders. There is also no consensus among readers on the question whether attackers or defenders are in view in v. 5(6). Such ambiguity in these three verses is likely deliberate, reflective of the chaos of war. By way of contrast, the clarity of v. 6(7) is all the starker, as decisive moments in the battle are described with a great economy of words. Before Nineveh is even named, it is already defeated, partly sobbing, partly on the run (vv. 7–8[8–9]). If v. 7 is correctly identified as a tricolon, it may mark thereby the opening of the section focusing on the aftermath, which concludes with a set of lines that spotlight the effect of the defeat on Nineveh's population. The last two lines of this unit take up *face* and *loins* from the beginning of the unit in reverse order. This *inclusio* is obscured in most translations, the present one included.[212]

The use of different verb forms has been explained in a number of ways. It is often thought that the *qatal* (perfect) forms need explaining given that the events are in the future. The *qatal* forms are explained as "prophetic perfect," a rhetorical device by which a future-time action is regarded as if already accomplished (cf. JM 112h; *IBHS* 30.5.1). Others explain the *qatal* forms as due to the fact that the vision (of future events) lies in the past.[213] In this case, it is the *yiqtol* (imperfect) forms that need to be explained (e.g., as iterative). The origin of the poetry possibly lies in a vision, and it is likely that the images were composed prior to the events they describe. In my view, however, the rhetoric of the discourse is neither retrospective (of a vision), nor prospective (as a prediction of future events). The images are presented in the "present tense," as it were, allowing readers to witness the events as they unfold. The use of imperatives, most clearly in v. 9(10), signals as much. *Yiqtol* (imperfect) forms are used for ongoing and repeated actions, *qatal* (perfect) forms for events that have just transpired and for their results. Thus the first verb (v. 1[2]) is *qatal*, not because the coming up of the *scatterer* has already happened in the prophet's vision nor because it is certain to happen ("prophetic perfect") but because the scene to which we are transported in our imagination is one in which the *scatterer has* already *come up* and readies his army before the gates of Nineveh. The same could be said about v. 5(6), in which we witness the running to the city wall as it happens but see the siege towers only after they have been set up.[214]

---

212. See the translation note on *brace yourselves* in v. 1(2) and note that *against you* renders ʿal-pānayik ("against your face").

213. Roglund, *Alleged Non-Past Uses*, 80–82.

214. The use of *qatal* for results is responsible for the fact that, typically in this chapter, impersonal subjects are construed with *qatal* while persons are observed in action with *yiqtol*. The *qatal* forms in v. 2b(3b) report past events.

Commentary

1(2) The MT speaks of a *scatterer*, someone who compels a group to disperse.[215] Many prefer a more obviously military term here (see the translation note), but the scattering motif seems to me suitable enough given that the focus of the attack is on a city—a place of gathering—rather than a country or empire. The running away of the population later in v. 8(9) shows that the attacker is successful as a *scatterer* (cf. 3:16–18). There is an old tradition of thinking that the city being addressed here is Jerusalem,[216] in which case the *scatterer* is the Assyrian king and the verse might be read as a retrospective. But the text makes much better sense with Nineveh as the addressee. The calls to *guard the guardpost* and so on are ironic and underline how useless the preparations will prove to be. The irony is all the stronger for the urgency with which Nineveh is addressed, with the lack of conjunctions producing a staccato effect. The move to high alert will prove useless because, in the light of ch. 1, the *scatterer* who *has come up against*[217] the city is YHWH himself as much as any human military commander acting on his behalf.[218] This is also underlined by the following verse.

2(3) The prophetic exposition in this verse, which provides the reason behind the events, makes explicit that Nineveh's downfall is YHWH's doing. The verse can be understood in various ways, depending on one's translation (see the translation notes). The LXX can be read as suggesting that YHWH is turning around the Assyrian arrogance toward Jacob.[219] But in my view, the Hebrew is better understood to say *YHWH has turned* or *is about to turn*

215. Reading *mēpîṣ* with its common meaning. The *hiphil* of this verb can also be used internally transitive (reflexive) for "spreading oneself" (e.g., Exod 5:12; 1 Sam 13:8), which may be equivalent to "invading" here. This is reflected in Tg., but such a meaning is rarer and does not recommend itself with an unspecified singular subject.

216. So Tg., in which the text is read as a retrospective until v. 2(3). Cf. Rashi, Kimchi. Jeremias argued in *Kultprophetie*, 25–28, that 2:1–2(2–3) was originally an announcement of judgment against Judah. But this has been abandoned in his commentary; see *Nahum*, 21, 124–32.

217. The phrase *come up against* (12× with place names, 8× with general designations) is often used for military action; cf. 1 Kgs 20:22; Isa 7:1; Joel 1:6; also 2 Kgs 23:29.

218. While *pûṣ hiphil* occurs with human agents (e.g., Jer 23:1–2; Hab 3:14), it often has YHWH as its subject. The most noteworthy passage to consider here is Isa 24:1 because of other verbal links between Isa 24 and Nah 2.

219. This depends on reading "arrogance of Jacob" as an objective genitive ("arrogance shown toward/against Jacob") with Theodore of Mopsuestia and Cyril of Alexandria. The Greek text could also be understood to refer to Jacob's pride being removed, which fits with other parts of the Book of the Twelve, for which cf. below under "Reflection." See BA 23.4–9, 212–13 for details.

the pride of Jacob as the pride of Israel. If the verb is read as a perfect form and understood negatively, the meaning would be that YHWH has repudiated Jacob's arrogance as he has repudiated the arrogance of Israel.[220] The devastation to which the second half of the verse refers would thus be the means of this repudiation.[221] The argument would be that now that the Southern Kingdom has been humiliated (by widespread devastation of its cities), just as the Northern Kingdom had been humiliated (by its complete destruction), YHWH can turn his attention to Assyria, which is no longer needed to remove Jacob's arrogance. It is difficult to choose between this reading and the one adopted in the translation above, which interprets the verb form as a participle and suggests that the turning refers to a restoration and that *the pride of Jacob* and *the pride of Israel* have positive connotations here. Without the phrase *as the pride of Israel*, the positive reading would clearly have the edge (*the pride of Jacob* nowhere else having negative connotations; the transitive use of the *qal* of the verb elsewhere referring to positive outcomes). The question is whether the final phrase subverts a positive reading. If it does not, and the first half of the verse does indeed refer to the restoration of Judah,[222] the second half of the verse highlights why restoration is necessary. On this reading, adopted here, the reestablishment of *the pride of Jacob* requires the removal of the oppressor (cf. 1:13–14). This implies the fall of Nineveh, because the Assyrians are the *devastators* who have *ruined* the vine, which is Israel, by breaking off *shoots*.[223] The language of devastation readily refers both to the end of the Northern Kingdom at the hand of the Assyrians (722) and also the destruction caused within Judah in 701 and perhaps later, whenever the Assyrians marched against Egypt from 674 onwards.[224]

During the time of the divided kingdom, the designations *Jacob* and *Israel* were used primarily for the Northern Kingdom. After the fall of Samaria,

220. Cf. Fabry, *Nahum*, 168–69, who argues for this reading not least on the grounds that *gə'ôn yiśrā'ēl* (*the pride of Israel*) is elsewhere negative (Hos 5:5; 7:10). As noted above, *gə'ôn ya'ăqōb* is more readily heard as positive.

221. Differently, Jeremias (*Nahum*, 129–32) sees a sharp contrast between divine chastisement in the first half of the verse and Assyria's culpable actions in the second half.

222. This is also the view of Jason LeCureux, who argues that the verb *šûb* ("turn," "return") is the thematic key for a coherent reading of the Book of the Twelve; see *The Thematic Unity of the Book of the Twelve*, HBM 41 (Sheffield: Sheffield Phoenix, 2012), 157–59.

223. The imagery of the vine is suggested by the reference to *shoots*, whether or not *gə'ôn* (*pride*) is emended to *gepen* ("vine"), which some propose (see translation note on *pride*).

224. This is one reason why the identification of *the pride of Jacob* with the city Samaria, offered by Joel S. Burnett in his impressive essay, "The Pride of Jacob," in *David and Zion: Biblical Studies in Honor of J. J. M. Roberts*, ed. Bernard F. Batto and Kathryn L. Roberts (Winona Lake, IN: Eisenbrauns, 2004), 319–50, is not persuasive.

however, *Israel* often designates the inhabitants of Judah, and sometimes even *Jacob* is used in this way (e.g., Mic 3; Obad). Here the terms *Jacob* and *Israel* refer to the whole people, embracing northerners and southerners. But the full phrases, *the pride of Jacob* and *the pride of Israel*, may refer to a part only, because the phrase *the pride of* most often refers to a prominent part of something.[225] If this is true here as well, *the pride of Jacob* may refer to Judah or, more likely, Jerusalem specifically,[226] namely on the grounds that Jerusalem is the only major city of the descendants of Jacob that had been left standing in the Assyrian onslaught.[227] If we then understand *the pride of Israel* as "the capital of the land of Israel," we can interpret the whole sentence as an announcement that God will restore "Jacob's glory," Jerusalem, to become again the glorious capital city of (all) Israel.

The unusual way of putting this idea (*the pride of Jacob* being restored *as the pride of Israel*) may be meant to recall the name change from *Jacob* to *Israel* (Gen 32:28–29; 35:10; cf. 2 Kgs 17:34). The glory of *Jacob* ("the supplanter, the hanger-on") shall be the glory of *Israel* ("El persists/contends"). Small *Jacob* (cf. Amos 7:2, 5), whose pride and glory has been greatly reduced by the Assyrians along with its territory, shall experience that God contends for it, and so *Israel* shall blossom again in all its *pride*. If this tentative reading is adopted, the verse specifically announces the restoration of Jerusalem to its former glory as the capital for all the tribes of Israel and thus implicitly promises the restoration of Judah and Israel in a united monarchy.

3(4) This verse probably portrays the splendid army that is set against Nineveh.[228] In this case, the personal suffix *his* on *heroes* in the first line and the phrase *on the day when he makes ready* ensure that the singular will behind this army is kept in focus. Once again it is possible to see YHWH as the one who *makes ready* (see above on the ambiguity of the *scatterer* in v. 1[2]). The army's colors are red. The shields are *mǝ'oddām* (*red*), a term that mod-

---

225. Thus, e.g., *gǝ'ôn hayyardēn* (Jer 12:5; 49:19; 50:44; Zech 11:3) "refers to the thick, lush vegetation along the banks of the river" (Burnett, "Pride of Jacob," 321).

226. Note that Burnett ("Pride of Jacob") argues that the phrase *the pride of Jacob* was originally coined as a designation for Jerusalem.

227. In other words, even northern Israelites could only look to Jerusalem with political pride, Samaria and the Northern Kingdom having been brought to an end.

228. The most forceful argument against this view has been put forward by Pinker in "Nahum 2,4 Revisited"; cf. his "Nineveh's Defensive Strategy and Nahum 2–3," *ZAW* 118 (2006): 618–25. Fabry, *Nahum*, 169–70, also thinks that we observe the army inside the occupied city, whose splendor will count for nothing in the end. For the following, see Thomas Renz, "The Colour Red and the Lion King: Two Studies in Nahum," in *Sprache lieben—Gottes Wort verstehen: Beiträge zur biblischen Exegese; Festschrift für Heinrich von Siebenthal*, ed. Walter Hilbrands, BWM 17 (Gießen: Brunnen, 2011), 163–69.

ifies rams' skins in Exod 25:5; 26:14; 35:7, 23; 36:19; 39:34 and may well do so here if the shields were made of hide.[229] The soldiers themselves are *dressed in crimson* (or "scarlet"). While it is obvious that there were expensive as well as more affordable colors in antiquity, the sources and manufacture of ancient dyes are not yet fully understood.[230] It is usually thought that *mətullā'îm* refers to the color of a very durable dye gained from the kermes insect,[231] whose use would have been confined to more luxurious textiles and apparel.[232] If that is correct, the soldiers are clad in expensive dress (cf. Lam 4:5, where the noun *tôlā'* is often rendered "purple" in English translation). Even if the term covered less expensive reds as well, Nahum likely wants to convey the notion of splendor.[233]

While Nahum does not provide a historical account, the poetic depiction of an army clad in red is probably not entirely fictional. There is a comment on the colorful outfit of Assyrian and Babylonian commanders in Ezek 23:5–6, 14–15, and red military dress is attested by Greek and Roman writers. Xenophon's romanticized description of the Persian army in red (or purple) garments[234] and the report by Claudius Aelianus that the Spartans had to wear a

229. Brenner (*Colour Terms*, 110) observes that *mə'oddām* is mostly understood as a synthetic rather than naturally reflected color effect. This makes it unlikely that the red color on the shields is that of spilled blood, for which *'ādōm* would seem more suitable (cf., e.g., 2 Kgs 3:22).

230. Cf. the comment in Carol Bier, "Textile Arts in Ancient Western Asia," in *CANE*, 1575.

231. There are a number of related scale insects producing similar red colors; cf. Dominique Cardon, "Mediterranean Kermes and Kermes Dyeing," *Dyes in History and Archaeology* 7 (1989): 5–8; "Le mystère résolu du kermès," *Archaeology and History in Lebanon* 19 (2004): 118–30; Zohar Amar et al., "The Scarlet Dye of the Holy Land," *BioScience* 55 (2005): 1080–83. It has been suggested that Tiglath-pileser I introduced oak trees to Assyria c. 1100 BC to act as hosts for the insects; see R. A. Donkin, "The Insect Dyes of Western and West-Central Asia," *Anthropos: International Review of Ethnology and Linguistics* 72 (1977): 847–80.

232. It would have been a lot less expensive than purple, however. One person can collect two pounds worth of color in a day, albeit only at the right time of the year for a few weeks. Contrast this with the need of some 12,000 snails to produce a mere 1.4 grams of purple pigment. See, e.g., Roland Gradwohl, *Die Farben im Alten Testament: Eine terminologische Studie*, BZAW 83 (Berlin: A. Töpelmann, 1963), 75.

233. Alternatively, the garments are sprinkled with blood from previous battles, portraying the soldiers as experienced veterans. But *mətullā'îm* probably denotes a brighter, stronger color than the one left by (old) blood stains. The broader term *'ādōm* would have been more suitable to denote the color of blood (cf. above and Isa 63:2–3 with reference to more recent blood), for which see Brenner, *Colour Terms*, 58–80.

234. Xenophon, *Cyropaedia* 6.4.1, cf. 7.1.2; 8.3.3. The Greek *phoinikis* refers etymologically to Phoenician purple but was used more widely for shades of red. *LSJ*, s.v. *phoinikis*, refers to a dark-red military cloak and offers further references.

red coat for battle suggest that "the colour had something superior about it, and when the blood from wounds spread it terrified the enemy still more, as the spectacle was more sombre and frightening."[235] Thus, ancient uniforms may well have been designed more to impress than to camouflage.[236]

The *coverings* of the *chariots* (or maybe of the horses or charioteers) are also *flaming-red*. These coverings would have to be of cloth. Pinker rightly points out that it is hard to think of a rationale for metal coverings. Metal plates would offer little additional protection but would increase the weight of the vehicle and thus reduce its speed and hamper its maneuverability.[237] Coverings of cloth were presumably used to offer a measure of protection against arrows to the lower body of the three or four members of the crew.

The translation of the last line of the verse remains very uncertain. Alternative versions could make the line refer to the flapping coverings of the chariot poles,[238] to veiled charioteers, or to restless horses. My translation still allows for different interpretations. The verse may refer to the rustling of trees as the army rushes past, to the shaking of the chariot poles, or to the "quivering of the wooden frames of the chariots as they rushed into battle." Perhaps most likely in the context of preparations being made (and completed), reference is made here to the "rippling or quivering effect in the sea of spears held aloft by the advancing spearmen," with stems of trees used as lances.[239] In any case, we get the picture of an army ready to do battle. Nineveh faces not a rag bag of soldiers but an organized and uniformly well-equipped army whose appearance is an aesthetic experience of color, brightness, order, and rhythm.[240]

---

235. Aelian, *Varia Historia* 6.6.6. The translation is from Aelian, *Historical Miscellany*, ed. Nigel Guy Wilson, Loeb Classical Library 486 (Cambridge: Harvard University Press, 1997), 233, 235. Note that the famous Chinese terracotta warriors were also originally painted.

236. Pinker ("Nahum 2,4 Revisited," 412) rightly objects to J. P. M. Smith's attempts to distinguish Assyrian defenders dressed in blue from scarlet-clad Babylonian and Median forces. His own argument that Assyrian officers must be in view relies too heavily on presumed historical plausibility. While Nahum may well have seen more Assyrian officers than Median soldiers in his life, this need not prevent a poet from painting the more obscure (to him) attacking forces in splendid colours. The same goes for his claim that the allied attacking forces would not all wear the same colors ("Nahum 2,4 Revisited," 413 = "Nineveh's Defensive Strategy," 622).

237. Pinker, "Nahum 2,4 Revisited," 414. On philological grounds already Manfried Dietrich and Oswald Loretz argued for a reference to cloth covering; see Cathcart, *Nahum*, 87–88.

238. See Spronk, *Nahum*, 90.

239. Both quotations from Roberts, *Nahum*, 58. Maier (*Nahum*, 237) points out that cypress wood is of a reddish hue, which fits well with other references to red color in the verse.

240. Lothar Perlitt, *Die Propheten Nahum, Habakuk, Zephanja*, ATD 25 (Göttingen: Vandenhoeck & Ruprecht, 2004), 20; cf. Roberts, *Nahum*, 65.

Dalley has observed that "by the middle of the seventh century, chariotry was waning as a main battle force, and cavalry took over its role as the main equestrian presence, although the chariot was still in evidence as a prestige vehicle for ceremonial occasions, including royal hunts."[241] This change may relate to the decline of the Neo-Assyrian Empire, which had historically used chariotry to the greatest effect,[242] but Noble argues that even the Assyrians "stopped using chariots to any effective extent in battle" after the reign of Sargon II (705 BC).[243] It is unlikely that chariots played a role in the final attack against Nineveh, although cavalry likely did. Chariots are best deployed in open space, and even the Assyrians would not have used them to attack fortified cities. Nahum's picture of the unidentified attacking forces is probably influenced by his experience of the Assyrian army more than by any knowledge of Median, Scythian, or Babylonian practice. Thus, he may have thought of the chariots exercising a role prior to the actual attack of the city. This role may have been either in warfare on the plains or as a means of transport to support the infantry and cavalry. Alternatively, the reference may be to the chariot of the chief commander or king.[244]

The phrase *on the day when he makes ready* need not refer specifically to the making ready of the chariot(s), although this is the impression given in some English translations. It may well be a more general reference to the arrangements being made in the move from approach (*has come up*, v. 1[2]) to attack.[245] It indicates that the attack has not yet begun, but this is soon to change.

4(5) The first half of the verse is beautifully constructed with *chariots* in the middle of the action, as the pivot of the bicolon.[246] The arrangement in the Hebrew is

241. Stephanie Dalley, "Ancient Mesopotamian Military Organization," in *CANE*, 419.

242. Cf. Angelika Berlejung, "Erinnerungen an Assyrien in Nahum 2,4–3,19," in *Die unwiderstehliche Wahrheit: Studien zur alttestamentlichen Prophetie, Festschrift für Arndt Meinhold*, ed. Rüdiger Lux and Ernst-Joachim Waschke, Arbeiten zur Bibel und ihrer Geschichte 23 (Leipzig: Evangelische Verlagsanstalt, 2006), 329.

243. Duncan Noble, "Assyrian Chariotry and Cavalry," *State Archive of Assyria Bulletin* 4 (1990): 61.

244. See Noble, "Assyrian Chariotry," 66. Note the prominence of the royal chariot on wall reliefs in Richard David Barnett, *Sculptures from the North Palace of Ashurbanipal at Nineveh (668–627 B.C.)* (London: British Museum, 1976), plates 28 (drawing; original now lost), 35 (BM 124946), 60 (Or. Dr. VI 24), 68 (Louvre AO 19904).

245. If the Assyrian army is depicted, *the day when he makes ready* is obviously the day of preparations to counter the expected assault.

246. This pivot-pattern may indicate the opening of a sub-unit, now focusing on the situation inside the city; cf. the discussion of v. 3(4) under composition.

> Through the streets
>   rush madly
>   the chariots
>   race each other
> through the plazas.

The use of a chiastic structure gives expression to the vehicles' back-and-forth movement. Standard usage demands that *the streets* and *the plazas* are inside the city.[247] Maier notes Bellino Cylinder 1.61, in which Sennacherib boasts of the streets and squares of Nineveh: "I widened its squares, made bright the avenues and streets and caused them to shine like the day."[248] Even so, the picture of chariots racing each other, presumably side-by-side, probably applies some poetic license.

The verse is generally understood to refer to the attackers.[249] Indeed, the reuse of *chariots* (cf. v. 3[4]) might suggest as much. If so, we have moved in a very short span from war preparations to the first success of the attackers with the chariotry already causing havoc in the city, presumably ahead of the foot soldiers. But we have noted above that chariots would not have been used to spearhead an attack against a fortified city, and even allowing for poetic license, one may question whether this is the impression Nahum seeks to convey here. Problems with identifying the protagonists are regularly noted for the following verse, and in my view, the confidence with which many scholars identify the protagonists in this verse as the attackers is misplaced. More likely, we are meant to contrast the chariotry of the attackers, which in the previous verse is part of a well-organized force, with the panic-stricken chariotry of the defenders in this verse.

As noted earlier, the Assyrians were famous for their chariots. Indeed, chariotry was Assyria's main strength, allowing for rapid movement, especially on the flat terrain of Mesopotamia. Pinker notes the importance of chariots for the defense of Nineveh itself given the nature of its surrounding terrain.[250] But the advantages of chariots are significantly reduced within a city, even a city with broad squares and streets. In a built-up area, the height advantage over foot soldiers is lost because chariots can be attacked from the roof-tops. Nineveh's city gates were comparatively broad but certainly

247. Cf., e.g., Isa 15:3; Jer 5:1; Amos 5:16; Prov 1:20. Contra BDB and a number of commentators; e.g., Samuel Driver, *Minor Prophets*, 31; Patterson, *Nahum*, 48.

248. Maier, *Nahum*, 244.

249. Unusually, Fabry (*Nahum*, 169–71) reads all of vv. 4–6 as descriptive of the Assyrian defenders.

250. See Pinker, "Nineveh's Defensive Strategy," 618–19.

not designed to let chariots quickly in or out, the construction forcing them to make a sharp turn at a slow pace in order to enter.[251] So, the picture is probably of "chariots rambling in the streets, from gate to gate, desperately trying to find a point of exit, to no avail."[252] If the Assyrian chariotry is still within the city walls by the time the attack has started, Nineveh is in trouble. The king of Assyria might have at his disposal the strongest chariot force in history, but it is no good to him inside the city.

5(6) The precise meaning of the opening clause (*He remembers his officers*) is debatable (see the translation notes), not least because of uncertainty about the identity of the one who calls upon his officers. A number of commentators think of the king of Nineveh because of the reference to stumbling later in the verse. If the above interpretation of the previous verse as a reference to Assyrian chariots is correct, it lends support to this view. But given that earlier masculine singular references in this unit refer to the leader of the attack, this remains a possibility here (see below). If the Assyrian king is in view, we see him turning to *his officers* at the very moment that he realizes that his chariots are not going to prevent the attack on the city. The term used to designate *his officers* ("his mighty/magnificent ones") is ironic here.

The use of *hasten* later in the verse is a strong argument in favor of interpreting *stumble* here as a result of hasty movement.[253] Stumbling in haste is probably also implied in Prov 4:12 ("If you run, you will not stumble") and Lev 26:37 ("They will stumble over each other as if from the sword").[254] Elsewhere, the verb always has negative connotations, and some have concluded that therefore the reference must be to the defenders.[255] Against this, one could argue that the reverse word order (*hasten* followed by *stumble*) might be more appropriate for the defenders. If the previous verse is interpreted as referring to the speed of the attackers, the attackers might still be in view in this verse.[256] A similar ambiguity is perhaps found in the stumbling over corpses in 3:3.[257]

---

251. The argument here does not presume that the poet offers historical reportage. It assumes that poet and audience were familiar with some basic facts of contemporary warfare.

252. Pinker, "Nineveh's Defensive Strategy," 623; cf. Fabry, *Nahum*, 170 (who compares Exod 14:23–25); already Kimchi.

253. While stumbling may be the result of weariness and weakness (e.g., Ps 109:24; Isa 5:27; 35:3), this would not happen at the beginning of the battle, whether on the side of attackers or defenders. Failure to notice stumbling blocks is another frequent cause for stumbling (e.g., Isa 59:10; Jer 6:21).

254. Lev 26:37 is usually understood as a reference to fleeing from the sword. In other places, reference to a quick retreat is at least plausible; e.g., Pss 9:3(4); 27:2.

255. E.g., Spronk, *Nahum*, 93; cf. Fabry, *Nahum*, 171.

256. So, e.g., Cathcart, *Nahum*, 94; Maier, *Nahum*, 248; Patterson, *Nahum*, 67–58; Roberts, *Nahum*, 59.

257. Many see the attackers stumble in 3:3 (e.g., Patterson, *Nahum*, 89; Roberts, *Nahum*, 73; Jeremias, *Nahum*, 158), which is perhaps more likely if a decision has to be made, but

The suffix of *ḥômātāh* (*her wall*) does not demand that those who rush to the wall are doing so from the outside. Outside observers may describe defenders rushing to their city wall in a detached manner, using *her wall* rather than "their wall." Maybe we are meant to hear an echo of *her place* (1:8). The shift to a passive perfect (*have been set up*) underlines the speed with which the attackers have put themselves in position. If we picture the way in which readers are guided to look at these scenes as the movement of a camera, we get a smoother movement if we read the first lines of the verse as a reference to the defenders. The first shot is of the king (in his palace?), maybe summoning his officers, the second shot is of stumbling runners. The camera follows them hastening to the city wall. The next shot logically lets us look over the wall: already *the siege towers have been set up*.[258]

6(7) *The gates of the rivers* have been variously understood as the sluices controlling the flow of the Khosr River into Nineveh,[259] the five gates facing the River Tigris,[260] or the fortified bridges that crossed the Tigris and other rivers.[261] One's choice between these relates to the question of how much knowledge about Nineveh's topography one may assume on the part of Judeans and how much poetic license one grants to Nahum. The fact that Nineveh was supported by an elaborate water system must have been well known beyond Assyria, not least because the system of canals supporting it

---

Spronk (*Nahum*, 121) suggests that the defenders are the subject of the verb. Maier (*Nahum*, 298) leans toward the latter, acknowledging the ambiguity.

258. By contrast, if those who run to the wall are pictured as attackers outside the city, the camera first moves toward the wall and then has to move back again to bring the siege towers into view, which have been overlooked or disregarded in the depiction of the infantry. While this is easier to describe in terms of camera movement, it is of course a description of the movement of the mental eye of readers. To me the movement described in the main text makes better (dramatic) sense.

259. So, e.g., Cathcart, *Nahum*, 89–90; Roberts, *Nahum*, 59–60. In this case, the plural *nəhārôt* ("rivers") might refer to various canals in addition to the Khosr. Aron Pinker ("Nahum and the Greek Tradition of Nineveh's Fall," *JHebS* 6 [2006]: art. 8, doi:10.5508/jhs.2006.v6.a8) suggests that *nāhār* refers to (large) rivers, not to (small) streams or canals, but the Pharpar (2 Kgs 5:12) is not a very large river and the Chebar (Ezek 1:1) is a canal.

260. So, e.g., Fabry, *Nahum*, 172–74. Gates are usually named after the direction in which they lead. This assumes that the plural *nəhārôt* may refer to a single river, but I am not convinced that this usage for the (arms of the) Nile (Exod 7:19; 8:5[1]; Isa 19:6; Ezek 32:2; references to the "rivers of Cush," i.e., the Blue Nile and the White Nile, in, e.g., Zeph 3:10) is appropriate here. The only example not involving the Nile is Ps 137:1, which likely refers to "the canals that crisscrossed the alluvial land of the lower Euphrates and Tigris" (Hans-Joachim Kraus, *Psalms 60–150* [ET 1989; Minneapolis: Fortress, 1993], 502; cf. Leslie C. Allen, *Psalms 101–150*, rev. ed. [Nashville: Nelson, 2002], 307).

261. Pinker, "Nineveh's Defensive Strategy," 624; cf. Tg. The use of the plural *rivers* is a chief plank in this argument; cf. "Greek Tradition." Pinker names the other rivers as Greater Zab, Khosr, and Gômel and thus must grant that *nāhār* can refer to smaller rivers (Khosr and Gômel).

stretched far to the north (cf. v. 8[9]).[262] It was probably also widely known that a river runs through Nineveh.[263] The observation that *the gates of the rivers are opened* signals either the failure of Nineveh's natural protection through the Tigris and maybe other rivers (on the second and third interpretation), or a situation in which Nineveh's famous water system turns or is turned against the city's inhabitants (on the first interpretation). The latter in particular carries great ideological significance (cf. the excursus below). The control of water to benefit Nineveh was an expression and sign of the ability of the Assyrian king, Sennacherib in the first instance, to control the watery forces of chaos and harness them for the end that he determined.

In this case, it may be possible to explain *the gates of the rivers* as a dramatic way of referring to the gates through which the Khosr passed the city.[264] This would be a means of saying that the city has been breached on two sides as well as of conveying an image of flooding in the use of the plural *nəhārôt* ("rivers"), which in more prosaic language would be inappropriate for the Khosr alone. If so, then the opening of *the gates of the rivers* leads to the collapse of *the palace* in two senses of the word. The physical building collapses, as its foundations are undermined by rushing water,[265] and the powers that reside in the palace despair.[266] The vivid picture of a palace dissolving as floods undermine its foundations would be part of the rhetoric of water turning against Nineveh rather than a description or prediction of the means by which Nineveh was destroyed. In this connection, it should be pointed out that the text does not specify which of Nineveh's palaces collapses.[267] The use of the definite article may suggest that Nahum was either unaware of

262. See Julian E. Reade's two-part "Studies in Assyrian Geography," *RA* 72 (1978): 47–72, 157–80; Stephanie Dalley, "Nineveh, Babylon and the Hanging Gardens: Cuneiform and Classical Sources Reconciled," *Iraq* 56 (1994): 45–58; Berlejung, "Erinnerungen," 330–31; Daniele Morandi Bonacossi, "Water for Assyria: Irrigation and Water Management in the Assyrian Empire," in Petit and Bonacossi, *Nineveh*, 132–36.

263. The Khosr River, which divides Nineveh into a northern and southern part, was apparently a perennial stream in antiquity. Today it seems to be dry for much of the year, and it would be more accurate to call it a wadi or riverbed.

264. Cf. Jeremias, *Nahum*, 138. The Khosr enters the city in the east, leaving it in the west. Nahum and his early readers need not have known the details to figure out that the river would leave the city through a part of the city wall at some remove from the place where it entered.

265. Cf. the use of the *hithpael* of the same root in 1:5 for the hills going to pieces. The *niphal* seems to refer to a swaying movement; cf. 1 Sam 14:16 for people moving back and forth.

266. See Exod 15:15; Josh 2:9, 24; Isa 14:31; maybe Jer 49:23 (all *niphal*, as here); and Ps 107:26 (*hithpolel*), to which can be added swaying hearts (Ezek 21:15[20]). About half of the occurrences of the verb refer to people who are terrified.

267. There were two main palaces on the Kuyunjik mound high above the plain: a south-

the existence of more than one palace or unconcerned about any specific building. If so, *the palace* would only be used as a metonymy for the king and maybe other people residing in palaces.

EXCURSUS: THE DESTRUCTION OF NINEVEH

Past scholarship has often appealed to the description of Nineveh's fall by the Greek writers Diodorus and Xenophon to illuminate the book of Nahum. Thus, it was sometimes believed that a succession of heavy rainfalls primed Nineveh for its fall. In this view, the rivers swelled, and the reservoir to the north of the city was breached (cf. *the gates of the rivers are opened*). The released waters severely damaged the city wall along a stretch of more than two miles and flooded the city. This allowed the conquerors to storm into Nineveh and conquer it.[268] But the texts on which this rough outline of events is based are confused and unreliable. Diodorus's blunder in referring to the Euphrates rather than the Tigris or Khosr is well known and could be explained on its own as a slip, but he also gives "three years" for the siege that took just under three months[269] and gets the names of the protagonists wrong. Xenophon does not even mention Nineveh, and it is doubtful that his account of the fall of "Larissa" is meant to refer to Nineveh.[270] The scenario is not corroborated by the archaeological evidence and is in fact implausible. The Khosr was not entirely irrelevant for the attack, but there is no evidence in sources contemporary to the events or in the archaeological record that water played any role in the fall of Nineveh.[271] Rather, the

---

west palace (Sennacherib's "Palace Without Rival," which Assurbanipal had restored) and a magnificent north palace (built during Assurbanipal's reign).

268. Diodorus Siculus, *Library*, 2.26–27; Xenophon, *Anabasis*, 3.4.12. See Paul Haupt, "Xenophon's Account of the Fall of Nineveh," *JAOS* 28 (1907): 65–83. Commentators accepting these accounts include Maier, *Nahum*, 253–54; Patterson, *Nahum*, 62. Others, like Elizabeth Achtemeier (*Nahum–Malachi* [Atlanta: John Knox, 1986], 18–20) seem positively inclined but are more cautious.

269. There were three years between the first and the last siege, but the impression given in Diodorus is that the siege continued throughout these three years.

270. Note also that Xenophon writes about two centuries after the fall of Nineveh and Diodorus some five centuries after the event. See Pinker, "Greek Tradition," for a fuller discussion.

271. See A. Kirk Grayson, *Assyrian and Babylonian Chronicles*, Texts from Cuneiform Sources 5 (Locust Valley, NY: Augustin, 1975), 90–96, for the record of the campaign in the Babylonian Chronicle (BM 21,901); cf. *ARAB*, 2:417–21. Cf. the essays by Peter Machinist ("The Fall of Assyria in Comparative Ancient Perspective," 179–95) and David Stronach ("Notes on the Fall of Nineveh," 307–24) in *Assyria 1995: Proceedings of the 10th Anniversary Symposium of the Neo-Assyrian Text Corpus Project, Helsinki, 1995*, ed. Simo K. A. Parpola and

evidence shows that only the Adad Gate in the extreme north and the Halzi Gate in the extreme south were actually attacked. Accordingly, it seems possible that the attackers sought to draw the Assyrian defenders towards the opposite ends of the elongated walled area before launching a critical assault at the most vulnerable point in the eastern defenses, i.e. at the precise spot where the River Khosr wound its way into the city.[272]

Nineveh was captured in the month of Abu (roughly August).[273] The rivers would have normally been fairly depleted at this time, approaching their low-water mark. A flood at this time of the year would have been highly unusual and surely reported in the contemporary chronicles that detail the fall of the city. Given the topography and the nature of the walls surrounding Nineveh, it is very unlikely that a manipulation of the water system could have led to widespread destruction of walls and buildings. If such a feat had been accomplished, one might expect the Babylonians to take credit for it in their chronicles, especially in the light of claims that Babylon itself had been flooded by a king of Nineveh (Sennacherib) at an earlier time.

Fire damage is evident from the archaeological records, and the Babylonians claim to have taken much spoil. Nineveh was never reestablished to anything like its former glory. It is thought to have been the largest city in the whole world at the time of its destruction, having taken this honor from Thebes in about 668. With its destruction, this honor fell to Babylon, which seems to have been the first city in the world with a population topping 200,000.[274] But Nineveh did not simply drop to second place. Unlike Thebes, Nineveh's demise was so spectacular that it did not recover its urban identity for centuries.

Robert M. Whiting (Helsinki: University of Helsinki Press, 1997); Gerlinde Baumann, "Die Eroberung Ninives bei Nahum und in den neubabylonischen Texten: Ein Motivvergleich," in *"Einen Altar von Erde macht mir . . .": Festschrift für Diethelm Conrad zu seinem 70. Geburtstag*, ed. Johannes F. Diehl, Reinhard Heitzenröder, and Markus Witte, Kleine Arbeiten zum Alten und Neuen Testament 4 (Waltrop: Spenner, 2003), 5–19.

272. David Stronach and Stephen Lumsden, "UC Berkeley Excavations at Nineveh," *Biblical Archaeologist* 55 (1992): 232. Albert T. Olmstead (*History of Assyria* [Chicago: University of Chicago Press, 1923], 137) claimed evidence for a successful attack on the northeastern corner, but no traces of this are visible today (Julian E. Reade, "Studies in Assyrian Geography, Part I: Sennacherib and the Waters of Nineveh," *RA* 72 [1978]: 68).

273. Note that Maier (*Nahum*, 253) claims that this period is "roughly parallel to the high-water period of the Khosr." (The opposite is true.) Some therefore appeal exclusively to manipulation of the water system; e.g., Jo A. Scurlock, "The Euphrates Flood and the Ashes of Nineveh (Diod. II 27.1–28.7)," *Historia* 39 (1990): 382–84.

274. Tertius Chandler, *Four Thousand Years of Urban Growth: An Historical Census* (Lewiston: St. David's University Press, 1987).

7(8) The beginning of this verse is a notorious crux. If the MT is retained at the beginning of the verse, the best rendering may be *he is positioned* in the sense of "standing tall, erect"—perhaps a reference to the attacking *scatterer*. The most attractive emendation is the addition of a *yod*, which, with different vocalization, produces *wǝhaṣṣǝbî*.[275] The word *ṣǝbî* may mean "beauty, ornament" or "gazelle" and is elsewhere used to designate a land (e.g., Isa 13:19) or cities (Ezek 25:9).[276] Given that the following two verbs and the suffix on *maids* require a feminine subject, it is attractive to supply this by emending to "the Beauty," even if this is not entirely without problems.[277] "The Beauty" could be a reference to the queen, the city, or the chief goddess of the city, Ishtar. Each identification has its strengths and weaknesses, but the focus throughout the book is on the city. The chief problem with finding a reference to the queen in this verse is the fact that the Assyrian queen plays no significant role in Assyrian or biblical literature.[278] It is possible to draw on cultural background for identifying the subject with a goddess or cult statue but, in my view, it seems that such a reference would need to be signaled more clearly in the text.[279] Without emendation, the subject remains unspecified. This has happened twice before in the book (*her wall* in v. 5[6]; *her place* in 1:8), and in both cases we have identified the implied subject as Nineveh. All things considered, the juxtaposition of an unspecified *he* who *is positioned* with an equally unspecified *she* who *is exposed* is perhaps tol-

275. Cf. Cathcart, *Nahum*, 96–98; F. W. Dobbs-Allsopp, *Weep, O Daughter of Zion: A Study of the City-Lament Genre in the Hebrew Bible*, BibOr 44 (Rome: Pontifical Biblical Institute, 1993), 128–30; Longman, "Nahum," 806.

276. See H. Madl, "צְבִי, *ṣ^ebî* I and II," *TDOT* 12:232–38; C. John Collins, "צְבִי," *NIDOTTE* 3:738–39. These are two distinct roots, differentiated in related languages (e.g., Aramaic; see *HALOT*, s.v. *ṣǝbî*). The Hebrew letter *ṣ* combines three originally distinct sounds, which resulted in a number of roots that look the same but are not identical (*ṣûr* may be the best-known example).

277. The term *ṣǝbî*, like similar noun formations, is grammatically masculine. Its reference—whether to the queen, the city, or a goddess—is, however, depicted as female, and this might be sufficient to explain the use of feminine verb forms and suffixes. Maybe cf. the use of feminine forms with (nongendered) names such as "Zion" (e.g., Pss 48:12–13[13–14]; 87:5; 97:8). I have not found a precise parallel (a masculine noun relating to feminine verb and suffix forms). See also the discussion in GKC 145; JM 148–151.

278. There is one woman who might have qualified for special mention, if the text was earlier: Naqia/Zakutu (c. 730–668), who came to prominence as queen mother of Esarhaddon and grandmother of Assurbanipal. See Sarah C. Melville, *The Role of Naqia/Zakutu in Sargonid Politics*, State Archives of Assyria Studies 9 (Helsinki: University of Helsinki Press, 1999).

279. But see the note on the translation and Timmer ("Boundaries," 181) who notes "the overlap between the characterisation of Nineveh as a prostitute and several of Ishtar's prominent features"; cf. *Non-Israelite Nations*, 131–32.

erable with (feminine) Nineveh and the (masculine) ruler of Assyria as the implied subjects.[280]

The short reference to the attacker being *positioned* echoes the end of v. 5(6)—*the siege towers have been set up*—although a different root is used. It stands in an appropriate place, after reference to breach of the city's defenses in the previous verse and before the description of the aftermath. It may also echo the erect stance of the Assyrian king on Assyrian reliefs, contrasting with the stooped posture of the defeated enemies.[281] The juxtaposition with the city being *exposed* might have suggested a sexual innuendo, but we do not know the cultural background well enough to be confident about this.[282] At any rate, the attacker *is positioned* in order to do the things that are being done to the city.[283]

What is being done to the city is described with two verbs, *she is exposed* and *offered up*. The first verb anticipates both the stripping of the city in the ransacking of v. 9(10) and the exposure of the prostitute in 3:5. Probably both levels of meaning are intended: the city is stripped of its goods and its women are humiliated by being treated like prostitutes. The verb *offered up* evokes the image of the city being presented as a sacrifice. Presumably, this alludes to the burning that often follows the looting. As noted above, there may be sexual overtones in the use of this verb, hinting at rape, in which case we may posit two levels of meaning here as well.

A problem with identifying the feminine subject as the city is the mention of *her maids*, which would seem to be more appropriate with reference to the queen or the goddess. There is no parallel for designating the inhabitants of

280. Cf. Spronk, *Nahum*, 96–98, with fuller discussion. Spronk himself follows the medieval commentator Yéfer ben Ély, interpreting *wǝhuṣṣab* as a reference to the Assyrian king and rendering as "he is put down." Cf. *CTAT*, 3:807–808. I do not find the alleged parallel in Ps 39:6 fully persuasive. Fabry's attempt is preferable: "He is put on display" (*Nahum*, 158).

281. Cynthia R. Chapman (*The Gendered Language of Warfare in the Israelite-Assyrian Encounter*, HSM 62 [Winona Lake, IN: Eisenbrauns, 2004], 26) argues that erect stance along with full beards, developed musculature, and unflinching gaze is part of the construction of masculinity on these reliefs. Cf. plate 5 (*Gendered Language*, 175) and Julian E. Reade, *Assyrian Sculpture*, 2nd ed. (London: British Museum, 1998), 83 (plate 98).

282. The verb used in *she is offered up* (*hō'ălātâ*) is used for the mating of animals in Gen 31:10, and it has been suggested that it may hint at rape; cf. Spronk, *Nahum*, 98; see further below.

283. We have observed that the *hophal* participle is used for things that stand tall, but it is also worth noting that the *niphal* participle is used for people looking after others, either in the sense of being in charge (e.g., Ruth 2:5–6; cf. *hanniṣṣābîm* in 1 Kgs 4–5 and 9:23 for "overseers") or in the sense of attending to someone (1 Sam 4:20), and that the *hiphil* is used for setting up an altar (Gen 33:20; cf. 35:14; 2 Kgs 17:10; cf. *she is offered up*). Thus, other connotations are (also) possible.

a city as *her maids*.[284] It is, however, possible that *'amhōtêhā* was chosen to allude to *'ummâ* ("people"), which is used three times in the Bible, always in the plural.[285] In addition, *HALOT* identifies a root *'ammâ* meaning "canal," to which the place name Ammah (2 Sam 2:24) is thought to be related, and this is another candidate for an allusion. It is even possible that the author prepares us for the picture of running people as flowing water in the next verse with a double allusion to "people" and "canals" in the reference to *maids sobbing*. Similarly, the use of the root *nhg* for *sobbing* may be designed to evoke the idea of forced removal, for which *nhg* is employed elsewhere.[286]

The *sound of doves* is commonly linked to the moaning only. This is presumably because the comparison of human moaning with the cooing of doves is found elsewhere in ancient Near Eastern literature and in the Bible (Isa 38:14; 59:11).[287] But maybe the position of the phrase allows it to go not only with the preceding (*sobbing* like *the sound of doves* cooing), but also with the following: people *beating on their breasts* sounding like fluttering *doves*. The verb for *beating on their breasts* is rare.[288] The *poel* stem here may indicate the intensity of repeated beating. Given that *breasts* are literally "hearts," the reference may also be to fast-beating (fluttering) hearts.[289]

8(9) The first half of this verse, too, has been the subject of much discussion with many commentators who consider the MT corrupt and meaningless. Pinker objects that *Nineveh* cannot be likened to *a pool of waters* and suggests an emendation to produce "Its waters are as a pool, and Nineveh is an isle."[290] This would link well with 3:8, which pictures Thebes situated on

---

284. Dobbs-Allsopp's suggestion that "Nineveh personified as a goddess figure is the subject" (*Weep*, 129) might further address this problem and introduces an irony to the picture of the city being *offered up* in sacrifice.

285. Gen 25:16 (*'ummōtām*); Num 25:15 (*'ummôt*); Ps 117:1 (*'ummîm*). Cf. the related and more common root *lə'ôm* ("people"; e.g., Prov 11:26), which occurs twenty-six of thirty-one times in the plural *lə'ummîm*, "nations" (e.g., Gen 25:23).

286. Cf. the apparent double rendering of the root in Tg. and Vulg. If *BHS* is followed in emending to *mənōhăgôt hōgôt* ("led away murmuring"), a comparable poetic effect is achieved. (For *mənuhăgôt* being elongated to *mənōhăgôt*, see *HGHS* 50l; cf. *yəgō'ălû*, Ezra 2:62 // Neh 7:64.)

287. See Cathcart, *Nahum*, 98–99; Dobbs-Allsopp, *Weep*, 130.

288. The root *tāpap* is used in the *qal* for beating tambourines in Ps 68:25(26) and has been conjectured for MT *tāwāh* in 1 Sam 21:13[14] in BDB and *HALOT*. See Cathcart, *Nahum*, 99–100, for examples in Ugaritic and Phoenician.

289. Imaginative readers may also be reminded of the prophet Jonah, whose name means "dove," and hear the *maids* pronouncing doom on Nineveh like Jonah.

290. Aron Pinker, "Nineveh—An Isle Is She," *ZAW* 116 (2004): 403–5. This requires a different word division at one point, the reversal of two letters, and the transposition of "Nineveh" to a different part of the sentence. The first change is entirely feasible, the second defensible, but the combination of all three asks for too much in my view.

waters (cf. Jer 51:13, where Babylon is described similarly). But the image of Nineveh as an isle stretches the imagination no less than the comparison with *a pool of waters*, even if one were to grant to Pinker the strategic importance of the four rivers enclosing the plain on which Nineveh was located (about 25 miles long and 14 miles wide). It may be more accurate from a military point of view to describe Nineveh as an isle,[291] but the comparison to a water pool is not absurd and has greater poetic effect. Nineveh's famous water system included a reservoir north of the city and wetlands and maybe even the (misnamed) "Hanging Gardens of Babylon."[292] Spronk suggests that the meaning of the name "Nineveh," namely "house of fishes," may have influenced the choice of this simile.[293]

The Hebrew phrase here rendered *since her days* is more literally "from the days of her." The translation interprets the phrase along the lines of the expression "from the days of PN" where PN is the name of a king (2 Chr 30:26; Ezra 4:2; Jer 36:2) or national leader (Samuel in 2 Chr 35:18 and Joshua in Neh 8:17). In this latter expression, the reference is not to someone's total lifetime but to the time of their prominence and power. Thus, *since her days* could be circumscribed as "ever since she rose to prominence and power." Indeed, Nineveh has not been *like a pool of waters* "throughout her days" (NASB) but throughout the days of her preeminence, ever since Sennacherib made the city the capital of Assyria and constructed the reservoir and wetlands habitat. Sennacherib's measures not only served to control the flow of rivers but also ensured that Nineveh was surrounded by lush and green countryside and that its orchards were well watered.[294]

If water that is channeled for human benefit is a sign of order, a reservoir whose waters run away is worse than useless. Some may object to the quick change from the image of waters flooding into the city and undermining the palace, hinted at in v. 6(7), to the image of waters draining away in this verse. There are ways around this. One may either disallow any watery connotations in v. 6(7) or interpret the second half of the present verse with exclusive reference to people. But this seems quite unnecessary. Nahum contrasts the concept of orderly confined waters (Nineveh at its height) with

---

291. Pinker's concern in a number of essays on Nah 2–3 is to demonstrate that Nahum reflects detailed knowledge of military-strategic factors relevant for the defence and capture of Nineveh. I am not persuaded that historical accuracy and precision is uppermost on Nahum's authorial mind(s).

292. See the references in the commentary on v. 6(7).

293. Spronk, *Nahum*, 100.

294. Cf. Julian E. Reade, "Studies in Assyrian Geography, Part II: The Northern Canal System," *RA* 72 (1978): 157–80, who notes (pp. 173–75) that the economic benefit of most of the canals was likely small. The principal aim was rather "to improve the landscape and living conditions of the two great cities [Kalhu and Nineveh]" (174).

the concept of water transgressing its boundaries (Nineveh's fall). The chaos of waters reflects the chaos among people as they flee in terror. Just as the water flow from a leaking reservoir is not stopped by shouting *"Stop! Stop!"* so the people running away from their homes are not stopped in their tracks by the shouts, as *no one* even *turns around* to see what is happening. The remarkable frequency of *m* sounds in this verse (9×), maybe along with five occurrences of *n*, is suggestive of the flowing movement this verse portrays. The Masoretes may have sought to imitate Nineveh's unstoppable draining away by reducing the number of poetic stops, accentuating the verse as two very long cola.

9(10) As the inhabitants flee, the raiders move in, and we hear more shouting. The direct speech is commonly limited to the two imperatives *"Plunder silver! Plunder gold!"* echoing the *"Stop! Stop!"* of the previous verse. But the whole verse may possibly be from the lips of the attackers as they see (note the contrast with those refusing to look around in the previous verse!) the marvelous and apparently unlimited assets of Nineveh for the first time. The extra-long line *wealth more than all precious objects* imitates poetically the weight of the treasures. The point of view from which Nineveh's possessions are described here is naturally different from the perspective offered later in v. 12(13).

10(11) The Hebrew words rendered *desolation, destruction, and devastation* hint not only at the damage done to the city but also the emptiness that results from the plundering the previous verse pictures. Interestingly, the same combination of the roots *bqq* ("devastate") and *bzz* ("plunder") comprise another example of soundplay in Isa 24:3: *hibbôq tibbôq hā'āreṣ wǝhibbôz tibbôz* ("utterly desolate the earth and utterly plundered").[295] Assonance and alliteration also provide great cohesion for this first line, which may encourage us to take it separately as a single-line summary of the result of the attack followed by a unit of three lines that focus on the physiological effect of this disaster.[296]

After the initial flood of hormones that put the body on high alert (cf. v. 8[9]) comes a general feeling of weakness.[297] The increased heartrate leads to palpitations or *fainting hearts*; muscle tensions and disturbances of the

---

295. Cf. *hinnê yhwh bôqēq hā'āreṣ ûbôlqāh* ("Look! YHWH is about to devastate the earth and to desolate it") in Isa 24:1.

296. Alternatively, it is possible to scan the verse as two bicola, the first summarizing the external and internal effect of the catastrophe, the second focusing on the internal effect and cohering in the use of *all.*

297. The "contradiction" between people running away from the destruction above and the picture of people rendered unable to function apparently in the midst of the desolation is similar to the "contradiction" observed above of waters flooding into the city and draining away from it.

nervous system make for *knees that totter*. Abdominal and intestinal discomfort as well as the need to urinate or defecate are frequently physiological responses to anxiety, here maybe referred to as *trembling in all loins*. With fear blood goes to the large skeletal muscles, making the face blanch. Thus, the common translation of the last line in terms of faces growing pale fits the context very well. But the justification in terms of the actual Hebrew wording (see translation note yy) is not unproblematic. The present rendering as *all their faces are flushed with fear*, playing on two senses of the English "flush" ("redden" and "wash out"), accepts the likelihood that the common physiological reaction of drained facial colors is in view, while accepting that if it were not for the context here and in Joel 2:6, the Hebrew might be rendered more naturally as "blushing."

Might the physical and emotional description offered in this verse reflect the metaphor of "a woman giving birth," which is used elsewhere to indicate a crisis (cf. Isa 13:7–8; 21:3; Jer 30:6)?[298] The text neither requires nor prevents this, but bringing the metaphor to bear upon it might risk reading the text against its grain.[299]

Reflection

We have observed that the images of the fall of Nineveh are painted in poetic colors that are suggestive of ideologies more than descriptive of actual military practice. Chariots were a status symbol, prestige vehicles that on numerous reliefs as well as in real life heralded the power of the Assyrian king. Chariots were used in royal lion hunts (cf. the following verses), but more importantly, the sight of the royal chariot was probably as close as most Israelites and Judahites would get to an encounter with the Assyrian king. Chariots symbolize Assyrian power. Nahum, therefore, relishes the uselessness of Assyrian chariots in the defense of Nineveh. The portrayal of feverish but futile preparations against the attack serves a similar purpose, revealing Assyrian powerlessness in the face of this *scatterer*. In stark contrast to Assyrian depictions, which invariably portray a well-ordered Assyrian army effortlessly putting its enemies to flight, Nahum's images show us the Assyrian army in disarray and confusion.

Read as the canonical word of God, these images can engender the confi-

298. Claudia Bergmann, "We Have Seen the Enemy, and He Is Only a 'She': The Portrayal of Warriors as Women," *CBQ* 69 (2007): 664.

299. Bergmann ("We Have Seen") argues that, unlike characterizing men as women (cf. 3:13), describing the crisis by utilizing the concept of a woman in labor is meant to evoke sympathy among the readers. See below for further reflection.

dence expressed in the words of the psalmist, "In God, whose word I praise, in God I trust; I shall not be afraid. What can flesh do to me?" (Ps 56:4[5]; cf. 27:1; 118:6). Those who have a proper assessment of God's power need not fear human powers (cf., e.g., Matt 10:16–39). Those who can be confident that God is for them need not fear even death itself (cf., e.g., Rom 8:31–39).

Images like these that portray the limits of Assyrian power are surely designed to convince us of the limits of all human power. This may be one reason why the human agent is barely in focus in the actual defeat of Nineveh. We see the preparations (v. 3[4]) and the plundering (v. 9[10]) but the action in between is described more indirectly. Nahum has sometimes been considered bloodthirsty, but there is in fact no description of the actual combat and bloodshed here. There will be more dead bodies in ch. 3, although even there the killing itself is not the focus. The function of poetry such as this is akin to a taunt. Nahum's "war poetry" does not celebrate heroic deeds but encourages its audience not to think too highly of the powers that threaten them.

Water is another motif of some significance in this chapter. In the ancient Near East, as in many other regions of the world, water is known to be precious. Assyria's wealth and power could be measured not least in its ability to manipulate water resources for its own good. But like the Egyptians, Mesopotamian peoples also knew something of the damage inundations can cause if they get out of control, and the sea was widely feared among them. Thus, water is symbolic in more than one way. While the (raging) sea is a symbol of chaos, the (gentle flowing) river is a symbol of provision. Inundations remind one of the forces of disorder; reservoirs are a sign of order. Assyria's elaborate water system can thus function as a symbol of the order Assyria imposes on the world. The opening of the gates of the rivers (v. 6[7]) and the depiction of Nineveh as a leaking water reservoir (v. 8[9]) signal the end of the Assyrian world order. Elsewhere, the Bible expands on this to state that all empires and dominions will come to an end "until the God of heaven will set up a kingdom that will never be destroyed" (Dan 2:44). At that time, "the kingdom, the dominion and the greatness of the kingdoms under the whole heaven will be given to the holy people of the Most High" (Dan 7:27).

As we muse over the text and its implications, we may be willing to explore additional readings, exploiting some of the poetic ambiguities. In this spirit, one can observe that *to restore the pride of Jacob* to become again *as the* former *pride of Israel*, YHWH has to "turn aside the pride of Jacob," namely the "pride of Jacob" that stands over against him (e.g., Amos 6:8).[300] Maybe

---

300. Similarly, *gə'ôn-mô'āb* ("the pride of Moab") in Isa 16:6 and Jer 48:29 is clearly a reference to arrogance, as is probably *gə'ôn-yiśrā'ēl* ("the pride of Israel") in Hos 5:5; 7:10. See further maybe *gə'ôn 'aššûr* ("the pride of Assyria") in Zech 10:11 and *gə'ôn pəlištîm* ("the

he has done this in the past through Assyrian oppression.[301] But if YHWH himself is the true "pride of Jacob" (cf. maybe Amos 8:7), then he will be zealous to be recognized as such, putting to shame those among Jacob whose pride is Assyria.

The defeat of evil brings with it humiliation. This motif is certainly present as far as the population of Nineveh is concerned (vv. 7[8], 10[11]). But because it features much more prominently in ch. 3, we will reflect about this further below. Witnessing such a humiliation, even if only in the world of the text, can be embarrassing, and the final verse in particular may invite our sympathy for Nineveh. But we are not invited by Nahum to esteem Nineveh highly; sympathy for its people should compel readers to action that avoids a similar fate. The text does not prevent sympathy for Nineveh of the sort that leads to resentfulness toward YHWH, the ultimate author of Nineveh's fate. But the text makes it very difficult to identify with both Nineveh and YHWH. Our identification with YHWH, however, need not produce glee either. In my view, the text is carefully balanced and can guide us toward an emotional response that is neither misplaced sympathy for Nineveh nor self-satisfied glee over its downfall.[302] Nineveh and other opponents of YHWH need not be feared, and their downfall brings relief to the oppressed.

VII. RIDICULE OF THE KING OF NINEVEH (2:11-12[12-13])

11(12) *Where is the dwelling place*a *of the lions*
   *and the feeding ground*b *of the young lions?*
*Where the lion went, the lioness*c *was there,*
   *the lion cub, and none to frighten them.*d
12(13) *The lion was tearing enough for*e *his cubs*f
   *and strangling*g *for his lionesses;*h
      *he filled his holes*i *with prey*
         *and his hiding places*j *with torn flesh.*k

a. Hebrew *məʿôn* (*dwelling place*) is usually rendered more specifically as "den" or "lair," but this may obscure the rhetoric of the verse (see commentary); *məʿôn* is elsewhere used for a den of animals only in Jeremiah's phrase *məʿôn tannîm* ("dwelling place of jackals") for a devastated city (9:11[10]; 10:22; 49:33; 51:37). Note the feminine *məʿônâ* in the next verse.

pride of the Philistines") in Zech 9:6, contra Burnett, "Pride of Jacob," 324, who considers the former a reference to Nineveh and the latter a reference to Ashdod.

301. As noted above, this is how Fabry, *Nahum*, 168–69, understands the text.

302. Cf. the commentary on 3:19. Those who have read Jonah as well as Nahum will have learned that the terror brought upon Nineveh does not reflect lack of concern on YHWH's part.

b. Hebrew *mir'ê* is used elsewhere only for the "pasture" of grass-eating animals. Wellhausen's suggestion to reverse the middle consonants, reading *mə'ārâ* ("cave"), is frequently accepted (e.g., *BHS*; Cathcart, *Nahum*, 105–6; Roberts, *Nahum*, 62), and it is reflected in some English translations (e.g., RSV, NRSV, NJB). But the change produces awkward syntax, unless *hû'* is also changed to *hî'*. If MT is retained (with all ancient versions), there may be a particular reason for identifying the lions' hunting ground as their "pasture"; see the commentary. Maier (*Nahum*, 279) tries to circumvent the problem by interpreting as "fodder," which he takes as the object of *lābî'*, understood in a verbal sense (see below).

c. Hebrew *lābî'* (*lioness*); see the excursus below for a discussion of the term. LXX, Syr., and Vulg. have a verbal form instead, and many adopt a change to *lābô'* ("to enter"; e.g., Roberts, *Nahum*, 62), found also in one medieval Hebrew manuscript (Spronk, *Nahum*, 105). Arnold B. Ehrlich (*Ezechiel und die Kleinen Propheten*, vol. 5 of *Randglossen zur Hebräischen Bibel: Textkritisches, Sprachliches und Sachliches* [Leipzig: Hinrichs'sche Buchhandlung, 1912], 296) and Alfred O. Haldar (*Studies in the Book of Nahum*, UUA 7 [Uppsala: Uppsala Universitet, 1947]) read *lābî'* as *hiphil* infinitive of *bô'* ("to bring"), written defectively as in 2 Chr 31:10; Jer 39:7. So also Maier, *Nahum*, 280, who identifies the object as *mir'ê*, understood as "fodder," thereby giving the *young lions* an unduly passive role (see below).

d. The masoretic accentuation of the second half of the verse (*Where . . .*) is unusual, suggesting that the whole sentence is considered one colon of nine feet (word units). Similarly, the next verse consists of only three poetic segments, reading the two verses as a set of two tricola rather than two quatrains, as in my translation.

e. Hebrew *bədê* is more literally "in the sufficiency of"—i.e., as much as the whelps needed.

f. Hebrew *gōrôtāyw* corresponds to *gûr 'aryê* in the previous verse (cf. *gôrê 'ărāyôt* in Jer 51:38). No semantic difference between *gûr* and *gôr* is evident.

g. Hebrew *məhannēq* (*piel* participle); the other occurrence of the root *ḥnq* in the Bible is in 2 Sam 17:23, for Ahithophel hanging himself (*niphal*).

h. Hebrew *lib'ōtāyw* is a plural of *ləbiyyā'* (elsewhere only Ezek 19:2), a variation on *lābî'* in the previous verse.

i. Hebrew *ḥōr* (*ḥūr/ḥûr* in Isa 11:8; 42:22) commonly designates a small hole (hole in chest, 2 Kgs 12:10; hole in wall, Ezek 8:7; eye socket, Zech 14:12; keyhole [?] in Song 5:4) or is used derogatively for human hiding places (1 Sam 14:11; Job 30:6).

j. The singular *mə'ōnâ* is used for God as dwelling place (Deut 33:27), for Zion as his dwelling place (Ps 76:2[3]), and for a lion's hiding place (Amos 3:4), for which see Edward R. Hope, "Problems of Interpretation in Amos 3.4," *BT* 42 (1991): 201–5. The plural *mə'ōnôt* always refers to the hideouts of animals (Job 37:8; 38:40; Ps 104:22; Song 4:8 and here), except for Jer 21:13 ("hiding places").

k. Hebrew *ṭərēpâ*, unlike *ṭerep* (*prey*) in the previous line, is never used with positive connotations.

Composition

These two verses can be closely connected to the surrounding material, but they also form a tightly knit poetic unit on their own. We have two quatrains (smaller units of four lines each) that together can be considered arranged as a palistrophe. The key words are as follows:

A dwelling place
B feeding ground
   C lioness
      D lion's cub
      D' his cubs
   C' his lionesses
B' his holes
A' his hiding places

The references to lionesses and cubs not only change from singular to plural but also employ slightly different forms (see the excursus below on the words used to refer to lions). The standard terms for a (male) lion are found in the first, second, and fourth lines of verse 11(12) and the first line of verse 12(13).[303] These are lines A, B, D, and D' above. Lines C', B', and A' refer to the (adult) male lion by pronouns. This suggests an emphasis on the (adult) male lion, presumably referencing the Assyrian king. There seem to be a movement from more open areas (see commentary) to a more confined area and a shift of focus from the lions in the first quatrain to more explicit references to their prey in the second quatrain. Maybe we are encouraged to imagine the lions hunting and returning to their hideout with prey. But the single word *'ayê* (*where is?*) acts like the minus sign in front of a high number. Gone are the Assyrian lions—and not only from the hunting grounds of their empire. They are not to be found in their hideout (Nineveh) either. And gone is all their prey.

Commentary

11(12) The rhetorical question in the first half of the verse implies that Nineveh, the place where the Assyrian "lions" devoured their prey, is gone. But the specific use of terms here suggests that more is going on. The *dwelling place* of the lions was no mere cave but broad, open country that served as their *feeding ground*. English translations that adopt the change to "cave" (see the translation notes) obviously produce a different sense. The same applies to a rendering such as "the place where they fed their young" (NIV; cf. LXX[304]), which misinterprets *young lions* as lions that are still being fed and so suggests an ordinary hideout. But *young lions* are no longer whelps

---

303. The very first occurrence is the plural of *'ărî*, the others are the singular of *'aryê*.

304. The LXX uses *skymnos* ("whelp") here. But in Ezek 19:2, *skymnos* renders both *ləbiyyā'* ("lioness") and *gûr* ("cub"), while *leōn* is used for *'ărî* ("lion") and *kəpîr* ("young

(see further below). Elsewhere in Scripture, we regularly encounter such *young lions* on the attack (e.g., Judg 14:5; Ps 35:17; Isa 5:29; Hos 5:14), and in Proverbs they are suggestive of danger (19:12; 20:2) and courage (28:1). The present verse either makes a point of the sheer size of this particular "lion's den" (cf. the regular use of *gǝdôlâ*, "great," with Nineveh in the book of Jonah and the reference to its size in Jonah 3:3) or does not distinguish between the place of hunting and the place of eating. In effect, it designates all the countries that the Assyrians conquered ("hunted") as their territory—space of which they were securely in control so that even their *cubs* could move freely. This at any rate is how the second bicolon (*Where the lion went . . . none to frighten them*) could be understood. The whole pride of lions moves freely, as if the whole world were their home. The Assyrians felt no need to withdraw to a hidden den to feel safe: wherever the lions went, there were *none to frighten them.*

EXCURSUS: DIFFERENT HEBREW TERMS FOR LIONS

Archaeological evidence documents the long history of human fascination with lions.[305] We do not know, however, how much Israelites knew about lions and how much of this knowledge is reflected in the various Hebrew terms for lions.[306] Some knowledge of leonine behavior would be helpful in a (semi-)pastoral society, whose flocks and herds were threatened by lions, even if the threat was only very occasional.[307] The lion that roamed the Jordan valley and other parts of the land was likely the Asiatic lion (*Panthera leo persica*),[308] which ranged in historical times from Turkey to India and

---

lion"). This suggests that translators in antiquity had similar problems with differentiating the Hebrew terms for "lion."

305. See Brent A. Strawn, *What Is Stronger Than a Lion? Leonine Image and Metaphor in the Hebrew Bible and the Ancient Near East*, OBO 212 (Göttingen: Vandenhoeck & Ruprecht; Fribourg: Presses Universitaires, 2005), 293–326. See also Renz, "The Colour Red and the Lion King," 163–77; and David J. A. Clines, "Misapprehensions, Ancient and Modern, about Lions (Nah 2,13)," in *Poets, Prophets, and Texts in Play: Studies in Biblical Poetry and Prophecy in Honour of Francis Landy*, ed. Ehud Ben Zvi et al., LHBOTS 597 (London: Bloomsbury T&T Clark, 2015), 58–76.

306. Hebrew terms for animals are often problematic for exegetes and translators; e.g., *šû'āl* is usually rendered "fox" (e.g., Judg 15:4) but is now often thought to refer to a *jackal* (*HALOT*). See the commentary on Hab 1:8 and Zeph 2:14.

307. Strawn, *Lion*, 28–29, argues that lions were more prevalent than some scholars believe; see also pp. 37–43 on the lion's habitat and, more indirectly, pp. 77–128 on the archaeological record.

308. So, e.g., Norman A. Khalaf-von Jaffa, "Felidae Palaestina: The Wild Cats of Pales-

from the Caucasus to Yemen. It is not clear whether the African lion spread eastward from Egypt,[309] but the Assyrians apparently brought African lions back from their Egyptian campaigns.[310]

Nahum makes use of all the main Hebrew terms for lions. Of these, the most common in the Hebrew Bible are *'ărî* (33×) and *'aryê* (47×).[311] It is not clear what if any difference there is between the two terms. Only the former is attested in the plural (*'ărāyôt*), once in the phrase *kəpîr 'ărāyôt* (Judg 14:5).[312]

Kəpîr occurs thirty-one times and may refer to a *young lion*, but it does not refer to a whelp, for which the term *gûr* is used. Ezek 19:2–3 (and 5–6) identifies the point at which a *gûr* (*cub*) becomes a *kəpîr* (*young lion*) as the time when it learns to catch its own prey.[313] Lions begin to display stalking behavior very early on but only begin to hunt effectively when nearing the age of two. As Packer observes, "Males show early signs of mane growth when they reach full body size at about 2 years of age, but their manes do not reach full size until they are about 4–5 years old."[314] This is the time at which

---

tine," *Gazelle: The Palestinian Biological Bulletin* 52 (2006): 1–15. Friedrich Simon Bodenheimer (*Animal and Man in Bible Lands* [Leiden: Brill, 1960], 42) seemed to think that African and Asiatic lions met in the Middle East; Strawn, *Lion*, 30–31, remains uncommitted. See now Annik E. Schnitzler, "Past and Present Distribution of the North African–Asian Lion Subgroup: A Review," *Mammal Review* 41 (2011): 220–43.

309. Several subspecies of the African lion are frequently distinguished. The North African type is the Barbary lion (*Panthera leo leo*) that was used in Roman circuses and is now extinct. Kristin Nowell and Peter Jackson observe that we seem to have "no record of contiguous populations of [this subspecies and the Asiatic lion] in historic times"; see their *Wild Cats: Status Survey and Conservation Action Plan* published by the International Union for Conservation of Nature and Natural Resources (Cambridge: Burlington Press, 1996), 37.

310. Cf. Eric William Heaton, *Everyday Life in Old Testament Times* (London: Batsford, 1956), 113; Roland K. Harrison, "Lion," *ISBE*, 3:141–42. For zoological parks in ancient Mesopotamia generally, see also Bodenheimer, *Animal*, 87.

311. In addition, *'ărî* occurs twice as *qere* for *ketiv 'aryê* (2 Sam 23:20; Lam 3:10), and Aramaic *'aryê* occurs ten times in Daniel. The two words are orthographically close, but there is no agreement about whether they are etymologically related; cf. Strawn, *Lion*, 294–95. A preference for the latter can be observed in Isaiah and Jeremiah, but the distribution does not follow any neat pattern.

312. Note that other terms for "lion" found in poetic texts whose meaning is less certain, namely *layiš* (attested only in Job 4:11; Prov 30:30; Isa 30:6) and *šaḥal* (Job 4:10; 10:16; 28:8; Ps 91:13; Prov 26:13; Hos 5:14; 13:7), are also only attested in the singular. See Strawn, *Lion*, 325–26 for the former, 322–25 for the latter.

313. Cf. Strawn, *Lion*, 309. Amos 3:4 also implies that the *kəpîr* has caught its own prey, and note the "young lion among the flocks of sheep" in Mic 5:8(7). Note that while lions are known to be the most social among cats, they hunt individually as well as together. The popular idea that only females hunt is not correct; see further below.

314. Craig Packer, "Lion," in *The Encyclopedia of Mammals*, ed. David W. Macdonald

young males leave their pride, if they have not been forced out earlier. If the Hebrew term *kəpîr* implies youth,[315] it seems most suitable as a reference to young lions that have reached full body size and are able to hunt independently. Such young (male) lions do not yet have any pride or territory commitments but form coalitions with other (male) lions with whom they will look out for a new pride and its territory. Once they succeed in taking over a territory and gaining tenure of a pride, they kill all the cubs and sire new ones. Maybe this is the point at which an *'ărî*/*'aryê* (*lion*) is no longer a *kəpîr* (*young lion*). In any case, the translation *young lions* must not obscure the fact that these are fully grown and dangerous animals. It is doubtful that YHWH would compare himself to a *kəpîr* (Isa 31:4; Hos 5:14) or that Pharaoh could be called *kəpîr gôyīm* ("a young lion among the nations," Ezek 32:2) if it were otherwise.

Gwr (*cub*), pointed in two different ways, occurs nine times.[316] Its Semitic cognates do not always refer to a lion's *cub*, but this seems to be always the reference in the Bible, maybe except for Lam 4:3. The decisive feature, as discussed above, seems to be that the *cub* is too young to hunt.

Lioness(es) translates two closely related Hebrew terms: the more common *lābî'* (v. 11[12]), which is always used in the singular,[317] and *lib'ōtāyw* (v. 12[13]), a plural form (with suffix) of the root *lib'â* (or possibly *lābā'*) not otherwise attested in the MT.[318] The view that *lābî'* and its derivatives, which are all found in poetic texts only, refers to the Asian type, contrasted with *'ărî* and *'aryê* for the African lion, is sometimes still contemplated.[319] But

---

(Oxford: Oxford University Press, 2006), 630. His entries "Lion" (pp. 628–33) and "Why Lions Roar" (pp. 634–35) provide a good summary of our knowledge of lions.

315. There has been little disagreement about this (see BDB; *HALOT*; G. Johannes Botterweck, "אֲרִי, *ʾrî*, etc.," *TDOT* 1:376), but the evidence is not decisive. *DCH* allows for Dahood's suggestion that the term refers to "tawny lion" instead (cf. *kōper*, "henna"), but Strawn (*Lion*, 309) considers this far-fetched.

316. The common form is *gûr* (v. 11[12]; cf. Gen 49:9; Deut 33:22; Lam 4:3; Ezek 19:2–3, 5); for *gōrōt* in v. 12(13), cf. *gōr* in Jer 51:38. Apart from Nah 2:12(13), the plural takes the masculine form (Jer 51:38; Lam 4:3; Ezek 19:2–3, 5).

317. Gen 49:9; Num 23:24; 24:9; Deut 33:20; Job 4:11; 38:39; Isa 5:29; 30:6; Hos 13:8; Joel 1:6. In addition, the MT reads *ləbiyyā'* in Ezek 19:2, which should be retained; cf. *HALOT* (a secondary formation); Strawn, *Lion*, 311–12 (the feminine form).

318. Cf. *ləbā'îm* in Ps 57:5, from *lebe'*, also not otherwise attested (so *HGHS* 72p' n. 1; cf. *HALOT*). The Samaritan Pentateuch has *lbyh* (*libyâ*) instead of *lby'* (*lābî'*) in Gen 49:9; Num 23:24; 24:9; Deut 33:20 (cf. *DCH*; it also reads *'aryê* for *'ărî* in the Numbers passages). BDB seems mistaken in deriving *lib'ōtāyw* from *ləbiyyā'* and *ləbā'îm* from *ləbî*.

319. E.g., G. Johannes Botterweck, "אֲרִי, *ʾrî*, etc.," *TDOT* 1:376–77. The view seems to go back to Ludwig Köhler, "Lexikologisch-Geographisches," *ZDPV* 62 (1939): 115–25, who appealed to the alleged Asiatic versus African origin of the words. But see Strawn, *Lion*, 296–97, 300–304.

one would expect in this case the more common terms, namely *'ărî* and *'aryê* (also Aramaic), to refer to the better-known animal, which is probably the Asiatic lion. In addition, passages like Nah 2 would then seem to imply that Asiatic and African lions were thought to live together in prides. If the Hebrews used different terms to distinguish subspecies, they would hardly have pictured Asiatic and African lions in one pride. It also needs to be remarked that the outward appearance of these two subspecies is not as distinct as is sometimes claimed.[320]

In my view, it seems more likely that the different terms preserve a distinction that was more easily observed. This lends plausibility to the view that *lābî'* (and its derivatives) refers to an adult lion without a mane—that is, usually the female of the species.[321] While it has to be admitted that the common translation as *lioness* is by no means certain,[322] it fits the context well in that the picture is clearly of a pride of lions, and so one might expect a reference to both males and females as well as cubs and adults. The popular idea that only females hunt seems to be based on the observation of lions in open areas like the Serengeti. But this is not correct for woodland savannas. There, male lions have been observed as active hunters. While lionesses do most of the hunting, male lions have to hunt during their bachelor stage (see above), and male involvement appears to increase in areas of high grass or thick foliage that allow surprise attacks.[323]

320. The two subspecies are genetically closer than some human ethnic groups. The Asiatic lion may have been slightly smaller. It has a fold of skin that runs along the belly, and the mane leaves the ears free, but both features are sometimes found with African lions. Already Bodenheimer (*Animal*, 42) remarked on the variations within the subspecies. Observations of Asiatic lions in the wild today are limited to one population and should be used only with caution for generalizations. Strawn (*Lion*, 32) also stresses the similarities.

321. Benno Landsberger (*The Fauna of Ancient Mesopotamia*, Materials for the Sumerian Lexicon 8 [Rome: Pontificium Institutum Biblicum, 1962], 76) observes that in Akkadian, *nēšu* (to which Hebrew *layiš* may be related) is the more prosaic and *lābu* (cf. Hebrew *lābî'*, etc.) the more poetic term but suggests that in old Semitic, the former was the male and the latter the female lion. But Strawn (*Lion*, 313–14, 318) points to the existence of masculine and feminine derivatives of the common Semitic root to argue against this.

322. Strawn (*Lion*, 311–19) concludes that only the feminine forms in Ezek 19:2 (see above) and here in Nah 2:13 refer to the lioness. Medieval commentators sometimes understood *lābî'* to refer to an older lion; see Abraham J. Rosenberg, *The Book of the Twelve Prophets: A New English Translation of the Text, Rashi, and a Commentary Digest*, vol. 2, Judaica Book of the Prophets (New York: Judaica Press, 1988), 249.

323. Male lions are 20 to 35 percent larger than the females and 50 percent heavier. It is therefore no surprise that a labor division has sometimes been observed, with male lions hunting particularly large prey such as buffalo and giraffe.

12(13) This verse focuses on the prey. The comment about *tearing enough for his cubs* is striking in the light of the observation that whelps are the last in the lion pride to get any food. In times of scarcity, lions have a high cub mortality rate because the weaker and smaller lions get to eat from the prey only after the strong lions have eaten their fill and only if there are any leftovers, which is not always the case. The second comment is surprising because it is much more common for *lionesses* to kill for their (male) lions.[324] It has been suggested that Nahum did not know this, which may be true, but the word *strangling* is particularly apt. It may indicate that the Israelites understood that lions usually kill their prey by strangulation, often suffocating their victims with a throat bite, and thus suggests some knowledge of lions. Assuming that the translation *lionesses* is correct (see the excursus above for discussion), the incongruity lends further support to the view that Nahum presents an allegory rather than just a general picture. The *lion* represents the Assyrian ruler, the *lionesses* may be his wives and concubines, the *young lions* might stand for the soldiers of the Assyrian army and maybe state officials, and the *cubs* would then represent the general population.[325]

Possibly, *məʿōnâ* (*hiding place*) describes a more closely circumscribed space than the *məʿôn* (*dwelling place*) used in the previous verse, but this is uncertain. The feminine *məʿōnâ* may have been chosen to match the gender of *ṭərēpâ* (*torn flesh*), just as masculine *ṭerep* (*prey*) matches the gender of *ḥōr* (*hole*).[326] If the precise connotation of the term *məʿōnâ* (*hiding place*) is unclear, *holes* certainly leads us to think of a narrow space and so affects our understanding of *hiding place*, especially since *holes* are mentioned first due to gender-matching parallelism and the needs of the palistrophe (see above). The description is not naturalistic. Lions do not live in narrowly circumscribed spaces like dens or lairs, except in zoos. They roam and rarely return to the same place to sleep for any length of time.[327] We have moved from the "pasture" of the previous verse to the hideout, Nineveh itself. The use of *torn flesh* in the last line keeps the focus on the violence involved in the kill as much as its food potential.

---

324. It was observed above that, while it is not true that male lions do not hunt, lionesses are responsible for the majority of kills.

325. Cf. Roberts, *Nahum*, 67, following Rudolph, *Micha*, 173. Cf. already Tg. ("kings," "princes," "consorts," "children") and medieval commentators (Rosenberg, *Twelve Prophets*, 249).

326. See Wilfred G. E. Watson ("Gender-Matched Synonymous Parallelism in the OT," *JBL* 99 [1980]: 321–41) for a discussion of the phenomenon, and note my discussion of the inversion of gender-matching in the commentary on the following verse.

327. This was pointed out by Hope ("Problems") for Amos 3:4; cf. Strawn, *Lion*, 38.

EXCURSUS: LION IMAGERY IN ASSYRIA

While lions play a part in the art and ideology of peoples throughout the ancient Near East,[328] they feature very prominently in Assyria. Lions are frequently depicted in Assyrian reliefs and decorations, the royal lion hunt was a potent symbol (only kings were permitted to hunt lions), and Assyrian monarchs liked to style themselves as "lions" with phrases like "I roared like a lion" or "raging like a lion."[329] Intriguingly, Assurbanipal (c. 668–627), the king who was likely on the Assyrian throne when these verses were composed, seems to have revived the royal sport of hunting lions. His annals produce more references to lion hunts than those of any other Assyrian king, and he boasted that he killed lions with bare hands, helped only by Ishtar.[330] Apparently, unusually high rainfalls provided more cover for lions and allowed them to expand their hunting grounds and increase their number.[331] It is no surprise, then, that the largest number of sculptures and murals depicting lion hunts are those Assurbanipal commissioned for his palace in Nineveh.[332] They show the Assyrian king as a mighty warrior to whom even "the king of the beasts" must submit and thus also represent his conquest over (human) enemies. Inscriptions confirm the close association made here between the Assyrian king and the divine realm. The royal lion hunt probably had ritual significance as well, designed to avert not only the harm of a lion plague but evil in all its forms.[333] Berlejung notes that Assurbanipal sought to symbolically secure the eighteen gates of the capital by killing eighteen lions.[334]

---

328. See, e.g., Izak Cornelius, "The Lion in the Art of the Ancient Near East: A Study of Selected Motifs," *JNSL* 15 (1989): 53–85; Strawn, *Lion*, 131–228.

329. Cf. Gordon H. Johnston, "Nahum's Rhetorical Allusions to the Neo-Assyrian Lion Motif," *BSac* 158 (2001): 287–307; Michael B. Dick, "The Neo-Assyrian Royal Lion-Hunt and Yahweh's Answer to Job," *JBL* 125 (2006): 243–70; Strawn, *Lion*, 163–72, 178–80; Chikako Esther Watanabe, *Animal Symbolism in Mesopotamia: A Contextual Approach*, Wiener Offene Orientalistik 1 (Vienna: Institut für Orientalistik, 2002), 42–56, 83–88; Davide Nadali, "Neo-Assyrian State Seals: An Allegory of Power," *State Archives of Assyria Bulletin* 28 (2009–2010): 215–44.

330. Cf. Johnston, "Lion Motif," 299.

331. See *ARAB*, 2:391–92. Cf. Bodenheimer, *Animal*, 89–90; Johnston, "Lion Motif," 300.

332. Cf. Johnston, "Lion Motif," 301. Reade, *Assyrian Sculpture*, devotes a whole chapter to "the hunts of Ashurbanipal" (pp. 72–79); cf. Strawn, *Lion*, 167–72.

333. See Strawn, *Lion*, 169–70, and Watanabe, *Animal Symbolism*, 76–88, for the evidence that points in this direction.

334. Berlejung, "Erinnerungen," 334.

Reflection

We have observed that the lion imagery was particularly apposite in an Assyrian context, and especially so during the reign of Assurbanipal, the time during which Nahum was likely written in my view. But the lion imagery is very well suited also for any prophecy that seeks further fulfillments; the lack of specific reference to Assurbanipal, or anyone else, both facilitates such seeking of further fulfillments and encourages us to apply the prophecy more widely. Lion imagery is used positively as well as negatively in other parts of Scripture. Its significance here must be governed by the literary context. *Lion* in this passage communicates dominating (v. 11[12]) and rapacious (v. 12[13]) behavior. With its predictive elements elsewhere (note the following verse!), the book of Nahum suggests that the rhetorical question *Where is . . . ?* can be asked both before and after the event. Certainly by the time that Nahum is read as part of the Book of the Twelve and part of a larger canon, readers will find themselves in both situations at the same time. Along the lines of the expression "after the game is before the game,"[335] the people of God may live "after" the fall of Nineveh but "before" the fall of Rome, and later on both "Nineveh" and "Rome" can be substituted until God's kingdom is fully established "on earth as in heaven" in the return of Christ.

As those who pray, "Your kingdom come," we may ask "Where is the kingdom that was Assyria?" as well as "Where is Hitler's Third Reich?" and do so with gladness and gratitude for the end of these powers (cf. 3:19). But there may also be a place for staring contemporary evil in its face and asking, "Where now is the place of exploitation and sex trafficking? Where now is the realm of the Grand Mullah?" and do so both in the knowledge that this place and time is still with us and in the knowledge that it has no future.[336] Saying such things in the face of evil can be difficult (cf. Habakkuk) but may help to provide release from the spell and hold that evil sometimes exercises over us. Without the prophecy, set within the whole of Scripture, this would be merely a bold attempt to put on a brave face. But the God to whom Nahum bears witness has proven his ability to deal with evil in the death and resurrection of Christ. If Christ has indeed ascended to heaven, the control room of the universe, as we believe, the rapacious lion always lives on borrowed time.

---

335. The phrase stems from Sepp Herberger (1897–1977), a German football player and manager who was famous for a number of short phrases summing up his philosophy of football (soccer).

336. Indeed, while sex trafficking is still a major force as the writing of this commentary draws to a close, Abu Bakr al-Baghdadi, "the Grand Mullah," has come and gone while work on this commentary proceeded.

VIII. PROPHECY OF COMPLETE DESTRUCTION (2:13[14])

13(14)*Look, I am against you—utterance of* [a] *YHWH of Hosts,*
 and I will burn up [your] chariotry[b] *in the smoke,*[c]
  and a sword will devour your young lions,
and I will entirely cut off [d] *from the earth your prey,*
 and no more shall be heard the voice of your messenger.[e]

a. Hebrew *nə'ūm* is either a noun or a passive participle. It is frequently used in prophetic texts to mark divine speech. See Meier, *Speaking*, 298–314, for a full discussion of the phrase *nə'ūm yhwh*.

b. Spronk (*Nahum*, 108–9) reviews proposals to emend the consonantal text, some with support from the versions. I agree with him that *rkbh* should be read here as a feminine equivalent to *rkb* (*rekeb*), the common word for chariots used earlier in the chapter (again understanding the singular as collective); cf. *ṭerep/ṭərēpâ* (*prey/torn flesh*) in the preceding verse; see further below. The Masoretes may not have recognized this noun formation, or else they seek to make doubly sure that the chariotry is understood to be Nineveh's by reading *rikbāh* ("her chariotry"). This is retained by Fabry, *Nahum*, 159. The suffix *your* is supplied by the context and maybe specifically by the suffix in the second colon; cf. Cathcart, *Nahum*, 109; see Mitchell Dahood, *Psalms III: A New Translation with Introduction and Commentary*, AB 17A (New York: Doubleday), 429–30, for further examples with suffix omitted in the first colon.

c. Hebrew *wəhib'artî be'āšān* (*and I will burn up . . . in the smoke*) may sound idiomatic but is attested only here. This influenced the decision to retain MT's definite article in translation.

d. Hebrew *wəhikrattî*. Cf. 1:14 (translation note k) for the use of *entirely* to express the *hiphil*.

e. Hebrew *mal'ākēkê* (with variations on the last two vowels in other codices) is interpreted here as equivalent to *mal'ākēk*. It may be the result of dittography (the following verse begins with *h*) or an unusual form of the suffix; maybe cf. *'ōtākâ* (second-person masculine singular) in Exod 29:35, to which Keil, *Minor Prophets*, 2:28, draws attention. See JM 94h–j for other examples of rare suffix forms in nouns and ambiguous forms. Some interpret the form as a plural "your messengers"; e.g., Spronk, *Nahum*, 109–10.

Composition

I am discussing this verse separately for two reasons. First, because the verse is especially marked as divine discourse: *utterance of YHWH of Hosts*. Second, because it could be considered a bookend together with 1:15 (2:1) to mark off the larger unit 1:15–2:13 (2:1–14). The verse echoes not only the immediately preceding verses with its reference to *lions* but also earlier motifs in mentioning *chariots* and a *messenger*. The combination of disparate motifs may be thought harsh, but mixed metaphors can be observed elsewhere in Nahum (see, e.g., 1:10; 3:15; the use of the water motif discussed in the previous section), and the combination of motifs allows the verse to better function as the culmination of the larger unit.[337]

The formula *hinnî 'ēlayik* (*Look, I am against you*), with which *nə'ūm yhwh ṣəbā'ôt* (*utterance of YHWH of Hosts*) is always connected in Nahum (2:13[14]; 3:5), is found elsewhere only in Jeremiah (21:13; 50:31; 51:25) and Ezekiel (21:3[8]; 29:10; 35:3; 38:3; 39:1). The discourse marker *utterance of YHWH of Hosts* is more prevalent in later literature, but the evidence is not unambiguous, and there is no need to assume that the formulae mark a later addition.[338] There are poetic elements to this verse (see below), but rhythmically it could be classified as prose, reminiscent in this respect of 1:15(2:1).

While the YHWH speech earlier in the book (1:12–14) included an address to the Assyrian king (1:14), the use of feminine suffixes in this verse indicates that the city is addressed, thus sidelining the king who featured so prominently in the immediately preceding verses, which allude to the time when Nineveh was at its height.[339]

Commentary

13(14) YHWH's involvement in the fall of Nineveh has not been made explicit in the preceding poem, except possibly in the remark in v. 2(3), depending on how that remark is interpreted. This is not surprising given that the nature and purpose of the poem was to dismantle the apparent powerfulness of Assyria in images depicting its helplessness. But this conclusion makes it perfectly clear that the challenge comes from *YHWH of Hosts*. Originally, the phrase *YHWH of Hosts* ("YHWH Zebaoth") may have referred to heavenly hosts, but here we may well consider YHWH as the one who in the final analysis commands all armies.[340] If he is *against* a city, the consequences are disastrous.

In the Hebrew, the first two lines spelling out the consequences are arranged in such a way that *chariotry* and *young lions* are surrounded by *smoke* and *sword*.

---

337. Note also the importance of the royal chariot in the Assyrian lion hunt; see, e.g., Watanabe, *Animal Symbolism*, 79–80.

338. The phrase *nə'ūm yhwh ṣəbā'ôt* is found outside Nahum in Isa 14:22–23; 17:3; 22:25; Jer 8:3; 25:29; 30:8; 49:26; Zeph 2:9; Hag 1:9; 2:4, 8–9, 23; Zech 1:3, 16; 3:9–10; 5:4; 8:6, 11; 13:2, 7. To this can be added *nə'um-yhwh 'ĕlōhê ṣəbā'ôt* in Amos 6:8, 14 (with article in the latter case).

339. Roberts (*Nahum*, 62–63) objects to this and supplies the text with different vowels to read second masculine singular throughout the verse.

340. The comparison of Nineveh with (Assyrian conquered) Thebes in 3:8 suggests that YHWH has used the Assyrian armies as well in the past.

> And I will burn up in the smoke
>   [your] chariotry
>   and your young lions
> will devour a sword.

Some suggest that the inversion of gender-matching in this parallelism (*smoke* and *young lions* are grammatically masculine in Hebrew, *chariotry* and *sword* feminine) underlines the destruction.[341] This would explain Nahum's choice (or creation?) of the feminine form for *chariotry*. The use of the definite article with *smoke* in the MT may also indicate that the burning of the chariots is considered part of a larger conflagration, but this must remain uncertain because the phrase lacks parallels. Lions were hunted down with arrows but, if Assyrian depictions of lion hunts are anything to go by, it was left to the king or crown prince to deal the deathblow to the lion with his sword.[342] It may be for poetic reasons that *sword* comes without a suffix ("my"),[343] in which case we should think of it specifically as YHWH's sword—the sword of the true king.[344]

I will entirely cut off from the earth your prey takes up the imagery of the preceding verse. This is the only instance in the Bible of *prey* being *cut off*. But significantly, in 1:14 the verb reports YHWH's entirely cutting off the idols from the Assyrian king's temples. Just as the king has been cut off from his presumed source of trust and provision, so the city is now cut off from its supply.[345] The phrase *from the earth* could alternatively be rendered "from the land," but the Assyrians caught prey in more than one land, and hence a broader perspective is more appropriate (cf. 3:19). If pressed further, the destruction of prey should not be thought of as the annihilation of Assyrian victims or of the booty it accumulated but, as it were, as the destruction of the victim-status of the victim and as the end to Assyrian possession of booty. Some suggest that changing the vocalization of the MT to produce

341. Wilfred G. E. Watson, "Gender-Matched Parallelism," 328; *CHP*, 127. Watson observes that inverted gender matching is used in parallelisms that report the unexpected or the abnormal and signal destruction; cf. the last two lines of Isa 41:2.

342. Fabry, *Nahum*, 178, has an excellent drawing of an alabaster from Nineveh; see also Barnett, *Sculptures*, plates 46, 49–50, 52 (all of BM 124875; cf. figure 4.130 in Strawn, *Lion*, 452). For textual evidence, see *ARAB*, 2:392 (par. 1024); Strawn, *Lion*, 38.

343. The MT reflects the pausal form of *ḥereb*, namely *ḥāreb*, which facilitates the sentence resting on *sword*. There would be no lengthening of the first syllable with the suffix, and the sound would be very different (*ḥarbî*).

344. Cf. Fabry, *Nahum*, 180, who comments that YHWH demonstrates here that he has always been able to fulfill the expectations directed at the Assyrian king.

345. The verb will reappear in the *hiphil* in 3:15. The *niphal* is used in 1:15 (2:1) to indicate that *the villain . . . is completely cut off*.

an infinitive ("your tearing") would be more appropriate.[346] But prey has already been accumulated in previous verses, and the verse is probably not concerned with the end of future preying only.

The last line does, however, focus on the positive consequences of Nineveh's fall for her victims: *No more shall be heard the voice of your messenger.* The word for *messenger* used here is different from the one in 1:15 (2:1), as the translation indicates. Fabry suspects negative connotations for the word used here but only by way of contrast to *herald*, which tends to be used positively. Etymologically, *mal'āk* (*messenger*) is related to "sending" and *məbaśśēr* (*herald*) to "bringing news." A differentiation along these lines is borne out by usage, here as elsewhere. The *messenger* in 2:13(14) is an emissary, a representative sent on behalf of the empire.[347] The *herald* in 1:15 (2:1) does not represent anyone. Thus, while in 1:15 it is the news that is important, not the sender, here the *messenger* is, first of all, Nineveh's representative. Once Nineveh has fallen, there will be news from the city (cf. 3:19), but there will not be any reports or instructions from a representative of Nineveh.

Reflection

The body of the poem has sought to deconstruct the pretensions of Nineveh. The divine speech rounding off the poem reminds us that Nineveh is seen to be weak and powerless only when YHWH, who commands the armies, comes in view. Once YHWH pronounces his opposition to the city, its inevitable end is in sight. Its status symbols (*chariotry*) go up in smoke and its strength (*young lions*) falls to the sword of destruction. YHWH leaves nothing for Nineveh to hold onto as its *prey*, and there will be no space left that could count as its sphere of influence.

As observed above under "Composition," this verse, which offers a summary statement of the destruction of Nineveh, could be seen as forming a bookend with 1:15 (2:1), which had focused on the implications of the fall of Nineveh for Judah—the *no more* here taking up the *never again* of the earlier verse (the Hebrew has *lō'* . . . *'ôd* in both instances). These bookends therefore both take a step back from the hustle and bustle of the images of the fall of Nineveh in vv. 1–10(2–11) to consider the long-term impact of Nineveh's destruction. The ridicule of the king in vv. 11–12(12–13) had already been in such a reflective mood. What is new here is the explicit description of the

---

346. Spronk, *Nahum*, 109. I am not aware of any other instances in which *krt* takes an infinitive as its object.

347. See Berlejung, "Erinnerungen," 335, for the importance of this motif in the cultural memory of peoples in Western Asia at the time.

event as an act of YHWH in line with 1:12–14. The author does not claim that the fall of Nineveh involved inexplicable, supernatural divine intervention. Rather, YHWH is said to claim responsibility for the disaster, now again spoken of as a future event. Just as YHWH claimed responsibility for the Assyrian oppression of Judah (1:12; cf., e.g., Isa 10:5–6), so now he takes credit for its end (cf. Isa 10:12). This reflects the widespread view within the Bible that human government exercises rule by divine mandate and that all such power is provisional and penultimate. This point is often and especially made in relation to superpowers and their leaders.[348]

In the New Testament, the divine mandate of governing authorities is affirmed most clearly in Rom 13:1–7, while Rev 13 draws on Dan 7 to describe the ugly side of human imperial power as an enemy of God. It is belief in the total sovereignty of God that requires us to see that human government is both under God's control (and therefore something for which God must accept some responsibility) and ultimately accountable to God. If employees of a business make a mistake that harms customers, the business owner usually has to accept responsibility for this vis-à-vis the customers, while the employees have to give an account to their employer. In a similar way, the Bible does not shy away from attributing human violence to God, even if the violence is disproportionate, as God accepts the actions of his agents as his own actions, but God is then described as taking his agents to task (cf. Isa 47:6; Zech 1:2, 15). See further the reflection on Hab 3:8–15.

IX. DOOM AND HUMILIATION FOR THE BLOODFLOW CITY (3:1-7)

[1]*Oy,*[a] *the*[b] *city of bloodshed,*[c]
  all of her falsehood,[d] *full of*[e] *plunder,*[f]
    prey does not cease.
[2]*Sound of whip,*[g]
  sound of rattling wheel,
horse galloping,[h]
  chariotry jolting.[i]
[3]*Cavalry charging,*
  blazing sword,[j]
lightning spear,[k]
  multitude of slain,

348. For wider discussion, see, e.g., Walter Brueggemann, *Theology of the Old Testament: Testimony, Dispute, Advocacy* (Minneapolis: Fortress, 1997), 492–527; John Goldingay, *Israel's Faith*, vol. 2 of *Old Testament Theology* (Milton Keynes: Paternoster; Downers Grove, IL: IVP Academic, 2006), 761–88, including a discussion of Nahum (pp. 779–82).

mass of corpses,
with[l] no end to the bodies;
they stumble[m] over their bodies.
[4]*Because of the multitude of the harlot's harlotries,*
graceful Beauty,[n] Lady of Sorceries,
she who sells off[o] nations for[p] her harlotries
and clans for her sorceries.

[5]*Look, I am against you—utterance of YHWH of Hosts,*
and I will strip your skirt[q] over your face,
and I will show[r] nations your nudity[s]
and kingdoms your shame.
[6]*I will throw filth[t] at you and declare you contemptuous[u]*
and make you just like a spectacle.[v]
[7]*And it shall happen that whoever sees you will run away from you*
and say "Nineveh is ruined.[w]
Who will grieve for her?"
Where can I find comforters for you?

a. Hebrew *hôy* is often translated "Woe!" There may be a somber quality to this interjection, as argued by Waldemar Janzen (*Mourning Cry and Woe Oracle*, BZAW 125 [Berlin: de Gruyter, 1972], 20), who sees a death-mourning-vengeance continuum at work. But "woe!" seems more appropriate for *'ôy*. While *hôy* is most often used as an expression of dismay, in a few places it is hardly more than an exclamation arousing attention (e.g., Isa 1:24; 17:12; 55:1). For a defense of the more mainstream view (that it is a "woe-cry" related to lament), see, e.g., the excursus in Daniel H. Ryou, *Zephaniah's Oracles against the Nations: A Synchronic & Diachronic Study of Zephaniah 2:1–3:8*, BibInt 13 (Leiden: Brill, 1995), 334–43. The participle or noun that follows *hôy* can be interpreted either as a vocative or as descriptive in the third person. Usage does not appear to be uniform. Delbert R. Hillers ("*Hôy* and *Hôy*-Oracles: A Neglected Syntactic Aspect," in *The Word of the Lord Shall Go Forth: Essays in Honor of David Noel Freedman in Celebration of His Sixtieth Birthday*, ed. Carol L. Meyers and Michael O'Connor [Winona Lake, IN: Eisenbrauns, 1983], 185–88) has pointed out that in Hebrew, the vocative often has third-person pronouns. This means that the use of the phrase *all of her* (rather than "all of you") is not decisive. The present translation renders third-person pronouns in the third person both here and in Hab 2:6–20. For Hab 2, this means that the vocative element is lost, which is regrettable, as it seems likely that *hôy* more often than not was linked with a second-person address. Here in Nahum, a transition from the vocative, as the English *city of bloodshed* (without the article) is likely heard, to third-person description seems workable.

b. The use or (more often) omission of the definite article after *hôy* appears to be a matter of style rather than substance. In English, the omission would signal the vocative, but *'îr dāmîm* does not seem to be a vocative here (see the previous note).

c. Hebrew *dāmîm*; see, e.g., GKC 124 for the significance of the plural.

d. Hebrew *kaḥaš* ("lie"), from a root that can also mean "to disappoint, to fail"; cf. Hab 3:17. For the syntax, see the note below.

e. This represents the standard interpretation of the syntax of this sequence of three nouns, "(her) totality" (*all of her*), *falsehood* (or "deception"), and *plunder*, followed by the adjective *full*; cf. the layout in *BHS*. The masoretic accentuation suggests the possibility of taking "deception" attributively with *plunder* ("deceptive plunder"), but this is not how the text has been read even in Jewish tradition; see Rosenberg, *Twelve Prophets*, 250.

f. Hebrew *pereq*. The noun is attested elsewhere only in Obad 14, with a disputed but obviously different meaning from here ("crossroads"?). The usage of the verb *prq* ("to tear") gives me confidence that the meaning of the noun here is parallel to *prey* in the next line.

g. All nouns in this and the following verse, apart from the last noun of v. 3 (*bodies*), are singular. Understood collectively, they could be rendered in the plural (see NIV), but the singular seems poetically more effective in English as well, except for the second half of v. 3, where this is no longer possible.

h. The reverse word order would be idiomatic in English, but imitating the word order of the Hebrew text allows me to reflect the variation found in the original.

i. The conjunction *waw* ("and") ties the various items together. A simple comma fulfills the same function in English. The absence of a *waw* before the next item (in v. 3) is reflected in the full stop there.

j. Hebrew *wəlahab ḥereb*, "and the flame of a sword." Again, the listed items are linked by *waw* ("and"); see above.

k. Hebrew *ûbəraq ḥănît*, "and the lightning of a spear." The noun *bārāq* is used metaphorically elsewhere with reference to "sword" (e.g., Deut 32:41) or "spear" (Hab 3:11) or "arrow" (e.g., Zech 9:14); see below.

l. Hebrew *wə'ên* is literally "and there is not."

m. The *ketiv* (*ykšlw*) is a *yiqtol* (imperfect) form, likely *niphal*, although the consonants allow for other possibilities; the *qere* (*wəkāšlû*) is *qatal* (perfect) with *waw*. There does not seem to be much difference in meaning between these forms.

n. Hebrew *ṭôbat ḥēn*, "good(ness) of grace/charm," whereby *ḥēn* ("grace/charm") qualifies *ṭôb* ("good," but also "pleasing, attractive, beautiful").

o. Hebrew *hammōkeret*, "the one [fem.] who is selling off." The Hebrew text has good support from the versions but is sometimes thought to make little sense. See, e.g., Cathcart, *Nahum*, 129–30, who, following Dahood, reads *hammukkeret* ("who is known"); Roberts, *Nahum*, 69–70, who emends to *hammašakkeret* ("who made drunk").

p. The precise nuance of the preposition here and in the next line is debatable. The *beth* could indicate a temporal ("in her harlotries" = "while she acted the harlot") or causal ("because of her harlotries") relationship, but it more likely refers to means or instrument, "by" (e.g., NIV), "with" (e.g., ESV), or "through" (e.g., NRSV). The verb and preposition are interpreted here along the lines of Joel 3:3 (4:3); Amos 2:6; Ps 44:12(13); so also Spronk, *Nahum*, 122.

q. Hebrew *šûlayik* refers to the lower part of either the body (i.e., the pubic region; so *HALOT*; Spronk, *Nahum*, 123) or the garment (i.e., the seams). In any case, the whole clause refers to lifting up the clothes so high that the whole body is exposed.

r. Hebrew *wəhar'êtî* is *hiphil* of *r'h*, "to see" (unusually, the long vowel in the first syllable is retained; see *HGHS* 57t" [p. 426]; JM 54a n. 2). NRSV interprets with a tolerative nuance ("I will let look"), which is unlikely to be accurate; see further below.

s. Hebrew *ma'rēk*. The root is used in 1 Kgs 7:36 for empty space but not found elsewhere in the Bible.

t. Hebrew *šiqqūṣîm*. The plural is maybe best understood as one of abstraction (cf. JM 136g). See below for the connection with idolatry.

u. Hebrew *wənibbaltîk*; for the interpretation of the *piel* as declarative, see *HALOT*; alternatively "treat with contempt." Patterson (*Nahum*, 92) suggests taking this verb together with the next as a hendiadys: "Make you a contemptible spectacle." I prefer the division of the verse reflected in the accentuation.

v. Hebrew *kərō'î* consists of the preposition *kaph* and the rare noun *rŏ'î* ("appearance, seeing"). 4QpNah reads *k'wrh* from the root *k'r = k'r* ("to be repulsive" in later Hebrew); cf. Tg.; see ArBib 14, 139–40, for fuller discussion. *Rŏ'î* is considered equivalent to *rə'î*, understood as "dung" (only attested as "pasture" in Classical Hebrew, 1 Kgs 4:23 [5:3]) among medieval commentators, based on *mur'â* ("crop, crissum") in Lev 1:16 for the organ containing the dung (see Rosenberg, *Twelve Prophets*, 251). Note also the discussion surrounding the translation of *mōr'â* in Zeph 3:1. LXX *paradeigma* ("precedent, example") seems to me closer to the original meaning of *rŏ'î* here. The likely demonstrative origin of the preposition *kaph* may have influenced its use here and in similar contexts; cf. Neh 7:2 (see GKC 118x for further examples).

w. Hebrew *šāddĕdâ* is *pual*. For the initial vowel, see GKC 52q; cf. *mə'oddām* in 2:3(4).

Composition

The *hôy* (*Oy*) with which the chapter opens marks the beginning of a new building block of the book. Like 1:15 (2:1), the introductory verse does not have the poetic rhythm of the following verses and could be considered a subunit in its own right. Verses 2–3 offer us another description of an army. As in ch. 2, the identification of the army is disputed. Some commentators see the Assyrian army depicted;[349] others, probably the majority, think of the attackers who come up against Nineveh.[350] Coggins provides an explanation that agrees with my reading of the text:

> The irony of the prophet's words is again apparent here. At face value this looks like an account of the power of the Assyrian armies, illustrated by the grisly sight of "hosts of slain, heaps of corpses, dead bodies without end." But in the context of the poem as a whole it is clear that the "slain" and the "corpses" are those of the Assyrian army themselves.[351]

Read in the light of v. 1, vv. 2–3 may at first seem to describe the *bloodshed* caused by the Assyrians. But v. 4 corrects this in retrospect. At the same time,

349. E.g., Jerome, *Commentaries on the Twelve Prophets*, vol. 1, ed. Thomas P. Scheck, Ancient Christian Texts (Downers Grove, IL: IVP Academic, 2016), 23–24; Achtemeier, *Nahum*, 22–23. Jeremias (*Nahum*, 166) notes B. Becking, "De Hymne van Nahum en de literaire Eenheid van het Boek" (diss., Utrecht, 1977), following Eaton and Van der Woude.

350. The disagreement goes back at least to medieval times. Abarbanel, like Jerome, sees a reference to the Assyrians while, e.g., Kimchi thinks the text has Nineveh's invaders in view; see Rosenberg, *Twelve Prophets*, 443.

351. Coggins, *Nahum*, 49.

v. 4 can be read as the rationale for vv. 5–7. Syntactically, the verse integrates fully neither with the preceding nor with the following. Read as a comment on vv. 1–3, we need to supply the thought "all this happens" *because of the multitude of the harlot's harlotries*. Read as the rationale for vv. 5–6 or vv. 5–7, we need to tolerate the shift from third person to second person.

My translation follows fairly standard procedure in its use of short lines in vv. 2–3 and thereby departs from the masoretic accentuation.[352] The rules of masoretic accentuation apparently do not allow division into such small units unless nearly each word is given a disjunctive accent, which might render fluent reading difficult.[353]

And it shall happen signals a new paragraph.[354] This means that the identity of the speaker of the last line (*Where can I find comforters for you?*) is ambiguous. If we tie this paragraph closely to vv. 5–6, YHWH is heard to ask this rhetorical question. If v. 7 is considered a separate paragraph within the section that opened with v. 1, it is possible instead that the prophet asks the question. The use of the root *nḥm* for the lacking comforters (*mənaḥămîm*; cf. "Nahum") may also suggest as much. In this case, it is possible to discern a palistrophic structure for this unit:

> A Prophetic taunt (v. 1)
> B Defeat described as a military event (vv. 2–3)
>   C The cause of taunt and defeat (v. 4)
> B' Defeat announced as a theological event (vv. 5–6)
> A' Prophetic taunt (v. 7)

Commentary

1 This verse may be elevated prose rather than poetry. The syntactical construction is not parallel, and the words used here for *plunder* and *prey* are

---

352. The Masoretes scanned vv. 2–3 as bicola with fairly long individual cola, with 3+3+3 disjunctive accents for the attack switching to 2+2+2 for the result, followed by 2+2 and 2+2 in v. 4. This gives a more unusual—for the book of Nahum—rhythm of 3+2 for the first half of v. 3, the point at which cola with three disjunctives give way to cola with two disjunctives.

353. See Renz, *Colometry*, for details; cf. James D. Price, *The Syntax of Masoretic Accents in the Hebrew Bible*, Studies in the Bible and Early Christianity 27 (Lewiston: Mellen, 1990).

354. Cf. *BHRG* 44.4, which speaks of a "paragraph or sub-paragraph." I am not convinced that it makes much sense to speak of "sub-paragraphs," but the point is that there is a subtle difference between *And it shall happen that whoever sees you*, which slightly sets off the following from the preceding, and the simpler "and whoever sees you," which preserves greater continuity.

not used elsewhere in parallelism.[355] The alliterations *k-k* (*kullāh kaḥaš*) and *m-l-l-m* (*mĕlē'â lō' yāmîš*) are noticeable but not particularly strong. The city is characterized, first of all, as violent, *a city of bloodshed*. Concerning the next phrase, most interpreters also see the city characterized as completely false. While it is possible to read "deceptive plunder" instead (see note on the translation), the theme of falsehood, referring to Assyrian propaganda, fits well. It can be connected to 1:11 (*advising villainy*) and to the immediately preceding verse (*no more shall be heard the voice of your messenger*). It also raises the key question: whose words and actions are trustworthy? The fake love of prostitution (v. 4) may also be in mind here, the falsehood consisting of the gap between appearance and reality. The *prey* that for the moment *does not cease* will be cut off (2:13[14]) and thus prove "deceptive plunder," so maybe the ambiguity of the syntax is not entirely accidental.

2 The next two verses lead us directly into a battle scene with the sound of cracking whips and the noise of rattling wheels. The Hebrew text draws pictures with the sound as much as with the meaning of the words. It begins with a series of dark *o* sounds (*qôl šôṭ wǝqôl raʿaš 'ôpān*) followed by a quick sequence of *u-o-e* vowels for the galloping horse (*wǝsûs dōhēr*) and the double *m-r-k(q)-b(d)* consonantal sequence of clattering chariot wheels (*ûmerkābâ mǝraqqēdâ*). It serves Nahum well that *raʿaš* (*rattling*) can also refer to an earthquake, something often associated with God's appearance (cf. 1:5), because it helps readers to discern YHWH behind the actions of the attacking armies.

The noise of Assyria's nail-studded chariot wheels was hardly considered a pleasant sound among those whom Assyrian forces had overrun at one time.[356] The root used for *galloping* is elsewhere only found in Judg 5:22 (as a noun). Spronk suspects it as "another example of the poet deliberately associating the attackers of Nineveh with YHWH and his heavenly host," but this remains speculative.[357] The Hebrew word translated *jolting* elsewhere describes dancing and jumping around (1 Chr 15:29; Job 21:11; Eccl 3:4) and the skipping around of calves and goats (Pss 29:6; 114:4, 6; Isa 13:21). But it

355. This is not only because the use of *pereq* for *plunder* is unique here but also because the motifs of plunder and prey are not paired elsewhere, as far as I know. Contrast, e.g., the "plunder" pair *mĕšissâ* and *baz* in Isa 42:22 (cf. v. 24 with the related verb *bzz*) and Jer 30:16; they are also used together in 2 Kgs 21:14.

356. Spronk (*Nahum*, 119) notes that "in the period of Sennacherib and Ashurbanipal the rims of the large wheels of war chariots were studded with nail-heads."

357. Spronk, *Nahum*, 119. He believes that the heavenly host is depicted in Judg 5:20ff. and compares *YHWH of Hosts* in 2:13(14). But the designation *YHWH of Hosts* is not used in Judg 5. Apart from *galloping*, we may note the use of *rā'āšâ* ("trembled") in Judg 5:4 (cf. *ra'aš*, *rattling*, here) and the name Barak ("lightning"; cf. v. 3).

characterizes the movement of chariots also in Joel 2:5 and surely suggests extreme speed.

3 The image of a rain of spears thrown by the Assyrian infantry must have evoked bad memories among the first readers. We cannot be entirely sure to what *lightning spear* refers. It could be the gleam of the metal tips of spears, which compares with the reference to the tip of an arrow in Job 20:25 and to a flashing sword in Ezek 21:10(15).[358] But perhaps the flying of the spear is compared to lightning across the sky, as arrows are probably compared to in Zech 9:14 (cf. Hab 3:11). The result is, in any case, *a multitude of slain, mass of corpses, with no end to the bodies; they stumble over their bodies*. The heaping up of words for bodies verbally reflects the *mass of corpses* in view. The *slain* (*ḥālāl*) could be the wounded who are still alive (e.g., Jer 51:52), but more often the word refers to those struck down dead (e.g., Num 19:18). The word rendered *corpses* (*peger*; here in pausal form, *pāger*) is also used for animal carcasses (Gen 15:11). Many references imply that the *corpses* lie exposed (e.g., Isa 66:24; Amos 8:3; 1 Sam 17:46), and none are in the context of proper funerary practices.[359] The verse twice uses the word for *bodies* (*gəwiyyâ*). Elsewhere it is used five times of living bodies (Gen 47:18; Neh 9:37; Ezek 1:11, 23; Dan 10:6) and five times of human (1 Sam 31:10, 12; Ps 110:6) or animal carcasses (Judg 14:8-9).[360] Possibly, attention to sound has kept Nahum from using *nəbēlâ*, a more common word for "corpse" or "carcass," in this verse.[361] Fabry notes that Assyrian kings sometimes boasted of having defeated their foes so decisively that enemy corpses filled the valleys and stopped up rivers.[362] Nahum suggests that it will be done to them as they have done to others.

4 According to its entry in *HALOT*, a *zônâ* (*harlot*) is a "woman occasionally or professionally committing fornication." But there is no clear instance in which the noun refers to an adulteress rather than a prostitute (someone

358. Ezek 21:15(20) probably also belongs here. Together with the references given in the footnote on the translation, these are all occurrences of this metaphorical usage of *bārāq*.

359. The related verb is attested twice in 1 Sam 30. It is used for people who are too exhausted to cross a brook (vv. 10, 21). This fits with the idea of bodies just lying around.

360. Perlitt claims that the word designates humans in their weakness (*Nahum*, 28) but this does not fit with Ezek 1 and Dan 10. A related Hebrew word means "back," and Robertson (*Nahum*, 106) wonders whether the reference is to bodies lying facedown. I suspect that this, too, reads too much into the text.

361. The word *nəbēlâ* is more common for "corpse" than any of the words Nahum has chosen, but *ḥālāl* fits after the reference to *sword*, and *pāger* goes with the sound of the preceding word (*kōbed*). Both have the advantage of being a syllable shorter. The only place for *nəbēlâ* here would be for one of the occurrences of *gəwiyyâ*, but the repetition of *gəwiyyâ* arguably imitates the stumbling better.

362. Fabry, *Nahum*, 190. Unfortunately, he gives no reference.

who offers sexual favors for pay), and there are a number of cases in which *zônâ* must refer to a prostitute rather than an adulteress.[363] While the verb is used more broadly and while it is true that a married woman who becomes a prostitute is also an adulteress,[364] this does not necessarily mean that the noun *zônâ* would have been used for an adulteress who is not a prostitute,[365] or perhaps at least the female head of a house of prostitution.[366] The use of a commercial term, *selling off* (assuming the text to be correct), implies that prostitution is in view here. Therefore the focus is maybe not on Nineveh's lack of faithfulness (with regard to a specific partner) but on its offer of merely superficial attractiveness and the promise of relations without relationship.[367] As the intimacy offered by a prostitute is a false one, so the relationships in which Nineveh engages are not true, intimate relationships, even between unequal partners, but fake ones built only on economic benefit. Nor is this prostitute/madam satisfied with a few tribute payments in exchange for favors; she is prepared to sell off clans and nations wholesale. This is obviously not a normal, realistic picture of prostitution because of the social status of Nineveh. In literal prostitution, the ones offering their services and receiving payment are most often the exploited ones. "Assyrian obsession with projecting an image of masculinity" may have played a role in casting Nineveh as a woman here,[368] as may be the fact that Ishtar, the patron deity of Nineveh, was worshipped as a prostitute.[369] The specific accusation may be that Nineveh completely subjects nations and then disposes of them

363. Note how Prov 6:26 contrasts the prostitute (*'iššâ zônâ*) and the adulteress (*'ēšet 'îš*); cf. the reference to a prostitute's appearance (*šit zônâ*) in 7:10. The adulteress is called *hā'iššâ hammənā'āpet* in Ezek 16:32.

364. Anselm C. Hagedorn ("Nahum—Ethnicity and Stereotypes: Anthropological Insights into Nahum's Literary History," in *Ancient Israel: The Old Testament in Its Social Context*, ed. Philip F. Esler [Minneapolis: Fortress, 2006], 223–39) speaks of "a subversion of the image of the fascinating and dazzling harlot" (238). When God's people are accused of harlotry, the implication is often that they are both adulterous and behave like a prostitute; see, e.g., Ezek 23:44.

365. The more precise verb for committing adultery is not *znh* but *n'p* as, e.g., in Exod 20:14; Lev 20:10; cf. Hos 4:14.

366. Gregory D. Cook ("Human Trafficking in Nahum," *HBT* 37 [2015]: 142–57) argues for "madam" in this sense, appealing to 2 Kgs 9:22 and suggesting that this might be the best description for Rahab in Josh 2 (pp. 147–48). In other words, Nineveh is selling others rather than herself.

367. This does not mean that accusations of disloyalty (and idolatry) cannot also be in the background but Jeremias (*Nahum*, 167–71) arguably overplays them.

368. The expression is Cook's ("Trafficking," 143); see Chapman, *Gendered Language*, 1. Assyrian treaties refer to recalcitrant vassal kings as prostitutes; see Hillers, *Treaty-Curses*, 58–60; cf. Timmer, "Boundaries," 181.

369. Cook, "Trafficking," 144–46; see *ANET*, 579–82.

at will. Second Kings 16 offers a paradigmatic example. Ahaz finds Assyria attractive as a means to keep the threatening Syro-Ephraimite alliance at bay and becomes ensnared by this superpower. Indeed, as Gregory Cook argued, Assyrian enslavement policies can be considered a case of human trafficking. "Nahum's charge shows that the incredible expansion Nineveh experienced came about because of the lives and deaths of thousands upon thousands of kidnapped people."[370] Cook believes that the kidnapped were considered sold to the Assyrian deities, not least when they were conscripted to construct buildings dedicated to Assyrian gods and goddesses. Assyrian kings thought that in return they received the favor of the Assyrian pantheon. Mindful and grateful of the aid received, these kings

> spare no effort or expense to give the gods and goddesses honor, worship, and luxury. This task required the resources and lives of foreign peoples and resulted in a cycle of military victory, plunder, kidnapping, extravagant building, and then the need for more conquest.[371]

The prostitute is bewitching not just because of her natural attractiveness (she is a *graceful Beauty*) but also because she is *Lady of Sorceries (ba'alat kəšāpîm)*. In terms of Old Testament law, the accusation of sorcery is more serious than that of prostitution. There are no sanctions for prostitution as long as it is not associated with the sanctuary (see below), but, "You shall not permit a sorceress (*məkaššēpâ*) to live" (Exod 22:18[17]; cf. Mic 5:12[11]; Mal 3:5). It may be worth noting that the combination of whoredom and sorcery is also attributed to Jezebel (2 Kgs 9:22; cf. also Isa 57:3). By way of establishing a contrast, it may be no accident that the two designations given to the city here echo the language of ch. 1. The *Lady of Sorceries (ba'alat kəšāpîm)* is opposed by one who is *Master of rage (ba'al ḥēmâ*, 1:2), and her *beauty* will prove anything but *graceful (ṭôbat ḥēn)* when *YHWH*, who is *good (ṭôb yhwh*, 1:7), takes action to oppose evil and falsehood.[372]

5 While the death penalty is specified for adultery, even if it was not necessarily executed,[373] prostitution was apparently not outlawed, except for the

---

370. Cook, "Trafficking," 152.

371. Cook, "Trafficking," 157.

372. Gregory D. Cook ("Naqia and Nineveh in Nahum: Ambiguity and the Prostitute Queen," *JBL* 136 [2017]: 895–904) takes the similarities between Nah 3:4 and 2 Kgs 9:22 as an encouragement to see here a portrait of Naqia, a queen mother (to Esarhaddon) who, like Jezebel, wielded significant power and had a reputation for engaging in magic.

373. There are indications that the cuckolded husband could substitute a heavy fine for the death penalty if he so wished, a procedure explicitly forbidden only for murder (Num 35:31; cf. Prov 6:35).

daughters of priests (Lev 21:9).[374] Fathers are, however, warned not to make their daughters prostitutes (Lev 19:29).[375] We do not have solid evidence to suggest that the actions described in this verse reflect a known punishment for prostitutes, although there is an Aramaic treaty (mid-eighth century BC) that threatens breach of covenant with the following curse:

> Just as a prostitute is stripped naked, so may the wives of Mati'ilu be stripped naked, and the wives of his offspring and the wives of his nobles. (Sefire IA, 40–41)[376]

How often such punishment was actually executed is unknown, but this treaty suggests that its authors considered public exposure of a prostitute a fitting judgment (cf. Isa 3:16–17, which arguably implies prostitution). Similar motifs are found in threats against Israel (Hos 2:3[5], 10[12]), Judah (Jer 13:26), and Jerusalem (Ezek 16:37–38; cf. 23:10, 29), but in these cases the prostitute was also an adulteress. Indeed, Ezek 16:38 specifically refers to the "judgment on those who commit adultery" (*mišpǝṭê nō'ǎpôt*). Still, it is by no means clear that the punishment was restricted to adulteresses, and its use here may be influenced by the brutalities of war. Note that other announcements of such punishment do not specify the sin committed, namely Isa 47:2–3 (Babylon); Jer 13:22 (Judah).

One might translate the second verb (*show*) with tolerative nuance, as in NRSV ("I will let nations look on your nakedness and kingdoms on your shame"). But given that YHWH declares that he *will strip* (in the preceding line) and *throw filth* (v. 6), *show* seems a more accurate translation, especially given the rarity of the tolerative nuance.[377] The metaphor conveys the idea that YHWH will discredit Nineveh by publicly exposing its true nature.[378]

374. Lev 21 also specifies that a priest is not allowed to marry a prostitute (vv. 7, 14), suggesting that other Israelites were permitted to do so. Cf. Deut 23:18(19) for another injunction designed to keep anything to do with prostitution away from the sanctuary.

375. Cf. Gen 34:31; Jer 3:3; and Amos 7:17 for the low regard in which prostitutes were held. The same appears to have been true in Mesopotamia, although law codes there tolerated and regulated prostitution; see Elaine Adler Goodfriend, "Prostitution (OT)," *ABD*, 5:506.

376. Cited from Johnston, "Treaty-Curses," 427; cf. Chapman, *Gendered Language*, 42. Johnston's claim that such public exposure happened often and that "prostitutes were punished severely in the ancient Near East" is not justified, however, based on the evidence cited. He also fails to acknowledge that this translation and the restoration of the text on which it is based are a (plausible) conjecture. See Hillers, *Treaty-Curses*, 58–59.

377. Note *IBHS* 27.5c. Cf. JM 54d, which notes the use of the *hiphil* for "conceding the thing expressed by the root" as, e.g., agreeing to a request. GKC 53 does not discuss the possibility of a tolerative sense.

378. Berlejung ("Erinnerungen," 337) rightly notes that this is different from the motif in

6 The singular *šiqqūṣ* (*filth*) always relates to idolatry, while the plural can perhaps also refer more broadly to detestable things or filth that makes one detestable.[379] This is a further step from the revelation of Nineveh's nature in the previous verse, the purpose being to besmirch and ruin Nineveh's beauty and attraction. But the frequent association of *šiqqūṣ* with idolatry may well suggest that YHWH is pelting Nineveh with her own idols.[380] In any case, the aim of this *spectacle* is for those formerly captivated by Nineveh's charm to turn away, acknowledging Nineveh to be *contemptuous*.

7 The ambiguity of the speaker of the last line (*Where can I find comforters for you?*) is briefly discussed above under "Composition" because it relates to the role of this short paragraph within the unit as a whole. I read the verse as Nahum's conclusion based on the divine speech in vv. 5-6.[381] The verse's playful use of sounds (*yiddôd, šāddĕdâ, yānûd*) arguably reflects a measure of delight in Nineveh's fall, and the question in the last line is of course asked by someone who has no intention of finding comforters (*mənaḥămîm*) for Nineveh. The prophet will not be a "Nahum" for both oppressor and oppressed.

Reflection

After the summary word of condemnation, Nahum conveys in a staccato manner both the action and the result of war. The heaping up of bodies forces us to face up to the reality of war. D. Stronach and S. Lumsden report that "the excavated portion of the central corridor of the Halzi Gate" of the city of Nineveh

> has revealed the presence of more than a dozen persons who died a vio-
> lent death—no doubt as they were caught in the fury of the assault. Each
> lies as he fell: one sprawled face down, one on his back with his arms

---

treaty curses that threaten the shaming of honorable women. She also questions the view of some that the exposure prepares for rape, given that in v. 7 the audience seems to turn away.

379. So, e.g., *HALOT* and Ges[18] s.v. *šiqqûṣ*. But a cultic background can plausibly be seen in (nearly) all occurrences of the noun, as observed by Fabry (*Nahum*, 196) and Jeremias (*Nahum*, 176-77).

380. Note the reference to *sorceries* above and cf. 1:14. In Leviticus, the related noun *šeqeṣ* is used for cultic abominations (cf. Isa 66:17; Ezek 8:10), and the verb for spurning something as unclean (cf. Deut 7:26). The verb is also used once for God (not) spurning someone (Ps 22:24[25]).

381. This is obviously meant to say something about the rhetoric of these verses, not about their divine inspiration. While some believe that in reality vv. 5-6 are no more "divine speech" than v. 7, I am persuaded that v. 7 is as much part of God's word as vv. 5-6.

outstretched, and still another (a mere 13-year-old boy) with a trilobite arrowhead lodged in his lower leg. Numerous bronze or iron arrowheads were found in the vicinity of these overlapping skeletons, together with the separate remains of a dagger, spearhead and pike.[382]

Nahum reminds us that violence (*bloodshed*, v. 1) calls forth further violence. Our cultures have their own iconic images of war—pictures that offer a window into the brutality of war. We may think of the noise of machine guns or artillery as encapsulating the sound of war.

It is worth observing how Nahum introduces God into this picture.[383] God is not portrayed here as the warrior who wields sword and spear. But neither is he someone who in the background merely tolerates what happens. His involvement is described in stark terms in vv. 5–6, but in a metaphor. The metaphor does not distance God from the events but should prevent us seeing him as the author of violence and bloodshed without a conceptual framework that puts the destruction into a larger context.

The main contribution of this section to the book may be the focus on humiliation. The book has previously conveyed the ideas that Assyria's power is a sham and that its evil will be countered with superior force. An element of humiliation may have been hinted at in the observation that the Assyrian lion king can no longer provide for his cubs, but only here does humiliation come into focus. Why must the ruin of the *city of bloodshed* involve humiliation? The answer is encapsulated in v. 4. Because Nineveh proved not only oppressive but also alluring, it is necessary to destroy her pretense. The assumption behind this is presumably that the Assyrians imposed treaties that delivered a lot more for them than for their vassals. If Nineveh promised protection but delivered exploitation, she will now be presented as being without protector herself. The one who was unwilling to fulfill her promises will be rendered unable to do so.

X. DENUNCIATION OF THE CITY'S COMPLACENCY (3:8–12)

[8] *Will you fare better*[a] *than No-Amon,*[b]
    dwelling at the streams [of the Nile],[c]
        water surrounding her,[d]
whose[e] *bulwark was the sea,*[f]

---

382. Stronach and Lumsden, "UC Berkeley Excavations," 231, 232. Cf. David Stronach, "The Last Days of Assyrian Nineveh: A View from the Halzi Gate," in Petit and Bonacossi, *Nineveh,* 228–42.

383. Cf. Fabry, *Nahum,* 190.

of the sea[g] *was her wall?*
[9]*Cush was her strength*[h] *and Egypt, without limit.*[i]
  Put and Libyans[j] *were against*[k] *your helpers.*[l]
[10]*She too*[m] *[was destined] for exile,*[n] *went into captivity,*[o]
  her children, too, being smashed[p] *at the head of every street;*
and for her public figures[q] *they cast lots,*[r]
  and all her dignitaries[s] *were bound in chains.*[t]
[11]*You too will become drunk; you will pass out;*[u]
  you too will seek a refuge from the enemy.[v]
[12]*All your fortifications are fig trees with firstfruits,*[w]
  when they are shaken, they fall into the mouth of the eater.

a. Hebrew *hătêṭbî* consists of the interrogative particle (*hă*) and what appears to be a mixed form of the root *ytb* (*têṭbî*), with the initial vowel suggesting a *hiphil* ("do good, do well") but the ending suggesting a *qal* ("go well"). This is perhaps a textual error, or it may be an alternative form of either (see *HGHS* 56u"). For the common translation, "Are you better . . . ?" see below.

b. For the LXX of this line, see Spronk, *Nahum*, 126–27; Fabry, *Nahum*, 201–2. Nesina Grütter ("A Tale of One City [Nah 3:8–9]: A Text-Critical Solution for an Often Discussed Problem Provided by a Reading Preserved in the Septuagint," *JSCS* 50 [2017]: 160–75) offers a careful argument in favor of an earlier reading that did not refer to any Egyptian city. But it seems implausible that the text originally contained a prophecy against Judah/Jerusalem here. Also, the language of watery destruction is apt; it seems designed to depict symbolically the political significance of the defeat of Thebes rather than to describe literally the nature and extent of the event. For the old equation of No-Amon with Alexandria, note ArBib 14, 140.

c. Hebrew *yə'ōrîm* most often refers to the streams of the Nile and may be an Egyptian loanword. The plural probably refers to the different watercourses of the Nile but may include canals and channels leading off from the river. Kenneth A. Kitchen thinks the reference here is "primarily to the East Delta defences of Egypt" (personal letter to author, September 10, 2001).

d. Hebrew *sābîb lāh*; cf. Ps 125:2; Song 3:7; see JM 103n. The substantive *sābîb* is regularly used as a preposition ("around") and more than thirty times with *lamed*.

e. The suffix on *ḥômātāh* (*her wall*) in the next line does double duty. For the concept of double-duty items, see, e.g., Francis I. Andersen, *Habakkuk: A New Translation with Introduction and Commentary*, AB 25 (New York: Doubleday, 2001), 99–102, who thinks that the device was much more common than is generally recognized.

f. Hebrew *yām* ("sea") can also refer to a large river; see, e.g., Isa 18:2; 19:5 for the Nile.

g. Hebrew *miyyām*, interpreted as "consisting of the sea," with the preposition indicating "material from which something is made" (*HALOT*). Alternatively, "on the west." There were settlements, temples, and palaces on both banks, but in Akkadian, "Ni" apparently referred to Thebes East only, and the same may have been true for Hebrew *No*; cf. Gen 12:8; Josh 11:2; 19:34. 8ḤevXIIgr and LXX read *mayim* ("water"), which is followed by many commentators; Vulg. suggests *mê yam* ("waters of the sea"). The reference stays the same in each of these cases.

h. Hebrew *'oṣmâ*. BHS suggests adding a *mappîq* (*'oṣmāh*), but see GKC 91e or JM 94h for similar cases without *mappîq*.

i. Hebrew *wə'ên qēṣê* ("and there was no end") alludes to 2:9(10) and 3:3 but sounds clumsy in English if translated literally.

j. Maybe "a doubled expression for Libya in poetic style" (cf. *HALOT*, s.v. *pûṭ*), unless *Libyans* refers to the rulers of Sais in upper Nubia, whose dynasty was of Libyan origin, and *Put* to the region west of Egypt toward Cyrenaica.

k. Hebrew *hāyû bə*. The adversative use of the preposition is common with verbs of fighting, etc. (see, e.g., BDB), but it is also found with *hyh* ("to be"); so twice in Josh 24:27 (*lə'ēdâ*, "as a witness") and in a similar context in Deut 28:46. It is the regular meaning where someone's hand (*yad*) is the subject of *hyh* (Gen 37:27; Deut 2:15; 13:9[10]; 17:7; Josh 2:19; Judg 2:15; 1 Sam 18:17, 21; 24:13-14); cf. the references to a plague/blow (*negep*, Exod 12:13; 30:12) or sin (*ḥēṭ'*, Deut 15:9; 23:21-22[22-23]; 24:15) being on/against someone; see 2 Kgs 24:3 ("upon Judah" = "against Judah"). In Nah 3:9, the preposition is usually rendered "among" (cf., e.g., Deut 7:14; 15:4, 7; Ps 81:9[10]; Dan 1:6); see further below.

l. Hebrew *'ezrātēk* is usually rendered "her helpers" (cf. LXX, Syr.), but MurXII, 8ḤevXII-Igr, Tg., and Vulg. confirm the second-person suffix of the MT; for *'ezrah* ("help, assistance") with reference to a group of helpers, cf. Isa 31:2.

m. Hebrew *gam* has the nuance of "nevertheless" here; see Casper J. Labuschagne, "The Emphasizing Particle *GAM* and Its Connotations," in *Studia Biblica et Semitica Theodoro Christiano Vriezen Quie Munere Professoris Theologiae per XXV Annos Functus Est, ab Amicis, Collegis, Discipulis Dedicata*, ed. A. S. van Unnik and Adam S. van der Woude (Wageningen: H. Veenman, 1966), 193-203. It is therefore usually rendered "yet," but the nuance in the next line is different, and it is worth preserving the fourfold repetition of *gam* in vv. 10-11.

n. Hebrew *laggōlâ* does not belong to the common idiom for going (*hlk*) into exile, which takes *baggōlâ* (cf. 4QNah); see Jer 48:11; 49:3; Ezek 12:11; 25:3; Amos 1:15; cf. Jer 29:16; 48:7; Zech 14:2, with *yṣ'* for *hlk*. If we have two clauses (see following note), the first clause is without verb and may be interpreted "became an exile" (e.g., NRSV, NASB), but the rendering above seems the more natural interpretation of the Hebrew; so also Fabry, *Nahum*, 200, and similarly Jeremias, *Nahum*, 183-84.

o. Hebrew *hālkâ baššebî* (*went into captivity*), as in Deut 28:41; Isa 46:2; Jer 20:6; 22:22; 30:16 (cf. 48:46 with *luqqəhû*, "taken"); Lam 1:18; Ezek 12:11; 30:17-18; Amos 9:4. The line could be read as one clause ("She too, as an exile, went into captivity"), but this seems to me less likely.

p. The *yiqtol yəruṭṭəšû* is not used here for imperfect, future action ("will be dashed to pieces") but expresses simultaneity (see *HALOT*) or maybe continuous, repeated action over a period of time. There is no need to emend the text, contra *BHS*. Patterson (*Nahum*, 99) considers the form a preterite.

q. Hebrew *nikbaddêhā*, "her honored ones."

r. Hebrew *gôral* is a collective singular and used in this way with *ydd* also in Joel 3:3(4:3) and Obad 11. The plural *gôrālôt* is used only ten times in the Bible.

s. Hebrew *gədôlêhā*, "her great ones."

t. Hebrew *ruttəqû* is a unique *pual* form of a root that is attested elsewhere only in Eccl 12:6 (*niphal*) and in Isa 40:19 (*rətūqôt*, a nominal form). The rare root *rtq* may have been chosen for its sound (Spronk, *Nahum*, 131).

u. Hebrew *təhî na'ălāmâ* (understood as "you will become hidden/concealed") probably refers to becoming unconscious (cf. *HALOT*). A connection with *'almâ* ("young woman"), either in the sense of "you will become young again" (Cathcart, *Nahum*, 137-38, following Dahood) or in the sense "you will be deflowered" (Seybold, *Nahum*, 39-40), seems to me less likely.

v. The line division follows the accentuation here. Some (e.g., *BHS*) suggest reading four cola. The same applies to the next verse.

w. The plural noun *ta'ēnîm* can refer to fig trees or figs. The former is suggested by the construction of the phrase, for which cf. *pardēs rimmônîm 'im pərî məgādîm* ("an orchard of pomegranates with choice fruits") in Song 4:13. For LXX *sykai skopous* ("fig trees with guards"), note Hos 9:10 (*hôs skopon en sykē*) and see Dogniez, "Fautes," 257–59, who points out that the translator knows that *bikkûrâ* refers to *ta prōtogona* (Mic 7:1) and argues that the choice of a metaphor for firstfruits is deliberate here; cf. BA 23.4–9, 227.

Composition

The rhetorical comparison of Nineveh with Thebes unifies this section. In interpreting the passage, it is important to remember that the fall of Thebes, to which Nahum alludes, was brought about by the Assyrians. Nahum's first readers and listeners would surely have known this. If the received Hebrew text is retained (*your helpers*, v. 9) and interpreted along the lines suggested below, each verse addresses Nineveh directly except for the middle verse, which focuses on the outcome of Thebes's defeat. In fact, we may wonder whether the unit was designed as a thematic palistrophe:

> A Rhetorical questioning of Nineveh's sense of security (v. 8)
> B Thebes's allies did not withstand Nineveh's helpers (v. 9)
>> C The fate of Thebes (v. 10)
> B' Nineveh will not withstand its enemy (v. 11)
> A' Statement about Nineveh's false sense of security (v. 12)

The correspondence of A and A', two verses that question the effectiveness of Nineveh's (natural) bulwark and (artificial) fortifications, seems straightforward enough. The correspondence between B and B' consists in the detail that only these two verses make explicit reference to third parties—to entities other than Nineveh and Thebes.[384] But in my view, this correspondence is not very strong, and the repetition of *too* can be used as an argument for taking vv. 10–11 more closely together. Hence, the palistrophe above is better considered a reading possibility than an intrinsic compositional feature of this unit.

Verse 12 presents a suitable conclusion whose burden it is to show that even mighty fortifications and cities may fall. The verse perhaps does not so much indicate that Nineveh's defenses are insufficient as v. 14 will do, but it

---

384. This presumes reading v. 12b as a general statement about the readiness for the taking of Nineveh's fortifications without specifically identifying *the* (fig) *eater* with Nineveh's enemy.

suggests in the language of harvesting that *fortifications* have a shelf life, as we might say. Thebes is not portrayed as having been weak and easy for the Assyrians to take. To the contrary, the points in favor of Thebes are enumerated in detail. But when the time came, Thebes was ripe for the taking, and so will be Nineveh. This line of argument unifies vv. 8–12 and separates it thematically from the following, which will have more to say about the people in Nineveh and the weakness of the city's defenses. It should also be noted that v. 10, by spelling out the fate of Thebes, implicitly offers more detail about the fate that awaits Nineveh than the following two units.

Commentary

8 The beginning of the verse is often translated "Are you better . . . ?" but this translation is not without problems. The meaning "to be good" not only requires us to identify the form as a *qal*, which is possible,[385] but also to face the objection that the *qal* of *ytb* is not used elsewhere with the meaning "to be good" without an indirect object being specified, most often with the complement "in the eyes of."[386] The question "Are you any better . . . ?" is asked in Judg 11:25 in the form *hăṭôb ṭôb* (with the *qal* infinitive and participle), and we might expect the same here.[387] The reference is thus more likely to an expected outcome (*Will you fare better . . . ?*), for which the verb is used regularly (e.g., Gen 12:13).[388]

No-Amon (*nō' 'āmôn*) is Thebes in Upper Egypt and translates as "City of Amon," whereby *nō'* probably reflects the Egyptian word for city.[389] Amon/Amun[390] is an Egyptian god who is often depicted with a human body and the head of a ram and who came to be identified with Ra, the sun god of

385. See the translation note on the form as pointed by the Masoretes (*têṭbî*).

386. In Neh 2:5–6, *lipnê* ("before") is used for something being pleasing to someone. First Samuel 20:13 has *'el* ("toward"), but most common is *ba'ênê* ("in the eyes of").

387. While *ṭôb* may refer to being likeable rather than (morally) good, when used absolutely (Num 24:5; 1 Sam 2:26; Song 4:10), it is evident that it can refer to a state of being good more easily than a *yiqtol* form (for which *ytb* is used), especially one that can easily be interpreted as a *hiphil* like the form employed here in Nahum.

388. The translation "Will you behave better . . . ?" could also be defended from usage elsewhere (cf. Gen 4:7), but it does not fit here.

389. The feminine ending *t* of the Egyptian word (*niwt*) is dropped; cf. *Ni* in Assyrian texts. The *aleph* in the Hebrew spelling is possibly a replacement of weakened *w* or simply a vowel-letter (Kenneth A. Kitchen, personal letter to author, September 10, 2001). J. Van Doorslear ("No Amon," *CBQ* 11 [1949]: 280–95) sought to defend the old identification of No with Alexandria, unsuccessfully in my view.

390. In the names of Egyptian Pharaohs, the deity is vocalised with "e" in the second syllable; thus Amenhotep or Amenophis ("Amun is satisfied").

Heliopolis. Thebes was the main city in Upper Egypt, and Egyptian texts sometimes refer to it simply as the "southern city" or even "the city."[391] Assurbanipal's conquest of Thebes in 663 BC was a remarkable and significant event.[392] Indeed, it has been suggested that Manasseh named his son Amon in commemoration of the Assyrian success, thus expressing his loyalty to Assurbanipal.[393] This may be one reason for giving the fuller name *No-Amon*, rather than simply *No*,[394] reminding readers that some Judeans identified and celebrated with the Assyrians.

Thebes is protected by *the sea* in more than one sense. The Nile delta could serve as an outer line of defense,[395] and the Nile itself, during the inundation season at any rate, acted as a *bulwark*. In fact, there are reports of campaigns that had to be abandoned even in later times because of the inundations of the Nile.[396]

The Nile sometimes divides into multiple courses, but because its course is unstable and has changed over the years, we cannot determine what the precise situation was in the seventh century BC. Schneider points to Greek ostraca that testify to the presence of at least four islands around Thebes in the later Ptolemaic and Roman period and produces evidence for an "island of Amenope" at an earlier time (1100 BC).[397] Thus it is a fair assumption that there were multiple river-courses in the seventh century. In any case, there were also canals that channeled water from the river to the temples. The picture of Thebes as surrounded by water is therefore not entirely implausible. The emphasis on water may, however, also owe something to the target of this comparison, Nineveh.[398] We might even suspect a mythological background. Like other Egyptian cult centers, Thebes was praised as the first

391. Cf. "No" in Jer 46:25 (the punishment upon Amon of Thebes) and in Ezek 30:14–16. Another Egyptian name indicates its political role, *w3st* ("[It of] the *Waset*-scepter").

392. See *ANET*, 295–97.

393. Dominic Rudman, "A Note on the Personal Name Amon (2 Kings 21,19–26 // 2 Chr 33,21–25)," *Bib* 81 (2000): 403–5. One may ask, however, whether the Assyrian overlords would have been thrilled with a vassal ruler who named his crown prince after the chief of the Egyptian pantheon. The Hebrew personal name is not unique to the (later) king of Judah (cf. 1 Kgs 22:26; Neh 7:59) and is usually derived from the Heb. root for "being firm, trustworthy, safe" (*'mn*); cf. Martin Noth, *Die israelitischen Personennamen im Rahmen der gemeinsemitischen Namengebung* (Stuttgart: Kohlhammer, 1923), 228.

394. Grütter ("A Tale of One City," 165–69) believes that the fuller designation only makes sense from the Hellenistic period. I do not believe that the evidence she presents requires this.

395. Any attack on Thebes at that time would have come from the north. The first Assyrian campaign against Egypt was in fact stopped in the Nile delta; see the excursus below.

396. See Schneider, "Nahum und Theben," 67, for campaigns in 373 and 306.

397. Schneider, "Nahum und Theben," 65.

398. John R. Huddlestun ("Nahum, Nineveh, and the Nile: The Description of Thebes in

place to have emerged from the primeval waters at creation: "The water and land were in her from the first times."[399] But there is no thought here in Nahum of Thebes being flooded and thus returned to chaos. The main point of comparison is that Thebes also had been thought to be secure from attack.

EXCURSUS: ASSYRIAN CAMPAIGNS AGAINST EGYPT

Esarhaddon and Assurbanipal between them are responsible for five campaigns against Egypt between 674 and 664,[400] at the time under the control of a Cushite dynasty.[401] The reason for the first campaign is uncertain, but it is likely that the Assyrians were concerned about Cushite-Egyptian influence in Syria-Palestine. The first campaign (674) failed at one of Egypt's border fortresses at the edge of the Eastern delta, possibly at Pelusium. Esarhaddon was more successful in 671, causing Pharaoh Taharqa's temporary retreat to Thebes and to Nubia. Taharqa's return prompted the third campaign in 669, which was not concluded due to Esarhaddon's death during the campaign. Exploiting Assyria's momentary weakness, Taharqa recaptured Memphis, his former place of residence, but Assurbanipal responded quickly and brought Lower Egypt back under Assyrian control in 667. His attempt to extend the Assyrian empire southward failed, however. Returning from Upper Egypt, Assurbanipal ended a conspiracy against the Assyrian occupation in Lower Egypt and secured Assyrian influence by putting loyal Egyptians in positions of power.

After the death of Taharqa, Tantamun (Tanutamani), the son of Taharqa's sister, came into power. He immediately attempted to recover Cush's sphere of influence in Lower Egypt but failed to persuade all the delta princes to rebel against Assyria. Among those who fled before Tantamun and awaited

Nahum 3:8–9," *JNES* 62 [2003]: 97–110) argues that the descriptions of Thebes here were inspired by Nineveh.

399. *ANET*, 8.

400. Esarhaddon seems to have led his three campaigns himself; Assurbanipal apparently did not. See *ARAB*, vol. 2, for primary texts. Especially important are par. 580 (pp. 226–27) for Esarhaddon and par. 770–775, 776–778 (pp. 292–96) for Assurbanipal's records of his two campaigns.

401. For this excursus, I have leaned on Hans-Ulrich Onasch, *Die assyrischen Eroberungen Ägyptens*, 2 vols., ÄAT 27 (Wiesbaden: Harrassowitz, 1994); and Kenneth A. Kitchen, "Egyptian Interventions in the Levant in Iron Age II," in *Symbiosis, Symbolism, and the Power of the Past: Canaan, Ancient Israel, and Their Neighbors from the Late Bronze Age through Roman Palaestina—Proceedings of the Centennial Symposium W. F. Albright Institute of Archaeological Research and American Schools of Oriental Research Jerusalem, May 29–31, 2000*, ed. William G. Dever and Seymour Gitin (Winona Lake, IN: Eisenbrauns, 2003), 113–32.

Assyrian intervention was Psamtik I, whom the Assyrians later installed as Pharaoh. Assurbanipal's second Egyptian campaign forced Tantamun to withdraw beyond Thebes to the south. Thebes, with its rich temples, was plundered but not destroyed. Among other things, the Assyrians took baboons and long-tailed monkeys and two obelisks back to their homeland.

Along with the rest of Egypt, Thebes appears to have recovered well. Psammetich I, the founder of the twenty-fifth dynasty, put an end to local chiefdoms and united Egypt. His centralized government brought Egypt renewed prosperity. It is generally thought that Egypt's independence was ended only in the fourth century BC by the Persian Empire under Cambyses.[402]

9 *Cush was her strength and Egypt, without limit* alludes to the fact that Egypt was governed at the time of the conquest of Thebes by a Cushite dynasty. The Pharaoh, with his power base in Upper Egypt, was in effect a suzerain to the various local princes in Lower Egypt. While Egypt was in a period of politically fragile disunity, its strength may have seemed unlimited given that the Assyrians had so far failed to bring the kingdom under their control.

Put and Libyans is a reference either to tribes in Libya or to powers to the south (Nubia) as well as the west of Egypt (see the translation notes). These were helping to defend Thebes against the Assyrian army. The preposition *bə* in the verse's concluding clause (*against*) is universally translated "among," which would suggest either that the author erroneously regarded *Put and Libyans* as Assyrian allies[403] or that the address suddenly shifts from Nineveh to Thebes.[404] As for the former, in my judgment such a mistake could only rest on ignorance rather than "false knowledge,"[405] but if the author was ignorant about these peoples, why would he mention them at all?[406] And what would be the rationale for giving such prominence to Assyrian allies? As for the latter, it is true that there are poetic, and especially prophetic, texts that

---

402. If true, this has implications for our understanding of Jer 46:13–26 and Ezek 30:1–19. But this is beyond the scope of a commentary on Nahum. See, in principle, Thomas Renz, "Proclaiming the Future: History and Theology in Prophecies Against Tyre," *TynBul* 51 (2000): 17–58.

403. Cf. Spronk, *Nahum*, 130.

404. So Maier, *Nahum*, 323 ("This abrupt change of person is for emphasis"); Robertson, *Nahum*, 115; Patterson, *Nahum*, 99.

405. In other words, while it is conceivable that someone might have no knowledge of *Put and Libyans*, it is difficult to think of a reason why anyone should have considered them Assyrian allies.

406. For similar reasons, it is unlikely that the change was introduced by a later scribe. Surely, scribes would "correct" texts only when they thought they knew better; i.e., they would change the text based on (false) knowledge rather than mere ignorance.

attest a more or less abrupt substitution of one person for another.[407] Sometimes a third-person statement about the addressee appears in the midst of a second-person address, perhaps rhetorically suggesting greater distance from author and reader. In other places a third-person statement may shift to direct address (accusation). But the situation in Nah 3:9 is different from these examples because, rather than a mixture of second and third person for the same referent, it would use the same person for different referents if the translation of the preposition is "among." Here, one would have to assume that within a rhetorical question addressed to a feminine singular entity, a feminine singular suffix is suddenly employed to refer to a different entity. This seems rhetorically implausible.[408]

These problems disappear if one translates the preposition as *against* (see the translation note). In this case, Nineveh is addressed, as in the other verses in this unit, and reminded that *Put and Libyans were against* her own *helpers.* To grant that the Assyrians had helpers does not reduce the force of the argument here, because it merely grants the obvious. It was, of course, known within Judah that the Assyrians employed auxiliary troops. Assyrian treaty obligations upon their vassals included the provision of soldiers for the Assyrian army. The real (Judean) audience may also have granted the superior force of the relatively independent desert tribes referred to as *Put and Libyans*, as compared with the Assyrian auxiliary troops conscripted from the peoples subjugated in Syria-Palestine.

10 In spite of everything it had going for it, Thebes, too, was marked out *for exile* and was brought *into captivity.* This Assyrian deportation of Cushites and Egyptians is dramatized in Isa 20:4 with the same words. The term *captivity* refers to the state of being captive, not to the place in which one is held captive.[409]

Being smashed refers to being dashed to pieces or hammered to death.[410] Such brutal acts are indeed attested for the Assyrians, although not for them alone. Possibly, the cruelty of killing children represents a calculated attempt to prevent the growth of a generation that will seek revenge for the murder of

---

407. See GKC 144p. Cf. 2:13(14) if the reading *rikbāh* ("her chariots") is followed; but see the discussion above. Nah 3:7 does not belong here because the shift of person relates to the citation. This must qualify Patterson's (*Nahum*, 99) claim, made with appeal to these two verses, that sudden shifts of person are typical for Nahum.

408. It is also rather different from the use of direct speech to liven up an exposition as in 2:8(9), for which see Alonso Schökel, *Manual*, 154–55.

409. Cf. *'ereṣ šibyām* ("land of captivity") in Jer 30:10; 46:27; 2 Chr 6:37–38.

410. The verb is used in Aramaic and later Hebrew also for "throwing away" or "casting out," but in the Bible, more violent action seems to be always in view; cf. Hos 10:14; 13:16 (14:1); Isa 13:16 for the *pual*; 2 Kgs 8:12 and Isa 13:18 for the *piel*.

their parents.[411] But it surely also expresses the fact that violence has its own dynamic. It may remind us that people get carried away in war in more than one sense of the word. The phrase *at the head of every street* (*bərō'š kol-ḥûṣôt*) probably refers to the intersections of narrower lanes with one of the city's main streets. These may well have been the places where young children played, given that the expression is used in connection with children in all four occurrences in the Bible.[412] The last two lines picture the most honored and powerful men (presumably) of Thebes as degraded and powerless.

11 The imagery of drunkenness for defeat needs little explanation. As those who had too much drink reel, stagger, and fall, so soldiers stumble and fall as they are overwhelmed by the enemy. A comment in the NET Bible goes further: "Drunkards frequently pass out and wine drools out of their mouth; likewise, slain warriors lie fallen and their blood flows out of their mouths."[413] But the parallel with 1:10 (*like their drink drunk*) may be more significant. Nineveh will get so drunk taking in the wealth of other nations that it will pass out and become helpless.[414] The idea of *refuge* also alludes back to ch. 1 (*he knows those who seek refuge in him*, v. 7).

12 The *fortifications* to which the text and its central metaphor refer are probably not the forts outside the city but the strongholds protecting the wall and gates of Nineveh itself, as in v. 14.[415] The *firstfruits* of the *fig trees* are those everyone is eager to get (cf. Isa 28:4; Mic 7:1). They are ripe for the taking; *when* the fig trees *are shaken*, the figs *fall into the mouth of the eater.*[416] This can be read as a conditional clause, expressing a general truth ("whenever fig trees that carry early ripe figs are shaken . . .") but also as a temporal clause with a predictive force ("when the fortifications will be shaken . . .").[417] In

---

411. More or less the same phrase is used in 2 Kgs 8:12; Isa 13:16, 18; Hos 10:14; 13:16 (14:1); cf. Amos 1:13.

412. Isa 51:20 and Lam 2:19 refer to children fainting for lack of food. The "sacred stones" in Lam 4:1 are likely also children (see v. 2). A different expression is used in Ezek 16:25, 31 for the place where prostitutes offer their services (*rō'š derek*). The locality may well be the same, presumably frequented by prostitutes at a different time of the day; but it is not necessarily so if *derek* ("main street") and *ḥûṣôt* ("side paths") were differentiated. The side roads in large cities may well have been broader than some main roads in smaller towns, which may explain the presence of chariots in such streets in 2:4(5).

413. Cf. Jer 25:27, which, however, refers to vomit. See also Isa 51:21–22 for numbness and staggering as a result of drinking from the cup of God's wrath.

414. See Perlitt, *Nahum*, 34. The concept of YHWH letting his enemies drink from the cup of his wrath seems to be later and may be dependent on this passage; cf. Spronk, *Nahum*, 132.

415. So also Spronk, *Nahum*, 133.

416. *Tə'ēnîm* (*fig trees*) is feminine; the masculine verbs agree with *bikkûrîm* (*figs*). Nevertheless, the trees are surely beaten for the figs to fall.

417. For the less frequent use of *'im* in a temporal clause, cf. JM 167p; GKC 164d. In this verse, the temporal-predictive sense is facilitated by the use of a *yiqtol* form in the protasis.

Mic 4:4, the fig tree is part of a picture of prosperity and peace. The early fruit, which grows on the shoots of the previous year, is especially succulent and hence desirable.[418] The simile therefore suggests that far from being intimidated by Nineveh's strongholds, the attackers will be only too eager to shake them and to plunder whatever Nineveh has to offer. The reference to *firstfruits* may also imply that Nineveh would fall easily and quickly, especially if the juicy *firstfruits* fall more easily from the tree than the later fruit, grown on that year's shoots.

Reflection

Who had really determined the fall of Thebes? The text does not spell it out, although the previous unit has prepared us for the idea that cities and fortifications and empires may have a limited shelf life. Those who saw in the fall of Thebes merely proof of Assyria's superior strength would have been tempted to answer the question *Will you fare better than No-Amon?* in the affirmative. Of course Nineveh will fare better. After all, it got the better of Thebes. But those whose eyes are trained by the theology expressed in the opening poem realize that Thebes did not find refuge because YHWH had not granted them refuge from the Assyrians. The echoes of ch. 1 observed above may encourage us to make such a link.

Patterson notes that the fourfold recurrence of *gam* (*too*) in vv. 10–11 "has the effect of the clarion peal of a bell dolefully sounding out the awful truth that Nineveh, too, must surely re-enact the tragic experience of Thebes."[419] This is possibly anachronistic, given that the analogy only works where low-pitch bells are known and heard as doleful. But the reading is evocative and true to the sentiments of the passage. If the use of the second person provides the passage with a personal note, the fourfold use of *gam* (*too*) strikes an impersonal note of "Time is up!"

The effect is a complete turnaround. The conquerors of Thebes are themselves conquered. *Public figures*, whose word carried weight in Thebes, had become the private property of various members of the Assyrian army, whose word they had to heed. The *dignitaries* who wore colorful robes and maybe chains of office had found themselves dressed in *chains* and fetters.[420]

---

418. Gustaf Dalman, *Jahreslauf und Tageslauf*, vol. 1 of *Arbeit und Sitte in Palästina* (Gütersloh: C. Bertelsmann, 1928), 378–80.

419. Patterson, *Nahum*, 100.

420. The way I phrase the contrast is anachronistic (public figure turns private property, chains of office become prison chains), but cf. *rətūqôt* (!) *kesep ṣôrēp* in Isa 40:19, which may refer to silver chains (on idols), and the golden necklace (*rəbîd hazzāhāb*) given by Pharaoh to Joseph in Gen 41:42.

Instead of looking back to this as a great success story, the Assyrians are now (rhetorically) invited to see their own fate prefigured in these events.

The killing of children is designed to eliminate the conditions for a new cycle of violence. People who kill even children may attempt to justify the exercise of such violence as a means to prevent revenge and further violence in the future—in short, to protect their own future progeny. But in God's economy, this does not work: those who live by the sword will die by the sword (cf. Matt 26:52). If the sword of Thebes is not lifted against Nineveh, the revenge comes from a different quarter. Nahum merely alludes to the idea that violence has a divine way of falling back upon its perpetrators, a truth affirmed more explicitly in Habakkuk.

We do not know whether the expression "drunk with/from violence" was known in Israel and Judah. Isa 49:26, which announces that Zion's oppressors will have to eat their own flesh and drink their own blood, suggests to me that in the past these oppressors reveled in the carnage and bloodshed that they caused, getting drunk with Zion's blood. If so, the idea may not be entirely foreign even in the context in which Nahum was written. But the book of Habakkuk is the place where military conquest is discussed further in terms of self-destructive greed.

XI. EXPOSITION OF THE USELESSNESS OF THE CITY'S DEFENSES (3:13-17)

13 *Look, your people*[a] *are women in your midst*
    for your enemies[b]*—wide open are the gates of your land;*[c]
        fire has consumed your bars.[d]
14 *Draw for yourself water for the siege;*
    reinforce your fortifications.
Go in the clay and tread the mortar;
    take hold [e] *of the brickwork.*
15 *There,*[f] *fire will consume you,*
    a sword will cut you down.
It will consume you like grasshoppers.[g]
    Growing heavy[h] *like grasshoppers, proliferate*[i] *like locusts!*[j]
16 *You have multiplied your merchants*
    more than[k] *the stars in the skies.*
        Grasshoppers shed [their skin][l] *and fly.*
17 *Your courtiers*[m] *are like a locust swarm,*
    and your officials[n] *like a horde of locusts.*[o]
They are camping[p] *in the walls*[q] *on a cold day:*

The sun rises and it^r has disappeared,
  and its place is unknown.
    Where are they?^s

a. Hebrew *'ammēk* is often rendered "your troops" (e.g., RSV, NIV) because *'am* sometimes refers to soldiers specifically, e.g., in Judg 20:10; 2 Sam 10:10; 2 Kgs 8:21; 13:7; Ezek 26:7. In many such places, the translation "people" is entirely feasible. See the commentary.

b. The suggestion in *BHS* to read *biqrōb* (*kōl*) *'ōybayik* ("when [all] your enemies draw near") for MT *baqirbēk lə'ōybayik* (in your midst for your enemies) is neither supported by the versions nor necessary. The dash reflects the belief that *lə'ōybayik* is pivotal; see the commentary.

c. It is not clear whether gates of your land (*ša'ărê 'arṣēk*) is equivalent to "gates of your city" (cf. the use of Akkadian *erṣetu* for the territory of a city) or to "cities of your land." See the commentary.

d. The *shewa* missing from the last letter of Nah 3:13 in Codex Leningradensis, and hence *BHS*, is present in the Cairo and the Aleppo Codices.

e. Note the double use of the root *hzq* ("to be strong") in the piel (*reinforce*) and hiphil (*take hold*). The line division here is debatable. The Masoretes seem to take the last three imperatives together in one colon; the layout in *BHS* suggests three cola.

f. Hebrew *šām*: "In poetry, pointing to a spot in which a scene is localized vividly in the imagination" (BDB), maybe shading into temporal "then"; cf. *HALOT*, where Dahood's proposal "Look!" for a number of passages in the Psalms, which would fit here, is also discussed.

g. The singular *yeleq* is always used collectively for a swarm of grasshoppers; *'arbê* (locusts) later in the verse is nearly always collective (exceptions: Exod 10:19b; Job 39:20; Ps 109:23). The plural is attested for neither. Aron Pinker ("On the Meaning of *HTKBD* in Nahum iii 15," *VT* 53 [2003]: 558–61) believes that *yeleq* (grasshoppers) refers to the younger form of the insect that does not multiply, and he takes it with the following line, translating *kayyāleq hitkabbēd* as "larva that grew heavy" (559); cf. LXX *barynthēsē hōs brouchos* ("you shall be weighed down like the locust larva"; *brouchos* can refer to the locust or its wingless larva, but the verb *barynō* suggests the latter). He considers the following *kayyeleq hitkabbĕdî* as a marginal correction (by a scribe who misunderstood the phrase) that later crept into the text, and he takes the final word of the verse (*kā'arbê*, like locusts) with the following line. But the identification of *yeleq* as larva that cannot fly is not secure (see the commentary). While the ferocious appetite of the developing larva would perhaps be a suitable image for a devouring sword, the way (adult) locust swarms fall upon a land is a more obvious image for military invasion.

h. Hebrew *hitkabbēd* could be analyzed as a masculine singular imperative but is best considered an infinitive. Some believe that the infinitive is used in place of the feminine singular imperative (cf. *hitkabbədî* later in the verse); so, e.g., Roberts, *Nahum*, 71. Jeremias (*Nahum*, 200–201), allows for this but suspects that the form is a spelling mistake for *hitkab-bədî*. Following Van der Woude, Spronk (*Nahum*, 137) argues that the infinitive is used as a noun functioning as an adverbial accusative ("numerous") and suggests the same for *hitkab-bədî* (with *yod compaginis*; cf. GKC 90l). The latter suggestion is implausible, given the origin of *yod compaginis* and the preposition in the following word; cf. also Meyer, *Grammatik*, 2:50–51. The precise meaning of the verb, which in any case is rarely attested in the *hithpael* (Prov 12:9 for someone who confers honor on themselves; *DCH* also gives occurrences in Sir 3:10; 10:26–27, 31; 4Q416, frag. 2) is disputed. Pinker ("Meaning of *HTKBD*," 559) designates "be heavy" as "the basic meaning," which he prefers to "a figurative derivative" such as "multiply" (often used by translators of this verse); cf. Christensen, *Nahum*, 382. I tentatively assume a play on two meanings of the verb.

i. The imperative is a feminine singular form. On the meaning of the verb, see the previous note. The roots *kbd* and *rbh* (multiplied, v. 16) are found in parallel in Jer 30:19 and Hab 2:6, but not as synonyms. The repetition of *kbd* is not reflected in the standard witnesses to LXX; a few later MSS supply *plēthynō hōs brouchos*, thus using two different Greek verbs for the same Hebrew verb. This later addition is irrelevant for evaluating the translation style of the original translator (see the commentary on 1:4). 8ḤevXIIgr apparently reflected the repetition, but it is insufficiently preserved for us to draw firm conclusions about what the text read; see *Biblia Qumranica* 3B:122. Grütter (*Nahum*, 190–217), argues that LXX reflects an earlier edition and the MT a conflation of two readings; cf. Pinker, "Meaning."

j. The precise identification of locusts is uncertain. With grasshoppers, difference in appearance is greater between the various life stages of one species than between different species compared at the same stage, and for this reason it is commonly assumed that the different Hebrew terms refer to different stages of development. In this case *'arbê* (locust) is perhaps the fully grown adult, *yeleq* (grasshopper) the younger insect. The fact that the same four terms for locust appear in both Joel 1:4 and 2:25 but in a different order arguably poses a difficulty for the notion that the Hebrew words clearly designate four distinct stages of the insect's development. See Ovid R. Sellers, "Stages of Locust in Joel," *The American Journal of Semitic Languages and Literatures* 52 (1936): 81–85.

k. Cat Quine ("Nineveh's Pretensions to Divine Power in Nahum 3:16," *VT* 69 [2019]: 498–504) observes that YHWH is always said to multiply his people "like the stars" rather than "more than the stars," which is used only here. She observes that "only a being of extraordinary power or extraordinary hubris could claim to multiply humans more than the stars" (500), although this verse is addressed to Nineveh rather than put on Nineveh's lips.

l. Hebrew *pāšaṭ* is here understood with most commentators in the sense of shedding skin, similar to its use for taking off clothes (e.g., Lev 6:11[4]; 1 Sam 19:24; Isa 32:11); see *HALOT*. Alternatively, one could read "stretch themselves" or "spread their wings," namely toward plunder and thus stripping the land (cf. Patterson, *Nahum*, 102), or simply "plunder." Keil (*Minor Prophets*) believes that the verb "never means anything else than to plunder, or to invade with plundering" (2:39), but its use for taking off garments provides a credible parallel, and shedding skin is a plausible step toward flying away. This is the only time that the verb has locusts as its subject.

m. Hebrew *minnazār* occurs only here in the Bible and appears to be an Akkadian loanword; see Kevin J. Cathcart, "Micah 2:4 and Nahum 3:16–17 in the Light of Akkadian," *Fucus* 58 (1988): 197–98; Spronk, *Nahum*, 140.

n. Hebrew *ṭapsarayik* (cf. *ṭipsār* in Jer 51:27) is from an Akkadian word ("tablet-writer") that seems to designate a record-keeper such as were employed in the army but also in other contexts.

o. Hebrew *kagôb gōbāy*. Given that *gōbāy* likely refers to a swarm of locusts (only found elsewhere in Amos 7:1; cf. *gēbîm* in Isa 33:4), as do other words for locusts, *gôb* (already attested in MurXII) either expresses the superlative by repetition (cf. Vulg.) or is the result of dittography.

p. Hebrew *haḥōnîm* ("those who encamp, the camping ones"). The plural masculine participle may have been used with reference to *your courtiers* and *your officials* (albeit pictured as locusts); so also the suffix at the end of the verse (*they*).

q. Hebrew *baggədērôt* could also refer to fences or hedges; cf. Cathcart, *Nahum*, 148.

r. The singular refers to the swarm or horde of locusts. The various collective singular terms for locusts invariably go with singular verbs and suffixes.

s. Hebrew *'ayyām* (cf. Isa 19:12) is an interrogative particle (*'ayyê, 'ê*) with suffix. Some take it with the following verse, often interpreting the *mem* as enclitic rather than as a suffix, but this would make it the only instance in which the particle on its own, rather than *'ê-mizzê* (e.g., 2 Sam 1:3) or *'ê-zê* (e.g., 1 Kgs 22:24), is followed directly by a verb. LXX *ouai autois* ("Woe to them") interprets as if from *'ôy*. James Nogalski (*Literary Precursors to the Book of the Twelve*, BZAW 217 [Berlin: de Gruyter, 1993], 44) reads *'āyōm* ("terrible"); Fabry (*Nahum*, 205) raises this as a possibility.

Composition

Nineveh continues to be addressed here, but vv. 13–17 bring us closer to the end of Nineveh than vv. 8–12. While the previous unit spoke of Nineveh as *fortifications* that are ready for the fate that had befallen Thebes, this unit leads us into the city and does so with a particular focus on the population (*people, merchants, courtiers, officials*). The first verse of the unit employs *qatal* (perfect) forms; v. 14 switches to imperatives and v. 15a to *yiqtol* (imperfect) forms. Thus, understanding the gates to be those of Nineveh,[421] it is possible to read 3:13 as a summary statement that looks already to the situation beyond the one described in the following verses. This would be analogous to 1:15 (2:1), which is also introduced with *hinnê* (*Look*).[422] If the verse presents a summary statement, we must not presume that there is a chronological sequence from v. 13 to v. 14. But the use of the phrase *gates of your land* rather than "gates of your city" could suggest that the reference is to Assyrian fortifications and cities that were meant to protect Nineveh and have already been overrun.[423] This, then, would allow for a chronological reading. Both readings seem possible, with the latter perhaps more likely, given that in the only other attested use of the phrase, in Jer 15:7, the *gates* are used by way of synecdoche for the cities of the land (of Judah).

Most commentators identify a sudden switch of metaphor in vv. 15–17, with the description *grasshoppers* being assigned to both the enemies of Nineveh and the Assyrians themselves. For some commentators, this has been one important datum among others for reconstructing the composi-

---

421. So, e.g., Cathcart, *Nahum*, 140–41 (including a reference to Jerome); Patterson, *Nahum*, 102; Spronk, *Nahum*, 135; Fabry, *Nahum*, 217.

422. By contrast, *hinnî* (*Look, I*) in 2:13(14) and 3:5 marks the beginning of a conclusion.

423. Thus Ralph L. Smith (*Nahum*, 347) believes the phrase must refer to "forts protecting the passes" because, in v. 14, Nineveh has not yet been breached. Cf., e.g., Maier, *Nahum*, 336; Roberts, *Nahum*, 75; Jeremias, *Nahum*, 197–98.

tion history of this unit.[424] As explained in the commentary on v. 15 below, it appears to be possible to read the metaphor in a way that would remove the inconsistency. But even if, as seems best, the double interpretation of the metaphor is retained, it is not clear whether this is the result of textual growth or a poetic device. Other problems have been identified in this unit, but most of them are more imaginary than real in my judgment. Thus, I see no reason to object to the use of different terms for locusts and believe that the use of masculine and feminine forms can be adequately explained. Nor am I troubled by a sunrise *on a cold day*.[425] The irregular rhythm may be the result of redactional changes, but it is not firm evidence of such changes.[426] The final clause in v. 15 is the most likely candidate for not being original, but a textual corruption may be more likely than redactional development (see the translation notes). *Grasshoppers shed [their skin] and fly* at the end of v. 16 looks like a marginal comment, which is perhaps original, preparing for the change of use of the metaphor in v. 17, but the remark may be an early gloss added to ensure that the multiplication of merchants is not read as an unambiguously positive statement.[427] If so, its attestation in every manuscript may encourage us to read it as a fully canonical "marginal comment."

Commentary

13 The *people* (*'am*) to which this verse refers may be specifically the defending "troops," as in a number of English translations. Elsewhere, the word describes units of military personnel (e.g., Judg 20:10; 1 Sam 14:17; 2 Sam 10:10; 2 Kgs 13:7). This rendering is plausible on the assumption that the statement *your people are women* is a metaphor that insults the army as incompetent and useless (cf. Jer 51:30; see further below).[428] Chapman observes that treaty

424. See, e.g., Spronk, *Nahum*, 139–40 (cf. "Synchronic," 185); Fabry, *Nahum*, 206–9.

425. Spronk (*Nahum*, 139) objects to *the sun rises* on the basis that *cold day* implies that the sun has already risen; cf. Fabry, *Nahum*, 208, 220. Note that Seybold (*Nahum*, 36–41; *Profane Prophetie*, 35–38), who confidently reconstructs an original Nahum text in 3:8–19 that deletes more than forty words from the MT, nevertheless seems to see no problem with this perceived incongruity.

426. Note the sensitive use of the length of lines in v. 17; see the commentary.

427. Jeremias (*Nahum*, 202–4) suggests that v. 16b belongs to the earlier text, with v. 16a having been added at a time when Judah felt the burden less of foreign officials than of foreign merchants. But foreign rule usually brings with it the presence of foreign merchants, as Jeremias appears to acknowledge, and I find it somewhat less likely that Nineveh was at first pictured as an administrative center only.

428. See Hillers, *Treaty-Curses*, 66–68; Chapman, *Gendered Language*, 48–59; Berlejung, "Erinnerungen," 338–39.

"curses that evoke images of feminization focus on the metaphorical domain of warfare."[429] She notes that "weapons of war came to signify masculinity."[430] Thus, men who metaphorically become *women* have lost the ability to fight. But there is no clear reference to soldiers in this unit and, as Floyd points out, *ʿam*, "when applied to a city or locality, normally refers to its entire population."[431] If this is the case here, *your people are women in your midst* is a way of saying that the men have been killed off, leaving only a female, noncombatant population in the city (cf. Isa 3:25–4:1). This would anticipate the disappearance of *courtiers* and *officials* (v. 17), and arguably *merchants* (v. 16), toward which this unit is headed (*Where are they?*). This makes good sense in terms of the structural considerations offered above.

If the statement is read as a metaphor (so the great majority of commentators),[432] we must proceed from the assumption that the "people" are male and likely soldiers. Given that the text is talking about the defenders, every able-bodied man would be a combatant, even if not a professional soldier. In this case, the troops are not given a more obviously military designation here either because they comprise all able-bodied men folk or because they are described as effectively nontroops. The metaphor of combatants as women is meant to evoke weakness and fear, maybe even defenselessness. Women did not ordinarily take up weapons in battle. Thus, to speak of combatants as *women* is to imply that they fail in their role as soldiers and thus in their role as men. They are *women* in that they are "failed men."[433]

Both ways of reading the statement are plausible. The former fits well in the context of this unit and exploits the fact that the text does not unambiguously refer to men.[434] The latter picks up a known metaphor, and

429. Chapman, *Gendered Language*, 48.

430. Chapman, *Gendered Language*, 52.

431. Floyd, *Minor Prophets 2*, 74. He draws attention to Jer 29:16, 25; Ruth 4:9; Zeph 1:11. All of these use *kol* ("all") with *ʿam*; cf. Jer 25:1–2; 26:18. Contrast *kol-ʿam yəhûdâ* ("all the people of Judah") in 2 Sam 19:41, which probably refers to Judah's militia; cf. 2 Kgs 14:21 and 2 Chr 26:1, where this is also possible. The people on the walls of Jerusalem in 2 Chr 32:18 are likely warriors. Examples for "people of PN" without *kol* ("all") referring to the entire population are Ezra 4:4; Isa 1:10; and probably Amos 1:5.

432. See also, tentatively, *DCH*, 6:431. Cf. LXX, which supplies *hōs* ("like"), and Tg., which elaborates "your people are as feeble as women." 8ḤevXIIgr, Vulg., and Syr. confirm the text of MT. The additions are evidence of early interpretation.

433. Cf. Chapman, *Gendered Language*, 7, 11–13, 48–50, 107–108; Bergmann, "We Have Seen," 671. Corinne L. Patton (" 'Should Our Sister Be Treated Like a Whore?': A Response to Feminist Critiques of Ezekiel 23," in *The Book of Ezekiel: Theological and Anthropological Perspectives*, ed. Margaret S. Odell and John T. Strong, SBL SymS 9 [Atlanta: Society of Biblical Literature, 2000], 235) wonders whether emasculation is in view, but there is no evidence that literal castration was a common practice; cf. Chapman, *Gendered Language*, 54.

434. Floyd (*Minor Prophets 2*, 74) argues in addition that "a sarcastic observation to the

it has to be said that there would have been less ambiguous ways of saying "only women are left" if that was all that was intended. We may allow for both meanings. They coalesce in the concept of failure to protect, either in the portrayal of the population as consisting of women left without protection or as men who fail to protect. I prefer the latter—the majority reading. Ishtar, the chief goddess of Nineveh, has an ambiguous gender identity and was believed to have "the power to change men into women and women into men."[435] The metaphorical reading is, thus, particularly appropriate in a speech against Nineveh.

The position of *for your enemies* in the verse deserves comment. If one takes it only with the following, the verse states that *the gates of your land* are wide open *for your enemies*. But the rhythm of the verse and the placement of the phrase *for your enemies* immediately after *in your midst* may also suggest that the enemies have already penetrated the city whose people are *women . . . for your enemies*. This develops sexual undertones if the next phrase (*wide open*) is taken with it.[436] The observation that *gates*, like other architectural openings, sometimes feature in ancient Near Eastern erotic poetry[437] adds plausibility to this view.[438] In this case, the defenders specifically fail to protect their women from physical and sexual harm. We may compare a threat in Esarhaddon's Succession Treaty: "May Venus, the brightest of stars, before your eyes make your wives lie in the lap of your enemy."[439] This would indicate the deepest level of shame and loss. If, however, *wide open* is read only with *gates of your land*, then the (separate) claim that the people are *women . . . for your enemies* might imply that the enemies take over the role of husbands, the women's protectors. This would fit with the ideology expressed in Assyrian palace reliefs depicting siege scenes.[440]

---

effect that Nineveh's troops have become cowardly and weak" is unlikely in the context of this unit. I do not see why. The verse speaks in the same breath of *gates* and *bars* as failing; cf. the need for reinforcing the *fortifications* in the next verse.

435. Chapman, *Gendered Language*, 56; Hillers, *Treaty-Curses*, 66.

436. Such a reading would be inescapable if the last phrase of this half verse (*gates of your land*) were missing. The question is therefore whether the introduction of the subject of *wide open*, namely *gates of your land*, invalidates the (initial) reading, which has *women* as the subject of *wide open*, or whether it supplements it.

437. Cf. Chapman, *Gendered Language*, 109–10.

438. Note also *pāthēn* in Isa 3:17, which is traditionally understood to refer to private parts (BDB; cf. KJV, NRSV, ESV). But *pāthēn* may be "their foreheads" (*HALOT*; cf. NASB; NIV, "their scalps"). *DCH* and Ges¹⁸ note the uncertainty.

439. Lines 428–29, cited from Chapman, *Gendered Language*, 42. Hillers (*Treaty-Curses*, 63) notes that this "is, to this writer's knowledge, unparalleled in other curse lists" but compares 2 Sam 12:11; 16:20–22; Jer 8:10; Job 31:10.

440. Cf. Chapman, *Gendered Language*, 46–47, who offers a convincing argument for reading the reliefs in this way. Note her definition of Assyrian ideology on p. 3 as "the in-

The *gates of your land* is an unusual phrase whose ambiguity has been discussed above. The only real parallel is found in Jer 15:7, where "gates of the land" (*ša'ărê hā'āreṣ*) probably refers to fortified cities. I prefer to read it this way here as well. Some readers would expect to first be told that *fire has consumed your bars* before hearing of the result of wide open gates.[441] The order in the text may be to strengthen the sexual undertones (see above), but it also makes sense logically. In this sequence, the verse does not speak of broken bars leading to open gates but of open gates that will assuredly remain open, unable to be closed again because their bars have been destroyed. In short, the verse moves from the city's vulnerability to its abuse by invaders to its utter defenselessness and complete defeat.

14 The imperatives in this verse are reminiscent of the ironic encouragement in 2:1(2) and fulfill the same function. It is well known that a besieged city must secure its *water* supply and *reinforce* its *fortifications*. Bricks are required because the supply of stones is not as abundant in Mesopotamia as in Israel and Judah. This is more than the (polemical) perspective from Jerusalem.[442] Scholars provide contradictory information about the walls of Nineveh, but most agree that there was a double wall. The main wall consisted of up to 180 layers of sun-dried mudbricks, reaching a height of more than twenty meters.[443] Deist claims that an imminent threat would not leave enough time to manufacture bricks and leave them to dry in the sun,[444] but a siege could be a protracted affair. Nineveh was under siege for three months, which leaves sufficient time to allow for the manufacture of new bricks for reinforcements. There is archaeological evidence for attempts to narrow the room within Nineveh's city gates, thus impeding the rapid progress of the attackers. "At the Halzi Gate . . . the width of the single entrance and that of an adjacent portion of the central corridor, was narrowed from 7 to 2 meters."[445] This could be one of the measures in the author's mind, but we should not

---

tegrated set of assertions regarding world view that the Neo-Assyrian kings actively promulgated in order to justify their socio-political program of conquering and annexing other peoples."

441. E.g., Fabry, *Nahum*, 217, who nevertheless considers the idea that the author employs a sexual metaphor "totally absurd" and seeks to explain the "strange" sequence with appeal to hendiadys.

442. Cf. Gen 11:3, using a different word for "bricks." Contrast the measures taken for reinforcing Jerusalem's fortification alluded to in Isa 22:10–11.

443. See, e.g., Julian E. Reade, "Ninive (Nineveh)," in *Reallexikon der Assyriologie und Vorderasiatischen Archäologie*, vol. 9, ed. Dietz O. Edzard (Berlin: de Gruyter, 2001), 388–433; Fabry, *Nahum*, 66; Pinker, "Greek Tradition."

444. Ferdinand E. Deist, *The Material Culture of the Bible: An Introduction* (Sheffield: Sheffield Academic Press, 2000), 200. Baked bricks were rarely used in Assyria.

445. Stronach and Lumsden, "UC Berkeley Excavations," 231. They refer to "a hastily installed blocking stone." Cf. p. 233 for the Shamash and Adad gates.

press Nahum for details as if we were presented with a war report rather than poetry designed to shape the audience's perspective on Nineveh.

15 This verse is intriguing in a number of ways. *There* focuses the imagination on a place we have been before. The place of hectic, even if ultimately useless, preparations (2:1[2]) is precisely the place of defeat. The first two lines use standard language to express this: *fire* destroying the city and the *sword* killing its inhabitants. Indeed, it has been observed that all words of this summary bicolon have been used before in the book.[446] But the third colon can be understood in different ways. Most interpreters (unless they change the text) assume that the consuming fire of the first line is now supplemented by consuming grasshoppers. A swarm of locusts is, of course, a potent and common image of destruction both in Scripture and beyond in ancient Near Eastern literature. But precisely for this reason, a swarm of locusts might also provide a good image for the (in their time) massive, seemingly unstoppable armies of the Assyrians. In this case it would be possible to construe the sense of the line not as "It will consume you like grasshoppers [consume the crop]," with *grasshoppers* being an image of the attackers, but as "It will consume you like [fire consumes] grasshoppers,"[447] with the *grasshoppers* an image of the defending army assembled in Nineveh. (Fire or, strictly speaking, the smoke it produces, may have been the main means of getting rid of locusts.) This would allow reading all references to *grasshoppers/locusts* in vv. 15–16 as relating to Assyrian soldiers, merchants, courtiers, and officials. But on balance, it is preferable to interpret (this first reference to) *grasshoppers* as the subject of the verb and hence a metaphor for the attacking troops.[448]

The feminine singular form of the imperative *proliferate* suggests that Nineveh is addressed, even if the simile of the *grasshoppers* is at first used for the attacking armies.[449] GKC 110a suggests that the imperative in the last line of the verse has concessive force ("though thou *make thyself many,* &c.").[450] But it may be better read as another mocking encouragement. Having grown heavy, feeding on other nations, the Assyrians may proliferate as much as they want to defend their territory, but it will do them no good. The coming doom can handle even the largest population! The next two verses elaborate on this idea. The Assyrians were indeed many compared to the

---

446. Spronk, *Nahum*, 136.

447. Cf. Maier, *Nahum*, 345–46. The reuse of *consume* would help such resorting to the first colon, jumping over the middle colon. "The sword consumes you like it consumes grasshopers," while grammatically possible, is not a reasonable alternative.

448. Cf. Christensen, *Nahum*, 380.

449. We would probably expect a masculine plural form to cheer on those who will bring Nineveh's downfall.

450. Cf. Maier, *Nahum*, 347.

smaller nations they had conquered (cf. 1:12), but their numbers will prove insignificant.[451]

16 This verse affirms that Nineveh has indeed multiplied its numbers (cf. 1:12), not least the number of its *merchants*, having become an active hub for trade with far-flung contacts.[452] Military expansion facilitated overland trade in that "royal roads" had to be kept in good repair, even if they were not paved at that time, and links were established between (Assyrian) settlements in the west and the Assyrian homeland.[453] In addition, the system of payment of annual tributes may have encouraged trade because the expected tribute payments were not always in the form of locally available produce, and hence homegrown goods had to be exchanged for produce asked for by the overlord. The focus here is on Assyria's merchants (*your merchants*),[454] or else merchants who play a willing part in Assyrian-controlled trade. Rephrasing the famous aphorism by Carl von Clausewitz according to which "war is a mere continuation of politics by other means," we may wonder whether trade is not sometimes experienced by conquered nations as a mere continuation of war by other means. In Nahum, at any rate, the proliferation of merchants in the Neo-Assyrian Empire is hardly seen in a positive light. Zephaniah seems to offer a similar perspective (see the commentary, e.g., on Zeph 1:8–11; 2:1–5). Quine notes the correlation between economic success and (false) claims to divinity in Isa 37:21–25 // 2 Kgs 19:20–24 and Ezek 28:1–6 and argues that this verse reflects Nineveh's pretensions to divine power. She observes that

> Nineveh's expansion of its merchant class—insofar as it affected Judah— could have been perceived as a challenge to Yahweh's authority on earth, as it came at the expense of Yahweh's people. Additionally, however, Nineveh's economic success reflected the success of its gods. . . . The issue

451. Christensen (*Nahum*, 382) translates "increase in substance" on the basis that the grasshoppers in question are too young to multiply. But this may be pressing the text too much, even if *yeleq* refers to locusts at the larval stage, which are too young to reproduce. The force of the comparison rests in the fact that locusts are usually encountered *en masse*, not that they breed many offspring at once.

452. Diederik J. W. Meijer, "Nineveh and Neo-Assyrian Trade: An Active Hub with Far-Flung Contacts," in Petit and Bonacossi, *Nineveh*, 170–73.

453. Sfronk (*Nahum*, 138) cites a text by Sargon II in which he boasts, "I opened the sealed borders of Egypt, mixed the inhabitants of Assyria and Egypt and made them trade" (*TUAT*, I/4, 382).

454. The reference may be specifically to the Assyrian *tamkare*, "large-scale entrepreneurs, who could become very rich in their own right, even to the extent that they lent money to the kings. . . . They often worked in the service of the kings and could combine business with diplomacy" (Meijer, "Nineveh," 172). The use of Assyrian terms in the next verse suggests some knowledge of Assyrian society.

at stake in Nah 3:16, therefore, was not an ethical concern about Nineveh's expanding economic practices, but rather the perceived challenge to Yahweh's authority created by them.[455]

The reference to *stars in the skies* to express extreme multitude is well known in the Bible but, as Quine observes, elsewhere YHWH alone has the power to multiply humans so that they will be as innumerable as the stars, and the multitude are always his people.[456] She also notes that in Neo-Assyrian royal iconography, "Ishtar was usually portrayed surrounded by stars or represented by them."[457]

The additional comment in this verse (*Grasshoppers shed [their skin] and fly*) seems premature in the flow of the passage. If we think of it as a marginal comment, its role is to ensure that readers at no point think too highly of Assyria's ability to increase business. Indeed, it casts the *merchants* in the role occupied in the previous verse by the attacking armies (following the interpretation advocated above). Just as an army falls over a land to raid it, the *merchants* are thus characterized as being in the trade for their own advantage rather than to enrich Assyria or Nineveh as such.[458] The merchants are like *grasshoppers* at the crawling larva stage, fairly stationary and hungry. Once they have eaten their fill, they lose their outer coat and fly away; they have no loyalty to the place in which they feed themselves. In the same way, Assyria's merchants will take what they can get and disappear in the face of grave danger to their livelihood (and lives), when there is nothing left for them from which to profit.

17 The terms *courtiers* and *officials* are both Akkadian loan words. They were probably not chosen here with reference to any specific tasks. Maybe

455. Quine, "Nineveh's Pretensions," 501.

456. Gen 15:5; 22:17; 26:4; Exod 32:13; Deut 1:10; 10:22; 28:62; 1 Chr 27:23; Neh 9:23; cf. Heb 11:12. The simile is found also in an Old Babylonian dialogue that refers to "my gossipy women, more numerous than the stars" (Cathcart, *Nahum*, 146). Quine ("Nineveh's Pretensions," 502) notes that "unlike locusts, the stars had a certain permanence to them." She believes that "the connection between Nineveh's merchants and the stars suggests that Nineveh's hopes for perpetual existence lay in its reliance on international trade and wealth." This is an interesting thought but perhaps reads too much into a description that is after all not put on the lips of Nineveh.

457. Quine, "Nineveh's Pretensions," 502. She suggests that the references to stars and to the sun (in the next verse) ironically invert Neo-Assyrian motifs of kingship and power. I am not fully convinced about this, nor about the claim that the sunrise in v. 17 should be read as making the stars disappear. The imagery has decisively shifted back to locusts by then.

458. The translation of *pāšaṭ*, here interpreted as *shed (their skin)*, with the verb "plunder" (see translation note) would make this more explicit but the more allusive rendering seems preferable.

they were chosen for sounding "official" or even pretentious.[459] They may be intended to depict Assyria as a highly bureaucratized state; Nahum's audience would have known that their tribute payments helped to make this possible. But Nineveh is merely providing *the walls* in which locusts take refuge *on a cold day*. (The insects apparently barely move on cold days, hiding in crevices instead, and get active again when the weather warms.) If the change of application of the *grasshoppers* metaphor from attacking armies to selfish merchants is bold, the designation of even *your courtiers* and *your officials*, whom one might expect to be the most loyal to the state, as a *locust swarm* is perhaps even bolder, apparently leaving no category of people in Nineveh willing to stay. It is noteworthy that the length of the first three lines increases (seven, nine, and eleven syllables), picturing the *camping* of the multitude of locusts. As *the sun rises* and the day gets hot, the whole multitude *has disappeared*.[460] If the whole population consists of self-interested profiteers (and this is what the *grasshopper* imagery suggests), then their departure, after having gotten out of the land what they could, leaves nothing of the city. The *place* where the swarm had settled *is unknown*, presumably because what is left is a desolation that is unrecognizable as the populated, prosperous place it had been. The shortening of line lengths at the end (nine and seven syllables) mirrors the increase in the first half of the verse if the concluding question (*Where are they?*) is allowed to stand on its own.[461]

Most translations don't render the final clause as a direct question (*Where are they?*) but combine it with *place* to result in something like "no one knows where they are." It is unlikely that the Hebrew presents anything other than a direct question here.[462] The implied answer to this rhetorical question is of course no one, but preserving the direct question in translation preserves

459. Cathcart ("Micah 2:4") reviews earlier proposals and argues that the passage refers to magicians (*merchants*), diviners (*courtiers*), and astrologers (*officials*). I am not persuaded, given the regularity with which *rōklîm* is used for *merchants* and the context of *ṭipsār* in Jer 51:27. The derivation from Akkadian *manzaz,* which Cathcart accepts for *minnəzārayik* (*courtiers*), need not suggest the narrow translation "diviners" (cf. his entry, "Nahum, Book of," in *ABD*, 4:998–1000, which, with reference to Parpola, indirectly acknowledges that the term may encompass palace officials more generally). Christensen (*Nahum*, 384–85) follows Cathcart's narrower translation of the latter two terms.

460. Quine ("Nineveh's Pretensions," 504) reckons that the rising sun "may be intended to evoke the winged sun as the symbol of Neo-Assyrian rule," in which case Assyria is depicted as "the architect of its own downfall." This is probably too subtle.

461. See the note on the translation for my affirmation that the question belongs to v. 17 rather than v. 18, as many commentators have it. If the question is counted with the final line, two lines of nine syllables follow the central line in this verse with eleven syllables.

462. *HALOT,* s.v. *'ê,* claims that this interrogative particle is only used in direct questions. It seems to me that indirect questions employ *'ê-mizzê* (so clearly in Judg 13:6; 1 Sam 25:11; but note that *'ê-mizzê* is also used more often in direct questions; e.g., 2 Sam 15:2).

the sharper tone of the rhetoric. It is noteworthy that the book also ends on a rhetorical question (3:19; cf. the rhetorical questions in 3:7 and 3:8).

Reflection

The opening reference to women (v. 13) is relative to the culture in and into which the text was written.[463] It is worth remembering that physical strength played a more important role in ancient than in contemporary life, including warfare. Also, remember that in the past, women at the prime of their strength were pregnant more of the time than most women living today—certainly in the West—due to both high infant mortality and the apparently greater desire for large families (more children, more workers, more prosperity). A population consisting of *women* only is an anomalous and unhealthy situation, arguably so even if *women* is understood metaphorically.[464] But the focus here is on lack of protection, a theme that continues into the following verses. The futility of Nineveh's protective measures is exposed in ironic commands (v. 14) followed by the prediction that fire and sword will do their work *there* (v. 15).

People often believe there is safety in numbers, and we may read the motif of proliferation and multitudes along such lines, developing the theme of protection. Ordinarily, of course, there are safety and strength in numbers, just as, in the normal run of things, walls that have been reinforced provide better protection than walls that have not been reinforced. But, as Prov 21:30 puts it, "there is no wisdom, no understanding, no counsel [that can avail] against YHWH." The psalmist recognizes that "no king is delivered by his vast army, no warrior is rescued by his massive strength; deceptive is the horse in terms of deliverance, its massive strength cannot save" (33:16–17). Notice that the psalmist three times invokes a word indicating multitude and abundance (*rob*, translated "vast" and "massive"). Nineveh may believe that the multitude of merchants, courtiers, and officials speaks in her favor, but "quickly come, quickly gone" is Nahum's message, as even the civil servants prove disloyal to the state.

For syntax similar to that represented here ('ê plus suffix as a question in its own right), cf. Exod 2:20; Job 14:10; 20:7.

463. While Christians affirm that "whatever was written in former days was written for our instruction" (Rom 15:4), we need to bear in mind that what was written *for* us was not written *to* us.

464. Without entering into a discussion about masculinity and femininity here, and without implying that masculinity and femininity must correspond to maleness and femaleness, I assume here that any society will function better if it consists of both people with more "masculine" and people with more "feminine" traits.

The metaphor of locusts is particularly potent in a society whose welfare is intimately linked to the annual success or failure of its agriculture. It also echoes a theme within the Book of the Twelve.[465] Fertility of the land is a gift from God that can be forfeited by rebellion against God. One of the ways in which God withholds the produce of the land from his people is through a plague of locusts (e.g., Joel 1:4; cf. 2:25), which may stand for a military invasion (e.g., Joel 1:6–7). Read in this context, the description of Assyrians as locusts reminds readers of the role of the Assyrian armies (and merchants) as a means of God's punishment on his people. Once God has decided no longer to afflict his people, the grasshoppers must disperse (cf. Nah 1:12). The end of Assyria's military dominance would have brought with it also the end of any Assyrian exploitation by trade. This may prompt reflection on the way in which economic dominance generally is supported by military strength. Throughout history, trade in slaves, oil, and diamonds has been most obviously related to warfare, but there are other trade opportunities and advantages that seem to have arisen or been supported by the deployment of armies, usually for the greater or even exclusive benefit of the nation with the superior military force.

The particular contribution of this passage to the general idea that no opposition can stand against YHWH may well be the warning against taking refuge in numbers. (According to one reading, Nahum may even be ironically encouraging Nineveh to go on proliferating, although this commentary has taken the imperatives as cheering on Nineveh's attackers.) The fate of the city no less than the fate of the whole world will not be decided by majority vote. Or rather, given that the merchants, courtiers, and officials will vote with their feet (cf. 2:8[9]), there will be no majority to stand with Nineveh against YHWH and his instruments. Because there is only one God and "no other," deliverance must be sought by "all the ends of the earth" from him (Isa 45:22). YHWH declares, "To me every knee shall bow, every tongue shall swear [allegiance]" (Isa 45:23; cf. Rom 14:11), and this will happen "at the name of Jesus" (Phil 2:10). Thus, to be precise, the warning is not so much against standing (kneeling!) with the majority, but against taking refuge in temporary numbers. And maybe there is an implicit warning here against putting one's trust in economic growth (the proliferation of merchants) or in a powerful state (the proliferation of courtiers and officials), certainly where such proliferation happens at the expense of other nations.

---

465. Cf. James D. Nogalski, "Recurring Themes in the Book of the Twelve: Creating Points of Contact for a Theological Reading," *Int* 61 (2007): 125–36, esp. 128–30 on the fertility of the land.

XII. EXPOSITION OF THE HELPLESSNESS OF THE CITY'S RULER (3:18-19)

[18]*Your[a] shepherds slumber,[b] king of Assyria;*
    your officers[c] are at rest.[d]
Your people are scattered [e] on the mountains,
    and there is no one to gather them.[f]
[19]*There is no relief [g] for your fracture,*
    your injury is severe.
All that hear the news about you
    clap [their] hands[h] over you.
For who has not been overwhelmed by your evil continually?[i]

a. The second-person suffixes in these verses are masculine in the MT, as one would expect given the vocative king of Assyria. *BHS* advises to read feminine suffixes instead, which leaves no place for king of Assyria. See further under "Composition."

b. Hebrew *nāmû* appears to have negative connotations; cf. its other occurrences in Pss 76:5(6); 121:3-4; Isa 5:27; 56:10.

c. Hebrew *'addîrêkā* (often "your nobles") is the same designation as in 2:5(6).

d. Hebrew *yiškənû* ("to settle"). The *yiqtol* (imperfect) form probably expresses the idea of continuing to be at rest. Many consider the verb *škn* here inappropriate and suggest a change to *yāšnû* ("they sleep"; cf. *BHS* and see Isa 5:27 and Ps 121:4 for the combination of this verb with "slumber"). Jeremias (*Nahum*, 206) wonders whether *yiškēbû* ("they lay down") may have stood in the text originally.

e. Hebrew *nāpōšû* is an otherwise unattested niphal of *pûš* (qal, "to spring about" in Jer 50:11; Hab 1:8; Mal 4:2[3:20]). The suggestion to read *nāpōṣû* ("being scattered") seems to me sound; cf. *BHS* and most commentators.

f. Hebrew, *wə'ên məqabbēṣ* ("There is no one who gathers"). The object is supplied by the context.

g. Hebrew *kēhâ* is not attested elsewhere (cf. *gēhâ* in Prov 17:22, also attested only there), but the verb is used half a dozen times in a medical context in Lev 13.

h. The pronoun *their* is added, as English usage demands. "Names of parts of the body do not require a suffix" in Hebrew, as Cathcart rightly notes (*Nahum*, 150).

i. Hebrew *kî 'al-mî lō'-'ābrâ rā'ātkā tāmîd* is more literally "for upon whom has not passed over your evil continually?" The last word could be taken with the immediately preceding ("continuous evil"), but taking it as an adverb seems to me the more obvious reading and agrees with the accentuation. For *'ābrâ* ("passed over"), cf. 1:8, 12; 1:15 (2:1).

Composition

The change of address to the Assyrian king sets these two verses apart from the preceding unit addressed to Nineveh. Several scholars object to the idea of a king having *shepherds* and, therefore, consider the vocative *king of As-*

syria in v. 18 an unfortunate gloss.[466] Deleting the phrase would pave the way for interpreting the suffixes as feminine, but I join those commentators who reject the necessity of this.[467] While it would be odd for the subordinates of a city-state ruler to be called *shepherds*, when addressing an emperor such a designation is not out of place.[468] What is said in this unit could have been addressed to the city, but the book is not narrowly focused on the city to the exclusion of the king. So, it is not altogether surprising that this unit should return to address the *king of Assyria* (cf. 1:14 for direct address and 1:11, 13; 2:5[6] for indirect references). It is, however, noteworthy that this marks the first use of the phrase *king of Assyria* in the book. This echoes the similar scarcity with which Nineveh is specified by name (after 1:1, only 2:8[9] and 3:7).

The vocative *king of Assyria* is in pivotal position, similar to *for your enemies* (or *for your enemies wide open*) in v. 13, which opened the previous unit. The rhythmic structure here is simpler than that of the preceding unit, with six bicola followed by a monocolon that concludes the unit and the book. This final monocolon is often also interpreted as a bicolon (see the layout in *BHS*), but it seems to me better to consider it an extra-long colon to mark closure. This seems to be the way the Masoretes scanned it as well.

Commentary

18 The term *shepherd* was frequently used in the ancient Near East to designate a king, but here it must refer to other political and military leaders. It is not entirely clear how unusual this is. There seem to be a number of cases in the Bible where the plural *shepherds* is used not with reference to the kings of different peoples or successively reigning kings but as a designation for contemporaneous leaders within one kingdom.[469] If in 2:5(6) the Assyrian king *remembers his officers*, here he is told that his *shepherds slumber* and his *officers are at rest*. The terms used are ambiguous, probably deliberately so, as sleep may refer to neglect of duties or the sleep of death. Thus, *slumber* is used for inattentive watchmen (Isa 56:10) as well as for people dying (Ps

---

466. E.g., Perlitt, *Nahum*, 34; Jeremias, *Nahum*, 207.

467. E.g., Spronk, *Nahum*, 142; Fabry, *Nahum*, 221.

468. Cf. the words put in the mouth of the king of Assyria in Isa 10:8 ("Are not my commanders all kings?").

469. See the discourses in Jer 21 and Ezek 34; cf. Isa 56:11; 63:11; Jer 2:8; 3:15 (?); 10:21; 12:10; 25:34–36; 50:6 (?); Mic 5:5(4); Zech 10:3. Doeg's title *'abbîr hārō'îm* ("chief of the shepherds") in 1 Sam 21:7(8) is sometimes thought to designate a political role that has no connection to "real" shepherds.

76:5[6]); similarly, *at rest* may hint at staying put (Judg 5:17) or at inhabiting the world of the dead (Job 26:5).[470] Maybe the leaders' neglect of shepherding duties led to the *people* being *scattered on the mountains* in the first place, while their death then leaves *no one to gather them*.[471]

19 If the previous verse implied that Assyria's leaders cannot be woken up because they are not merely inattentive but dead, this verse underlines the irreversibility of the disaster. The incurable wound and fatal disease is a common theme in ancient Semitic literature and frequently attested for Neo-Assyrian treaties of the eighth and seventh century BC and for the Hebrew prophetic literature of the time.[472] What the Assyrian kings, in the name of their gods, threatened would happen to nations that proved disloyal to Nineveh becomes, Nahum affirms, the fate of the Assyrian king. This is especially poignant here, given that Ishtar of Nineveh was "particularly famed as a goddess of healing and magic."[473] There is no hope for recovery. The king will not restore his once-magnificent city, nation, and empire. The focus on the king himself toward the end of the book is fitting in the light of 1:11 as interpreted in this commentary, with reference to Nineveh from which has come forth *someone scheming evil against YHWH, someone advising villainy*. The clash is ultimately between two rulers: YHWH, characterized in the opening poem, and the king of Nineveh, introduced in 1:11. The Assyrian king (rather than Assyria or Nineveh) is spoken of as the oppressor in YHWH's verdict (1:12–13) and directly addressed in 1:14. The summary good news in 1:15 (2:1) focuses on his destruction rather than the city's. The belittling of the city's ability to defend itself includes ridicule specifically directed against its ruler (2:11–12[12–13]).

The final lines return to the theme of hearing news of events in Nineveh (cf. 1:15 [2:1]). While clapping hands may denote a variety of things, here it is clearly an expression of joy and celebration.[474] We may even detect a note of glee here if we so wish, but it is possible to experience the joy of relief that comes from liberation without giving room to glee. The big news here

470. Cathcart (*Nahum*, 149) points to Isa 26:19 (*šōknê ʿāpār*, "dust dwellers") and Ps 94:17 (*šāknâ dûmâ*, "dwelled in silence") for the verb referring to repose in death and to Isa 22:16 and Ps 49:11(12) for *miškān* ("abode") used with reference to a tomb.

471. Cathcart (*Nahum*, 149) thinks that the gathering is for burial, but the use of *shepherds* earlier in the verse suggests the gathering of sheep scattered on the mountains as an image of national restoration.

472. See Johnston, "Treaty Curses," 429–30. While the prophets use the motif of the incurable wound with reference to the whole people (Isa 1:5–6; Jer 8:22; 14:17, 19; 30:12–15; 46:11; 51:8–9; Hos 5:13; Mic 1:9), the Assyrian treaties seem to address the vassal king.

473. John MacGinnis, "Ištar of Nineveh," in Petit and Bonacossi, *Nineveh*, 217.

474. See Nili Sacher Fox, "Clapping Hands as a Gesture of Anguish and Anger in Mesopotamia and in Israel," *JANES* 23 (1995): 49–60, esp. 54.

is, strictly speaking, not the end of the city but the demise of its king. The text does not specify which king, whether Sin-sharra-ishkun, whose end in 612 is not entirely certain,[475] or Ashur-uballit II, the last attested Assyrian king, who survived the sack of Nineveh and fled to Harran.[476] Again, we see that the book of Nahum is not so much interested in historical details as in views of the world that are in conflict with each other. The Assyrian king, as much as and maybe even more than the city of Nineveh, embodies the evil that has for so long cruelly plagued the peoples of the Levant. This evil has been *overwhelming* (cf. *pass through*, 1:15 [2:1]), but YHWH will make an end of it with a *sweeping* flood (1:8).[477] The Assyrian king had boasted of control over water (see the commentary on 2:6[7], 8[9]) and, symbolically speaking, had overwhelmed the region with waters of chaos. His downfall is, for Nahum, evidence that YHWH is in ultimate control of the forces of chaos and of creation and hence worthy of worship. The focus on the king at the end of the prophecy may suggest the question of who can be trusted to rule and to provide, a question to which Nahum provided an answer in the opening poem.

Closing the book with a question is an effective way of stimulating a response. The generality of the question *For who has not been overwhelmed by your evil continually?* widens the horizon beyond Judah, signaling wider applicability of Nahum's message. The evil seemed not only overwhelming but unstoppable. To this many peoples could bear witness. By attributing responsibility for the end of this evil to YHWH, Nahum testifies to YHWH's sovereign authority over all rulers (and their idols, 1:14) and invites readers to worship YHWH alone as a *stronghold in the day of distress* (1:7).

Reflection

The books of Nahum and Jonah are the only prophetic books to end with a rhetorical question. Jonah ends with a question that challenges the audience to reflect on the character of YHWH. Nahum ends with a question that stresses the character of the evil emanating from the Assyrian king. This final question does not so much serve to justify the military acts against Nineveh but to stress their inevitability. Because evil proceeded continuously from

475. The relevant line in the Babylonian Chronicle (44) is broken at this point. Grayson (*Chronicles*, 94) suggests "died," which is plausible but conjectural.

476. See Amélie Kuhrt, *The Ancient Near East c. 3000-330 BC* (London: Routledge, 1995), 540-46; and the entries in Gwendolyn Leick, *Who's Who in the Ancient Near East* (London: Routledge, 1999); cf. Fabry, *Nahum*, 225, whose reconstruction is more confident.

477. The italicised verbs all translate the root *'br*, whose reuse here is surely deliberate.

the villain who set forth from Nineveh (1:11), passing through the lands (1:15 [2:1]), therefore it was going to be impossible for this villain to stand in the face of God's inevitable anger. The joy at the end of the book anticipates the joy of Easter in the realization that whoever and whatever brings death and destruction cannot last.

It had been affirmed earlier that *distress will not arise a second time* (1:9). These verses spell out the same message. The Assyrian flock will not be regathered; the blow is final, the wound is fatal. "Where, O death, is your victory? Where, O death, is your sting?" (1 Cor 15:55).

The Book of
HABAKKUK

Introduction

I. THE PROFILE OF THE BOOK

A. THE SUPERSCRIPTIONS

There are two headings in the book of Habakkuk (1:1 and 3:1). The presence of the second heading, which even reuses the prophet's name, invites us to read the first heading as covering the first two chapters in particular.[1] The heading designates chapters 1–2 as a *maśśāʾ that Habakkuk the prophet saw*. The term *maśśāʾ* is discussed in the commentary on Nah 1:1. The understanding outlined there is that it refers to a prophetic exposition of divine revelation, which would be appropriate for the book of Habakkuk and is especially fitting for the first chapter, in which prayer frames the quotation of an earlier divine revelation.[2] Together, chapters 1–2 form a prophecy in which a human question (ch. 1) arising from an earlier prophecy (referenced in 1:5–11) and its devastating fulfillment is given a divine answer (ch. 2). The concluding chapter then offers a response to the prophecy. As pointed out in the introduction to Nahum, the reference to seeing (*which Habakkuk the prophet saw*) need not imply an actual visionary experience involving the eyes. It is unlikely that it does so here, although there is an interesting interplay between the motifs of seeing and hearing in the book of Habakkuk.

Like the first chapter, the final chapter embeds divine revelation, this time

---

1. Cf. Gert T. M. Prinsloo, "Reading Habakkuk as a Literary Unit: Exploring the Possibilities," *OTE* 12 (1999): 520.

2. See David Cleaver-Bartholomew, "An Alternative Approach to Hab 1,2–2,20," *SJOT* 17 (2003): 212–13. Cf. Marvin A. Sweeney, "Structure, Genre, and Intent in the Book of Habakkuk," *VT* 41 (1991): 63–83. This is based on the work of Weis (*Definition*), referenced above in the commentary on Nahum, which I do not find as persuasive for other contexts.

in the form of an account of a theophany (albeit one that may be heard and imagined more than seen; note the references to hearing in vv. 2, 16), set inside a prayer. While the first heading (1:1) points in the direction of reading the prayer in ch. 1 as part of a prophecy, the heading in ch. 3 suggests reading the prophecy in ch. 3 as prayer. The designation *tapillâ* ("prayer") is echoed and stressed in the subscript, which suggests that the prayer of *Habakkuk the prophet* (3:1) has become a public prayer, as it is available *to the music director* (3:19). In this way, the headings encourage us to read the book as a prophecy in chapters 1 and 2 followed by public prayer in chapter 3 in response to God's revelation. In other words, the opening prayer is part of the revelation to which the concluding prayer responds.

The book of Habakkuk's dialogical character is maybe its best-known characteristic. This remains true even if the role of 1:5–11 is here perceived differently than in the common reading, according to which 1:5–11 is a response to 1:2–4. While the first two chapters incorporate the prophet's prayer into the presentation and exposition of God's revelation, ch. 3 incorporates divine revelation into the prophet's (and the congregation's) prayer.

B. MACROSTRUCTURE

After the superscription, the main body of the text opens with a prayer about a general state of affairs expressed in the third person (1:2–4).[3] The change in subject to a second-person plural address in v. 5 with God as the first-person speaker indicates the beginning of a new section (1:5–11).[4] While it is not inconceivable that all or part (e.g., v. 11) of the third-person description of *the Chaldeans* in vv. 7–11 is spoken by the prophet rather than God, the passage seems closely tied to v. 6, and there is no textual marker to suggest a different speaker. In particular, vv. 7 and 9 link this second section closely to the preceding. Such a close connection could be either, as traditionally understood, because 1:5–11 is God's first answer to the prophet's complaint in 1:2–4, or (my preference) because the oracle in 1:5–11 provides the cause for the prayer in 1:2–4.[5] This will be discussed more fully in the commentary, in the composition sections of the respective passages. For now, it is

3. The person praying need not have been directly, let alone exclusively, affected. The prepositional phrase *before me* more likely has the common meaning "in my presence" rather than the specific meaning "against me," which is found in Job 10:17; Eccl 4:12.

4. Strictly speaking, the shift to first-person divine speech occurs in v. 6. See the discussion in the commentary on v. 5.

5. So also, e.g., Michael H. Floyd, "Prophetic Complaints about the Fulfillment of Oracles in Habakkuk 1:12–17 and Jeremiah 15:10–18," *JBL* 110 (1991): 397–418; *Minor Prophets* 2, 85–86; Cleaver-Bartholomew, "Alternative Approach"; Prinsloo, "Reading Habakkuk as

sufficient to note that, in contrast to what we find at the beginning of ch. 2 and again at the beginning of ch. 3, there is no introduction to a new major section in 1:5.[6]

Verse 12 reverts back to direct address to YHWH in the second-person masculine singular.[7] Again, a third-person description of *the Chaldeans* in vv. 15–17 (not specified as such, but the personal pronouns link with the earlier section) is part of the address that extends to the end of the chapter. The opening of the section has strong links to the earlier part of the chapter. One noteworthy feature is the double use of *nbṭ* ("to see") in v. 13, at first with the same direct object as in v. 3 and then in close conjunction with a similar form to that in v. 5 (*baggôyīm/bôgdîm*).[8]

In 2:1–2, the use of the third person to refer to YHWH within the first-person discourse spoken by the prophet suggests the beginning of a new section within the first major part of the book.[9] Thus, ch. 1 is the first section of the book, consisting of heading (1:1), complaint (1:2–4), citation of divine oracle (1:5–11), and further complaint (1:12–17). The language used may suggest a development from "injustice at a local level (1.2–4) to injustice at an international level (1.5–11) and finally to injustice at a cosmic level (1.12–17)."[10] But this may be either because, as often understood, God is thought to deal with local problems by way of international developments or, as I will argue along with others, because the prophet in effect zooms out from a focus on local injustice to its cause in (divinely sanctioned) imperial aggression.

No Hebrew manuscript that I know of marks subdivisions in ch. 1, but a *setumah* break divides chs. 1 and 2 in the Aleppo, Leningrad, and Reuchlin Codices, and a *petucha* break does so in the Cairo Codex. Habakkuk 2:2 introduces YHWH's answer to the prophetic complaint. The answer certainly continues into vv. 3–4. Given the lack of any subsequent signal of discontinuity, it may continue right to the end of the chapter, although from v. 6 onward

---

a Literary Unit"; Francis Watson, *Paul and the Hermeneutics of Faith* (London: T&T Clark International, 2004), 139–42.

6. Note also the citation formulas at 2:2aα and 2:6bβ. The absence of such a citation formula in 1:5 casts doubt on the traditional interpretation of ch. 1 as a dialogue between the prophet and YHWH; cf. Floyd, *Minor Prophets 2*, 95.

7. Note that if vv. 5–11 are a quotation within the prayer that is ch. 1, as I will argue, vv. 5–11 are indirect speech to God because God's word is quoted back to him.

8. The LXX translator apparently read the same form (*bôgdîm*) in both verses. See the commentary on 1:5.

9. Some take 2:1 with the first chapter, including Carl E. Armerding, "Obadiah, Nahum, Habakkuk," in *Daniel and the Minor Prophets*, vol. 7 of *The Expositor's Bible Commentary*, ed. Frank E. Gaebelein (Grand Rapids: Zondervan, 1985), 505; Robert D. Haak, *Habakkuk*, VTSup 44 (Leiden: Brill, 1992), 49; and Loren F. Bliese in a rather eccentric essay, "The Poetics of Habakkuk," *JOTT* 12 (1999): 47–75.

10. Oskar Dangl, "Habakkuk in Recent Research," *CurBS* 9 (2001): 153.

the speaker is citing the speech of the nations.[11] Thus, the key components of YHWH's answer are as follows: v. 2 gives an instruction to the prophet (to write down a revelation); v. 3 gives the reason for the instruction (that the revelation will surely be fulfilled); vv. 4–5 present the actual revelation,[12] v. 5 being closely tied to the preceding verse by its opening *wəʾap* ("and furthermore").[13] The rhetorical question in v. 6, which stands as an introduction to the subsequent collection of *hôy* sayings, is closely linked to v. 5 because it uses a pronoun (third-person plural) whose antecedent is in v. 5. Verses 6b–20 present the speech of the oppressed nations—speaking as one.[14] But the speech is a quotation within the elaboration on the vision that is part of YHWH's answer. In other words, the overall speaker remains YHWH.

The first four *hôy* sayings are clearly demarcated (2:6b–8, 9–11, 12–14, 15–17). Each exclamation characterizes the wicked using a participle and is followed by an accusation with second-person finite verbs.[15] What is usually identified as the fifth and final *hôy* saying deviates from this pattern. Verse 18 consists of a rhetorical question concerning the value of idolatry. This is thematically connected with the *hôy* exclamation in v. 19 which lacks a following accusation with second-person finite verbs. Whether v. 18 comprises a subsection on its own or not,[16] it obviously shares the theme of idolatry with v. 19 and is therefore here taken together with vv. 19–20.

The heading in 3:1 marks out ch. 3 as the second major part of the book. The prayer opens with a first-person statement of awe and a petition for activation of God's work in v. 2. Verses 3–7 narrate in the third person God's march from the southeast, concluding with a resumption of the first person in the last verse. Verse 8 refers to YHWH in the vocative and thus switches to direct address in the second person up to and including v. 15. This section talks about God's attack on his enemies. Verse 16 switches back to the first person, and the first verb used (*šmʿ*) picks up the first verb of v. 2. The statement of

---

11. G. Michael O'Neal (*Interpreting Habakkuk as Scripture: An Application of the Canonical Approach of Brevard S. Childs*, StBibLit 9 [New York: Peter Lang, 2007], 105) is right to note that 2:6a "acts to contextualize the woe imprecations and to heighten their effect" and does not constitute a separate heading.

12. Note that the third-person pronouns employed in v. 4 do not stand in continuity with v. 3 but refer back to ch. 1.

13. Alternatively, v. 5 could be read as introducing additional support for the revelation, which links it more explicitly with ch. 1. See especially vv. 9 and 15 for the gathering motif.

14. 1QpHab and ancient Greek and Syriac versions read the plural: "And they will say."

15. The participles are traditionally rendered in the third person ("woe to the one who . . ."), but a case can be made for reading a vocative ("woe to you who . . ."). See the commentary and note the use of the second person in v. 15.

16. For the *setumah* break after v. 18, see the excursus below on traditional paragraph divisions.

confidence in the midst of distress that extends to the end of the chapter (excluding the subscript) takes up the reference to salvation in v. 18 (cf. v. 13).

This results in the following structure:[17]

A. The Pronouncement (1:1–2:20)
 1. The Superscription (1:1)
 2. Habakkuk's Complaint (1:2–17)
   (a) The First Part of Habakkuk's Complaint (1:2–4)
   (b) The Citation of an Earlier Oracle (1:5–11)
   (c) The Final Part of the Complaint (1:12–17)
 2. The Prophet's Resolve to Get an Answer (2:1)
 3. YHWH's Reply (2:2–20)
   (a) The Instruction to the Prophet (2:2–3)
   (b) The Revelation (2:4–5)
   (c) The Agreement of the Oppressed Nations (2:6–20)
     (i) Introduction (2:6a)
     (ii) The First Saying (2:6b–8)
     (iii) The Second Saying (2:9–11)
     (iv) The Third Saying (2:12–14)
     (v) The Fourth Saying (2:15–17)
     (vi) The Fifth Saying (2:18–20)
B. The Prayer (3:1–19)
 1. The Heading (3:1)
 2. The Prayer (3:2–19a)
   (a) The Opening Part of the Prayer (3:2)
   (b) A Reflection on YHWH's Appearance (3:3–7)
   (c) Expression of Marvel at YHWH's Attack on His Enemies (3:8–15)
   (d) Expression of Confidence in the Midst of Distress (3:16–19a)
 3. The Postscript (3:19b)

In broad outline, the book moves from Habakkuk's anguished crying out to YHWH in ch. 1 via his silence before YHWH in ch. 2 to his prayer-song in ch. 3. In my view, in ch. 1, Habakkuk cries out as a representative of God's

---

17. O'Neal (*Interpreting Habakkuk*, 125) presents a lament framework for the book in which address (1:2) is followed by complaint (1:2–17), turning to God (2:1–20), petition (3:2–15), and vow of praise (3:16–19). This is suggestive but is not entirely plausible with regard to 2:1–20 and probably assumes too much identity between ancient and modern genre expectations, for which see Harry P. Nasuti, *Defining the Sacred Songs: Genre, Tradition and the Post-Critical Interpretation of the Psalms*, JSOTSup 218 (Sheffield: Sheffield Academic, 1999). Note also the suppression of the second heading in this scheme.

people, or at least as a spokesman for its faithful members. His expectant silence before YHWH in ch. 2 enacts what is required of all the earth (2:20), and his song in ch. 3 is to be shared among God's people (3:19).

Such structural analysis is helpful for getting a grasp of the overall movement of the book but seems of little benefit in the actual commentary on individual sections. The commentary will therefore proceed by analyzing the following sections without hierarchical ordering:

A. The Superscription (1:1)
B. The First Part of Habakkuk's Complaint (1:2–4)
C. The Citation of an Earlier Oracle (1:5–11)
D. The Final Part of the Complaint (1:12–17)
E. The Prophet's Resolve to Get an Answer (2:1)
F. The Instruction to the Prophet (2:2–3)
G. The Revelation (2:4–5)
H. The Agreement of the Oppressed Nations, First Saying (2:6–8)
I. The Second Saying (2:9–11)
J. The Third Saying (2:12–14)
K. The Fourth Saying (2:15–17)
L. The Fifth Saying (2:18–20)
M. The Heading for Habakkuk's Prayer (3:1)
N. The Opening Part of the Prayer (3:2)
O. A Reflection on YHWH's Appearance (3:3–7)
P. Expression of Marvel at YHWH's Attack on His Enemies (3:8–15)
Q. Expression of Confidence in the Midst of Distress (3:16–19a)
R. The Postscript (3:19b)

EXCURSUS: TRADITIONAL PARAGRAPH DIVISIONS

A brief introduction to traditional paragraph divisions can be found in the introduction to the book of Nahum (pp. 35–36). The Leningrad Codex opens new paragraphs in Hab 2:1 (*setumah*), 9, 12 (both *petucha*), 15, 18, 19 (*setumah*); 3:1 (*petucha*), 8 (*setumah*), 14 (*petucha*). The Aleppo Codex opens new paragraphs in 2:1, 5 (*setumah*), 9, 12, 15 (*petucha*), 19 (*setumah*); 3:1 (*setumah*), 8 (*setumah*), 14 (*petucha*). The Cairo Codex and the Babylonian Codex of Petrograd support Leningradensis in opening a paragraph at 2:18 and the Aleppo Codex in opening a paragraph at 2:5.[18]

---

18. The Reuchlin Codex has *setumah* breaks before 2:1, 9, 12, 15, 18, 19 and a *petucha* break before 3:1. It has no paragraph breaks in Hab 1. Chapter 3 has a *petucha* break before v. 14.

Gert T. M. Prinsloo gathered data not only from masoretic texts but also from manuscripts coming from other scribal traditions (Qumran, Wadi Murabba'at, Naḥal Ḥever) that revealed a fairly consistent convention of delimiting the text over the three chapters: 1:1–17; 2:1–4; 2:5–8; 2:9–11; 2:12–14; 2:15–17; 2:18; 2:19–20; 3:1–7; 3:8–13; 3:14–19.[19] The following points are noteworthy. First, ch. 1 is never subdivided. This fits well with my reading of the chapter as a single complaint rather than a dialogue. Second, while this is not reflected in the Leningrad Codex, which forms the basis of most modern editions of the Hebrew text, there is commonly a division between 2:4 and 2:5. The opening of v. 5 establishes an obvious link with v. 4, so the paragraph division is likely a move to make 2:4 stand out more prominently. Third, the other paragraph divisions in ch. 2 set apart the different *Oy* sayings. The additional division at 2:18 acknowledges the different construction of the fifth saying, in which *Oy* is preceded by a verse. Verse 18 clearly belongs with what follows rather than what precedes, given its content. Finally, the agreement on concluding a paragraph with 3:13 is noteworthy. The Greek tradition also notes a pause here (*diapsalma*).[20] This is probably to highlight the purpose of God's coming, which is summed up in this verse. Verse 13 does in fact make for a good conclusion, and v. 14 already refers to the person praying by way of a first-person object suffix, so that it would be defensible to take vv. 14–15 with the following as a summary statement of confidence.

C. LANGUAGE AND STYLE

Similarities between the opening of Habakkuk and complaint psalms are obvious, and there are similarities of motifs with other prophetic literature.[21] The perceived importance of the issue of theodicy has also led many to compare Habakkuk with Job and encouraged the exploration of similarities with wisdom literature. Robert Haak rightly notes that there is "no inherent reason why wisdom influence on Habakkuk should be denied if he in fact was a prophet associated with the temple in Jerusalem." But he adds the observation that "there does not seem to be anything within the basic structure or thought of the prophecy that is not common to prophetic writings."[22] If, however, God's earlier announcement of the Babylonians as his instrument

19. Gert T. M. Prinsloo, "Petuhot/Setumot and the Structure of Habakkuk: Evaluating the Evidence," *The Impact of Unit Delimitation on Exegesis*, ed. Raymond de Hoop, Marjo C. A. Korpel, and Stanley E. Porter, Pericope 7 (Leiden: Brill, 2009), 196–227.

20. There is a *diapsalma* also after the first couple of lines in v. 3, highlighting the theme statement, and in v. 9 for *selah*.

21. See Fabry, *Habakuk/Obadja*, 126–35, for lists of intertextual connections.

22. Haak, *Habakkuk*, 148. Haak was probably concerned to stress the specific political situation (with "the wicked one" and "the righteous one" identified as royal figures)

is what gives Habakkuk's complaint its edge, the issue of divine justice is more to the foreground than Haak allows. Haak does in fact acknowledge the frequency in the book of terms associated with the legal and judicial sphere.[23] This feature has been explored more fully by Kevin Cathcart, who notes similarities with Job and Jeremiah as well as lament psalms.[24]

Stylistically, we can detect in Habakkuk a penchant for using similar- or identical-sounding words in immediate succession. Vanderhooft offers the following examples: *wəhittamməhû təmāhû* ("astonish yourselves, be astonished") and *pō'al pō'ēl* ("one is about to do a deed") in 1:5; *hammar wəhannimhār* ("the sharp and swift") in 1:6; *llō'-lô* ("not his") in 1:6 and 2:6; *ûpāšû pārāšāyw ûpārāšāyw* ("his cavalry is restless. And his cavalry") in 1:8; *bōṣēa' beṣa'* ("one who takes takings") in 2:9; *yōṣēr yiṣrô* ("a fashioner of its form") and *'ĕlîlîm 'illəmîm* ("dumb nothings") in 2:18; *'āmad wayəmōded* ("he stood and sized up") in 3:6; and *'eryâ tē'ôr* ("fully uncovered") in 3:9. To this can be added the repetition of the same or similar words in adjacent clauses or sentences.[25] He further observes that "the fact that these literary characteristics appear throughout the book (with the exception of the opening complaint in 1:2–4), including the hymn of chapter 3, may suggest a deliberate and overarching literary technique for the book," which in turn may "suggest that the book is the product of a singular design." They certainly give the composition a distinctive feel. The implied author likes to play with words, and we may suspect deliberate ambiguity in some places (e.g., in 3:6). Maybe the surprising absence of a personal pronoun with the participle in both 1:5 and 2:10 is also the result of a penchant for ambiguity that seeks to engage readers by forcing a double-take at words and phrases.[26] It can be difficult, however, to ascertain whether Habakkuk's prophecy at times appears to us as equivocal because we are not native speakers of Habakkuk's language or

---

over against more general reflections on theodicy as one might find emanating from a wisdom school.

23. Cf. Brian Peckham, "The Vision of Habakkuk," *CBQ* 48 (1986): 617–36, who writes: "The language of the book is imaginative and abstract: the abstract language is mostly forensic; the imaginative language defines specific legal problems and occurs in logical discourse and arguments" (624).

24. Kevin J. Cathcart, " 'Law Is Paralysed' (Habakkuk 1.4): Habakkuk's Dialogue with God and the Language of Legal Disputation," in Day, *Prophecy and the Prophets*, 339–53.

25. David Stephen Vanderhooft ("Habakkuk," in *The Oxford Encyclopedia of the Books of the Bible*, ed. David Stephen Vanderhooft, *Oxford Biblical Studies Online*, http://www .oxfordbiblicalstudies.com/article/opr/t280/e99) offers a dozen examples in that category. Cf. Robertson, *Nahum*, 188, on the rhyming of phrases in 2:7–8.

26. Andersen (*Habakkuk*, 199) sees a pattern of unconventional parallelism as a feature of Habakkuk's style. He may well be right; it would fit the picture of an implied author who makes words work extra hard. Robertson (*Nahum*, 186–87) notes possible cases of double entendre in 2:6.

whether he crafted genuine ambiguity into the discourse. But there seem to be more such instances in Habakkuk than in other collections of similar size, so one may conclude that the implied author exploits ambiguity more fully than others.

D. REDACTION HISTORY

I find it difficult to outline a redaction history of the book or to accept any of the diverging proposals on offer.[27] Instead, what follows sketches briefly what some scholars have read as signs inviting us to explore the book's textual history and explains why I have not taken up the invitation. First, the search for redactional layers was often prompted by the view that the book allegedly shows a mixture of pro- and anti-Babylonian passages. But I find no truly pro-Babylonian material in the book and see coherence where others have seen conflict. The commentary will show that it is not only possible but reasonable to read the allegedly pro-Babylonian passages as part of a book that is consistently critical of the empire.

Second, many consider the sayings in chapter 2 as more suitable to condemn sins within Judah, and specifically those of Jehoiakim, rather than, as in the received version of the book, to condemn Babylonian hegemony. Rhetorically, however, the chapter's language can be read as entirely coherent within the development of the argument in the book. The metaphorical use of a range of sinful behavior to condemn imperial aggression relates to the core revelation in 2:4-5 that categorizes the Babylonian conquest as an instance of the type of behavior that leads to its own downfall. It would be counterproductive to describe imperial aggression as behavior that is entirely in a class by itself. It is far more effective to picture it as a form of greed and drunkenness, of robbery (the taking of goods to which one has no right and that one therefore has to return), and of idolatry. It is for this very reason it cannot be successful in the end according to the revelation in 2:4-5, which promises life to those whose trust continues to be in God but announces death to all who proudly turn away from God. The fact that this encourages readers to condemn Babylon on grounds that would also condemn behavior and attitudes within Judah is an added bonus, not least because Babylonian

---

27. See, e.g., Peter Jöcken, *Das Buch Habakuk: Darstellung der Geschichte seiner kritischen Erforschung mit einer eigenen Beurteilung*, BBB 58 (Cologne-Bonn: Hanstein, 1977); Dangl, "Habakkuk in Recent Research"; Eckart Otto, "Habakkuk/Book of Habakkuk," *RPP*, 5:625-27; cf. Henrik Pfeiffer, *Jahwes Kommen von Süden: Jdc 5; Hab 3; Dtn 33 und Ps 68 in ihrem literatur- und theologiegeschichtlichen Umfeld*, FRLANT 211 (Göttingen: Vandenhoeck & Ruprecht, 2005), 125-28.

hegemony and the fight against it had seriously compromised the functioning of law and order within Judah.

Third, it is the condemnation of idolatry on the lips of foreign nations (2:18–20) that is considered particularly implausible. One could read only the first four sayings as "cited" speech and the fifth as a commentary by the prophet. But one must bear in mind that the whole section is not cast as a report of what other nations have actually said but as the imagined sayings of all the victims of Babylonian aggression speaking as one. It is a poetic device to underline the reversal motif and was arguably never meant as a realistic description of the response that the nations surrounding Judah were expected to give in the future. There is in any case no clear conception as to when the nations will take up this saying. The implied time is clearly one during which the Babylonian hegemony is still in full swing, and yet the sayings seem to be future rather than present. Within the present form of the book, the sayings outline the response everyone who believes in the revelation offered in 2:4–5 should make. The reference to other nations is both a way of acknowledging that Judah is only one of many nations suffering under the Babylonians and a way of affirming that YHWH rules the nations, not only Judah. The scholarly view that objects to references to idolatry, and indeed to the use of the divine name in other sayings, rests on a questionable assumption. It assumes that an earlier version of the material depicted more realistically how nations other than Judah would respond with new confidence to Babylonian domination at some unspecified future point. This is not at all likely, not least because it remains unclear what would have prompted such sayings. The reason why the oppressed can respond with confidence rather than despondency to Babylonian might is found in the revelation in 2:4–5, which assures that greed cannot last and that those who keep faith with YHWH will live. Those who respond in faith to this revelation will have no trouble naming YHWH and condemning idolatry.

Fourth, the special nature of ch. 3 has given rise to reflections on the book's textual history. Scholars have often wondered whether the poem is archaic or uses archaizing language. In either case, its earlier versions would not be part of the redaction history of the book itself; the author would simply have used preexisting material. More recently, Henrik Pfeiffer argued that the poem is in fact from the early Hellenistic period.[28] This is based on a comparison of Hab 3 with similar texts, supposing that the author of Hab 3 no longer understood the symbolic significance of "Edom" (Judg 5:4) and transformed it into Teman and Mount Paran (Hab 3:3) and that the poem was

---

28. Henrik Pfeiffer, *Jahwes Kommen*, 117–77. For a critical discussion, see Martin Leuenberger, *Gott in Bewegung: Religions- und theologiegeschichtliche Beiträge zu Gottesvorstellungen im alten Israel*, FAT 76 (Tübingen: Mohr Siebeck 2011), 10–33.

originally an eschatological poem that spoke of universal judgment. Pfeiffer's caution against the view that YHWH's origin from the south (Teman) presents an archaic tradition needs to be heard.[29] His view that the theophany out of Edom is rooted in a concept of divine judgment on Edom is worth considering, although it is not necessary or even plausible that this tradition is older than the Sinai traditions. More importantly, two supporting claims simply fail to convince: first, as Pfeiffer argues, that Hab 3 presupposes Isa 34 and Isa 63:1–6 (judgment *on* Edom in the presumed original layer but on the nations *in* Edom in later revisions);[30] and second, given the ongoing transmission of the relevant texts, that the connection between "Edom" and divine judgment would have been forgotten by the late fourth century BC. Finally, the broad, large-scale perspective of Hab 3 fits the concern of the book with the Babylonian Empire and its near-universal dominance as seen from a Judahite perspective. Such a judgment obviously makes more than one nation tremble, but this is different from the concept of an apocalyptic day of judgment on each individual person or even an eschatological judgment of every nation under heaven. In short, nothing here calls for a date later than the one proposed for chs. 1–2 in the very late seventh or early sixth century BC.

Fifth, the fact that the book contains a variety of genres that use different language registers, in my view, does not warrant the assumption that it, therefore, cannot be a unified composition.[31]

Finally, one must mention redactional proposals that are linked to views about the origin and development of the Book of the Twelve.[32] There is no space here to discuss these adequately and in detail. I have examined some of the key arguments that concern Habakkuk in my essay "Habakkuk and Its Co-Texts." See also the general introduction above (pp. 4–16).

29. Note that Richard J. Clifford (*The Cosmic Mountain in Canaan and the Old Testament*, HSM 4 [Cambridge: Harvard University Press, 1972], 114–20) argues that this group of passages refer to a march *in* the south, not from the south, and that Haak (*Habakkuk*) suggests that it may be better to term them "March from the East" (84). My exegesis of Hab 3 does not presume an archaic tradition of YHWH's movement in or from the south.

30. This is to say that I am not convinced that there is enough evidence to assume a literary relationship, quite apart from the question of the direction of influence, which, as Henrik Pfeiffer admits, is difficult to establish (*Jahwes Kommen*, 176). The same goes for other parallels that Pfeiffer interprets in terms of literary dependence (e.g., Hab 3:3a, allegedly using Ezek 1:4 and Job 37:22 as well as [an earlier version of] Judg 5:4), which seem to me to simply share motifs.

31. Contra Fabry, *Habakuk/Obadja*, 114–15, who adds observation of various details that in his view demand a redactional layering of the text (115–16) before discussing different redaction-critical hypotheses and models (117–23).

32. See, e.g., Redditt, "Recent Research"; Albertz, Nogalski, and Wöhrle, *Perspectives on the Formation*.

E. TEXTUAL WITNESSES

The well-preserved Habakkuk Pesher from Qumran (1QpHab) contains the text of the first two chapters along with a detailed commentary interpreting the book as pointing to the ultimate destiny of the righteous and the wicked.[33] Radiocarbon dating suggests it was written in the second or first century BC.[34] This makes it the earliest surviving textual witness to the book of Habakkuk, but not the most reliable. The belief within the Qumran community that these ancient prophecies were only then, in their time, properly understood meant that contemporary interpretation was more important than the actual wording of the text. The latter could be changed to better bring out the sense as understood within the community.[35] The Scroll of the Minor Prophets from Wadi Murabba'at dates from the second century AD and contains 1:3–2:11 and 2:18–3:19. In addition to the Greek Scroll of the Minor Prophets from Naḥal Ḥever and the LXX tradition, mentioned in the introduction to the Nahum commentary, there is a special Greek version of Hab 3, the Barberini text, which is attested in six medieval manuscripts from the eighth to the thirteenth centuries. It was apparently originally translated no later than the mid-third century AD and at first independent of the Septuagint, but it offers little promise for establishing an earlier version of the text than MT.[36] A fuller description and evaluation of the text of Hab 3 is given by Andersen,[37] and James A. E. Mulroney offers a full introduction to and discussion of the Old Greek text of Habakkuk.[38] Good examples of the LXX's literal translation style are also offered by Radu Gheorghita.[39]

33. See the scroll of 1QpHab with commentary at http://www.moellerhaus.com/habdir.htm; also see Donald W. Parry and Emanuel Tov, *The Dead Sea Scrolls Reader, Part 2: Exegetical Texts* (Leiden: Brill, 2004). For a much fuller overview of Habakkuk's textual history, see Fabry, *Habakuk/Obadja*, 82–104.

34. Cf. Géza Vermes, *The Complete Dead Sea Scrolls in English*, rev. ed. (London: Penguin, 2004), 13.

35. Cf. Oskar Dangl, *Das Buch Habakuk*, NSKAT 25 (Stuttgart: KBW, 2014), 133–34.

36. So Joshua L. Harper, *Responding to a Puzzled Scribe: The Barberini Version of Habakkuk 3 Analysed in the Light of the Other Greek Versions*, LHBOS 608 (London: Bloomsbury T&T Clark, 2014).

37. Andersen, *Habakkuk*, 264–68.

38. James A. E. Mulroney, *The Translation Style of Old Greek Habakkuk: Methodological Advancement in Interpretative Studies of the Septuagint*, FAT 2/86 (Tübingen: Mohr Siebeck, 2016). See also BA 23.4–9, 231–310; Heinz-Josef Fabry, "Ambakuk/Habakkuk," in Karrer and Wolfgang Kraus, *Septuaginta Deutsch*, 2413–28.

39. Radu Gheorghita, *The Role of the Septuagint in Hebrews: An Investigation of Its Influence with Special Consideration to the Use of Hab 2:3–4 in Heb 10:37–38*, WUNT 2/160 (Tübingen: Mohr Siebeck, 2003), 193–208, 212–18.

II. THE HISTORICAL SETTING OF THE BOOK

No historical setting is claimed in the superscription in 1:1. The violence and strife that trouble Habakkuk are sadly characteristic of many times and places. Most scholars consider the reference to the rise of *hksdym* (*hak-kaśdîm*) in 1:6 the only firm historical clue. This reference is now generally accepted to be to the Neo-Babylonian Empire.[40] The prediction of the rise of the Babylonians fits best within the period near the end of the Neo-Assyrian Empire. But even if we take this at face value, and there is no good reason why we should not, this only gives us an estimated date for the basic content of 1:5–11. In the commentary on the passage, I will suggest that 1:5–11 is likely a later, polemic rewriting of an earlier prophecy such as Jer 5:15–17.

It was in the reign of Josiah that prophets in Judah announced the rise and devastating impact on Judah of what today we call the Neo-Babylonian Empire (cf. 2 Kings 22; Jeremiah), although it is not inconceivable that such prophecies already circulated in Manasseh's time (the early seventh century BC; cf. 2 Kgs 21:12). The majority of scholars date Habakkuk's ministry sometime in the seventh century, from the time of Manasseh right down to 600 BC or the very early years of the sixth century BC.[41]

Apart from considerations surrounding 1:5–11, a key factor in dating the book or the individual parts of it has been the identification of "the wicked" in different parts of the book and the attempt to separate "pro-Babylonian" from "anti-Babylonian" passages. This attempt seems misguided, however, because 1:5–11 cannot be simply classified as "pro-Babylonian." While it affirms that the Babylonians are YHWH's instrument, it does so in language that characterizes them negatively. The following discussion will seek to show that it is perfectly possible to read the first two chapters as a coherent whole, a prophecy that responds to the effects of the fulfillment of an earlier oracle (1:5–11). While "the wicked" need not be identified exclusively as external enemies (i.e., the Neo-Babylonian Empire), on my reading, the Babylonians are never portrayed in the book as the divine answer to Judean

---

40. The explanation "Kittim" (most likely a reference to the Romans) in the Habakkuk Pesher (1QpHab col. 2, line 11) is obviously a contemporary application. The citation *hks-d'ym* confirms the received text, its spelling (with an additional *aleph*) reflecting an Aramaic accent (cf., e.g., Dan 3:8; 5:11).

41. See Jöcken, *Habakuk*, 3–14, for a review of earlier scholars who link Habakkuk with the time of Manasseh. Patterson (*Habakkuk*, 115–17) appears to be the only recent commentator attracted to this early date. Perlitt (*Nahum*, 41–43) offers 600 BC for the ministry of Habakkuk, considering the book itself postexilic. Others are skeptical about finding any words of a seventh-century prophet and content suggesting a postexilic date for the compilation of the book; see James D. Nogalski, *The Book of the Twelve: Micah–Malachi*, SHBC 18b (Macon, GA: Smyth & Helwys, 2011), 649.

wickedness. In fact, if anything, they are a direct as well as an indirect cause of the violation of Torah within Judah. This means that the origin of the book needs to be sought in a time when the impact of Babylonian tyranny on Judah was already being felt. Given the reputation of Josiah as a promoter of Torah, it is not likely that the strong statement about the ineffectiveness of Torah in 1:4 was made during his lifetime. While there may have been prophets who were highly critical of the effectiveness of Josiah's reforms, we would imagine their complaint to be more nuanced, condemning the superficiality of reforms rather than the ineffectiveness of Torah itself. The words we find in Habakkuk are, after all, perhaps the most despondent concerning Torah we find in the Hebrew Bible.

The book could be read as a response to the end of Judah's statehood, composed from the perspective of survivors in Jerusalem and Judah. But the lack of specific reference to the destruction of the temple and the end of the monarchy suggests an earlier date. The treatment that the prophet Jeremiah received at the hand of the authorities in Jerusalem and the very threat to the survival of the people of God at that time would seem a suitable backdrop to Habakkuk's complaint in ch. 1. It thus seems likely that Habakkuk and Jeremiah were contemporaries, with Jeremiah already prophesying before Habakkuk arrived on the scene and continuing to do so beyond Habakkuk, given the lack of signs of the 587/586 BC catastrophe in Habakkuk.[42] While Jeremiah tells King Zedekiah to surrender to the Babylonians, the executors of divine judgment on Judah, the book of Habakkuk seems more concerned with the evil perpetrated by the Babylonians themselves.

Some scholars have argued that earlier parts of Hab 2 go back to judgment oracles first proclaimed against Judah and specifically against Jehoiakim.[43] On the one hand, it is clear that in its present form, the material is used above all for a different purpose, namely the condemnation of imperial abuse of power. On the other hand, it is evident that deletion of some phrases and verses makes it possible to construct a form of the text that would be well suited to the condemnation of the Judean upper class. The use of local imagery to condemn international crimes, however, is not restricted to Habakkuk.[44] The question is whether the fit of the material with the anti-imperial intent communicated in the book is so poor as to demand that we postulate

---

42. Dominik Markl ("Hab 3 in intertextueller und kontextueller Sicht," *Bib* 85 [2004]: 99–108) speaks of Habakkuk as a critical disciple of Jeremiah. This seems to me right conceptually, regardless of the length of Jeremiah's ministry. "Habakkuk" here refers to the voice associated with the book, as we have no real evidence outside the book for this prophet.

43. E.g., Jeremias, *Kultprophetie*, 55–110; Haak, *Habakkuk*, 130–49; William L. Holladay, "Plausible Circumstances for the Prophecy of Habakkuk," *JBL* 120 (2001): 123–42.

44. Cf. the use of the image of a disgraced adulteress for condemning national (e.g., Ezek 16:37–41) and international (e.g., Nah 3:5–7) crimes.

a different original design. I remain unconvinced of that. If one allows for the use of traditional motifs and a rhetorical agenda that is a little more complex than offering a condemnation of Babylon, there seems little reason to assume that the sayings in ch. 2 had an earlier life as anti-Judean oracles. This is not to say that we must exclude the possibility, but there seem no strong textual grounds for postulating such an earlier use.[45] The use of traditional material stresses the inevitability of Babylon's downfall rather than merely announcing it, and it serves up Babylon as a paradigm of overreach. The paradigmatic nature of the condemnation thus allows for reapplication to others who could be characterized in the words of Hab 2:4a. Indeed, the fact that the book names a human protagonist only once suggests that it is concerned with a more principled critique of a system of violence and abuse.[46]

Just as Babylon is never portrayed in the book as good or even a necessary evil, given that 1:5-11 partakes of the complaint character of ch. 1, so Judah is not portrayed as unambiguously righteous over against its wicked oppressors. Judah is "righteous" only in comparison with Babylon, and largely because it is a victim rather than an agent (see 1:13-14). The breakdown of law and order, the violation and ineffectiveness of Torah, may well be related to living in the shadow of Babylonian hegemony (cf. 1:4b with 1:13b),[47] but the portrayal does not inspire confidence in Judah's leadership (cf. Jer 23:1-2, 9-11). There is no implicit claim here that all would be well with Judah and the royal and priestly authorities in Jerusalem were it not for Babylonian imperialism.[48] It is, therefore, not inconceivable that the condemnation of Babylonian overreach in ch. 2 has a secondary eye on the infringements of Judean authorities. There is, however, little evidence to allow us to place Habakkuk firmly in one of the political camps that might have existed toward the end of the seventh century (see further below).

45. There are reasons outside the text of Habakkuk itself that lend plausibility to the view that Habakkuk would have preached against his own people prior to the communication we now have in written form under his name. See below.

46. Cf. Dangl, *Habakuk*, 43.

47. King Josiah had acted on the assumption that faithfulness to Torah and the proper functioning of Torah required political independence from both Egypt and Babylon. Jehoiakim was pro-Egyptian and may have opposed Josiah's earlier reforms for a mix of pragmatic-political and more specifically theological reasons, while Jeremiah proclaimed that failure to live by Torah now left submission to Babylon as the only feasible option. While I do not fully agree with Haak's (*Habakkuk*) portrayal of the setting and place of Habakkuk (see esp. 139-46 on major political groupings), I consider it likely that Habakkuk would have been against the pro-Egyptian policy pursued by Jehoiakim, as was Jeremiah.

48. It is worth noting already here, as will be further explored below, that 1:5-11 nowhere suggests that the Babylonians were raised as God's instrument to punish evil in Judah. This is proclaimed in Jeremiah; its absence here suggests that the focus in Habakkuk remains on the Babylonians as such.

Holladay argues that Hab 3:17–18 can be linked to the drought described in Jer 15. He dates the public fasting in response to it to November/December 601 BC.[49] But Haak's critique of this proposal is compelling, especially his observation that the stereotypical language used in Hab 3:17 means that the verse "probably cannot bear the weight which Holladay suggests."[50] Holladay's proposal rests on linking several passages, each of which is given a defensible but by no means uncontroversial reading. With questions about each link in the chain, the plausibility of the overall proposal is reduced.

Habakkuk's prayer in ch. 3 seems impossible to date on its own. Its distinctive character does not demand that its origin be separate from the preceding chapters. I join other contemporary scholars who are impressed with its close rhetorical fit with the preceding.[51] Taken at face value, the heading in 3:1 invites us to read the prayer as the prophet's own response to the prophecy in chs. 1–2. We are neither asked to imagine further historical developments nor compelled to look beyond the chronological setting of the preceding chapters. This means that Holladay's suggested date fits well even if he has not offered incontrovertible proof for his view. The liturgical instructions are a different matter; they may well be postexilic.[52]

In sum, the book seems to fit well into the period after the death of Josiah (609) and maybe (but not necessarily) before the deportation in 597.[53] An earlier prophecy is alluded to in 1:5–11, and one need not exclude later editorial work a priori, although in my view evidence for different redactional layers seems harder to come by than many other scholars believe. It is possible that earlier material in the form of proverbs was incorporated in ch. 2 and that ch. 3 makes use of earlier hymnic material, but this would seem more a case of authorial creativity with existing material than part of the history of the book of Habakkuk. The question of to what extent an oral message preceded the writing down of Habakkuk's prophecy is difficult to answer. There is no reference to an oral performance of the material within the book other

49. Holladay, "Plausible Circumstances."

50. Haak, *Habakkuk*, 134.

51. See, e.g., Markl, "Hab 3." Cf. the quick overview in Marvin A. Sweeney, "Habakkuk," *ABD*, 3:4–5.

52. It may have been difficult for a prophetic voice close to Jeremiah to get a hymn into the official temple collection during the closing years of the Kingdom of Judah, although I will suggest below that Habakkuk may have been able to move a little more freely than Jeremiah. It is not inconceivable that the prophet designated the prayer for official, public use even if he felt that there was little chance of this happening in the short run. Still, my guess would be that the closing notice is a later addition.

53. The pursuit of the Egyptians for more than 150 miles after the Battle of Carchemish in 605 BC would have fit the description of the Chaldeans in 1:5–11 and maybe intensified the complaint.

than in the context of prayer and revelation given to the prophet. Some of the cited material (1:5–11 in the complaint, 2:6ff. in the revelation, and perhaps 3:3–15 in the prayer) would have been suitable for oral preaching in contexts other than the one given in the book. But we have no evidence that it ever saw use like that, and for 1:5–11 this seems highly unlikely. It is perfectly possible, and maybe likely, that the complaint in Hab 1 was preceded by a prophetic ministry that left no clear traces in the book itself. A prophet who calls out to God like this can be expected to have preached against injustice.[54] There is no reason to assume that the book of Habakkuk is a representative sample of the ministry of the prophet whose name it bears. It may well represent only one aspect of the prophet's ministry.

III. THE RHETORICAL FUNCTION OF THE BOOK

A. HABAKKUK'S MESSAGE IN ITS ORIGINAL CONTEXT

As suggested above, in about 600 BC, Habakkuk composed a prayer in which he reflected on the catastrophic effects of the Babylonian success story. Unlike Jeremiah's complaints, Habakkuk's is not narrowly personal. While "he is speaking in the work as an individual . . . his complaint as an individual has implications for a wider community."[55] Habakkuk was concerned about widespread injustice in the wake of the ultimate failure of Josiah's attempts at political independence and Torah-shaped communal living. Habakkuk feared for the very survival of the people of God. He could not blame YHWH for the failure of monarchy and priesthood, but given the extent to which experience and policy were shaped either by Babylonian hegemony or by way of response to Babylonian hegemony, he could complain to YHWH about the Babylonians. After all, earlier prophecy (by Jeremiah) had claimed that the empire was God's instrument. The book enters the implied story without indication of the length of time passed since the complaint was first raised. The opening *How long?* suggests a climax to the prayer; the prophet has become impatient waiting for a response. The beginning of ch. 2 conveys a definite sense of expectation that finally the prophet will receive an an-

---

54. It was Martin Luther who alerted me to this. See Thomas Renz, "Martin Luther as an Example of Participatory Exegesis," forthcoming in *The Book of the Minor Prophets* [provisional title], ed. David G. Firth and Brittany N. Melton (Bellingham: Lexham Press).

55. Haak, *Habakkuk*, 111. Haak is right, however, to observe that this does not demand a public communal setting.

swer. The narrative thus focuses on the climactic point at which Habakkuk's prayers received an answer.

As Habakkuk's complaint includes a free rendering of an earlier prophecy that claims God's agency in the rise of the Neo-Babylonian Empire, so YHWH's reply includes a free rendering of (future) sayings from the victims of Babylonian aggression who thereby, finally, become agents rather than victims who are acted upon. The reply does not offer any justification for the divine use of imperial force in the present but affirms that the future does not belong to violent idolaters. Rather than escape justice, the Babylonians' greed will lead to their death; the righteous, by contrast, in remaining faithful, will live. The prophecy does not elaborate on what loyalty to YHWH looks like, but the allusive sayings that expose Babylonian aggression as self-destructive indirectly show how the righteous are not to live. And the conclusion of the prophecy indicates that to hush before YHWH is an appropriate response to the realization that YHWH is ultimately in charge.

In one sense, silence seems an apt response to YHWH's revelation and, hence, an appropriate conclusion to the book; but in another sense, it is not. Silence speaks volumes only in a context in which the silence is clearly identifiable as one of defiance or awe, resignation or respect. Habakkuk's prayer in ch. 3 portrays the right kind of "hush" and models what faithfulness to YHWH looks like in a situation of distress. It would do so even without the explicit instruction for the prayer to be used in public worship, but the liturgical instructions stress the model character of the prayer.

The book of Habakkuk implies a narrative, sketched in a few verses (1:1; 2:1-2; 3:1). Much of the material could have had an earlier setting outside this narrative, although, as indicated above, this is difficult to pin down. The book is what it is only because of the implied narrative, and it is doubtful that there was much Habakkuk-related material *written* prior to this narrative. God's response to the prophet is the hinge on which the book opens for us. Without this response, Habakkuk's complaint may never have been passed on to future generations, and without God's response to Habakkuk's prayers, there would not have been the response we know as Habakkuk's prayer. The hinge is encapsulated in 2:4-5, the heart of the divine reply that affirms that evil, including imperial greed, is self-destructive and that the righteous hold on to life by steadfast faith. This revelation was to be documented on tablets.

We may think that the book of Habakkuk originated with the document that contained what we now know as Hab 2:4-5. The purpose of the tablets to which 2:2 refers apparently was not to ensure widespread dissemination of the message but to affirm its certainty by legally documenting it. One could describe it as a sign act. The tablet could have come into existence without any of the other material we now find in the book having been written down yet. The message of 2:4-5 includes no names and no reference to YHWH, but an earlier version may have made indirect reference to YHWH with an allusion back to 1:5 (see the commentary). If so, one might speculate that (a form of) the complaint in ch. 1 that cites 1:5–11 was already publicly known before the publication of the tablet. In any case, the content of the tablet would have invited elaboration, using the sort of material now embedded in chs. 1–2, even if not necessarily in precisely those words. It is impossible to know whether Habakkuk functioned as a prophet or worship leader within the context of the temple, either before or after receiving this revelation. On the one hand, it seems likely that the liturgical forms used and developed in the temple of Jerusalem were well known beyond the confines of the temple. Also, use of a friendly scribe would have allowed even dissident prophets to compose material that could look formally similar to material produced within the temple. On the other hand, the material in the book of Habakkuk is not as obviously critical of the establishment as is much of the material in the book of Jeremiah. If Habakkuk was a disciple of Jeremiah (possible, in my view), he might have felt able to preach more freely than Jeremiah himself by being less direct about the failings of the Jerusalem hierarchy. The book of Jeremiah gives insight into the oppressive regime of Jehoiakim (e.g., 22:13–19; 26:20–23), but it also indicates that Jeremiah had friends and sympathizers in high places (26:24). Not all his supporters were in hiding, although presumably they had to move cautiously.[56]

Habakkuk's complaint, once made public, is no longer only an address to YHWH. What would it communicate to those in Judah overhearing the prophet's complaint? First, it conveys a message about YHWH—namely, that in some way he can and should be thought responsible for the havoc caused by the Babylonians. Habakkuk's negative portrayal of the Babylonians (even in 1:5–11!) arguably creates some critical distance from Jeremiah's "pro-Babylonian" prophecies, which employ less hostile language when they depict the Babylonians as God's instrument to punish Judah. Still, Habakkuk's complaint proceeds on the assumption that Jeremiah's prophecies about Nebuchadnezzar are correct. And what Habakkuk implies about the Babylonians agrees with Jeremiah also in its claim of unstoppable effectiveness. Hence, secondly, Habakkuk's complaint conveys the message that the people of God are indeed in desperate straits. This could have been self-evident by the time Habakkuk uttered his complaint around 600 BC, but the human ca-

---

56. Haak (*Habakkuk*, 151–52) concludes that Habakkuk's prophecy was likely a written composition from the start. He considers the critique of Judah's leadership to be more overt than I do, seeing Habakkuk as specifically a sympathiser of exiled King Jehoahaz. Even in my reading, Habakkuk comes close to criticizing the regime directly. Protesting to God about the failure of Torah could be heard as an indirect criticism of the king, whose responsibility it was to uphold and promote Torah, and the language with which the Neo-Babylonian Empire is condemned could easily find application in condemning Jehoiakim, as observed above.

pacity for denying the obvious is great when such a denial fulfills a need. The opposition to Jeremiah recorded in the book that bears his name suggests that such denial was widespread even on the very eve of Jerusalem's downfall. Habakkuk's complaint undercuts the tendency to deny the accuracy of Jeremiah's preaching. Any who wished to complain to God alongside Habakkuk would have to agree with Jeremiah's analysis of the situation rather than join in with the maneuvers of the political elite that put its hope in receiving help from other nations.

In the same way, those who accept the prophecy in ch. 2 that claims that the atrocities committed by Nebuchadnezzar will prove self-destructive in the end cannot then promote similar behavior at home. In other words, those who wish to believe in the downfall of Babylon on the grounds offered in Habakkuk may have to accept the long-standing prophetic critique of Judean society, because the language that in Hab 2 is put in the mouths of the victims of Babylonian hegemony might well borrow from earlier prophetic denunciations of homegrown injustice.[57] In any case, the motifs used are applicable to local contexts, and it would have been inconsistent for any who denied the truthfulness of Jeremiah's condemnations to affirm the sayings in Habakkuk. At the very least, listening to Habakkuk would be a big step toward taking Jeremiah seriously. Discussing the origin of the book above (pp. 203–5), I drew two conclusions: that the reasons for thinking that these sayings originally condemned Jerusalem's leadership are not compelling and that the language used would have been well suited to indirectly address some of the things that were wrong with Judean society. In other words, if the sayings point the finger at Nebuchadnezzar's campaigns, there are three fingers pointing back to the greed and oppression within Judah.

While there is preaching potential in the book of Habakkuk, the final chapter reminds us that the first context of Habakkuk's words is prayer, and so perhaps it was a desire to offer guidance for prayer that first prompted the writing down of Habakkuk's message beyond 2:4–5. Overall, the book is a record of a dialogue between the prophet and God, not the record of a ministry of a prophet addressing a nation, even if the dialogue employs forms that could have been used as part of a prophetic ministry among the people. As a liturgy, the book would have retained direct relevance after the destruction of the Southern Kingdom, even if it contains no hint of the final catastrophe. In terms of its function, Habakkuk's book is closer to the book of Lamentations than the book of Jeremiah. The lack of reference to the end of temple and monarchy suggests a date earlier than that of the book of Lamentations, but the two books complement each other. Lamentations focuses on

57. This remains difficult to establish; see esp. the commentary on Hab 2:15–17 under "Composition."

Zion, which is named fifteen times (Jerusalem is named seven times, Judah five, Jacob and Israel three times each). Its personification is essential for the poems, with barely a side glance at the instrument of God's punishment. Habakkuk, by contrast, focuses on the Babylonians, their role in the divine plan, and the appropriate human response, with Judah or Jerusalem not even named once. Lamentations is largely backward looking, while Habakkuk is forward looking from the second verse onward (*How long?*). In terms of their concern, Lamentations encourages those who have strayed from YHWH to repent; Habakkuk encourages the faithful to remain loyal to YHWH.

B. HABAKKUK'S PLACE IN THE BOOK OF THE TWELVE

The masoretic arrangement of individual books within the Twelve seems to be broadly motivated by the implied chronological setting of the books. So, Habakkuk could have been placed after Zephaniah. It is possible that the compilers thought Habakkuk's implied setting is earlier than Zephaniah's, but it seems more likely that the chronological consideration was not decisive. A desire to pair Habakkuk with Nahum may have overruled it.[58] This pairing has been discussed above, and in another essay I lay out the reasons against thinking that Nahum and Habakkuk were conceived (composed or redacted) as a single two-volume work.[59] The desire to place Zephaniah last among the pre-destruction prophetic writings may have been more determinative for Habakkuk's penultimate position. In their canonical sequence, Nahum, Habakkuk, and Zephaniah envisage the end of the Neo-Assyrian Empire, the Neo-Babylonian Empire, and the Judean Kingdom. The Kingdom of Judah obviously came to an end prior to the disintegration of the Neo-Babylonian Empire, but the move from the end of foreign empires to the end of one's own nation makes rhetorical sense in preparation for the postexilic prophets, and it echoes Amos 1–2.[60]

Within the anthology of the Minor Prophets, Habakkuk is unique in being linked to the Neo-Babylonian setting that is the major backdrop of two of the three major prophets (Jeremiah and Ezekiel) and the major turning point in

58. Later Jewish tradition that dates Habakkuk in the time of Manasseh seems to me the result of interpreting settings in line with the order of the Book of the Twelve.

59. See Renz, "Habakkuk and Its Co-Texts."

60. A. Joseph Everson ("The Canonical Location of Habakkuk," in Reddit and Schart, *Thematic Threads*, 165–74) relates Habakkuk specifically to reflection upon the death of Josiah in 609 BC and Zephaniah to the later destruction of Jerusalem. While I am not persuaded by the specific link to the death of Josiah, his analysis is similar to my view that the key themes of the two books are decisive for the chronological ordering rather than their implied setting.

the other (Isaiah). If Nahum can be linked with the book of Isaiah, notably in its use of *maśśā'* and in the use of Nah 1:15 (2:1) in Isa 52:7,[61] Habakkuk arguably belongs more closely with Jeremiah, even if links to Isaiah need not be denied.[62] In 1:5–11, it uses language similar to Jeremiah (see the commentary), and it prominently features the motif of the prophet in prayer. (Zephaniah has the closest verbal links with Ezekiel.) This focus on the prophet speaking to God as well as receiving messages from God, which is even more prominent in Habakkuk than in Jeremiah, is arguably a unique contribution of Habakkuk to the anthology. It enables the anthology to present a rounded picture of prophecy, while the book's setting supports the anthology's suggestion of a continuous history of prophetic ministry through the ages.

C. HABAKKUK'S PLACE IN THE BIBLICAL CANON

The previous section highlighted the unique contribution of Habakkuk as well as links to Jeremiah and similarities and differences with Lamentations. The prophet's complaint is similar to complaint psalms in the Psalter, but it has a distinct focus on prophecy (1:5–11) as part of the complaint. The word about Torah being "numbed" (1:4) is striking and probably unique in its negativity.[63] This context may well have been the reason why the statement about the righteous living by faith(fulness) in Hab 2:4 became so important to the apostle Paul among others (for details, see the commentary below). Hab 3 probably presents a development of motifs from Exod 15, Deut 33, Judg 5, and possibly Pss 68 and 77, although scholars disagree on the dating of these different passages.

D. HABAKKUK IN THE HISTORY OF INTERPRETATION

The scroll of Habakkuk may be minor in length, but its reception easily competes with two of the three major prophets, Jeremiah and Ezekiel.[64] Its critique of an oppressive system was important to commentators such as

---

61. For further links, see the excursus "The Relationship between Nahum 1:15 (2:1) and Isaiah 52:7" (pp. 106–9); Fabry, *Nahum*, 113.

62. Walter Dietrich, "Habakuk—ein Jesajaschüler," in *Nachdenken über Israel, Bibel und Theologie*, ed. H. Michael Niemann, Matthias Augustin, and Werner H. Schmidt (Frankfurt am Main: Peter Lang, 1994), 197–215. See the list in Fabry, *Habakuk/Obadja*, 132–33, and note the similarity between Hab 2:1 and Isa 21:6.

63. See Renz, "Torah in the Minor Prophets," 73–94.

64. See Richard J. Coggins and Jin H. Han, *Six Minor Prophets through the Centuries: Nahum, Habakkuk, Zephaniah, Haggai, Zechariah, and Malachi*, Blackwell Bible Commen-

Theodore of Mopsuestia and Martin Luther but also influenced people who were not professionally engaged with biblical literature, such as novelist Harriet Beecher Stowe (1811–1896), who used Hab 1:11 as the epigraph for the thirty-first chapter of *Uncle Tom's Cabin*. The physicist and poet Wilbur Morris Stine (1863–1934) even composed a book-length allegory, *Habakkuk: A Poem*, based on the biblical character.[65] The apocryphal addition to the book of Daniel, Bel and the Dragon, recounts how an angel transported Habakkuk to bring a stew the prophet had prepared for reapers to Daniel in the lions' den. The incident may be a narrative dramatization of the significance of the prophet Habakkuk as one who lives face to face with the people who bring judgment (reaping is a symbol of judgment) but offers nourishment to the victims of oppression. In medieval times, Habakkuk was often depicted with Daniel (e.g., in illustrated books).[66]

The importance of Hab 2:4 within the New Testament, noted above, carries over into Christian reception history.[67] But the verse is apparently "one of the most frequently quoted in the rabbinic writings" as well, most famously as the one-verse summary of the whole Torah.[68] Also, the combination of theophany and harvest motifs in Hab 3 may have been responsible for the chapter becoming one of the Haftara readings on Shavuot within the Jewish tradition.[69] The motif of God remembering (Hab 3:2; Gen 8:1) seems to have prompted the appointment of the chapter as the Haftara for the Torah lesson of Gen 8:1–14 in the Palestinian three-year cycle.[70] In Christian liturgy, Hab 1–2 became one of the Old Testament readings for the Thursday of Holy Week in a sixth-century East Syrian lectionary,[71] and Hab 3 was associated with Christ's resurrection in the Byzantine liturgy, apparently on the strength of the interpretation of Hab 2:1 as an anticipation of the resurrection of Christ in an Easter homily by Gregory of Nazianzus (fourth century AD).[72] The Coptic liturgy also appoints the

---

taries 29 (Chichester: Wiley-Blackwell, 2011), 37. Fabry (*Habakuk/Obadja*, 153–82) focuses on Habakkuk's reception in antiquity.

65. Coggins and Han, *Six Minor Prophets*, 39.

66. See Coggins and Han, *Six Minor Prophets*, 45–46.

67. By way of example, see Han's excursus on the reception history of the verse in Augustine's work (Coggins and Han, *Six Minor Prophets*, 71–73).

68. Coggins and Han, *Six Minor Prophets*, 62. See b. Makkot 24A.

69. See H. St. John Thackeray, *The Septuagint and Jewish Worship: A Study in Origins*, Schweich Lectures 1920 (London: British Academy, 1921), 47–55. Thackeray believed that the poem had been composed for the festival liturgy prior to being incorporated into Habakkuk.

70. See Coggins and Han, *Six Minor Prophets*, 48, with reference to Jacob Mann, *The Bible as Read and Preached in the Old Synagogue*, vol. 1 (New York: Ktav, 1971), 69–70.

71. F. Crawford Burkitt, *The Early Syriac Lectionary System* (London: The British Academy; Oxford University Press, 1923), 29.

72. Coggins and Han, *Six Minor Prophets*, 48.

chapter to be read on Holy Saturday (the Saturday of Light, Joyous Saturday in the Coptic church).[73] It has found a home in other liturgical contexts as well, as will be noted at the end of this commentary on the book.

The Greek translation of Hab 3:2b ("You will be known between two living creatures") seems to have played a role in the depiction of ox and ass in the nativity scene,[74] although Isa 1:3 must have been the original source of the motif. Several expressions or phrases from Habakkuk other than "the righteous shall live by faith" have entered common parlance in some cultures, namely "evening wolves" (Hab 1:8; cf. Zeph 3:3) and "who runs may read"—a mistranslation of Hab 2:2 that likely goes back to Martin Luther.[75]

The beautiful, large-scale anthem "For lo, I raise up" by Charles Villiers Stanford (opus 145) deserves a special mention. It has Hab 1:6–12; 2:1–3, 14, 20 (Revised Version, slightly altered) as its source text. It was composed in 1914, the year World War I began, but remained unpublished until 1939, the year World War II began, fifteen years after Stanford's death.

E. HABAKKUK'S PLACE IN THE CHURCH TODAY

Habakkuk invites us to reflect on the breakdown of good order, the weakness of Torah in this context as unable to restore justice, and the role of God in all this. The commentary will invite a distinction between God's characteristic and his alien work as well as between his direct and indirect work, cautioning against naivete in praying for God's intervention in human affairs. Sometimes God's wrath is evident in his lack of intervention, in his handing over of humanity to its own devices. Habakkuk establishes that the answer to the problem of overwhelming wickedness ultimately cannot lie in the Torah, nor in the use of imperial force. The prophecy assumes and communicates that God knows beforehand the shape of even the most serious disaster and even has a hand in it. This proves comforting and frightening at the same time. The book invites us to respond to God in a combination of fear with trembling and rejoicing with confidence.

Maybe more so than other books in the Bible, Habakkuk suggests that thoughtful, engaged prayer, informed by Scripture, can help us to discern what is truly going on in a situation, given the inescapability of interpreta-

---

73. Mikhail E. Mikhail, *Focus on the Coptic Family: A Scriptural and Liturgical Guide Based on the Coptic Orthodox Lectionary (Katamaros)* (Cleveland, OH: St Mark's Coptic Orthodox Church, 1993), 311.

74. Coggins and Han, *Six Minor Prophets*, 42, 76.

75. Coggins and Han, *Six Minor Prophets*, 40–41. On the mistranslation, see Thomas Renz, "Reading and Running: Notes on the History of Translating the Final Clause of Hab 2:2," *VT* 69 (2019): 435–46.

tion. It thus stresses the importance of words, reminding us of the need for prayer prior to our action as well as our need for divine words to discern (recognize and understand) divine action. Habakkuk finds that God not only responds but enables the prophet's response to God.[76] The mature posture toward God is firm hope in his future coming, trusting that God's deeds must ultimately speak of his justice and compassion because God cannot be made known in random acts of aggression. While God is associated with devastation and disaster, his work and aim are not identified with it. Renewed energy comes with confidence in God's good purposes and his ability to bring them about. It can therefore encourage us to keep going, not abandoning confidence in God. It may challenge those among us who are lax in seeking justice to desire it more earnestly and may challenge those of us who long for divine justice to long for his mercy as well.

The revelation ultimately affirms the prophet's hunch that unjust means cannot lead to justice. The means the Babylonians employ will lead to the end determined for such evil; the greed with which they pursue their conquest will be their downfall. While the book's focus is on empire, the rhetoric used underlines a principle that is more generally true: evil falls back on the one who commits evil. Being reminded that life has to be received from God and that we cannot ourselves sustain it, we should not read the sayings in ch. 2 as directed against others only but instead use them to diagnose ourselves as well. If we do so, we will be encouraged to reflect on what the movement of goods in which we participate says about our underlying relationships and whether our toil is for this lifetime only or for something more lasting. We are warned against greed, gluttony, and seeking security in material possessions. Stepping back and looking at the chapter vis-à-vis Babylonian propaganda, we may again reflect on the power and weakness of words. While the sayings in ch. 2 are imagined rather than reported, they may nevertheless hint that there is more prophecy in the perception of subjugated communities than in the imperial propaganda that seems to shape events for a while. And Habakkuk would certainly affirm that there is more truth in the old traditions that inform the prayer of ch. 3 than the words of those who cry the loudest in the present. In this sense, Habakkuk may help us gain a new and better perception and interpretation of our lives, if read prayerfully.

76. Han (Coggins and Han, *Six Minor Prophets*, 87) notes the prominent use of Hab 3:16 "in the early church's polemic against the Pelagians, who taught that salvation could be attained by the exercise of free will." Such a use could appeal to the flow of the book of Habakkuk as a whole.

Text and Commentary

I. THE SUPERSCRIPTION (1:1)

¹The pronouncement that Habakkuk the prophet saw.

Composition

Because of the way a superscription potentially shapes the reading of a whole book, the superscription has been discussed above in the introduction, where we explored the profile of the book. The MT divides the verse into two units, which each have two disjunctive accents ("The pronouncement that saw / Habakkuk the prophet"). Perhaps this is meant to encourage a solemn recitation of the verse.

Commentary

There is a constant interplay between divine revelation and prophetic response in the book of Habakkuk. The superscription in 1:1 probably covers the first two chapters (see p. 195). These two chapters constitute the pronouncement to which ch. 3 is the response in the form of prayer. Just as the pronouncement incorporates prayer (ch. 1), so the prayer incorporates an account of divine revelation. While this is my preferred reading, it is possible to read it as covering all three chapters or, maybe less likely, as introducing only ch. 1, with 2:1 introducing ch. 2. We can imagine three ways in which *the pronouncement* (see the commentary on Nah 1:1 for discussion of this term) *that Habakkuk the prophet saw* unfolds. First, the complaint in ch. 1, which focuses on an earlier problematic oracle (1:5–11), could be considered a *pronouncement* in its own right that receives a reply in ch. 2. But it is possible, second, to read the complaint (ch. 1) and its reply (ch. 2) together as forming *the pronouncement that Habakkuk the prophet saw*, which in turn elicits the prophetic response in ch. 3. Finally, the pronouncement of chs. 1–2 and the prayer in ch. 3 can be read together as Habakkuk's *pronouncement*. While I prefer the second option, little is gained by firmly deciding for one of these options to the exclusion of the others.

The name *Habakkuk* is not a typical Hebrew formation. While there have been attempts in the tradition to link the name to a Hebrew root,[1] it is more likely that the name relates to an Akkadian root for a garden plant (cf. the English names Briar, Jasmine, Rose).[2] The name is apparently not attested independently of the book.[3] Thus the designation *the prophet* was probably not necessary to distinguish this Habakkuk from other persons of that name. The designation is found elsewhere in a superscription only with the postexilic prophets Haggai and Zechariah. This makes it plausible that the title, which is also used in 3:1, is meant to indicate that Habakkuk was a professional prophet. The book bearing his name contains two sections that are specifically marked for public promulgation: the writing on the tablets (2:4–5) that is elaborated upon by the outcry of the nations (2:6–20) and the prayer in ch. 3 whose subscript marks it for public use. Neither is what one would traditionally expect by way of prophetic speech. The only more traditionally shaped oracle is the prophecy concerning YHWH's role in the rise of the Neo-Babylonian Empire in 1:5–11, but this forms part of a prayer or prayer-dialogue that is again somewhat unusual. The designation *prophet* may have been added here to suggest that Habakkuk exercised a ministry beyond what is reflected in the book. Indeed, the prayer in ch. 1 could be heard as a complaint whose roots lie in frustration about a preaching or teaching ministry that seems to bear no fruit.[4]

Habakkuk *saw* (or "perceived") *the pronouncement*. The verb, which is also found in other headings (Isa 1:1; 2:1; Amos 1:1; Mic 1:1; Nah 1:1), may include experiencing visions but seems to have been used more widely for receiving divine revelation in whatever form it was provided.[5] The visual element is

---

1. See, e.g., Rosenberg, *Twelve Prophets*, 257, for the link to 2 Kgs 4:16.

2. Roberts (*Nahum*, 86) rightly lists Tamar, Elon, Keziah, and Hadassah as Hebrew examples and notes that the presence of an "Akkadian loanword in seventh-century Judah is not surprising, given Assyria's domination of Palestine since the late eighth century."

3. The tradition in the apocryphal writing Bel and the Dragon (vv. 33–39), according to which the prophet Habakkuk provided Daniel with food in the lions' den, is obviously dependent on the book of Habakkuk. Habakkuk is also mentioned in 4 Esd 1:40 in a list of the Twelve Prophets, and the name is also found in later Jewish tradition (cf. Rosenberg, *Twelve Prophets*, 257), again obviously dependent on the biblical book.

4. This is how Luther interpreted it.

5. For seeing an oracle, cf. Isa 13:1; Lam 2:14.

prominent in ch. 3, but it features already in v. 3 of this chapter, where the experience of iniquity is interpreted as, in a sense, a divine revelation. The use of the verb is thus very appropriate here.

Reflection

The book of Psalms is sometimes considered a unique part of Scripture in that words addressed to God in prayer are read also as words of revelation from God. This superscription suggests that the same is true here in the book of Habakkuk. It is the responsibility of a prophet to offer intercessory prayers (cf. Gen 20:7; 2 Chr 32:20; Jer 37:3; 42:1-4).[6] In the case of Habakkuk, as well as Jeremiah, such prayer is divine revelation. This feature testifies to a God who draws close to his people and makes their concerns his own. It thus prefigures Jesus, the Word of God that comes from the Father, who offered up prayers and supplications while he dwelled on earth (Heb 5:7) and returned to the Father. In its fullest sense, "word of God" is not only the Word that brings everything into existence and addresses human beings but also the Word that incorporates human experience into its life.

II. THE FIRST PART OF HABAKKUK'S COMPLAINT (1:2-4)

[2]*How long, O YHWH, do I shout for help*[a] *but you will not hear?*
I cry out to you, "Violence!"[b] *but you will not save.*
[3]*Why do you make me see iniquity and trouble?*[c]
You look on[d] *while destruction and violence are before me,*
while it happened that strife and contention arose.[e]
[4]*That is why the law*[f] *is numbed*[g]
and justice never[h] *comes forth.*
Because the wicked surrounds[i] *the righteous,*[j]
that is why justice comes forth perverted.[k]

a. The question *How long?* is commonly asked not with a *qatal* form as here but with a *yiqtol*, which would lend itself to the translation "shall I cry" (e.g., NRSV, ESV) or "must I call" (e.g., NIV). The only other occurrence of *'ad-'ānâ* with a *qatal* is in Exod 16:28. Once, it takes a participle (Josh 18:3). The more common *'ad-mātay* ("How long?") is used on its own in nominal clauses, with *yiqtol*, with a participle, and three times with *qatal* (Exod 10:3; Ps 80:4[5]; Prov 1:22), always with the implication of continuing to do something. (Note

6. Cf. 2 Macc 15:14 on Jeremiah and the role of Moses, the archetypal prophet, as intercessor, for which see, e.g., Michael Widmer, *Moses, God, and the Dynamics of Intercessory Prayer: A Study of Exodus 32–34 and Numbers 13–14*, FAT 2/8 (Tübingen: Mohr Siebeck, 2004).

that in Prov 1:22, the *qatal* form is used between two *yiqtol* forms.) It is therefore probably not advisable to translate "have I cried" (e.g., Keil, *Minor Prophets*, 2:55; Patterson, *Nahum*, 141; F. F. Bruce, "Habakkuk," in McComiskey, *Minor Prophets*, 843; Andersen, *Habakkuk*, 108–10).

b. It is possible that *how long* carries over into this sentence, as, e.g., in NRSV, NIV; cf. Job 8:2; 19:2. In other places, *how long* is repeated (Num 14:11; Ps 13:1–2[2–3]). Ps 62:3(4) is similarly ambiguous. Likewise, *why* in the following verse may carry over into the next sentence.

c. This line division disagrees with the accentuation, which makes *trouble* the object of the following verb. With Roberts (*Nahum*, 87–88), I prefer to read the following two clauses introduced by *wə-* ("and") as circumstantial (*while*).

d. KJV has "cause *me* to behold" (cf. Calvin, Geneva Bible, NKJV, NASB, NAB), but a causative meaning of the *hiphil* of this verb is not apparent in any of the other sixty-eight occurrences in the Hebrew Bible. The juxtaposition of *make me see* and *you look* was apparently perceived as awkward by ancient translators. LXX and Vulg. read the infinitive, Syr. and Tg. the first person. Elliger (*BHS*) finds the latter attractive, but see Roberts, *Nahum*, 87–88.

e. Reading with the accentuation; cf. 2 Kgs 4:8 (with a single subject) for the syntax. Or "while there is strife and contention arises." For the unusual intransitive sense of *nśʾ qal* ("arises"), see the note and commentary on Nah 1:5.

f. Hebrew *tôrâ* is used for "instruction" as well as "law" and here refers to "Torah" in my view; see Renz, "Torah in the Minor Prophets." The rendering *the law* allows for connotations of "law and order," which are appropriate in context.

g. The verb is used elsewhere in Gen 45:26; Pss 38:8(9); 77:2(3) and conjectured for 88:15(16) (see *BHS*); cf. the nouns *pûgâ* and *hăpûgâ* ("relaxation, stopping") in Lam 2:18 and 3:49.

h. This rendering reflects the traditional understanding. Alternatively, *lāneṣaḥ* may suggest here that justice "does not come forth successfully." For this nuance, see Prov 21:28; cf. Bruce K. Waltke, *The Book of Proverbs, Chapters 15–31*, NICOT (Grand Rapids: Eerdmans, 2005), 164.

i. Hebrew *maktîr* is *hiphil* of *ktr* (the *qal* is not attested), which is used positively in Ps 142:7(8) for "the righteous gather around me." The use in Prov 14:18 ("crowned"?) is identified in *HALOT* as the single occurrence of *ktr* III ("wear as a headdress"; cf. *keter*, "headdress," in Esth 1:11; 2:17; 6:8). The *piel* is attested in Judg 20:43 and Ps 22:12(13) for "surround" in a threatening manner and in Job 36:2, which *HALOT* identifies as the single occurrence of *ktr* I ("be patient with").

j. Or, in a forensic sense (as, e.g., in Exod 23:7), "the guilty . . . the innocent." The singular appears to be generic.

k. Hebrew *məʿuqqāl* (lit. "bent"). This is the only occurrence of the verb, but two adjectives are known: *ʿăqalqall*, used in Judg 5:6 for winding paths and in Ps 125:5 on its own for "crooked ways"; and *ʿăqallātôn*, used in Isa 27:1 of Leviathan, the coiling serpent.

Composition

Habakkuk's complaint is similar to complaints found in the Psalter. Psalms 13:1–2; 74:10; and 89:46(47) feature Habakkuk's opening question (*How long?*). Psalms written in relation to a situation of distress can be usefully categorized as either plea or complaint psalms, depending on whether God is addressed as the helper who is opposed to the evil encountered or as the opponent who causes it. In Hab 1:2-3 the distress is described in three sets of paired words (*iniquity and trouble, destruction and violence, strife and contention*) for which God is not made directly responsible.[7] But Habakkuk accuses YHWH of failing to *hear* and to *save* in v. 2 and holds him indirectly responsible in v. 3 for making the prophet witness evil, which would not be necessary if YHWH did not look on (i.e., tolerate) it. Verse 4 traces the root cause of the *destruction and violence* and *strife and contention* back to the fact that the wicked have the upper hand and the law is unable to do anything about it.

Habakkuk's complaint is commonly read as focusing on the general social situation rather than his own suffering. This is correct in my view, although others disagree.[8] The prophet fulfills his role as an intercessor and complains on behalf of all those suffering innocently at the hands of *the wicked*. This may have included personal suffering, but such is not highlighted here.[9] The prepositional phrase *before me* commonly means "in my presence," and only rarely does it specifically mean "against me" (Job 10:17; Eccl 4:12). Just as YHWH is not made *directly* responsible for the evil, so Habakkuk is not described as *directly* affected. YHWH looks on evil, countenancing it, and Habakkuk is made to see evil, witnessing it.

This unit does not specify whether the evil is primarily an internal or an external problem. When the following verses (1:5-11) are read as a response to this opening complaint, it is often assumed that the wickedness about which Habakkuk complains is exclusively internal. In this case, "the cry for God to act against the parochial violence within Israel is answered with the announcement that God will do so by sending imperial violence from beyond Israel."[10] But even on the traditional reading of ch. 1 as a dialogue, this should not be a foregone conclusion. Vasholz recognized that the last section of the chapter (vv. 12-17) does not easily qualify as a *different* complaint.

7. For *iniquity and trouble*, cf. Ps 55:10(11) and, in reverse order, Ps 10:7; 90:10; for *destruction and violence* (always in reverse order), cf. Jer 6:7; 20:8; Ezek 45:9; Amos 3:10; for *strife and contention* (together but not as one phrase), cf. Prov 15:18; 17:14; 26:21; Jer 15:10.

8. J. Gerald Janzen, "Eschatological Symbol and Existence in Habakkuk," *CBQ* 44 (1982): 394–414; Andersen, *Habakkuk*, 112; Cleaver-Bartholomew, "Alternative Approach," 207–8. These scholars *inter alia* point to a perceived autobiographical tone and similarity of language with petitionary prayers in the psalms and suggest that there is no group with which Habakkuk could have readily identified.

9. Janzen ("Eschatological Symbol," 398–99) connects *tôrâ* and *mišpāṭ* to prophetic instruction and on this basis finds in this text opposition to Habakkuk specifically. I do not think that the context warrants such a narrowing of the reference of these terms; see Renz, "Torah in the Minor Prophets."

10. Rickie D. Moore, "The Prophetic Path from Lament to Praise," *The Living Pulpit* 11 (Oct–Dec 2002): 26.

Indeed, it is characteristic for laments to elaborate at greater length on the distress after a brief summary statement. Vasholz also noted that the language of (apparently) local violence can be used to refer to international turmoil. He concluded that this first section of the book has the Assyrian oppression of Judah in view.[11] This would imply an early date for this part of the book. Széles suggests that Egyptian pressure may have contributed to the crisis.[12] The text does not allow us to identify the oppressor as local or foreign. Thus, as noted above, rhetorically there may be a development from "injustice at a local level (1.2–4) to injustice at an international level (1.5–11) and finally to injustice at a cosmic level (1.12–17)."[13] But in fact, the injustice focused upon may be the same, albeit looked at with different lenses that consecutively widen the horizon. I assume that the prophet saw the oppression within Judah as related to the wider political situation.

The line division of v. 3 adopted here highlights the occurrence of three word pairs to describe the crisis. This results in a tricolon that arguably stresses YHWH's tolerance of evil (*You look on*). Alternatively, it would be possible to scan this unit as three times two bicola. But such regularity would be more apparent than real, given the vastly different lengths of cola that would result: from four (v. 2aβ) or five (vv. 2bβ, 3aβ) syllables in the second half of the first three bicola to nine syllables in the last three cola (v. 4aβ, 4bα, 4bβ).

A few scholars express more unease about the juxtaposition of *justice never comes forth* (v. 4a) and *justice comes forth perverted* (v. 4b) than seems warranted.[14] The text is hardly incoherent; the second statement does not correct the first but explicates it. There are two different ways in which it might be true that *justice never comes forth*. A lack of justice could be the result of a complete breakdown of judicial institutions or of their perversion. The second statement (*justice comes forth perverted*) clarifies that the latter is in view.

Commentary

2 *How long* introduces a rhetorical question that is usually directed toward the future ("How much longer?"), expressing impatience. The use of a *qatal*

11. Robert I. Vasholz, "Habakkuk: Complaints or Complaint?" *Presbyterion* 18 (1992): 50–52.

12. Mária Eszenyei Széles, *Wrath and Mercy: A Commentary on the Books of Habakkuk and Zephaniah* (Edinburgh: Handsel; Grand Rapids: Eerdmans, 1987), 19–20.

13. Dangl, "Habakkuk in Recent Research," 153.

14. Seybold, *Nahum*, 56; Perlitt, *Nahum*, 51; Andersen, *Nahum*, 119; cf. Fabry, *Habakuk/ Obadja*, 190, 195.

("perfect") form has led some to interpret Habakkuk's opening sentence instead as an exclamation directed toward the past ("How long have I . . . !"), expressing exasperation. This is unnecessary and probably inadvisable in the light of the *yiqtol* (imperfect) form *you will not hear*.[15] The *qatal* shifts to *yiqtol*, emphasizing the continuous nature of the action in *I cry out to you, "Violence!"* This expression has a parallel in Job 19:7 and Jer 20:8.[16] The latter has *ḥāmās wāšōd* ("violence and destruction") as its object (cf. *destruction and violence* in v. 3); the former also has the verb *šawwaʿ* (*shout for help*). In both instances, as here in Habakkuk, crying out, "Violence!" means calling attention to violence, whether the focus falls on suffering, as in Job, or on perpetration, as probably in Jeremiah.[17] Drawing God's attention to unjust suffering and violence is, of course, asking him to intervene; *but you will not save* indicates YHWH's apparent refusal to do so.

3 Habakkuk sees *iniquity and trouble* and witnesses *destruction and violence*, but he is unable to do anything about it.[18] This surely implies that he would want YHWH to intervene but must tolerate these scenes because he is powerless to do anything about them himself. For God to tolerate and *make . . . see* such scenes is different, because he is expected to be able and willing to do something about such injustice. Habakkuk does not allow for the possibility that YHWH looks on because he is powerless to do anything about the situation. For YHWH to countenance evil is in some ways to endorse it. Hence the question *why?* The last line may suggest a further development (*it happened*). If so, it probably implies that *strife and contention* could have been avoided if *iniquity* had been dealt with promptly as it arose. YHWH's continuing (cf. *How long?* in the preceding verse) toleration of evil has apparently made things as bad as they can be.

4 *That is why* at the beginning of the verse implies that *the law* can function properly only as long as YHWH intervenes to stop evil getting out of hand.[19] This may be true in two senses. First, it could be argued that as long

15. See the translation note. Andersen (*Habakkuk*, 110) allows for a future reference only where absolutely required and demands that the *yiqtol* form is read in the light of the *qatal* form. The question *kammâ* ("how often") is more obviously used both for rhetorical questions (e.g., Pss 35:17; 119:84) and for exclamations (e.g., Ps 78:40, with a *yiqtol* form expressing iterative action).

16. Job 19:7 uses the version of the verb with *tsade* (*ṣʿq*) rather than *zayin* (*zʿq*).

17. The phrase "violence and destruction" (Habakkuk's reverse order in v. 3 is the exception) refers to actions committed rather than suffered in Jer 6:7 and Ezek 45:9. This is probably also true for Amos 3:10, which, however, may be deliberately ambiguous—a possibility that cannot be excluded for Jer 20:8 either.

18. See 2:17 for a reuse of these last two terms, clearly in an international context; cf. *destruction* in 1:9 and 2:8.

19. It also hints at the covenantal context of this *law*. YHWH is considered to have a

as the God of the covenant blesses the righteous and curses the wicked, and does so visibly and promptly, there is an incentive to abide by *law*, understood as Torah, and this renders Torah effective. But the covenant was never designed to function in this way. The implementation of Torah was put in human hands, with divine blessings promised and curses threatened for the people as a whole rather than individually allocated. Second, *the law* may be *numbed* because *strife and contention* prevent a consistent and prompt application of *the law* in the judicial realm. This, in turn, encourages people to neglect and violate the covenant regulations (cf. Eccl 8:11 for the general principle, not expressed in covenant terms). In this case, the divine instruction has been rendered ineffective and powerless because its human component has broken down. First, Torah needs to be properly taught and implemented in court. Second, it needs to be taken to heart by the people. We may wonder whether the problem was more the former or the latter. Was Torah appropriately given but widely ignored, or has "the lying pen of the scribes" turned YHWH's Torah "into a lie" (Jer 8:8)? The corruption of the judicial system to which Habakkuk alludes may suggest that Torah was hampered at all levels, but because there are no specific accusations against the priests (or the judges), we cannot be certain. In any case, it seems that Torah is only able to guide a functioning society. It is unable to fulfill its purpose when *the wicked surrounds the righteous*, which is to say when the righteous are hedged or hemmed in by the wicked, unable to escape their grasp.[20]

It is not entirely clear how specific the complaint that *justice never comes forth* is. Does it refer more generally to the absence of good order and thus the breakdown of the fabric of society,[21] or is specifically the perversion of the judicial system in view, as the majority of commentators believe? The verb *comes forth* may suggest the pronouncement of verdicts, as in Pss 17:2; 37:6; Mic 7:9. But in all these cases *mišpāṭ* (*justice*) has a pronominal suffix and refers to the justice due to someone (cf. Hos 6:5). In fact, the verb *comes forth* can also designate the promulgation of law and the establishment of

---

stake in *the law* and in *justice*, suggesting that *the law* that defines *justice* is Torah, divine law. I do not believe that *tôrâ* in 1:4 refers to the prophetic word, as J. Gerald Janzen argues in "Eschatological Symbol," 397-98. While both *mišpāṭ* ("judgment") and *tôrâ* ("instruction") are found in a variety of contexts, the unqualified use (the prophet does not say "my instruction") and combination of the two terms lead one naturally to think of Torah. Strong signals to the contrary would be required if another referent were intended. (Further alternatives would be a reference to priestly instruction or [parental or wisdom] teaching, neither of which easily fits the context, or to royal legislation, for which there is no parallel.)

20. The consonantal text could be read as "wickedness surrounds the righteous," but already LXX attests the more concrete reading *the wicked*.

21. So, e.g., Keil, *Minor Prophets*, 2:57, followed by Patterson, *Nahum*, 142-43; Haak, *Habakkuk*, 33-34.

justice more generally. This is probably the case in Isa 42:1, 3, where the *hiphil* of the verb ("bringing forth") is used for the activity of the servant of YHWH and in Isa 51:4 where *tôrâ* (Torah) is the subject of the verb but *mišpāṭ* (*justice*) is also referenced (cf. Isa 2:3 with *šāpaṭ*, "judge," in v. 4).[22] The last line (*that is why justice comes forth perverted*) probably refers specifically to the perversion of judicial verdicts but the reuse of the phrase *justice comes forth* in v. 7 likely lacks such a narrow focus.

Reflection

Habakkuk's prayer here and elsewhere in the book is personal, but it is not narrowly concerned with him individually. Habakkuk does not voice worry about being vindicated himself but outrage at the impact of miscarriages of justice on society at large. The social picture he draws is dark indeed, suggesting a general breakdown of righteousness, integrity, and honesty in society. Injustice appears to pervade the whole of society. Nevertheless, these opening verses show a specific concern with the workings of law and order. The logic needs to be carefully discerned. Habakkuk could have complained that a situation of widespread injustice is not being rectified by the pronouncement of sound judgments, the failure of human judges mirroring God's refusal to set things right. But the thrust of the argument is not so much that evil triumphs because good men do nothing[23] or because the authorities fail to respond appropriately to evil. Habakkuk cries out because the violence is so overwhelming and the grip of the wicked so strong that law and order have been overpowered. The focus is not on the *cause* of violence but on its *effect*. This may be the reason for leaving the Babylonians out of the picture at this stage.[24]

The effect is that good order has broken down and Torah has been rendered inoperative. It is not so much that justice and order have been obscured but that their very existence is in question. As day follows night when the sun comes forth, so justice is meant to shine forth again and again to set things right. But as in a land of permanent darkness, where the sun does

22. Apart from Hab 1:4, "law" (*tôrâ*, sg. or pl.) and "justice, judgment" (*mišpāṭ*, sg. or pl.) are together in Lev 26:46; Num 15:16; Deut 4:8; 17:11; 33:10; 1 Kgs 2:3; 2 Kgs 17:34, 37; 2 Chr 19:10; 30:16; 33:8; Ezra 7:10; Neh 8:18; 9:13, 29; 10:30; Ps 89:30(31); Isa 42:4; 51:4; Ezek 44:24; Mal 3:22.

23. For the saying to which this alludes, wrongly attributed to Edmund Burke, see Martin Porter's study (January 2002) at http://tartarus.org/~martin/essays/burkequote.html.

24. The wider impact of Babylonian occupation is in view in subsequent verses. For now, it does not matter who causes the violence; refusing to lay the blame at the foot of the Babylonians too quickly may encourage self-examination among those who listen.

THE BOOK OF HABAKKUK

not rise, *justice never comes forth*. How can God tolerate this? A world that knows both good and evil has long been a reality, but does not a society disintegrate where the judicial system is altogether corrupted? And has not a people's relationship with YHWH completely broken down where Torah is ineffective? The *strife and contention* that Habakkuk perceives around him seem to threaten the very fabric of life (cf. Lev 18:5).

In the onslaught of evil, Habakkuk experiences the truth that Torah can describe the shape of obedience but cannot create it. This is arguably true for all law. Law can describe and even shape human behavior, but it is powerless against widespread disregard and violation. Good order cannot be legislated out of chaos. In such situations, law can only be upheld by force. The prayer does not outline what precisely God could or should have done. Should Torah have been shored up with the help of a more authoritarian regime on God's part? If Torah is powerless on its own, how much force should be expended to uphold it? Raising these questions leads naturally to a consideration of God's use of imperial forces.

It is no surprise that the apostle Paul and others used Habakkuk to reflect on the power of God in the face of Torah's incapacity. If Habakkuk's complaint about God's passivity is understood as a complaint about the lack of God's anger in the face of wrongdoing, Paul's answer at the beginning of his letter to the Romans seems to be that God's wrath is evident precisely in his lack of intervention, in his handing over of humanity to its own devices. This relates to the answer that unfolds in Hab 2. The punishment of sin is experiencing sin and its consequences. But such an answer looks at humanity as undifferentiated. If it is possible to distinguish the righteous and the wicked, more needs to be said about the suffering of the righteous at the hand of the wicked, but both Habakkuk and Paul will have more to say. What the prophet establishes first is that the answer to the problem of overwhelming wickedness cannot lie in the Torah. The following verses highlight that the answer cannot ultimately lie in the use of imperial force either. Just as Torah is of use but only limited use against evil, so foreign armies can at best be a limited, temporary solution.

III. THE CITATION OF AN EARLIER ORACLE (1:5-11)

⁵*Look at*ᵃ *the nations*ᵇ *and observe,*
   *and astonish yourselves, be astonished!*ᶜ
*For one is*ᵈ *about to do a deed in your days*
   [that] you would not believe if it were told.
⁶*For look, I am raising up the Chaldeans,*ᵉ
   *the sharp*ᶠ *and swift*ᵍ *nation,*

one going across[h] the length and breadth of the earth[i]
  to take possession of dwellings not his[j] own.[k]
[7]*He is dread-inspiring and fearsome;[l]*
  it is from him[m] that his justice and exaltation[n] comes[o] forth.[p]
[8]*And faster than leopards[q] are his steeds,*
  and quicker[r] than wolves at dusk,[s]
    and his cavalry is restless.[t]
And his cavalry[u] comes[v] from afar;
  they fly[w]—like a vulture[x] swooping to devour.
[9]*All of them[y] come[z] to do violence;[aa]*
  the mass of their faces[bb] is [directed] forward.[cc]
    And he gathers[dd] captives like sand.
[10]*He—scoffs at the kings,[ee]*
and rulers[ff] are an object of derision to him.
He—laughs at every fortified city.
  He piles up dust and captures it.[gg]
[11]*Then he sweeps along,[hh] a wind,[ii] and passes through*
and transgresses[jj]—he whose[kk] strength is for his god.[ll]

a. With *r'h qal* ("to see"), the preposition *beth* usually introduces the object, hence *at* rather than "among" (e.g., Vulg., RSV, ESV, NASB). Where *beth* indicates the realm of vision, the object is otherwise specified within the same sentence; see, e.g., Deut 21:11; 23:14[15]; Josh 7:21; Judg 14:2; 1 Sam 16:1. While the looking *at the nations* soon focuses on one "among" *the nations*, other nations remain in view, explicitly in v. 10. Note that *look* in v. 6 translates the particle interjection *hinnē*. Traditional translations distinguish the interjection from the verb by the use of "lo" or "behold" for the former, but these are now archaic.

b. LXX *hoi kataphronētai* ("you scoffers") apparently reads *bōgdîm* for MT *baggôyim* (*at the nations*); cf. 1QpHab (in the commentary; the text itself is not preserved), Syr., Acts 13:41. 8HevXIIgr is not preserved at this point; the *alpha* that is preserved may have belonged to *hoi kataphronētai* but *[eis] ta ethnē*, reflecting *baggôyim*, cannot be excluded. The MT is supported by MurXII, Aquila, Symmachus, Theodotion, Vulg., and Tg. See the excursus below.

c. Hebrew *wǝhittammǝhû tǝmāhû* uses the *hithpael* and the *qal* of the root *tmh* ("to be astounded, shocked, horrified"). The precise force of the *hithpael* is uncertain. It occurs only here and in a conjectured version of Isa 29:9. One could translate "and be horrified, be astounded," but it seems worth retaining the repetition of the root.

d. The active participle lacks a subject pronoun; cf. 2:10. The omitted pronoun in such cases is nearly always in the third person. For omission of the first-person pronoun, GKC 116s compares Zech 9:12, where the participle is followed by a first-person *yiqtol*, and Mal 2:16, which the Masoretes did not interpret as a participle; cf. JM 154c. The first-person pronoun is provided in LXX (cf. Syr., NIV, NASB, ESV). Other translations offer a passive rendering (e.g., NRSV, NAB, TNK, HCSB; cf. already Vulg. and Tg.), which preserves the lack of identified agent. The alternative translation, "he is about to do a deed," might suggest that the prophet is the speaker, in which case the citation of divine speech would open with *kî* (*for*) in the next verse, which seems to me less plausible.

e. See Andersen, *Habakkuk*, 145–48, for a defense of the reading *Chaldeans* with reference to the Babylonians, particularly against the view that "Kasdim" with reference to the Greeks (1QpHab) is original; cf. Sellin, *Zwölfprophetenbuch*, 388–89, who changed his mind between the first and second edition. In the commentary, "Babylonians" will be used interchangeably with *Chaldeans*. For the addition of *tous machētas* ("the warriors") in Greek MSS, see Mulroney, *Translation Style*, 117–18.

f. Hebrew *mar* is clearly attested as "bitter" in a literal or metaphorical sense. The possibility of a second meaning "strong" is recognized, with hesitation, in *DCH* but not in *HALOT* and Ges[18]; cf. Laurence Kutler, "A 'Strong' Case for Hebrew MAR," *UF* 16 (1984): 111–18; Ehud Ben Zvi, *A Historical-Critical Study of the Book of Zephaniah*, BZAW 198 (Berlin: de Gruyter, 1991), 119. I take *mar* here as a reference to a harsh or hostile attitude. The word alliterates with the following *wəhannimhār* (*and hasty*); cf. "fierce and fiery" (NJB, followed by Patterson, *Nahum*, 150) or "hostile and hasty." Cf. Dennis G. Pardee, "The Semitic Root *mrr* and the Etymology of Ugaritic *mr(h) // brk*," *UF* 10 (1978): 249–88.

g. Hebrew *nimhār* ("hasty, swift, impetuous") is sometimes considered to have the nuance "skilled" here (e.g., Haak, *Habakkuk*, 38; this is usually only contemplated for the adjective *māhîr*), but the motif of swiftness is both much more common to the root and more prominent in this chapter. As an indication of eagerness, the term itself is neutral; cf. Andersen, *Habakkuk*, 149; see *DCH* references to Qumran texts.

h. Apart from the idiomatic expression *lipnê* ("before"), the participle of *hlk* is followed by a noun with *lamed* only rarely. Elsewhere, the noun in question indicates the *manner* of movement (2 Sam 15:11; Isa 8:6; Song 7:9[10] second noun) or its *direction* (Num 24:14; Ezek 7:14; Song 7:9[10] first noun; cf. Neh 12:28).

i. Hebrew *merḥābê-'ereṣ* is more literally "the wide places of the earth" (or "land"). The noun *merḥāb* ("wideness") is used for a large (and safe?) meadow in Hos 4:16 and has connotations of safety in 2 Sam 22:20 // Ps 18:19(20); Pss 31:8(9); 118:5. It is used in the plural only here, where the idea seems to be that the Chaldeans can move unhindered wherever they please. Cf. *raḥăbê-'āreṣ* ("the expanse of the earth") in Job 38:18; see also Isa 8:8.

j. The pronoun here raises an acute problem for translating the book of Habakkuk. Its antecedent is the *nation*, and English usage would therefore demand "its" or maybe "hers," but this is not easily sustained throughout the book. English translations therefore usually switch to the masculine singular in ch. 2, thus obscuring the link to ch. 1, where masculine singular pronouns, suffixes, and verb forms refer to the personified Neo-Babylonian Empire. To preserve consistency, I will use "he" and "his" throughout.

k. Cf. the same phrase, *llō'-lô* ("not his/its"), in 2:6; see GKC 155e for the construction generally and 13e for the dagesh.

l. Dogniez ("Fautes," 248–51) argues that the use of *epiphanēs* ("conspicuous, notable, formidable, splendid") here and in a few other places in the LXX of the Minor Prophets is not the result of a misreading of the Hebrew root (*r'h* for *yr'*) but a deliberate choice, playing on the graphic similarity of the roots, to suggest an awe-inspiring dread; cf. BA 23.4–9, 263–64.

m. Hebrew *mimmennû* (*from him* or "because of him/us") is traditionally taken with the second half of the verse; cf. the masoretic accentuation and LXX *ex auto*. Connecting it with the first half would result in "He is too dread-inspiring and fearsome for us" (cf. Num 13:31 for a similar construction), which would require a change of speaker (back to Habakkuk) and is therefore unlikely.

n. Both *justice* and *exaltation* have a pronominal suffix (*his*) in the Hebrew. Halévy (*Recherches Bibliques*, 387) thinks that the suffixes refer back to YHWH. This is unlikely. I believe that they, in conjunction with *mimmennû*, stress that the prevailing justice is that of the

Babylonian empire; see the commentary. I added *it is . . . that* to bring out this emphasis but retained the use of the pronoun (*his*) with *justice*, which, while awkward in English, facilitates the discussion in the exposition below.

o. The use of a singular verb with more than one subject is rare but possible where the nouns form a single idea as, e.g., in Deut 8:13; Prov 27:9; Isa 9:5(4); Hos 4:11; see JM 150p; cf. GKC 146e. For alternative explanations, see the following note.

p. LXX reads as two phrases: "His judgment shall be of himself, and his oracle [*lēmma*, as in 1:1] shall come out of himself." Andersen (*Habakkuk*, 152–53) translates Symmachus as "He will decide for himself and by his own decision he will march out" and considers this the best interpretation.

q. Hebrew *nəmērîm* cannot be defined with zoological precision. The reference may even be to cheetahs, the fastest land animal (adopted in NLT).

r. Hebrew *ḥdd qal* ("be sharp, i.e. be quick," *DCH*; cf. *HALOT*). Only the *hophal* of the verb is securely attested elsewhere, referring to sharpened swords in Ezek 21:9–11(14–16). Note also the two occurrences of *ḥdh hiphil* in Prov 27:17, where BDB accepts *ḥdh* as an alternative for *ḥdd* and *HALOT* suggests emendation to *ḥdd*. The hiphil of *ḥdd* has been conjectured also for Zech 1:21 (2:4), the hithpael for Ezek 21:16(21). See the commentary.

s. Hebrew *mizzə'ēbê 'ereb* is literally "than wolves of the evening," but English usage of "evening" means that the term does not convey the implied threat; hence *dusk*. LXX interprets as "wolves of Arabia," reading *'ărāb* (the Arabian desert) instead of MT *'ereb* (evening). In Ancient Hebrew, *'ărāb* could probably designate the desert or steppe more generally alongside the longer form *'ărābâ* (for which cf. Jer 5:6, *zə'ēb 'ărābôt*). It is possible that we should understand "wolves of the desert," but see, e.g., Perlitt, *Nahum*, 55; Fabry, *Habakuk/ Obadja*, 200. Cf. Zeph 3:3. Adele Berlin (*Zephaniah: A New Translation with Introduction and Commentary*, AB 25A [New York: Doubleday, 1994], 128) and Johannes Vlaardinger-broek (*Zephaniah*, HCOT [Leuven: Peeters, 1999], 174–75) note that Zalcman's rendering "ravening wolves" cleverly captures sound and wordplay. Cf. Zalcman's suggestion of an allusion to the Midianite leaders Oreb and Zeev (Judg 7:25; 8:3; Ps 83:11[12]), which is ingenious but implausible.

t. The precise nuance of the verb *pûš* here is uncertain. The *qal* is attested twice more, with reference to frisking calves (Jer 50:11; Mal 4:2 [3:20]). The *niphal* refers to people being scattered in Nah 3:18.

u. Hebrew *ûpāšû pārāšāyw ûpārāšāyw* (*and his cavalry is restless. And his cavalry*) is (1) textually uncertain (see the discussion in *BHQ*, 13:115*–116* and *CTAT* 3:826–28; cf. *BHS*; *HALOT*; Roberts, *Nahum*, 92–93; Haak, *Habakkuk*, 42–43; Fabry, *Habakuk/Obadja*, 200) and (2) ambiguous, if one allows that *pārāš* may refer either to "horse" or to "horseman." Franz Delitzsch (*Der Prophet Habakuk*, Exegetisches Handbuch zu den Propheten des Alten Bundes [Leipzig: Tauchnitz, 1843], 13) only allows the latter; cf. KJV.

v. Hebrew *yābō'û* is plural. The collective noun "cavalry" (cf. previous note on horsemen and horses) requires the singular verb; retention of the plural *they fly* in the following line seems to me tolerable, however. From here onward, *yiqtol* forms are used for repeated action.

w. Hebrew *yā'upû* (*they fly*) has been accented with *zaqef parvum* by the Masoretes. My translation seeks to reflect the same rhythm with a dash.

x. Hebrew *nešer* apparently refers to a griffon-vulture in Mic 1:16 but is probably less specific elsewhere and may designate any bird with a large wingspan. The swiftness of a *nešer* is a common motif; cf. Deut 28:49; 2 Sam 1:23; Jer 4:13; 48:40; Hos 8:1; Prov 23:5; Job 9:28; Lam 4:19.

y. Hebrew *kullô* is "all of it" or "the whole of it," and hence "each one of them" or *all of them*. Alternatively, "all of it" could mean "entirely" (e.g., Ps 139:4; Prov 24:31; Jer 2:21; Job 21:23; cf. JM 146j; GKC 128e), but the word order probably counsels against this.

z. *kullô* governs singular verbs, even when the discourse continues with plural verb forms (e.g., Ps 53:3[4]; Isa 1:23), but the translation *all of them* requires a change to the plural in English.

aa. Hebrew *ləḥāmās* could alternatively be rendered as an adverb ("violently," which seems to be how it is taken in 1QpHab; cf. William H. Brownlee, *The Midrash Pesher of Habakkuk*, SBLMS 24 [Missoula: Scholars Press, 1979], 69) or "against violence" (with reference to *violence* in v. 3), but the traditional understanding ("for violence"; i.e., *to do violence*) is the most obvious.

bb. The meaning of the first term in this difficult phrase (*məgammat pənêhem*), a hapax legomenon, is uncertain; *DCH* offers "multitude"; *HALOT* suggests "totality." Some medieval Jewish commentators linked the noun to the root *gm'* (Gen 24:17; Job 39:24), which may suggest interpreting the noun as a reference to "eagerness" or "craving" (cf. Rosenberg, *Twelve Prophets*, 260). This is defended by Franz Delitzsch, *Habakkuk*, 15–16. Others wonder about a connection with similar Arabic roots referring to desire or to glowing/burning (see Fabry, *Habakuk/Obadja*, 201). An idea of opposition is reflected in LXX and apparently Boharic (Andersen, *Habakkuk*, 155); this may reflect the reading *məgôrat* ("terror of"; cf. Prov 10:24) for MT's *məgammat*; cf. *BHS*.

cc. Hebrew *qādîmâ* with directive *he* elsewhere means "eastward" (fourteen times, all in Ezek 40–48, except for Ezek 11:1), a meaning also attested for *qādîm* without *he* (e.g., Ezek 43:17). This is adopted by Abarbanel and interpreted in terms of eagerness to bring booty home (Rosenberg, *Twelve Prophets*, 260). Duhm suggested a Babylonian advance from Cappadocia, reading *miggōmer* for *məgammat* (see Andersen, *Habakkuk*, 155). But the rendering *forward* seems possible and preferable (cf. Franz Delitzsch, *Habakkuk*, 16). 1QpHab has *qdym* (*qādîm*), most likely a reference to the east wind; cf. Tg., Vulg., Syr., Symmachus.

dd. Hebrew *wayye'ĕsōp*. The masoretic vocalization of *yiqtol* forms with *waw* here and in the following verse (*wayyiṣbōr*, "piles up"; *wayyilkədāh*, "captures") is surprising. They are generally interpreted as parallel to the *yiqtol* forms without *waw*; cf. GKC 111t; JM 118q.

ee. The dash here and in the third line seeks to bring out the use of the personal pronoun *hû'* with the two *yiqtol* verbs, which singles out and puts emphasis on the subject (*He*).

ff. Hebrew *rōznîm* (always in the plural) appears to be a poetic designation for *rulers*. It is used parallel to *kings* also in Judg 5:3; Ps 2:2; Prov 8:15; 31:4 and parallel to *šōpṭê 'ereṣ* ("judges of the earth") in Isa 40:23. Cf. Haak, *Habakkuk*, 45, for Phoenician and Punic parallels.

gg. Hebrew *wayyilkədāh*. The feminine suffix is frequently emended with 1QpHab to a masculine, *wayyilkəduhû* (cf. *BHS*). The MT's feminine suffix (cf. MurXII) may interpret the masculine *mibṣār* ("fortification") as elliptical for the feminine *'îr mibṣār* ("fortified city"); cf. Franz Delitzsch, *Habakkuk*, 16. The singular *mibṣār* is often used in the expression "fortified city/cities" (16×). It is used without *'îr* five times (Isa 17:3; 25:12; Jer 6:27; Amos 5:9; and *mibṣar-ṣōr*, "fortress of Tyre," in 2 Sam 24:7), of which two have been queried (see *HALOT* for the suggestion to read *məbaṣṣēr*, "grape-picker," in Jer 6:27; Amos 5:9).

hh. The use of a *qatal* (perfect) form indicates the switch from the vivid description of the Babylonian progress to reflection on it; cf. Fabry, *Habakuk/Obadja*, 210–11.

ii. Andersen (*Habakkuk*, 160–65) demonstrates that *rûaḥ* ("wind, spirit") sometimes governs masculine verbs (e.g., Exod 10:13b; Hos 4:19, with a feminine pronominal suffix referring back to it). According to his analysis, the gender of *rûaḥ* is 227 times indeterminate,

116 times feminine, and 54 times masculine. It is thus possible that *wind* is the subject for the first two verbs (see NJB; Patterson, *Nahum*, 153), but this is unlikely for the last line.

jj. Hebrew *wə'āšēm* is taken by the Masoretes with the first half of the verse and could be either verbal or adjectival. 1QpHab has *wysm*, which can be interpreted in different ways (see further below) and is favored by some (cf. *BHS*); Andersen (*Habakkuk*, 159) suggests the original text may have contained both. LXX has *kai exilasetai* ("and he will appease / make atonement"). For the reading "and devastates," see the commentary.

kk. Hebrew *zû* is sometimes taken as a demonstrative here (e.g., LXX, "this strength is [= belongs] to my God," rendered in BA 23.4-9 [266-67] "telle est la force de mon Dieu" ["such is the strength of my God"]), but it is better read as introducing a relative clause, for which it is used more often; cf. JM 145c; Meyer, *Grammatik*, 2:12, 15; 3:97. It probably specifies the subject, as in Job 19:19. GKC 138h interprets the relative clause as an accusative, as in Job 15:17.

ll. Hebrew *lē'lōhô*. Uniquely, the pronominal suffix is attached to *'ĕlôah* (singular of *'ĕlōhîm*; cf. 3:3), here spelled defectively, rather than *'ēl*. This is likely for euphonic reasons to produce *zû kōḥô lē'lōhô*.

Composition

This section is traditionally read as a response to the complaint in vv. 2-4, but two features of the text render such a dialogical reading problematic. Both have been noted in commentaries before, but their force has not always been recognized. First, the opening imperatives are plural. This is a particular problem for those who identify Habakkuk as an individual whose complaint in vv. 2-4 focuses on his own suffering. Andersen, for example, comments, "Habakkuk's opening prayer is ignored or, rather, the response is not supplied as an answer that explicitly takes up the issues in that prayer."[25] But this also applies to some extent when Habakkuk is identified as an intercessor, as I have done, because even then one might expect an answer to be addressed to the person praying. Habakkuk has not led a communal lament in vv. 2-4 but put forth a personal appeal, even if that appeal was not focusing on his personal distress.[26]

Second, there is no hint in vv. 5-11 of comfort or assurance or deliverance. Verses 12-17 are traditionally read as complaining that God's answer is not satisfactory. But the point to be made here is that vv. 5-11 do not even

25. Andersen, *Habakkuk*, 139; cf. p. 167, where he concludes that "one may gravely doubt that vv 5-11 are intended to be a response to Habakkuk's prayer in any cogent sense."

26. Cleaver-Bartholomew ("Alternative Approach," 208) identifies problems with considering Habakkuk a "spokesman for the people" or a representative of "a specific group within the overall nation." But he does not address the possibility of prophetic intercession. The "intensely personal tone" of the book need not suggest that Habakkuk's appeal is of a "private character."

pretend to be an answer to the situation outlined in vv. 2–4.[27] The oracle in vv. 5–11 does not claim that *the Chaldeans* are God's instrument to deal with evil. It nowhere suggests that God means to deliver the righteous or punish the wicked through *the Chaldeans*. In fact, the oracle has nothing positive to say about the coming of *the Chaldeans*. It focuses entirely on their fearsome and effective destructiveness.[28] In particular, the reference in v. 7b to the coming forth of the *justice* and *exaltation* of *the Chaldeans* would be odd if the thrust of vv. 5–11 was to designate the Babylonians as instruments of God's justice.

In addition, one must note that vv. 12–17 do not read well as Habakkuk's reply to vv. 5–11. While Habakkuk acknowledges, or at least hopes, that the Chaldeans were appointed to chastise rather than destroy (see the commentary on v. 12), he continues to complain about YHWH's looking on and being silent in the face of evil (v. 13; cf. v. 3). Such a complaint about God's inaction would make little sense on the assumption that it responds to news about a major divine intervention. One would have to postulate a significant chronological gap between vv. 11 and 12, which would undermine the idea of a dialogue.[29] In other words, we must note that vv. 12–17 do not complain about the injustice of God's action but continue to complain that God is passive in the face of unrelenting evil. In this respect, little has changed from vv. 2–4. In sum, the oracle in vv. 5–11 is not a reply to Habakkuk's complaint. Its fulfillment is what the complaint is all about.[30] YHWH had in the past announced that he would *raise up* the Babylonians, but this has led to the situation about which the prophet complains.

Catchwords and phrases that are repeated in 1:2–17 provide cohesion to the chapter.[31] The imperative plural in v. 5, moving away from address to

27. Fabry (*Habakuk/Obadja*, 202) believes that, formally, 1:2–4 and 1:5–11 are a dialogue but accepts that in terms of narrative logic, 1:5–11 cannot be seen as an answer to 1:2–4. He wonders whether both texts derive from the prophet but were originally not related to each other (212).

28. Cf. Marshall D. Johnson, "The Paralysis of Torah in Habakkuk I 4," *VT* 35 (1985): 261; Rex Mason, *Zephaniah, Habakkuk, Joel*, OTG (Sheffield: JSOT Press, 1994), 86–87.

29. Franz Delitzsch (*Habakuk*, 22) suggests that the future announced in vv. 5–11 is present to the mind of the prophet in vv. 12–17, even if not yet experienced reality. I do not think that this explains the continuing complaint about divine inactivity.

30. So Floyd, *Minor Prophets 2*, 96; cf. Donald E. Gowan, *The Triumph of Faith in Habakkuk* (Atlanta: John Knox Press, 1976), 36; Cleaver-Bartholomew, "Alternative Approach," 212. Note also Cathcart, "Law Is Paralysed," 340. A similar proposal had already been made by Abraham Kuenen in 1889; see Jöcken, *Habakuk*, 123. Note also the commentators mentioned below who concluded that 1:5–11 was the earliest part of the book.

31. Cf. Floyd, *Minor Prophets 2*, 95–96. Notable are *ḥāmās* (*violence*) in vv. 2, 3, 9; *mišpāṭ* (*justice*) with *yṣ'* (*come forth*) in vv. 4, 7; the pair *r'h* (*see*) and *nbṭ* (*look on*) in vv. 5, 13; the use of *rāšā'* (*wicked*) and *ṣaddîq* (*righteous*) in vv. 4, 13. To this we can add the reuse of *'āmāl*

God, and the vocative in v. 12, resuming the direct appeal to God, mark out vv. 5–11 as a subunit. These signals are obvious, and there was therefore no need for additional markers. Haak appears to be alone in restricting the divine speech to vv. 5–6, which he identifies as an oracle of salvation, but this results from his imposition of a questionable form-critical scheme on the text.[32] The description of the personified Neo-Babylonian Empire in vv. 7–11, echoed in vv. 15–17, should be considered part of the oracle. The fact that this description is entirely negative does not argue against this conclusion, because already the short description in v. 6 is negative without a hint of what the positive significance of the divine rising up of the Babylonians might be.[33] Already in v. 6, the Babylonians are described as conquerors grabbing territories for themselves rather than liberators of the oppressed or agents of punishment. This observation raises questions of a different sort about the literary integrity of the divine oracle.

At least conceptually, one may consider vv. 5–11 the earliest part of the book,[34] which has been incorporated into a complaint (ch. 1) to which YHWH responds in ch. 2. If we take it this way, we must ask, did these verses ever exist independently of the complaint? In other words, should vv. 5–11 be considered (1) a previously delivered oracle, (2) an excerpt from a previously available oracle,[35] or (3) the prophet's précis of earlier revelation

---

(*iniquity*) in v. 13 (cf. v. 3) and *'sp* (*gather*) in v. 15 (cf. v. 9) and maybe the use of the root *qdm* in both v. 9 (*qādîmâ, forward*) and v. 12 (*qedem*, here temporal: *old*).

32. Haak, *Habakkuk*, 14. Andersen (*Habakkuk*, 166) contemplates this possibility but observes that "assigning vv 7–11 to Habakkuk makes it even harder to find continuity between v 11 and v 12." Andersen's insistence that vv. 7–11 describe the Babylonians in the past tense might have made it attractive to him to restrict the divine speech to vv. 5–6, but he rightly questions Haak's criteria, and the past reference is compatible with the unity of the passage if vv. 7–11 are seen as elaborating on the description of *the sharp and swift nation* in v. 6.

33. Contra Haak, *Habakkuk*, 130, whose own translation and notes on vv. 5–6 (pp. 35–40) offer only two hints that may serve as a basis for his assessment of the passage as pro-Babylonian: *mar* ("bitter") is interpreted in terms of (righteous) anger "provoked by the political actions within Judah," and *nimhār* ("skilled") is interpreted as "able and willing to carry out the effects of its anger" (38). Skill can be exercised for good or evil, and thus all depends here on the question whether the fierceness of the Babylonians is justified. The first half of the verse, at best, does not exclude this possibility, but the second half seems to me to undermine it.

34. Following Friedrich Giesebrecht (1890), several older commentators concluded that vv. 5–11 constitute the oldest part of the book. This proposal was also taken up by Julius Wellhausen, *Skizzen und Vorarbeiten—Fünftes Heft: Die kleinen Propheten übersetzt, mit Noten* (Berlin: Reimer, 1892), 163, and J. Halévy, *Recherches Bibliques: Les Livres de Nahum, de Sophonie, de Jonas, de Habacuc, d'Obadia; Antinomies d'Histoire Religieuse; La Date Du Récit Yahwéiste de la Création* (Paris: Leroux et Geuthner, 1907), 383–86. Cf. Jöcken, *Habakuk*, 127–28, 139–40.

35. Cleaver-Bartholomew, "Alternative Approach," 212–13, following the work of Rich-

written specifically for the purpose of the complaint? If, with some commentators, we detect a note of irony in this passage, the last is arguably the best option. Markl has put forward the case that the earlier revelation used in Habakkuk can be found in Jer 4–5 with its references to a "scorching wind" (4:11) and to "horses swifter than eagles" (4:13).[36] We may think of Jer 5:15–17 in particular:[37]

> "Look, I am bringing against you a nation from afar, O house of Israel," utterance of YHWH. "An enduring nation is he, a nation from of old is he, a nation whose language you do not know, nor can you understand what he says. His quiver is like an open grave; all of them are heroes. And he will devour your harvest and your food; they will devour your sons and your daughters; he will devour your flocks and your herds; he will devour your vines and your fig trees. He will demolish—with the sword—your fortified cities in which you trust."

The personification of the Babylonian nation, the notion of distance traveled (cf. Jer 4:16), and the purpose expressed as "devouring" are all reminiscent of Habakkuk, but here the "destroyer of nations" (Jer 4:7) is more specifically said to be brought against the people of God, something perhaps assumed but not stated in Habakkuk. Markl points to the change from the less specific "in those days" in Jer 5:18 (cf. 4:9, 11) to *in your days* (Hab 1:5) as one of the indications that Habakkuk is dependent on Jeremiah rather than vice versa.[38]

There is no need to come to a definite conclusion as to whether Hab 1:5–11 is directly dependent on Jeremiah. It is sufficient to observe that prophecies such as those by Jeremiah may well form the background for this section and that it is therefore not necessary to assume that the passage in the wording found here ever existed independently of the complaint. This makes it easier to account for the particular features of the passage—not only the absence of accusation and vocabulary of punishment, but also the description of the Chaldean nation as bringing its own justice (v. 7) and serving its

---

ard D. Weis on *maśśā'* (*pronouncement*) as prophetic exposition of previous revelation more closely than I do (see the commentary on Nah 1:1), argues that 1:5–11 reports a previously delivered oracle, but he acknowledges that it is probably incomplete.

36. Markl, "Hab 3," 105–6. Markl notes shared vocabulary between Hab 1 and Jer 4–5 (cf. "violence and destruction" in 6:7). He also observes that 46 of 80 occurrences of *kaśdîm* (*Chaldeans*) in the Hebrew Bible are in Jeremiah.

37. Also noteworthy are the association of evil and bitterness in Jer 4:18 (cf. 2:19); the questions "How long must I see?" in 4:21 and "YHWH, your eyes—are they not toward steadfast faith?" in 5:3 (cf. *steadfast faith* in Hab 2:4); the "I looked" sequence in 4:23–26; and the breakdown of *mišpāṭ* (*justice*) in 5:1.

38. Franz Delitzsch (*Habakuk*, xi) argued that Jeremiah was dependent on Habakkuk.

own god (v. 11).[39] The account of previous revelation is phrased in such a way as to highlight the problematic side, which is spelled out further in the following section.

Commentary

5 The motif of seeing (*look*) is important in all three sections of the chapter (cf. vv. 3, 13) and recurs beyond (cf. 2:1; 3:6, 7, 10). It may well have its conceptual origin here, if, as argued above, the oracle in 1:5–11 is a citation within the prophetic complaint. The oracle asks for a close inspection of *the nations*. That inspection will bring with it utter amazement and shock. God's call to watch and be amazed finds a reaction in the prophet's complaint that, in effect, challenges YHWH: "No, *you* look, and take note of all the wrongdoing this has caused!" This, in turn, is answered in a new prophetic vision within the prayer in ch. 3, in which Habakkuk, in effect, acknowledges that he has been the blind one.

One will not be able to overlook the *deed* about to be done, a *deed* so incredible that people will need to see it for themselves to believe it. But intriguingly, the agent of this deed is left unspecified at first and creates suspense concerning the origin of the events to come. Can it really be that YHWH is behind all this? Indeed, he is, as the next verse claims.

EXCURSUS: "LOOK, YOU SCOFFERS" OR "LOOK AT THE NATIONS"?

The traditional Hebrew text *rə'û baggôyīm* (*look at the nations*) is well supported by some of the versions and seems to be attested also in MurXII. The mainstream Greek (LXX, but not Aquila, Symmachus, and Theodotion) and Syr. tradition, however, do not reflect the consonants *bgwym*. Instead, they presume a different Hebrew text, to which 1QpHab may also bear witness—most likely *bwgdym* (*bôgdîm*, "treacherous ones"), which is found in the commentary in 1QpHab.[40] The passage containing the biblical text

---

39. The problem is not the negative description as such, to which we may add the notions of taking what does not belong to him (v. 6) and coming for violence (v. 9), but the lack of any indication that, somehow through this, YHWH's justice is exercised and that *the Chaldeans* are working for YHWH.

40. The text is also broken in the commentary part with *bwgdym* being the first visible letters. The letters are preceded by something which suggests to me the presence of the definite article (*hbwgdym*). The use of the definite article in the commentary in a different syntactical context does not allow us to deduce its presence in the biblical text. Neither does the presence of the article in the Greek text demand its presence in the Hebrew source, as

is unfortunately missing. Gelston rightly points out that we cannot simply reconstruct the missing text citation from the commentary part,[41] and it is entirely possible that the text on which 1QpHab commented read *bgwym* (*at the nations*).[42] The semantic shift from Hebrew *bôgēd* ("treacherous") to Greek *kataphronētēs* ("despiser, scoffer") is noteworthy, but *kataphronētēs* is also used in Hab 2:5 for Hebrew *bôgēd*, and the plural participle of the related verb *kataphroneō* is used for *bôgdîm* in 1:13.[43] This makes it plausible that early on, there were some manuscripts that read *bgwym* and others that read *bwgdym*.[44] The difference in the Hebrew consonantal text could have arisen by mistake in either direction.[45] In the case of *bwgdym*, the *beth* is not the inseparable preposition but part of the root, and the word could be either the direct object ("see the treacherous ones") or the vocative ("you treacherous").[46] LXX takes it as the latter and adds another imperative, *kai aphanisthēte* ("and be removed"; cf. Acts 13:41).[47]

Andersen (*Habakkuk*, 140) seems to assume. (Note that in Hebrew as in Greek, the article can be used to mark a vocative; cf. n. 46.)

41. *BHQ*, 115*. The commentary exhibits knowledge of different readings and some interpretative liberty in other places as well. Thus, the text for the next verse has *hkśd'ym* ("the Chaldeans"), but the commentary reads *hkty'ym* ("the Kittim"; for the spelling with *aleph* in both cases, see Brownlee, *Midrash*, 60). Commenting on v. 3, the pesher interprets *'ml* (*trouble*) with *m'l* ("treachery"); cf. Andersen, *Habakkuk*, 141.

42. So, e.g., Shemaryahu Talmon, "Aspects of the Textual Transmission of the Bible in the Light of Qumran Manuscripts," *Textus* 4 (1964): 131–32; contra Brownlee, *Midrash*, 54.

43. Cf. Prov 13:15; Hos 6:7; Zeph 3:4. The *qal* participle of *bgd* is rendered in different ways in the LXX. The participle of *atheteō* ("to reject") is used in Isa 21:2; 24:16; 33:1; Jer 9:1; 12:1. The idea of faithlessness is stressed in Jer 3:8, 11 (*asynthetos,* adj.) and Ps 119:158 (participle of *asyntheteō*), but lawlessness is to the fore in Ps 25:3 (LXX 24:3, *anomeō*; cf. Ps 59:5 [LXX 58:6]); Prov 2:22; 11:6; 13:2; 22:12; 23:28 (*paranomos,* adj.); 21:18 (*anomos,* adj.). Prov 11:3 uses *asebōn* ("impious, godless").

44. The Hebrew root *bwz* (the verb "to despise" and the noun "contempt") would seem to be a more suitable basis for *kataphronētēs,* but the only occurrence of *kataphronētēs* unrelated to Habakkuk renders *bōgdôt* ("faithlessness") in Zeph 3:4, and even the verb *kataphroneō* relates to *bwz* only thrice (Prov 13:13; 18:3; 23:22).

45. It is also possible that originally both were present (cf. Andersen, *Habakkuk*, 141), challenging "the scoffers" to look "at the nations" ("at the treacherous nations" would require the definite article, *bgwym hbwgdym*). But the combination could also be parsed in terms of seeing *bwgdym* ("scoffers") *bgwym* ("among the nations"; cf. the references in my note on the translation), which is ill-suited to the context. Such ambiguity may be considered a problem for this third possibility.

46. The definite article to mark the vocative could have disambiguated the text, but it is often omitted, especially in poetry and where the addressee is not physically present (cf. JM 137g).

47. I suspect that Acts 13:41 follows the lead given in LXX in reading "you scoffers," but

A previous generation of scholars gravitated to *bwgdym* as the original reading, but among recent commentators, Bruce seems the only one to prefer *bwgdym* over MT's *bgwym*.[48] The reference to *the nations* is suitable given the introduction of the *nation* that overruns other nations, while an address to "the treacherous ones" creates several difficulties in context. First, it sidelines Habakkuk, as he is hardly to be included among the treacherous, and thus makes a coherent reading of the chapter more difficult. Given the anguish of the opening complaint, it would be entirely surprising for the righteous not to be addressed at all. Second, while it is surprising on any account that the speech lacks any condemnation and makes no reference to punishment (see the discussion under composition), this would be even more peculiar on the view that the unfaithful are directly addressed. Third, it stands to reason that the double call to *look at* and *observe* is better motivated by an intervening *bgwym*, providing the object of the inspection.[49]

While an accident in the transmission of the text could have led to a change from *bgwym* to *bwgdym* or vice versa, the change from *bgwym* to *bwgdym* can be explained as an interpretative move in the light of 1:13 and 2:5. Such a move seems likely for 1QpHab, and the addition of *kai aphanisthēte* ("and be removed") in LXX and Acts 13:41 suggests the same for this tradition. The reading "you scoffers" is therefore considered further in the reflection section rather than in the commentary section, which interprets the presumed earlier reading.

6 The initial *for* may introduce a reason for the astonishment, but it could also be attached to the initial challenge to *look* around, in which case it would be parallel to the *for* in the second half of v. 5. The use of *look* arguably points in this direction. YHWH offers a vision to behold, and it is not in a dream but in the historical arena of international affairs. *I am raising up the Chaldeans* relates to the rise of the Babylonians but is not a reference to the establish-

---

the addition *kai aphanisthēte* ("and be removed") in turn may have been imported into our LXX MSS from Acts 13:41.

48. Bruce, "Habakkuk," 847. Haak's (*Habakkuk*, 35) remark about commentators being "nearly equally divided over the reading at this point" is hardly true in our generation, which shows a preference for reading *bgwym* in contrast to the former preference for *bwgdym*. William Hayes Ward ("Habakkuk," in *A Critical and Exegetical Commentary on Micah, Zephaniah, Nahum, Habakkuk, Obadiah, and Joel*, ed. J. M. Powis Smith, William Hayes Ward, and Julius A. Bewer, ICC [Edinburgh: T&T Clark, 1911], 10) considered himself in agreement with "critics generally" in correcting MT; cf., in 1938, Junker, *Zwölf*, 42. In 1930, Sellin (*Zwölfprophetenbuch*, 389) argued for MT against "many interpreters" who follow LXX and Syr.

49. This last argument is from Sellin, *Zwölfprophetenbuch*, 389.

ment of the Neo-Babylonian Empire. Delitzsch rightly argues that the description of the Chaldeans presumes that they are already a powerful force. The nation is already *going across the length and breadth of the earth*.[50] While this does not require that the conquest has been completed, the characteristics of the Babylonians are already in evidence. Delitzsch concludes that the reference is specifically to the *raising up* of the Babylonians as adversaries of Judah.[51] Indeed, the two closest parallels, Amos 6:14 and Jer 5:15, add *'ălêkem* ("against you").[52] Thus, the astonishing thing to which v. 5 refers is that an empire such as that of the rapacious Chaldeans described in vv. 6–11 should be raised up against Judah.[53] The use of the designation *Chaldeans* may have been prompted by the fact that the currently reigning dynasty in Babylon was Chaldean.[54]

The absence of "against you" is, however, noteworthy.[55] The *sharp and swift nation* is not in fact explicitly said to be sent against Judah. While this is arguably implied, the focus remains on *the Chaldeans*. Their aim is *to take possession of dwellings* that do not belong to them. The root *yrš* (*take possession*) is used regularly for nations dispossessing other nations (e.g., Deut 2:12) and does not imply a "right of inheritance."[56] The objective is described in

---

50. Note the use of the participle (with definite article) rather than a consecutive form, which would indicate future conquest ("and it will go across . . ."). The translation *earth* (rather than "land") is confirmed by the reference to *kings* and *rulers* in v. 10.

51. Franz Delitzsch, *Habakuk*, 11. He compares *hinnî mē'îr* ("look, I am going to stir up") in Isa 13:17; Jer 50:9; 51:1 (cf. Ezek 23:22) and *hinnî mēbî'* ("look, I am going to bring") in Jer 5:15, and some of the references given below. But these are all followed by the preposition *'āl* ("against").

52. Cf. 2 Sam 12:11 ("raise up evil" against David) and narrative accounts of YHWH's raising up of adversaries (1 Kgs 11:14; 14:14) or deliverers (Judg 2:16, 18; 3:9, 15); cf. YHWH's raising up of watchmen in Jer 6:17. The raising up of rulers (positively in Jer 23:4–5; 30:9; Ezek 34:23; negatively in Zech 11:16) need not be for specific punishment or deliverance, although it is still for the people's benefit or disadvantage. The same could be said of the raising up of prophets (Deut 18:15; Jer 29:15; Amos 2:11, "prophets" and "Nazirites") and maybe of (faithful) priests (1 Sam 2:35).

53. There is therefore no need to be troubled by alleged ignorance of the character of the Babylonians in one verse (v. 5) and knowledge of their ferocity in the next.

54. So Fabry, *Habakuk/Obadja*, 206, with reference to Nabopolassar (626–605 BC). Nabopolassar was succeeded by his son Nebuchadnezzar II, who was responsible for the fall of Jerusalem. See the outline of the late Neo-Assyrian and early Neo-Babylonian period in the general introduction (pp. 18–20).

55. Some Greek MSS add *eph' hymas* ("against you"); see the Göttingen edition of the LXX.

56. Aron Pinker ("Better Bitter River," *ZAW* 114 [2002]: 112–15) claims that the root is "used in the Bible mostly for acts of possession that entail the right of inheritance" (115), but the evidence does not suggest to me that *yrš* intrinsically suggests a "right of inheritance"

striking language that does not seem to correspond to historical realities. As Pinker observes,

> The purposes of military campaigns were either punitive or economic not occupational. The goal was either to punish a recalcitrant vassal state or to conquer, plunder, exact a ransom, and secure fealty and annual payments, not occupy the dwellings of others.[57]

Pinker is right to draw attention to the fact that imperial forces by and large did not *take possession of dwellings*—not in the sense of settling in them anyway[58]—even if this is not always true for smaller tribes, peoples, and nations, some of which might get incorporated into an empire. Pinker in particular objects to the use of *dwellings* rather than "cities" or "nations." But if taking possession is understood as inhabiting, "cities" would just as much imply settlement, and the same would be true for "nations" as the object of *yrš* (cf. Exod 34:24; Deut 4:38; 7:17; 9:1; etc.). The surprising feature is therefore not the object *miškānôt* (*dwellings*)—which suggests inhabited regions in the broadest sense and may have been chosen as befitting *merḥābê-'ereṣ* ("the wide places of the earth," *the length and breadth of the earth*)[59]—but the use of the verb *yrš* (*take possession*).

The verb *yrš* is frequently used for Israel's conquest of the promised land.[60]

---

any more than the English *take possession*. The word is used for conquest also in the Mesha Stele (line 7); cf. Haak, *Habakkuk*, 40.

57. Pinker, "Better Bitter River," 114. He concludes that the text must refer to something other than what is generally thought, and with the emendation of *hmr whnmhr* (*the sharp* ["bitter"] *and swift*) to *mhnr hmr*, he reads, "Because, here I raise the Chaldeans, a nation from the Bitter River, dispersed in the world, to inherit dwellings not theirs" (115).

58. According to Jöcken (*Habakuk*, 43–44), Wilhelm Caspari ("Die Chaldäer bei Habakuk," *Neue Kirchliche Zeitschrift* 18 [1907]: 156–75) argued on the basis of archaeological evidence that, far from being incongruous, the phrase shows that Habakkuk had more intimate knowledge of the Chaldeans than his Judean contemporaries. I have no access to Caspari's essay, but it seems doubtful that excavations at Babylon and Borsippa, on which he apparently relies, are relevant here.

59. The term can refer to the dwellings of semi-nomadic people, like Israel in the wilderness (Num 24:5; Ps 78:28) or shepherds (Song 1:8), or to the barren land inhabited by the wild donkey (Job 39:6). Well over half of the occurrences of the singular *miškān* refer to YHWH's abode, the central sanctuary, a meaning also found with the plural (Pss 43:3; 46:4[5]; 84:2; 132:5, 7), but I am not convinced that we may therefore assume cultic connotations; note, e.g., Job 18:21; 21:28 for the abode of the wicked. Closer parallels to our passage are in Jer 9:18; 30:18; 51:30; Ezek 25:4.

60. Most prominently in Deuteronomy but also in, e.g., Lev 20:24; Num 13:30; 21:24; cf. Gen 15:7; 28:4 and passages like Exod 34:24; Num 14:12 (YHWH dispossessing in favor of Israel). In the Book of the Twelve, note Amos 2:10; 9:12 and the use of the root in Obad (vv.

In this and other contexts, it is evident that the nations (*gôyīm*) that are the object of *yrš* are dispossessed and driven out rather than ruled.[61] Thus, a change of ownership of a land or city entails a change of inhabitants when the conflict is between smaller tribes and peoples. It is not clear, however, that *yrš* intrinsically requires this. In other places, the verb concerns questions of authority, inheritance, and ownership. In my view, therefore, the use of *yrš* here need not imply the (foreign) occupation of dwellings, and there is no other verb to imply that the Chaldeans are living in the places of which they *take possession*. If the verb is not entirely unsuitable to the idea of conquest of territories with subjugation of rulers and their peoples, it is nevertheless important for understanding the rhetoric of the verse to note that there would have been alternative ways of referring to imperial conquest. Different verbs would have put the emphasis elsewhere. The Babylonians are not said to "subdue,"[62] "destroy,"[63] or "trample on" nations, verbs that would stress the violence involved, but to *take possession* of them. The idea being highlighted is of an empire appropriating territory, *dwellings not his own*. Maybe this verb more than the others also hints at questions of legality, thus echoing vv. 2–4. In any case, the phrase *not his own* points to the injustice and becomes significant for God's response in ch. 2, especially for the first woe oracle (2:6b–8; cf. v. 5).

7 *He* has the personified empire in view here and throughout the book. Its use in English is awkward here but seems necessary for the sake of consistently rendering the personification. In Hebrew, masculine adjectives, verb forms, and pronouns are used with *gôy* (*nation*). In English, "it" or maybe "she" is more appropriate than "he" for an empire or nation, but from v. 10 onward, "it" would seem odd, and "she" might create problems in ch. 2.[64]

17, 19, 20). Other occurrences of *yrš* in the Minor Prophets are for YHWH's dispossession of Moresh (Mic 1:15) and Tyre (Zech 9:4).

61. Apart from the references already given, cf. Ps 44:2(3); Ezek 35:10. The situation is no different when the object is *'am* ("people"; e.g., Deut 2:21). But note that Isa 54:3 and maybe Amos 9:12 allow for a more "imperial" sense without requiring it, and passages like 1 Kgs 9:20–21 know of dispossessed people who remained in the land.

62. Cf. *kbš piel* (2 Sam 8:11; cf. 2 Chr 28:10; elsewhere for the enslaving of individuals, Neh 5:5; Jer 34:11, 16, but in the *niphal*, regularly with "land" as the subject); *rdd* (Ps 144:2; Isa 41:2; 45:1); *dbr hiphil* (Pss 18:47[48]; 47:3[4]; in the *piel*, the meaning is closer to "destroy," see 2 Chr 22:10). Note that *'bd hiphil* ("make serve," Exod 1:13; 6:5; cf. Jer 17:4) is never used for conquest.

63. Note *hrg* (*kill*) in v. 17. Deut 9:3 uses *'bd hiphil* ("wipe out") and *šmd* ("exterminate").

64. To switch to masculine forms in ch. 2 would weaken the link between the chapters, and to persevere with feminine forms might streamline the woe oracles too much, suggesting an original and exclusive application to the empire. It would also introduce an

The use of the plural "they" (most English translations, except for NAB)[65] obscures the consistency with which the use of singular forms invites us to think of the empire as a single entity, sometimes embodied in the army or the person of the king. This must be remembered in relation to 2:4–5, where the contrast encapsulated in the saying is thus between communities as well as individuals.[66]

The empire can be pictured in the form of the king, the will of the empire, or in the form of the army, the force of the empire. But while the king, as distinct from the city and empire, is of some importance in Nahum, this is not true for Habakkuk. There is also no attempt in Habakkuk to distinguish between the empire and its army. We may think of the king as the heart and mind of the empire and the army as its face and arm. Either may be more in view in one place or the other, but they are never distinct from the empire as such. The description of this nation as *dread-inspiring and fearsome* echoes the call to be astounded in v. 5. The word translated *dread-inspiring* (*'āyōm*) is used for an "awesome" army in Song 6:4, 10, illustrating the terrific beauty of the woman.[67] The word translated *fearsome* (*nôrā'*) also carries the nuance of "awesome" or "awe-inspiring" in some contexts (e.g., Exod 34:10), although the connotation of fear is often present (e.g., Gen 28:17), and sometimes the referent seems to be plain terrifying (e.g., Deut 1:19).[68] The rising up of *the Chaldeans* (against Judah) is not just amazing but shocking given their potential to induce dread and horror. "They are cruel and have no mercy," as Jer 6:23 puts it.

The precise understanding of the second half of the verse is debated. Andersen reads it in terms of the nation making its own decisions and setting out on military expeditions in its self-exaltation.[69] It is indeed possible to divide this long line into two phrases and translate "from him [is] his justice/

---

unintended contrast of sexes in 2:4, unless the righteous is also feminine, which obscures the use of the verse in the New Testament and in 2:15.

65. This seems more natural because *the Chaldeans* are mentioned first. NJB switches to the singular in vv. 11–12 but is back to the plural from v. 15 onward, the place at which a number of translations switch to the singular (NIV, NRSV, ESV, JPS Tanakh; cf. the NET, which uses the singular also in v. 11b but not in v. 12).

66. Most English translations use the singular in 2:4–5. NRSV is an exception. Its use of the plural is particularly unfortunate in the light of its use of a singular in 1:15–17.

67. These are the only other occurrences of *'āyōm* in the Bible, but cf. the noun *'êmâ* ("terror") and the Aramaic *dəḥîlâ wə'êmtānî* ("frightening and terrifying") in Dan 7:7 of the fourth kingdom.

68. YHWH, his name, and his deeds are often described as "awesome" or "fearsome" (e.g., Zeph 2:11, where a verbal rendering "is feared" is also possible; cf. Mal 1:14). Elsewhere in the Book of the Twelve, the Day of YHWH is "[very] awesome" (Joel 2:11; 2:31 [3:4]; Mal 4:5 [3:23]).

69. Andersen, *Habakkuk*, 152–53. Cf. Symmachus; see the translation notes.

decision" and "his exaltation comes forth" or "in exaltation he comes forth." But the double use of *comes forth* with *justice* in v. 4 rightly inclines most readers to read *his justice* as the subject of *comes forth*. This invites us to understand *his justice and exaltation* as a compound subject, which is how most interpreters take it. The line could then be understood to make the point that the Babylonians are a "law and authority" to themselves.[70] But the parallel with v. 4 suggests an alternative, with *his justice* being more the justice he imposes on others than the justice assumed (*from him*) for himself. In this case, the phrase declares that the currently prevailing justice and authority (*exaltation*, or "majesty") are *his justice* and *his exaltation*. The initial *from him* need not indicate the origin of *his justice and exaltation* but may stress the pronoun, as if to say "*it is from him*, the dread-inspiring and fearsome nation, *that* justice and exaltation comes forth—*his justice and* his *exaltation comes forth*."[71] There is no justice and dignity but his. Any local judicial system or dignity in opposition to this nation is suspended (cf. the complaint about Torah being numbed, v. 4).

The word *exaltation* (*śə'ēt*) is not very common.[72] It refers to the eminence or rank of Reuben in Gen 49:3, to the terrifying majesty of God in Job 13:11; 31:23, and to the high position of someone, perhaps the king, in Ps 62:4(5). It is used in a verbal sense for the raising up of Leviathan in Job 41:25(17) and refers seven times to a "swelling" in Lev 13–14.[73] The *exaltation* of the Babylonian nation is its prominence and dominance over others,[74] "swelling" like a mountain that arises on the earth's skin and towers over other nations that are mere lowlands by comparison. The choice of this particular noun may hint at the manifestation of this exaltation in decisions about who rises to (subordinate!) prominence. In this case, the wicked of v. 4 could be the Judean leadership installed by the Babylonians, but this is speculative.

8 The swiftness of the Babylonian army, to which v. 6 alluded, now comes into focus. The statement about *steeds* being *faster than leopards* is obviously hyperbolic but may reflect actual advances in military technique. The Assyrian dominance had been gained by their chariotry, but a slow move away from chariotry was already under way in the late Neo-Assyrian period. It is

---

70. Cf. Patterson, *Habakkuk*, 150. This is also the understanding widely reflected in translations, except for NIV's "they are a law to themselves and promote their own honor."

71. Cf. Franz Delitzsch, *Habakuk*, 12.

72. Tg. interprets *śə'ēt* as a *decree* (cf. *maśśā'*, pronouncement, in v. 1), unless the source text was different, which seems less likely; see ArBib 14, 146. A different vocalization would produce "his devastation" (cf. Lam 3:47), but it is noteworthy than none of the versions adopted this.

73. This last use forms an interesting subtext; cf. the use of *'ōpel* for a tumor in Deut 28:27; 1 Sam 5:6, 9, 12; 6:4–5, to which *'uppəlâ* (*presumptuous*) in 2:4 is related.

74. Cf. the use of the *hithpael* of *nś'*, e.g., in 1 Chr 29:11; Ezek 29:15.

not clear at what point proper cavalry units emerged.[75] The Assyrian confidence about Judah's inability to muster competent riders for 2,000 horses (2 Kgs 18:23 // Isa 36:8) suggests their superiority in this area, but whether such horsemen constituted an extensive cavalry unit is less certain. The lack of stirrups, metal bridles, and, at least in earlier days, proper saddles, made it difficult to ride and fight at the same time. In addition, horses are sensitive, vulnerable animals, and cavalry thus does not always provide an advantage over infantry.[76] Most riders probably still dismounted for the actual fighting for some time after effective and sustained horseback riding had been developed.[77]

Iranian nomadic pastoralists seem to have been the first to be truly comfortable on horseback.[78] Their skill was renowned, and the best known of these were the Scythian tribes.[79] The Scythians may have contributed to the fall of Nineveh as allies of the Babylonians,[80] and it is possible that mercenary troops on horseback are primarily in view here (see further below). But Habakkuk is interested in the empire as such, not the component parts of its army, and there is no need to question the designation *Chaldeans* in v. 6.[81] The simple remark made twice about the Babylonians in Jeremiah, "they ride

75. Assyrian soldiers on horseback are known from the ninth century onward. Some use the term cavalry for this time; e.g., Wolfram von Soden, *The Ancient Orient: An Introduction to the Study of the Ancient Near East* (Grand Rapids: Eerdmans, 1994), 84; Azar Gat, *War in Human Civilization* (Oxford: Oxford University Press, 2006), 327. Perlitt (*Nahum*, 55) believes that proper cavalry was deployed only from the Persian period onward. This likely understands cavalry as a fighting unit of significant size, while others would use the term for horsemen providing reconnaissance and intelligence. Alan Millard ("On Some Alleged Anachronisms in the Books of Samuel," *TynBul* 71 [2020]: 65–73) provides evidence for horsemen even before the ninth century.

76. This is pointed out by Gat, *War*, 328.

77. In addition, *pārāš* can refer to charioteers (e.g., probably Exod 14:9, 23; 15:19) as well as riders on horseback. See Daniel I. Block, *The Book of Ezekiel: Chapters 1–24*, NICOT (Grand Rapids: Eerdmans, 1997), 739, for translating *pārāšîm rōkbê sûsîm* in Ezek 23:6, 12 as (Assyrian) "charioteers, men driving horses." Note the different description of the Babylonian army in Ezek 26:7: *basûs ûbərekeb ûbəpārāšîm* (lit. "with horse and with chariot and with horsemen").

78. For fuller background, see P. R. S. Moore, "Pictorial Evidence for the History of Horse-Riding in Iraq before the Kassite Period," *Iraq* 32 (1970): 36–50; Mary Aiken Littauer and Joost H. Crouwel, *Wheeled Vehicles and Ridden Animals in the Ancient Near East* (Leiden: Brill, 1979).

79. See Karen S. Rubinson, "Scythians," *ABD* 5:1056–57.

80. Kuhrt, *Ancient Near East*, 546, notes that the often-asserted involvement of the Scythians in the fall of Nineveh is not certain.

81. Contra Seybold, *Nahum*, 58–59.

on horses" (6:23; 50:42), may indicate significant progress in this area in the seventh and sixth centuries BC.[82]

The verb that describes the horses as *quicker than wolves at dusk* (*ḥdd qal*) is elsewhere used in a different stem in connection with the sharpening of swords.[83] The notions of "sharp" and "quick" were apparently associated in Semitic languages as well as in English,[84] but whether this extended to "mentally agile" (i.e., "quick-witted") is uncertain.[85] Delitzsch observes that wolves are called "sharp" (*ḥad*) in Arabic with reference to their vehemence and atrocity, not their keen sensibilities.[86] Many English translations opt for fierceness as the point of comparison.[87] But it is more likely that the main point of the comparison is speed, as is the case with the other animal metaphors here.[88] This understanding is also reflected in the ancient Greek and Latin translations.[89] Maybe we should even discern a progression to greater suddenness in the movement from leopards to wolves to vultures. The ferocity of wolves is, of course, an important subtext for the comparison. Wolves are primarily active at night. They generally commence hunting *at dusk* and therefore could be imagined as being at their most hungry and eager for prey at evening time.[90] Note that v. 9 spells out the attackers' eagerness for violence. Perhaps the excellent cooperation of wolves in packs hints

82. Cf. Ezek 23:6, 12, 23 with reference to the Assyrians. Isaiah was already impressed by the speed of the Assyrians (5:26–28).

83. See the translation note and cf. the adjectives *ḥad* ("sharp"), used in Ps 57:5; Prov 5:4; Isa 49:2; Ezek 5:1, always in connection with *ḥereb* ("sword"), and *ḥaddûd* ("sharp, pointed") for potsherds in Job 41:30(22).

84. Cf. especially the reference to a swift horse in (Aramaic) Ahiqar, line 38. See Marcus Jastrow, *A Dictionary of the Targumim, the Talmud Babli and Yerushalmi, and the Midrashic Literature* (London: Luzak; New York: Putnam, 1903), 425, for later Aramaic references.

85. The use of the root to indicate sharpness of mind is found in later Aramaic; cf. Jastrow, *Dictionary*, 425. Perlitt (*Nahum*, 55) apparently interprets "sharp" along these lines, as he insists that the characterization does not fit horses, arguing for a different colon division on this basis.

86. Franz Delitzsch, *Habakuk*, 12–13. Note that NAB and NASB interpret "sharp" here as "keen." The NET offers "alert." Cf. Patterson, *Nahum*, 151.

87. So already KJV and Geneva Bible and still NIV, NJB and ESV; cf. NRSV, "menacing."

88. So also, e.g., Haak, *Habakkuk*, 42; Roberts, *Nahum*, 96–97.

89. It has been adopted by only very few English translations that are not based on LXX or Vulg., namely the Darby Bible (1884/1890), JPS Tanakh (1985), and God's Word to the Nations (1995).

90. The image is presumably based on the observation that wolves are nocturnal and on the human experience of hunger. In fact, the bodies of wolves are designed for feast or famine. Wolves can go without a meal for several days if need be before gorging on up to 10 kg of meat when they make a kill. See, e.g., L. David Mech, Douglas W. Smith, and Daniel R. MacNulty, *Wolves on the Hunt: The Behavior of Wolves Hunting Wild Prey* (Chicago: University of Chicago Press, 2015), 9.

at the idea of a proper cavalry—especially if quick, well-organized troops on horseback were indeed a recent development in ancient Near Eastern military technology.

The text in the middle of the verse (*cavalry is restless. And his cavalry comes from afar*) is uncertain, as indicated in the translation notes above. Fortunately, the uncertainties do not affect the overall sense.[91] Horses were in high demand in the ancient world, first for chariots then for cavalry. They were sometimes imported from afar. Tyre received horses from Beth-togarmah in the remote north (Ezek 27:14; cf. Ezek 38:6); the Assyrians traded them from and via the Zagros foothills to their east.[92] The reference to the nation's *cavalry* coming *from afar* perhaps alludes to the use of Iranian horses and horsemen (see above on the Scythians). But it is also possible that the reference to distance serves to underline their speed again: *his cavalry comes from afar*, and yet in no time at all they are on top of their prey. The masoretic accentuation suggests that we pause on the phrase *they fly* for a moment, maybe to imagine the movement of a vulture, at first circling then swiftly *swooping to devour*; cf. "his horses are swifter (*qallû*) than vultures" (Jer 4:13).

9 *All of them*, the cavalry as a unit but perhaps now the whole army, *come to do violence*. The speed of the leopard, wolf, and vulture serves a specific purpose, and so does the speed of the Babylonian army. The difficult phrase *the mass of their faces is [directed] forward* (see the translation note) probably further underlines the purposefulness of this war machine. An ancient tradition interprets *forward* (*qādîmâ*, elsewhere "eastward") as a reference to the east wind.[93] This is suggestive, given the destructive, crop-damaging nature of the hot wind blowing from the east (cf., e.g., Isa 27:8; Ezek 17:10; 19:12). The reference to *a wind* in v. 11 and a possible interplay with ch. 3 reinforce this.[94] The use of *qādîmâ* recommends reading *forward* as the surface meaning of the text, but an allusion to the desert wind from the east (*qādîm*) is probably intended. Like the east wind, the destructive advance of the Babylonian army cannot be stopped.

As the east wind gathers up *sand* in its wake, so does the Babylonian nation. In fact, it *gathers captives like sand*—effortlessly.

---

91. See, e.g., Ralph L. Smith (*Micah–Malachi*, 100) who translates closer to 1QpHab: "His horses paw the ground, they spring forward, they come from afar."

92. Kuhrt, *Ancient Near East*, 480. Other regions were also required to supply horses. Kuhrt counts 2,720 horses for Tukulti-ninurta II's campaign in 885 "around the southern and western frontiers of Assyrian-controlled territory" (482–83).

93. Hebrew *rûaḥ qādîm* (e.g., Jer 18:17; Jonah 4:8), or just as often *qādîm* (which means "east" only in Ezekiel), elsewhere refers to the east wind (e.g., Gen 41:6, 23). Cf. 1QpHab *qdym* (*qādîm*) and Tg., Vulg. ("burning wind"), Syr., Symmachus.

94. Hab 3 alludes to the exodus and God's advance against "the sea" (i.e., from east to west), with which we may compare the references to the east wind in Exod 10:13 and 14:21.

10 Next to this empire and its king, other kings and rulers *are an object of derision. He* opens the bicolon and *to him* concludes it, as if to say that the first and last word belong to this irresistible force that finds it difficult to take others seriously. *He—laughs at every fortified city.* No fortifications are safe against this nation. They are all a bit of a joke to this army. The prevalence of *s* sounds in this verse may imitate contemptuous hissing, further driving home the derision. The earth piled up for ramps is described as mere dirt or *dust* to emphasize how little effort it requires to move. Before one looks, the invader has already captured the city.[95]

11 The sense of this verse hangs on two short words that again employ an *s* sound, *'āz* (*then*) and *zû* (rendered with the following pronominal suffix, *he whose*).[96] It works at more than one level.[97] It compares the personified nation to *a wind* that *sweeps along* (cf. Isa 21:1; Job 4:15) *and passes through* (cf. Gen 8:1; Job 37:21; Ps 103:16) with devastating effect. This "devastation" is, indeed, an alternative meaning for *and transgresses* if one allows that *'šm* ("be guilty" or "pay for one's guilt" elsewhere) is here a dialectical variant of *šmm* ("to devastate"; cf. *yšm*, "be deserted").[98] Thus, on a first reading, the verse follows up v. 10 by describing the Babylonian army as a destructive force that has effortlessly passed through countries like *a wind.* Appropriately, the second verb in the verse (*passes through*) is associated elsewhere with military invasions (Isa 51:23; Dan 11:10, 40; cf. Judg 12:3; 1 Sam 14:1, 6, 8). Indeed, Isa 8:8 employs both *ḥālap* (*sweeps along*) and *'ābar* (*passes through*) for the Assyrian invasion of Judah.

But a nation that shows as little concern for boundaries as a wind (cf. *dwellings not his own*, v. 6) *transgresses* and becomes guilty. This is the more regular meaning of the third verb, which in this case could also be under-

---

95. I wonder whether this nuance of "watch them doing it—see it done" is the significance of the change of forms, as reflected in MT, in 1:9 (*yiqtol* and noun-clause to *wayyiqtol*), 10a (*yiqtol* to noun-clause) and 10b (*yiqtol* to *wayyiqtol*), with *qatal* and *wayyiqtol* forms in v. 11.

96. Arguably *wayya'ābōr* (*and passes through*) echoes *wayyiṣbōr* (*He piles up*). Cf. the remark in *CHP*, 227 n. 19 about interline linkage through alliteration in vv. 10–11.

97. Another reading, which, due to the lack of a suffix on *rûaḥ* (*wind* or "spirit" or "mind"), I consider less plausible, is to see a reference to a change of mind on the part of the Babylonian nation with the first verb; cf. LXX, Vulg., KJV. Bruce ("Habakkuk," 850) suggests that the text refers "to a change in tactical or strategic planning"; cf. Cleaver-Bartholomew, "Alternative Approach," 218–19.

98. This was proposed by Godfrey Rolles Driver, "Linguistic and Textual Problems: Minor Prophets, III," *JTS* 39 (1938): 394–98; cf. Isa 24:6; Hos 13:16 (14:1); Ps 34:21(22). Ezek 6:6 and Joel 1:18 seem to me other good examples. See further Haak, *Habakkuk*, 46–47. It seems to be one way in which the text was read in 1QpHab; cf. Brownlee, *Midrash*, 81–83.

stood as an adjective.[99] The accentuation, which keeps the verb in the same colon with the preceding two verbs, therefore may intend to facilitate the less common reading presented above. The root *'šm* designates a number of ways in which people become guilty.[100] Here we may think specifically of the guilt incurred in laying hold of other territories and peoples (cf. Jer 2:3; 50:7) but then also of the idolatry involved in the process: *he whose strength is for his god.* This is regularly understood to be equivalent to "whose strength is for him god"[101]—in other words, "whose own strength is his god" (cf. most English translations). But in my view, the syntax suggests that the nation's strength is exercised *for his god,* notwithstanding the description in v. 16.[102] In any case, *the Chaldeans,* whom God says he is *raising up* (v. 6), are not mindful of fulfilling YHWH's purposes.

Once the Babylonian nation is identified as guilty, it is noteworthy that the earlier verb *'br (passes through)* is used elsewhere also for overstepping and contravening (mostly God's) commands, although rarely so without the object being specified (maybe only Ps 17:3). If one accepts this as a secondary meaning of the verb here, it strengthens the notion that invading nations constitutes the Babylonian "overstepping": the military passing through is a moral trespassing; to transgress boundaries is to become guilty. Thus, this last verse is the perfect climax of the ambiguous citation of divine revelation in 1:5-11. At one level, one may read the verse as a divine announcement of the devastating impact of the Babylonian army, the "scorching wind" of Jer 4:11. But at another level, Habakkuk's summary of the divine announcement reveals misgivings about a nation that *passes through* other nations like a wind—a nation that *transgresses.* Such transgression should normally lead to punishment, but this is not explicitly promised, and the prophet does not take it for granted.[103]

---

99. Interpreted as a verb, the form can function in both ways indicated above. This is therefore my preference. The *waw* should probably be considered non-consecutive.

100. It is noteworthy that 42 of 103 occurrences of words related to the root are in Leviticus, but few of these are in specifically "cultic" contexts. Cf. Lev 4:13, 22, 27.

101. So explicitly Franz Delitzsch, *Habakuk,* 20-21, who then compares Exod 6:7.

102. If *wǝ'āśēm (and transgresses)* were emended to *wayyāśem (and made),* the situation would be different. Similarly, the rendering "imputing this his power unto his God" (KJV), which also suffers from taking *zû* as demonstrative (see the translation note), would work better with (an additional?) *wayyāśem.* Fabry (*Habakuk,* 202) hears, "His strength becomes his god," which would be more plausible with the verb *hyh* ("to be, become").

103. Contra Thomas Krüger, "Prophetie, Weisheit und religiöse Dichtung im Buch Habakuk," in *Schreiber als Weisheitslehrer und Propheten? Prophetische und weisheitliche Traditionen in den Weisheitsschriften und im Zwölfprophetenbuch,* ed. Jutta Krispenz, BZAW 496 (Berlin: de Gruyter, 2018), who concludes from the fact that the root *'šm* can mean not only

Reflection

The realm in which YHWH's Torah functions properly is the realm in which YHWH reigns. It is therefore difficult to conceive how YHWH's raising of *the Chaldeans* (against Judah) might establish YHWH's justice. Surely as the Babylonians take possession of other countries, they expand the realm of *Babylonian* justice and of the chief *Babylonian* deity (Marduk, not referenced by name in the book). The world thus established is one of violence and strife. Not only is Torah no longer operable, but the promised land is no longer Israel's inheritance, it seems, and, along with other habitations, up for grabs for the Babylonians. The speed and ease with which they conquer fortresses indicate that nothing is able to stand in their way. The fact that, like wind, they ignore boundaries and seem able to sin with impunity underscores that YHWH does not stand in their way either. By incorporating this material into his prayer in the form of a citation of divine revelation, Habakkuk claims that YHWH's toleration does not spring from lack of awareness of Babylonian fierceness or its consequences. The Judean population might at first not have known what the results of Babylonian expansion into their territory would imply, but YHWH did. The thought that God knows beforehand the shape of even the most serious disaster—and even has a hand in it—is comforting and frightening at the same time. It is comforting in that it implies that God is still in charge even where his word is disregarded. It is frightening in that God is implicated in the atrocities committed.

In the Book of the Twelve, we read this as a reflection on the establishment of the Neo-Babylonian Empire after the fall of Nineveh that Nahum has celebrated. Habakkuk does not complain about the establishment of the Neo-Babylonian Empire as such but about the violence that it brings. There is no question in Nahum that the fall of Nineveh comes about through violent means, but the violence is not discussed as a problem. It is in Habakkuk, even if not specifically in relation to Assyria.[104] The violence that was Assyria had been brought to an end with violence from another source, leading to the establishment of another empire that Habakkuk considers no less violent.

Looking beyond the Old Testament, we may think of the Satanic forces that are said to have "marched up over the breadth of the earth" in Rev 20:9. The book of Revelation picks up Ezekiel 38–39 as well as Hab 1:6, and maybe also the sequence of Isaiah 24–27,[105] in its description of a final onslaught of

---

"to be guilty" but also "to pay for one's guilt, to be punished" that the verse anticipates the punishment of the Babylonians.

104. The impact on Judah is the focus in Habakkuk, but other nations are in the picture in vv. 5–11 and later on in ch. 2 (note vv. 5–6!).

105. J. Webb Mealy, *After the Thousand Years: Resurrection and Judgment in Revelation 20,*

violence. The fiery defeat of these forces at first appears to suggest that the end of violence only comes with a divine act of violence that is unmediated and all-consuming, finally separating the realms of violence and peace. But as Richard Bauckham has observed, the most important contrast between the army of evil and the power of the Lamb is between deceit and truth (cf. Rev 20:8, 10).[106] The juxtaposition of earthly and heavenly perspectives and the use of military imagery in both enable the seer "to pose most effectively the issue of how one sees things. Is the world a place in which political and military might carries all before it, or is it one in which suffering witness to the truth prevails in the end?"[107] Fire from heaven symbolizes divine judgment, but fire is also a metaphor for powerful speech (cf. Rev 11:5); it is the faithful testimony, especially of martyrs, that belongs to heaven and which judges and defeats Satanic deceit. "As with the fire from the mouth of the two witnesses (11:5), this must be a symbolic destruction, since the nations will in the end bring their glory into the holy city in 21:24–26."[108] It would undermine the overall biblical vision if the final victory of truth over falsehood were won by physical violence. The sharp sword with which Christ defeats his enemies is in his mouth (Rev 1:16; 2:16; 19:15, 21); it is not a physical weapon in his hand. Those who belong to him overcome the evil one not by shedding the blood of others but "by the blood of the Lamb" and not by a sword in the hand but "by the word of their testimony" (Rev 12:11). Habakkuk did not yet have this vision, and the final part of his complaint in ch. 1 therefore juxtaposes the contradiction between a belief that the imperial violence must serve some good (v. 12) and the recognition that it appears to be unmitigated and indiscriminate bad news (vv. 13–17). This agrees with 1:5–11, which suggests that the Babylonians only bring their own justice, which is in fact no justice at all. What the prophet intuits correctly is that the announcement of the rise of an empire that is going to bring violence cannot be God's final word.

IV. THE FINAL PART OF THE COMPLAINT (1:12–17)

^{12}*Are you not from of old, O YHWH?*
   My God, my Holy One,[a] *we should* [b] *not die!*[c]
O YHWH, for justice you established him,

JSNTSup 70 (Sheffield: JSOT Press, 1992); cf. Jan Fekkes III, *Isaiah and the Prophetic Tradition in the Book of Revelation: Visionary Antecedents and Their Development*, JSNTSup 93 (Sheffield: JSOT Press, 1994), 226.

106. Richard Bauckham, *The Climax of Prophecy: Studies on the Book of Revelation* (London: T&T Clark, 1993), 234.

107. Bauckham, *Climax*, 236.

108. Ian Paul, *Revelation*, TNTC (Downers Grove: IVP Academic, 2018), 330.

and, O Rock,^d to adjudicate^e you founded him.

¹³Eyes^f are too pure to see evil,

and to look upon trouble you are not able.

Why do you look upon treacherous ones,

keep silent^g when a wicked one swallows one more righteous than
them,^h

¹⁴and so made people like fish of the sea,

like a swarm without anyone ruling over it?

¹⁵Every one of them, with a hook, he brings up;ⁱ

he drags them with his net and gathers them with his seine.^j

Therefore he is glad and rejoices.^k

¹⁶Therefore he sacrifices to his net

and burns incense^l to his seine,

for by them his portion is plump

and his food is rich.^m

¹⁷Shall he therefore empty his netⁿ—

and continually be slaying^o nations unsparingly?^p

a. In LXX, the consonants are read as *qodšî* ("my holiness," often used in attributive phrases); hence, "my holy God." I follow MT's unique *qədōšî* (*my Holy One*), which is also reflected in Vulg.

b. The first-person plural is also attested in LXX. It is often considered the result of a scribal correction from an original second-person singular ("you will not die"); see the commentary for this and for the modal nuance.

c. The masoretic accentuation keeps these two lines closely together in one colon, contra my layout in Renz, *Colometry*, 111. This may reflect a different understanding of the syntax; see the commentary.

d. Or, less likely, "as a rock" (cf. the rock for stumbling in Isa 8:14), with the *lamed* of the previous line doing double duty. See Franz Delitzsch, *Habakuk*, 25–26, for cogent arguments against identifying the rock with the Babylonians. *BHS* suggests reading *ṣûrî* ("my rock"), deleting the conjunction (as dittography), and adding the personal pronoun; cf. Fabry, *Habakuk/Obadja*, 215. LXX reads a verb (*eplasen me*, "he has formed me") which suggests a Vorlage that read *yṣry* for (proto-masoretic) consonantal text *wṣwr*.

e. Hebrew *ləhôkîaḥ* can have connotations of rebuke or punishment, but the context suggests *to adjudicate* as in mediating justice (cf. Isa 2:4 // Mic 4:3). The consonants in 1QpHab suggest *ləmôkîḥô* ("as one who rebukes him").

f. Translations usually add the personal pronoun to fit with the address to YHWH, but the prophet may be making a general point: eyes are not meant to see things like that, including YHWH's eyes. So also the LXX, which uses the singular; cf. Dangl, *Habakuk*, 55.

g. The division of lines follows the lead of the Masoretes; cf. *BHQ*.

h. The MT suggests a comparison (*more righteous than them*); the LXX contrasts more starkly the ungodly (*asebēs*) with the righteous (*dikaios*).

i. The form of the *hiphil* found here is not otherwise attested. The opening vowel is nevertheless short; cf. *HGHS* 11m. See Meyer, *Grammatik*, 1:57–58, on *tsere* not always being long.

j. This is usually scanned as two lines (cf. *BHS* and *BHQ*), which is certainly possible, but I find it more poetically satisfying this way. Note that the following line also has two verbs in parallel and that the Masoretes provided the first sentence here with only one disjunctive accent.

k. LXX reads *hē kardia autou* ("his heart") as the subject of *rejoices*. Gelston (*BHQ*, 13:117*) allows for the possibility of assimilation to Isa 66:14 and Zech 10:7 (twice); cf. *CTAT* 3:cxlix.

l. The *piel* of *qtr* is not used with worship the biblical authors considered legitimate; the *hiphil* serves to refer to legitimate burning of incense, e.g. Exod 29:13, 18, 25; 30:7–8.

m. The adjective *rich* translates *bərî'â* ("fat"), which must be a noun here, as the feminine form of the adjective does not fit with *ma'ăkālô* (1QpHab reads the masculine form). Interpreted as equivalent to *bərî'â* in Num 16:30, it could be rendered "unheard of," but the evidence is too tenuous for that. "Plump" in the previous line could also be translated "fat" (adj.), but the references are to desirably rich food; the negative connotation fatty food often has in the modern West is inappropriate in this context.

n. Wellhausen and others suggested a small emendation of *ḥermô* ("his net") to *ḥarbô* ("his sword"), an object that is regularly used with *rîq* ("to empty"): "unsheathe his sword" (cf. Exod 15:9; Lev 26:33; Ezek 5:2, 12; 12:14; 28:7; 30:11). We now have manuscript evidence for this in 1QpHab and 8ḤevXIIgr. The image of uninterrupted slaughter would suggest that the sword is already unsheathed and leads me to prefer MT; the variant can be explained as an assimilation to a common expression just as MT could be an assimilation to the context.

o. For the use of the infinitive with *lamed* here, cf., e.g., Jer 19:12; and see the discussion in Franz Delitzsch, *Habakuk*, 31–32, alongside standard reference works (e.g., GKC 114o).

p. The adverb renders a circumstantial clause in the Hebrew. 1QpHab and the versions do not take this verse as a question, maybe by way of assimilating to the context, as suggested in *BHQ*.

Composition

The rhetorical question addressed to YHWH clearly marks the beginning of a new stanza after the description of *the Chaldeans* in vv. 6b–11. It would be an abrupt opening if vv. 12–17 were a separate prayer.[109] But I have argued above that ch. 1 should be read as a single prayer-complaint that includes the citation of earlier revelation (most likely in new words) in vv. 5–11. This earlier revelation is in some sense the basis for the prophet's protest. Its citation intensifies the complaint and thus prepares for the rhetorical question about God himself. Another rhetorical question at the end of this passage marks an effective conclusion. The first verse of ch. 2 expresses a resolve that becomes part of a first-person narrative in the following verse and should hardly be considered "the concluding verse of Habakkuk's complaint."[110] It marks the transition between the prophet's prayer and the divine response.

109. Cf. Andersen, *Habakkuk*, 175, who remarks: "Nothing could be more abrupt than the beginning of Habakkuk's second prayer. There is nothing like it anywhere else in the Bible."
110. Haak, *Habakkuk*, 15.

Commentary

12 Prinsloo observes that the renewed lament in 1:12–17 "again commences with a temporal question" (v. 12; cf. v. 2), followed by "why?" (v. 13; cf. v. 3).[111] The syntax of the first half of the verse is usually taken in such a way that the divine name and the following designations for God are understood as vocatives, as reflected in my translation. Some prefer to interpret the syntax differently: "Are you not from of old YHWH?" Interpreted thus, the rhetorical question would not assert, "You (YHWH) are from of old," but, "You are YHWH (from of old)." The Masoretes accented this first half of the verse in such a way that no major disjunction is encouraged.[112] This is sometimes interpreted to support the inclusion of *YHWH, my God, my Holy One* in the predicate.[113] But while the assertion that God has been YHWH, the covenant God, for a long time fits the context well, this sense would be the more obvious if the word order were different. As it is, *from of old* seems to take the place of the predicate.

The rhetorical question *Are you not from of old?* follows the reference to a different divinity in the preceding verse. It challenges YHWH to assert his privileges and rights as someone who is *from of old*.[114] The specific phrase used (*miqqedem*), while not unusual, is noteworthy. On its own, it is ambiguous, unlike comparable phrases that might have been used instead,[115] and it could also be rendered "in the east" or "from the east" (cf. Isa 2:6).[116] This is not its meaning here, but the allusion to *qādîmâ* (*forward*) in v. 9 may be deliberate and could prepare the reader for YHWH's coming from Teman in ch. 3. Habakkuk asks in effect:

111. Gert T. M. Prinsloo, "Life for the Righteous, Doom for the Wicked: Reading Habakkuk from a Wisdom Perspective," *Skrif en Kerk* 21 (2000): 626.

112. The *atnach* segment, which constitutes the first half of the verse, governs only one subordinate disjunctive accent (*tifcha*), which in turn governs two, establishing a *revia* segment (up to *from of old*) and a *tebir* segment (from *YHWH* onward). The *revia* segment contains no subordinate disjunctive accents and should therefore not be considered a colon, which means that the *tebir* segment cannot constitute a colon either.

113. Franz Delitzsch, *Habakuk*, 23.

114. The notion that something being *from of old* implies established rights or privileges probably lies behind other passages as well (e.g., Ps 74:2; Isa 19:11; 23:7; Mic 5:2[1]).

115. Two alternative phrases to indicate the same concept, *mē'āz* and *mē'ôlām*, are used in Ps 93:2, of which the latter is more common. Cf. *gôy mē'ôlām hû'* ("he is an ancient nation") in Jer 5:15.

116. Discussing the phrase *mîmê-qedem* in Isaiah, Peter Leithart ("Days of the East," Patheos.com, September 23, 2010, https://www.patheos.com/blogs/leithart/2010/09/days-of-the-east/) observes: "East is the direction of the sunrise, so 'days of east' would presumably [be] early days, morning days, in the morning of the world. That is the way most translators take the phrase, using 'ancient days' or 'ancient times.' "

Are the Chaldeans not taking the place that rightfully belongs to you, YHWH, when they come from the east to establish their justice here? Surely this can only be a temporary situation. You would not allow us to die, our identity as the people of God extinguished, would you?

The prophet appeals to YHWH as *my God, my Holy One*, thus stressing the relationship between YHWH and those who belong to him and doing so by putting himself in the place of those who belong to YHWH. YHWH is, of course, the "God of Israel" and "the Holy One of Israel" in other parts of Scripture, but strikingly, Habakkuk never uses the term "Israel" (or "Judah" or "Jacob"). He never even uses the plural "our" and only in 3:13 speaks of "your people" in addressing God. It is as if the identity of Israel has been erased already.[117] Of course, Habakkuk does not pray as a private individual concerned for himself only. When he says *my God, my Holy One*, he speaks as one interceding for his people, but the choice of the singular *my* highlights the personal involvement of the prophet. It may also reflect the conviction that YHWH has to prove to be Habakkuk's God and Habakkuk's Holy One before he can be perceived again as Israel's.

The reading *lōʾ nāmût* (*We should not die*) is sometimes considered secondary to an original *lōʾ tāmût* ("You will not die"), because the passage is in traditional *Tiqqune Sopherim* ("Emendations of the Scribes") lists that register places where the received text allegedly does not reproduce the text intended by the author.[118] The Targum reflects awareness of the reading "you will not die" with reference to God, but 1QpHab and the Old Greek and Latin translations confirm the antiquity of the first-person plural.[119] Contemporary commentators and translators are divided on the merits of either reading.[120] It must be borne in mind that the *Tiqqune Sopherim* do not necessarily reflect

---

117. Cf. Markl, "Hab 3," 107.

118. See Ginsburg, *Introduction*, 358, who argues in favor of the second person singular as the better text; and Carmel McCarthy, *The Tiqqune Sopherim and Other Theological Corrections in the Masoretic Text of the Old Testament*, OBO 36 (Göttingen: Vandenhoeck & Ruprecht; Fribourg: Presses Universitaires, 1981), 105–11, who argues in the opposite direction. Andersen (*Habakkuk*, 176–78) offers further considerations.

119. McCarthy (*Tiqqune Sopherim*) argues that even Tg. does not reflect a different reading from MT; cf. the review by Robert P. Gordon, *VT* 32 (1982): 361; ArBib 14, 147. See Brownlee (*Midrash*, 85) for 1QpHab, contra Fishbane, *Biblical Interpretation*, 69, who is inclined to the view that 1QpHab reflects a third-person singular (an alternative *tiqqun*). The evidence of the Peshitta is discussed controversially. In medieval times, Rashi believed "you shall not die" to be original (Rosenberg, *Twelve Prophets*, 261), but others, e.g., Ibn Kaspi (*Adne Kesef*, 2:117), only read *we shall not die*.

120. The first-person plural is adopted by, among others, Haak, *Habakkuk*, 48–49; Perlitt, *Nahum*, 57–58 (considered a later addition); and Fabry, *Habakuk/Obadja*, 215, 220, and found in NIV, NASB, ESV. The second-person singular is accepted as original by Ralph L.

actual textual variations but may attest to different exegetical traditions. In fact, many scholars now believe that this is the rule rather than the exception.[121] In my view, the opening of the verse (*Are you not from of old?*) either occasioned a misreading of *we should not die* as "you will not die" in a few manuscripts or suggested an alternative exegetical tradition. In the light of the best and oldest evidence, it seems most likely that the original text read *we should not die.*

An assertion of YHWH's immortality ("You shall not die") would echo *from of old* and suitably support YHWH's reliability as a *rock* within the verse. That might explain the mistake, but *we should not die* is also appropriate here. As someone who is *from of old*, YHWH should be expected not to give up quickly on his claims. These include his claims on Israel, or at any rate on the faithful covenant members among them, as the prophet reminds YHWH by addressing him as *My God, my Holy One.* It should therefore be inconceivable that this is the end of the people for whom Habakkuk intercedes. Those who accept the first-person plural reading *lōʾ nāmût* are not agreed on the nuance. Some interpret it as a confident assertion ("We will not die," or "We cannot die"),[122] but others consider it a supplication ("We shall not die, shall we?"), or even an expression of despair (*We should not die*).[123] We could also render it, "We do not want to die," with hints of supplication or despair. None of these nuances can be decisively excluded. Maybe it is best to read *we should not die* as an implied supplication that has its place between hope, generated by the assertions implied at the beginning of the verse, and despair, expressed throughout the complaint. It finds its answer in the promise of life given in 2:4 to the righteous who persist in their loyalty.[124]

The following two cola make a single assertion formulated in closely parallel syntax. The two vocatives, *YHWH* and *Rock*, pick up the grounds of hope from the preceding. Given who God is, it is inconceivable in the final analysis

---

Smith, *Micah–Malachi*, 103; and Roberts, *Nahum*, 101, among others, and adopted in NRSV, NJB, JPS Tanakh, HCSB, NET.

121. Cf. Carmel McCarthy, "Emendations of the Scribes," *IDBSup*, 263–64; E. J. Revell, "Scribal Emendations," *ABD* 5:1011–12; Page H. Kelley et al., eds., *The Masorah of Biblia Hebraica Stuttgartensia* (Grand Rapids: Eerdmans, 1998), 37–40; Tov, *Textual Criticism*, 64–67; Moshe A. Zipor, "Some Notes on the Origin of the Tradition of the Eighteen Tiqqûnê Sôperîm," *VT* 44 (1994): 77–102. Note also the appendix in Franz Delitzsch, *Habakuk*, 206–8, which offers material from J. S. Nurzi.

122. E.g., Franz Delitzsch, *Habakuk*, 24, followed by Keil, *Minor Prophets*, 2:64.

123. See A. J. O. van der Wal, "*Lō Nāmūt* in Habakkuk I 12: A Suggestion," *VT* 38 (1988): 480–83, who himself opts for this last interpretation. Prinsloo ("Life," 626) considers it "an ironic confession of faith."

124. Cf. Dangl, *Habakuk*, 55.

that the Babylonians could have *established* themselves. (It is clear in context that the reference must be to the Chaldeans, the use of the singular either abstractly personifying the empire or seeing it embodied in its king as the prophet embodies the faithful among the people of God.) More specifically, the oracle in vv. 5–11 clearly accepts that, ultimately, the Babylonian rampage is YHWH's doing. However sweeping the change may have been in the experience of the people of Judah, the Neo-Babylonian Empire is now firmly *established* on strong foundations. The verbs in question tend to be used for permanent fixtures, most ironically—given the sense here—in Isaiah 23:13, which refers to Assyria having destined the land of Babylonia to a wilderness of ruins.[125] But if the establishment of the Neo-Babylonian Empire cannot lead to the annihilation of the people of God, there must be a larger agenda with a more positive result in the end. It is identified in the word *justice*, reinforced by the verbal form in the following colon, *to adjudicate*.

13 The opening parallelism in the next verse does not explain wherein this justice might consist but, at first sight, offers another reason to think that the end result must be positive. If the purity of eyes, and certainly YHWH's eyes, demands that they do not see such evil, then surely YHWH cannot countenance a wicked mess, and the present disaster cannot be unqualified evil. In fact, however, the assertion that YHWH cannot tolerate looking upon evil is made to give force to the accusing question that follows. The prophet affirms that YHWH is unable to see evil and trouble without being moved to do something about it. He then asks why, inexplicably, he does precisely that, looking upon treacherous ones without reaction, keeping silent when the wicked overwhelms the righteous. The use of *treacherous* as a broad designation for a foreign enemy, apparently without specific reference to the breach of a treaty, is found also in the book of Isaiah.[126] More commonly, the prophets apply the designation in accusing the people of God of disloyalty. Here the term *treacherous* is likely meant to evoke not so much betrayal of a specific relationship but ruthlessness and recklessness in relating to others (cf. the targumic use of *'nws*, "oppressor, one who acts violently"), and maybe *treacherous* in the sense of taking what is not their own.

The terms *wicked* and *righteous* are not simply placeholders for Babylonia and Judah. It is true that *the wicked* finds expression in the Babylonian army, but this is not to say that Habakkuk necessarily considered the whole of Judah, let alone neighboring peoples—even compared with Babylonia—as

---

125. See Renz, "Proclaiming the Future," 40–41, for a brief defense of interpreting this verse as a reference to the destruction of Babylon foreshadowing the fate of Tyre.

126. Isaiah 21:2; 24:16; 33:1; cf. Prov 2:22; 21:18; Jer 12:1 for the parallel use of *bôgēd* ("treacherous") and *rāšāʿ* ("wicked").

more righteous.[127] The text remains opaque on the question of how strong the righteous component of Judah was considered to be; it is sufficient for Habakkuk's complaint to stand that the righteous suffer under the onslaught of the wicked. Nor does the text imply that the righteous are *more righteous* than the Babylonians are righteous; the prophet does not grant any genuine righteousness to the Babylonians. At best, the sheer wickedness of the Babylonians makes others look *righteous* by way of contrast,[128] whether or not they would be classified as "righteous" if seen on their own. The motif of swallowing will be picked up in 2:4–5, albeit with different terminology.

14-15 The gulping up in v. 13 may have evoked the image of dragging up a haul of fish, which is developed in vv. 14–15. On the one side, people are a seething mass of swarming animals without governmental structure.[129] On the other side, someone is deliberate (*every one of them, with a hook*) as well as comprehensive (*with his net . . . with his seine*) in his catching fish. The picture is not unique in the ancient Near East. Conquered peoples are depicted as caught in a net both in ancient Mesopotamia and Egypt, the net being "a symbol of absolute sovereignty and control, and of ultimate world dominion."[130] The motif is also used in Amos 4:2 and Jer 16:16 (cf. Eccl 9:12).[131] What does the comparison of human beings with a school of fish imply? Many note that, within the Bible, ants (Prov 6:7) and locusts (Prov 30:27) are also said to have no ruler.[132] The point is probably not lack of order as such. In large quantities, swarming animals can appear very coordinated and orderly even to the scientifically untrained eye. Rather, the point is likely the lack of an order and command structure based on verbal communication. Maybe unlike mammals, which communicate with noises that can be interpreted as words, fish, as well as ants and locusts, are not ordered by words.[133] By

127. Franz Delitzsch, *Habakuk*, 28. Contra Timmer, *Non-Israelite Nations*, 140, it is not clear that the prophet thinks Judah "morally superior to Babylon."

128. Cf. Franz Delitzsch, *Habakuk*, 28, who compares the phrase *ʿāmōq min-hāʿôr* ("deeper than the skin") in Lev 13 (vv. 4, 25, 30) to this use of the preposition, as the flesh is not deeper than the skin is deep but deep by contrast to the skin, which is not deep. Similarly, Andersen (*Habakkuk*, 184) sees the binary relationship in personal litigation in view and defines it as "righteous in relation to the wicked in this particular suit."

129. English does not use *swarm* with sea creatures, but "school" is too narrow, as the Hebrew term is not used for fish only and, more importantly, does not convey the lack of hierarchy that seems implied here.

130. Cf. Othmar Keel, *The Symbolism of the Biblical World: Ancient Near Eastern Iconography and the Book of Psalms*, trans. Timothy J. Hallett (Winona Lake, IN: Eisenbrauns, 1997), 89–93. The quotation is from page 90, which also offers the two most relevant illustrations.

131. For a detailed discussion of Amos 4:2, which includes some difficult terms, see Shalom M. Paul, *Amos*, Hermeneia (Minneapolis: Fortress, 1991), esp. 134–35.

132. E.g., Franz Delitzsch, *Habakuk*, 29; Haak, *Habakkuk*, 50.

133. Maybe "subhuman creatures" were generally considered to "have no ruler" (so Gel-

suggesting that any order based on words has broken down, this picks up the concern expressed earlier about Torah's (lack of) effectiveness. Without an effective implementation of Torah, Judah has become a society without guidance. Its people have become like creatures without words, *a swarm without anyone ruling over it*. Addressed to God, this clearly implies that YHWH does not govern either (cf. Isa 63:19). This is the complaint in a nutshell: the absence of God's rule. The people are helpless and defenseless against the fisherman who works with hook, throwing net, and dragnet.[134] That the two Hebrew terms specifically refer to a throwing *net* (with a diameter of only a few yards) and a *seine* (a dragnet with a diameter of about three dozen yards) is not certain but plausible.[135] If so the fisherman gets *every one of them* in ever increasing quantities, a few fish with a *hook*, more fish with a throwing *net*, many fish with a *seine*. No wonder *he is glad and rejoices*.

Now, comparison of a people with fish (rather than sheep) is unusual in the Bible. Also, other Biblical and wider ancient Near Eastern references to the capture of peoples with nets and similar implements do not make a point about a lack of leadership. These observations lead Richard Whitekettle to argue that the nonstandard phrasing in this verse must specifically refer to a lack of governmental structure and therefore conceptually assumes the collapse of the (Davidic) monarchy.[136] Whitekettle leaves it open whether the complaint is therefore to be dated after 586 or whether the prophet anticipates what is going to happen. Certainly, in retrospect it is easy to make a link between the imagery used here and the total collapse of Judah in the destruction of Jerusalem. But Habakkuk's complaint centers on the failure of Torah rather than the absence of a Davidic king on the throne in Jerusalem.[137] It is really God's governance that is questioned in the Babylonian

---

ston, *BHQ*, 13:117*), in which case one might argue that no other animals were considered to communicate in more than rudimentary ways.

134. Andersen (*Habakkuk*, 184) points out that the Akkadian word *bā'iru* refers to soldiers as well as fishermen and hunters and wonders whether this usage suggested the comparison. There is no way of knowing.

135. Franz Delitzsch (*Habakuk*, 30) considers *ḥerēm* (*net*) to be the more general term and *mikmeret* (*seine*) to be specifically the fishing net alongside *mikmār*, the hunting net (Isa 51:20). *DCH* also suggests that *mikmeret* is perhaps specifically a fishing net. LXX already reflects this distinction between the smaller casting net (*amphiblēstron*) and the larger drag net (*sagēnē*).

136. Richard Whitekettle, "How the Sheep of Judah Became Fish: Habakkuk 1,14 and the Davidic Monarchy," *Bib* 96 (2015): 273–81. He actually makes four points, but the first two seem decisive for his argument. The third and fourth are that elsewhere Israelite authors talk about a "leadership crisis as a matter of episodic leaderlessness" and that "structural leaderlessness in animals is mentioned in the Israelite textual record (Prov 6,6–8; 30,27)" (276).

137. In this sense, the explanation reported in the Talmud (b. 'Abodah Zarah 6a) is more apposite: "Just as fish in the sea, when they come up on dry land, forthwith begin to die,

onslaught, with the culmination of the attack in the loss of the kingdom and the destruction of the temple never directly in view. I therefore suspect that we should not press the imagery used in vv. 14–15 to the extent that we see here a prediction of the abolition of the Davidic monarchy or a reflection of the experience of being fully absorbed into the Neo-Babylonian Empire. In a different essay, Whitekettle argues that the reference to both *fish* (clean aquatic animals) and *a swarm* (interpreted as unclean aquatic animals, cf. Gen 1:21) makes the point that the onslaught affects the righteous and the wicked indiscriminately.[138] This fits the context well. He notes:

> The use of fish and other aquatics to convey this idea would have been an especially powerful image if, during the deportation(s) of which Habakkuk was thinking, the righteous and the wicked of Jerusalem were taken out of that city into exile through the Fish Gate (2 Chr 33:14; Neh 3:3; 12:39), a location that Zephaniah specifically mentions as a place of anguish during the Babylonian attack (Zeph 1:10).[139]

16 The gratitude of the fisherman goes to the wrong address. The picture of sacrifices being made to a fishing net may have been inspired by the use of a weapon to represent the god of war, as the Scythians are said to have made sacrifices to an iron scimitar. Similarly, a dagger stuck in the ground could represent Nergal to the Assyrians.[140] But this is hardly a necessary assumption. It seems very doubtful that "Hab 1:16 alludes to an actual cult of weapons."[141] The point is that the conquering monarch worships the means of his success rather than the one who, according to the prophecy, is the true author of this success.[142] The conqueror does not see himself as an instru-

---

so with human beings, when they take their leave of teachings of the Torah and religious deeds, forthwith they begin to die" (Jacob Neusner, *The Babylonian Talmud: A Translation and Commentary*, 22 vols. [Peabody: Hendrickson, 2011], 17b:9).

138. Richard Whitekettle, "Like a Fish and Shrimp Out of Water: Identifying the *Dāg* and *Remeś* Animals of Habakkuk 1:14," *BBR* 24 (2014): 491–503.

139. Whitekettle, "Fish and Shrimp," 503.

140. For the latter, see Keel, *Symbolism*, 238. The former is reported in Herodotus, *Histories*, 4.62. See Franz Delitzsch, *Habakuk*, 30, for further examples. David Stephen Vanderhooft (*The Neo-Babylonian Empire and Babylon in the Latter Prophets*, HSM 59 [Atlanta: Scholars Press, 1999], 157) wonders whether the imagery chosen points to a "caricature of the royal provision of fish offerings in the cult," but there would be no reason for such a caricature here in spite of Hab 2:18–19.

141. Keel, *Symbolism*, 235. Andersen (*Habakkuk*, 185) agrees: "We need not suppose that this description was intended to describe any actual ceremony in Babylonian religion, because the fishing tackle is only a metaphor." Verse 11 already claimed that for the Babylonian, it is *his strength* that is *his god*. *Net* and *seine* are metaphors for Babylonian power.

142. Cf. the threat against Egypt in Ezek 32:3, where YHWH says the attackers bring the conquered people up "in my net."

ment in YHWH's hands but is only interested in satisfying his own hunger and desires, and perhaps deities.

17 The rhetorical question that concludes the opening complaint underscores that in the prophet's mind, this cannot possibly continue unchecked. Everything is wrong about the picture that presents itself to him. The successful campaigns against other political entities merely encourage the Babylonians to keep going. The first half of the verse captures the moment in which the net is emptied. It is the moment of life and death for the fish. If not immediately returned to the water, the fish will die. With this image, Habakkuk returns to the urgency evident in the opening words of the complaint.[143] The second half stresses the observation that the Babylonians appear to be able to continue unhindered and unchecked. The word for continuity (*tāmîd*) is the same as the final word of the book of Nahum. In Nahum, the conquered nations had been overwhelmed by Assyrian evil *continually*, but the prophet celebrates the end of this as much as Habakkuk desires an end to the continuing slaughter—a slaughter that to his eyes continues without pity, *unsparingly*.

Reflection

This section continues the complaint and brings it to a conclusion. The first few verses of the chapter had already assumed that YHWH could (and should) intervene and asked why he did not. Verse 4 gave a reason why it was high time to do something about the situation, as the prophet observes the ineffectiveness of Torah and a breakdown of justice. The citation of the oracle that claims that YHWH is the ultimate author of Babylonian success highlighted the incredible freedom of the Chaldeans to impose their own order and justice upon the rest of the world, the description itself offering an indirect argument for stopping the rampage. But it is this final part of the complaint that drives the argument home. The impunity with which the Babylonians are able to enforce their will demonstrates that other peoples, including the people of God, are, bereft of orderly government, merely food for the appetite of the empire. The picture of a ravenous empire swallowing up others is not yet developed here, but its introduction sows the seed for the answer in ch. 2.

The term *swallow* (*bl'*) is regularly used in the Hebrew Bible in highly destructive contexts, such as when the earth swallowed up Korah and com-

143. Assuming that the nets are emptied to be filled again, the NET renders, "Will he then continue to fill and empty his throw net?" Cf. Fabry, *Habakuk/Obadja*, 225–26, who also wonders whether the emptying is an allusion to the practice of deporting the upper classes. The latter seems doubtful.

pany in Numbers 16. In military contexts, swallowing up is used in effect as a synonym for destroying (e.g., 2 Sam 17:16; 20:19–20; cf. Lam 2:2), which is also often its sense in contexts involving individuals (e.g., Job 2:3; Ps 35:25; Prov 1:12).[144] Such devouring is never said to satiate.[145] But the reference to food in v. 16 ensures that the swallowing is not merely a dead metaphor for full-scale destruction. While the effect on the victims (destruction) is at the forefront of the complaint, the action itself—unconstrained greed leading to worship of that which enables consumption—is horrendous, even before one considers its consequences. The motif of fishing may add to this a notion of "harvesting what one did not sow," especially since the chapter throughout stresses that the conquests do not require any real effort on the part of the Babylonians. The rationale for describing the Babylonian modus operandi in such striking imagery is to underscore the gap between what is and what should be. YHWH should never tolerate such treacherous behavior, so why does he? The prophet does not appeal to YHWH's pity but to his sense of what is right and proper. "Habakkuk's problem is that he is horrified at the atrocities" committed by the Babylonians, "whereas God is apparently in-different, unresponsive."[146] The complaint is an attempt to get YHWH to face the facts in a way that demands a response. When God seems absent, even absent-minded, some turn their back on God. Habakkuk does what all those who pray the Psalms have done throughout the ages—namely, turn to God with renewed vigor. Neither of these opposing responses is necessarily more linked to further action than the other. Those who turn away from God may do so accommodating themselves to a situation they feel powerless to change, or they may do so rebelling against the status quo without the help of God. Similarly, those who turn to God may do so fatalistically, and Christians have sometimes misused prayer as a substitute for campaign and action. But as long as people truly turn to God in complaint, they will not easily give in to resignation and accommodate themselves to an unjust status quo. Habakkuk not only turns to God, but his prayer seeks to turn God to the situation at hand. Such prayer will not allow the person praying to avert their eyes from injustice and evil. Naming evil is an important first step in opposing it.[147]

144. Some passages that were traditionally interpreted like this, such as Isa 3:12; 9:16(15); 19:3, are now derived from the homonym "to confuse."

145. In fact, probably the only instance in which the result of the swallowing up is positive is in Isa 25:8, where YHWH is said to swallow up death itself, a motif taken up in 1 Cor 15:54; cf. 2 Cor 5:4, another rare instance of *katapinō* (the Greek verb regularly used to translate *blʿ*) having a positive connotation.

146. Andersen, *Habakkuk*, 190.

147. The Duke University symposium essays collected in Ruth W. Grant, ed., *Naming Evil, Judging Evil* (Chicago: University of Chicago Press, 2006) consider the question

Later readers can take Habakkuk's complaint as a template but should be careful to do so with integrity, prayerfully exploring whether the description of evil offered in these verses applies to a present-day situation.[148] The language of this prayer can help us to discern what is truly going on in a situation we perceive as unjust, either by way of highlighting certain issues (failure of Torah, greed) or by way of revealing to us that the situation we bring to God in prayer is more complex than the description offered here. Accepting with Habakkuk that the Babylonians were on a violent rampage that ignored God's good order and that God was somehow responsible for this need not imply that we depict a present-day aggressor in the same terms. In the light of patterns of empirical behavior in the Scriptures, we will be prepared to detect similarities today, but we should remain alert to differences as well. "Trying out" a prayer like Habakkuk's can be a way of discerning whether the description fits.

Habakkuk's was, of course, not a private prayer in the end. We do not know at which point in time this became a public prayer, whether already in the midst of the events described and without what we now know as Hab 2 or only later as a package together with its response in ch. 2. Even on its own, in being made public, the prayer in Hab 1 becomes a prophecy; the liturgy cannot but be political. It is the same for the church. Private prayer may wrestle with issues, weighing up to what extent complaint is justified; public prayer takes a stand. Public prayer therefore requires greater confidence in the truth of what is implicitly or explicitly asserted in the prayer. This makes it difficult, in my view, to use Hab 1 in Christian public prayer today. Habakkuk's complaint is in part fed by an expectation that the law should not be as ineffective as all that and that Babylonian aggression should serve some good in punishing wrongdoing. The revelation brought by Christ has taught us more about the intrinsic limits of what the law or military force can do to establish justice, and we will therefore want to pray accordingly, still lamenting oppression and injustice but with a greater realism about law and violence and greater confidence in the power of faithfulness gained from Hab 2 and, e.g., the Beatitudes of Christ.

---

whether it is more dangerous to call something "evil" (because doing so oversimplifies matters) or more dangerous not to do so (since to address evil, one must acknowledge it). I incline to the latter view but believe that naming "evil" in private prayer first of all can help one discern its nature and decide how to name it in public.

148. Early Christian commentators were more reluctant to commend this as an exemplary prayer, and their hesitation is not without good reason. It would be wrong to ignore the further development in the book and indeed beyond the book in the revelation of Jesus Christ.

V. THE PROPHET'S RESOLVE TO GET AN ANSWER (2:1)

¹*At my watch*ᵃ *I will stand,*
*and I will station myself on the rampart;*ᵇ
*and I will keep watch to see what he will say about*ᶜ *me,*
*and what I will answer*ᵈ *when I am reprimanded.*ᵉ

a. Hebrew *mišmeret* "refers widely to any responsible job that requires watchfulness" and often to the priestly task of "looking after" something (Andersen, *Habakkuk*, 192). Marvin A. Sweeney (*The Twelve Prophets*, vol. 2, Berit Olam [Collegeville, MN: Liturgical Press], 454) suggests that the use of the term here gave rise to the tradition of identifying Habakkuk as a Levite (Bel and Dragon 1:1). But *mišmeret* is used with specific reference to a lookout or guard post in Isa 21:8, and the next line confirms that we are to picture (metaphorically) a city wall rather than the inside of the temple at this point. This leaves open the question whether the prophet was actually in the temple, maybe even in a professional capacity. Later Jewish tradition saw the image of a prison implied (cf. *bêt-mišmeret* in 2 Sam 20:3); see Rosenberg, *Twelve Prophets*, 263.

b. 1QpHab has a final *yod*, suggesting "my rampart," which could also be understood if the suffix in the previous colon is thought to do double duty. Some prefer to vocalize *maṣṣôr* ("guard post") for MT *māṣôr* (*rampart*), arguing it offers a closer parallel; e.g., Cathcart, "Law Is Paralysed," 346.

c. The translation of the preposition is tricky and will require detailed comment below (see the commentary).

d. This is the common understanding of *'āšîb* ("I will bring back") here; cf. the idiom *'āšîb dābār* ("I will bring back a word," i.e., "I will reply") in 2 Sam 3:11; 24:13; etc. At first, the elliptical variant seems well attested, but corpus and usage are narrow. Most instances are in Job, usually with a pronominal suffix for the one to whom an answer is given (e.g., 13:22), except in 20:2 ("[My thoughts] cause me to answer"). In Est 4:13, 15, the recipient of the answer is introduced with *'el* (cf. Aramaic Dan 2:14). Prov 26:16 uses "answer" without specifying to whom the answer is given. Still, the usual understanding is to be preferred to "I will get back" (cf. Rudolph, *Micha*, 212, followed by Fabry, *Habakuk/Obadja*, 229), as the verb commonly relates to giving back rather than receiving back. Roberts (*Nahum*, 105) suspects that the Peshitta's third-person reading ("He will answer") was the original and that "the text was altered to avoid the idea that the prophet could reprove God." Rashi manages to avoid the idea by assuming that the reproof comes from people who contend with Habakkuk (Rosenberg, *Twelve Prophets*, 264).

e. Literally "my reprimand," but the nuance of *tôkaḥat* is a matter of interpretation, relating to decisions about the subject of the verb and whether the suffix is taken as indicating agent or recipient. See the commentary.

Composition

The switch to speaking about YHWH in the third person is noteworthy and marks a break from the complaint in ch. 1. The prophet maybe addresses himself more than anyone else, but the audience or readers of the text are still listening in on this soliloquy. The layout above shows the parallelism between lines, but it is debatable whether this verse should be considered poetry or elevated prose.[149] The chiastic arrangement in the first two lines (nominal phrase, verb, verb, nominal phrase) puts the prophet at the center and may evoke the idea of being enclosed in a fortress-city. The more usual frontal position of the main verb going with the next two lines introduces a forward movement from watching and seeing the reply to contemplating the answer to the reply. If the suffix with the last word were to be understood as subjective ("my argument") rather than objective (*when I am reprimanded*), it would refer back to the preceding chapter, but otherwise the verse looks forward, and v. 2 will pick up the narrative. A case could be made for keeping vv. 1–2 together on the basis of the relationship of the verses to Isa 21:6–8, which Fabry examines in detail.[150] But the links to v. 2 that he tabulates are not as strong as they appear in his table: *And YHWH answered me and said* overlaps with Isa 21:6 only in the word *said*. *Write down a revelation* has a conceptual parallel in "what he sees he must report" in Isa 21:6, but there is no lexical overlap. The admonition "let him be fully attentive" in Isa 21:7 is only vaguely similar to Hab 2:2, even if one were to understand *document it on tablets* as "write down clearly." This makes it a little less certain that there is a literary dependence rather than just a parallel of motifs, even if the parallels between Isa 21 and Hab 2:1 are more impressive, with actual lexical overlap: the noun *mišmeret* (*watch*, Isa 21:8); the verb *'md* (*stand*, Isa 21:6, 8); the verb *ṣph* (*keep watch*), whose piel participle is used in Isa 21:6 to designate the guard/lookout, with a related noun designating the watchtower in Isa 21:8 (instead of the word for *rampart* in Hab 2:1).

Commentary

The prophet is pictured on a rampart, suggesting a military context, as is appropriate for the subject matter of his complaint. The prophet as watchman is a motif found also in Jeremiah (6:17) and in Ezekiel (chs. 3 and 33), where it is well developed and of particular significance. In Ezekiel, the prophet in exile is portrayed as a watchman first of all because he sees the enemy forces approaching Jerusalem, although he is unable to usher an appropriate warning. Once news of the fall of Jerusalem arrives in exile, the prophet, who had been unable to function as "a man who reproves" (*'îš môkîaḥ*, 3:26), is freed to usher warnings to his community by arguing with them and calling them

---

149. Cf. Andersen, *Habakkuk*, 191. The masoretic accentuation suggests division into three units only, taking the first two lines together.

150. Fabry, *Habakuk/Obadja*, 237–39, leaning toward dependence of Isa 21 on Hab 2.

to repent. He thus becomes a watchman for his community in a fuller sense.[151] The symbolism is used with a twist in Habakkuk as well, as the prophet and his community already know about devastation caused by the military aggressor. Habakkuk offers his argument, a complaint that is in effect a call for repentance, but it is addressed to God. From the prophet's point of view, the proper reply must come in the form of a reversal of fortunes between the wicked and those they oppress. The watchman is not anxiously looking to see whether an enemy force approaches but whether it will be turned back before it is altogether too late for the victims.

Just as the Babylonian onslaught had been preceded by an oracle announcing that YHWH would do something unbelievable in the world of nations, so now the first sign of a reversal would be a word from God. But does Habakkuk expect a word spoken "in" him,[152] "to" him,[153] "with" him,[154] "against" him,[155] "through" him,[156] or "about" him?[157] All of these options could have been expressed equally well, but not necessarily less ambiguously, in other ways: namely, "to" with the preposition *'el* (see, e.g., Num 31:3; Deut 1:43),[158] "against" with the preposition *'al* (e.g., 2 Kgs 22:19; Ps 35:20; Jer 29:32; Hos 7:13; Amos 3:1),[159] and prophetic agency with the

151. See Renz, *Rhetorical Function*, 101–3, 158–62, for details.

152. Franz Delitzsch, *Habakuk*, 35–36; Keil, *Minor Prophets*, 2:69 ("since the speaking of God to the prophets was an internal speaking, and not one perceptible from without"). Cf. Naomi G. Cohen, "ר‎בד ... ב‎י: An 'Enthusiastic' Prophetic Formula," *ZAW* 99 (1987): 219–32, who argues that the prophet expects God's speaking to happen within a vision and the prophet's reply to be offered "in nebiatic trance" (229).

153. Cf. maybe Num 12:6, 8 (first instance). As the communication in v. 6 is *baḥălôm* ("in a dream"), "in him" would seem possible here, but the parallel with v. 8 makes this inadvisable, and "with him" is probably preferable.

154. See previous footnote and Zech 1:9, 13, 14, 19 (2:2); 2:3(7); 4:1, 4, 5; 5:5, 10; 6:4.

155. Cf. Num 12:1, 8 (second instance); 21:5, 7; Job 19:18; Pss 50:20; 78:19; Jer 31:20. So Haak, *Habakkuk*, 54.

156. Cf. Num 12:2; 2 Sam 23:2. So, e.g., Andersen, *Habakkuk*, 193; Fabry, *Habakuk/Obadja*, 228.

157. Cf. Deut 6:7; 11:19; Pss 87:3; 119:46; Ezek 33:30 (also Song 8:8?). Note 1 Sam 19:3: "I will speak about you (*bəkā*) to my father (*'el-'ābî*)."

158. While "to" is the appropriate translation of *'el* in most places, in 1 Sam 3:12 and Job 42:7 the preposition may be better rendered "concerning," and in 1 Kgs 16:7 "against." The preposition *'im* can also be used for "to" (e.g., Gen 31:24; Exod 19:20, 22). Note that *lipnê* is only appropriate when speaking "to" a superior (cf. Esth 8:3).

159. But *'al* is also used for "about" (e.g., Josh 14:6), even with the nuance "on your behalf" (e.g., 1 Kgs 2:18), whereby *'al* is differentiated from *'el* ("to"), as in Jer 36:2, where the nuance of *'al* is "against." In Jer 11:2, it is not clear whether the prepositions should be distinguished (cf. 18:11, with *'mr*). Psalm 109 uses *'ittî* for "against me" in v. 2 (v. 20 uses *'al-napšî*, "against my life"). But note that *'al* is also used in the positive expression *dibbēr 'al-lēb* ("speak to the heart" = "speak tenderly" or "speak encouragingly," e.g., Gen 34:3; Isa 40:2).

phrase *dibbēr bəyad* ("speak through [the agency of]").[160] The Greek translation (*en emoi*) imitates the Hebrew and is similarly ambiguous. The church fathers saw a reference to the internal reception of the divine communication,[161] but the sense "in" is nowhere clearly attested and could have been expressed more unambiguously by *bəlibbî* ("in my heart") or *bətôkî* ("within me").[162] All in all, a decision is difficult to make. The translation "through me" is maybe the least likely, as this use of the preposition with *dibbēr* is rarely found and has a well-attested alternative in *dibbēr bəyad*. The rendering "to me" would be similarly unusual for this preposition, although it could be said to have the advantage of incorporating the more specific "in me." On balance, I opt for "about me," not least because it is less specific than "against me," which some may prefer on the basis of their understanding of the next line.[163]

The final line of the verse is similarly open to different understandings. If *what I will answer* is correct (see translation note), the suffix attached to *tôkahat* ("reprimand, reproof, rebuke") does not indicate the author of the reproof but its recipient, which in English may be better expressed with a verbal phrase (*when I am reprimanded*).[164] If the suffix refers to Habakkuk as author, "complaint" or "argument," which allows for the nuances of reasoning (cf. Job 13:6; 23:4) as well as disagreement or criticism, would be among the possible renderings.[165] Floyd claims that *tôkahat* cannot refer back to Habakkuk's complaint in ch. 1 because this would require another

160. Cf. Exod 9:35; Lev 10:11; 16:21; 26:25; Num 16:40 (17:5); 27:23; Josh 20:2; 1 Sam 28:17; 1 Kgs 8:53, 56; 12:15; 14:18; 15:29; 16:12, 34; 17:16; 2 Kgs 9:36; 10:10; 14:25; 17:23; 21:10; 24:2; 2 Chr 10:15; Isa 20:2; Jer 37:2; 50:1; Ezek 38:17. Hos 12:11(12) uses *bəyad* with *dmh* piel for prophetic speech. The idiom is also regularly used with *dabar-yhwh* ("word of YHWH," e.g., Hag 1:1) and with other verbs (e.g., *qārāʾ*, "cry out," in Zech 7:7).

161. BA 23.4–9, 272. Cf. Franz Delitzsch, Keil, and Naomi G. Cohen (see n. 152). Cf. Kimchi's gloss, "with the spirit of prophecy" (Rosenberg, *Twelve Prophets*, 264).

162. The use of a pronominal suffix with a finite verb would seem to be impossible here; this construction is used in Deut 18:21–22 to refer to an internal object and in Jer 11:2 to anticipate addressees who are introduced with prepositions.

163. The preposition *ʿal* may have been avoided because of its heavy use elsewhere in the verse.

164. Haak (*Habakkuk*, 54–55) translates "my prosecutor," appealing to occurrences in Proverbs (cf. Prov 29:1) and to the individual asked to adjudicate in Hab 1:12.

165. Prinsloo ("Reading Habakkuk as a Literary Unit," 532; "Life," 630) opts for "protest" in view of the legal context in Job; cf. Andersen, *Habakkuk*, 194; Fredrik Lindström, "'I am rousing the Chaldaeans'—Regrettably? Habakkuk 1.5–11 and the End of the Prophetic Theology of History," in *The Centre and the Periphery: A European Tribute to Walter Brueggemann*, ed. Jill Middlemas, David J. Clines, and Else Holt, HBM 27 (Sheffield: Phoenix Press, 2010), 51.

term.[166] While not as confident as Floyd about it being impossible for *tôkaḥat* to refer to Habakkuk's complaint, I agree that it is rather more likely that the pronominal suffix is to be understood as indicating an objective genitive. In this interpretation, the prophet fully expects that what YHWH will say about him will take the form of a counterargument that will in effect be a rebuke to the prophet who in turn expects to offer a reply to this reprimand. The verse thus looks forward to the remainder of the book. The divine reply (rebuke) is given from 2:2 to the end of the chapter, the prophet's response to this in ch. 3.

Reflection

Regardless of the precise interpretation of the preposition (*what he will say about [?] me*), the prophet expects a divine response to come to him from the outside,[167] and he expects the response to be confrontational, as the use of *tôkaḥat* ("reprimand, reproof, rebuke") indicates. The watchtower motif is fitting, therefore, not only in the light of the military conquests that inform Habakkuk's complaint in ch. 1 but also, in a secondary sense, with regard to the way in which the prophet perceives his relationship with God. Just as in ch. 1, the earlier divine word (vv. 5–11) led to the prophet's protest, so he expects his prophetic word to lead to a divine protest. It looks as if the prophet and his God cannot walk together, as they are not agreed (cf. Amos 3:3). That the prophet, metaphorically, stations himself on a rampart suggests determination not to move until this situation has been resolved.

What seems peculiar is that Habakkuk watches to see not only what YHWH will say but also how he himself in turn will answer YHWH, as if Habakkuk's reply will come to him from the outside, as something to be observed on a rampart. In the end, this can be said to happen in the book. The rest of this chapter will give us YHWH's reply, only indirectly a reprimand of the prophet but even so a rejoinder to the prophet's protest. Chapter 3 tells of Habakkuk's answer; its visionary context allows us to say that, in a sense, the prophet's reply comes to him from the outside.[168] This does not mean

---

166. Floyd, *Minor Prophets 2*, 111. He states that *tôkaḥat* cannot be used for "complaint" generally, let alone specifically for what he terms Habakkuk's "cultic complaint," for which he suggests *śîaḥ* (cf. 1 Sam 1:16; 2 Kings 9:11; Job 9:27) would be appropriate.

167. This is not contested by those who argue that the preposition indicates that the prophet receives the word inside himself. Franz Delitzsch (*Habakuk*, 36) makes a point of the prophet's ability to distinguish between his own thoughts and what comes to him from God.

168. This would be true even if ch. 3 predated the prophet, as some believe; cf. Theodore

that the prophet is merely a passive recipient, but it links with a common theme in Christian theology that God not only provides the object of faith but also brings about the obedience of faith (Rom 16:26). God not only asks us to work out our salvation but also brings forth in us the desire and the effort to do so (Phil 2:13). With Habakkuk as our model, we may find a way of combining protest against God with the expectation that he will provide us with an answer when we are challenged by him. It is striking that Habakkuk made international issues his personal business, as the frequent use of the first person highlights. The first question to us, therefore, may be whether we ourselves are called to make such broad issues our own in prayer.

Jason T. LeCureux reckons that "Habakkuk offers two key applications," one at the level of the book of Habakkuk ("internally") and one at the level of the Book of the Twelve ("externally"). He anchors these in Hab 2:1 because of the use of *šûb* (*turn*), the verb that is the key for his thematic reading of the Book of the Twelve:

> Internally, the writing asks whether the reader can accept by faith Yhwh's control of the Babylonians in particular, and that the destruction of [Jerusalem in] 586 was the will of Yhwh. Externally, however, this question can be reapplied to Yhwh's interaction with the nations all the way back to Obadiah. Will the audience accept by faith that Yhwh is in control of the nations and will bring about their destruction (Obadiah, Nahum), or salvation/prosperity (Jonah, Micah), both aspects of which are portrayed in Habakkuk? In this way, Habakkuk acts as a referendum on what Yhwh has been doing throughout the Twelve in regards to the punishment/restoration of his own people and the nations.[169]

The liturgical notes at the end of the book commend Habakkuk's response to wider use. As Habakkuk comes to accept that success is given to the Babylonians for a while before they, too, come under God's judgment, so, LeCureux argues, the readers of the Book of the Twelve are invited to adopt a similar stance in relation to the Persian Empire. In my view, this invitation to consider one's own response to the divine "rebuke" in ch. 2 is present in the text even without consideration of the co-texts of Habakkuk within the anthology. The formulation of God's response in paradigmatic language, suggesting patterns, rather than with specific and exclusive reference to the Babylonians, ensures as much.

Hiebert, *God of My Victory: The Ancient Hymn in Habakkuk 3*, HSM 38 (Atlanta: Scholars Press, 1986).

169. LeCureux, *Thematic Unity*, 164.

VI. THE INSTRUCTION TO THE PROPHET (2:2–3)

[2]And YHWH answered me and said:
  Write down a revelation[a] and document it[b] on tablets[c]
    so that one will run who reads[d] it.[e]
[3]For still[f] there is a revelation for the appointed time,
  and it[g] is a testifier[h] to the end; and it does not lie.
If it lingers,[i] wait for it,
  for it will surely come; it will not be late.[j]

    a. For the translation of *ḥāzôn* as *revelation* rather than "vision," see the commentary here and on Nah 1:1. There are disadvantages with translating *revelation*, particularly when talking about this "vision" alongside the Torah. I will therefore use "vision" (in its looser English sense) as well as *revelation* in the commentary.

    b. The object is only implied in the Hebrew text, but English usage demands it to be made explicit. The verb is more commonly understood as "make plain," referring either to the clarity of the message or, more likely in view of the reference to tablets, to legibility, in which case the hendiadys could be rendered "write down plainly." But legal connotations have been discerned by David T. Tsumura, "Hab 2:2 in the Light of Akkadian Legal Practice," *ZAW* 94 (1984): 294–95, who suggests "confirm" with a legal sense; see also Vanderhooft, *Neo-Babylonian Empire*, 157–59, to whom I am indebted for the rendering *document* (for promulgation). Cf. Cathcart, "Law Is Paralysed," 348.

    c. LXX uses the singular, maybe assuming that the tablets were bound together as one (Franz Delitzsch, *Habakuk*, 38). A single tablet is insufficient either because of the length of the inscription (so, e.g., Andersen, *Habakkuk*, 204; Tsumura, "Hab 2:2," 294) or because of the need for more than one copy for proper attestation. "The use of the article in Hebrew is rather loose" (JM 137f); here it falls in the category of imperfect determination (JM 137m) and is desirable, too, for euphonic reasons. It is therefore inadvisable to see a reference to tablets that were already determinate prior to the act of writing, as suggested by some (see the commentary).

    d. There really is no good reason for changing the syntactical places of running and reading as happens in a number of modern translations; cf. Renz, "Reading and Running," 435–46.

    e. Andersen, *Habakkuk*, 204, surprisingly claims that "the sense of the preposition is hard to establish." The preposition goes with *qr'*, with which it is regularly used for reciting or reading from a source (cf. *HALOT*, s.v. *qr'*, B:1). There are no grounds for contemplating "by means of it" as an alternative. Commenting on Neh 8:3, Hugh G. M. Williamson (*Ezra, Nehemiah*, WBC 16 [Waco: Word, 1985], 288) distinguishes between *qr'* with the preposition *beth* ("reading from") and *qr'* with accusative ("reading"), suggesting that the former indicates that only extracts were read. This is unlikely here, whatever one decides about the extent of the "vision."

    f. The emendation of *'ôd* (*still*) to *'ēd* ("witness"), apparently first suggested by Samuel E. Loewenstamm in 1962, is attractive in light of the next line; see Roberts, *Nahum*, 106; Patterson, *Nahum*, 174; Seybold, *Nahum*, 63; Vanderhooft, *Neo-Babylonian Empire*, 159. But others believe that the external evidence for the traditional text is too solid to allow for the emendation (Perlitt, *Nahum*, 64; Andersen, *Habakkuk*, 205–6). Prinsloo ("Life," 631) suggests regarding ʿôd as a *hiphil* infinitive or participle of ʿwd ("to witness"), but either would look very different orthographically.

g. The subject of this and the following statements is not entirely clear; see the commentary.

h. Hebrew *yāpēaḥ* is either an apocopated *hiphil* verb, jussive in form but not meaning (GKC 72dd suggests a shortening for rhythmical reasons), or maybe a verbal adjective functioning as a noun like *yāpîaḥ* in Prov 6:19, 12:17, 14:5, 14:25, 19:5, 19:9 (cf. 1QHab) where it is always parallel to ʿēd ("witness"); cf. Ps 27:12. The root is now often understood to refer to testifying, a sense that is also possible for the verbs in Pss 10:5 and 12:5(6). See, e.g., Dennis Pardee, "YPḤ 'Witness' in Hebrew and Ugaritic," *VT* 28 (1978): 204–13; J. Gerald Janzen, "Habakkuk 2:2–4 in the Light of Recent Philological Advances," *HTR* 73 (1980): 58–78; Andersen, *Habakkuk*, 205–7; Cf. Cathcart, "Law Is Paralysed," 348–49.

i. Alternatively, this could be read as an oath, as argued by James W. Haring, "'He will certainly not hesitate, wait for him!': Evidence for an unrecognized oath in Habakkuk 2,3b, and its implications for interpreting Habakkuk 2,2–4," *ZAW* 126 (2014): 372–82. See the commentary.

j. The verbs *lingers* (*mhh hitpalpel*) and *be late* (ʾḥr *piel*) overlap in meaning. For expressing a paradox, we might expect the same verb to be used twice. The translation assumes that the author either exploits an already existing difference in nuance between the two verbs, with the latter indicating a failure to turn up on time, or asks readers to differentiate them in such a way that the claim makes sense.

Composition

The instruction to the prophet follows straight on from the preceding verse and introduces the following verses. (On the parallels between Hab 2:1–2 and Isa 21:6–8, see the comments on the composition of Hab 2:1.) Andersen argues that vv. 2–5 make up a poem, and he points to several features suggesting that they are verse rather than prose, such as the rhythmic quality of the text, the presence of parallelism, and the rarity of prose markers. He admits, however, that the style is rough.[170] Verses 2–5 certainly do not stand out as poetry in relation to the rest of the chapter. The prosody in vv. 6–20 is also "quite mixed," with both more poetic and more prosaic elements, as acknowledged by Andersen.[171] Verse 4 could easily be attached to this section, and the opening of v. 5 ties it closely with v. 4. It would therefore be defensible to take 2:2–5 as one section, as Andersen does. But in my judgment, the break between vv. 5 and 6 is no greater than the break between

---

170. Andersen, *Habakkuk*, 199–202. His discussion occasionally includes reference to v. 1 as if it were part of the poem, but in fact he considers v. 1 a little poem in its own right.

171. The designation "quite mixed" is from Andersen (*Habakkuk*, 225), who concludes that "the author was aspiring to poetic expression." While he sees vv. 6–20 as an editorial rather than a necessarily original unity and allows for corruptions, he does not attempt to separate an original poetic core from later accretions.

vv. 3 and 4. In any case, it would be unwise to draw exegetical conclusions from adopting one subdivision over another of the possible subdivisions of this text. The whole of ch. 2 belongs together. The subdivisions presented here are meant to help us focus on each of the movements (the prophet's stance, the divine instruction, the revelation, the elaboration of the revelation) without implying that we are dealing with sections that should be read separately from each other.

Commentary

2 Kevin Cathcart observes that the sequence of verbs in vv. 1–2 (*yədabber, he will say*; *'āšîb, I will answer*; *wayya'ănēnî, and he answered me*; *wayyō'mer, and said*) is similar to one found in Job 13:22. The verbs are in and of themselves unremarkable, and I am more reluctant than he is to speak of specifically "forensic language" here.[172] But we likely should hear it as formal, official language, such as language that might be used in a court setting.

As the translation notes indicate, the instruction given to the prophet stresses the importance of the content and its official nature (*document*), not its legibility ("make it plain" in many translations). Some commentators see a reference to *tablets* that were "customarily erected in marketplaces,"[173] appealing to 1 Macc 14:25–49, which, however, does not provide evidence for a widespread practice.[174] But it is interesting to note the legal context of 1 Macc 14:25–49 and the production of duplicates. The use of the plural here in Habakkuk is similarly best explained as a reference to duplicates, ensuring the documentation of the witness. One could also think of the need of multiple copies for wide promulgation of the revelation through several messengers, but the legal symbolism of duplicate copies seems to me a more likely concern of the text than the practicalities of its distribution. It is unwarranted to base a specific allusion to the tablets of the covenant here on the use of the plural form and the definite article. Still, the context and the use of the verb (*document it*) encourage some readers to see an allusion to the tablets of the Torah.[175] I do

---

172. Cathcart, "Law Is Paralysed," 346. On the next page, he observes that Pietro Bovati (*Re-establishing Justice: Legal Terms, Concepts and Procedures in the Hebrew Bible*, trans. Michael J. Smith, JSOTSup 105 [Sheffield: JSOT Press, 1994], 334) includes Hab 2:1 in his examples of the forensic use of *hēšîb* but surprisingly omits *'ānâ* in v. 2 from a similar list.

173. So, e.g., Patterson, *Nahum*, 173, with reference to earlier commentators. The use of the direct article is sometimes thought to support this, but see the translation note.

174. Cf. Andersen, *Habakkuk*, 202–4, who argues at length against this proposal; and more briefly, already Franz Delitzsch, *Habakuk*, 37.

175. E.g., Robertson, *Nahum*, 168–69; Markus Witte, "Orakel und Gebete im Buch Habakkuk," in *Orakel und Gebete: Interdisziplinäre Studien zur Sprache der Religion in Ägypten,*

not object to it, but I do not believe this to be well secured.[176] Whether we are meant to think of metal plates as in 1 Macc 14 or tablets made of clay, stone, or wood cannot be decided. Following Hengstenberg, Keil adopts a figurative understanding for the tablets while retaining the idea of a writing prophet:

> The words simply express the thought, that the prophecy is to be laid to heart by all the people on account of its great importance, and that not merely in the present but in the future also. This no doubt involved the obligation on the part of the prophet to take care, by committing it to writing, that it did not fall into oblivion.[177]

But the context points to a concern with documentation as a witness and transmission because of the expected delay. Written tablets serve both official documentation and transmission over time; without them one would expect specific persons to be mentioned as witnesses and "the tablets of the heart" (memory) as a repository for long-term transmission. Isaiah 30:8 is therefore arguably a more relevant parallel than Keil allows.[178]

One will run has been understood by some commentators metaphorically with reference to living obediently (cf. Ps 119:32; 1 Cor 9:24-27; Phil 3:13-14).[179] Haak reads it as running away in terror and cites Amos 5:19; Isa 2:10, 19-21 for comparison.[180] But none of the parallels he offers employ the verb used here. A general association of the day of the Lord with fleeing in terror is hardly sufficient grounds on which to interpret the running in Hab 2:2 as running away.[181] An older interpretation is that the writing is to be

---

Vorderasien und Griechenland in hellenistischer Zeit, ed. Markus Witte and Johannes F. Diehl, FAT 2/38 (Tübingen: Mohr Siebeck, 2009), 72; cf. the rendering in Tg.: "The prophecy is written and expressed clearly in the book of the law" (ArBib 14, 150; the editors suggest that "MT's reference to tablets not unnaturally suggests an association with the tablets of the law").

176. The verb is elsewhere in the Bible found only in Deut 1:5 and 27:8 (cf. 1Q22 II, 8), both times in connection with the Torah promulgated through Moses but without reference to tablets. Deuteronomy 27:8 speaks of *hā'ăbānîm* ("the stones").

177. Keil, *Minor Prophets*, 2:70, rejecting the parallels Franz Delitzsch (*Habakuk*, 38) offered in support of a literal understanding as not decisive. Patterson (*Nahum*, 173-74) also toys with the idea of understanding the tablets figuratively.

178. Michael H. Floyd ("Prophecy and Writing in Habakkuk 2,1-5," *ZAW* 105 [1993]: 470-71) argues that the texts are not comparable because in Habakkuk the writing happens alongside prophetic activity, while Isaiah's placarded saying is a public symbolic action. I do not think the differences invalidate the comparison.

179. John Marshall Holt ("So He May Run Who Reads It," *JBL* 83 [1964]: 298-302) promoted this understanding.

180. Haak, *Habakkuk*, 56.

181. Haak refers to Robert Bach, *Aufforderungen zur Flucht*, WMANT 9 (Berlin: de Gruyter, 1962), 15-50, but there is no such call to flee anywhere in Habakkuk.

distinct enough so that even a hurried passerby can read it easily (Martin Luther, influencing others).[182] This seems to be a development of the still earlier interpretation that links the running with the reading itself and so finds a comment about readers being able to read the message fluently.[183] But with legal documentation rather than legibility being the issue in this verse, a metaphorical reference to proclamation is more probable. Running was a less widespread activity in the ancient Near East than it is in Western cultures today, and in the Hebrew Bible it is regularly associated with messengers, as, e.g., in 1 Sam 4:12; 2 Sam 18:19; Jer 23:21; 51:31; Zech 2:4(8); cf. the use of the motif in Gal 2:2.[184]

There are two passages in Habakkuk that may be relevant here, namely, the numb ineffectiveness of Torah on the one hand (1:4) and the fruitless effort of the nations' wearying on the other (2:13). The prophetic *revelation* ("vision"), by contrast, energizes those who read it so that they spring into action. Such vigor contrasts with the limpness of Torah in 1:4. It may be tempting to conclude that this *revelation* is more effective than the Torah, but the situation is more complex than that and the vision of course does not replace the Torah. Habakkuk does not directly compare Torah and vision. The *prophet's* depiction of Torah as numbed contrasts with the *divine* portrayal of the *reader* of the vision as running. Still, the new revelation may be the answer to the complaint about Torah's ineffectiveness—perhaps especially so if we look forward to v. 13 of this chapter. The verbs for toiling (yg') and wearying ($y'p$) in Hab 2:13 are contrasted in Isa 40:31 with running.[185] In this light, the running may suggest not only an energized life but a productive

---

182. Luther (*LW* 19:194) speaks of such "large letters that a person could read it on the run." Similarly, Calvin (*Habakkuk, Zephaniah, Haggai*, vol. 4 of *Commentaries on the Twelve Minor Prophets*, trans. John Owen [1848; repr. Grand Rapids: Christian Classics Ethereal Library]): "Write it in large characters, that any one, in running by, may see what is written." Cf. William H. Brownlee, "The Placarded Revelation of Habakkuk," *VT* 82 (1963): 320, but he does not commit himself to a literal understanding of running (contra Haak, *Habakkuk*, 56) and leaves it open whether this or the interpretation by Driver given below is the correct one. See Holt, "So He May Run," 299-300, for further references, although he conflates advocates of this interpretation with those advocating the one below, as does, e.g., Patterson, *Nahum*, 171.

183. This seems to have been the dominant view among interpreters in antiquity and in medieval times. It is succinctly expressed more recently, e.g., by Samuel R. Driver, *Minor Prophets*, 75.

184. Nah 1:15(2:1) // Isa 52:7 allude to the same idea without using the verb "run." In some places, the running of a messenger may be explained by excitement (e.g., Gen 29:12) or urgency (e.g., Josh 7:22). Another occurrence of running in non-military contexts is to welcome someone (see Gen 18:2; 24:17; 29:13; 33:4; 1 Sam 17:48; 2 Kgs 4:26). Similarly, Floyd, "Habakkuk 2,1-5," 473.

185. Sirach 11:11, however, pairs yg' ("toil") and $'ml$ ("labor") with $rûṣ$ ("run"): "Some

one. The one who reads the vision is able to keep going, running up to *the end* to which the vision bears witness.

Drawing these perspectives together, we can exclude the possibility that the running is a running away in terror. The energy evident in running is likely positive. If the running is a reference to something more than a promise that the readers of the *revelation* will "keep going," which for readers who trust the "vision" would certainly imply continuing to run in God's commandments, the reference is likely to the running of those who have been given a message to pass on. The careful documentation of the *revelation* in the first half of the verse would then be supplemented by the expectation that its message would be promulgated widely.

But what is the *revelation*? What is the content of the *tablets*? The proposals range all the way from nothing that we now find written in the book of Habakkuk[186] to the whole book of Habakkuk.[187] More often, the proposal is made that it is v. 4, vv. 4–5, most of ch. 2, or ch. 3.[188] Krüger argues for 1:5–11.[189] Locating the *revelation* in ch. 3 is popular in the light of the theophany in 3:8–15.[190] But ch. 3 is at some distance from 2:2 and clearly set apart with a heading that designates it as a prayer (v. 1) rather than a *revelation*. Within the flow of the book, ch. 3 is more likely to present Habakkuk's answer to the revelation than the revelation itself. Floyd points out that while 3:8–15 are

> obviously visionary in the sense that it is the product of a vivid imagination . . . there is no vision report formula nor any other indication that it originated from visionary experience in the strict sense. On the contrary,

---

people toil, labor, and run and come up short" (the idea of coming up short being expressed with the lemma *'ḥr*, which we encounter in Hab 2:3 as "be late").

186. So Kimchi, who contrasts what is written in the book for all generations with what is written on the tablets specifically for Habakkuk's generation (Rosenberg, *Twelve Prophets*, 264). Luther also distinguishes between the revelation and what is written on the tablets, but he finds the latter in v. 4, which he reads as a commentary on the vision. The vision itself is "not the one Habakkuk beheld, but the vision of all prophets who foretold of the Christ" (*LW* 19:193; cf. *LW* 19:121).

187. Junker, *Zwölf*, 47.

188. Jöcken (*Habakkuk*, 520) lists the various proposals on offer among nineteenth and early twentieth century commentators. As far as I am aware, more recent interpreters have neither increased the options nor offered more decisive arguments in favor of one of them.

189. Krüger, "Prophetie." He objects to the view that 2:4–5 or 2:4–20 constitute the *revelation* on the grounds that one would expect the relevant actors to be named in the document. Karl Budde thought 1:5–11 along with 2:2–3 to be the *revelation* (Jöcken, *Habakkuk*, 520).

190. This is the view, among others, of Elliger, *Die Propheten*, 40, who nevertheless describes 2:4 as the quintessence of the "vision"; Roberts, *Nahum*, 116, 128; Bruce, "Habakkuk," 859.

YHWH's mighty works are explicitly said to be things about which the prophet has "heard" (*šm'*, 3,2.16).[191]

It is clear that the term *revelation* must not be pressed to refer to material that appeals to the eye rather than the ear.[192] Hebrew *ḥāzôn* can refer to revelation in a broader sense, and in the final edition of the book, at any rate, this *revelation* must be found in ch. 2. Chapter 1 has given us Habakkuk's challenge to YHWH. In 2:1, the prophet puts himself in position to receive a reply. The continuation of the narrative in vv. 2–3 gives us the divine answer that centers on a vision or *revelation* whose content must be sought in what follows. With its new heading, ch. 3 brings us the prophet's response to God's answer. How much of 2:4–20 constitutes the actual vision is difficult to decide and may not matter too much, as we need not assume that the revelation was proclaimed on its own, without further explanation. If 2:4–5 constitute the *revelation* that presents a general truth, then 2:6–20 would be the exposition and application to the present situation.

3 This verse offers the reason for the confidence that those who read the *revelation* can run with it. There is an *appointed time* at which the truth of the *revelation* will be vindicated. The subject of the following lines is debated. It seems best in the first instance to assume that the *revelation* introduced in the first line is the subject of the third-person verbs that follow and the antecedent of the pronominal suffix in the phrase *for it*. This is also the common rendering in English translations. Alternatively, one could think of *the appointed time* as the subject. The overall sense would remain the same.[193] Earlier commentators have sometimes interpreted the breathing out in the second line as "panting," which was then understood to refer to the vision being breathless in its fast movement toward its fulfillment. This is reflected in NEB ("It will come in breathless haste") and NASB ("It hastens toward the goal"). Andersen is probably right when he says that this is "too fanciful to be taken seriously."[194] It seems clear that the breathing out in question refers to speaking, as in most English translations, and most likely specifically to testifying. As indicated in the translation note above, the word may

---

191. Floyd, "Habakkuk 2,1–5," 472.

192. Cf. the commentary on Nah 1:1.

193. In Greek, the "vision" is feminine but the pronominal suffix is masculine (or neuter) and the coming one is masculine, usually understood in reception history as a reference to the Messiah or, more recently, to God. See BA 23.4–9, 274, where the authors express a preference for relating it to *kairos*, the Greek equivalent of *appointed time*. This is also the view taken by Albert Pietersma and Benjamin G. Wright in NETS, 808.

194. Andersen, *Habakkuk*, 206. See already Franz Delitzsch's strong refutation of the panting interpretation in *Habakuk*, 40–41. Delitzsch may have been the first commentator to note the significance of the parallels in Proverbs.

be interpreted as a verb or an adjective functioning as a noun; in the light of the Ugaritic evidence, the latter is my preference.

The *revelation . . . is a testifier* not to present times but *to the end*. In other words, the truth of the vision will not be immediately evident. But if the truth claim of the vision looks implausible now, there is nevertheless an *appointed time* at which such a reversal of the current situation will take place that the time can be designated *the end*—namely, the end of the current state of affairs. This is the end of the imperialism and oppression and lawlessness of which Habakkuk complained in ch. 1. In a sense, the opening question *How long?* has found an answer, but not by way of an actual time frame. There is no indication of how far or near the appointed time for the end is. (We need not assume that a developed concept of "the end-times" lies behind the use of *the end*.) But it is clear that in the meantime the reliability of this witness will not be obvious; to stress the truthfulness of the testifier, *it does not lie* is added. This is to say that the *revelation* will not fail and thus prove false but will come about and thus be shown to be true.

Two verbs indicate a delay in the coming of the (that is, the fulfillment of the) *revelation* (see the translation note). No evidence allows us to sharply differentiate between these two verbs, but readers throughout history were able to make sense of the statements along the following lines: "On the one hand there is a tarrying, a waiting; on the other hand, this tarrying is not of a sort that constitutes a reluctance to come, a failure to keep rendezvous, a breach of promise."[195] I express this by saying that the vision *lingers* but *it will not be late*. The delay will raise the question whether what is promised in the new *revelation* will ever happen. This calls for patient waiting, *for it will surely come*. Andersen objects to the idea of the vision coming since it has already been given. Because he also believes it more appropriate for a person to be the witness who is said not to lie, he argues that the referent is not in fact the vision but God himself.[196] God is indeed sometimes asked not to delay (*'al-tə'aḥar*, Pss 40:17[18]; 70:5[6]; Dan 9:19), but salvation can also be said not to delay (*lō' tə'aḥēr*, Isa 46:13). These instances are all using the second verb for delaying in Hab 2:3. Employing the first verb used in Hab 2:3, Sir 14:12 says that death will not delay (*wĕl'ō māwet yitmahmāh*).[197] It is therefore clear that these verbs can be used with impersonal subjects. Grammatically, the subject could also be the *appointed time / end*, which

---

195. J. Gerald Janzen, "Habakkuk 2:2-4," 72. Haak (*Habakkuk*, 57) interprets *'im* as "an emphatic negative" (cf. BDB 50a) and translates, "He tarries?!" which he paraphrases as "He tarries? You've got to be kidding! He surely comes!"

196. Andersen, *Habakkuk*, 206-7.

197. Manuscript A, page VI recto; see Pancratius C. Beentjes, *The Book of Ben Sira in Hebrew: A Text Edition of All Extant Hebrew Manuscripts and a Synopsis of All Parallel Hebrew Ben Sira Texts*, VTSup 68 (Leiden: Brill, 2003), 46.

would amount to the same thing.[198] It is, of course, not the knowledge of the *revelation* that is coming at the appointed time—the *revelation* is about to be made known—but its fulfillment. This was understood by readers throughout reception history. By way of example, we may quote the dynamic-equivalent, interpretative rendering in the Tg.: "For the prophecy is ready for a time and the end is fixed, nor shall it fail; if there is delay in the matter wait for it, for it shall come in its time and shall not be deferred."[199] As it is only in the fulfillment that the *revelation* is truly established—in the coming true of the referent of the *revelation*—it can fairly be said that the *revelation* has only really arrived when the appointed time to which it testifies has arrived.

While it seems to be perfectly possible to read the whole of v. 3 as speaking of the *revelation*, a number of commentators nevertheless prefer a change of subject to YHWH in the second half of the verse.[200] The coming of God in 3:3 is often adduced as an argument.[201] But the fact that there is nothing to indicate a change in subject presents a serious hindrance to introducing YHWH (or the messiah) as the subject in a primary reading of the text. This is true even if further theological reflection may suggest that the coming of the *revelation* will be accomplished by the coming of God (on which see further below in the reflection). Janzen identifies "If he tarries, wait for him; he will surely come, he will not delay!" as the content of the vision.[202] But one might expect this bicolon to be marked out more clearly to function as "the vision." The opening word of v. 4, by contrast, is well suited to mark the beginning of the vision.

Alternatively, James W. Haring identifies the herald (the one who reads the vision and runs) as the one who testifies "at the end" and whose reliability (faithfulness) enables the righteous to live. He offers good but not decisive arguments for interpreting the beginning of 2:3b as an oath (with the apodosis left unexpressed, as is not uncommon in Classical Hebrew): "He

---

198. Cf. J. Gerald Janzen, "Habakkuk 2:2–4," 72–73; cf. "Eschatological Symbol," 404. Janzen presses *mô'ēd* (*appointed time*) too hard in the direction of "rendezvous," from which he concludes two persons must be involved, the reader and God.

199. ArBib 14, 150. Tg. continues very freely into v. 4: "Behold, the wicked think that all these things are not so, but the righteous shall live by the truth of them" (150–51).

200. As hinted above, Andersen switches to a personal subject even earlier, translating, "And he is a witness to the end . . ." on the basis that the witness is a person in other occurrences of the term (*Habakkuk*, 198, 206–7). Others have rightly not seen any problem with speaking of the "vision" as a testifier. He is wrong to conclude from the Greek rendering with a masculine that the translators must have thought of a person (208); see above, where it is pointed out that the pronoun may refer to *kairos*.

201. E.g., J. Gerald Janzen, "Eschatological Symbol," 404.

202. J. Gerald Janzen, "Eschatological Symbol," 404.

will certainly not hesitate."[203] Haring compares this figure to the messenger announced in Malachi as precursor of YHWH's coming and the herald in Isa 40:1–8 (a heavenly messenger in the interpretation of Frank Cross, who is followed by Haring). If we take the wider context of Habakkuk into consideration, this interpretation of 2:2–4 is less plausible. First, the question of when God will finally intervene (i.e., the issue of delay) marks the beginning and the end of Habakkuk's complaint (1:2, 17). The more traditional translation of 2:3 is therefore more fitting for the book than Haring allows. Second, the prophet who is the one who documents the revelation here in ch. 2 is also, in my reading, the one who responds to this revelation in ch. 3. It is not clear how another figure legally testifying to the revelation "at the end" fits into this picture. The situation in Malachi and Isaiah 40 seems quite different.

Reflection

In ch. 1, the prophet took issue with God's word. An earlier prophecy, related in 1:5–11, albeit probably in a new, polemically recast form, had proven all too true with its description of Babylonian aggression. But it raised serious questions about God's purposes and the morality of using the Neo-Babylonian Empire as an instrument for establishing law and order. In the meantime, and likely in part as a consequence of Babylonian aggression, Torah was proving unable to order the life of God's people. The effect of (the coming true of) the prophecy appeared to be to render God's basic word, the Torah, ineffective. Habakkuk nevertheless expects that God's answer will not come in a new deed only but in another word that will reprimand him (2:1). And, indeed, YHWH's reply comes first of all in words—words that point beyond themselves to a vision that the prophet is to document carefully.

Just as the earlier prophecy (1:5–11) led to activity, so will this revelation. The earlier prophecy prompted a new deed that used the Babylonians as its active ingredient, who likely never heard the prophecy. But the new revelation will energize those who read it (cf. Isa 40:31), maybe not least in the direction of promulgating the vision further, as it is often messengers who do the running. The revelation itself, by contrast, will be moving rather more slowly and so may give the appearance of being another numb Scripture. But

---

203. Haring, "Evidence"; see the translation notes. Haring's discussion of *bā'ēr* builds on work that has been critiqued by Eckart Otto, "Mose, der erste Schriftgelehrte: Deuteronomium 1,5 in der Fabel des Pentateuch," in *L'Ecrit et l'Esprit: Etudes d'histoire du texte et de théologie biblique en hommage à Adrian Schenker*, ed. Dieter Böhler, Innocent Himbaza, and Philippe Hugo, OBO 214 (Göttingen: Vandenhoeck & Ruprecht; Fribourg: Presses Universitaires, 2005), 273–84.

God underlines that the vision's testimony is reliable and that it will certainly come to pass; "it will not miss its appointment."[204]

Up to this point in the book, readers have not yet heard the revelation, but they may have certain expectations. The earlier prophecy, while announcing a deed of YHWH, arguably brought the coming of the Babylonians, not the coming of YHWH. In fact, Habakkuk's complaint centers on the inactivity of God in the face of evil. If the earlier prophecy set off Babylonian action and this fresh revelation springs its readers into action, then the fulfillment of the revelation hopefully will make those who put their trust in the revelation see some divine action. The coming of the vision (i.e., its fulfillment in all its glory) must therefore imply a coming of God. This will not in fact be the content of the vision. While the distinction between God's passivity and his active intervention reflects human experience, it is not a distinction God himself affirms in the book of Habakkuk. God does not directly promise his *future* coming, which would concede that he had been absent and inactive in the recent past and present. Such a concession is not found in divine speech in Habakkuk. YHWH stands by the claim made in the earlier prophecy that the Babylonian aggression is his work. In this sense, the expansion of the Neo-Babylonian Empire has been a coming of YHWH, but it is a coming that will lead to a countermovement in which the true character of YHWH may be better revealed. We may compare talk about YHWH's "strange work" in Isa 28:21 to designate a deed that, in some ways at least, is uncharacteristic. The hope is for the revelation of a new deed of YHWH that sees him act more in character, so to speak.

Looking beyond the book of Habakkuk, the canon of Scripture has led numerous readers to expect one great coming of God at the end of history.[205] Many such readers expected this decisive intervention to come soon in their own time and saw themselves confronted with the problem of the delay of God's coming. For some of them, Hab 2:3 offered a way to reflect and come to terms with this delay, as Strobel demonstrated in a comprehensive study.[206] In effect, the verse was understood as fundamentally true not only in relation to the specific revelation communicated in Habakkuk but also in relation to the overall vision of an eschatological future offered by the broader canon of Scripture. But if this is so, then the statements in the second half of the verse can indeed be applied secondarily to God or Christ: "If he lingers, wait for

---

204. This is Bruce's rendering ("Habakkuk," 858).

205. This is true both for some non-Christian readers, whose biblical canon only includes the Hebrew Scriptures, and for Christian readers, both Jewish and non-Jewish, whose canon includes the New Testament.

206. August Strobel, *Untersuchungen zum eschatologischen Verzögerungsproblem: Auf Grund der spätjüdisch-urchristlichen Geschichte von Habakuk 2,2ff*, NovTSup 2 (Leiden: Brill, 1961).

him, for he will surely come, he will not be late."[207] Such a move was facilitated by the switch of pronouns in the Greek text of Hab 2:3, which, e.g., the
author of Hebrews exploited in 10:37–38, conflating Isa 26:20 (*mikron hoson
hoson*, "a very little while") and Hab 2:3–4.[208] The addition of the definite
article (*ho erchomenos*, "the coming one"; cf. Matt. 11:3 // Luke 7:19–20; Rev
1:4, 8; 4:8) unambiguously marks the subject as a person. In the context of
the letter to the Hebrews, this person is clearly Christ. Many interpreters
believe that "the Septuagint interpretation of this passage is essentially messianic" and that the author of Hebrews "is but dotting the i's and crossing
the t's" when he makes the identity of the expected deliverer clearer.[209] Dependence on the Greek text is even more evident in the citation of Hab 2:4.[210]
Whereas the Hebrew text marks a contrast between two people or groups
of people, the author of Hebrews uses the verse to outline two options open
to the addressees: to shrink back[211] or to continue forward in faith. What is
clear and relevant for our discussion of Hab 2:3 (for Hab 2:4, see below) is
the close correlation between faith and hope, and maybe even specifically
the expectation of the end being near, without which there would be no
concern about a delay.[212] The right posture toward God is firm hope in his
future coming. The characterization of the righteous as those who faithfully
endure and wait for an end is common to both Habakkuk and the early Christians. In Habakkuk, the end is first of all the end of Babylonian injustice and
oppression; in Hebrews, the end of all injustice and oppression will come
with the second coming of Christ. "The promised coming of the Lord with
earth-shaking judgment on the Chaldeans has become a foreshadowing of
Christ's return and the final Judgment."[213]

207. Cf. the Jewish creed Ani Ma'amim, based on Maimonides's *Thirteen Articles of Faith*,
which opens, "I believe with a complete faith in the coming of the Messiah. Though he may
tarry, I will wait for him—every day—for his coming."

208. See George H. Guthrie, "Hebrews," in *Commentary on the New Testament Use of the
Old Testament*, ed. Gregory K. Beale and Donald A. Carson (Grand Rapids: Baker Academic;
Nottingham: Apollos, 2007), 981–84, for a fuller discussion.

209. F. F. Bruce, *The Epistle to the Hebrews*, rev. ed., NICNT (Grand Rapids, Eerdmans,
1990), 273. Gary L. Cockerill (*The Epistle to the Hebrews*, NICNT [Grand Rapids, Eerdmans,
2012], 507) is rightly more cautious; he still thinks the masculine pronoun must refer to a
person (God), even though he realises that *kairos* (appointed time) is masculine.

210. See also Gheorghita, *The Role of the Septuagint in Hebrews*, 175–79, 218–24.

211. It is rather less clear what the translators of the LXX had in mind. The text from
which they worked likely had *'lph* rather than the sequence of consonants attested in the
MT (*'plh*), possibly a copying mistake that the translators did not spot because *'plh* is so rare
that it seems to have presented other ancient translators with problems (see *BHQ*, 118*). See
further below on the text of 2:4.

212. Cf. Strobel, *Untersuchungen*, 301–5.

213. Cockerill, *Hebrews*, 508, although a more exact parallel may be between coming

It would be wide of the mark to consider this posture of waiting mere passivity. The need for patient waiting is presented in both Habakkuk and Hebrews not as an alternative to a faith that is active in works of justice and mercy but as an alternative to giving up in the face of persecution.

VII. THE REVELATION (2:4-5)

[4]*Look, swollen, not judicious is his appetite within him,*[a]
   but the righteous: in his[b] *faithfulness he will live.*
[5]*And furthermore,*[c] *the wine*[d] *deals treacherously;*
   a proud man[e] *will not abide.*[f]
One who like Sheol enlarges his appetite.[g]
   Indeed, he is like the death and is not sated.
He gathers to himself all the nations
   and collects to himself all the peoples.

a. There are many proposals for reading this difficult text with and without emendations. Apart from the major commentaries and Haak, *Habakkuk*, see John A. Emerton, "The Textual and Linguistic Problems of Habakkuk II. 4–5," *JTS* 28 (1977): 1–18, for a valuable overview of some earlier studies; and subsequently, e.g., J. Gerald Janzen, "Habakkuk 2.2–4"; James M. Scott, "A New Approach to Habakkuk II 4–5A," *VT* 35 (1985): 330–40; Klaus Seybold, "Habakuk 2,4b und sein Kontext," in *Zur Aktualität des Alten Testaments: Festschrift für Georg Sauer zum 65. Geburtstag*, ed. Siegfried Kreuzer and Kurt Küthi (Frankfurt: Peter Lang, 1992), 99–107, repr. in Seybold, *Studien zur Psalmenauslegung* (Stuttgart: Kohlhammer, 1998), 189–98; Aron Pinker, "Habakkuk 2.4: An Ethical Paradigm or a Political Observation?" *JSOT* 32 (2007): 91–112. See the commentary.

b. It is also possible to read "its faithfulness," with reference to the *revelation*, although it is more likely that the pronoun refers to the immediately preceding ṣaddîq (*the righteous*) than the more distant ḥāzôn (*revelation*) of v. 3. But see, e.g., J. Gerald Janzen, "Habakkuk 2:2–4"; Roberts, *Nahum*, 107; and, more cautiously, Haak, *Habakkuk*, 59. It is rare for 'ĕmûnâ (faithfulness) to be predicated of anything other than a person. The only biblical exceptions are Exod 17:12 ("hands") and Ps 119:86 ("commandments"). In Proverbs, the faithful testifier is always a person. The LXX reflects a first-person suffix, presumably an objective genitive ("faith in me" = "faithfulness with regard to me").

c. The compound particle 'ap kî, with or without preceding waw, occurs twenty-six times in the Hebrew Bible (in prophecy elsewhere only in Ezek 14:21; 15:5; 23:40), usually in the sense "how much more" or, with preceding negation, "how much less." Genesis 3:1 appears to be the only instance where 'ap kî does not link with the preceding; likely, it is the one instance in which 'ap and kî function not as a compound but separately, in an abbreviated form of "is it also ('ap) true that (kî) . . . ?" Fabry (*Habakuk/Obadja*, 253, but

judgment on the Babylonians (with vindication of the righteous) and the final judgment (with vindication of the righteous) rather than God's coming and Christ's coming, as discussed above.

note 261) suggests that MT makes no sense because it must be translated "and how much less does the wine deceive" (following the negation in 2:4a) or "how much more does the wine deceive" (connecting with 2:4b). But his own rendering (following emendation of the text) is, "And how much more: woe to the one who is faithless," which seems to allow for a similar understanding of the syntax to the one I adopt, reading *'ap kî* against standard usage as a separate introduction or heading for what follows rather than linking it with the verb.

d. 1QpHab has the orthographically similar *hwn* ("wealth") for *hyyn* ("wine"). Following M. T. Houtsma (1885), Patterson (*Nahum*, 180–81) reads *hwn* or *hyn* in the sense of "presumption," arguing that this best explains the other readings; cf. Gelston in *BHQ*, 13:118*–19*. Haak (*Habakkuk*, 60–61) suggests reading *hywn ybgd* ("as the mire he deals treacherously") for *hyyn bwgd*. Cf. William H. Brownlee, *The Text of Habakkuk in the Ancient Commentary from Qumran*, JBL Manuscript Series 11 (Philadelphia: Society of Biblical Literature, 1959), 45–49; Andersen, *Habakkuk*, 216–18. Wellhausen (*Skizzen*, 5:164) speculated that the "woe oracles" begin in v. 5, reading *hayyayin* ("wine") as *hôy* (*Oy*, "woe"); cf. Dietrich, *Nahum*, 141–42; Fabry, *Habakuk/Obadja*, 253–54.

e. Interpreted in line with the masoretic accentuation, *geber yāhîr* ("a proud man") stands outside the sentence to which it belongs. This cannot easily be reproduced in English because the more literal "a proud man—he will not abide" would suggest a personification of the wine, which is probably not implied in the Hebrew. The implied subject of the verb anticipates the next line. See below for fuller discussion of the syntax.

f. The *hiphil* of a verb with the same root letters appears in Exod 15:2 but seems to be unrelated to the verb used here. A related noun that designates a grazing place or a settlement suggests a meaning for the verb parallel to "live" in v. 4. *HALOT* suggests "to reach a result" (cf. LXX) but is also open to emendations.

g. Or "opens his throat" (cf. Isa 5:14). The decision in favor of translating *appetite* is made in conjunction with decisions about the translation of v. 4. *Napšô* should probably be translated in the same way in both verses, either as "his throat" or *his appetite*.

Composition

We observed above that the whole of Hab 2 belongs together; v. 4 could easily be attached to the preceding section, and v. 6 closely follows v. 5. It is nevertheless useful to look at these two verses together as a miniature section. In my view, the opening *hinnê* (*look*) signals the beginning of the *revelation* ("vision"). Verse 6 introduces the speech of the nations that had become victims of Babylonian expansion; it looks forward to what will be said once the revealed prophecy is being fulfilled. This gives vv. 6ff. the character of an elaboration of the consequences of the revelation. Probably, vv. 4–5 are meant to be read as the actual vision that is to be documented. The Aleppo Codex, unlike the Leningrad Codex that forms the basis of most modern editions of the MT, marks the end of a paragraph after v. 4. This perhaps marks v. 4 alone as the vision or, given that the opening words of v. 5 link this verse clearly with the preceding, it aims to give greater emphasis specifically to v. 4. The latter may reflect the importance of v. 4 in the history of interpretation as the most succinct summary of the 613 commandments given to Moses: "Habakkuk further came and based them on one, as it is said, 'But the righteous shall live by his faith' " (b. Makkot 24a).[214]

The text of the first half of v. 4 is difficult, and some have argued that the MT must be corrupt. It is possible that an earlier text of the vision referred not only to the righteous in 2:4b and the Babylonian aggressor in 2:5 but also to YHWH, the cause behind the Babylonian oppression according to the prophecy cited in 1:5-11. This assumes that the text transmitted by the Masoretes is the result of accidental changes to the text in the form of wrong word divisions and a reversal of two letters in the second word.[215] If so, an earlier version of the text may have asked: "Consider the doer: Is not his desire in him right?"—a reference back to 1:5-6.[216] If so, the earlier form of the text has been lost in the mists of time. The LXX offers a significantly different text: "If he/it should draw back, my soul has no pleasure in him/it" (with variations surrounding the positioning of the personal pronoun *mou*), which in 8ḤevXIIgr has been corrected in the direction of the proto-MT. Lacking an equivalent for the opening *hinnê* (restored in 8ḤevXIIgr and Aquila), v. 4 follows more directly from v. 3 in the LXX.[217] The Targum similarly offers two contrasting responses to the prophecy: "Behold, the wicked think that all these things are not so, but the righteous shall live by the truth of them."[218] This likely reflects not a different source text but an attempt to make sense of an obscure text. Among modern commentators, Fabry sees a contrasting response to the vision portrayed here. He assumes a casus pendens construction and renders v. 4a, "If she is heedless, she is not upright, his soul in him" ("she" = his soul in him).[219] Whether or not the Masoretes transmitted to us

---

214. Neusner, *Babylonian Talmud*, 17a:122.

215. The reconstructed text is *hn hpʿl hlʾ* for the consonants *hnh ʿplh lʾ* in the MT. Alternatively, the MT could have come into being through haplography (and the above-mentioned reversal of letters) from *hnh hpʿlh hlʾ*. The changes are all minor, but the fact that three are required advises caution.

216. For fuller discussion, see Renz, "An Emendation of Hab 2:4a in the light of Hab 1:5," *JHebS* 13 (2013): art. 11, doi:10.5508/jhs.2013.v13.a11.

217. For details, see BA 23.4-9, 275-76; Andersen, *Habakkuk*, 210-12; and Fabry, *Septuaginta Deutsch*, 2:2416-17, 2421.

218. ArBib 14, 150-51. As in the MT, the reference of the suffix in the second part of the verse is not unambiguous. The editors note that T. W. Manson translated the latter part of the verse as "shall be established on their uprightness (truth)" but argue in favor of the translation adopted above.

219. Fabry, *Habakuk/Obadja*, 243, with reference to an Arabic root for "heedless" (Germ. "unachtsam"); cf. Ges¹⁸. *HALOT* renders the Arabic root "to be foolish, impudent." Neither dictionary adopts this for Hab 2:4.

the text in the form in which its first author intended it, the MT has proven a canonical and fruitful version of Hab 2:4 that is worth commenting upon.[220]

The composition of v. 5 is not unambiguous and will be discussed in more detail below.[221] It is clear that the verse ends with a bicolon that climactically and in effect identifies the referent of the metaphorical statements in the preceding lines and prepares for v. 6. Translation note d above hinted that some commentators separate v. 5 from v. 4 and with an emendation make v. 5 the beginning of the *Oy* sayings. Given that v. 6a presents vv. 6b–8 and the following sayings as the speech of the oppressed nations, this would make for an odd relationship between the first (vv. 5–6a) and the subsequent *Oy* sayings, unless one assumes that some of the original text went missing.

Commentary

4 The MT gives us a picture of two very different persons. The first is characterized by *appetite*. The line simply focuses on the nature of the appetite: it is *swollen* without constraint, a desire that does *not* know the limits set by *judicious* moderation. This picture of swollen appetite suggests that the first person will come to grief, a fate that the next verse spells out. It is possible to translate this half-verse more concretely: "Look, swollen, not smooth, is his throat in him."[222] Read thus, the line echoes the swallowing motif in 1:13 and links more specifically with the theme of not getting sated in the following verse.[223] Little hangs on our decision whether to translate the word as "appetite" or "throat," especially if we are able to hear both. I prefer the former because a swollen throat is not the result of overeating, and a smooth or straight throat is perhaps not readily understood as an image for moderation and good health. Also, the qualification *yāšrâ* (*judicious* here) seems to go more easily with the notion of desire or *appetite*, contrasting presumptuous desire with desire that is kept in check.

Janzen strongly objected to traditional renderings of *yāšrâ* (vocalized as

220. See Renz, "An Emendation," for an interpretation based on my reconstruction of a possible earlier text.

221. There is more textual variety in the ancient versions than indicated in the translation note. The Peshitta omits the beginning of the verse; for the LXX, see especially BA 23.4–9, 276–77.

222. Cf. Haak, *Habakkuk*, 57–59.

223. Andersen (*Habakkuk*, 208) interprets "throat" with reference to (crooked) speech because he thinks that the verse contrasts two responses to the "vision," with the "vision" itself being found in ch. 3. This identification of the revelation seems to me unlikely and may be the result of too specific and narrow expectations of the contents of a *ḥāzôn* (*revelation* or "vision").

a verb, as in the MT), which are close to the meaning of the related adjective (*yāšār*, "right, straight, righteous").[224] He claims that "verbal forms *in every other instance* have to do, literally or figuratively, with locomotion along a path, or making straight such a path."[225] In fact, only fifteen other occurrences of the *qal* are attested, three of which are outside the Hebrew Bible.[226] Of the biblical occurrences outside Habakkuk, all but one are with the phrase "in the eyes of," a phrase that refers to a positive value judgment; it is not at all clear that locomotion is implied in any of these cases.[227] This leaves 1 Sam 6:12, which speaks of young bulls going straight on the road to Beth-Shemesh, as the basis for Janzen's demand for distancing the verb in the *qal* from the related nominal and adjectival forms. Of the three extrabiblical occurrences, only one suggests locomotion, namely 11QShirShab, which in col. VII refers to the celestial chariotry not turning but going straight.[228] In sum, while the verb in the *qal* can refer to locomotion, the standard dictionaries are correct in offering the gloss "be straight, be upright, be level, be right" alongside "go straight ahead," seeing that frequently no locomotion is implied. As with the adjective, the reference to something being even, level, straight, and right need not imply a moral judgment, although it can do so. Here, disapproval is surely implied in the judgment that *swollen, not judicious is his appetite within him.* The verse may echo the only other biblical occurrence of the verb *ʿpl* (here *ʿuppǝlâ*, swollen), which is in Num 14:44, also in a context of disapproval (*wayyaʿpilû laʿălôt*, "they presumed to go up"). An immoderate, enlarged appetite is a presumptuous desire because it ignores boundaries. It is an appetite that is not moderated by recognition of the need to balance it with the needs and desires of others.

The implied contrast suggests that the righteous person is marked by restraint, someone prepared to delay gratification. Boundless greed finds its opposite in patient trust; a life governed by appetite contrasts with a life of integrity. It is noteworthy that Prov 28:20 contrasts "a man of faithfulness [pl., complete faithfulness?]" with someone who is in a hurry to get rich. The *faithfulness* of the *righteous* is loyalty to YHWH and trust in his providential

224. The feminine form required here, *yǝšārâ*, differs from the MT only in its vocalization.

225. J. Gerald Janzen, "Habakkuk 2:2–4," 63; cf. Pinker, "Habakkuk 2.4," 101 n. 39.

226. Sir 39:24; 4QJub[d] 21:15; 11QShirShabb 3:6 are listed in *DCH* 3:339.

227. J. Gerald Janzen claims an implicit reference to a "way" or "path" that is straight, but the noun most commonly used is *dābār* ("word, matter"). There is not a single instance of a (metaphorical) path or way being straight in someone's eyes.

228. Sirach 39:24 claims that to the faithful, God's ways are straight. While it is implied that the faithful will walk on God's ways, the reference itself is not to locomotion or to a path being made straight but to the contrast between smooth ways and ways that are full of pitfalls. 4QJub[d] speaks of Abraham asking Isaac to carry out God's commandment so that he will be "upright" in all his deeds.

care. This also implies trust in the reliability of God's revelation. Much of the debate about the precise reference of the pronoun attached to *faithfulness* ("his" or "its") is therefore of little consequence for describing the dynamics involved; one implies the other: The loyalty of the righteous rests on the dependability of YHWH, which finds expression in the reliability of the revelation. The righteous will live because they faithfully cling to the reliability of the revelation given by a faithful God.[229]

Likewise, the contrast between (a) the "righteous by faithfulness" shall live and (b) the righteous shall "live by faithfulness" may be smaller conceptually than syntactically. The revelation is not given in answer to the question how someone becomes righteous but in answer to the question how the righteous can live in the face of brutal assault. The expression "by faithfulness," therefore, surely goes with "live" as the Masoretes correctly accentuate the verse. But there is little doubt that any who abandon faithfulness would no longer be considered "righteous" in accordance with this prophecy. And it would be no overstatement, certainly not in the crisis that Habakkuk addresses, to say that the righteous are characterized precisely by this faithfulness to the covenant God, even if this is not the precise statement being made in this verse.

The question at hand is arguably one of basic commitment, and this may justify the translation "faith" for *faithfulness*. In fact, in the original entry on "Faith" for James Hastings's *A Dictionary of the Bible*,[230] Benjamin B. Warfield argued that Hab 2:4 is the only place where the translation "faith" for 'ĕmûnâ is demanded:

> For throughout this prophecy the Chaldean is ever exhibited as the type of insolent self-assertion (i. 7, 11, 16), in contrast with which the righteous appear, certainly not as men of integrity and steadfast faithfulness, but as men who look in faith to God and trustingly depend upon His arm.[231]

But do we need to assume a somewhat unique use of the term here? On the one hand, 'ĕmûnâ, as applied to the character and conduct of persons, including God, elsewhere carries the notion of "honesty, integrity, dependability, steadfastness"—trustworthiness more than trustfulness. On the other hand, Warfield is right to observe that trusting faith in God forms a more apt

229. But see the translation note for some reasons why I think it is not likely that the text specifically refers to the revelation's reliability as life-giving.

230. Vol. 1 (Edinburgh: T&T Clark, 1898), 827–38. The essay has been reprinted numerous times and is cited here from Benjamin B. Warfield, *Biblical Doctrines*, vol. 2 of *The Works of Benjamin B. Warfield* (Grand Rapids: Baker Book House, 1981; orig. New York: Oxford University Press, 1929), 467–508.

231. Warfield, *Biblical Doctrines*, 470.

contrast to arrogant self-sufficiency than integrity understood as a general virtue. Habakkuk 2:4 certainly focuses on steadfastness in keeping loyalty with God rather than on honesty and dependability in social dealings.[232] But to be precise, it seems to be *faithfulness* in continuing to trust God and his word more than this basic attitude of "faith" itself that is specifically in view. As important as the contrast between the self-sufficient arrogance of the Babylonians and the trustfulness of the righteous is the contrast between abandoning one's trust in God and remaining faithful to him. The revelation promises that the innocent victims of aggression who remain loyal to God will live while the swollen appetite of the oppressors will be their downfall. The promise does not so much call the arrogant to repent and adopt faith in God as urge those who put their trust in God to continue to do so. In other words, it calls for *faithfulness*. It does not directly address the temptation to imitate Babylonian greed and arrogance but the temptation to give up trust in God in the face of the earlier prophecy's disastrous outcome in the Babylonian devastations and Torah's inability to tackle injustice. Clearly, faith and *faithfulness* are here intricately related: it is impossible to remain faithful to YHWH without having faith in him and his revelation; it is impossible to have faith in YHWH and not remain faithful to him. One need not draw too sharp a distinction between the two.[233]

5 More is now said about the downfall of the greedy. It is possible, maybe even probable, that the text originally referred to "presumption" dealing treacherously.[234] This would be a true statement in this context, as is the statement that "wealth is treacherous" (1QpHab), certainly if acquired in the way in which the Babylonians acquired it (cf. Prov 13:11 and 28:8). Bruce, who follows the lead of 1QpHab in opting for "wealth," is certainly right in observing that greed is denounced here, not strong drink.[235] But if greed

232. Cf. Franz Delitzsch (*Habakuk*, 50–54) who argues at length that the understanding of faith here is no different from that in the New Testament because it is not the reliability and integrity of the righteous *per se* that is in view here but their steadfastness in waiting (v. 3) for the prophecy's fulfillment.

233. Cf. Achtemeier, *Nahum*, 46 ("faithfulness here means trust . . . clinging to God"); and E. Ray Clendenen, "Salvation by Faith or by Faithfulness in the Book of Habakkuk?" *BBR* 24 (2014): 505–13, who recently reaffirmed the view that "faith" is the better translation. The allusion to Gen 15:6 does not seem to me as obvious as he and others make it out to be. On 1QpHab, in which the phrase is interpreted to indicate faith in the Teacher of Righteousness, see Pieter B. Hartog, "Re-Reading Habakkuk 2:4b: Lemma and Interpretation in 1 QpHab VII 17– VIII 3," *RevQ* 26 (2013): 127–132.

234. See the translation note.

235. Bruce, "Habakkuk," 863. Franz Delitzsch (*Habakuk*, 55–56), with reference, e.g., to the *Histories of Alexander the Great* (5.1) by first-century Roman historian Quintus Curtius Rufus, insists that *wine* is not a metaphor here but refers to the well-known drunkenness of the Babylonians; cf. Robertson, *Nahum*, 184. This does not seem likely to me.

is condemned in the picture of a swollen appetite in the preceding verse (as argued here), *wine*, as an object of consumption, is a suitable object for developing the metaphor. If "presumption" was in the original text, the MT offering of "wine" (also adopted in Vulg.) gives us an enriched text.[236] Wine is treacherous because at first it gratifies the drinker, increasing elation. But consumed in greater quantities, it turns against drinkers and leads to their downfall. Wine may also be treacherous in that, like wealth, the more one has of it, the more one desires, and so it does not fulfill the promise of satisfaction. Drinking wine starts pleasurably but—uncontrolled—ends bitterly (Prov 23:32); it may make one feel good and strong to begin with, but in the end one staggers and struggles to stand firm. Drunkenness is, therefore, an apt image for someone whose unbounded appetite will lead to their downfall. It is possible that the motif of the cup of wrath, which in Jer 25:15 is a "cup of the wine of wrath" (cf. Ps 75:8[9]),[237] plays a role here as well. Receiving judgment is sometimes described as having to drink from the cup of wrath.[238] The Babylonians gave this cup to others to drink (see below 2:15–17; cf. Jer 51:7) but, as this verse would imply, got drunk themselves on the violence.[239]

If, along with greed, v. 4 also hints at arrogance with *ʿuppəlâ* (*swollen*), the designation *a proud man* in v. 5 brings it to the fore.[240] The use of *geber* (*man*) instead of the more general *ʾîš* emphasizes strength and suggests the arrogance of power. But the place of the designation *a proud man* within the sentence is not entirely clear. There are three options. First, *a proud man* might function as an apposition that further characterizes *the wine* with the help of a personification. This is syntactically without problems but does not yield a clear meaning. In what sense could wine be spoken of as *a proud man*? To attribute treachery to wine is one thing (see above); arrogance is a different matter. One can imagine a drinker proudly consuming wine without fear of consequences, but it is harder to see in what sense wine itself could

236. Conversely, if MT represents the earlier text, the reading "presumption," while less imaginative, is not truly misleading.

237. Cf. Rev 14:8, 10, 19; 18:3; 19:15. See also Isa 63:3 for the association of wine with wrath.

238. See, e.g., Gerald L. Keown, Pamela J. Scalisle, and Thomas G. Smothers, *Jeremiah 26–52*, WBC 27 (Dallas: Word Books, 1995), 278–79; David T. Lamb, "Wrath," *DOTP*, 880.

239. Prinsloo ("Life," 633) claims that wine "is sometimes used in the Old Testament as a metaphor for the lust for power," but in the passages in question, wine stands for the exercise of power (violence, punishment), not the lust for power, and drinking from the cup is an image of being at the receiving end of aggression.

240. The only other occurrence of *yāhîr* in the Hebrew Bible is in Prov 21:24, which links it with *zēd* (cf. the related noun *zādôn* later in the verse: "presumptuous," elsewhere only in the pl.).

be spoken of as arrogant. Similar considerations would apply for alternative understandings of the text as "wealth" or "presumption" (on which see notes above).

The second option is to take *a proud man* as the object of the verb, in which case the participle would function as a verb, not as an adjective ("wine betrays a proud man").[241] This is possible and would yield the sense that an arrogant strongman can be overcome by drunkenness, as he underestimates the power of the alcohol. Translated into the political situation, which is what truly concerns Habakkuk, this would imply that the Babylonians in their might misjudge the way their infatuation with power will make them victims of it. But apart from Ps 73:15, the object of the verb is always introduced with the preposition *beth*.[242] Its omission in Ps 73:15 is arguably facilitated by the more indirect relationship between the (hypothetical) disloyalty and the offended party:[243] "Look—the generation of your sons, I would have betrayed." The use of the participle in Hab 2:5, the regular word order, and the more direct relationship between grammatical object and conceptual object of the treachery all seem to make the omission of the preposition here harsher and, thus, less likely.

This leaves us with the option of following the masoretic accentuation, taking the phrase with the subsequent rather than the preceding clause. In this case, positioning *a proud man* outside the sentence beginning with *waw* ("and") serves to stress the phrase as the topic of the sentence.[244] This would be problematic only if we assumed that the sentence already has a lengthy subject in the form of the relative clause, *who like Sheol enlarges his appetite.* That would leave us with two competing contenders for topic of the sentence.[245] But this can be avoided by taking *who like Sheol enlarges his appetite* as the subject of *indeed he is like the death and he is not sated*, which agrees with the masoretic accentuation. We thus have two statements: one about

241. E.g., Patterson, *Nahum*, 179. Bruce seems to think that this is only possible if the imperfect (*yiqtol*) is read instead of the participle, as in 1QpHab. His commentary appears to lean in this direction ("Habakkuk," 863) although this is not reflected in his translation (862). Cf. Roberts, *Nahum*, 112–13.

242. See Exod 21:8; Judg 9:23; Isa 33:1 (twice); Jer 3:20b; 5:11; 12:6; Lam 1:2; Hos 5:7; 6:7; Mal 2:10, 14, 15.

243. The disloyalty would have been against God in the first instance and therefore secondarily a treachery with regard to God's loyal followers.

244. So Franz Delitzsch, *Habakuk*, 56, comparing Job 23:12; 25:5; 36:26; Ps 115:7. For the phenomenon and further examples, see GKC 143d and JM 156.

245. The two designations obviously refer to the same person, and the second designation could be the resumption of the first, but it would be unusual for the resumptive designation (often just a pronoun) to be as elaborate as this, and the two different angles would rather overload the sentence.

a proud man (he *will not abide*) and one about someone who is greedy like death (he will never be satisfied).[246] *Sheol* and *death* are equivalent here; the point is that death eats away at human (and other) life from generation to generation with no sign of it getting to the point of having had its fill.[247]

The third bicolon juxtaposes the voraciousness of the Neo-Babylonian Empire (*all the nations . . . all the peoples*) with the gluttony of death. The Babylonians are not named, but, following on from ch. 1, there can be no doubt who is gathering and collecting nations.[248] *He*—the empire embodied in its ruler—is the glutton who like death will always be hungry for more. *He* is *a proud man* who will not be able to enjoy living in rest and peace. *He* is the one whose intoxication will be his downfall.

Reflection

The message is not dissimilar to "What you sow, so shall you reap" (Gal 6:7; see also Hos 10:11–14; Lev 26; Deut 19:21). Those who pursue greed will finally be overcome by it; those who remain loyal to God will live. Wellhausen asked whether this needed revelation and suggests that Habakkuk received precious little here.[249] But the anguish expressed in ch. 1 arose from the fact that the Babylonians did not simply act on their own accord; they were said to be God's instrument. It seemed to the prophet as if God was prepared to overlook the atrocities the Babylonians committed, probably on the grounds that they were his instrument. In this light, the revelation in effect affirms that the ends do not justify the means. God uses the Babylonians for his own ends, but the means they employ will lead to the end determined for such evil; the greed with which they pursue the conquest will be their downfall. The elaboration of the principle that evil falls back on the one who commits

246. Note the reuse of the verb *śbʿ* in v. 16, where someone will have his fill—of dishonor.

247. Cf. the allusions to Death's devouring of enemies in the Baal cycle, e.g., *KTU* 1.5 col. I; 1.6 col. II, col. V (see Simon B. Parker, ed., *Ugaritic Narrative Poetry*, WAW 9 [Atlanta: Scholars Press, 1997], 141–42, 155–56, 162).

248. Note that the verb *ʾsp* ("gather") is used in connection with death in a number of places, including the double uses in 2 Kgs 22:20 and Isa 57:1. Cf. Wilfred G. E. Watson, "The Hebrew Word-Pair *ʾsp // qbṣ*," *ZAW* 96 (1984): 426–34; repr. in Watson, *Traditional Techniques in Classical Hebrew Verse*, JSOTSup 170 (Sheffield: Sheffield Academic Press, 1994), 301–12.

249. Wellhausen, *Skizzen*, 5:163. So also Lindström, "I Am Rousing," 51: "But is this really revelation, 'vision' (2.2–3)? Is it not rather experience?" Brownlee ("Placarded Revelation," 325) agrees that "Habakkuk's 'revelation' represents timeless truth: 'Blessed are the meek for they shall inherit the earth.' " But he adds, "To see that this is really true, Habakkuk was counseled to be patient and wait." This acknowledges that a general truth may still be contested and its repetition may be pertinent to a particular situation.

evil in the following verses confirms that we are not dealing here with some new truth. But it was nevertheless important in this context to reaffirm the validity of this principle and so to exhort the righteous (in the words of Acts 11:23) "to remain faithful to the Lord with steadfast devotion."

Who are the righteous in Habakkuk? Chapter 2 will continue to offer a fuller description of its opposite, the arrogant, who is no other than the wicked in the words of the oppressed nations. But the righteous are characterized negatively only—they are the oppressed innocent ones (1:4, 13) whom the law proves unable to declare innocent. The wicked are the Babylonians in the first instance. But given that the Babylonian oppression made internal injustice only worse, it would be a mistake to identify the righteous with the whole of Judah. The righteous are those who have become victims of injustice and of the inability of Torah to set things right. They are characterized by weakness. Their only other distinguishing mark is that they cling steadfastly to God. While the text in Habakkuk does not tell us explicitly how righteousness and faith are related, taking *faithfulness* (steadfastness in faith; see above) with *live* rather than with *righteous*, it is clear that those who abandon their trust in God would no longer be counted among the righteous.

The ultimate outcome of the Babylonian domination is not spelled out in the book of Habakkuk. But the breakdown of Torah as the governing instrument for the people of God (1:4) prefigures the end of the Davidic monarchy and the destruction of the temple. In other words, the revelation given here had to be able to address a spiritual crisis even deeper than the one reflected in the text itself. With the temple in ruins and much of Torah legislation in abeyance insofar as it related to and depended on a central sanctuary, the exiles had to face the question whether it was still possible to live faithfully in relation to God—that is, to be righteous. Habakkuk would have given grounds for believing that even those who live in a society not governed by Torah and unable to access the provisions made in the Torah (e.g., for expressing repentance and receiving forgiveness) can still remain loyal to God.

This, along with the theme in ch. 1 of Torah's inability to declare the innocent righteous, makes the verse attractive to the apostle Paul and others. As in Habakkuk, the Spirit-receiving faith of which Paul speaks belongs to a persistent habit of trusting in God. It is not a one-off posture in which assent is given to a truth that can then be compromised by subsequent attitudes without loss. "Having started with the Spirit, are you now ending with the flesh?" (Gal 3:3). It is faith from the beginning and throughout one's life (cf. Gal 2:20, also implied in Rom 14:23). But Paul expands the argument beyond Habakkuk by drawing explicitly on Deut 27:26 rather than Hab 1:4 in his letter to the Galatians. The phrase *ek pisteōs eis pistin* in Rom 1:17 could be understood to stress the centrality of faith: righteousness from God is a matter of faith from beginning to end (cf. "from strength to strength" in Ps 84:7[8; LXX 83:8]; "from evil to evil" in Jer 9:3[2]). But the phrase could also imply a movement of faith from one person or group to another (cf. "from town to town" in Sir 36:35[26]; "from your [sg.] generation to your [pl.] generations" in Lev 21:17), and there are still other interpretations on offer.[250]

In Habakkuk, continuing trust in God surely implies a continuing clinging to God's commandments in spite of the apparent uselessness of such obedience in the face of Torah's numbness. This means arguably that the obedience flows out of trust in God and his promises rather than faith in Torah's rewards. Even in Habakkuk, the call is not for Judeans to find their identity anew in Torah but to keep faith in spite of the inability of Torah to reward such faith. Paul goes beyond this in arguing that Torah was not merely ineffective in bringing about righteousness but even brought a curse on God's people due to their disobedience. Paul's premise is that Israel as a whole is not "in the right" with God but that God has done something about this. God has demonstrated his righteousness in another event, part of which from one angle can be described as unspeakable wickedness.[251] If Torah as such is used as the defining factor of the community, it defines a community under the curse of the law. It must be faith in God that defines the community. In Christ, God has done another deed one would hardly believe but that commands a response of faith for salvation (Rom 1:17).

Given that the martyrdom and resurrection of Christ are decisive here, another reading of the phrase *ek pisteōs eis pistin* in Rom 1:17 is worth considering. Some have proposed that Paul sees the righteousness of God revealed in the gospel "by means of faithfulness (namely, of Christ), with the goal of faith or faithfulness (in the Christian)."[252] God's righteousness (and, indeed, perhaps his faithfulness), is demonstrated in the faithfulness and vindication

---

250. See further below and, e.g., Nijay K. Gupta, *Paul and the Language of Faith* (Grand Rapids: Eerdmans, 2020), 156–70, as well as commentaries on Romans; e.g., Colin Kruse, *Paul's Letter to the Romans*, PNTC (Grand Rapids: Eerdmans, 2012), 71, 74–78. The literature concerning the use of Hab 2:4 in the New Testament is vast and complex. See, e.g., Desta Heliso, *Pistis and the Righteous One: A Study of Romans 1:17 against the Background of Scripture and Second Temple Jewish Literature*, WUNT 2/235 (Tübingen: Mohr Siebeck, 2007).

251. The gospel event is the death, resurrection, and ascension of Christ. On the cross, we see the death of an innocent victim at the hand of an oppressor, aided and indeed promoted by internal enemies, with Torah unable to provide vindication.

252. Building on important contributions by Richard B. Hays and Glenn N. Davies among others, see, e.g., Douglas A. Campbell, "The Faithfulness of Jesus Christ in Romans and Galatians (with Special Reference to Romans 1:17 & 3:22)" (paper presented at the SBL Annual Meeting, San Diego, CA, 16 Nov 2007); cf. Campbell, *The Righteousness of God: An Apocalyptic Rereading of Justification in Paul* (Grand Rapids: Eerdmans, 2009), esp. 601–38, 1091–98; cf. 323–26, 350–53, 377–80, 1033–34.

of Christ. This in turn evokes a response in us.[253] Christ's fidelity is the source, the Christian's fidelity the goal. This suggests a Christological rereading of Hab 2:4. Christ is "the righteous one" (so also in Acts 7:52; 22:14; cf. Acts 3:14; 1 Pet 3:18; 1 John 2:1)[254] who lives by faithfulness, namely the one whose fidelity brought him (and those who are "in him") resurrection life.[255] While *ek pisteōs* ("by faith") in the citation of Hab 2:4 in Rom 1:17 has often been read as adjectival (belonging with *dikaios*, "righteous") rather than adverbial (belonging with *zēsetai*, "will live"), there are compelling arguments for allowing the phrase to modify the verb in Romans just as in Habakkuk.[256]

Jesus's act of righteousness, undergoing suffering and death in faithfulness to God, effects righteousness leading to life for all (cf. Rom 5:18-19). Those who are "in Christ" are vindicated not through Torah, which proved unable to prevent the death of Christ, but by his resurrection into the new

253. One of the arguments against taking the first *pistis* as faith in Christ is that such faith is better considered a *response* to God's righteousness rather than something that *reveals* God's righteousness. The same would be true for Habakkuk, where God's justice is not revealed in human faith but in God's word and deed. But in the New Testament, the decisive acts involve the one who is both human and divine; i.e., God acts in and through the faithfulness of Christ. For a defense of reading "faith in Christ" here, see Watson, *Paul and the Hermeneutics of Faith*, 50-53.

254. Cf. Richard B. Hays's 1988 essay, reprinted as "Apocalyptic Hermeneutics: Habakkuk Proclaims 'The Righteous One'," in *The Conversion of the Imagination: Paul as an Interpreter of Israel's Scripture* (Grand Rapids: Eerdmans, 2005), 119-42; see his *The Faith of Jesus Christ: An Investigation of the Narrative Substructure of Galatians 3:1-4:11*, SBLDS 56 (Chico: Scholars Press, 1983), 151-57, for the question in relation to Galatians. It is of course not necessary to accept "the Righteous One" as a known title for Jesus in order to allow that "the righteous one" in Rom 1:17 refers to Jesus, "the paradigm for the life of faith" (Hays, "Apocalyptic," 134, on one of the roles of Jesus in Hebrews; see Heb. 12:2). N. T. Wright (*Paul and the Faithfulness of God* [London: SPCK, 2013], 1466-71) thinks that identifying the righteous one with Christ "is probably a bridge too far" (1470) but argues against Watson (see n. 253) for a reference to divine faithfulness.

255. Cf. Walter Zorn, "The Messianic Use of Habakkuk 2:4a in Romans," *Stone-Campbell Journal* 1 (1998): 213-30. On the tradition of reading Hab 2:4 as a messianic prophecy, see also Strobel, *Untersuchungen*; Dietrich-Alex Koch, "Der Text von Hab 2.4b in der Septuaginta und im Neuen Testament," *ZNW* 76 (1985): 73 n. 25. Already, C. H. Dodd (*According to the Scriptures: The Sub-Structure of New Testament Theology* [London: Nisbet & Co., 1952], 49-51) argued that Hab 2:3-4 belonged to the key Old Testament passages considered to testify to Christ "from the earliest period" and was therefore agreed ground between Paul and others.

256. See D. Moody Smith, "ὁ δὲ δίκαιος ἐκ πίστεως ζήσεται," in *Studies in the History and Text of the New Testament in Honor of Kenneth Willis Clark*, ed. Boyd L. Daniels and M. Jack Suggs (Salt Lake City: University of Utah, 1967), 13-25, for a detailed argument, summarized in Douglas A. Campbell, *The Deliverance of God: An Apocalyptic Rereading of Justification in Paul* (Grand Rapids: Eerdmans, 2009), 1094-95. The phrase is sometimes taken by commentators on Romans to apply both ways.

creation. This new creation is characterized by life in the Spirit rather than by adherence to the Mosaic law. Those who today insist on defining God's people with reference to the Torah are still arguing from within the old creation and thus implicitly denying the new work God has done. Already in Habakkuk, the righteous live in their loyalty to YHWH, not in meritorious accomplishment of the law. Obedience to divine law does not lead to a right relationship with God; being right with God leads to obedience. The righteous are those who keep faith with God and therefore seek to do his will. Such faithfulness and obedience were expressed in Habakkuk's days in obedience to the Torah and are today expressed in Christian discipleship. Habakkuk did not yet reckon with God's supremely new work, which effected a change in the law. This is why the apostle has to do more than simply repeat Habakkuk. And so do we. With more revelation comes a responsibility to say more.

Habakkuk may have also inspired Paul to see a double antithesis to true loyalty to God. One antithesis is to stop trusting God, the lack of faithfulness against which Hab 2:4 implicitly warns (and which is picked up in the use of the verse in Hebrews). Another is the contrast that can be seen in Hab 2:4 between pride and faith, which may have inspired Paul's references to false boasting (Rom 2:17, 23; 4:2).[257] The idea that God's wrath is not an alternative to salvation but in fact its vehicle can be found elsewhere in Scripture. But it may have been Habakkuk who specifically prompted Paul to link the revelation of the gospel with the revelation of God's wrath.[258] Without speculating about what went on in the apostle's mind, it is certainly possible to draw numerous links between his letters and Habakkuk and to read them together as mutually enriching one another in a harmonious whole. Both allow for the possibility of being "righteous" without (yet) being publicly vindicated as such and so encourage faithfulness, even if Habakkuk is only concerned with how the righteous are to live (and implicitly how to remain righteous) while Paul explores the question how we become righteous.

Like Habakkuk we live "in the midst of the years" (Hab 3:2), between two mighty acts of God. The first, astonishing, act in Habakkuk's days numbed Torah in its effect (cf. Rom 8:3) and in our days has set it aside as law with the establishment of a new priesthood (Heb 7:12). The further, still future, act

257. My reading of "swollenness" above stressed allusions to the overconsumption of food and wine and so interpreted it as a symbol of greed. But I noted the link with Num 14:44, and the reference to *a proud man* suggests that swollenness can also be read as a symbol of pride.

258. This is explored in Mark A. Seifrid, "Paul's Use of Habakkuk 2:4 in Romans 1:17: Reflections on Israel's Exile in Romans," in *History and Exegesis: New Testament Essays in Honor of Dr. E. Earle Ellis*, ed. Sang-Won Son (London: T&T Clark, 2006), 133–49.

of God will judge the proud, wicked oppressor and prove the righteousness of those who in loyalty to God find life. (In Habakkuk, too, the designation "righteous" would not be worth much, if there was no difference of outcome between the righteous and the proud.) All these acts of God can be read as an expression of God's wrath and judgment, the conquests of the Babylonians as well as their downfall, the cross of Christ as well as the final judgment. God vindicates the righteous when he reveals that injustice and wickedness will not have the last word. He has done so supremely in the cross and resurrection of Christ but will confirm this in the final judgment. Our faith is therefore, like Habakkuk's, forward looking ("wait for it," v. 3). It will be fully vindicated only in the future when it will be evident that its end is life rather than death.

In the meantime, the good news is proclaimed in a context in which God's wrath is revealed against human society and God's people suffer (cf. Rom 1:18-25 and Heb 10:32-34 with Hab 1). There is therefore still need for the encouragement "not to abandon that confidence of yours" (Heb 10:35), trusting the promise that such confidence has a great reward when "the coming one" will come (Heb 10:37, citing Hab 2:3 in a modified version of the Greek Bible; see the reflection on 2:2-3 above). Faithfulness is still expressed in doing the will of God (Heb 10:36). This is, however, no longer understood in terms of obedience to the Mosaic Torah (cf. Heb 7:12, mentioned above). Using a verb found in the Old Greek tradition (*hypostellō*, "to draw back"), Heb 10:39 implies that the alternative to keeping faith is to shrink back. By reversing the two clauses, the letter to the Hebrews makes it easier to see not so much a contrast between two groups of people but two actions open to "my righteous one."[259] Of these, only the former is appropriate for the Christian community: "But we are not people of hesitancy toward destruction but of faithfulness toward the preservation of our lives." This contrast is in fact a fundamental pastoral concern in the letter to the Hebrews.[260]

Life has to be received from God. It cannot be sustained by greed, nor even by obedience to God's Torah.

---

259. Unlike MSS A and C, which read the same text as Heb 10:38, most LXX MSS have the pronoun not with "righteous" but with "faith." The genitival relationship could be understood as objective ("faithfulness toward me") or subjective ("my faithfulness"), with the former maybe being the more natural reading here. 8ḤevXIIgr, Aquila, and Symmachus are closer to the MT, reading the third-person pronoun. There are manuscript differences in the text of Heb 10:38 as well, assimilating the text either to MT by omitting the pronoun or to the majority LXX tradition by shifting the place of the pronoun.

260. So, e.g., Cockerill, *Hebrews*, 510.

VIII. THE AGREEMENT OF THE OPPRESSED NATIONS, FIRST SAYING (2:6-8)

[6] *Will not all of these[a] against him take up a veiled saying,*
   allusive speech,[b] and riddles[c] about him?[d]
And one will say:[e]
   Oy[f] the one[g] who increases what is not his own—how long?[h]—
      and the one who[i] loads upon him heavy pledges.
[7] *Will not those who bite you[j] suddenly arise,*
   and those who make you tremble[k] awake?
      Then you will become spoil[l] for them.
[8] *Because you have plundered many nations,*
   all that are left among the people will plunder you
      on account of shedding human blood and violence to[m] land,
         city, and all who inhabit[n] it.[o]

a. Literally "these, all of them." 1QpHab abbreviates by omitting *these* (which is, however, attested in MurXII and 8HevXIIgr). Haak (*Habakkuk*, 63) interprets the consonants *'lh* as the preposition with the archaic third-person suffix used elsewhere in Habakkuk.

b. A good English equivalent for *māšāl* (*veiled saying*) is difficult to find, and the precise connotation of *məlîṣâ* (*allusive speech*) is debatable; see the commentary. The closest parallels in which *māšāl* is used with the verb *nś'* as here are Isa 14:4; Mic 2:4. Elsewhere, the phrase is prominent in the Balaam narrative (seven times in Num 23–24); cf. Job 27:1; 29:1.

c. *CHP*, 325, reads as a hendiadys ("scoffing derision") to parallel "taunt" (*veiled saying*) in the previous line. But in the two other places in which *məlîṣâ* (*allusive speech*) is used, it is similarly connected with *māšāl* (*veiled saying*) and a third term (*riddles*, as here, in Prov 1:6; "songs" in Sir 47:17). This counsels against insisting that the second line must parallel the first by offering a single (combined) expression.

d. This rendering follows the interpretation of the syntax in the LXX and the masoretic accentuation. A possible alternative would be: "Are not all of these against him? A veiled saying they will take up—allusive speech and riddles about him."

e. Gelston (*BHQ* 13, 119*) observes that the singular in MT "is probably to be understood impersonally. There was an obvious tendency to render it as a pl. by way of assimilation to the context, or as a passive to facilitate a similar interpretation."

f. Hebrew *hôy* is most often used in the context of actions or events of which the speaker disapproves and occasionally in expressions of mourning (1 Kgs 13:30; Jer 22:18; 34:5). "Woe" is too specifically threatening. While a threat is often expressed subsequently in the second-person accusation, as in this series of *hôy* sayings, the *hôy* clause itself arguably expresses dismay more than threat (cf. Jer 47:6), sometimes even with a touch of pity (e.g., Isa 18:1). "Ah" is maybe not somber enough. In British English, "Oy!" is used to get someone's attention (similar to "Hey!") but also by way of rebuke ("Oy, you spilled your drink all over me!"). See the commentary on Nah 3:1 and Zeph 2:5; 3:1.

g. Strictly speaking, this could well be a vocative that, as Hillers ("*Hôy* and *Hôy*-Oracles") points out, is often linked in Hebrew with third-person pronouns. There is probably an element of (rhetorical) direct address here, which, however, cannot be rendered into English without changing the pronouns. See also the note on Nah 3:1.

h. The question arguably stands outside the poetic structure—a pivot between two cola.

The Masoretes apparently align it more closely with the following line, but the accentuation may have been used to mark a pivot; cf. Renz, *Colometry*, 41–42, 44, 112.

i. For the use of an indeterminate participle following on from, and parallel to, a determinate participle, cf., e.g., Isa 5:20; 10:1; Ps 57:8(9). See Franz Delitzsch, *Habakuk*, 64.

j. Cf. LXX, KJV. Arguably, both this and either the sense "those who take interest from you" ("your creditors") or maybe "those who give interest to you" ("your debtors") are implied; see the commentary below. Haak (*Habakkuk*, 64) sees "the image here of a dog harassing an enemy" (cf. Dahood), but the subject of the verb is usually a snake (Gen 49:17; Num 21:6, 8–9; Prov 23:32; Eccl 10:11; Jer 8:17; Amos 5:19; 9:3; prophets in Mic 3:5).

k. The verb appears to be the *pilpel* of a medium *waw* verb that is attested in the *qal* in Eccl 12:3, Esth 5:9; and Sir 48:12 in the sense of trembling. Following his mistaken association of biting with dogs (see previous note), Haak (*Habakkuk*, 64) ignores these passages in favor of "howling."

l. The plural of *məšissâ* (*spoil*) is attested only here in the Hebrew Bible; it is presumably intensifying.

m. The genitival relationship likely refers to violence perpetrated against land and city (cf. Gen 16:5; Judg 9:24; Jer 51:35; Joel 3:19[4:19]; Obad 10) rather than violence perpetrated by land and city (for which cf. Pss 7:16[17]; 58:2[3]; Ezek 12:19).

n. It is possible that 1QpHab read "and all in it" only (without *who inhabit*), "whether by error or in preserving a genuine variant" (Gelston, *BHQ*, 13:119*). This would facilitate reading the last two lines as one colon. With fifteen syllables, it would still be a very long colon. (The preceding two lines have ten and nine syllables.)

o. The feminine singular of the Hebrew for *it* could refer to *city* or *land*; the former is closer and in the same line and hence more likely.

Composition

The demonstrative pronoun *these* along with the reuse of *all* establishes a close link between v. 6 (and thus the whole unit governed by this introduction) and v. 5 (and thus the revelation in vv. 4–5 on which the book centers). The revelation in effect promised a reversal of fortunes: the greedy proud, who at present have the upper hand, will be destroyed by their greed; the righteous, who at present suffer at their hands, will find life in remaining faithful. The speech of the oppressed nations gives expression to this reversal and so expands the revelation in vv. 4–5. The speech comprises five sayings. The first two (vv. 6b–8 and 9–11) have a similar surface pattern: a *hôy* (*Oy*) exclamation with a description of the evildoer in the third person is followed by direct (second-person) address and concluded with a sentence introduced by *kî*. In the first saying, the second-person sentence voices a rhetorical question, and the *kî* sentence offers a rationale for the judgment. As we will see below, the second saying uses the same surface structure rather differently and, while the first saying expands as it proceeds from bicolon to tricolon to quatrain, the second saying contracts from an initial tricolon to two bicola.

The third saying (vv. 12–14) starts in the same way but focuses on YHWH in place of a second-person accusation. A concluding theological rationale is introduced with *kî*. The fourth saying (vv. 15–17) switches to second-person address already within the exclamation, as if to make up for the lack of a second-person address in the preceding saying. The repetition of a line (bicolon) from the first saying may nevertheless reestablish a sense of conformity to a pattern. If so, the completely different arrangement of the fifth saying is even more striking. There, an introduction in v. 18 precedes the actual exclamation in v. 19, which does not lead to a second-person accusation, and the rationale statement is not introduced with *kî*.

As a rule, *hôy (Oy)* exclamations use the third person to specify the object of attention,[261] but this is sometimes followed by a second-person accusation (e.g., Jer 22:13–15; 23:1–2; Zeph 2:5).[262] The use of rhetorical questions, as here in 2:7, 13, 18–19, is not unusual in this context (Isa 10:1–4; 29:15–17; Ezek 13:18; 34:2; Amos 5:18). Haak notes that, outside of Habakkuk, when a *kî* clause follows *hôy* it "invariably describes the poor conditions which will be the cause of the woe for the evildoer."[263] He appears to have overlooked, however, that the *kî* clauses in Habakkuk do not immediately follow the (third-person) exclamation but the (second-person) accusation. A similar pattern is found in Isa 29:15–16 and 30:1–4. But Haak is certainly right to point to the fluidity of the form. He argues further that "the author of Habakkuk has broken with the tradition of beginning the woe oracle with the announcement *hôy*," not only in v. 19 but in other places as well.[264] On thematic grounds, he suggests that the units are vv. 5–7 (the insatiable appetite and its result), vv. 8–10 (the plunder of nations/peoples), vv. 11–13 (the one building by wickedness), vv. 14–17 (covering and uncovering), and vv. 18–20 (the ineffectiveness of idols). To my mind, the double transition that he implies (from direct address to indirect "Woe" [better: *Oy*] and back to direct

261. Sometimes the object of attention is introduced with a preposition; e.g., Jer 48:1; 50:27; Ezek 13:3, 18. Isaiah 33:1 switches to the second person within the exclamation, and Zech 2:7(11) is altogether couched in direct address. In Zech 2:6(10), the imperatives belong to the next clause, *hôy* (doubled) being used on its own without a specified object of attention.

262. Isaiah 55:1 uses this pattern to rhetorical effect when the second person is used for an invitation rather than an accusation. David L. Petersen (*Haggai and Zechariah 1–8*, OTL [London: SCM, 1985], 173) suggests that *hôy* means "listen" here and in Isa 18:1; Jer 47:6; and Zech 2:6–7(10–11).

263. Haak, *Habakkuk*, 21. Even excluding clauses where *kî* is used incidentally (e.g., Isa 31:1), the statements in Jer 30:7 and 34:5, and probably also 50:27, seem to me different enough from those in Isa 5:10 and Jer 48:1 to suggest that there is no standard pattern outside Habakkuk either.

264. Haak, *Habakkuk*, 21.

address in vv. 8–10) would be rather harsh. Furthermore, v. 14 reads better juxtaposed with v. 13 than contrasting with v. 15.[265] It therefore seems advisable to retain the traditional division into units, as already indicated in medieval Hebrew manuscripts. Haak's main argument in favor of his proposal is that it does not require any repositioning of verses. But such a repositioning is not required in any case if one allows for a certain fluidity of the form.

The singulars *veiled saying* and *allusive speech* may point us to the unity of these sayings, while *riddles* points to their plurality. The references to YHWH may seem inappropriate in the mouth of a multitude of nations. If so, one could read the verses as a combination of *Oy* sayings (minimally vv. 6b, 9, 12, 15, 19a) and prophetic commentary, but this would not remove the difficulty of seeing nations other than Israel renounce idolatry in the way suggested in the final *Oy* saying. More likely, the author was not interested in painting a realistic picture of the oppressed nations but uses their "speech" as a stylistic means for further underlining the reversal aspect so prominent in these sayings.[266]

Some commentators argue that the unit 2:6–19 was originally a critique of Judean society that was then reinterpreted and applied to the Babylonians.[267] This is indeed possible but more likely on the traditional view that ch. 1 reflects a dialogical development than on the view adopted here that ch. 1 presents a single complaint that cites an earlier oracle (1:5–11). On my reading of the book, Habakkuk is from the start primarily concerned with injustice and the breakdown of a Torah-faithful society as a consequence of Babylonian domination, although it is implied that the Judean leadership largely participated in the injustice. Even then, it is not inconceivable that the prophet used preexisting material that in a different context accused a Judean audience. Regardless of their origin, I am convinced that the wide applicability of these sayings is deliberate and rhetorically significant. It is precisely not the intention here to speak a specific and unique word of condemnation but to affirm the downfall of the Babylonians with appeal to a pattern that holds true in other situations too. Therefore, one may rightly expect that many of

---

265. Haak (*Habakkuk*, 68), too, sees in v. 14 a "contrast between the ineffective and empty results of the work of 'the peoples' [v. 13] and the effective and filling presence of the 'glory of YHWH' "—but without explaining how the verse might introduce vv. 15–17.

266. It is theoretically possible that the prophet envisaged the conversion of the nations to YHWH, but it would seem odd not to spell this out as a precondition for their speech.

267. E.g., Jeremias, *Kultprophetie*, 57–75; Eckart Otto, "Die Stellung der Wehe-Worte in der Verkündigung des Propheten Habakuk," *ZAW* 89 (1977): 73–107; Rainer Kessler, *Staat und Gesellschaft im vorexilischen Juda: Vom 8. Jahrhundert bis zum Exil*, VTSup 47 (Leiden: Brill, 1992), 91–94. Cf. Fabry, *Habakuk/Obadja*, 251–53, whose translation graphically distinguishes between presumed redactional layers.

the phrases used are open-ended enough to offer suitable material for the denunciation of different individuals and communities.

Commentary

6 The victims of Babylonian expansion to which the previous verse referred will not keep quiet.[268] The rhetorical question seems to assume that at present the nations suffer silently but that one day they will open their mouths. We are not told what will prompt them to speak. The expressions *veiled saying, allusive speech and riddles about him* suggest that it may not yet be safe to talk plainly and directly (although see, e.g., v. 8), and the words spoken look forward to the downfall of the aggressor rather than celebrating it as a fact. The Babylonians are still oppressing nations, it seems. But speak they will. Janzen speaks of *māšāl* (*veiled saying*) as "a good prophetic term, with a range of meaning capable of spanning the whole continuum from taunting lamentation to bitter invective."[269] While the term is often neutral outside the prophetic literature ("proverb, parable, discourse"), the prophets use it most frequently to make a point against someone. *Məlîṣâ* (*allusive speech*) is found only one other time in the Hebrew Bible, in Prov 1:6, also paired with *māšāl* and alongside *riddles*. Its use in Proverbs, and Sir 47:17, where it is paired with *māšāl* and "songs," suggests a derivation from the root *mlṣ* ("to be smooth") for a well-crafted saying, a word that goes down well with the audience.[270] At least as common, however, is a derivation from *lîṣ* ("to brag, to scorn"; cf. *HALOT*).[271] It is clear that there are no negative connotations

268. Timmer (*Non-Israelite Nations*, 143) points out that the focus on their victimhood does not imply the innocence of these peoples.

269. Waldemar Janzen, *Mourning Cry*, 65. Gowan (*Triumph of Faith*, 62) suggests the translation "parody."

270. The verb is attested in Ps 119:103; some, after emendation, find the root also in Job 6:25 (cf. Tg.). For the pattern of noun formation, see Meyer, *Grammatik*, 2:28. A derivation from the noun *mēlîṣ* ("mediator, interpreter") with the gloss "trope, saying that puts things in different words" is one of five options offered in *DCH*. Two of the other four are related to *mlṣ*, interpreted once as "be smooth" and hence "allusive saying, slippery saying" and once as "be pleasant" and hence "sweet saying." The other two are *lîṣ* ("scorn," hence "mocking poem, figure"; see the following footnote) and the variant *lûṣ* (interpreted as "turn astray," for which cf. a related Arabic root; hence "sharp saying, obscure saying").

271. For this pattern of noun formation, see Meyer, *Grammatik*, 2:32–33. Haak (*Habakkuk*, 63) interprets the form not as a feminine noun but as a *hiphil* participle with the archaic third-person masculine singular suffix also used in 1:9, 15 and adopts the translation "his ambassador," as suggested by Maurice A. Canney in 1924. The parallels in Prov 1:8 and Sir 47:17 advise treating it as a noun.

of scorn associated with it in Prov 1:6 and Sir 47:17, but such a connotation would be appropriate here. It is speech latent with possibilities—possibilities that will need to be teased out and figured out, and in this sense the nations speak in *riddles*. These are not *riddles* in the sense of a specific speech form; they are enigmatic sayings. Hearers and readers should expect that there is more than at first meets the eye, or ear. Maybe the Babylonians would hear these sayings only as smooth, well-crafted discourses, although some phrases (*the cutting off of many peoples*, v. 10) and verses (8, 17) do, of course, reveal the target and give the game away. The nations will certainly intend these well-crafted sayings as taunting invectives by way of parables.[272]

The nations know that there will be an end to the oppression—and to the oppressor. How so? There are two possibilities to consider. First, perhaps those who read the revelation and run with it bring the message to the nations, who, believing it, express their faith in this revelation in the form of a *veiled saying* announcing the downfall of the voracious empire. Second, perhaps cracks will appear in the Babylonian armor, which will give the nations the courage to hope for an end to come upon their tormentors. In the latter case, the proclamation of this *allusive speech* will strengthen the faith of those within Israel who have put their trust in the revelation. The prophetic discourse does not specify when and on what basis the nations will gain a voice. In truth, while *all of them* are said to raise their voice, they might do so in unison only toward the end of Babylonian dominance. The rhetorical question in the prophecy hides a challenge for those who read these words. Will they make *the veiled saying* that follows their own? The *allusive speech* offers words that form an appropriate response to the revelation in vv. 4–5; it also offers help in believing these words by alluding to other, more local situations in which truths similar to the one proclaimed in vv. 4–5 are demonstrated.

Finally, one should note that the specific verb used for the speech of the peoples (*take up*) is the root from which the first word in the book (*pronouncement*) derives (*nś'*). The nations echo the prophet, whose *pronouncement* had incorporated an earlier divine revelation. Like the prophet's complaint in ch. 1, the nations' taunt in ch. 2 is related to divine revelation and in some ways a response to it, whether or not the nations are fully aware of this.

The first parable draws attention to a creditor who becomes a debtor. Increase is good, but not when the abundance consists of *what is not* your *own*. Weinfeld comments, "In contrast to taxes paid to the local government which were given in exchange for services to the local population, the taxes

---

272. Unambiguously negative terms would have been available: *mangînâ* ("mocking song," Lam 3:63), *ḥerpâ* ("taunt, reproach"), *šәnînâ* ("taunt"); these last two are used together with *māšāl* in Jer 24:9. The exclusive use of ambiguous terms appears to be deliberate.

and corvée work for the empire were given for no exchange, and thus were rightly considered by the prophets robbery."[273] But in this parable, the nations do not think of themselves as peoples who have been robbed but as peoples who are in a creditor-debtor relationship. At first, the robbed goods are considered *heavy pledges*, which the Babylonians heaped upon them. The tribute payments to the empire are like securities on a loan—allegedly. But the word used to describe the Babylonian debts, *'abṭîṭ*—maybe an Akkadian loanword—can be heard as *'ābṭîṭ*, possibly "a heap of muck."[274] This double entendre is likely intended and may be the reason for the choice of *'abṭîṭ*, which is not found elsewhere in the Hebrew Bible.[275] The nations will not accept that they are indebted to the empire. The *heavy pledges* are stolen property. The next verse suggests not only an end to the understanding of the subjugated peoples as debtors to the empire but a reversal of the relationship.

7 The oppressed nations have been trod upon by the Babylonians, but they will bite Babylonian heels. The enmity is not unlike the one pictured in Gen 3:15, but the movement reverses the one in Gen 3. The groveling snake in the dust, biting at heels, will *suddenly arise* and claim that it is time for payback. The verb for biting, or maybe a homonym,[276] is used in the *hiphil* for "charging interest" (Deut 23:19-20[20-21]).[277] "Interest" (*nešek*) was the "bite" a creditor took from a debtor. It is not clear whether the *qal* of the verb *nšk* means to "to give interest" or "to take interest." Its use in Deut 23:19(20) can be reconciled with either understanding. Some

273. Moshe Weinfeld, "The Protest against Imperialism in Ancient Israelite Prophecy," in *The Origins and Diversity of Axial Age Civilizations*, ed. Shmuel N. Eisenstadt (Albany: State University of New York Press, 1986), 173.

274. Already 8HevXIIgr reads the text in this way (*pachos pēlou*; cf. Peshitta, Vulg., Tg.), so also medieval Jewish exegetes, who often reversed the word order to yield "thick mud" (see Rosenberg, *Twelve Prophets*, 267). Cf. Franz Delitzsch, *Habakuk*, 65. *'Āb* is usually "cloud," but for a non-meteorological "density," see Jer 4:29, where the plural refers to thickets.

275. In Deut 24, the related (and broadly equivalent, it seems) *'ăbōṭ* is used. The use of the verb *'bṭ* for entering into a relationship of giving and taking pledges is found in Deut 15:6, 8; 24:10; Joel 2:7.

276. Ges[18] lists the two meanings of *nšk* in one entry; *HALOT* and *DCH* offer two different entries. The noun only occurs with the meaning "interest" (Exod 22:25[24]; Lev 25:36-37; Deut 23:20; Ps 15:5; Prov 28:8; Ezek 18:8, 13, 17; 22:12).

277. The people of Israel were forbidden to charge interest within their own polity, whether from their own people or resident aliens, presumably because such loans were always to people in desperate need, and the people of God are not to exploit the needy (see, e.g., Exod 22:25[24]). Charging interest was permitted on loans to nonresident foreigners, presumably because foreigners who were not living among them were merchants and the loans commercial loans.

scholars believe that it must be the former, given the reference to pledges in v. 6.[278] But if there is a link with "biting," it seems more plausible that the *qal* is largely equivalent to the *hiphil* "to charge interest" and means "to take interest."[279] As suggested above, it is questionable whether the nations would have accepted an understanding of themselves as debtors to Babylon. They are not in debt to the Babylonians. Quite the reverse: it is the imperial force that did the taking by robbing them, and it is therefore the Babylonians who are in debt to the nations they oppressed, who now demand their money back.

The saying pictures the Babylonians as trembling in the knowledge that one day there will be a reckoning, presumably all the while hoping that *those who make you tremble* will keep ignoring them. But they will *awake* and make their demands, as creditors are wont to do. The Babylonians may well claim that they provide security and peace in return for taxes and forced labor, but such benefits are at best interest payments on the loans, or maybe collaterals. When the time comes to claim back the loan, *you will become spoil for them.*[280]

8 Now without metaphor, the facts are stated plainly. The Babylonians have been plundering and will be plundered in turn. The contrast between *many nations* in the first line and *all that are left among the people* hints at bloodshed and violence.[281] Both of the final lines suggest the double cost of the Babylonian invasion, to human lives as well as to agriculture (*shedding human blood and violence to land*), to infrastructure as well as human life (*city, and all who inhabit it*). In the middle of this bicolon, countryside and city lie violated, and spread across on either side are the human victims. The whole bicolon recurs unchanged at the end of v. 17.

278. Jeremias, *Kultprophetie*, 70–71; cf. Kessler, *Staat*, 92–93. So also BDB.

279. So *HALOT*; Ges[18]. *DCH* offers "pay interest" for the *qal* but comments on the use of the participle as a noun: "creditor, or perh. debtor."

280. Much borrowing in the ancient world was presumably seasonal, without regular interest payments between the taking out of the loan and its repayment. Where there was interest payment, "there seems to have been a long tradition of considering the loan to be amortized when its interest payments had fully reproduced the principal," as Michael Hudson observes in "How Interest Rates Were Set, 2500 BC – 1000 AD," *Journal of the Economic and Social History of the Orient* 43 (2000): 132–61.

281. The view that *all that are left among the people* refers to nations that the Babylonians have not subjugated is not to be countenanced. Such a division of nations is unknown in Habakkuk and would soften the strong *lex talionis* aspect. Cf. the extensive discussion in Franz Delitzsch, *Habakuk*, 68–70.

Reflection

As in ch. 1, so in ch. 2: earlier revelation plus response form a fuller revelation. What the nations will say is an appropriate response to vv. 4–5—the revelation itself or its fulfillment—but in turn it becomes divine revelation for us along with Habakkuk's complaint in ch. 1. Critical for the perspective expressed in the first "riddle" is the view the oppressed nations have of themselves in relation to the empire. No doubt the subjugated nations have been trembling in the face of the Babylonian onslaught, but now they picture the Babylonians as trembling. The empire has overreached itself in swiping the wealth of the nations. The nations know themselves to be exploited; they are oppressed like debtors by creditors. But knowing that what the Babylonian emperor grasped does not belong to him allows the nations to see themselves instead as the creditors and the robbed goods as loans that lie heavy on Babylonian shoulders. The fearsome empire is now pictured as laden with muck. The great reversal is just, because those who plundered deserve to be plundered in turn and because the violent destruction that they caused calls for reparations.

This first strophe of the parable can encourage us to reflect on what the movement of goods in which we participate says about our underlying relationships. The Babylonians did plunder, but Nebuchadnezzar saw himself as the protector of the nations under his sway. He claimed to "gather" populations for their own good, although there is no doubt that the system worked best for the heartland of the empire. Vanderhooft observes:

> The procedure of funneling resources from the subject populations of the empire to the heartland through seizure and exaction was no less important to the Babylonians than it had been to the Assyrians, and the massive building projects of the Neo-Babylonians, and those of Nebuchadnezzar II in particular, indicate how well these practices were refined in the sixth century. Nebuchadnezzar campaigned almost yearly in the west, in part to insure [sic] order, but also to fill the royal coffers.[282]

The receipt of foreign tribute was justified in imperial propaganda by the alleged benefits that the subjugated nations received and by the divine vocation of Babylonian supremacy.

> The assumption of the imperial creed . . . is that the populations of the empire benefit from the king's divine commission to rule them: he is their

---

282. Vanderhooft, *Neo-Babylonian Empire*, 160. See the whole of ch. 1 for the portrayal of imperial rule in the Neo-Babylonian royal inscriptions.

shepherd, leads them justly, gathers them peacefully into the shadow of Babylon, and causes them to prosper. Their recognition of Babylon's pre-eminence therefore justified the one-way flow of goods into the heartland. This was not, however, the perception of the subjugated communities.[283]

It is the perception of the subjugated communities, however, as expressed in these verses, which becomes prophecy. Those who are oppressed today may be strengthened by this congruence of the perspective of the exploited peoples and the divine revelation in vv. 4–5. Others, closer to the heart of today's empires, may be challenged to listen to the voice of people at the suffering end of contemporary economic and political forces, asking whether their perception of things can help us see truths we would rather ignore, believing instead our self-serving propaganda.

IX. THE SECOND SAYING (2:9-11)

[9]*Oy the one who takes evil[a] takings[b] for his house,*
   to set his nest on high,
      to escape from the clutch[c] of evil.
[10]*You have devised ignominy for your house,*
   the cutting off[d] of many peoples, and so you are going to sin[e] against
      your life.
[11]*Indeed, stones[f] from the wall will cry out,*
   and rafters[g] from[h] the woodwork will respond.

   a. Because *beṣaʿ* in itself refers to "evil gain" (*takings*, see the following footnote), some believe that *rāʿ* (*evil*) should be read with "for his house" as a separate clause (e.g., Jeanette Mathews, *Performing Habakkuk: Faithful Re-enactment in the Midst of Crisis* [Eugene, OR: Pickwick, 2012], 211), but this is unnecessary. *Rāʿ* (*evil*) may have been added to prepare for its use at the end of the verse. I prefer to read the text in line with the accentuation; cf. Franz Delitzsch, *Habakuk*, 71.

   b. The verb *bṣʿ* is used for breaking away and regularly takes its related noun, *beṣaʿ* ("severing"), as its object (see *HALOT*: "to make one's cut"). Even without the addition of *rāʿ* (*evil*), *beṣaʿ* refers to illicit profit. Cf. P. J. Garland, "*Bṣʿ*: Bribe, Extortion or Profit?" *VT* 50 (2000): 310–322.

   c. The *kap* is literally the palm (the hollow or flat of the hand; also used for the foot's sole).

   d. Reading the MT as the *qal* infinitive construct, this serves as a further explication of the object of *you have devised.* 1QpHab reads a plural noun, which is favored by, among others, Haak, *Habakkuk*, 64–65, who translates "terminations." The versions vocalize this as a finite verb form ("You have cut off").

283. Vanderhooft, *Neo-Babylonian Empire*, 161.

e. The subject *you* before the participle is omitted in the Hebrew. Franz Delitzsch (*Habakuk*, 73–74) points to Ps 7:9(10) as a close parallel; cf. Ps 55:19(20), with omission of the third-person pronoun. The participle suggests the immediate future rather than the present, for which a finite form might have been used. Haak (*Habakkuk*, 65) interprets the *waw* as pleonastic or vocative (my translation tends toward epexegetical) and the participle as a noun ("o sinner"), rendering the complete line as "Terminations for great peoples, o sinner, is your desire."

f. I interpret the singular nouns here as collective. The singular "stone" is regularly used in this way, as in the contexts of stoning to death (Lev 20:2, 27; 24:23; Josh 7:25; 1 Kgs 12:18; etc.), throwing stones (Lam 3:53), committing adultery with stones (and trees, Jer 3:9), clearing a path of stones (Isa 62:10), precious stones (1 Kgs 10:2, 10, 11, passim), and rows of stones (Exod 28:17; 39:10).

g. This word is not attested earlier or elsewhere in the Bible. I adopt what is probably the most widespread understanding today; see, e.g., Aron Pinker, "Castanets," *ZAW* 114 (2002): 618–21, for more details. His suggested emendation to *kpym m'ṣ*, understood as wooden clappers, seems to me to offer a solution with at least as many uncertainties and problems as the more common understanding.

h. The preposition *min* (*from*) could conceivably introduce a genitive of material ("wooden [rafters]"), but the parallelism recommends the translation above.

Composition

The second saying, or second strophe of the discourse of the nations, is broadly patterned in the same way as the first. The first *Oy* exclamation there consisted of a bicolon (3+3) with two extra elements (the introductory *and one will say* and the question *How long?*). Here, the exclamation consists of a tricolon (4+2+2 beats) instead, with the second and third colon focusing on the intention of the evildoer. The following second-person address is a direct accusation rather than a rhetorical question as in the first strophe; the reuse of *house* links the exclamation with the accusation more tightly. Andersen claims that it is impossible to make coherent sense of this paragraph if the text is read continuously, as in the translation above. He argues that "two staccato curses are inserted into other clauses" by way of parentheses.[284] This would introduce exclamations within an exclamation, which to my mind read awkwardly, especially in v. 10. If one allows, contra Andersen, that an ironic commentator might speak of someone scheming shame for their own house (*You have devised ignominy for your house*), there is no need to assume that we are dealing with a section that is "contrariwise, nervous, disjointed, and rough in its grammar."[285]

284. Andersen, *Habakkuk*, 239.
285. Andersen, *Habakkuk*, 240.

Commentary

9 The characteristic of the evil condemned is again presented in the *Oy* exclamation. The Babylonian acquisitiveness that had already been condemned in the first saying is now presented in the form of *one who takes evil takings for his house*, one who creams off others to make dishonest gain for his household. The English phrase "to make a killing" is poetically appropriate here, as the verb *bṣʿ* is also used for finishing off someone, cutting off the threat of their life as it were (Isa 38:12; Jer 51:13; Job 6:9; 27:8). Those characterized in this way take for themselves without concern for those from whom they profit. The *takings* are characteristically profit gained through violence (e.g., Gen 37:26; Judg 5:19) or extortion (Isa 33:15; Ezek 22:12) or in the form of bribes that pervert justice (Exod 18:21; 1 Sam 8:3). The addition of *evil* underlines the wickedness of this greedy gain but also highlights the irony of trying to keep oneself safe *from the clutch of evil* by *evil* grasping of the possessions of others.[286]

The aim is *to set his nest on high*, that is, in a safe place (cf. Job 5:11; Isa 33:16). The *nest on high* evokes the image of an eagle, as in Jer 49:16, where Edom (cf. Obad 3–4) is said to attempt to build its nest high up like an eagle. The related verb (*rwm*) is also used for an eagle setting up a nest on high in Job 39:27.[287] In Jer 51:53, the possibility of Babylon reaching to the sky in strengthening fortifications is raised only to be dismissed as futile when YHWH comes to judge. People cannot get themselves out of harm's way by building higher, seeking to remove themselves from the realm of disaster. The Babylonians will find out, like others before and after them, that *evil* has a way of catching up with those who perpetrate it.

10 The second-person accusation spells out that the planning and decision-making based on the reasoning in v. 9 have put the accused on the road to *ignominy*, bringing trouble on their household, as evil gain tends to do (cf. Prov 15:27a). The use of *ignominy* rather than another word for disaster suggests a contrast to the seeking for honor that was surely a part of the Babylonian emperor's motivation in the conquest of other nations. It is therefore not so much a subjective feeling of embarrassment as the objective experience of public disgrace that is in view here.[288] The emperor had

286. The KJV preserved the wordplay, as did, e.g., the Old Greek and Latin versions, but modern translations render the second occurrence of *rāʿ* with "harm" (e.g., RSV), "disaster" (NET), "calamity" (NASB), or "ruin" (NIV).

287. Cf. Sennacherib's use of the nest simile for his enemies in campaign reports against the hill tribes east of the Tigris (*ARAB*, 2:122, 139, 144).

288. Yael Avrahami ("בוש in the Psalms—Shame or Disappointment?" *JSOT* 34 [2010]: 295–313) argues that the verbal forms found in lament psalms more often refer to disappointment.

in mind *the cutting off of many peoples*, but in fact he was thereby planning to do wrong to himself, forfeiting his own life (see Prov 20:2 for the same expression and Prov 8:36 for a similar thought). The *ignominy* consists in the discrepancy between intent (escaping from evil) and result (forfeiting one's life).

11 The emphatic *indeed* at the beginning of the verse could also be interpreted as providing the foundation for the *Oy* exclamation. Even *stones* and *woodwork* will serve as witnesses, accusing the evildoer and thus filling the complainants with confidence. If so, it is not the responsorial accusation by *stones* and *woodwork* itself that causes the *Oy* exclamation but the firm hope and expectation that even the building materials of the Babylonian emperor will side against him in the end. The use of wooden rafters may suggest a palace, or at any rate a rather luxurious house,[289] as the roofs of ordinary houses in Mesopotamia, as in Israel, likely consisted largely of reeds and leaves along with a layer of mud, although they may have included "planks of palm tree wood" for support.[290] But it is in any case by no means certain that the reference is to beams supporting the roof, and it has been suggested that layers of wood were used in stone walls "to minimize earthquake damage."[291] It seems rash to exclude the possibility that ordinary houses would have both stone and wood elements, but in all likelihood, wooden pillars and beams would have been more prominent in larger houses. In any case, while v. 9 can be applied more widely, the immediate focus here remains on the Babylonian conqueror of foreign nations. The reference to *stones* rather than bricks makes us think of houses in Israel rather than Mesopotamia. By way of metaphor, this fits the motif of appropriating foreign goods.[292] But

289. Cf. Pinker, "Castanets," 620, who believes that "in that case, the verse would lose much of its intensity." Not so; the proverb is not focused on ordinary homeowners. This homeowner is engaged in imperial conquest; cf. v. 10.

290. Karen Rhea Nemet-Nejat, *Daily Life in Ancient Mesopotamia* (Westport, CT: Greenwood Press, 1998), 122. Wood was also used to help with the establishment of doors and passageways. See Stephen Bertman, *Handbook to Life in Ancient Mesopotamia* (New York: Facts on File, 2003), 186–90. Oded Borowski (*Daily Life in Biblical Times*, SBL Archaeology and Biblical Studies 5 [Atlanta: SBL, 2003], 20) speaks of the use of crossbeams in connection with ceilings and roofs of typical four-room houses in Israel.

291. Joyce G. Baldwin, *Haggai, Zechariah, Malachi* (Leicester: Inter-Varsity Press, 1972), 41. She is confident that this was customary, but without indicating a source. Amihai Mazar (*Archaeology of the Land of the Bible: 10,000 – 586 B.C.E.* [New York: Doubleday, 1990]) lends some support, claiming that wooden as well as stone pillars "were deployed in various ways" (343), although the specific examples cited are of larger structures (see 473 fig. 11.6).

292. The account in Gen 11 suggests Israelites knew that Mesopotamian buildings used bricks in the absence of stones. Ephraim Stern (*Archaeology of the Land of the Bible*, vol. 2 [New York: Doubleday, 2001], 18–31) documents the Assyrian influence on the material culture of Palestine, including increased use of bricks.

there is no suggestion that Babylonian architecture changed as a result of importing stones from the Levant!

The responsorial nature of the outcry of wood and stone underscores their agreement in the complementary witness they provide. The outcry is a call for redress and implies that someone, surely God, will respond to the cry for justice. Thus, while there is some emphasis on the self-destructive nature of evil in this chapter, this should not be pictured as an automatic, impersonal act-consequence connection. Both the hint of a law court here and the use of *ignominy* in the previous verse suggest personal dimensions to the claim that evil will catch up with the evildoer.

Reflection

There are a number of similarities between the first and second strophe, both structurally and thematically. But while the first *Oy* speaks of evil incurring a debt that will have to be paid in the end, the second *Oy* stresses that evil and its fruit do not provide a secure foundation for one's household. The following *Oy* will extend this to the realm of society. This second *Oy* speaks against our tendency to seek security in material possessions, as does the parable of the rich fool in Luke 12:13-21. Augustine's comment on the rich fool (in a sermon on Prov 13:7) is an apt description of the Neo-Babylonian Empire as well: "He was planning to sate his soul with excessive and unnecessary feasting, and proudly disregarding all those empty bellies of the poor. He didn't realize that the bellies of the poor were much safer storerooms than his barns."[293] The empire is rejoicing in its big catch (1:15-16) without regard for its victims. But *cutting off* peoples in this way means in fact cutting off one's own life thread. The frequent "I" in Luke 12:17-19 indicates how the possessions have cut off the rich fool from (concern for) others. Life does not consist in abundance of possessions (Luke 12:15) but in rich—that is, loving—relationships, and ultimately in being rich to God (Luke 12:21), the source of life and love. This is why possessions at the expense of relationships cut life short rather than enhancing it. Giving to the poor builds up a treasure in heaven (cf. Luke 12:33; Prov 19:17). This is because wealth is to be found in our relationship to God, which finds expression in our relationship with others. It is love that offers the true security on the day of judgment—God's love for us, which has found a response in our love for him and others (cf. 1 John 4:16-21). Resources are a means for strengthening or weakening relation-

293. Augustine, *Sermons* 36.9; quoted from *Sermons 20-50*, trans. Edmund Hill, ed. John E. Rotelle, The Works of Saint Augustine III/2 (New York: New City Press, 1990), 180. Cf. Thomas C. Oden, *The Good Works Reader* (Grand Rapids: Eerdmans, 2007), 40; Arthur A. Just, *Luke*, ACCS NT 3 (Downers Grove: InterVarsity Press, 2003), 208.

ships; security is not found apart from relationships. The fact that stones and rafters cry out as witnesses may suggest the absence of human witnesses (cf. Luke 19:40), and so the absence of human relationships, at least beyond the narrow confines of the household that seeks safety in distance from others. But those who adopt this *Oy* saying likely expect that there will be someone in the end to overhear the witness of stones and rafters and redress the wrong done to them by their appropriation for evil. The next saying is more explicit about the one who guarantees the necessary processes.

X. THE THIRD SAYING (2:12–14)

¹²*Oy the one who builds a city with bloodshed,*
    *and establishes a town*ᵃ *with injustice.*
¹³*Is it not, indeed,*ᵇ *from YHWH of Hosts,*
    that peoples toil only for fire
        *and nations*ᶜ *only for nothing grow weary?*
¹⁴*Yes:*ᵈ *the earth shall be filled*
    with the knowledge of the glory of YHWH
        *as the waters cover over the sea.*ᵉ

a. Hebrew *qiryâ* (*town*) is almost exclusively used in poetry (but see Deut 2:36; 1 Kings 1:41, 45) and in place-names. No substantial distinction between the much more common *'îr* (*city*) and *qiryâ* (*town*) commends itself. The latter, like the former, can certainly refer to fortified cities (e.g., Isa 25:2).

b. Cf. 2 Chr 25:26 for the combination *hălô' hinnê* (there with suffix).

c. *Lə'ummîm* appears to be an archaic or poetic term. The translation *nations* is not entirely satisfactory. If I had not used "peoples" in the preceding colon, this would be better. It is sometimes suggested that in contrast to the more common *'ammîm* (*peoples*), this term "emphasizes the group considered as a whole unit" (Patterson, *Habakkuk*, 197).

d. The particle *kî* is often taken here in an adversative sense ("but"), for which see, e.g., Anton Schoors, "The Particle *kî*," *OTS* 21 (1981): 251–52, 256–59. Franz Delitzsch (*Habakuk*, 84) argues that the more common causal use of the particle applies here as well. Probably less likely, although not impossible, is a temporal connection ("when"). The translation above reflects a broad emphatic use of the particle without suggesting a specific link to the preceding. It might also simply introduce the quotation, although this use of the particle (*recitativum*) is denied by some.

e. Franz Delitzsch (*Habakuk*, 85) notes that just as *'ăpîq* can designate a stream or its bed, so *yām* can refer to the sea or, as here, to the seabed.

Composition

Verse 14 (and similarly maybe v. 20) could be read as a comment outside the *Oy* sayings. But every *Oy* saying apart from the final one (vv. 18–20), in which

v. 20 does indeed mark the end of the collection as well as of the specific say-ing, ends with a *ky* statement, so we might expect the third saying to do so as well. Also, if we exclude v. 14, the third *Oy* saying would be much shorter than the others in the series. It is therefore advisable to keep these three verses together. On this assumption, the third saying consists of three parts that, separated from each other, are also found elsewhere in the Hebrew Bible. With minor changes throughout, v. 12 runs parallel to Mic 3:10, which speaks of Zion and Jerusalem rather than *city* and *town*; v. 13 is parallel to the second half of Jer 51:58, where the changes include a reversal of *fire* and *nothing*; and v. 14 is parallel to the second half of Isa 11:9. The textual variations do not offer a sufficient basis for establishing dependence.

The parallel of v. 12 with Mic 3:10 is less often noted in commentaries; it might reflect shared access to a proverbial complaint against rulers rather than direct dependence of one on the other. The surprising use of the singu-lar in Micah, within an oracle addressed to a plurality of rulers, could be the result of such proverbial influence and does not clearly signal dependence on Habakkuk.[294] Even if dependence on Hab 2:12 were considered plausible, this could be the result of an editorial process as part of the transmission of the Book of the Twelve. It would therefore not offer sufficient grounds to assume Habakkuk's priority. Read synchronically, our interpretation of Micah perhaps gains more from an observation of this intertextuality with Habakkuk than the other way around. Read with an awareness of Hab 2:12, the denunciation of the rulers of Jerusalem in Micah is both sharpened by an implicit comparison to the Babylonian oppressor in Habakkuk and made more secure through the support of this more general saying in Habakkuk. By contrast, knowing that Jerusalem's rulers had been denounced similarly in Micah does not seem to add much to the condemnation of Babylon in Hab 2:12. But it might encourage applying the condemnation in Habakkuk to sit-uations other than the international one in focus (see "Habakkuk's Message in Its Original Context," pp. 211–15).

Jeremiah 51:58 concludes the collection of oracles against Babylon and, indeed, the collection of oracles about other nations that makes the conclud-ing saying about nations (generally) toiling for nothing most appropriate. In the LXX of Jeremiah, this material comes much earlier in the book (after what we know as 25:13), and the statement that parallels Hab 2:13 is negated: "The peoples shall not labor in vain, nor shall nations fail in their rule" (28:58 LXX). This is at first surprising, given that the preceding oracles promise even less hope to other nations than they do in the masoretic version.[295] In

---

294. Vocalizing the consonantal form as an infinitive absolute is another popular solu-tion; so, e.g., Waltke, *Micah*, 178.

295. Indeed, the final words of restoration for Egypt (46:26), Moab (48:47), and Ammon

addition, the second part is phrased differently, with "rule" instead of "fire" — the two words are orthographically closer in (unvocalized) Hebrew (r'š for 'š) than in Greek. Maybe the LXX promise that "the peoples shall not labor in vain, nor shall nations fail in their rule" seeks to affirm that opposition to Babylonian rule will be successful in the end (cf. 51:27–33 MT // 28:27–33 LXX). Again, the duplication of this saying in Jer 51 and Hab 2 could indicate that we are dealing with an old proverb.[296] But the many verbal variations do not point to a fixed saying, and the fact that the context in both is the futility of Babylonian building works might suggest that one may be quoting the other. If so, it could be argued that the more perfectly formed saying in Hab 2:13 quotes and improves on its source.[297] Delitzsch, by contrast, argues that Jeremiah modified Hab 2:13, turning a statement that is quite specifically linked to the building of cities (Hab 2:12) into a more general comment, with the second verb (*grow weary*) no longer the result of labor but of God's punishment.[298] This may be overly subtle, but it reminds us of the possibility that Hab 2:13 is not in fact citing anything and that the parallel in Jeremiah could belong to Habakkuk's reception rather than composition history.

To Andersen's ears, Hab 2:14 "sounds like a slogan that could be put anywhere."[299] In Isa 11:9, we can read it as a development of the striking statement in Isa 6:3. The latter both programmatically sets apart YHWH from everything else ("Holy, holy, holy is YHWH of Hosts," which anchors Isaiah's frequent designation of YHWH as "the Holy One of Israel") and claims that "the whole earth is full of his glory" already (cf. Num 14:21).[300] Yet it is only when this glory is recognized and the whole earth is full of the knowledge that is given to the new branch out of Jesse's root (Isa 11:1–2) that human relationships will reflect the divine will and disharmony in creation will be resolved. It is intriguing to note that violence done to Lebanon is spoken

---

(49:6) are absent in LXX. Only the restoration for Elam (49:39) is promised in both MT and LXX. In LXX, it concludes the first oracle about another nation (25:19 LXX) and is thus far removed from the verse in question (28:58 LXX).

296. So, e.g., Jack R. Lundbom, *Jeremiah 37–52*, AB 21C (New York: Doubleday, 2004), 500; Andersen, *Habakkuk*, 245.

297. Even if the book of Jeremiah is later than the book of Habakkuk, this need not be the case for individual oracles within the book of Jeremiah.

298. Franz Delitzsch, *Habakuk*, 79.

299. Andersen, *Habakkuk*, 245. Less kindly, Ward (*Habakkuk*, 17) speaks of "a pious reflection thrown in at hazard."

300. Note that the first half of Isa 11:9 also has a parallel elsewhere, namely in Isa 65:25b. Joseph Blenkinsopp (*Isaiah 1–39*, AB 19 [New York: Doubleday, 2000], 265) argues that the "fact that Isa 65:25 combines phrases from vv 6–7 and 9 of our poem [Isa 11:1–9] and that Hab 2:12–14 alludes to Mic 3:10 in addition to Isa 11:9b points to the originality of 11:9 rather than the opposite, and we have seen that the sentiments it expresses are in any case not out of place in the poem."

of nearby (Isa 10:34; cf. Hab 2:17).[301] But the use of the "slogan" in Isaiah is quite different from its use in Habakkuk, even though a tentative, or maybe creative, case for exegetical use of Isaiah can be made (see the commentary). As with Mic 3:10, even if we consider Habakkuk the younger text, it is not at all certain that there is a specific, rhetorically significant allusion to the earlier text.

At first sight, it might look as if this section was strung together with the help of three quotations. But all things considered, it is by no means definite that all three sayings are older than their context in Habakkuk. Even those that are older need not have been firmly tied to the one other text of which we are aware today. It is possible that one, two, or all three sentences were common sayings without a specific setting. The use of such adages does fit well with the introduction to the series in 2:6, and we shall not go far wrong if we read this section with a sense of received wisdom being applied to a specific new setting.

Commentary

12 Building projects feature prominently in Neo-Babylonian inscriptions. The conscription of prisoners of war seems to have played a significant role in the many building projects of the time and may have prompted the use of this saying. City building also forms a logical broadening from the focus on (gathering for) oneself in vv. 6b–8 and (*evil takings* in setting up) one's house in vv. 9–11. Our text is more interested in the means than the ends of these building projects. The *bloodshed* relates to *the cutting off of many peoples* in v. 10 and the reference to bloodshed in v. 8b; the *injustice* could relate to the *evil takings* in v. 9 and the plundering in v. 8a. But if the building blocks are bloodshed and injustice, the establishment cannot possibly last—a thought that is, intriguingly, not spelled out. The *Oy* here suggests, and the following verse assumes, that building with bloodshed is untenable, but the assumption is left for readers to make. Verse 13 hints at the eventually inevitable destruction of such cities (*fire*), but without stating this explicitly.

13 The rhetorical question in this verse serves to affirm strongly that the futility of the nations' labor has its cause in the decision of *YHWH of Hosts*. The second and third line of my translation, which parallel Jer 51:58, explicate the subject (*it*) of the opening line's sentence.[302] In Jeremiah, the phrase

---

301. Widely differing interpretations of 10:33–34 have been offered, with some commentators seeing a closer relationship to Isa 11 than others.

302. See Franz Delitzsch, *Habakuk*, 78, for discussion and for parallels of the construction with *waw* after the fronting of the stressed part of the sentence.

serves to underline an oracle specifically predicting the downfall of Babylon (see "Composition"). The couplet suggests not only the futility of Babylonian efforts but with it the futility of the labors of the nations that the Babylonians made subservient. Their toil will just be enough to keep the fire going—presumably the fire that will destroy the Neo-Babylonian Empire. In the end, they will have become exhausted for nothing because all they have to show for their labor will be destroyed. This links with the reality of forced labor. Paid laborers would at least have their wages to show for their toil, while these builders will have labored *for nothing* after the eventual destruction of what they have been forced to build.

14 In the book of Isaiah, the promise that the earth shall be filled with the knowledge of YHWH is for the distant future.[303] Here, it is less obvious that this is expected to happen in the distant future, even though the picture of comprehensive and extensive *knowledge of the glory of YHWH* throughout the earth is extravagant. It would be possible to translate *earth* as "land," but the international context throughout these verses advises against doing so. What is the significance of the reference to knowledge of the *glory* of YHWH? It may not be wise to differentiate sharply between knowledge of YHWH (Isa 11:9) and knowledge of his glory (here), but one could imagine a difference between becoming aware of someone's glory on the one hand and an intimate knowledge of the person on the other. When YHWH's power and presence are conspicuous (*glory*), it will not take much for everyone to realize who is in charge and to act accordingly. We can imagine various relationships between the picture in this verse and the one in the preceding verse. There is a contrast between *the glory of YHWH* and the power and presence of Nebuchadnezzar, and we would be justified to conclude that just as those who labor for Babylon's glory labor for nothing, those who know YHWH's glory and labor for him do not labor in vain, although this contrast is not explicitly drawn. There is arguably a temporal and causal relationship between YHWH revealing his glory on the one hand and the vanity of other empires (and the uselessness of toil for them) becoming evident on the other hand. Even so, it is not so much the *knowledge* of God's glory that is the cause of the futility expressed in the previous verse, but God's glory itself, in which case a causal translation of the opening particle of v. 14 is not advisable. *Yes*, this verse suggests that the peoples who have come to experience the empty glory of the Neo-Babylonian Empire will come to know YHWH's glory, and so futility will emphatically not have the last word.

---

303. Note how Isa 11:6–9 is paralleled in 65:25; cf. the discussion in Richard L. Schultz, *The Search for Quotation: Verbal Parallels in the Prophets*, JSOTSup 180 (Sheffield: Sheffield Academic Press, 1999), 240–56.

Reflection

The downfall of an oppressive regime remains something for which to hope and in which to rejoice, but these verses alert us to the extent to which even involuntary participation in an oppressive regime brings people under a negative divine decree. For a while, there was nothing to do for the nations but to submit to the Babylonian yoke (cf. Jer 27:1–15) that meant condemnation to futility (cf. Rom 8:20). The peoples who are forced to labor for the Babylonian emperor are victims of the regime, and yet the Babylonian rule means that their toil, too, is for nothing. But we must qualify this. Those who submitted to Nebuchadnezzar *as an act of obedience to YHWH* already lived in the hope that one day YHWH's glory will appear and such hope will not disappoint. This was not Habakkuk's concern to point out, but v. 14 encourages us to think along more hopeful lines. Habakkuk reminds us that it is the larger context that will determine whether our labor will be in vain. As Christians, we hold on to the promise that in the Lord Jesus our labor is not in vain (1 Cor 15:58). Those who toil only for themselves will produce what lasts for their lifetime only. Those who toil for their families or communities might achieve something of benefit for two or even three generations. The labor of a few extraordinary people has a lasting impact on generations. But only what is done in and through the Lord, in whom God's glory has become manifest, will last forever. This is possible even for slaves (e.g., Eph 6:5–8) because it is a question of mindset and integrity.

Stephen Langton, the thirteenth-century Archbishop of Canterbury, told a story "about a king who built a grand house with money acquired through robbery and extortion." When the king asked a clerk to compose a "memorial inscription" for the gate of the house, the clerk wrote:

> A house built on wrong
> Will not last for long.[304]

XI. THE FOURTH SAYING (2:15-17)

[15]*Oy the one who gives drink to his companion,*
  who attaches your[a] *passion*[b] *and even making drunk,*[c]
    so as to look on their private parts.[d]
[16]*You have sated yourself with disgrace rather than honor.*
  Now, drink yourself and show your foreskin![e]

---

304. Coggins and Han, *Six Minor Prophets*, 67. The source is Beryl Smalley, *The Study of the Bible in the Middle Ages* (Oxford: Blackwell, 1952), 257.

The cup of YHWH's right hand shall come around to you,
    and utter disgrace[f] will be on[g] your honor.
[17] *Yes,[h] the violence done to Lebanon[i] will overwhelm[j] you,*
    and the destruction of animals will terrify you[k]
        on account of shedding human blood and violence to land,
        city, and all who inhabit it.[l]

a. Some textual witnesses offer a stylistically easier third-person pronoun, but the consonantal text of MT here and throughout the line is well attested; see *BHQ*, 13:120*, for details.

b. Or "heat." While the hot excitement to which this word points is most often anger, this is not always the case (see the commentary). The root *ḥmh* can be used for the glow of the sun (Ps 19:6[7]) and, indeed, as a designation for the sun (e.g., Isa 24:23; 30:26). Maybe the meaning "venom" (e.g., Deut 32:24, 33) is derived from the human response to venom (inflammation, raised temperature). With different vocalization, others derive from *ḥēmet*, a bottle for holding liquid made of skin.

c. There are a good number of interrelated ways of reading the different phrases combined here, either by way of small emendations (e.g., "from the bowl of your anger"; so *BHS*, *HALOT*) or by way of reading a different homonym (e.g., "venom" for *anger*). The opening verb can maybe also mean "to pour out" (not firmly attested), but this seems ill-suited as a reference to forcing someone to drink *from* a cup and, alternatively, not at all suited for pouring *into* a cup.

d. The expression *private parts* translates a word that is attested only here but is surely equivalent to the more common *'erwâ* ("nakedness"). The plural form need not require that we read *the companion* collectively, although this remains a possibility (so Franz Delitzsch, *Habakuk*, 87, who defines this sense more precisely as distributive); it may well be a plural similar to the English plurals *private parts* and "genitals."

e. The reading "and stagger" in a number of versions is obtained by the reversal of two letters—likely an exegetical move. See *BHQ*, 13:121*.

f. This assumes a derivation from the root *qll* (cf. *HGHS* 499l), or at any rate that the first syllable serves to heighten the meaning of *qālôn*. Alternatively, a derivation from a root meaning "vomit" (*qy'*; cf. Isa 28:8; Prov 26:11 without *y*) combined with *qālôn* ("disgrace") has been proposed; cf. Vulg. (*vomitus ignominiae*); KJV ("shameful spewing"); and Andersen, *Habakkuk*, 250–51.

g. This reflects the common view that the verb "to be" is to be supplied. In the absence of parallels in which disgrace is "upon" honor, it also seems possible that the verb of the previous line carries over so that *utter disgrace* shall come around to honor or maybe surrounds or turns against honor.

h. I take the particle *kî* here to have the same force as at the beginning of v. 14 (see the translation note on that verse).

i. Haak (*Habakkuk*, 71) proposes to read *lbnwn* (*Lebanon* in my translation) and *bhmwt* (*animals* in the next line) "as subjective genitives seen in reference to ancient mythology in which mountain deities act as agents of destruction."

j. Literally "cover."

k. English usage requires the addition of the pronoun here, which in Hebrew is understood from the previous colon.

l. These last two cola are identical to the second half of v. 8. See the notes on that verse.

Composition

Unless v. 18 is treated as a separate saying or the text rearranged, this is the last saying to open with *Oy* and, so far, the longest of them. Alliteration with heavy use of *m* increases the cohesiveness of v. 15. The use of *wə'ap*, here understood as emphatic (*and even*; cf. Ps 68:18[19]), along with *ḥēmâ* for passion is likely also the result of playing with the sound of words, as both *'ap* and *ḥēmâ* elsewhere refer to anger. This links with *the cup of YHWH's right hand* mentioned in the next verse, a cup that is elsewhere described as the cup of God's anger or wrath and often linked with reeling from drunkenness.[305] God's cup is never offered to punish an individual on their own but always deals with communities (Ps 75:8[9]; Isa 51:17, 22; Jer 25:15, 17, 28; 49:12; 51:7; Lam 4:21; Ezek 23:31–33). The reference to *the cup of YHWH's right hand* therefore already signals the international context that is further spelled out in v. 17.

The reuse of the second half of v. 8 can be heard as an *inclusio*, which makes the subsequent fifth saying stand out even more clearly. While all the sayings concern Nebuchadnezzar's oppression of the nations, the focus of the picture widened in the first three sayings from the individual (loading upon himself heavy pledges, first saying) via his household (second saying) to city building (third saying). The fourth saying goes back to the individual, now in company with a friend or neighbor. Significantly, it also seems to pick up the metaphors used in 2:4–5, adding to a sense of closure.

Commentary

15 The translation of the middle line of the tricolon in this verse is much debated, but it is clear from the first and third colon that the verse refers to an attempt to make someone drunk in order to expose and so disgrace them. The choice of the word *passion*, most often used in the Hebrew Bible to refer to anger, may seem odd. But the agitation to which the word refers need not necessarily relate to anger (it is unlikely, e.g., for Ezek 3:14). Indeed, wine can be said to produce "heat" (Hos 7:5). The hot passion mixed in with the drink may be sexual. Sexual passion can link with violence just as well as anger. The passion and sexual fantasy lived out in sexual abuse is very often about reinforcing dominance, with physical violence sometimes being an

---

305. For an examination of this motif, see, e.g., Theodor Seidl, *"Der Becher in der Hand des Herrn": Studie zu den prophetischen "Taumelbecher"-Texten*, ATSAT 70 (St. Ottilien: EOS Verlag, 2001); and, briefly, G. Mayer, "בּוֹס, *kôs*," *TDOT* 7:101–4; Edwin C. Hoistetter, "בּוֹס," *NIDOTTE* 2:617–18. The reference to YHWH's *right hand* seems to be unique.

integral aspect of the abuse. The Neo-Assyrian and Neo-Babylonian practice of stripping prisoners of war, documented in their own illustrations,[306] may have inspired this saying, but the prior intoxication adds a twist that opens up several lines of thought, pursued further below. As pointed out above, the use of *ḥēmâ* (*passion*) prepares for the reference to *the cup of YHWH's right hand* in the next verse, which is generally a cup of wrath (see further below). In such a context, intoxication is an image of becoming incapacitated and defeated by YHWH (Isa 51:17–20; Jer 13:12–14; 25:15–29; 48:26; Pss 60:3[5]; 75:8[9]). For a while, YHWH's cup was Babylon, making the nations drunk (Jer 51:7; cf. Rev 14:8; 17:2; 18:3) and stripping countries of their population and vegetation.[307] With knowledge of this motif, it is not too difficult to see that the verse is not primarily aimed at individuals literally engaging in these activities but a reference to imperial aggression.

16 *Sated yourself* apparently refers to the "looking" of the previous verse. Trying to satiate oneself in connection with looking is attested in Eccl 1:8 and 4:8.[308] The accused has found satisfaction in bringing *disgrace* on others. Now, the tables are to be turned, and it is the aggressor who drinks and is exposed. He is exposed as uncircumcised, thus revealing himself as someone not belonging to the covenant people. This is not new information, but it highlights the reversal from master to outsider. Just as the nudity is worsened by showing *foreskin*, so *disgrace* becomes *utter disgrace*.

The verb *come around* is used only here in connection with God's cup. It is not explicitly stated that the cup given to the victim in the preceding verse was *the cup of YHWH's right hand* as well as being the cup of a human aggressor. But given that God's use of the Babylonians is the main concern of the book, we may be justified in concluding that at some level, the cup given to intoxicate the companion was also the cup of God's wrath. If so, that same cup is now taken out of the hand of the companion and given to the aggressor, an idea also found in Isa 51:22–23 and Jer 25:15–17 (cf. 49:12).[309] The reference to *YHWH's right hand* rather than a simple reference to "the

---

306. See, e.g., *ANEP*, 124–25; Vanderhooft, *Neo-Babylonian Empire*, 182–83.

307. Cf. Laurie J. Braaten, "Violence Against Earth: Moving from Land Abuse to Good Neighbor in Habakkuk" (paper presented at the SBL Annual Meeting, Atlanta, GA, 22 November 2015).

308. In German, one can "sich satt sehen" ("have one's fill looking") at something. In English, one can "drink in" a sight and "devour" with one's eyes. See John Newman, "Eating and Drinking as Sources of Metaphor in English," *Cuadernos de Filología Inglesa* 612 (1997): 213–31. For other languages, see John Newman, ed., *The Linguistics of Eating and Drinking*, Typological Studies in Language 84 (Amsterdam: John Benjamins, 2009).

309. As noted above, in Jer 51:7, Babylonia itself is the (golden) cup in God's hand: "From its wine the nations have drunk; on that account the nations have gone senseless." In the very next verse, Babylonia has suddenly fallen.

cup in YHWH's hand" or even just "YHWH's cup" stresses God's power and so hints at enforced drinking.

The preposition with *honor* (*on your honor*) could suggest either substitution, as in suffering disgrace instead of honor, or the image of (a person of) honor being covered with something disgusting (e.g., vomit; see the translation note). Because the disgrace of the emperor has already been depicted in terms of being stripped naked (cf. Isa 47:3), the former is maybe more likely if we have to decide between the two possibilities, even if the next verse speaks of being "covered" (overwhelmed) by committed violence. But Delitzsch may well be right not only in deciding against the etymological derivation from "vomit" as well as "shame" for the word translated *utter disgrace* but also in insisting that *utter disgrace* should nevertheless be heard as implying the vomit following drunkenness (cf. Jer 25:28). If the verb from the previous line is to be heard (see the translation note), then the emphasis is that it is now the turn of *your honor* to receive the *utter disgrace* previously handed to others.

17 *Violence* is not elsewhere said to cover (*overwhelm*) anyone. The closest parallel may be in Ps 140:9(10): "As for the head(s) of those who surround me, may the harm done by their lips overwhelm them!" The verb *overwhelm* maybe echoes v. 14, whose reference to YHWH's *glory* contrasts with the disgraced *honor* in v. 16 (twice).

Lebanon is not chosen at random. Vanderhooft observes that

> the heroic conquest of the Lebanon and acquisition of its prized cedars, is a well-known topos in Akkadian royal inscriptions beginning in the Old Babylonian period, and it receives special attention in Assyrian and Neo-Babylonian texts. The emphasis in this tradition about the conquest of the Lebanon is precisely that such conquest demonstrates the king's imperial achievement.[310]

The forested, mountainous nature of Lebanon made it harder to bring under the control of a single party than the plains of Mesopotamia. To be able to say that one has secured peace for its inhabitants from marauders was, therefore, all the more impressive. The prominent role of the Lebanon is also reflected in biblical literature (e.g., Isa 14:8; 37:24) and an indication here of a concern for the whole earth, not just humanity.[311] The *destruction of animals*

---

310. Vanderhooft, *Neo-Babylonian Empire*, 153. He notes that "in addition to the symbolic affirmation of the king's might, an important motive for Nebuchadnezzar's Lebanon campaign was to maintain the supply of cedar for Babylonian building projects. The use of cedar is often emphasized in Nebuchadnezzar's inscriptions" (153–54).

311. So rightly Braaten, "Violence Against Earth."

may refer to the heavy use of animals for the transportation of wood from Lebanon to Babylon, to the death of animals through the destruction of their habitat by extensive logging, and perhaps to the hunting of animals for sport, given the prominence of the royal hunt motif in Mesopotamian reliefs.

Reflection

Rape and sexual abuse were an aspect of military conquest in ancient warfare as much as in the modern world. Sexual violence continues the assault on the militarily defeated victim. It is used as a weapon of war to "feminize" the enemy.[312] Many of the early recipients of this text would have experienced military defeat, seeing their public figures led away naked into captivity and their homeland stripped of a significant part of its population.[313] They may well have remembered a sense of disorientation in defeat, as if intoxicated. Others, including in all likelihood the very first recipients of this message, would have had at least an indirect knowledge of such experiences. Virtually all recipients of this text in the century of its origin would have been all too familiar with warfare and the abuse it brought with it. Such an audience would have heard this saying differently than the many recipients today who, thankfully, have not suffered rape in warfare and may more readily think of spiked drinks and date rapes. But something like the military reality behind this text is still experienced by many today. There are still readers today who hear or read the book of Habakkuk in the midst of strife, aggression, and warfare.[314] The sense of betrayal hinted at by the use of *companion* and the motif of spiking a drink suggest bad faith in covenant relationships. It finds an echo in more recent conflicts that saw neighbors violate and kill each other—for example, in the former Yugoslavia (1991–2001), in Rwanda (most notoriously in 1994), and in a number of places in the Middle East.

The revelation earlier in the chapter (vv. 4–5) pointed to the insatiable ap-

312. For different ways of conceptualising sexual violence with regard to twentieth-century conflicts, see Inger Skjelsbæk, "Sexual Violence and War: Mapping Out a Complex Relationship," *European Journal of International Relations* 7 (2001): 211–37. See also Joshua S. Goldstein, *War and Gender: How Gender Shapes the War System and Vice Versa* (Cambridge: Cambridge University Press, 2003), 332–402, esp. 359–66.

313. Note that the Hebrew word for "exile/deportation" relates to the verb "to uncover/strip." See also Daniel L. Smith-Christopher, "Ezekiel in Abu Ghraib: Rereading Ezekiel 16:37–39 in the Context of Imperial Conquest," in *Ezekiel's Hierarchical World: Wrestling with a Tiered Reality*, ed. Stephen L. Cook and Corinne L. Patton, SBL SymS 31 (Atlanta: Society of Biblical Literature, 2004), 141–57.

314. E.g., Riad A. Kassis, *Frustrated with God: A Syrian Theologian's Reflections on Habakkuk* (self-pub., 2016), Kindle.

petite of the aggressor, depicted also as a greedy desire for wine, as the cause of his downfall. This present saying is more explicit in pointing to YHWH as the ultimate source of the retributive justice so prominent in this chapter. The companionship offered by the Neo-Babylonian Empire by means of vassal treaties was designed for imperial gratification (cf. Hab 1:16b; 2:6b, 8a, 9) and left the empire's vassals disgraced and vulnerable. It is understandable that the victims have a desire for seeing their oppressor disgraced, but it is YHWH who ensures that it will happen. Because the cup bringing disaster is in YHWH's right hand, it is he who determines whose turn it is to drink it.

Verse 17 widens the horizon beyond atrocities on humans to the ravaging of lands and forests and cruelty against animals. It is not too difficult to think of contemporary examples in which greed leads to cruelty against animals and to vicious deforestation and pollution. The saying can therefore serve us, too, as a warning against satiating ourselves without regard for the negative impact of our greed on life on this planet. Non-human creation is included in the covenant God made with Noah and his descendants. This both implies that God takes care of all of his creation and reaffirms human responsibility to do likewise as beings made in his image.[315]

Satiating, here used for drinking one's fill (cf. Isa 66:11 for a suckling child and Amos 4:8 for drinking water), more commonly refers to eating. Habakkuk 2:4–5 first made us think of eating before supplementing the image with reference to wine. Eating initiated and desired by the eater involves destruction and disappearance (of food) and thus proves a useful metaphor for imperial conquest. First, there is desire—the hunger for power and expansion. Then the intake and mastication (the crushing and grinding of other nations) followed by swallowing and digesting. The empire is "nourished" as "food" (other nations) become part of its body. The hope of the nations here is that their incorporation will turn out to be a form of intoxication.

In a different but comparable way, the voluntary suffering of the church at the hand of its oppressors for Christ's sake can lead to the downfall of the oppressor. The oppressor is defeated not by encountering a violent resistance that is too powerful to overcome but by apparently succeeding in crushing and swallowing its victims. This is not spelled out here, but we may want to note that while the plundering earlier found its counterpart in being plundered—victims getting their own back—the shaming and degradation here does not have a direct counterpart. The reference to YHWH's right hand and the command *drink yourself* are not linked with any human agent. This

---

315. Note the several uses of "with you" in Gen 9:10, 12, which stresses the connection between humanity and the animals listed. In Gen 9:13, the covenant is said to be between God and "the earth" (or "the land," *hā'āreṣ*), later spelled out as "all flesh" on the earth (vv. 15–17).

suggests that by God's plan and power, the degrader, who shamed others, will degrade himself without the need for anyone else shaming him. Victims who are eager for and tempted to revenge but who trust in this promise can thereby moderate their passion for revenge. For those who trust that such evil brings its self-degradation with it, there is no need to adopt the means and methods of one's degraders, even if one is finally able to do so. Indeed, there is a warning for those who would repay evil with evil.

XII. THE FIFTH SAYING (2:18–20)

[18]*What profit is[a] a carved image that its shaper carved it,*
   a cast image and a teacher[b] of falsehood,
      that one who shaped its shape puts his trust in it,
         making dumb nothings?
[19]*Oy the one who says to wood, "Arise!"[c]*
   "Rouse yourself!" to still stone.[d]
It shall teach?[e] Look, it is caught in gold and silver
   and there is no breath inside it at all!
[20]*But YHWH is in his holy temple;*
   hush[f] before him all the earth.

a. The *hiphil* is understood here as inwardly transitive, partly in view of instances where the subject of the verb gains rather than confers profit. The alternative understanding "What profit does . . . confer?" would not alter the sense.

b. LXX renders *môrê / yôrê* (*teacher / teach*) in 2:18–19 as *phantasia* ("display, illusion"), as if from the word for seeing.

c. Hebrew *hāqîṣâ* is the masculine singular imperative of *qîṣ*, which always has the paragogic *hê*. It goes with *'ēṣ* (*wood*), which is a masculine noun. The following imperative is feminine to go with the feminine noun *'eben* (*stone*).

d. LXX does not render the chiasm but reads both imperatives as addressing the wood, creating a new address for the stone out of *dûmām* (*still*). Haak (*Habakkuk*, 26, 76) suggests a similar division of lines and reads, "Woe to the one saying to wood, 'Awake! Stir up!'/ to still stone, 'Make the early rain fall!' " See also following note.

e. Or "It shall [let it] rain?" (cf. Hos 6:3; 10:12; Prov 11:25) with reference to the early rain (cf. the noun in Deut 11:14; Jer 5:24). There is no interrogative particle here, but its absence is not unusual in Biblical Hebrew. The personal pronoun is used for emphasis. Andersen (*Habakkuk*, 252–53, 256) interprets the phrase as a statement rather than a question, with the pronoun referring to the priest who speaks to wood and stone. Haak (*Habakkuk*, 78) interprets the verb as a *piel* imperative: "Fall!" (cf. Job 37:6, with snow as the subject).

f. The rare interjection *has* (6× in the Hebrew Bible) sounds similar to the English *hush* and has a parallel also in Arabic, Syriac, and Egyptian, where it is used to encourage animals to stand still; see Friedrich Schulthess, *Zurufe an Tiere im Arabischen* (Berlin: Verlag der Königlichen Akademie der Wissenschaften, 1912), 64.

Composition

The fifth saying differs from the others in not referring to peoples and nations or bloodshed and violence. It is set apart from the other sayings also by the presence of an introductory quatrain (v. 18) prior to the actual *Oy* saying.[316] This helps to mark it as the concluding saying and underlines that the Babylonians can expect no help from their gods once the time has come for the reversals spelled out in the previous sayings. Sweeney reads it as a commentary on the preceding four sayings, pointing to the repeated refrain between the first and the fourth saying as marking an *inclusio*.[317] This is possible and helps to avoid any perceived difficulties of attributing anti-idol polemic to other nations. But as suggested above, the presentation of the *Oy* sayings as speech of the nations is a literary device to underscore the reversal motif. It no longer plays any noticeable role from v. 8 onward, so there is no need to postulate a change of speaker here. I read the unusual structure as a way to mark the climax of the sayings. Putting v. 18 prior to the *Oy* saying arguably helps to link it (and maybe the fifth saying as a whole) more closely to the preceding. The preceding four sayings described Babylonian conquest and imperialism in different images. The fifth proceeds to characterize not the conquest but the ultimate powerlessness of the conqueror, who cannot expect help from his gods. Prinsloo finds here "the basic cause for the failure of the arrogant man—he does not recognise the sovereignty of Yahweh."[318] As Andersen points out, the received order of vv. 18–19 also makes for a good juxtaposition, contrasting the presence of YHWH in his holy temple at the beginning of v. 20 with the absence of spirit from the idol at the end of v. 19.[319]

The final verse is an appropriate conclusion not only to this last saying, which features speech or lack thereof prominently, but also to the whole series of sayings, which are after all introduced as the speech of the nations (v. 6). Indeed, it can be read as bringing the whole of chs. 1–2 to a (preliminary) conclusion. As Andersen notes, "The whole matter began with the frantic prayers of the prophet to his silent God. Now the whole world is reduced to silence before the majesty of Yahweh."[320] Whether this verse could ever have functioned as a conclusion to the book is harder to tell. It

---

316. Masoretic MSS consistently mark a paragraph break after v. 18 with a closed space. The Cairo and Leningrad Codices also have a closed space before v. 18, Codex Petropolitanus an open space. Only the Aleppo Codex does not have a space before the verse. Thus, in most masoretic MSS, the verse is given prominence by a space before and afterward.

317. Sweeney, "Structure, Genre, and Intent," 73; *Twelve Prophets*, 473, 475.

318. Prinsloo, "Reading Habakkuk as a Literary Unit," 525.

319. Andersen, *Habakkuk*, 257.

320. Andersen, *Habakkuk*, 256.

seems to raise an expectation, not unlike the first verse of the chapter. But ch. 3 does not follow on from ch. 2 as 2:2 follows 2:1. The new title in ch. 3 marks it clearly off from ch. 2. But on the other hand, ch. 3 arguably defines or redefines the *hush* that is asked for in this final verse of ch. 2. Habakkuk is not silent in ch. 3, but his speech is very different from the complaint in ch. 1. We may compare the "hush" in Neh 8:11, which stills the mourning and makes space for the mirth of Neh 8:12. The movement of the book is from a prophet's complaint (ch. 1, citing divine speech) via God's answer (ch. 2, citing the speech of the nations) to a prophet's prayer (ch. 3, again reflecting traditional material). The function of 2:20 may be to ensure that readers do not move on from divine speech, as if to give human speech (even in the form of prayer, ch. 3) the last word, but to read (and pray, 3:19) the following chapter as a means of keeping the "silence" of submission and expectation.

Commentary

18 The prophets describe idols or foreign deities (Isa 44:9–10; Jer 2:8, 11; 16:19; cf. 1 Sam 12:21) as well as political powers (Egypt in Isa 30:5–6) as entities that do not *profit*. Absence of profitableness is also linked explicitly to *falsehood* in Jer 7:8 and 23:32. Isa 47:12 offers a challenge to the Babylonians to see whether they can get any benefit out of their magic. It is the *falsehood*, which implies a lack of dependability, that ensures that there will not be any *profit*. In fact, there seems to be only one biblical reference that points to a reliable source of *profit*: "I am the LORD your God, who teaches you how to gain profit" (Isa 48:17, with a different root used for the "teaching" than in Hab 2:18).

The two words used (*pesel, massēkâ*) may suggest idols crafted from wood or stone and metal. They form a stock phrase in Deut 27:5; Judg 17:3–4; 18:14; and Nah 1:14, maybe to indicate any sort of idol or as a hendiadys for a wooden or stone image with an overlay of metal.[321] The latter fits with the observation that the terms are always found in the order in which they appear here (and in Isa 42:17). The term rendered above as *carved image* appears on its own in passages where the idol is made of metal (Isa 40:19; 44:10; Jer 10:14; 51:17)—although there, too, the metal is perhaps to be thought of as an overlay. Only small figurines would have been *cast* entirely out of metal. But the more important point here is that the idol-maker is the one who gives *shape* to the idol and then wants to allow it to shape his or her own life. This can only lead to disappointment, as the idol is a *teacher of falsehood* (less likely,

---

321. See also Jer 10:3–4, which does not use the term *pesel* (*carved image*) for the procedure, referring to wood, silver, and gold.

"a false/deceptive teacher").[322] The references to dumbness and absence of breath suggest that the emphasis is not so much on the presence of lies as on the absence of truth, if such a distinction makes sense. The teacher is deceptive in that there is no reliable teaching to be had from an idol. The idols are *dumb nothings* (*'ĕlîlîm 'illĕmîm*, a wordplay that puns with "God/gods"); there is no teaching here at all. The only words that could come forth from an idol are those put in their mouths by a human, and Hab 2:18–19 lacks even a hint of such words. The only words here are words addressed to the idols.

19 The Psalms allow for the covenant God of Israel to be addressed with the words *"Arise!"* and *"Rouse yourself!"* (35:23; 44:23[24]; cf. 73:20), but it is ridiculous to expect lifeless *wood* and *stone* to respond to such a call. Exodus 15:16 suggests that *"still* as a *stone"* was proverbial in ancient Israel. In my view, *It shall teach?* is a rhetorical question. The pronoun here probably has a different referent from the same pronoun after *look* (contra Andersen). *Look* expresses the sort of surprise that fits well with taking the previous words as a rhetorical question to which the presumed answer is no. The idol cannot teach because *it is caught in gold and silver*. The word translated *caught* (*tāpûś*) may be a neutral reference here to being overlaid with *gold and silver* (Isa 40:19; 44:10; Jer 10:14; 51:17). It seems to be the only use of the passive *qal* for this verb; the *niphal* is used for being seized, captured, or trapped. Maybe the use of a *niphal* would imply an intent on the part of the sculptor to trap the idol, which is avoided by the use of the passive *qal*, but the notion of the idol being "trapped" is inappropriate only insofar as it suggests that the idol may be a living being. Yet *there is no breath inside it at all* (cf. Jer 10:14; 51:17), and so there is a complete absence not only of speech but of life. Idols are therefore completely unable to offer rain. It is unlikely that this is the primary reference here (contra Haak, see translation note on *teach*). But given that ch. 3 attributes responsibility for weather phenomena to YHWH, it is fortuitous that the word for *teach* (*yôre*) reads and sounds exactly like the noun "early rain" (also *yôre*; e.g., Deut 11:14) and the *hiphil* of the related verb "to (send) rain" (Hos 10:12). The double entendre may well be intentional. Idols will not bring a change of season ("It shall send rain?"), but YHWH can do so.

20 The possible allusion to rain in the previous verse lends support to the view that *his holy temple* here refers to heaven, the place from which rain and

---

322. Franz Delitzsch (*Habakuk*, 99–100) argues correctly that the designation belongs to the idol rather than the priest or prophet (cf. Isa 9:15[14] for a prophet as a *teacher of falsehood*). In my view, the second half of the verse explains what makes the idol a *teacher of falsehood*, namely the trust of the worshiper by which the idolater takes the idol as their guide. Delitzsch believes that the rhetorical question does not deny that the idol teaches; he thinks that the question uses "teach" in the full sense of teaching what is right.

snow also come (e.g., Isa 55:10). This seems to be the case in Ps 11:4, where *YHWH is in his holy temple* is parallel to "YHWH—in heaven is his throne." This is also true for the reference to *his holy throne* in Mic 1:2, as the subsequent verse confirms with its reference to YHWH's coming down to march on the heights of the earth.[323] The alternative, that *his holy temple* refers to the temple in Jerusalem, is possible but less likely, as the earthly sanctuary does not clearly come into view at any point in Habakkuk. The Jerusalem temple may well be the implicit setting of chs. 1–2 and is the most likely setting for the communal use of ch. 3. But YHWH is more readily seen in the book as in the process of coming to his people rather than being in their midst. The affirmation that *YHWH is in his holy temple* offers reassurance not so much of divine presence but of divine rule. YHWH has not been displaced from his palace; he remains very much in charge. This is to be acknowledged by everyone—hence *hush before him all the earth*. The hushing is a sign of respect (encouraged by the addition of *holy* to *temple*) and probably also of expectation. The two subsequent uses of a similar phrase in the Book of the Twelve (Zeph 1:7; Zech 2:13[17]) are in relation to a theophany.[324]

The evidence does not allow us to conclude with confidence that *hush before him all the earth* was a liturgical call that prepared for a divine word or action, but the phrase is eminently suited for marking a conclusion that is only preliminary, awaiting a further word. The judgment has been announced out of the mouths of the oppressed nations, so we now await its execution (cf. Ps 76:8[9]). Mark Boda noted that while there are several instances of people addressing God from Hosea to Habakkuk, this becomes rare in the Book of the Twelve after this point, excepting divine citation of inappropriate words of the people (Zech 11:5; Mal 1:2, 6, 7; 2:14, 17; 3:7, 8, 13).[325] Boda must allow "for one final and climactic expression of direct and indirect human address to Yahweh in Hab 3" and acknowledges that Mal 1:5 reflects "norma-

---

323. The "holy temple" in Ps 79:1 and Jonah 2:4(5) is clearly a reference to the sanctuary in Jerusalem. The "worship toward your holy temple" in Ps 138:2 may be in the direction of Jerusalem, although in Ps 5:7(8) the psalmist seems to "come" to the earthly sanctuary ("your house") to "bow down" toward the heavenly one ("your *holy temple*"), and in Jonah 2:7 the prayer is more likely thought of as having risen "to your holy temple" in heaven than to the one in Jerusalem. In other words, nothing can be deduced from the usage of the expression *holy temple* itself.

324. The lines between earthly and heavenly temple are similarly blurred in Zech 2:13(17). As the action is "from his holy dwelling" in favor of Jerusalem, it seems to me again more likely that the focus is on the heavenly dwelling.

325. Mark J. Boda, "A Deafening Call to Silence: The Rhetorical 'End' of Human Address to the Deity in the Book of the Twelve," in *The Book of the Twelve and the New Form Criticism*, ed. Mark J. Boda, Michael H. Floyd, and Colin M. Toffelmire, SBLANEM 10 (Atlanta: Society of Biblical Literature, 2015), 183–204.

tive human address."[326] It might be more accurate to say that from now on, prophetic complaint, challenge, or even intercession is no longer allowed within the Book of the Twelve, although the angel of YHWH is allowed to ask questions of YHWH (Zech 1:12). As this may well be part of a general move from complaint to penitence within the restoration community, this feature need not go back to specific editorial activity within the Twelve.[327]

Reflection

Moshe Weinfeld observes,

> The empire is the embodiment of idolatry which is doomed to failure. End of idolatry is end of empire. Bowing down to idols made out of gold and silver means worshipping the work of one's own hand and is tantamount to prostration and submission to the imperial power.[328]

This, in a nutshell, teases out one of the implications for Habakkuk's audience and offers one reason for putting this saying last. Now that the empire is on its way out, it is high time to get rid of any idols associated with it. It was YHWH who had announced the rise of the Neo-Babylonian Empire (cf. 1:5–11), and it is YHWH who guarantees its end. The dumb dummies worshipped as deities cannot compare with YHWH—a theme developed in Isa 40–48 in the context of the end of the Neo-Babylonian Empire.

What one pays homage to reveals what one ascribes power to. This does indeed affect the whole earth. In ch. 1, the Babylonians were portrayed as worshipping their tools (1:16), but the prophet knew that it was YHWH's plan and purpose that gave the Babylonians their power—hence the com-

---

326. Boda, "A Deafening Call," 201 and 200 respectively. Zechariah 1:6 is indirect speech, and in Zech 1:21 (2:4), the prophet addresses the deity merely "to seek an interpretation of elements in the vision" (199). The absence of prayers directed to YHWH in Obadiah and Nahum (i.e., prior to the call to silence in Hab 2:20; Zeph 1:7; Zech 2:13[17]) is explained with appeal to the observation that these books are "on the surface" not addressed to an Israelite audience (203). Given that Obadiah and Nahum were written for the people of God as much as Hosea, Joel, Amos, and Micah, this seems to me a feeble argument. Habakkuk is "on the surface" not addressed to the people of God either, and the same is arguably true for Jonah, a narrative without an explicit recipient.

327. Note that the book of Jonah, whose chronological setting and place within the Twelve are before Habakkuk but which was most likely written later, does not contain any valid prophetic complaint either.

328. Weinfeld, "Protest," 179.

plaint. The end of ch. 2 underlines again that the aggressors did not truly receive guidance and power from anyone else but YHWH.

So it is for us. Whatever we worship, whatever we put at the center of our lives, will give shape and direction to our lives, but the center can only hold if it is the living God himself. Everything else will let down its worshippers. Ultimately, all will bow their knees to the one who alone is perfectly true and reliable (Isa 45:23; Rom 14:11; Phil 2:10).

XIII. THE HEADING FOR HABAKKUK'S PRAYER (3:1)

¹*A prayer of*ᵃ *the prophet Habakkuk, besides vehement protests.*ᵇ

a. For the vowel with the preposition, see JM 22d. It does not represent the definite article, which does not occur with a name referring to a person; cf. JM 137b.

b. Or "according to Shigionoth," indicating a mode of performance; see further in the commentary. The traditional derivation of *šigyōnôt* from a root meaning "to stray, to do wrong (inadvertently)" is reflected in the rendering in the Stone edition of the Tanach, "for erroneous utterances" (cf. Vulg.; Tg.; Rashi); cf. *šagî'ôt* in Ps 19:12(13).

Composition

It will be good to say a few things here about this chapter as a whole. The heading sets it apart from the preceding two chapters, although we have already observed that the end of ch. 2 can be read as setting up a continuation. Such a continuation might be expected in the form of divine speech. Yet this is not what we get in ch. 3. As before in the book, what we now receive as divine revelation is clothed in the speech of someone else. Habakkuk's complaint in ch. 1 incorporated earlier divine speech. The divine revelation in ch. 2 was expanded in the form of speech attributed to the nations conquered by the Babylonians. In ch. 3, one senses that, in an act of worship, the prophet either received further revelation or has come to a deeper appreciation of God's revelation. It may be ill advised to make a strict distinction between human prayer and divine revelation within Habakkuk; not only do the prophet's prayers cite revelation, but the prayers are now presented as divine revelation (cf. 1:1).³²⁹ Nevertheless, if we think of the book as a whole, we can discern a development from prayer to prayer. The prayer in ch. 1 is mulling over divine revelation in the form of an earlier but recent prophecy; the prayer in ch. 3 is mulling over more ancient divine revelation (and what it

329. Even granted that 1:1 may or may not extend to cover ch. 3, as part of Scripture, the final chapter has been received as divine revelation just as much as, e.g., the Psalms.

suggests about the future). The movement from the earlier complaint-prayer to the later petition-prayer is facilitated by God's revelation in ch. 2, encapsulated in 2:4–5 and expanded (mulled over) in 2:6–20.

Habakkuk 3 offers a fascinating mix of traditions and motifs. There are echoes of biblical texts portraying YHWH as storm god (e.g., Ps 29) and divine warrior (e.g., Judg 4–5), riding on the winds (e.g., Ps 18), and fighting the forces of chaos (e.g., Ps 77). There are also parallels in extrabiblical West Semitic as well as Mesopotamian and Egyptian descriptions of various deities. The likelihood that the author of Hab 3 knew many of the inner-biblical parallel texts, either in the form we know them today or in an earlier but similar form, is strong, especially if one believes (as I do, albeit tentatively) that the poetic material in Hab 3 does not date earlier than Hab 1–2.

The links with extrabiblical traditions may similarly be the result of knowledge of specific texts and traditions. Thus, for example, Nili Shupak argues for a close link between Hab 3:3–7 and the worship of the sun god Aten at Amarna.[330] But in broad terms, all these traditions seem to have been part of Israel's heritage or cultural knowledge well before the sixth century. Mark S. Smith rightly argues that the application of solar imagery to YHWH (e.g., also in Ps 84), other than in general terms, came relatively late, arising within the royal cult in the Southern Kingdom.[331] This would still be much earlier than the composition of the book of Habakkuk.

It may be useful here to recap Smith's influential study of the early history of Israel's religion. He suggests that "the original god of Israel was El" and that YHWH was "originally a warrior-god from Sinai/Paran/Edom/Teiman" who came to be identified with El early on in Israel's history.[332] Smith thinks that storm imagery, such as we find in the latter half of Hab 3, likely came to be applied to Israel's chief god secondarily but already before the establishment of the monarchy. Further, he avers that from the ninth century onward, such imagery was used in conscious polemic against the worship of Baal (Adad), the Phoenician (and Canaanite) storm god whose mythical conflict with Yamm (Sea) and Mot (Death) reflects the agricultural seasons as well as political concerns.[333] As Smith says,

330. Nili Shupak, "The God from Teman and the Egyptian Sun God: A Reconsideration of Habakkuk 3:3–7," *JANES* 28 (2001): 97–116.

331. Mark S. Smith, *The Early History of God: YHWH and the Other Deities in Ancient Israel*, 2nd ed. (Grand Rapids: Eerdmans, 2002), 148–59. Note also the discussion in Leuenberger, *Gott in Bewegung*, 34–71.

332. Mark S. Smith, *Early History*, 32. Cf. his *The Origins of Biblical Monotheism: Israel's Polytheistic Background and the Ugaritic Texts* (Oxford: Oxford University Press, 2001), 142–46.

333. Mark S. Smith, *Early History*, 91–101. The enthronement of Baal was thought to establish fertility and supported the political claims of the local monarchy.

Israelite tradition modified its Canaanite heritage by molding the march of the divine warrior specifically to the element of YHWH's southern sanctuary, variously called Sinai (Deut 33:2; cf. Judg 5:5; Ps 68:8[9]), Paran (Deut 33:2; Hab 3:3), Edom (Judg 5:4), and Teiman (Hab 3:3 and in the Kuntillet 'Arjûd inscriptions; cf. Amos 1:12; Ezek 25:13).[334]

This commentary is not the place to engage in detail with Smith's reconstruction, but I will simply observe from this and similar proposals that the motifs found in Hab 3 were likely not employed to characterize YHWH and his work for the first time here.

How relevant is it for readers of Habakkuk to have knowledge of this background? On the one hand, it is very useful. It may explain some otherwise surprising or puzzling features, such as the appearance of pestilence in YHWH's entourage in Hab 3:5. This seems to have a Ugaritic antecedent in *KTU* 1.82, lines 1–3, "which perhaps includes Reshep as a warrior with Baal against *tnn*, related to biblical *tannînîm*."[335] As a traditional element, one need not, therefore, explain the choice of pestilence to signal the threatening nature of YHWH's approach as describing or anticipating actual outbreaks of illness. The parallels also alert us to the possible interrelationships between geographical, theological or mythological, and political realities, because geopolitical and theological agendas are frequently combined in similar ancient Near Eastern texts. On the other hand, there is the possibility that we may fail to see what is going on in Hab 3 itself by pressing the parallels too much. Thus, for example, the parallels to theophany reports from early in Israel's history have often led to a reading of vv. 3–15 as purely retrospective— in my view a rather problematic approach.[336] The parallels with conflicts between various deities in Babylonian, Canaanite, and Egyptian sources should not mislead us into thinking that Hab 3 presents aspects of the divine on both sides of the conflict. The use of the tradition about YHWH's southern sanctuary (Sinai/Teman) is a good example of Habakkuk's creativity. Habakkuk does not refer to "YHWH from Teman" as in the Kuntillet 'Arjûd inscriptions but uses the comparatively rare designation Eloah (*God*), a name or title not linked with Teman in any other text known to us today. More strikingly, vv. 8–11 reflect traditions about a battle between a god aspiring for kingship and the Sea, itself personified as a god. The rhetorical question in Hab 3:8, however, expects a negative answer (YHWH is not battling the River and

---

334. Mark S. Smith, *Early History*, 81.

335. Mark S. Smith, *Early History*, 81; cf. 77n. 43; Smith, *Origins*, 67–68.

336. The arguments against reading these verses essentially as historical narrative were presented already by Franz Delitzsch, *Habakuk*, 137–39; cf. John H. Eaton, "The Origin and Meaning of Habakkuk 3," *ZAW* 76 (1964): 164–65.

the Sea). This should be allowed to stand, contra those scholars and translators who emend the rhetorical question to its opposite to conform it to expectations brought to the text from a knowledge of these other traditions. In other words, these various biblical and extrabiblical traditions may well help us see from where the various ideas and motifs used in Hab 3 derive but not necessarily what is made of them here and what purpose they serve. The text of Hab 3 is often difficult, but recent scholars seem, on the whole, more reluctant than a previous generation to emend the MT extensively.[337]

Commentary

1 The heading designates the following poem as a *prayer*. The Hebrew term *təpillâ* seems to function similarly to the English word "prayer" as a broad and general term for speech addressed to God that is nevertheless more commonly used for petition than praise (*təhillâ*; cf. v. 3).[338] The basic petition is expressed in the next verse, which rhetorically governs the verses that follow, even if vv. 3–15 are considered a hymn that is incorporated into petitionary prayer. In other words, whatever other material is employed here, at its heart, Hab 3 is a prayer of supplication. The reference to *Habakkuk* here could be a reference either to the author or simply to the person praying. As was the case for the prayer in ch. 1, we need not choose between these two options. The heading in 1:1 covers chs. 1–2 (or maybe the whole book) and thus attributes responsibility for them to the prophet Habakkuk while at the same time designating him as the one who prays the complaint, eagerly expecting an answer from God (cf. 2:1). The reuse of the prophet's name with the label *the prophet* suggests that we should consider Habakkuk not only the person responsible for the communication conveyed in ch. 3 but also, implicitly, the person who first prays the prayer, which is then offered for communal use (cf. 3:19).

The translation *besides vehement protests* is a tentative proposal. It assumes, with ancient interpreters, that the preposition *'al* introduces the content or context of the prayer. It also assumes that the feminine plural *šigyōnôt* is related to *šiggāyôn* in the title of Ps 7, where it indicates a type of composition. The derivation of *šiggāyôn* and *šigyōnôt* from the root *šgh* should be

---

337. This reluctance is, e.g., reflected in the detailed textual study by Christopher R. Lortie, *Mighty to Save: A Literary and Historical Study of Habakkuk 3 and Its Traditions*, ATSAT 99 (St. Ottilien: EOS, 2017).

338. See, e.g., 1 Kgs 8, where the term is used half a dozen times, and again in 9:3, nearly always associated with and apparently parallel to *təhinnâ* ("plea for grace"); cf. Pss 6:9(10); 55:1(2).

uncontroversial,[339] even though Rembert Sorg proposed a derivation from
gnn ("to cover, protect").[340] The verb related to this root is used for straying
(e.g., of sheep in Ezek 34:6), staggering (from drunkenness, e.g., in Isa 28:7),
doing wrong (1 Sam 26:21), and sinning unintentionally (e.g., Lev 4:13; Num
15:22; Job 6:24; 19:4). The by-form *šgg* is also used for sinning inadvertently
(Lev 5:18; Num 15:28) as well as going astray (Job 12:16; Ps 119:67). The root
also underlies the noun *šəgāgâ*, which refers to inadvertent wrongdoing (e.g.,
Lev 4:2, 22, 27; Num 15:24–29), e.g., homicide (Num 35:11, 15; Josh 20:3, 9)
and hasty speech (Eccl 5:5); and the noun *šəgî'ôt* ("errors") in Ps 19:13. The
traditional interpretation of *šigyōnôt* in Hab 3, as well as *šiggāyôn* in Ps 7
(see the Psalms Midrash), thus relates the term to inadvertent wrongdoing
either in relation to Habakkuk (e.g., Jerome, Rashi), in which case the prayer
springs out of penitence for the prophet's impetuous speech recorded earlier
in the book, or in relation to the sins of God's people, in which case the prayer
springs from gratitude that a delay in God's judgment gives them opportunity
to repent. The latter is expressed in the Tg.:

> A prayer which Habakkuk the prophet prayed when it was revealed to
> him about the extension he grants to evildoers that if they return to the
> Torah with a perfect heart they will be forgiven, and all their sins that they
> committed before him will be like inadvertent errors.

Modern scholars have appealed to cognates from Arabic to render *šiggāyôn* as either an ecstatic song or an elegy or to cognates from Syriac to
render it as a hymn of praise. None of these, however, seem suitable for Ps 7.
The same applies to the popular derivation from the Akkadian *šigû*, which
designates a minor genre of incantations and cries for mercy, usually or always in the context of sin.[341] These prayers have a very different feel from Ps

---

339. Cf. the similar noun formations *higgāyôn* (from *hgh*, "to meditate, murmur, make
a soft noise"), *ḥizzāyôn* (from *ḥzh*, "to see"), *killāyôn* (from *klh*, "to annihilate"), and
several others.

340. Rembert Sorg, *Habaqquq III and Selah* (Fifield: King of Martyrs Priory, 1968), 12.
He proposes a "shaf'el formation" and thinks of it as a prayer for (God's) protection. But
vestiges of the causative *šap'el* (attested in Akkadian, Ugaritic, and Aramaic) are exceedingly
rare in the Hebrew Bible. Meyer (*Grammatik*, 2:35) allows for the prefix *ša* with two or
three nouns (cf. *HGHS* 61kε), but Sorg offers no explanation for the first vowel, which one
would expect to be a *patakh* (as in *šalhebet*, "flame") or reduced to *shewa* (as in *šəqa'ărûrâ*,
"depression, hollow").

341. See *CAD* 17:413–14. Werner Mayer's major study *Untersuchungen zur Formensprache
der babylonischen Gebetsbeschwörungen* (Rome: Pontifical Biblical Institute, 1976) lists *šigû*
prayers among the smaller genres specifically pleading for liberation from sin ("Bitte um
Befreiung von Sünde," 15, 111–13); cf. already Walther Schrank, *Babylonische Sühnriten*,
Leipziger Semitische Studien 3/1 (Leipzig: J. C. Hinrichs, 1908), 47–50. See also the dis-

7 or Hab 3, which renders an equation of the terms problematic.[342] But the insight that *šiggāyôn* is likely a technical term indicating a type of composition, an insight recovered from the tenth century onward among Jewish exegetes and linguists, should be affirmed against the regular interpretation found in antiquity and still dominant in medieval times that relates *šiggāyôn* to ignorance or inadvertent wrongdoing. In Ps 7:1, *šiggāyôn* occupies a place that is regularly taken by designations such as *mizmôr* ("psalm," probably a song accompanied by instruments), *miktām* (maybe "inscription," emphasizing that a firm record is made of something), and *maśkîl* (maybe "instruction" to refer to a didactic poem or "artful song," emphasizing artistic endeavor). While we do not know what these terms truly signified to those who first used them, it is clear that they are terms similar to and maybe more precise than "song" (*šîr*), "prayer" (*təpillâ*), or "hymn" (*təhillâ*). The *šiggāyôn* in Ps 7 may be a prayer that pleads for the righting of a wrong, vaguely similar to the Akkadian *šigû* but without the penitential aspect, but this is true for many a complaint psalm. There is, however, arguably a greater sense of outrage and agitation than found in some psalms, as the psalmist fiercely rejects accusations against him, solemnly swearing his innocence. Alternatively, or in addition to this, many have suggested that *šiggāyôn* refers to a "staggering" or "straying" rhythm, expressing either agitation or ecstasy, with *šigyōnôt* possibly referring to rapid changes of rhythm.[343] The suggestion, however, that Ps 7 (or Hab 3) has a noticeably more erratic rhythm than other poems in the Psalter is unconvincing; in any case, our reconstruction of the rhythm of ancient Hebrew poetry remains so beset with difficulties that this would be hard to demonstrate. It is also worth observing that in similar designa-

---

cussion in Karel van der Toorn, *Sin and Sanction in Israel and Mesopotamia: A Comparative Study*, SSN 22 (Assen: Van Gorcum, 1985), 117–21, who stresses that the lighthearted use of the penitential word *šigû* was considered dangerous and suggests that over time the prayers were "increasingly restricted to royal usage" (119), with the misfortunes to be averted "usually of national importance" (120). Whether the term was also used for cries for mercy outside a context of sin is less clear. For discussion of an example in detail, see Takayoshi Oshima, *Babylonian Prayers to Marduk*, ORA 7 (Tübingen: Mohr Siebeck, 2011), 296–327.

342. Cf. M.-J. Seux, "*Šiggāyôn = šigû?*," in *Mélanges bibliques et orientaux en l'honneur de M. Henri Cazelles*, ed. André Caquot and Matthias Delcor, AOAT 212 (Kevelaer: Butzon & Bercker; Neukirchen-Vluyn: Neukirchener Verlag, 1981), 419–38, who prints several examples of Akkadian *šigû* prayers in (French) translation and agrees with an earlier suggestion that Ps 51 might be considered the best example of a biblical *šigû* prayer. See also Andersen, *Habakkuk*, 271–72.

343. See the detailed argument in Franz Delitzsch, *Habakuk*, 126–27. Cf. Robert Sinker, *The Psalm of Habakkuk* (Cambridge: Deighton, Bell and Co., 1890), 9–10, who speaks of "a wild, wandering strain" in view of "the melody," presumably a reference to the tune as opposed to the rhythm, which he identifies as pretty regular "ternary *stichi*" throughout most of the poem (11).

tions, the subject of the implied verb seems to be the poet or performer. It is the poet who prays (*pll*) and so the *təpillâ* comes about, who sings (*šyr*) or praises (*hll*) and so a *šîr* or *təhillâ* is heard, who plucks a stringed instrument (*zmr piel*) and so produces a *mizmôr*. In the same way, the *miktām* possibly results from the poet's writing (*ktb piel*, with *b* exchanged for *m*?),[344] perhaps documenting a petition that has received a positive response. Similarly, the *maśkîl* flows from the poet's instructing (*śkl hiphil*). Only in this last case could it be said, alternatively, that the *maśkîl* itself offers instruction. Just as it is not the song that sings but the singer, so here it seems more likely that the subject of the implied verb (*šgh/šgg*) is the poet himself rather than the verse or rhythm of the *šiggāyôn*.

Herbert G. May argued that the preposition *'al* in superscriptions of the Psalms should normally be read as referring to a tune.[345] He suggested that the rubric in Hab 3 either imitates the one in Ps 7, although he does not explain how or why, or indicates another melody.[346] Others allow that *'al* may be used in titles in a variety of ways but always in relation to music (tune, mode of composition, instrument, voice) and assume that the same must be true for *'al šigyōnôt* in Hab 3, which is then understood as "in the mode typical of a *šiggāyôn*." This is the understanding most commonly adopted today, and it may be correct. But it is not clear how "in the mode of *šigyōnôt*" would be different from "a *šiggāyôn*" and hence why the prayer is not simply called a *šiggāyôn*. Further, it is not likely that the reference is to instruments typically used with a *šiggāyôn* given that there seems to be a reference to instruments in the postscript (v. 19). As pointed out above, *šiggāyôn* in Ps 7 takes the place of a genre designation, not unlike *təpillâ* (*prayer*) here in Hab 3:1. Interestingly, when *təpillâ* is used in the title of a psalm (17:1; 86:1; 90:1; 102:1), it is always coupled with a reference to the person praying (usually a name, but "one afflicted, when faint and pleading before YHWH" in Ps 102) and never with a musical notation. Nor do any of the psalms that bear the title *təpillâ* feature *selâ* or any reference to singing or making music in the body

344. See, very tentatively, *HALOT* and Ges[18]. The alternative derivation, from *ktm* ("to cover [with stain], conceal"), would similarly suggest a derivation from the poet's activity rather than the poem's literary characteristics.

345. Herbert G. May, " "AL . . .' in the Superscriptions of the Psalms," *AJSL* 58 (1941): 70–83. He argues that this is true also for *'al-haššəmînît* in Pss 6 and 12 and *'al-'ălāmôt* in Ps 46, which are sometimes interpreted as indicating tuning or voices, and suggests that the ascriptions in 53:1 and 88:1 also do not refer to occasion but to a melody. In addition, he believes that one tune ('*al-tašḥēt*, Pss 57; 58; 59; 75) is indicated without use of the preposition.

346. May, "'AL . . . ," 83. On the analogy of the cases he considers clear, this is his default option and therefore his conclusion also for *'al-yədûtûn* in Pss 62:1 and 77:1, which "little can be made of" otherwise.

of the psalm. This does not mean, of course, that a *təpillâ* cannot be put to music, not least as Hab 3 plainly is presented as a musical piece, but it may register with us a caution against simply assuming that *'al šigyōnôt* must be a musical notation. The separation of title (Hab 3:1) and colophon (Hab 3:19b) may be rhetorically significant. Perhaps we are invited to read the chapter first as Habakkuk's prayer then as a musical composition for wider use, even if the threefold use of *selâ* within the poem does prepare for the subscript.

If it is true that the preposition *'al* in Psalm superscriptions generally refers to an aspect of the music—maybe the tune—it is also true that it always follows *lamnaṣṣēaḥ* (usually translated "for the musical director" or similarly) and usually immediately (8:1; 12:1; 22:1; 45:1; 53:1; 56:1; 60:1; 61:1; 62:1; 69:1; 77:1; 81:1; 84:1; 88:1).[347] Indeed, only twice is an element allowed to come between *lamnaṣṣēaḥ* and the *'al-* designation (6:1; 46:1). In Ps 6:1 *bingînôt* ("on stringed instruments"?) intervenes, presumably because in titles, *bingînôt* always follows *lamnaṣṣēaḥ* immediately (Ps 4:1; 54:1; 55:1; 67:1; 76:1; cf. 61:1). In Ps 46:1, no reason for the unusual order of designations is evident, but there too, *'al* follows *lamnaṣṣēaḥ*, even if not immediately and *'al-'ălāmôt* is in turn immediately followed by *šîr*, putting it into a musical context. Indeed, in the light of Ps 68:25(26), it is possible that *'al-'ălāmôt* should be understood as a reference to performers ("alongside the young women [playing drums]"), which would seem possible for 1 Chr 15:20 as well, but this must remain speculative.

There is only one instance of *'al* in a psalm title where it does not follow *lamnaṣṣēaḥ*—namely Ps 7:1, "the *šiggāyôn* belonging to David that he sang to YHWH concerning (*'al*) the words of Cush, the Benjaminite." This is also the one instance in which *'al* is surely meant to indicate the subject matter, not an aspect of music.[348] This need not mean that *'al* functions in the same way in Hab 3:1 but, along with the preceding considerations, it demonstrates that, in spite of first appearances, the common usage and patterns in psalm titles do not clearly point us in the direction of expecting *'al* to introduce a reference to the music of the poem. The use of *təpillâ* (*prayer*), which is nowhere else linked to a musical notation, and the use of *lamnaṣṣēaḥ* ("for the musical director") in the colophon rather than the title and thus separated from *'al šigyōnôt* can all be read as evidence pointing away from reading *'al šigyōnôt* as a musical notation. In this context, it is worth mentioning that in 1904, James Thirtle argued, taking his lead from Hab 3, that many designations

---

347. This remains true also for Pss 9:1 and 80:1 if the preposition *'al* is read in those cases.

348. This is the general understanding. Brevard S. Childs ("Psalm Titles and Midrashic Exegesis," *JSS* 16 [1971]: 137–150) translates "according to the words of Cush" and understands it as a reference to the manner in which the psalm is to be rendered, having overlooked the pattern of the usage of *'al* in psalm titles.

that appear as superscriptions in our editions of the Psalter were originally subscriptions of the preceding psalm.[349] Among other pieces of evidence are the superscript of Ps 88, which seems overloaded, and the echo of Ps 55:6(7) in the notation now attached to the superscription of Ps 56. He suggested that the superscripts for the most part describe genre, authorship, and sometimes a historical setting, while the postscripts describe (for the most part) musical directions.[350] He deduced from the inclusion of 'al šigyōnôt in the superscript rather than with the musical notations at the end that it served some special literary or liturgical function rather than indicating a musical type.

Andersen believes that Ps 7 and Hab 3 "do not have much in common apart from being prayers."[351] This is true in terms of modern genre classifications, but thematically it is not difficult to see a number of parallels between Ps 7 and the book of Habakkuk. Both prayers are prayed by an individual but seem to have the fate of the nation in view. In Ps 7, the references to "the assembly of the peoples" (v. 7[8]) and YHWH's judging of the peoples (v. 8[9]) suggest a wider context, as would be especially appropriate if the individual under attack is a king.[352] This leads to the general plea: "May the evil deeds of the wicked come to an end! But make the righteous one secure, O, you who examine hearts and kidneys, righteous God!" (v. 9[10]). We have here essentially the same plea that runs through the book of Habakkuk. But the plea gives way to a lengthy statement of faith, not unlike what we find in Hab 3. The psalmist expresses confidence that the one who does not turn from evil ways will ultimately be the target of God's wrath (vv. 12–13[13–14]) and with a well-known proverb affirms that the evil committed by the evildoer will be their own downfall (v. 15[16]; cf. Pss 9:15[16]; 35:8; 57:6[7]; Eccl 10:8).

---

349. James W. Thirtle, *The Titles of the Psalms: Their Nature and Meaning Explained* (London: Henry Frowde, 1904). Haim M. I. Gevaryahu ("Biblical Colophons," in *Congress Volume: Edinburgh, 1974*, ed. George W. Anderson et al., VTSup 28 [Leiden: Brill, 1975], 42–59) argued on the basis of a comparative study with Akkadian hymns and ancient Greek literature that the superscriptions were first colophons and later deliberately transposed to the beginning of psalms. But the Akkadian evidence is not directly comparable because the colophons are concerned with different matters.

350. Thirtle's proposal has largely been overlooked—neither accepted nor opposed. Bruce K. Waltke ("Superscripts, Postscripts, or Both," *JBL* 110 [1991]: 583–96) has taken it up and offers further support.

351. Andersen, *Habakkuk*, 269. He is right to observe that the meaning of psalm titles cannot be worked out on the basis of modern form-critical classifications.

352. The heading in Ps 7 invites us to hear King David as the person pleading with YHWH, apparently linking the psalm with events surrounding Absalom's rebellion, which seem to be the background for Pss 3–7; see Beat Weber, " 'An dem Tag, als JHWH ihn rettete aus der Hand aller seiner Feinde und aus der Hand Sauls' (Ps 18,1): Erwägungen zur Anordnung der biographischen Angaben zu David im Psalter," *VT* 64 (2014): 284–304. Traditionally, the psalm was more often linked to the time of David's persecution under Saul.

The following verse reaffirms this idea: "His mischief returns upon his own head, and on the crown of his head his violence descends." YHWH's bow and arrows may be incidental parallels between Ps 7 and Hab 3,[353] but the ideas that evildoers cannot escape punishment in the long run and that the seeds of their destruction lie in their behavior are the points Hab 2 stresses and to which therefore Hab 3 responds.

If *šiggāyôn* were to signify a prayer that revolves around a specific wrong that needs correcting (committed by someone other than the one praying), then a prayer *'al šigyōnôt* might be one that concerns several wrongs (committed by someone other than the one praying), or more likely one that relates to more than one previous prayer concerning wrongdoing. But this derivation faces the difficulty that, as suggested above, the "straying" or "reeling" that makes for a *šiggāyôn* is most likely that of the poet. If a *šiggāyôn* is a composition of someone who is reeling with fury at wrong committed by someone else, this could fit Hab 1 as well as Ps 7. It would also seem possible that *'al šigyōnôt* does not in fact describe Hab 3 but refers back to his earlier prayers.[354] The plural would not be a problem. The "How long . . . ?" at the beginning of the book clearly implies more than one prayer. The absence of the definite article or a suffix could be explained as generalizing; Habakkuk's prayer is offered to all who are similarly reeling and protesting. In connection with the verb "to pray," the preposition *'al* is used most commonly to indicate the people for whom intercession is offered (e.g., Job 42:8; 2 Chr 30:18; 32:20; Neh 1:6), and on this basis one might expect it to indicate the theme or concern of the prayer, given that *šigyōnôt* clearly does not refer to people. This would bring it close to the traditional interpretation because a prayer about *šiggāyôn* compositions would likely be a penitential prayer.

But this faces the problem that Hab 3 includes no acknowledgement of wrongdoing on the part of the person praying. In any case, the verb "to pray" is not used in the title, unless the phrase is understood as linked to the verbal element implied in *prayer*. In fact, alongside information about the type of composition (here *a prayer*) and the author (here *of the prophet Habakkuk*), the third element offered in superscriptions, separate from musical notations, usually indicates circumstances. If we follow this here, it seems better to take the preposition as indicating that a new prayer is now offered alongside (not necessarily "against") the previously offered *šigyōnôt*. The *besides* could maybe be understood as "in place of," but a different preposition would have been available for this (*taḥat*, cf. v. 7). James W. Watts observes that "Habakkuk 3 uses the language and forms of laments to frame the victory hymn rather than those of the thanksgivings found uniformly in [hymns set within]

---

353. Ps 7:12(13) and Hab 3:9 for bow; Ps 7:13(14) and Hab 3:11 for arrows.
354. Cf. the noun *šiggā'ôn* for mental imbalance (Deut 28:28; 2 Kgs 9:20; Zech 12:4).

narratives" and notes that while "most of the lament's traditional elements appear" in this psalm (in vv. 2, 16–19), "the complaint itself is missing, probably because it is already voiced in 1.2–4, 12–17."[355] On the understanding of the superscript offered here, the title explicitly acknowledges the presence of complaint earlier in the book, which makes it redundant for the prayer in ch. 3 to specify the nature of the distress. What the prayer offers instead is renewed petition and an expression of confidence in God's salvation.

The interpretation offered here has affinities with the reading of the verse in antiquity, but I do not think that the prayer is one of penitence for erroneous or hasty utterances or any wrong committed on the part of the person praying.[356] Nor do I see a reference to the wrongdoing of others. What the traditional understanding has rightly grasped, however, is that the prophet has moved on from ch. 1. The complaint has been silenced (cf. 2:20). To continue complaining now would be wrong. Still, there is no obvious expression of regret on the part of the prophet for having voiced his objections previously. It seems that within Habakkuk, as in the Psalter, there is a rightful place for complaint, even if it must give way before it turns into grumbling. The prophet does not express sorrow for it, but he enacts a turning toward praise and confidence. Habakkuk's concern is still the overall situation that was the focus in the preceding chapters; it is not his own previously spoken (and written) words as such. YHWH's raising of the Babylonians has led to much wrong (the wicked oppressing the innocent, Torah being ineffective). This was the initial complaint. God's answer, and the expansion in 2:6–20, offers a wider, long-term perspective, but it does not deny that there has been a departure from the good way. It is therefore conceivable that Habakkuk offers a further prayer *besides* the many *vehement protests* previously offered, now informed by the revelation in Hab 2, which has opened up new horizons for Habakkuk that lead him to take a further step back. That backward step enables him to reflect more widely on God's history with his people and the ways in which harsh things are followed by good things in the cycle of the seasons, as the summer drought must give way to winter rains or as northwest winds bring refreshment after the oppressive heat of the east wind.

---

355. James W. Watts, "Psalmody in Prophecy: Habakkuk 3 in Context," in Watts and House, *Forming Prophetic Literature*, 214.

356. See the Stone edition of the Tanach (see the translation note) and Jerome (who in *Against the Pelagians* 1.39 refers to this chapter as Habakkuk's "Canticum poenitentiae"— "Canticle of Penance," or maybe better in Jerome's understanding, "Canticle of Penitence"), believing that the heading refers to "sins of ignorance"; see Alberto Ferreiro, ed., *The Twelve Prophets*, ACCS 14 (Downers Grove: InterVarsity Press, 2003), 198. Luther reads "on behalf of the ignorances" and sees, instead, innocence signified, appealing to Job 9:21 (which on his reading links blamelessness with not knowing) and Ps 7 (*LW* 19:133, cf. *LW* 19:227).

Reflection

One thing we surely have in common with the prophet Habakkuk is an awareness that lots of things have gone and are going wrong in the world at large, in
our communities, and in our own lives. If Hab 1 might have encouraged us to
lay the blame, at least for some of those disasters, at God's feet, the heading
here invites us to use a different sort of prayer to reflect on what has gone
wrong. While vv. 3–15 will involve an element of remembrance, the heading
and the opening plea in v. 2 invite us to read Hab 3:3–15 not merely as a report
but as a prayerful reflection and maybe even as a present (liturgical/mystical)
experience of a future event that has been foreshadowed in the past.

Habakkuk 2 comes close to suggesting an automatic deed-consequence
connection that will ensure that evil will not win out in the end, although
a number of references to YHWH guard against this. While the following
prayer in some ways offers a more explicitly God-centered account of the
defeat of evil, it, too, hints that there are "natural" patterns, now drawn from
meteorology. But whatever natural and historical events shape the contents
of Hab 3, it is in prayer that these patterns are discerned and considered.
A (true or false) prophet is a (true or false) witness to God's ways in the
world. Habakkuk is presented to us as a prophet who became a witness
out of prayer. This link between prophecy and prayer seems to have been
understood as generally true by the author of the New Testament letter of
James among others. As an example of a man of *prayer* in connection with
the prophetic announcement of a drought, he points to Elijah, who within
first-century Judaism was apparently considered second only to Moses as a
prophet.[357] In the Old Testament narrative, Elijah appears quite suddenly
on the scene in 1 Kgs 17 announcing the drought without any hint in the text
itself of prayer having preceded it. This suggests that James (who also refers
to "the prophets who spoke in the Lord's name" as examples of suffering and
patience in 5:10—a very fitting designation of Habakkuk as much as Elijah)
could assume that a prophet making such an announcement would not have
done so without prayer preceding the public declaration.

More recently Henri J. M. Nouwen expressed in new words the need for
Christian leaders to be men and women of prayer if they are to articulate
God's work in their own lives and the lives of others. It is not our regular

---

357. First Kings recounts instances of Elijah praying but not clearly in connection with
the end of the drought and certainly not with the beginning of the drought. Douglas J. Moo
sees "evidence for an association between the drought and Elijah's praying" in Sir 48:2–3
and 2 Esd 7:109 (*The Letter of James*, PNTC [Grand Rapids: Eerdmans, 2000], 248), but
the former makes no reference to prayer, and the latter refers to the end of the drought, not
a prayer for it to start.

experience that everything becomes suddenly clear when we pray, but the Christian leader who offers true discernment, being in the words of Nouwen "a contemplative critic," cannot do so apart from prayer.[358] Studying the book of Habakkuk should help ministers to witness to the truth about God and our world, but without prayer it is not likely that the truth will be truthfully spoken.

While the prayer neither expresses contrition nor confesses sins and thus should not be considered a prayer of penitence, it could be used in an act of penance—an act that helps to heal and mend fractured relationships after sin has been forgiven. The relationships underlying ch. 1 were not harmonious. There was, on the one hand, agony over what God was doing and, on the other hand, fear of the Babylonians. It would have been easy to slide into thinking and doing wrong, questioning the God of Israel from a position of mistrust and fearing the empire more than God. The final chapter can help mend those relationships, whether or not actual sin has crept into them, and it is apparently only this second prayer that is handed over for public performance. While the prayer in ch. 1 seems permissible with the right attitude and in the right context, it is the prayer in ch. 3 that is commended for public use.

XIV. THE OPENING PART OF THE PRAYER (3:2)

²*YHWH, I have heard the report about you;*ᵃ
  *I am alarmed;*ᵇ
YHWH, your work—
  *in the midst of years,*ᶜ *renew it;*ᵈ
*in the midst of years, you shall make it*ᵉ *known;*
  *in turmoil you shall remember to have compassion.*ᶠ

a. "The news about you" (as *šim'ăkā* was rendered in Nah 3:19) would wrongly imply that what Habakkuk heard was largely new to him. Alternatively, "your renown" (e.g., NRSV; cf. NIV "fame") is a defensible translation (cf. Isa 66:19), but the flow of the book leads me to expect something more specific, whether the report refers to what follows (vv. 3–7 in particular; so, e.g., Andersen, *Habakkuk*, 276) or to what preceded (either in ch. 1 or ch. 2; for the latter, see, e.g., Prinsloo, "Life," 628).

b. Hebrew *yārē'tî* is often understood to refer to "awe" here. This is possible, but the

358. "Having said all this, I realize that I have done nothing more than rephrase the fact that the Christian leader must be in the future what he has always had to be in the past: a man of prayer, a man who has to pray, and who has to pray always" (Henri J. M. Nouwen, *The Wounded Healer* [London: Darton, Longman & Todd, 1994], 47; the text was first published in 1979, and in the acknowledgements, Nouwen apologizes for his "male-dominated language").

trembling later in the verse suggests a fearful element to the awe. The frequently proposed emendation of *yārē'tî* to *rā'îtî* ("I saw" as in v. 7; see, e.g., *BHS* and *HALOT*) was already suggested by one of the three equivalents offered in LXX (*katenoēsa*, "I considered"; see n. f). But the other two clearly (*ephobēthēn*, "I feared") or likely (*exestēn*, "I was astonished") render *yārē'tî*. Hearing and fearing are parallel also in Ps 76:8(9).

c. Reading different vowels, one could translate "when the years draw near" (cf. Deut 15:9), which is one of the equivalents offered in the LXX (see n. f).

d. Hiebert (*God of My Victory*, 13) emends to read the *piel* ("You sustained life!"); Haak (*Habakkuk*, 80–81) divides the word differently to read, "May Yahu live!"; cf. Andersen, *Habakkuk*, 281. See also Michael L. Barré, "Habakkuk 3:2: Translation in Context," *CBQ* 50 (1989): 184–97.

e. The translation seeks to reflect the change from imperative (*renew*) to *yiqtol* forms (*shall make . . . known . . . remember*). The suffix in the preceding colon does double duty. LXX and Tg. read the *niphal* (passive form) instead.

f. LXX of this verse is expansive. Rather than reflecting a longer Hebrew text, it seems to incorporate different ways of understanding its source: "O Lord, I have heard of your renown and feared; I considered your works and was astonished. You will be known in the midst of two living creatures; you will be recognized when the years draw near; you will be displayed when the right time comes; you will remember mercy when my soul is troubled in wrath" (NETS).

Composition

The Masoretes divide this very long verse into two rather unequal parts, the second part consisting of the last line *in turmoil you shall remember to have compassion*, which could be said to sum up the plea. It stands alongside the preceding two requests, only the first of which is expressed with an imperative. The accentuation highlights the parallelism of the three circumstantial phrases introduced with the preposition *beth* (*in*), although the first line belongs closely with *YHWH, your work*, which the translation above graphically separates to reflect the high incidence of disjunctive accents following each other. Alternatively, it would be possible to translate

> YHWH, I have heard the report about you;
> I am alarmed, YHWH, about your work.

This arrangement of the text—adopted in *BHQ* and its predecessors—smooths the rhythm and results in an a-b-c // b-a-c pattern with "your report" (objective genitive = the report about you) paralleling "your work" (subjective genitive = the work you do). It is attractive, but in my view, the division in my translation, with its rougher rhythm, does greater justice to the significance of a number of key terms. Its double placing of the divine name in first position corresponds to and contrasts with the use of *God* (*'ĕlôah*) and

344

the Holy One in the next verse. The reuse of the root *pʿl* ("work/deed") harks back to 1:5 (*one is about to do a deed in your days [that] you would not believe, if it were told*) and 2:4, if emended (see the translation note there). The double use of the root *šmʿ* in the first line (*šimʿākā*, "what is heard about you" = *the report about you*) prepares for its reuse in v. 16 (along with the recurrence of *rgz* twice in v. 16; also in v. 7). The echo of the opening verse of Habakkuk's first prayer (*you will not hear*, 1:2) may well be deliberate given that the double reference to *years* in 3:2 takes up the motif of the progress of time, which is important in Habakkuk's complaint. The double fronting of the divine name is also reminiscent of the poem in Nah 1 (see v. 3). This perhaps reflects the importance of the divine name among YHWH-alone worshippers at the time. The way the poetry, as understood by the Masoretes, further highlights the object of the verbs *renew* and *make known* (picked up with pronominal suffixes on the verbs) stresses its importance in interaction with 1:5.[359]

The happy coincidence, if that is what it is, that the roots involved in the final line (other than the preposition) have not been used previously in the book nicely highlights what is new in the prayer following the revelation of ch. 2. The evil experienced by Habakkuk and God's people generally is now interpreted as *turmoil*, and the plea has moved from the urgent wake-up calls of ch. 1 to the more submissive *remember to have compassion*.

Commentary

2 The opening prayer of the book concerned the question whether YHWH would ever hear and thus heed the pleas of his people. The prophet accused his God, "You will not hear!" (1:2). Chapter 2 concluded with a call to the whole earth to keep silence before YHWH. At the beginning of this prayer, the prophet confesses that he has *heard*. But what has he heard? The complaint in ch. 1 centered on an earlier revelation about an incredible deed YHWH announced he was going to do. Habakkuk had heard this earlier report about YHWH but prior to the interaction to which this writing bears witness had not understood its wider context and implications. These are spelled out in ch. 2. Having been offered this wider perspective, focused in the revelation in 2:4–5, the prophet is awestruck—but in fear as much as admiration. After all, while there is the promise of the ultimate victory of good over evil, this is a long-term prospect without the promise of an easing up of pressure or any amelioration in the short run. Delitzsch overlooks this when he argues that the reference must be to the earlier revelation in 1:5–11

---

359. See Renz, "Emendation," and the commentary on 2:4 for the possibility that an earlier form of the text of Habakkuk gave even greater prominence to the *pʿl* root.

because news about the downfall of the Babylonians could not but produce joy in the prophet.[360] Alongside this, it is possible that the prophet heard the recital of God's deeds of old, which are echoed in vv. 8–15. Such a recital would be a plausible reference for *the report about you* in addition to the revelation recorded in ch. 2. Habakkuk has been reassured that YHWH is indeed from of old (*miqqedem*, 1:12), sovereign over the whole of time and not without purposes for his people (*we shall not die*, 1:12). But if the doer of this deed could indeed be trusted, it was nevertheless a fearsome thing that has come upon God's people and—for the time being—remains upon them and that therefore calls for faithfulness.

If, however, it was the Neo-Babylonian Empire that was depicted as fearsome in ch. 1 (v. 7), now fear is, as it should be in biblical thought, directed toward YHWH rather than humans. This redirection changes the quality of the fear. Fear of an unremitting enemy is sheer fright and horror, but proper fear of YHWH is trepidation with trust. Renewed trust in YHWH and his purposes leads the prophet to change his tack. If in ch. 1 Habakkuk saw the root of the problem in a divine deed that needed stopping (the rise of the Neo-Babylonian Empire), he now asks YHWH to give new vitality to his deed—to *renew it*. The prophet is now content; indeed, he desires that YHWH go through with his deed until it finds its completion. The earlier prophecy spoke of the *days* in which YHWH would bring about this deed (1:5); now Habakkuk refers to the *years* that pass in the progress. There may be a sense of being in the midst of times between the marvelous deeds of the past of which tradition speaks and to which the following verses allude (cf. the reference to "the days of old" in Isa 63) and the eagerly anticipated deeds of deliverance in the future. The hope might be that a renewal of YHWH's deed, allowing it its full effect, would ensure that it more faithfully reflects YHWH's character, encapsulated in the reference to *compassion*. Perhaps the renewal of the deed would ensure that it comes quicker to its glorious conclusion in the day to which 3:16 alludes. But the use of *years* also prepares for the agricultural references later, and this may be the more important reason for the switch from *days* to *years*.[361]

---

360. Franz Delitzsch, *Habakuk*, 128. He argues that fear of the immediate future leads the prophet to pray for the renewal of God's age-old deed of salvation. But the (double) use of the *p'l* root in 1:5 (*doing a deed*) makes it difficult to narrow the meaning of *deed* in 3:2 to God's salvific action.

361. Andersen (*Habakkuk*, 278) argues that the MT needs emending here because "the more abstract idea of a stretch of time" would demand the feminine form of the plural, *šānôt* (as, e.g., in Deut 32:7). He does not consider that time may not be abstract here but patterned in analogy to agricultural years; cf., e.g., Gen 1:14; 41:35; 1 Kgs 17:1. His objection to the masculine form is in any case unjustified given the use of *šānîm* for unmeasured time in places like 2 Chr 18:2; Neh 9:30; Job 32:7. Note that, contra Andersen, Diethelm Michel

The reference to the *midst of years* is probably, first of all, to a time somewhere between the early days of Israel's history and its culmination in a messianic reign of peace and justice, which probably entered the horizon of Israel's prophets from the eighth century onward (Isaiah) if not before. But there may also be an allusion to the middle of the calendar year(s). There are two strong possibilities for determining the beginning and end of years in ancient Israel and, consequently, their middle. The first possibility calculates the beginning of the year from Rosh Hashanah (New Year) in the seventh month, followed by Yom Kippur and Sukkoth, which marks the final agricultural harvest; the middle part would occur in the first month, the month of Passover, when winter ends and spring starts with the beginning of the barley harvest. In this case, renewal of God's deed *in the midst of years* suggests renewed protection and deliverance (Passover) and some first indication of a good harvest. The second possibility is to count Nisan, the first month, as the beginning of the year; the middle would be the seventh month and speak of repentance and forgiveness (Yom Kippur) as well as harvest, fasting, and feasting. Either way, the middle of the year is a significant time in the biblical and Jewish calendar.[362] It is also possible that the reference is to the agricultural cycle more generally, *the midst of years* being the time between planting and harvesting. In this case, planting would refer to God's deed of old in establishing Israel and harvesting to the time when God's people are brought to full fruition and prosperity. The time in between, then, is the time in which God must work in hidden ways through the provision of sun and rain.[363] The use of the plural *years* is warranted because Habakkuk does not speak of any specific year and, in any case, the events of which he speaks and that he anticipates span several years at least.

The petition to *make known* his deed is presumably a petition to reveal

---

(*Grundlegung einer hebräischen Syntax*, vol. 1: *Sprachwissenschaftliche Methodik. Genus und Numerus des Nomens* [Neukirchen: Neukirchener Verlag, 2004], referenced in *HALOT*) claims that *šānîm* "is to be understood as a mass or a group plural," while *šānôt* "is to be considered as a quantity of items collected together."

362. Exod 12:2 asks Israel to consider the month of deliverance the first month of the year, and this is how the months are counted in the Bible. But if the *religious* year ended and began in spring, the *agricultural* year still ended and began in autumn, and the celebration of Rosh Hashanah as the New Year festival indicates the prominence of thinking of a year along those lines. It seems likely that the Israelites allowed for different "years" alongside each other just as we do. (E.g., in my culture the church year, the academic year, and the tax year are all different from each other and from the calendar year and by no means less important for it.)

363. Even more generally, we could consider *baqereb* (*in the midst of*) a mere ballast variant of the preposition *beth* and translate "throughout the years" (so Hiebert, *God of My Victory*, 12; cf. *CHP*, 345). But while it is true that rhythmic considerations alone would suggest the use of the trisyllabic *baqereb* in these cola, the repetition of the phrase invites a search for a fuller meaning.

that both the historical events that frighten Habakkuk now and the expected future events that will encourage him as the Babylonians are defeated are indeed YHWH's deed. It is a deed by which he can be known and so *the earth shall be filled with the knowledge of the glory of YHWH as the waters cover the sea* (2:14). For the deed to be truly characteristic of YHWH, there must be *compassion* in the rage or turmoil, taking up the first designation of YHWH from the creedal statement in Exod 34:6–7.[364]

Turmoil renders a noun from the root *rgz* that requires comment. Typically, the verb refers to violent, often involuntary shaking. It is used for earthquakes (1 Sam 14:15; Joel 2:10) and for physical trembling (e.g., caused by fear) as well as for raging against someone and, hence, for wrath and for the destabilizing of nations. Here it could conceivably refer to God's wrath, to the trembling of those who feel the impact of divine intervention (cf. its use later in the chapter in vv. 7 and 16) or to the general situation of instability that gave rise to Habakkuk's complaint in the first place. The LXX renders *rgz* in effect twice, *en tō tarachthēnai tēn psychēn mou en orgē* (when my soul is troubled in wrath). Elsewhere, a term expressing anger (*orgizō, orgē, thymoō*) translates about a third of the occurrences of *rgz*. In quite a few of these, the connotation of anger is at the least doubtful (e.g., Exod 15:14; Isa 13:13; 32:10), perhaps the most surprising instance being the use of a passive form of *pikrainō* ("becoming embittered") to render what seems to be in the Hebrew text a trembling for joy in Jer 33:9 (LXX 40:9). A reference to trembling with fear or awe is common in the Psalms (probably 4:4[5]; 77:16[17], 18[19]; 99:1) and found elsewhere (e.g., Exod 15:14; Deut 2:25; 28:65). Mental distress expresses itself in physical shaking (e.g., Isa 32:10–11; cf. Joel 2:1; Amos 8:8; Mic 7:17). The shaking of the ground or earth (e.g., 1 Sam 14:15) or the foundations of heavens (e.g., 2 Sam 22:8) or mountains (e.g., Ps 18:7[8]) is a common theme, especially in Isaiah (e.g., 5:25; 13:13) where the motif is also used for instability caused among the nations (14:16; 23:11). The root is used also for people agitating against someone, provoking them to anger (e.g., 2 Kgs 19:27–28 // Isa 37:28–29). Given this broad usage, we should probably not deduce notions of anger in *rgz* without further indications from the context. The opposite of *rgz* is being at ease, at rest (e.g., Deut 28:65; Job 3:17, 26; Jer 50:34). The roots most often found in parallel to *rgz* are *rʿš* ("to convulse, shake"; 2 Sam 22:8 // Ps 18:7[8]; Ps 77:18[19]; Joel 2:10) and *pḥd* ("to tremble with fear"; Deut 2:25; Jer 33:9; Mic 7:17).

As for *rōgez*, the noun used here, elsewhere in the Hebrew Bible it appears only in Isa 14:3 and, prominently, in Job (3:17, 26; 14:1; 37:2; 39:24).

---

364. For the importance of Exod 34:6–7, see "Nahum's Place in the Book of the Twelve" (pp. 49–52) and the commentary on Nah 1:2–10.

The translation *turmoil* fits most of these instances.[365] Verse 8 refers to God's anger, but as this chapter begins, there is nothing much to suggest that the trembling/turmoil here is God's rage. The *compassion* is, of course, God's *compassion*, and from this one might deduce that the *turmoil* or agitation might be God's as well. This argument would be stronger if the root *rgz* more regularly carried connotations of wrath and perhaps if a verbal form of *rgz* (rather than the noun) had more forcefully compelled us to imagine a subject to which the action applies. As it is, the root *rgz* can refer to a range of unsettling things, including shaking and trembling later in the chapter, and there is no intrinsic reason to adopt a connotation of rage or anger here. (Also, we may be contrasting anger and compassion too readily. Depending on the object of the anger, it can be a form of compassion, and the question of the object of divine wrath is raised later on.) The noun *rōgez* is in fact well suited to sum up the topsy-turvy world in which Habakkuk finds himself, where law and order has ceased to offer a firm foundation. The revelation in the previous chapter suggests that the world will be in flux for a little longer, and so it makes perfect sense for Habakkuk to pray that in such *turmoil* God would *remember to have compassion*. As in any prayer asking God to *remember*, the petition is not so much for a calling to mind as for action. God is to activate his compassion in a situation in which those who plead with him struggle to find a safe ground, security, and peace. While all three verbs used in the last lines can be read as petitioning, the switch from the imperative form to the use of *yiqtol* (imperfect) and infinitive forms might suggest a note of confidence, a plea for renewal of God's work in the confidence that he will make it known and remember to have compassion.[366]

Reflection

The opening verse of this prayer holds trepidation and trust together. There is no pretense here that God's deed brings only good things and ease to his people. Divine use of the Babylonian army remains alarming, even if the prophet no longer fears that this will lead to complete destruction and the end of God's people. What the prophet now knows is that turmoil is not all there is to it. If God causes turmoil, there are good grounds for appealing to

---

365. In the phrase *barōgez qōlô* (Job 37:2) *rōgez* apparently refers to the "thunder" of the voice. Job 39:24 refers to the fierceness and restlessness of the horse.

366. There are a number of examples for the use of an imperative at the end of a verse with a preceding object; see, e.g., Jer 17:18; Ezek 3:10; Mic 1:10; Zech 8:19. Examples of the use of the imperative of *zkr* following its object in Neh 4:14(8) and 13:22 suggest that this would have been possible with the root in question.

and trusting in his compassion because God could not be made known in random acts of aggression. God's deeds must speak of his justice and compassion; otherwise God's wrath would seem to be spite or malice, which is not acceptable as a canonical description of God. It is, of course, notoriously difficult, not to say impossible, to discern God's specific deeds simply by observing events. This is perhaps no less true for events that affect nations than it is for events that affect individuals. Personal misfortunes and national disasters indicate divine disapproval no more reliably than good fortune indicates divine approval (see, e.g., Job 42:8; Luke 13:4; John 9:2–3). A good example in biblical narrative of someone wondering about God's plan in relation to foreign aggression is found in 2 Kgs 19, in which Hezekiah wrestles with the consequences of Sennacherib's invasion of Judah.

The Greek rendering of the verse includes "You will be known in the midst of two living creatures; you will be recognized when the years draw near; you will be displayed when the right time comes" (NETS). These words prompted reflection among early Christians about the coming of Christ in between the Old and New Testaments (Caesarius of Arles),[367] about the voice from heaven at the transfiguration of Christ between Moses and Elijah (Tertullian), and about Christ enthroned by angels (Gregory of Nazianzus).[368] Origen interpreted the verse with reference to the Trinity. Appealing to Luke 10:22; 1 Cor 2:10; John 14:26; 16:12–13, he wrote:

> For all knowledge of the Father is obtained by revelation of the Son through the Holy Spirit, so that both of these beings which, according to the prophet, are called either "living things" or "lives" exist as the grounds of the knowledge of God the Father.[369]

Most of us today are reluctant to make similar interpretive moves, but the idea that the birth, life, death, resurrection, and ascension of Christ are the works that supremely reveal God in the midst of years—between the beginning of time in creation and the closure of this age in the arrival of the new heavens and the new earth—is an important part of Christian

367. The phrase "when the right time comes" (*en tō pareinai ton kairon*) could evoke Gal 4:4 (*ēlthen to plērōma tou chronou*), but there are no significant links at the level of wording.

368. See Bogdan C. Bucur and Elijah N. Mueller, "Gregory Nazianzen's Reading of Habbakuk [*sic*] 3:2 and Its Reception: A Lesson from Byzantine Scripture Exegesis," *Pro Ecclesia* 20 (2011): 86–103, which discusses images in three codices from the eleventh and twelfth centuries that "depict a majestic Christ resplendent with glory, escorted by two angels; or Christ enthroned on a platform upheld by four creatures; or an angelomorphic Christ, surrounded by angels that form a living throne; or a vision of Christ shared by Habakkuk and Ezekiel" (88). The others are cited in Ferreiro, *Twelve Prophets*, 198–200.

369. Origen, *First Principles* 1.3.4; cited in Ferreiro, *Twelve Prophets*, 199–200.

confession. Therefore, it seems appropriate to allow this verse to prompt reflection on the compassion of God revealed in Christ in the midst of our turmoil. We believe that God is known by his deeds, that such deeds must reflect his life-giving compassion to be fully recognizable as God's deeds, and that the miracles and sufferings of Christ reveal God's glory. That belief should inspire us to pray for the continuing revival of such works and should give us confidence that God will indeed show compassion. It also suggests guidelines for discerning God's work today. The pattern confirmed by Christ is one of victory through self-sacrificial suffering rather than self-assertive conquest.

XV. A REFLECTION ON YHWH'S APPEARANCE (3:3-7)

³*God!ᵃ From Teman he comes,ᵇ*
  the Holy Oneᶜ from Mount Paran. Selah.
His majesty covers the heavensᵈ
  and the earth is full of his praiseworthiness.ᵉ
⁴*And haze becomes like bright light.*
  Twin rays [horns]ᶠ from his handᵍ are his,
    and there is the hiding place of his strength.ʰ
⁵*Before his faceⁱ goes Pestilenceʲ*
  and Burning Plague goes forth at his feet.
⁶*He stands and surveys [shakes]ᵏ a land,*
  he looks and spies out [startles] nations,
    and the everlastingˡ hills are shattered,ᵐ
      the eternal hills bow down—
the ancient triumphal procession belongs to him.ⁿ
⁷*In place of iniquity,ᵒ I see the tents of Cushan*
  trembling,ᵖ the tent curtains of the land of Midian.

a. Hebrew *'ĕlôah* is rare outside the book of Job, where it is found more than forty times. It is not used in Jeremiah or Ezekiel, and is it used only once in Isaiah (44:8). The only other occurrence in the Book of the Twelve is in Hab 1:11. Here in 3:3, the parallelism with *the Holy One* and the implied identification with YHWH rule out the translation "a god." *God* (*'ĕlôah*) stands in initial position with a disjunctive accent. The form without *mappîq* is less common but identical in reference and meaning.

b. It is unfortunate that the translation obscures the distinction between *yiqtol* and *qatal* forms in this chapter. The poem seems to use *yiqtol* forms to vividly describe actions and *qatal* forms to refer to states and results. There is no satisfactory way of reflecting this in English (e.g., by consistent use of the progressive present for the former). The use of the present tense in English is discussed below.

c. The adjective without definite article is also found elsewhere in cases where English must use the noun with the definite article to convey the correct sense, *the Holy One* (Isa

40:25; Hos 11:9; Job 6:10). The coordinating *waw* ("and") is not represented here because in English the use of "and" would be unnatural. The singular verb, not repeated in the second colon, ensures the identity of *God* and *the Holy One*. There is clearly only one agent in view.

d. English uses two words ("sky" and "heaven") to render the same Hebrew word. Either would work here, as we may think of the geographical contrast (sky/earth) or the contrast between the divine and the human world (heaven/earth). The Hebrew noun does not have a singular form and could be rendered "heaven" (or "sky"). The plural *the heavens* seems poetically more satisfying.

e. The singular verb form *covers* suggests that *the heavens* are the object rather than the subject in spite of the position in the sentence. The final colon is ambiguous and could also be read as "his praise(worthiness) fills the earth." I follow, e.g., Franz Delitzsch, *Habakuk*, 147, in taking *the earth* as the subject on the grounds that the verb is used more often intransitively. For the translation *praiseworthiness*, see further below.

f. The related verb *qrn* apparently means "to shine, radiate" in Exod 34:29–30, 35. The noun here is to be understood first as rays (in light of the preceding), then (retrospectively, in light of what follows) as horns; see David Toshio Tsumura, "Janus Parallelism in Hab. III 4," *VT* 54 (2004): 124–28. Modern English translations usually opt for "rays"; KJV followed LXX and Vulg. in translating "horns"; see the commentary. The use of the dual is natural with "horns" in preference to the plural form (*qərānôt*); the added *twin* is meant to signal the use of the dual.

g. We should probably think of both hands here, the singular being used for euphonic reasons, but this remains uncertain. The translation "from his side" would be defensible in my view, even if *yād* is not used elsewhere in this precise sense in connection with living beings (although cf., e.g., 1 Sam 19:3; Neh 13:13). The translation preserves the allusion to different parts of the body; see n. i.

h. The regular form would be *'uzzô*. The form here (*'uzzōh*) is archaic and may have been used to strengthen association with the first word of the verse (*nōgah*, *haze*).

i. Because the enclosure of reference to the attendants by YHWH's *face* and *feet* seems deliberate, the translation *before his face* is favored on this occasion over the more idiomatic "before him," which is appropriate elsewhere.

j. The Greek translator, using *logos*, vocalized as "word." The capitalization of *Pestilence* and *Burning Plague* is discussed in the commentary.

k. Several lexemes in this verse can be interpreted in two different ways. We cannot be certain that this is deliberate, but a play on meanings seems plausible here. Cf. maybe *'rh*, *'wr* in v. 9. This chapter has an unusual potential for ambiguity that may well be deliberate; see Eric N. Ortlund, "Intentional Ambiguity in OT and Ugaritic Descriptions of Divine Conflict," *UF* 38 (2006): 543–57.

l. Both *'ad* (*everlasting*) here and *'ôlām* (*eternal, ancient*) in the next two lines refer to long duration; *'ad* nearly always looks forward while *'ôlām* as often refers to the distant past as to the distant future. The ambivalence of *'ôlām* is exploited here: its first occurrence (rendered *eternal*) parallels *everlasting*. The idea that mountains would last forever makes their destruction all the more striking. With the second use of *'ôlām*, the poet seems to be looking back more than forward; hence the rendering *ancient*.

m. This rendering reads the verb as a *hithpolel* of *pṣṣ* (so also *HALOT*, *DCH*, and Ges[18]); cf. Meyer, *Grammatik*, 1:112–13, on dissimilation of consonants in intensive stems of geminate roots (cf. 2:146). The form is not otherwise attested, but cf. the *polel* in Jer 23:29. An alternative derivation from the *pwṣ* root would give "scattered, dispersed." This would require us to postulate a *hithpolel* form for a root with a regular *niphal* form, something that is attested with other roots (cf. *kwn, mwg, mwṭ, ywr*). So, there is perhaps another deliberate ambiguity at play here.

n. The meaning of this line, traditionally rendered "his ways are eternal," is not entirely clear. It is sometimes taken with what follows (see already the LXX) or deleted as a gloss. Many, with emendation, interpret it as eternal orbits being shattered (see *HALOT* and, e.g., Bruce, "Habakkuk," 883). Cf. Gert T. M. Prinsloo, "Reading Habakkuk 3 in its Literary Context: A Worthwhile Exercise or Futile Attempt?" *JSem* 11 (2002): 95. The word *hălîkôt* (*triumphal procession*) is only found four more times in the Hebrew Bible, always in the plural. The grammatical plural probably designates a single entity (consisting of a plurality of elements; cf. the Hebrew words for "life, lifetime," *ḥayyîm*; and "youth [as a stage of life]," *nĕ'ûrîm*). The word refers to a triumphal procession in Ps 68:24(25), which seems appropriate here; cf. Fabry, *Habakuk/Obadja*, 283. Elsewhere it refers to a convoy or caravan (Job 6:19), the way a household is run (Prov 31:27), and the movement of fighters (Nah 2:5[6]).

o. When not emended, this is often translated "under affliction," which is also possible; see perhaps Prov 30:21–23 for suffering *taḥat* ("under/on account of") something. Among others, Roberts (*Nahum*, 137) and Prinsloo ("Reading Habakkuk 3," 95) opt for "instead." It may be that both meanings are intended. The most popular emendation is Albright's (William Foxwell Albright, "Two Letters from Ugarit (Ras Shamra)," *BASOR* 82 [1941]: 43–49; "The Psalm of Habakkuk," in *Studies in Old Testament Prophecy*, ed. H. H. Rowley [Edinburgh: T&T Clark, 1950], 1–18, 15; apparently first suggested in "The North-Canaanite Poems of Al'êyân Ba'al and the Gracious Gods," *JPOS* 14 [1934]: 101–40; cf. Andersen, *Habakkuk*, 310–11; G. R. Driver, "Critical Note on Habakkuk 3:7," *JBL* 62 [1943]: 121) taking the phrase as a verb that goes with v. 6 and speaks of shattering (see *BHS*). It has attracted various criticisms; e.g., Baruch Margulis, "The Psalm of Habakkuk: A Reconstruction and Interpretation," *ZAW* 82 (1970): 417–18. But it has been defended, e.g., by Haak, *Habakkuk*, 91. The emendation does not seem compelling to me because I understand the end of v. 6 to refer to God's ancient movements rather than highways or celestial paths, and I do not consider the problems in v. 7 insurmountable. Another emendation would be to read *taḥat 'ôn* ("instead of strength").

p. For the paragogic *nun*, see, e.g., JM 44e. It is likely here for poetic reasons. The *yiqtol* is appropriate for a noncompleted action. The gender signals that the verb is a two-way middle. See the commentary.

Composition

For an introduction to the motifs used in this chapter, see above on 3:1. The two epithets for YHWH in the opening verse echo Hab 1:11–12, where both had been used with pronominal suffixes, contrasting the Babylonian *god* with Habakkuk's *Holy One*. The use of *God* (*'ĕlôah*) rather than YHWH suggests that the echo is deliberate. This means that if an earlier hymn was incorporated into this prayer, it was likely adapted to its new context in the process.

The interpretation of the verbal forms in this chapter is controversial.[370]

370. See, e.g., Hiebert, *God of My Victory*; Yitzhak Avishur, *Studies in Hebrew and Ugaritic Psalms* (Jerusalem: Magnes Press, 1994), 111–205.

The parallel use of *yiqtol* (imperfect, prefixed) and *qatal* (perfect, suffixed) forms has been variously explained with an appeal to the origin of the chapter. Some trace the chapter to a vision that has been seen in the past (explaining the *qatal* forms) but anticipates future events (explaining the use of *yiqtol* forms). Others see the mixture as a consequence of the chapter's relationship with liturgy (past or future events presently experienced). Still others take a position that has become increasingly popular, appealing to the historical development of the Hebrew language (with the prefix conjugation functioning as a preterit form). Thus, Andersen states, "It is in keeping with the archaic character of the poem that prefixed and suffixed verb forms are intermingled, with no distinction in tense."[371] He concludes his discussion with the following claim:

> With the exception of the personal framework, which is obviously contemporary, we can now be confident that all of the core of the poem (vv 3–15) is intended to be past tense. The use of both prefixed and suffixed verbs with this meaning is now better understood ... and this makes clearer the archaic, not merely archaizing, character of the composition.[372]

I do not share Andersen's confidence. Granted, Old Canaanite had several prefix conjugations,[373] and it is not inconceivable that the *yiqtol* (imperfect) forms in this chapter originally functioned differently from how they are employed elsewhere in the Hebrew Bible. But within its new context, a pure past reference seems less plausible. We should reckon with the possibility that the citation of an old hymn subtly changed its reference in the process. But in any case, it may be that the archaic or archaizing character of Hab 3 has been overstated.[374]

There are probably three main factors that suggest to many that we should translate this passage with English verb forms suggesting a focus on the past. First, there is the *report* the prophet has received in v. 2. This, however, is likely not a reference to what follows but to what precedes ch. 3 within Habakkuk's prophecy and forms the grounds for the prayer in that verse. It does not indicate that what follows refers to events in the past. The prayer concerns the present and the future.

Second, there are the allusions to past events. The question is whether

---

371. Andersen, *Habakkuk*, 263.

372. Andersen, *Habakkuk*, 264. The appeal is to David A. Robertson, *Linguistic Evidence in Dating Early Hebrew Poetry*, SBLDS 3 (Missoula, MT: Society of Biblical Literature, 1972).

373. See Meyer, *Grammatik*, 2:97, for a list.

374. See Henrik Pfeiffer, *Jahwes Kommen*, for a challenge to the consensus that these texts reflect an ancient tradition. It will become apparent that I see no reason to date Hab 3 as late as Pfeiffer does (in the Hellenistic period).

vv. 3–15 offer further motivation for the prayer by way of an appeal to God's past deeds or whether, with the use of traditional motifs, this main part of the chapter anticipates God's future intervention by way of describing the promise offered in the previous chapter. It may be that the future is described in the language of past events. As winter rains have followed the summer drought before, so they will do again. In a similar way, God's deeds in the past may be thought to indicate reliably what he is going to do in the future. In other words, the visionary might see the future by looking into the past. Past events foreshadow (maybe we should say "cast light on") the future. In my view, the chapter as a whole focuses on the future glimpsed in ch. 2 rather than on the archaic past. I agree with Delitzsch's comment that Mic 7:15 could serve as a motto for Hab 3:3–15 ("As in the days when you came forth from the land of Egypt, I will show him miraculous deeds").[375]

The third reason is that it seems easier to make the *yiqtol* forms conform to the *qatal* forms (by way of appealing to a Canaanite preterit) than the other way around. But this is only so if one insists that *yiqtol* and *qatal* mark tense and that *qatal* cannot be used for future events. In the light of the function of the chapter, and allowing that the Hebrew verb forms here do not indicate tense, I suggest tentatively that the verb forms in Hab 3 differentiate between events that are vividly described as progressing, as if happening now, and the effects of these events. In other words, the *yiqtol* forms carry the dynamics of unfolding events, the *qatal* forms mark effects and completed actions. This distinction could work for describing past or future events and, therefore, depending on our overall interpretation of the chapter, we could consistently use either past or future tense in an English translation of vv. 3–15. But the way the chapter draws us into the prophet's vision (cf. the reference to his seeing in v. 7 and the question in v. 8) encourages the use of the vivid present in this translation. This does not determine whether the present is used dramatically to describe the past or visionarily to describe the future or whether it refers to contemporary events.

In the light of the context (anticipation of things to come, prayer for the revitalization of God's work), it seems ill advised to read all of vv. 3–15 as looking back to the distant past only. Given that there is no indication of a switch to a different time frame in vv. 8–15, we should allow that any historical reminiscence serves to portray and interpret present or future events. Indeed, Markl argues that the author of Hab 3, in using Deut 33, switched the opening verb form to *yiqtol* precisely to signal that a new theophany "in the midst of years" is in view, not the old theophany of the distant past.[376] The

---

375. Franz Delitzsch, *Habakuk*, 139.

376. Markl, "Hab 3," 102. Roberts (*Nahum*, 151) interprets the *yiqtol* as a signal of a present visionary experience. But this experience could be a vision of the past. Thus Prinsloo

prophet remembers the past to anticipate the future. If he does so by citing a theophany poem, the hymn's past reference is not decisive for its function in the prayer.[377] Given the use of citation in earlier chapters (the divine speech in 1:5–11 as part of the prophet's complaint and the sayings of the nations in 2:6ff. as part of the elaboration of God's answer to the prophet), it is attractive to read the prayer here as citing an earlier text as well. But in truth, it is just as possible that the author employs traditional motifs rather than a text that had already been known in Jerusalem.

Following v. 2, the division of the chapter is controversial, but there is agreement about vv. 3–7 forming the first stanza. Verse 3 clearly opens a new section in which the main actor, God, is consistently referred to in the third person. Verse 8 opens in a different mood, with a (rhetorical) question addressed to YHWH. In addition, Hiebert suggested that the four geographical names in this chapter form an inclusion, as they are found in v. 3 (Teman, Paran) and 7 (Cushan, Midian). The link is reinforced by the fact that they all consist of two syllables and end on -an.[378] The remainder of the chapter is now often divided into vv. 8–15 and vv. 16–19a (excluding the postscript in v. 19b), and this is my approach as well.[379] As observed in the introduction to Habakkuk (see "Macrostructure," p. 201), the first person already features by way of a pronominal suffix in v. 14, and ancient manuscripts regularly mark a division between verses 13 and 14. This can be justified on the grounds that, with v. 13, the divine warrior's victory has been won; vv. 14–15 are then read as summary statements. However, I read the first two suffixes in v. 14 as referring back to "the wicked" in v. 13. This counsels against following the masoretic tradition of having a paragraph break between these verses.

This division of the chapter, along with Haak's subdivision of the last part into vv. 16–17 and 18–19, is defended by Michael L. Barré with appeal to anagrams and repetitions.[380] His is an intriguing proposal, although, as he acknowledges, "this appears to be the only example of an extensive use of anagrams in an ancient Hebrew poem as a structuring device discovered thus

---

("Literary Context," 102) opts for a present tense translation yet thinks that the prophet "remembers the great salvation acts of Yahweh in the past" in vv. 3–7 (cf. 105: "By recalling the great saving acts of Yahweh in the past, the prophet has experienced that Yahweh is his strength").

377. Cf. Seybold, *Nahum*, 78.

378. Theodore Hiebert, "The Use of Inclusion in Habakkuk 3," in *Directions in Biblical Hebrew Poetry*, ed. Elaine R. Follis, JSOTSup 40 (Sheffield: JSOT Press, 1987), 122–23; cf. Michael L. Barré, "Newly Discovered Literary Devices in the Prayer of Habakkuk," *CBQ* 75 (2013): 454.

379. See, e.g., Hiebert, "Use of Inclusion"; Andersen, *Habakkuk*, 261; Fabry, *Habakuk/Obadja*, 195; Dietrich, *Nahum*, 175.

380. Barré, "Literary Devices," 455–62.

far."[381] Barré also offers no examples of anagrams functioning as a structuring device in extrabiblical texts. There is no question that anagrams can be a powerful rhetorical device in the case of significant puns, as with the play on Noah (nḥ) and "grace" (ḥn) in Gen 6:8,[382] but it is doubtful that anagrams can support a division of the text that cannot be secured in other ways. But the use of anagrams to tie together subunits and distinguish them from each other might work if the words used are prominent or in an already clearly marked, prominent position.

It is widely recognized that vv. 3-7 and 8-15 form separate stanzas, as observed above, and Barré makes a case for the division of vv. 16-19 into two stanzas apart from any anagrams (see below on the composition of vv. 16-19). His division of the chapter, therefore, does not rely on anagrams. Nor does he take into account every possible anagram within the poem. He focuses on repetitions and anagrams of words found in the last three lines of v. 2, the prophet's actual petition.[383] This is a plausibly important tricolon. It is interesting to observe, however, that the first two lines of v. 2 are also taken up later. The verb in the first colon (šāmaʿtî, I have heard) is repeated in v. 16, and the verb in the second (yrʾty, I am alarmed) is anagrammatized in v. 7 (rʾyty, I see). In modifying Barré's proposal, I suggest that one take these into account as well, along with noting that the divine name is used in vv. 2, 8, 18-19. Anagrams that have no relationship with v. 2, such as the relative particle ʾšr in v. 16, which takes up rʾš (head, vv. 13-14) are rightly ignored. Barré sees no reason to exclude anagrams that cross word boundaries. This allows him to identify ḥōmer (heap, v.15) not only as an anagram of raḥēm (compassion, v. 2) but also of a sequence of letters crossing the first two words of v. 8, thus binding vv. 8-15 as a unit by way of an anagram inclusio. I am not convinced that such anagrams are sufficiently recognizable to be a useful poetic device. Any appeal to anagrams should be limited to examples that use the roots of words with the possible addition of prefixes or suffixes; they should not include examples using, say, the prefix and only part of the root.[384]

---

381. Barré, "Literary Devices," 458. Paul G. Mosca ("Psalm 26: Poetic Structure and the Form-Critical Task," CBQ 47 [1985]: 212-37) identified anagrams between the first and last verses of Ps 26 (lōʾ ʾemʿād, raglî ʿāmdâ) and Ps 90 (māʿôn, nōʿam), but these cannot be said to be structural, even if one recognises them, in that they do not signal a subdivision within a poem.

382. In addition, the opening of this verse (wanōaḥ māṣāʾ ḥēn) may have been phrased to echo the use of nḥm ("to be sorry") in the preceding two verses; cf. Gen 5:29.

383. The only repetition is of the root rgz (as noted already).

384. By way of example, note that the last three consonants of dāraktā (you trample, v. 15) are an anagram of the first three consonants of tirkab (you mount, v. 8). Barré might have been willing to make use of this in support of defining vv. 8-15 as a unit if the sequence were present in the petition in v. 2. Another word-crossing anagram, in addition to the one

With these modifications, we may observe that anagrams of words in v. 2 appear in v. 7 (*r'yty*, *I see*, taking up *yr'ty*, *I am alarmed*), v. 11 (*bəraq, lightning*, taking up *qereb, midst*), v. 15 (*ḥōmer, heap*, taking up *raḥēm, compassion*) and in vv. 16–17 (*rāqāb, rot*, and *bāqār, cattle*, taking up the two occurrences of *qereb, midst*; *gāzar, cut off*, taking up *rōgez, turmoil*) and that repetitions appear in v. 7 (the root *rgz*) and in v. 16 (*šāma'tî* and the root *rgz*). Anagrams and repetitions of words from v. 2 therefore mark the end of the first stanza (v. 7), the end of the second stanza (v. 15), and the end of the poem (beginning with vv. 16–17), as well as the middle of the middle section (v. 11),[385] if one takes vv. 16–19 as a single unit (as I do). The lack of further anagrams in vv. 18–19 suggests that these verses, if they are not a later addition, belong with vv. 16–17 to the conclusion of the poem. The question whether vv. 16–19 should be divided into two stanzas will be further discussed below. Here it is sufficient to note that Barré's observations strengthen the division of the prayer into v. 2, vv. 3–7, vv. 8–15, and vv. 16–19 (or vv. 16–17 and vv. 18–19) and, as importantly, strengthen the links between v. 2 and what follows.

Commentary

3 The word for *God* used in this verse (*'ĕlôah*) is rare in the Hebrew Bible outside the book of Job. But it was used already in 1:11 (with pronominal suffix) with reference to Marduk, Babylon's chief deity—or perhaps, in the interpretation of others, with reference to the divinization of imperial power. Its reuse here (without suffix or further qualification) is as if to say that there is only one who truly deserves to be called *'ĕlôah* (*God*), namely *the Holy One*. The latter designation also does not have a pronominal suffix (unlike its use in 1:12), and the covenant name of the God of Israel is not used. In this way God's transcendence and independence are magnified. The disjunctive accent discourages reading the divine title as "the God from Teman" in analogy to inscriptions that speak of "YHWH from Teman"; instead it encourages us to interpret the parallelism as A-B-C // A-B with ellipsis of the verb in the second colon.[386] The alternative (*God of Teman* // *Holy One*) with ellipsis of the place of departure in the first colon and of the verb in the second, while not impossible, is less compelling. Thus, strictly speaking, *Teman*, like *Mount*

---

identified by Barré, is the sequence *lamed-yod-kaph* in *the tents of Cushan* (v. 7), taking up *yēlek* (*goes*, v. 5), which is seven lines from the beginning of the unit and followed by seven lines before we get to *the tents of Cushan*. This sequence, too, is not found in v. 2.

385. For *bəraq* as the midpoint of vv. 8–15, see Barré, "Literary Devices," 457.

386. Thus, *God* in the first colon is specified as *the Holy One* in the second and *Teman* is parallel to *Mount Paran*.

Paran, indicates the starting point of God's coming rather than his home necessarily.

The *selah* might indicate a musical interlude, offering a pause to reflect on this opening statement.[387] If we allow ourselves to discern the significance of God's coming from the southeastern desert regions in the light of the preceding chapters in Habakkuk, then one could possibly relate the coming of God in 3:3 to the coming to fruition of the revelation (cf. 2:3), which answers the coming of the Babylonians (cf. 1:8-9). The revelation in ch. 2 claims that the overreach of the empire will lead to its downfall. It asserts that the movement of the attacking force will lead to a countermovement: the plunderer will be plundered, the one who brought shame on others will be shamed, the one who intoxicated others will be intoxicated. As the Babylonians invaded from the north, it makes sense for the countermovement to be described as coming from the south. *Teman* is a word meaning "south" that sometimes designates the south wind (e.g., Ps 78:26; Song 4:16), a region within Edom (the southernmost Canaanite state at the time), or Edom as a whole. *Paran* designates a wilderness region to the south of Judah that is difficult to pinpoint with precision. Deuteronomy 33:2 is the only other text to refer to *Mount Paran* rather than "the wilderness of Paran."[388] There, the designation is parallel to both Seir (the hill country east of the Arabah) and Sinai (further south, whether east or west ["Midianite hypothesis"] of the Gulf of Aqaba), thus indicating a broad wilderness region rather than a precise location.[389] Similarly, in Hab 3:3, *Mount Paran* and *Teman* are not different terms for the same place; together they broadly suggest a mountainous area in the far south. Because Teman (like Seir, Deut 33:2) also evokes Edom, a country to the east as well as to the south of Judah, it may allow for an association with the east as well. Together they sketch a more extensive, or less precisely defined, region as the place of origin of God's march.

As will be indicated below, the next verse is capable of more than one interpretation. In my reading, v. 4 evokes a sunrise and leads us to think of an east-west movement toward the sea (v. 8) rather than a south-north movement. This means that we should not read the poem as a simple description

---

387. Yelena Kolyada (*A Compendium of Musical Instruments and Instrumental Terminology in the Bible* [London: Equinox, 2009]) notes that "the exegesis of the term is rich but very diverse" (164). She, too, finds the explanation that *selah* indicates a pause in the singing—maybe filled by a musical interlude—the most convincing of the musical explanations. There are also poetic and liturgical explanations, which Kolyada reviews on pp. 164-65.

388. Gen 21:21; Num 10:12; 12:16; 13:3, 26; 1 Sam 25:1; cf. "Paran," Deut 1:1; 1 Kgs 11:18 (2×).

389. This is the only place in Deuteronomy in which Sinai rather than Horeb is used to refer to the mountain on which YHWH revealed himself. The parallelism and our inability to identify the sites with confidence do not allow us to establish a direction of movement from the sequence Sinai-Seir-Mount Paran.

of a south-north movement (of God) that counters the previous north-south movement (of the Babylonians). The more complex use of motifs perhaps guards against the notion of a dualistic battle between the Babylonians, who made the first move when they invaded the country from the north, and God, who comes to the rescue of his people from the south. Such a dualism would dissociate God from the earlier north-south movement when, in fact, Habakkuk's complaint precisely arose from the conviction that YHWH must bear some responsibility for the Babylonian aggression. In other words, in some sense, the Babylonian invasion was also God's coming, a coming in judgment against his people. YHWH is not simply a "southerner," a "God of Teman" who had nothing to do with the movement from the north; the coming from Teman could be thought of as God coming a second time, now for salvation. But it may also be fair to see here a closer association of YHWH with the south than the north, suggesting that this second movement from the south is more characteristic of the God of Sinai than the earlier movement from the north, which is to say that it speaks more clearly of YHWH's character than the earlier events. As the poem unfolds, the east-west movement (from the desert toward the place where the people of God are oppressed) appears to be followed by a west-east movement. The reference to heavy rainfall (v. 10) implies such a movement, as it is the west wind that brings rain to Israel.[390] So, alternatively, the poem could suggest that those who now suffer under the hot winds blowing from the east (cf. 1:11; the Babylonians invaded from the north but they originated from the east) will experience anew the blessings of western winds blowing from the Mediterranean and bringing rain, making rivers flow again (v. 9). In this case, vv. 3-7 could be read as a poetic description of the Babylonian invasion as step one of two in God's coming to—ultimately—rescue his people. The poem's reference would be to the recent past.[391] See the reflection.

From a place in the east that has mountains, the sun illumines first the sky (*the heavens*) before spreading quite suddenly (once the sun has risen beyond the mountain) across *the earth*. Whether or not "the chief associations" of *majesty* (*hôd*) would have been "with radiance" for a native speaker, as some claim,[392] we are probably right to think of brightness here. We are invited to picture God's coming as the appearance of a bright light, as in Deut 33:2,

390. See 1 Kgs 18:41-46; Luke 12:54. For the north wind (unexpectedly) bringing rain in Prov 25:23, see Waltke, *Proverbs 15-31*, 332-33.

391. Cf. Jeremias, *Kultprophetie*, 85, who takes the whole poem in this way, anticipating rescue for a remnant along with judgment on God's people: "Die an altisraelitische Tradition anknüpfende hymnische Theophanieschilderung voll mythischer Motive (V. 3-12.13-15) meint ein Kommen Jahwes, das sich im Auftreten der Babylonier als Strafwerkzeug realisiert."

392. Andersen, *Habakkuk*, 293.

where the specific verbs used encourage an association with sunrise. While the imagery of Deut 33:2 need not be determinative for Hab 3:3, there is no evidence to the contrary here, and the following verse fits with this interpretation. In short, the splendor to which this verse refers is the splendor of light as evoked by a sunrise observed from a place west of some high mountains. Andersen sums up the various geographical references in this way: "The revelation of the splendour of Yahweh at Mount Sinai is like that of the rising of the sun between the peaks of Edom as viewed from Sinai."[393] Given that this is hardly meant as a literal and realistic description, it may be better to say "as viewed from Egypt"—namely, from the land of slavery. The people of God are oppressed, but God is on his way to their rescue. If vv. 3–7 suggest the Babylonian invasion, then the very oppression would be the preliminary act, the coming of God that precedes his engagement in a decisive act of salvation.

No such association with radiance is found in *təhillātô* (*his praiseworthiness*; more often translated "his praise"), which may suggest a verbal response to the appearance of God. Andersen points to Mesopotamian and Egyptian parallels of the splendor of the god in the sky evoking praise on earth.[394] Just as the sun rising above the top of the mountain range cannot but illuminate the earth as well as the sky, so the appearance of God as light cannot but evoke praise on earth. If so, this line makes it unlikely that God's coming from Edom is to be thought of as a picture of his involvement in the Babylonian invasion. For this, the reference to "praise" comes too soon. In the words of Isa 28:21, the Babylonian invasion is God's "strange" and "alien" work, his appearance in darkness as it were, which prompted complaint. Complaint will only give way to praise with the appearance of the light of salvation. But the translation as "praise" is not certain. It is possible that here *təhillâ* refers not to verbal adoration given to God but to his *praiseworthiness*, as is the case in Ps 102:21(22) and other places.[395]

4 The *haze* of early morning before sunrise *becomes like bright light*. The verse seems to be painting a picture of the first rays of sunshine (quickly) becoming bright as broad daylight,[396] as when the morning sun finally ascends

---

393. Andersen, *Habakkuk*, 292, apparently locating Sinai west of Edom.

394. Andersen, *Habakkuk*, 294.

395. Or in the plural, "praiseworthy deeds" (e.g., Isa 63:7). See the standard dictionaries. Robertson (*Nahum*, 223; "the word *praise* is referring to the attributes of God worthy of spontaneous praise of all his creation") compares Exod 15:11.

396. The more common Hebrew word translated *dawn* (*šāḥar*) apparently refers to the gray or reddish glow of morning twilight before dawn. This may be true even in Isa 8:20, which could be understood as "there is not even the gray of morning light in them." The word used here, *nōgah*, apparently never refers to broad daylight but rather to various other forms of light; e.g., of the moon (the related verb in Isa 13:10) or stars (Joel 2:10; 3:15 [4:15])

from behind a high mountain range. The word translated *bright light* can refer more generally to *light*; e.g., the light of dawn in the phrase *'ôr habbōqer* ("morning light"). It can also refer to lightning (e.g., Job 36:32; 37:3, 11, 15), and some believe that the context suggests this here as well.[397] But I understand this verse in a way similar to Judg 19:26, where a distinction is made between *bōqer* (morning light) and *'ôr* (full daylight),[398] except that the picture in Habakkuk is of morning light (*haze*) turning quite suddenly into the *bright light* of the rising sun when it becomes visible above the horizon.

The word rendered here doubly as *rays [horns]* elsewhere always refers to horns only. The root likely indicates a certain shape.[399] The plural is most often used where the four "horns" of an altar are in view.[400] The dual refers to the horns of an animal, which obviously come in pairs as long as they are affixed to the animal.[401] Although the noun is not attested elsewhere with reference to *rays*, the related verb describes the shining of Moses's face in Exod 34:29, 30, 35.[402] The reference to *his strength* later in the verse shows that the widespread use of horn as a metaphor for strength is relevant for the use of *qeren* here and may explain the use of the dual rather than the plural (*twin*).[403] But the rising sun as a symbol for God is not to be pictured as a horned head that appears from behind a mountain. It is perhaps to avoid such a crass zoomorphism that the *twin rays [horns]* are said to be *from his hand*

---

or indeed the light of the sun at its rising (Isa 60:3; Prov 4:18). Here it is probably best understood as a reference to the rays of light mentioned in the next colon.

397. E.g., Roberts, *Nahum*, 153.

398. Andersen (*Habakkuk*, 295) believes that "there should be no doubt that *ôr* here means 'sun' (NRSV)." He adds that "in most places where the sun is called *ôr*, it is at its rising." The fuller phrase *'ôr habbōqer* ("morning light," Judg 16:2; 1 Sam 14:36; 25:34, 36; 2 Sam 17:22; 23:4; 2 Kgs 7:9; Mi. 2:1; cf. *'ôr nōgah* in Prov 4:18) seems to account for the vast majority of the places. On its own, *'ôr* refers to the sun at dawn in Job 24:14 and Neh 8:3 but not in Job 31:26; 37:21.

399. Cf. the use of *qeren* in Isa 5:1 for a hill (or part of a hill), presumably imagined shaped like a horn and likely influenced by the wordplay with *kerem*, vineyard. The association with the material of a horn rather than its shape is not unknown in Hebrew (see esp. 1QM 5:14), although this may be a later development. Tsumura ("Janus Parallelism," 126) observes that the Sumerian sign SI is associated with Akkadian words for "horn" as well as "ray."

400. Exod 27:2; 29:12; 30:2–3, 10; 37:25–26; 38:2; Lev 4:7, 18, 25, 30, 34; 8:15; 9:9; 16:18; 1 Kgs 1:50–51; 2:28; Ps 118:27; Jer 17:1; Ezek 43:15, 20; Amos 3:14. The exceptions are the use of the plural in Ezek 27:15 to refer to ivory tusks and the metaphorical use in Ps 75:10(11) (second instance) and Zech 1:18–19, 21 (2:1–2, 4).

401. Gen 22:13; Deut 33:17; Pss 22:21(22); 75:10(11) (first instance); Dan 8:3, 6–7, 20; metaphorically in Ezek 34:21; in imitation of the horns of an animal in 1 Kgs 22:11; 2 Chr 18:10.

402. The pictorial representation of Moses with horns in western European Renaissance art interprets the verb with reference to material rather than shape.

403. Cf. the reference to the two horns of the moon in an Eblaite incantation text; see Tsumura, "Janus Parallelism," 126.

or side rather than from his head.[404] Alternatively, *hand* may suggest work and so would imply that God's glory is seen in his works. Appealing to the Amarna religion, Shupak argues that the meaning of the verse is that "God's rays are his hands," but the analogy with the Egyptian representations would be stronger if the hands bestowed some favor or grace on someone, which is not the case here.[405] Also, solar imagery for a deity seems to have been common enough in the ancient world for us to be cautious about associating its use here with specific instances in Egyptian religion. After all, a temporal distance of several hundred years falls between the Amarna religion and our text.[406] As Andersen comments, "Poetic comparison of God with the sun is a literary resource, a commonplace, but it is going too far to find behind such language either an original hymn to the sun transferred to Yahweh or traces of an ancient identity of Yahweh and the sun god."[407]

The word for *hiding place* occurs only here in the Hebrew Bible, but its derivation from a root meaning "to hide oneself" (*ḥbʾ*; by-form, *ḥbh*) is likely.[408] The root is not used elsewhere for God hiding himself or his strength.[409] Andersen considers the heavens in v. 3 to be the most likely referent of *there*.[410] But in my view *there* refers to the splendor of light, which

404. Othmar Keel and Christoph Uehlinger (*Gods, Goddesses, and Images of God in Ancient Israel* [Edinburgh: T&T Clark, 1998]) refer to a stamp seal recovered from Beth Shemesh that shows a god, "perhaps . . . a local sun god," with "notched bows ('horns,' possibly light beams; see Hab 3:4) [which] jut out from his side" (140; see the illustration on p. 139).

405. Shupak, "God from Teman." Shupak considers the preposition that goes with *his hand* to be the result of dittography and deletes it.

406. Cf. Keel and Uehlinger, *Gods*, 277, for extrabiblical evidence from Judah.

407. Andersen, *Habakkuk*, 298.

408. Impressed by the reference to twin horns, Cyrus H. Gordon ("ḤBY, Possessor of Horns and Tail," *UF* 18 [1986]: 129–32) sees a reference to a Ugaritic deity here; cf. Haak, *Habakkuk*, 90 ("the Crawler"); Paolo Xella, "HABY," *DDD*, 377; Koert van Bekkum, " 'Is Your Rage Against the Rivers, Your Wrath against the Sea?' Storm-God Imagery in Habakkuk 3," in *Playing with Leviathan: Interpretation and Reception of Monsters from the Biblical World*, ed. Kurt van Bekkum, Jaap Dekker, Henk van de Kamp, and Eric Peels, TBN 21 (Leiden: Brill 2017), 55–76. This association requires a fair bit of imagination. In Hab 3, the horns (rays) are linked to *the Holy* One, not to any companion. Also, the Ugaritic deity is known to us from a single text (*KTU* 1.114, lines 19–20) whose implied setting is very different.

409. YHWH is the subject of the verb in Isa 49:2 and, according to *DCH*, in 1QH 5:11, 25, but in these cases the verb is used transitively. The idea of YHWH concealing himself is expressed with the root *ʿlm* in Ps 10:1 and *str* in Ps 89:46(47). Pss 13:1; 88:14(15); 143:7; Ezek 39:29; Mic 3:4 use the language of YHWH turning his face away.

410. Andersen, *Habakkuk*, 298. A reference to the heavens might better be achieved by substituting *šāmayim* (heaven[s]) for *šām* (there), as proposed by Godfrey Rolles Driver, "Linguistic and Textual Problems," 396, arguably resulting in something rather prosaic and anticlimactic.

is a *hiding place* in the sense that God's real, full *strength* is not revealed even in the most powerful light humans can see. Just as we cannot look directly toward the sun in full blaze, so *his strength* is hidden from us precisely in the light. In biblical tradition, God's presence can be signaled by both a pillar of fire and a pillar of cloud (cf. Exod 13:21–22; 14:24); God can be thought of as dwelling in thick darkness (Exod 20:21; 1 Kgs 8:12) as well as wrapped in light as in a garment (Ps 104:2).[411] The reference in 1 Tim 6:16 to God as dwelling in unapproachable light captures well the aspect of tradition that comes to expression here in Hab 3:4. While it could be said that in this case, light, which normally illumines things, obscures them instead, it may be more appropriate to think of the analogy of increased knowledge revealing one's ignorance (i.e., the hiddenness of full knowledge).

5 The previous verse possibly invites us to picture rays of light to both the left and right of God, even though *hand* is used in the singular. This verse paints *Pestilence* (*dāber*) and *Burning Plague* (*rešep*) as going ahead of and following God respectively. The references to *face* and *feet* link with the reference to *hand* in v. 4, but they also suggest that *Pestilence* and *Burning Plague* are in God's presence (*before his face*) as his attendants (*at his feet*). *Pestilence* was the fifth plague upon Egypt (Exod 9:3–7) and is elsewhere a (threatened) divine judgment on God's own people (e.g., Lev 26:25; Num 14:12; Deut 28:21; Amos 4:10). Jeremiah and Ezekiel often list it in conjunction with sword or bloodshed and famine (e.g., Jer 14:12; Ezek 6:11).[412] *Burning Plague* is used much more rarely within the Hebrew Bible, and only once more refers to plague, in Deut 32:24.[413] The word can evoke flames ("burning heat, lightning"), which goes well with the light motif here in Hab 3 and accounts for my use of *Burning* with *Plague*. A deity of that name is known in early northwest Semitic religion and occasionally associated with the sun goddess, and this may have left a few traces in the Bible.[414] With an

---

411. Cf. Franz Delitzsch, *Habakuk*, 151.

412. More rarely, *pestilence* is spoken of as God's judgment on other nations (e.g., Jer 28:8).

413. The other occurrences are Job 5:7 ("sons of flame" = sparks); Pss 76:3(4) ("flames of the bow" = arrows); 78:48 ("flames," usually interpreted as a reference to lightning bolts); Song 8:6 ("Its flames are flames of fire"). Some occurrences in the Dead Sea Scrolls refer to pestilence rather than flame; see *DCH*. Among others, Maciej Münnich believes that the god Resheph is referenced in these three verses as well as in Deut 32:24; 1 Chr 7:25; Job 5:7; Sir 43:18. See his *The God Resheph in the Ancient Near East*, ORA 11 (Tübingen: Mohr Siebeck, 2013), 215–37, 216–19 for Hab 3.

414. In addition to (some of) the texts mentioned in the previous footnote, Susanne Rudnig-Zelt ("JHWH und Ræšæp—Zu JHWHs Umgang mit einem syrischen Pestgott," *VT* 65 [2015]: 247–64) thinks that the reference to an arrow that flies by day (Ps 91:5) indicates knowledge of the Syrian deity among the writers of the Hebrew Bible.

eye to Deut 33:2 and other texts, Andersen seeks to reconstruct an ancient tradition of four attendants, an ensemble of bodyguards in which individual destroyers are not always clearly distinguished from one another. He suggests that Hab 3 evokes plague, pestilence, fire, and maybe sword as quasi-divine beings surrounding God.[415]

This seems, however, to make a great deal out of very little, given that there is no reference to fire and the *twin rays [horns]* in the previous verse are not personified. In fact, the *twin rays [horns]* are not distinguished from each other, even if we picture them to the left and right. Thus, in my view, to differentiate between *Pestilence* and *Burning Plague* as if they are two clearly distinct entities is questionable. The use of capitalization reflects the belief that these illnesses are personified here and may interact with a possible mythological background. Even so, caution is advisable against overinterpretation, given that knowledge of the god Resheph (*Burning Plague*) and a separate god Deber (*Pestilence*) is not unambiguously attested in the Bible.[416] Indeed, it remains a matter of debate whether even at Ebla "Deber" (Dabir) is an independent deity or an epithet designating an aspect of Resheph.[417] In addition, we should note that bringing plague was only one feature of the god Resheph, and there is nothing here or in other biblical texts that demonstrates an awareness of the other features of Resheph.[418] It remains difficult, therefore, to be confident about whether the line between personification (maybe even inspired by the knowledge of the deification of numerous forces in ancient pantheons) and reference to known characters has been crossed. The terms *Pestilence* and *Burning Plague* in my translation rather than "Deber" and "Resheph" reflect the belief that it probably has not. In any case, if *Pestilence* and *Burning Plague* are to be considered actual beings here— Resheph and Deber rather than instances of personified diseases—they must be thought of as angels of judgment rather than demons, given that they are

---

415. Andersen, *Habakkuk*, 300–306.

416. The two other texts in which some see knowledge of a "Deber" in the Hebrew Bible are Ps 91:3 and Hos 13:14; see Gregorio del Olmo Lete, "Deber," *DDD*, 230–31.

417. For the latter, see Robert R. Stieglitz, "Ebla and the Gods of Canaan," in *Eblaitica: Essays on the Ebla Archives and Eblaite Language 2*, ed. Cyrus H. Gordon (Winona Lake, IN: Eisenbrauns, 1990), 84; Francesco Pomponio and Paolo Xella, *Les dieux d'Ebla: Étude analytique des divinités éblaites à l'époque des archives royales du IIIe millénaire* (Münster: Ugarit-Verlag, 1997), 123–24.

418. Paolo Xella, "Resheph," *DDD*, 700–703. John Day, "New Light on the Mythological Background of the Allusion to Resheph in Habakkuk iii 5," *VT* 29 (1979): 353–55, draws attention to a Ugaritic text (*KTU* 1.82) "in which Reshep participates alongside Baal in conflict with the dragon" (354), which is considered relevant because Day believes that Baal's conflict with the sea forms the background for the whole of Hab 3:3–15. This is very doubtful; cf. David Toshio Tsumura, "Ugaritic Poetry and Habakkuk 3," *TynBul* 40 (1989): 24–48.

in God's entourage.[419] They are not independently acting forces; the presence of *Pestilence* and *Burning Plague* indicates God's power and strength, to which the previous verse alluded. As God marches forth from Teman, he means business.

6 As indicated in the translation, the first bicolon can be read in two ways. God *stands and surveys a land, he looks and spies out nations*, mapping out the lay of the land and examining the state of nations. But in doing so he also *shakes a land* and *startles nations*.[420] The close attention paid by God cannot but have an effect on the land so that even *everlasting hills are shattered*, which is to say that even the strongest opposition gives way.[421] There will be nothing to obstruct God's march. The next colon makes the same point by saying that *the eternal hills bow* or sink *down*.[422] The verb does not so much suggest bowing down in an act of worship as having to bend low in submission. The last three words are difficult to interpret (see the translation note). Some believe that the line specifically alludes to God taking the same route he did in days of old.[423] In my view, *hălîkôt* (*triumphal procession*) draws attention not to geography but to the way in which God's movements are consistent with what he has done in the distant past: "Ancient movements are his."[424] Indeed, the translation expresses a more specific sense in which God's movement is typical. While *hălîkôt* could be used for the movement of troops (Nah 2:5[6]), the portrayal here is not of a battle but of a movement no one dares to oppose. It is therefore more like a *triumphal procession* of the sort we find referenced in Ps 68:24(25). This is a suitable way to sum up

419. Cf. Rudnig-Zelt, "JHWH und Ræšæp," who makes the point that in biblical literature, in contrast to post-biblical literature, Resheph is not treated as a demon. See also Judit M. Blair, *De-demonising the Old Testament: An Investigation of Azazel, Lilith, Deber, Qeteb and Reshef in the Hebrew Bible*, FAT 2/37 (Tübingen: Mohr Siebeck, 2009).

420. The former reading derives the relevant verbs from the roots *mdd* and *trr* (a by-form of the medium *waw/yod* root, which as such cannot have a *piel* form), the latter from *mwd* (maybe a by-form of *mwṭ*) or *myd* (accepted in *HALOT* and *DCH*; Barr, *Comparative Philology*, 252, is right to reject the claim that the use of *saleuō* by the Greek translator provides firm evidence for the existence of this Hebrew root) and *ntr*.

421. If we are supposed to hear in the *shattered* also a "scattered" (see the translation note), there is a further intensification, but the basic meaning remains the same.

422. The verb in the *qal* has an impersonal subject also in Isa 2, namely in v. 11 ("the height/arrogance of men") and v. 17 ("human haughtiness").

423. E.g., Roberts, *Nahum*, 154.

424. Cf. Avishur, *Studies*, 170. Avishur believes that the phrase has the same meaning in Ps 68. Franz Delitzsch (*Habakuk*, 156–57) similarly considered the parallels in Pss 68:24(25) and 77:13(14) decisive (relating them to the exodus and interpreting *baqqōdeš* in both places as "in holiness" rather than "in the sanctuary"). See also Prinsloo, "Literary Context," 103, who speaks of "a reminder that it is God's everlasting way not to remain silent, but to appear in his full heavenly majesty when his people call for help!"

what precedes. The word translated *ancient* (*ʿôlām*, rendered *eternal* in the previous line; see the translation note on *everlasting*) refers to long duration reaching either back to the distant past or forward to the distant future. The former links well with the following verse.

7 The last line of v. 6 gave us something like a summary, and so it would not be unreasonable to expect that we are coming to the end of the first stanza of the poem. The return of the first person at this stage, therefore, is not odd, even if many commentators consider it alien.[425] The verse rounds up the report of the divine march by focusing on its impact on humanity. Some interpreters note the parallels between the opening of this verse and 1:3, *Why do you make me see iniquity . . . ?* Habakkuk's complaint was that he had to see iniquity and that God was looking on and so, by his inaction, apparently condoned the violence. Now God is on the march and *in place of iniquity* the prophet sees something else.[426] There may be a double entendre here, and the above translation seeks to hint at this. What the prophet sees may be happening "on account of" (a possible nuance of the preposition) *iniquity* (i.e., responding to the iniquity found in a place) or "instead of" iniquity. It is also possible that *iniquity* here can be heard as "misfortune" so that, on the one hand, the nomads are trembling, suffering "under misfortune" (and "because of iniquity"—theirs or someone else's?) while, on the other hand, the prophet now sees something else "instead of iniquity." In my view, the primary sense is that the prophet's eyes, which had been focusing on evil and disaster within Judah, are now directed to another reality instead. Or perhaps more precisely, they look at this same reality as part of a wider picture and in this sense see something else.

What the prophet now sees is *trembling*. The verb is masculine, while *the tent curtains of the land of Midian* are feminine. In my view, this indicates that the verb goes with *the tents of Cushan* (masc.) as well as *the tent curtains of the land of Midian*.[427] *Tents* and *tent curtains* are found together in poetic texts on five other occasions, always in this order, either with positive connotations (Song 1:5; Isa 54:2) or, as presumably here, in the context of judgment (Jer 4:20; 10:20; 49:29).[428] Interestingly, the reference is not necessarily to nomadic living. Thus, mention of Kedar (a nomadic tribe) is linked with Solomon in Song 1:5 (arguably signaling urbanity as well as royalty) and

---

425. E.g., Hiebert, *God of My Victory*, 22; Andersen, *Habakkuk*, 311.

426. E.g., Roberts, *Nahum*, 155; Prinsloo, "Literary Context," 89.

427. Others take the verb only with the second subject (e.g., NRSV, NIV), in which case the discrepancy of gender must be explained as a "dislike of using the 3rd plur. fem. imperf" (GKC 145p; cf. JM 150b).

428. Elsewhere, the terms are used together with reference to the tabernacle; so in Exod 26:7, 9, 12–13; 36:14; Num 4:25.

with Hazor in Jer 49:29, a well-known fortified city.[429] The term *Cushan* is known elsewhere only in connection with King Cushan-Rishataim (Judg 3:8, 10).[430] It was most likely formed here for poetic reasons (cf. the sounds ending Midian and, in the opening verse of this section, Teman and Paran), in which case it would be equivalent to Cush. Cush normally refers to Nubia, called "Ethiopia" in antiquity (e.g., in Nah 3:9), and Greek translations of Hab 3 accordingly render it as "Ethiopians" (Nubians). But Midianites and Nubians are not usually thought to have lived near each other.[431] Andersen and many others are, therefore, convinced that the reference here is to "the Cush associated with Midian (and Moses), not Ethiopia or any other place," and Andersen points to "the Kushu that is mentioned in Egyptian texts of the Middle Bronze Age" for further support.[432] The identification of Moses's Cushite wife (Num 12:1) with Zipporah, his Midianite wife (Exod 2:16–22; 4:25–26; 18:1–12) is by no means certain. Nevertheless, a reference to Nubia seems unlikely here. If two such different regions were covered in this verse, one would expect them to be mentioned in reverse order, given that the divine approach is from the East and Midian would therefore be reached first and then Cush. Thus, while the evidence is not as strong as sometimes claimed, we should probably interpret both *Cushan* and *Midian* as references to Arabian nomadic tribes.

In either case, however, the *trembling* of tents cannot but be preliminary only. If the reference is to nomadic tribes in the wilderness, it evokes the wilderness wanderings of the people of God. In this case, one expects the equivalent of the conquest of Jericho and other cities as the climax of the movement, not the trembling of tents in the wilderness. If, however, *Cushan* and *Midian* are referenced as the two southernmost regions in the consciousness of Habakkuk's contemporaries, then it is similarly clear that a trembling in the south cannot yet be the answer to the military forces that have devastated Judah from the north. This means that Habakkuk does not see the end. He is still *in the midst of years*. But instead of focusing on iniquity, which God

---

429. Note also the phrase "tents of Ham" (parallel to "Egypt") in Ps 78:51. Avishur (*Studies*, 171–72) appeals to this as an argument for accepting the emendation *teḥat 'ōn wetīrā'* (his transliteration): "On (= Heliopolis) will fear and be frightened."

430. The link is made in the Tg. ("I gave them into the hand of Cushan the Wicked"), which reads these verses as a historical review in which reference to the Midianites evokes deliverance at the hand of Gideon; see ArBib 14, 158.

431. Midian covers a large territory east of the gulf of Aqaba. Lower Egypt was at times governed by Cushites from Upper Egypt. Franz Delitzsch (*Habakuk*, 159) therefore reckons that the two terms can be seen as in close affinity, even with Cushan being interpreted to refer to Cush as usually understood.

432. Andersen, *Habakkuk*, 312. He does not offer references to Egyptian texts.

apparently tolerates without concern for the victims, the prophet now sees signs of God's being on the move as he was in times of old.

Reflection

The picture drawn in these verses is evocative; its historical reference is left imprecise. Verse 3 offers the summary: God comes, and heaven and earth are affected by it. Verses 4–5 elaborate on the coming of God with his retinue while vv. 6–7 focus on the effect of God's coming. This is all described metaphorically; God is not seen and felt like an actor alongside other actors on the historical stage. We may infer this from the similarities with imagery that is used elsewhere in looking back on God's deliverance of Israel out of Egypt. Judges 5 speaks of mountains melting at the presence of the God of Sinai, Ps 114 of mountains skipping like rams.[433] Reading these poems alongside the narrative texts that refer to the same events guards against postulating massive geological changes at the time of Israel's exodus and conquest of the land. The claim made is that nothing can get in God's way when he is on the march, not that one can trace God's movements with a seismograph. (This is not to say that there is no measurable effect at all; see below.) In other words, the divine march described in vv. 3–6 is not readily visible to human eyes. The prophetic testimony is required to discern the cause behind events that are described in indirect metaphorical or mythological language.[434] Even the reference to pestilence does not demand an actual outbreak of bubonic plague but is likely poetic language to indicate grave danger to human life. Only the trembling of nomadic tents in v. 7 might be something that can be observed by human eyes, and it is only this event that Habakkuk is said to be seeing. But if God's appearance here is pictured in terms of a sirocco that makes tent curtains flutter, the language is nevertheless surely still metaphorical. What is indicated is the panic among nomadic tribes, reminiscent of the panic among the inhabitants of Philistia and Canaan to which Exod 15:14–16 refers. In modern terms, this might be described as a widespread rise in anxiety levels, which, in principle, would have been verifiable. The fear among the nations is reported as a sign both that God is at work and that he will bring his people securely into the land that he has chosen as his own residence.

433. Cf. Isa 63:19b–64:3 (63:19b–64:2), where recollection of the past is explicitly a part of the plea for future intervention.

434. In this respect, the identification of the solution is not dissimilar to the identification of the problem. The rise of the Neo-Babylonian Empire was visible enough; what was not readily observable is that this was God's raising up of the Chaldeans.

It may be fruitful to note that both hearing and seeing are involved. Hearing seems to be linked with tradition or revelation that has been received and needs to be trusted (v. 2) while seeing appears to relate to events one can experience, indeed in some cases that one can hardly fail to experience (cf. 1:3, 5). Nevertheless, this is no mere passive receiving of sounds and sights. Decisions are involved as to what to hear and see and how to interpret what is heard and seen. The divine response in ch. 2 urges us to keep faith with YHWH, which includes giving the tradition a proper hearing. And in ch. 3, the prophet, therefore, sees differently. Having heard God's promise and remembering the tradition of God's deeds in the past, the prophet notices, or sees imaginatively, one of two things. He either (1) sees the first signs of God's intervention for the salvation of his people (i.e., God's approach from the east to save his people from oppression in "Egypt," the trembling of the nomadic tribes being a sign that God is already on the move) or (2) reinterprets Babylonian aggression (a move that has people in southern regions trembling) as merely the first leg of God's approach, to be followed by the second leg as rains from the west follow a sirocco from the east. In any case, the prophet does not see the full picture yet. He still only sees the *turmoil* (note the reuse of the root from v. 2 in v. 7). There is little in the scenario painted so far that in itself offers hope, but (renewed) faith in what he has heard about God leads the prophet to expect that the divine march will lead to something good in the end.

So far, we have been told from where God is coming but not yet where he is going, even though the reuse of geographical designations ending in *an* marks a first resting point in the poem. The last phrase, *the land of Midian*, may well evoke Sinai (Horeb), the mountain of God (Exod 3:1).[435] When the prophet complained about seeing iniquity (1:3), it was in the context of observing that the law was numbed, unable to bring forth justice (1:4). Now he sees disarray near the place where the law was given to the people of God. This could be a poetic description of the chaos the prophet experienced and complained about in the first place, but if so, it would be from a different vantage point. YHWH is no longer seen as inactive or on the defensive but as someone who is on the march. In his complaint, Habakkuk had linked the experience of injustice and disaster with YHWH, citing a prophecy that claims divine agency behind the immediate cause of Judah's distress (1:5–11). But at the same time, he separated YHWH from the evil by suggesting that YHWH merely looks on without intervening to save the righteous. In ch. 3,

---

435. Cf. Shmuel Aḥituv, "The Sinai Theophany in the Psalm of Habakkuk," in *Birkat Shalom: Studies in the Bible, Ancient Near Eastern Literature, and Postbiblical Judaism Presented to Shalom M. Paul on the Occasion of His Seventieth Birthday*, ed. Chaim Cohen et al. (Winona Lake, IN: Eisenbrauns, 2008), 231.

the weight falls on acknowledging God's involvement. Even now, however, a little gap is left between what is experienced and God's "work" (3:2). Plague and pestilence are God's companions. They are closely associated with God, but their personification allows for a little distance. Plague is not directly the work of God but accompanies it. Above all, what these verses describe is surely not the sum of God's work, of which the opening verse of the prayer speaks, but a preliminary move toward it—the march has not yet reached its destination. This means that while God is associated with devastation and disaster, as in 1:5–11, his work and aim are not identified with it. If in ch. 1 the prophet nearly went as far as to characterize the destruction he witnessed as an unintended consequence of God's initiative in raising the Babylonians,[436] there is now no hint of unintended consequences. But maybe it would be fair to speak of terrifying side-effects of God's coming. They are side-effects in the sense that they are not the purpose and content of God's coming. The main message is that when God is on the march, nothing can get in his way; all opposition will be vanquished. To the extent that God is trusted to move for good rather than evil, justice rather than iniquity, this is good news.

XVI. EXPRESSION OF MARVEL AT YHWH'S ATTACK ON HIS ENEMIES (3:8-15)

[8]*Is it against streams[a] that it burns, YHWH,[b]*
  indeed,[c] against the streams your anger,
    against the sea your fury[d]
  when you mount your horses,
    your chariots of deliverance?[e]
[9]*Fully uncovered is your bow,[f]*
  oaths are the rods, a word.[g] Selah.
    With rivers you divide the earth.[h]
[10]*The mountains see you, they tremble;*
  a torrent of water passes through.[i]
The abyss gives forth its voice,
  high[j] it raises its hands.[k]
[11]*Sun, moon stand at the zenith[l]*
  at[m] the light of your arrows going forward,[n]
    at the brightness of the lightning of your spear.

436. The way the prophet's complaint in 1:5–11 is phrased does not really allow YHWH to reply that the consequences were not intended, and thus this is not an option the prophet puts on the table even in ch. 1. Nevertheless, the complaint implies that the relationship between God's initiative and the negative consequences it produced is unfathomable.

¹²*In indignation you stride the earth;*
in anger you trample nations.
¹³*You have gone out for the salvation of your people,*
for the salvation of ° *your anointed one.*^p
You crush the head of ^q *the house of the wicked,*
laying bare^r *the foundation*^s *to the neck.*^t *Selah.*
¹⁴*You penetrate*^u *with his own*^v *rods*^w *the heads*^x *of his hordes*^y—
they storm in to scatter^z *me,*^{aa}
  their exultation^{bb} *as of one devouring in secret*^{cc} *someone poor.*
¹⁵*You tread*^{dd} *through the sea on*^{ee} *your horses,*
a heap^{ff} *of mighty waters.*

a. While *nāhār* ("river" or "stream") is a masculine noun, the feminine plural form is commonly used, maybe to more clearly differentiate the plural from the dual form used in *'ăram nahărayim* ("Aram of the two rivers" = Mesopotamia), whose consonantal form would otherwise look the same. While rare, the masculine plural form is found elsewhere (Job 20:17; Isa 18:1, 2, 7; 33:21; Zeph 3:10). Hiebert, *God of My Victory*, 23, prefers to interpret the final consonant as an enclitic *mem*. Samuel R. Driver (*Minor Prophets*, 90) suggests dropping the first syllable to avoid the repetition and so reads "mountains," which fits with v. 6. There are other places in which hills are affected by God's wrath (Deut 32:22; Job 9:5; Ps 18:7[8]; Isa 5:25) but generally as part of a cataclysm rather than as the specific target.

b. The idiomatic use of the verb with impersonal subject demands that the divine name be considered a vocative here with the subject of the verb being given in the next colon. Many find the text of the first three cola problematic, especially with the double reference to *streams*. For a discussion of this and similarly constructed verses, see Samuel E. Loewenstamm, "The Expanded Colon in Ugaritic and Biblical Verse," *JSS* 14 (1969): 176–96, esp. 190–92; repr. in *Comparative Studies in Biblical and Ancient Oriental Literatures*, AOAT 204 (Kevelaer: Butzon & Bercker; Neukirchen: Neukirchener Verlag, 1980), 281–309 (see 297–302 for a discussion and defense of the integrity of Hab 3:8).

c. This and the following colon are introduced by *'im*, which I have left untranslated in the next colon. It could be translated "or" in both instances, but no genuine alternatives are distinguished here. The verse presents a threefold rhetorical question to which the answer is no. See the commentary.

d. The expansion of double questions to triple questions was examined by Yitzhak Avishur, "Patterns of the Double Question in the Bible and in Ugarit," in *The Zolman Shazar Jubilee Volume* (Jerusalem: Kiryat Sefer, 1973), 421–64, esp. 421–24. Cf. Avishur, *Studies*, 175, where he notes that the *hă* . . . *'im* . . . *kî* sequence is found elsewhere as a unit, "confirming that our verse is a pentacolon" (cf. "Pattern," 456–58).

e. Or "your victorious chariots"; but while *tašûʿâ* can refer to victory without the notion of deliverance (e.g., 2 Kgs 5:1), it is not clear that *yəšûʿâ* (the form used here) ever does. While the plural *horses* can be explained with reference to a chariot drawn by more than one horse, one would not expect anyone to mount more than one chariot. Many therefore emend the plural *chariots*. But Jamie Aislinn Banister ("Theophanies in the Minor Prophets: A Cross-Analysis of Theophonic Texts in Micah, Habakkuk, and Zechariah" [PhD diss., Catholic University of America, 2013], 141) points out that the plural is used also in the only other place where the chariotry (*merkābâ*) is clearly God's (Isa 66:15); cf. Ps 68:17(18), where

God's chariotry (*rekeb*) is said to number thousands. Only in Ps 104:3, which declares the clouds to be God's chariot, is a single vehicle (*rəkûb*) in view.

f. Deriving the verb from '*rh* and interpreting the noun "nakedness" (here *fully uncovered*) as an internal object, for which see David Toshio Tsumura, "Niphal with an Internal Object in Habakkuk 3:9a," *JSS* 31 (1961): 11–16; cf. Andersen, *Habakkuk*, 320. It is possible that the text originally read as emended in *BHS* ("You bared your bow"); see Michael L. Barré, "Yahweh Gears Up for Battle: Habakkuk 3,9a," *Biblica* 87 (2006): 75–84. Others derive from '*wr* ("to arouse, wake up"); e.g., Eaton, "Origin," 151, already attested in the Greek Barberini manuscript and 8HevXIIgr (and Latin and Syr. renderings). Other Greek MSS use *enteinō* ("to stretch out"), which could be an idiomatic rendering of either. Whether the protective cover is removed or the bow "aroused" or "stretched," these are all different ways of saying that the bow is ready for action.

g. This line is notoriously difficult to interpret. The first word can mean "seven" or "sevenfold" (or, less plausibly here, "weeks"). Franz Delitzsch (*Habakuk*, 165–71) argues at length for reading the passive participle here, used predicatively. He is followed by Eaton, "Origin," 151–52. BDB and JPS ("Sworn are the rods of the word") reflect a similar understanding, but the lack of congruence between predicate (fem.) and subject (masc.) might stand in the way of this interpretation, unless it is to be explained by accommodation to the feminine-looking form of the subject. The middle word most likely indicates weaponry (*rods* or "maces") rather than "tribes" and is the word least often emended; cf. v. 14 (there with a masculine-looking form). It is often thought that the context demands that the reference is to arrows, but this is not likely; see David Toshio Tsumura, "The 'Word Pair' *qšt* and *mṭ* in Habakkuk 3:9 in the Light of Ugaritic and Akkadian," in *Go to the Land I Will Show You: Studies in Honor of Dwight W. Young*, ed. Joseph E. Coleson and Victor H. Matthews (Winona Lake, IN: Eisenbrauns, 1996), 353–61. Tsumura reads the plural as one of intensity, hence "a majestic mace." The noun '*ōmer* (*word*) is found elsewhere only in Job 22:28; Pss 19:2–3(3–4); 68:11(12); 77:8(9) with varying connotations. Assuming that a *tav* went missing due to haplography, "you have said" could be read (cf. Vulg.).

h. Reading a *niphal* instead of a *piel*, the LXX makes *the earth* the subject ("of rivers will the earth be torn asunder"), which could be understood either as flagging up YHWH's (future) action or as describing a reaction to the threat from YHWH. The LXX is followed by, e.g., Hiebert, *God of My Victory*, 28–29; Alexa F. Wilke, *Die Gebete der Propheten: Anrufungen Gottes im "Corpus Propheticum" der Hebräischen Bibel*, BZAW 451 (Berlin: de Gruyter 2014), 354.

i. Andersen (*Habakkuk*, 265) points out that Wellhausen's 1893 emendation to *zōrmû mayim 'ābôt* ("the clouds pour forth water," as in Ps 77:17[18]) was subsequently attested in an ancient manuscript (MurXII). Even so, not everyone is persuaded. Maybe an ancient scribe came up with the same adjustment to the text as Wellhausen.

j. Hebrew *rôm* ("height") seems to function here as an adverb; cf. the use of *mārôm* in Isa 37:23; 40:26. It is also possible to take it as the subject of the verb, making a high-low chiasm: mountains-water-abyss-height; cf. Gareth J. Wearne, "Habakkuk 3:10–11: In Defence of a Masoretic Unit Division," *VT* 64 (2014): 515–18. But the abyss is more readily pictured as raising its hands (in the form of waves) than the height(s) are. Others take the final line with v. 11, making *sun* the subject (cf. LXX, which, however, only takes the verb; Peshitta and Vulg. keep *sun* and *moon* together, adding a coordinating "and"). In addition, the middle letter of the verb is sometimes changed; see BHS and HALOT (entry 8709 on *rôm*).

k. The form *yādêhû* is unique, with only a few similarly formed parallels (cf. *HGHS* 29v);

the standard form for "his hand" is *yādô*. It may be "a genuine archaism" (Andersen, *Habakkuk*, 332) or chosen for euphonic reasons, avoiding the presence of another *ô*, of which there were four in the preceding three words. Avishur (*Studies*, 182) suggests dividing *yādêhû* into two words and translates, "YHW [*sic*] has raised His hand to the heavens," as if the author of the psalm construed Josh 10:12 as an oath.

l. I assume that the *he* of direction has (nearly) lost any notion of direction or motion here, as happens in some idiomatic expressions (JM 93e) and names of cities (JM 93f). See, e.g., 1 Sam 23:15 (Horesh) and 1 Kgs 4:12 (Zarethan). Otherwise: "toward the zenith" or "toward [their] lofty habitation." Others interpret the final *he* as a feminine suffix (agreeing with *sun*); so Patterson, *Nahum*, 245.

m. Andersen (*Habakkuk*, 332) argues that the preposition introduces the targets of the divine arrows, namely *light* (sun) and *brightness* (moon). Others suggest an adverbial use (e.g., Haak, *Habakkuk*, 92, translating "brightly" and "brilliantly").

n. The verb is sometimes taken as relating to *sun* and *moon* (*HALOT* suggests the meaning "vanish"), but in Ps 77:17(18), the same verb (in the *hithpael*) has *your arrows* as the subject. Given how close the motifs here and in Ps 77 are, this seems the better reading.

o. The MT *'et* is often rendered as a preposition ("with") in ancient versions, but I take it as the direct object marker with the verbal noun functioning as a pseudo-infinitive (cf. JM 49ca). The preposition is commonly used in the sense of "together with" or "alongside" but could be instrumental (e.g., Gen 4:1; Judg 8:7). A reference to the Davidic king as instrumental for the people's salvation would be totally unexpected here, and a reference to Cyrus (Isa 45:1) or the Babylonian king (bringing salvation to the people by destroying the wicked Judean royal house) is similarly unlikely. David Noel Freedman identified this as an example of "the broken construct chain" in an article so titled; see *Bib* 53 (1972): 535; cf. *IBHS* 9.3d. Freedman is undecided whether the intruding element represents the object marker or the personal pronoun (defectively written). Alternatively, Andersen (*Habakkuk*, 335) suggests that the two consonants stand for the poetic verb *'ātâ* ("to come"; cf. Deut 33:2); the overall meaning of the colon would be the same. The object marker is very rare in poetry and may have been used here for emphasis (see GKC 117m). Indeed, *'et* is apparently sometimes used to stress a noun that is not the direct object (see JM 125j; Meyer, *Grammatik*, 3:71–73).

p. Most LXX MSS have the plural *tous christous sou* ("your anointed ones"; cf. Barberini *tous christous sotous eklektous sou*, "your chosen ones"), thus probably referring to the people, which does not seem very plausible (notwithstanding Ps 105:15, where the reference is to the patriarchs) and would make for a highly redundant bicolon. The translator may have wanted to avoid the suggestion that the Messiah needed saving; cf. Eaton, "Origin," 154; Fabry, *Habakuk/Obadja*, 286–87.

q. A similar construction (*māḥaṣ* with *min*) is found in Ps 68:21(22); cf. Isa 9:14(13) with the verb *krt* ("cut"), which elsewhere takes "head" as its direct object (e.g., 1 Sam 31:9).

r. The ancient versions have a second-person singular verb form here (e.g., Gk. *ebales*, Lat. *percussisti*).

s. Or "laying bare from base to neck." NRSV interprets this as the house being laid bare "from foundation to roof," but *neck* can hardly stand in for the topmost part of the building, which would be "the head." Other translations take *the head*, understood as the leader, as the object, "laying him bare from thigh to neck" (RSV, ESV; cf. NIV, NASB). The ambiguity relates to the fact that *neck* refers generally to the neck of humans or animals and is never used of a building, while *yəsôd* always refers to the foundation of a building (outside the Pentateuch) or the base of the altar (in Exod 29:12 and throughout Leviticus). On the basis of a similar expression found twice in Ugaritic, David Toshio Tsumura (*Creation and Destruction: A Reappraisal of the Chaoskampf Theory in the Old Testament* [Winona Lake, IN: Eisenbrauns, 2006], 177) argues that '*ad-ṣawwā'r* means "*up* to the neck," not "*down* to the neck" (cf. following note), but the nuance may well be determined by the movement in context. While waters naturally rise *up* to the neck, a blow to the head could be readily pictured as a *down*ward movement.

t. Avishur (*Studies*, 187–88) sees two variant readings conflated here, one concerned with striking a body, the other with destroying a house. He does not attempt to explain how the second "inappropriate" reading might have come about. Tsumura (*Creation and Destruction*, 176–77) suggests that the verse can be analyzed as four lines, with the middle two being read as an "inserted bicolon" that results in an outer bicolon, "You crushed the head/ up-to-the-neckness" (= "You crushed the head/ to be headless"), and an inner bicolon, "From the house of the evil one/ (you) laid bare the foundation." A similar reading had been adopted by Luzzatto in the 18th century (see Avishur, *Studies*, 186). Not having come across such an inserted bicolon before, I find his alternative proposal that the verse depicts the smashing of a statue preferable (178); see the commentary.

u. Tsumura ("Word Pair," 361) points out that the Akkadian cognate means "to butt, gore, abut; knock down" and compares the Hebrew noun *maqqebet* ("hammer") so that an arrow-like movement need not be implied. As observed above on v. 9, it is unlikely that *maṭṭôt/maṭṭîm* refers to arrows (see n. g). Still, the verb is used elsewhere in the Hebrew Bible for piercing or boring (e.g., 2 Kgs 12:9[10]; 18:21).

v. I interpret the first two suffixes as referring back to *the wicked* in v. 13; cf. Franz Delitzsch, *Habakuk*, 185. The addition of *own* brings out the meaning more clearly in English. Some emend to read a second-person suffix (cf. *BHS*) but with scant support from the versions (see Barberini *meta dynameōs sou*, "with your power"). MT is not improbable; cf. Eaton, "Origin," 155.

w. It is interesting to observe that the form used here presumes the -*îm* formation of the plural though, in v. 9, the standard -*ôt* form was used. Is this a deliberate echo of the *nəhārîm* (v. 8) / *nəhārôt* (v. 9) variation? More likely, it reflects the author's penchant for echoing sounds (see "Language and Style," p. 202), here with two words in close succession ending on -*āyw*. This explanation could also hold for the use of *nəhārîm* and *nəhārôt*. In this latter case, however, the two different forms also suggest a difference between broad, empire-building rivers and smaller streams dividing the land. By contrast, there seems to be no basis for distinguishing between, say, "sticks" (*maṭṭîm*) in v. 14 and "rods" (*maṭṭôt*) in v. 9. Aaron Pinker ("On the Meaning of מטיו in Habakkuk 3,14a," *Bib* 86 [2005]: 376–86) suggests a small emendation to read "into the spun of [the head]" instead of *with his own rods* and reads this as a reference to the braids of long hair so that the attack would in effect be on the nape from behind (as the enemy is fleeing).

x. I interpret the singular attested in MT and MurXII as collective. The translators of LXX, Barberini, Peshitta, and Tg. also opted for the plural. 8ḤevXIIgr and Vulg. render with the singular.

y. *Ketiv* suggests the singular, *qere* the plural. The meaning of the word is uncertain; it seems to be related to *pərāzôn* in Judg 5:7, 11, which is traditionally thought to refer to the rural population (cf. KJV, here "villages"). LXX *dynastōn* interprets as "rulers" (cf. JPS). A more likely alternative reading would be "horsemen," but in the light of Judg 5, it seems best to see a reference to the bulk of the army rather than any elites. The translation "warriors" is a popular and possible alternative to my *hordes*. Against the accentuation, some take the word with the following line, which creates a more balanced bicolon; see NIV. The plural *rods* (changed into the singular in NIV) counsels against this.

z. Pinker ("Meaning of מטי," 384) believes that the verb could be the *hiphil* infinitive of either *pwṣ* (*scatter*) or *npṣ* ("smash"), but the latter is not attested in the *hiphil* and the masoretic vocalization suggests the former. Eaton ("Origin," 156) points to Job 18:11 (also with a singular!) and Ezek 46:18 for the nuance "chase away" rather than *scatter*.

aa. 8ḤevXIIgr has the plural ("us"). The use of the singular *me* is peculiar with the verb *scatter* but takes up the way in which the prayer in Hab 1 used the first-person singular to describe the impact of injustice that affected the whole people.

bb. The noun *ʿălîṣūt* is attested only here (*ʿārîṣ* in Ps 37:35 is often emended to read a similar noun); it relates to the verb *ʿlṣ* ("to exult"), which in its alternative, softer spelling (*ʿlz*) is found in v. 18. Eaton ("Origin," 155) follows G. R. Driver's explanation based on an Arabic root to read *ʿălîṣâ* as "throat," seeing this attested in the LXX *chalinos* ("bit, bridle").

cc. The translation takes *bammistār* (*in secret*) with the verb, as suggested by the accentuation. Alternatively, it could be taken with *ʿānî* to refer to a poor man "in hiding." But note that *mistār* is regularly the hiding place of the wicked (Pss 10:8–9 [parallel to *maʾrab*, "ambush"]; 17:12; 64:5; cf. Jer 23:24; 49:10, Lam 3:10). The only positive reference is in Isa 45:3 (riches hidden in secret places).

dd. LXX, Barberini, Vulg. apparently read the *hiphil*, which would give "you caused [your horses] to tread."

ee. Franz Delitzsch (*Habakuk*, 87–88) observes that the instrumental accusative without preposition is used elsewhere only for the body part used (e.g., Pss 44:2[3]; 60:5[7]) or inanimate instruments (Ps 17:13) and concludes that *your horses* must be an explanatory permutation of the subject here, like *ʿammô* in Deut 32:43. I understand *sûsêkā* as an adverbial accusative (accusative of means) or accusative of specification.

ff. For this meaning, reflected also in Tg., cf. *ḥŏmārîm ḥŏmārîm* in Exod 8:14(10) and probably *ḥămôr ḥămôrātāyim* in Judg 15:16 (punning with *ḥămôr*, "donkey"). LXX and Barberini reflect a verb here (different forms of *tarassō*) whose meaning approximates to the use of the verb *ḥmr* for the foaming of waves in Ps 46:3(4). On this basis, many postulate the meaning "churning" or "surging" for *ḥômer* here. This is possible and more likely than "mud" (Vulg., *luto*; cf., e.g., Isa 10:6), but the phrase is apparently in apposition to *the sea* (cf. Ps 77:19[20]), for which *heap of mighty waters* seems more suitable, perhaps with an allusion to Exod 15:8 (cf. Ps 78:13; both with *nēd* for "heap"; see also Josh 3:13, 16). Another possibility would be to read the singular *ḥămôr* ("donkey") parallel to the plural *sûsêkā* (*your horses*), with the plural *mighty waters* being parallel to the singular *sea*, resulting in a chiastic arrangement (a-b-b-a) with preposition and suffix in the first colon doing double duty. But the ceremonial use of donkeys for kings in procession is quite different from the military use of horses (and chariots, v. 8) in warfare; I am not convinced that the two ideas would mix well here.

Composition

The switch back to second-person address marks out this section from vv. 3–7. But the opening question is prompted by what precedes and so connects vv. 8–15 with vv. 3–7. It is therefore not advisable to think of two separate and independent compositions. We may think of "two distinct traditions

(vv. 3–7 and vv. 8–15) which together are also a coherent literary unit."[437] In a sense, v. 7 is the pivotal turning point. God's approach, described in vv. 3–6, along with its effects on everything, is in v. 7 experienced by the prophet in a visionary, imaginary, or liturgical way. The now-present God is addressed in the second person.[438] The portrayal of YHWH changes from the sun to a chariot-riding warrior, as the light imagery gives way to references to water. A number of commentators hear various echoes of ancient myths in this section.[439] On closer examination, they seem to be faint echoes at best that add color to Habakkuk's description for those familiar with these stories but without being employed as a rhetorical strategy designed to shape our reading of this passage to any significant extent. The two occurrences of *selah* (vv. 9, 13) remind us that this passage is now part of a liturgical composition. The first appears to function as a dramatic pause not unlike the *selah* in 3:3.[440] But while in 3:3 the interlude encouraged thought about the summary statement in the first bicolon prior to its elaboration in subsequent lines, here the first bicolon that immediately precedes the *selah* indicates readiness for battle, which is then followed by scenes that seem to belong to the actual battle. Thus, the tricolon in v. 9 could also be read as a bicolon followed by a monocolon—the two distinct poetic units perhaps combining to a larger unit much as v. 8 joins a tricolon and its following bicolon to form a pentacolon. This colometry is unusual and interesting but not in need of correction.[441] The further *selah* in v.13 marks the point at which everything seems to have been accomplished, with the enemy having been comprehensively beaten.

---

437. John E. Anderson, "Awaiting an Answered Prayer: The Development and Reinterpretation of Habakkuk 3 in Its Contexts," *ZAW* 123 (2011): 59. Anderson describes them as "a theophany and a refashioning of Canaanite epic with YHWH as the divine warrior" (61).

438. Cf. Eaton, "Origin," 165: "This change [to second-person address] powerfully conveys the effect of his having now arrived and being present in some way to the speaker."

439. See the discussion of *streams* and *sea* below; *sun and moon* were worshipped as deities in the world surrounding Habakkuk and his people, and Hiebert (*God of My Victory*, 99), e.g., believes that "in the cry of Tehom [v. 10], there may be a distant echo of Tiamat's cry of fury when challenged by Marduk in battle." For a skeptical view, see Tsumura, *Creation and Destruction*, esp. 164–81.

440. For an evaluation (and rejection) of Henry St. John Thackeray's intriguing suggestion that the sequence of three words preceding the *selah* in v. 9, whose meaning here is notoriously difficult to interpret, presents a series of catchwords to Torah lessons, see David Marcus, "Does the Enigmatic Phrase שְׁבֻעוֹת מַטּוֹת אֹמֶר (Hab 3:9) Represent Liturgical Glosses?" in *In the Shadow of Bezalel: Aramaic, Biblical, and Ancient Near Eastern Studies in Honor of Bezalel Porten*, ed. Alejandro F. Botta, CHANE 60 (Leiden: Brill, 2012), 277–88.

441. For tricola that could be analyzed as bicolon plus monocolon, see *CHP*, 180–81; for the pentacolon see *CHP*, 187–88. Amos 5:5 has a similar tricolon plus bicolon structure.

A paragraph break is indicated in masoretic and earlier manuscripts here[442] but not followed in this commentary, as discussed above (p. 356).

Commentary

8 The question in v. 8 is prompted by what precedes. The divine march in vv. 3–7 becomes ever more ominous, from images of light to pestilence to trembling. It is now clearly interpreted as an expression of God's anger. The question in v. 8 is not whether YHWH is angry but against whom his anger is directed. The identification of the subject of the verb (*your anger*) is delayed until the end of the second colon (and paralleled at the end of the third with *your fury*), while the object is positioned as early as possible in each of the first three cola. Syntactically, the question could be a real one that asks God whether his anger is directed against (1) *streams* in general, (2) *the streams*, or (3) *the sea*. If *the streams* is read as a dual, or at least as an allusion to Mesopotamia (see below), the question would be whether God's anger is directed against (1) all flowing water, (2) the land along the streams in the east, or (3) the regions in the west,[443] maybe specifically Egypt.[444] But the distinction between the first two seems too subtle, and *yām* (*the sea*) can also be used of a large river other than the Nile (e.g., Jer 51:36). If the question were genuinely disjunctive, one would expect the different options to be laid out more clearly. One might also expect to be given an answer as to which of the three alternatives is the real target of God's anger.[445]

A note on the translation above points out the unusual masculine plural forms used for *streams* (contrast the use of the regular plural form in v. 9). In fact, with different vocalization, they could be read as dual forms, which is defensible also for other occurrences of this consonantal form.[446] Thus, in Isa 18:1 and Zeph 3:10, the reference is to Cush and, therefore, a dual form could refer to the two great tributaries of the Nile found in this region, the Blue and the White Nile. The references in Isa 18:2, 7 likely either continue

442. Mostly in the form of a *petucha* space (see 8ḤevXIIgr), but the Cairo Codex has a *setumah* space.

443. Hebrew *yām* (*the sea*) is often the Mediterranean and can designate its regions or the west generally; e.g., Gen 12:8; 13:14; Zech 14:4.

444. When *yām* is used for a large river, it is most often the Nile (Isa 18:1; 19:5; Nah 3:8; see the plural for the branches of the Nile in Ezek 32:2).

445. This objection applies also to S. R. Driver's (*Minor Prophets*, 90) suggested emendation mentioned above.

446. A number of these are in the construct state, in which plural and dual forms are indistinguishable even with vowels (Isa 18:1; Zeph 3:10; Job 20:17). Aron Pinker ("Problems and Solutions of Habakkuk 3:8," *JBQ* 31 [2003]: 7) suggests reading the dual here.

the reference to Cush or switch to Assyria. In the latter case, the two rivers would be the Tigris and the Euphrates. In Job 20:17, if the text is correct,[447] the two streams are of honey and cream. Isaiah 33:21 speaks of Jerusalem's security as found in God who is "a place of broad rivers and streams."[448] John Oswalt elaborates:

> Jerusalem had no great rivers to contribute to its defense such as Babylon or Nineveh had. Better to have God. With him one has all the benefits of a great river with none of its liabilities. For while a river makes crossing from side to side difficult, it also provides an excellent highway for a concerted naval attack. Not so with God.[449]

This is a fair comment except that Isa 33:21 specifically refers to more than one river. If interpreted as a dual form, the allusion to Mesopotamia (probably, or maybe Cush) would be stronger. Even if one resists reading all the *yod-mem* endings as dual, this brief overview of all its occurrences in the Hebrew Bible demonstrates that the form ending in *îm* is more evocative here than the standard plural form (*nəhārôt*) would have been, given the book's concern with oppression from the direction of "the land between the two rivers." Andersen objects to "the strain of having two different plurals (masculine and feminine) of the same stem so close to each other."[450] On the contrary, the *streams* apparently being attacked by YHWH in v. 8 are clearly different from those in v. 9, which result from YHWH's approach. In addition, the *streams* in v. 8 seem to be perennial and broad, parallel to *the sea* and politically a means of unifying territory, while the streams in v. 9 are probably formed by a downpour of rain (v. 10) and divide the land rather than unify a country. It makes good sense to exploit the availability of two different forms to speak of two rather different types of *streams*. In my view, we should not see a reference to (two or more) specific rivers in this verse. The language is allusive rather than precise. But we are probably justified in seeing large, empire-supporting rivers evoked here.

Are there also allusions to ancient myths? Andersen appeals to the ab-

---

447. The received text in its masoretic division is problematic. See, e.g., David J. A. Clines, *Job 1–20*, WBC 17 (Dallas: Word, 1989), 475; Choon-Leong Seow, *Job 1–21: Interpretation and Commentary* (Grand Rapids: Eerdmans, 2013), 853–54.

448. It is possible to take the descriptors as a reference to Jerusalem itself. In this case, it is still a poetic metaphor, and the sense is similar in that the presence of majestic YHWH prevents the presence of majestic (war)ships.

449. John N. Oswalt, *The Book of Isaiah, Chapters 1–39*, NICOT (Grand Rapids: Eerdmans, 1986), 604.

450. Andersen, *Habakkuk*, 318. He therefore prefers to read the singular (with enclitic *mem*) or the dual.

sence of historical identification and "the cosmic scope of the passage" and finds "the identical vocabulary and parallelism" in the *Ugaritic Epic of Baal and Anat* "striking." Against him, however, stand the following: (1) *yām* ("sea") and *nāhār* ("stream/river") are not exactly uncommon lexemes, (2) their use in parallelism is not altogether surprising (cf., e.g., Pss 24:2; 66:6; 80:11[12], Jonah 2:3[4]; Nah 1:4), (3) the order in the Baal Cycle is sea // stream (as nearly always in the Hebrew Bible) rather than *streams // sea* as here, and (4) the epic uses the singular "river" rather than a dual or plural form.[451] To his credit, Andersen acknowledges that "the identical vocabulary and parallelism . . . should not be allowed to control the interpretation of the Israelite poem."[452] Later, he introduces two other possible allusions to myth but must admit that

> neither the dual streams of Babylonian cosmogony nor the twin rivers of Canaanite mythology [in connection with describing the home of El rather than the enemy of Baal to which reference was made above] are the objects of an assault by a chariot-riding warrior god, in any story we now have.[453]

In any case, an allusion to an attack on the home of El is entirely implausible here, as YHWH would more likely be identified with El than with an enemy of El. Allusion to cosmogony might suggest a reference to sweet and saltwater streams as original elements of creation. If so, the first two cola could be interpreted as questioning whether YHWH is intent on undoing creation by attacking two of its constituent elements. But this would not fit with the reference to *sea* in the third colon that, read mythologically, would have to be a reference to the chaos that threatens creation (cosmos) rather than to forces that sustain it. So, the first *'īm* would have to be rhetorical ("is it the case that . . . ?," implying a negative answer), while the second would offer a genuine alternative ("or," asking for a decision).[454] This is all quite implausible. A consistent use of *'īm* could be safeguarded if instead one read all three cola as referring to forces threatening creation unless subdued. But in this case, we might expect the use of the regular feminine plural form for *streams* as in Pss 24:2 and 93:3–4. In sum, the parallels to other biblical and non-biblical texts are not strong enough for us to claim allusions to specific mythological stories or concepts in this verse.[455]

451. An enclitic *mem* is used with the form in *KTU* 1.2, line 37 (text reconstructed); see Mark S. Smith, *The Ugaritic Baal Cycle*, vol. 1 (Leiden: Brill, 1994), 268.

452. All from Andersen, *Habakkuk*, 317.

453. Andersen, *Habakkuk*, 318.

454. In the translation, the first instance of *'īm* is rendered *indeed*, the second left untranslated. See the translation notes.

455. Cf. Tsumura, *Creation and Destruction*, 164–66, also summarised in "The 'Cha-

In poetry, formally disjunctive questions often do not offer a choice of genuine alternatives,[456] and this seems to be the case here. The first three lines are poetic parallels that ask one question. But is it a real or a rhetorical question? If he is asking for real, the prophet presumably dares to hope that the answer is yes—God's march is not directed toward nomads in the wilderness, but the ultimate target of his anger is Babylon, the civilization sustained by streams. But disjunctive questions that do not explore genuine alternatives are elsewhere always rhetorical questions. Without evidence to the contrary, we must assume that this is the case here as well. Such disjunctive rhetorical questions, however, require the negative particle (*lōʾ*) for the answer to be yes (as, e.g., in Isa 10:9).[457] Without a negative particle, such questions require the answer no (e.g., Isa 10:9; 49:24; Amos 6:2).[458] The examination of parallel patterns recommends that we read the verse as posing a single rhetorical question, expressed in three ways, to which the answer is no.[459] The divine anger is not directed against *streams* and *sea*, or anything they represent, at least not at present.[460] Given that the rhetorical question is, in effect, a forceful denial of the possibility that YHWH's wrath is directed against *streams* and *sea*, it seems very unlikely that *streams* and *sea* should be understood in purely naturalistic terms, as if anyone would seriously wonder whether YHWH is angry with forces of nature that involve water.

While the mention of *streams* and *sea* cannot be unambiguously resolved to refer to historical forces of chaos, Babylonia, or Egypt, it is clear that *streams* and *sea* are potential opponents of YHWH that are "other" than the people of God. If the answer to the rhetorical question were yes, Judah might be considered safe. The answer no suggests that the impact of YHWH's march in anger is to be felt beyond the realms of chaos (and maybe empire) and so to affect parts of the creation (cosmos) that would not be considered

oskampf' Motif in Ugaritic and Hebrew Literatures," in *Le Royaume d'Ougarit de la Crète à l'Euphrate: Nouveaux axes de Recherche*, ed. Jean-Marc Michaud, Proche-Orient et Littérature Ougaritique 2 (Sherbrooke: GGC, 2007), 487–88.

456. So, e.g., in Isa 10:15; 66:8; Jer 3:5; Pss 77:9[10]; 78:20. Cf. Franz Delitzsch, *Habakuk*, 162.

457. Simple (rather than disjunctive) rhetorical questions are sometimes introduced with the interrogative only, even when the answer yes is expected (e.g., 1 Kgs 22:3; Job 20:4), but even they more commonly include the negative particle, as in English usage (so, e.g., Josh 10:13). See Meyer, *Grammatik*, 3:87, with further examples. Cf. *CHP*, 338–42.

458. Rebecca S. Watson's detailed study ("הֲ ... אִם: A rhetorical question anticipating a negative answer," *JSOT* 44 [2020]: 437–55) should put an end to any claims to the contrary.

459. The use of *mē* in the ancient Greek translations (and of *numquid* in Latin) indicates that this is also how ancient translators read the verse.

460. Contra, e.g., Haak, *Habakkuk*, 92, who introduces a negation in his translation without offering a note in support of this reading; Roberts, *Nahum*, 155, who connects the verse with Canaanite mythology; Pinker, "Problems," who suggests a historical interpretation.

YHWH's natural opponents, including his own people. This fits with the prayer and expectation that *in turmoil* God *shall remember to have compassion* (v. 2). It also fits with the earlier protest in ch. 1. The observation in 3:8 that the divine anger is not targeted at mighty forces of chaos chimes with the observation in the complaint that YHWH looks on, apparently without getting angry, as chaos engulfs the righteous.

The reference to *chariots of deliverance* anticipates the salvation to come (cf. v. 13). Because the root in question is often used in the Bible for the deliverance given by YHWH, we should discern a hint of salvation, even if we were to render the phrase as "victorious chariots" (see the translation note). But the rhetorical question with which this reference to salvation is connected precludes the idea that this is simply a matter of divine anger against the enemies of God's people equating to salvation for God's people. The actual target of God's anger remains for now unidentified, except for the claim that the objects of God's anger are not, at least not primarily, the forces threatening to overwhelm God's people. This raises the possibility that God's anger is directed against his own people and only so brings salvation to them.

9 This verse is especially difficult to translate. The translation of the first colon as *fully uncovered is your bow* is reasonably straightforward, and even scholars who disagree on the details nevertheless arrive at basically the same interpretation: God's bow is unsheathed, ready for action. The second colon is far more controversial, with many believing that it cannot be given an intelligible reading. Of the various emendations on offer, the one by Michael L. Barré may be the most attractive. He translates, "You removed your bow (from its case), // you poisoned (your) seven arrows."[461] In this case, the second line, with a slight development, underlines the first line, and so the whole bicolon speaks of God's readiness for action. In terms of the overall meaning of the discourse, we would be safe to leave it at that. But the ancient versions seem to reflect the consonantal text of the MT, and the chain of inferences that Barré's reconstruction requires is uncomfortably long. Also, the claim that *maṭṭôt* can refer to "arrows," however well this would fit the context, is unpersuasive. Perhaps we should be content with the MT after all. It seems to poetically describe *the rods* that belong to God as *oaths*, which is to say that they are a sign of God's firm intention.[462] The construction that adds *a word* to *oaths* is similar to *šəbū'at hā'ālâ* in Num 5:21, an "oath" made by "the curse," and maybe *šəbū'at 'iṣṣār* in Num 30:14 ("an oath of bond"). Tsumura urges a similar interpretation, referring to *oaths* of *word* as an

---

461. Barré, "Yahweh Gears Up," 75–84.

462. We may compare the oath in Deut 32:40–42, in which the sharpening of the divine sword fulfills a similar function.

example of the AXB pattern in poetic parallelism, in which a composite unit (AB) retains its grammatical dependency within itself even if X (an additional element) is inserted between A and B, thus violating the normal grammatical rule of adjacency, and X holds a grammatical relationship with [A . . . B] as a whole.

He argues that once we recognize that *your bow* is polysemous (suggesting both a weapon and the rainbow as a sign of God's covenant with Noah), this syntactical analysis is not merely possible but probable.[463] So he translates the first two cola as "Your bow is unsheathed/ (your) mace is the oaths of (your) word."[464] The word order "oaths of your word are your maces" may better reflect the emphasis of the line.[465] Alternatively, we could render "oaths are the rods with a word," which is to say that God's word turns his weapons into a binding commitment to attack. God's *rods* are a firm promise of things to come. But what does this mean in the context of Habakkuk's anguish? Babylonia had arguably been experienced as a rod of God's anger (cf. Isa 14:3–23, anticipating the downfall of Babylon, the empire that has oppressed nations with its "rod of rulers" [v. 5]). It had been sworn in for the task with the *word* that is reflected in Hab 1:5–11. The use of the plural *rods* could be seen as taking a step back to take in a wider perspective. Not only is Babylonia a rod of God's anger, but prior to the Babylonians, Assyria was "the rod of my anger" (Isa 10:5). If God's involvement in the calamities brought about by these empires is affirmed over against the view that God's passivity in the face of evil is the problem, there may be a hint that just as Assyria was a rod for a while before it had to drink the cup of YHWH's anger, so Babylonia's role as a sworn-in rod of God's anger will come to an end. Habakkuk 2 suggests that the end comes through overreach. In a sense, the Babylonians provide the means for their own destruction. The reuse of *rods* in v. 14 is, therefore, entirely in keeping with this message.

With rivers you divide the earth is probably meant to evoke flash floods given what follows in the next verse, even if perennial streams and the valleys through which they flow also divide lands. The use of the root in connection

463. Tsumura, *Creation and Destruction*, 173.

464. Tsumura, *Creation and Destruction*, 174. He suggests "the seven-headed mace *is* (your) word" as another possibility but it is not entirely clear what this would mean. Is it a claim that from now on God will speak through his weapon only? Tsumura's interpretation of the plural *rods* as one of intensity referring to a single mace seems possible, but the plural *oaths* may go better with a plurality of *rods*.

465. Imitating the word order in the Hebrew text makes it inadvisable to render "of (your) word," as this could be read as indicating a construct relationship between *rods* and *word*, in my view an implausible reading. This is why the translation uses *a word* in apposition to *oaths*.

with military invasions (e.g., Isa 7:6; 2 Chr 32:1) and other violent events suggests that the positive effects of rain falling upon the earth are not (yet) in view here, even if an ancient audience of the book would have been aware of the transformative effect of flash floods on desert land. For now, the primary association is with the speed and danger of flash floods.

10 The verse imitates the waves as the eye moves to the *mountains* and then down to see a *torrent* (downpour) *of water* and deeper into *the abyss*, which, after shouting out, tosses *its hands* upward, starting an upward movement that continues into the next verse with references to *sun* and *moon*. *The mountains* are not enemies; they are a symbol of stability, now threatened as the mountains *tremble* upon seeing YHWH's approach (cf. Judg 5:5; Nah 1:5). Rain is, of course, on the whole a positive feature, certainly in arid countries, but the heavy rain responsible for the *torrent of water* described here is a threat from which one seeks shelter (so in all occurrences of *zerem* in the Hebrew Bible; e.g., Isa 4:6; 28:2). The great deep (*abyss*) designates subterranean waters or the sea, a traditional symbol of chaos and enmity to YHWH. Here the latter is likely in view, or a combination of the two (cf. vv. 8, 15).[466] Lifting the hands occurs very often in the context of oaths,[467] less often for giving a blessing (Lev 9:22), petitioning or praising God (Pss 28:2; 134:2), or acting against someone (2 Sam 18:28; 20:21; Ps 10:12).[468] The context and the fronted *high* (accusative of direction) suggest panic combined with a loud cry, maybe a cry for mercy as in Ps 28:2 (and Lam 2:19, with "palm" [*kap*] rather than "hand" [*yad*]). The image of the *abyss* lifting high its hands evokes massive waves, accompanied by the raucous roaring of the sea. None of these entities are described as the actual targets of YHWH's attack.[469] It is noteworthy that in a similar way, *the abyss* is an instrument in God's final triumph over Pharaoh and his army during the exodus of God's people from Egypt (Exod 15:5, 8) rather than an image of the targeted opponent.

11 Delitzsch urges that the beginning of the verse must refer to a retreat of sun and moon to their dwelling because the traditional interpretation that sees a reference here to Josh 10 does not fit with the darkness that the second half of the verse presumes.[470] But *zəbūlâ* (*zenith*) is a lofty dwelling place and

466. Andersen (*Habakkuk*, 326) sees a reference to subterranean waters (only) here as well as in v. 9 (*nəhārôt*), surrounded by references to a terrestrial ocean (*yām*, vv. 8, 15) and heavenly streams (*nəhārîm*, vv. 8, 15). But I interpret the reference to *streams* differently and therefore cannot follow him in seeing such a palistrophic structure here.

467. Exod 6:8; Num 14:30; Deut 32:40; Neh 9:15; Ps 106:26; Ezek 20:5–6, 15, 23, 28, 42; 36:7; 44:12; 47:14.

468. Maybe Isa 49:22 could be interpreted along those lines, but it is more likely a summoning.

469. Cf. Fabry, *Habakuk/Obadja*, 311–12.

470. Franz Delitzsch, *Habakuk*, 175–76.

would most naturally be understood as a reference to sun and moon at their height rather than hidden away.[471] Delitzsch appeals to (later?) "oriental" notions of stars living in houses and fortresses (citing Arabic phrases but not texts) and to Ps 19:6. It is true that Ps 19 paints a more restful picture of the sun at night than other ancient Near Eastern traditions. Whereas elsewhere the setting sun enters the netherworld from which it emerges in the morning, Ps 19 pictures God as providing the sun with overnight accommodation in a tent. Still, this seems insufficient grounds for identifying *zəbūlâ* as the sun's (nighttime) home, for which *məʿôn* ("dwelling"), *miškan* ("abode"), *bayit* ("house"), *môšāb* ("dwelling place"), *mənûḥâ* ("resting place"), or maybe *ḥădar* ("dark room," or more fully *ḥădar miškābkā*, "bedroom") would all seem more appropriate than a term suggesting height. The same goes, of course, for the moon's home.[472] The fact that reference is made to both sun and moon and the use of *ʿāmad* (*stand*) give better ground for linking the verse with Josh 10:12 than with Ps 19:6(7). Hence, Avishur, linking the first half of the verse with Josh 10 and in effect agreeing with Delitzsch about the problem relating this to the second half of the verse, comments:

> Here the poet confused the motif of the sun and moon standing in mid-heaven to lengthen the day—which, in essence, means that they continued to *give off light*—with another motif, the prophetic motif of the darkening of the sun, moon, and other celestial bodies as the warrior God reveals Himself on the "day of the Lord" (Ezek. 32:7–8; Joel 4:15; [Joel 2:31; cf. 2:10]). The author of Hab. 3 twisted the verse in Josh. 10 out of its plain meaning by interpreting the "standstill" of the sun and moon in Joshua as referring to the cessation of their activity. What is common to both descriptions—continued illumination and darkening—is the suspension of the sun and moon's natural activity as the warrior God reveals Himself.[473]

471. The only other references in the Hebrew Bible are *bêt zəbūl* ("a lofty house," referring to the temple in Jerusalem) in 1 Kgs 8:13 and 2 Chr 6:2, *zəbūl qodšəkā* ("the habitation of your holiness" parallel to *šāmayim*, "heaven") in Isa 63:15, and the more difficult *mizzəbūl lô* at the end of Ps 49:14(15), which I interpret as "away from their impressive homes" (lit. "away from [or without] the impressive home that was its" whereby "its" refers to "their form"), again a lofty place by contrast to going down to Sheol. See also Staffan Olofsson, "Death Shall Be Their Shepherd: An Interpretation of Psalm 49.15 in the Masoretic Text and the Septuagint," in *The Interpretation of Scripture in Early Judaism and Christianity*, ed. Craig A. Evans, JSPSup 23 (Sheffield: Sheffield Academic Press, 2000), 75–105.

472. Delitzsch may have been led by Ps 19 to picture the sun as going to work at sunrise, having been in his chamber at night. But this is a singular metaphor. More commonly, sun and moon are given ruling functions (Ps 136:8–9; cf. Gen 1:16), and rulers might well work "from home" (the palace) as well as in the gates. There is therefore nothing incongruous with picturing sun and moon at the zenith exercising their work while being at home.

473. Avishur, *Studies*, 183.

To see the poet transforming the motif from Josh 10 here by turning it into a total solar eclipse (moon and sun standing at the same place in the zenith) seems to me more plausible than Delitzsch's view that sun and moon stayed at home. But perhaps the poet was less interested than some of his readers in a dark-light contrast and did not worry about conveying a "realistic" picture. Perhaps, all he wanted to reference was "the suspension of . . . natural activity" (to use Avishur's words). Just as it is characteristic for *mountains* not to be active but to stand unmoved (and yet now they *tremble*, v. 10), so it is natural for *sun* and *moon* to go their course (and yet now they *stand* still). Why? In my view, the following two lines offer the cause. The words for *light* and *brightness* are readily associated with *sun* and *moon* (see Isa 60:19). Indeed, Andersen believes that the words designate sun and moon here.[474] More likely, they designate the function of *sun* and *moon*. As God's arrows and spears of lightning illuminate the world, *sun* and *moon* find themselves out of a job and *stand* still, stunned. If this is the thought here, it may explain why there is no reference to sun and moon turning dark. If the motif of darkness had been used, the lightning could be interpreted as a response to the darkness. But throughout this section of the poem, it is the natural world responding to YHWH, not the other way around. We might even go so far as to speak of day and night, previously ruled by sun and moon, as being now under YHWH's direct rule. Given that YHWH's indirect, delegated rule (through the Neo-Babylonian Empire) is the central problem of the book, a move to direct rule would be desirable and promising. The allusion to Josh 10 may suggest that sun and moon will resume their normal functions again only after the victory has been won.

12 From the height of sun and moon we rapidly come down as YHWH *strides* the *earth*. *Earth* renders the same Hebrew word as in v. 9, where the translation "land" could also be justified. Here *earth* is more appropriate given the reference to *nations* in the second colon. Finally, there is an answer to the question in v. 8. The target of YHWH's *anger* has been found, or at any rate the passive object of the activities in this part of the poem ("land"/*earth*, *nations*) is specified. Other entities responded to YHWH's approach, but *the earth* and *the nations* are affected directly.[475] The first verb, *stride*, does not suggest that *the earth* is necessarily affected by the movement, although v. 9

---

474. Andersen, *Habakkuk*, 332, citing Isa 60:19. In fact, while '*ôr* can stand in for the sun on its own (Job 31:26; 37:21; maybe also Job 24:14 and Neh 8:3 where, however, it is possible to see a reference to the light of dawn more generally), I know of no example in which *nōgah* on its own stands in for the moon.

475. The contrast should not be overdrawn; the trembling of the mountains is not truly a voluntary response nor the outcry of the abyss. Nevertheless, these entities are the grammatical subjects of verbs and could be seen as getting out of God's way more than being the target of his approach.

has already suggested an impact.[476] The second verb, *trample*, is, however, clearly more forceful and is used a number of times for the destruction of a community or nation.[477] How does the identification of the target of God's anger relate to v. 8? The reference to *nations* here paints on a broad canvass. We may think of the *nations* in Hab 1:5, 17; 2:5, 8—all those peoples who suffered under the impact of the Neo-Babylonian Empire.[478] But here, the term need not exclude the Babylonians themselves. They probably come into view in the next verse, which spells out the ultimate purpose of the angry attack.

13 As v. 12 picks up the first half of v. 8 by answering the question concerning the target of YHWH's *anger*, so this verse picks up the second half of the verse with its intimation of *salvation*.[479] It is interesting to note that in none of the thirty-six occurrences of *yēša'* in the Hebrew Bible is the source of salvation anyone other than YHWH.[480] This seems to reflect a conviction that *salvation* (deliverance, decisive help, victory) is something YHWH characteristically has to bring (cf. the use of the verb in 1:2, *save*, which assumes that YHWH is the one responsible for deliverance). This verse now underlines that God's march is indeed for this purpose. Having translated the various verb forms earlier in the poem with the simple present tense, as discussed

476. The verb is actually rare. Of the seven occurrences in the Hebrew Bible (Gen 49:22; Judg 5:4; 2 Sam 6:13; Job 18:14 [*hiphil*]; Ps 68:7[8]; Prov 7:8; Jer 10:5), two also concern YHWH's approach, accompanied by rain (Judg 5; Ps 68). As the heavy rain divides the land, it is fair to say that the ground is not left unaffected by the one who marches on it.

477. Judges 8:7; 2 Kgs 13:7; Isa 25:10; Amos 1:3; Mic 4:13. Cf. Isa 41:15, where YHWH is said to crush mountains and hills, symbolic obstacles to the return of the exiles. The verb is used elsewhere for treading or threshing grain (Deut 25:4; 1 Chr 21:20; Isa 28:27–28; Hos 10:11; cf. the treading down of straw in a manure pile in Isa 25:10, symbolic of the destruction of Moab) and for an animal's trampling (Job 39:15). Jeremiah 50:11 is usually, and rightly, corrected.

478. Timmer (*Non-Israelite Nations*, 143–47) believes that because the nations are helpless victims of Babylonian aggression in chs. 1–2 but (wicked) objects of God's aggression in ch. 3, the latter must present a shift to the eschatological future. But this is not required if, in response to the divine revelation in ch. 2, the prophet adopts a new perspective on Babylonian aggression and its end in ch. 3.

479. Verse 8 uses *yašû'â*, v. 13 the shorter and less common form *yēša'* (twice; the second occurrence is sometimes emended to a form of *yašû'â* to avoid the surprising use of the object marker *'et*). There does not seem to be a semantic difference between the two forms.

480. Job 5:4 refers to safety in general, but v. 11 attributes it to God. Of the seventy-eight occurrences of *yašû'â*, only two or three refer to anyone other than YHWH bringing victory (Jonathan in 1 Sam 14:45, but explicitly with the help of God) or help (Joab and Abishai to each other, 2 Sam 10:11) or deliverance (Ps 20:5[6], if we read the suffix as indicating the agent; the following verse may lead us to prefer seeing the king as the recipient of God's deliverance). Job 13:16 and 30:15 are more general; Isa 26:18 and 59:11 refer to the absence of deliverance.

above, here the present perfect seems required. God's march has been described from v. 3 onward; now, looking back, we are told for what purpose he has *gone out*. With the question about the purpose of God's anger, and hence of the whole divine march, answered, the second bicolon graphically describes the destruction of the enemy. This is the other side of the coin. God's compassion for his people becomes evident in the angry destruction of *the house of the wicked*. In failing to identify the Babylonians specifically, the general designation makes the broader point that God's anger is directed toward the elimination of wickedness in whatever form. Unless one opts for a strict differentiation between mythical and historical foes (v. 8: YHWH is not angry with mythical forces; vv. 12–13: YHWH strides against human enemies), a differentiation that is implausible,[481] this seems to reverse the claim made in v. 8. The apparent reversal perhaps explains why so many commentators have misread v. 8 as a rhetorical question to which the answer must be yes (see above). But the implicit claim made in v. 8, that YHWH's anger does not burn against *streams* and *sea*, was confirmed in subsequent verses as other parts of creation, and what they stand for, were shown to be impacted by YHWH's campaign. In retrospect, what v. 8 affirms can be understood in two complementary ways. First, when YHWH sets out to bring deliverance, it is not a simple case of his anger burning up the waters of chaos. The impact will be felt much more widely than that. Second, the ensuing chaos, the churning of waters (cf. v. 15), is not where it will end. The ambiguity this presents (YHWH's anger is not neatly directed at chaos [v. 8] but nevertheless has the wicked as its target [vv. 12–13]) is perhaps parallel to the ambiguity explored above with which YHWH's march from Teman can be read both as a metaphorical way of describing the terror brought by the Babylonians (moving from east to west) and as a countermovement (from south to north) to the Babylonian advance from the north.

Both halves of the verse focus on leadership. *Your anointed one* is most likely a reference to the (Davidic) king, as nearly everywhere else in the Hebrew Bible,[482] and *the head of the house of the wicked* is likely also a king,

481. What, after all, would be the point of emphatically denying that YHWH is angry with mythical foes? A denial of their existence would be more effective rhetorically. In any case, a strict separation of the world of deities and demons from the world of politics would be unusual in an ancient Near Eastern context. For similar reasons, as observed above, we must reject the idea that v. 8 stresses that YHWH's anger is not directed against the natural world.

482. The term is used in reference to a priest in the expression *hakkōhēn hammāšiaḥ* (Lev 4:3, 5, 16; 6:22[15]; cf. Num 3:3) and maybe in Dan 9:25–26, where the identification is uncertain. Unusually, the patriarchs are referred to as "anointed ones" (and prophets) in Ps 105:15 // 1 Chr 16:22. This may suggest royal status (cf. the reference to Abraham as a mighty prince in Gen 23:6). While kings were not the only ones to have been anointed, it

with *the house* indicating the royal household (the dynasty) or, less likely, the whole kingdom.[483] The final colon, with its surprising mix of nouns (see the translation note) is often thought to refer to the leader, with *yəsôd* (*foundation*) being interpreted as a reference to the lower body (the thigh or backside). Tsumura suggests that the verse can be read to depict the destruction of a statue of the king.[484] Delitzsch sees *the house of the wicked* pictured in three parts: *head* (the upper part), *foundation* (the lower part), and *neck* (the middle part left after the destruction of the upper part).[485] As the *laying bare* is described from the bottom up, we should maybe picture the attack as twofold, from the top (*head*) down as well as from the foundation up. But no second weapon is mentioned for the bottom-up movement, and the use of the infinitive in the Hebrew, albeit not in the ancient translations, subordinates the *laying bare* to the crushing so that one may better conclude that the smashing of the *head* is at the same time an attack on the foundation of the royal family. The point is that the destruction of the king leaves the royal household, and ultimately the empire, completely exposed.

The reference to the salvation of the Davidic king may seem surprising given the book's historical context and could support the hypothesis that Habakkuk uses a preexisting poem. Whichever precise date one suggests for the book of Habakkuk in general or for the composition of Hab 3 as a prayer

---

is exceedingly rare for *māšîaḥ* on its own to be used for anyone other than a king, usually an Israelite king (exceptionally Isa 45:1 of Cyrus). Hiebert (*God of My Victory*, 107) argues from the use of the verb in 1 Sam 9:16; 10:1 that *māšîaḥ* here is "the title for the military commander of the league militia," but this assumes that the poem reflects premonarchic political structures and that the supreme commander was not the leader of the people/league. Hiebert also does not address the obvious question why Hab 3:13 does not use the same title as 1 Sam 9:16; 10:1 (*nāgîd*, "leader").

483. The phrase *bêt rāšāʿ* ("house of the wicked") is also used in Prov 3:33; 21:12. A further reference in Mic 6:10 is often thought corrupt. Bruce Waltke (*A Commentary on Micah* [Grand Rapids: Eerdmans, 2007], 398) considers but ultimately rejects emendation. He thinks the reference there is to "the king's and his official's [*sic*] granaries." The use of "house" for a kingdom would be unique, and so it is more likely that the reference is to the dynasty, as in 2:9–10; so also Franz Delitzsch, *Habakuk*, 182.

484. Tsumura, "Ugaritic Poetry," 44–45. He suggests to translate, "You crushed the head to be headless," or, "You crushed the head of the evil one so that there might be no house; (You) laid bare the base up to the neck." See the translation note above. Prinsloo ("Literary Context," 97) notes that J. C. de Moor (*The Rise of Yahwism: The Roots of Israelite Monotheism*, 2nd ed., BETL 91 [Leiden: University Press, 1997], 202–3) "indicates that the body is often likened to a house in Ancient Near Eastern literature." He adds, "Probably the wicked is here conceptualised as the mythical monster of chaos," which might allow interpreting *foundation* as the belly (on which the monster crawls).

485. Franz Delitzsch, *Habakuk*, 182. Rashi reads *neck* as a specific reference to the walls and the towers (Rosenberg, *Twelve Prophets*, 279), but Delitzsch is right to observe that the word is occasioned by the allegory rather than specific architectural features.

(i.e., adding a frame to the core, if vv. 3–15 are considered earlier), it does not seem plausible that the prophet who railed against the complete breakdown of justice in ch. 1 would consider the currently reigning Davidic king a suitable object of deliverance from the wicked. The king would seem to be one out of whose hands the people need to be saved. If this is a problem, it is in my view not readily solved by assuming that the core of the poem dates to an earlier time, because one would also need to make the quite unwarranted assumption that the one who used the hymn in his prayer was unable to make the necessary modifications. But the problem may be more apparent than real. In Hab 1–2, the evil empire was personified and spoken of as if one person. In a similar way, the singular was used for the righteous who lives by steadfast faith. Here, again, the empire is embodied in the emperor, and so by analogy the people of God are embodied in their king, God's *anointed one*. As the salvation is not expected for the near future, the king in question will not be the currently reigning king (e.g., Jehoiakim). The expectation is that when God's people will be saved, there will be a (faithful) Davidic king, embodying his people, who will be saved as well. For now, the one speaking for the people, and in this sense embodying them, is the prophet himself (see v. 14)

Verse 13 could have brought the poem to a dramatic conclusion. This may be the reason the *selah* at its end, suggesting to me a musical interlude to offer space for further reflection, is reinforced by a paragraph division in many ancient manuscripts. The following two verses are in a sense a recapitulation of the attack in less symbolic language.[486] They also reintroduce the first person (cf. vv. 2, 7)

14 There is much that is uncertain about the original wording and the best translation of this verse. Avishur comments that

> this is one of the most difficult verses in the psalm, and no two commentators agree about its text and interpretation. Even such radical exponents of bold emendation as Ehrlich and Tur-Sinai despaired of satisfactorily explaining or emending this verse.[487]

The translation notes above barely hint at the many emendations that have been proposed. Any interpretation must remain tentative, but it is clear that YHWH is smiting an enemy. Hiebert notes that the primordial monster was struck with a twofold blow in Ugaritic and Akkadian literature, a blow to the body followed by a blow to the head. Patterson adds the example of

486. Cf. Prinsloo, "Literary Context," 97, who speaks of "a deviation from the language of myth to the language of reality" in v. 14.

487. Avishur, *Studies*, 189.

"the Egyptian's Sinuhe's dispatching of his Amorite foe by an arrow to the neck followed by a deathblow with his battle-axe."[488] Whether or not we meet a well-known ancient Near Eastern topos here,[489] the parallel with Goliath (1 Sam 17:51), which Patterson also mentions, suggests that Israel was not unfamiliar with the idea of a battle ending with the decapitation of the enemy using his own weapon. We may be justified in seeing in the use of the enemy's *own rods* (*his* probably refers back to *the wicked* in v. 13; the spears used by his army could be said to be *rods* belonging to the emperor) and in the reference to *heads* a picture of the decisive end of the battle. As with Goliath, it is possible that the blows to which this verse refers are not dealt in combat but mutilate an already-dead foe.[490]

The use of singular suffixes and the collective noun "head" (rendered as a plural in this translation) continues to depict wickedness embodied in one entity as throughout the book of Habakkuk. The use of *his own rods* is in keeping with the message of ch. 2 that the deeds of the wicked carry the seeds of their destruction and so bring a reversal of fortunes. While the coming like a *storm* was not described in the same language in ch. 1, a thematic allusion to the speed and destructiveness of the Babylonian army described in 1:5–11 (cf. Jer 4:13) is supported by further thematic links to ch. 1. The *exultation* could make one think of "he is glad and rejoices" (1:15); the *devouring* features the same verb as 1:8 and connects thematically with 2:4a. If the Hebrew word used for *exultation* made some think also of a word relating to gullet, so much the better, but this is quite uncertain (see the translation note). The enemy army is compared to a bandit or highwayman ambushing *someone poor*, which is to say someone without protection rather than someone completely destitute. It is possible that the comparison with devouring the poor was proverbial (cf. Prov 30:14). The juxtaposition of a picture of the decisive blow defeating the enemies with experiencing them like a violent storm is striking. It encapsulates the chapter. The prayer looks forward to the victory over evil while still very much experiencing its current dominance. Delitzsch suggests that the use of the abstract noun *exultation* instead of a verb form points to a habitual character trait of the enemy forces.[491] The first-person singular *me* characteristically makes Habakkuk speak as the one who embodies the people, as the fate described is clearly that of the people (cf. ch. 1). In my view, it is likely that Habakkuk knew that renewed freedom

488. Hiebert, *God of My Victory*, 38; Patterson, *Nahum*, 252–53. Both refer to these examples in connection with suggested emendations.

489. The expression "strike/smite the head of somebody" on its own is identified as a likely cliché in Ugaritic literature by Tsumura, *Creation and Destruction*, 175.

490. Anderson, *Habakkuk*, 336.

491. Franz Delitzsch, *Habakuk*, 187. He also notes that the use of the form with the harder sound (see the translation note) is fitting and deliberate.

and justice would only be experienced beyond exile. Huldah, Zephaniah, and probably Jeremiah had already pointed in this direction, speaking of the end of nationhood. But in any case, those who used the prayer later would not be wrong in seeing in this picture of a chase an image of the scattering into exile resulting from the Babylonian storm.

15 This verse is a remarkable conclusion to the description marveling at YHWH's attack on his enemies because it stops in the middle of events, thus echoing *the midst of years* to which v. 2 referred. We have learned that *the sea* is not truly the targeted enemy, not even as a personification of God's opponent. The rhetorical question with which this section opened in v. 8 suggested a negative answer, and the actual target was introduced in v. 12. The *sea* is, rather, the place of battle as in the Exodus narrative. Parallels in the book of Isaiah are instructive, not least for how they differ from Habakkuk. Isaiah 11:15–16 reads:

> Then YHWH will utterly destroy [= dry up] the tongue of the Sea of Egypt, and he will wave his hand [= shake his fist] against the River with his strong [= scorching] wind, and he will smite it into seven streams so that people will make their way across in sandals. And there will be a highway from Assyria for the remnant of his people who remain, just as there was for Israel on the day when they came up from the land of Egypt.

Isaiah 43:16 speaks of a way through the sea, a path through strong waters (cf. Zech 10:11).[492] There, as here, the future is described in images of the past, but the role of the sea and river is ambiguous (a place of deliverance, but maybe also an opponent), and the climax is in the renewed deliverance of God's people. In Hab 3, however, the salvific effects of the way through the sea are not mentioned, and this sets the prayer up for the expression of confidence in the midst of distress we have in the following verses rather than a song of celebration in victory.

Reflection

As the prayer moves on from reflecting on God's approach to contemplating his presence, the prophet engages with the question of the target of the divine anger. Two things seem to be clear. First, there can be no let-off for the people of God. YHWH's attack is not partisan, directed against others only. The impact is felt widely. The divine anger is not, or not primarily, directed

---

492. See Franz Delitzsch, *Habakuk*, 179, who also compares the drying up in Isa 42:15 and the rivers in the desert in 43:19.

against the waters of sea and rivers but against the earth and the nations that inhabit it. But second, the aim is salvation for God's people, and the attack, however broadly felt, is targeted specifically against *the house of the wicked*. The memory to which appeal is made here is the dividing of sea and river in the exodus from Egypt and the entry into the promised land. This was not an expression of anger against waters but something that served a salvific purpose. It also demonstrated YHWH's sovereignty over all powers, whether these are thought of as natural forces (as usually conceived in modernity) or supernatural ones (as usually conceived in the ancient world). The prayer confesses that God is battle-ready and committed—indeed sworn—to attack, but this is not simply good news. When God deals directly with evil, normality is suspended, and this is described as something terrifying, as even sun and moon are eclipsed. Nor does the poem offer the comfort of resting on "all shall be well in the end." The only glimpse of an actual battle scene, which may be, strictly speaking, an after-battle scene (see the commentary on v. 14), shows the divine warrior victorious over hordes of enemies. But juxtaposed to this is a reminder of the glee and success of those who come like a storm and ambush like a highwayman. The description of the battle ends in the midst of action. The only place in which the prophet describes the impact on himself as embodying the people is in being scattered (v. 14), not in being snatched out of the hands of evildoers. This is the opposite of an opium of the people, in the words of Karl Marx's famous description of religion. The poem does not divert eyes from the current distress to dwell on salvation, victory, and the good life to come. The only comfort it offers is the claim that in all the tragedy and violence, God is there and in charge and can be addressed as such.

The English proverb "better the devil you know than the devil you don't" is in more ways than one inappropriate in this context. Yet it may be worth reflecting here on the thought that it is often better to deal with someone or something with whom one is familiar and whom one knows, even if they are not ideal, than take a risk with an unknown person or thing. Ultimately, in faith, Habakkuk confesses that it is good dealing with, or being dealt with by, YHWH, and so he prays for the renewal of YHWH's deed (v. 2). This is because God has made himself known as the one committed to redeem his people from slavery, to guide them by his good laws, to bring them to a good land. But in many ways, YHWH must remain "an unknown person." God cannot be readily defined by mere humans. There can be a certain naivete in praying for God's intervention in human affairs. Much of the time, we do so thinking that we know who the good and the evil are and what God ought to do to make things better. This prayer is a reminder that when God makes his presence known, the impact is not easily contained. To join in this prayer is to acknowledge that we do not control God. The ambiguities we have explored above (see especially the commentary on v. 13) arguably have a theological basis. They arise from the decision to accept neither a dualism that would make God responsible for good and pleasant things only, nor a version of panentheism that sees God *equally* involved in all things (or its negative: equally uninvolved). The worldview assumed here is different: the Creator God is indeed involved in, and in some sense responsible for, all things, but not in the same way. It may be helpful to tease this out by distinguishing between God's characteristic and his alien work, and between his direct and his indirect work.

God's usual modus operandi is delegated rule. He created humanity in his image to rule his world as his representative. He establishes governing authorities to wield the sword for him (cf. Dan 2:21; 4:17; Rom 13:1; 1 Pet 2:14). Because human institutions fail and disappoint, as do individuals, we may well long for God to rule more directly. This is why Habakkuk complained that, having appointed the Babylonians, God seemed to sit back and just watch the disaster unfold. But this world is not designed for God's direct rule. When God makes his presence and rule felt more directly, therefore, things fall apart, mountains tremble. In other words, there is a cost to God's direct intervention. This is in many ways an unsatisfactory way of putting it. The deliverance of God's people from Pharaoh's oppression in the exodus is described in various places as an unfolding of miraculous, supernatural events. It is not at all clear, however, that what Habakkuk expects to happen in the future is a supernatural divine intervention that transcends "normal" history. In fact, ch. 2 made a point of both attributing the downfall of the wicked to YHWH and describing it as in some ways a natural outworking of the nature of evil. In other words, this is not a zero-sum game, as if divine and human involvement compete with each other on the same level. In the previous reflection, we followed the distinction between God's characteristic and his alien work suggested in Isa 28:21, differentiating between works that reflect God's character more or less clearly. Maybe it is possible to distinguish in a similar way between God's direct and his indirect work. But the distinction is arguably not between supernatural and natural events, as if God is necessarily less directly involved in events that could also be explained without reference to God. The destruction of Jerusalem at the hand of the Babylonians is widely attributed to God in the Bible and yet it did not involve any miraculous or unexplainable events. Having been announced beforehand by God's prophets, it is arguably one of the events in which God could be said to be more directly involved. But if it is not possible to measure God's increased, direct involvement by observing a diminished human role, does it make sense to distinguish between God's direct and indirect work? I think it does because (1) the biblical description of God makes it inconceivable that there are events that have nothing to do with him—God cannot ever be truly uninvolved in human and other affairs—but (2) the language of God's silence and passivity in the Psalms as well as in Hab 1 and other places suggests that it is helpful, even necessary, to distinguish between different kinds of divine involvement, or at least different ways in which God's involvement is experienced. The distinction between God's direct and his indirect work is in some respects a distinction between ordinary and extraordinary events. When people complain about God's silence or absence, they usually feel the need for something extraordinary to happen—something that turns a situation around. People praying for such an intervention usually hope for a turn of events that reflects God's character and promises better than their current situation. And yet, God's direct work cannot be simply equated with his characteristic work. From many angles, the fall of Jerusalem, so often described as in effect "an act of God" in the literal sense, was an ordinary event (deliverance would have required an extraordinary intervention) and an alien work of God. Maybe we should think of God's "direct" work as the work that is accompanied by his word, a revelation that specifically identifies God's doing, while God's "indirect" work is the events that happen under his sovereign care and oversight but without specific revelation that pinpoints God's involvement.

In any case, Habakkuk's theophany affirms that when God takes charge more directly, which in truth need not mean that humans are any less involved, the *ultimate* result will be salvation. But it also affirms that such a direct work is no less frightening than the ordinary experience of injustice and oppression. We should remember here that the rise of the Neo-Babylonian Empire has been specifically identified as God's doing (1:5–11) and should therefore be classified as his "direct" work, even if Habakkuk has distanced God from some of the disastrous effects by complaining about God's inactivity. God established the Babylonians for a purpose (1:12) but looked on when iniquity arose as a result (1:13). God made people helpless like fish before the Babylonians (1:14) and yet surely can only be said to be tolerating the idolatrous celebration of violence (1:15–17) rather than causing it. How will the enslavement to wickedness come to an end? If, because of a lack of human cooperation in readiness to allow injustice to be untangled, the knot into which human wickedness has entangled itself cannot be patiently undone, the knot has to be cut. But this will come at a cost.

Christians contemplate that cost when they look to the cross. The crucifixion of Christ was very much a human event, explainable with reference to human motives and agendas without recourse to supernatural intervention. But it was also God's direct work in that it was announced beforehand (e.g., Isa 53, whether directly or typologically) and claimed by God as his doing (e.g., Col 2:13–15). Maybe it can be described, along with the resurrection, as the most direct act of God in human history and one that transcends the distinction between God's characteristic and his alien work. It is a frightful scene; in Christ God himself is bruised as he crushes the serpent's head (cf. Gen 3:15). In the wake of this event, the striking juxtaposition in v. 14 takes on a deeper significance. In the final defeat of the wicked one, the good shepherd was struck and the sheep were scattered (cf. Zech 13:7; Matt 26:31) and it looked as if evil had triumphed over goodness, as if "to be restored, our sickness must grow worse" (in the words of T. S. Eliot's poem "East Coker"). No wonder that the expression of confidence that follows is not triumphalist but remains realistic about the cost. As is often said, "Salvation is free, but it wasn't cheap."

XVII. EXPRESSION OF CONFIDENCE IN THE MIDST OF DISTRESS (3:16–19A)

[16]*I have heard and my stomach churns;*[a]
  at the sound, my lips quiver;
    rot enters my bones;
      in my place,[b] *I tremble,*
    where[c] *I settle down*[d] *for the day of distress*
      to[e] *come up for*[f] *the people who*[g] *invade*[h] *us.*
[17]*When*[i] *the fig tree will*[j] *not blossom*[k]
  and there is no yield[l] *on the vines,*[m]
the produce of[n] *the olive has failed,*[o]
  and the groves[p] *produced*[q] *no food,*
when he[r] *cuts off the flock from the fold*
  and there is no cattle in the stables,
[18]*I will nevertheless*[s] *exult in YHWH,*
  I will rejoice in the God of my salvation.
[19a]*YHWH, the Lord, is my might;*
  he makes[t] *my feet like those of*[u] *deer;*[v]
    on high places[w] *he will enable*[x] *me to tread.*

a. The verb *rgz* is translated *tremble* later in the verse and in v. 7, but a trembling stomach is not idiomatic English. The meaning is better conveyed by *my stomach churns* than, e.g., "my body trembles" (ESV). Note that the verb is related to the noun *turmoil* in v. 2.

b. For this use of *taḥat* with pronominal suffix, meaning *in my/his/their place* (= "where I/he/they stood"), cf. 2 Sam 2:23; Job 40:12.

c. The particle is usually emended and taken with the preceding, as, e.g., reflected in NIV ("my legs") and NRSV ("my steps"); cf. *BHS*; Andersen, *Habakkuk*, 344–45; Lortie, *Mighty to Save*, 52–53. But the alleged support from the LXX is dubious. For fuller discussion, see Robert D. Holmstedt, "Habakkuk 3:16—Where Did the אֲשֶׁר Go?" *HS* 44 (2003): 129–38. Holmstedt's research also raises serious questions about the causal and concessive understandings of the particle reflected in other translations (e.g., NASB, ESV). The rendering here follows his analysis of the particle.

d. Others interpret the verb as a by-form of *'nḥ* ("to sigh, groan"; see *HALOT*; *DCH*), or they emend the text.

e. NASB, in the main text, interprets this *lamed* as parallel to the previous ("for the people to arise who will invade us"); cf. Franz Delitzsch, *Habakuk*, 193–94; Sinker, *Psalm*, 40. But within the book's argument *the day of distress* has already arrived for God's people; it is future only for the oppressors. Albright's suggestion to read the preposition with infinitive here as "when . . . came up" (cf. "at the turning of the evening/morning," Gen 24:63; Judg 19:26; "at the sending of the king's servant," 2 Sam 18:29) is adopted by Hiebert, *God of My Victory*, 53; cf. Avishur, *Studies*, 205.

f. The translation "come to(ward)" or even "come upon" (reading the preposition as equivalent to *'al*) would be entirely defensible. The rendering *come up for* makes the specific verb employed (*'ālâ*) more transparent; cf. the following note.

g. Franz Delitzsch (*Habakuk*, 194–97) argues that the relative clause is the subject of *come up*. He interprets the suffix as third-person singular rather than first-person plural and reads "for those who invade it to come up against the people." He notes that the thirteenth-century commentator Tanchum ben Joseph ha-Yerushalmi read the text in the same way. This relates to his decision to coordinate this line with *for the day of distress* rather than assume subordination (see n. e) and is defended by the observation that *come up* (*'ālâ*) nowhere else has as its subject *day*. It is true that a *day* is commonly said to "come" (e.g., Isa 13:9; Jer 46:21; Joel 2:1), but dawn can be said to *come up* (e.g., Gen 19:15) as well as, e.g., death (Jer 9:21[20]) and battle (1 Kgs 22:35) so that it does not seem inconceivable that a *day of distress* can *come up* against someone. If this is rejected, an alternative is to take YHWH as the implied subject and translate "at his coming up to the people [against the enemy host or possibly for the benefit of his people], he will invade them." The NASB apparently ignores the *lamed* before *people*, which makes it possible for *the people* to become the subject; cf. Hiebert, *God of My Victory*, 53, who suggests the *lamed* may have arisen by dittography.

h. The verb *gwd* is found only twice more in the Hebrew Bible, both times in Gen 49:19; cf. *gdd* in the sense of "band together" (Ps 94:21; *hithpolel*, "flocking to a place," Jer 5:7; maybe "muster," Mic 5:1[4:14]) and in the sense of "to make an incision" (always *hithpolel*: "to cut oneself," Deut 14:1; 1 Kgs 18:28; Jer 16:6; 41:5; 47:5; Mic 5:1[4:14]; if not "muster," as above]). For suggested derivations and emendations, see the standard dictionaries and Franz Delitzsch, *Habakuk*, 196, who argues for a meaning along the lines of "attack in force"—i.e., with many troops.

i. Most interpret *kî* as concessive here; others take it as causal (e.g., Franz Delitzsch, *Habakuk*, 196); cf. LXX *dioti*. Hiebert (*God of My Victory*, 53) deletes it. The temporal *when* has the advantage that it can work with different ways of understanding v. 17 as describing either the distress that is to fall on the Babylonians or the distress suffered by God's people. The latter seems more likely. It raises the question how v. 17 relates to the preceding or following verse. The punctuation in the present translation and the addition of *nevertheless* in the next verse reflects the decision to read v. 17 with v. 18. See further below under "Composition."

j. The *yiqtol* suggests a modal sense—not future time but a habitual aspect; see the commentary.

k. LXX (*ou karpophorēsei*, "shall not bear fruit"; cf. Barberini: *ou mē paradō ton karpon autēs*) either renders freely or reads *tiprāh* for *tiprāḥ*. Vulg. supports the MT. *Prḥ* is used elsewhere with various trees (e.g., Isa 11:1; 17:6; Ezek 17:24; Job 14:9; Ps 92:12[13]). It is also found in the Thanksgiving Hymn at Qumran for cypress, pine, and cedar putting out shoots (1QH col. 16). There seems to be no good reason to object to the MT.

l. Based on the use of *yabûl* in Job 20:28, Aaron Pinker ("Infertile Quartet of Flora," *ZAW* 115 [2003]: 622) translates "no flow" rather than *no yield*, suggesting fruit is shriveled up rather than completely absent. Elsewhere the noun refers to produce (e.g., Lev 26:4, 20). While many postulate a different meaning in Job 20:28, translating "flood" (see, e.g., NIV; cf. *mabbûl*), the standard meaning is by no means implausible for Job 20:28 as well (*yabûl bêtô*, the produce of the household). Even if one allows that *yabûl* refers to a destructive flood in Job 20:28, Pinker must assume that the same word can alternatively refer to the life-giving "flow" or sap of plants (here in Hab 3:16). This seems implausible.

m. The use of the rare plural here seems influenced by the decision to alternate singular (*fig, olive, fold*) with plural (*vines, groves, stables*) in these lines, as Andersen (*Habakkuk*, 346) observes.

n. Cf. the expression *ʿśh pərî* ("bear fruit," Gen 1:11–12; 2 Kgs 19:30; Isa 37:31; Jer 12:2; 17:8; Ezek 17:23 [cf. growing branches in v. 8]; Hos 9:16) and the use of *ʿśh* for getting produce from fields (Ps 107:37). While the verb *ʿśh* is also used for "making" (planting) gardens (Eccl 2:5; Amos 9:14), it is unlikely that the noun here refers to "the labor on" (the olive).

o. Building on Hiebert's (*God of My Victory*, 54) suggestion that the meaning "cringe, draw back, cower" (Deut 33:29; Ps 18:44[45]) is fitting here, Pinker ("Infertile Quartet," 622) suggests "became scrawny." But it is not obvious that we should expect here an image of "nature recoiling at a theophany" (Hiebert), let alone that enemies fawning (Deut 33:29; Ps 18:44[45]) provides a fitting template for this. In addition, it seems quite a leap from this image to the meaning "became scrawny."

p. Or "plantations." The plural of the rare *šədēmâ* (also Deut 32:32; 2 Kgs 23:4; Isa 16:8; 37:27) is widely understood to refer to "fields" (for the cultivation of food). Andersen considers it "the poetic word for cultivated fields" (*Habakkuk*, 347). The word is attested in Ugaritic, e.g., for terraces on which vines are grown. This precise meaning would fit Deut 32:32 and perhaps Isa 16:8, but the plantations in the Kidron valley (2 Kgs 23:4) are not likely to be vines. In any case, the reference to *vines* earlier in the verse suggests that something else is in view here. Pinker ("Infertile Quartets," 619–22) has made a good case for translating "groves" (of fruit trees).

q. A masculine singular verb is used with this feminine plural noun also in Isa 16:8; cf. JM 150l. The noun is not attested elsewhere as the grammatical subject of a verb.

r. Gelston (*BHQ*, 13:125*), noting the intransitive forms in LXX, Barberini, and Peshitta and the passive in the Vulg., suggests that *gāzar* may be best construed impersonally ("one cut off"). The book's emphasis on the work of YHWH suggests that YHWH could be considered the subject in the sense of being ultimately responsible, even though human agents are at work. English style requires the repetition of *when* here.

s. The addition of *nevertheless* is meant to reflect the use of the personal pronoun for emphasis and contrast and assumes that the situation described in the previous verse affects the prophet's people rather than their oppressors.

t. Or "and so he makes" (cf. *IBHS* 33.3.4 with further examples of *wayyiqtol* taking the implied time frame of the nominal clause). English idiom seems better served by not imitating the *wayyiqtol* form. The parallel in Ps 18:33[34] // 2 Sam 22:34 uses the *piel* of *śwh*, which perhaps more readily refers to making something like something else.

u. Or "like deer." In other words, it is not entirely clear whether the *feet* (or possibly legs) are compared to deer or to the feet/legs of deer. With a different verb, the latter is most likely for Ps 18 (see previous note). A similarly shortened comparison is found in Ps 55:6(7): "wings like a dove," which surely means "wings like a dove's wings." The comparison is, therefore, likely with the feet/legs of deer.

v. The feminine form is used, presumably as more fitting to suggest light-footedness. The masculine form is understandably used for the (male) beloved in Song 2:9, 17; 8:14 (cf. Isa 35:6 for "the lame" [masc.], where in any case the focus on leaping is not exactly the same as here). The fact that the point of comparison is not the prophet but his *feet* facilitates the use of the feminine form. In English, the gender-neutral "deer" does not suggest the (relative) heaviness of "stags, harts" and is therefore just as suited as "hinds, does," and maybe better suited, being the more general term. Haak (*Habakkuk*, 104–5) relates *'ayyālôt* to a Ugaritic noun for army or strength and interprets *rgly* (*raglay, feet*) as footmen, translating, "He constitutes my footmen as a force." In other places in which *rgly* (*raglî*) designates people (usually soldiers) "on foot" (footmen), the term is connected with the numeral *'elep* ("thousand," Exod 12:37; Num 11:21; 1 Sam 4:10; 15:4; 2 Sam 10:6; 1 Kgs 20:29; Jer 12:5; with the addition of *'îš*, "men," in Judg 20:2; 2 Sam 8:4; 1 Chr 18:4; 19:18; the plural *'ălāpîm* is used in 2 Kgs 13:7).

w. Or "on my high places." The form *bāmôtay* looks as if it has the first-person suffix, but it may be an unusual plural form in which the construct form is (1) influenced by the dual (*HGHS* 64f) and then (2) used as an absolute (*HGHS*, "Nachträge und Verbesserungen [Schluß]," 203); cf. *nəginôtay* later in the verse and in Isa 38:20. The same applies to *bāmôtay* in 2 Sam 22:34 // Ps 18:33(34). If instead the suffix is read, the *heights* perhaps belong to the one praying by virtue of him being able to walk upon them. Markl ("Hab 3," 102) sees in the use of the first-person suffix a deliberate change from Deut 33:29 (with the suffix "their" relating to enemies) to greater modesty, but note that Deut 33:29 uses the term differently anyway, referring to "their backs" rather than "their high places," and *bāmôtay* is also used in 2 Sam 22 // Ps 18.

x. This modal nuance seems appropriate in context. The alternative rendering "he makes me tread" could be (mis)read as "he forces me to tread." For the use of the future tense, see the commentary.

Composition

This section is an integral part of the prayer and is discussed separately only because it moves beyond the contemplation of God's coming and God's work to the prophet's response. Nogalski claims that "the direct address to YHWH in much of 3:8–15 does not call for a prophetic response."[493] He points out that "YHWH never speaks in chapter 3" and that v. 16 "does not respond . . . to the contents of the theophanic prayer in more than general terms." Instead, he suggests, "it reinterprets the theophany to one of judgment, in spite of the reference to salvation mentioned in 3:13."[494] In my reading of the

493. Nogalski, *Redactional Processes*, 174. Later he observes, however, that 3:16a, 18 "form a consistent ending to the theophanic poem of 3:3–15" (179).

494. Nogalski, *Redactional Processes*, 175.

book, the prophet responds to the revelation in ch. 2 by immersing himself in prayer based on an understanding of "the work of God" (the deed of YHWH) that is informed by the accounts of what YHWH has done in the past. Whether this involved a visionary experience or a recitation of tradition within the temple, we do not know. But even the direct address in 3:8–15 is meditative. From v. 3 onward, the prophet is not pleading with YHWH but reflecting on YHWH's presence and action, first in third-person and then in second-person address. Exploring propositions prayerfully in direct address to God is a mode of speaking made famous later by Augustine's *Confessions*. While vv. 16–19a switch back to the third person, this section can still be read as prayerful in the same way. Similar switches are found in the Psalms. See, e.g., Ps 18, which shares with Hab 3 the use of theophanic descriptions of YHWH and the motif of moving securely on heights like a deer (v. 33[34]). Verse 15 is, in my view, no more a satisfactory conclusion to Hab 3 than v. 7. Just as vv. 3–7 and vv. 8–15 are clearly distinct stanzas that are unable to stand on their own, so vv. 16–19a feel distinct but still belong to the prayer. The commentary on vv. 3–15 above suggested that the coming and action of YHWH is depicted as frightening. In this sense, it involves an element of "bad news" even with the affirmation that there is salvation at the end. In this, it is like ch. 2, which promises that evil does not have a longterm future but also refrains from offering hope for a quick end to the bad situation in which God's people find themselves. It is, therefore, appropriate that the conclusion here mixes trembling with joy.

As the translation notes hint, one's overall interpretation of the chapter and indeed the book as a whole plays a role in the identification of *the day of distress* (Is it for Judah or Judah's oppressors?) and in one's understanding of the syntax of the last line of v. 16. It might also predispose one to link the description in v. 17 with either Judah or Babylon in present or future times. From the Tg. onward, Jewish tradition understood v. 16 as the words of Babylon. Babylon is said to be trembling at the remembrance of God's judgment against Egypt. But the incipits in the Tg. that attribute different parts of the speech in these verses to Babylon and the prophet do not, in my view, reflect a plausible reading. Others, reading the chapter in isolation from Hab 1–2, see the prayer anticipate *the day of distress* that is to come upon Judah at the hand of the Babylonians. But the book can be read sequentially. In this case, *the day of distress* for Judah has already begun, producing Habakkuk's complaint in ch. 1. God's reply in ch. 2 suggests that the oppressor will fall due to overreach, but this means that things might well get worse for Judah before they get better. This prospect calls for faithfulness—ongoing faith in God (2:4)—while the downfall of the oppressor is still future (2:5–20). The interpretation below suggests that Habakkuk now knows that *the day of distress* will also come to Babylon one day and is prepared to wait calmly for this turn of events while suffering the ongoing distress of the people of Judah.[495]

Alternatively, one might read v. 16 in the sense of "I am trembling, and I will only be at rest when the day of distress comes up for Babylon."[496] Verse 17 would then read as a description of what will happen to Babylon. This is, for example, how Barré reads the text,[497] supported by the division of vv. 16–19a into two stanzas, and his view requires additional comment. Barré argues that three standard structuring devices show that vv. 18–19a do not belong with v. 17. First, there is a shift from no references to YHWH in vv. 16–17 to third-person references in vv. 18–19a.[498] But it remains debatable whether a switch of second-person address to YHWH to third-person reference to him and vice versa is used much as a structuring device in Hebrew poetry.[499] While in Hab 3, such a change helps to mark vv. 3–7 (third person) and vv. 8–15 (second person) as distinct units, it is doubtful that "no reference to YHWH" should be accepted as a separate category.[500] Verses 16–17 readily go with vv. 18–19a, with no sense of discontinuity in the way YHWH is referenced. Second, Barré argues that the mood shift between vv. 16–17 and vv. 18–19a suggests a break. But this disallows the possibility that the juxtaposition of fear and fascination is precisely the point of these verses, as Hiebert argued, not least on the grounds that the combination is also found in v. 2.[501] Third, he suggests that the use of the divine name in the first bicolon of v. 2, the first line of v. 8, and in the first lines of v. 18 and v. 19a is structurally significant. But this seems unlikely, especially since the divine name in v. 18 is not a vocative, unlike the other occurrences, and the one in v. 19a comes too late to signal the beginning of a new unit.

As noted above (see on the composition of 3:3–7), I have adopted Barré's observations concerning the use of anagrams and repetition as structural devices in Hab 3. I have accepted his proposition that direct and anagrammatized reuse of words from v. 2 occurs at significant points, but I have modified his proposal in two ways. First, I have allowed for the use of words later in the poem as a structural device from not only the tricolon but also the opening

---

495. Fabry (*Habakuk/Obadja*, 145–46) speculates that v. 16b is part of a Day of YHWH redaction of the Book of the Twelve, although this is not taken up later in the commentary (293–94, 318).

496. Or "I sigh for the day of distress to come up for Babylon"; see the translation note.

497. Barré, "Literary Devices," 455–62.

498. This requires that the implied subject of *gāzar* (*cuts off*) must not be identified as YHWH; see the translation note.

499. The question is relevant also in relation to Zephaniah and will be taken up further in the commentary on that book below.

500. Barré ("Literary Devices," 449) appeals to Ps 6 as evidence.

501. Hiebert, "Use of Inclusion," 133–34.

bicolon of v. 2. This further strengthens the divisions between vv. 7 and 8 and between vv. 15 and 16. It also makes the observation more noteworthy that vv. 18–19a, other than employing the divine name, do not participate in this reuse of words from v. 2. Even drawing on the whole of v. 2, there is no further link to be made. Second, I expressed skepticism about acknowledging anagrams that cross word boundaries. This disallows the identification of an anagram in v. 8 by way of an *inclusio* with v. 15. The proposed segmentation of the chapter remains unaffected because vv. 8–15 can be identified as a stanza on other grounds, not least the presence of a different, more straightforward *inclusio* in the reference to the *sea*, which is not found anywhere else in the poem.[502] But it does mean that words from v. 2 are reused at the end and not at the beginning of the stanzas in vv. 3–7 and 8–15. As noted above, there is a further anagram in the middle of vv. 8–15, namely *bəraq* (*lightning*) in v. 11. It forms an anagram not only of *qereb* (*midst*, used twice in v. 2) but also of *rāqāb* (*rot*) in v. 16 and *bāqār* (*cattle*) in v. 17, but not of any word (or sequence of letters) anywhere else in the chapter. Thus, we should arguably think of v. 11 as the middle of the middle stanza of the whole poem rather than merely as the midpoint of vv. 8–15. This does not resolve the question whether vv. 16–19a should be subdivided. Verses 8–15 could be considered the middle stanza of five within the chapter (vv. 2, 3–7, 8–15, 16–17, 18–19a). Alternatively, separating off the petition in v. 2 (the source of the anagrams and repetitions) from the actual poem, vv. 8–15 could be the middle stanza of three within the poem (vv. 3–7, 8–15, 16–19a). The latter has the advantage of greater balance because vv. 3–7 and 16–19a are roughly of equal length.[503] If v. 2 is included in the scheme, the first half is noticeably longer than the second.

Barré argues for vv. 16–17 as a distinct unit by observing that *rāqāb* and *bāqār* are not only anagrams of *qereb* (*midst*, v. 2) but also of each other. He observes that *gāzar* not only links with the root *rgz* in v. 2 but also with the reuse of the root at the beginning of v. 16 (*churns*), arguing that these anagrams tie vv. 16–17 together to the exclusion of vv. 18–19a.[504] In a further move, Barré then points to the similarities between v. 2 and vv. 18–19a (bicolon + tricolon structure, double use of the divine name, word count, two

---

502. In fact, vv. 8 and 15 use the same preposition with *yām* in Hebrew (*bayyām*, *against/through the sea*).

503. A precise determination is impossible because of the many factors involved in reconstructing and scanning the text, but the MT has fifty accentuated units in vv. 3–7 and forty-nine in vv. 16–19 (without the musical notation). There are forty-one accentuated units in the lines of vv. 8–11 up to the line that contains *bəraq* (which is in the middle of its line) and thirty-five such units in 3:12–15.

504. Barré, "Literary Devices," 456–58.

predications in the first person followed by three in the second person).[505] The features that Barré has identified can be read as giving to vv. 16–17 and vv. 18–19a each their separate cohesion. But even if one accepts this (an alternative will be proposed below), it is worth discussing whether we should identify two stanzas here, as Barré does, or a two-part stanza. A few observations argue for the latter.

First, given the suggested significance of anagrams for the identification of stanzas in this poem, the absence of such an anagram in vv. 18–19a makes it more problematic to identify these verses as a separate stanza. For my modification of Barré's proposal, I argue that all three stanzas (vv. 3–7, 8–15, 16–19a) anagrammatize words from v. 2, whereas with Barré's division only three of the four do. Second, the beginning of v. 2 is already picked up at the beginning of v. 16 (*I have heard*). It would therefore not be true to say that vv. 16–17 reuse words from the tricolon in v. 2 while vv. 18–19a (alone) go further back to the bicolon of v. 2. One feature that distinguishes vv. 16–19a from the previous two stanzas is that the repetition and anagrams, previously placed at the end of stanzas, now occur at the beginning and in greater quantity.[506] This suggests that the conclusion of the poem is signaled from v. 16 onward, which implies that vv. 16–17 do not add a third stanza that is roughly parallel to the first two but with vv. 18–19a comprise the poem's final stanza, offering the prophet's response. Third, the use of the personal pronoun at the beginning of v. 18 suggests a contrast with what precedes. Because the reaction of the Babylonians to their day of distress is not reported, the prophet's rejoicing does not contrast with their wailing. Rather, the contrast is between the prophet in his rejoicing and the absence of fruitful life in the land in the immediately preceding verse.[507] This suggests that the land is the prophet's rather than the land of the oppressor and that vv. 17–18 should not be separated. To this, finally, we can add the observation about length made above. While v. 2 and vv. 18–19a are of the same length, vv. 16–17 are significantly shorter than vv. 3–7, creating an imbalance within the poem. If vv. 16–19a are kept together, they correspond in length to vv. 3–7,[508] the two stanzas thus surrounding the longer stanza in vv. 8–15. Verse 2 then falls outside this

505. Barré, "Literary Devices," 460–62.

506. This means that the switch to first-person verbs and suffixes in v. 16, including the reuse of *šāma'tî* (*I have heard*) from v. 2, is critical for marking the break between vv. 15 and 16, which would otherwise be obscured by the presence of anagrams of roots from v. 2 in both verses.

507. Alternatively, but in my view less likely, the contrast is with the prophet's trembling in v. 16. In this case, a separation of vv. 18–19 from vv. 16–17 would be equally ill advised.

508. While the lengths of these stanzas correspond to each other, the rhythm is different, as the two lists in vv. 16 and 17 make for more extended units, even though this commentary scans v. 17 as a series of bicola.

balanced structure, but this merely serves to highlight the significance of v. 2 as the petitionary heart of the prayer and the treasury providing words to be reused in significant ways later in the poem.

If, as argued here, we keep vv. 16–19a together, we may ask further whether a subdivision into vv. 16–17 and vv. 18–19a is advisable. If v. 17 describes further *the day of distress to come up for the people who invade us* (v. 16), then vv. 16–17 must be read together. But most readers understand v. 17 to speak of the desolation of God's people. In this case, v. 17 could either go with v. 16, further explaining the reason for the prophet's anguish, or with v. 18. The latter seems to account better for the opening of v. 18, which suggests a contrast with something that precedes. The bicolon in v. 18 is very similar to the first two cola in Mic 7:7, which likewise follows a list of undesirable circumstances introduced with *kî* (usually rendered "for" in Mic 7:6). Banister argues that Mic 7:7 is later than Hab 3:18,[509] while others reckon that Mic 7:1–7 belongs to the basic layer of Micah.[510] In the latter case and if there is a literary dependence, it would be more likely that Hab 3 cites Mic 7 than the other way round.[511] The fact that *ṣph* is also used in Mic 7:4 makes it less likely that its use in v. 7 was inspired by Hab 2:1. Markl makes a good case for the dependence of Hab 3 on Ps 18 and Deut 33 and points out that the tradition is significantly reshaped in Hab 3.[512] This would also be true of any use of Mic 7:7.

If vv. 17–18 are read together,[513] they echo the movement from distress to resolve in v. 16 and heighten it. The distress is now described in terms that affect the whole land rather than just in relation to an individual, and the resolve is now to rejoice, not merely to settle down calmly. The poem concludes with a hymnic confession of faith in v. 19a in the form of a tricolon that parallels Ps 18:33(34) // 2 Sam 22:34 and takes up a motif from Deut 33:29 (cf. Deut 33:2 with Hab 3:3).

Commentary

16 This verse picks up *I have heard* from v. 2 as well as the root translated *turmoil* there and *churns* and *tremble* here (cf. *trembling* in v. 7). The two verbs

509. Banister, "Theophanies," 242–44. Cf. William McKane, *Micah: Introduction and Commentary* (Edinburgh: T&T Clark, 1998), 214–16, who considers v. 7 a postexilic addition.

510. E.g., Jakob Wöhrle, *Die frühen Sammlungen des Zwölfprophetenbuches: Entstehung und Komposition*, BZAW 360 (Berlin: de Gruyter, 2006), 178–80.

511. Franz Delitzsch (*Habakuk*, 198) thinks that, independently from each other, both are indebted to similar expressions in the Psalms.

512. Markl, "Hab 3," 100–104.

513. Floyd's outline in *Minor Prophets 2*, 149, reflects the same decision.

occur together also, for example, in Exod 15:14, in which Moses and the Israelites sing of the trembling of the peoples who hear about Israel's deliverance from Egypt. Earlier I suggested that in v. 2, the primary reference is to the revelation in ch. 2 but that this could be heard alongside a secondary reference—a recital of God's deeds of the sort reflected in vv. 3–15. Here, following on from vv. 3–15, this secondary reference gains greater prominence. The visual imagery of vv. 3–15 does not stand in the way of this, as it is possible that the vision was received while God's deeds of old were recited in the liturgy (see the reflection on seeing and hearing above, p. 370). Delitzsch thinks that the prophet's fear had been assuaged by the depiction of deliverance in vv. 3–15 but now reasserts itself; after the focus on the ultimate salvation, the prophet becomes again mindful of the current distress.[514] The promise of future deliverance in ch. 2 implied a period of continuing distress that calls for faithfulness. So here, the promise of salvation may well also induce fear and trembling (see the commentary on v. 2). If so, the stomach-churning anguish of the prophet is likely a response to the coming of the warrior God just like the trembling of the tents of Midian and Cushan in v. 7. God's intervention is a fearful thing, even if it is for salvation. The whole body is affected, the soft tissue (*stomach*) as well as the *bones*, from top (*lips*) to bottom (*in my place*, using a word that elsewhere is often used in the sense of "under, beneath, below"). The use of the same verb in the first and last of the first four lines (*churns, tremble*) makes the point that the whole body is shaking. The quivering of the lips may well indicate a chattering of teeth. It is usually the ears that are said to reverberate ("tingle"), always at the hearing of calamitous news (1 Sam 3:11; 2 Kgs 21:12; Jer 19:3).[515] Following the mention of hearing in the first colon, we might have expected that same expression here. The unique variation may aim to leave us with an ambiguity about *at the sound*. If it were the ears that reverberated, *the sound* would certainly be equivalent to *the report* in v. 2—namely, what the prophet hears. Even with the variation here, this is the most likely reference. Still, the reference to his *lips* makes one wonder in retrospect whether *the sound* might not in addition be the prayer the prophet utters in response to what he has heard.[516] The image of decaying bones is also found in Prov 14:30 (cf. 12:4), where its opposite (*lēb marpēʾ*) seems to be inner calmness. Fabry objects to *rot*, seeing instead a reference to paralysis on the grounds that necrosis is the result of long-term illness rather

514. Franz Delitzsch, *Habakuk*, 189. He adds that nevertheless the picture of the future presents a weapon against fear to the prophet so that confidence asserts itself in the fear.

515. These are all occurrences of the verb. Homonyms are used in Exod 15:10 ("sink," likely a by-form of the root *ṣwl*), Neh 13:19 (*qal*, "becoming dark"), and Ezek 31:3 (*hiphil*, "giving shade"), probably a denominative of *ṣēl* ("shade").

516. Franz Delitzsch (*Habakuk*, 191), by contrast, is convinced that it can only be the voice of God.

than shock,[517] but the phrase does not designate a literal illness. Rather, the prophet feels as if his body has been ravaged by an illness that spread to his very bones. The picture of security in 2 Sam 7:10 and 1 Chr 17:9 uses both *taḥat* for *place* with pronominal suffix and the same verb that this verse has, but there the verb *rgz* is negated to denote a lack of disturbance.

The *place* might still be the same on which the prophet is imaginatively positioned in 2:1, a place of expectancy and a place from which military developments might be seen. This link is more explicit in the LXX, which has *ephylaxamēn* ("I watched," the verb related to the noun in 2:1, *phylakē*) at the beginning of the verse instead of *I have heard*.[518] It is not clear whether this is the result of a mistake, reading *šmrty* for *šmʿty*, or an exegetical decision linking the hearing with the listening in 2:1. But there is probably no need to think of a specific place unless one feels compelled to do so by the addition of the relative clause. The expression *in my place, I tremble* probably indicates that the prophet can hardly hold himself upright in the place where he stands.[519]

The reaction this verse describes is sometimes thought to be a characteristic response to the experience of a theophany,[520] but, as Hillers notes, it is arguably better categorized as a conventional reaction to bad news.[521] In other words, the reaction is not simply to the inspiration *per se* but to its contents. The content is frightful even if the ultimate outcome is salvation. It is, therefore, not necessary to see the prophet here as embodying the distress that will befall the Babylonians rather than his own, as argued by Barré.[522] In ch. 1, the distress of the prophet reflects and embodies the distress of the righteous among God's people. The first-person singular in 3:14 similarly has the prophet embody the fate of his people (cf. *the God of my salvation* in v. 18). It is, therefore, more natural to read the description here with reference to God's people rather than their oppressors.

To *settle down* is not simply to "wait" but to "wait quietly."[523] Waiting

---

517. Fabry, *Habakuk/Obadja*, 317.

518. Barberini has *etaxamēn* ("I position myself"), which probably also refers back to 2:1 (so Fabry, *Habakuk/Obadja*, 317), although LXX has *histēmi* rather than *tassō* in 2:1.

519. Cf. Franz Delitzsch, *Habakuk*, 192.

520. E.g., Eaton, "Origin," 16. He compares Isa 21:3–4 and Jer 23:9 (cf. Jeremias, *Kultprophetie*, 107). The former is in response to "a distressing revelation" (*ḥāzût qāšâ*, v. 2); the latter is in the context of evil within society and deceit among its leaders.

521. Delbert R. Hillers, "A Convention in Hebrew Literature: The Reaction to Bad News," *ZAW* 77 (1965): 86–90.

522. Barré, "Literary Devices," 461.

523. The verb is often translated "waited" in 1 Sam 25:9, where it could be rendered "paused" (NET), understood as cessation of speaking (cf. Vulg. *siluerunt*). The notion of settling down is the one most frequently ascribed to the verb.

could involve a great deal of agitation. Here, the stress falls on being composed rather than agitated in the expectation of what is to come (contrast *vehement protests* in 3:1 to characterize the preceding prayers). The prophet knows that there is worse to come before it gets better, but he is now convinced that it will end well and, therefore, he is content to *settle down* even while trembling for the time when *the day of distress* will reach the oppressors, as ch. 2 promised. If one assumes that *the day of distress* is indeed the subject of *come up for the people who invade us* (see the translation note), the unusual *come up* (*ʿālâ* rather than the standard verb for "come," *bôʾ*, which is frequently used with *day*) was perhaps chosen because it seems to carry a military sense in some places ("mounting an attack")—a connotation that is fitting here.

17 It is not inconceivable that this verse further describes *the day of distress* that is to befall the Babylonians. If so, the contrast between vv. 16–17 on the one hand and vv. 18–19 on the other would be one of patiently waiting now (while the people of God continue to suffer) and rejoicing then (when *the day of distress* has arrived for the Babylonians). But, as explained above, I prefer reading the desolation of v. 17 as depicting the situation of the people of God, and I take it with v. 18. This juxtaposes the trembling and determination to settle down of v. 16 with the resolve to rejoice in vv. 17–19 (see further under "Composition"). The emphasis found in ch. 2 on retribution as suffering what one inflicts on others allows reading the description, in a secondary sense, as a depiction of the fate of the Babylonians whose gluttonous greed (1:8; 2:5; 3:14) will meet lack of provisions. The verse is often thought to depict a drought, and in the introduction to the commentary, I referred to Holladay's proposal that the verse can be linked to the drought described in Jer 14, which he dates to 601 BC.[524] But the language is too stereotypical for such precision. Pinker argued that what lies behind the loss of productivity is not a drought but neglect.[525] This, too, is pressing the text to be more specific than it is. What is described is a catastrophe, the economic collapse of a community. The land that was given as a blessing to Israel no longer offers this blessing (see Deut 8:8 for a similar agricultural list in a context of blessing). The immediate cause for this is perhaps not sufficiently relevant to be mentioned here, maybe in contrast to Joel 1 (vv. 10–12, 16–18), for example,

---

524. Holladay, "Plausible Circumstances."

525. Pinker, "Infertile Quartet." Andrew T. Abernathy ("Eating, Assyrian Imperialism, and God's Kingdom in Isaiah," in *Isaiah and Imperial Context: The Book of Isaiah in the Times of Empire*, ed. Andrew T. Abernathy and Mark G. Brett [Eugene, OR: Pickwick, 2013], 35–50) notes "Assyria's practice of harvesting the crops of those they were invading" and destroying food sources they did not use (41). Babylon's practice may have differed little. This also would be too narrow as a specific explanation for our verses but is probably a relevant context.

which explicitly refers to drought (vv. 19–20), although the drought may be symbolic given the earlier reference to locusts (v. 4, possibly a metaphor for foreign armies). There are a number of texts that describe such a disaster, mentioning some of the same things (e.g., Amos 4:9 and Hag 2:19, both the result of blight and mildew as well as locusts [Amos] or hail [Haggai]). Habakkuk's context and strong verbal links suggest that we should look to Jer 5:17 as the closest parallel.[526] (Jeremiah 5:15–17 was already mentioned earlier as a parallel and possible source for Hab 1:5–11.) Jeremiah 5:17 uses the verb 'ākal ("eat up, devour"), which relates to 'ōkel (*food*) in our verse, and the list of items consumed features four that make an appearance in our verse: flocks, herds, vines, and fig trees. Jeremiah describes the greed of the Babylonians, eating up the land of Judah, and this seems to be the primary reference here, with the implication that the same is going to happen to Babylon in the future.[527] It is possible that the prayer does not claim such a collapse as already present. Interpreting the opening particle as concessive ("though") rather than temporal (*when*; see the translation note) and reading the verbs as hypothetical, one could even allow for the possibility that the worst might not happen. But the renewed allusion to Jer 5 suggests that the situation continues to be bad and that the prophet accepts that it might get worse before salvation comes. Thus, the conclusion of the prayer turns from the expected end of God's work back to the present situation, the midst of years between YHWH's deeds of old and the completion of his current work.

Fig trees generally blossom more than once a year with different flowering on old wood and on new shoots. In colder climes, this still leaves only one edible crop at best, but there are kinds of fig trees that in some regions produce two crops, the first in spring, the second and main crop in late summer or early autumn. The use of the *yiqtol* (imperfect) suggests that the fig trees have failed more than once to produce flowers. For various reasons, it is not possible to fix with precision the timing of this or of the states of affair subsequently described. Crop failure can often be determined well before the crop is due to be harvested. Nevertheless, we may be able to see a movement

---

526. The parallels with Jer 5:17 and the fact that these clauses of lack and loss negate elements that are used to signal Israel's prosperity in Deut 8:8 (note also oliveyards, vineyards [kərāmîm], flocks, and cattle in 2 Kgs 5:26) is in my view not sufficiently taken into account by those who believe that the verse is a later addition (e.g., Rudolph, *Micha*, 240–41), sometimes linked to the redactional transmission of the Book of the Twelve (e.g., Nogalski, *Redactional Processes*, 176–78). A specific allusion to Judg 9:8–15 (considered by Fabry, *Habakuk/Obadja*, 318) is not likely.

527. This is also supported by the use of *cut off*, which suggests active destruction rather than the languishing and dying of sheep. Fabry (*Habakuk/Obadja*, 318) points to archaeological evidence for the impact of warfare on agriculture.

through subsequent months in this verse.[528] While the precise timings are debatable, the sequence seems (chrono)logical, and we may note the absence of any reference to barley or wheat, which would be harvested earlier in the year and that in terms of dietary calories are the most important.[529] Roughly speaking, in May the fig trees may have failed (again) to flower. In June, the vine harvest could be called off. In July, one would be able to determine that there will be no olives this year. In August, any pistachios, walnuts, almonds, dates, or other produce one might have hoped for in the *groves* could be written off. Instead of the great festival of ingathering (Sukkoth), there would be lamenting in early autumn not only with regard to the past months but with regard to the future, as there are no flocks and herds of animals, which are meant to prosper over the rainy winter months.

18 The exulting and rejoicing is not prompted by the experience of salvation as evil befalls the oppressors. It is a taking delight in YHWH in the face of suffering, trusting that in the long run he will show himself to be *the God of my salvation*. Habakkuk again embodies the people (cf. v. 14). In my interpretation, the *nevertheless* is in the face of (potential) disaster for God's people, as described in the preceding verse. If, instead, v. 17 is interpreted as the description of the disaster to come upon the oppressors, there would arguably be still an implied *nevertheless*, namely with the trembling in v. 16, so that even in this interpretation one could not say that the suffering of the invaders prompts the prophet's exulting.

The exultation of the attackers had been linked with plundering (v. 14). The two instances of *exult* here echo the contrast made in 2:4–5 between the greedy and those whose loyalty remains to YHWH. Avishur thinks that the parallelism between Hab 3:18–19 and Ps 18:46(47) and 32–33(33–34) "proves that they are actually a single text, transmitted with stylistic variants." He argues from this that the verses are a later addition to the prayer of Habakkuk,[530] while I instead see the use of a common motif (cf. also Deut 33:29). Even if these verses were a later addition (unlikely in view of the discussion above under "Composition"), the prayer is better for having them. As the opening of the prayer combined fear with trust, the latter expressed in the petition that presumes that God's work is a good work, so in this conclusion to the prayer, trembling is combined with trust, now expressed in delighting in YHWH anyway. The prophet accepts that the downfall of the oppressors that

---

528. See, e.g., Borowski, *Daily Life*, 27–30.

529. Note that in a similar list (but of blessings) in Deut 8:8, wheat and barley are mentioned first, and Hag 2:19 refers to seed in the barn before referencing the vine, the fig tree, the pomegranate, and the olive tree. If *groves* is translated "fields" instead (see the translation note), one could see a reference to grain, although the word is nowhere else in the Bible linked with wheat or barley.

530. Avishur, *Studies*, 202.

will bring salvation to God's people will come at a time of God's choosing. A close parallel is found in Mic 7:7, where we find the only other occurrence of the phrase *God of my salvation* outside the Psalms.[531] McKane describes it as "a 'nevertheless,' an affirmation of hope in Yahweh in the face of the unpropitious signs of the times: the speaker will keep a look-out for Yahweh and nourish his hope in God, his saviour, to answer his prayer."[532] The first two lines of this verse are structured in the same way as Hab 3:18: *wa'ănî byhwh* (verb) / (verb) (*l/b*)*ē'lōhê yiš'î*. In both verses, the verbs are in the first person and cohortative in meaning, the second requiring a different preposition in Micah and Habakkuk.[533] The verbs in Mic 7:7 are "watch" (*sph*; cf. Hab 2:1) and "wait" (*yḥl*), and the contrast is with a corrupt society. Micah compares the absence of righteous people to the absence of fruit because the harvest has been taken in (vv. 1–2). Whatever their literary relationship, Mic 7:7 is conceptually earlier from the point of view of Habakkuk. Micah expresses a hopeful watching for God in the context of being at odds with the people so that the use of *my* in *the God of my salvation* might be polemical (*my* not "your"). Such a contrast was more to the fore in Hab 1, leading to the watching and waiting at the beginning of ch. 2. But the divine reply has moved the prophet to a different place, where there is rejoicing with the trembling and the expression *the God of my salvation* is not likely to have a polemical edge.

19a This verse further spells out the reasons for rejoicing in YHWH. He is the army and strength of his people. The prophet again embodies the people, using the first-person singular. But now the full significance of this device becomes clearer.[534] The prophet takes up the literary testament of King David (2 Sam 22 // Ps 18), citing a complete bicolon about the king nearly exactly (2 Sam 22:34; cf. *ḥāyil, might*, in the preceding verse). He changes the verb for close equivalents. The first verb, *he makes . . . like* (see the translation note) was possibly changed to establish a link with 2:9, where the same verb was used in connection with an animal metaphor and height, thereby highlighting again the contrast between the greedy and the faithful. The second verb (*tread*) is changed to allude to Deut 33 ("But you shall tread on their high places," v. 29), whose beginning (v. 2) inspired Hab 3:3. In this way, the literary testament of Moses, the paradigmatic prophet, is also taken up.

---

531. The three occurrences in the Psalms are in 18:46(47); 25:5; 27:9. We may compare *'ēl yəšû'ātî* ("God is my salvation") in Isa 12:2 and *'ĕlōhê yiš'ēk* ("God of your salvation") in Isa 17:10.

532. McKane, *Micah*, 214.

533. The preposition *beth* in the first colon in Mic 7:7 is odd with *sph*. Waltke (*Micah*, 429) suggests to mentally add a verb such as *bṭḥ* ("trust"): "I will watch [and trust] in YHWH." Cf. *IBHS* 11.4.3d.

534. The following is indebted to Markl, "Hab 3," 102–4.

Habakkuk is like both a new Moses and a new David. No longer are the people of God embodied in their king who experiences divine deliverance of a kind that enables him to exercise authority over other nations (2 Sam 22:44), destroying all who oppose him (vv. 38–41). Now the people of God are concentrated in the pleading and suffering prophet. The *feet* are made like *those of deer*, able to stride freely without slipping on the heights (2 Sam 22:34; cf. v. 37), but the hands are not made ready for battle (v. 35). The blessing (Deut 33) has become a prayer (Hab 3), and the prayer does not express a desire to see enemies cringe. The prophet is content simply to be able to negotiate rugged terrain. He does not pray for or anticipate trampling on his enemies' backs (Deut 33:29).[535] The similarities with Deut 33 toward the beginning and end of the chapter highlight the poem's movement from a mountain range (*Teman, Mount Paran*) to *heights*. This influenced the decision to use the future tense for the *yiqtol* (imperfect), rendering *he will enable me to tread*, which could alternatively be translated with the present tense, following on from *he makes my feet like those of deer*. The image of treading on heights is one of victory and security, one of undisputed and therefore undisturbed possession of the land. This will be true for God's people only after God's work has been renewed and completed. God's coming from the heights of *Teman* and *Mount Paran* (v. 3) once led through the water (v. 15) to the promised land. The prophet now trusts that the turmoil of sea, rivers, and water will again not be the last word but will lead to undisturbed possession of the *heights* (and thus the land). So even now the prophet knows YHWH to be the might of his people who enables his faithful ones to tread securely on their journey as a token of ultimate victory. In the present, having feet like deer means being surefooted on difficult terrain; in the future it will mean leaping freely upon the high hills.

Reflection

There are a number of different options for understanding and interpreting these verses. Decisions on some of the details may influence how one reflects on this passage as a whole more strongly than is the case with many other passages. My reading sees the prophet tremble in shock as the full, existential impact of God's revelation and work sinks in, and yet he rejoices in God. The situation calls for patient waiting as the people of God anticipate that things might get a lot worse for them before the day of distress comes for the invaders and the faithful can walk freely and securely again. But there

---

535. The expression is used in a similar sense in Sir 9:2: "Do not give your soul to a woman for her to trample upon your back."

is confidence that even in disaster, YHWH is a strength and enables one to walk securely. There is a defiance here that is similar to Ps 27:1 ("YHWH is my light and my salvation; whom shall I fear? YHWH is the stronghold of my life; whom shall I dread?"). Much later, the apostle Paul recounts how he received a message about the sufficiency of God's grace and of power being made perfect in weakness (2 Cor 12:9). Renewed energy comes with such confidence in a powerful God who has good purposes (cf. Isa 40:28–31).

I have argued that the prophet's response is related to the content of the revelation more than the experience of theophany. With this qualification, it is worth citing Hiebert to the effect that

> fear and fascination are to be taken together as representing the response to the recitation of the theophany. . . . The way in which these emotions are combined with one another suggests that they are to be understood as aspects of a single experience, the confrontation with God through the account of his theophany. The contrasting emotion of terror at God's appearance and rapture at God's salvation are conventional elements in the human response to theophany.[536]

Fear and fascination are a proper response not merely in a context of any particular experience of God ("theophany") but also to the way in which God has revealed himself to us, as a fearful and merciful God, and to the way this world is: deeply corrupt, deeply loved by God, and in the process of being redeemed. For the apostle Paul, paradox seems to have been a daily experience, "sorrowful, yet always rejoicing" (2 Cor 6:10). Andersen comments:

> It is only a bloodless rationalistic analysis that finds contradiction between the reverence of v. 16a, the delight of v. 18, the devastation of v. 17 and the tranquility of v. 16b. The ancient pieces that are closest to Habakkuk 3 in genre—Exodus 15, Judges 5, Psalms 18 and 68—contain a lyrical synthesis of the fear of Yahweh with admiration and confidence, a synthesis of faith and love that is the height of adoration—Yahweh, terrible and compassionate.[537]

Dividing the trembling and the rejoicing onto two different stanzas (vv. 16–17, 18–19) would not separate them altogether, as the poet affirms them both at the same time. It is not trembling now and rejoicing later. The only

---

536. Hiebert, "Use of Inclusion," 133–34. He points to Rudolf Otto, *The Idea of the Holy* (Oxford: Oxford University Press, 1923), as testimony for how typical these contrasting emotions are in encounter with the holy.

537. Andersen, *Habakkuk*, 345.

separation that could be made would be redactional. But even if the original unity and coherence of these verses is denied, I believe that the larger canonical context is guiding readers of the received text toward the combination of fear with trembling and rejoicing with confidence. Reciting the works of God with an awareness of this paradox can help us discern what aspects of the tradition we might need to pay closer attention to so that our own appreciation of God and his work is not lopsidedly one of fear or rejoicing only. Do we lack confidence that evil will really be defeated in the end? Or are we naïve about the costs involved in dealing with evil? In a song released in 1997 ("Once Again"), Matt Redman sees the horror of Christ becoming nothing, "poured out to death," and marvels at this amazing gift of life. Looking at the cross, he confesses, "I'm humbled by Your mercy and I'm broken inside." Throughout the ages songs and hymns have celebrated Christ's achievement with a combination of joy and trembling, seeing desolation and ultimate victory. If the (faithful) prophet rather than the (currently reigning unfaithful) king embodies the people, it is because the path through death to life lies in faithfulness to God's word, not in political and military might. In Isa 53, the idea of royal triumph (e.g., 2 Sam 22 // Ps 18) and victory through faithfulness in suffering are combined, if the suffering servant who embodies Israel is the anointed king. In any case, in Christ Jesus the promised king (Isa 9, 11) and the suffering servant (Isa 53) are one.

The Vulg. renders the second line of Hab 3:18, *exultabo in Deo Iesu meo* ("I will exult in God my Jesus"). The linking of this chapter with God's most marvelous work in the death and resurrection of Jesus Christ flows from the conviction that the prophet knows the future work of God because he knows God's past work. In the light of the revelation in ch. 2, the prophet trusts that the characteristic features of God's work will be seen again. Christians can see the glorious fulfillment of this chapter in the death and resurrection of Christ. But because this work of God was typical (characteristic) as well as unique, it provides a model for our lives in the expectation that the righteous who remain loyal to God will live (Hab 2:4)—will triumph—while arrogance, greed, gluttony, and imperial conquest will ever have God as their opponent.

XVIII. THE POSTSCRIPT (3:19B)

¹⁹ᵇ*For the leader.*ᵃ *With string music.*ᵇ

a. See, e.g., Marvin E. Tate, *Psalms 51–100*, WBC 20 (Dallas: Word Books, 1990), 4–5, for a discussion of *lamnaṣṣēaḥ*, found fifty-five times in the Psalms and only here outside the Psalms.

b. This seems to be an unassimilated plural form without suffix (cf. *nəgînôtay* in Isa 38:20); see the translation note on *high places* in v. 19a. Franz Delitzsch (*Habakuk*, 203–4) argues persuasively that the term does not refer to stringed instruments themselves but to the music of stringed instruments. This is also how it is glossed in *DCH*; other standard dictionaries (e.g., *HALOT*, and Ges¹⁸) allow for either.

Composition

These final words were sometimes read as integral to the poem, as in the LXX ("to be victorious in his songs") and in the Vulg. ("victorious in singing psalms"). Delitzsch runs through the various options for reading *lamnaṣṣēaḥ bingînôtāy* as an integral part of the poem and shows why they fail.[538] There is no need to rehearse his arguments here, as it is now widely recognized that these final words are annotations separate from the poem. We may compare *lamnaṣṣēaḥ bingînôt* in the Psalms.[539] In the Psalms, the Masoretes have given *lamnaṣṣēaḥ* a conjunctive accent, linking the two instructions more closely. Here, however, *lamnaṣṣēaḥ* is given a disjunctive accent, perhaps suggesting that the Masoretes read *bingînôtāy* as having a first-person pronominal suffix (see the translation note). Delitzsch insists that this is the correct reading, disallowing the use of a construct form here in place of an absolute (see the translation note). He explores what the meaning of the suffix could be and concludes that the prophet is directing that he himself should accompany the performance of the prayer with his string playing.[540] This would seem to imply that Habakkuk was a Levite, which is possible, and claimed in some manuscripts of the apocryphal work Bel and the Dragon (1:1). Delitzsch points out that Jeremiah and Ezekiel were priests too, although without observing that neither of them ministered in the temple. The psalmlike features of the book of Habakkuk in the first and third chapter suggest great familiarity with the composition of psalms. If the instruction were original, and if the first-person suffix were to be read, one could speculate that Habakkuk felt the need to ensure proper performance of the prayer given political opposition to faithful YHWH prophets (cf. Jer 26). But in my view, even then it seems implausible that Habakkuk would have planned for this prayer to be performed in the temple only as long as he was available to pull (pluck) the strings.

More likely, the musical instructions here and the three occurrences of *selah* in the prayer are later additions, part of the transmission of the text as

538. Franz Delitzsch, *Habakuk*, 200–202.

539. Superscripts of Pss 4; 6; and with defective spelling (*bingînōt*), 54; 55; 67; 76; cf. *lamnaṣṣēaḥ 'al-nəgînat* (maybe: "alongside string music") in Ps 61.

540. Franz Delitzsch, *Habakuk*, 203–5.

part of the worship life of the people of God, presumably after the destruction of temple and city.[541] Nogalski believes that "the tendency of scholars to assume this chapter exhibits a literary unity with the remainder of the book is extremely difficult to reconcile with the peculiar transmission history it has received."[542] He struggles to imagine that anyone would give this chapter a "cultic treatment" without also reworking other parts of the book, of which there is no trace.[543] But this should not be difficult at all. On the contrary, why should a decision to use part of a prophetic book in liturgical ways only be permissible if the whole book was given a liturgical (or priestly) makeover? The *Book of Odes*, which collects prayers and songs (canticles) from the Old and New Testaments, testifies to such secondary use of portions of biblical books, even if this did not lead to the addition of liturgical notes in other places (see further below in the reflection). In my reading of Habakkuk, there are indeed close links between its three chapters, and there is development in the book. The prophet moves from vehement protest (ch. 1) to a prayer that combines petition, awe, and rejoicing (ch. 3) in response to a revelation that reaffirms that faithfulness will have its rewards (ch. 2). If the prayer with which the book receives its climax is commended for public use, this does not mean that the opening protest must also be sung as part of cultic worship or that *selah* notations should be added to ch. 2 as well. There is, of course, an added complexity in the view that Hab 3 has a significant place both within the book of Habakkuk and within the liturgical life of God's people. But such complexity exists with any view, whether the setting within the book or the one within the cult is considered the original.

Commentary

19b *For the leader* likely means that the prayer enters a collection that belongs to the official who oversees the worship of God's people with regard to its music. It is possible that in some of its occurrences in the Psalms the meaning of *lamnaṣṣēaḥ* is narrowed by the phrase that follows it, but in spite of the use of a conjunctive accent, this seems unlikely for *binginôt* in Pss 4:1 and 6:1, given the preposition used. The disjunctive accent on *lamnaṣṣēaḥ* here

541. Cf. Nogalski, *Redactional Processes*, 155–58. I am not convinced that the superscription necessarily belongs in the same category, although this is possible.

542. Nogalski, *Redactional Processes*, 158. Cf. the observations in Fabry, *Habakuk*, 88–89, 96–101, which, however, he relativizes later (124–26) in favor of differentiating between material that the prophet himself included in a first redaction of the basic layer on the one hand and the hymn in 3:3–7 on the other hand, which, he believes, was added in a late-exilic or early postexilic redaction.

543. Nogalski, *Redactional Processes*, 159.

confirms that the Masoretes did not read the phrase as designating a leader of the string playing.

With string music reminds us of the prominence of strings in ancient Judah. While it is likely that horns, flutes, tambourines, shakers/rattles, and cymbals all played a role in Judah's sung worship (suggested possibly by 2 Sam 6:5 and Ps 150), string music seems to have been the most typical to accompany the performance of psalms.[544] *With string music* is used in musical notations with half a dozen psalms (see the translation note). In addition, one of the unclear musical terms, often transliterated "Sheminith" (Pss 6:1; 12:1), might refer to a lyre with eight strings or perhaps tuned an octave higher or lower (cf. 1 Chr 15:21).[545] Strings were presumably used to stir as well as calm emotions (see 1 Sam 16:14–23 for the latter). They can certainly be used with thanksgiving songs (cf. Isa 38:20).[546] But enthusiasm might have been conveyed musically more readily by the use of trumpets and horns (cf. 2 Chr 15:12–15), maybe accompanied by cymbals, harps, and lyre (cf. 1 Chr 15:28) rather than *string music* alone.[547] String music is well suited to more meditative prayer (cf. Ps 49:4[5]; 77:6[7]).[548] In Hab 3, the music might make space for such meditation. It probably served to fill in the pauses (interludes) indicated with *selah* and also to accentuate the drama of the theophany. Were the latter its primary intention, however, a wider range of instruments would probably have been specified. Of course, all this must remain speculative, and one must acknowledge that none of the annotations in the Psalms specify an orchestra.

Reflection

The annotations at the end of ch. 3 encourage us not only to read the prayer in the context of the book of Habakkuk but to imagine it as part of the sung worship of God's people. Indeed, it is no surprise that the chapter is found among the odes appended to the Psalms in Codex Alexandrinus and a few

---

544. The Hebrew word translated "psalm" (*mizmôr*) designates a song accompanied by instrumental music. Maybe the main alternative to strings were flutes.

545. See Kolyada, *Compendium*, 141–43, for an overview of explanations.

546. I am not aware of any study examining whether the psalms that carry a musical notation referring to *string music* share any characteristics. Note that if Thirtle (*Titles*) is right, these notations belong to the psalms preceding the ones to which they are now attached. This would give us Pss 3; 5; 53; 54; 60; 66; 75 as the relevant group.

547. In other places, too, mirthful and celebratory music is accompanied by tambourine as well as lyre (e.g., Gen 31:27; Neh 12:27), and a fuller range of instruments is used in the martial context of Isa 30:31–32.

548. Strings are also used with taunt songs in Job 30:9; Ps 69:12(13).

other manuscripts along with prayers from, for example, Exod 15, Deut 32, 1 Sam 2, and Isa 26.[549] This collection is usually thought to reflect Christian liturgical practice or traditions of prayer, although this may not have been its origin, and the relationship between the odes collected and odes used in liturgy is not entirely straightforward. Jeremiah T. Coogan recently argued that the anthology was originally designed to retell the biblical story in Scripture's own words.[550] In the early Latin tradition, Hab 3 was appointed for Matins on Fridays, suggesting that it was used to meditate on the cross more than to celebrate the resurrection.[551] In the Mozarabic Breviary (1502), the canticle of Habakkuk is appointed for Advent, hence in the context of anticipation rather than triumph.[552] This may have been prompted by the tradition of seeing in LXX Hab 3:2 ("You will be known between two living creatures") an expectation of the revelation of God in the fullness of time between the ox and ass of the nativity scene (cf. Isa 1:3).[553] The LXX rendering is reflected in the Old Latin text[554] but not in the Vulg. of Hab 3, which instead reflects the traditional Hebrew text here (*in medio annorum*, "in the midst of years"). The text was in fact interpreted in a number of ways by Latin-writing Christians (e.g., "between two covenants," namely Old and New Testament; "between two thieves" on the cross; "between Moses and Elijah" at the transfiguration).[555] The use of the prayer in more meditative than exuberant contexts agrees with my interpretation above of the use of strings to accompany it.

The church apparently never felt itself bound by the musical instructions in the Psalms. In any case, it could not readily follow the instructions in the postscript to Hab 3 because the Greek, Syriac, and Latin versions did not

549. James Mearns (*The Canticles of the Christian Church Eastern and Western in Early and Medieval Times* [Cambridge: Cambridge University Press, 1914], 22–23) offers a convenient list of MSS.

550. For a summary, see Jeremiah T. Coogan, "Biblical Odes," in *Textual History of the Bible*, ed. Matthias Henze and Frank Feder, vol. 2C (Leiden: Brill, 2019), 533–66.

551. Mearns, *Canticles*, 51. Meinrad Stenzel ("Altlateinische Canticatexte im Dodekapropheton," *ZNW* 46 [1954]: 31–60) notes use on Easter Eve (34) and in the Easter Vigil (35).

552. Mearns, *Canticles*, 74.

553. There is no reference to ox and ass in the canonical gospels, but "the fifth-century Gospel of Pseudo-Matthew (a Latin adaptation of the Proto-Evangelium of Pseudo-James) identifies an ox and ass as the fulfillment of 'what was spoken by Kabam (Habakkuk) the Prophet' (14:2)" (Coggins and Han, *Six Minor Prophets*, 76).

554. *In medio duorum animalium cognosceris*. See Stenzel, "Altlateinische Canticatexte," 45. The Old Latin text continued to be transmitted among the canticles so that there are some notable differences between the Song of Habakkuk and the Vulg. text of Hab 3.

555. See, e.g., Augustine, *City of God* 17. Readers in antiquity readily accepted a plurality of interpretations as legitimate.

render them.[556] I am familiar with settings of Hab 3:17–18 to music—for example by Jesse Strickland (Hymn of Habakkuk, for SATB choirs, premiered September 2014). These verses also inspired hymns such as Charles Wesley's "Away My Unbelieving Fear!" and the fourth verse of William Cowper's "Sometimes a Light Surprises." But the chapter as a whole is not prominent in the church liturgies with which I am familiar.[557] Boniface Ramsey, the editor of the New City edition of Augustine's *City of God*, expresses surprise at the detailed explanation Augustine offers for "the relatively uncelebrated prayer of Habakkuk, while giving much less attention to better-known passages from other prophets."[558] This likely exposes the relativity of "better-known" and suggests that Augustine expected his first readers to be more familiar with Hab 3 than many of his readers today would be. One of the roles of hymns and songs is arguably to commit to our memories truths that we hope will nourish us again and again. The postscript suggests that this chapter belonged in this category for many who transmitted it early in its history. Today, it can still train and strengthen an analogical imagination and teach us typological thinking. A similar function is fulfilled by the allusions to the crossing of the Red Sea found in some liturgies and music written for baptism services. Habakkuk 3 links past and future in the belief that there are characteristic ways in which God acts. It is appropriate for Christian hymns and preaching to extend the lines further to include explicitly what we believe to be the most marvelous fear- and joy-inspiring news of all: God's coming in Christ.

A former student of mine and now pastor of a Baptist church wrote a hymn based on Hab 3. With his permission, I conclude this reflection with his version, sung to the tune Finlandia:[559]

> O Lord, your fame has long been known to me;
> Your deeds have made me stand in holy awe.
> And yet today we offer you this plea:

556. Habakkuk is depicted with a stringed instrument in the 1709 engraving *The Great Tableau of the World* by Romeyn de Hooghe; see Coggins and Han, *Six Minor Prophets*, 89. The Protestant artist would have had access to a Dutch Bible translation from the Hebrew text.

557. The postscript does not provide a rationale for considering Hab 3 more important than any of the psalms. But some psalms and Scriptural canticles have greater prominence than others in the church (e.g., by being used weekly), and Hab 3 seems to have been one of those in some parts of the church at some times.

558. Boniface Ramsey, ed., *The City of God, Books 11–22*, trans. William S. Babcock, The Works of Saint Augustine I/7 (New York: New City Press, 2013), 311.

559. The repetion of the final line arguably fulfills an equivalent function within hymn writing to the use of *selah* in Hab 3: letting selected phrases or thoughts sink in.

Your mighty deeds renew! Your fame restore!
In wrath remember mercy we implore,
In wrath remember mercy we implore.

Your glory fills both earth and highest heaven:
Your splendour burns, you send forth flashing rays;
Before your gaze the ancient hills lie broken;
From everlasting are your holy ways;
Your foes are left in sickness and dismay,
Your foes are left in sickness and dismay.

Was it the streams that caused your awesome wrath?
Was it the sea that fired your holy rage?
With brandished bow and quiver you went forth
As through the earth you strode your war to wage
Till you had slain the ruler of this age,
Till you had slain the ruler of this age.

It is for love that Christ fights in our stead;
It is for grace he waged that war of wars;
It is for us he pierces Satan's head
As on the cross our sentence he endures.
It is our victory that our Lamb secures,
It is our victory that our Lamb secures.

When I perceive the workings of the Lord,
My heart is quickened, and my limbs are numb.
Though harvest fails and no supplies are stored,
I will rejoice, and to His Strength succumb,
And patiently cry, "Come, Lord Jesus, Come!"
And patiently cry, "Come, Lord Jesus, Come!"

The Book of
ZEPHANIAH

Introduction

I. THE PROFILE OF THE BOOK

A. THE SUPERSCRIPTION

The most common superscription in the Book of the Twelve is "The word of YHWH that came to . . ." (Hos 1:1; Joel 1:1; Mic 1:1; Zeph 1:1; cf. Mal 1:1), a formula that is also used in three prophetic books that open with a narrative introduction rather than an actual superscription (Jonah 1:1; Hag 1:1; Zech 1:1; cf. Jer 1:2). It puts the emphasis on the divine origin of the message. An alternative superscription ties the material more closely to the prophet: "The words of Amos . . . that he saw" (1:1; cf. Jer 1:1, but note the continuation in v. 2), "the vision of Obadiah" (1; cf. Isa 1:1),[1] "the oracle that the prophet Habakkuk saw" (1:1; cf. Isa 2:1; 13:1).[2]

Because the superscription of Zephaniah is more typical than those in Nahum or Habakkuk, it has often been seen as evidence of Zephaniah's membership in an earlier collection of prophetic books. This is by no means certain, however. Because the argument depends in part on the (alleged) presence of Deuteronomistic phrasing, it will be more useful to take this up below in the commentary on 1:1, after the introduction to the historical context.

---

1. It is possible that "Obadiah" is not meant to properly identify the recipient of the revelation but is a kind of stage-name, in which case this heading would belong with the first category.

2. I have used the traditional renderings "vision" and "oracle" here, but they are not without problems; see fuller discussion in the introduction to Nahum (pp. 23–26) and in the commentary on Nah 1:1.

B. MACROSTRUCTURE

The segmentation of the text in masoretic manuscripts tends to follow formal criteria, with connecting phrases like "and it shall happen on that day" (e.g., 1:10) marking a new paragraph. Berlin follows the divisions of the Leningrad Codex except for separating the superscription from the body of the work, but she explicitly notes that in her view these do not reflect "compositional units" and implicitly denies that they shed any light on the literary structure of the book.[3] Levin observes, "Usually the literary nature of the book is explained as being a collection of short prophetic sayings, composed by pupils of the prophet or by later editors."[4] This seems to be true for much of German scholarship in particular, in which Zephaniah and other prophetic books are treated as anthologies of short, independent sayings. The isolated sayings are then interpreted, first of all, apart from their cotexts, and the resulting thematic diversity is seen as further proof of the theory. Irsigler claims that modern research must not give up this insight, which he attributes to Carl Steuernagel.[5] Steuernagel appealed to the opening phrases in 1:8, 10, 12 and the change between divine speech in the first person and speeches that refer to YHWH in the third person as proof that there are no extended prophetic speeches in Zephaniah.[6]

But his interpretation of the evidence is by no means universally accepted, and Irsigler overlooks the extent to which "the notion of prophets as 'maniacs' who cry out a few words and disappear" has been challenged.[7] Sweeney claims the precise opposite of Irsigler in concluding, "The interpretation of prophetic texts can no longer be based exclusively on the short, well-defined oracular unit, but requires the analysis of much longer rhetorical compositions that may or may not represent prophetic speeches."[8] Floyd notes that "the final compositional form often serves precisely to integrate the kinds of thematic contrasts that historical criticism has usually attempted to dissociate" and that "the book as a whole is no less dependent than its

---

3. Berlin, *Zephaniah*, 17–23.

4. Christoph Levin, "Zephaniah: How This Book Became Prophecy," in *Constructs of Prophecy in the Former and Latter Prophets and Other Texts*, ed. Lester L. Grabbe and Martti Nissinen, SBLANEM 4 (Atlanta: Society of Biblical Literature, 2011), 117.

5. Hubert Irsigler, *Zefanja*, HThKAT (Freiburg: Herder, 2002), 58.

6. Carl Steuernagel, *Lehrbuch der Einleitung in das Alte Testament mit einem Anhang über die Apokryphen und Pseudepigraphen* (Tübingen: Mohr Siebeck, 1912), 636.

7. Marvin A. Sweeney, "Zephaniah: A Paradigm for the Study of the Prophetic Books," *CurBS* 7 (1999): 132, with specific reference to Arvid S. Kapelrud, *The Message of the Prophet Zephaniah: Morphology and Ideas* (Oslo: Universitetsforlaget, 1975), 29.

8. Sweeney, "Zephaniah," 120.

individual units on forms that are typical of oral prophetic speech."[9] Levin
believes that the model that proceeds from the assumption that "a prophetic
tradition started with the preaching of an individual prophet in a particular
historical setting" and that any meaningful order within a book must derive
from secondary arrangement "does not fit in explaining the composition of
most prophetic books, because the single sayings are closely interwoven."[10]
His own criteria for separating layers, however, seem hardly different from
those he critiques. Floyd is skeptical about our ability to establish even the
endpoint of the production of the book (which might have been completed
in the early sixth century or later by an exilic or postexilic author), let alone
our ability to allocate phrases to different layers.[11] My own understanding and
approach to the book is similar to that of Berlin, Floyd, and Sweeney.[12] Like
them, I am disinclined to isolate smaller units from the overarching literary
context of the book of Zephaniah.

The superscription (1:1) is obviously a unit in its own right. It is followed
by a divine declaration of sweeping judgment on the world and then specifically on Judah and Jerusalem (1:2–6). A first address to the audience by the
prophet follows in v. 7, with an interjection that functions as an imperative,
before the sweeping judgment is described as a Day of YHWH (vv. 8–18).
This section reverses the order of the divine declaration, focusing first on
Jerusalem, then on the wider world. The second part of this speech can be
subdivided either by separating the poetic passage about the Day of YHWH
on humanity (vv. 14–18) from the more specific description of the situation
in Jerusalem (vv. 8–13) or by separating a *hush* section (vv. 7–10) from a
wail section (vv. 11–18). The latter option takes the (rhetorical) imperative
at the beginning of v. 11 as parallel to the interjection at the beginning of
v. 7.[13] It would highlight the double response expected of the people (hushed
reverence before YHWH; anguished realization of judgment). The former
option would give us a chiastic structure for 1:2–18 that focuses on the call
to silence:

---

9. Floyd, *Minor Prophets 2*, 174–75.

10. Christoph Levin, "Zephaniah," 117–18.

11. Cf. the caution expressed by Johannes Vlaardingerbroek, *Zephaniah*, HCOT (Leuven:
Peeters, 1999), 47. The assumed ability of (mostly German) scholars to sift out a dozen or so
redactional layers originating over several centuries in a text of fifty-three verses stretches
the credulity of many other scholars, mine included.

12. Apart from the commentaries, see Marvin A. Sweeney, "A Form-Critical Reassessment of the Book of Zephaniah," *CBQ* 53 (1991): 388–408; *King Josiah of Judah: The Lost
Messiah of Israel* (New York: Oxford University Press, 2001), 185–97.

13. See the discussion on the composition of 1:7–18 below. I also interpret *qôl* in vv. 10 and
14 as functionally imperative (*Listen!*), rhetorically grabbing the attention of the audience.

YHWH will cut off humanity (1:2–3)
YHWH will cut off sinners in Judah and Jerusalem (1:4–6)
    Call to silence (1:7)
Day of YHWH against Jerusalem (1:8–13)
Day of YHWH against humanity (1:14–18)

The two possibilities highlight different but equally valid aspects of the text. In my view, 1:2–18 looks like a single speech in which the judgment on Jerusalem is framed by judgment on the region. The rhetoric is meant to induce shock at the scale of the disaster to which both wailing and silence before YHWH are appropriate responses. It is perhaps worth pointing out that apparently none of the ancient and medieval manuscripts support a division between vv. 10 and 11, and only 8ḤevXIIgr supports a division between vv. 13 and 14. More commonly, and not without reason, phrases like *It shall happen on that day* (v. 10; cf. v. 12) are combined with paragraph breaks. The commentary below will keep vv. 7–18 together but offer a separate discussion for vv. 2–6.

The more substantial response to the announcement of punishment in 1:2–18 is spelled out in the next section. In masoretic manuscripts, 2:1–4 is set out as a paragraph,[14] but this is not uncontroversial. Because the opening speech (1:2–18) sets the scene for the imperatives in 2:1–3, and because v. 4 mentions the Philistines, as do the following verses (2:5–7), there has been some debate within scholarship about the delineation of units. (For further discussion, see the relevant composition sections below.) The imperatives in 2:1–3 are a climax in the book. Not only are they prepared for by the announcement in 1:2–18, but they are also in a sense motivated by much of what follows. Verse 4 can be seen as a placeholder for 2:5–15, which speaks of divine punishment on the world around Judah. The two instances of *Oy* in the book (2:5; 3:1) echo the bipartite description of the judgment, again first on the nations (2:5–15), then on Jerusalem (3:1ff.).

The segmentation of ch. 3 is also controversial. In the commentary, I will argue that 3:8, with its reuse of language and motifs from earlier in the book, seems to round off the section that predominantly speaks of judgment. Because 3:1–5 speaks to the same situation as 1:2–2:15 while 3:6–7 assumes a different rhetorical situation (i.e., after a substantial part of the threats in 2:5–15 had been realized), I take 3:1–5 and 3:6–8 as separate units. The im-

---

14. I have checked Codex Cairensis, Codex Babylonicus Petropolitanus, the Aleppo Codex, the Leningrad Codex, and Codex Reuchlianus. This division is already found in MurXII but not 8ḤevXIIgr.

peratives in 3:14 suggest to me, as well as to many others, that the final part of the book is best separated into 3:9–13 and 3:14–20.

Other than the superscription and perhaps 2:10–11 and 3:18–20, the book consists of poetry that mixes prophetic speech referring to YHWH in the third person and divine speech in which YHWH refers to himself in the first person. The presence of third-person references within divine speech (enallage), however, blurs the distinction.[15] The *utterance* formula (1:2, 3, 10; 2:9; 3:8) and *says YHWH* in 3:20 also remind readers of the presence of the prophet as the mediator of the divine word.[16] The distinction between prophetic and divine speech gives a richer texture to the communication, but it seems unwise to press the distinction. House, for whom this distinction is of great structural importance, ends up postulating a sharp break between 1:17 (the end of act one) and 1:18 (beginning of act two), treating all of 1:18–2:7 as a single soliloquy and claiming a change of scene in the middle of a sentence in 1:8. To my mind, these decisions are obviously wrong and demonstrate that the hypothesis is flawed. They are the result of his conclusion that the book of Zephaniah is a drama because it is not a work of epic or lyrical poetry. But it is not clear why Zephaniah must conform to one of these three genres.[17] It is difficult to make sense of his claim that it is "the shifting between characters in Zephaniah that produces the action" rather than YHWH's decision to punish and restore. Equally problematic is House's thesis that it is this alternating of divine and prophetic speech that causes "the conflict and resolution" in the drama.[18] The latter may relate to his observation that "while Yahweh announces judgment, it is the prophet who

15. See 1:5–6, 17; 3:9, 12. Paul R. House (*Zephaniah: A Prophetic Drama*, JSOTSup 69, BLS 16 [Sheffield: Almond Press, 1989], 122, 130) also considers 2:10 part of divine speech, in which case there would be another case of enallage; but 2:10–11 is better seen as a unit in analogy to other summary appraisals. See the commentary.

16. House (*Unity*, 60) treats these phrases as stage (or reader) directions separate from the prophetic voice, but there is no equivalent "says the prophet" (or similar) direction. His interpretation of the book as a drama forces him to postulate a third, narratorial voice above or behind those of YHWH and the prophet, ending up with three characters that are omniscient and omnipresent (cf. *Zephaniah*, 86–87). This seems to me one of the weaknesses of his theory.

17. House (*Zephaniah*, 106) also claims that, unlike "Ezekiel, Daniel, or Jeremiah," the book of Zephaniah "observes the three unities of drama: unity of place, unity of action, and unity of time." I am not convinced that the address to rebellious Jerusalem in ch. 1 and to "a bewildered remnant" in ch. 3 does indeed suggest unity of place and time (cf. *Zephaniah*, 67). But if true, this would raise the question about the character of Ezekiel, Daniel, and Jeremiah. These books can surely not be classified as epic or lyrical poetry either.

18. House, *Zephaniah*, 102. It may be relevant here that House eschews historical analysis, distancing himself from Luther and Calvin (10–11).

is the forerunner of kindness."[19] But this seems an exaggerated conclusion from the observation that the call to repentance and the first reference to a remnant come in prophetic rather than divine speech, even if the first indication of life beyond judgment among the nations in 2:11 is also in prophetic speech. House seems to consider 2:11 the complication that ushers in the crisis in his analysis of the plot as exposition (1:2–7), complication (1:8–2:11), crisis (2:13–3:5), resolution (3:6–13), and falling action (3:14–20).[20] None of these divisions are self-evident or well argued, and the analysis completely obscures the importance of 2:1–3, a passage that clearly occupies a climactic position within the book. In distinction from the book of Habakkuk, the prophet in this book is only ever heard as conveying a message from God. The shift between formally direct divine speech (which is also heard through human writing) and prophetically mediated divine speech is not without rhetorical effect in creating impressions of immediacy or mediation. It seems unwise, however, to consider it of decisive structural significance in this book. It makes sense to put the opening declaration of sweeping judgment in the mouth of God to give full force to it, and it makes sense that the *hush* is on the lips of the prophet, as is the call to seek YHWH in 2:1–3. But it is difficult to gainsay that the prophetic speech against Philistia (2:5–7) belongs more closely with the oracle against Moab and the Ammonites (2:8–11) and other announcements of the fate of nations than with 1:18 and 2:1–3, despite the fact that 2:8–9 are couched as divine speech.[21]

Earlier, Ivan J. Ball had argued for a different way of conceptualizing the unity of the book of Zephaniah.[22] He proposes that 2:1–7 imitates the shape of the book as follows:

> Warning of impending Day of YHWH (2:1–3 // 1:2–18)
> Destruction of the enemy (2:4 // 2:8–15)
> Woe and salvation (2:5–7 // 3:1–20)

19. House, *Zephaniah*, 81.

20. House, *Zephaniah*, 98–99. The omission of 2:12 appears to be a mistake. House here includes the verse in his discussion of 1:8–2:11 but considers it to open scene 3 of the second act (123), and in his summary on p. 126, he includes it in the "climax of crisis" section. (He reads it as a future threat—wrongly in my view.)

21. I do not object to including the first-person divine speech in 2:5 in the prophetic soliloquy because it can be heard as a citation. I object to the view that 1:18–2:7 is a single speech that belongs to a different scene from what precedes and follows.

22. His 1972 ThD dissertation (Graduate Theological Union, Berkeley, CA) was published as *A Rhetorical Study of Zephaniah* (Berkeley: BIBAL, 1988); cf. Ivan J. Ball, "The Rhetorical Shape of Zephaniah," in *Perspectives on Language and Text: Essays and Poems in Honor of Francis I. Andersen on His Sixtieth Birthday*, ed. Edgar Conrad and Edward Newing (Winona Lake, IN: Eisenbrauns, 1987), 155–65.

He was able to find some interesting correspondences throughout (e.g., eight "significant terms" in the same sequence in the last section and four other "key words" not in sequence). Nevertheless, his proposal has not won a following. "The main problem," notes Floyd, "is that Ball's approach lacks any criteria for determining which of the many things noted by him are more salient indications of how the composition is organized."[23] The four "key words" shared by 2:5–7 and 3:1–20, even if not in sequence, are indeed nothing of the sort.[24] More interesting are the eight "significant terms" that all have a high frequency rating in Zephaniah compared with other biblical books. They include two phrases (*without inhabitant, restore fortunes*), two verbs (*to pasture, to lie down* [also 2:14]), an interjection (*Oy*, "Woe"), and a noun (*remnant* [also 2:9]), which Ball combines with the verb *to leave a remnant* (1:4; 3:12; not in 2:5–7), and an admittedly very common noun, *nation* (8× in Zephaniah). The expression "YHWH their/your God" (2:7; 3:17) also has a higher density in Zephaniah than in any of the major prophets; Jonah and Haggai, two shorter books, also have two occurrences, Micah has four and Joel seven.[25] If Ball offers no clear criteria for deciding which verbal parallels are structurally significant, the words are nevertheless not randomly chosen. (See the excursus below.) Still, one wonders whether the signal character of the eight "significant" verbal parallels is strong enough to cover the diversity of material in ch. 3.

In fact, for both 2:5–7 and 3:1–20, "woe and salvation" looks like a big, catch-all phrase that tells us little about the nature of these two sections. In 2:5–7, the woe is for one group, salvation for another. The situation in 3:1–20 is more complex. While both sections begin with "woe" (*Oy* in my translation) and end with a reference to fortunes being restored, the units in ch. 3 (prophetic *Oy* speech in vv. 1–5, divine judgment speech in vv. 6–8, divine announcement of salvation in vv. 9–13, the prophetic call to rejoice in vv. 14–18, and the final divine speech in vv. 18–20) have no corresponding parts in 2:5–7. All in all, Ball's division of Zephaniah into 1:1; 1:2–18; 2:1–7; 2:8–18; 3:1–20 is most questionable in those places where it is most unusual, namely

---

23. Floyd, *Minor Prophets 2*, 168.

24. Two are extremely common words—one a shared root (*word, speak*), another used with different references (*land/earth*). *Pqd* (also 1:8–9, 12) is a significant word but used in a different sense in 2:7 (*attend*; cf. Ball: "visit") and 3:7 (*appointed*; cf. Ball: "entrusted"), and only one (*evening*) does not also occur elsewhere in the book.

25. Density is counted as number of occurrences in relation to number of words in the book. Thus the 40 occurrences in Jeremiah (the longest book of the Bible at about 30,095 words) give a density of 0.133%. I used BibleWorks 10 to ascertain this, and the results should be accurate for the Leningrad Codex. Zephaniah's two occurrences count as 0.192% of the book's 1,044 words. In Jonah, the divine name followed by *'ĕlōhîm* with pronominal suffix counts for more than 0.5% of words, in Deuteronomy more than 1.5%.

in the proposed strong disjunction between 2:7 and 2:8 combined with the lack of subdivisions in the last third of the book. In my view, the warning of the impending Day of YHWH is more closely coupled with the destruction of the nations because the decisive divine intervention is from the beginning said to affect nations other than Judah and Jerusalem while being focused on the latter. The unit that presents the book in a nutshell is more plausibly 2:1–4, which combines the warning to the elites (2:1–2) with hope for the poor (2:3) and an appeal to see the signs of judgment in other nations (2:4). We have a similar combination of motifs in long form in 1:2–18 with 2:5–18 (omitting the "nutshell" passage 2:1–4) and in shorter form in 3:1–13, the latter with a significant expansion of what salvation implies, which had previously only been hinted at. This future hope is then elaborated in 3:14–20.

Dorsey identifies seven major units in symmetric configuration.[26] This highlights that the book begins with "coming judgement upon the wicked of Jerusalem" (1:2–6) and ends with "coming restoration of Jerusalem and its fortunes" (3:8–20).[27] It underscores that the judgment is focused on corrupt leaders (1:7–13; 3:1–7)[28] and includes in it "all nations" (1:14–18; 2:4–15).[29] Plausibly, it makes the "call to repentance" (2:1–3)[30] the center of the book. If we judge the design by the question whether it accurately reflects the emphases of the book, this is not far wrong. But the symmetric design obscures that judgment and restoration are in fact asymmetrical. The judgment is a divine act that has a rationale in human doing. This is why there are motivated imperatives in 2:1–4. But the promised restoration does not flow from human repentance. It is therefore problematic to include 3:9–20 in a structure centered on 2:1–3. This also fails to give proper weight to the new imperatives in ch. 3.

I am not convinced that Zephaniah has an intricate design in which different units clearly correspond to each other in a way that is rhetorically significant. The hierarchy of the different units and subunits is debatable because it is not clearly marked. Thus, 1:2–18 could be seen as at the same level as 2:1–4 and 2:5–15, but subunits in either or both 1:2–18 and 2:5–15 could be seen as on the same level as each other and 2:1–4. The outline adopted

26. David A. Dorsey, *The Literary Structure of the Old Testament: A Commentary on Genesis – Malachi* (Grand Rapids: Baker Academic, 1999), 310–14.

27. Note that 1:2–3 have a wider perspective than (Judah and) Jerusalem and that 1:2–6 does not specifically single out "the wicked" (i.e., it is not made clear that there are any in Jerusalem who are not wicked); 3:8 speaks of judgment, and there is salvation for people beyond Jerusalem in 3:9ff.

28. Note that 3:6–7 seem to go beyond a focus on leaders.

29. The wider perspective, beyond Judah and Jerusalem, is only evident in 1:17–18. Arguably, 2:4 belongs with 2:1–3, and note the hints of a positive future in 2:5–15, absent in ch. 1.

30. Only 2:1–2 is a call to repentance; 2:3 is a call to endurance.

in this commentary follows what seem to be clear divisions of the text, but the decision to treat some divisions as marking distinct units (e.g., 1:2–6 treated separately from 1:7–18), while others are ignored in favor of a larger unit (2:5–15) has as much to do with the rhetoric of the commentary as the rhetoric of Zephaniah. This division offers a convenient way of highlighting various features of the book:

A. Superscription (1:1)
B. Declaration of Sweeping Judgment (1:2–6)
C. Announcement of the Day of YHWH (1:7–18)
D. Call to Submit to God's Judgment (2:1–4)
E. Announcements of the Fate of Nations (2:5–15)
F. Jerusalem Will Share the Fate of Nations (3:1–5)
G. Reaffirmation of Comprehensive Judgment (3:6–8)
H. Announcement of a Future Beyond Judgment (3:9–13)
I. Celebration of Life Beyond Judgment (3:14–17)
J. Promise of Salvation (3:18–20)

EXCURSUS: SIGNIFICANT WORDS IN ZEPHANIAH

The words that are notable due to their relative density in Zephaniah are *yôm* (*day*), which is used twenty-one times; *qārôb* (1:7, 14 [2×]) and *qrb* (3:2–3, 5, 11–12, 15, 17) to speak of nearness three and seven times; the combined five occurrences of *'ādām* (*humanity*) and *'ădāmâ* (*ground*) in 1:2–3, 17; *šəmāmâ* (*desolation*, 1:13; 2:4, 9, 13) and *'ap* (2:2–3, 8), both used four times; the punning roots *'sp* (*to gather*, 1:2; 3:8, 18) and *swp* (*to make an end*, 1:2–3); the words for assembling (*qbṣ*, 3:8, 19–20) and lying down (*rbṣ*, 2:7, 14; 3:13), as well as *r'h* (*to pasture*), are used three times each, as is the noun *hebel* (*portion*, 2:5–7); *pqd* in its various senses (1:8–9, 12; 2:7; 3:7), for which Zephaniah has the highest density within the Hebrew Bible; Zephaniah also has this distinction for the root *ksp*—used twice for *silver* (*kesep*, 1:11, 18) and once as a verb (2:1, translated *longing* by me)—and for (*bə*)*terem* (*before*, 3× in 2:2); *krt* (*to cut off*, 1:3–4, 11; 2:6; 3:6–7), which within the Minor Prophets is used more often only in Zechariah (7×), a book more than four times the size of Zephaniah; *mišpāṭ* (*decree/justice*, 2:3; 3:5, 8, 15; cf. *špṭ* in 3:3). Zephaniah is also in the top five in terms of density for using *šēm* (*name*, 1:4, 14; 3:9, 12, 19–20) and *nə'um-yhwh* (*utterance of YHWH*, 1:2–3, 10; 2:9; 3:8).[31] Because *dāg* (*fish*) is not a common word, its two occurrences in Zephaniah (1:3, 10) are

---

31. Also for *nə'um* considered on its own. While *'ereṣ* (*land/earth*) is used eight times in the book (1:18; 2:3, 5, 11; 3:8, 19–20), this is not particularly unusual.

noteworthy. It is found more often (3×) only in Jonah (unsurprisingly, given the narrative) and Nehemiah (two of which are references to the Fish Gate). Zephaniah's use of *dāg* can be added to a group of terms relating to water, namely *yām* (*sea*, 1:3; 2:5–6), *nahăr* (*river*, 3:10) and *'iy* ("coastland," 2:11).

II. THE HISTORICAL SETTING OF THE BOOK

The most detailed case for an early date of the earliest material within Zephaniah has been made by Irsigler.[32] He believes that the (Assyrian-Aramean inspired) syncretism of which 1:4–5 speaks was no longer an issue after Josiah's reforms. Jeremiah, however, seems to have condemned similar practices later (2:8; 8:2; 19:5, 13; 32:35). Irsigler also believes that the failure to address the king is best explained by assuming that he was still a minor. In my view, the absence of the king in the prophecy of punishment is an argument, even if not a decisive one, against dating the material to the time of Jehoiakim, as has been urged by some.[33] But Josiah's piety could well be an alternative reason for leaving him out of the condemnation so that the king's absence from the list does not offer any real clue to fixing the prophecy early or late in Josiah's reign. Like Irsigler (and others), I read 1:12 as looking back to an event that has already happened—the destruction of Thebes with which the Nubian rule of Egypt came to an end—and 1:13 as anticipating the fall of Nineveh. This puts Zephaniah's prophecy in a similar timeframe as Nahum's. But unlike Irsigler, I do not believe that there are firm grounds for dating the prophecy to a specific decade between 663 and 612. Irsigler even wonders whether the report that Josiah consulted Huldah rather than Zephaniah or Jeremiah (2 Kgs 22:13, 14–20) indicates that Zephaniah was no longer active at the time. Others might see it as an indication that Zephaniah had not yet been active. It is doubtful, however, that we should conclude anything from the non-consultation of Zephaniah (note the reference to a plurality of prophets in 2 Kgs 23:2). Perhaps the best argument for a pre-reform dating in relation to activities that are condemned in the book is the observation that 1:8–9 suggest cultivation of a foreign lifestyle even among government officials, which one would expect Josiah to have ended. But the accounts of Josiah's reforms make no reference to the specifics mentioned in 1:8–9, and it is therefore by no means certain that these were stopped by Josiah, who

---

32. Irsigler, *Zefanja*, 67–70; cf. Roberts, *Nahum*, 32–34; Patterson, *Nahum*, 275–77.

33. See Irsigler, *Zefanja*, 68. I also agree with Irsigler that neither 1:4 (misunderstood as presuming that some action against Baal worship has already been taken) nor 1:12 (misunderstood as expressing disappointment with Josiah's reform) is evidence that the prophecy has to be dated subsequent to Josiah's reform.

may either not have seen the urgency to do so or felt unable to pursue the reform so far.

The presence of Deuteronomic language is often adduced as an argument for a date subsequent to the reemergence of "the Book of the Law." But this is not as decisive as it may seem at first, even if we allow for a relationship between the Book of the Law and Deuteronomy.[34] First, while Josiah appears to have started the reform prior to the discovery of the Book of the Law,[35] the discovery was a major impetus shaping the course of the reforms, and it is not inconceivable that Zephaniah's prophecies went alongside the reform movement rather than preceding or following it. Second, phraseology that is particularly associated with Deuteronomy need not have been unknown in the absence of Deuteronomy. Third, the possibility that Deuteronomic phrases belong to a later layer that supplemented or revised pre-reform prophecies cannot be excluded. In any case, the identification of such language is not straightforward. Thus, to destroy "from the face of the earth" in 1:3 has been identified as Deuteronomic (cf. Deut 6:15),[36] but Zephaniah is more often considered to be indebted to the story of the flood here (Gen 6:7; 7:4; cf. 8:8; see also 4:14). In fact, the distribution of the thirteen uses of the phrase does not suggest a specific influence, and the enumeration of animals in v. 3 similarly can be found in a wide variety of contexts.[37] The reference to "those who bow down . . . to the host of heaven" and do so (possibly burning incense) "on the roofs" in 1:5 may be Deuteronomistic,[38] but the phraseology is not indebted to Deuteronomy itself. The "frustration formula" in 1:13 does have a close parallel in Deuteronomy (cf. 28:30, 39),[39] but "[not] to receive correction"

---

34. The hypothesis that "the book of the law [of YHWH given through Moses]" (2 Kgs 22:8 // 2 Chr 34:14) that the priest Hilkiah passed on to King Josiah via the scribe Shaphan bears a close relationship to what we know of as the book of Deuteronomy is not securely established. See the short excursus below.

35. This is often considered the perspective of 2 Chronicles only but seems to me implied in 2 Kings as well, which reports repairs to the temple prior to Josiah's encounter with the document. This is not to deny the differences between the accounts.

36. Moshe Weinfeld, *Deuteronomy and the Deuteronomic School* (Oxford: Clarendon Press, 1972; repr., Winona Lake, IN: Eisenbrauns, 1992), 346–47. Weinfeld's list of instances of "Deuteronomic phraseology" (320–65) includes more than 200 phrases, of which only three are listed as finding an echo in Zephaniah.

37. Vlaardingerbroek, *Zephaniah*, 56–57; cf. Irsigler, *Zefanja*, 99–100, and see below.

38. Weinfeld, *Deuteronomy*, 321–22. For worship to the host of heaven, cf. Deut 4:19; 17:3 and 2 Kgs 17:16; 21:3, 5; Jer 8:2; 19:13. Reference to incense is absent in Zephaniah; "on the roofs" compares with incense burning in Jer 19:13 (to the host of heaven) and 32:29 (to Baal).

39. This is Vlaardingerbroek's expression (*Zephaniah*, 22–23). Cf. the first two items in Robertson's list (*Nahum*, 254), but note my comment on Amos 5:11 below. For a differently phrased frustration formula, see, e.g., Mic 6:14–15.

in 3:2, 7 does not, with parallels found in Jeremiah instead.[40] Indeed, even on its own, *mûsar* is used only once in Deuteronomy (11:2). The portrayal of the Day of YHWH in 1:15 has similarities in Deut 4:11; 28:53, 55, 57 but need not be indebted to it, not least given that the similarities are not exclusive. Thus, for example, use of the phrase *a day of distress and anguish* hardly requires knowledge of Deut 28. It is arguably closer to Job 15:24; Pss 25:17; 107:6, 13, 19, 28, although it need not be dependent on them either. The words *darkness and gloom* (*ḥōšek wa'ăpēlâ*) occur together in Exod 10:22 (and Isa 58:10; 59:9; Joel 2:2) but not in Deuteronomy; only *cloudiness and cloudy blackness* (*'ānān wa'ărāpel*) has a direct parallel in Deuteronomy (4:11).

Vlaardingerbroek, stressing the difference in style between Zephaniah and Deuteronomy (prophetic versus homiletical), invites us to consider further "examples (cf. Zeph 1:18 with Deut 32:21f.; Zeph 3:5 with Deut 32:4; Zeph 3:17 with Deut 28:63; 30:9; Zeph 3:19 with Deut 26:19)."[41] Dietrich discerns Deuteronomic language only in secondary additions in 1:6, 13b; 2:8; 3:2.[42] Hadjiev offers a careful examination of claims about the Deuteronomistic character of Zeph 1:2–3:13 and finds them wanting.[43] He considers it "safe to conclude that Zephaniah, unlike Amos, never underwent any significant Deuteronomistic redactions . . . and is unlikely to have been part of a Deuteronomistic corpus of prophetic books during the exile."[44] We may

---

40. Weinfeld, *Deuteronomy*, 352. Weinfeld compares these verses and Jer 2:30; 5:3; 7:28 with Jer 17:23; 32:33; 35:13 but notes that the phrase "seems to be rooted in the didactic sphere," comparing Prov 1:3; 8:10; 24:32. Jeremiah 7:28 offers a particularly close parallel to Zeph 3:2.

41. Vlaardingerbroek, *Zephaniah*, 23; cf. Robertson, *Nahum*, 254–55, with more examples, of which the motif of walking like the blind (Zeph 1:17; Deut 28:29) is worth considering, as it is not clearly attested earlier in the Bible, except without use of the word "blind" in Prov 4:19 (cf. Job 5:14; 12:25) and assuming that Zephaniah had no access to Isa 59:10.

42. Walter Dietrich, *Nahum, Habakkuk, Zephaniah*, IECOT (Stuttgart: Kohlhammer, 2016), 190. Dietrich holds to the idea of a Deuteronomistic book of the four (Hosea, Amos, Micah, Zephaniah), for which the similarities of the respective headings are allegedly an indicator. He does not interact with scholars questioning the idea, such as Tchavdar S. Hadjiev, "'Book of the Twelve' Hypothesis," 325–338, or Christoph Levin, "Das 'Vierprophetenbuch': Ein exegetischer Nachruf," *ZAW* 123 (2011): 221–35.

43. Hadjiev, "Zephaniah," 326–28.

44. Hadjiev, "Zephaniah," 328. Cf. Nicholas R. Werse, *Reconsidering the Book of the Four: The Shaping of Hosea, Amos, Micah, and Zephaniah as an Early Prophetic Collection*, BZAW 517 (Berlin: de Gruyter, 2019), 250–84. On the Deuteronomistic movement, see, e.g., Rainer Albertz, *A History of Israelite Religion in the Old Testament Period*, vol. 1 (London: SCM Press, 1994), 195–231; Norbert Lohfink, "Gab es eine deuteronomistische Bewegung?" in *Studien zum Deuteronomium und zur deuteronomistischen Literatur III*, SBAB 20 (Stuttgart: KBW, 1995), 65–142.

note that already Laato had concluded his comparison of the relevant texts with the observation that "the pictures of the religious life of Judah at the beginning of Josiah's reign given in 2 Kgs, Jer and Zeph correspond quite well even though the terminology used in them is different."[45] In sum, while it is possible to discern from the language used indications in favor of dating (some of) Zephaniah before or after Josiah's reform, none of them constitute firm evidence in either direction.[46]

EXCURSUS: FINDING THE BOOK OF THE LAW

The story of how Hilkiah found the (or "a") Book of the Law[47] in the temple while money was handed to the workers engaged in repairing the temple (2 Kgs 22:3–13; 2 Chr 34:14–21) raises a number of questions.[48] Many readers are convinced of at least one thing: "Finding the Book of the Law means finding Deuteronomy"[49] or an earlier incarnation of the work known to us as Deuteronomy. Apparently already Athanasius, Chrysostom, Jerome, and Theodoret identified the Book of the Law with Deuteronomy,[50] while Jo-

---

45. Antti Laato, *Josiah and David Redivivus: The Historical Josiah and the Messianic Expectations of Exilic and Postexilic Times*, ConBOT 33 (Stockholm: Almqvist & Wiksell, 1992), 42.

46. Cf. Vlaardingerbroek, *Zephaniah*, 15–17. Note that Werse (*Reconsidering*, 261–67) argues against dependence of Zeph 1:4–5 on 2 Kgs 23.

47. The literature on Josiah's reform and the Book of the Law is extensive. See, e.g., Gary N. Knoppers, *The Reign of Jeroboam, the Fall of Israel, and the Reign of Josiah*, vol. 2 of *Two Nations Under God: The Deuteronomistic History of Solomon and the Dual Monarchies*, HSM 53 (Atlanta: Scholars Press, 1994), 121–69 (on the scroll), 171–228 (on the reforms); W. Boyd Barrick, *The King and the Cemeteries: Towards a New Understanding of Josiah's Reform*, VTSup 88 (Leiden: Brill, 2002); various contributions in Lester L. Grabbe, ed., *Good Kings and Bad Kings: The Kingdom of Judah in the Seventh Century BCE*, LHBOTS 393 (London: T&T Clark, 2005); Nadav Na'aman, "The 'Discovered Book' and the Legitimation of Josiah's Reform," *JBL* 130 (2011): 47–62; Lauren A. S. Monroe, *Josiah's Reform and the Dynamics of Defilement: Israelite Rites of Violence and the Making of a Biblical Text* (New York: Oxford University Press, 2011). Monroe argues that the original account of Josiah's reforms in 2 Kgs 23 was composed by the same group that was responsible for the Holiness Code (Lev 17–26), later edited by Deuteronomists. This has the potential to reshape the discussion significantly.

48. Cf. David Henige, "Found But Not Lost: A Skeptical Note on the Document Discovered in the Temple Under Josiah," *JHebS* 7 (2007): art. 1, doi:10.5508/jhs.2007.v7.a1; Henige focuses on 2 Kings.

49. Johannes Bugenhagen (1485–1558), cited from Derek Cooper and Martin J. Lohrmann, *Reformation Commentary on Scripture: Old Testament*, vol. 5 (Downers Grove: IVP Academic, 2016), 501.

50. Jack R. Lundbom, "The Lawbook of the Josianic Reform," *CBQ* 38 (1976): 293, citing Eberhard Nestle, "Das Deuteronomium und 2 Könige 22," *ZAW* 22 (1902): 170–71, 312–13. Cf.

sephus pluralized it to *tais hierais biblois tais Mōuseos* ("the sacred books of Moses"), presumably understanding the reference to be to the entire Pentateuch.[51] Critical scholarship since the nineteenth century has sought to define a *Urdeuteronomium*, an earlier, shorter form of Deuteronomy that could more readily fit on a scroll that could be "lost" and "found" somewhere in the temple.

Philip R. Davies comments:

> The language and ideology of the framework of 2 Kings is Deuteronomistic, and even before Noth's theory of the 'Deuteronomistic History' it could have been realized that any *Deuteronomistic* account of the finding of a law book would present that law book as *Deuteronomy* (rather than, say, Leviticus, or the 'Covenant Code' of Exodus). The writer of the law book story wishes to make it clear that in the days of the kings of Judah, the scroll of Deuteronomy, which had been lost temporarily, was recovered and used as the basis of a religious reform, and with the full authority of a Davidic king, no less.[52]

But while one can expect that a history whose language is shaped by Deuteronomy would describe a king's enthusiastic response to the word of God in terms borrowed from Deuteronomy, it is less clear that this means that the author necessarily wishes us to identify the Book of the Law specifically with Deuteronomy.

The account in 2 Kgs 22–23 does indeed place most of the reforming action in the wake of Josiah's encounter with the Book of the Law, thus portraying him as responsive to the word of God. But the narrative need not be and arguably "cannot be an exact historical account of the order of events in Josiah's time."[53] Readers who are aware of the literary conventions that would have allowed the author to be flexible with chronology in ways that would not be acceptable in modern historiography do not need to believe that Josiah was completely ignorant of the requirements of ortho-

---

Marco Conti, ed., *1–2 Kings, 1–2 Chronicles, Ezra, Nehemiah, Esther*, ACCS (Downers Grove: InterVarsity Press, 2008), for Isho'dad of Merv as identifying the book with Deuteronomy (230). Lundbom argues that the scroll that Hilkiah found was Deut 32.

51. Josephus, *Ant.* 10.58; cf. John Mayer, *Many Commentaries in One: Joshua–Esther* (London: Legatt & Coates, 1647), 310: "all the books of *Moses* here called the book of the Law."

52. Philip R. Davies, "Josiah and the Law Book," in Grabbe, *Good Kings*, 69–70. See Knoppers, *Reign of Jeroboam*, 123–24, on the issue of Deuteronomy, which narrowly circumscribes royal power, being forcefully implemented by a king.

53. Laato, *Josiah*, 44, following Würthwein und Hofmann in this respect. He notes that the author "followed the order of presentation used in Deut. 12."

dox YHWH worship prior to having the Book of the Law read to him. The account in 2 Chr 34, which has Josiah being presented with this document in the midst of being engaged in reform, may well present the historical order of events more exactly.[54] In modern times, the identification is often based on the similarities between the requirements in Deuteronomy and the reforms undertaken by Josiah, although not always.[55] But even the narrative in 2 Kings does not link the two quite so tightly. The alternative designation, "the book of the covenant" (2 Kgs 23:2), suggests an emphasis on the covenant between YHWH and his people. Its contents suggested to the king that YHWH must be very angry with his people, who had clearly failed for generations to keep the terms of the covenant (2 Kgs 22:13; 2 Chr 34:21). Readers may thus assume that the document contained some serious threats to covenant breaking as well as stipulations for God's people (cf. 2 Kgs 23:3), including an injunction to keep Passover (2 Kgs 23:21). The removal of mediums, wizards, and so on is described as a consequence of following God's law (2 Kgs 23:24), and so readers may wonder whether the document contained specific references to some of these practices. Focusing only on what the narrative implies about the contents of the document, it seems that something like the Covenant Code (Exod 20–23) or the Holiness Code (Lev 17–26) would be just as suitable as the book of Deuteronomy or a corpus such as Deut 5–26. The only place where one could attempt to identify definite verbal links between what the narrative implies about the contents of the book and a specific law code is 2 Kgs 23:24, but this does not offer conclusive evidence.[56]

In my view, the accounts in 2 Kings and 2 Chronicles do not imply that the document must have been (accidentally) lost rather than (deliberately) hidden, nor that it was necessarily an autograph of great age rather than a credible copy, or even that its contents had been completely unknown to everyone at the time. Ancient readers did not seem to think so either. Those in antiquity who identified the temple scroll specifically with Deuteronomy would have assumed that other parts of the Pentateuch had been available. Josephus speaks of Josiah making use of "his natural wisdom and discern-

54. Cf. Laato, *Josiah*, 44–47. Note that the decision to stress Josiah's responsiveness to the word of God represented by the document leads to an account in which all the major acts seem to take place within a very short span of time (2 Kgs 22:3; 23:23). See already, e.g., John Mayer, *Commentaries*, 304; Donald W. B. Robinson, *Josiah's Reform and the Book of the Law* (London: Tyndale Press, 1951), 5–15.

55. Cf. Robinson, *Josiah's Reform*, 26–34.

56. The list contains "mediums" (*'ōbōt*) and "wizards" (*yiddə'ōnîm*), both of which are found in Lev 19:31; 20:6, 27; Deut 18:11; "teraphim" (*tərāpîm*), which are not mentioned in Exodus–Deuteronomy; "idols" (*gillūlîm*), which are referenced in Lev 26:30 and Deut 29:17(16); and "abominations" (*šiqqūṣîm*), again found in Deut 29:17(16).

ment" and being guided by "the counsel and traditions of the elders; for it was by following the laws that he succeeded so well in the ordering of his government," even before the discovery of the books of Moses.[57] A natural reading of the biblical narrative coheres with the plausible assumption that the law of God was known at various points in Israel's history to a greater or lesser extent, not least depending on willingness to understand and obey it, and that the cultural memory embedded among the faithful was backed up by only a very limited number of written documents.[58] It could, therefore, happen that during the reign of an unsympathetic king, documents were destroyed (by the authorities) and/or hidden away (by those whose loyalty was with these documents) and thus became unavailable for a time. A seventeenth-century Anglican scholar notes that "some of the Hebrews say, that [king] Amon had burnt the books of the Law, which he could find, in so much as it was thought, that they had all perished." He finds this plausible but comments that even without such an action there would be at any time so few books that it can well be believed that for a time no one knew where to locate a copy. At least, not until the high priest "lighted accidentally upon which [happily] his predecessor had hidden here from wicked *Amon*, and then dying left it, no man knowing thereof."[59]

Within modern scholarship, the identity of the scroll has often been closely tied up with the question of the origin of Deuteronomy. This is increasingly questioned as scholars debate the historicity and extent of Josiah's reforms and of any discovery of any scroll. This is not the place to enter such a discussion, and it is not my intention to offer an alternative proposal concerning the identity of the temple scroll within the two narratives. Several scenarios are possible, including some in which the contents of Deuteronomy were basically known before Hilkiah passed on a Book of the Law to Josiah and others in which no written document like Deuteronomy was put together until after Josiah's reign. In my view, the language used in Zephaniah does not seem to point decisively in either direction. What the narratives in 2 Kings and 2 Chronicles, as well as the prophetic books, do imply is that YHWH's will could be known in basic outline and acted upon. For this reason, it may be best not to look at the Book of the Law that the high priest presented to

---

57. Josephus, *Ant.* 10.51. See Christopher Begg, *Josephus' Story of the Later Monarchy*, BETL 145 (Leuven: Leuven University Press. 2000), 457–97, for an analysis of the way Josephus presents Josiah's reign.

58. This aspect seems to have been overlooked by Robertson, *Nahum*, 254–56, who assumes that Zephaniah could not have had access to phraseology from Deuteronomy without access to the book itself. With regard to his first two examples (Zeph 1:13 and Deut 28:30, 39), there is also the question whether Amos 5:11 was already in existence and available to Zephaniah.

59. John Mayer, *Commentaries*, 309–10.

the king as filling an information deficit. Rather, its physicality carried the symbolic power of a covenant agreement with binding obligations.

Josiah's reform has often been interpreted in conjunction with wider political developments, especially the weakening of the Neo-Assyrian Empire. This is not without problems. While there is a certain logic to the idea that a strong emphasis on religious distinctiveness would go along with an ardent desire for national independence, there is no biblical or extrabiblical evidence to suggest that there was a straightforward relationship between the political decision about whether or not to continue paying tribute to one of the major powers of the time and national religious life.[60] There would have been scope for Manasseh to pursue a less heterodox course (from the point of view of the biblical testimony) while remaining a loyal vassal of Assyria. Conversely, Josiah's religious reform did not require that he also pursued Judah's political independence. While we cannot reconstruct the political history of the Levant at this time with full confidence, not least because the annals of Assurbanipal (668–627) do not extend beyond 639, the view that the Assyrian decline left a power vacuum that Josiah might have filled with national ambitions of his own is open to serious questioning.[61] It seems that Egypt smoothly morphed from being a vassal of Assyria into an Assyrian ally on a more equal footing, being able to claim some control over Syria-Palestine with tacit or explicit Assyrian approval. Judah may have moved from being an Assyrian vassal early in Josiah's reign to being an Egyptian vassal later in it. Others have argued that Judah was an Egyptian vassal throughout the reign of Josiah.[62] Among those who argue that Judah was neither a vassal of Egypt during the reign of Josiah nor allied with Assyria, Laato offers a succinct discussion of the different ways in which the relationships between King Josiah and the major powers to the west (Egypt) and east (Assyria) have been conceptualized by a number of historians.[63] He concludes:

60. Cf. Mordechai Cogan, "Judah under Assyrian Hegemony: A Reexamination of *Imperialism and Religion*," *JBL* 112 (1993): 403–14; contra Hermann Spieckermann, *Juda unter Assur in der Sargonidenzeit*, FRLANT 129 (Göttingen: Vandenhoeck & Ruprecht, 1982). See also Laato, *Josiah*, 43–44; Carly L. Crouch, *Israel and the Assyrians: Deuteronomy, the Succession Treaty of Esarhaddon, and the Nature of Subversion*, SBLANEM 8 (Atlanta: Society of Biblical Literature, 2014), esp. 167–78.

61. For an exposition of this earlier view, see Bustenay Oded, "Judah and the Exile," in *Israelite and Judean History*, ed. John H. Hayes and J. Maxwell Miller (London: SCM Press, 1977), 458–69.

62. J. Maxwell Miller and John H. Hayes, *A History of Ancient Israel and Judah* (London: SCM Press, 1986), 388–90 (cf. pp. 451–53 in the 2nd ed., published in 2006). See further below.

63. Laato, *Josiah*, 74–80.

Josiah seems to have been a clever politician who attempted to find a viable way to lead Judah to freedom from foreign domination. At the beginning of Josiah's reign (630's and 620's) close contacts were maintained with Egypt (as indicated in Jer 2) and it is plausible to assume that Judah and Egypt had drawn up a treaty concerning the division of Palestine. We may characterize Josiah's policy at that time as anti-Assyrian and pro-Egyptian. However, the situation changed radically at the end of the 620's and certainly by the 610's when the Babylonians appeared on the bank of the Euphrates. This led to an Egyptian and Assyrian alliance against Babylonia which in turn led Josiah to reevaluate his former policy. From this time onwards Josiah could no longer be a whole-hearted ally of Egypt because he realized that if an Assyrian-Egyptian alliance managed to defeat Babylonia then Judah would again be subjugated. Therefore Josiah attempted to pursue a more independent policy and it is not impossible that Josiah's Deuteronomic reformation in 622 B.C. was integrated with his political aim to strengthen Judah religiously and to provide an ideological basis for the new policy that Judah must put its confidence in YHWH alone (cf. the central motif of Deut: YHWH war).[64]

This is a possible scenario, but in consideration of all the evidence, it may not be a likely one.[65] Others have strengthened the argument that Judah was in fact an Egyptian vassal from 610 onward at the very latest and quite possibly earlier on the basis of some ancient Hebrew inscriptions and an ostracon that refers to tribute payments.[66] We do not know whether there was any written arrangement between Egypt and Judah following the fading away of Assyrian control over the region. What is clear is that the Egyptians were able to move up and down the Mediterranean coast without Judean interference, and it is probable that Judah, being entirely or largely without access

64. Laato, *Josiah*, 79–80. Cf. Gösta W. Ahlström, *The History of Ancient Palestine from the Palaeolithic Period to Alexander's Conquest*, JSOTSup 146 (Sheffield: Sheffield Academic Press, 1993), 766–67, who assumes political alliances with Egypt and Assyria and allows for the possibility that Josiah sought to meet Neco II to lend him support.

65. For this discussion, see Brad E. Kelle, "Judah in the Seventh Century: From the Aftermath of Sennacherib's Invasion to the Beginning of Jehoiakim's Rebellion," in *Ancient Israel's History: An Introduction to Issues and Sources*, ed. Bill T. Arnold and Richard S. Hess (Grand Rapids: Baker Academic, 2014), 350–82, esp. the section on the status of Judah within Syria-Palestine.

66. See Bernd U. Schipper, "Egypt and the Kingdom of Judah under Josiah and Jehoiakim," *Tel Aviv* 37 (2010): 200–226; Dan'el Kahn, "Judean Auxiliaries in Egypt's War Against Kush," *JAOS* (2007): 507–16; "Why Did Necho II Kill Josiah?," in *There and Back Again—the Crossroads II: Proceedings of an International Conference Held in Prague, September 15–18, 2014*, ed. Jana Mynářová, Pavel Onderka, and Peter Pavúk (Prague: Charles University in Prague, 2015), 512.

to the coast, did not present a threat to the Egyptians. The lack of confrontation between the two before 609 could suggest that Josiah did not annex former Israelite territories. It is conceivable that Egypt and Judah came to an arrangement that allowed Josiah to claim some of the territory in the Israelite highlands, with Egypt retaining control of the main trading route.[67] Schipper notes, "One thing can be said for certain, though: Egypt was interested in the Coastal Plain and in the Negev and not in the Kingdom of Judah as such."[68] Judah was of interest only with regard to its control of trading routes in the Negev. Nevertheless, the archaeological evidence has been interpreted by some to suggest that Judahite control did not extend northward beyond Bethel,[69] and it should be noted that the accounts in 2 Kgs 23 and 2 Chr 34 focus entirely on desecrating worship places in Samaria without giving any indication that Josiah established a political or military presence north of Bethel. It is likely that Egypt was content to leave Josiah some room for maneuver, at least as far as the Judean heartland was concerned and maybe including Israelite highlands.[70] But it is not plausible that Josiah would have been able to take over Philistine territories without facing opposition from Egypt, nor does it seem probable that Judah sought to expand into Transjordanian territory.[71] Ahlström notes, "It is inconceivable that the biblical writer would not mention anything about Josiah's extension of the kingdom, had it occurred, for such military-political success would have been a very important factor in his glorification of Josiah as the most important king after David."[72]

To what purpose Josiah went to meet Pharaoh Neco II remains a matter of dispute, not least because of the significant differences between the accounts

67. Megiddo, e.g., was likely an Egyptian garrison city. See Ahlström, *History*, 779 (the latter reference seems to contradict the former slightly). Nadav Na'aman, "The Kingdom of Judah under Josiah," *Tel Aviv* 18 (1991): 41–44, 57 (repr. in lightly rev. form as "Josiah and the Kingdom of Judah," in Grabbe, *Good Kings*, 217–19, 231), allows that Josiah may have extended his rule into Samaria but without annexing its territory beyond Bethel and nearby towns. Note also the reference in 2 Kgs 23:8 to Geba, some 18.5 miles (30 km) south of Megiddo, as apparently the northernmost point of Josiah's intervention.

68. Schipper, "Egypt," 212; cf. Kahn, "Why?," 519.

69. Raz Kletter, "Pots and Polities: Material Remains of Late Iron Age Judah in Relation to Its Political Borders," *BASOR* 314 (1999): 19–54; cf. Schipper, "Egypt," 214. But see the following note.

70. Michael Heltzer ("Some Questions Concerning the Economic Policy of Josiah, King of Judah," *Israel Exploration Journal* 50 [2000]: 105–8) notes one clay seal that indicates that 'ărubbôt (identified as Tel Narbeta, southwest of Megiddo) had been annexed to Judah. This remains the only evidence for any northward expansion.

71. Cf. Na'aman, "Kingdom," 42–44; "Josiah," 217–19.

72. Ahlström, *History*, 766. Cf. the summary in Lester L. Grabbe, *Ancient Israel: What Do We Know and How Do We Know It?* (London: T&T Clark, 2007), 204–7.

in 2 Kings and 2 Chronicles. As is widely recognized, the account in the latter portrays Josiah as disobedient to a divine word and suffering a similar fate to Ahab.[73] This concern may have overridden any desire to give a matter-of-fact portrayal of the political-military situation of the time. Many now think that Josiah, as an Egyptian vassal, presented himself to the new ruler of Egypt, who may have been personally present in the Levant for the first time, and that Neco II executed Josiah for treachery.[74]

Regardless of the extent of Josiah's political power between 640 and 609 vis-à-vis the other powers of the time, we may want to ask whether Zephaniah's prophecy, especially the oracles about other nations in ch. 2, fits more readily into the early period still under the shadow of the Assyrians or into the middle and later period under greater Egyptian influence. In this respect, it is noteworthy that ch. 2 contains an oracle against Assyria but apparently not against Egypt. The reference to Cush (2:12) is sometimes read as an oracle against Egypt, but this is unlikely to be correct. While "Cush" is sometimes used in parallel with "Egypt" (e.g., Isa 20:3–5), to my knowledge there is not a single instance in which "Cush" (or "Cushites") on its own refers to Egypt.[75] Cush means Nubia, whose kingdom occupied a large area of the region of modern Ethiopia, Sudan, and Somalia. During the eighth century, Nubia extended its control also into Lower Egypt, but Cushite rule came to an end with the fall of Thebes, to which 2:12 likely refers (see the commentary). Subsequently, Lower Egypt, and within less than ten years a reunified Egypt, was ruled by a dynasty from Sais in the Delta region, and there is evidence to suggest that relationships between Cush and Egypt were not peaceful at the time.[76] It would therefore be very odd for "Cush" to stand in as a designation for Egypt "in the days of Josiah" or at any time later. (It is worth noting here that Berlin discusses five interpretations of "Cush," herself opting for a reference to Mesopotamia, specifically Assyria [cf. Gen 10:7].[77] I find this improbable, but it would not affect the argument at hand.)

Other pronouncements in ch. 2 are against the Philistine principalities and against Moab and Ammon. The Philistine cities were in a situation sim-

---

73. See, e.g., Ralph W. Klein, *2 Chronicles*, Hermeneia (Minneapolis: Fortress, 2012), 516–18, 524–28.

74. Kuhrt, *Ancient Near East*, 543; Grabbe, *Ancient Israel*, 207; Na'aman, "Kingdom," 51–55; "Josiah," 226–29; Schipper, "Egypt," 218. Kahn ("Why?") examines the main proposals and himself concludes that Josiah was beheaded for having ceased to pay tributes following Neco's failure to defeat the Babylonians in the previous year.

75. Cf. Ben Zvi, *Zephaniah*, 176–77; Irsigler, *Zefanja*, 288–92. (Irsigler does, however, believe that at a later point "the Cushites" in Zeph 2:12 were understood as designating, *pars pro toto*, Egypt; see p. 293 and discussion below.)

76. Kahn, "Judean Auxiliaries," 509.

77. Berlin, *Zephaniah*, 111–13.

ilar to Judah vis-à-vis Assyrian and Egyptian hegemony, but due to their geopolitical position, they were possibly of greater interest to Egypt than Judah was. The latter two were likely still Assyrian vassals during much of the reign of Josiah. It is sometimes argued that the oracle against Moab and the Ammonites comes from a later period, but it does not seem inappropriate in the context of Josiah's reign.[78] There is nothing in Zephaniah to suggest any particular sympathy for Egypt that could explain its absence from condemnation, nor for Edom, which is also left unmentioned. Given the stark words against Jerusalem as well as against Egypt's Philistine allies, it is also not plausible that Egypt was omitted for fear of the authorities. Zephaniah 2 reflects no desire to cover the ground comprehensively with oracles against all the political powers of the region, and we must therefore be careful to base any firm conclusion on the omission of this or that entity. But given that Egypt kept growing in significance throughout the days of Josiah, its absence in the book suggests a date earlier rather than later in Josiah's reign. Even if the material in the middle of the book were older than that at the beginning and end, which is plausible, we might have expected the addition of an oracle against Egypt in ch. 2 at a later point during Josiah's reign. In other words, if its absence in ch. 2 is a reason to date the oracles in ch. 2 before 616, by which time the Levant seems to have been under Egyptian hegemony, then it also suggests that the book, at least as far as its basic argument concerning judgment is concerned, was completed before that time—even on the view that the book grew from the middle. This does not rule out the later addition of a supplement (e.g., elaborating on the future beyond the judgment), but in my view, no recasting of the message of judgment in the light of later events can be ascertained.

Dating biblical texts is notoriously difficult, and it would be foolish to commit to a specific date. But everything considered, it seems more likely than not that much of Zephaniah took its shape in the 630s or 620s. There is nothing in the text to rule this out, and the absence of any reference to Josiah's reforms (positively or negatively) or to the growth of Egyptian hegemony in the region arguably fits better with an early date, given that these important political developments are of significance to Zephaniah's message.[79]

---

78. See the commentary and Dan'el Kahn, "The Historical Setting of Zephaniah's Oracles Against the Nations (Zeph 2:4–15)," in *Homeland and Exile: Biblical and Ancient Near Eastern Studies in Honour of Bustenay Oded*, ed. Gerschon Galil, Markham J Geller, and Alan R. Millard, VTSup 130 (Leiden: Brill, 2009), 439–53; and, in earlier scholarship, e.g., Klaus-Dietrich Schunk, "Juda in der Verkündigung des Propheten Zefanja," in *Alttestamentlicher Glaube und biblische Theologie: Festschrift für Horst Dietrich Preuß zum 65. Geburtstag*, ed. Jutta Hausmann and Hans-Jürgen Zobel (Stuttgart: Kohlhammer, 1992), 174–79.

79. The first scroll of Jeremiah's prophecies came to be recorded in the fourth year of King Jehoiakim (Jer 36:1–4) and destroyed a year later (36:22–23). If Jeremiah had commented

III. THE RHETORICAL FUNCTION OF THE BOOK

A. ZEPHANIAH'S MESSAGE IN ITS ORIGINAL CONTEXT

Zephaniah's message in its original context is intimately related to the question, discussed in detail in the preceding section, of the relationship between the prophet and Josiah's reforms. The prophet announced the end of the Neo-Assyrian Empire, but as part of the annihilation of the socioeconomic and political order of the whole region, focused on Jerusalem. The idea that the downfall of Nineveh might give space to a renewed flourishing of a more independent Jerusalem is thereby quashed. Judah is given no hope of escaping the disaster. Its hope lies in YHWH's plans for a remnant, and the people are therefore urged to seek justice and humility. Aligning oneself with Josiah's reforms would arguably be one way to pursue this. The prophet may or may not have made this specific link in any oral ministry; in the book it is not made.

Human agency in bringing the destruction is not highlighted, and there was no updating of the book to establish that it was the Babylonians who brought an end to the Southern Kingdom and other political entities. Along with other prophetic messages, such as Jeremiah's and Ezekiel's, Zephaniah's would have made the point that the fall of Jerusalem was YHWH's doing. I believe that a hint of a positive future for a remnant not only of Judah but of other nations as well was part of Zephaniah's message from early on. This will be discussed in the commentary at the relevant places. After the disaster had occurred, this was developed further with regard to a glorious future for a purified Jerusalem in particular.

B. ZEPHANIAH'S PLACE IN THE BIBLICAL CANON

Related to the historical context is a key aspect of Zephaniah's place in the biblical canon—namely, the relationship between Deuteronomy and Zephaniah. This is, in turn, relevant for the question of Zephaniah's place within the Book of the Twelve, as Zephaniah is sometimes reckoned to have belonged to a "Book of the Four,"[80] which was allegedly shaped in interaction with

---

on Josiah's reforms in the early days of his ministry, there may have been little reason to reproduce such preaching in a scroll written long after it had become clear that the reforms had not changed the life of the nation.

80. This is the reason why, in the case of Zephaniah, I have combined the sections on the book's place in the Book of the Twelve and its place in the biblical canon.

the book of Deuteronomy or the Deuteronomistic History.[81] This, too, was already mentioned above. As I have not been persuaded about the existence of a Book of the Four, on which others have written in sufficient detail (see p. 434 n. 42), I see no need to discuss this further here.[82] The issue will be briefly brought up in the commentary on 3:11–13, which is read by proponents of the theory as the conclusion to this Book of the Four.

In my judgment, Zephaniah was composed as an individual scroll rather than a chapter within the Book of the Twelve or within one of its precursors. There seem to be only a few signs of redactional activity designed to link Zephaniah with other writings, namely in the summons to joy in the final section of the book. This may have been contributed by redactors responsible for the book of Zechariah who sought to integrate the Haggai–Malachi corpus into the Book of the Twelve. The link between Zephaniah and Haggai is strengthened by the threefold "time" references both at the end of Zephaniah and at the beginning of Haggai (see the commentary on 3:18–20).

Zephaniah anticipates the fall of Jerusalem and describes it as the end of a world, the end not only of the Southern Kingdom of Judah but of the entire region's socioeconomic and political system. This comprehensiveness may be its unique contribution. It is not difficult to hear echoes of Genesis 1–11 in Zephaniah that support this sense of universality.[83] Allusions to the patriarchs or to the exodus and Sinai (Horeb) tradition, by contrast, are absent, although the designation *my people* (2:8–9) and *people of YHWH of Hosts* (2:10) presume the covenant between YHWH and Israel. The use of *YHWH of Hosts* (2:9–10) and the notion of YHWH as king (3:15, and arguably implied in ch. 1; see the commentary) may be indebted to the Zion tradition.[84]

---

81. Seen not necessarily in affirmative ways, e.g., Jakob Wöhrle, " 'No Future for the Proud Exultant Ones': The Exilic Book of the Four Prophets (Hos., Am., Mic., Zeph.) as a Concept Opposed to the Deuteronomistic History," *VT* 58 (2008): 608–27.

82. Werse's careful study (*Reconsidering*) appeared too late for me to give it full and detailed consideration.

83. Of any commentator, Berlin (*Zephaniah*, 13–14) probably makes the most of these; cf. Michael De Roche, "Zephaniah I 2–3: The 'Sweeping' of Creation," *VT* 30 (1980): 104–9. David Melvin ("Making All Things New (Again): Zephaniah's Eschatological Vision of a Return to Primeval Time," in *Creation and Chaos: A Reconsideration of Hermann Gunkel's Chaoskampf Hypothesis*, ed. JoAnn Scurlock and Richard H. Beal [Winona Lake, IN: Eisenbrauns, 2013], 269–81) believes that "Zephaniah's eschatology is shaped by the primeval history in a manner that anticipates later apocalyptic eschatology and its recasting of themes of creation/re-creation and the antediluvian epoch as foreshadows of the end of time" (281). I will indicate in the commentary that the allusions to Gen 1–11 may have been overplayed.

84. See Thomas Renz, "Use of the Zion Tradition in the Book of Ezekiel," in *Zion, City of Our God*, ed. Richard S. Hess and Gordon J. Wenham (Grand Rapids: Eerdmans, 1999), 82–83.

The designation of Jerusalem as *my holy mount* (3:11) implies the election of Zion, as does the notion of YHWH's presence in Jerusalem in 3:14–20. There is no allusion to the Davidic covenant, however. This is in keeping with the fact that YHWH's instrument of judgment (the Babylonians) does not feature explicitly either. The strong focus on YHWH means that human agents are outside the field of vision.

Ezekiel, too, has announcements of destruction for a range of nations, and its oracles about other nations (chs. 25–32, but also chs. 21 and 35) are arguably all related to Babylonian campaigns, as are the oracles in Zephaniah.[85] Indeed, Ezek 7 (note v. 2: "The end is coming on the four corners of the land/earth") paints a similar picture of comprehensive judgment. But Zephaniah's striking opening, its succinctness, and the way the impeding destruction of Jerusalem frames short oracles about surrounding political entities give Zephaniah a sharpness that Ezekiel arguably lacks.[86] This final reckoning is suitably placed within the anthology of the Book of the Twelve just prior to the restoration prophecies in Haggai–Malachi, which the end of Zephaniah anticipates. Some of the language of Zephaniah has close parallels with Isaiah and Jeremiah as well as Ezekiel and writings in the Book of the Twelve.[87] Along with cross-references to Genesis 1–11, Deuteronomy, and the prophetic literature, a few links to the Psalms and the wisdom literature can be observed (e.g., in the focus on the humble).[88]

The concept of the Day of YHWH as a day of decisive and comprehensive punishment may have fed into New Testament language that links the end of the world as we know it with the Day of the Lord (e.g., 1 Cor 1:8; 5:5; 1 Thess 5:2; 2 Pet 3:10). The focus of the message of judgment on the wealthy elite is echoed in Jesus's warning that it is hard for the rich to enter God's kingdom (e.g., Mark 10:23; cf. Jas 1:9–11; 2:5–6; 5:1–6). The glimmer of hope for the humble and poor is fanned into flame by Christ's beatitudes on the poor and meek (Matt 5:3, 5). Echoes of Zephaniah may be detected in Matt 13:41 (Zeph 1:3); Rev 6:17 (Zeph 1:14–15); and possibly Rom 15:6 (Zeph 3:9); Rev 14:5 (Zeph 3:13); 16:1 (Zeph 3:8).

---

85. Ezek 38–39 is in a different category; see Daniel I. Block, *The Book of Ezekiel, Chapters 25–48*, NICOT (Grand Rapids: Eerdmans, 1998).

86. Ezekiel's length works in favor of a more relentless argument that leaves hardly a stone unturned, answering possible objections to the message of judgment in some detail; see Renz, *Rhetorical Function*.

87. See the list in Berlin, *Zephaniah*, 15–16.

88. Berlin, *Zephaniah*, 16–17. See also the discussion of intertextual references in Irsigler, *Zefanja*, 49–54.

C. ZEPHANIAH IN THE HISTORY OF INTERPRETATION

Only fragments of the Qumran pesher remain (4Q170; 1Q15), but they suggest that Zephaniah was read as speaking into the situation of the Qumran community. In addition, the attribution of an apocalypse to Zephaniah suggests popularity with eschatological-apocalyptic groups in early Judaism. (Its final redaction may have been undertaken by Coptic Christians.[89]) The triannual cycle of Torah readings featured Zeph 3:9-17, 20 as the Haftara to the portion of Torah beginning with Gen 11:1, suggesting a universal language.[90] Zephaniah 3:7-15, 20 was read with the portion that begins with Num 4:17.[91] The claim that the key word connection is "shoulder" is questionable, as Zeph 3:9 uses šəkem, while Num 7:9 has kātēp. Perhaps the shared notion of following divine instruction in order not to be cut off (Num 4:17-20; cf. Zeph 3:7) prompted the pairing.

Zephaniah was not very often cited in early Jewish or Christian literature.[92] The verses from Zephaniah cited more than four times in early Christian literature of the first three centuries are 1:1; 2:11; 3:8; 3:9.[93] Apart from 1:1, which is cited to situate Zephaniah, these are the verses that lend themselves to speak about the universal worship of the one God of Israel. John Chrysostom (c. AD 347-407), too, makes reference only to Zeph 2:11; 3:3, 9-10.[94] But these verses are important for the Christian vision of a world mission and the unity of the church.[95] While for Christians, the time of fulfillment is now, the Talmud reads the verse as a promise for the future conversion of the gentiles (b. Berakhot 57b; cf. b. 'Abodah Zarah 24a), which will bring about the unity of the world (Genesis Midrash Rabbah 88:7).[96]

89. Irsigler, *Zefanja*, 77. The Apocalypse of Zephaniah paints a picture of the final judgment on individuals, with visions of heaven and hell.

90. Mann, *Bible in the Old Synagogue*, vol. 1, 91–95; cf. Ben Zvi, *Zephaniah*, 24–25; BA 23.4–9, 329; Irsigler, *Zefanja*, 383–84.

91. Cf. BA 23.4–9, 329; Irsigler, *Zefanja*, 384, with reference to Jacob Mann, *The Bible as Read and Preached in the Old Synagogue*, vol. 2 (Cincinnati: HUC, 1966), 201–8.

92. Cf. Ben Zvi, *Zephaniah*, 25–27.

93. See the Index of Biblical Quotations in Early Christian Literature at http://www.biblindex.mom.fr/. This does not include the New Testament. Alongside at best very vague allusions, e.g., to a day of wrath, J. G. Schomerus (in Kurt Aland et al., eds., *Novum Testamentum Graece*, 26th ed. [Stuttgart: Deutsche Bibelgesellschaft, 1979], 768), identifies one citation from Zephaniah in the NT, namely 3:13 in Rev 14:5.

94. Ben Zvi, *Zephaniah*, 25, with reference to Robert A. Krupp, *Saint John Chrysostom: A Scripture Index* (Lanham: University Press of America, 1984). Cf. Irsigler, *Zefanja*, 384, focusing on Origen and Jerome.

95. Cf. Coggins and Han, *Six Minor Prophets*, 111–12, 118–19; BA 23.4–9, 332–35.

96. The reference to the Genesis midrash is from Irsigler, *Zefanja*, 384. Cf. the reference to Maimonides in Coggins and Han, *Six Minor Prophets*, 118.

In later times, the poem *Dies irae* ("Day of Wrath"), often attributed to Thomas of Celano (c. AD 1185–1260), which was chanted for many centuries in the Western church as part of requiem masses, was likely the most prominent representation of a part of Zephaniah (1:14–18).[97] The indebtedness of the poem to Zephaniah may be overstated, but it seems that Zephaniah was valued for much of its reception history as a witness to eschatological judgment and the universality of the people of God.

> Luther thought that among the Minor Prophets, Zephaniah 'makes the clearest prophecies about the kingdom of Christ' (319). He saw in the prophet someone who, like himself, proclaimed a divine message unacknowledged as such by the authorities. For Luther, Zephaniah ruthlessly rejects human righteousness and religion, preparing the kingdom of Christ. The gathering of kingdoms and nations he sees fulfilled through the spread of the gospel (355), which is a message of repentance that declares the outpouring of God's wrath (356). Zephaniah agrees with all of Scripture in its battle against 'the powerful, the wise, and the holy' (326), and in addressing the promise to the 'humble, oppressed, . . . those who lack honor and wealth,' like Christ and Mary in the NT (339).[98]

In spite of this conviction, I am not aware that Luther referred much to Zephaniah in his sermons. This suggests that Zephaniah contains hidden treasures for the church, texts that have been prominent here and there but often overlooked.

Max Thurian studied the resemblance between Zeph 3:14–17 and the words of the angel Gabriel to Mary in Luke 1:28–31, bolstering the identification of "the daughter of Zion" with Mary commonly found in Roman Catholic tradition.[99] He is particularly impressed with the pleonastic *en gastri* ("in the womb") in Luke 1:31 (cf. *en tē koilia* in 2:21), which, he believes, takes up the emphasis of "in your midst" (*bəqirbēk*) in Zephaniah (3:15, 17; cf. *bəqirbāh* in Gen 25:22).

---

97. Coggins and Han, *Six Minor Prophets*, 96–99.

98. Thomas Renz, "Zephaniah," in *Theological Interpretation of the Old Testament: A Book-by-Book Survey*, ed. Kevin J. Vanhoozer (Grand Rapids: Baker, 2008), 293; orig. "Zephaniah," in *Dictionary for Theological Interpretation of the Bible*, ed. Kevin J. Vanhoozer (Grand Rapids: Baker Academic, 2005). The citations are to Luther's "Lectures on Zephaniah," in *LW* 18:317–64.

99. Max Thurian, *Mary: Mother of All Christians* (New York: Herder and Herder, 1962), 15–19; published in London under the title *Mary: Mother of the Lord, Figure of the Church* by The Faith Press, 1963.

D. ZEPHANIAH'S PLACE IN THE CHURCH TODAY

As indicated by its reception history, Zephaniah may make particular contributions in three areas: first, the comprehensiveness and finality of divine judgment; second, the relationship between poverty and humility;[100] third, the universal outlook for the people of God. These three focal points can be combined in the motif of salvation for a purified remnant as the goal of God's judgment. While there are implications for individuals, close attention to Zephaniah encourages us to take corporate aspects seriously. It is a society and a regime that is under judgment, and it is a community that forms the remnant.

We will see the seriousness of idolatry. When God is not represented and worshipped faithfully, the world is deprived of true knowledge of God and of the blessings that flow from it. True worship concerns not only what is confessed but also the question to what extent our thoughts and actions reflect what we confess with our lips. Falsehood in worship relates to unjust living (the political and the religious are related to one another) and is hazardous. Reading Zephaniah will remind us of the importance of integrity in our worship and that worship means acknowledging God as our king with and in our whole lives.

Zephaniah also highlights the fact that wealth and power, however significant they seem to be today, count for nothing in the face of God's judgment. It can raise some challenging questions about the extent to which our attitudes and behavior may be shaped by the cultural systems of which we are a part, and maybe especially with regard to economic activity. Zephaniah can be helpful in teasing out the risk factors of being well-off and apparently able to shape one's destiny. It suggests that there can be benefits to being powerless because those who have no resources of their own may be more likely to entrust themselves to God, who has a preferential option for the lowly.[101] It stresses the need to continually seek after justice and humility and the dangers of arrogant pride.

Where the message of Zephaniah is believed, it can ultimately be reassuring, as it emerges that the divine judgment has the establishment of a just society as its end and that God's presence is a source of joy for

---

100. So already, e.g., Luther and Augustine. Cf. Norbert Lohfink, "Zephaniah and the Church of the Poor," *Theology Digest* 32 (1985): 113–18; Michael Weigl, *Zefanja und das "Israel der Armen"*, Österreichische Biblische Studien 13 (Klosterneuburg: Österreichisches KBW, 1994); Coggins and Han, *Six Minor Prophets*, 110, 120.

101. There is, however, no glorification of poverty, as I will point out in my reflections below; nor is there condemnation of wealth as such.

those who seek refuge in him. As elsewhere in Scripture, the picture at the end of the book is of a future more glorious than the past had ever been—not least because it brings those who have been far off into the worshipping community.

Text and Commentary

I. SUPERSCRIPTION (1:1)

[1]*The word of YHWH that came to Zephaniah son of Cushi son of Gedaliah,*[a] *son of Amariah son of Hezekiah,*[b] *in the days of Josiah*[c] *son of Amon, king of Judah.*

a. The comma indicates the major break within the first half of the verse according to the masoretic accentuation. We may consider it the point at which a long version of the name expands to a short genealogy. The name Gedaliah is found in Jeremiah (applied to different persons) in both its short form as here, ending on *-yah* (40:5–6, 8; 41:16), and in its long form, ending on *-yahu* (38:1; 39:14; 40:7, 9, 11–16; 41:1–4, 6, 9–10, 18; 43:6). In 2 Kings and 1 Chronicles, only the longer form is used; Ezra 10:18 uses the shorter form in the same list in which the name Shelemiah is used in both forms (vv. 39, 41), albeit for different persons. Amariah is used another dozen times with the short ending as in Zeph 1:1; the long ending is found in 1 Chr 24:23; 2 Chr 19:11; 31:15. Hezekiah, by contrast, is attested more often with the longer form (more than seventy times); the shorter form is found only a dozen times outside Zeph 1:1. The presence of long or short forms does not offer good grounds for dating a text. See the comment on Josiah below.

b. The Peshitta and a few masoretic MSS read "Hilkiah." This reading has been attributed to Bar Hebraeus, identifying Hilkiah as the father of the prophet Jeremiah. But it may more likely be the result of a misreading. For discussion, see Sweeney, *Zephaniah*, 48.

c. In spite of the English rendering with *Josiah*, only the longer form ending on *-yahu* is attested with reference to the king (another fifty times in 1–2 Kings, 1–2 Chronicles, and Jeremiah). The short form is used for another Josiah in Zech 6:10.

Composition

The opening verse of Zephaniah can be compared to the opening verses of Hosea, Joel, and Micah within the Book of the Twelve. The exact opening phrase is not found outside the Book of the Twelve. Hosea and Micah, but not Joel, similarly include a reference to the kings in whose time the prophet is situated. The resemblance may suggest a common editor for these four minor prophets.[1] But the absence of the component "in the days of . . ." in Joel, the fact that the word is said to be seen in Micah (cf. Hab 1:1) but not in the other three, and the presence of a genealogy with Zephaniah means that none of the introductions is phrased in exactly the same way. It is perfectly possible for an editor to vary such introductions, but if the argument for a common editor rests on the similarity of these opening verses, their differences must weaken the argument.[2] It is just as possible that different redactors of prophetic writings worked with the same phraseology for indicating divine revelation. Ben Zvi observes that the phrase "may be considered a superscriptional variant of narrative openings like the 'word event formula' (i.e. . . . 'the word of YHWH came to X') and of similar expressions."[3] Jeremiah 1:2 and Zech 1:1 do not use the exact wording found here but have very much the same phraseology, as does Zech 4:6 within a prophetic scroll.[4]

Other than within the narrative of 2 Chr 20:14, this is the only place in the Hebrew Bible where a prophet is given a genealogy. Prophets are sometimes not named, sometimes given a pen name (possibly Nahum and Malachi), and sometimes given a full name that includes the name of father (and grandfather in the case of Zechariah). Here we are given in addition the names of great-grandfather and great-great-grandfather or, if intervening names were omitted, earlier ancestors.[5] Vlaardingerbroek questions the need to find a reason "for the mention of four preceding generations," pointing out that this "also occurs in 1 Sam 9:1 (Kish), cf. Bar 1:1 (five generations)."[6] But it stands to reason that the more detailed information in 1 Sam 9:1 is not without reason either. Here, after all, begins the story of the choice of the first king of Israel whose genealogy one would expect to be of significant interest. This

1. For discussion see, e.g., Aaron Schart, *Die Entstehung des Zwölfprophetenbuchs: Neubearbeitungen von Amos im Rahmen schriftenübergreifender Redaktionsprozesse*, BZAW 260 (Berlin: de Gruyter, 1998), 30–46; Christoph Levin, "Das »Vierprophetenbuch«."

2. The argument relates to a broader discussion of a Deuteronomistic school that is thought to have edited a number of biblical books. Cf. the introduction to the book of Zephaniah above.

3. Ben Zvi, *Zephaniah*, 41.

4. A variation is found in Hag 1:1. Jeremiah 1:1 in the LXX (*to rhēma tou theou ho egeneto epi*) suggests a wording closer to Zeph 1:1 and its parallels than MT. For a fuller discussion of prophetic superscriptions, see Francis I. Andersen and David Noel Freedman, *Hosea: A New Translation with Introduction and Commentary*, AB 24 (New York: Doubleday, 1980), 143–49.

5. For a broader examination of short genealogies, see Francis I. Andersen, "Israelite Kinship Terminology and Social Structure," *BT* 20 (1969): 29–39.

6. Vlaardingerbroek, *Zephaniah*, 13.

may also be true for other references.[7] The commentary below will explore possible reasons for the extended genealogy given to Zephaniah.

The reference to *the days of Josiah son of Amon, king of Judah* is often considered secondary. The fact that it has a parallel in Jer 1:2 hardly seems sufficient ground for this belief, especially given that associating Jeremiah with Josiah raises more difficulties than Zephaniah's association with Josiah, suggesting, as it does, a decades-long gap between the first and subsequent phases of Jeremiah's ministry. It is probably the sheer size of the book of Jeremiah that leads some to think that an editor of Zephaniah wanted to make a comparison with Jeremiah rather than the other way around.[8] But there is nothing peculiar about the phrasing, and in my view, it seems likely that the information given here reflects historical fact.

Commentary

1 *The word of YHWH* refers to the content that follows. Ben Zvi notes that the idiom does not claim that all that follows is direct divine speech, given that books with this superscription contain passages that speak of YHWH or the prophet or both in the third person.[9] This is certainly true even if divine speech sometimes uses "YHWH" in the third person. A canonical reader (i.e., a reader who receives Zephaniah as part of a wider biblical canon) will likely not limit the recognition of a text as God's word to direct divine speech given that other texts (e.g., the Psalms and the prayers in Habakkuk) also came to be received as a word from God even where they address God, and it is possible that such a broader understanding is already operative here. Deuteronomy is largely cast as a speech of Moses but could well have been received as divine word by the author of Zeph 1:1 whether or not it was identified as "the Book of the Law of YHWH" (cf. 2 Chr 34:14). Berlin observes that the syntax, with *the word of YHWH* at the head of the clause, suggests that the function of this verse is apparently not "to emphasize the process of communication to the prophet as much as to specify ownership of the oracle to follow."[10]

The name Zephaniah means "YHWH has hidden/protected/treasured" (from the verb *ṣpn*; cf. Ps 31:20–21) or "YHWH's treasure" or possibly

---

7. See below on Jer 36:14. Sean A. Adams (*Baruch and the Epistle of Jeremiah: A Commentary Based on the Texts in Codex Vaticanus*, Septuagint Commentary Series [Leiden: Brill, 2014], 51) comments regarding Bar 1:1, "The author clearly felt the need to fill in Baruch's ancestral history," but he does not suggest why.

8. Christoph Levin, "Zephaniah," 123.

9. Ben Zvi, *Zephaniah*, 42.

10. Berlin, *Zephaniah*, 64.

"YHWH's observation point" (the latter from a root *ṣph* with this presumed meaning).[11] There are four people in the Hebrew Bible who bear this name, and the name is also known from sources outside the Bible.[12] If the name was a popular one, which seems a reasonable assumption, the addition of the father's name would be important to clarify the prophet's identity. It is not likely, however, that the fuller *Zephaniah son of Cushi* was so popular that the editor felt a need to add further genealogical information to avoid ambiguity.

Scholars who accept that the genealogy asks for an explanation (contra Vlaardingerbroek; see above under "Composition") have focused on two. Some argue that it was occasioned by the name Cushi, which, if read as a gentilic noun rather than a proper name ("a Cushite"; see, e.g., Jer 13:23; cf. the plural in Zeph 2:12), is thought to raise questions about the status of Zephaniah as a member of YHWH's covenant people.[13] The addition of three clearly Judean names would have ensured that *Cushi* was understood as a proper name. But one such name (*Gedaliah*) would have been sufficient to signal that *Cushi* is a proper name here,[14] so the addition of two more names (*Amariah, Hezekiah*) remains unexplained. Without clear evidence for discrimination based on skin color in ancient Israel of the sort painfully familiar to us in modern times, there seems to be no reason to think that embarrassment was felt about the presence of *Cushi* in Zephaniah's genealogy.[15]

Another person mentioned in biblical prophetic literature who is identi-

11. See Irsigler, *Zefanja*, 84–85, who argues that the Latin and Greek traditions derive from interpreting the name as a noun construction. Among others, cf. Vlaardingerbroek, *Zephaniah*, 30–31, for the more typical explanation.

12. Irsigler, *Zefanja*, 85–86; Vlaardingerbroek, *Zephaniah*, 10–11; Berlin, *Zephaniah*, 64–65.

13. Sellin (*Zwölfprophetenbuch*, 419) appears to have been the first to propose this, with reference to the law in Deut 23:7–8(8–9) about Edomites and Egyptians (which may have been applied to Cushites) and Jer 36:14, where another Cushi is found within a short genealogy. But in Jer 36:14, Cushi has three descendants; Zephaniah, by contrast, is a first descendant of a Cushi, in which case Deut 23:7–8(8–9) cannot be relevant. I suspect that people were more concerned about (alleged) racial purity in Sellin's time than "in the days of Josiah." Jan Heller, "Zephanjas Ahnenreihe: Eine redaktionsgeschichtliche Bemerkung zu Zef 1,1," *VT* 21 (1971): 102–4, argues that a postexilic redactor was inspired by Deut 23: 7–8(8–9) but did not dare to add names between Zephaniah and Cushi and therefore added them further back in the genealogy.

14. Cf. maybe Cush the Benjaminite in the superscription to Ps 7, unless this was an African adopted into the tribe of Benjamin. A Cushite would be a Nubian or, less likely, a member of the tribe Cushan (associated with the Midianites).

15. As pointed out in the commentary on Hab 3, Moses' Cushite wife (Num 12:1) was unlikely to be Nubian. Miriam and Aaron's objection to the marriage was likely ethnic, but there is no reason to believe that it was based on skin color.

fied beyond patronymic (father) and extended household (grandfather) is Jehudi in Jer 36:14, and there the reference ends with a great-grandfather named Cushi, which is certainly not meant to put Jehudi in a bad light.[16] The idea that *Cushi* received his name on account of his darker skin color seems plausible and may be more likely than the suggestion that the name was given to express sympathy for the Nubian rulers of Egypt (cf. the name Amon) or simply awarded at random.[17] It is furthermore credible, even if not demonstrable, that Cushi's skin color was dark because *Gedaliah*, Zephaniah's grandfather, had married a Nubian woman.[18] If so, Zephaniah's Nubian ancestry may have providentially stimulated a particular interest in the area. While the reference to Cush in 2:12 is not in itself surprising and can be explained by other rhetorical considerations, it is linked with an interest in distant nations (2:11), and the singling out of Cush in 3:10 is noteworthy.[19] But this remains impossible to prove. All in all, it seems unlikely that any presence of Cushite (Nubian) blood in the prophet occasioned the genealogy.

The older explanation is that the specific purpose of the genealogy is found in the last name mentioned, *Hezekiah*, who is then usually but not always identified as the king of that name.[20] Some scholars have questioned the chronological feasibility of this identification. But there are various considerations that show that it would have been possible for Josiah and Zephaniah to have been contemporaries, even if they were in the third (Josiah) and fourth (Zephaniah) generation after Hezekiah. *Amariah* may have been Manasseh's older brother by a concubine, thus starting this genealogical line

---

16. The main reason for the extended identification in Jer 36:14 is probably rhetorical, marking the seriousness and significance of this point of the story. Jehudi's ancestor "shares his name with Ebed-melech, the man who saved Jeremiah from the cistern, for whom it is used as a gentilicum (Jer 38:7, 10, 12; 39:16)" (Christoph Levin, "Zephaniah," 123). This fact would ensure that the name evokes positive rather than negative associations in the mind of the ideal reader.

17. Vlaardingerbroek (*Zephaniah*, 12) compares contemporary surnames such as Black, Brown, and De Moore (cf. 31). But surnames, even if chosen in distant times for a reason (e.g., Black for a blacksmith, De Moore for someone deriving from the Muslim population of the Maghreb, Iberian Peninsula, Sicily, or Malta), today do not describe a specific individual in the way a "first" name might. Cushi is attested as a proper name not only in Hebrew but also in Phoenician and Aramaic; see Irsigler, *Zefanja*, 87; Ben Zvi, *Zephaniah*, 44.

18. Gene Rice, "The African Roots of the Prophet Zephaniah," *The Journal of Religious Thought* 37 (1979): 28; cf. Irsigler, *Zefanja*, 87–88.

19. There is of course the question whether these verses go back to the prophet himself. I consider this likely for 2:11–12 and possible for 3:10. Note that not all scholars identify Cush in these places as Nubia; some look to a place in Mesopotamia instead.

20. So Ibn Ezra; Kimchi said he did not see it that way but thought that Zephaniah's ancestors must have been "great men" to have been mentioned; see Rosenberg, *Twelve Prophets*, 283; cf. Ben Zvi, *Zephaniah*, 43; Sweeney, *Zephaniah*, 48.

earlier. Given that Amon was twenty-two years old when he became king (2 Kgs 21:19) and Manasseh died aged sixty-seven (2 Kgs 21:1), Amon was born to Manasseh when the latter was already forty-five. This could explain the jump in generation. Josiah was thirty-nine when he died (2 Kgs 22:1), and three months later one of his sons became king under the name Jehoiakim, aged twenty-five (2 Kgs 23:36). This means, taken at face value, that Josiah would have become a father at age fourteen. Similar calculations suggest that Amon was sixteen when he became a father (2 Kgs 21:19; 22:1) and Jehoiakim eighteen (2 Kgs 23:36; 24:8). If the named ancestors of Zephaniah all became fathers at about the age of sixteen—the average for Amon, Josiah, and Jehoiakim—the birth of Amon late in Manasseh's life would explain how Josiah ended up in an earlier "generation" from Zephaniah.[21] Similarly, the objection that claims that *Hezekiah* would have been given the title "king" if this is who he was is not cogent. Gene Rice reverses the argument:

> The memory of King Hezekiah would certainly have been alive in the time of Josiah and Zephaniah. If the Hezekiah of Zephaniah's ancestry were not King Hezekiah, it would have been incumbent upon the author of Zeph 1:1 to distinguish the two Hezekiahs in order to avoid misunderstanding and the displeasure of the Davidic dynasty, especially since Zephaniah is highly critical of Jerusalem and the royal house (cf. 1:8–9, 10–11, 12–13; 3:1–8).[22]

This could have been accomplished by not mentioning the name or by adding a further ancestor to disambiguate. As it is, there are no good reasons for rejecting the identification of *Hezekiah* with the reforming king of that name. But the cogency of Rice's argument in favor of the identification depends on the popularity of the name at the time. Are there other reasons for making the identification?

Robert Wilson argues that any genealogy of such length asserts a claim to power and that therefore the reference must be to King Hezekiah, thus claiming royal blood for Zephaniah.[23] But there are problems with this assumption. Hezekiah certainly had a good reputation among those who were responsible for and transmitted the biblical texts, but if Zephaniah as well as Josiah were his descendant, so were Manasseh and Amon. It is very doubtful

---

21. Cf. Rice, "African Roots," 21–22. See also Berlin, *Zephaniah*, 68–69, taking up an observation by David Noel Freedman about the relatively high average age at which Josiah's predecessors came to the throne (calculated at 34.3 years), which only needs an average age of the father at the birth of his firstborn of 25.75 years to fit in another generation between Hezekiah and Zephaniah.

22. Rice, "African Roots," 22.

23. Robert R. Wilson, *Prophecy and Society in Ancient Israel* (Minneapolis: Fortress, 1980), 279–80.

that the prophetic message would gain credibility among postexilic readers through an alleged connection with the royal house. The verdict is similar when we consider possible audience reception in preexilic times. A royal connection might help with the promulgation of the message, but it might hinder its reception if the critique of society is read and exposed as a manifesto for Zephaniah's own political aspirations. Put differently, if Zephaniah was a supporter of Josiah's reforms, being associated with the royal house might give his prophetic critiques of society less credibility, not more. There is no reason to think that ancient people were incapable of a hermeneutic of suspicion. Therefore, the thought that a link to the royal house is designed to lend weight to the prophetic message fails to convince here. It also overlooks that the identification of the *Hezekiah* in Zephaniah's genealogy with the king of that name is not explicit and therefore remains uncertain.

What, then, is the reason for tracing Zephaniah's genealogy that far back? In my view, it is to bring to mind King Hezekiah and his zeal for reform,[24] whether or not Zephaniah's ancestor was the king or someone who bore his name. While this could be seen as claiming Zephaniah as a true heir of Hezekiah's legacy, the rhetorical reason for mentioning Hezekiah may have had more to do with the themes of the book than with Zephaniah himself.[25] It may be the small beginnings of a "kingship" thread (see the commentary on 1:5), but it certainly can serve to highlight the necessity as well as the rather limited effectiveness of royal reform. The first readers may have also remembered that it was during Hezekiah's reign that Assyria brought an end to the Northern Kingdom. The destruction of Israel could be seen both as prefiguring the "end of the world" scenario outlined in Zephaniah for Judah and the region and as heralding the height of the Neo-Assyrian Empire (reached a few decades later). It was the largest empire the world had seen up to that day, and its end will be a fundamental part of Zephaniah's message.

There is another possibility overlooked by commentators so far but worth considering. Genealogies are especially important in tribal societies. Since we find in Zephaniah a condemnation of the urban elite in particular, an extended genealogy could signal allegiance to an older ideal based on kinship. Tribal identity contrasts with the identity of the urban elites, whom the prophet portrays arrayed in foreign attire (see the commentary on 1:8).

---

24. Cf. Christoph Levin, "Zephaniah," 123. Others argue for a reference to King Hezekiah based on perceived redactional links with Hos 1:1 and Mic 1:1; see Nogalski, *Literary Precursors*, 86, 181–83; Byron G. Curtis, "The Zion-Daughter Oracles: Evidence on the Identity and Ideology of the Late Redactors of the Book of the Twelve," in Nogalski and Sweeney, *Reading and Hearing*, 171–72.

25. Werse (*Reconsidering*, 287–90) believes that the reference to King Hezekiah picks up from Mic 1:1, establishing a chain linking Hosea, Amos, and Micah with Zephaniah.

Zephaniah's ministry is placed *in the days of Josiah* (ca. 640–609 BC).[26] A more precise dating is not usually given for preexilic prophets (Jer 1:2–3 gives us the exception to the rule: a more precise date, and one associated with Josiah in v. 2), although the mention of Josiah raises the question whether Zephaniah ministered before or after the reform. On the common assumption that the superscription in its current form is postexilic, or at least could have been revised in postexilic times, the absence of further precision is noteworthy. In a discussion above concerning the relationship between Zephaniah's prophecy and Josiah's reform (see pp. 432–33), I suggested that the oracles concerning other nations favor a date earlier in Josiah's reign. Even so, the book does not allow us to confidently date the prophet before, alongside, or toward the end of Josiah's reforms, and this may be for a reason.[27] The book of Zephaniah has a broader perspective that takes in the destruction of Jerusalem announced by Huldah during the reign of Josiah. The prophet can be seen as supporting Josiah's agenda but looking beyond it in the knowledge that Josiah's reforms will at best help to delay the inevitable. Seeking YHWH is the means to preserve a remnant rather than avert the coming disaster.

The addition *son of Amon* to *Josiah*, while probably not strictly necessary, is not unusual (cf. Jer 1:2). It merely gives *Josiah* his full name. Robertson observes that it "underscores the perilous situation in which Zephaniah prophesied. For Amon had been assassinated in an action of political intrigue by his own officials (2 K. 21:23)."[28]

Reflection

The superscription invites us to hear the content of the following as a word from Israel's covenant God mediated through a certain Zephaniah back in the days of King Josiah. Floyd observes well that the book, in the superscription, "presents the revelation to Zephaniah retrospectively, from the standpoint of an unidentified author for whom 'the days of Josiah' are at least to some extent past history," but, in the following, "addresses its readers in much the same way that a prophet would have addressed a live audience of hearers."[29] We are asked imaginatively to enter *the days of Josiah* but also to hear these

---

26. See Dan'el Kahn, "Revisiting the Date of King Josiah's Death," in Botta, *Shadow of Bezalel*, 255–64, for an argument in favor of May/June 609 as the time of Josiah's death.

27. Vlaardingerbroek, *Zephaniah*, 15–24.

28. Robertson, *Nahum*, 256.

29. Floyd, *Minor Prophets 2*, 170, 171. The latter point is well made against Ben Zvi's (*Zephaniah*, 349) characterization of the author of the book as not assuming a prophetic role.

words as addressed to us. Zephaniah's prophecies are anchored in the world of the final king on the throne of Jerusalem to be evaluated positively within the Bible as well as apparently the first king to have been confronted with the message of the now inevitable destruction of Jerusalem (2 Kgs 22:14–20 // 2 Chr 34:22–28).[30] As those looking back to the days of Josiah, we know that the reforms did not fundamentally alter the relationship between the people of Judah and YHWH and that Jerusalem did not accept correction (3:2) and was finally overthrown in the Babylonian reordering of the world of the fertile crescent. But this does not mean that Josiah's reforms were useless or fruitless. If it is true that Zephaniah supported Josiah's reforms, it may also be true that we have Josiah's reforms to thank for this book. Without the galvanization of the YHWH-loyal in the days of Josiah, prophetic messages like those of Zephaniah might have been lost.

If it was available in the early days of Josiah's reforms, Zephaniah's message could have been heard as encouraging a seeking for God in the face of the coming disintegration of the whole world. Such a seeking for God would not carry the promise of being able to avert disaster but would offer the possibility of surviving the conflagration. To the extent that some might have expected Josiah's reforms to herald the return of a glorious greater Davidic kingdom, Zephaniah's prophecy would have poured cold water on the excitement, affirming Huldah's prophecy more strongly than Josiah's reforms. Vlaardingerbroek distinguishes between three related movements at the time of Josiah, a "nationalistic-reformational school of thought" (Josiah), a "prophetic school which had long ceased to see any benefit in political and religious reformation" (Huldah), and "the deuteronomistic movement which combined prophetic influence with cultic and reformational interest." He associates Zeph 1:2–3 and 3:1–8 with the second current and 2:4–15 with a more positive attitude toward Josiah's reforms.[31] Sweeney reckons that 1:2–18 "was written to support Josiah's program and efforts."[32] Irsigler believes that the prophet cannot be identified as a supporter of Josiah's reform but that the reform movement nevertheless received his message as motivating and inspiring.[33] In the end, this remains guesswork. But what is clear is that Zephaniah overlaps with the accounts of Josiah's reign in the announcement of disaster, in stressing the urgency of the need to seek God, and in holding out the possibility of survival for a remnant, expressed in Huldah's prophecy by

30. Cf. my discussion of Ezek 1:1 in Renz, *Rhetorical Function*, 133–35, suggesting that Huldah's prophecy was decades later remembered as the beginning of the end.

31. Vlaardingerbroek, *Zephaniah*, 20. For the view that Zeph 2 supports Josiah's political ambitions, cf. Anselm C. Hagedorn, "When Did Zephaniah Become a Supporter of Josiah's Reform?" *JTS* 62 (2011): 453–75; see also the comments below on the composition of 2:4–15.

32. Sweeney, *Zephaniah*, 53.

33. Irsigler, *Zefanja*, 70.

the sparing of Josiah himself. Josiah's premature death, however, may serve as a reminder that nothing can be taken for granted.

Floyd observes how difficult it is to distinguish between any original words of Zephaniah and possible secondary additions. He notes that a number of scholars have "supposed that the book simply reports what Zephaniah said without much, if any, secondary reworking," but he believes that "if the author were merely a transcriber of Zephaniah's words . . . there would be no need for the self-consciously retrospective viewpoint created by the superscription."[34] This apparently assumes that the author of 1:1 is the author of the book, but this need not be the case. It is conceivable that 1:1 is an annotation by someone other than the author of the book's prophetic message.

II. DECLARATION OF SWEEPING JUDGMENT (1:2–6)

^{2}*I will make a sweeping end*[a] *of everything*
   from[b] *the face of the ground, utterance of YHWH.*
^{3}*I will make an end of human*[c] *and animal;*
   I will make an end of the birds of the air[d] *and the fish of the sea,*
      and what causes the wicked to stumble.[e]
I will cut off humanity from the face of the ground, utterance of YHWH.
^{4}*I will stretch out my hand against Judah*
   and against all the inhabitants of Jerusalem.
I will cut off from this place any vestige[f] *of "the Master,"*[g]
   the names of the cult attendants[h] *with the priests,*
^{5}*and those who offer obeisance*[i] *on the roofs to the host of heaven,*
   namely[j] *those offering obeisance who swear to YHWH*[k]
      and those who swear by their King,[l]
^{6}*and those who turn aside from following YHWH,*[m]
   and who do not seek YHWH and do not inquire of him.

a. The MT reads the *qal* infinitive absolute of *'sp* ("to gather") with what appears to be the *hiphil* short *yiqtol* form of *swp* ("I will make an end"; cf. Jer 8:13; see *HALOT*). The use of two different roots in such a construction is highly unusual and therefore often considered objectionable. The most popular among alternative proposals may be to read the second verb with different vocalization as the *qal* participle of *'sp* (*'ōsēp*), as suggested in GKC 72aa (so, e.g., *BHS*; Rudolph, *Nahum*, 261; Vlaardingerbroek, *Zephaniah*, 58; Irsigler, *Zefanja*, 95, 97–98; Dietrich, *Nahum*, 200). See the fuller discussion in Vlaardingerbroek, *Zephaniah*, 57–59, who adopts this, and Sweeney, *Zephaniah*, 58–62, who retains the MT. Jason S. DeRouchie ("YHWH's Future Ingathering in Zephaniah 1:2: Interpreting אָסֹף אָסֵף," *HS* 59 [2018]: 173–91) argues that the second form can be read as a *hiphil yiqtol* of *'sp*, with the customary dropping of the first *aleph* (cf. GKC 68g). Note that the form *'ōsēp* is attested both as a *qal*

34. Floyd, *Minor Prophets 2*, 175.

participle of 'sp (Num 19:10) and elsewhere as a form of ysp (Deut 18:16; Ezek 5:16; cf. Gen 4:12; Num 22:19; Deut 12:32 [13:1]; the plene form in Joel 2:2; see JM 75f).

b. Or "from upon" (also in v. 3); mēʿal is idiomatic in Hebrew with pənê hāʾădāmâ, but "from upon" is not idiomatic in English.

c. All Hebrew nouns designating groups in the first two lines are collective, which is difficult to imitate because English does not have a collective noun for animals corresponding to humanity ("animal kingdom" does not seem a good substitute here) or for birds corresponding to *fish* (which in English doubles as a collective). The use of the singular seems to work in the first colon, but the plural is required for "birds" in the second colon.

d. Literally "bird(s) of the sky" to poetically match *fish of the sea*; the phrase distinguishes flying birds from those more at home on land and in water, such as chickens and ducks. Strictly speaking, the phrase encompasses all creatures that fly, including bats and insects (see Lev 11). In English, *air* seems to match better with *sea*, and *bird of the air*, while not idiomatic English, probably makes more sense in English than "bird of the sky." For the use of the plural, see above.

e. Interpreting *makšēlôt* as an unusual form of the *hiphil* participle (fem. pl.), my translation seeks to preserve the openness of the Hebrew, translating neither "those who . . ." (Sweeney), which would imply personal agents, nor "the things that . . ." (Patterson), which would imply the opposite. The verb is used in this sense in Ezek 36:15; Mal 2:8; Prov 4:16. Alternatively: "the stumbling blocks with the wicked." The noun is used in Isa 3:6 to refer to a rubble of ruins. The whole phrase is usually considered a late gloss. Its absence in many LXX MSS is often adduced as evidence that the phrase originated after 200 BC. Gelston, by contrast, suggests that the Greek translator deliberately omitted the phrase as unintelligible (*BHQ*, 13:126*), and it should be noted that something like this phrase appears in several recensions of the Greek text and among its commentators (cf. BA 23.4–9, 339–40; Jerome, *Twelve*, 116; Theodoret of Cyrus, *Commentaries on the Prophets*, trans. Robert Charles Hill, vol. 3 [Brookline, MA: Holy Cross Orthodox Press, 2006], 341–42). Tov claims that there is enough space in the damaged 8ḤevXIIgr for the phrase; cf. Sweeney, *Zephaniah*, 55. Sidney Zandstra (*The Witness of the Vulgate, Peshitta and Septuagint to the Text of Zephaniah* [New York: Columbia University Press, 1909], 43) considers the testimony of the versions "contradictory and entirely inconclusive."

f. The LXX has "the names" (*ta onomata tēs Baal*) as with the next phrase. The LXX construes "Baal" with both the feminine and (more regularly) the masculine article in narratives; in prophetic literature, only the feminine is used (Hos 2:8[10]; 13:1; Jer 2:8, 28; 7:9; 11:13, 17; 12:16; 19:5; 23:27; 32:29 [LXX 39:29], 35), maybe for polemical reasons, orally substituting *aischynē* ("shame") for the name (*BHQ*, 13:126*).

g. The use of the definite article with *baʿal* here, as elsewhere in the Hebrew Bible (e.g., 1 Kgs 18:21; Jer 19:5; cf. the use of the plural), indicates that *baʿal* is, strictly speaking, an epithet rather than a name, although it came to be used as a name for the Canaanite god of storm and fertility par excellence. In Ugaritic religion, it is used as a proper name for a deity, with the appellative "lord" having a different spelling. Designations like Baal-Peor ("the Master worshiped in Peor," Num 25:3) likely refer to specific, local manifestations of the one deity rather than to strictly distinct beings. The title is used also to indicate status within human relationships (e.g., for landowners and husbands). The related verb ("to be the master") can be applied to YHWH (Jer 3:14; 31:32), but the use of the title for YHWH is avoided in Scripture (cf. Hos 2:16[18]). For fuller discussion see, e.g., Wolfgang Herrmann, "Baal," *DDD*, 132–39, and some of the subsequent entries in *DDD*.

h. The standard Greek text renders *hakkəmārîm ʿim-hakkōhănîm* with *tōn hiereōn* ("of the priests") only, likely omitting what was unintelligible to the translator (so also Zandstra, *Witness*, 42). In Hos 10:5, the translator derived *wkmryw* (MT *ûkəmārāyw*) from the verb *mrh* ("to be rebellious"), not reading the *yod* and interpreting the *kaph* as a preposition. The only other occurrence of the noun, in 2 Kgs 23:5, is transliterated in the LXX. Note that, as with the phrase in v. 3, there is evidence of the presence of two designations in parts of the Greek tradition; see BA 23.4–9, 341; cf. Theodoret of Cyrus, *Commentaries*, 208.

i. This is the first in a series of participles with the definite article. Only the final line of v. 6, which begins with the relative particle, has finite verbs. A fivefold use of "the ones" (with offering obeisance [2×], swearing [2×], turning aside) would be clumsy in English, and I have therefore not tried to imitate the Hebrew syntax in translation.

j. Interpreting the duplication as introducing a clarification, whether redactional or original.

k. Dietrich (*Nahum*, 200), among others, alters to "those who bow down before the moon" (cf. *BHS*), but where "moon" and "host of heaven" are mentioned elsewhere, the latter comes second.

l. Ancient versions and modern translations often read the name of the Ammonite god Milcom here, which the consonants allow. (The NIV uses "Molek" [= Molech] to render "Milcom" throughout the Bible. Other translations distinguish between the two.) The main Greek MSS support the vocalization in MT, but a number of MSS read "Milcom" or "Molech." On the relationship between the two, see further below, and for the wider context, see Wilfred H. van Soldt, "The Vocalisation of the Word *MLK*, 'King', in Late Bronze Age Syllabic Texts from Syria and Palestine," in *Hamlet on a Hill: Semitic and Greek Studies Presented to Professor T. Muraoka on the Occasion of His Sixty-Fifth Birthday*, ed. Martin F. J. Baasten and Wido Th. van Peursen, OLA 118 (Leuven: Peeters, 2003), 449–71. See also Nicholas R. Werse, "Of Gods and Kings: The Case for Reading 'Milcom' in Zephaniah 1:5bβ," *VT* 68 (2018): 505–13.

m. Literally "from after YHWH." The phrase is used more than a dozen times in the Hebrew Bible; it is elliptical for "from walking after YHWH" (for "walking after YHWH," see Deut 13:4[5]; 2 Chr 34:31; Hos 11:10).

Composition

The first major section following the superscription is 1:2–18. It can be read as a single speech announcing a comprehensive conflagration that focuses on Judah and Jerusalem. It prepares the ground for the exhortation in 2:1–3, on which the remainder of ch. 2 at least depends. Zephaniah 2:1–3 is the central hinge on which much of the book turns. It is therefore not advisable to take 2:1–3 with 1:2–18 as a number of scholars do on the grounds that both mention the Day of YHWH.[35] Within the announcement in 1:2–18, we can distinguish between a prophecy of punishment in 1:2–6 and an elaboration that opens with the first address to the audience in v. 7, signaled by a particle interjection that functions as an imperative.

In contemporary scholarship, Zeph 1 is often considered the product of

---

35. I agree here with Sweeney, *Zephaniah*, 50–51; cf. Floyd, *Minor Prophets 2*, 186.

a skillful weaving together of two different themes: judgment against Jerusalem and judgment against all humanity. In this case, the latter is usually
considered a later development. Earlier commentators typically did not recognize a theme of universal judgment here. Yerushalmi, whose commentary
seeks to offer the traditional Jewish interpretation, notes on 1:2 that Zephaniah "foresaw the destruction of all living things in the Land of Israel."[36]
Luther similarly comments that this is said about the Babylonian captivity.[37]
It is true that 'ădāmâ can be used to refer to the land of Israel (e.g., Deut 4:40;
5:16), but in this case 'ădāmâ is usually further qualified, and the expression
appears to be universal in nearly every other instance. Only in three places
(1 Kgs 8:40; 9:7; 2 Chr 6:31) does the phrase denote the promised land, as
clarified in the attached relative clause. In Jer 35:7, it refers to Babylonia.
In several places, the reference is to the ground, either generally (Jer 8:2;
16:4; 25:33) or in view of a drought-ridden region extending beyond Israel
(1 Kgs 17:14; 18:1). Most often, the reference can be said to be so broad as to
be universal.[38] Mention of fish and birds (cf., e.g., Ps 8:8[9]; Ezek 38:20) is
suggestive of such a broader reference.

Nevertheless, this need not imply that the author envisaged a literal, universal judgment. Gowan rightly comments: "It appears that we are not to take
the destruction of the whole earth literally, for later the book does not speak
of restoration in terms of re-creation, as would seem to be necessary, and as
other prophets did."[39] Certainly, the theme is not sufficiently developed to
warrant the assumption that redactors turned an earlier localized judgment
into an eschatological judgment of the world. In other words, 1:2–3 could
give expression to an apocalyptic perspective if considered in isolation, but
this is not an easy reading to sustain when the verses are read in their context.
Dietrich thinks that the "preexilic original layer" (identified as 1:2, 4–5, 7,
8aβb, 9, 10aβb, 13a, 14–16, 17aαb; 2:1–3, 4–6, 9, 13–15; 3:1, 3–4, 5) announces
that "the entire political system at that juncture needed to be eliminated." But
following Irsigler, he believes that 1:3, 17aβb, 18, which he identifies as "postexilic accretions" (along with 2:7, 9b–11; 3:9–20), suggest a world judgment
of the sort that belongs to a developing apocalyptic worldview.[40] The prob-

36. Shmuel Yerushalmi, *The Book of Trei-Asar (2)*, trans. Zvi Faier (New York: Moznaim,
1997), 219. Cf. Rashi's comment on v. 17, explicitly explaining *ādām* as a reference to Israel.
37. *LW* 18:320.
38. See Gen 2:6; 4:14; 6:1, 7; 7:4, 23; 8:8, 13; Exod 32:12; 33:16; Num 12:3; Deut 6:15; 7:6;
14:2; 1 Sam 20:15; 2 Sam 14:7; 1 Kgs 13:34; Isa 23:17; Jer 25:26; 28:16; Ezek 38:20; Amos 9:8.
39. Gowan, *Theology*, 81. Irsigler, by contrast, insists that vv. 2–3 speak of the end of the
world with the elimination of all life, beyond which no new life is in sight (*Zefanja*, 98).
40. Dietrich, *Nahum*, 188, 191, 212. See Irsigler, *Zefanja*, 101–2, 186–88. Irsigler also counts
v. 2 as belonging to the postexilic layer; cf. Christoph Levin, "Zephaniah," 124–25. Werse
(*Reconsidering*, 267–71) argues that only v. 3 is dependent on Genesis and that it is late. The

lem is that the postulated redactors left us a text that as a whole focuses on Judah and Jerusalem, the final verse of the chapter notwithstanding. If they had wanted to develop the message into a worldwide judgment, this might have been done better by adding the universalizing passages later, having *I will stretch out my hand against Judah* followed by something like "and then I will stretch out my hand against all nations, and so I will make a sweeping end to everything." This is not simply to complain that the redactors did not write what one would have expected them to write but to observe that it is difficult to read 1:2–3 as apocalyptical if one reads on. It seems methodologically problematic to seek to reconstruct the meaning redactors wanted to communicate by paying attention to the added texts only rather than the text they would have transmitted—namely, the basic text plus the additions.

If 1:2–6 or even 1:2–18 communicated a clear vision of universal judgment, we might be able to discern an earlier version of the text that focused on Judah and Jerusalem. Because 1:2–6 and even 1:2–18 as a whole do not sound apocalyptic to me, this commentary prefers the reading of scholars like Floyd, who interpret Zephaniah in terms of an announcement of "the disintegration of the present world order" in which Josiah's purge takes on "mythic connotations," marking "a cosmic turning point."[41] Rhetorically, the sweeping opening judgment is focused on Jerusalem, and the universal language does not detract from this. As Vlaardingerbroek observes, "There is actually nothing that points to a world judgment. The indefiniteness and lack of concreteness of the language used in vss. 2, 3 and 14ff. is certainly something other than speaking of world judgment."[42] The universal language can be explained in relation to theological concepts underlying the message.[43] It also prepares for the notion of a comprehensive reshaping of the world order that does not merely affect Judah and Jerusalem and that finds expression in ch. 2. Nothing in 1:2–18 leads readers to expect a universal judgment separate from the sixth century, with some verses applying to the events surrounding the Neo-Babylonian campaigns and others to a different, later event. Furthermore, the idea is unwarranted that the absence of any reference to the Babylonians or another human instrument means that the

---

argument for v. 3 being a later addition is weakened if the Priestly source of the Pentateuch (P) is (largely) preexilic.

41. Floyd, *Minor Prophets 2*, 170, 177, 176.

42. Vlaardingerbroek, *Zephaniah*, 50.

43. Sweeney, *Zephaniah*, 52, 57; cf. Floyd, *Minor Prophets 2*, 186, 190–91. Vlaardingerbroek (*Zephaniah*, 50) suggests that "a certain universality was possibly inherent in the idea of the Day of the Lord."

author must have thought that the events would be brought about directly by YHWH himself.[44]

More plausible is the suggestion that the reference to those who cause stumbling is a later note, although its absence in the LXX may just as well be explained by the translator having failed to make sense of it. But the extent to which the phrase necessarily reshapes the meaning of the verse has been overplayed. The shift from divine speech to speech about YHWH is also sometimes thought to indicate the different origin of the latter. Indeed, Levin considers the terminology of v. 6 to be that of late piety, which proves that the addition "cannot be earlier than the late Persian era."[45] This is a bold and surprising claim. To "seek YHWH" (*biqqēš 'et-yhwh*) is attested in Exod 33:7; Deut 4:29; Hos 3:5; 5:6; 7:10 (cf. 2 Sam 12:16; Hos 5:15; Ps 40:16[17]), as well as Zeph 2:3; to "enquire of YHWH" (*dāraš 'et-yhwh*) appears in Deut 4:29; Isa 9:13(12); 31:1; Hos 10:12; Amos 5:4, 6; Pss 9:10(11); 22:26(27); 34:4(5), 10(11), as well as in the account of Josiah's reign in 2 Kgs 22:13, 18 and 2 Chr 34:21, 26. If vv. 5b–6 were a later expansion, the addition could have been inspired by Zeph 2:3 and the account of Josiah's reign. But as Hadjiev notes, "the motif of seeking Yahweh is not exclusively Deuteronomistic," being "frequent in prophetic literature and the Psalms." Further, "the connections between Zeph. 1:4–6 and the narrative in 2 Kings 23 are confined mainly to the list of persons and practices condemned as idolatrous." This, he observes, could be the result of referring to the same historical situation, and "the divergences between the two texts suggests that this is the more likely solution."[46] Hadjiev also examines alleged closeness of Zeph 1:6–8 to Mic 5:10–14(9–13) and the idea that the motif of seeking YHWH connects Zeph 1:6 (and 2:3) with Hosea and Amos. But he finds strong grounds for excluding a literary relationship.[47] Given that the mix between cited divine speech and prophetic speech about YHWH is so common in prophetic literature, it may well be a stylistic feature of biblical prophecy that modern convention dislikes rather than an indication of the different origin of various verses and half-verses.

The utterance formula at the end of v. 2 sets this verse apart as the opening statement on which vv. 3–6 elaborate. The utterance formula in v. 3 is best applied to vv. 3–6, as no similar formula marks off vv. 4–6 as a separate paragraph. As noted above, v. 7 opens another section, which employs the Day

44. Contra Dietrich, *Nahum*, 188.
45. Christoph Levin, "Zephaniah," 127; cf., e.g., Irsigler, *Zefanja*, 118.
46. Hadjiev, "Zephaniah," 327. The divergences include some significant omissions.
47. Hadjiev, "Zephaniah," 328–29. In particular, the function of the motifs is quite different in the various texts.

of YHWH motif to develop the prophecy of punishment in 1:2–6 and builds apprehension prior to the exhortation in 2:1–3.

Commentary

2 The first *utterance of YHWH* makes for a striking beginning. The opening infinitive is from a verb that is also used for gathering in the harvest. This motif is echoed in the word *ground*; the term designates the land on which and from which one lives (Dietrich translates specifically "farmland") and is linked with the word for "human" (cf. Gen 2:7; 3:19).[48] Sweeney suggests that "the statement presupposes a setting in relation to the Festival of Sukkot . . . the concluding harvest festival of the year" that "completes the harvest and therefore presupposes the removal of the entire range of agricultural produce from the land."[49] This would fit with the festival call in v. 7. In any case, the latent harvest motif readily interacts with the stubble/straw gathering motif in 2:1.[50] But the verb "to gather" can also be used in the sense of "to take away, remove" (see standard dictionaries), and here the imagery of harvest is used to announce a comprehensive annihilation *from the face of the ground* (an ominous phrase in other places as well; cf. Gen 4:14; 6:7; 7:4; 8:8; Exod 32:12; Deut 6:15; 1 Sam 20:15; 1 Kgs 9:7; 13:34; Jer 28:16; Amos 9:8). Just how comprehensive the action will be is spelled out in the following verse.

If the MT vocalization is followed, the main verb probably derives from *swp* ("to make an end"). Infinitive absolutes are usually paired with finite verbs of the same root. A combination of two different verbal roots in such a construction is, therefore, unexpected, although it is found with the same two roots also in Jer 8:13 (*'āsōp 'ăsîpēm*), where many question its originality. A combination of two other roots sharing two root letters is found in 2 Sam 1:6 (*niqrō' niqrêtî*, "I just happened to be").[51] This may be enough evidence to allow for such a play of roots, especially given that the harvest associations of "to gather" fit well and *I will make an end* is repeated in the following verse.[52] The infinitive, therefore, does not underline the certainty or decisiveness of the event as is often the case with this construction (e.g., *'āsōp 'e'ĕsōp*, "I will

---

48. Dietrich, *Nahum*, 198. Cf. the discussion in Irsigler, *Zefanja*, 97–98.

49. Sweeney, *Zephaniah*, 62; cf. Roberts, *Nahum*, 177 (with regard to v. 7, understood as part of the same unit).

50. Note the use of the root in 3:18.

51. As noted by Sweeney, *Zephaniah*, 59.

52. As pointed out in the translation note, DeRouchie ("YHWH's Future Ingathering") also derives the second verb from *'sp*. He interprets the ingathering as separate from the punishment (cf. 3:8) and argues that it is the same event as the ingathering for salvation (cf. 3:18).

surely gather," in Mic 2:12).[53] Instead, it enriches the elimination motif with that of (harvest) gathering, thus preparing for the different gathering in 2:1. The use of two different roots that can be used to refer to elimination is arguably no less effective than the repetition of a single root would have been. For the phrase *utterance of YHWH*, see the commentary on Nah 2:13(14).

3 The total, albeit not necessarily universal, destruction is now explained both in its comprehensiveness and in its focus on humanity. The expression *'ādām ûbəhēm* (*human and animal*) is a common merism, often used in the context of disaster, with *animal* probably indicating all embodied creatures, but certainly wild as well as domesticated animals.[54] It is therefore not advisable to translate "humans and cattle" as Dietrich does.[55] In none of the other occurrences of this combination in the prophetic literature is the reference point universal rather than regional.[56] The second colon develops this into an implicit triad (earth, sky, sea), another way of speaking of totality. Such a tripartite division of the world is implied elsewhere in the Bible (Deut 4:16–19; 30:11–13; Pss 8:7–8[8–9]; 69:34[35]; 96:11; Job 12:7–8; Hos 4:3), and there are reasons to doubt specific influence from the flood story in Genesis.[57] Repetitions of words and roots echo the gathering motif. Hearing in *'āsēp* (*I will make an end*) an allusion to the root *'sp* ("to gather," see above) is surely appropriate, especially in connection with fish, for whom gathering leads to the end of their lives (cf. Num 11:22; Hos 4:3). The way the comprehensive nature of the destruction is spelled out here is very similar to Hos 4:3, again in a context focusing on human misconduct. All creation suffers as a consequence of human sin.[58]

The phrase *what causes the wicked to stumble* may be later than the main composition of the text.[59] It is often understood to explain the totality of the judgment by implying that the animals caused people to stumble because they gave rise to idolatry.[60] But the idea that failings in the human

53. Indeed, the certainty of "making an end" is never underlined with this construction. The verb is emphasised by the addition of *yaḥdāw* ("altogether") in Isa 66:17 and by the addition of the verb *tmm* ("to be complete") in Ps 73:19.

54. Cf. Ben Zvi, *Zephaniah*, 56; Sweeney, *Zephaniah*, 63.

55. Dietrich, *Nahum*, 198. Cf. Vlaardingerbroek, *Zephaniah*, 59–60, for the broader range of meaning.

56. See Jer 7:20; 21:6; 27:5; 31:27; 32:43; 33:10, 12; 36:29; 50:3; 51:62; Ezek 14:13, 17, 19, 21; 25:13; 29:8, 11; 32:13; 36:11; Jonah 3:7–8; Hag 1:11; Zech 2:4(8); 8:10. A more universal meaning may be assumed in Ps 36:6(7).

57. See Ben Zvi, *Zephaniah*, 55–58; cf. Vlaardingerbroek, *Zephaniah*, 56–57.

58. Cf. Sweeney, *Zephaniah*, 63.

59. See, e.g., Ben Zvi, *Zephaniah*, 58–60; Vlaardingerbroek, *Zephaniah*, 55.

60. E.g., Roberts, *Nahum*, 167. Irsigler (*Zefanja*, 100–101) urges that humans are included as well given the human-shaped idols condemned in places like Deut 4. He considers it an early Hellenistic gloss.

realm and the punishments associated with them disrupt all of creation is not unusual within the Bible (e.g., Jer 9:10[9]; Hos 4:3), and I am not convinced that any transmitter of the tradition would have seen an urgent need to explain the comprehensiveness of the judgment here. While nearly everything could become an occasion for idolatry, birds and fish would seem to be among the less plausible candidates for stimulating idolatry.[61] Later on, in v. 5, *what causes the wicked to stumble* are the stars and maybe sun and moon (cf. Jer 8:2), whose elimination would mean the end of the world (cf. Jer 31:35–36). A student of mine, Tim Ambrose, suggested an allusion to Gen 1, with the land animals in the first colon relating to the sixth day of creation, the birds and fish in the second colon to the fifth, and consequently *what causes the wicked to stumble* to the fourth day, on which sun and moon were created. Going through the list of populations backward underlines the undoing of creation.[62] This reading is too subtle to be claimed confidently as the original meaning of the text, but it is in the spirit of the passage.[63] This colon, like the preceding ones, serves to underline the comprehensiveness of the elimination, not unlike the references to *vestige* and *names* in the following verse. Not only are *the wicked* destroyed but also what causes them to stumble.

Maybe it is not necessary to specify *what causes the wicked to stumble* as a reference to one thing rather than another. A list of suspects would include: animals and humans (elaborating on the preceding), sun, moon and stars (developing the preceding and anticipating what follows), high places (reading with a knowledge of the accounts of Josiah's reforms), priests (note the reference to priests in the next verse, and see Mal 2:8; cf. Ezek 44:12), or even iniquity in the abstract (cf. Ezek 14:3, 4, 7). The reference to *the wicked* does not necessarily imply that only a part of humanity is targeted; prophecies of punishment often address the people as a whole, characterizing them as evil. In the same way here, *the wicked* may well be shorthand for the whole population. Such broad-brush language does not usually imply that there were none that might be considered "righteous"

61. Animals featured prominently in Egyptian cults, but even in that context, fish feature relatively rarely. I do not know whether the worship of the fish goddess Hatmehit was still extant in Persian, let alone Hellenistic, times. Neither fish nor birds find a mention in the polemic against idolatry in the Epistle of Jeremiah or in the Wisdom of Solomon.

62. For the general idea that Zephaniah reverses the sequence of creation in Gen 1 see De Roche, "The 'Sweeping' of Creation," 106; J. Alec Motyer, "Zephaniah," in *The Minor Prophets: An Exegetical and Expository Commentary*, ed. Thomas Edward McComiskey, vol. 3 (Grand Rapids: Baker, 1998), 911–12; cf. Melvin, "Making All Things New (Again)," 274–76.

63. The fact that *fish* are not explicitly mentioned in Gen 1:20–23 (but see v. 28) is not an insurmountable obstacle given that the work of day five is very clearly the populating of the world with flying creatures and water creatures.

but rather that the number of "the righteous" is negligible and unable to prevent national disaster.

The logic behind such an announcement of elimination presumes the presence of evil to which YHWH responds, and in the Hebrew Bible this evil is always, or nearly always, laid at the feet of humans. It is entirely consistent with this that the wicked are presumed to be human and that the *utterance of YHWH* concludes with *I will cut off humanity from the face of the ground*, thus specifying the actual target. The switch to the more common verb *cut off*, which is more at home in judicial contexts than the verbs "to gather" and "to make an end," might facilitate a distinction between the specifically intended target and the broader category of objects affected.

There is a Jewish tradition of reading the first (longer) part of v. 3 as a question that is answered negatively in the second part, which declares that God will only eliminate humans.[64] But linguistically, this seems implausible. While questions are not always marked in Biblical Hebrew, good communication would surely require disambiguation in this case. Thus, in so far as it is a possible reading, it is not a reading that can be claimed as natural or intended by the author. A similar objection must be raised to Levin's proposal that v. 3b was added "to limit the punishment to humankind only" by way of correcting vv. 2–3aα (v. 3aβ being a still later gloss).[65] The text as it stands still implies that the catastrophe includes fish and birds, as readers are hardly invited to choose whether to give credence to the first or the second part of the verse. A redactor who felt unable to delete clauses could not hope to succeed in undoing them by merely adding an alternative. The final statement does not correct the preceding but underlines the target of the judgment: *humanity* is to be removed from the *ground* (the "humus," if we were to imitate the wordplay).

4 Given the use of connection formulae at the beginning of vv. 8, 10, and 12, the absence of such a formula here is noteworthy. Stretching out his hand against Judah and Jerusalem is not something YHWH also does "on that day" but proves to be that which the comprehensive elimination vv. 2–3 speak of. Verses 2–3 implied that the destruction of humanity cannot but have an impact on the wider creation. In the same way, punitive action against God's chosen people and city cannot but have wider ramifications. In addition, both the placement of Zephaniah within the anthology and the anchoring of the prophecy in the reign of Josiah (v. 1), during which the coming destruction of Jerusalem was prophesied, puts the punishment of Judah and Jerusalem in the context of the Neo-Babylonian western campaigns, which were directed against other nations as well. The implication

---

64. See Yerushalmi, *Trei-Asar (2)*, 221–22.
65. Christoph Levin, "Zephaniah," 125.

is that all this is happening because YHWH acts against his people. Ben Zvi notes that the expression "to stretch out the hand against X" is prominent in the plague narratives, where X refers to the natural elements from which the disaster comes rather than the target. He notes that the only exception appears in Exod 7:5 "in an explanatory note concerning the reasons for the plagues that is not part of the narrative as such."[66] But this is also the only instance in Exodus where it is YHWH who stretches out his hand (against Egypt), which makes it of more direct relevance than the other references, in which Aaron and Moses stretch out their hands, often with a staff, to perform a symbolic action. In the prophetic literature, YHWH is always the agent, and the hand is always outstretched in readiness for a destructive strike, including in Zeph 2:3.[67] There is thus no question: *Judah* and *the inhabitants of Jerusalem* are the prime object of the threatened strike. But reuse of *I will cut off* again specifies the target more precisely, whereby *from this place* may refer back to Judah and Jerusalem or continue the progressive narrowing down of the target (humanity, Judah, Jerusalem) with a reference specifically to the temple.[68] As in Huldah's prophecy (2 Kgs 22:16–17, 19–20), *place* probably refers to Jerusalem.

The use of quotation marks around *"the Master"* is meant to signal that the epithet is regularly used with specific reference to the Canaanite deity Baal. The common translation as a proper name, already found in antiquity, is entirely justifiable even if the name Baal may have been used in a more general sense, but it obscures an ambiguity that may well be deliberate. Not translating the Hebrew as a proper name leaves it open that *"the Master"* interacts with the reference to *their King* in the next verse and *their lord* in v. 9. All these designations could be used with reference to YHWH, whom Zephaniah proclaims as the true master, king, and lord who is, however, not acknowledged as such by those who have chosen other lords for themselves. The extent to which Baal was worshipped alongside YHWH and other deities in seventh-century Judah is debated. Ben Zvi points out that while inscriptions testify to many Judean personal names that make reference to YHWH, no clear example of a name making reference to Baal has been found in Judah.[69] This does not prove that Baal was not worshipped in Judah, merely that YHWH was the national deity and as such most prominent

---

66. Ben Zvi, *Zephaniah*, 60. Actually, the expression is also used in Exod 14:16, 21, 26–27 for the division of the sea to be crossed, beyond the plague narratives as such. Cf. the similar symbolic act in Josh 8:18–19, 26.

67. Isa 5:25; 9:12, 17, 21(11, 16, 20); 10:4; 14:26–27; 23:11; 31:3; Jer 6:12; 15:6; 21:5; 51:25; Ezek 6:14; 14:9, 13; 16:27; 25:7, 13, 16; 35:3.

68. The latter is advocated, e.g., by Sweeney, *Zephaniah*, 66.

69. Ben Zvi, *Zephaniah*, 68–69; cf. Sweeney, *Zephaniah*, 67. This is strikingly different from the findings in Samaria, where about a quarter of theophoric names relate to Baal.

among Judeans, and certainly among the upper classes. What is clear is that those who worshipped YHWH did not necessarily do so exclusively. The presence of many figurines in late monarchic layers of archaeological sites throughout Jerusalem and Judah that are commonly interpreted as representing Asherah indicate widespread veneration of this Canaanite goddess.[70] In the same way, astral worship (cf. v. 5) and (prior to Josiah's reign) possibly worship of the Assyrian state god Assur was likely practiced alongside YHWH worship rather than as an alternative to it. It is possible that Baal was similarly worshipped alongside YHWH. But biblical authors seem to have used "Baal" not only to refer to a specific deity but also in a more abstract sense and polemically to designate any unacceptable worship.[71] This may be true here, so that the threat of cutting off *every vestige of "the Master"* in effect would be an announcement that anything associated with illegitimate worship will be removed. If those who engaged in this worship thought of themselves as worshippers of YHWH but venerated him as a god in the mold of Baal—maybe addressing YHWH as "Master" but more importantly treating him, say, as a dying-and-rising fertility god whose power is enhanced by sacrifices—then in the eyes of the biblical authors, they would have been Baal worshippers, idolaters. Such a perspective should not be dismissed as unduly polemic. It was common in the ancient world for gods and goddesses from different cultures to be identified with each other and for deities to be worshipped under different names. Even from a non-polemical phenomenological perspective, such practices could be described as essentially a Baal cult in which the name YHWH was used. The polemical or theological question is whether from a different perspective it could also be described as a YHWH cult. Zephaniah's prophecy shows no interest in carefully distinguishing between YHWH cults and non-YHWH cults; its interest lies in the legitimacy of worship. Such legitimacy is not guaranteed by a declared intention to have YHWH as its object.

The use of *vestige* parallel to *name* indicates that the cutting off is so comprehensive that nothing will be left as a reminder of what was (cf. Isa 14:22; 2 Sam 14:7). The phrase, therefore, does not imply that the Baal cult "has already been reduced in number or influence" and so "cannot be used to

---

See the studies by Mitka R. Golub, e.g., "Personal Names in Judah in the Iron Age II," *JSS* 62 (2017): 19–58.

70. Cf. the famous Kuntillet Ajrud inscriptions that mention "YHWH and his Ashera," where Ashera likely refers to the deity. (An Ashera is also a cult object.) See Nicholas Wyatt, "Ashera," *DDD*, 99–105.

71. See, e.g., Ben Zvi, *Zephaniah*, 66; Irsigler, *Zefanja*, 109. Carefully weighing the argument, Vlaardingerbroek (*Zephaniah*, 64–66) nevertheless thinks that veneration of Baal is in view here, given the specific references in v. 5 with which this is paired.

date Zephaniah after Josiah's reforms."[72] Nor does the expression suggest that "the people of Judah did not worship the Baal idol with the same zeal as the Ten Tribes had done,"[73] although this may be true in the light of the onomastic evidence if we define Baal worship more narrowly as worship of a deity distinct from YHWH. The equivalent in other Semitic languages of the term translated *cult attendants* (*kəmārîm*) appears frequently to designate priests but is found elsewhere in the Hebrew Bible only in Hos 10:5 and in the account of Josiah's reforms in 2 Kgs 23:5—in both cases for (Israelite/Judean) idolatrous priests.[74] Uehlinger proposed that *kəmārîm* refers to priests of the astral cult, maybe specifically attendants of the moon god.[75] But there are no such connotations in Hos 10:5, nor are the *kəmārîm* linked with the astral cult rather than the worship of Baal and Asherah in 2 Kgs 23:5. The related Aramaic term is not restricted in this way either.[76] In my view, the Hebrew term is attested too rarely to judge confidently whether it carried negative connotations in and of itself for biblical authors, although its absence in connection with legitimate worship is noteworthy. The term *priests*, by contrast, is regularly used to designate cult officials offering acceptable worship. Given that this second term can also designate (Israelite or non-Israelite) priests engaging in illegitimate worship (e.g., Judg 17:5), including priests serving other deities (e.g., 2 Kgs 10:19; 11:18; Jer 48:7; 49:3), it is not plausible that the complete phrase *the names of the cult attendants with the priests* is meant to distinguish between priests that seek to serve other gods and priests engaged in YHWH worship. Unless *the priests* derives from an early marginal note explaining the meaning of *cult attendants*, whose inclusion in the main text requires the addition of *with*,[77] the phrase is probably again a way of stressing completeness: not only will *the priests* be *cut off* but with them even *the*

72. Roberts, *Nahum*, 171. Similarly, among others, Irsigler, *Zefanja*, 104.

73. Yerushalmi, *Trei-Asar (2)*, 222.

74. The only other extant occurrence of the Hebrew term is in 4Q372, which, intriguingly in the light of the reference to high places in Hos 10:8 and 2 Kgs 23:5, polemizes against the "high place" of the Samaritans; see Matthew Thiessen, "4Q372 1 and the Continuation of Joseph's Exile," *DSD* 15 (2008): 380–95, esp. 390.

75. Christoph Uehlinger, "Astralkultpriester und Fremdgekleidete, Kanaanvolk und Silberwäger—Zur Verknüpfung von Kult- und Sozialkritik in Zef 1," in *Der Tag wird kommen: Ein interkontextuelles Gespräch über das Buch des Propheten Zefanja*, ed. Walter Dietrich and Milton Schwantes, SBS 170 (Stuttgart: KBW, 1996), 49–83. This is followed by Irsigler, *Zefanja*, 109–10; Dietrich, *Nahum*, 200.

76. The term is used, e.g., in the Elephantine papyri to refer to priests of the Egyptian god Khnub (Khnum), a god of fertility symbolised by the ram, namely in *AP* 27 (U. of Strasbourg Library, P. Aram. 2 [2×]) and *AP* 30 (Berlin, St. Mus. P. 13495). For Jewish priests, the standard term from the root *khn* is used in these documents.

77. E.g., Roberts, *Nahum*, 167–68; rejected, e.g., by Sweeney, *Zephaniah*, 68–69. Cf. Ben Zvi, *Zephaniah*, 69–72.

names of . . . the priests. The use of the rare word for *cult attendants* may then be explained by a desire to avoid the repetition of *priests.* The *priests* in view here are priests whose "Master" is Baal but, as argued above, this may well include priests who worship YHWH as a manifestation of Baal or possibly even priests serving the moon god or another deity. The question whether there are also those who worship YHWH faithfully in *this place* is not raised; if so, they are obviously not included in the implicit condemnation, even if they may be affected by the overall judgment.

5 In Hebrew, *and* is employed much more frequently—not only for the final item but usually for all items in a list, and also in places where English usage demands a different connector because what follows presents an alternative, a specification, or an emphasis (see GKC 154). In my view, the first occurrence of the conjunction introduces an additional item.[78] To the elimination of priests and every memory of them and of the cult, this verse adds the elimination of worshippers, *those who offer obeisance on the roofs to the host of heaven.* While it is included in the summary explanation for the end of the Northern Kingdom in 2 Kgs 17:16, the veneration of heavenly bodies is condemned specifically in connection with Judah rather than Israel (see, e.g., 2 Kgs 21:3, 5; 2 Chr 33:3, 5; Jer 19:13). Twice, sun and moon are mentioned before the reference to *the host of heaven* (Deut 17:3; Jer 8:2), which could suggest that the latter refers to the smaller lights (only). But twice, sun, moon, and stars are mentioned before *the host of heaven* (Deut 4:19; 2 Kgs 23:5). This indicates that *the host of heaven* is a summary phrase that can encompass sun and moon as well as stars (see especially 2 Kgs 23:4-5).[79] Even if *cult attendants* in the previous verse does not specifically refer to priests engaged in the worship of heavenly bodies, the main interest of Zephaniah does not lie in expanding the list of deities (if that were the intention, the absence of Asherah would seem odd) but in broadening the reference from cult officials to worshippers generally. Manasseh is reported to have built altars "for all the host of heavens" in the temple courtyards (2 Kgs 21:5)—that is, right at the heart of Judah's cultic center, and widely accessible. The reference to *the roofs* here suggests even more widespread veneration (cf. 2 Kgs 23:12; Jer 19:13), perhaps inspired by Manasseh's act.[80]

The relationship of the various participle phrases to each other is not

78. Sweeney (*Zephaniah,* 69) thinks that the absence of the conjunction before *the name of the cult attendants with the priests* in the previous verse "indicates that v. 5a and 5b specify this phrase in particular." I do not know why this should be so.

79. In 1 Kgs 22:19 // 2 Chr 18:18 and presumably Neh 9:6, *the host of heaven* refers to YHWH's court attendants. Isa 34:4; Jer 33:22; and Dan 8:10 probably refer to the natural world.

80. See Irsigler, *Zefanja,* 110-14, for discussion and archaeological evidence that can be interpreted as suggesting an increase of the worship of sun and moon in seventh-century Judah (but see his note on p. 120).

entirely straightforward.[81] Tentatively, one may take the repetition of *those offering obeisance* as indicating that the second half of the verse offers an explication and the following participles as characterizing *those offering obeisance* further. For this reason, *namely* translates the second occurrence of the conjunction here. In other words, among those bowing down on the housetops to sun, moon, and stars are people *who swear to YHWH and those who swear by their King*. At first sight, the answer to the question whether these are two groups or one depends on who the *King* is. Most likely *their King* is, like *"the Master"* in the previous verse, a god who in the eyes of the author is a different deity from YHWH (regardless of the self-understanding of its devotees).[82] The change of preposition, however, would nevertheless allow for the two characterizations to apply to the same group: people who pledge loyalty (*swear to*) YHWH but whose confidence (*who swear by*) is in someone else, *their King*—either a different deity or a conception of YHWH so heterodox as to effectively be a different god. As is clear in examples where both prepositions are used with persons for the same oath, *lamed* (*to*) introduces the party to whom an oath is made and *beth* (*by*) the party who is thought to guarantee the oath,[83] usually YHWH/God.[84] In other contexts, however, the oath formula "as X lives . . ." is used, with X being a person of authority (cf. 1 Sam 1:26; 17:55; 20:3; 25:26; 2 Sam 14:19; 15:21), and so *their King* could refer to Josiah or to the Assyrian overlord.[85] But neither a reference to Josiah nor a reference to the Assyrian king fits the context well.[86] Capitalizing *King* is meant to signal that a reference to a human king is less likely.

Many translations take *mlkm* (here rendered *their King*) to refer to the chief Ammonite god Milcom (e.g., RSV, NRSV, ESV, NAB, NASB), as

---

81. See Ben Zvi, *Zephaniah*, 73–74, for the interface between text-critical and redaction-critical perspectives here; cf. Sweeney, *Zephaniah*, 70.

82. Werse ("Of Gods and Kings," 508) dismisses this possibility too quickly on the grounds that the application of this title to gods other than YHWH would be unusual in the Hebrew Bible. But this is only to be expected, given that the authors do not grant what others apparently believed, namely that there are deities other than YHWH that are to be acknowledged as kings.

83. Gen 21:23; Exod 32:13; Josh 2:12; 9:18–19; 1 Sam 24:22; 28:10; 30:15; 1 Kgs 1:17, 30; 2:8.

84. Note that Jer 5:7 laments people swearing "by them that are not gods" and 12:16 speaks of those who swear by Baal. Amos 8:14 condemns those who swear "by the guilt of Samaria," i.e., the deities worshiped there. Ps 63:11(12) is ambiguous and might commend people who swear by the Davidic king; alternatively, the preposition refers to YHWH.

85. Amos 8:14; Jer 5:7; 12:16 suggest but do not prove that swearing was usually by a deity. Sweeney (*Zephaniah*, 71) argues that the Davidic monarch is in view here. In (rightly) rejecting this, Werse (*Reconsidering*, 264) fails to take the usage of oath formulas into account.

86. Uehlinger ("Astralkultpriester," 53 n. 10) argues that it is unlikely that the Assyrian king was intended.

in Amos 1:15; Jer 49:1, 3, where MT also vocalizes it *malkām*. In 1 Kgs 11, "Molech" seems to be an epithet for the Ammonite chief god (cf. v. 5 with vv. 7, 33).[87] But in 2 Kgs 23, Milcom appears to be distinguished from a deity "Molech" who is associated with the ritual of passing children through fire at the Tophet in the valley of Ben Hinnom (vv. 10, 13).[88] The ancient Greek and Latin versions never reflect a distinction between Molech and Milcom and are followed in this by NIV and NLT.[89] It is probably a mistake to see here a specific reference to either Milcom or Molech.[90] The text allows for different people to have adopted different royal deities, maybe even a heterodox version of YHWH, whether worshipped as *"the Master"* equivalent to Baal/Hadad or not. Note also the use of "their lord" in v. 9, which is similarly open in reference. Vlaardingerbroek observes that people might have used the actual formula "I swear by my king," allowing them to invoke inconspicuously whatever deity they worshipped as supreme.[91] This would imply that there are people who prostrate themselves before *the host of heaven* while pledging loyalty to YHWH. Some of them may have worshipped YHWH as king among other important deities, but Zephaniah likely suggests that both in their actions (prostrating to heavenly bodies) and their confidence (swearing by *their King*), those who are sworn to YHWH prove disloyal to him. Deuteronomy 6:13 enjoins the people of God to swear only by the name of their God. This means that YHWH alone is to be called upon as the arbiter and guarantor. Those who swear by God's name submit to his judgment. Swearing by anyone else, unless maybe this other person is strictly the ex-

---

87. Berlin (*Zephaniah*, 75–77) recognises this and favors the rendering "their Melekh," meaning "their Molekh god."

88. Cf. Lev 18:21; 20:2–5; Jer 32:35. See George C. Heider, "Molech," *DDD*, 581–85. Heider considers the presence of a deity Molech established and its equation with Milcom or Melqart "unlikely" (583); cf. John Day, *Molech: A God of Human Sacrifice in the Old Testament*, University of Cambridge Oriental Publications 41 (Cambridge: Cambridge University Press, 1989), 31–33. Differently, Francesca Stavrakopoulou, *King Manasseh and Child Sacrifice: Biblical Distortions of Historical Realities*, BZAW 338 (Berlin: de Gruyter, 2004), 207–15. Alternatively, if "Molech" is an epithet for various deities, Milcom could be one of them.

89. Both NIV and NLT use "Molek" throughout, never "Milcom," including in 1 Kgs 11:5, 33; 2 Kgs 23:13 where the MT has *milkōm*. LXX and Vulg. interestingly offer a double translation of *malkām* in 1 Chr 20:2 as a name (of the deity, presumably, Molech = Milcom) and "their king."

90. Cf. Irsigler, *Zefanja*, 116–18. Reading "Molech" would require changing the consonantal text; "Milcom" is arguably not a prominent enough deity to be singled out here, even if we allow that there are a few more instances in the Bible than recognised by the Masoretes; e.g., Amos 1:15; Jer 49:3; 2 Sam 12:30 // 1 Chr 20:2 (so, e.g., Emile Puech, "Milcom," *DDD*, 575–76, who considers the reading "Milcom" in Zeph 1:5 [misidentified as 3:5] as "almost certain"). Cf. Ben Zvi, *Zephaniah*, 75–78.

91. Vlaardingerbroek, *Zephaniah*, 70.

ecutor of YHWH's will, is a sign of disloyalty to YHWH, whatever else one may profess in worship.

The subtle shift from first-person speech of YHWH to speech about YHWH does not coincide with any structural break. It might be formulaic or reflect the prophet's identification with YHWH, or it could be identified as a more general instance of illeism (reference to oneself in the third person), which is not unusual in divine speech (e.g., Jer 2:19; 3:12–13; Hos 1:2; 2:20[22]).[92]

6 This verse is sometimes considered a later addition that updates the condemnation implied in the previous verses to include anyone turning away from true YHWH worship. I am not convinced that the terminology used here is late, but it is true that the verse could function as a summary that offers an application beyond the groups specified in the preceding verses.[93] In a sense, all the preceding groups, insofar as they belong to God's people, are *those who turn aside from following YHWH and* consequently *do not* truly *seek YHWH and do not* truly *inquire of him.* Alternatively, one could read this as widening the circle to include specifically those who have abandoned any pretense of being YHWH worshippers in the condemnation, alongside idolatrous priests (v. 4) and syncretistic worshippers (v. 5). But, rhetorically, this would be anticlimactic because it is unremarkable that a YHWH prophecy should condemn those who openly do not care for YHWH. The earlier claim that even those who have the name of YHWH on their lips fall under condemnation seems to have greater rhetorical force. It is, therefore, preferable to read *those who turn aside from following YHWH* as a more generalizing statement that includes the previously mentioned categories of people.

The final two verbs are the first two finite verbs after a series of participles beginning with v. 5, which may be a way of highlighting them. They overlap significantly in their more general usage ("to serve YHWH") and in more specific connotations. But Vlaardingerbroek observes that to *seek* YHWH refers most often to praying, while *to inquire* most often refers to

92. For more general discussion, see Meier, *Speaking of Speaking*, esp. ch. 4 on the latitude of marking direct discourse in prophetic literature and ch. 5 on problems in the marking of divine speech. For illeism, specifically, see chs. 3 (on the OT) and 4 (on other ancient Near Eastern texts) in Rod Ellege, *Use of the Third Person for Self-Reference by Jesus and Yahweh: A Study of Illeism in the Bible and Ancient Near Eastern Texts and Its Implications for Christology*, LNTS 575 (London: Bloomsbury T&T Clark, 2017), esp. 67–84, 155–58. Excluding phrases that could be categorized as fixed in nature (e.g., "before YHWH" and the use of the divine name in construct such as "mouth of YHWH"), Ellege counts 178 examples within divine speech.

93. Among those unpersuaded that this is a later addition are Rudolph, *Micha*, 266; Roberts, *Nahum*, 173; Vlaardingerbroek, *Zephaniah*, 63–64; Sweeney, *Zephaniah*, 72.

seeking an oracle.⁹⁴ This matches well with the attitude that seems to be condemned in v. 12. If *those who turn aside from following YHWH* is a summary characterization of those against whom YHWH's hand is stretched out, then the second half of the verse ensures that it is understood that this sin is committed by omission as well as by the pursuit of idolatrous worship highlighted earlier.

Reflection

This text came into being in the context of the prophetic announcement of the end of the Southern Kingdom and the destruction of city and temple. Every trace of heterodox worship is going to be removed, as God announces a root-and-branch attack on Judah and Jerusalem. If the worship in Jerusalem proves unacceptable, what chance is there for the rest of the world? The opening verses speak of the coming destruction in terms of a universal, all-inclusive judgment that, in its comprehensiveness, includes every kind of animal in any kind of environment. In my judgment, vv. 2–3 are not intended to develop the sixth-century disaster that befell Judah and Jerusalem into an apocalyptic vision of a literal judgment on all individuals or nations of the earth. Rather, they describe the sixth-century events as the collapse of a world order and affirm that the judgment will be inevitable and total, as well as hinting that the attack on Judah and Jerusalem will be part of a more comprehensive divine action (cf. Jer 51:7, describing the events retrospectively). Details of this broader action will be given in ch. 2. Theodoret of Cyrus interprets the reference to the elimination of animals: "Just as I made the creatures that fly and swim and the cattle, so I shall also destroy them along with the people, there being no need for them when those benefiting from them are no more."⁹⁵ Calvin notes that it sharpens the threat against humanity: "What will become of you when God's wrath shall be thus kindled against the unhappy creatures who have committed no sins? Shall ye indeed escape unpunished?"⁹⁶

Given that common rather than unusual terms are used, a specific allusion to either the creation or the flood story is more difficult to establish than many commentators believe. But as noted above, the reversal of the order of creation is suggestive and can be noted with profit even in the absence of

94. See Vlaardingerbroek, *Zephaniah*, 77–78, with statistics.
95. Theodoret of Cyrus, *Commentaries*, 208. Cf. Calvin, *Commentaries*, 4:188–89: "because all things were created for the sake of man." Along similar lines but argued on more pragmatically economic grounds see Martin Luther, *LW* 18:320–21.
96. Calvin, *Commentaries*, 4:189.

clear evidence of citation. (An allusion to the flood story could have been strengthened by the use of the water motif for destructive judgment, as, e.g., in Isa 8:7–8; Jer 46:7–8; 47:2; Nah 1:8.) I suspect that birds and fish are introduced to spell out that there is no place in the universe (earth, sky, or sea) where one could be safe from this sweeping judgment. The real target is in any case humanity. The comprehensive language may also suggest that there is no power that can withstand this God when he comes to judge, a motif picked up at the end of the chapter with the reference to silver and gold.[97] In addition, theologically, a threat against God's people gathered around God's word and sacrifice, as they should be in the temple, is a threat against all humanity.[98] If God's people fail to represent God faithfully, the whole world is deprived of true knowledge of God. The iniquity of God's people comes to ruin others.

Ezekiel speaks of how idolatry and every iniquity come between people and God, preventing communication (14:3, 4, 7), and lays the blame at the feet of the Levites among others (44:12). Here, too, professionals are singled out, but the cutting off is not limited to them. God pays attention to *what causes the wicked to stumble*, but there is no hint that anyone might be excused as having been made to stumble. This interacts with the broader biblical theme that "we all have sinned and fall short of the glory of God" (Rom 3:23) and with the idea that an essentially universal judgment is in fact executed in one specific place on one (group/person) embodying all, finally, at Golgotha. In the context of the whole of Zephaniah, the punishment is the means by which a remnant of those who have gone through the judgment will be restored and saved. There is no greater sweeping, comprehensive, total judgment than the one executed on the cross of Christ, in which our idolatry is crucified and the old world comes to an end for the new creation to be inaugurated in the resurrection of Jesus. "Now, if we have died with Christ, we believe that we will also live with him" (Rom 6:8).

There is no uncontroverted evidence to suggest that the Assyrians imposed religious obligations on other nations, but vassal oaths had to be sworn in the name of Assyrian along with local deities, and there are examples of "prescribed sacrifices for Assyrian gods in connection with the reorganization of a subdued country."[99] Ahlström suggests that "because the territory that the king ruled over was the territory of his god, the realms of religion and politics were considered to be two related aspects of the nation's life.

---

97. Cf. Christoph Uehlinger, "Astralkultpriester," 50.

98. Floyd (*Minor Prophets 2*, 190) speaks of "Jerusalem as the microcosmic representation of the macrocosmic reality."

99. Ahlström, *History*, 762.

To organize the nation was therefore to organize the religion and its cult."[100] But there was likely a difference between, on the one hand, vassal states and, on the other hand, territories that became Assyrian provinces, with less pressure on vassals to worship Assyrian deities on a regular basis.[101] There is little reason to believe that syncretism had been imposed on Judah by outside forces.[102] In any case, by the time Josiah came to the throne, Assyria had begun to lose its grip on the Levant. Nevertheless, political circumstances had for some time favored syncretistic worship, including the revival of older homegrown versions of paganism.[103] Josiah sought to put an end to this, although even where he seemed to be successful, he may have driven such worship underground rather than eradicating it altogether. Zephaniah's prophecy could offer succor to the reform movement; it would certainly affirm its necessity. Even if reforms were no longer able to prevent the disaster, Zephaniah offers no grounds for a defeatist tolerance of heterodox worship. Some of the material in the following chapter may or may not have offered specific support to the more nationalist side of Josiah's reform. The prophet would certainly not have recommended reliance on other nations and likely not even willing subservience to the doomed Neo-Assyrian Empire in the way Jeremiah would a few decades later counsel submission to the Babylonians. The political and the religious cannot be put into separate, independent compartments, but neither is their interrelationship necessarily straightforward. In any case, truly acknowledging YHWH as king recognizes that all realms are governed by him and puts other would-be masters and kings in their place. The text is a challenge also to us today: do our thoughts and actions reflect what we confess with our lips?

Syncretistic worship remains an issue across the world and can take on monotheistic forms. The implicit claim that not all ostensible YHWH worship is truly YHWH worship would apply today, for example, to worship of "the Supreme Being" among freemasons of different religions. It also challenges an easy equation of the God worshipped in spirit and in truth with Allah as worshipped by Muslims.[104] Such clear marking of differences

---

100. Ahlström, *History*, 763.

101. Among others, Yifat Thareani ("The Empire and the 'Upper Sea': Assyrian Control Strategies along the Southern Levantine Coast," *BASOR* 375 [2016]: 77–102) emphasises the flexibility and diversity of Assyrian control strategies, including the impact of annexation on religious practice (79).

102. The classic studies are John McKay, *Religion in Judah under the Assyrians*, SBT 2/26 (London: SCM Press, 1973) and Morton Cogan, *Imperialism and Religion: Assyria, Judah and Israel in the Eighth and Seventh Centuries B.C.E.*, SBLMS 19 (Missoula, MT: Scholars Press, 1974).

103. Cf. Vlaardingerbroek, *Zephaniah*, 69.

104. Cf. Vlaardingerbroek, *Zephaniah*, 70. This is a complex question relating to issues

need not be harsh or vicious. Probably most people would recognize the potentially constructive aspect of distancing oneself from apparent fellow coreligionists in the context of condemning violence. Thus, for example, certain Christians/Muslims declare that Christians/Muslims who maim and kill in the name of God/Allah do not truly worship God/Allah. Such disowning is not dissimilar to the way that the reformers in seventh-century Judah disowned those who offered their children in a fire ritual to their god-king, addressed by the epithet Molech. Purity of religion is no mere academic concern. But the text does not specifically target the worst forms of idolatry only or only those whose rituals are widely considered criminal or distasteful. In truth, any departure from faithful, acceptable worship of the true God, any failure to seek his will is hazardous—and not only for human life—and therefore needs to be challenged. And yet, church history has also given us the experience of the excommunications and mutual condemnations that later generations have had reason to regret. Sometimes, diverging church communities have come to recognize later that their conflicts were not in fact straightforwardly between those who faithfully sought the Lord God and those who had turned their backs on him. This passage cannot tell the whole story, but it can serve as a reminder of the importance of integrity in worship. There is no reason to criticize the passage's focus on ritual as opposed to ethics, as if love of God and neighbor were separated. The following section broadens the picture, and even if this passage once stood as a text in its own right, which I very much doubt, it would have done so only for a moment. If a prophet or preacher focuses on one thing at one time, this need not imply that other things are of no importance.

III. ANNOUNCEMENT OF THE DAY OF YHWH (1:7-18)

[7]*Hush before the Lord YHWH,*[a]
  for the Day of YHWH is near;
for YHWH has prepared a sacrifice;[b]
  he has consecrated [c] *his invitees.*
[8]*It shall happen on the day of YHWH's sacrifice*
  that I will punish[d] *the officials and the royal household,*[e]
    namely[f] *all those clothed in foreign clothing.*[g]
[9]*I will punish everyone who hops*[h] *over the threshold on that day,*

---

of unique reference (there is only one Creator) and specific characterisation in worship (the Trinity is not worshipped by Muslims) more than language (Allah being the general Arabic word for "God"). Allah as depicted in the Qur'an may be considered a fictional character based on the true and living God. But see, e.g., Miroslav Volf, *Allah: A Christian Response* (San Francisco: HarperOne, 2011).

the ones who fill the house of their lord ⁱ with violence and fraud.

¹⁰It shall happen on that day, utterance of YHWH,
  Listen!^j An outcry from the Fish Gate,^k
    wailing from the Second Ward,
      and a great crash from the hills.

¹¹Wail,^l inhabitants of the Mortar,
  because all the merchant people^m are wiped out,ⁿ
    and all who are laden with silver^o are cut off.

¹²And it shall happen at that time,
  I will search out Jerusalem with lamps,^p
and I will punish the men^q who congeal on their wine lees,^r
  the ones who say in their hearts
    "YHWH will cause neither good nor evil."

¹³Their wealth shall become a plunder,^s
  and their houses a desolation.
Though they build houses, they will not settle;
  though they plant vineyards, they will not drink their wine.

¹⁴Near is the great Day of YHWH,
  near^t and coming very fast.^u
Listen!^v The Day of YHWH:
  fiercely^w screams the warrior then.^x

¹⁵A day of fury is that day,
  a day of distress and anguish,^y
  a day of devastation and desolation,^z
  a day of darkness and gloom,
  a day of cloudiness and cloudy blackness,

¹⁶a day of shofar blast ^{aa} and loud sound ^{bb}
  against the fortified cities
    and against the lofty corner towers.

¹⁷And I will bring distress to humankind, and they shall walk like the blind,
  because they have sinned against YHWH.
Their blood shall be spilled ^{cc} like the dust
  and their guts^{dd} like dung.

¹⁸Neither their silver nor their gold will be able to save them
  on the day of YHWH's fury.
And in the fire of his passion
  shall the whole land ^{ee} be consumed,
for a full end—surely a terrifying^{ff} one—he will make
  of all the inhabitants of the land.

a. Sweeney believes that the suffix indicates the first person ("my L-rd," which he capitalizes and renders without vowel as a reverential reference to God; *'ădōnāy*, "my Lord" with reference to God, is distinct from *'ădōnî*, "my lord" with reference to a man). But there are many passages in which it seems very unlikely that the suffix functions in this way; see, e.g., Ps 68:20(21); Amos 5:16; Job 28:28 and the use of the word in Ezekiel.

b. The last two words have only one disjunctive accent, suggesting that the Masoretes read a tricolon in v. 7; see Renz, *Colometry*, 116. This is understandable given the preponderance of long poetic lines in Zephaniah, but it seems to me more natural in English to divide the last line in two.

c. The verb is also used in the phrase "to prepare for battle" (Jer 6:4; Joel 3:9[4:9]), but in those cases the *piel* is used. I accept the argument by John Hans de Jong, "Sanctified or Dedicated? הקדיש in Zephaniah 1:7," *VT* 68 (2018): 94–101, that the use of the *hiphil* indicates that the guests (*invitees*) will be the sacrifice; see the commentary.

d. The verb has a wide range of meaning and can, e.g., refer to "taking care of" in a positive sense. The preposition used here suggests a threatening "taking care of" as elsewhere when *'al* introduces a single object (e.g., Jer 25:12; 29:32; Hos 4:14) or is used with "transgressions" (or "evil" or "guilt" or similar terms) as the direct object (cf., e.g., Jer 36:31; Hos 2:13[15]; Amos 3:2, 14; differently where the direct object is something else, as in Num 4:17; Job 34:13; 36:23; cf. Ezra 1:2 // 2 Chr 36:22).

e. Literally "sons of the king." This is unlikely to be a merely titular designation without connection to the royal house; cf. Ben Zvi, *Zephaniah*, 92–93; Irsigler, *Zefanja*, 141; Kessler, *Staat*, 62. Many or most *bǝnê hammelek* may have been children sired by the king, but the term probably also included, e.g., brothers and other relatives of the king. The title is also attested on seals, as is "daughter of the king," and signals someone's high status, which does not necessarily mean that each bearer of the title belonged to the highest rank of administration.

f. I interpret the *waw* ("and") as introducing an explication here.

g. The translation reflects the double use of the corresponding Hebrew root.

h. The verb is rare in the Bible, and elsewhere it is in the *piel* (2 Sam 22:30 // Ps 18:29[30]; Song 2:8; Isa 35:6). Sweeney (*Zephaniah*, 87) argues that the *qal* should be translated "step/cross over," but its rarity perhaps counsels against treating it as a simple equivalent to the more common verb *dārak* (used in 1 Sam 5:5). LXX renders with an adverb (*emphanōs*, "openly, publicly") that the Vulg. may have interpreted as "arrogantly," taking it with the verb for stepping over (cf. Symmachus, *epibainontas*); cf. Sweeney, *Zephaniah*, 73; Irsigler, *Zefanja*, 136.

i. The plural form might be distributive (different people serve different masters; thus the lower case here), but as a plural of majesty, it also regularly refers to a single lord; see *HGHS* 63z; JM 136d–f; Irsigler, *Zefanja*, 136. LXX specifies as "the house of their Lord God." Vlaardingerbroek (*Zephaniah*, 90) interprets as "their lordly houses," but the interpretation of *'ādōn* as adverbial is not justified by assuming a rare case of pluralizing a construct relationship by putting the second noun in the plural (on which see, e.g., GKC 124r and JM 136n; often both items are implicitly plural; thus *bêt habbāmôt* is "houses [shrines] of the high places").

j. The noun *qôl* ("voice") likely functions as an interjection here (cf., e.g., Gen 4:10); see *DCH*; Irsigler, *Zefanja*, 146; Sweeney, *Zephaniah*, 89.

k. LXX has *pylēs apokentountōn* ("the gate of men slaying"), reading the letter *resh* for the very similar *dalet* either by mistake (facilitated by unfamiliarity with Jerusalem's gates during the monarchy) or as a deliberate, interpretative move to stress the motif of slaughter; see Sweeney, *Zephaniah*, 73, 89.

l. The verb is only attested in the *hiphil*, and its form could be read here as a third-person masculine plural perfect (so, e.g., NRSV, Sweeney). With most readers ancient (LXX, Tg.,

Peshitta) and modern, I read the verb as an imperative in conformity with its most common usage (see the commentary). A *waw* would have facilitated reading the form as an indicative here, and its absence therefore favors reading the imperative.

m. The root *knʿn* most often refers to the land and inhabitants of Canaan (*kanaʿan*) but is sometimes employed for traders and those who handle money (note "land of Canaan" in Ezek 16:29; 17:4 to refer to Babylonia; cf. Isa 23:8; Hos 12:7(8); Zech 14:21; Prov 31:24; Job 41:6[40:30]). Here *kol-ʿam kanaʿan* is not "all the people of Canaan" but *all the merchant people*. Nevertheless, the link with 2:5 should not be missed.

n. On the ancient versions, see Sweeney, *Zephaniah*, 74, 92, and the commentary below.

o. Hebrew *naṭîlê kāsep* can be interpreted as "those laden with silver" (preferred, e.g., in *DCH*) or "those who weigh out silver" (preferred, e.g., in *HALOT*). The ancient versions tended to the former, modern English translations to the latter. Commentators are divided. With, e.g., Vlaardingerbroek, *Zephaniah*, 95–96; Irsigler, *Zefanja*, 153, I opt for the passive sense.

p. The standard Greek text and the Lucianic MSS have the singular, also found in the Peshitta, presumably to conform more easily with the singular subject of the verb. The use of the definite article in the MT is probably best explained by analogy with other cases in which items are considered determinate through the action described; e.g., "write on a scroll/in a book" (Exod 17:14; 1 Sam 10:25; Jer 32:10); see GKC 126q–s; JM 137m.

q. Hebrew *ʾîš* is often used without emphasis on maleness, as may well be the case here. The clause would work with just the participle ("those who . . ."); the addition of *men* possibly adds a note of (presumed) distinction (cf. the exhortation "behave like men/a man" in 1 Sam 4:9; 1 Kgs 2:2; maybe 1 Sam 26:15); so Vlaardingerbroek, *Zephaniah*, 99. Contextually, I think a reference to upper-class men likely, although Amos 4:1 knows of women of whom similar things could be said.

r. The versions struggled with the noun *šemer* for the dregs of wine, attested elsewhere only in Ps 75:8(9); Jer 48:11; and (used for the mature wine itself) Isa 25:6. See Sweeney, *Zephaniah*, 94, for details.

s. The terms in both lines are most often understood as abstract ("subject to plunder . . . subject to destruction"; i.e. "plundered . . . destroyed"), which is reflected in the majority of English translations; but as Vlaardingerbroek (*Zephaniah*, 101) argues, it should be understood concretely, referring to the result rather than the action.

t. Hebrew *qārôb* could be interpreted as an infinitive ("coming close") rather than the adjective *close*, in line with *mahēr* (see the following note). But it is so common for the Day of YHWH to be announced as imminent (*close*) that it seems better to treat this as a fixed phrase. The meaning is in any case the same.

u. I read *mahēr* as a *piel* infinitive here, used as an adverb; cf. Meyer, *Grammatik*, 3:62. See Ben Zvi, *Zephaniah*, 117–18, for a discussion of other proposals.

v. Or "the sound of the Day of YHWH"; see on v. 10. A double translation is also defensible ("Listen! The sound of the Day of YHWH"), so Ben Zvi, *Zephaniah*, 118–19.

w. The line division follows the accentuation, with *mar* functioning as an adverb (as in Isa 33:7). Alternatively, "fierce" is taken with the first line, then as an adjective (cf. *yôm mār*, a pausal form, in Amos 8:10). It is probably in pivotal position to allow for both: the sound of the Day of YHWH is fierce because of the screaming of the warrior. See Vlaardingerbroek, *Zephaniah*, 106–7, for other ways of construing the sentence. In antiquity, translators struggled (see Sweeney, *Zephaniah*, 98), and in modern times, a number of emendations have been suggested (see Vlaardingerbroek, *Zephaniah*, 102–3).

x. The particle is most often spatial ("there") but on a few occasions seems to be temporal (*then*), as, arguably, in Job 35:12; Ps 14:5 // 53:5(6); Ps 36:12(13); Hos 6:7 (cf. *DCH*; *HALOT*; *IBHS* 39.3.1h; but not BDB); so also Ben Zvi, *Zephaniah*, 120. The more common word for "then" (*'āz*) may have been unsuitable because, as far as I know, it never follows the verb that it qualifies (except in Eccl 2:15?), and the poetic rhetoric desired did not allow placing it before the verb (see note above).

y. The pairing of terms of similar meaning and, in the first two instances, of similar sound may convey superlative meaning here; so GKC 133l; Ben Zvi, *Zephaniah*, 121.

z. Giving the preceding line only one disjunctive accent, the Masoretes apparently take this line with the preceding; cf. Renz, *Colometry*, 117. Contra MT, the decision here is in favor of a more regular arrangement.

aa. The word *blast* is added because *shofar* here stands for giving a signal by blowing a ram's horn.

bb. Hebrew *tərû'â* here could indicate the sounding of the horn or the intimidating roar of the soldiers.

cc. Ancient grammarians read *šuppak* as a *pual*. Today, it is often considered a *qal* passive because the root is not attested in the *piel*; see JM 58. *HALOT*; *DCH*; Ges[18] give both options. This does not affect the meaning of the verb.

dd. Hebrew *ləḥūm* is similar to the common noun for bread/food, *leḥem*, and its related verb "to eat" (Deut 32:24; Ps 141:4; Prov 4:17; 9:5; 23:1, 6). Its apparent use in Job 20:23 is often queried or related to a homonym root ("warfare"), while Isa 47:14; Job 6:7; 30:4 are occasionally emended to yield this noun. My translation reflects the understanding already found in the ancient versions. Cf. Sweeney, *Zephaniah*, 103, for the versions, and Vlaardingerbroek, *Zephaniah*, 112, for suggested emendations. Irsigler among others suggests "Lebenssaft" ("the sap of life," which he considers securely established for Jer 11:19), maybe in the broader sense of "Lebenskraft" ("vitality"); see his discussion in *Zefanja*, 180.

ee. Or "earth" both here and in the last line. In the second part of the book, *'ereṣ* is better translated "earth" (2:11; 3:8, 19–20); in the next couple of references, it is better translated "land" (2:3, 5). Identifying these lines as part of a proto-apocalyptic addition, Irsigler (*Zefanja*, 181), e.g., claims that *hā'āreṣ* can only mean "the earth" here, while, e.g., Vlaardingerbroek (*Zephaniah*, 113) sees no reason to translate "earth," as the Day of YHWH is so clearly directed against Judah and Jerusalem. In 3:8, the reference is indeed broader, but here the literary context cautions against the assumption that the verse makes universal claims. (In line with his methodology, Irsigler offers an interpretation of 1:17–18 as an independent unit that comments on the preceding but is not read in the light of the preceding.) See further under "Composition."

ff. The *niphal* participle *nibhālâ* functions here as an adjective. It is understood as "swift, speedy" in the LXX and Vulg., which is defended by some moderns (cf. RSV); more often today it is understood in relation to the most common meaning of the verb; cf. Ben Zvi, *Zephaniah*, 133–34.

Composition

The opening exclamation (which is not syntactically joined to the preceding) and a thematic shift mark a new beginning, even if vv. 2–6 prepare us for this section and should not be completely separated from it (see the comments on the composition of 1:2–6). The section that begins with 2:1 similarly assumes ch. 1, or something like it, but its opening imperative begins a section that spells out the response urged on those who have heard the preceding announcement. The reuse of the Day of YHWH motif has led many commentators to include 2:1–3 with ch. 1, but what follows in ch. 2 offers a more detailed rationale for the exhortation in 2:1–3. Further, 2:4 is syntactically linked to the first three verses through the opening *kî* (*For*), unless the particle is interpreted as asseverative ("indeed"; see the discussion below). Floyd, taking his lead from the commands at the beginning of vv. 7 and 11, subdivides this section into two major portions: one linking the approaching Day of YHWH with the expectation of a day of festive sacrifice (vv. 7–10), the other linking it with a day of solemn lamentation (vv. 11–18).[105] More often, v. 14, with its renewed declaration of the imminence of the Day of YHWH, is seen as opening a new section that begins by characterizing the Day of YHWH in a list-like enumeration of its features.[106] But while vv. 15–16 do indeed offer a list, what follows does not, and already v. 10 has list-like character. First-person divine speech and prophetic speech about YHWH are found in both.[107] Vlaardingerbroek suggests that we have "a much more general and less concrete portrayal" of the Day of YHWH in vv. 14–18 than in the preceding verses.[108] This is true as far as the condemnation of specific groups is concerned; in other ways, however, vv. 14–18 leaves us with some very concrete pictures. The shift from the condemnation of specific groups to a more general depiction could also be interpreted as part of a parallel structure. Note that twice an imperative (vv. 7a, 11a) and the rationale for it (vv. 7b, 11b) is followed by attention to specific groups (vv. 8–9, 12–13) before a more general reference to sound enters (vv. 10, 14, 16). In the second instance, the reference is expanded (vv. 15, 17–18) in a way that is appropriate for concluding the whole section, indeed the whole chapter, rather than just a part of it. Note also that *silver and gold* in v. 18 seems to pick up the reference to merchants in v. 11 (cf. v. 13). I prefer to discuss vv. 7–18 as one unit.

Phrases like *it shall happen on that day* (vv. 8, 10; similarly v. 12)[109] allow the identification of individual paragraphs but do not, in my view, necessarily

105. Floyd, *Minor Prophets 2*, 185–86. The *form* at the beginning of v. 7 is an interjection, but this does not gainsay its imperative *function*. The form at the beginning of v. 11 could be interpreted as indicative, but this is less likely; see the commentary below.

106. E.g., Roberts, *Nahum*, 162; Irsigler, *Zefanja*, 93, 165; Sweeney, *Zephaniah*, 75.

107. Sweeney, *Zephaniah*, 77, believes that the first-person speaker in v. 17 is the prophet on the grounds that the verse refers to YHWH in the third person. But see the comments on 1:5–6 regarding the use of the third person in divine speech.

108. Vlaardingerbroek, *Zephaniah*, 49.

109. In line with standard English usage, I have omitted the conjunction "and" in my translation.

indicate self-contained units or secondary elaborations.[110] The first of them, with its reference to *the day of YHWH's sacrifice* (v. 8), is especially closely connected to the preceding verse. Indeed, v. 7 demands further explication, so we would be ill-advised to allow for a strong break between vv. 7 and vv. 8–9. The phrase *on that day* (v. 10) also links with what precedes, whether this is a compositional or redactional device, as does *at that time* (v. 12). Thus, if vv. 7–18 are to be subdivided, it makes best sense to see a break either at v. 11, with the second command, or at v. 14, with the second announcement of the imminence of the Day of YHWH. But neither of these breaks seems very pronounced.

Because *on the day of YHWH's fury* in v. 18 could form a fitting conclusion with a reference back to v. 15, it is possible that the following lines (*And in the fire of his passion . . .*) are an editorial addition designed to facilitate a broader application of the passage.[111] Even if not understood to make claims about all the inhabitants of the "earth" (see the translation note), the progressive narrowing characteristic of this chapter is reversed here with the reference to *the whole land* and *all the inhabitants of the land*. After all, the focus has very much been on Jerusalem's upper class. But even ch. 2 allows for the possibility of escape for the lower classes only with a "perhaps," and alternatively it could be argued that by way of *inclusio*, the chapter is rounded off with a renewed widening of scope (cf. vv. 2–3) to ensure that no one feels secure too readily. In addition, as pointed out below, v. 13 speaks of *desolation* of a sort unlikely to be precisely targeted. If the wealthy are punished by the capture and destruction of Jerusalem, the less wealthy will not remain unaffected. It can certainly not be claimed that the text does not cohere well as it stands.

---

110. Simon J. DeVries (*Yesterday, Today and Tomorrow: Time and History in the Old Testament* [London: SPCK, 1975]) saw in these verses "a number of epexegetical interpretations" added by "a disciple-redactor" (299), but I question the idea that we are dealing here with "new acts of judgment" (300) that expand on the groups already said to be affected by the punishment in vv. 7–9. In *From Old Revelation to New: A Tradition-Historical and Redaction-Critical Study of Temporal Transitions in Prophetic Prediction* (Grand Rapids: Eerdmans, 1995), DeVries distinguishes "the punishment on Jerusalem's leaders" (vv. 8–9) from "the sounds of siege and the plundering of the complacent" (53; cf. 47). The separating of these as distinct events strikes me as artificial.

111. Many commentators consider parts or all of v. 18 a later addition; see, e.g., Vlaardingerbroek, *Zephaniah*, 104–5. As noted above, Irsigler (*Zephaniah*, 181) interprets 1:17–18 as a later commentary on the preceding. Even so, he does not believe that 1:17–18 came into being all at the same time. Dietrich (*Nahum*, 209) appears to recognise in his synchronic analysis that vv. 17–18 simply refer to "the people embroiled in the catastrophe" without any hint that the catastrophe should be considered a global one. But in his diachronic analysis, he assumes "a universal cosmic judgement" and therefore sees "apocalyptic colors flame up" in most of v. 18 (215).

Commentary

7 The opening call to silence (*Hush*) is a command to acknowledge the presence of God (*before the Lord YHWH*)[112] or, more precisely, to prepare for an encounter with him; the given rationale is that *the Day of YHWH is near* (cf. the same or similar clauses in Isa 13:6; Ezek 30:3; Joel 1:15; 2:1; 3:14[4:14]; Obad 15). The collocation *Lord YHWH* is especially frequent in Amos (21×) and Ezekiel (217×).[113] Here, it arguably adds weight to the line. The verse is often considered a cultic invocation or an imitation thereof on the grounds of the opening formula.[114] This is difficult to ascertain. The differences between Hab 2:20; Zeph 1:7; and Zech 2:13(17) do not suggest a fixed formula, and unlike Hab 2:20 and Zech 2:13(17), Zephaniah does not mention God's dwelling place. The call to silence uses an everyday onomatopoetic word that is not limited to the cult.[115] The exact phrase *before the Lord YHWH* is not attested elsewhere in the Hebrew Bible; *before . . . YHWH* is found a few times, but a cultic context is plausible only twice for the use of the phrase with *mippǝnê* as here (Zech 2:13[17]; Mal 3:14).[116] By contrast, *millipnê yhwh* is more readily at home in a cultic context, although it is also used more widely (2 Chr 19:2; 33:23; Ps 97:5).[117] There is no firm evidence from which we could deduce that *the Day of YHWH* motif played a traditional role in the cult.[118] The reference to *sacrifice* may lead one to think of the temple or even specifically of a celebration such as Sukkoth (given the harvest theme noted above) or Passover (given the memory of Josiah's celebrated Passover in 2 Kgs 23:21–23; 2 Chr

112. See also the commentary on Hab 2:20.

113. Elsewhere in the Book of the Twelve only in Obad 1; Mic 1:2; and Zech 9:14. Jeremiah has fourteen occurrences, Isaiah has twenty-five (spread across the book).

114. E.g., Christoph Levin, "Zephaniah," 127–29; cf. Irsigler, *Zefanja*, 123–24.

115. See Sweeney, *Zephaniah*, 78–79, for a discussion of the various occurrences in the Hebrew Bible.

116. The other references are Gen 3:8; Exod 9:30; Judg 5:5; 2 Kgs 22:19; Jer 4:26; 23:9; Hag 1:12.

117. *Millipnê yhwh* is used in a cultic context in Lev 9:24; 10:2; 16:12; Num 16:46; 17:9(17:11, 24); 20:9; 1 Sam 21:6(7); 1 Chr 16:33. In a secondary sense, one could add Gen 4:16 and, more indirectly, Jonah 1:3, 10, where the reference is to the promised land. The situation is similar for the use of *millipnê* with first-person suffix in divine speech (Lev 22:3; 1 Kgs 8:25; Isa 57:16; Jer 16:17; 31:36; 33:18) and with other designations of God (2 Chr 6:16; 33:12; 34:27; Ps 114:7; Eccl 8:13).

118. Sweeney, *Zephaniah*, 80–81, thinks differently; cf. Irsigler, *Zefanja*, 129, 134. I do, however, agree with his strong insistence that the Day of YHWH "does not represent the end of time" (81). Martin Beck (*Der "Tag YHWHs" im Dodekapropheton: Studien im Spannungsfeld von Traditions- und Redaktionsgeschichte*, BZAW 356 [Berlin: de Gruyter, 2012], 103–4) argues that talk about the nearness of the Day of YHWH did not originate in a war or cult setting and that Zeph 1:7, 14 are the earliest references of the phrase.

35:1–19).[119] But readers or hearers get to the reference to *sacrifice* only after having heard about the imminence of *the Day of YHWH*.[120] The verse does not invite its recipients to interpret a sacrificial feast (celebration) retrospectively as a *Day of YHWH* (devastation) but *the Day of YHWH* as a day of sacrifice.[121] All in all, I remain agnostic about the possibility of ancient readers having heard an (ironically subverted) call to worship behind v. 7.

The Day of YHWH is a time, indeed any time, at which YHWH decisively intervenes in events such that people come to encounter him. It is arguably always a day of judgment—a day on which the divine judge executes his verdict, a day on which YHWH defeats his enemies and thus the enemies of the order instituted by him. This is good news for those who suffer injustice and consequently are vindicated on such a day; it is bad news for those who until then "got away with murder" or other wrongdoing. Along with the innocent, the complacent might eagerly expect such a day (cf. Amos 5:18–20), but in prophetic preaching during the time in which the Kingdom of (Israel and then) Judah was still in existence, the Day of YHWH seems to have featured most often in threats against God's people. It is only beyond the Day of YHWH that brings about the destruction of Jerusalem (cf. Lam 1:12; 2:1, 21–22; Ezek 34:12) that such a Day of YHWH can be looked forward to again with hopeful expectation because it brings calamity on one's enemies (cf. Lam 1:21). This seems to be the case for Isa 13:6, 9; 34:1 (assuming that these passages look beyond 587 BC) and maybe the prophecy of Obadiah (depending on its date). But this does not mean that after the fall of the Southern Kingdom the Day of YHWH is invariably a day of vindication for all God's people. The announcement in Mal 4:5–6(3:23–24) calls for preparation in repentance so that the Day of YHWH would not be experienced as a curse. Zephaniah's *Day of YHWH* is, first of all, the time at which YHWH decisively judges Judah and Jerusalem by, as it will turn out, bringing destruction through the Babylonians (cf. Ezek 7:19; 13:5).[122]

---

119. N. M. Nigolsky ("Pascha im Kulte des jerusalemischen Tempels," *ZAW* 45 [1927]: 171–90, 241–53) argues that the following points to Passover: (1) YHWH himself prepares the sacrifice; (2) YHWH searches victims at night in 1:12; (3) people "becoming fat on yeast" in 1:12 as a sign of not keeping the feast of unleavened bread (188–89). He suggests that use of the actual word *pesaḥ* ("Passover") would have unveiled the threat (189), ruining its allusive character, and that the use of *zebaḥ* (*sacrifice*) here might even have influenced later understanding of the ritual (243).

120. Unless v. 7 is considered an independent saying as, e.g., in Klaus Seybold, *Satirische Prophetie: Studien zum Buch Zefanja*, SBS 120 (Stuttgart: KBW, 1985), 23–25.

121. Cf. the use of sacrificial language for YHWH's punishment in Isa 34:6; Jer 46:10; Ezek 39:17–19; arguably Jer 50:27.

122. Note that in ch. 30, Ezekiel uses the motif in relation to Egypt's punishment in the Babylonian campaign.

The Day of YHWH is a day of divine initiative, and so it is appropriate that it is *YHWH* who *has prepared a sacrifice*, turning the day into a day of sacrifice (so explicitly in the next verse). Its imminence is underlined by the observation that *YHWH has* already *prepared a sacrifice, he has* already *consecrated his invitees*—the preparations have been made. The term for *sacrifice* (*zebah*) is the common one to designate a rite in which the flesh of the victim is eaten by the worshippers and the deity receives the blood and fat. As such, it is distinguished from the sacrifices from which the worshipper did not eat, namely sin and guilt sacrifices—offerings that were wholly burnt up on the altar—and maybe also from tribute offerings in which only the priests and Levites had a share. It is conceivable that *zebah* could be used to refer to "slaughter" in a non-cultic context, given that the verb is sometimes used in preparation for apparently non-sacrificial eating (e.g., Deut 12:15, 21; 1 Sam 28:24; 1 Kgs 19:21). This is in fact how the Tg. reads our verse, maybe for theological reasons.[123] But the meaning "slaughter" without sacrificial overtones is not securely established for the noun (Isa 34:6; Jer 4:6, 10; Ezek 39:17 all refer to slaughter in the context of divine punishment, and the notion of sacrifice may still be relevant).[124] And the expression "prepare a slaughter" seems less appropriate than "prepare a sacrifice" (the combination of this verb and noun is not attested elsewhere).[125] So, here the translation *YHWH has prepared a sacrifice* seems secure. But if a festival meal is being prepared, who is the sacrifice and who are the invited guests? The slaughtered sacrifice will turn out to be the various groups condemned later. Read in the context of the chapter, readers could already expect the sacrifice to be *Judah* and *the inhabitants of Jerusalem* (v. 4), or at any rate a substantial part of these entities, so that within the book there is little chance of any readers at first thinking that they might be the guests only to discover that they are the meal.[126]

If *consecrated* could be understood in the sense of "being ready for the cultic meal" (rather than "being permanently set apart for YHWH"), we

123. Cf. Sweeney, *Zephaniah*, 82. Seybold (*Satirische Prophetie*, 24–25) notes the shock of YHWH acting like a lay member of the community. (He also thinks that YHWH brings foreigners as guests into the temple, but this is unlikely once *consecrated* is understood not as "sanctified for the feast" but "given over to YHWH [as sacrifice]," on which see the translation note and comments below.)

124. Ancient Near Eastern parallels for sacrifice as a metaphor for divine annihilation are noted by Irsigler, *Zefanja*, 133.

125. The use of "prepare" in Gen 43:16 and 2 Chr 35:6 includes the slaughtering but is broader; there is no sense of the slaughter itself being prepared. In Num 23:1, 29, the root *kwn* is used for getting animals ready to be sacrificed, in 2 Chr 33:16 for the restoration of the altar prior to the sacrifice.

126. Differently Sweeney, *Zephaniah*, 81, 83.

might think of the invading armies as the unspecified *invitees*.[127] While they remain very much in the background in Zephaniah so as not to detract from the focus on YHWH, this is no reason to think that the disaster would come in some supernatural way. The language of *invitees* being *consecrated* fits the context of guests at a sacrificial meal. More commonly, people are said to consecrate themselves prior to participating in a sacrifice, but in 1 Sam 16:5, which uses both expressions, consecrating oneself is also expressed as Samuel, the priest, "consecrating" those he has "invited" to the "sacrifice" (using the same three roots as here).[128] On the *Day of YHWH*, the only agent that truly matters is YHWH, and it is in keeping with this that he is said to be doing the consecrating. There is an interesting parallel in Isa 13:3, where YHWH speaks of armies as "my consecrated ones" and warriors being "summoned" (the root behind *invitees* here). God has already set apart those whom he has summoned to benefit from the sacrifice he will make. But against this line of interpreting the text, a good case has been made that the specific verb form used here suggests that the consecration is in fact permanent, in which case it must be a reference to the sacrifice.[129] If so, there is little question who the invitees are. Instead of accepting his people's sacrifice, YHWH makes a sacrifice of his people. He has already *consecrated* them for this purpose.

8 In my view, the suggestion that the linking expression at the beginning of this verse "removes (or at the very least strongly tempers) the sense of imminence that v. 7 brings to the text"[130] is unconvincing. But I agree that the reuse of *day* here (and more so in vv. 9–10), along with the linking phrase in v. 12, somewhat attenuates the sense of imminence simply by focusing on and taking the time to spell out what will happen *on that day* rather than continuing to urge its nearness. It is perhaps for this reason that v. 14 revives a sense of imminence. The *Day of YHWH* is a time when YHWH finally takes care of matters that he seems to have left unattended, and so *it shall happen . . .*

---

127. See Ben Zvi, *Zephaniah*, 82–86, for a fuller discussion of the options. He concludes that there is deliberate ambiguity, causing uncertainty: "The reader/hearer cannot but leave the verse with a clear sense that something terrible is about to happen, but he/she does not know for sure what" (86). Cf. Irsigler, *Zefanja*, 132–34.

128. For consecrating oneself, the *hithpael* is used; for consecrating something else, the *piel* is used. The "consecrated ones" in Isa 13:3 are described with a *pual*.

129. De Jong ("Sanctified or Dedicated?," 97) notes that the *hiphil* stem "never expresses the idea of bringing someone or something into a temporary state of holiness in order to participate in cultic activity. Rather, it describes the causing of an object to become holy and therefore the property of Yahweh."

130. Ben Zvi, *Zephaniah*, 277; cf. Kapelrud, *Message*, 30. Kapelrud assumes that expressions like "on that day" were added to put events into the distant future, apparently following Hugh Gressmann's (mistaken) view of the phrase as an eschatological *terminus technicus*.

that I will attend to (i.e., *punish*) *the officials and the royal household, namely all those clothed in foreign clothing.*

The designation "sons of the king" (*royal household*) is often thought to include important court officials who are not part of the royal family.[131] There is no clear example in the Hebrew Bible of a "son of the king" exercising an official role (e.g., Jer 36:26; 38:6) who cannot also have been a biological son of the king. Seals with the inscription "son of the king" identify their owners as people of high status but do not make clear whether this status derives from their family connection or from an appointment to a significant role in the royal administration. The question of the precise connotation of the phrase cannot be resolved fully. Most likely, the reference is to (male) members of the royal family in an extended sense; other high officials may or may not have been included in the household. If the phrase were taken in the strictest sense only, then there would have been no "sons of the king" when Josiah became king at eight years old and not very many even a few years later. It thus seems more likely that, unless specifically booted out, those who were considered "sons of the king" in one reign would have retained the title in the following reign, especially within the Kingdom of Judah, which was ruled by one dynasty throughout its existence. The translation *royal household* is meant to allow for a fairly broad reference without demanding it. The absence of any mention of the king himself in the condemnation of the elite is probably not as significant as it appears to some (cf. Ezek 22:23–31),[132] although the minority or piety of King Josiah could have been a relevant factor.[133] The prophecy in any case came to be fulfilled in a disaster beyond Josiah's lifetime (cf. 2 Kgs 22:20), a disaster that very much engulfed the then reigning king as well as his family and officials (cf. 2 Kgs 25:7).

The reference to *foreign clothing* is unique in the Bible. The rare word used for *clothing* suggests expensive, high-status garments, as Isa 63:3 implies,[134]

---

131. E.g., Seybold, *Satirische Prophetie*, 26–27; Uehlinger, "Astralkultpriester," 55. Sweeney speaks of "the king's inner circle of advisors" (*Zephaniah*, 76); see his discussion in which he also points out that "son of the king" appears as a title in other ancient Near Eastern texts (84–85). He concludes that the phrase refers to biological sons of the king who had some official role. See the translation note.

132. See Ben Zvi, *Zephaniah*, 93, 280–81.

133. Kessler (*Staat*, 68) insists that the king would have been responsible for the behavior of the royal household and that the only reason for the lack of mention of the king must lie in his minority. Seybold (*Satirische Prophetie*, 26) considers the king's minority or his busyness the reason for insufficient attention to the affairs of his household, prompting YHWH to take care of it.

134. The other references are 1 Kgs 10:5; 2 Kgs 10:22; 2 Chr 9:4; Job 27:16; Ezek 16:13, all with reference to clothing worn by people of high status or, in Ezek 16, specified as "of fine

and the addition of *foreign* certainly makes it so. "Dress provides important social and cultural information concerning status, power, group identity, manufacture, and trade." In the ancient world, "except for luxury goods, most clothing and ornaments were made and circulated locally."[135] It is therefore possible that typifying people as *clothed in foreign clothing* first of all characterizes them as parading their wealth, but it likely also portrays them here as being at home in an alien culture or at least as being unconcerned about preserving a distinct identity. Archaeologists observe with regard to the seventh century that

> the economies of both Judah and Philistia were well integrated in the period's larger economic system and should be seen as almost one economic unit (or region) within the system, the driving force behind which was the Phoenician maritime trade.[136]

Arguably, this does not sufficiently take into account that, on the whole, Judah did not benefit from these economic developments nearly as much as others, especially the Philistine cities.[137] Nevertheless, those with large land holdings were likely able to reap benefits from increased opportunities for trade. To say that the people condemned in this prophecy did not support the local economy might seem to reflect a modern concern, but beyond narrowly economic considerations there is probably a sense here of an elite that associates and identifies itself more with the elites of other nations than with their own people and so compromises the cohesion of society and its values.[138] Such foreign clothing may well have ignored injunctions against mixed fabrics (Lev 19:19; Deut 22:11) and is unlikely to have had "tassels on the four corners of the cloak" in the way prescribed in the Torah (Deut 22:12; cf. Num 15:37–41). There is a question about the extent to which these

---

linen and silk and embroidered cloth." A more common word for outer garment (*śimlâ*) is used 35×. Cf. Ben Zvi, *Zephaniah*, 94.

135. Douglas R. Edwards, "Dress and Ornamentation," *ABD* 2:232, 235. But note that wool and textiles are found in Assyrian tribute lists alongside metals, suggesting that these were sufficiently valued to warrant the cost of long-distance transportation; see Craig William Tyson, "Israel's Kin Across the Jordan: A Social History of the Ammonites in the Iron Age II (1000–500 BCE)" (PhD diss, University of Michigan, 2011), 292–93.

136. Avraham Faust and Ehud Weiss, "Judah, Philistia, and the Mediterranean World: Reconstructing the Economic System of the Seventh Century B.C.E.," *BASOR* 338 (2005): 71.

137. Seymour Gitin, "The Neo-Assyrian Empire and Its Western Periphery: The Levant, with a Focus on Philistine Ekron," in Parpola and Whiting, *Assyria 1995*, 87–103; "Neo-Assyrian and Egyptian Hegemony over Ekron in the Seventh Century BCE: A Response to Lawrence E. Stager," *Eretz-Israel* 27 (2003): 55*–61*.

138. Cf. Irsigler, *Zefanja*, 139–42, with epigraphic evidence.

covenantal injunctions were known and adhered to at the time, but it seems likely that the prophet knew of them and approved of clothing that included signs of God's covenant with his people.[139] Because 2 Kgs 10:22 suggests that Baal worshippers wore special clothing, commentators have sometimes wondered whether the concern here is specifically with "foreign apparel" that "was donned for religious purposes."[140] In my view, such a narrowing of the connotations of alien clothing is not justified. Foreign clothing signals a foreign value system and here most likely went along with a departure from "covenantal economics"—the sort of socioeconomic life that is an expression of being YHWH's covenant community.[141]

9 The expression *everyone who hops over the threshold* created problems for ancient translators, and the significance of the action implied continues to be debated.[142] The most common interpretation today, found already in antiquity, is to see a reference to pagan, superstitious behavior, possibly in a cultic context (cf. 1 Sam 5:4–5), albeit not necessarily so.[143] But as Ben Zvi has demonstrated, despite being the majority view, this cultic or magical interpretation is not securely established. He argues that the negative evaluation only comes with the next line, just as in the previous verse the targets of the punishment are first mentioned in neutral language (*the officials and the royal household*) before the negative characterization *namely all those clothed in foreign clothing.* Sweeney developed this further by suggesting that "those who cross over the threshold" (see the translation note for his rendering of the verb) is a roundabout way of designating the priests, assuming *the threshold* to be that of the temple.[144] The use of the rare verb and the ambiguity of *the house of their lord* (see below), which means that *the threshold* is not obviously that of the temple, argue against this specific proposal. But the

139. On the significance of clothing more generally, see S. David Sperling, "Pants, Persians and the Priestly Source," in *Ki Baruch Hu: Ancient Near Eastern, Biblical and Judaic Studies in Honor of Baruch A. Levine,* ed. Robert Chazan, William W. Hallo, and Lawrence H. Schiffman (Winona Lake, Indiana: Eisenbrauns, 1999), 373–85.

140. Roberts, *Nahum,* 179; cf. Robertson, *Nahum,* 276.

141. For the term "covenantal economics," see ch. 6 of Ellen F. Davis, *Scripture, Culture, and Agriculture: An Agrarian Reading of the Bible* (Cambridge: Cambridge University Press, 2009), 101–19. The following chapter ("Running on Poetry: The Agrarian Prophets," 120–38) focuses on Amos and Hosea. Zephaniah's prophecy seems to have grown on the same soil, even if his critique of the new economy may be less explicitly agrarian.

142. See esp. Ben Zvi, *Zephaniah,* 95–102; Vlaardingerbroek, *Zephaniah,* 87–89; Irsigler, *Zefanja,* 142–44; Sweeney, *Zephaniah,* 85–88.

143. Following Van der Woude, Vlaardingerbroek (*Zephaniah,* 89) even thinks "that the people practising it were barely conscious of its religious background." The MT of 1 Sam 5:4–5 does not use the verb *dlg,* but a retranslation of the longer LXX text into Hebrew could yield *dlg.*

144. Sweeney, *Zephaniah,* 87–88.

general idea that the main characterization comes only in the second half of the verse is plausible, even if the construction is not exactly parallel to that in v. 8. This interpretation, which keeps the focus of the entire verse on "crimes in the social sphere" apparently has a similarly long pedigree ("see Peshitta, Ibn Ezra, Radak, Abrabanel, Altschuler, Calvin"[145]). The use of a verb for hopping or leaping suggests the self-assuredness and confidence of those who enter the house.

But which house is it? Like Sweeney, already the LXX and Vulgate interpreted *the house of their lord* as a reference to the temple, and we could appeal to the presence of *'ădōnāy* (*the Lord*) in v. 7 for support. But this particular expression is never used to refer to the temple. The lord of the house is elsewhere always human (Gen 39:2; 40:7; 44:8; 2 Sam 12:8; 2 Kgs 10:3; Isa 22:18), and only few of the numerous occurrences of the plural of *'ădōn* with suffix in the Hebrew Bible refer to YHWH. Ben Zvi counts six (Pss 8:1[2], 9[10]; 135:5; 147:5; Neh 8:10; 10:29[30]), but he seems to have considered only instances with the first-person plural suffix.[146] There are nearly two hundred instances with the first-person singular suffix, of which none refers to YHWH. Of thirty-five occurrences with the second-person suffix (sg. or pl.), only one relates to YHWH (Isa 51:22). Of the fifty-seven instances with the third-person suffix (as here), the only one that can refer to YHWH is in Hos 12:14(15).[147] This evidence suggests that *the house of their lord* here does not refer to the temple. In view of the preceding verse, we are probably to think of the royal palace in particular, but a more general application cannot be excluded and is supported by the openness of the phrase *their king* earlier (v. 5). The judgment against the elite in v. 8 is now broadened to include those who serve the elite, unless *their lord* is specifically understood with reference to the king only, in which case the group of people mentioned here could be identical to the group in v. 8. Verse 8 would then condemn them for having an alien cultural reference point, while v. 9 adds injustice as a further basis for condemnation. But even on my preferred reading, namely, that v. 9 adds another group of people, the charge of injustice would apply to *the officials and the royal household* as well. The servants that violently and fraudulently acquire wealth for their masters are likely not thought to do so without the knowledge of their masters.[148] There is nothing here to exonerate the high officials.

Ben Zvi points out that the combination of *violence* and *fraud* occurs else-

---

145. Ben Zvi, *Zephaniah*, 95.

146. Ben Zvi, *Zephaniah*, 101.

147. Twice a comparison with a relationship to YHWH is made (Ps 132:2; Mal 1:4), but the expression itself still refers to human masters.

148. This is so unless *their lord* is read as a specific reference to Josiah, in which case sympathetic readers would likely assume that the king is not implicated, maybe being unaware of the goings on because of his young age.

where only in Isa 53:9b ("on the grounds [or notwithstanding?] that he had done no *violence* and *fraud* was not in his mouth"), which combines an emphasis on social wrongdoing and speech (cf. Zeph 3:9, 13).[149] For the idiom of filling a house with violence and fraud, we can compare Amos 3:10 (storing up violence and robbery in strongholds) and Jer 5:27 (houses full of deceit).

10 The opening, *It shall happen on that day*, connects this verse to the preceding verses, and the use of *wailing* connects this verse to the following one. This more impersonal *utterance of YHWH* in v. 10 rounds off the condemnation of the elite by focusing on the (sound) effect of the judgment. There is no truly new action in view here, nor new conditions.[150] These verses merely fill in the picture and add sound to it. The *Fish Gate* (cf. 2 Chr 33:14; Neh 3:3; 12:39), perhaps the Middle Gate mentioned in Jer 39:3,[151] implies the presence of a fish market nearby, maybe primarily supplied by Tyrians (cf. Neh 13:16), which might explain its northern location. But we know little about any gates on the west, let alone their road connections, and it is perfectly possible that roads led from the *Fish Gate* to the coastal plain as well as to Samaria and beyond or that other gates offered not enough space for a market.[152] It is entirely conceivable, therefore, that the fish mongers included people from the Philistine coastal region mentioned in ch. 2. Faust and Weiss observe:

> An analysis of the large selection of fish bones found in the City of David and in the Ophel at Jerusalem, the capital of Judah, indicates intensive trade with the Mediterranean and the southern coastal plain. In the words of Lernau and Lernau (1992: 136): "the archaeological evidence . . . suggest[s] that different kinds of fish were popular food in the city, and that the trade in fish was well organized."[153]

149. Ben Zvi, *Zephaniah*, 102.

150. This is worth noting contra the implication in DeVries, *Yesterday*, 324. In *From Old Revelation*, 203, he speaks of "the divine punishment on the unruly upper classes, the noise of destruction within the city, and Yahweh's search for the self-satisfied" as "events in the same proximate future." In my view, they are not in fact separate events from the sacrifice of v. 7—i.e., the punishment of vv. 8–9.

151. Sweeney (*Zephaniah*, 89) reports that the gate is sometimes identified with the Ephraim Gate (2 Kgs 14:13; 2 Chr 25:23; Neh 8:16; 12:39), but in Neh 12:39, the two are distinguished. The Fish Gate may have been designated as the "Middle Gate" for its location among the (newer?) northern gates beyond (?) the (older?) Ephraim Gate, namely the Yeshanah Gate (Neh 3:6; 12:39) to the west and the Sheep Gate (Neh 3:1, 32; 12:39) to the east, close to the temple mount.

152. It seems likely that there was no gate between the Yeshanah Gate, maybe at the northwestern corner of the city (identical with the Corner Gate in 2 Chr 26:9?), and the Valley Gate further south.

153. Faust and Weiss, "Economic System," 75 (with further references). The citation in

The *Fish Gate* probably stood somewhere across the Central (Tyropoeon) Valley and provided a northern access point to the city. The *Second Ward* (cf. 2 Kgs 22:14 // 2 Chr 34:22) was the newer residential quarter to the west across the Central Valley (in today's Armenian and Jewish quarters of the Old City).[154] The expansion of the city by more than a hundred acres had probably become necessary, not least as a result of an influx of refugees into Judah after the destruction of the Northern Kingdom in 722/721.

The *great crash from the hills* is a suitable climax, as we can imagine the hills echoing with the sound of destruction: the breaching of walls and the breaking of pots and jars alongside anguished cries. The *hills* are likely those on either side of the Central Valley, namely the Western Ridge with (today's) Mount Zion, Mount Moriah (the Temple Hill), and Mount Ophel with the Eastern Ridge (the ancient city of David), unless the reference is to the (higher) western hills of the new city only.[155] Even in the latter case, the expression would seem to be a *pars pro toto* reference to Jerusalem as a whole.

Why are *the Fish Gate* and *the Second Ward* singled out? The *Fish Gate* was likely the most prominent gate in the north, from which any attack on the city would come, and *the Second Ward* would be considered more vulnerable than the ancient city, which was famed for its invincibility. The *outcry* thus signals the breach of the city, the *wailing* accompanies the conquest, and the *great crash* relates to the havoc caused by the invading army. We should not be too quick to think of *the Second Ward* as a well-to-do living area popular with royal officials on the grounds that Huldah lived there (see 2 Kgs 22:14). Hillel Geva, publisher of the Jewish Quarter excavations, even claims that the nature of the settlement was "essentially rural-agricultural" and sparsely populated.[156] This is, however, contested by others. Faust believes that the

---

the quotation is from H. Lernau and O. Lernau, "Fish Bone Remains," in *Excavations at the City of David 1978–1985*, ed. A. De Groot and D. T. Ariel, vol. 3, Qedem 33 (Jerusalem: Hebrew University of Jerusalem, 1992).

154. Today, a section of the Broad Wall (cf. Neh 3:8) built at the end of the eighth century to protect the new city against the Assyrian threat is visible to passersby in the Jewish quarter of the Old City. For the identification of the various locations mentioned, see, e.g., Irsigler, *Zefanja*, 149–52, and standard reference works. Cf. Hillel Geva, "Western Jerusalem at the End of the First Temple Period in Light of the Excavations in the Jewish Quarter," in *Jerusalem in the Bible and Archaeology: The First Temple Period*, ed. Andrew G. Vaughn and Ann E. Killebrew (Atlanta: Society of Biblical Literature, 2003), 183–208.

155. The latter is argued by Seybold, *Prophetie*, 31, and Irsigler, *Zefanja*, 152. It seems less likely that *the hills* are those beyond the Hinnom and Kidron Valleys, as suggested by Sweeney, *Zephaniah*, 90, and very unlikely that *the hills* are another specific (to us unknown) part of the city distinct from the areas already mentioned, as Vlaardingerbroek (*Zephaniah*, 94) believes.

156. Hillel Geva, "Jerusalem's Population in Antiquity: A Minimalist View," *Tel Aviv* 41

building of the wall "served as an incentive for the transfer of royal structures (and the rich) to the empty new quarters." He concludes that "the western part of the Western Hill was populated by *all* social classes."[157]

Listen! An outcry is paralleled (only) in Jer 48:3, where it also relates to *a great crash*. Indeed, *a great crash* is found elsewhere only in Jeremiah (also 4:6; 6:1; 14:17; 50:22; 51:54) where it always speaks of the horror of invasion. The noun *wailing*, rarer than the verb of the same root (used in the next verse; see below), is attested three more times in the Hebrew Bible, always in the context of war (Isa 15:8; Jer 25:36; Zech 11:3).

11 The *Mortar* is often identified as the low-lying area between, on the one side, Mount Moriah and Mount Ophel with the Eastern Ridge and, on the other side, *the Second Ward* and the Western Ridge with what is today called Mount Zion. (Due to centuries of building on the debris of previous destructions, the ground is no longer as depressed as it used to be.) It is then thought to have received its name from the shape of the terrain, which may have brought to mind a tool for grinding grain (cf. Prov 27:22; the only other occurrence is in Judg 15:19). But as the name is not attested elsewhere, we cannot discount the possibility that Zephaniah freshly coined the term as a designation that applies to the whole city, which is to be ground like grain in the coming judgment. The failure to consider this alternative is likely due to the tendency to take vv. 10–11 closely together and discuss the geographical references as if they occur in exactly the same context. The *Mortar* is then made out to be the special area in which the merchants and money changers did their business.[158] This is possible, although one could ask who would be left to wail if the *inhabitants of the Mortar* are the same people who are said to have been *wiped out* and *cut off*.[159] But in an urban environment, few if any people would be self-sufficient, and the end of trade would therefore affect the whole city. It is therefore entirely possible that *the inhabitants* of

---

(2014): 140 (with further references). Geva reckons that about 2,000 (or at most 3,000) people lived in the Second Ward, with Jerusalem's overall population being no higher than 8,000 at its pre-destruction peak at the end of the eighth century, from which it declined and then recovered to about 6,000 on the eve of its destruction by the Babylonians.

157. Avraham Faust, "The Settlement on Jerusalem's Western Hill and the City's Status in the Iron Age II Revisited," *ZDPV* 121 (2005): 104, 105. The emphasis in the second citation is his.

158. Seybold (*Satirische Prophetie*, 28–32) is alert to the possibility that Zephaniah may have coined the term. Like others, he assumes that the reference is to a specific area but does not seem to think that the merchants necessarily lived there, as he allows that the suburb may have been a slum (29).

159. Cf. Uehlinger, "Astralkultpriester," 61. Even opting for the assertive use of the particle *kî* here ("indeed, surely") could not altogether avoid the implication that the action in the first line follows the events described in the following lines.

the whole city are called to wail *because all the merchant people are wiped out, and all who are laden with silver are cut off,*[160] or at any rate those most disastrously affected by it, namely the more prosperous parts.

It is possible that *the Mortar* designates an area on which commercial activities were centered, perhaps as "the city" functions for London as a reference to its pulsating, economic heart. But my preference is for the alternative view, which sees the whole city addressed broadly, or in any case not a group different from the people listed in vv. 8–9. The great outcry in v. 10 in response to the effects of the Day of YHWH offered a marked contrast to the *hush* in v. 7 in preparation for the Day of YHWH. We may consider the references to noise as concluding a paragraph that began with a call to silence. That call turns out not to be viable. The imperative at the beginning of this verse can be seen as something of a new beginning, even if it recaps v. 10 by the reuse of the root for *wail*. Thus, vv. 7–10 stand under the call to keep quiet before YHWH's approach, a call that proves impossible to sustain once the effects of the Day of YHWH are felt. Verses 11–18 stand under the call to howl in the aftermath of the disaster. One could say that this is similarly a call that will not be sustained, because by the end of v. 18, *a full end* will have been made and, rhetorically, no one is left to wail. The two sections, if analyzed thus, are closely tied together (see also my comments under "Composition").

The verb *yll* (*wail*) is only attested in the prophetic literature and always in connection with a communal catastrophe.[161] Its most common use is as an imperative.[162] The use of *yiqtol* forms is more common in the indicative (9×) than *qatal* forms (3×: Jer 47:2; 48:39; Amos 8:3), all of which are unambiguous and could not be mistaken for an imperative. It is therefore most likely that the imperative is intended here. As such, a summons to lament stands in

160. Cf. Robertson, *Nahum*, 279. See also Ben Zvi's (*Zephaniah*, 105) comments on the pattern of describing distress in a series of places (also Mic 1:8–16; Isa 10:28–29). He suggests that Isa 15:1–2; 16:7–8 make it obvious that in this pattern, "the entire geographical area is described as struck (or going to be struck) and not only the particular places explicitly mentioned."

161. The related noun *yəlēl* is attested once for the "howling" wasteland of the wilderness in Deut 32:10.

162. Elsewhere in Isa 13:6; 14:31; 23:1, 6, 14; Jer 4:8; 25:34; 48:20; 49:3; 51:8; Ezek 21:12(17); 30:2; Joel 1:5, 11, 13; Zech 11:2 (twice). Christopher S. Tachik (*"King of Israel" and "Do Not Fear, Daughter of Zion": The Use of Zephaniah 3 in John 12* [Phillipsburg: P&R Publishing, 2018], 89) makes the odd comment that none of the *hêlîlû* occurrences "require" interpretation as an imperative. It would be very forced to translate *hêlîlû* as indicative where it follows (e.g., Isa 23:6) or precedes (e.g., Jer 51:8) another imperative. In places like Isa 23:14, in which the causal statement uses a second-person suffix, the indicative is well-nigh impossible. A comparison of translations reveals few difficulties distinguishing the indicative (Jer 48:39) from the imperative (elsewhere).

contrast to the *hush* in v. 7. It indeed makes sense to me to see the beginning of a new paragraph here, even if this is a minority view.[163]

The reference to *merchant people* (lit. "people of Canaan"; see the translation note) may evoke the coastal region specifically,[164] or at any rate foreigners, thus harking back to the condemnation of *all those clothed in foreign clothing* (v. 8). Along with structural changes, "trade brought with it cultural and religious orientation to foreign countries."[165] Sweeney concludes, "Overall, the passage employs the term 'Canaanites' to convey a combination of ethnic, religious, and economic associations in an effort to prompt the audience to dissociate itself with everything that the term 'Canaanite' entails and to identify more closely with Judean interests as articulated by Zephaniah and Josiah's reform."[166] Indeed, the reference to *the Fish Gate* in the preceding verse may have facilitated similar associations, as fish mongers were most likely foreigners (Phoenicians, Philistines; see above).[167] In this way, we may be subtly prepared for the logic of 2:1–4, where a call is based on what YHWH is going to do abroad. This observation should not detract from the fact that the targets here are within Jerusalem, but it underlines that those within Jerusalem who are most closely involved in dealings with foreigners are the prime target. It is possible that, rather than being ignorant of the meaning of *nidmâ* (*wiped out*) here,[168] the Greek translator who rendered *hōmoiōthē pas ho laos Chanaan* ("all the people were made like Canaan") exploited the fact that there is a homonym that allows for a contextually fitting translation that brings out an element of alienation. The Tg. combines the two with a double translation of *nidmâ*: "Because all the people whose works are like the works of the people of the land of Canaan are utterly destroyed, all those rich in property."[169] The use of *conticuit* ("be silent," cf. Hos 4:6; Obad 5) in the Vulg. could be read as reversing the *hush* to *wail* movement of vv. 7–10. This is unlikely to be deliberate (*silete* is used in v. 7), but the mul-

---

163. But see Floyd, *Minor Prophets* 2, 192–200. Following the opening calls, Floyd identifies a movement from YHWH's action to the effects of his action within the respective narrations, doubled in the second section (described first from Judah's and then from a cosmic perspective).

164. So Uehlinger, "Astralkultpriester," 61.

165. Vlaardingerbroek, *Zephaniah*, 95.

166. Sweeney, *Zephaniah*, 92; cf. Irsigler, *Zefanja*, 153.

167. I do not expect that the Sea of Galilee yielded much trade at the time from any Israelites remaining in the area, nor did the Salt Sea (Dead Sea) yield any fish.

168. While *homoioō* is by far the most common LXX equivalent for these Hebrew homonyms, within the Book of the Twelve, *aporiptō* ("throw aside," Hos 10:7, 15 [2×]; Obad 5; cf. Jer 47:5) is found as often as *homoioō* (Hos 4:5–6; 12:10[11]), suggesting that the translator knew an alternative.

169. Cf. Sweeney, *Zephaniah*, 92. The use of "works" highlights that the question is one of (cultural) behavior rather than (biological) ethnicity.

tiple possibilities for interpreting *nidmâ* allow for an allusiveness that makes it an especially fitting verb here. It is the parallel *nikrətû* (*cut off*) in the next line, which should ensure that ultimately *nidmâ* is read (also) as *wiped out*.

Kol-'am kəna'an (*all the merchant people*) are parallel to *kol-nəṭîlê kāsep*, either "all those who weigh out silver" or *all those laden with silver*. Sweeney translates the LXX rendering *pantes hoi epērmenoi argyriō* as "all those who lift up/exalt silver" and interprets it as perhaps implying "a value judgment on those who are greedy for money."[170] But the passive form with the dative is better rendered as in NETS: "all those buoyed by silver."[171] Those who translate the Hebrew in the sense of weighing out silver think of trading middlemen or "money" exchangers. Sweeney notes that "coinage is believed to have begun in Asia Minor during the seventh century BCE,[172] and the Assyrians are frequently credited with having established a cash basis for trade during the period of their rule."[173] Even so, in picturing the situation in monarchic Judah, we should not think of actual coins, which were not introduced there until the Persian period, but silver ingots. The parallelism does not mean that the active meaning has to be preferred.[174] Both meanings would fit with the parallelism because the merchant people can either be linked with their middlemen and associates or be parallel to all those who profit from the trade. In my reading, *all those who are laden with silver* in the third line are more or less the same group as *all the merchant people* in the second line. We may compare the way in which *foreign clothing* in v. 8 has connotations of both cultural otherness (*merchant people* or "Canaanites" here) and wealth (*laden with silver* here).

12 This verse is responsible for the standard artistic depiction of Zephaniah with a lamp, although it is of course YHWH who is searching out *Jerusalem with lamps*.[175] The phrase *at that time* is not as common a formula as *on that day*;[176] in fact, nowhere else is it used with *and it shall happen*, and

---

170. Sweeney, *Zephaniah*, 92.

171. Cf. BA 23.4–9, 345.

172. Per Sweeney (*Zephaniah*, 92 n.), see John W. Betlyon, "Coinage," *ABD* 1:1076–89 (esp. 1079, 1082).

173. Sweeney, *Zephaniah*, 92.

174. Contra Ben Zvi, *Zephaniah*, 105.

175. The Tg. avoids the anthropomorphic image by having YHWH appoint searchers. I am not convinced that the iconography implies that in medieval tradition, Zephaniah was considered the subject of the verb. The item may be just a convenient link to the text, distinguishing him from other prophets. (Note that the Vulg. preserves the plural for lamps.)

176. Cf. 3:19–20 and Isa 18:7; Jer 3:17; 4:11; 8:1; 31:1. Three other occurrences in the prophetic literature are clearly not formulaic in this sense (Isa 20:2; Amos 5:13; Mic 3:4). Even the longer phrase "and it shall happen on that day" (32×) is far more common than *at that time* (with or without *and it shall happen*).

the LXX emends the unique expression to the more common one. "And it shall happen on that day" is typically followed by a clause with a *yiqtol* (imperfect) verb, as is *and it shall happen at that time* here.[177] In a quarter of cases, *utterance of YHWH* or its equivalent with "Lord YHWH" or "YHWH of Hosts" is placed between the introductory phrase and the verb.[178] The question whether the beginning of the verse belongs inside the divine speech or is to be read as the prophet's introduction before the citation of the divine speech, which then begins with the verb, cannot and need not be decided, as the blurring of "prophetic" and "divine" speech is common in prophetic literature.

In any case, *at that time* does not signal strict contemporaneity, and we are certainly not to picture the search as happening in the rubble after the disaster described in v. 10 and most likely not after the events of lines 2–3 of the previous verse. The latter would only be possible on the assumption that *the merchant people* and *all who are laden with silver* are exclusively foreigners trading with the inhabitants of Jerusalem. In that case, the call to wail would be intended to disturb the complacent in Jerusalem who have not yet realized that their allies have already been *wiped out*. But given the focus on Jerusalem in this chapter, it is better to think of v. 12 as going back to the beginning of the disaster. This time, its inescapability for the intended recipients is underlined. While the search could be interpreted as a careful and thorough investigation prior to the punishment, it more likely speaks of the thoroughness of finding the intended targets. The use of the plural *lamps* is in all probability designed to stress this further. The use of *lamps* need not imply a nighttime scenario, as some commentators believe, but rather suggests that the search goes into every hidden corner of the city. Ben Zvi points out that the most probable hiding places within a city are dark places such as caves, cisterns, and inner rooms.[179]

I suggested above that the call to wail goes to all inhabitants of Jerusalem, because in one way or another they will all be affected. But just as the punishment had a specific target in vv. 8–9, so it does here. The target is described in two ways. The first apparently paints a picture of people who had been left undisturbed like wine quietly maturing on its lees. The second offers the reason for their complacency: they think, "*YHWH will cause neither good nor evil*," which is to say they do not expect YHWH to do anything much. There

---

177. *Wə*-qatal is used in Isa 22:20; 23:15; Hos 1:5; Amos 8:9. Zeph 1:10 is unusual in not employing a verb.

178. Jer 4:9; 30:8; Ezek 38:18; Hos 2:16(18); Amos 8:9; Mic 5:10(9); Zech 13:2.

179. Ben Zvi, *Zephaniah*, 108; cf. Weigl, *Zefanja*, 49; Seybold, *Satirische Prophetie*, 32; contra Sweeney, *Zephaniah*, 93–94, who goes on to link the nighttime with drunkenness, which he sees clearly implied in the verse. Jerome (*Twelve*, 125–26) notes that Josephus mentions underground caverns (e.g., *Jewish War* 3.336; 6.370–72; 7.35).

is, therefore, no advantage in seeking him and no harm in failing to do so. YHWH's search is, however, so comprehensive that even the most hidden place, the human mind, is illuminated by his lamps so that thoughts and attitudes are revealed (cf. Prov 20:27 where "the lamp of YHWH . . . searches out all the inner rooms of the body"[180]). Thus, he will reach those who think themselves out of reach and deal with those who think that he will have no effect on their lives.

Exactly how the metaphor implied here works is, however, debated. The verb *congeal* is not used with wine elsewhere, and so it is not entirely clear whether the image is (1) of wine "sitting" on its dregs, with which people are compared who are "congealing" (i.e., the congealing does not apply to the wine itself), or (2) of wine "congealing" on its lees, with which people are compared. If the latter, it is also not clear whether congealing is a good or a bad thing. Is the wine spoiled by congealing or matured and so now ready to drink? Sweeney refers to "the ancient method of making wine by letting grapes sit and ferment in water until they form a thick, sticky, and unmoving conglomeration that must be mixed with water before it can be drunk." (In fact, it may need to be strained beforehand as well.) He comments, "In effect, those who drink the wine become exactly like the wine that they drink."[181] Isaiah 25:6 uses *wine lees* for the refined, aged wine itself (the part being used for the whole), and Jer 48:11-12 compares Moab to a wine left undisturbed until now. These suggest that leaving a wine to sit on its lees does not have negative connotations in and of itself. But perhaps wine can be left for too long in that state, and the reference to congealing might then indicate either that the wine is now ready to be moved into different vessels or that it has stood for too long.[182]

A substantial system of seventh-century wine presses and cellars has been discovered at Gibeon, north of Jerusalem, and there is evidence for

180. YHWH's lamp is apparently the human breath going through every part of the body. Prov 20:27 has been interpreted in different ways. Thus, e.g., Waltke (*Proverbs 15-31*, 157-58) argues that "breath" is a metonymy for "words" or "speech" here, while Tremper Longman III (*Proverbs* [Grand Rapids: Baker, 2006], 385) thinks "the point of the saying is that the person lives only because of Yahweh."

181. Sweeney, *Zephaniah*, 94. Dietrich (*Nahum*, 208) refers to two methods: "Wine was at that time, as a rule, siphoned off after the fermentation process—in effect, filtered. However, it could also be left 'with the yeast,' in which case it would become cloudy and heavy." Others are not convinced that in the second case the wine would remain desirable; cf. Vlaardingerbroek, *Zephaniah*, 100; Irsigler, *Zefanja*, 160.

182. See also William D. Barker, "Wine Production in Ancient Israel and the Meaning of שמרים in the Hebrew Bible," in *Leshon Limmudim: Essays on the Language and Literature of the Hebrew Bible in Honour of A. A. Macintosh*, ed. David A. Baer and Robert P. Gordon, LHBOTS 593 (London: T&T Clark, 2013), 268-74.

"industrial-scale wine production" at Ashkelon in the same period.[183] Wine was therefore available nearby. Irsigler points out that the wine imagery for the judgment on Moab in Jer 48:11–12 is very fitting because Moab was well known for its wine production (cf. Isa 16:8–10; Jer 48:32–33).[184] In the same way, he suggests, the use of the metaphor in this verse indicates the importance of wine in the life of the rich and prominent men condemned here.[185] This is plausible, but it does not mean that the people should be pictured as drunk, as some have argued.[186] The complacency condemned here need not be pressed too far in the direction of sloth. The metaphor does not suggest wine that is "passive" as opposed to active (slothful) but wine that is left "undisturbed" as opposed to being moved (at ease). These people felt that they could go about their business in tranquility, without taking God's demands into account and without worrying that YHWH might get in the way. Read with the earlier part of the chapter, we may be allowed to suspect that these men, too, acquired riches *with violence and fraud* (v. 9) and through foreign associations at the expense of local norms (v. 8). Their punishment will refute the idea that *"YHWH will cause neither good nor evil."*

13 This verse consists of two parts. The first two lines announce the consequences directly, interestingly focusing on *their wealth* and *their houses* rather than the persons themselves. Sweeney notes that "there is nothing in this verse that points to the despoliation or destruction of the entire city," and it is certainly true that the threat is focused and indirectly calls people to turn from the attitudes condemned here.[187] The words used nevertheless suggest indiscriminate action on a large scale: *plunder* is found elsewhere in the context of national catastrophe (2 Kgs 21:14; Isa 42:22, 24; Jer 30:16;

---

183. Michal Dayagi-Mendels, *Drink and Be Merry: Wine and Beer in Ancient Times* (Jerusalem: The Israel Museum, 1999), 25–26.

184. We already noted that *qôl ṣəʿāqâ* (*Listen! An outcry*; v. 10) is paralleled (only) in Jer 48:3, also in connection with *šeber gādôl, a great crash*. In addition, *mahēr* is qualified by *məʾōd* only here in v. 14 (*coming very fast*) and in Jer 48:16, both in connection with *qārôb* (*near*). Along with the motif of wine settling on its lees, this makes for three exclusive connections between the two chapters to which other, less significant links could be added (e.g., the use of *ṭebaḥ*, "slaughter," in Jer 48:15). It is possible that Zeph 1 was an inspiration for Jer 48.

185. Irsigler, *Zefanja*, 160. Jeremy D. Smoak ("Building Houses and Planting Vineyards: The Inner-Biblical Discourse on an Ancient Israelite Wartime Curse," *JBL* 127 [2008]: 19–35) notes "the increase in viticulture industries in the environs of Jerusalem and adjacent regions" at the time (29); cf. Faust and Weiss, "Economic System," 75–76, 80.

186. E.g., Sweeney, *Zephaniah*, 94. See Ben Zvi, *Zephaniah*, 111–12, for further references and the observation that it is quite a way from *qpʾ* ("congeal") to "being in a (drunken) stupor."

187. Sweeney, *Zephaniah*, 95. A less focused description might have given rise to defeatism.

arguably also in the only other occurrence, in Hab 2:7);[188] *desolation* speaks not only of destruction but also of an area that has been deserted. One does not get a sense of a select group of people being dispossessed while their neighbors are left in peace. In the latter case, we would probably expect the houses being taken over rather than made a *desolation*.

The second set of two lines cites common images for futility. We should probably think of these as proverbial motifs more than formulaic phrases given that even those passages whose wording is most similar to that in Zephaniah are not couched in exactly the same way (Deut 28:30, 39; Amos 5:11; Mic 6:15; and for the removal of the curse, Isa 62:8; 65:22; Ezek 28:26; Amos 9:14). These and similar images for frustrated efforts appear frequently in the prophetic literature, presumably influenced by traditional motifs found in biblical and extrabiblical treaty curses.[189] There is a temporal disruption between these two sets. With wealth gone and *houses a desolation*, any new building of houses and planting of vineyards would need to be in the more distant future, and it would take a few years between planting vines and producing fruit. Some have argued that the verse is a later addition, maybe adapting or extending the threat to new circumstances or creating editorial links to other parts of the Book of the Twelve. But the parallels with Amos 5:11 (cf. 9:14) and Mic 6:15 are arguably not strong enough to function as sign-posts within the Book of the Twelve, and Vlaardingerbroek's proposal that someone who "witnessed the beginning of reconstruction . . . wanted to remove the illusion that apparently the Day of YHWH did not turn out all that badly" is entirely implausible.[190] No rebuilding in Persian times could make anyone seriously think that what happened a few decades earlier was not so bad after all. The proposal only makes sense on the mistaken idea that people would have equated the Day of YHWH with the end of the world beyond which nothing could be expected.

The futility motif is well suited to the context. Those who think that YHWH makes no difference to what they do will in turn experience that nothing they do will make any difference. The specific way the futility motif is phrased here is well-adapted for its immediate literary context with reference to houses and wine. It is therefore fair to speak of "thematic completion.

---

188. Cf. the use of the related verbs *šss* (Judg 2:14; 1 Sam 17:53; Ps 89:41[42] [defeat of the king]; Isa 13:16; Jer 30:16; Zech 14:2) and *šsh* (Judg 2:14, 16; 1 Sam 14:48; 23:1; 2 Kgs 17:20; Ps 44:10[11]; Isa 10:13; 17:14; 42:22; Jer 50:11; Hos 13:15). This may simply reflect the nature of events spoken of in the Bible, but note that Ps 109:11 uses the more common verb *bzz*, which, along with its related noun *baz*, is elsewhere too only used for national catastrophes.

189. Smoak, "Building Houses"; Melissa Ramos, "A Northwest Semitic Curse Formula: The Sefire Treaty and Deuteronomy 28," *ZAW* 128 (2016): 205–20; Laura Quick, *Deuteronomy 28 and the Aramaic Curse Tradition* (Oxford: Oxford University Press, 2017).

190. Vlaardingerbroek, *Zephaniah*, 97.

The wealth of the indicted is to be destroyed and their efforts to restore it will be in vain."[191] It is very well conceivable, therefore, that the second half of the verse came into being at the same time as the first. While it is also, in principle, possible for these two lines to belong to a later edition, no strong motive for such an updating presents itself.

14 A new paragraph begins with this verse. After the look into the more distant future at the end of v. 13, this verse renews the sense of urgency that goes with the announcement of the proximity of the Day of YHWH in v. 7. It also heightens the sense of danger. Now the day is twice said to be *near* and, in addition, *coming very fast*. The Day of YHWH is also described as *great* in Malachi and twice in Joel,[192] always in connection with being "fearsome" (*nôrā'*).[193] Here, too, the greatness of *the Day of YHWH* consists in the extent to which it is threatening. It will be an experience of overwhelming destruction, as is soon spelled out.

Regardless of the exact rendering of the opening *qôl* (*Listen!*), the second bicolon draws attention to what the *Day of YHWH* sounds like: *Fiercely screams the warrior then*. The verb used here (in the *qal*) is found elsewhere only in Isa 42:13 (in the *hiphil*), where YHWH, going forth "like a warrior," raises a warcry. This is likely its meaning here as well—it is the yelling of a warrior going forth into battle rather than the crying out in terror of soldiers fleeing the battle. This is not to claim that *ṣrḥ* ("to scream fiercely") always has such narrow connotations[194] or that the sound of the Day of YHWH could not be described in terms of cries of fear coming even out of the mouths of warriors. But the reuse of *warrior* in 3:17 looks like an allusion to this verse, and a meaning along the lines of Isa 42:13 is also fitting here. In this case, just as it is YHWH who shapes the events of that day, it is his warcry that makes the Day of YHWH sound fierce.[195]

15 The list that opens here uses repetition for dramatic effect. It poetically portrays the overwhelming nature of *that day*, reinforced in the Hebrew text by the use of alliteration (especially in the first two sets) and assonance (with *a* and *o* sounds). Irsigler observes the gradual buildup of syllables in each

---

191. Ben Zvi, *Zephaniah*, 116.

192. Joel 2:11; 2:31(3:4); Mal 4:5(3:23); cf. "Certainly, the day of Jezreel will be great" in Hos 1:11(2:2).

193. The two terms are together also in Deut 1:19; 7:21; 8:15; 10:17, 21; 1 Chr 16:25; Neh 1:5; 4:14(8); 9:32; Pss 47:2(3); 96:4; 99:3; Dan 9:4. Cf. Mal 1:14 and see *nôrā'* with *gədûllâ* ("greatness") in 2 Sam 7:23; 1 Chr 17:21; Ps 145:6.

194. *DCH* cites 1QHa XI, 33 and 4Q418 frag. 69, II, 7 for the meaning "scream, cry out for help" (and interprets Zeph 1:14 along those lines). Unless it is a later development, this suggests that the word could refer to shouting more generally.

195. So also, e.g., Ben Zvi, *Zephaniah*, 120–21.

line (1–2–4).[196] We find similar use of repetition in descriptions of distress elsewhere (Isa 37:3 // 2 Kgs 19:3 is often noted), but the length of the list here drives home the point in the most forceful way. The sevenfold use of *day* in vv. 15–16 suggests completeness, stressing the totality as well as the devastating impact of the destruction. If an allusion to the creation story is picked up, the sevenfold use (six times *day of* as the predicate of *that day*) can be read as reverting the seven (six plus one) days of creation, painting a picture of de-creation.[197]

Syntactically, *that day* functions as the once-mentioned subject of six nominal clauses. The day is first characterized as *a day of fury*, using a word (*'ebrâ*) that features elsewhere in Day of YHWH passages, although the actual phrase *day of fury* is only attested once more in this context as "the day of the fury of YHWH"—in Ezek 7:19, which may be influenced by our passage.[198] The opening line sets the descriptions of extreme devastation in the following lines in the context of something personal. Even if not spelled out explicitly, the fury is YHWH's, given that it is his day. Thus, the destruction is first said to arise from YHWH's judgment before it is characterized as a day of the most distressing anguish, absolutely devastating desolation, complete darkness, thoroughly black clouds, and (in the next verse) blasting noise that signals an attack on fortifications. The reference to dark clouds following a picture of extreme darkness may feel anticlimactic, but we seem to have a twofold movement from the more general/abstract/atmospheric to the more specific/concrete/visual, which perhaps depicts the move from the less accessible divine realm to more tangible earthly realities. Also, the reference to clouds at the end of the verse guides our imagination upward so that *the fortified cities* and *lofty corner towers* in the next verse are seen in the imagination from the outside looking down—in a sense, from YHWH's point of view.

Darkness is a common motif in descriptions of the Day of YHWH (cf. already Amos 5:18, 20) and indeed generally in connection with an appearance of YHWH (e.g., Exod 19:16; Deut 4:11).[199] The final two pairs of the verse (*a day of darkness and gloom, a day of cloudiness and cloudy blackness*) are also found in Joel 2:2. The abundance of cross-references within Joel is usually

---

196. Irsigler, *Zefanja*, 168.

197. Cf. Peter C. Craigie, *Twelve Prophets*, vol. 2 (Philadelphia: Westminster John Knox, 1985), 116; David W. Baker, *Nahum, Habakkuk and Zephaniah*, TOTC (Leicester: InterVarsity Press, 1988), 100.

198. Without the Day of YHWH motif, the phrase is used in Prov 11:4 and Job 21:30 (pl. *yôm 'ăbārôt*).

199. Sweeney (*Zephaniah*, 100) notes the association of darkness with YHWH's presence in the temple in particular (1 Kgs 8:12 // 2 Chr 6:1; Ps 97:2), which in his view "aids in establishing the ironic character of the event."

considered a sign of Joel's late date.[200] It is, therefore, more likely that Joel cites Zephaniah than the other way around.[201] Assuming that Joel cites Zephaniah, the description of the Day of YHWH in these verses reflects a creative use of traditional motifs rather than stereotypical phrases.[202] Zephaniah, in turn, may be indebted to Amos 5:18–20 for the motif of darkness, and the list-like character of Isa 2:12–17 may have inspired the structure of the text.

16 The final description of *that day* in this list is expanded and takes up the reference to sound. The interpretation of the sound in v. 14b as a warcry was rejected by Irsigler on the grounds that it prematurely anticipates the specific war language found here in v. 16.[203] But there is a logical movement from YHWH's warrior scream in v. 14, which puts into motion the events that v. 15 describes. The report begins in general and "abstract" terms (in the sense that the target of the devastation is not specified) before the disaster specifically and concretely reaches *the fortified cities* and *the lofty corner towers* under a *loud sound* that is also more specific and concrete than YHWH's warrior cry of v. 14. Both *shofar blast* and *loud sound* feature in warfare as well as liturgical celebrations (note, e.g., the sound of the shofar in Lev 25:9). Here, the *shofar* blast gives the signal to attack, as in Judg 7:20 and other places. Because the blowing of rams' horns was a common way to signal assembly or retreat in various contexts, we should be cautious about hearing any allusions to a specific text here. Given the use of parallel terms defining each other in preceding lines, it may be preferable to identify the *loud sound* as the blast from the shofar. Alternatively, the warcry of attacking soldiers is implied (cf., e.g., Josh 6:5, 20 for the people's shouts alongside the shofar sound). But no specifics are given about the approaching army; the focus remains on YHWH. *Bāṣûr (fortified)*, the adjective that qualifies *cities*, has connotations of inaccessibility and suggests fortifications that are (nearly) impregnable. It is paired with *lofty corner towers* (cf. 3:6) only here,[204] although height is

---

200. See, e.g., James L. Crenshaw, *Joel: A New Translation with Introduction and Commentary*, AB 24C (New York: Doubleday, 1995), 27; cf. the section on "Joel and prior prophecy" in Christopher R. Seitz, *Joel*, ITC (London: Bloomsbury, 2016), 25–29.

201. So also, e.g., Beck, "*Tag YHWHs*," 106–8, critically interacting with Nogalski's hypothesis of a Joel-related redactional layer.

202. Various commentators have examined the use of these words and phrases elsewhere; e.g., Ben Zvi, *Zephaniah*, 121–26; Vlaardingerbroek, *Zephaniah*, 108–10; Sweeney, *Zephaniah*, 98–101; Irsigler, *Zefanja*, 173–74.

203. Irsigler, *Zefanja*, 166–67. The sound of fleeing warriors would be equally premature. Irsigler accepts an emendation that makes the text speak of the day of YHWH being faster than a (war) hero; cf. *BHS* (and already *BHK* but—with reference to *CTAT* 3:884–86—no longer *BHQ*).

204. Indeed, *pinnâ* more often simply means "corner." Corner towers are in view also in 2 Chr 26:15 and possibly in Neh 3:24, 31–32. The word is also used metaphorically for leaders, pictured as either corner towers or corner stones; so, e.g., in Isa 19:13.

a feature mentioned in other places as well (Deut 3:5; 28:52; 2 Chr 33:14; Isa 2:15). If even these strong defenses are under attack, there is going to be no place for anyone to hide.

17 Now that the human target of the attack is specified, we are back to divine speech in the first person as the consequences are spelled out. *I will bring distress to humankind* means that YHWH will act with such hostility toward people that they will be in great panic and agony. Jeremiah speaks similarly of YHWH causing distress (10:18) and elsewhere employs the same verb for comparing the anguish of the mighty men of Moab and Edom with that of a woman suffering labor pains (48:41; 49:22). The collective noun *humankind* need not mean every man, woman and child alive on the earth but the people implied by the context. Ben Zvi points to the expression *'ādām ûbəhēmâ* ("people and animals") in Exod 8:17–18(13–14); 9:10; 13:2; Num 8:17; 18:15; 31:11, 26.[205] Nonuniversal references to a specific population are also found with *'ādām* on its own (e.g., Isa 6:11–12; Hos 9:12; Mic 7:2). One of the most interesting verses for comparison is Jer 4:25 because there, too, "the judgment that is to fall on Judah takes on the aspect of a cosmic conflagration."[206] Even those who consider the vision of total desolation in Jer 4:23–26 a later "apocalyptic" insertion seem to acknowledge that "the poem reflects the disaster of Jerusalem's destruction."[207] But McKane rightly cautions against "the antithesis between particular and universal, or historical and cosmic" as a possible "over-simplification." A "prophet who is also a poet and who is stretching his powers of expression to the limit may find that the universalizing of the anticipated moment of historical disaster is the ultimate power he possesses to convey the totality of the coming catastrophe."[208] While *humankind* allows for a creative rereading of the passage along universal lines, there is nothing in the verse to suggest that the reference must be to humanity as a whole, and the content of the preceding verses speaks against it.[209] It is at best

205. Ben Zvi, *Zephaniah*, 128. See also the references for use of the combination in prophetic literature in my commentary on 1:3.

206. John A. Thompson, *The Book of Jeremiah*, NICOT (Grand Rapids: Eerdmans, 1980), 229–30; cf. Jack R. Lundbom, *Jeremiah 1–20: A New Translation with Introduction and Commentary*, AB 21A (New York: Doubleday, 1999), 356–63; Leslie C. Allen, *Jeremiah: A Commentary*, OTL (London: SCM Press, 2008), 69.

207. Robert P. Caroll, *Jeremiah: A Commentary*, OTL (London: SCM Press, 1986), 168.

208. William McKane, *Jeremiah I-XXV*, ICC (Edinburgh: T&T Clark, 1986), 108. Michael A. Fishbane, "Jeremiah iv 23–6 and Job iii 3–13: A Recovered Use of the Creation Pattern," *VT* 21 (1971): 151–67, sees in such language a form of incantation. Even if this is rejected for Jer 4 and Zeph 1, the use of cosmological motifs in other ancient Near Eastern texts whose focus is specific and local is instructive.

209. So also, e.g., Ben Zvi, *Zephaniah*, 127–28; Roberts, *Nahum*, 182; Sweeney, *Zephaniah*, 102.

arguable that retrospectively, having read v. 18, a wider application suggests itself. But as will be shown below, the language of v. 18 is not unambiguously universal either.

The metaphor of walking *like the blind* is presumably inspired by the imagery of darkness in v. 15 (cf. Deut 28:29; Isa 29:18; 42:16). The Torah acknowledges the hazards of blindness (Lev 19:14; Deut 27:18; cf. Job 29:15), which in ancient times would have been at least as great as today. The same comparison serves as a portrayal of helplessness in Isa 59:10. We may also hear an echo of the Jebusite taunt against David: "You shall not come in here [Jerusalem], but the blind and lame will turn you away" (2 Sam 5:6, 8).

The next line gives the rationale for this distress and loss of orientation. It can be read as another instance of illeism (see the commentary on 1:5) rather than as a gloss or an indication that the whole verse is in the voice of the prophet-narrator.[210] The object *against YHWH* is positioned before the verb, which probably adds emphasis to it (cf. Jer 3:25; 50:14 [but not LXX 27:14] with Jer 8:14; 40:3). We could translate "because against YHWH they have sinned" (but this sounds harsh in English) or "because it is against YHWH that they have sinned" (which is cumbersome). The emphasis is fitting in connection with the Day of YHWH motif. It is not merely a case of wrong behavior being followed by disaster but of sin against YHWH being followed by the Day of YHWH. Ben Zvi claims that "a clear stress on the culpability of those who are punished by YHWH . . . is pointless if there were no (explicit or implicit) doubts about divine justice in the community."[211] But this supposition is unwarranted. It seems implausible that a later editor was worried about the lack of a rationale for the judgment. In any case, read as a whole, the chapter has already indicated reasons for the punishment. Maybe more plausible is the suggestion that a later gloss ensures that subsequent readers include themselves under the threat.[212] But the claim that the human population of Jerusalem and Judah (*humankind*) could be characterized in a blanket way with the clause *they have sinned against YHWH* does not itself give notice to later readers that they are included as well. On the one hand, the doctrine that all have sinned, for which Irsigler rightly cites 4 Esd 7:46, 68; Rom 5:12, is not explicitly taught here and cannot be communicated by the simple addition of *they have sinned against YHWH*. On the other hand, those who affirm this doctrine have no need for an editorial intervention to ensure that they do not read the threats as of historical interest only.

The verb *spilled* is frequently used for the shedding of *blood* (e.g., Gen 9:6;

---

210. For the former, see Vlaardingerbroek, *Zephaniah*, 104; Irsigler, *Zefanja*, 181; Dietrich, *Nahum*, 212; the latter is argued by Sweeney, *Zephaniah*, 102.

211. Ben Zvi, *Zephaniah*, 129.

212. Irsigler, *Zefanja*, 182–83.

Jer 7:6) and is readily associated with killing and warfare; here it also serves as the verb for the following line with *their guts* as the subject. This is more likely than the view that the last line characterizes *their guts* as *dung*. The translation *their guts* is not secure, but it seems probable that the reference is to the fleshy parts that are responsible for digestion, the intestines, although it may be a broader term for internal organs (see the translation note). Sweeney thinks that "the primary function of the verse is to depict the gutting of sacrificial victims and the removal of their intestines and internal organs as part of the process by which sacrificial animals are prepared for burning on the altar."[213] This is an intriguing suggestion in view of the sacrificial imagery above, but the general word for internal organs in the context of sacrifice is consistently *qereb* (e.g., Lev 1:9, 13; 3:3, 9, 14), with kidneys and liver named specifically in some places (e.g., Lev 3:4, 10, 15). *Qereb* does not look like an overly technical term, and it would be possible for Zephaniah to employ a different word to designate the same thing, perhaps from a desire to restrict use of the *qrb* root to the announcement of the imminence of the Day of YHWH (*qārôb*, "near"). But the use of a different word nevertheless means that an allusion to the sacrificial system cannot be established securely.

The verb for spilling or pouring out is used with *'āpār* (*dust*) also in Lev 14:41, where it refers to moldy plaster that has been scraped off houses. In more than half a dozen cases, unspecified items—presumably stones (cf. Lam 4:1), earth, and rubble—are poured out (cast up) to make a siege-mound (so, e.g., in 2 Sam 20:15; Jer 6:6).[214] In 2 Sam 20:10, the object being *spilled* is *mē'ê* ("bowels"), in Job 16:13 *mərērâ* ("gall"), in Lam 2:11 *kābēd* ("liver"). There is therefore no reason to object to the comparisons made in this verse with *dust* and *dung* on the grounds that these cannot be *spilled*. The point of the comparison in any case lies not in the act of spilling but in the worthlessness of *dust* and *dung*. There was an expectation that spilled *blood* would be covered by *dust* (Lev 17:13; Ezek 24:7; cf. Isa 26:21). In addition, *dung* relates easily to *guts* (assuming the reference is indeed to intestines).[215] The two substances, *dust* and *dung*, are therefore suggested by the two items being spilled, *blood* and *guts*. Finally, it is worth noting that the comparison with *dust* so soon after the reintroduction of *'ādām* (cf. 1:3) at the conclusion of this chapter evokes the sentence that those who have been taken from dust (*'āpār*) must return to it (Gen 3:19; cf. 2:7).

213. Sweeney, *Zephaniah*, 103. He also points to the reference to *fire* in the following verse (104).

214. Elsewhere, "ashes of fat" are poured out (1 Kgs 13:3, 5), and note *šepek* in Lev 4:12 for the dumping ground of ashes.

215. See the note on the translation of *ləḥūmām* with *their guts*. The word for *dung* is attested elsewhere only once, in 1 Kgs 14:10 (sg.; here it is plural), where it is burned.

18 On that day, when human blood and entrails will be considered worthless (see v. 17), valuable items such as *silver* and *gold* will not be able to ward off the judgment. The thought is developed further in Ezek 7:19, where *silver* and *gold* are discarded by their owners like something unclean, maybe because they were among the things that caused the people of God to stumble.[216] One can well imagine an attacking army that cannot be bought off if its leaders are confident of success at not too high a price. They will be able to plunder any valuables after the capture of the city anyway. But in keeping with the Day of YHWH motif, the rationale is simpler: this is *the day of YHWH's fury*. This hints at two reasons for the failure of *silver* and *gold* to redeem lives: (1) *on the day of . . . fury*, it is too late to pacify one's opponent with treasures (cf. Prov 11:4); and (2) *YHWH* can never be bought (cf. Ps 49:7[8]).

Ben Zvi notes that while both *fire* and *passion* are associated with YHWH and his appearance in many other places, the expression *in the fire of his passion* occurs only here, later in 3:8, and in Ezek 36:5 (likely dependent on Zephaniah). Zephaniah 3:8 repeats the full sentence but in first-person speech and following a reference to nations and kingdoms, thus universalizing it (*in the fire of my passion shall the whole earth be consumed*). Here, the preceding verses indicate that we should translate *hā'āreṣ* as *land* (see above). The expression *a full end* for complete termination is found elsewhere (note especially Isa 10:23; Jer 4:27). In Jer 30:11 (first instance) and 46:28 it is used in relation to all the nations to which the people of God had been scattered; elsewhere the target is narrower.[217] Nowhere is the expression used for the annihilation of the whole world. Similarly, *kol-yōšbê hā'āreṣ* could be universal only in Ps 33:14 ("all the inhabitants of the earth"). In Jer 25:29-30 the phrase also encompasses more than one nation, but everywhere else it means *all the inhabitants of the land*.[218] In other words, none of the phrases employed here demands that we picture the destruction of the entire world in this verse rather than a large but geographically limited destruction.[219] The emphasis of the text does of course not lie in the (implicit) geographical

---

216. The phrase repeated in Ezek 7:19 in MT and most versions ("silver and gold cannot save them") is not found in LXX. It may be a later addition in Ezekiel, but even the first edition of Ezekiel seems to have been inspired by Zephaniah, especially in its use of the Day of YHWH motif (but also, e.g., in 22:5; 25:16; 36:5); cf. also the use of "stumble" in Ezek 7:19 with Zeph 1:3.

217. Also Jer 5:10, 18; 30:11 (second instance); 46:28; Ezek 11:13; 20:17; Nah 1:8-9; cf. Neh 9:31.

218. Num 33:52; Josh 2:9, 24; 7:9; 9:24; Jer 1:14; 13:13; 47:2 (sg.); Joel 1:2, 14; 2:1.

219. Cf. the discussion in Ben Zvi, *Zephaniah*, 134-36, who thinks that the most conspicuous feature of the text is that it is ambiguous. He notes that the ambiguity could have been resolved by the use of *tēbēl* ("world") instead of, or alongside, *'ereṣ* ("land, earth").

limitation to Judah and Jerusalem (and maybe surrounding nations) but in the totality of the destruction, which for those involved will be the end of their world.

Reflection

The commentary has traced two movements (vv. 7–10, 11–18), both of which describe the imminent disaster as a Day of YHWH and consistently focus on YHWH as the agent of the day's events. There are two challenges here for our reflection: one relating to the depiction of YHWH and one relating to our view of ourselves. Taking the second challenge first, we do well to remember that the people condemned here probably saw themselves "in a much less negative light" than portrayed by the prophet; "like the rich at all times, they would have seen themselves as especially proficient and successful, having earned and deserved their wealth."[220] They would hardly have thought of themselves as areligious people, let alone atheists, but in practice they did not reckon with God—an attitude also portrayed elsewhere (cf. Isa 5:19; 29:15). The injunction in 1 Tim 6:17 suggests that it is a perennial danger for those who are rich in this world's goods to be haughty, to tell themselves that they deserve to be better off than others without asking to what purpose God has given them more than others. James 4:13–17 also warns about immersing oneself in business and trade without acknowledging God's sovereignty. The thought about YHWH's absence in human affairs spelled out in v. 12 may well have gone unspoken in ancient Judah (*in their hearts*) and maybe even unacknowledged by the people themselves, but God acts in response to who we truly are. He probes our minds and examines our thoughts (see, e.g., 1 Sam 16:7; Jer 17:10; 20:12; 1 Chr 28:9). His word raises questions about our true inner drives.

In Zephaniah's time, God's people were apparently compromised by participation in a wider socioeconomic system. When God's people were defined along ethnic-national lines, adherence to a specific culture was required. But in the fullness of time, one born under the law came not only to reconcile us to God but also to tear down the wall between Jews and non-Jews (see Gal 4:4; Eph 2:14). Today, the life of God's people finds expression in a wide range of cultures. The growing interconnectedness of the modern world, therefore, need not be a threat to us in and of itself.[221] But it is still worth pondering to what extent the structures of our society foster particular

220. Dietrich, *Nahum*, 208.
221. The COVID-19 pandemic reveals both the increased risks of such interconnectedness, as the virus spread more quickly across the globe than it would have in a less inter-

virtues or vices. It may be that dependence on God is more readily acknowl-edged in places where most families are engaged in subsistence farming than in societies in which goods are traded in ways that obscure our relationship with the rest of creation. People in self-sufficient rural communities are likely more aware of their dependence on each other and on a network of relationships. By contrast, our interdependence is obscured in societies in which producers and consumers are not personally known to each other. The move toward such economic systems has arguably also led to a greater gap between rich and poor. Unless counteracted by taxation or something like the Torah's Jubilee legislation, this easily creates haughtiness and pride with some and despondency and resentment with others. The prophetic critique of urban living cannot be applied to modern societies without adaptation, but it reveals the possible connection between the structure of a society and its preeminent values, and therefore it reveals that the people of God face particular temptations with respect to their particular societies.[222]

In most cultures today, foreign clothing does not have the connotations it had in ancient Judah, although in parts of the world it does raise similar issues—for example, where the donation of clothes from overseas hampers local trade in textiles, thus potentially doing more harm than good. This commentary cannot spell out in detail what today's challenges are in various contexts, but it can highlight the issues. Our economic activity (1) is driven by motives and reflects values that should be examined; (2) is of interest to God, whose norms should govern our activity and whose judgment is com-ing; and (3) has a social aspect and impact that should not be ignored.

The application of Zeph 1 to the final day of judgment derives from the con-viction that this day, too, will be entirely determined and shaped by YHWH. It will be a terrifying day on which the thoughts and intentions of our hearts will be revealed, a day of comprehensive reckoning. The Latin translation of vv. 15–16 is widely thought to have inspired the medieval hymn "Dies irae, dies illa" ("A day of wrath that day"), although apart from its opening line and the reference to a trumpet (*tuba*; cf. 1 Thess 4:16), specific verbal connections are hard to discern. The hymn also incorporates images from other biblical texts that are worth reflecting on in this context (Matt 25:31–46; Luke 21:26; 2 Pet 3:7; Rev 20:11–15).[223] Such a use of biblical imagery seems entirely

---

connected world, and its opportunities, as the human response to the pandemic draws on research and materials sourced from across the world.

222. See Eric O. Jacobsen, *The Space Between: A Christian Engagement with the Built Environment* (Grand Rapids: Baker Academic, 2012) for an eye-opening exploration of the relationship between the structure of urban spaces and the way we live our communal life that demonstrates how certain values can be promoted or hindered by specific forms of the built environment.

223. A similar poem has long been a part of the Rosh Hashanah and Yom Kippur lit-

appropriate, but it is not the same as to claim that the material in Zeph 1 was read as depicting universal judgment at the time of its composition. Also, while the Day of YHWH motif is relevant for doctrinal consideration of the final judgment, there is more to be said about this judgment than can be deduced from Zephaniah. In particular, the final day is "the day of our Lord Jesus Christ" (1 Cor 1:8 [cf. 5:5]; 2 Cor 1:14; Phil 1:6, 10; 2 Thess 2:2) when he makes his royal appearance with his saints (1 Thess 3:13; 5:23), and so our knowledge of Christ will color our understanding of this day. References to a final day of judgment in the Gospels (e.g., Matt 10:15; 11:22, 24; 12:32) and elsewhere (e.g., 1 John 4:17; 2 Pet 2:9; 3:10) are relevant.[224]

Potential imminence is expressed in the New Testament by the motif of the day's sudden appearance (e.g., 1 Thess 5:2); delay offers opportunity for repentance (e.g., 2 Pet 3:9). Vlaardingerbroek points out that "nearness is integral to the preaching of judgment."[225] But this need not be a problem for preachers. Our lives are short, and death can overtake us at any time, after which we face God's judgment (Heb 9:27). In this sense, for individuals, judgment is always imminent—or nearly so. As Vlaardingerbroek points out, the response to the claim here that "no real action ever proceeds from God" is not argumentation but "preaching: the end will tell us."[226]

The original referent of Zephaniah's *Day of YHWH* is the destruction of Jerusalem in the sixth century, a communal event that, for the vast majority of readers Zephaniah has ever had, has lain in the past.[227] It is possible that something like the contents of ch. 1 was preached by Zephaniah as early as 630 BC. Judah's end would then have been less than sixty years away—maybe not imminent, but not far off either. Huldah's prophecy is reported as announcing that the disaster was inevitable but would not happen in Josiah's days. The nearness of the Day of YHWH could well be understood in this way: the judgment is about to come, but how close it is may depend on a range of factors. This would imply that the announcement of imminent total

---

urgy in some traditions of rabbinical Judaism (*"Unethanneh Toqeph,"* "Let us speak of the awesomeness").

224. I realise that such a list of New Testament references is not sophisticated, but it serves a purpose as a signpost pointing toward a fuller discussion of the kind that is beyond the scope of this commentary.

225. Vlaardingerbroek, *Zephaniah*, 36: "The preacher who cries out: 'Repent, for after thousands of years judgment will come!' does not make a strong impression."

226. Vlaardingerbroek, *Zephaniah*, 41.

227. As indicated above, I do not believe that the lack of reference to human armies and the "eerie" language in 1:14–18 suggests that no real, "ordinary" war is in view here (contra Vlaardingerbroek, *Zephaniah*, 39). The topographical references in any case seem to evoke an enemy from the north, as is characteristic of "ordinary" war against Jerusalem; cf. Irsigler, *Zefanja*, 153–54, 176, 186.

disaster need not be antithetical to attempts at reformation. Even those who are convinced that the disaster can no longer be prevented are not thereby excused from doing what is right and stopping the things that cause the stumbling and the judgment. This is so not only because one never knows exactly how "close" the judgment is but also because any preaching of judgment is implicitly also a call to repentance. In retrospect, sixty years could be considered close enough to preserve the prophecy as accurate and to do so without removing references to imminence.

Christian preachers today may not be able to announce the end of a socioeconomic system with greater accuracy than anyone else, but they have the warnings of Jesus about "how hard it will be for those who have wealth to enter the kingdom of God!" (Mark 10:23), reinforced by the saying "It is easier for a camel to go through the eye of a needle than for someone who is rich to enter the kingdom of God!" (Mark 10:25). Zephaniah can help to tease out the risk factors of being well-off. The condemnation of the powerful reminds us that with great power (and resources) comes great responsibility. We also see here that wealth and power often disconnect people from those who are less well-off and that there can be an easy relationship of wealth and greed with violence and fraud. It is of no little significance that wealth creates an illusion of independence and safety. These are warnings that remain pertinent.

The claim that the end of the Davidic monarchy, the destruction of the temple and city, and the exile of the upper class to Babylon all belonged to a Day of YHWH is integral to biblical theology. The Bible offers a variety of perspectives on those events (e.g., in Jeremiah and the book of Lamentations), but the idea that they were outside YHWH's control or happened while he did not pay attention (cf. 1 Kgs 18:27) is never contemplated. The Bible claims that there is such a thing as punitive divine justice and that it did not come unannounced. This brings us to the other major challenge presented by this section: the depiction of YHWH as a furious God bringing distress to people in specific, horrendous events.

Franz Rosenzweig's short essay, "A Note on Anthropomorphism" (1928), offers a helpful caution against misreading biblical anthropomorphisms. Batnitzky summarizes the argument:

> Properly speaking, Rosenzweig argues, there is no 'anthropomorphism' in the Bible. Rather, 'the "anthropomorphisms" of the Bible are throughout assertions about meetings between God and man.' Once we understand that the Bible's descriptions of God are about meetings that take place in time, rather than about essences that are eternal, we can understand that the Bible does not 'assert something either about God or about man, but only about an event between the two.' Rosenzweig argues that the philo-

sophical problems created by 'biblical anthropomorphisms' are a result of a category error. The Bible is not concerned with what God *is*, but rather with how God *acts*, in time, in God's relation to the human being.[228]

The image of a sacrificing God is intended to shock and to say something about God's relationship to a group of people without making a direct, ontological claim about God. The horrendous pictures of spilled blood and entrails need not be interpreted as depicting a sadistic deity but can be seen as preparing the people for what was actually to come. It would do no good to gloss over or sugarcoat the terrors of war and destruction. Seen in this way, it is not so much the language used here that offers a theological challenge but the assertion that God was intimately involved in the terrors anticipated in the text. God claims overall responsibility for the events surrounding the fall of Jerusalem. He is the one who conceived the punishment and used human agents to execute it.

Taking into account the full biblical witness, we can add to this that while, vis-à-vis his people, God takes full responsibility for the way his agents act without showing pity, he nevertheless takes them to task for their ferociousness and lack of compassion (Isa 47:7; Zech 1:15), with the result that judgment comes to them as well (e.g., Jer 50). Also, while God deals with his people corporately, this does not mean that everyone within Judah must be considered guilty. The target in Zeph 1 is specific, even if the chapter makes no space for a category of people who are innocent (see v. 17). Taking seriously both the general character as well as the specific targets mentioned, Vlaardingerbroek observes, "The groups referred to seem to be more or less representative for the society as a whole or at least so to structure and qualify that society that it cannot continue to exist as it is."[229] This chapter offers little ground for hope to those parts of society that are not specifically mentioned. The appropriate response may be the same as the one given by bystanders to Jesus's warning about how difficult it is for the rich to be saved: "Then who can be saved?" (Luke 18:26). But the chapter does not stand on its own, and with the remaining material in Zephaniah, it becomes clearer that there remains some hope for survivors, that the judgment includes other nations, and that the judgment will purify rather than annihilate God's people.

Beyond the issue of God's acts in the past, the question may be raised

---

228. Leora Batnitzky, *Idolatry and Representation: The Philosophy of Franz Rosenzweig Reconsidered* (Princeton, NJ: Princeton University Press, 2009), 21. I am indebted to Peter Leithart for bringing this passage to my attention in "Rosenzweig on Anthropomorphismm," *Patheos*, May 4, 2018, http://www.patheos.com/blogs/leithart/2018/05/rosen zweig-on-anthropomorphism/.

229. Vlaardingerbroek, *Zephaniah*, 37.

to what extent the Day of YHWH motif can be applied to historical and contemporary events not spoken of in the Bible. We must bear in mind that our situation is in significant ways not analogous.[230] The time of preparation until the coming of Christ was a time in which God's promises and threats were focused on one ethnic group and, by the time of the monarchy, on the house of David and the temple in Jerusalem. Today, Christ fulfills the central role for God's people that Jerusalem once played, and his kingship is of a different nature from the Davidic monarchy of old. This is not to say that we cannot speak of general principles that apply to individuals as well as societies. Certain consequences likely follow from certain attitudes and acts. It remains generally and ultimately true that "righteousness exalts a nation, but sin is a disgrace to any people" (Prov 14:34) and "pride goes before destruction, and a haughty spirit before a fall" (Prov 16:18). But specific correlations between behavior and consequences are more difficult to make with confidence. James 5:14–15 urges those who are seriously unwell to ask for prayer and promises that the prayer of faith can ensure them that if they have committed sins, they will be forgiven (forgiveness being more important than physical health in this life). James seems to assume that serious illness should raise the question of sin, but the use of "if" indicates that illness is not a sure indicator of sin. In the same way, organizations and nations in distress should raise the question of corporate wrongdoing but without assuming that their sin must have caused the calamity.

Finally, we should note that we live with the Day of YHWH, the day of divine wrath and judgment, both ahead of us (e.g., Rom 2:5 and references above) and, in a sense, behind us, as the darkness surrounding the death of Christ on the cross shows (Matt 27:45; Mark 15:33; Luke 23:44).[231]

IV. CALL TO SUBMIT TO GOD'S JUDGMENT (2:1–4)

[1]*Act like those who scrape together and scrape up,*[a]
   O[b] *nation without longing,*[c]
[2]*before the birthing of the prescribed*[d]—
   like chaff passes a day[e]—
before[f] *there comes upon you*
   YHWH's burning anger,[g]

---

230. Note also that the motif is arguably only suited for a disaster on a grand scale—a judgment that could not fall upon God's people without prior warning through his prophets (cf. Amos 3:7).

231. See Géza Vermes, *The Passion* (New York: Penguin, 2005), 108–9; J. Bergman Kline, "The Day of the Lord in the Death and Resurrection of Christ," *JETS* 48 (2005): 757–70.

before there comes upon you
  the day of YHWH's anger.
[3]*Seek YHWH, all you[h] humble of the land[i]*
  who act upon his judgment.[j]
Seek righteousness, seek humility—
  perhaps you will be hidden[k]
    on the day of YHWH's anger.
[4]*For[l] Gaza will be forsaken,[m]*
  Ashkelon become a desolation.
Ashdod: at midday they will drive her out,
  and Ekron will be uprooted.[n]

a. My translation assumes a simulating nuance for the *hithpolel* (cf. Seybold, *Satirische Prophetie*, 35–36; Weigl, *Zefanja*, 100; see JM 53i for other examples) and little difference between *qal* (*scrape up*), *polel* ("scrape together"), and *hithpolel* (*scrape together*). The main alternative is to interpret the *hithpolel* as reflexive ("gather or assemble yourselves") as in the ancient versions, with the *qal* imperative understood as intensifying the command; cf., e.g., Irsigler, *Zefanja*, 195–96. A. Vanlier Hunter (*Seek the Lord! A Study of the Meaning and Function of the Exhortations in Amos, Hosea, Isaiah, Micah, and Zephaniah* [Baltimore: St Mary's Seminary & University, 1982], 259–71) offers, "Gather yourselves as stubble, and remain as stubble" (261), appealing to the analogy of combinations of identical roots in Isa 29:9 and Hab 1:5 for the reflexive-denominative meaning in an ironic command to do something to oneself that YHWH will soon produce (267). But this requires a complete disjunction between the two audiences of vv. 1 and 3, which I consider unlikely (see further below).

b. On the use of the article with a vocative, see, e.g., JM 137g.

c. Literally "O nation that does not long," following the usual meaning of the verb *ksp* in the Hebrew Bible, both in the *qal* (Job 14:15; Ps 17:12) and, as here, in the *niphal* (Gen 31:30; Ps 84:2[3]). In the other instances, the verb always has an object specified, and many therefore argue that the verb has a different sense here. Very often "growing pale" or "being ashamed" is adopted (so most English translations)—a meaning found in Mishnaic Hebrew and Aramaic. Others make a closer connection with the pale metal silver (*kesep*; cf. 1:18); so, e.g., Weigl, *Zefanja*, 101, who thinks of "people that do not strike silver." Tg. and Vulg. reflect the standard meaning, although the latter adopts a passive sense (*gens non amabilis*, "a people that is not loveable"); the Greek *to ethnos to apaideuton* ("you uneducated nation"; cf. Peshitta) could relate to the sense given in the Tg. (not desiring the law of God, hence uninstructed) or be linked to being put to shame (cf. Isa 26:11 LXX). See Ben Zvi, *Zephaniah*, 139–43, for a fuller discussion of the various options.

d. Hebrew *ḥōq* (*the prescribed*; or "something prescribed," as there is no definite article) could also be rendered, e.g., "decree" or "moment" and related to the infinitive as the implied subject ("the decree gives birth," namely to the events decreed) rather than the object ("the giving birth of the moment"). For the numerous proposals for emendations of this line and the next, see, e.g., Vlaardingerbroek, *Zephaniah*, 118–20. Ludwig Köhler's emendation, promoted in *BHS*, is reflected in RSV's "before you are driven away like the drifting chaff" (also NRSV; cf. NAB, NJB) and has also been adopted, e.g., by Irsigler, *Zefanja*, 197. The addressees are also compared to chaff (Peshitta, Tg.) or a passing flower (LXX; see next note) in renderings from antiquity; cf. Sweeney, *Zephaniah*, 117–18.

e. For these two lines, LXX has *pro tou genesthai hymas hōs anthos paraporeuomenon* ("before you become like a transient flower"). Jong-Hoon Kim ("Text und Übersetzung des griechischen Zephanjabuches," in *Die Septuaginta—Entstehung, Sprache, Geschichte: 3. Internationale Fachtagung veranstaltet von Septuaginta Deutsch (LXX.D), Wuppertal 22.-25. Juli 2010*, ed. Siegfried Kreuzer, Martin Meiser, and Marcus Sigismund [Tübingen: Mohr Siebeck, 2012], 155–66) suggests that the translator had *bṭrm ldtkm kmw ṣyṣ 'br* in front of them rather than *bṭrm ldt ḥq kmṣ 'br ywm*.

f. The double negative in the form *baṭerem lō'* (twice in this verse) is unique. As in similar cases, this does not cancel the negation. The *lō'* should be considered pleonastic here (JM 160p), unless it makes the negation more emphatic (GKC 152y).

g. The great similarity between this bicolon and the following, along with its absence in some MSS, has led various commentators to the conclusion that the original text was shorter. But the versions attest to the longer text and "the question why someone would add an almost identical verse segment is not easy to answer" (Vlaardingerbroek, *Zephaniah*, 116). In my view, the repetition works well as poetry, and its absence in some MSS can be explained as the result of a scribe's eye jumping to the wrong place in the text.

h. Rudolph (*Micha*, 271, 273–74) argues that a letter was lost by accident and that *kl-'nwy h'rṣ* (*kol-'anwê hā'āreṣ*, all you humble of the land*) originally read *kkl-'nwy h'rṣ* (*kəkōl-'anwê hā'āreṣ*, "like all the humble of the land"); cf. Günter Krinetzki, *Zefanjastudien: Motiv- und Traditionskritik + Kompositions- und Redaktionskritik*, RST 7 (Frankfurt: Lang, 1977), 257; Rainer Edler, *Das Kerygma des Propheten Zefanja*, Freiburger Theologische Studien 126 (Freiburg: Herder, 1984), 18. This seeks to solve the problem of diverging audiences in vv. 1 and 3, which I think is better addressed differently; see the commentary below.

i. The phrase is used with definite article only here in MT, without definite article in Ps 76:9(10); Isa 11:4; Amos 8:4 (written *'nwy*; read *'ăniyyê*); cf. *'ăniyyê-'āreṣ* in Job 24:4. Note that the definite article is missing in MurXII as well as some later Hebrew MSS and also not reflected in LXX. The phrase could be translated "the afflicted/oppressed of the land," which is appropriate in the other references; cf. *'ăniyyê-'ām* ("the oppressed among the people") in Ps 72:4 (cf. v. 2, "your poor") and Isa 14:32, where it is perhaps possible to interpret *'ăniyyê-'ām* as "the (spiritually) humble among the people" and furthermore maybe *'ăniyyê haṣṣō'n* ("the weakest among the flock") in Zech 11:7, 11 (see commentaries for the textual problems).

j. The LXX renders *p'lw* (*pā'ālû*; *act upon*) as an imperative. This requires ignoring the particle *'ăšer* (*who*), for which I find no good reason. See, e.g., Sweeney, *Zephaniah*, 110–11, for discussion of this and other changes later in the verse as a smoothening of the text in "an effort to strengthen its exhortative character" (111).

k. This follows the usual interpretation of the form as a *niphal* imperfect of the root *str*. Patterson (*Nahum*, 332–33) takes the verb as an infixed-*t* form from *swr* ("turn aside") in the sense of "turn oneself aside"—hence "escape," "be delivered." Cf. Dahood, *Psalms 3*, 389, suggesting "do not turn away your face" is more accurate than the traditional rendering "do not hide your face"; and, more generally on the *t*-stem, cf. W. Randall Garr, *Dialect Geography of Syria-Palestine: 1000–586 B.C.E.* (Philadelphia: University of Pennsylvania Press, 1985; repr. Winona Lake, IN: Eisenbrauns, 2004), 119–20. Such forms are attested in Moabite, a language very closely related to Hebrew, and likely in a few geographic names (see *HGHS* 38f). Garr (*Dialect Geography*, 119–20) notes that there is no trace of such *t*-forms in Hebrew inscriptions and observes that they seem to have disappeared from Hebrew very early. Given also that the combination of *str* (or infixed-*t* form from *swr*) with *pnym* ("face") is semantically distinct (see Samuel E. Balentine, "A Description of the Semantic Field of Hebrew Words for 'Hide'," *VT* 30 [1980]: 147–53), it seems safer to follow the traditional derivation.

l. *For* is the traditional, and I believe correct, rendering of the opening particle; cf. LXX (*dioti*). But the particle is sometimes taken as emphatic here ("Indeed"), e.g., by Vlaardingerbroek, *Zephaniah*, 136 (with the particularly doubtful rendering as an exclamative, "Behold"). Irsigler (*Zefanja*, 219) allows that this may have been its function at an earlier stage (if original, prior to being incorporated into its present context); he acknowledges that within the text as transmitted, *kî* is best understood as causal. While *kî* can be used at the opening of a speech (cf. Isa 15:1), it is not clear in relation to what the assertion would be made, even if one took v. 4 on its own. Where *kî* is emphatic outside vows, it is usually in relation to the word it immediately precedes, but it is not clear why Gaza (or even the sentence on Gaza) should be emphasized. For general discussion, see, e.g., JM 164b; Takamitsu Muraoka, *Emphatic Words and Structures in Biblical Hebrew* (Jerusalem: Magnes Press; Leiden: Brill, 1985), 158–64; Anneli Aejmelaeus, "Function and Interpretation of כִּי in Biblical Hebrew," *JBL* 105 (1986): 193–209, 204–5. See also Carl M. Follingstad, *Deictic Viewpoint in Biblical Hebrew Text: A Syntagmatic and Paradigmatic Analysis of the Particle Kî* (Dallas: SIL International, 2001), esp. 46–56, 277–79, 305–306, 569–79.

m. The consonants of the city names *Gaza* and *Ekron* are used to describe their fate (*'azzâ 'āzûbâ; 'eqrôn tē'āqēr*). It would have been possible to do something similar with *Ashdod*, using the verb *šdd* ("to devastate") or the noun *šōd* ("devastation"), and with *Ashkelon*, e.g., by using *qālôn* ("shame, dishonor"). The author possibly felt that such an abundance of paronomasia would have been tawdry, and the *Ash*kelon-*Ash*dod assonance in the two middle lines supplements the puns with Gaza and Ekron in the outer lines. Lawrence Zalcman, "Ambiguity and Assonance at Zephaniah II 4," *VT* 36 (1986): 365–71, has offered a largely persuasive argument for assonance having been sacrificed in favor of double entendre; see further below. Sweeney (*Zephaniah*, 111) notes attempts in the versions to imitate the wordplay.

n. Eric Lee Welch ("The Roots of Anger: An Economic Perspective on Zephaniah's Oracle against the Philistines," *VT* 63 [2013]: 471–85) sees a double entendre here that highlights the agricultural context. I am not fully convinced. He himself points out that what would be critical for seventh-century Judean farmers is the destruction of Ekron's oil presses, not the uprooting of olive trees supplying Ekron, many of which would have been Judean. Welch may be right, however, in claiming that the verse accurately reflects widespread seventh-century Judean sentiments toward Ekron and other Philistine cities.

Composition

The relationship of 2:1–3 to what precedes and follows is a matter of controversy. There are thematic links on the one hand between 2:1–3 and ch. 1 with reference to the Day of YHWH and on the other hand between 2:4 and the remainder of ch. 2, with a focus on political entities other than Judah and Jerusalem. In the present reading, the announcement of the Day of YHWH in ch. 1 did not include any genuine exhortation. The call to silence before the presence of YHWH (1:7), the invitation to hear (1:10, 14), and the summons to wailing in response to the disaster (1:11) were rhetorical in the sense that they drew attention to the content of the announcement itself more than any actual response to it. Only here in 2:1–3 does the objective announcement move into exhortation. (As will be seen further below, I do not read the imperatives in 2:1 as ironical.) The second-person exhortation in 2:1–3 is, within the book, based on the general announcement in ch. 1 and, hence, belongs closely with it. Nevertheless, it is not syntactically linked with the preceding, and thematically there is development and even discontinuity alongside the resumption of the motif of the Day of YHWH. While ch. 1 stressed the totality and inescapability of the coming disaster, here there is a glimmer of possible survival. Vlaardingerbroek suspects that these verses, "though originating with Zephaniah," are later than the message of doom and may have been offered in answer to questions the earlier message had raised.[232] This may be so, although it seems equally likely that the message of the Day of YHWH in ch. 1 was from its start proclaimed with an exhortation along the lines we find here. While the exhortation modifies the all-inclusiveness of the judgment, it does so only tentatively and ultimately only for a group that was not in focus in ch. 1. Still, the summons to repentance is not syntactically attached to the proclamation of the Day of YHWH in the way that, say, Joel 2:12–14 is attached to Joel 2:1–11. The announcement in ch. 1 was essentially presented as divine speech in spite of some third-person references to YHWH. In 2:5ff., divine first-person speech is mixed with third-person references, which are especially prominent toward the beginning (vv. 5, 8, 9). By contrast, 2:1–4 is best read as a prophetic exhortation that does not cite YHWH. Ben Zvi notes that "the emphasis on the possible, but not necessary, character of any specific divine response to human behaviour . . . occurs only in units in which the prophet is the speaker (e.g., Exod 32:30; 2 Kgs 19:4 // Isa 37:4; Am 5:15)."[233]

Verse 4 is a hinge verse.[234] It is ill-advised to separate it from 2:1–3 merely because it focuses on the Philistine cities. After all, these cities are not addressed, not even rhetorically (unlike in v. 5). Something is said in the third person about them that motivates the call to seek YHWH, righteousness, and humility. The above translation note voices doubt about the likelihood that the particle at the beginning of v. 4 ever functioned in a way other than to mark a relation to what precedes.[235] Thus, I follow the ancient tradition that

---

232. Vlaardingerbroek, *Zephaniah*, 115. Irsigler (*Zefanja*, 210) similarly believes that the original version of 2:1–3 is later than the primary material in ch. 1 but can be attributed to the prophet.

233. Ben Zvi, *Zephaniah*, 296.

234. So also, e.g., Ryou, *Oracles*, 203–4.

235. Roberts (*Nahum*, 195–96) accepts that treating *kî* as emphatic here is "dubious" but considers the link thereby established between 2:1–3 and 2:4–15 "superficial" and suggests that v. 4 "came originally after v. 5, where it would fit very well." He attributes the current

sees a paragraph break after v. 4 rather than before it.[236] The thematic link with vv. 5–7 helps to identify the oracles about nations as a further, expanded rationale for the exhortation to repent.

Commentary

1 The text at the beginning of this chapter is very difficult to construe, but its consonants are well attested in the earliest manuscripts known to us. The opening imperatives have been understood from antiquity as a call for gathering, the first imperative as "gather together" and the second mostly as intensifying the first (see the translation note). Ben Zvi seeks to downplay any connection of these imperatives to the noun *qaš* ("stubble") on the grounds that the verb does not mean "gathering straw" but simply "gathering," and in the *hithpael* "to gather together," following a pattern that he also claims for semantically related roots.[237] The evidence for this pattern, however, is not clear-cut.[238] What is clear is that the poet did not use one of the more common words for people gathering.[239] Instead, he employed a rare word that is used elsewhere in the Hebrew Bible for gathering straw (*teben* in Exod 5:7, 12) and firewood (*'ēṣîm* in Num 15:32–33; 1 Kgs 17:10, 12)—that is, for very menial activities[240]—and never for the assembling of people. The present interpretation of the verb in terms of "scraping" and "scraping up" rather than more generally "gathering" seeks to express the likely connotations of

---

order of verses to "a later, secondary editorial rearrangement," which he is willing to ignore in commenting on the text in favor of "the presumed original order."

236. Cf., e.g., Ryou, *Oracles*, 27–28, 97, 135, 186–87, 203–4; Sweeney, *Zephaniah*, 120–21.

237. Ben Zvi, *Zephaniah*, 139.

238. The root *kns*, which in the *qal* and *piel* stems means "to gather," is used only once in the *hithpael*, and that for wrapping oneself in a cover (Isa 28:20); *qbṣ* means "to assemble, gather" in its various stems, and the nuance "gather together" is barely more distinctive for the *hithpael* than the *niphal*; *'sp* also occurs only once (Deut 33:5) or twice (Deut 33:21, if the text is emended) in the *hithpael*; elsewhere the *niphal* serves for "gathering together."

239. It is therefore unlikely that we should look for a background in a traditional ritual gathering for penitence here. A call for such a gathering would more likely employ *'sp* (cf. Joel 1:14; 2:16) or *qbṣ* (cf. 2 Chr 20:4, with the purpose clause "to seek YHWH") or maybe *qhl* (see, e.g., Lev 8:3; Deut 4:10).

240. Thus, while it is true that the verb does not mean "gathering straw," the occurrence of *mōṣ* (*chaff*) in the next verse is very fitting. Weigl (*Zefanja*, 110–11) presses this point too far when he insists that the activity is involuntary, and probably even when he claims that it is the activity of the oppressed, but his overstatement should not detract from the general point that the verb is elsewhere only used for the sort of activity that one would not normally associate with the well-off.

the verb, given its usage elsewhere. The verb would be an odd choice to refer to a gathering of people.

The long-established understanding of the imperatives in terms of people being asked to assemble creates an additional problem. One would expect a call to "gather together" to be followed by a more specific instruction as to what to do once gathered. Some German commentators and translations sought a solution in a metaphorical understanding of "gather together" as a moral appeal along the lines of "get your act together,"[241] but this seems difficult to justify from the Hebrew idiom.[242] Nor can a further specification of what to do when gathered be easily added from v. 3, because we seem to have a new addressee there.[243] Certainly, *haggôy lō' niksāp* (*O nation without longing*) encompasses a larger, and perhaps altogether different, group from the one qualified as the *humble of the land* who *act upon* YHWH's *judgment* in v. 3. But the difference is not a simple opposition, as if there are two fixed, contrasting groups. Indeed, my reading assumes that the first imperatives encourage movement. The prophet's call goes to the nation as a whole, asking people in effect to *act like* and so become (like) the humble of the land *who scrape together and scrape up*. The attitude called for here is the opposite of resting content in one's possessions (cf. 1:12, 18), and for rich people, inside the city and beyond, it may even suggest a renunciation of wealth. Thus, the *nation without longing* is, by way of wordplay with *kesep* in 1:18 (see the translation note), to become a nation that is not "silvered," which is to say a people that works the land rather than enriching itself in trade with foreign powers. Perhaps it was to facilitate this pun that the object of the *longing* was not stated. The context suggests that what is absent is specifically a *longing* for God rather than desire more generally.[244]

An alternative is to read the command not as a genuine exhortation but

241. E.g., Elberfelder Bibel 2006: "Rafft euch zusammen, rafft euch auf!" (Witten: SCM R. Brockhaus, 2006), similarly already in its 1871 and 1905 editions ("Gehet in euch und sammelt euch!").

242. So, rightly, Irsigler, *Zefanja*, 196.

243. The main alternative is to interpret *haggôy lō' niksāp* as a designation for the poor, thus conforming the reference of the first vocative to the second. This requires one to assume that the poor of the land as a whole are seen as implementing God's will. Others propose that an original "like" dropped out in v. 3, thus conforming the reference of the second vocative to the first (see the translation note). Many consider neither attempt at equating the addressees successful and seek a diachronic solution. See further Ryou, *Oracles*, 326–28; Irsigler, *Zefanja*, 198–99.

244. I agree with Irsigler, *Zefanja*, 196, that the absence of an object does not render irrelevant the fact that the verb elsewhere in the Hebrew Bible refers to longing, but he opts for the interpretation that sees the people as indifferent, without aspirations. Similarly, Edler, *Kerygma*, 209, although he acknowledges that the desired alternative is a YHWH-oriented aspiration (210).

as an ironic call to get ready for the coming judgment in words designed to imitate a call to gather in the city for refuge (cf. Lev 26:25 and especially Jer 4:5–6; 8:14). Read this way, the verse would urge, "Be gathered together like straw or firewood, ready for the fire of judgment to burn you away." But the haunting and insistent repetition of *before* in the next verse makes the call sound more like an earnest plea that the addressees use what little time is left than a sarcastic taunt that gleefully points out that there is nothing more that can be done. Nevertheless, readers looking back to Jerusalem's destruction as a "harvest" may see a hint of gathering stubble in this verse that suggests that the exhortation would only be fulfilled once the Day of YHWH had come and gone, just as stubble is gathered after the harvest.

In sum, the prophet calls the nation to *scrape up*, which is to gather leftovers or goods of little value—"scrape a living" as we might say in English. The use of the *hithpolel* stem at the beginning of the verse (with its simulating nuance) signals that this is meant metaphorically: *Act like those who scrape together*. The *nation without longing* for God, in particular those within it laden with silver, is to climb down from its arrogant position of undisturbed wealth and act as if it belonged to the humble of the land.

2 The parallel clauses in this verse underline the threat. As a birth is expected to follow a pregnancy, so what God has *prescribed*, his decree, will before long give birth to the decisive moment. The time until then will pass quickly *like chaff* being blown away by the wind. The comparison with *chaff* (the noun is never used without *like*) elsewhere refers to the judgment of the wicked who are blown away by the wind (Job 21:18; Pss 1:4; 35:5; Hos 13:3) as well as the tumult of war (Isa 17:13 [defenders]; 29:5 [attackers]) and the ease with which major obstacles are overcome (Isa 41:15). It therefore seems possible, even without changing the text (see the translation note), to hear an allusion to the ease with which Judah and Jerusalem will be blown away in God's judgment. What is coming upon Judah and Jerusalem is *YHWH's burning anger* (cf. *the fire of his passion*, 1:18) and therefore the day that is coming, the Day of YHWH, is *the day of YHWH's anger* (cf. *a day of fury*, 1:15; *the day of YHWH's fury*, 1:18).

3 The first summary complaint about the targets of God's judgment in ch. 1 spoke of people *who do not seek YHWH and do not inquire of him* (1:6). *Seek YHWH* here picks up this summary and so puts its finger on the heart of the problem. Such a call will not be heeded by those who are in focus in ch. 1 unless they first dissociate themselves from the class of those who profit from the socioeconomic developments that made for greater integration at the margins of the Neo-Assyrian Empire and associate instead with the lowly (v. 1).[245] Then they, too, might be addressed along with *the humble of the land*.

---

245. The Assyrians seem to have benefitted from this economic integration rather than

Who are these *humble of the land*? It is sometimes argued that the relative clause attached to the main clause (*who act upon his judgment*) demands that we understand them as spiritually humble rather than socially oppressed. But this is not so, because the relative clause could be restrictive as easily as nonrestrictive.[246] In other words, *the humble* are either equated with those *who act upon* YHWH's *judgment* or those *who act upon* YHWH's *judgment* are addressed as a subgroup among *the humble of the land*. Usage elsewhere counsels against a purely spiritualized understanding of *the humble of the land*. While in some places a distinction between *'ānāw* and *'ānî* is possible, with the latter referring to someone who is socioeconomically humble and the former designating someone as spiritually humble, the distinction is far from clear-cut. It is noteworthy that *'ānāw* occurs only once in the singular, where it is traditionally understood to designate Moses as humble before God (Num 12:3),[247] while *'ānî* is more common in the singular, with a third of its plural occurrences (8 of 24) in a *ketiv-qere* relationship with the plural of *'ānāw*. It is therefore not advisable to build an argument about the exact meaning of the word on the presence of *waw* instead of *yod* in the plural form.

In 3:12, *a humble and powerless people* are left in Jerusalem. A number of commentators believe that *the humble* have found their way from 3:12 into this text at a later stage, but two things are worth noting. First, while a more "spiritualized" understanding of the term is often considered more likely with a later date, reading the term in view of *'ānî wādāl* in 3:12 suggests that even at this later stage we are not dealing with a label for God-fearers that is entirely disconnected from the socioeconomic connotations of lowliness (cf. Job 34:28; Ps 82:3; Prov 22:22; Isa 10:2).[248] Second, the addition of the qualifier *of the land* (see the translation note) draws our attention to the countryside beyond Jerusalem. This is not to say that the text assumes a contrast between city and land that exactly coincides with the contrast

---

having promoted it themselves; see Shawn Zelig Aster and Avraham Faust, eds., *The Southern Levant under Assyrian Domination* (University Park, PA: Eisenbrauns, 2018).

246. See Robert D. Holmstedt (*The Relative Clause in Biblical Hebrew*, Linguistic Studies in Ancient West Semitic 10 [Winona Lake, IN: Eisenbrauns, 2016]) for the syntax and semantics of relatives. None of the syntactical features that would remove ambiguity are present here.

247. Cleon Rogers ("Moses: Meek or Miserable?" *JETS* 29 [1986]: 257–63) suggests instead that Moses is called "miserable" (cf. Luther's 1545 translation as "geplagt," "afflicted").

248. Only Isa 26:6 could conceivably refer to the humble and lowly in an exclusively spiritual sense, but this is unlikely because *dāl* elsewhere refers to the poor and powerless more than forty times. The only two instances of a possible wider use attested in the Bible are Gen 41:19, where the adjective is used for the weak, thin cows of Pharaoh's dream, and 2 Sam 13:4, where it describes lovesick Ammon as dejected.

between the arrogant rich of the city who are condemned in ch. 1 and the humble poor of the countryside who are exhorted here. Nevertheless, rhetorically, the prophecy in ch. 1 made no space for any who are humble and lowly (and innocent) inside Jerusalem, and the horizon seems deliberately widened here, leaving open the question whether any of *the humble of the land* might be found in Jerusalem itself. There is a sense in which the city has to become countryside, and it is therefore only beyond the disaster that will destroy the city that the poor and lowly will definitely be found inside Jerusalem. To recap, the whole nation, but specifically the upper classes in Jerusalem who have been condemned in ch. 1, needs to identify with and become like the poor who bend down for humble pickings from the land. Only if they renounce their upper-class status can they be included in the exhortation here in v. 3, which offers a glimpse of hope. A positive response to v. 1 might even qualify as *acting upon* God's *judgment*. But what is needed is, of course, not merely a one-off positive response to a specific judgment but a general carrying out of God's ordinances. The combination of this verb (*p'l*) and object is unique to this verse. The more common verb "to do" (*'śh*) is used very frequently with *mišpāṭ* (*judgment*, "justice," "ordinance") in a range of meanings that include executing or administering justice, maintaining the cause of the innocent, and executing judgment[249] alongside doing what is right and acting justly with others (e.g., Jer 5:1; 7:5; Mic 6:8). Thus, while the reference here is best understood as acting in line with God's judgment as expressed in his ordinances (cf. Lev 18:4-5),[250] if *p'l* here is equivalent to *'śh* elsewhere, there may be a hint of being entrusted with implementing God's judgment, as if (some of) *the humble of the land* are seen in a position of (true) authority. If so, this would not be to say that the oppressed are expected to be the ones to bring the catastrophic divine judgment on the city but that the sort of faithful administration of justice that might have prevented the destruction of the city was not found in the place where one looks for it. It is *the humble of the land* who are responsive to God's judgment and therefore might have ensured that justice was done, if only they had been in authority (cf. Eccl 9:15 for a similar thought). But it is possible that *p'l* was chosen rather than *'śh* precisely because any connotations of executing justice were considered inappropriate.

The imperative of *bqš* (*seek*) is attested in the Hebrew Bible only nine

---

249. The following list is not complete but offers a cross-section: Deut 10:18; 2 Sam 8:15; 1 Kgs 3:28; 8:45, 49, 59 (and par.); Pss 9:4[5], 16[17]; 103:6; 119:84; 149:9; Ezek 5:8; Mic 7:9.

250. Milton Schwantes ("'Jhwh hat Schutz gewährt': Theologische Anmerkungen zum Buch des Propheten *Zefanja*," in Walter and Schwantes, *Der Tag wird kommen*, 134–53) believes the reference of living in YHWH's *mišpāṭ* is to clan and family solidarity (140). I struggle to see the basis for this.

times outside this verse; *drš*, which was used in 1:6 in parallel with *bqš*, is the more common of the two verbs in the imperative (41×), even though *bqš* in general is more common than *drš*. With *YHWH*, the imperative of *bqš* is not found elsewhere, but a few times "YHWH's face" is used with the imperative as the object of the seeking (Pss 27:8; 105:4; 1 Chr 16:11) and once the personal pronoun referring to YHWH (Isa 45:19). Only once is the object abstract (*šālôm* in Ps 34:14[15]). The reuse of the imperative of *bqš* with *righteousness* and *humility* is, therefore, noteworthy. Even in the indicative, neither of the two terms occurs anywhere else as the object of *seek*. *Righteousness* is sometimes "pursued" (*rdp*; Deut 16:20 and Isa 51:1 with *ṣedeq*; Prov 15:9; 21:21 with *ṣədāqâ*); *humility* is a rare noun (see references below). There are two plausible explanations for the lexical choice of *bqš* here, and both seem relevant. First, the threefold use of *seek* is poetically effective in conveying urgency and in echoing the (sound of the) two imperatives of v. 1 with the use of a similar root (*qšš, bqš*). In this sense, the act of humbling oneself in v. 1 (or "gathering" in most translations) is truly fulfilled only in this seeking.[251] Second, the threefold use of the same imperative highlights the close relationship between the three commands, which in a sense are one command. Seeking *YHWH* involves seeking *righteousness* (cf. Isa 51:1), and *righteousness* is sought along with *humility* (cf. Ps 45:4[5]), both of which are seen in social relationships. *Humility* stands in contrast to a haughty heart in Prov 18:12. It is associated with fearing YHWH in Prov 15:33 and 22:4 and attributed to YHWH himself in Ps 18:35[36]. In this latter case, it suggests either condescension or gentleness, unless the text is emended or without emendation somehow linked to *'nh* ("to answer").[252] In the three places in Proverbs, *humility* is a prerequisite of honor, a theme that is developed in Sir 3:17–29. The focus does not seem to be on internal attitude so much as on a gentle, non-coercive behavior, not pushing for one's own standing but fitting in with what is required for healthy community. The focus on behavior is also evident in the two instances in Psalms, where *humility* is ascribed to God (Ps 18) and king (Ps 45), unless *'anwâ* is emended or otherwise distinguished from the occurrences of the root outside Psalms.[253] *Humility* does

251. Note again that in my interpretation, the larger group of addressees in v. 1 can be included in the smaller group addressed in v. 3 if and when they respond positively by implementing the injunction in v. 1.

252. The parallel passage in 2 Sam 22:36 has *'ănōtkā* ("your answering")

253. Among others, Stephen B. Dawes ("'Ānāwâ in Translation and Tradition," *VT* 41 [1991]: 38–48) points to Mic 6:8 as the only other clear injunction to humility in the Hebrew Bible (42), but it is not in fact clear that *haṣnēa' leket 'im-'ĕlōhêkā* is best rendered as "walk humbly with your God" (NRSV and many others). It may be better rendered as "walk circumspectly with your God" in the sense of behaving wisely; see, e.g., Waltke, *Micah*, 364–65, 394.

not mean considering oneself insignificant but is a considered attention to others and so, like *righteousness,* serves the well-being of the community.

The pursuit of YHWH, righteousness, and humility is encouraged without the promise that this will turn away God's anger from the community. There is no question that *the day of YHWH's anger* will come, but there may be the possibility of remaining *hidden*—protected amid the onslaught (cf. the LXX's use of a verb that suggests being sheltered or protected, *skepazō*). Balentine observed that *str,* the verbal root used here for *hidden,* in contrast to some of its alternatives, appears in over half of its occurrences in the context of "hiding with reference to God" rather than humans or objects, more often with reference to God hiding someone or something than to being hidden from God.[254] Not least in the light of 1:12, we should probably not contemplate here the possibility of being hidden from YHWH himself but rather being hidden from the attack. We may even think of being hidden by God from God's attack. The *perhaps* guards against any presumption and indicates that there is nothing anyone can do to secure their future.[255] Seeking YHWH, therefore, also means seeking his grace and mercy.

4 In the discussion under "Composition" above, I sided with those who consider the opening particle (*for*) as a means of linking this verse closely with the exhortation. Sweeney observes that this verse, "with its definite statement of the impending threat to the Philistine cities, provides an unambiguous demonstration of YHWH's intentions; that is, the fate of the Philistines portends the fate of Jerusalem and Judah."[256] Indeed, the order in which the cities are listed traces an approach to Jerusalem: *Gaza* is the farthest (southwest) from Jerusalem, *Ashkelon* is further north from Gaza on the coast, *Ashdod* is on nearly the same latitude as Jerusalem and slightly inland, although the reference here might be to Ashdod-Yam (Ashdod by the sea, the port city that by then had become more prominent in status), and with *Ekron* we move further inland toward Jerusalem. The linear distance ("as the crow flies") between Jerusalem and Gaza is about 50 miles (80 km); Ekron is about 23 miles (37 km) west of Jerusalem. This is the only time that the four cities are listed in this order. It is a fact sometimes explained as a hint that the attack will come from the south (i.e., Egypt) rather than the north, although the scenario of deportation fits better with Mesopotamian practice.[257] But nowhere does the book of Zephaniah reveal any interest in

254. Balentine, "Description," 140, 143.
255. LXX reads *perhaps* as "in such manner" and thus removes the uncertainty about the positive outcome; see Sweeney, *Zephaniah,* 113, for discussion.
256. Sweeney, *Zephaniah,* 112. He characteristically adds "if the people do not follow the prophet's instructions," but 2:1–3 offer no hope that the disaster can be altogether averted, merely that there might be the possibility of escape for some.
257. Cf. Irsigler, *Zefanja,* 227–29. He contrasts this with Jer 47:2–7, where disaster falls

the identity of the attacking armies. Where the attacker is in view, it is always YHWH. It is preferable to see the saying ordered to press home the image of a rapid approach toward Jerusalem rather than to communicate the expected course of the attack.[258]

The use of assonance and paronomasia in this verse is impressive (see the translation note). G. A. Smith suggests "For Gaza ghastful shall be" for the opening line by way of an English imitation, and Ivan J. Ball adds "And Ekron shall be extirpated" for the final line.[259] Some modern interpreters have been keen to add to the wordplay by way of emendation, while medieval commentators such as Rashi and Kimchi were content to allude to Ps 91:6, where disease "devastates" (*yāšûd*, which could pun with *Ashdod*) at midday. The fact that the same collocation of verb and temporal qualifier is found in Jer 15:8 may suggest that the phrase was proverbial.[260] In this case, it would have been possible for the prophet to allude to a pun with *Ashdod* without actually making it. Zalcman sees a reason for the specific lexical choices that do not fully exploit the potential for puns in a desire to portray "an elaborate sequence of *double entendres*, in which the cities of the Philistines are personified as women and consigned to four of the most bitter fates a woman can endure: abandonment, spinsterhood, divorce, and barrenness."[261] With modification, this may well be plausible:[262] Gaza will be like a (betrothed or married) woman abandoned by her man, Ashkelon will be like a desolate wife following desertion by her husband, Ashdod will be driven out like a divorced woman, and Ekron will be like a barren woman. "What then might happen to the daughter of Zion?" is the unspoken question that motivates the call to seek YHWH.

It is also noteworthy that the first two lines speak of results (*forsaken, desolation*), using only the verb "to be" (once), while the latter two lines focus on the action with the use of main verbs for driving out and uprooting. This

---

upon the Philistines from the north. Note that this oracle nevertheless mentions Gaza before Ashkelon and that v. 1 refers to a Pharaoh's conquest of Gaza.

258. It should be noted that the order speaks against the proposal that the saying was given to support Josiah's foreign policy, as Duane L. Christensen argues in "Zephaniah 2:4–15: A Theological Basis for Josiah's Program of Political Expansion," *CBQ* 46 (1984): 669–82.

259. Ivan J. Ball, *A Rhetorical Study of Zephaniah* (Berkeley: BIBAL, 1988), 101, 120; cf. Christensen, "Josiah's Program of Political Expansion," 673.

260. Zalcman, "Ambiguity," 366–67.

261. Zalcman, "Ambiguity," 367. Seybold (*Satirische Prophetie*, 43–44) independently argued that the form *'ăzûbâ* (*forsaken*) was chosen to facilitate a double entendre.

262. Cf. Robert Gordis, "A Rising Tide of Misery: A Note on a Note on Zephaniah ii 4," *VT* 37 (1987): 487–90; Berlin, *Zephaniah*, 101–2; Vlaardingerbroek, *Zephaniah*, 136–37; Sweeney, *Zephaniah*, 122–23; Irsigler, *Zefanja*, 221–22; Dietrich, *Nahum*, 226. Ryou (*Oracles*, 204–5) is not convinced.

fits the tracing of a movement toward Jerusalem, suggesting that the action is drawing closer to Judah's capital. The reference to *midday* in the line about Ashdod could be understood as a way of underlining the ease with which the attack happens, either because it happens "in broadest daylight" or because the city's conquest happens so quickly that, already at noon, its inhabitants are driven out.[263] Vlaardingerbroek suggests that misfortune was traditionally associated with midday (cf. Jer 15:8; Ps 91:6), like salvation and rescue with dawn (cf. Pss 30:5[6]; 46:5[6]),[264] but this is very unlikely. In Ps 91:6, "noon" is parallel to "darkness" in the first line, picking up the "night" and "day" parallelism of the previous verse. In the psalm, it is clearly part of a poetic scheme to indicate every time. In Jer 15:8, *baṣṣāhŏrāyim* ("at midday") could be parallel to *pitʾōm* ("suddenly") and so may be an idiom for "unexpectedly," which would lend support to the proposal that a sudden surprise attack during a time of siesta is in view. An emphasis on the surprise of the attack seems unlikely in Zephaniah, given that Ashdod is the third city mentioned. All in all, the phrase is maybe best explained as a claim that it will only take half a day for the city to be conquered. According to Herodotus (*Histories* 2.157), Ashdod was taken by Pharaoh Psamtik I (664–610) after a twenty-nine-year siege, the longest siege in history known to him. If Herodotus is to be believed,[265] Ashdod would have been under siege during much of Josiah's reign.[266] Indeed, it is possible that the reference to "the remnant of Ashdod" in the list of Philistine cities in Jer 25:20 reflects such a siege by suggesting that Ashdod was in a weaker place than the other Philistine city-states by the time Nebuchadnezzar conquered them. But the reference in Jeremiah does not require that the siege was a long one; it merely suggests that Ashdod held out against Assyria/Egypt when other Philistine cities did not and suffered for it (see below). There are problems with allowing for a twenty-nine-year

263. See, e.g., Robertson, *Nahum*, 298, for the former, and Roberts, *Nahum*, 198, for the latter.

264. Vlaardingerbroek, *Zephaniah*, 137.

265. Herodotus is widely acknowledged as a useful source whose accounts deserve a careful and critical hearing. Cf. Lester L. Grabbe, "Of Mice and Dead Men: Herodotus 2.141 and Sennacherib's Campaign," in *"Like a Bird in a Cage": The Invasion of Sennacherib in 701 BCE*, ed. Lester L. Grabbe, JSOTSup 363 / European Seminar in Historical Methodology 4 (London: T&T Clark, 2003), 119–40.

266. In this case, we do not have much by way of corroborating evidence, and Herodotus does not indicate whether Ashdod was destroyed at the end of the siege or not. It would therefore be very speculative to correlate the text with any destruction layers of the city. Moshe Dotan, one of the directors of the Ashdod excavations, speculates that Ashdod may have been conquered by Josiah (cf. Stern, *Archaeology*, 107). He attributes the final destruction of the city gate in the relevant stratum (VII), "most probably around 600 B.C.," to either Psametik I or Nebuchadnezzar; see "Ashdod," *ABD* 1:481. The latter seems more likely.

siege, and Tadmor's suggestion that we should instead think of Psamtik I's twenty-ninth year has been followed by a number of scholars.[267]

A short historical aside further illumines the historical background of v. 4. The Assyrians exercised a measure of control over Philistine cities as well as Israel and Judah. They may have been responsible for the establishment of processing centers for olives and grapes in the area, which saw four of the five traditional Philistine city-kingdoms flourish.[268] Neither olive oil nor wine features among the Philistine tribute payments known to us from textual sources. The establishment of these economies, therefore, would not have been a case of Assyrian desire for these specific products but a move toward economic rationalization. Greater specialization would increase the interdependence of different political entities and arguably make it more difficult for any of those political entities to stand on their own. In fact, Philistine flourishing may have been actively promoted by the Assyrians as a counterbalance to the power of Judah.[269] Sennacherib's annals state that territory he had captured from Judah during his third campaign was parceled out to Ashdod, Ekron, Gaza, and Ashkelon.[270] Archaeological evidence suggests that most Judahite settlements in the Shephelah were not rebuilt but left abandoned,[271] while Ekron suddenly grew to over two hundred dunams after more than two hundred years of decline.[272] The reason for this parcel-

---

267. Cf. Ahlström, *History*, 751, 758–59. Others think that Herodotus believed that Ashdod surrendered after the defeat of the Scythians by the Medes and that the twenty-nine-year siege arose out of a speculation in relation to the length of the Scythian rule in Asia, which he had earlier measured as twenty-eight years. Cf. Na'aman, "Kingdom," 39–40; "Josiah," 215–16.

268. Following its conquest by Sargon II in the late eighth century, Gath seems to have come under the domain of Ashdod, or possibly Judah, no longer having a king of its own. Cf. Irsigler, *Zefanja*, 222; Stern, *Archaeology*, 102. Note that the record of Esarhaddon's Syro-Palestinian campaign mentions the kings of Gaza, Ashkelon, Ekron, and Ashdod along with Manasseh, king of Judah, and other kings, but not Gath (*ANET*, 291).

269. Thareani ("Empire," 90) notes that "the empire generally pursued a tolerant policy toward Philistia, mostly allowing its cities to survive as client kingdoms."

270. *ARAB* 2:120, 143 (pars. 240, 312); cf. *ANET*, 288.

271. Israel Finkelstein, "The Archaeology of the Days of Manasseh," in *Scripture and Other Artefacts: Essays on the Bible and Archeology in Honor of Philip J. King*, ed. Michael David Coogan, J. Cheryl Exum, and Lawrence E. Stager (Louisville: Westminster John Knox, 1994), 169–87; Avraham Faust, "Settlement and Demography in Seventh-Century Judah and the Extent and Intensity of Sennacherib's Campaign," *PEQ* 140 (2013): 168–94.

272. Cf. Na'aman, "Josiah," 224 (slightly corrected from "Kingdom," 49). Ekron became a huge olive oil production center capable of producing at least a thousand tons of oil annually, as well as a site for the mass production of textiles; see Gitin, "Neo-Assyrian Empire," 87–88; cf. the contributions by Seymour Gitin, "Tel Miqne-Ekron in the 7th Century B.C. City Plan Development and the Oil Industry," and David Eitam, "The Olive Oil Industry at Tell Miqne-Ekron in the Late Iron Age," in *Olive Oil in Antiquity: Israel and Neighbouring*

ing was surely not an expectation of greater compliance on the part of the Philistines but more likely a desire to prevent the growth of a single strong power in the region.[273] The Philistine principalities were not a single political entity, and their foreign policy was not always coordinated. They had likely all succumbed to Assyrian rule after Tiglath-pileser III's 734 campaign but, apart from Ashkelon, rebelled against Assyria in 721. Ashdod also rebelled in 712, and Gath, which at that time likely belonged to Ashdod, may have been destroyed the following year. The king of Ashkelon, in turn, was part of Hezekiah's alliance against Assyria. Sennacherib would have been under no illusions about the potential of any of these cities rebelling again.[274] Nevertheless, the massive growth of Ekron may be related to Padi's loyalty to him. (Padi, the king of Ekron, had been deposed by the anti-Assyrian alliance; see the commentary on 2:7.)

In the latter part of the seventh century, the Assyrians had increasing problems in the east. Assurbanipal was engaged in a civil war with his brother, the viceroy of Babylon, in 652–648 and then with Babylon's ally Elam in 647–646.[275] The Assyrians either allowed the Egyptians to exercise greater influence and control over the area or were unable to do much about it. Assurbanipal still responded to rebellions in Tyre and Akko in the 640s.[276] Stern thinks that "the Assyrian administration in Palestine collapsed totally around 640 BCE" with the Egyptians exercising a measure of control shortly afterward.[277] To Na'aman, "it seems that no one managed to oust Assyria from Syria and Palestine before Ashurbanipal's death in 631 B.C.E. and the outbreak of the revolt in Babylonia in 626 B.C.E."[278] It is not altogether clear whether Egyptian campaigns were "more of a diplomatic nature than

---

Countries from the Neolithic to the Early Arab Period, ed. David Eitam and Michael Heltzer, HANE 7 (Padova: Sargon, 1996), 219–42 and 166–96 respectively.

273. Joshua T. Walton ("Assyrian Interest in the West: Philistia and Judah," *Eretz-Israel* 33 [2018]: 175*–82*) stresses the importance of military reasons for the Assyrian expansion westward.

274. Cf. Nadav Na'aman, "Ashkelon under the Assyrian Empire," in *Exploring the Longue Durée: Essays in Honor of Lawrence E. Stager*, ed. J. David Schloen (Winona Lake, IN: Eisenbrauns, 2009), 351–59; Stern, *Archaeology*, 104–6; Mazar, *Archaeology*, 532; Douglas L. Esse, "Ashkelon," *ABD* 1:488.

275. A. Kirk Grayson, "Mesopotamia, History of (Assyria)," *ABD* 4:732–55, 746; cf. Schipper, "Egypt," 202. Grayson comments, "Assyria never recovered from that conflict. Although to all appearances it was the victor" (747).

276. Na'aman, "Kingdom," 35; "Josiah," 212; Schipper, "Egypt," 202.

277. Stern, *Archaeology*, 107; cf. Kuhrt, *Ancient Near East*, 643; David Vanderhooft, "Babylonian Strategies of Imperial Control in the West: Royal Practice and Rhetoric," in *Judah and the Judeans in the Neo-Babylonian Period*, ed. Oded Lipschits and Joseph Blenkinsopp (Winona Lake, IN: Eisenbrauns, 2003), 236–37.

278. Na'aman, "Kingdom," 38; "Josiah," 217.

real conquests,"[279] concerned with retaining free access to trade routes, or whether there was an attempt to establish an Egyptian "successor state" to Assyria in the Levant, possibly with the agreement of the Assyrians.[280] Psamtik I, who besieged Ashdod, "may have been an ally of Assyria most of the time" who considered Ashdod's attempts to gain independence from Assyria a hindrance to his own interests.[281] Alternatively, if Egypt was not yet an ally of Assyria, the relationship between the two powers may have been cool without being hostile.[282] In any case, there is no reference in Egyptian or classical sources to Egyptian-Assyrian rivalry at the time; nor is there any reference to hostilities between the two in Assyrian sources.[283] Assyria may have been content with Egyptian control in this region because Egypt did not threaten to establish an empire closer to the Assyrian heartland, and Egypt, at least over time, preferred Assyria to act as a buffer against expanding Babylonian forces. Thus, when Egypt sought to assist Assyria against Babylon in 609, this may have been as "a favour paid for being allowed to take over control of former Assyrian territory."[284] But it is also possible that the Egyptians did not so much feel obliged to Assyria as compelled by the desire for a weak Assyrian empire in the east rather than a resurgent Babylonian one.

In the light of this historical background, v. 4 does not point to a specific military campaign, whether from the north (against which is the order of the list), from Judah (against which are both the order and the lack of any evidence for an attempt on Josiah's part to take over Philistine cities),[285] or even from Egypt (against which stands the likelihood that they already exercised some control over the area at the time and put Ashdod under siege). The verse hints at a still-future disaster to fall upon the Philistines. The in-

---

279. Ahlström, *History*, 750–51.

280. Na'aman ("Kingdom," 39; "Josiah," 215) suggests that "the Egyptian entry into Asia was not a forcible conquest, but part of an Assyrian retreat by agreement, with Egypt (gradually or rapidly) taking the place of Assyria in the vacated areas." Cf. Schipper, "Egypt."

281. Ahlström, *History*, 751. Abraham Malamat (*The History of Biblical Israel*, CHANE 7 [Leiden: Brill, 2001], 282–98) thinks that Psametik I sought to undermine Assyrian rule at the time and argues that the Egyptian-Assyrian alliance came into existence after 622.

282. Laato, *Josiah*, 69–74.

283. Cf. Na'aman, "Kingdom," 38–39; "Josiah," 215.

284. So Anselm Hagedorn, "When Did Zephaniah Become a Supporter of Josiah's Reform?" *JTS* 62 (2011): 471.

285. Moshe Dotan and Ephraim Stern's speculation that Ashdod may have been conquered by Josiah (see fn. 266) has little to commend itself. Note that Stern is elsewhere more cautious (*Archaeology*, 140), merely allowing that "Ashdod may have been an ally of Josiah." Judean pottery at the site more likely testifies to trading relationships than Judean conquest (cf. 144). On the Meṣad Ḥashavyahu fortress south of Joppa, which plays a role in this discussion, see Ahlström, *History*, 767–68; Na'aman, "Kingdom," 44–48; "Josiah," 220–23 (with further references); Schipper, "Egypt," *passim*, esp. 209–12, 215, 221.

strument by which YHWH, who must be seen as the ultimate source of the ruin, would make these cities desolate remains unspecified. What is more important is that it will herald the end of Jerusalem and thus should motivate people to seek YHWH.

Reflection

The inevitable storm of judgment will be devastating, and there is no pleading here with God to turn away the disaster. Instead, the people are called to anticipate the tragedy—in a sense to act as if it had already been realized by disregarding (gold and) silver and adopting the posture of the humble poor of the land. This is commended on the grounds that there are still those who act in accordance with God's will among those at the bottom of the social heap. They, and any who associate with them, are affirmed in their loyalty to YHWH and encouraged to continue to seek him and his righteousness— and humility. A poetic glimpse of the destruction of the Philistine city-states as heralding the fall of Jerusalem is given to underline the seriousness and urgency of the call to seek YHWH. It is likely that economic links between Judah and its neighbors, especially the Philistines, had been strengthened under Assyrian guidance and that this interrelationship of economies continued even as Assyrian influence waned.[286] But if ch. 1 put the emphasis on the economic impact of the destruction of the "Canaanites," here the focus probably shifts onto an unspecified military campaign, which sees devastation draw ever closer to Jerusalem. In fact, the cities mentioned here, as well as the nations mentioned later in the chapter, all fell to Nebuchadnezzar, who proved to be the divine instrument that is left unmentioned here. As Egypt and Babylonia vied for dominance over the area,[287] at least some of the Philistine cities suffered attack also from the Egyptians (for Ashdod, see above on the siege by Psamtik I; for Gaza, see Jer 47:1), but in every case their destruction seems to have come at the hand of the Babylonians. It was presumably only once Nebuchadnezzar had become enthroned that he was specified as the one who would bring "the cup of God's wrath" to the nations, including Jerusalem (note the reference to Nebuchadnezzar's first year in Jer 25:1). While we lack sufficient knowledge to establish with certainty at

286. Gitin ("Neo-Assyrian Empire," 99–100) does, however, see evidence for a reduction in output as Assyrian dominance gave way to Egyptian dominance, suggesting some upset in the market trading systems.

287. See the Saqqara Papyrus (Cairo, Eg. Mus. J. 86984 = 3483), an Aramaic letter to Neco II from the king of one of the Philistine cities (probably Ekron) appealing for help against the Babylonians; see James M. Lindenberger, *Ancient Aramaic and Hebrew Letters*, 2nd ed., WAW 14 (Atlanta: Society of Biblical Literature, 2003), 23.

what point the various Philistine cities were conquered by Nebuchadnezzar, what we know suggests that Ashkelon fell to the Babylonians in November or December of 604 and Ekron, Ashdod, and Gaza sometime between 604 and 598/597.[288]

Nebuchadnezzar "deported all Jerusalem, that is all the officials, all the valiant soldiers, ten thousand captives, all the craftsmen and the metal-workers; no one remained, except the poorest people of the land [*dallat 'am-hā'āreṣ*]" (2 Kgs 24:14; cf. 25:12). The Babylonian armies did not distinguish carefully between those who sought YHWH and those who did not. While Jeremiah was released from prison and not exiled (Jer 39:11–14), Ezekiel had been. While Jeremiah's scribe Baruch survived the onslaught on the city, he was told not to expect great things for himself under the circumstances (Jer 45). A national disaster cannot but make an impact on the godly as well as the ungodly, and for all the greater freedom Jeremiah enjoyed after Jerusalem's conquest, it came with much sorrow for his people. The book of Lamentations testifies to the grief of the surviving YHWH-faithful over the destruction. The glimmer of hope offered in this passage is, therefore, not to be read as an expectation that those who remain faithful to YHWH will have less sorrow than others. The overall biblical testimony is that such vindication is ultimately not to be found, let alone clearly discerned, in historical events. But the upper class was hit harder in the sense that their lives were changed more dramatically (or ended), and so we see in 3:12 that it is indeed a *humble and powerless people* that are left in Jerusalem.

Retaining life is not a matter of merit any more than receiving life in the first place. Life is not an inalienable possession. Similarly, as Weigl points out, righteousness and humility are not objects that one can possess like silver or gold; they need to be enacted and thus realized again and again.[289] In this sense, our passage speaks both of grace and of our ongoing need for repentance. Our experience demonstrates that there is nothing peculiar about calling those who already act upon God's judgment to the pursuit of

---

288. Esse, "Ashkelon," *ABD* 1:489; Lawrence E. Stager, "Ashkelon on the Eve of Destruction in 604 B.C.," in *Ashkelon 3: The Seventh Century B.C.*, ed. Lawrence E. Stager et al. (Winona Lake, IN: Eisenbrauns, 2011), 3–11; Alexander Fantalkin, "Why Did Nebuchadnezzar II Destroy Ashkelon in Kislev 604 B.C.E.?" in *The Fire Signals of Lachish: Studies in the Archaeology and History of Israel in the Late Bronze Age, Iron Age, and Persian Period in Honor of David Ussishkin*, ed. Israel Finkelstein and Nadav Na'aman (Winona Lake, IN: Eisenbrauns, 2011), 87–111; Trude Dothan and Seymour Gitin, "Ekron," *ABD* 2:420; Moshe Dotan, "Ashdod," *ABD* 1:481; H.-J. Katzenstein, "Gaza (Pre-Hellenistic)," *ABD* 2:914. Stern (*Archaeology*, 109) believes that all Philistine cities had been destroyed and their inhabitants deported by 603 or so. Cf. Vanderhooft, "Babylonian Strategies," 239–40.

289. Weigl, *Zefanja*, 109.

righteousness or about enjoining the humble to seek humility.[290] Jesus similarly enjoins his disciples, those who have already responded to his call, to seek God and his kingdom (Matt 6:33). He motivates this instruction with a promise rather than a threat, but we must not overplay any contrast between Jesus and Zephaniah.[291] Zephaniah's call to seek YHWH is grounded in the knowledge of an approaching disaster but not exclusively so. Those who believed the announcement of a coming Day of YHWH that would make an end of Judah and Jerusalem could not hope to secure their physical safety by seeking YHWH. They would have known, as we do, that in any such disaster, the innocent suffer as well as the guilty and those who survive are not necessarily the most righteous. The people are called to entrust themselves to the hands of God, (1) knowing that there is ultimately no other place in which to put one's confidence and (2) in the hope that God's purposes are not exclusively destructive. In other words, it would be a misreading to interpret these verses along individualistic lines, as if now it is everyone for themselves and as if there were a direct link between personal piety and individual survival. Nor would it be right to see fear as the decisive motivating factor to which appeal is made. The hope is that God still has some positive purposes for the community beyond the disaster, and the encouragement is to live in a way that would be pleasing to him and build up such a community. Other biblical texts also testify to the insufficiency of fear alone as a motivating factor for seeking YHWH. Rahab claims that all inhabitants of the land were terrified in anticipation of what YHWH might do to them, having heard reports of what happened to the Egyptians and the Amorites, but only in Rahab's case was the fear paired with hope of survival in claiming allegiance to YHWH (Josh 2:9–13). If we accept the double entendre in the description of the fate of the Philistine cities, we may begin to see an implicit contrast between, on the one hand, these city-states that will be entirely abandoned and desolate, and, on the other hand, Lady Zion, who may still have progeny left and might be taken back as a wife. But it will be for subsequent passages to spell this out.

The theme of future hope cannot come fully to the surface here because it might compromise the stress on submission to the mighty hand of God, an aspect of faith in God that remains an important feature of the life of believers (cf. 1 Pet 5:6). Calvin notes that the relationship between affliction and humility is no coincidence, "for men grow wanton in their pleasures, and abundance commonly produces insolence; but by adversity they learn

290. There is in any case a difference between having humility thrust (forced) upon oneself and seeking (desiring) humility.

291. Note also how Jesus's decision to focus his ministry on Galilee, based in the comparatively large Capernaum but not stationary there, echoes Zephaniah's rejection of the Jerusalem elite in favor of the rural population.

to become meek."[292] When future hope comes into view in ch. 2 and especially ch. 3, it is with a clear understanding that salvation lies on the other side of judgment and is for a remnant. In this way, the announcement of the possibility of salvation still urges repentance on the ungodly (cf. Rom 2:4). Following the death and resurrection of Christ, the call to seek God and his rule is more firmly rooted in an act of both judgment and salvation and goes to all the world with greater hopefulness (see, e.g., Acts 17:30–31).

V. ANNOUNCEMENTS OF THE FATE OF NATIONS (2:5–15)

[5]*Oy,*[a] *inhabitants of the coastal portion,*[b] *nation of Cherethites.*[c]
　The word of YHWH is against you.[d]
"Canaan,"[e] *land of the Philistines,*[f]
　I will destroy you[g] *until no inhabitant is left.*[h]
[6]*And the coastal portion*[i] *shall become herders' camps,*[j]
　grazing lands of shepherds and sheepfolds for flocks.
[7]*And it shall be the portion*[k] *for the remnant of the house of Judah;*[l]
　by the sea[m] *they shall graze.*[n]
In the houses of Ashkelon, in the evening, they shall lie down,
　for YHWH their God will attend to them[o]
　　and restore their fortunes.[p]
[8]*I have heard the taunting*[q] *of Moab*
　and the insults of the Ammonites[r]
　　with which[s] *they have taunted my people*
　　　and made boasts against their territory.[t]
[9]*Therefore, as I live,*[u] *utterance of YHWH of Hosts, the God of Israel,*[v]
　surely[w] *Moab shall be like Sodom,*
　　and the Ammonites like Gomorrah,[x]
　　　a place of weeds and a patch of salt[y] *and a permanent desolation.*
The remnant of my people will despoil them;[z]
　the survivors of my nation[aa] *will possess them.*
[10]*This*[bb] *will happen to them in return for their pride,*
　for they taunted and made boasts[cc]
　　against the people of[dd] *YHWH of Hosts.*[ee]
[11]*Fearsome*[ff] *is YHWH,*[gg] *more than they,*[hh]
　for he demotes[ii] *all the gods of the earth*[jj]
　　so that to him will offer obeisance, each[kk] *in*[ll] *their place,*
　　　all the coastal[mm] *nations.*[nn]
[12]*You, yes*[oo] *you Cushites,*[pp] *are*[qq] *slain by*[rr] *my*[ss] *sword!*

292. Calvin, *Commentaries*, 4:235.

[13]*And he shall[tt] stretch out his hand against the north,*
 and he shall destroy Assyria,[uu]
  and he shall make Nineveh a desolation,
   a parched land,[vv] like the desert.
[14]*Then[ww] flocks[xx] will lie down in her midst, every wild animal[yy] of the field.[zz]*
 The owl as well as the jackdaw[aaa]
  shall lodge on her capitals.[bbb]
Listen! The sound[ccc] of singing[ddd] at the window[eee]—devastation[fff] on the threshold,
 because he has exposed [ggg] the cedar work.[hhh]
[15]*This is the exultant city that [iii] dwelled in safety,[jjj]*
 that said in her heart,
  "I am—and I only."[kkk]
What a desolation she has become,[lll]
 a lair for wild animals!
Everyone who passes by her
 will hiss[mmm] and shake his fist.[nnn]

a. The fact that the interjection is regularly connected with a designation that is also an indictment leads Roberts (*Nahum*, 197) to suggest that the Philistines may be condemned for being *inhabitants* of the promised land; cf. Rudolph, *Micha*, 280. This seems far-fetched to me. One other instance of *hôy* introducing a threatening speech without indictment is Isa 29:1. The participial phrase that follows along with the appositional noun phrase is probably best interpreted as a vocative here. See the translation notes on Nah 3:1 and Hab 2:6.

b. Or "coastal allotment," which seems to me more likely than "narrow strip of land" (see further in the commentary). Cf. *schoinisma* in LXX, which is arguably a piece of land measured out by the *schoinion* ("rope, cord") here as elsewhere (and like *schoinismos*). Takamitsu Muraoka (*A Greek-English Lexicon of the Septuagint* [Louvain: Peeters, 2009], 667) gives "long, narrow area" for the occurrences in Zephaniah (cf. LEH), although he notes that "σχοῖνος is used in Egypt in the sense of 'land-measure' (LSJ, s.v., III)." Franco Montanari (*The Brill Dictionary of Ancient Greek* [Leiden: Brill, 2015], 2071), like LSJ, only gives "allotment of land"; cf. BDAG.

c. LXX renders this gentilic term *paroikoi Krētōn* ("aliens of the Cretans"; cf. Peshitta "people of Crete"), which may reflect a misreading of *gwy* (*nation*) as *grym* ("aliens"); cf. *BHQ*; Irsigler, *Zefanja*, 233. But it could also be a free rendering of a phrase designed to stress further that the Philistines were immigrants (cf. following note). Other (Greek, Aramaic, Latin) versions derive *kərētîm* from *krt* ("to cut off"), either anticipating annihilation or condemning the Philistines; cf. Irsigler, *Zefanja*, 233. Vulg. *gens perditorum* should probably be rendered "nation of the ruined," reading *perditorum* as a passive participle (cf. Jerome, *Twelve*, 1:134–35) rather than in an active sense as "nation of destroyers." Ben Zvi (*Zephaniah*, 153) believes that the expression *gôy kərētîm* "is an intentional play on words."

d. This first *you* translates a masculine plural suffix; the *you* later in the verse translates a feminine singular suffix, whose antecedent is *land*. The whole phrase is widely considered a later addition (see *BHS*), but I see little reason to think so; cf. Ben Zvi, *Zephaniah*, 153–55;

Ryou, *Oracles*, 29–30; contra Irsigler, *Zefanja*, 234–35. The masoretic accentuation links this line with the following rather than the preceding line, as does, e.g., Sweeney, *Zephaniah*, 124. The use of the phrase as a heading in the only other occurrence (Zech 12:1, where *'al* functions similarly to *'el*; cf. Mal 1:1) may have influenced the Masoretes, but the agreement of suffixes suggests to me a different understanding here (where *'al* means *against* rather than "about").

e. The Philistine cities could be seen as part of Canaan (see, e.g., Num 13:29; Josh 13:3), although *Canaan* here is unique as a designation for the *land of the Philistines* and therefore often emended or considered a later addition. None of the ancient versions support an emendation, and it seems to me that the obvious link to 1:11 is just as likely to be original as redactional; cf. Ryou, *Oracles*, 30–31; Ben Zvi, *Zephaniah*, 155–56.

f. LXX renders *gē allophylōn* ("land of foreigners"), using the standard rendering of *pǝlištîm* outside the Pentateuch and Joshua, where *Phylistiim* is used exclusively (as also in 1 Macc 3:24; Odes 1:14; Sir 46:18; 47:7; 50:26), except for *Gerarōn* in Gen 26:8. In Judges, both renderings are found.

g. The feminine singular suffix agrees with *'ereṣ* (*land*). LXX has the plural form (*hymas*), referring to the inhabitants rather than the land. The MT is to be preferred because the subsequent phrase always follows reference to a place rather than a people; cf. Ivan J. Ball, *Zephaniah*, 102; Ryou, *Oracles*, 31.

h. Ben Zvi (*Zephaniah*, 156) notes that *mē'ên yôšēb* (*until no inhabitant is left*) regularly occurs with *šammâ* or *šǝmāmâ* ("desolation"), namely in nine of eleven occurrences outside Zephaniah. Of the two exceptions, Jer 33:10 uses the related verb *šmm*, and only Jer 26:9 goes entirely without reference to this root (it uses the verb *ḥrb*, "to lie in ruins"). He believes that this suggests that v. 5 is not independent of v. 4 (which uses *šǝmāmâ* with Ashkelon). It certainly helps to strengthen the link, confirming the Janus-like character of v. 4 (contra Irsigler, *Zefanja*, 244). Note that the other occurrence of *mē'ên yôšēb* in Zephaniah (3:6) also comes with use of the verb *šmm*.

i. Hebrew *ḥebel hayyām* (*coastal portion*) picks up the phrase from the preceding verse. LXX avoids the repetition and reads "Crete" instead. The use of the feminine form at the beginning of the verse (*And ... shall be*) is surprising because *ḥebel* is usually masculine, although *DCH* allows that it might be feminine here; cf. Ivan J. Ball, *Zephaniah*, 103, who notes that *'ereṣ* ("land," usually feminine) can be either as well, followed by Ryou, *Oracles*, 32; Sweeney, *Zephaniah*, 128 (who argues from the context). An alternative rendering would be, "And it [the land], the coastal portion, shall be" (cf. Berlin, *Zephaniah*, 106, who thinks *ḥebel hayyām* may have crept in later). A change of the MT to render as a direct address (NRSV: "And you, O seacoast, shall be"; cf. *BHS*) does not seem warranted, contra Irsigler, *Zefanja*, 234.

j. The exact meaning of *nǝwōt kǝrōt rō'îm* already caused difficulties to translators in antiquity. Expressions similar to *nǝwōt rō'îm* are found in Amos 1:2 and Jer 33:12. I take *kǝrōt* as an alternative plural form of *kar* II, with the meaning "pasturage, grazing land" (Isa 30:23; Ps 65:13[14]; maybe 37:20), chosen instead of the masculine form to facilitate a wordplay with *Cherethites*. Others derive *kǝrōt* from the verb *krh* ("to dig"), giving "wells" in NIV (2011 and already TNIV; the 1986 version rendered as "Kerethites") and "caves" in NASB and HCSB. I have taken the first word (*nǝwōt*) as a sort of heading; the plural is used elsewhere for "pasturages." The unusual spelling without *aleph* here might be designed to facilitate the reading "habitations" (attested in the singular, e.g., in Exod 15:13; Jer 10:25), which is then developed in a merism as daytime habitation (*grazing lands of shepherds*) and nighttime habitation (*sheepfolds for flocks*), but in context, we should also hear "pasturages" because the point of the statement is that the land will not return to having ordinary habitations; hence *herders' camps* ("sheilings" in Scotland and the north of England). The overlap in meaning between *nəwōt* and *kərōt* has led some to suggest that one is a gloss to explain the other, but neither term is unambiguous enough to render the other explicit. (*Kərōt* would be more likely to be original, chosen for its allusion to *Cherethites*, but one would expect the form *nə'ôt* as a gloss, not the more difficult *nəwōt*.)

k. Alternatively, *hebel* is the subject ("And the portion shall belong to the remnant of the house of Judah"); so, e.g., Sweeney, *Zephaniah*, 124. See Ryou, *Oracles*, 103–4, for a fuller discussion of the syntactical options.

l. The accentuation suggests keeping this and the following line together in an extraordinary long line. In my reconstruction of masoretic colometry, the MT has only three lines in this verse; see Renz, *Colometry*, 118; also *BHQ*. While I am generally inclined to follow the MT's predilection for longer lines (and disinclined to change the text to regularize its rhythm, which would be difficult to accomplish in this verse anyway), here it seems to me preferable to divide the text into five lines—a bicolon and a tricolon, with the final colon in each case climactically short.

m. Assuming that the expression *hebel hayyām* (used both in v. 5 and v. 6) is here broken up, with *hebel* used in the first line and *hayyām* in the second, I accept the emendation of *'lyhm* (*'ălêhem*, "upon them") to *'lhym* (*'al hayyām*, "by the sea"), which goes back to Julius Wellhausen (*Skizzen*, 5:150; cf. *BHS*). There is admittedly no substantial support from the versions. Among recent commentators, Vlaardingerbroek (*Zephaniah*, 133, tentatively) and Dietrich (*Nahum*, 221) also follow the emendation accepted here, which assumes a reversal of two consonants early in the history of the text.

n. The context suggests that the subject of the verb is *the remnant of the house of Judah*. The use of the plural form is a *constructio ad sensum*; cf. GKC 145be; JM 150e; *IBHS*, 109.

o. Cf. the note on *punish* in 1:8 for the different uses of this verb. Only here in Zephaniah is the verb used with a suffix indicating its object. In the other occurrences, in which the activity is hostile, the preposition *'al* introduces the object (1:8–9, 12; 3:7).

p. The consonants *šbwt* are vocalized here to be read *šəbît*, as also in Pss 85:1(2); 126:4. There has been a longstanding debate about the question whether *šəbût* (*šəbît*) should be derived from *šwb* ("to turn/bring back") or *šbh* ("to deport") and whether the expression as a whole typically refers to a reversal of fortunes or more specifically to a return from captivity. Within what we have read so far in Zephaniah, *restore their fortunes* seems to fit better, given that readers were led to distinguish between those who are swept away on the Day of YHWH and a *remnant* of the poor and lowly who remain "hidden" on the day of judgment. Later, the returnees from exile understood themselves as *the remnant*, and the phrase could be reread as a reference to a return from captivity, as is readily possible in 3:20.

q. Or "taunt." LXX has the plural. Of more than seventy occurrences in the Hebrew Bible, the plural of *herpâ* is used only in Ps 69:9–10(10–11) and Dan 12:2, which leads me to conclude that it often functions as a collective, suggesting my translation as *taunting*. Its pairing with the plural of *giddûp* (found elsewhere only in Isa 43:28, also in the plural) is not objectionable; cf. the pairing with the plural of *gədûpâ* in Isa 51:7 (equivalent to *giddûp* and used as a collective singular in its other occurrence, Ezek 5:15).

r. Literally "sons of Ammon"; see the commentary. The (standard) use of this construct expression commends the order *Moab . . . Ammonites*, with the shorter *Moab* in the first colon. Using *taunting* in the first colon and *insults* in the second arguably gives a more poetic ring, with the echo *giddûpê bənê*, and results in two lines of a pretty much equal number of syllables (if *bənê* is enunciated as one rather than two syllables). The next two lines would again have roughly the same number of syllables (depending on whether *gəbûlām* is read as two or three syllables).

s. The particle *'ăšer* is construed as taking the role of the indirect object in this sentence and translated *with which*, relating to the taunting and reviling; cf. Ps 79:12. Alternatively, it could be rendered as the relative pronoun "who," referring to *Moab* and *the Ammonites* or, more controversially, taken as a conjunction ("because, when").

t. Or "aggrandized themselves on their territory" in the sense of encroaching on their territory (Patterson, *Nahum*, 346–47: "violated their borders"), or with the suffix related to Moab-Ammon, as in "expanded upon their border" (Sweeney, *Zephaniah*, 133). Most LXX MSS have *ta horia mou* ("my borders"), which was probably influenced by "my people" earlier in the verse. LXX-W (Ms. Washington, third century AD) and other versions reflect the MT; cf. Irsigler, *Zefanja*, 256. Given the context and the fact that *gdl* (*hiphil*) *'al-* nowhere else refers to territorial expansion but in most cases clearly refers to boasting against or vilifying someone, this is surely the meaning here as well, contra Berlin, *Zephaniah*, 109, who postulates an idiom *gdl* (*hiphil*) *ph 'al* ("make [one's] mouth great against"). Usage elsewhere (e.g., Pss 35:26; 38:16[17]; Jer 48:28, 42; Ezek 35:13 with the specification *bəpîkem*, "with their mouth") suggests that the suffix is not reflexive, contra NJB ("boast of their own domains"). But there may be a deliberate ambiguity.

u. Only YHWH swears by his own life in the Old Testament, which would seem to be equivalent to saying that he swears by his holiness (Amos 4:2) or by his own self (*nepeš*, Amos 6:8; the use of "the pride of Jacob" in 8:7 seems to be sarcastic). There are more than forty occurrences of others swearing by the life of YHWH (e.g., Judg 8:19; Hos 4:15); cf. the commentary on 1:5 on swearing "by their King."

v. The longer expression *utterance of YHWH of Hosts* (26× in prophetic literature) is used only here with the oath formula. Elsewhere, *utterance* in connection with the oath formula takes just the divine name (Num 14:28; Isa 49:18; Jer 22:24) or, in Ezekiel, "Lord YHWH" (13×). Another variation is found in Jer 46:18, which uses a single noun that is then expanded ("utterance of the King, whose name is YHWH of hosts").

w. I accept that the particle *kî* in the context of an oath here and in some other places conveys emphasis; cf. Isa 49:18; Jer 46:18; Ezek 35:6; see JM 165; *IBHS*, 679. For a different view, see Barry L. Bandstra, "The Syntax of the Particle KY in Biblical Hebrew and Ugaritic" (PhD diss., Yale University, 1982), 25–61 (on emphasis), 142–46 (on oaths). Note also the literature in the annotation on the first word of v. 4. Ryou (*Oracles*, 108; cf. 145–46) here translates, "when Moab will become like Sodom."

x. Irsigler (*Zefanja*, 265) suggests that the similarity of sound is responsible for linking the Ammonites with Gomorrah. This may be so, but the order *Moab . . . Ammonites* is the same order as in v. 8, again likely for poetic reasons (the verb being taken together with the single word *Moab* rather than the construct "sons of Ammon" = *Ammonites*, again resulting in lines of roughly seven syllables), and *Sodom* and *Gomorrah* are always mentioned in this order.

y. Hebrew *mimšaq ḥārûl ûmikrê-melaḥ*. The translation is tentative, as *mimšaq* and *mikrê* are not elsewhere attested, and *ḥārûl* is attested only twice more. We can be confident that *melaḥ* means *salt* here (cf., e.g., Lev 2:13; Num 18:19; Deut 29:23[22]), but *mikrê-melaḥ* could be "a salt pit" (deriving the noun from the verb for digging) or "a heap of salt" (based on Akkadian, Aramaic, and later Hebrew equivalents; cf. LXX, Vulg.). Job 30:7 and Prov 24:31 suggest that *ḥārûl* (as a collective singular here) refers to nettles or thistles or wild vetchlings.

It is possible that *mimšaq* is related to *ben-mešeq* (Gen 15:2, perhaps "son of possession"); *mimšaq ḥārûl* might then be "a place possessed by weeds" (see Sweeney, *Zephaniah*, 139; cf. Ivan J. Ball, *Zephaniah*, 107; Ryou, *Oracles*, 38; Irsigler, *Zefanja*, 257). My translation uses relatively non-specific terms. The general meaning is in any case not in question.

z. For the use of plural verbs with a singular collective noun, see, e.g., GKC 145b–g; JM 150e.

aa. The *qere* suggests, surely rightly, to read *gwy* as *gôyî*, as if it had two *yôd*s. The defective spelling is either deliberate (facilitated by the presence of "my people" in the previous line, which leads one naturally to read "my nation"), avoiding a sequence of three *yôd*s, or it is the result of an error; see Ben Zvi, *Zephaniah*, 169.

bb. The proposal that *zō't* is here a noun meaning "shame" is seriously considered by Vlaardingerbroek, *Zephaniah*, 149, but rejected (rightly, in my view) by others; e.g., Ben Zvi, *Zephaniah*, 172; Ryou, *Oracles*, 39.

cc. Sweeney (*Zephaniah*, 142) allows that the idiom with *gdl hiphil* usually refers to making boasts but reads his understanding of v. 8 (see on that verse above) into v. 10 and renders "expanded against." I agree that the idiom likely means the same here as in v. 8 and see here further confirmation that the reference is to verbal swagger.

dd. LXX does not read *'am* (*the people of*), either as a result of haplography or deliberately; see Ryou, *Oracles*, 39. Note that in Jer 48, Moab's arrogance is said to be directed against YHWH (vv. 26, 42).

ee. This verse is more prosaic in that it does not exhibit parallelism, but in scanning it like this (cf. MT), we again have three lines of roughly seven syllables, as in vv. 8–9—except for the oath formula and the long and somber colon describing the desolation.

ff. Many LXX MSS and Peshitta derive *nôrā'* not from *yr'* ("to fear") but from *r'h* ("to see") and speak of an appearance of YHWH "against [or to] them." This is commended in *BHS*. While retaining the MT, many nevertheless speak of a theophany; e.g., Rudolph, *Micha*, 282; Robertson, *Nahum*, 307; Vlaardingerbroek, *Zephaniah*, 150; Irsigler, *Zefanja*, 273–74. See the commentary for possible implications.

gg. My understanding of this line could lead to a translation such as "YHWH is fearsome above them" or "YHWH is more to be feared than they," but I want to retain "fearsome is YHWH" as the main statement, which could stand in its own right.

hh. Or "above them" or "against them." Ivan J. Ball (*Zephaniah*, 138) proposed that the suffix anticipates *all the gods of the earth* from the next line; cf. Daniel C. Timmer, "The Non-Israelite Nations in Zephaniah: Conceptual Coherence and the Relationship of the Parts to the Whole," in Boda, Floyd, and Toffelmire, *Book of the Twelve*, 253. But such a prospective use of the pronominal suffix is extraordinarily rare. The common understanding that relates the suffix back to *Moab* and *the Ammonites*, the subjects of the previous verse, is the most plausible. See 1 Chr 16:25 and Ps 96:4 for the comparative use of the preposition with *nôrā'*.

ii. The verb is attested elsewhere only in Isa 17:4 (*niphal*) for the shrinking away of flesh and bones; cf. the adjective *rāzâ* ("lean") in Num 13:20 and Ezek 34:20 and the noun *rāzôn* ("emaciation, leanness"; for the formation of a noun ending in -*ôn* from a III-*hê* root, cf. *ḥāzôn*, "vision," from *ḥzh*, "to see") in Ps 106:15; Isa 10:16; Mic 6:10. This leads to renderings along the lines of "make lean, weaken, diminish" (for which some emend to a *piel* form; cf. Roberts, *Nahum*, 193; Irsigler, *Zefanja*, 271–72). Most English versions use a future tense, for which one would expect a *yiqtol* form; cf. already LXX. *BHS* proposes to emend the text; Patterson (*Nahum*, 348) achieves the same result by assuming that the final letter of *kî* (*For*) does double duty. In my view, the *qatal* form is used to describe a characteristic action.

jj. Or "land."

kk. Or "everyone." Irsigler (*Zefanja*, 277, following Marco Striek, *Das vordeuterono-mistische Zefanjabuch*, BET 29 [Frankfurt: Lang, 1999], 161) insists that the reference is to each individual person rather than each nation. While the prophecy does not envisage any dissenters, it is more likely that *each* relates directly to the subject of the verb. For similar use of distributive *'îš* for a group, see, e.g., Num 26:54; 35:8.

ll. Or "from," but likely not in the separative sense of "coming from" (to go to, e.g., Jerusalem). The verse does not seem to envisage a pilgrimage to the temple but peoples worshipping YHWH in their homeland; cf. Ryou, *Oracles*, 43, 236–37; Irsigler, *Zefanja*, 277.

mm. The plural of *'iy* refers to lands bordered or surrounded by water—coasts and pen-insulas as well as islands. The traditional English rendering is "isles/islands," used nearly exclusively in KJV (except for "country" in Jer 47:4). The translators of KJV presumably took their lead from the Vulg. (which has "insula" wherever *'iy* is identified as a geographical term) and the LXX (which regularly has *nēsos*—but *ethnos*, "nation," in Isa 41:5; 42:4). By contrast, NASB uses "coastland(s)" thirty times and "islands" only six times. Ben Zvi (*Zephaniah*, 175) even considers "habitable lands" contextually more appropriate here and in Isa 40:15; 41:1, 5; 42:4, 10; 49:1; 51:5 (misprinted as 51:1), or else the addition of an implied "even" (176).

nn. For a defense of the reading adopted here against alternative understandings of the syntax, see Ryou, *Oracles*, 112–13.

oo. Or "even." If *gam* is interpreted as associating what follows with what preceded, it could be translated "also," but there are cases in which it is best to think of the particle as em-phasizing at the expense of associating (see Gen 32:19; Jer 8:12; Job 2:10; Ps 52:5[7]), which seems to be the case here; see *HALOT*, s.v. *gam* IV (which does not mention this verse).

pp. Ivan J. Ball (*Zephaniah*, 140–41) interprets *kûšîm* as "Kassites" (also in 3:10) and an instantiation of *all the coastal nations* (v. 11), perhaps facilitated by an implied merism designating, respectively, the western and eastern limits of the world. But the switch to the second person and the use of *gam* (*even*) argue against taking vv. 11–12 together.

qq. Or "you are [the] ones slain by my sword"; "the slain by my sword are they." Analysis of the syntax of this verse is controversial. In my view, the pronoun here is copular, although this possibility is rejected by some eminent scholars. For a fuller discussion of such clauses with reference to earlier literature, see Robert D. Holmstedt and Andrew R. Jones, "The Pronoun in Tripartite Verbless Clauses in Biblical Hebrew: Resumption for Left-Dislocation or Pronominal Copula?" *JSS* 59 (2014): 53–89; cf. the contributions in Cynthia L. Miller, ed., *The Verbless Clause in Biblical Hebrew: Linguistic Approaches* (Winona Lake, IN: Eisen-brauns, 1999). For the use of the third person in a modifying phrase or clause after a vocative (also, e.g., in Mic 1:2; Isa 54:1), see *IBHS*, 77. An analysis of the grammar is also offered, e.g., by Ryou, *Oracles*, 43–44, 113–14; Irsigler, *Zefanja*, 284–85.

rr. The construct form *ḥalalê ḥarbî*, like the more general *ḥalalê-ḥereb* ("slain of the sword" = "slain by the sword"; e.g., Isa 22:2; Jer 14:18; Ezek 31:17–18) is best understood as a genitive of instrument; cf. *IBHS*, 144. A reference to "my sword" (*ḥarbî*) in a divine oracle is also found in Isa 34:5; Ezek 21:3–5[8–10]; 30:24–25; 32:10 (cf. Deut 32:41–42).

ss. In *BHS*, Elliger suggests reading "slain by the sword of YHWH," which would fit better with the third-person references to YHWH in both the preceding (vv. 9–10) and the following verses (vv. 13–15); cf. Ben Zvi, *Zephaniah*, 177–78; Irsigler, *Zefanja*, 285–86. But there is no real necessity for changing the text; cf. Ryou, *Oracles*, 43–44.

tt. The shorter (apocopated) form of the *yiqtol* here (*yēṭ* rather than *yiṭṭê*) and with the third verb (the second does not have two different *yiqtol* forms) is read as the jussive by Rudolph, *Micha*, 276; Robertson, *Nahum*, 310; Berlin, *Zephaniah*, 104; cf. NEB ("So let him stretch out his hand . . ."), changed in REB to the indicative ("He will stretch out his hand . . ."). But the shorter form does not invariably indicate a jussive (and sometimes the longer form is used for the jussive; see *tērā'ê* in Gen 1:9). It is hard to see what could motivate a jussive here. Recent research suggests that jussives were marked by position rather than morphology in Biblical Hebrew; see Peter J. Gentry, "The System of the Finite Verb in Classical Biblical Hebrew," *HS* 39 (1998): 7–38, 22–24. The variation seems to be stylistic; cf. "He causes the clouds to ascend" in Jer 10:13 (long form) and 51:16 (short form).

uu. Or "Assur." In Akkadian, and presumably in Hebrew, the name of the land and empire is the same as the name of its (historically) most important city and deity, although there is no clear instance in Hebrew in which *'aššûr* refers to the city.

vv. Or "drought." The word is often used in the phrase "land of dryness" (*'ereṣ-ṣiyyâ*, Pss 63:1[2]; 107:35; Isa 41:18; 53:2; Jer 2:6; 51:43; Ezek 19:13; Hos 2:3[5]; Joel 2:20). In view of *like the desert*, a more concrete rendering (cf. Job 30:3; Pss 78:17; 105:41; Isa 35:1) is preferable. Even so, the comma is meant to signal that *like the desert* qualifies *Nineveh* rather than *parched land*, resulting in three ways in which Nineveh is described (cf. the threefold description in v. 9). The disjunctive accent on *ṣiyyâ* suggests that the Masoretes read the text similarly.

ww. *Then* is used in the translation to signal the shift to a *wǝ-qatal* form. Irsigler (*Zefanja*, 294) does the same; cf. Ryou, *Oracles*, 303 n. 32.

xx. Or "herds." The term *'ēder* (like, e.g., German "Herde") can be used for herds of big cattle as well as flocks of small animals (sheep and goats); see both in Joel 1:18. English usage requires a decision; the pastoral references earlier in the chapter prime us for *flocks*.

yy. The final *waw* on *ḥaytô* does not function like a true suffix but is in effect an alternative to the more common form of the construct *ḥayyat* (cf. Gen 1:24 with Gen 1:25, 30); see *HGHS* 65i and GKC 90e for further examples.

zz. Or "every animal of a nation." It may be possible to interpret *gôy* ("nation") here in the sense of "every kind of animal one might find in a nation" (all species of beasts; cf. BDB) or metaphorically along the lines of "every animal living in a group," but I follow Israel Eitan's suggestion (*A Contribution to Biblical Lexicography* [New York: Columbia University Press, 1924], 32–33) of a homonym here meaning "field"; cf. James Barr, *Comparative Philology and the Text of the Old Testament* (Oxford: Clarendon Press, 1968), 144, 324; *DCH*. The three words of this clause are joined by *maqqep* in the MT, giving the line a single accent and keeping it with the preceding in a single colon in MT. Maybe this is meant to smooth the semantic tension between *flocks* and *every wild animal*. The Masoretes allow for a colon of only four syllables, but only rarely (e.g., Nah 3:1a; 3:7aγ). Alternatively, we could scan it as a bicolon.

aaa. The precise identity of the two wild animals that have been singled out is uncertain, and the ancient versions are of little help. The first (*qā'āt*) is an unclean species of bird (Lev 11:18; Deut 14:17) found in the wilderness (Ps 102:6[7]; cf. Isa 34:11). The second (*qippōd*) is only attested in descriptions similar to the one here (Isa 14:23; 34:11), which do not allow further precision. The *qippōd* was often understood to be a hedgehog. However, Michael L. Barré (*The Lord Has Saved Me: A Study of the Psalm of Hezekiah [Isaiah 38:9–20]*, CBQMS 39 [Washington: Catholic Biblical Society of America, 2005], 95–100) demonstrates that there is no evidence for the meaning "to roll/fold up" for a verb *qpd* in Hebrew or cognate languages, on the basis of which some have argued for the meaning "hedgehog." Most likely, *qippōd* indicates another species of bird. Perhaps the terms refer to two types of owls (e.g., long- and short-eared owls). See esp. Vlaardingerbroek, *Zephaniah*, 159–60, for a fuller discussion.

bbb. The meaning of this term is also uncertain and apparently was guessed already by translators in antiquity. I follow the standard rendering (BDB, *HALOT, DCH*). Others suggest "doorframe" (e.g., Sweeney, *Zephaniah*, 149).

ccc. Hebrew *qôl* can function as an interjection ("Listen! Someone is singing") or a noun ("voice, sound"). While many take *qôl* as the subject of the verb (e.g., Ben Zvi, *Zephaniah*, 181; Sweeney, *Zephaniah*, 149; Dietrich, *Nahum*, 219), I am not certain that this is permissible. Keil (*Minor Prophets*, 2:148) rightly argues that this would require a meaning ("resonate") that the verb does not have. Although I opt for understanding *qôl* as an interjection here as in 1:10, 14, I exploit the fact that in English "sound" can be the subject of singing (whether or not it could in Ancient Hebrew), because the more literal rendering "someone is singing" puts more emphasis on the person singing than the Hebrew warrants.

ddd. The *polel* form is often used as a participle in relation to Levitical singers.

eee. Dividing here, we could scan as a bicolon. The Masoretes did not read the following four syllables in the Hebrew as a separate line (cf. n. zz on another four-syllable unit). My division of the verse (tricolon followed by bicolon) underlines the presence of two distinct ideas; see the commentary. Scanning as a tetracolon followed by a tricolon would achieve the same.

fff. Or "rubble." See the commentary for the multiple meanings to be heard here. As ravens feature in LXX and Vulg., some propose to read *'ōrēb* ("raven") for *ḥōreb*, often alongside a change of *qôl* (see n. ccc) to *kôs* (a kind of owl; cf. Lev 11:17; Deut 14:16; Ps 102:6[7]) so that the verb is understood as referring to the hooting of owls and the croaking of ravens; cf. *BHS*; RSV. See Ben Zvi, *Zephaniah*, 181–82, for an argument in favor of retaining the MT against this and other suggestions for emendation; cf. Vlaardingerbroek, *Zephaniah*, 49–50. The translators clearly struggled with the text (as I do). The similarity of sound (*'ōrēb/ḥōreb*) and the reference to a *window* may have inspired thought of a raven (cf. Gen 8:6–7). A homonym for *ḥōreb* (relating to an Akkadian root) with the meaning "bustard" has also been proposed (see *DCH*).

ggg. The subject is often considered indefinite, and many English translations render with the passive, but I see a return to the language of v. 13 with YHWH as the implied subject (see the commentary).

hhh. Hebrew *'arzâ* is not otherwise attested but obviously related to *'erez*, which is traditionally rendered "cedar" but may refer to other conifers as well. The final letter likely indicates not a suffix but a feminine noun, perhaps indicating a collective; cf. *'ēṣâ* ("the wood, trees") in Jer 6:6 in place of the common *'ēṣ*. The context suggests that what is exposed are things made of wood, so if it is a collective, it would stand for *the cedar work(s)*. Others see a specific reference to wainscot (e.g., *HALOT*) or decorative wood paneling (e.g., Berlin, *Zephaniah*, 116).

iii. Literally "the one dwelling" (or "the dweller"). Similarly in the next line, "the one that said."

jjj. This is another long line in the MT and could be divided into two, creating a tetracolon.

kkk. The exact expression *'ănî wə'apsî 'ôd* is also found in Isa 47:8, 10. It is not clear whether the final *yod* indicates a suffix as in *'epes bil'ādāy* ("no one apart from me," Isa 45:6) and *'epes kāmônî* ("no one like me," Isa 46:9) or is an archaic form of the construct. GKC 90l opts for the latter; I find the former slightly more likely, in which case "the expression can be translated literally as 'Me, and my exclusivity still (is),' that is to say 'I, and I exclusively (= I alone), I exist!' " (JM 160m; cf. 93q).

lll. Or "How did she become a desolation?" *'Ēk* is found both as an interrogative to introduce simple (e.g., Jer 36:17) and rhetorical (e.g., Judg 16:15) questions and as an interjection expressing the enormity of a catastrophe as, e.g., in the well-known "How have the mighty fallen!" (2 Sam 1:19; cf., e.g., Isa 14:4, 12; Jer 3:19; Ezek 26:17).

mmm. The *yiqtol* forms may either indicate that the hissing and fist-shaking lie in the future (cf. v. 13) or signal an ongoing, repeated action (whenever people pass by, they hiss and shake their fist).

nnn. Literally "hand." The expression is unusual. Roberts (*Nahum*, 204) interprets it as "scoffing" and translates "waves his hand" (191). Robertson (*Nahum*, 312) offers the less ambiguous rendering "and dismiss her with a wave of the hand." Martin Holland (*Die Propheten Nahum, Habakuk und Zephanja*, WStB, 2nd ed. [Wuppertal: Brockhaus, 1997], 129) thinks of an apotropaic gesture. My translation assumes that the gesture of derision is forceful and maybe threatening (cf. Berlin, *Zephaniah*, 117); see the commentary. The specific Hebrew word for *fist* is probably *'egrōp* (unless this refers to a club with which one strikes), which is only attested in the Bible in Exod 21:18 and Isa 58:4. Note that *yād* is used for shaking the *fist* also in Isa 10:32 and Sir 48:18, albeit with different verbs (*nwp po'lel, nṭh qal*).

Composition

The opening *hôy* (*Oy*) marks the beginning of a new segment here as well as in 3:1. In Habakkuk, we found a collection of *hôy* sayings that belonged closely together (2:6–20), although the commentary treated them in separate sections, as each has a distinctive theme. Here there are only two such *hôy* sayings, and again they likely belong together. Indeed, the opening of ch. 3 is phrased in a way that facilitates the transition from the condemnation of Nineveh to the condemnation of Jerusalem. There is therefore an argument for keeping 2:5–15 and the following section together, but Jerusalem is not like any other regional political entity under YHWH's judgment, and so it seems appropriate to reflect separately on 2:5–15.[293]

This section of the book has three parts: the *hôy* saying about the Philistines (2:5–7), the combined oracle about Moab and the Ammonites (2:8–11), and the saying about Cush and Assyria (2:12–15). But each of these delineations has been contested. As for the first unit, others take 2:4 with 2:5–7 because it, too, concerns Philistia, but this seems to me a mistake. I have already explained why this commentary takes v. 4 with vv. 1–3 (see on the composition of 2:1–4). As for the second part (2:8–11), v. 10 is often considered a later addition and v. 11 a still later saying unrelated to the oracle in vv. 8–9. With Floyd and Sweeney, I read vv. 10–11 as a summary-appraisal.[294] This need not imply that the verses originated at the same time as vv. 8–9, but it means that vv. 10–11 can and should be read as belonging to the prophecy about Moab and the Ammonites; they are not barely related or isolated fragments. While

293. The extent of the first section in ch. 3 is debatable; see on the composition of 3:1–5 below.

294. Floyd, *Minor Prophets 2*, 224; Sweeney, *Zephaniah*, 141–42.

v. 10 could have functioned on its own as a summary-appraisal in terms of its length (cf. Isa 17:14b; 28:29), the length of vv. 10–11 is not without parallel (cf. Isa 14:26–27), and it is characteristic of the form to generalize from the specific, which only happens with v. 11.[295] This suggests that vv. 10–11 originated together. The summary-appraisal might have been added when the oracles in 2:5–15 were put together as a collection.

As for the third unit (2:12–15), many separate 2:12 (Cush) from 2:13–15 (Assyria) on thematic grounds and to highlight the implied reference to the four points of the compass, namely west (2:5–7), east (2:8–11), south (2:12), and north (2:13–15). But v. 12 is rather short to function as an oracle in its own right and not likely to be future-oriented, given the absence of a verb. (A verbless clause usually refers to a present state. This would be the result of a past event, not of something still to happen.) Irsigler acknowledges that the verb forms used in v. 13 suggest that vv. 13–15 originally followed v. 12, which referred to a past event. But he argues that in its present form, v. 12 fulfills a different role in the book and must be understood as future-oriented.[296] The verse was allegedly given a new role with a slight change that produced a first-person divine speech in v. 12 (see the translation note) distinct from the third person speech in vv. 13–15. But there are problems with making v. 12 refer to the future, not least the necessity for reading the designation "Cushites" as a reference to Egypt,[297] or maybe another term for Assyria.[298] It seems better to accept that the verse does indeed refer to a past event. The shift from the divine first person in v. 12 to the third person in v. 13 has parallels in analogous shifts in the earlier sections and is not itself a reason to separate v. 12 from v. 13.[299] The link between the destruction of Cush in v. 12 and the announcement of the future destruction of Assyria in vv. 13–15 can also be argued on thematic grounds (see below), and this supports the conclusion

295. See Brevard S. Childs, *Isaiah and the Assyrian Crisis*, SBT II/3 (London: SCM Press, 1967), 128–36, for the summary-appraisal form. Sweeney (*Isaiah 1–39*, 529) adds Jer 13:25, but this is in divine speech, which is different from Childs's examples in Isaiah.

296. Irsigler, *Zefanja*, 212, 283–93. See also Vlaardingerbroek, *Zephaniah*, 151–52, for a weighing up of different perspectives; he is inclined to read v. 12 as a prophecy of judgment against Egypt, but see below.

297. Irsigler, *Zefanja*, 293. He shows at length (288–90) why such an equation is hugely problematic; his claim that what was impossible for the author (using "Cush" as a reference to Egypt) could become feasible for a later reader and redactor is not persuasive.

298. As noted above, Ivan J. Ball (*Zephaniah*, 140–41) identifies the *kûšîm* as "Kassites." Berlin (*Zephaniah*, 113) also sees a reference to "the descendants of the forebearer of the Assyrian empire."

299. Note that Irsigler (*Zefanja*, 293) allows that the earliest form of 2:12–14 (with YHWH in the third person) may have been originally attached to the earliest form of 2:4–6, in which he includes the first-person divine speech in v. 5bβ.

that vv. 12–15 form a single paragraph. Verse 15 seems to function in a way similar to vv. 10–11, which means that we should take it with the preceding rather than the following.[300] Its perspective is post-judgment. It is possible that the verse was added after 612, maybe alongside 3:6–7 (see below), but given its climactic position at the end of the oracles against other nations, it is also conceivable that a future situation was here rhetorically assumed in order to stress the certainty of the coming punishment.

The references to the *remnant* of Judah and God's people (vv. 7, 9) do not, as often argued, require a post-monarchic date for these parts of the text. It is possible that the reference to *the remnant of my people* (and *the survivors of my nation*) in v. 9 alludes to the fall of the Northern Kingdom, as argued by Sweeney. In my view, however, it is less plausible that *the remnant of the house of Judah* in v. 7 reflects the extent to which Sennacherib had decimated Judah's territory, as Sweeney also argues.[301] More likely, both references to a *remnant* assume the judgment announced in ch. 1. This does not require actual experience of the disaster; it only involves the firm conviction that the disaster is going to happen. The thematic development from apparently total annihilation in the announcement of the Day of YHWH (ch. 1) via the glimmer of hope offered in 2:1–4 ("perhaps") to the firm expectation that a remnant would survive seems rhetorically plausible. It thus does not necessitate that the material derives from different times, although this remains a possibility.[302] Suppose that something like 2:5–3:8 was at one point delivered as a public address, with 3:1 intended to shock the audience, who at first might have thought that the condemned city is still Nineveh before realizing that Jerusalem is the real target. This would have worked better if Judah's decimation and restoration had not yet been anticipated by references to a remnant. On such a reconstruction of the oral history of these oracles, it would be plausible that the references to a remnant are later additions. But there are many other possibilities, and there is no way for us to know which parts of the book of Zephaniah featured in any public oral address. Within the book, 2:5–15 does in any case follow the announcement of comprehensive judgment on Judah and Jerusalem. Consequently, the rhetorical effect of hearing or reading 3:1ff. after 2:5–15 cannot be quite the same as the one usually claimed for Amos 1:3–2:16, which surprises an audience that gladly heard about judgment on other nations with an announcement of judgment

300. In the Göttingen Septuagint, the verse is numbered 3:1 and apparently taken with what follows.

301. Sweeney, *Zephaniah*, 130, 140; cf. *King Josiah*, 194–95.

302. Irsigler (*Zefanja*, 193) thinks that 3:2, 6–7 demonstrate that the hope expressed in 2:3 came to nothing. See my comments on the composition of 3:1–5.

on their own. Within its literary context, the ambiguity at the beginning of ch. 3 is not designed to shock but to drive home the equation of Jerusalem with Nineveh.

The diversity of language and form in this section suggests that the various sayings collected in this chapter might have been formulated at different times for different occasions. But whether they once formed independent addresses or were developed only in written form over time is impossible to tell. Specific rhetorical situations for the various oracles are difficult to reconstruct. Christensen argues that Zephaniah's prophecy offered a basis for Josiah's political ambitions,[303] but this is unlikely to be correct, certainly as far as any specific foreign policy objectives are concerned. The lone possible exception might have been supporting a desire for independence from Assyria (early in Josiah's reign). There is little evidence in either the biblical text or archaeological research for the expansionism sometimes attributed to Josiah.[304] Even apart from Josiah's politics, there is probably nothing in this section that is specific to the time of Josiah's reign until we get to v. 12, which, in my reading, looks back to the fall of Thebes in 663 and forward to the destruction of Nineveh in 612. In other words, it points to a similar timeframe as the prophecy of Nahum (see Nah 3:8–13). But there is also nothing, in my view, that would be out of place *in the days of Josiah*. Indeed, the focus on the Philistines without reference to the Phoenicians and especially on Moab and the Ammonites without reference to Edom seems more at home in the seventh century than at a time after the destruction of Jerusalem.

Ben Zvi, who believes the book of Zephaniah to be a post-monarchic composition, explains the absence of Edom and Egypt among the targets in Zeph 2 with the observation that these, unlike the entities mentioned, had not been conquered by Nebuchadnezzar II.[305] He does not directly address the question why such a concern should be operative in the composition of Zephaniah but not of other prophetic books like Jeremiah that do contain such oracles (Jer 46:1–26; 49:7–22). Perhaps he hints at an explanation when he observes that the Edomite kingdom seems to have come to an end in ca. 553 and Egypt was conquered in 525. The final redaction of the book of Zephaniah would have taken place in the Babylonian period, at a time when the community might have been aware of the movements Nebuchadnezzar did and did not make. Ben Zvi does not say so, but he might well date the final

---

303. Duane L. Christensen, "Zephaniah 2:4–15," 669–82; cf. Ryou, *Oracles*, esp. 314–15; Vlaardingerbroek, *Zephaniah*, 128–29, 134, 143; Sweeney, *Zephaniah*, 126, 135–36.

304. Cf. Floyd, *Minor Prophets 2*, 205–6; Irsigler, *Zefanja*, 215. See "The Historical Setting of the Book" (p. 432).

305. Ben Zvi, *Zephaniah*, 298–306.

composition of the book of Jeremiah to a later time, when Nebuchadnezzar's movements were a more distant memory.[306] This must remain uncertain because we are not in a position to reconstruct Nebuchadnezzar's Transjordanian campaigns with confidence, let alone what Judeans may have known or thought about them. Ben Zvi's claim that Babylon conquered Moab and the Ammonites but not Edom is largely based on the fact that Josephus only says that Nebuchadnezzar subjugated Moab and the Ammonites but is silent about Edom (*Antiquities* 10.181–82).[307] We have no Babylonian records to confirm such a Transjordanian campaign. Some have argued that Edom, unlike her neighbors, remained intact politically until the mid-sixth century,[308] when the last Babylonian king, Nabonidus (555–539 BC), in the third year of his reign "besieged and probably captured the '[town of A]dummu' (i.e., town of Edom), most likely Busayra."[309] At this stage, we cannot be certain that Moab and the Ammonites had been conquered and ceased to be recognizable political entities before that, as Ben Zvi assumes.

The earlier view that the Ammonites ceased to exist in the sixth century was based on Nelson Glueck's survey work and has been rejected in the light of more recent archaeological work. Burnett observes that "the archaeological record at Tall Umayri . . . shows no evidence of destruction but rather a thriving economy in the Ammonite heartland continuing under the Babylonian Empire." He also points out that Josephus used *hypēkoa* ("subjugated") rather than a word indicating conquest and destruction.[310] But this is only a single site, and Lipschits suggests that it may have served as a local administrative center like Mizpah in Judah (after the destruction of the capital?).[311] It is possible that the king of the Ammonites became a vassal in 604 and his land a Babylonian province in 582.[312] If the Ammonites offered less resis-

---

306. Irsigler (*Zefanja*, 217–18) is both critical and appreciative of Ben Zvi's proposal (215–16) and in the end follows him in arguing that the book of Zephaniah was essentially completed between ca. 580 and ca. 550.

307. See John Lindsay, "Babylonian Kings and Edom, 605–550 BC," *PEQ* 108 (1976): 28–29, for a discussion of this text.

308. Lindsay, "Babylonian Kings," 23–39.

309. Joel S. Burnett, "Transjordan: The Ammonites, Moabites and Edomites," in *The World around the Old Testament: The People and Places of the Ancient Near East*, ed. Bill T. Arnold and Brent A. Strawn (Grand Rapids: Baker Academic, 2016), 338. Burnett notes some archaeological evidence consistent with this. Cf. *ANET*, 305, for the text and Lindsay, "Babylonian Kings," 33–36, for a detailed defense of the identification of the region as Edom. Lindsay argues that the city might have been Elath (36–38).

310. Burnett, "Transjordan," 320 (cf. 328–29 for Moab). Cf. Oded Lipschits, "Ammon in Transition from Vassal Kingdom to Babylonian Province," *BASOR* 335 (2004): 38.

311. Lipschits, "Ammon," 44.

312. Lipschits, "Ammon," 39–41. He acknowledges, however, that it is possible that Ammonite royalty was retained by Babylon as a vassal after 582 (44).

tance to the Babylonians than others, their capital might have suffered less destruction than Jerusalem and the Philistine cities. The evidence available to us allows that the Ammonites and Moab alongside Judah and the Philistines lost their status as kingdoms sooner than Edom. Lipschits stresses that there is evidence of discontinuity in the Ammonite region and that we do not yet know the fate of Rabbat-Ammon, the capital of the Ammonites.[313]

In the final analysis, we lack the historical and archaeological data to reconstruct Babylonian policy in Ammon, Moab, and Edom. The reconstruction required on Ben Zvi's hypothesis remains a possibility, if one allows that readers would not have expected the words against Moab and Ammon to be fulfilled to the letter. This seems a fair assumption, given the prevalence of hyperbolic and formulaic language in prophetic oracles. Note that Jer 48:47 and 49:6 speak of a restoration of fortunes after desolation and that Zech 9:5-6 contains a word against the four Philistine cities that suggests that the Babylonians had not made a complete end to them.

Another possibility for explaining the absence of Edom arises from considering the likely reason for the exceptionally hostile attitude to Edom found in much prophetic literature. Assis argues that this was the result not only of the events surrounding the fall of Jerusalem and Edomite encroachment on Judean territory in the sixth century but also of the way these were perceived by Israel through the prism of the struggle between Esau and Jacob for their father's birthright and control over the promised land. Consequently, "anti-Edomite oracles were meant to instil into the hearts of the people that, despite the destruction, Israel is still the chosen people and the sins of Edom against Judah will not remain unpunished."[314] Such a message would not fit Zephaniah's prophecy, in which the judgment on various political entities is presented as part of one comprehensive, punitive action of YHWH that includes Judah. The future inheritance, therefore, cannot be promised to Judah over against Edom but only to a remnant of Judah over against the nation as a whole. In addition, the very fact that Edom could stand for all of humanity by way of a wordplay (*'ĕdôm-'ādām*) might have made it less suitable to be named as (just) one further instance among other entities.

There are thus a number of possible explanations for the absence of an oracle against Edom, so it would not be safe to draw any firm conclusions from it. Still, in my view, the absence of an oracle against Egypt is probably best explained by an early date for this material (630s?).[315] This would also explain the absence of an oracle against Edom and maybe also against the

---

313. Lipschits, "Ammon," 42-44.

314. Elie Assis, "Why Edom? On the Hostility Towards Jacob's Brother in Prophetic Sources," *VT* 56 (2006): 19.

315. See "The Historical Setting of the Book" (pp. 432-43).

Phoenicians, all of whom come more into prophetic view as the fall of Jerusalem draws closer (cf. Ezek 25–32, 35).

Zephaniah 2:5–7 lacks any rationale for the judgment, and this would be true even if v. 4 were added. This may suggest a dependence on ch. 1, if we read ch. 1 as an announcement of the destruction of the entire region for attitudes and behavior relating to the socioeconomic structures of the time.[316] The reuse of *kənaʿan* (*Canaan*, 2:5; cf. 1:11, *merchant people*) facilitates this, and we may note that the punishment in ch. 2 is described throughout in terms of depopulation, which picks up 1:2–3. The oracle against the Philistines in Jer 47 likewise lacks a specific accusation. In Jeremiah, the "rising water" motif links the condemnation of the Philistines with the oracle against Egypt in the preceding chapter (47:2; cf. 46:7–8) and suggests, similarly to Zephaniah, that the devastation of the Philistines is part of a more comprehensive movement. Moab and the Ammonites, like Assyria later, are condemned for arrogance and pride that, by way of contrast, links with the call to humility in 2:3.[317] A rationale for the destruction of Cush is also absent, but this is the least surprising, given that on the present reading the verse is a historical flashback that prepares for the oracle against Assyria rather than an announcement of future punishment. Insofar as the defeat referenced here marked the humiliation of the empire the Nubians had established, this again fits with the motif of the contrast of pride and humility. While this is a common enough motif in oracles about other nations (as well as oracles concerning Israel and Judah), it is nevertheless noteworthy that the chapter does not offer any other specific condemnation of the kind one finds occasionally elsewhere (e.g., in Amos 1). But even if the lack of specific accusations in oracles about foreign nations is unremarkable and therefore does not suggest that these oracles could not have existed without the preceding material, the function of 2:5–15 and the following section within their literary context is to support the exhortation of 2:1–4. These sayings add detail to the description of the catastrophe to come upon the whole region rather than dealing with the specific culpability of various nations. The ultimate addressees are Judahites. They were most likely the actual addressees from the inception, even if rhetorically the oracles address foreign entities. (It is conceivable that in some historical contexts, oracles about other nations were delivered to their

---

316. A rationale is offered in Amos 1:6–8 (assuming that the accusation against Gaza also holds for the other cities) and in Ezek 25:15–17 but only implied in Zech 9:5–8 (v. 7!) where Philistine towns are linked with northern cities (vv. 1–4). Isa 14:28–32 apparently addresses Philistine plotting against Assyria.

317. Irsigler (*Zefanja*, 213, 217, 261) believes that the original oracles contained no accusations. He sees historical events of a later period reflected in the accusations. I relate the accusations to the Neo-Assyrian rather than the Neo-Babylonian period.

representatives—e.g., foreign delegates negotiating common political action in gatherings in Jerusalem—but this would have been the exception rather than the rule. The vast majority of oracles ostensibly addressing foreign entities were from the beginning designed to be heard by the people of God rather than the nations addressed.)

Adele Berlin argues that Gen 10 "serves as the conceptual undergirding, and to a large extent the literary model, for Zeph. 2:5–15."[318] She points out that *Canaan* "is never used during the monarchic period to refer to contemporary Philistines" and notes that the exact phrase *coastal nations* is used only here (2:11) and in Gen 10:5, where it refers to descendants of Japheth. She proposes that Zephaniah's prophecy made the contemporary political reality "to look like a realization of the tradition of Gen. 9:26–28: Canaan will become subservient to his brothers, and Japheth will reside in the tents of Shem."[319] It is an intriguing proposal, especially as it takes up Oded's idea that Ham represents city dwellers in contrast to nomads (Shem) and seafarers (Japheth).[320] The latter idea would fit well with the polemic against urban elites in Zephaniah and the stress in ch. 2, also noticed by Berlin, on pastoral elements, with greater focus on the aftermath of destruction in deurbanization than on the act of destruction itself. Nevertheless, as others have pointed out, there are a number of problems with the details of her proposal.[321] For example, the mention of Sodom and Gomorrah in both Zeph 2:9 and Gen 10:19 is hardly enough to associate Moab and the Ammonites with Ham. This is especially so since any who know Gen 10 are likely also familiar with the story of the origin of Moab and the Ammonites in Gen 19:30–38 in the aftermath of the destruction of Sodom and Gomorrah, which associates them with descendants of Shem. Ashur (Zeph 2:13) is also explicitly associated with Shem rather than Ham in Gen 10:22.

---

318. See Adele Berlin, *Zephaniah*; "Zephaniah's Oracle against the Nations and an Israelite Cultural Myth," in *Fortunate the Eyes That See: Essays in Honor of David Noel Freedman in Celebration of His Seventieth Birthday*, ed. Astrid B. Beck et al. (Grand Rapids: Eerdmans, 1995), 175–84. This and the following citation are from the essay (178).

319. Berlin, "Zephaniah's Oracle," 183.

320. Bustenay Oded, "The Table of Nations (Genesis 10)—A Socio-Cultural Approach," *ZAW* 98 (1986): 14–31; cf. Ellen van Wolde, *Stories of the Beginning: Genesis 1–11 and Other Creation Stories* (London: SCM, 1996), 162. Yigal Levin ("The Family of Man: The Genre and Purpose of Genesis 10," in *Looking at the Ancient Near East and the Bible through the Same Eyes—Minha LeAhron, A Tribute to Aaron Skaist*, ed. Kathleen Abraham and Joseph Fleishman [Bethesda: CDL Press, 2012], 303) rightly notes: "This theory leaves landlocked Madai (Media) son of Japeth, tribal Havilah and Sheba of Ham and Shem's definitely urbanized Elam and Ashur in need of explaining."

321. See Floyd, *Minor Prophets 2*, 206–11; cf. Irsigler, *Zefanja*, 214.

Commentary

5 The Philistines were a people whose roots may have been in the Balkan peninsula or possibly in Anatolia. They emigrated from the Aegean region during the transitional period between the Late Bronze Age and the Early Iron Age and settled on the southern coastal strip of Canaan in the early twelfth century,[322] becoming *inhabitants of the coastal portion*. Their arrival was apparently part of a wider movement of "sea peoples" (so in Egyptian documents) who came into conflict with Ramses III. *Cherethites* is here an alternative term for *Philistines*, as also in Ezek 25:16.[323] If "Pelethites" reflects an alternative pronunciation for *Philistines*, the expression "the Cherethites and the Pelethites" (singular forms used with collective meaning, always in this order) in 2 Sam 8:18; 15:18 (with Gittites); 20:7, 23; 1 Kgs 1:38, 44; and 1 Chr 18:17 suggests that *Cherethites* and *Philistines* were, at least formerly, distinct groups although closely associated with each other.[324] The designation *Cherethites* stresses the foreign origin of the *Philistines* and may be related to Crete (cf. Amos 9:7; Deut 2:23).[325] Indeed, there is some archaeological evidence that links the Philistines more closely to Crete and Cyprus than to Mycenaean culture in the Aegean.[326] It may be that some migrated from the Aegean to Crete and Cyprus, others toward Egypt (where they were repelled). Over time, there was likely some interchange between groups in the Eastern Mediterranean coastal regions and the Mediterranean islands as well as Phoenicia. This may have led to secondary migrations, but the details of the origin of the Philistines are not relevant here. It is sufficient to note that people in Judah knew that the Philistines were not originally from the Eastern Mediterranean, and this knowledge is likely reflected here. The expression *ḥebel hayyām* (*coastal portion*) is unique to Zephaniah; elsewhere *ḥôp hayyām* ("seacoast") is used (Jer 47:7; Ezek 25:16). Because *ḥebel* can also

322. For a detailed discussion, see Assaf Yasur-Landau, *Philistines and Aegean Migration in the Late Bronze Age* (Cambridge: Cambridge University Press, 2010), esp. chs. 6–8.

323. Cf. 1 Sam 30:14, where "the Negev of the Kerethite(s)" apparently distinguishes the Philistine-controlled part of the Negev from parts controlled by others.

324. But see the discussion in Carl S. Ehrlich, *The Philistines in Transition: A History from ca. 1000–730 BCE*, SHCANE 10 (Leiden: Brill, 1996), 37–41. The evidence for the view that the Cherethites and Pelethites are equivalent to Cretans and Philistines is at best circumstantial, as he notes. It still seems more plausible to me than the proposed alternatives.

325. See Irsigler, *Zefanja*, 239–41. It also enables wordplay with *kərōt* (*herders' camps*) in the next verse.

326. See especially Aren M. Maeir and Louise A. Hitchcock, "Absence Makes the *Hearth* Grow Fonder: Searching for the Origins of the Philistine Hearth," *Eretz-Israel* 30 (2011): 46–64, on the variability in Philistine hearth construction techniques that finds parallels on Crete and Cyprus but not among Mycenaean hearths.

mean "rope," it has been argued that it refers here to a long, narrow strip of land, but this is an inadequate description of Philistine territory. More likely, the connection with "rope" is that ropes were used as measuring lines, not least for allocating territory (cf. Amos 7:17; Ps 78:55; metaphorically Deut 32:9; Ps 16:6).[327] Combined with the use of the designation *Cherethites*, the use of *ḥebel hayyām* hints that the coastal region was apportioned to the Philistines as other parts of the land had been apportioned to Israel/Judah. This is strengthened by the use of the term *Canaan* in the direct address, *against you. "Canaan," land of the Philistines*, which in addition provides a link with 1:11. The idea of apportionment prepares for the redistribution of the region to *the remnant of the house of Judah* in v. 7.

Stern rightly observes that the

> rich Philistine towns managed to retain their semi-independent status and their commercial and internal freedom by paying high tributes to the Assyrian court. Caught between Assyria and Egypt, they developed a particular flexibility, continually adapting themselves to the fluctuating political situation, at times swearing allegiance to both sides. They thus had the capacity to endure, while greater, stronger kingdoms elsewhere were totally annihilated.[328]

They certainly needed greater flexibility than the Transjordanian kingdoms. Egypt dominated them for forty years, and gradually the kings ruling various Philistine political units shifted their loyalty from Assyria to Egypt.[329] Moab and Ammon, by contrast, were of less interest to Egypt and, therefore, did not need to negotiate different imperial powers in the same way, although for them, too, the question arose every now and again whether it might be safe to stop paying tribute. The destruction announced for the Philistines is attributed directly to YHWH but, as in ch. 1, this does not mean that the oracle envisages a divine punishment without human agency; it merely means that the focus remains entirely on the ultimate cause. One might expect a political commentary to identify the agent of destruction as Egyptian or Mesopotamian, given the Philistines' place on the map, but the oracle is not intended as a political commentary of that sort. We do not know whether the prophet had an inkling of the human agent. The final oracle in the chapter suggests that it was not going to be Assyria, but the lack of an oracle against Egypt leaves it open whether the comprehensive judgment would come from

---

327. The same considerations apply to the LXX's use of *schoinisma* (see the translation note). Sweeney (*Zephaniah*, 126–27) sees a multifaceted play on words.

328. Stern, *Archaeology*, 104.

329. Stern, *Archaeology*, 107.

the south (Egypt) or from the north (Babylon). Post-monarchical readers would have known that it was the latter, and the canonical placement of Zephaniah following Habakkuk underlines this.

The verse first addresses the *inhabitants* with a declaration that *the word of YHWH* is against them; then it addresses the *land*, announcing destruction *until no inhabitant* is left. It thus forms an *inclusio* (*inhabitants—no inhabitant*) that highlights the movement from existence to non-existence.[330] The first bicolon is in effect the prophet's introduction to the divine speech cited in the second bicolon. This may have suggested the use of *the word of YHWH is against you* rather than, for example, "YHWH of hosts is against you." But within the context of the book, the phrase *the word of YHWH* echoes 1:1 and so encourages the idea that *the word* we have already heard in ch. 1 is (also) against *the nation of Cherethites*.[331] In other words, at the level of the book, *the word of YHWH* is not only found in what follows but also in what has preceded.

As noted under "Composition," *Canaan* provides another link with ch. 1. While it is not likely that it should be rendered "merchant" here, the use of this designation for the *land of the Philistines* enables the prophet to accomplish two key tasks: (1) to mark the Philistines (like Israel) as immigrants who were apportioned part of the land of Canaan, and (2) to characterize them as traders. For the same reason, *Canaan* is used in Isa 23:11 in an oracle against Tyre (cf. "merchants" in v. 8), and in Ezekiel, even Babylon is called "land of Canaan/merchants" (16:29; cf. 17:4). There are a few instances in which *kənaʿan* is used for a trader in a neutral context (cf. Job 41:6[40:30]; Prov 31:24), but *rôkēl* may have been the more common term for "traders" without negative associations (cf. 1 Kgs 10:15; Neh 3:31–32; 13:20; Song 3:6; Nah 3:16). By contrast, the cheating trader in Hos 12:7(8) is readily termed *kənaʿan*.

6 At first one may think that the references to *shepherds* here and to *the house of Judah* in the next verse, the latter taking possession of the land, contradicts the message of complete annihilation in v. 5 (and v. 4). But this is not so, and not only because the message in v. 5a is specifically against the Philistines, none of whom are expected to return in vv. 6–7. The removal of the population in v. 5b refers to the complete destruction of the Philistine cities. This does not preclude a return of people or even require the absence of any survivors. We may compare the use of the phrase *mēʾên yôšēb* (*until no inhabitant is left*) in announcements of Judah's destruction (Isa 5:9; 6:11; Jer 4:7; 26:9; 33:10; 34:22; 44:22). They make it difficult to argue that the phrase

---

330. Cf. Ryou, *Oracles*, 209.

331. If 1:1 is redactional, as usually assumed, this may strengthen the idea that *the word of YHWH is against you* is a later addition (see above). I am open to this possibility, although I am not entirely convinced that 1:1 has to be editorial.

was meant to imply that no one would live again in the place under judgment since the ultimate outlook for Judah and Jerusalem in the prophetic books is clearly more hopeful.[332] Neither should we assume that Jer 46:19 implied that Egypt would be uninhabited in the future. The announcement of complete annihilation leaves it open what might happen afterward.[333] It is nevertheless significant that there is no hint of city building here. Urban life gives way to the nomadic life of shepherds, and this underlines that it is not simply a question of Judeans replacing Philistines. No, the main change that needed to happen has nothing to do with ethnicity but with a question of different ways of life. For Zephaniah, the life of the urban elites embodies pride and arrogance; the life of the poor who glean leftovers and of shepherds who live in the fields embodies dependence and humility.[334] To support this general theme, Zeph 2 focuses more on the aftermath of destruction than on describing the act of destroying itself. It is worth bearing in mind that in this culture, shepherds took their sheep out to graze free range rather than in enclosed fields, and often the wilderness was the pasturage. We should not think of a modern, Western rural idyll of meadows and green pastures.[335] The *sheep-folds* too are enclosures with rough, dry-stone walls, often quickly thrown together to provide temporary shelter while in transit. The overall picture is not a romantic one but one of relative desolation. The motif is picked up in 2:13–15, probably not so much to create a close link between the Philistines and the Assyrians[336] but by way of *inclusio*, giving prominence to that theme within ch. 2. Granted, it is true that the Philistines and the Assyrians (with specific reference to Nineveh) represent urban culture better than Moab and the Ammonites. That means that the motif of cities becoming countryside that is only able to sustain grazing flocks fits better with these oracles than with the oracles about the less urbanized Moabites and Ammonites. But it is also true that there is a logic independent of the *inclusio* that demands

---

332. Jer 33:10, which in addition uses *mē'ên 'ādām ûmē'ên bəhēmâ* ("without human or animal"), is especially noteworthy. See also Jer 2:15, which uses a different particle (*mibbəlî yōšēb*; cf. 9:11[10]), looking back to an event that has already happened to Israel, indicating that this language could be used also for a heavy decimation of the population short of complete eradication.

333. Cf. Jer 48:9 (with reference to Moab, which is promised restoration in v. 47, albeit probably in a later oracle) and 51:29, 37 (with reference to Babylon, which may have been expected to remain a perpetual ruin).

334. There is no hint here of sheep-owners who live in towns and cities while shepherds watch their flocks, nor of the rearing of oxen and cows. The word *flock* only refers to smaller animals: goats and sheep.

335. Contra Ryou, *Oracles*, 217, who evokes serenity and tranquillity and speaks of "a joyful life without fear."

336. Irsigler, *Zefanja*, 246.

that the Philistines be mentioned first (linking with v. 4, which portrays the judgment as being on its way to Jerusalem) and the Assyrians last (being the climax and the point of comparison with Jerusalem).

7 Developing the motif in v. 6 metaphorically, the flock is now identified as *the remnant of the house of Judah* who will be given *the coastal portion* as their allotment; it will now be their *portion . . . by the sea*.[337] It is they who *shall graze* (typically the predicate of "flock") and *lie down* (often the predicate of "flock"; cf. Ps 23:2). The reference to *Judah* may draw attention to the tribal allotment in Josh 15:12.[338] It includes this territory, which, however, had never been held in possession by Judah. The line *by the sea they shall graze* is short compared with those surrounding it. Rudolph suggests that *yômām* ("by day"), corresponding to *in the evening* in the next line, has dropped out.[339] But *in the evening* does not require a corresponding phrase in the preceding line because grazing is arguably the unmarked normality for a flock and need not be qualified further. Also, *in the evening* may subtly pick up *at midday* from v. 4, perhaps further underlining the speed of events, even though there the temporal qualification goes with *Ashdod* rather than *Ashkelon*. Following the line division adopted here, the shortness of the line *by the sea they shall graze* corresponds to the shortness of the last line of the verse; in this way both the bicolon and the tricolon in this verse end with an extra-short line that poetically suggests finality. Even without the addition of *yômām* ("by day"), there is an implicit merism that corresponds to the combination of *grazing lands* (during the day) and *sheepfolds* (for the night) in the previous verse. This combination suggests (1) that the whole time, day and night, there is nothing present but shepherds and flocks (v. 6); and (2) that the *remnant of the house of Judah* that takes permanent possession is not at any time to be driven away. Irsigler believes that such an expectation of rehabilitation must be postexilic, even though such a takeover of Philistine, Moabite, and Ammonite territories (vv. 9–10) looks no more realistic in the Persian period than earlier. He acknowledges that these verses do not reflect a desire for power and possession, but he detects in them a sense of compensation for lost territories,[340] a sense I do not share in the same way.

The phrase *šə'ērît yəhûdâ* ("remnant of Judah") is found a few times in

337. The elegant breakup of the phrase *coastal portion* from vv. 5–6 (which could also be rendered "portion by the sea") into *portion* and *by the sea* in this verse is reconstructed; see the translation note.

338. With thanks to Bob Hubbard, the NICOT series editor, for pointing this out.

339. Rudolph, *Micha*, 277. Orthographic similarities between *ywmm* and the word preceding it would be responsible for the loss.

340. Irsigler, *Zefanja*, 250–54. There are many other commentators who are inclined to see later redactional insertions here; cf. Vlaardingerbroek, *Zephaniah*, 132. See also the discussion under "Composition" above. My point is not so much to claim that the text did

Jeremiah with reference to the community left after the destruction of Jerusalem (40:15; 42:15, 19; 43:5; 44:12, 14, 28; cf. 40:11 and "remnant of Jerusalem" in 24:8) but never in the form used here with *house*, even though *bêt-yəhûdâ* ("house of Judah") is attested in Jeremiah (3:18; 12:14; 13:11; 31:27, 31; 33:14; 36:3). The inclusion of *house* in the phrase anticipates the reference to *the houses of Ashkelon* later in the verse. But why is *Ashkelon* singled out among the Philistine cities? With sometimes one, sometimes another Philistine principality trying to secure greater independence, Ashkelon was not atypical or special among the Philistines as far as relationships with imperial powers are concerned. The leaders of the Leon Levy expedition to Ashkelon summarized its recent history up to the days of Josiah:

> Assyrian sources indicate that after the Assyrian monarch Tiglath-pileser III invaded Philistia in 734 B.C., Mitinti I, king of Ashkelon, acknowledged his suzerainty, but revolted shortly thereafter (*ANET*, 283). Mitinti was then replaced by his son Rukibtu, who headed a pro-Assyrian regime. Ashkelon remained loyal to Assyria until late in the eighth century B.C., when Ṣidqa usurped the throne in Ashkelon and joined Hezekiah, king of Judah, in an alliance against Assyria (*ANET*, 287f.). Together they deposed Padi, king of Ekron, who, like Mitinti of Ashdod and Ṣillibel of Gaza, had remained loyal to Assyria. In 701 B.C. Sennacherib brought an end to the rebellion and restored Padi to his throne. He deported Ṣidqa to Assyria, replacing him with Šarruludari, son of Rukibtu, the king who had earlier followed a pro-Assyrian policy. But Ashkelon lost and never regained a substantial part of its kingdom, which at one time included Joppa, Bnei-Brak, Azor, and Beth-Dagon. This coastal region (in the vicinity of modern Tel Aviv) was annexed to the directly administered Assyrian province of Dor in the north.[341]

There is some debate about the extent to which Ashkelon experienced a period of renewed prosperity in the latter part of the seventh century, as may be suggested by the creation of a large marketplace only a decade or so before its destruction. But at the moment, we have little to suggest that Ashkelon stood out in terms of economic or political success. Its importance may have been more of a strategic nature. Its proximity to the Egyptian border arguably gave it greater political and military significance than Ashdod or Ekron:

---

not undergo any changes over time but to indicate that I do not find the specific arguments and identification of glosses compelling.

341. Lawrence E. Stager and J. David Schloen, "Introduction: Ashkelon and Its Inhabitants," in *Ashkelon 1: Introduction and Overview (1985–2006)*, ed. Lawrence E. Stager et al. (Winona Lake, IN: Eisenbrauns, 2008), 8. Cf. Na'aman, "Ashkelon."

through it, Egypt could exercise a considerable amount of control in the region. (Gaza is closer to Egypt but maybe a little too far inland and too far south to act as a convenient springboard into the region?) Indeed, it is possible that by the late seventh century, the heavily fortified port town hosted an Egyptian garrison mainly consisting of Greek mercenaries.[342] In any case, Nebuchadnezzar's complete destruction of the city shows that he was keen to make it impossible for Egypt to retain or reestablish a foothold there.

Some argue that Ashkelon was the heart of the integrated local economic system referred to previously.[343] For some part of the seventh century at least, there seem to have been specialized zones of production for wine (Ashkelon and the coastal plain), olive oil and textiles (the inner coastal plain and Shephelah), grain (the Judean highlands), and sheep and goat herding (the Judean desert). The port of Ashkelon would have facilitated maritime trade of the Philistine-Judean region to the north with the Phoenicians and maybe south to Egypt.[344] Gaza was located slightly inland and may not have had much of a port, while Ashkelon was the southernmost Eastern Mediterranean port city. Presumably, for this reason it proved critical for trade between, on the one hand, Egypt and Edom (and maybe Arabian tribes via the Negev) and, on the other hand, Tyre, Sidon, Cyprus, Crete, and maybe the Aegean and beyond. In sum, it seems that singling out *Ashkelon* keeps our focus on the to-and-fro of trade with which the lying down of animals stands in marked contrast.

YHWH their God in effect takes on the role of shepherd to the flock of the remnant of Judah. As he paid close attention to the Jerusalem elites to *punish* them (1:8, 9, 12; cf. 3:7), so he is attentive to *the remnant of the house of Judah* now, taking up the same verb.[345] This favorable attentiveness of YHWH is the truly decisive gain, as Irsigler rightly points out.[346] Interestingly, Isaiah's oracle concerning Philistia, dated to the year King Ahaz died (Isa 14:28; around 715?), uses the same verbs as here to speak of "the firstborn

---

342. As argued by Fantalkin, "Why Did Nebuchadnezzar II Destroy Ashkelon?" But see Jane C. Waldbaum, "Greek Pottery," in Stager et al., *Ashkelon 3*, 127–338, for an argument against the supposition that the presence of Greek pottery in the Levant suggests the presence of Greek mercenaries.

343. Alexander Fantalkin, "Neo-Assyrian Involvement in the Southern Coastal Plain of Israel: Old Concepts and New Interpretations," in Zelig Aster and Faust, *Southern Levant*, 162–85, argues to the contrary that Ashkelon came to prominence only under Egyptian domination subsequent to the fall of Assyria.

344. See Faust and Weiss, "Economic System"; Faust, "Settlement and Demography"; cf. Gitin, "Neo-Assyrian Empire."

345. Cf. Ryou, *Oracles*, 219–21. He notes the use of the verb in Jer 23:2–4 in the context of shepherd imagery.

346. Irsigler, *Zephaniah*, 254.

of the poor" as grazing and the needy lying down in safety (Isa 14:30).[347] The verbs are again used in Zeph 3:13, after the *remnant of Israel* is described as *a humble and powerless people* in v. 12 (using *dāl*, as in Isa 14:30, but with *'ānî* for Isaiah's *'ebyôn*). These cross-references help to draw 2:7 and 3:12–13 together as complementary images of the ideal society.[348] For now, the destruction of urbanity and commerce with no prospect of rebuilding cities leaves space only for the humble life of shepherds. In 3:12–13, we will learn that it is not urban life as such that was the problem but the pride and arrogance that was typically found there.

8 Assyrian records of tribute payments suggest that both *Moab* and *the Ammonites* were Assyrian vassals over an extended period of time.[349] From all we know, the Ammonites were loyal Assyrians vassals from 734 onwards,[350] while *Moab*, along with Judah and others, was once part of an unsuccessful alliance against Assyria during the reign of Sargon II (722–705).[351] *Moab*, however, proved itself a faithful vassal of Assurbanipal (668–627) in a successful campaign against Arab tribes in Transjordan and Syria.[352] There may be evidence for an increase in Ammonite economic and political power and the expansion of the Ammonite borders in the seventh century. "Ammonite remains have been reported at Hesban [Heshbon] in the south, [Tell el-] Mazar in the Jordan Valley, and the Baqʻa Valley in the north."[353] A region's

347. The term "firstborn of the poor" is presumably a superlative ("the poorest of the poor"). It is possible that the text originally read *bkry* (*bəkārāy*, "on my pastures") and was changed by accident to *bkwry* (*bəkôrê*, "firstborn of"); see *HALOT*. In this case, there would also be a link with the word for *pastures* in Zeph 2:6.

348. Cf. Ben Zvi, *Zephaniah*, 307, who notes the cross-references between the two places in Zephaniah but not the contribution Isa 14 might make toward minimising the differences between Zeph 2:7 (pastoral) and 3:12–13 (urban).

349. We have a fragmentary receipt dated to the period between Sargon II (722–705) and Esarhaddon (681–669) recording that the Ammonites paid two minas of gold and the Moabites one (*ANET*, 301), a record of their submission to Sennacherib (705–681) during his third campaign (*ARAB* 2:119, par. 239), a record of their assistance to Esarhaddon in the rebuilding of his palace (*ARAB* 2:265), and a record from the first campaign of Assurbanipal (668–627) that refers to Moab and Ammon as tribute-paying vassals (*ARAB* 2:340, par. 876) and from his ninth campaign that refers to Moab as a victorious vassal (*ARAB* 2:338, par. 870).

350. So, e.g., Tyson, "Israel's Kin," 258.

351. *ARAB* 2:105, par. 195. Tiglath-pileser III (744–727) reports having received tribute from Moab and Ammon (*ANET*, 282).

352. *ARAB* 2:314, par. 818. Cf. Ahlström, *History*, 750. For more information on the little we know about the Moabites, see, e.g., Gerald L. Mattingly, "Moabites," in *Peoples of the Old Testament World*, ed. Alfred J. Hoerth (Grand Rapids: Baker, 1994), 317–33.

353. Randall W. Younker, "Ammonites," in Hoerth, *Peoples*, 313; cf. Burton MacDonald, "Ammonite Territory and Sites," in *Ancient Ammon*, ed. Burton MacDonald and Randall W. Younker, SHCANE 17 (Leiden: Brill, 1999), 30–56, esp. 43–46. But it is difficult to date some

prosperity must be ascertained largely by archaeological study. The amount of tribute to be paid to the Assyrians is likely not a reliable indicator of a region's wealth, as other political factors come into play, such as punishment for previous rebellion. In addition, there is a question about the reliability of the numbers given in tribute lists.[354]

The designation "sons of Ammon" (*Ammonites*) reflects a self-designation of a people group or confederation whose kings styled themselves as "kings of the sons of Ammon" rather than referring to themselves as rulers of a territory like other kings. This may be a useful reminder that in the ancient world political boundaries were defined as much or more by allegiance to a ruler or confederation than by precise geographical delimitations. (This applies to Moab, Judah, and Edom as much as to the Ammonites, and we should not conclude from their designation that the political structure of the Ammonites was fundamentally different from that of Moab.) Ben Zvi observes that "announcements of judgment against Ammon tend to refer to territorial encroachment (e.g., Am 1:13–15; Jer 49:1–6; cf. Judg 11:12–28), announcements of judgment against Moab tend to mention its pride, its boastful attitude (e.g., Isa 16:6; 25:11; Jer 48:26)." Hearing a double entendre in the last line of the verse (cf. Ezek 35:12 for boasting against a territory as reflecting a hope of future possession), he thinks that the two themes are combined here.[355] This is a possible reading, especially in a post-monarchic context. But the boasting *against their territory* could also look back to the devastations the Assyrians had caused to Israel (732) and Judah (701) in the light of boasting about the integrity of one's own territory. Such boasting was therefore not necessarily expressing a desire to expand one's own borders, or even, in the light of the observations above on the nature of tribal kingdoms, a matter of having secure, clearly marked borders.[356] Instead, it speaks of established loyalties and the ability to live without outside threat. It may be objected that, by then, these were events of a previous generation, but the pain of the eradication of the Northern Kingdom was surely still felt in Judah. Further, Judah's security and "territorial integrity" (using the term loosely) arguably remained under greater threat vis-à-vis Assyrian and Egyptian demands and maybe from the Philistines (and Edomites in the Negev?) than that of Moab

---

of the findings more precisely than Iron Age II, and Tyson ("Israel's Kin") seems to put more emphasis on growth in the sixth and fifth century (e.g., 51–54, 71–72, 265–74).

354. See Marco De Odorico, *The Use of Numbers and Quantifications in the Assyrian Royal Inscriptions*, SAAS 3 (Helsinki: The Neo-Assyrian Text Corpus Project, 1995).

355. Ben Zvi, *Zephaniah*, 166. Ben Zvi notes, however, that "Ammon, because of its geographical position, was not able to annex Judean territory."

356. Cf. the excursus on "Salient Features of Iron Age Tribal Kingdoms" by Øystein LaBianca in Macdonald and Younker, *Ancient Ammon*, 19–23, esp. the concept of "overlapping territorial units" (22).

and the Ammonites. The *pride* (cf. v. 10) consists in a sense of security that, as *the taunting* would have implied, eluded the people of God. The *insults* could have been combined with raids into (former) Israelite and (current/former) Judahite territory, but this does not seem a necessary implication to draw.[357] The opening *I have heard* indicates that v. 9 is in response to verbal attacks rather than territorial encroachments, which YHWH might be said to "have seen" more than to have *heard*.

The use of *my people* is sometimes thought to reflect "a very different climate from that of 1:2–2:3."[358] It is true that the earlier distinction between the targets of divine punishment and those who might be hidden on the Day of YHWH is ignored here, but this is rhetorically unremarkable; it would be difficult to think of a suitable alternative. Nothing here implies that *my people* are considered broadly faithful. YHWH's name is associated with them regardless. There is no reason to think that here or elsewhere YHWH takes *the insults* against his people to heart only when his people are faithful. Even in 1:2–2:3, YHWH's judgment is part of a comprehensive reckoning with the world rather than a disowning of his people over against others. YHWH is here responding to an outside (verbal) attack with respect to which YHWH and his people are a unity. This leaves open the question how healthy the relationship is on the inside when considered apart from the outside attack. There are places in which YHWH in effect disowns his people (e.g., Exod 32:7; Hos 1:9), but these are not in a context of outside threat, and there are many more places in which the language of "my people" is used in oracles of judgment (e.g., Isa 1:3; 5:13; Jer 2:11, 13; 4:22; Hos 11:7; Amos 7:8; 8:2). Oracles against Moab and the Ammonites are often paired, but only here do we have a fully integrated single oracle against both entities.[359]

9 The destruction of *Moab* and *the Ammonites* is announced with an oath.[360] Such an oath nearly always introduces a curse or threat (except in Num 14:21; Isa 49:28; Ezek 33:11). An unusually lengthy, solemn designation, *YHWH of Hosts, the God of Israel*, is attached to the oath (see the translation note). It is possible that the formula was originally shorter and that it expanded under the influence of Jeremiah, a conclusion that some have drawn from the pattern of usage.[361] Note that *utterance of YHWH of Hosts* is used,

---

357. Cf. Ryou, *Oracles*, 36–37; Irsigler, *Zefanja*, 260 (but see 266); contra Vlaardingerbroek, *Zephaniah*, 146.

358. Vlaardingerbroek, *Zephaniah*, 146.

359. Ezekiel 25:8–11 is an oracle against Moab that refers to the Ammonites. It may well have been influenced by Zephaniah.

360. On the use of oaths in predictive prophecies, see Richard L. Pratt Jr., "Historical Contingencies and Biblical Predictions," in *The Way of Wisdom: Essays in Honor of Bruce K. Waltke*, ed. J. I. Packer and Sven K. Soderlund (Grand Rapids: Zondervan, 2000), 186–87.

361. Cf. Ben Zvi, *Zephaniah*, 168, who sees "a convergence of Jeremianic style with some relatively typical expressions of late prophecy."

for example, fifteen times in Haggai and Zechariah but never, say, in Hosea, Amos, and Micah, which use *utterance of YHWH* instead (22×, but expanded only once, in Amos 6:8). Even if we consider the distribution of the designation *YHWH of Hosts* on its own, we find that it appears four times in Micah–Habakkuk but ninety-one times in Haggai–Malachi. On the other hand, there seems no reason to consider the use of *utterance of YHWH of Hosts* in Nah 2:13(14); 3:5 to be late, and the expansion in Amos 6:8 reads "utterance of YHWH, God of Hosts" ("God of Hosts" is found six times in Amos). While the designation *YHWH of Hosts* became popular with postexilic prophets, it was surely familiar to Zephaniah from the Zion tradition[362] and from Isaiah.[363] Within the Zion tradition, it may have been already connected with *God of Israel*,[364] a designation that is evocative here,[365] as *Israel* reminds one of the most disastrous loss of territory God's people had suffered—when the Northern Kingdom collapsed and was annexed to become an Assyrian province.[366] It therefore seems plausible to me that this longer phrase could have been used with an oracle prior to the destruction of Jerusalem.

The announcement sees *Moab* and *the Ammonites* become totally destroyed like *Sodom* and *Gomorrah*, evoking Gen 18–19 (cf. Deut 29:23[22]). Similar comparisons are made in oracles against Israel (Amos 4:11), Judah and Jerusalem (Isa 1:9–10; Jer 23:14), Babylon (Isa 13:19; Jer 50:40), and Edom (Jer 49:18). But the geographical proximity and the story of the origin of Moab and Ammon in the aftermath of the destruction of Sodom and Gomorrah (Gen 19:30–38) makes the announcement here especially apt. In the same way, *salt* has a special resonance given that Sodom and Gomorrah became the Dead Sea, which was formerly known as the Salt Sea (*yām hammelaḥ*; e.g., Gen 14:3; Deut 3:17) and given the memory of Lot's wife's turning into a pillar of salt (Gen 19:26).[367]

362. See Renz, "Zion Tradition," 77–103. The two other likely monarchic-period occurrences within the Minor Prophets, other than in Nahum, are Mic 4:4 and Hab 2:13.

363. The designation is most often used in chs. 19 and 22, but see also, e.g., Isa 3:1, 15; 5:7, 9, 16, 24; 6:3, 5; 8:13, 18; 9:7, 13, 19 (6, 12, 18); 10:16, 23–24, 26, 33.

364. Cf. 2 Sam 7:27; 1 Chr 17:24; Isa 21:10; 37:16; see Roberts, *Nahum*, 200. The expression is used thirty-two times in Jeremiah, which led Ben Zvi (*Zephaniah*, 168) to think of it as "Jeremianic style."

365. The designation *God of Israel* is found in Isaiah (12×), Jeremiah (49×), and Ezekiel (7×) but only once more in the Book of the Twelve, in Mal 2:16.

366. *Israel* in the expression *God of Israel* arguably refers to the socio-religious people group of twelve tribes seen as a unity even in the face of political divisions. On the different meanings of "Israel," see Silvio S. Scatolini Apóstolo, "On The Elusiveness and Malleability of 'Israel'," *JHebS* 6 (2006): art. 7, doi:10.5508/jhs.2006.v6.a7; cf. Renz, *Rhetorical Function*, 118–22.

367. See also "salt land" (*'ereṣ məlēḥâ*, Jer 17:6) or "salt marsh" (*məlēḥâ*, Ps 107:34) for an uninhabited, barren wilderness; cf. Deut 29:23(22) and the symbolic action in Judg 9:45.

Some readers hear in the use of the verb *despoil* (*bzz*) an echo of a Hebrew verb for "despise" (*bzh*),[368] suggesting a motif of poetic justice. In this case, the despoiling need not be specifically in return for having been despoiled previously, "repaying [Moab and the Ammonites] for the territorial encroachment against Israel in which they had engaged from the ninth century on."[369] Rather, the despising is answered in the despoiling.

But having given us such a vivid picture of *permanent desolation*, what does the text leave for the remnant of God's people to *possess*? It may be unwise to press this question, but it is worth observing that in other places in which the verb *bzz* (*despoil*, "plunder") has as its object a people (Isa 17:14) or a city (Gen 34:27; 2 Chr 14:13), the emphasis seems to be on pillaging rather than on taking over the land or city itself. In fact, the latter is sometimes explicitly excluded. Raiding is also implied in the more frequent passages in which the grammatical objects of the verb are people, livestock, and goods, such as Num 31:9 and Deut 20:14.[370] It is likely that the objects of the despoiling in our verse are (the people of) *Moab* and *the Ammonites* rather than *a place of weeds and a patch of salt and a permanent desolation*. Much more readily than *bzz*, the verb *nḥl* (*possess*) takes places as its direct object (e.g., *'ereṣ*, "land," in Exod 23:30; Num 18:20; Isa 57:13 and elsewhere). But more rarely, it can also take people as its object (Exod 34:9; Isa 14:2; Zech 2:12[16]), which may be the best option here because it avoids having the pronominal suffixes of the two verbs refer to different entities.[371] If, instead, we were to think of the territory of Moab and the Ammonites as the inheritance,[372] we should perhaps allow for a mix of metaphors that need not be pressed too hard,[373] unless the *desolation* is inherited to be transformed.[374] Irsigler thinks the tension is too great and can only be resolved by assuming that the final bicolon is a later addition.[375] But it seems implausible that a later redactor would have overlooked that the area was not a well-watered valley

---

368. Sweeney, *Zephaniah*, 140–41.

369. Sweeney, *Zephaniah*, 141, having interpreted the last sentence in v. 8 as a reference to territorial expansion at Israel's expense (cf. 136–38), although he accepts that v. 10 presents the idiom as a reference to boasting (134).

370. The references in Isa 42:24 and Jer 30:16 can be read in the same way, with emphasis on pillaging, although the Babylonians did for a while annex Judah.

371. Cf. Ryou, *Oracles*, 231, taking up Keil, *Minor Prophets*, 2:143.

372. Cf. Ben Zvi, *Zephaniah*, 169–70.

373. Cf. Jer 48:47, where the restoration of fortunes for Moab follows a similar desolation, and Jer 49:2, where, using the root *yrš*, Israel is promised "to take possession of its possessors" after the capital of Ammon had become "a desolate heap" and her towns burned down.

374. Note *naḥălôt šōmēmôt* ("desolate heritages") as the object of *nḥl hiphil* in Isa 49:8.

375. Ryou, *Oracles*, 300–301; Irsigler, *Zefanja*, 258–59.

"like the garden of YHWH" (Gen 13:10) just because he had not written the words *permanent desolation* himself.[376]

10 This summary statement keeps the focus on the verbal attacks received from Moab and the Ammonites and identifies them as springing from *pride*, making explicit the contrast to what is commended in 2:3. Pride (*gā'ôn*) is condemned also in oracles against Moab in Isa 16:6 (twice) and Jer 48:29, but the motif is also found in oracles against other nations—for example, Tyre (Isa 23:9) and Egypt (Ezek 32:12), as well as other nations generally (e.g., Isa 13:11).[377] The reference to *my people* is now developed into *the people of YHWH of Hosts*. The point is that the boasts threatened YHWH's reputation, regardless of how healthy or unhealthy his relationship to his people was at the time (see above). Indeed, the following verse invites us to hear the taunts as likely having made reference to gods. Moab and the Ammonites were able to sustain their vassal relationship with Assyria without ever being annexed into an Assyrian province like Israel (732) or experiencing significant devastation like Judah (701). This seems to have led them to boast of Chemosh (see, e.g., Num 21:29; Judg 11:24; Jer 48:46) and Milcom (1 Kgs 11:5, 33; 2 Kgs 23:13)[378] respectively as more powerful and faithful than YHWH. Thus, by accident or design, the LXX rendering, which has Moab and the Ammonites scoff and boast directly "against the Lord, the Almighty" (*epi ton kyrion ton pantokratora*), correctly conveys one aspect of the ridicule.

11 There are different ways of understanding the first line of this verse (see the translation note). The present rendering implies that the Moabite-Ammonite boasting and reviling made the implied addressees afraid. They are now instructed that YHWH is the one who is truly *fearsome*, the one who is more to be feared than the peoples (cf. Deut 7:21) or their gods who seemed so powerful. YHWH *demotes* these gods. Many commentators see a specific reference to making *the gods of the earth* "lean" by reducing their territory and the number of worshippers who would bring them food.[379] But this thought is not convincing. The verb refers to a diminishing that need not have anything to do with starving. Following from v. 10, we may think rather of a diminishment of status, respect, and power. In the context of the idolatry condemned in ch. 1, we should first observe that the loss of Moabite and Ammonite power would render worship of their gods in Judah and Je-

---

376. Questions of plausibility of course relate to one's assumptions; cf. my comments on redaction criticism in the introduction to the commentary (p. 10).

377. Sweeney (*Zephaniah*, 141) sees a reference to Isa 2:6–21, where the Day of YHWH is a day against all that is proud and lofty. This is thematically appropriate, but *gā'ôn* is used rather differently there (vv. 2, 19, 21).

378. See the commentary on 1:5, where many see a reference to Milcom/Molech.

379. E.g., Robertson, *Nahum*, 308; Berlin, *Zephaniah*, 110–11; Dominic Rudman, "A Note on Zephaniah," *Bib* 80 (1999): 109–12; Ryou, *Oracles*, 235; Irsigler, *Zefanja*, 273–74.

rusalem less attractive. Here it is worth bearing in mind that *all the gods of the earth* could also be heard at first as "all the gods of the land" (all the gods worshipped in the land/region). But the *all* prepares for the wider perspective opened up in the following two lines.

Some suggest that "YHWH's diminishing [of] 'all the gods of the earth' and the worship of YHWH by 'all the coastlands of the nations' simply refers to worldwide recognition that YHWH is responsible for the defeat of Moab and Ammon."[380] But the demotion of the gods of Moab and the Ammonites is surely presented here only as an instance and maybe even as a pledge of YHWH's ultimate demotion of *all the gods of the earth*. *All the coastal nations* are the most far-flung peoples.[381] This precise expression is found elsewhere only in Gen 10:5 for the descendants of Javan, son of Japheth (see the discussion under "Composition"). On its own, *'iyyîm* is used as a term for the coasts and islands of the Mediterranean Sea, which came to represent the most distant parts of the world known in ancient Judah. While specific places (Crete, Cyprus, the island of Tyre) are in view in some verses, often *'iyyîm* refers to distant lands more generally (e.g., Ps 72:10; Isa 42:4, 10, 12). This prepares nicely for vv. 12–15, which refer to some of the most distant places from the perspective of ancient Jerusalem, namely Cush and Assyria, which could therefore broadly fall in the conceptual category of *the coastal nations* understood as distant political entities.[382] Cush is among the southernmost places mentioned in the Old Testament; only the kingdom of Sheba can compete with it. Assyria could count among the furthest political entities known in the northeast at the time.[383] The link between the Mediterranean coastlands and islands and the Philistines (see the commentary on 2:5; note that in Isa 20:6, *'î* apparently refers to the Philistine coast itself) allows vv. 10–11 to look back not only to vv. 8–9 but also to the preceding verses; v. 11 then looks back but also forward to vv. 12–15.[384] Its position within the chap-

380. Sweeney, *King Josiah*, 195; cf. Berlin, "Zephaniah's Oracle," 179. Sweeney's commentary, however, offers a broader, more accurate perspective (*Zephaniah*, 142–44).

381. Cf. Sweeney, *Zephaniah*, 144; Irsigler, *Zefanja*, 276–77.

382. Berlin (*Zephaniah*, 124) thinks that "the islands of the nations are the descendants of the sons of Japheth," among them Cimmerians, the Medes, and the Scythians, and comments: "Perhaps Zephaniah is making a veiled reference to these groups and others like them who figure in Assyrian history, sometimes as friends and sometimes as foes, beginning in the time of Esarhaddon."

383. Later, the Median and Persian empires extended further to the north and east. A reference to the land/mounts of Ararat (Gen 8:4; 2 Kgs 19:37; Isa 37:38; Jer 51:27) or Minni (Jer 51:27), a kingdom possibly within or near Armenia, might have been best suited if the intention had been to mention the place furthest away in the northeast, but Judeans likely had little if any interaction with peoples from these regions.

384. Cf., with different nuances, Sweeney, *Zephaniah*, 141–42; Irsigler, *Zefanja*, 272–73.

ter is, therefore, most appropriate as a hinge between the material on the neighboring nations to the west and east (vv. 5–8) and the distant lands south and north referenced in vv. 12–15.

The verse appears to make a link between political-historical events and the worship of YHWH. This seems true, even if one were to follow some of the ancient versions in rendering "YHWH will appear" (cf. the translation note). If this is a theophany, it should not be understood as a mystic or cultic revelation. It is through political events that YHWH *demotes* other *gods* and shows himself to be more *fearsome* than anyone else.[385] Only subsequent to such a revelation of YHWH as supreme over other gods, proving himself "God of gods and Lord of lords" (cf. Deut 10:17), *each in their place*—even those furthest away—*will offer obeisance* not to the gods they used to worship but *to him*. The verse thus envisages a process by which people come to recognize the sovereignty of YHWH as he subdues the nations.[386] Do the nations *offer obeisance* in grudging submission or genuine worship? The question is not raised and hence not directly answered here. The verb generally refers to the act of prostrating oneself before someone in authority (cf. the use of the verb twice in 1:5). Here it implies a recognition of YHWH's authority, following an awareness of the lack of alternatives, now that other gods have been weakened and diminished. It is clear that what has sometimes been suggested for Mal 1:14, unconvincingly in my view—namely, that YHWH is thought to be feared among the nations anonymously—cannot work here.[387] Those who are predicted to *offer obeisance* to YHWH in this verse do so in the knowledge that the gods to whom they used to bow down are not worthy of their worship.

12 Following the summary-appraisal in vv. 10–11, which is best characterized as a prophetic reflection rather than a divine oracle,[388] v. 12 resumes divine speech.[389] Because the verse does not contain a verb, its temporal

385. Irsigler (*Zefanja*, 274) separates the demotion of gods from political events and contrasts them, but he does not elucidate how in his reading the text envisages that the nations come to the realization that their gods have passed away. This is all the more puzzling, as he relates the diminishing of gods to the cessation of food contributions from worshippers (275) and yet claims that it is the destruction of the gods that makes their cults disappear (276).

386. Sweeney (*Zephaniah*, 143–44) thinks that it is *the gods* who *offer obeisance*, but *all the islands of the nations* surely does not refer to deities, and even *each in its own place*, while not impossible as a reference to each deity's major cult shrine, would seem odd in relation to *the gods*.

387. So, rightly, Irsigler, *Zefanja*, 277–78.

388. The distinction is sometimes, like here, rhetorically relevant, even if in other cases prophetic and divine speech are interleaved. See the remarks on prophetic books in the introduction to the commentary (pp. 2–3, 427–28).

389. Sweeney (*Zephaniah*, 145) apparently resists this conclusion in spite of the use of *my sword*, which he correctly identifies as YHWH's sword. The Buber/Rosenzweig translation

reference can and has been understood in different ways, but the future orientation reflected in many translations is unlikely for two reasons.[390] First, as the introduction to Zephaniah argued (p. 442), it is implausible that *Cushites* stands for "Egypt" here, and the relative political obscurity of the *Cushites* from the mid-seventh century onward would make them a surprising target of a future attack. Cush is still mentioned in later oracles, but only alongside other peoples, mostly in oracles against Egypt (e.g., Jer 46:9; Ezek 30:4–5).[391] Second, both the subject and the predication as *slain by my sword* are stressed (through the emphasized pronoun and through fronting respectively), which suggests a statement about status rather than about an event. The unmarked default of such statements would be reflected in the use of the present tense. In other words, a statement about someone's status is most readily understood as a statement about their present status; if the status were the result of an event that is yet to happen, one would expect this to be indicated in some way. The oracle apparently claims the destruction of the Cushite Empire by the Assyrians with the fall of Thebes in 664/663 as YHWH's doing. This assumes that "Cush" refers to Nubia, the region along the Nile encompassing the area between Aswan in southern Egypt and Khartoum in central Sudan, an area that the ancient world called "Ethiopia" (Greek *Aithiopia*, Latin *Ethiopia*).[392] The terse statement should not be pressed to claim that all Cushites are dead.[393] Indeed, the rhetorical direct address presumes that the reference is to death in battle and the defeat of a military power rather than the elimination of a people.[394] I scan the verse as one clause (see the translation note). If it is scanned as two clauses (e.g., "Also you, the Cushites—the slain of the sword are they!"),[395] one might see the ones being addressed at the beginning of the verse being already spoken of in the third person at the end of the verse

---

has the prophet address the Cushites with a citation of a divine speech that seems rather abrupt; cf. Irsigler, *Zefanja*, 284.

390. A future orientation is already found in the Vulg. (*eritis*) and reflected in the Tg. By contrast, the LXX has *este* (present), not *esesthe* (future).

391. In Ezek 30:9, Cush is presumably mentioned as a people that (used to) live in security because of their distance from events (cf. 29:10), but "the day of Egypt"—i.e., Egypt's downfall—will be so great that it will frighten even them. Again, Cush and Egypt are clearly distinguished.

392. See Berlin, *Zephaniah*, 111–13, for a discussion of alternative proposals, none of which seem to me a plausible fit here. Cf. Sweeney, *Zephaniah*, 146–48, who, having advocated a reference to Egypt previously, now accepts that "Ethiopia" (Nubia) is in view.

393. Rudolph (*Micha*, 278, 283) considers reading *'ittəkem* ("with you") for *'attem* ("you") to avoid the implication of total annihilation, but this is unnecessary. (Rudolph, in any case, thinks that the reference is specifically to Cushite auxiliary troops used by Psametik I. This is unlikely to be correct.)

394. Irsigler, *Zefanja*, 287.

395. Ryou, *Oracles*, 114, and many others.

as a special rhetorical effect underlining the insignificance of the Cushites. But because the use of the third-person pronoun in such a statement is not too surprising (see the translation note; a reuse of *'attem*, "you," would be rather odd), it seems unwise to make too much of it.

The end of Cushite rule over Egypt made quite an impression on Judah, which may have had closer relationships with Cush than is sometimes recognized.[396] YHWH claims here that instead of being an example of Assyrian power, the end of the Cushite Empire was the work of his sword. It is noteworthy that the Saite dynasty governing Egypt in the days of Josiah was associated with Assyria against the Cushite ruler, even if it is not clear whether the Delta Egyptians offered military support to the Assyrians in the defeat of the Cushites.[397] The (in Josiah's days) resurgent Saite dynasty may have been tempted to claim a slice of this victory for themselves. If so, the polemic against Assyrian claims could be heard at the same time as rejecting Egyptian claims to holding power. If Assyria's power, evident in the defeat of the Cushites, had been given to them only to wield the sword of YHWH (cf. Ezek 30:24–25; John 19:11), they will be powerless when YHWH stretches out his hand against them, even if they call on assistance from Egypt as they did in the late seventh century. In this way, v. 12 prepares for the announcement in vv. 13–15. A direct comparison between the fall of Thebes and the fall of Nineveh is made in Nah 3:8–11, which may have originated at about the same time (see the commentary on Nah 3:8–11).

It has been said that "the conquest of Egypt can be labelled the beginning of the end of the Assyrian empire. With this victory Assyria had reached its limits. It had overextended itself."[398] Whether or not this is strictly true— alternatively the seeds of its downfall were in the conflicts with Babylon and Elam mentioned above in the commentary on v. 4—the fall of Thebes marked a high point for the Neo-Assyrian Empire. From then on the empire declined until its collapse.

13 The opening *and* may seem harsh, as it links the third-person speech in vv. 13–15 to the first-person divine oracle in v. 12. But on the positive side,

---

396. See Norma Franklin, "The Kushite Connection: The Destruction of Lachish and the Salvation of Jerusalem," in *Tell It in Gath: Studies in the History and Archaeology of Israel— Essays in Honor of A. M. Maeir on the Occasion of His Sixtieth Birthday*, ed. Itzhaq Shai et al., ÄAT 90 (Münster: Zaphon-Verlag, 2018), 680–95.

397. Assurbanipal does not acknowledge any Egyptian help but speaks of Neco and other kings as having deserted their posts and being reinstalled by him; see *ARAB* 2:293–94. The Delta Egyptians may not have been able or willing to offer much help, but there is no punishment mentioned for having fled before Taharqa, the Cushite king; it is also possible that Assurbanipal did not want to detract from his own glory and that of his gods by mentioning Egyptian support.

398. Ahlström, *History*, 748.

it encourages readers to see the thematic connection between the fall of the Cushites (at the hand of the Assyrians) in the past and the announcement of Assyria's downfall in the future (see above).[399] The fact that the subject of the verbs of destruction is never specified is rhetorically very interesting and may reflect the hiddenness of divine action—the fact that YHWH's sword is wielded by human agents who act as his instruments, often without knowing it. As I pointed out in the comments on 1:4, the idiom within the prophetic literature of "stretching out one's hand against someone" always has YHWH as the one whose outstretched hand signals readiness for a destructive strike. While this does not imply that no human means will be employed, as if the destruction of Nineveh would occur in fundamentally different ways from the destruction of Thebes, *his hand* in this verse surely refers to YHWH's hand as much as *my sword* in the previous verse referred to YHWH's sword. Following on from v. 12, we may even picture a sword in YHWH's outstretched hand here.

As in previous oracles in this chapter, we move without any description of the attack (contrast Nahum!) quickly to destruction and *desolation*. The verb *destroy* was used in connection with the Philistines at the beginning of this section (2:5; there in the *hiphil*, here in the *piel*), and *desolation* is something of a Leitmotif in Zephaniah (cf. 1:13; 2:4, 9, 13; and the verb in 3:6). Readers alert to wordplay and aware that the name *'aššûr* may be used not only for city, land, and empire but also for the chief Assyrian deity might make a link between the desolation of Nineveh and the destruction of another god (cf. v. 11).[400] As in previous oracles, the *desolation* is poetically evoked in a series of images. There is an intensification as we move through the chapter. In v. 6, the urbanized Philistine areas were reduced to *herders' camps* (*grazing lands* and *sheepfolds*). In v. 9, the territory of Moab and the Ammonites became *a place of weeds and a patch of salt*, and the *desolation* was designated *permanent*. This verse speaks of *a parched land, like a desert*, and we may wonder what sort of life it might sustain. The answer comes in the next verse.

14 There is no surprise that the destruction brings all urban life and culture to an end, but this verse seems to be poetically teasing. At first *flocks will lie down in her midst* may make us think of the fate of the Philistine cities—no rebuilding of cities, but at least there are shepherds and their flocks. Alas, the next line (or, in the MT, the second half of the same line) clarifies that the animals that will be flocking or herding are wild animals. So, in retrospect, readers are led to reevaluate *flocks* and read it as a metaphorical term for a

---

399. It also discourages reading the short *yiqtol* form as a jussive; see the translation note.

400. As it happens, the city Assur was destroyed about two years before Nineveh, so the order of terms would be fitting even if the name were applied to the city. The primary reference is, however, surely the land and empire.

more random collection of animals: herds without herders, flocks without a shepherd.[401] The next line may bring further disintegration, depending on the identification of the animals in question. If the verb at the beginning of the verse (*lie down*) made us think of sheep, it would also be appropriate for animals such as lions, which have lairs, and maybe for hedgehogs or porcupines or even pelicans, which some suspect are behind *qā'at* and *qippōd*. But it is very doubtful that *lie down* would be used in normal speech for *owl* and *jackdaw* (the more likely translations for *qā'at* and *qippōd*). Indeed, they are not pictured as making nests. They are given a separate verb at the end of the line: they *lodge* on the *capitals* of the former city's pillars (if the translation is correct), evoking a picture of the pillars still standing, like eerie ruins.[402] Among the ruins, there is still a *window*, and from there a sound is heard. This may be the only evidence of human presence; singing elsewhere in the Hebrew Bible is always human singing.[403] We do not know whether the verb *šîr* was ever used in ancient Judah to refer to birdsong. On the one hand, our familiarity with the idiom in English and other languages may lead us to presume too quickly that speakers of Ancient Hebrew would have readily linked birds with singing. On the other hand, it seems that already translators in antiquity supposed that the singing here was that of animals. It is worth exploring this in more detail.

First, it is notable that in Eccl 12:4 we read of *qôl haṣṣippôr* ("the sound of the bird") in a context in which we would likely speak in English more specifically of birdsong. In Ps 104:12, the birds give voice (*yittanû-qôl*), again with the most general term for making a sound. Song 2:12 attests an appreciation of the sound (some) birds make and comes closest to associating the voice (*qôl*) of a bird (the turtledove) with singing, as the first half of the verse speaks of the time for *zāmîr*. But *zāmîr* is often understood here to refer to "pruning," and if there is a play on the homonym, it is more likely that the "singing" is done by the same people who do the "pruning" (of vines?). Even if *zāmîr* is understood exclusively as a reference to singing, the structure of the verse suggests that three unrelated signs of springtime are listed, so the human singing is not to be equated with "the voice of the turtledove."

Second, there is a Hebrew verb that refers to the sound of birds chirping or tweeting (*ṣpp*, always *pilpel*). It is used in Isa 10:14 directly of birds and in

401. For other readers, the tension is too great and resolved by emending the text; e.g., Irsigler, *Zefanja*, 295; see translation notes.

402. If the animals are identified as hedgehogs and pelicans, the *capitals* would presumably be pictured as having fallen down, unless a different translation is adopted.

403. In the same way, the noun *šîr* always designates human song. It is only in Sirach that the term comes to be used for melody or music made by instruments (flutes and harps); see *HALOT* and *DCH*.

Isa 38:14 for Hezekiah's moaning "like a swallow" (*kǝsûs 'āgûr*),[404] parallel to the cooing of a dove, for which the general verb for making low sounds (*hgh*) is employed (cf. 59:11). In Isa 8:19, *ṣpp* refers to the sounds spiritists make, which is probably also the background in 29:4. Hugh Williamson points out that "elsewhere in the ancient Near East there is some evidence that the dead were thought to adopt a bird-like appearance and, indeed, to sound like them."[405]

Third, we should analyze the Aramaic fragments found in a twenty-room sanctuary at Deir 'Alla relating to Balaam to see whether they offer a parallel. Combination I portrays the desolation with a number of birds alongside sheep and rabbits and other animals. In Baruch A. Levine's translation, a part of the text reads, "It shall be that the swift and crane will shriek insult to the eagle, / And a nest of vultures shall cry out in response."[406] The first line has only three words:[407] the words for "swallow" (which Levine interprets as two birds, but there is no word divider; cf. above on Isa 38:14), for "reproach" in the construct state (the form is the same as in Zeph 2:8), and for "eagle" (*nšr*, as in Hebrew). The verb "shriek" in Levine's translation reflects the preference in English for verbs indicating a specific sound, like "moan" for doves in passages in which Hebrew uses a more general word.[408] While the second line is partly illegible,[409] the verb comes at the end and is clearly legible. It is the verb for "answer," also found in Hebrew (*'nh*), rendered "cry out in response" by Levine. It seems that we have here a parallel for the presence

404. Many English translations have two birds, but the space in MT seems to have crept in by mistake. The bird is attested in the Deir 'Alla inscription to which I refer below, as pointed out by Barré, *The Lord Has Saved Me*, 119–23.

405. Hugh G. M. Williamson, *A Critical and Exegetical Commentary on Isaiah 1–27*, vol. 2, ICC (London: Bloomsbury T&T Clark, 2018), 336, with references to primary and secondary literature.

406. "The Deir 'Alla Plaster Inscriptions," *COS*, 2.27:140–45. In Victor H. Matthews and Dom C. Benjamin, *Old Testament Parallels*, 3rd ed. (New York: Paulist, 2006), 133, the text seems to be reconstructed differently and rendered, "Let the sparrow hunt carrion like a vulture, / Let the vulture chirp for its food like a sparrow" (133).

407. For the Aramaic text, I have consulted Baruch Margolis, "עלילות בלעם בר-בעור מעמק מעמק סוכות," *AlHaperek* 15 (1998): 3–10, offers the Aramaic text; see http://lib.cet.ac.il/Pages/item.asp?item=7595.

408. Even allowing for the fact the Hebrew Bible only gives us a glimpse into Classical Hebrew as spoken in ancient Israel and Judah, it is unlikely that there was anything like the number of verbs that are used in English for bird sounds (e.g., caw, cark, croak, cheep, chirp, chirrup, hoot, squawk, peep, tweet, twitter, quack).

409. The initial word ("a nest") has been alternatively reconstructed as "the voice"; see P. Kyle McCarter Jr., "The Balaam Texts from Deir 'Alla: The First Combination," *BASOR* 237 (1980): 49–60.

of wild animals as a motif to underline the absence of human population, but no sounds are registered as especially significant.

Finally, it is worth bearing in mind that song thrushes and nightingales do not feature in the Bible, and we do not know how people in ancient Judah referred to their sound. But even if, unusually, they used the more specific term *šîr* in their case, the animals mentioned in Zeph 2 are not songbirds, which is why English translations that assume that it is birds that are singing here often translate with "hoot" or similar terms that are considered more apposite for owls.

The evidence just noted suggests that some bird sounds were linked with moaning and maybe with the dead. This would be evocative in a context such as ours. Such connotations could have been activated with the use of the only Hebrew verb known to us to designate primarily sounds made by birds: *ṣpp*. The use of the verb *šîr* probably does not achieve this. There is no evidence that the sound birds make is elsewhere associated in Ancient Hebrew with "singing," and it seems unlikely that the verb used here suggests that "all kinds of sound (e.g., that of animals, birds, wind) are in view here, all contributing to the solemn state of desolation in this passage."[410] Rather, the specific sound evoked is that of human singing. But is it in fact human singing? It would be fanciful to look for an analogy in the destruction of Jericho, in which but one house survived. While a *window* plays a critical role in that narrative (Josh 2:15, 18, 21), Rahab is not a lone singer who was spared. Nor does the lament of Sisera's mother out of the *window* (Judg 5:28) offer a true analogy. Indeed, it is uncertain that *šîr* is ever used in connection with plaintive singing.[411] The picture in Zephaniah is of still greater desolation than the one in Judg 5 and, as noted already, the presence of wild animals rather suggests the absence of humans in this picture. The reason for excluding human singing is contextual. It is hard to conceive who should be singing in these ruins and for what purpose. I conclude that we must seek the singer among the animals inhabiting the ruins after all. But my interpretation differs from the standard view in two or three ways.

First, the use of *singing* here is not a dead metaphor as it might be in English, where talk about birdsong is pervasive, even if not in connection with owls. It is very much a live metaphor in which animals are anthropomorphized. Second, this *singing* is not mentioned to conjure up mournful

---

410. Ryou, *Oracles*, 49, "taking the mood and atmosphere of the passage" into consideration but not the fact that the subject is elsewhere always human, including in Job 36:24, to which he appeals for his rendering "a sound shall echo."

411. Note that the verb *rnn*, which also never has animals as its subject as far as I know, is regularly used for joyful shouting or singing, but once for crying out in distress in Lam 2:19. This should make us reluctant to draw firm conclusions based on the absence of evidence.

sounds of desolation. For all we know, the animals might be singing songs of praise (for which *šîr* is used regularly), maybe in gratitude for their new habitations. Third, the source of the singing remains unidentified. The text is suggestive rather than definite in linking any subject with the verb. It stands to reason that there would be a closer connection with *owl* and *jackdaw* if the line *Listen! The sound of singing at the window* had come earlier, because the interjection seems to go more naturally with a forward movement. In other words, after coming across *Listen!* readers will naturally seek to find the source of any sound in the following sentence(s) rather than going back to what has already been said. In addition, the new location, *at the window*, distances the sound from the animals *on her capitals*. The same distancing is at work in the reference to yet another setting in the following line, *on the threshold*, where one might hear another possible source.

What is said to be *on the threshold* is *devastation* (*ḥōreb*). If the Hebrew text had something different at an earlier point, it is hard to imagine what could have caused the change. It is possible that we should understand a homonym meaning "bustard," but if there was such a homonym, it is probably best to hear "bustard" alongside *devastation*, "ruin" (Jer 49:13) and maybe even "heat, drought" (the most common meaning of *ḥōreb*). This last sense echoes the *parched land* of v. 13. Note another link with v. 13 in that *devastation* is paired with *desolation* in Isa 61:4 (and in Ezek 29:10 alongside the plural of the more concrete feminine form, *ḥorbâ*), suggesting that in its abstract sense, *ḥōreb* goes well with the word found throughout vv. 5–15: *šəmāmâ* (*desolation*). If the (in Hebrew) unattested homonym "bustard" is not accepted, we may hear an allusion to ʿōrēb ("raven"). Indeed, it may be to facilitate the pun that the poet did not choose the more concrete feminine form *ḥorbâ* for the rubble.

Singing suggests cultural activity. Maybe we should think of three strophes in vv. 13–14: a first strophe of four lines that speak of action that leaves Assyria devastated (v. 13), another strophe of three lines suggesting depopulation by way of painting a picture of animals inhabiting ruins (v. 14a), and a strophe of two (or three, if v. 14bα is subdivided) lines that sums up the desolation in terms of the end of cultural life (v. 14b). The first line of this last strophe reminds us of *the sound of singing*, but readers who imaginatively follow the call to listen realize that all they can hear are animals. If they listen hard, they may hear a raven croak, facilitated by the wordplay with *threshold* and perhaps evoked by the sequence of *r* with *a/e* sounds in *ʾarzâ ʿērâ* at the end of the verse. The reference to a *threshold* (mentioned alongside the capitals of pillars also in Amos 9:1) suggests a building, but the building no longer stands, as there is only rubble and *devastation* on the stone on which the doorframe should be. The last line explains why the *threshold* holds rubble rather than a door: *the cedar work* has been stripped away from the walls and threshold that had surrounded and "clothed" the door. We can imagine, however, that *the cedar work* applies not only to wooden doors but to wooden paneling as well, none of which is imagined to still be in its place.

15 The verb for being *exultant* can be used for rejoicing in God (e.g., Ps 28:7) and for God's own triumphant exulting (Ps 60:6[8]) as well as for rejoicing in evil (e.g., Jer 11:15). When the adjective is used with a city, the exultation seems to be something that should be evaluated negatively, both here (*hāʿîr hāʿallîzâ*) and when the designation is used for Jerusalem in Isa 22:2 (*qiryâ ʿallîzâ*; cf. 32:13) and for Tyre in Isa 23:7 (*ʿallîzâ*, with the adjective used substantively).[412] In a similar way, dwelling *in safety* is a positive thing. Indeed, it is promised to Israel as a blessing for covenant faithfulness (Lev 25:18–19; 26:5; cf. 1 Kgs 4:25 [5:5]) but turns negative when it is paired with arrogant self-confidence of the sort expressed in the following lines. *"I am—and I only"* is a claim that no one else matters and implies that one does not need anyone else to, for example, be able to continue to dwell *in safety*. A similar arrogance is claimed later in the book for parts of Jerusalem, presumably the leadership (3:11). Such overconfidence is always misplaced, and the following bicolon expresses the contrast, either in a rhetorical question or maybe, more likely, as translated here, in an exclamation: *What a desolation she has become, / a lair for wild animals!*

Berlin notes that "a passerby viewing the destruction" is "a common literary figure for presenting an external view of a destruction."[413] The "hissing" is a typical response on the part of those who pass by a ruin. The verb (*šrq*) is often employed alongside one for being appalled or horrified (*šmm*, 1 Kgs 9:8; Jer 19:8; 49:17; 50:13), and the same is true for the related nouns.[414] This suggests that hissing expresses horror at what happened (cf. Ezek 27:36). It can be accompanied by shaking of the head to express derision (Lam 2:15–16).[415] Similar is the clapping of hands for gleeful joy (cf. Nah 3:19). The shaking of the hand, distinct from clapping or the shaking of the head, may be more threatening—thus the translation *and shake his fist* (see the translation note). Note that the noun for hissing is used with cursing in Jer 25:18.[416] It

---

412. The use of the adjective is rare. It is possible that Zephaniah here (and in 3:11) is indebted to Isaiah (see 13:3; 22:2; 23:7; 24:8; 32:13), but this is difficult to establish because the verb is used more widely, and Isa 13:3 and 24:8 may be later than Zephaniah.

413. Berlin, *Zephaniah*, 117. She offers for comparison Isa 34:10; 60:15; Jer 9:10, 12 (9, 11); 18:16; 19:8; 49:17; 50:13; Ezek 5:14; 14:15; 16:15; 33:28; 35:7; 36:34; Zeph 3:6; Lam 2:15; 2 Chr 7:21. Cf. Hillers, *Treaty-Curses*, 76–77.

414. See 2 Chr 29:8; Jer 18:16; 19:8; 25:9, 18; 28:18; 51:37; Mic 6:16.

415. For shaking of the head as mocking, see 2 Kgs 19:21; Job 16:4; Pss 22:7(8); 109:25; Isa 37:22; Lam 2:15.

416. Cf. Jer 29:18, where the implied curse might use the ruined entity as an example ("May you be like . . .") rather than being directed against what the ruin represents.

might be objected that it makes little sense to utter threats and curses against an entity that is already ruined, but it is not unknown for people to express hostility against a regime after its downfall. It is a small gesture of taking sides (when it is safe to do so). In our times, pent-up hostility to an authoritarian regime may be expressed in the toppling of statues after the rule has come to an end.

Reflection

Commentators have often seen a stark contrast between the destruction of Judah's enemies and an expectation of universal YHWH worship, but the contrast is not nearly as great when the relevant passages are read within the context of the book rather than on their own. I have argued that it is historically implausible that the oracles about other nations were ever proclaimed as a way of supporting any political-military moves on the part of Josiah against the Philistine cities in the west or Moabite and Ammonite territories in the east. In addition, it needs stressing that Zephaniah's prophecy is not nationalistic. The judgment against the entire region announced in ch. 1 focuses on Judah and Jerusalem. The envisaged beneficiary of the Philistine and Transjordanian lands that are made desolate in the judgment is not the Kingdom of Judah but a remnant of the house of Judah. The repeated use of the remnant motif is a reminder that Judah, too, is under judgment and that any future inheritance will be received the other side of destruction and decimation. In the same way, the nations are said to worship YHWH only after having experienced the demotion of their gods in the devastating judgment that is to fall on their lands and peoples and so, by implication, it is a remnant of the peoples that will worship YHWH.[417] The focus in v. 11 on far-flung peoples also mitigates against seeing any conflict between this promise and the promise that the remnant of Judah will take over neighboring territories. While, in a sense, the announcement in v. 11 comes out of the blue, it is in keeping with the stress in Zephaniah's prophecy on future hope (only) beyond the judgment to come and does not actually contradict anything said elsewhere.

This section of the book continues to support the call to seek righteousness and humility (v. 3). No reason is given for the punishment of the Philistines. Arguably, no reason is necessary because Philistine city life could easily be associated with the attitudes condemned in ch. 1 in relation to the Jerusalem elite ("Canaan" = "merchant people"). The future lies with the humble, and this is expressed in the pastoral imagery, which does not portray

417. Cf. Timmer, "Non-Israelite Nations," 256–57. See Isa 45:20–22.

a rural idyll but freedom from the trappings of urban life. Moab and the Ammonites, whose kingdoms included cities but were not focused on cities to the same extent, do not readily fall under the same condemnation. They are punished because of their arrogant pride in the integrity of their own realms vis-à-vis the dispossession and devastation that first the Northern and then the Southern Kingdom experienced at the hand of the Assyrians. The Assyrians are similarly condemned for a false sense of security in their presumed uniqueness. It seems that once Nineveh has been destroyed, onlookers can show their true feelings (cf. Nah 3:19). The chapter focuses not on the way the various entities mentioned will find their end but on the aftermath, giving us three pictures of desolation. No fallen warriors and no dead bodies are found in this picture. The only reference to the slain is in the retrospect of v. 12, whose purpose is to claim YHWH as the true actor behind the scenes. The focus is on the end of urban life and commerce, the end of arrogant boasting, the destruction of cultural accomplishments. It is as if YHWH prefers shepherds to traders, wild animals to human civilization. Why is this? I am not competent to write on the interrelationship between urbanization and (changes in) religious outlook. I do not know whether the view is true that rural people have a greater predilection for superstition while city people (especially the prosperous?) tend to sit light on any religious commitments. There are certainly plenty of exceptions. But it may be that different lifestyles hold particular temptations. People who work the land or tend animals may recognize more readily their dependence on nonhuman factors beyond their control. They also work year by year to ensure their survival and the survival of their families and do not create monuments that they hope will last for generations. By contrast, people involved in creating cultural accomplishments that are meant to last for generations may tend more readily to pride and the rich (including landed gentry) to self-sufficient arrogance.[418]

Within the overall biblical context, it would not be warranted to denigrate culture in favor of "the simple life" of shepherds and farmers. The biblical narrative ends in a city after all. But this chapter can serve as a warning about the typical temptations of urban life and commerce (Philistines, taken with Jerusalem in ch. 1), about the dangers of experiencing relative peace and security (Moab and the Ammonites), and of having success in shaping the world to one's own advantage (Assyria). We must not forget that life is a gift. If we enjoy security, riches, and success, it is easy to forget to be grateful to the one who has enabled this and to be mindful of the needs of others. If we suffer abuse at the hands or from the mouths of the better off, the "I have heard" of v. 8 may be an encouragement to remember that the status quo

---

418. This is not to deny various forms of culture in nonurban settings, as expressed in song and music, garments, and lived traditions.

is not the ultimate reality; God is. This is not to encourage quietism but a continuing seeking of righteousness and humility, trusting that an unjust and arrogant world order will not have the last word.

VI. JERUSALEM WILL SHARE THE FATE OF NATIONS (3:1–5)

1 *Oy, rebellious*[a] *and defiled*[b] *one,*[c]
city[d] *that oppresses.*[e]
2 *She*[f] *does not pay heed to*[g] *any voice;*
she does not accept correction.[h]
In YHWH she does not trust,
to her God she does not draw near.
3 *Her officials in her midst are growling*[i] *lions,*[j]
her judges wolves at dusk:[k]
they do not scrunch in the morning.[l]
4 *Her prophets are insurrectionists,*[m]
men of treachery;[n]
her priests profane what is holy,
do violence to the Torah.[o]
5 *YHWH is righteous in her midst;*
he will not commit iniquity.
Morning by morning he gives his judgment[p] *as light,*[q]
at daylight[r] *it does not fail to appear;*[s]
but the iniquitous[t] *does not experience disgrace.*[u]

a. Hebrew *mōrʾâ* should probably be identified as a *qal* participle from *mrh* ("to be rebellious"). Some forms of III-*he* verbs are treated as if *aleph* was their final root letter (see *HGHS* 57t″; GKC 75rr; JM 79l). An alternative derivation as a *hophal* participle of a verb related to the noun *rʾy* ("excrement, filth"), which medieval commentators postulated based on *murʾâ* in Lev 1:16 ("crissum"; see note on Nah 3:6), is responsible for "filthy" in KJV and "soiled" in NRSV; cf. Berlin, *Zephaniah*, 126. The Greek rendering *epiphanēs* (cf. Peshitta) is usually thought to reflect a derivation from *rʾh* ("to see," *hophal* participle: "the one who gets shown, makes an appearance"); the translator may have thought of *yrʾ* ("to fear") as well; see the translation note on Hab 1:7. Vulg.'s *provocatrix* apparently derives from *mrr* ("to be bitter"; see Jerome, *Twelve*, 1:145), although it is not far from *mrh* as I understand it. A derivation from *mrʾ* in the sense of "to fatten, graze," understood as a metaphor for arrogance, is also occasionally defended; for details, see Ben Zvi, *Zephaniah*, 184–85; Irsigler, *Zefanja*, 318.

b. The *niphal* participle of *gʾl* can mean *defiled* (cf. the perfect in Isa 59:3; Lam 4:14) or "redeemed" (cf. the perfect in Lev 25:49). The latter is adopted in LXX (*apolelytrōmenē*), Vulg. (*redempta*), and Peshitta. The ambiguity could have been prevented by choosing *gʿl* for *defiled* (used in the *niphal* in 2 Sam 1:21). Given that *mōrʾâ* can also be read in more than one way (see the note above) and the fact that the form translated *oppressive* in the following line can also refer to a dove, which is how LXX and the Vulg. render it (*peristera*, *columba*), we should surely conclude that "the description/indictment of the city in v. 1 is built around ironical puns on words" (Ben Zvi, *Zephaniah*, 184; cf. B. Jongeling, "Jeux de Mots en Sophonie III 1 et 3?" *VT* 21 [1971]: 541–47; Seybold, *Satirische Prophetie*, 55–56).

c. Or "Oy the rebellious and defiled one, the oppressive city." See the translation notes on Nah 3:1 and Hab 3:6 regarding the use of the second or third person. The participles in this line function as nouns rather than adjectives modifying *city*. The use or (more often) omission of the article after *hôy* appears to be a matter of style rather than substance.

d. Or "you city." In Hebrew, the definite article can be used with the vocative. In English "the city" would not convey the vocative.

e. Or "that is destructive." For the *qal* participle, see also Jer 25:38; 46:16; 50:16. The only occurrence of a finite form of the *qal* is in Ps 74:8. In these other cases, the *qal* may be better rendered "destructive" rather than "oppressive," a meaning that is otherwise associated with the *hiphil*. But here, the destructive nature of the city presumably finds expression in oppression, and I take the *qal* participle as in effect equivalent to the *hiphil* participle, which is attested only once (Isa 49:26).

f. It may well be best to understand these lines as unmarked relative clauses ("who refuses to pay heed . . ."); cf. Roberts, *Nahum*, 206–7. But it is common for *hôy* sayings to shift into third-person description, even if the first clause is understood as a vocative; see Hillers, "*Hôy* and *Hôy*-Oracles"; see the translation notes on Nah 3:1; Hab 2:6. English style probably demands that we revert to independent clauses at some point in v. 2. Roberts translates the second half with independent clauses. Like Berlin (*Zephaniah*, 125, 127), I have decided to begin a new sentence at the beginning of v. 2.

g. The Hebrew *šm'* ("to hear") often, as here, carries connotations of listening attentively, even in the sense of obeying.

h. The first two lines have a close parallel in Jer 7:28, which speaks of the nation and not just of Jerusalem. In Jeremiah, the voice is explicitly "the voice of YHWH their God." This is only implied here, with *voice* parallel to *instruction* in the first bicolon and *YHWH* to *her God* in the second bicolon. Ben Zvi (*Zephaniah*, 188) notes that the idiom *lqḥ mûsār* ("to accept/receive correction") is found within the prophetic literature only in this chapter (see also v. 7) and in Jeremiah (Jer 2:30; 5:3; 7:28; 17:23; 32:33; 35:13). Other references are in Prov 1:3; 8:10; 24:32.

i. The usual rendering of *š'g* as roaring is inappropriate in several places; e.g., Judg 14:5 (lions do not roar when attacking) and Amos 3:4 (lions do roar when they have no prey); see Hope, "Problems," 201–5. Here, either roaring (e.g., after a period of rest to locate each other) or growling (e.g., to frighten off competitors after successful hunt) would be appropriate.

j. This could be scanned as a bicolon. Scanning as a single colon, as in the MT, draws the *officials* and *judges* closer together. Note that Ezek 22:27, which draws on Zeph 3:3, speaks of the officials as wolves (judges are not mentioned as a group in Ezekiel). For Ezekiel's dependence on Zephaniah, see, e.g., Irsigler, *Zefanja*, 325–26.

k. As in Habakkuk, the LXX and the Old Latin have "wolves of Arabia," but Vulg., Peshitta, and Tg. support MT. See the translation note on Hab 1:8 and, e.g., Ben Zvi, *Zephaniah*, 190–93; Sweeney, *Zephaniah*, 163–64; Dietrich, *Nahum*, 222.

l. The meaning of this line is uncertain. The verb appears only here in the *qal*; it is used in the *piel* in Num 24:8 (*wə'aṣmōtêhem yəgārēm*, "and will break their bones") and Ezek 23:34 (*wə'et-ḥărāśêhā təgārēmî*, "and you will break/gnaw [?] its shards"). The related noun, *gerem*, means "bone, strength" (Gen 49:14; Job 40:18; Prov 17:22; 25:15; the noun in 2 Kgs

9:13 may be a homonym: "landing"?). The LXX and Vulg. interpret it as leaving nothing for the morning in line with a meaning attested for the verb in later Hebrew; cf. Sweeney, *Zephaniah*, 157, 164. Ben Zvi (*Zephaniah*, 193–94) argues for the meaning "to be strong" by analogy to *'ṣm*, a root with which *grm* significantly overlaps in meaning. Those who adopt a rendering like gnawing, as I do, usually interpret the preposition in *labbōqer* as equivalent to *'ad*, which is used with *bōqer* both for "by the morning" (Judg 6:31) and, more often, "until the morning" (e.g., Judg 19:25); so, e.g., KJV; Berlin, *Zephaniah*, 128–29. But *labbōqer* also often overlaps with *babbōqer* ("in the morning"), with different nuances at best only minimally discernible. See, e.g., Exod 34:2 (*wehəyê nākôn labbōqer wə'ālîtā babbōqer*, "Be prepared in the morning and go up in the morning") and 1 Chr 9:27 (*labbōqer labbōqer*, "every morning"). The latter is elsewhere more than a dozen times expressed by *babbōqer babbōqer* as well as a few times by *labbəqārîm* (Job 7:18; Pss 73:14; 101:8; only in Isa 33:2 and Lam 3:23 would it be feasible to render "for each morning"). I take the preposition in this second sense, *in the morning*, maybe with a nuance of "for" the morning, which in terms of overall meaning comes close to leaving nothing for the morning; see the commentary.

m. Or "reckless." For my translation, see Armin Lange, "Die Wurzel *PHZ* und ihre Konnotationen," *VT* 51 (2001): 497–510, who argues that in preexilic times, "to rise up against someone" developed from an earlier meaning "to get up," which was then used later also in a wider sense for behaving recklessly. This remains debatable, and others remain unconvinced; e.g., Irsigler, *Zefanja*, 320–21, who opts for something like "(arrogant) rattlers."

n. Or "treacheries." The root *bgd* is well attested, but the form *bōgdôt* is found only here. See *HGHS* 61qβ and 61tι for its formation. As with, e.g., *ḥokmôt* ("wisdom") and *hôlēlôt* ("foolishness," also only attested in the plural: Eccl 1:17; 2:12; 7:25; 9:3; 10:13), the singular may be more appropriate in English, using an abstract noun to convey characterization.

o. Or "to instruction/teaching."

p. Namely, he gives his sentence, his decision; alternatively, he assigns his judgment. This combination of verb and object is used elsewhere for giving the afflicted their right (Job 36:6) and for assigning divine judgment to a human ruler (Ps 72:1; Ezek 21:27[32]; 23:24). With the object in the plural, the reference seems to be always to YHWH giving his ordinances (and statutes, *ḥuqqîm*) to his people (Deut 4:8; 11:32; Ezek 20:11, 25).

q. Berlin (*Zephaniah*, 130) understands the first part of the verse to mean that each morning, "God makes his judgment visible in the light (= sun)." She notes the use of the construction for turning one thing into another (e.g., Jer 9:11[10], and many other places), presumably meaning that the decree, when it is enacted, becomes the rising sun. Note that the construction works differently in Jer 31:35, where the sun is arguably not turned into light but given as light. (In Isa 51:4, decree/justice is also given as a light, but with a different verb, and the light is metaphorical. I take it to be concrete here.)

r. I interpret *lā'ôr* as a pivot and render it twice; it is missing in most LXX MSS. For this temporal function of the preposition with other nouns, see, e.g., Gen 3:8; 49:27; Amos 4:4. (*At daylight* is a possible but disputed rendering of *lā'ôr* in Job 24:14.) The masoretic accentuation keeps what I have scanned as two lines in one line. Other commentators disagree on whether to take *lā'ôr* more closely with the preceding (e.g., Berlin, as in the previous note; Sweeney, *Zephaniah*, 167; Dietrich, *Nahum*, 220) or with what follows (e.g., Vlaardingerbroek, *Zephaniah*, 178; Ryou, *Oracles*, 124–25; Irsigler, *Zefanja*, 317, 321–22).

s. This verb is regularly used in negated statements to indicate that something is not missing: material things (1 Sam 30:19), food (1 Kgs 4:27[5:7]), creatures (Isa 34:16), or stars (Isa 40:26). It is similarly used for people not being left behind (2 Sam 17:22). In the only statement that is not negated, truth/honesty has disappeared (Isa 59:15). Here, the morning light proves that YHWH's *mišpāṭ* "has not disappeared" (*qatal* form); in the form of sunlight it "is not missing." Regarding the line as a whole, the Greek Washington Papyrus and Codex Venetus have no equivalent; see Kim, "Text und Übersetzung," 156–57, and the following two notes.

t. LXX (with significant differences among MSS; cf. the preceding note) apparently keeps YHWH as the subject, departing noticeably from the received Hebrew text, when it renders *kai ouk eis neikos adikian* ("not [will he give/permit?] unto victory injustice"). Instead of *bōšet*, the translator apparently read *bašaḥat* ("with ruin, into destruction," as in Ps 9:15[16]; Ezek 19:8) or maybe *bǝšē't* (cf. Lam 3:47) and took it with the next verse. For fuller discussion, see BA 23.4–9, 360–61; cf. Irsigler, *Zefanja*, 322. See below under "Composition."

u. Or "does not know shame." In some places (e.g., 1 Sam 20:30; Ezra 9:7), *bōšet* can only refer to objective disgrace and humiliation rather than subjective feelings of shame. In fact, it seems feasible to read it this way in all occurrences in the Hebrew Bible. Cf. the commentary on Hab 2:10 ("ignominy"). Berlin (*Zephaniah*, 130–31) renders "ignores condemnation," which is possible, although it stretches the meaning of both parts of the clause. See Isa 42:25, where *lō' yādā'* ("does not know" = "ignores") is parallel to *lō'-yāśîm 'al-lēb* ("does not take to heart"). In the Greek codices Vaticanus and Sinaiticus, this word is taken with the next verse and read with an additional letter (*bšḥt* for *bšt*), rendered *en diaphthora* ("with ruin").

Composition

The oldest Hebrew manuscript, MurXII, has 3:1–13 as a distinct paragraph, and this is largely followed in the masoretic tradition. The chapter is divided differently in Codex Babylonicus Petropolitanus, namely into three paragraphs: vv. 1–7, 8–15, 16–20. (Verses 16–20 also form the final paragraph in the Aleppo Codex, but not in the Leningrad Codex.) A division between vv. 13 and 14 is widely agreed upon in modern scholarship, but the subdivision of vv. 1–13 into smaller units is controversial.[419] Irsigler divides the whole book into three major parts consisting of 1:2–18; 2:1–3:8; and 3:9–20, seeing a greater caesura between vv. 8 and 9 than between vv. 13 and 14. This does full justice to the role of v. 8 as a concluding statement (cf. my comments on the composition of 3:6–8).

While the opening verses do not constitute a typical *Oy* saying—there is no reference to the fate that lies in store for the accused—it is unproblematic to think of at least vv. 1–4 belonging together. Sweeney argues that v. 5 introduces the next section because it no longer focuses on the guilt of Jerusalem.[420] This depends on the translation of the last line of v. 5, which Sweeney renders as a statement about YHWH: "And he does not know iniquity, shame."[421] He

419. Irsigler, *Zefanja*, 41–42.
420. Sweeney, "Form-Critical Reassessment," 401–2.
421. Sweeney, *Zephaniah*, 167; cf. 174–75. His appeal to LXX and Vulg. also reading

suggests that ʿwl, which he needs to vocalize as ʿāwel ("iniquity"), might be a gloss. But the MT's ʿawwāl (*the iniquitous*) is not really problematic. If it is retained, v. 5 still refers to the guilt of Jerusalem. In addition, it is very debatable that the verse specifically speaks of Jerusalem's restoration, as Sweeney implies, rather than more generally about YHWH's pure justice (*morning by morning*), contrasting with Jerusalem's leadership, which had been arraigned in the previous two verses. Sweeney points to the parallel between *he will not commit injustice* in v. 5 and *the remnant of Israel will not commit injustice* in v. 13, but he is also aware that *in her midst* links v. 3 and v. 5.[422] All in all, v. 5 could work well as a fitting conclusion to the first paragraph. Among others, Sabottka identifies vv. 1–5 as the first unit, but he allows that v. 5 might also serve to introduce the divine speech in vv. 6–8, his second unit.[423]

It could be argued that v. 6 more obviously opens a new subsection with its change from prophetic to oracular speech, from YHWH being spoken of in the third person to first-person divine speech. Sweeney seeks to rebut this by claiming that "although vv 6–13 are primarily a speech by Yhwh, the oracular formula in v 8 indicates the dominant perspective of the prophet's speech which corresponds to the perspective of v 5, likewise a speech by the prophet."[424] In my view, however, the parenthetical *utterance of YHWH* cannot carry the weight it is given by Sweeney. All divine speech within prophetic literature is mediated. The addition of the utterance formula (Sweeney's "oracular formula") does not fundamentally alter the character of a section that is otherwise consistently phrased as first-person divine speech. Nevertheless, divine and prophetic speech cannot and should not always be neatly distinguished. Floyd, who takes vv. 1–7 as the first unit,[425] argues that the move from prophetic speech in vv. 1–5 to divine speech in vv. 6–13 does not indicate a major break, pointing to the alternation between the two in ch. 2.[426] This seems a more plausible argument. While the first unit in ch. 2 (vv. 1–4) is entirely in the third person, subunits of the collection in vv. 5–15 use a mixture of genres. After the opening *Oy* call, which introduces the word of YHWH in the third person, vv. 5–6 are first-person divine speech, but v. 7

YHWH as the subject is problematic for two reasons. First, LXX (in its best MSS) departs significantly from the received Hebrew text (*kai ouk eis neikos adikian*, "and not unto victory injustice"), not reading the participle *yôdēaʿ* but, apparently, *lāʿad*, understood as equivalent to *lānesaḥ*, interpreted in the Aramaic sense of the noun (cf. Rudolph, *Micha*, 286). Second, in the Vulg., *iniquus* ("the unjust") appears to be the subject of the last clause, as in MT.

422. It also relates to *draw near* (*qārēbâ*) in v. 2.

423. Liudger Sabottka, *Zephanja: Versuch einer Neuübersetzung mit philologischem Kommentar*, BibOr 25 (Rome: Biblical Institute, 1972), 198.

424. Sweeney, "Form-Critical Reassessment," 402.

425. Cf. Ivan J. Ball, *Zephaniah*, 199.

426. Floyd, *Minor Prophets 2*, 230–31.

has a third-person reference. The saying against Moab and the Ammonites in vv. 8–9 is, apart from the utterance formula, divine speech, but a prophetic summary-appraisal is attached to it in vv. 10–11. The saying about Cush and Assyria moves from first person (v. 12) to third person (vv. 13–15). The last two examples show, however, that a change of person can coincide with and indicate a break within a unit, and Floyd rightly acknowledges such a minor division between vv. 5 and 6. He discerns a twofold accusation in v. 2: of the city's incorrigibility and of its faithlessness. In reverse order, vv. 3–5 then offer specific indications of faithlessness, vv. 6–7 of incorrigibility. This is an attractive reading. While "faithlessness" may seem thematically too broad a category to establish a link between v. 2a and vv. 3–5, the connection is strengthened by the use of the *qrb* root both in v. 2a (*draw near*) and vv. 3–5 (*in her midst*, twice). The exposition of incorrigibility in vv. 6–7 is obvious. Nevertheless, there is an aspect that seems insufficiently addressed in Floyd's analysis. Verse 6 appears to be looking back to events that were still future in ch. 2.[427] This suggests that the "prophetic charge of failure to repent" (Floyd's genre definition for 3:1–7) is not generic, as v. 2 on its own can be understood, but in vv. 6–7 relates specifically to the call to repentance in 2:1–4.[428] Irsigler recognizes this, although he overstates the hope implied in these earlier verses and therefore the disappointment resulting from failure to repent.[429] On my reading, only the addressee of 2:1 was called to repentance, which was to be expressed in becoming like the *humble of the land who act on* YHWH's *judgment* (2:3). The *humble*, the addressees of 2:3, were encouraged to continue to seek YHWH. The prophetic charge of failure to repent in 3:6–7 only applies to the larger group; it says nothing about the *humble of the land*.

Floyd divides Zephaniah into three major sections, the middle being 2:1–3:13, which he further divides into two major units (2:1–3:7; 3:8–13).[430] Given the relationship between 3:6–7 and the preceding chapter as just outlined, it is not advisable to include 3:1–7 as the last unit of the "exhortation to repent," which Floyd sees extending from 2:1 to 3:7 (followed by the exhortation to await the Day of YHWH in 3:8–13). The "prophetic charge of

427. Sweeney (*Zephaniah*) seems to think that v. 6 still "anticipates the downfall of Assyria" (175). He also argues that v. 7 "provides the justification for Jerusalem's past punishment" (178), namely in pre-Josianic times. I find this reconstruction of relevant timeframes implausible.

428. Roberts (*Nahum*, 208) avoids this conclusion by changing the text; see translation note on 3:6.

429. Cf. Irsigler, *Zefanja*, 193. I also disagree with Irsigler about v. 2, which in my view cannot be said to look back to ch. 2 specifically. (Irsigler acknowledges that vv. 6–7 are stronger.)

430. Floyd, *Minor Prophets 2*, 201–4.

failure to repent" (3:1–7)[431] is not part of the "exhortation to repent." Does this mean that all of 3:1–7 should be put into the second major unit? No. Floyd's genre description of 3:1–7 actually does not fit the early part of the chapter very well. While v. 2a can be interpreted as a "prophetic charge of failure to repent" with its reference to failure to accept correction, this could still be said generally about a history of prophetic challenges. It is only vv. 6–7 that specifically refer to the (forthcoming) events that, earlier in the book (see esp. 2:5), were meant to motivate repentance in this generation. We therefore have in vv. 6–7, along with the change to divine speech, a thematic narrowing and a setting that is different from ch. 2 and arguably from 3:1–5. (There are likely diachronic implications here, but the issue is one of synchronic reading as well.) I am therefore inclined to define 3:1–5 only as the saying that puts Jerusalem in a line with the entities that were specified in ch. 2 as specific targets in the divine judgment of the world of which ch. 1 spoke. They include the Philistine principalities, Moab and the Ammonites, and Nineveh (Assyria), with Cush having been an early casualty.

In the introduction to Zephaniah above (pp. 432–43), I suggested that its bulk dates to the 630s or 620s. If this is so, and if my reading of vv. 6–7 is correct, at least 3:6–7 and possibly subsequent verses (see further below) are to be dated later. To my mind, Zeph 1:2–3:5 offers a coherent message, calling Judah broadly but the well-off in Jerusalem specifically to repentance in the light of a comprehensive judgment YHWH has decreed on their world while encouraging the humble faithful to continue to pursue YHWH and what is right. The end of the Cushite Empire is claimed as YHWH's deed, and the coming devastation of the Philistine cities is singled out as a warning to Jerusalem and hence a motivation for repentance. First, 1:2–18 stressed both the comprehensiveness of the judgment and its specific focus on the wheelers and dealers of the time. Then, 2:5–15 spelled out the comprehensiveness by specifying the political entities that were of major interest in Josiah's days, with the absence of Egypt suggesting an early date for the section. These oracles also highlighted the focus of the judgment by describing the aftermath in greater detail, stressing that there is a future only for the humble survivors of the conflagration. In their current form, probably more or less their original form, there is no trace of nationalistic fervor: on the one hand, only a remnant of Judah comes to take possession, and on the other hand, other nations come to worship YHWH, realizing the worthlessness of their gods. Finally, 3:1–5 rounds this off. It ensures that the spotlight remains on Jerusalem and on its leadership, where it was in ch. 1. What moderns might separate as "social" and "religious" concerns are combined both in ch. 1 and in 3:1–5.

If vv. 6–7 are spoken from a later perspective, the question is whether 3:5

431. Floyd, *Minor Prophets 2*, 231.

was the end of the first edition, as it were, or whether there are verses beyond v. 7 that also belong to this earlier part. Given that v. 8 reuses '*sp* ("gather"), the key verb of the motto statement in 1:2, *yôm* (*day*), which is employed seventeen times in 1:2–2:3, and *ḥărôn 'appî* (*my burning anger*, cf. 2:2), which features in the central section along with *mišpāṭ* (cf. 2:3), and ends with a clause from the end of ch. 1 (*ba'ēš qin'ātî tē'ākēl kol-hā'āreṣ*, *in the fire of my passion shall the whole earth be consumed*; cf. 1:18),[432] it seems likely that v. 8 once formed the conclusion of a work centered on 2:1–4. See the section on 3:6–8 for further discussion.

Commentary

1 The opening verse of this section is carefully crafted in an ambiguous way that leaves hearers wondering where the saying is going (see the translation notes). In Isa 55:1, *hôy* (*Oy*) calls for attention to a message that is positive and hopeful.[433] The terms under which the unnamed city here is addressed could be read in a similarly positive way. This is reflected in the LXX: "Ah, distinguished and ransomed, the city, the dove!" The dove may evoke freedom (cf. Ps 55:6[7]) and security (cf. Jer 48:28) or senselessness and thus vulnerability (cf. Hos 7:11),[434] or it may simply be a term of endearment (cf. Song 2:14; 5:2; 6:9). But while most occurrences of *yônâ* in the Hebrew Bible should be identified as a noun, there are three other places in which it is in fact the *qal* participle of the verb "to oppress" (cf. Jer 25:38; 46:16; 50:16), none of which are recognized as such in LXX or Vulg.[435] Most often, of course, *Oy* announces a saying that characterizes an entity (negatively) before offering condemnation (cf. 2:5 and, e.g., Nah 3:1; Hab 2:6, 9, 12, 15, 19). Here, it is easy to read the characterizing terms as negative: *rebellious*

432. The only textual differences here and in relation to 2:2 are the necessary changes from "his" in prophetic speech to "my" in divine speech. I rendered '*ereṣ* in 1:18 as "land" to guard against the assumption that an apocalyptic world judgment is in view; the reference to nations and kingdoms in 3:8 makes it difficult to translate "land" here, but the reference need not be broader than in 1:18; it is possible to think of '*ereṣ* in both places as roughly corresponding to the lands controlled by the Assyrians.

433. Cf. Zech 2:6–7(10–11) for the use of *hôy* as a call to attention without overtones of threat or mourning. Irsigler (*Zephaniah*, 236) believes this to be a later development that is not relevant here.

434. So Symmachus, who renders *anoētos* ("devoid of understanding") here (cf. Rudolph, *Micha*, 285).

435. The Vulg. has *columba* ("dove") in all three places. LXX has a shorter text at Jer 25:38 (LXX 32:38) and renders the *ḥereb hayyônâ* ("oppressing sword") in 46:16 (LXX 26:16) and 50:16 (LXX 27:16) as *machairas Hellēnikēs* ("Greek dagger"), understanding *yônâ* as a gentilic (Ionians as a term for Greeks generally).

and defiled one, city that oppresses. This is confirmed in the following verses that, surprisingly, bring further accusations rather than an announcement of judgment.[436] These opening lines could be thought of as encompassing the whole chapter (or 3:1–13 at any rate). Alternatively, the author may have chosen these specific words to highlight that the city that should be worth presenting and that has experienced redemption (having heeded warnings; see below) is in fact *rebellious and defiled.*

The use of *yônâ* could participate in this logic with the connotations above for "dove," but the Peshitta's rendering *mdynth dywnn,* "city of Jonah" (the noun for "dove" is identical to the personal name "Jonah") is also worth considering as bringing a possible pun to the fore. This need not mean that the speech is directed against Nineveh. Jerome rejects the then widespread idea that the oracle is about Nineveh on the grounds that "never would Scripture have called Nineveh a *dove.*"[437] He is, of course, right to think that Jerusalem is addressed here, and it is indeed unlikely that "dove" would be used as a term of endearment for Nineveh. But the expression "city of Jonah" could make one think of Nineveh even in an address to Jerusalem.[438] This saying comes straight on the heels of an oracle against Assyria that, in turn, followed other oracles whose target had been named at the beginning. Thus, the omission of the city's name here may well suggest that the defilement consists precisely in this erasure of sacred identity: Jerusalem (the holy) has become like Nineveh (the profane, the wicked)—that is, similar things could be said about either. Indeed, the first bicolon of the next verse still omits any names so that only the reference to *YHWH* as *her God* in the second half of the next verse finally resolves the potential ambiguity. What's more, the one way Jerusalem is not like Jonah's Nineveh—responding positively to a prophetic call to repentance—is very much the issue in the verses that follow. Once alerted to it, it should not be difficult for readers of the canon of Scripture to see an interesting and thought-provoking pun here. The question whether this was intended by the author is more difficult to answer, as we do not know whether the author would have known the story of Jonah's mission to Nineveh. Given the most probable scenario for the book of Jonah's origin,[439]

436. The Vulg. combines negative and positive characterizations: "Alas, the provoking and redeemed city, a dove." It has a form of *polluo* ("to stain, defile") for relevant occurrences of *g'l* in other places (e.g., Isa 59:3; Lam 4:14; Mal 1:7, 12), which suggests that "redeemed" was a deliberate choice, not a matter of ignorance.

437. Jerome, *Twelve,* 1:145.

438. This would be by association with the story for which he became most famous; the prophet was from Gath Hepher and may have been active in Jerusalem (2 Kgs 14:25).

439. That the book of Jonah is postmonarchic and the story told therein was unknown before its composition; Zeph 3:1, by contrast, is likely to have been formulated pre-destruction.

this seems unlikely, but if any of a number of relevant factors is evaluated differently, it would not be impossible.[440]

In any case, to speak of Jerusalem as a *city that oppresses* is unusual. More commonly it is individuals who are said to oppress (or warned against oppressing) other individuals, or else nations and empires oppress other nations. If the city of Jerusalem as a body can be said to oppress, who are the oppressed? Zephaniah does not spell it out, but Ezekiel has an answer: *ʿānî waʾebyôn*, "the poor and needy" (22:29), including the orphan and the widow (22:7). This is a fair reading of Zephaniah.[441] When Zephaniah announced judgment on Jerusalem (and Judah) in ch. 1, the specific target proved to be the upper class. The same will prove true here in v. 3. Ezekiel's focus is similar. His condemnation of Judah also focuses on Jerusalem, and his condemnation of Jerusalem on those who are in charge.[442]

2 This verse makes it unambiguously clear that the preceding is to be understood negatively. Thus, for example, paying heed to YHWH's voice is contrasted with being rebellious in a number of other places (e.g., Exod 23:21; Deut 1:43). If the city *does not pay heed to any voice*, it should be clear that the first participle of v. 1 is to be understood as her being *rebellious*. The portrayed stubbornness and willfulness, spelled out in the second half as lack of concern for and engagement with YHWH, is reminiscent of 1:6, 12b. The reported attitudes are considered so widespread that they are seen to characterize the whole city. In the first instance, the opening bicolon can be read as a general description of recalcitrance. In vv. 3–4, this is specified as failure to pay heed to YHWH's judgments. Verses 6–7 will take up this motif and focus on the failure to heed the call to repentance that was motivated by the destruction soon to come over the region (see the discussion under "Composition" above). The disloyalty of which the second bicolon speaks is also illustrated in the behavior listed in the two verses that follow. It is therefore possible to read vv. 3–4 as teasing out each half of v. 2.[443]

---

440. That is, if Zeph 3:1 (or even just the phrase *hāʿîr hayyônâ*) is later or the story about Jonah was known earlier than I suppose.

441. Ezekiel characteristically expands on Zephaniah. In the verses just referenced, e.g., he does so not only by providing objects for *ynh* but also by adding the oppression of foreigners (using the root *ʿšq*, not used in Zephaniah).

442. Ezekiel includes in his condemnation *ʿam hāʾāreṣ* ("the people of the land"), which may function as a general designation for Judahites in 12:19 but in 7:27 and 22:29 (as is common in Jeremiah) more likely designates the group of property owners with political influence; cf. Daniel I. Block, *The Book of Ezekiel, Chapters 1–24*, NICOT (Grand Rapids: Eerdmans, 1997), 270.

443. This means that the fact that vv. 6–7 develop the first half in a certain direction does not prove that these verses were an original unit with vv. 1–5; see further under "Composition" above.

3 The condemnation of specific groups in Jerusalem pulls no punches. If Nineveh faces a future of being inhabited by wildlife only, Jerusalem already hosts wild animals *in her midst*. Her leaders, whose duty it is to protect others, are spoken of as predatory animals. Lions growl, snarl, and roar for different reasons. Whichever is chosen for the translation here, the sound is likely meant to suggest aggressive behavior. The expression *wolves at dusk* serves in Hab 1:8 to characterize the wolves as especially sharp and quick, ready for the hunt. Here, the emphasis lies as much on wolves being nocturnal animals as on their eagerness to hunt. Ben Zvi notes that "judging is related to morning in other places in the OT (see 2 Sam 15:2–5; Jer 21:12; Ps 101:8; cf. Ps 37:6)."[444] The evidence he cites, however, can be debated. In 2 Sam 15, the reference to early morning may be suggesting Absalom's eagerness, reflected in an early start. He is probably judging all day rather than in the morning specifically. Similarly, the injunction to execute justice in the morning in Jer 21 may be a way of urging that justice be done promptly. Nevertheless, he is right to observe that, metaphorically, justice and light are connected in the Hebrew Bible and to suggest that comparing judges to animals that are most active when it is dark implies that they are not doing their job properly. Nighttime may also imply underhandedness, but to see here a specific reference to nocturnal bribery that makes a mockery of the judgment spoken in daylight probably goes too far.

Benjamin is described in Gen 49:27 as a ravenous wolf who devours the prey in the morning and (still) divides spoil in the evening. There, too, it is assumed that wolves hunt at night, and the greatness of Benjamin's exploits is underlined by speaking of him as enjoying his success all day ("morning" and "evening" serving as a merism). By contrast, the *judges*, and maybe the *officials*,[445] in our verse *do not scrunch in the morning*. This probably more realistic picture is not given to suggest failure but rather to imply that they are done eating by the time morning comes and do not leave anything for the morning (cf. the translation note). Wolves do not always eat immediately after fatally wounding or killing their prey.[446] They sometimes rest for a while

444. Ben Zvi, *Zephaniah*, 191; cf. Irsigler, *Zefanja*, 331. See also Exod 18:13–14, where the judging takes place all day—i.e., during daylight hours.

445. Scanning the verse as a tricolon, it seems possible to read the line as applicable to the officials of the first line as well as the judges of the second line. Lions also typically begin to get active at dusk, although, as opportunity arises, they might also hunt by day—maybe more often than wolves. The perception of people in ancient Judah was presumably shaped by the experience of shepherds. The risk to flocks must have been much greater by night than by day.

446. Wolves are not equipped to deliver killer blows and will often let their victims die of shock, muscle damage, or blood loss rather than risk injury to themselves by trying to bite, e.g., the neck.

after the exertion of the hunt and before gorging themselves on the meat. Wolves can devour up to ten kilograms in one meal and then sometimes go for days without food if the subsequent hunt is not successful. They do not keep anything for later eating; any leftovers are for carrion eaters to finish off.[447] We are therefore invited to picture the *judges* as hungry and ready to hunt in the evening, *at dusk* (cf. Hab 1:8), and all done with hunting and eating by the time morning comes. The general implication is that *officials* and *judges* are not concerned with the well-being of the community but exploit their powerful positions for their own advantage.

4 It is easy to imagine prophets being accused of recklessness. Prophets are "reckless" when they offer false hopes, saying, "All is well," when things are not well, in effect coating with whitewash rather than repairing the damaged wall. They are "reckless" also when they discourage the righteous and encourage the wicked (cf. Ezek 13; Jer 8:10–11) and when they offer judgments and oracles in relation to the income they receive (cf. Mic 3:5, 11; Jer 6:13–14). Such may well be the background of Zephaniah's condemnation, but this bicolon specifically highlights the rebelliousness and disloyalty of the prophets. They are *insurrectionists* against the one who allegedly sent them, *men of treachery* vis-à-vis the God who has covenanted himself to Israel and in whose name they speak.[448] Given the reference to Josiah in 1:1, they could also be thought of secondarily as treasonous vis-à-vis the reforming king, maybe in condoning practices that he condemned and sought to abolish.

Priests are entrusted with the *holy*, and one of their roles is to teach the difference between the sacred and the profane (cf. Lev 10:10–11). Therefore, the accusation made here could hardly be more damning.

5 While Habakkuk describes the breakdown of justice and order as indicative of Torah's weakness (1:4) and the result of YHWH's action, here YHWH is contrasted with and thus distanced from the priests and prophets, the judges and officials who speak in his name. The reuse of *in her midst* underlines the contrast and should probably not be pressed to suggest a divine action that is specific to Jerusalem. The first bicolon declares YHWH's righteousness; it is inconceivable that he partakes in iniquity. The second bicolon uses the standard phrase *'ôr habbōqer*, "morning light" (Judg 16:2; 1 Sam 14:36; 25:34, 36; 2 Sam 17:22; 2 Kgs 7:9; Mic 2:1) and separates it onto two

---

447. See, e.g., Mech, Smith, and MacNulty, *Wolves on the Hunt*. I consider it likely that the general behavior of wolves was better known in ancient Judah than by many of today's readers of Zephaniah.

448. It is not likely that they are called *insurrectionists* and *men of treachery* because they speak in the name of other gods, as one might expect idolatry to be specifically named, and the *priests* in the next bicolon are surely to be thought of as priests of YHWH.

lines.[449] The appearance of *daylight* is the result of YHWH's ordinance (his *judgment*; cf. the juxtaposition of the motifs of sun and Torah in Ps 19 with reference to his ordinances/judgments in v. 9[10]). YHWH shows his dependable justice in the order of day and night. He unfailingly brings new light each morning, implicitly condemning the "nocturnal" behavior of officials and judges (see above). Others have given various institutional explanations for how YHWH *gives his judgment morning by morning*.[450] But vv. 3-4 suggest that all institutions have failed. The *judgment* he has assigned to humans to implement is obscured. YHWH can be seen to be righteous only in those areas of his established order that operate without human intermediaries. These areas show that YHWH is consistently righteous and that therefore the misapplication of his name and law by the city's leadership cannot be blamed on him.

While the natural order unfailingly enacts YHWH's decree, no judicial or prophetic light falls on *the iniquitous*, who consequently *does not know disgrace*.[451] On this understanding of the final line, it takes up the motif of justice not being done as implied in vv. 3-4. Alternatively, we may think that the deeds of the iniquitous are implicitly shown to be blameworthy and thus condemned by the fact that they are typically done at night, in secret, away from the light. And yet the iniquitous ignores this implicit condemnation that is daily received from the rising of the sun (see the translation note).

Reflection

The focus of this section is on Jerusalem and in particular on its leadership not being what it should be. There are ways in which Jerusalem is inevitably and rightly like other cities and the people of God like other people. There are also distinctions one should not make (e.g., by oppressing foreigners). But there is a special calling on God's people. Zion has been elected to be different. It should appear glorious, a picture of redemption, innocent like a dove. Instead, it partakes in humanity's rebellion against God. Moab and the Ammonites mocked Israel and Judah, as if YHWH was simply another national god or tribal deity rather than the one supreme God; Assyria failed to acknowledge YHWH as the true source of all power.[452] Shockingly, even Jerusalem fails to recognize YHWH for who he is and so to bear true witness

---

449. Cf. Irsigler, *Zefanja*, 321. This is a popular stylistic device, often with the components of a phrase used in reverse order; see Watson, *CHP*, 328-32.

450. See Irsigler, *Zefanja*, 335-36.

451. See Jer 2:26 for a thief's disgrace at being found out.

452. Cf. Ben Zvi, *Zephaniah*, 334-35.

to him. She has become defiled by failing to be distinct, having had more reason than Nineveh to give heed and accept correction because God's revelation is more fully present within her. YHWH could be more readily known in Judah than in Assyria as the giver of light and life, and yet in the story of Jonah's preaching, it is Nineveh, not Jerusalem, that responds to the call for repentance. The words of Jesus are apposite here: "From everyone who has been given much, much will be required; and to whom they entrusted much, of him they will ask all the more" (Luke 12:48). This applies to the people of God as a whole, as they have been entrusted with a knowledge of God's will. It also applies to the particular abilities and calling given to individuals, such as officials, judges, prophets, and priests. They are all condemned here for failing to exercise their responsibilities properly. Power was given to leaders of the community to uphold justice and help the weak, not to exploit the powerless like wild animals. Insight is given to some in order to guide others, not to advance their own interests. Ezekiel develops this further in a less poetic and more elaborate passage (22:25–29), spelling out the deadly consequences of pursuit of gain for oneself becoming one's overriding interest.

YHWH's ability and reliability in bringing about his decree is evident in the parts of creation not compromised by human mediation, specifically in the daily rising of the sun over the evil and the good (cf. Matt 5:45). A basic sense that some things are not to be done is widespread, and one way in which this is evident is in the use of the cover of night for immoral deeds. While this experience is universal (cf. Rom 1:18–23), the call to repentance was specific at that time (cf. Acts 17:30–31), which is why YHWH's righteousness is contrasted specifically with the iniquity of Jerusalem's leaders. While the judgment announced in ch. 1 is comprehensive, and ch. 2 spells out how other entities will be affected, there is no hint of a call to repentance along the lines of 2:1–4 having been ushered to any other nation. This gives rise to the specific accusation that is going to be added in vv. 6–7.

Today, the difference between Judah and other nations is minimized, as God now commands all people everywhere to repent. The call to repentance goes out in the present day not in view of the impending end of a (regional) world order but in view of the appointment of the first human being to be resurrected as the judge over all the world and everything that brings death. This does not necessarily mean that the judgment will look the same whether people had access to God's written revelation or not, even if the result is (cf. Rom 2:12).

This passage may also serve as a reminder of the extent to which the leadership can shape the character of a community. The characterization of the city as oppressive implies the existence of people who were oppressed as well—maybe in surrounding towns and villages but most likely also within Jerusalem itself. The powerlessness of the oppressed means that the humble and poor do not get to shape the nature of the city. In these verses, they are barely visible, but they will take center stage later in the chapter. Christians have specific responsibilities to look out for the powerless and poor (e.g., Luke 14:12-14; Gal 2:10); they also have specific responsibilities for leaders, namely to pray for them (1 Tim 2:2), not least because communities are shaped and characterized by those within them who hold power (by God's authority; cf. Rom 13:1-7).

VII. REAFFIRMATION OF COMPREHENSIVE JUDGMENT (3:6-8)

⁶*I have cut off nations;*[a] *desolate are their corner towers.*[b]
  I have devastated their streets, empty of any passerby.
    Their cities are laid waste,[c] *empty of anyone, without inhabitant.*
⁷*I thought,*[d] *"Surely,*[e] *you will fear me,*
  you will accept correction,"[f]
    and her dwelling[g] *would not be cut off*
      [according to][h] *everything that I appointed against*[i] *her.*
But in fact,[j] *they eagerly corrupted*[k]
  all their deeds.
⁸*Therefore, wait*[l] *for me, utterance of YHWH,*
  when I arise for prey.[m]
For my decree is to assemble nations, for me[n] *to gather kingdoms,*[o]
  to pour out upon them[p] *my indignation,*
    all my burning anger.
Indeed,[q] *by the fire of my passion shall the whole earth be consumed.*

a. LXX *hyperēphanous* ("arrogant ones") suggests *gē'îm* for *gôyīm*. Roberts (*Nahum*, 208) reads *gôyām* ("their nation") for *gôyīm* (*nations*) and makes a similar change in v. 9. He recognizes that there is no support for this from the versions and that suffixed forms of *gôy* are rare. He points out that a suffixed form is found in 2:9 and that the rarity of such forms would have given rise to the misunderstanding (*gôyām* is not in fact attested at all). But the perspective of previous chapters gives good reason to think of the plural *gôyīm* here, and any ambiguity in the consonantal text could have been avoided by using *hgwy* (*haggôy*, "the nation").

b. Taking my lead from the masoretic accentuation, I keep these four Hebrew words together in one line. Alternatively, they and the next two lines could be scanned as bicola. To my ears, the longer lines convey gravity while shorter lines of three bicola would produce an undesirable staccato effect.

c. This hapax legomenon is likely an Aramaic loanword. The occurrences of *ṣdh* in Exod 21:13 and 1 Sam 24:12 are of a homonym related to *ṣwd*.

d. Or "I said." *'Āmartî* is probably best understood here as equivalent to *'āmartî bəlibbî* ("I said in my heart" = "I thought"; cf. 1:12; 2:15 above; occasionally the preposition *'el* ["to"] is used instead; so in Gen 8:21, the only instance of the full phrase in which YHWH is the subject), as clearly, e.g., in Judg 15:2 (*'āmōr 'āmartî* within reported speech) and Ruth 4:4. Cf. Jer 3:7.

e. Or "Above all fear me and receive correction!" Cf. the use of *'ak* in Exod 31:13. When Ben Zvi (*Zephaniah*, 215) and others think that *'ak* has a restrictive meaning here ("only," cf. LXX *plēn*), this is presumably what they have in mind. But *surely* seems to fit the context better. Cf. Muraoka, *Emphatic Words*, 129–30.

f. LXX and Sweeney (*Zephaniah*, 167) translate the verbs in these lines as imperatives. In this case, the opening is understood as "I said" rather than *I thought*. The second-person forms are firmly attested in the versions as well as MT; a change to third-person forms (cf. *BHS*, NRSV) is unwarranted.

g. LXX *ex ophthalmōn autēs* ("out of sight," lit. "out of her eyes," although rendered in NETS as "before its eyes") reads *m'ynyh* instead of *m'wnh* (cf. Peshitta *mn 'ynyh*). 8ḤevXIIgr has *[p]ēgē [au]tēs* ("her fountain"), which also reflects *m'ynyh* (cf. Prov 4:21). It is thus well attested as an ancient reading, and many prefer it to MT (e.g., Elliger in *BHS*; Rudolph, *Micha*, 286; Ryou, *Oracles*, 65–66; Irsigler, *Zefanja*, 341). On balance, MT seems preferable to me; cf. Weigl, *Zefanja*, 158–59; Ben Zvi, *Zephaniah*, 216–18.

h. The relationship between this line and the preceding is not clear. Some consider it the subject of *cut off*. More likely, the bicolon refers to (avoiding) punishment. Either the negation carries over from the previous line or "according to" is implied. The latter is my interpretation. It is unnecessary to assume that a *kaph* dropped out from an original *kkl* to produce *kl* (*kōl*), but this is possible.

i. Hebrew *pqd 'āl* can also be used for appointing a task for someone (Num 4:27; Job 36:23; 2 Chr 36:23 = Ezra 1:2). If "out of sight" is read instead of *her dwelling* (see previous note), this rarer use of the phrase is sometimes adopted, but Roberts (*Nahum*, 209) recognizes the difficulties of taking the phrase in anything other than its common, hostile sense here—the sense it also has in LXX (*exedikēsa ep' autēn*); cf. its use for "punish" in 1:8–9, 12. Vlaardingerbroek (*Zephaniah*, 183) opts for "despite everything that I have against her," comparing 2 Sam 3:8.

j. Hebrew *'ākēn* is an exclamation to emphasize the unexpected; cf. Muraoka, *Emphatic Words*, 132. It is often used after the verb *'mr* ("to say"), either at the beginning of the cited speech, in which case it is strongly affirmative ("surely," Gen 28:16; Exod 2:14; 1 Sam 15:32; Jer 4:10 after the vocative), or later in the speech, in which case it is strongly contrastive ("nevertheless," "but in fact," Pss 31:22[23]; 82:7; Job 32:8; Isa 49:4; Jer 3:20).

k. Literally, "they got up early, they corrupted." The verb for rising early is also used idiomatically in Hebrew for expressing eagerness. Vlaardingerbroek (*Zephaniah*, 179) translates "they consistently made all their deeds corrupt."

l. The MT has a masculine plural imperative, presumably addressing the inhabitants of Jerusalem (cf. the end of v. 7). The LXX and Vulg. render it as a singular imperative, presumably addressing the city itself (cf. the beginning of v. 7).

m. Depending on the vocalization, *l'd* can be read as *for prey* (*lə'ad*; so MT), "as a witness" (*lə'ēd*; cf. LXX, *eis martyrion*, and Tg., "for judgment"), or "forever" (*lā'ad*; cf. Vulg. *in futurum* and the citation in Exodus Rabbah 17, "for a time," quoted in Sweeney, *Zephaniah*, 180 n. 36), which maybe carries the nuance "once for all" (Berlin, *Zephaniah*, 133). Another meaning, "to the throne," has been postulated based on Ugaritic *'d* for throne or throne room, but a number of lexicographers remain skeptical; see recent dictionaries. I will discuss the options further in the commentary.

n. Many ancient and modern translations omit the suffix. Some scholars interpret the final *yod* as a paragogic vowel, but this would be highly unusual with an infinitive (cf. *HGHS* 65j-m; JM 93l-q). Sabottka (*Zephanja*, 114) interprets the suffix as a dative, "to gather for myself." In either case, YHWH's role is stressed.

o. LXX has "kings" instead, maybe to distinguish nations gathered for judgment (where they might receive pardon) from kings gathered for punishment (experiencing the full force of divine wrath); cf. Jerome, *Twelve*, 1:150. Sabottka (*Zephanja*, 114) believes that this is indeed the meaning of *mamlākôt* here.

p. For the reference, see the commentary. Rudolph (*Micha*, 290) argues for an emendation to *'ălêkem* ("upon you"); cf. *BHS*. Irsigler (*Zefanja*, 345-46), who had earlier agreed with Rudolph, now considers the emendation unnecessary.

q. Or "for."

Composition

The discussion of the composition of the previous section (Zeph 3:1-5) reviewed the reasons for thinking that there is a smaller or greater caesura at v. 6. My decision to treat vv. 6-8 separately rather than as a paragraph within 3:1-8, which would also be defensible, reflects my desire to underline that vv. 6-7 speak from a later perspective. Verse 6 picks up *corner towers* from 1:16, *without inhabitant* from 2:5, and *passerby* (although now absent) from 2:15; *heḥĕrabtî* (*I have devastated*) relates to *ḥōreb* (*devastation*) in 2:14. The choice of vocabulary in the verse is presumably designed to echo the judgment of which the previous two chapters spoke. An explicit link in v. 7 with 3:2 is established by the use of the idiom "accepting correction," which is not elsewhere found outside Jeremiah and Proverbs (see the translation note on 3:2). The verse also picks up the expression *pqd 'al*, which ch. 1 featured, albeit with a different nuance, three times for the punishment appointed (1:8-9, 12; cf. 2:7). These last two links do not, however, establish 3:1-7 as a literary unit but result from the general character of this passage as a response to what had been said previously.

Verse 8 is linked to the preceding by the opening *therefore*, which introduces something that follows from the preceding. *Therefore* should be seen as marking a minor break, a transition from premise to conclusion, but not a major division. The content of v. 8, however, does not seem to fit with the preceding. In its received form, the verse speaks of judgment on nations and kingdoms, but the preceding verses accuse Jerusalem.[453] A common solution

---

453. Floyd (*Minor Prophets 2*, 202-4) believes that the command to wait can only be understood positively (hope for YHWH) and that therefore v. 8 neither focuses on Judah nor even announces punishment. He considers it parallel to 2:1-3. Sweeney (*Zephaniah*,

for this problem is to postulate that parts of the verse are later or that the assembling of the nations was originally to pour out wrath on Jerusalem. This solution often entails changing the prepositional phrase *upon them* to "upon you" (the city). To my mind, the solution lies in the opposite direction. The concluding demonstration of Jerusalem's guilt (3:1–5) did not need a specific announcement of judgment parallel to that for the other political entities in 2:5–15 because ch. 1 had already announced the disaster at great length, focusing on Jerusalem. It is likely that v. 8 was originally the conclusion not only of 3:1–5 but of 2:5–3:5. It echoes the comprehensive language of ch. 1 because the judgment on Jerusalem is at the heart of a more wide-ranging judgment. Preconceived notions of alleged eschatological schemes (judgment on the people of God followed by judgment on the nations, which ushers in salvation for God's people) prevent some from seeing that in the light of 1:2–3:5 (or 1:2–3:7), the judgment on the nations very much includes Judah and Jerusalem.[454] This is reinforced by the way v. 8 is phrased, only establishing with the very last line that the nations are gathered to experience rather than execute judgment. Because he reads v. 8 as the consequence specifically of vv. 6–7, Irsigler reckons that a judgment in which Jerusalem is only implicitly included would have to be attributed to a redactor.[455] He believes instead that *upon them* originally referred to the people of Jerusalem (cf. the change of person in v. 7) and that the final line that speaks of *the whole earth* was added later.[456] But the echoes of ch. 1 are found from the first line onward and suggest that v. 8 always had this wider scope.

Floyd argues that the opening command is not meant to threaten but "to foster a particular attitude toward Yahweh, in connection with what is happening on the day when Yahweh acts." On this basis, he takes it with what follows rather than what precedes.[457] This understanding of the imperative seems wrong and will be discussed in the commentary on the verse. But the problem with beginning a major new section in v. 8 not only lies in the

---

167–92) also reads the command positively, addressed to the remnant of Judah, but believes that earlier verses are about restoration as well and so keeps vv. 5–13 together.

454. Contra Sweeney, *Zephaniah*, 179. While Sweeney persistently argues against the threefold eschatological scheme, he nevertheless separates judgment on Judah from judgment on other nations in a way that Zephaniah does not.

455. Irsigler, *Zefanja*, 344. He rightly rejects the view that a postulated change of an earlier "upon you" to *upon them* would have served to detract judgment away from Jerusalem (345).

456. Irsigler, *Zefanja*, 345–46; cf. Vlaardingerbroek, *Zephaniah*, 179–80. Roberts (*Nahum*, 216) argues that *upon them* refers to the people of Jerusalem and that the last line merely reflects the fact that "a judgment on Jerusalem would inevitably affect the inhabitants of its larger territory outside the city."

457. Floyd, *Minor Prophets 2*, 203.

opening *therefore*, which invites a link with the preceding, but also in the fact that v. 7 seems to ask for a continuation, spelling out YHWH's response to the continuing rebellion. This would be one of the reasons for adding vv. 6–7 between 3:5 and 3:8 rather than after 3:8. Another reason would be that the next section more appropriately follows v. 8 rather than vv. 6–7.

Dating such an addition is extremely difficult. There is one small piece of evidence to suggest that vv. 6–7 are also pre-597. This will be discussed below with regard to the composition of 3:9–13. The new edition may have been produced in response to the fall of the Philistine cities in about 600 BC.

Commentary

6 Each of the three lines emphasizes the absence of a population.[458] The phrase *mibbəlî-ʾîš* is attested also in Jer 9:11(10). There, the full phrase is *mibbəlî-ʾîš ʿōbēr*, "empty of anyone passing through"—that is "[the pastures are so scorched that] no one travels through them." The author of Zeph 3:6 may have known Jer 9:10 and split up the phrase, distributing it onto two lines: *empty of any passerby . . . empty of anyone*. There is no other context for this statement than the one given in the book. The allusions to earlier parts of the book (1:16; 2:5, 14–15; see above under "Composition") suggest that the verse refers to the beginning fulfillment of the disaster announced in previous chapters.[459] The following verse indicates that *the nations* does not include Judah. If it has been affected by the comprehensive judgment, it is not yet devastated and desolate. But the judgment is under way, presumably having by now engulfed Assyria (614 fall of Assur, 612 fall of Nineveh, 609 fall of Harran, 605 final defeat of the Assyrians in the battle of Carchemish) and the Philistine cities (604 Ashkelon and subsequently Ekron, Ashdod, and Gaza). By the end of 597, many cities had been destroyed, from their military installations (*corner towers*) to their places of public life (*streets*), and Jerusalem had experienced the deportation of a significant part of its population.[460] The fact that Jerusalem did not belong to the cities that had been devastated could either have strengthened the mistaken belief in Zion's inviolability or been taken as a final, gracious moment for repentance. The author of vv. 6–7 would have urged the latter.

458. Note that *šmm* ("be desolate," *niphal*, similar to *qal*) often has the connotation of "made uninhabited" as a result of violence; see Jer 33:10; Zech 7:14 among others.

459. Note that the allusions are to oracles against the Philistine cities and Assyria but not Moab and the Ammonites. The Transjordanian nations may not have seen destruction as a result of the rise of the Neo-Babylonian Empire by the time these verses were composed.

460. Having changed *nations* to "their nation" (see the translation note), Roberts (*Nahum*, 214) thinks instead of the Assyrian devastation of Judah during Hezekiah's reign.

7 The presence in one verse of second-person feminine singular address, third-person feminine singular references (to the city), and third-person masculine plural references (to the inhabitants), all indicating essentially the same group of people, is remarkable. The use of the second person in the initial bicolon conveys a sense of (internal) pleading with the addressee, the shift to the third person a certain wistfulness, as the imagined pleading trails off but the feminine singular is retained. The third-person plural forms complete the distancing and highlight the plurality of evildoers within the city. A desire to poetically trace such a movement may be behind the use of the pronoun with *dwelling*, which some consider unnecessary and illogical, given that the city is addressed.[461] The address to the city is of course an address to its population, so the reference to *her dwelling* is not absurd. Jerusalem stands under the same sentence as Assur, Nineveh, Ashkelon, and the other cities mentioned above, but it has not yet been *cut off*. This verse suggests that there is yet the possibility of *everything that I appointed against her* not being implemented.

8 Much turns on the question whether *wait for me* can be understood in a threatening sense. Floyd thinks that it is difficult to imagine so and that the exhortation must be positive, asking those addressed (Judah) to wait in hope for YHWH to act.[462] Now it is only to be expected that with YHWH as the object of waiting or hoping, the connotations are regularly positive. But the claim that the verb could not possibly be negative is more difficult to establish, and not only because it discounts the possibility of irony. There are in fact verbs that are more common for waiting upon and hoping for YHWH (*yḥl*, *qwh*), and it may be that the choice of a rare verb facilitates a more negative meaning. Schibler concludes his examination of the verb by claiming that "like *śbr*, but unlike *qwh* and *yḥl*, *ḥkh* does not necessarily denote hope. Given its main usages in the Latter Prophets and in Psalms, its main idea is mere waiting, albeit expectantly or with patient endurance."[463] In other words, if the intention had been "to foster a particular attitude toward Yahweh,"[464] *yḥl* or *qwh* would have been more suitable. The sense here is more along the lines of "just wait and see what I will be doing," which in

---

461. Notably Rudolph, *Micha*, 286.

462. Floyd, *Minor Prophets 2*, 202. Cf. Sweeney, *Zephaniah*, 179–80.

463. Daniel Schibler, "חכה," *NIDOTTE* 2:130. While Christoph Barth ("חָכָה, *chākhāh*," *TDOT* 4:359–63) at one point seems to resist drawing such a distinction, he acknowledges that in narrative texts, "the word is used only in a neutral sense" (362; see 2 Kgs 7:9; 9:3; cf. Job 32:4) and that in the prophetic literature, the focus is on patient waiting and endurance (363), the opposite being changing or becoming active (361).

464. Floyd, *Minor Prophets 2*, 203.

other contexts could very well be positive, but following on from v. 7, we need not be surprised that it turns out to be more threatening.[465]

As indicated in the translation note, *l'd* was already understood in various ways in antiquity. First, and most straightforward, the judicial sense "as a witness" (cf. LXX) fits well, evoking the image of a court in which YHWH is accuser and judge (cf. Mal 3:5).[466] It is interesting to observe that the Greek translation of the Minor Prophets shows a predilection for the phrase *eis martyrion* ("for a testimony/witness"). The phrase renders *lə'ēd* in Mic 1:2, as one might expect, but it is also found in three more places where the Hebrew text transmitted in MT gives no reason to use it, namely in Hos 2:12(14); Amos 1:12; Mic 7:18.[467] One might therefore expect the translator to take the opportunity given here with *l'd*, regardless of any other possibilities of understanding the phrase. Second, maybe the least straightforward reading is the one that understands the phrase to have a decisive future reference. If it is possible to understand "for perpetuity" here as meaning "once for all," this would add an appropriate nuance, especially following vv. 6–7. But in my view, the phrase cannot carry this nuance very readily. Last but not least, the MT *lə'ad* (*for prey*) seems to allude back to v. 3; note that Gen 49:27 speaks of Benjamin as a wolf (*zə'ēb*) who "in the morning" (*babbōqer*) eats prey (*'ad*). A double entendre is plausible here: YHWH will (once for all?) go for *prey/ booty*, but "as a witness"—which is to say as a judge who enacts justice in accordance with evidence, unlike Jerusalem's judges. This link back to v. 3 helps readers to include Jerusalem's leaders in the phrase *upon them*,[468] just as the final line of the verse ensures that the nations are included as objects rather than executors of the judgment. Ben Zvi correctly observes, "It is almost self-evident that the existence of multiple possible meanings is the main stylistic feature of the phrase." He concludes that "the communicative meaning of the phrase is not exhausted by the translation 'for the booty,' 'as a witness, as an accuser' or 'forever,' but embraces all of these meanings."[469]

At first, the assembling of *nations* and gathering of *kingdoms* may be for

465. Cf. Vlaardingerbroek, *Zephaniah*, 184. Ivan J. Ball (*Zephaniah*, 231) suggests that the use of *wait for me* "continues the tension and irony of the passage."

466. See also Jer 29:23; Mic 1:2; Ps 50:7. Where YHWH is witness for the prosecution, he is almost inevitably also the judge. This is presumably also the implication in Gen 31:50.

467. Outside the Book of the Twelve, by contrast, it usually corresponds to MT *lā'ēd* (Gen 31:44; Deut 31:19, 26; Job 16:8) or *lə'ēdâ* (Gen 21:30; Josh 24:27 [2×]). In Prov 29:14, the MT has *lā'ad*. LXX 1 Sam 9:24 has *eis martyrion* for MT *lammô'ēd*; cf. *hē skēnē tou martyriou* for *'ōhel mô'ēd* ("the tent of meeting") numerous times in the Pentateuch.

468. Cf. *my burning anger* with *YHWH's burning anger* against Jerusalem in 2:2.

469. Ben Zvi, *Zephaniah*, 222, 223. Cf., more cautiously, Ivan J. Ball, *Zephaniah*, 171–72; Ryou, *Oracles*, 277–78.

the purpose of executing YHWH's *decree* or judgment on Jerusalem.[470] But the use of *'sp* (*assemble*) right at the beginning of the book (1:2; see the translation note on *I will make a sweeping end*) prepares for the final line, which includes the *nations* and *kingdoms* as objects of YHWH's *indignation* and *burning anger*. To pour out upon them my indignation, all my burning anger is similar to Ps 69:24(25) and finds an echo in Ezek 22:31.[471] As argued above, the original announcement of comprehensive judgment is not eschatological. It speaks of the end of the world as Judah knew it, of a punishment YHWH would bring that would encompass the whole region. This could be seen as fulfilled in the end of the Neo-Assyrian Empire and the widespread destruction brought by the Babylonians, out of which arose a new political order.[472] It seems possible to read this verse in analogous ways, at least at first. Allusions to the Tower of Babel story in vv. 9–10 and reference to Cush in retrospect may broaden this so that the reference to the entire region becomes *the whole earth*.

Reflection

Hadjiev observes:

> The structure and the main idea of this passage parallels Amos 4.6–12 in a striking way. In both places we have actions of Yahweh in history designed to lead his people to repentance but which ultimately fail to achieve their goal. Both passages culminate with a brief final description of judgment introduced with 'therefore'. In both cases the description is cryptic and, ironically, uses somewhat ambiguous verbs that can be taken in a positive sense. Both times the punishment is in fact the personal appearance of God, and readers are challenged to expect that appearance with all its terrible but not clearly stated consequences (more so in Amos than in Zephaniah). The parallels in structure, thought pattern and technique between these two passages are so strong that it does not seem very likely that they were formulated completely independently from one another.[473]

470. Vlaardingerbroek (*Zephaniah*, 187) objects to the idea that "the peoples pour out YHWH's wrath upon Judah" on the grounds "that one can hardly pour out someone else's wrath," but he misunderstands the view of Rudolph and others here; it would of course still be YHWH's anger that he would pour out in his judgment, even if he used the nations as his instrument. Sweeney (*Zephaniah*, 181) lists and gives references for the different contexts in which the verbs are used.

471. Cf. Kapelrud, *Message*, 57.

472. Cf., e.g., Isa 10:14, 23; 13:5; Jer 4:23–28; 8:16; and the reference to Babylon as "the hammer of the whole earth" (*paṭṭîš kol-hā'āreṣ*) in Jer 50:23.

473. Hadjiev, "Zephaniah," 330.

He also points out that "the influence is on the level of ideas rather than on the level of specific words and expressions."[474] This makes it less likely that we are dealing with a redactor of the Book of the Twelve here. The vocabulary used in this section is in fact very much indebted to earlier parts of Zephaniah. Pfeiffer called Amos 4:6–12 "far more impressive" than the passage in Zephaniah.[475] This may be so from the point of view of poetic rhetoric, but our passage fulfills its apparent purpose very effectively. It reports that the judgment Zephaniah has prophesied about has begun and that even now Jerusalem has not taken warning. The parallel in Amos 4, whether or not it helped to inspire this passage, highlights that this was not unpredictable. While Amos focuses on divine castigation not leading to repentance, here the action has been against other nations, at least primarily, and the link with what precedes also throws a spotlight on the limits of what preaching can achieve, even if we need not assume that Zephaniah had great hopes of what his call to repentance might accomplish. Christians may be reminded of Matt 23:37: "Jerusalem, Jerusalem, who kills the prophets and stones those who are sent to her! How often I wanted to gather your children together, the way a hen gathers her chicks under her wings, and you were not willing!"[476] But this does not mean that the proclamation was pointless. Those who preserved and passed on the book of Zephaniah clearly did not think so. The prophetic proclamation makes it possible to identify divine action and motives and to respond to YHWH accordingly.

Even without 3:9–20, it is evident from what has been said so far in the book that the consuming fire of God's wrath will not be the end of the story. There are those who believe that the references to a Judahite remnant and to YHWH's acknowledgement by the nations in ch. 2 are later additions, maybe influenced by 3:9–20, as if the presence of survivors were at odds with the picture painted in the opening chapter. But I see no reason to believe that Zephaniah proclaimed the destruction of the world in an apocalyptic sense, nor the annihilation of God's people, nor the end of YHWH's relationship with Judah and Jerusalem. To be sure, the proclamation spoke of a complete disaster, but the focus has been on the urban elites for whom this judgment will indeed be the end. Just as 3:1–5 characterized Jerusalem in terms of its leadership and in a way that implied the existence of victims of injustice and oppression, quite possibly within Jerusalem itself, so vv. 6–7 do not require us to believe that absolutely no one responded. They speak of Jerusalem in broad terms and may have the response of the elite particularly in mind. Nor does 3:8 undo what—synchronically at least but also chronologically in my

474. Hadjiev, "Zephaniah," 330–31.

475. Robert H. Pfeiffer, *Introduction to the Old Testament* (London: Adam and Charles Black, 1952), 601.

476. Cf. Vlaardingerbroek, *Zephaniah*, 165.

view—has already been said in 2:11. The ultimate aim of the judgment is not annihilation but the acknowledgement of YHWH in the humiliation of all that is proud and lofty.

Vlaardingerbroek draws attention to our need for balancing the desirability of being specific, naming groups of sinners concretely, and recognizing at the same time that we are all under sin and judgment, a concept he finds more prominently in the NT.[477] It is noteworthy that while Zephaniah consistently locates the cause for the coming disaster among the elites, he does not adopt the voice of a spokesperson for the oppressed. He assumes that those who seek God's kingdom and justice are at present only to be found among the humble poor but in my reading of the critical verses he (a) had called on the elites to humble themselves and join the group of those who want to see God's justice implemented (2:1) and (b) urged the humble poor to (continue to) seek justice and humility (2:3), thereby assuming that low socioeconomic status does not guarantee a seeking for justice and humility. While the assumption is that the rich tend to be arrogant and the materially humble tend to be also spiritually humble because YHWH is the only help left to them, the boundaries between the two groups is not fixed.

Finally, and again following Vlaardingerbroek's lead, we may observe how the rhetoric of God not knowing (*I thought . . . but . . .*) is used to offer an insight into YHWH's heart.[478] While some may prefer to read God's internal monologue in more literal ways as indicative of a change of divine attitude or perspective, this does not seem advisable here. The previous material in Zephaniah gives no grounds for believing that the prophet, let alone God, held any great hope of a turnaround in Jerusalem, and it is by no means necessary to do so based on v. 7.[479] We have here a rhetorical device that stresses the logic of repentance.[480] It is arguably a characteristic of all sin and of all failure to repent that ultimately it makes no sense. In addition, the anthropomorphic description of a divine monologue serves to highlight that God is not a neutral dispenser of justice who indifferently rewards the good and punishes the evil. His desire is for a positive outcome, which means a restored relationship.

But if the first instances of judgment have had no such positive result, what is the point of reaffirming and maybe extending the wide-ranging punishment, as v. 8 does? An answer is only forthcoming in the following verses, but if, as v. 5 claimed, God unfailingly executes his righteous decree, the suspension of judgment cannot be the answer to lack of responsiveness on

---

477. Vlaardingerbroek, *Zephaniah*, 165.
478. Vlaardingerbroek, *Zephaniah*, 182.
479. Contra Irsigler, *Zefanja*, 346, who speaks of YHWH's deep disappointment.
480. Similar things could be said of Jer 3:19–20.

the part of Jerusalem or indeed the nations. For the sake of the powerless and oppressed, for all those who suffer under the current regime, there has to be a reckoning, and v. 8 promises it. But if YHWH's desire is for a positive outcome, as suggested in v. 7, there is going to be a future beyond this comprehensive judgment, even if this has been barely sketched out so far in Zephaniah through the references to a remnant and to the demotion of other gods that comes with international judgment and the subsequent acknowledgement of YHWH among the nations.

VIII. ANNOUNCEMENT OF A FUTURE BEYOND JUDGMENT (3:9-13)

^{9}*Surely then^a I will transfer to^b the^c peoples^d pure^e speech,^{f}*
so that all of them will call on the name of YHWH^g
to serve him with one accord.^{h}
^{10}*From beyond the rivers of Cush,*
my supplicants,^{i} the daughter of my dispersed,^{j}
will bring my tribute.
^{11}*On that day, you shall not be disgraced because of all your deeds*
by which you have rebelled against me.
For then I will remove from your midst
those of you exulting^k with pride
and you shall no longer continue to be haughty^l on my holy mount.^{m}
^{12}*And I will leave [a remnant]^n in your midst,*
a humble and powerless people,^{o}
and they shall seek refuge in the name of YHWH.
^{13}*The remnant of Israel:^{p} they^q will not commit iniquity,*
and they will not tell lies;^{r}
no deceitful tongue^s will be found^t in their mouths.
It is they who^u will graze and lie down;
no one will make them afraid.

a. Hebrew *kî-'āz* is found here and in v. 11. Elsewhere the phrase, sometimes with and at other times without *maqqep*, always has a close relationship with what preceded. It follows a negated statement in Deut 29:20(19) and Josh 1:8 and introduces the apodosis of a conditional sentence in 2 Sam 2:27 and 19:6(7) and a causal clause in 2 Sam 5:24. The occurrences in Zephaniah may be best compared with Job 11:15; 22:26; and Jer 22:22, where *kî-'āz* introduces the ultimate result of an if-then sequence. (In Job 38:21, the two particles *kî* and *'āz* arguably fulfill separate roles even though a *maqqep* connects them in MT.)

b. Or maybe "I will change in consideration of the peoples [their impure into] pure speech." The Hebrew expression is difficult to imitate in English. For "in consideration of" as a rendering of the preposition, cf. 2 Sam 1:24; 24:16. *HALOT* suggests "restore pure language" for this verse, but while the verb can refer to a turning around/back, and especially retreating in battle (e.g., Judg 20:39, 41; 2 Kgs 5:26), glossing "restore" presumes a notion of return to an earlier state for which there does not seem to be any parallel.

c. MurXII has the definite article (with the preposition ʿal, "upon," rather than ʾel as in MT), which in MT is omitted. This seems to me a stylistic matter without any difference in meaning. In English, the sentence reads better with the article, especially given the continuation.

d. Roberts (Nahum, 210) again thinks that the context requires ʿammām ("their people") rather than ʿammîm (peoples); cf. above on v. 6. Cf. Elliger's proposal in BHS to read ʿammî ("my people"), which is adopted, e.g., by Vlaardingerbroek, Zephaniah, 189, 192, 196.

e. Tg., Peshitta, Vulg., Aquila, and Theodotion interpret bərûrâ as "chosen." This may reflect the view that the confusion of languages (Gen 11:1–9) is here reversed; see the commentary. LXX has eis genean autēs, presumably reflecting the visually very similar bdwrh instead of brwrh.

f. The singular śāpâ ("lip") does not usually refer to the physical organ. Here it denotes the "manner of speaking," namely speech as, e.g., in Job 12:20; Prov 12:19; 17:4, 7; cf. the use of the singular in Isa 19:18 and four times in Gen 11:1–9 for "language." It would be nonsensical to have one "lip" pure but not the other, and the singular never stands for the plural "lips" (understood literally) as far as I know; cf. Ben Zvi, Zephaniah, 225. Elsewhere the singular is used, e.g., for the seashore or the edge of a piece of a fabric.

g. Given the standard use of the phrase (e.g., Gen 4:26; 12:8; Joel 2:32[3:5]) and the preceding reference to speech, this rendering is more likely than the alternative "to call, all of them, in the name of YHWH," which is adopted by Sweeney, Zephaniah, 167.

h. Literally "shoulder"; hence some translate "shoulder to shoulder" (e.g., NIV, NASB). The notion that the unique phrase refers to the idea of sharing under one yoke (LXX hypo zygon hena) is old, unless the LXX translator merely rendered idiomatically. Sabottka (Zephanja, 117) points out that in Hebrew, a yoke is said to be carried on the neck (ṣawwāʾr; cf. Gen 27:40; Deut 28:48; Isa 10:27; Jer 27:8, 11–12; 28:11, 14; 30:8; Lam 1:14), not the shoulder (šəkem). This is true even where šəkem appears in parallel constructions with ʿōl ("yoke," Isa 9:4[3]; 10:27; 14:25). The image is more likely derived from jointly carrying a burden; cf. Vlaardingerbroek, Zephaniah, 197.

i. The meaning assumed here is based on the verb, the noun not being attested otherwise with this meaning (cf. Ezek 8:11, "fragrance"). The form is rather unexpected, as nouns of this formation do not usually designate persons (cf. HGHS 61s″). If ʿātār is distinct from the (unattested) participle ʿôtēr, it may designate a collective of supplicants, in which case we could think of communities of supplicants here, but it is just as likely that the noun is an alternative form with the same meaning as the participle. Against the accentuation, the verse could be scanned as a bicolon: From beyond the rivers of Cush will be my supplicants / the daughter of my dispersed will bring my tribute. See Vlaardingerbroek, Zephaniah, 199; cf. Ben Zvi, Zephaniah, 229. In this case my supplicants would clearly be parallel to the daughter of my dispersed and refer to the peoples of v. 9.

j. This line is missing in early Greek and Syriac texts and is often considered a later gloss. It is attested in MurXII. An alternative understanding of the syntax would allow the rendering "my supplicants will bring the daughter of my dispersed as my tribute." Some read batəpûṣâ ("in the dispersion"), but apart from the textually difficult təpôṣôtîkem in Jer 25:34 (with holem!), təpûṣâ appears to be attested only in post-Talmudic Hebrew. For other emendations, see, e.g., Vlaardingerbroek, Zephaniah, 195; and for fuller discussion of the options Ben Zvi, Zephaniah, 227–30. Departing from his earlier view (Literary Precursors,

202), Nogalski (*Book of the Twelve*, 744) now proposes that *the daughter of my dispersed* is "a vocative referring to Lady Zion." This is implausible because, if anything, Jerusalem is the mother, not the daughter, of the exiles.

k. LXX *ta phaulismata tēs hybreōs sou* does not refer to persons but to "the contemptible acts of your pride."

l. On the *qal* infinitive construct with feminine *-â* ending, see GKC 45d; JM 49d.

m. Given that *qōdeš* is used in Biblical Hebrew much more often to designate something as holy than to refer to the sanctuary, for which *miqdāš* is the standard word, "on the mount of my sanctuary" is unlikely as an alternative translation.

n. Hebrew *wəhiš'artî* is usually just rendered *I will leave*. I have added *[a remnant]* to signal the use of the root taken up at the beginning of the next verse.

o. The accentuation keeps the first two lines more closely together than I have done.

p. In LXX and some modern translations, this is connected with the previous verse, an option favored by a number of commentators as well; e.g., Vlaardingerbroek, *Zephaniah*, 189. The overall sense of the passage is not affected, as *the remnant of Israel* is surely to be identified with *a humble and powerless people* and the subject of the relevant verbs. In neither case is seeking refuge clearly established as a condition for being rescued (contra Vlaardingerbroek, *Zephaniah*, 204).

q. The use of plural verbs with a collective singular noun is unobjectionable; cf. 2:9. It would therefore be possible to translate, "The remnant of Israel will not commit iniquity . . ." My belief that this verse serves to define the remnant (implied in the verb in the previous verse) suggested this more complex rendering to me.

r. The accentuation again suggests longer lines both here and in the second half of the verse, which has only two disjunctive accents, maybe treating the passage as prose.

s. Hebrew *ləšôn tarmît* only appears here; cf. Job 27:4, "my lips shall not speak iniquity and my tongue (*ləšônî*) not whisper deceit (*rəmiyyâ*)"; *ləšôn rəmiyyâ* in Mic 6:12; Ps 120:2–3.

t. Hebrew *lāšôn* is usually construed as a feminine noun, but it is treated as a masculine here.

u. *Kî* here probably further emphasizes the personal pronoun. This presents a good case for asseverative *kî*; it would seem forced to read the statement as either giving the cause or offering a contrast to the preceding; see the commentary.

Composition

The previous section (3:6–8) was like an appendix to 1:1–3:5. As argued above, this results from the addition of vv. 6–7, which noted (the beginning of) the fulfillment of the specific announcements in 2:5–15 and stated Jerusalem's failure even then to respond to the announcement of judgment. This confirmed that Jerusalem's destruction was indeed inevitable. It seems unlikely that Zephaniah ever expected this to be the complete end of God's people, and I argued earlier that the verses speaking of a remnant in ch. 2 were likely not later additions.[481] Even more controversially, I also decided

---

481. Nor did I consider *all you humble of the land who act upon his judgment* in 2:3 a later gloss introduced from the end of the book.

against identifying 2:11 as a later addition. This shapes my interpretation of the relationship of this earlier material to the final paragraphs of the book. I interpret them as exegetical supplements (*Fortschreibung*), whether by the prophet himself or a disciple. I am skeptical about our ability to reconstruct the redaction histories of biblical books in detail with any degree of confidence, but my view is that a first edition of the book did not include 3:6-7, 9-20.[482] The first supplement (3:6-7) was added as Jerusalem's failure to turn to YHWH, following the defeat of the Neo-Assyrian Empire and the Babylonian conquests of Philistine cities, confirmed the earlier condemnation and announcement of judgment. This would have taken place before the destruction of the city, possibly after 597 and the first exile of Judahites to Babylon (but see below). Verses 9-20 are presumably later, though likely not as late as Vlaardingerbroek argues on the grounds that prophecies like 3:9-20 would be "counterproductive in preaching that still faces judgment."[483] It is not inconceivable that (an earlier form of) 3:9-13 was part of pre-destruction proclamation, but it seems unlikely, considering the different tone adopted for Jerusalem. While in 1:2-3:8, Jerusalem is identified with the rebelliousness of its elite, from v. 9 onward, Jerusalem and its elite are clearly distinguished. Given this and the eminent suitability of v. 8 as the conclusion of a first edition by way of inclusion, it seems probable that all of 3:9-20 is later than the body of the book. This also suggests that Ezekiel, who more than once drew on Zephaniah, would have been familiar with Zeph 1:1-3:5, 8 but likely not 3:9-20. As for vv. 6-7, it is interesting to observe that '*ălîlâ* is used in 3:7 and 3:11. This word is rare in prophetic literature. It is used for God's deeds in Isa 12:4 but otherwise only in Zephaniah and Ezekiel.[484] If Ezekiel, who is responsible for a third of all occurrences of '*ălîlâ* in the Hebrew Bible, is indebted to Zephaniah, this may argue for a pre-597 composition of vv. 6-7.[485] It would not have been necessary for Ezekiel to have had access to the occurrence in v. 11 as well.[486] The claim in Ezek 16 that the restoration of Jerusalem would in all fairness also require restoration of Sodom and Go-

---

482. In response to, e.g., Robertson, *Nahum*, 335, it needs pointing out that verses that were not part of the original composition are not to be eliminated; they are as canonical as the other verses. While there is no manuscript evidence for the existence of Zephaniah without 3:9-20 (which is not at all surprising, given that the earliest MSS are centuries younger than the final edition), neither is there any manuscript evidence for the existence of Zeph 3:9-20 without Haggai. Few would think that the latter means that there cannot have been a book of Zephaniah without Haggai at an earlier point.

483. Vlaardingerbroek, *Zephaniah*, 166.

484. Ezek 14:22-23; 20:43-44; 21:24(29); 24:14; 36:17, 19. Most other occurrences are in the Psalms (9×). Other than that, the word is used in Deut 22:14, 17; 1 Sam 2:3; 1 Chr 16:8.

485. For the date of Ezekiel, see Renz, *Rhetorical Function*, 27-55.

486. Note that Ezek 16:50 does not take up '*allîz* (*exultant*), which might have suggested

morrah can be compared to the way the purification of Jerusalem is set in the context of the purification of the nations in Zeph 3:6–7. Nevertheless, there are no lexical links to suggest dependence.

The remaining verses divide into two main sections: 3:9–13 and 3:14–20. It would be possible and defensible to subdivide the text further, but there are elements that tie the smaller units together. Thus, in my view, it makes sense to distinguish two main groupings: one focusing on YHWH's salvific action beyond judgment (vv. 9–13) and one focusing on the desired response to this action (vv. 14–20). *On that day* (v. 11) marks a paragraph break in the first section. On the reading offered here, vv. 9–10 pick up the wider, international focus of v. 8 before vv. 11–13 revert to concentrate on Jerusalem.[487] This second paragraph (vv. 11–13) has been considered by some the conclusion of a Deuteronomistic "Book of the Four," but Hadjiev rightly observes that the "literary horizon of 3.11–13 seems in the main to be the book of Zephaniah itself."[488] He concludes, "It seems that the point of 3.11–13 is to draw a parallel between the sins of the Judean upper class and those of the heathen nations."[489] The tribute-bearing in v. 10 leads naturally to a consideration of Jerusalem in vv. 11–12, and the concern with language (*pure speech*, v. 9; *not tell lies, no deceitful tongue*, v. 13) binds vv. 9–10 and vv. 11–13 together.

Ben Zvi notes that three times in the Psalms, those who *seek refuge* in YHWH call on him not to *be disgraced* (v. 11; see Pss 25:20; 31:1[2]; 71:1). Here, this pair of phrases is broken up and used in reverse order right at the beginning of v. 11 (after the necessarily first-positioned *on that day*) and right at the end of v. 12.[490] This strengthens the cohesion of this subunit and might argue against taking *the remnant of Israel* as the subject of seeking refuge.[491]

Commentary

9 The above translation of *surely then* assumes that *kî* functions here to add emphasis rather than to define a link with what precedes and that *kî 'āz*,

---

dependence on Zeph 3:11, although Zephaniah used the root already in 2:15 to characterize Jerusalem as Nineveh-like.

487. With a changed text (see the translation note), Vlaardingerbroek (*Zephaniah*, 193) sees here a "promise of conversion of dispersed Judeans."

488. Hadjiev, "Zephaniah," 331.

489. Hadjiev, "Zephaniah," 332.

490. Ben Zvi, *Zephaniah*, 231. He also compares Pss 22:5(6) and 25:2 (both with *bṭḥ*, "trust"; cf. trust in idols in Isa 42:17).

491. Sweeney (*Zephaniah*, 191) points out that a conjunction would be expected with *lō'-ya'ăśû* (*they will not commit*) if *šə'ērît yiśrā'ēl* (*remnant of Israel*) belonged with *shall seek refuge* in v. 12.

therefore, only indicates a temporal transition. This reading concurs with many grammarians and lexicographers who allow for this asseverative function, although it remains controversial among some. Alternatively, *kî* could perhaps be understood as adversative ("but then"), although this function usually follows a negative statement. An interesting reading results from discerning a causal nuance, maybe along the lines of "All this will be happening because . . ." If vv. 9–10 indicate the reason for the judgment in v. 8, they do so in the sense of introducing the ultimate purpose of all these events.[492] The description of the judgment in v. 8 with the language of *fire* and the notion of purification through fire (see Num 31:23, with *ṭhr* for "purify") could support this interpretation. But the root *brr* is nowhere linked with *'ēš* (*fire*), so it seems unwise to build too much on a possible rendering of the opening of the verse as causal. Isaiah 6, where a burning coal is used to purify Isaiah's lips, is sometimes adduced as a parallel and possible source of this verse, but neither *brr* nor *'ēš* is used there. In Isaiah, "unclean lips" (6:5) appear to relate to "evil" and "sin" generally (6:7), which compromise the worship offered (cf. 29:13).[493] Here, there is a greater focus on *speech* itself, with which we may compare Hos 2:17(19), which speaks of the removal of the names of Baals from the lips of Israel (cf. Zeph 1:4–6).[494] *I will transfer to the peoples pure speech* means that the speech of the peoples will be changed from being impure to being pure and that this is entirely YHWH's doing. Note that the verb chosen does not merely speak of "giving" *pure speech*; it "implies overthrow, destruction of the establishment, and abolition of the old status quo."[495] Transferring—turning over—to peoples *pure speech* is an overturning of the old order. Pure speech refers to integrity; it is sincere and truthful speech. We may compare Ps 15:2–3 for *pure speech* as a requirement for true worship.[496] (See also v. 13.)

This verse and the following are clearly related to 2:11. All three verses are sometimes seen as belonging to the same redaction.[497] Others see a de-

---

492. In Jer 22:22, such an appeal to ultimate purpose may be the only way to avoid the conclusion that *kî* in *kî 'āz* is asseverative.

493. Williamson, *Isaiah 1–27*, 63–66.

494. Cf. Timmer, *Non-Israelite Nations*, 161, although Timmer conflates Isa 6:5–7; Hos 2:17; and Zeph 3:9 to erase the distinctive emphasis on (idolatrous) speech, stressing (with Irsigler, *Zefanja*, 374) comprehensive moral-religious purification. The purification of all of life is surely presumed as well, but the emphasis here is on speech.

495. Judith Gärtner, "Jerusalem—City of God for Israel and for the Nations in Zeph 3:8, 9–10, 11–13," in *Perspectives on the Formation of the Book of the Twelve*, 276.

496. Cf. Ben Zvi, *Zephaniah*, 226; Berlin, *Zephaniah*, 133. In spite of this link, and overlooking the connection with earlier parts of the book, Berlin focuses on idolatrous or unintelligible speech as the antithesis to pure speech.

497. Tchavdar S. Hadjiev, "Survival, Conversion and Restoration: Reflections on the Redaction History of the Book of Zephaniah," *VT* 61 (2011): 579.

velopment, often from 3:9–10 to 2:11, with the latter being more universal-
istic because everyone worships YHWH in their own place. I have argued
that 2:11 has an integral place in the earlier part of the book. It speaks of
an acknowledgement of YHWH even in distant countries once YHWH has
demoted other gods through political events. Beyond what appears to have
been the original conclusion of the book, what we have here is an exegetical
development. It takes up the condemnation of the taunting and insults of
Moab and the Ammonites (2:8, 10). It reaffirms that there is no future for
such impure speech, but it expresses this in a more positive way: YHWH *will
transfer to the peoples pure speech*. Verse 10 also picks up the reference to the
Cushites in 2:12, thus combining allusions to 2:10 and 2:12 in its development
of 2:11. To some, perhaps especially to Christian readers with John 4:21 in
mind, 2:11 may look theologically more advanced, but within Zephaniah the
advancement seems to be in the other direction. While 2:11 merely speaks
of YHWH being acknowledged by distant nations as the true sovereign, in
3:9–10 there is a stronger implication that all nations will be involved (note
how the speech motif links with Moab and the Ammonites—i.e., neighboring
nations, not distant ones). In addition, there is now the thought of unity of
worship and service. The reference to this prior to the purification of Zion
itself arguably underlines its importance. YHWH not only seeks worshippers
in every place but seeks their unity as well. The promise here is for the sake of
YHWH and for the sake of true worship, not for the sake of Zion as such.

  10 *From beyond the rivers of Cush* seems inspired by 2:11 but heightens
the notion of distant lands with its use of *beyond*.[498] It is often thought that
this verse is indebted to Isa 18, which uses *from beyond the rivers of Cush* in
the opening designation (v. 1) and speaks of tribute-bearing to YHWH in its
concluding verse with the verb *ybl* (*bring*; *hiphil* in Zeph; *hophal* in Isa 18:7).[499]
In Isa 18, the tribute-bearing is all the more remarkable for coming from a
people that used to be "feared far and wide, a nation mighty and conquering"
(vv. 2, 7). But here, the stress falls on their distance, although maybe with a
different function than in ch. 2. While 2:11 could be read as marking a contrast

---

498. In the commentary on 1:1, I noted that interest in *Cush* may have been inspired by
Zephaniah's ancestry, but this must remain speculative. While such a connection might
suggest that these verses reproduce words of the prophet himself, it is not inconceivable
that a disciple developed the Nubian connection. I am content to leave the question open.

499. See, e.g., Sweeney, *Zephaniah*, 183; Irsigler, *Zefanja*, 372–73; John Hans de Jong,
"Making Sense in Zephaniah: An Intertextual Reading" (PhD diss., Auckland University
of Technology, 2015), 209–13. De Jong argues that *šay*, the typical word for "tribute," was
changed to *minḥâ* in Zephaniah to allude to Gen 4. Isa 18:7 is often, although not universally,
considered a later addition to an eighth-century oracle. Paul M. Cook (*A Sign and a Wonder:
The Redactional Formation of Isaiah 18–20*, VTSup 147 [Leiden: Brill, 2011], 66–70) dates it
to the end of the exilic period.

between distant lands such as Cush (and Assyria) and neighboring lands such as Moab, Ammon, and the Philistine territories,[500] here the tribute-bearers from the most distant region presumably stand in for all the peoples who worship and serve YHWH with one accord. If there are *supplicants* even *from beyond the rivers of Cush,* we may assume that those closer by will not be slow in bringing tribute either. In the light of v. 9, it seems most likely that the supplicants are not Judean exiles but non-Judeans.[501] Berlin argues for a Mesopotamian location of *Cush,* which suggests the rivers of the garden of Eden.[502] Nogalski follows this and adds that the eastward direction makes the promise more poignant as "an oblique allusion to exiles in Mesopotamia."[503] This interpretation is not out of the question, but it fails to persuade me. First, it is not securely established that Cush in Gen 2:13 refers to a Mesopotamian place rather than to Nubia. Second, Gen 2:13 links only one of the rivers to Cush. If the Cush of Zeph 3:10 and Gen 2:13 are the same, the single river in Gen 2:13 could be the Nile and the plural in our verse a reference to the Blue and the White Nile. If, however, "Gihon" in Gen 2:13 refers to a river near the Persian Gulf,[504] the use of the plural here is more problematic. It would seem necessary to identify *Cush* in broader terms than in Gen 2:13. Third, against Berlin's claim that *Cush* in Zeph 2:12 is Mesopotamian, I believe that it refers to the Nubian Empire. In this case, it is not likely that *Cush* refers to a completely different place here in 3:10.

Some have argued that *my supplicants, the daughter of my dispersed,* which is missing in some ancient versions, or *the daughter of my dispersed* only, is a later gloss that changes the tribute-bearers from non-Judean peoples (v. 9) to Judeans.[505] But the syntactical ambiguities argue against this. Surely someone

---

500. This would be the result of reconciling the statement about distant peoples acknowledging YHWH with a literal reading of the fate of Philistine, Moabite, and Ammonite territories. But note that Assyria is also described as annihilated, and there is no hint in ch. 2 of Cush having fared differently. The near-distant contrast may therefore be more rhetorical to underline that the Judahite remnant will have no competitors to fear.

501. Cf. Timmer, *Non-Israelite Nations,* 162–63.

502. Berlin, *Zephaniah,* 134, accepting the identification of Cush in Gen 2:13 as Mesopotamian argued for in Ephraim Avigdor Speiser, "The Rivers of Paradise," in *Festschrift Johannes Friedrich zum 65. Geburtstag gewidmet,* ed. Anton Moortgat and Richard von Kienle (Heidelberg: Carl Winter, 1959), 473–85, and accepted by others. See already Friedrich Delitzsch, *Wo lag das Paradies? Eine Biblisch-Assyriologische Studie* (Leipzig: Hinrichs'sche Buchhandlung, 1881), 51–59, 72–73; cf. Ivan J. Ball, *Zephaniah,* 244–52.

503. Nogalski, *Book of the Twelve,* 744.

504. E.g., Speiser ("Rivers," 480–82) suggested the Diyala or the Kherka River. Yehuda T. Radday ("The Four Rivers of Paradise," *Hebrew Studies* 23 [1982]: 23–31) argues that such identifications miss the purpose of the story and that "Gihon" evokes the rivulet near Jerusalem (as elsewhere in Scripture, namely 1 Kgs 1:33, 38, 45; 2 Chr 32:30; 33:14).

505. E.g., Perlitt, *Nahum,* 140.

with the intention of ensuring that the worshippers are Jewish would have created a text that cannot be read as referring to gentile tribute-bearers.[506] In addition, if both *my supplicants* and *the daughter of my dispersed* were to designate Jewish exiles, the verse would paint a picture of a diaspora community that offers worship in Jerusalem without returning from exile. This would be unique within the prophetic literature. While books like Ezra-Nehemiah and Esther assume the existence of a diaspora community that has the freedom of returning to settle in the land of Judah without using it, such a situation is, to my knowledge, nowhere reflected upon in the prophetic literature.[507] As the book of Zephaniah does not even anticipate an exile, it would be a most surprising host for such a glimpse of diaspora life.

If *the daughter of my dispersed* refers to the exiles, the children of those who had been deported, it is more plausible that *my supplicants* are the nations who bring the exiles back home as their tribute to YHWH. It would make for an interesting contrast to the human sacrifice in 1:7. In this case, the phrase could not be a gloss designed to deflect attention from salvation for the nations. Instead, it would combine the notion of the nations' pilgrimage to Zion with that of the return of Judahites from exile. Given that elsewhere it is YHWH who brings back the exiles himself,[508] this would be an unusual way of speaking about the return of the exiles, but it would not be unique (cf. Isa 49:22; 66:20).[509] Gärtner observes that the complex reflection assumed to have given rise to these verses "exceeds the framework of a singular prophetic book" and postulates that the verses belong to a Book of the Twelve redactional layer whose literary horizon included Isaiah.[510] However, I am skeptical about the existence of redactional work that operates on this scale but apparently ignores the more immediate cotext.[511] More likely, the additions in 3:9–20 are a development of motifs within Zephaniah in the light of changed circumstances and likely with an awareness of other writings. Note

506. Roberts (*Nahum*, 218) observes that "the tendency in later readings of the text is toward highlighting the role of the nations and increasing the universalism" and on this basis also objects to the view that a gloss was designed to undercut an earlier universalism in favor of attention to the Judean exiles.

507. This also raises further questions about the plausibility of the proposed emendation to "my worshippers in the dispersion" (see the translation note).

508. Deut 30:3–4; Isa 11:12; 43:5; 54:7; 56:8; 62:11; Jer 23:3; 29:14; 31:8, 10; 32:37; Ezek 11:17; 20:41; 28:25; 34:13; 36:24; 37:21; 39:27; Mic 2:12; 4:6; Zech 10:8, 10.

509. Cf. Gärtner, "Jerusalem," 280.

510. Gärtner, "Jerusalem," 281, having failed to see links between 3:9–10 and other parts of Zephaniah.

511. Note the negative attitude to exiles one might detect in the next verse. Gärtner ("Jerusalem," 278) ascribes vv. 11–13 to a different, earlier layer that, in her view unlike vv. 9–10, is "woven into the literary context of the book of Zephaniah."

that elsewhere, the root *glh* is commonly used to refer to the exiles (*gôlâ*, *hammuglîm*, *gālût*, *gōlîm*); their return would typically be expressed with the regular word for return (*šûb*) or with the word for going up (*'lh*, both, e.g., in Ezra 2:1). Where YHWH's initiative is foregrounded "to bring up" (*bw' hiphil*) and "to gather" (*qbṣ piel*) are also used (e.g., in v. 20). Indeed, Isa 49:22 and 66:20 both have *bw' hiphil* with gentile nations as the subject and describe the exiles with family terms ("your sons . . . your daughters," "your brethren"). In other words, there would have been ways a reference to the exiles could have been made here in terms that are more typical and more recognizable; the use of the *glh* root in particular would have made such a reference unambiguous. Another possibility of understanding the phrase *the daughter of my dispersed* is therefore worth considering.[512]

While *pûṣ* is occasionally used for the scattering of Judeans in exile,[513] it also features three times in the Tower of Babel story (Gen 11:4, 8–9). This is noteworthy because the sequence *śāpâ bərûrâ liqrō' kullām bəšēm yhwh* (*pure speech, so that all of them will call on the name of YHWH*) in the previous verse shares all of its vocabulary with Gen 11:9 except for the prepositions and *bərûrâ*.[514] While the use of *qārā' šəmâ* in Gen 11:9 is very different from *liqrō' . . . bəšēm* in Zephaniah, the Tower of Babel story also concerns (the abuse of) worship, given that, as is widely recognized, "the tower with its top in heavens" (v. 4) is a ziggurat, a sacred space. In the light of this story, it is possible to think of the peoples as YHWH's dispersed.[515] Is *the daughter of my dispersed* a reference to the community of worship YHWH forms for himself from the descendants of those he had scattered in Gen 11 rather than a reference to Israel in the dispersion? Ben Zvi rightly points out that one would expect such an ambiguity, if it is deliberate, to be resolved in what follows. And yet what follows in v. 11 is not the answer to the question of who *the daughter of my dispersed* is but to the question where the offering

---

512. Note that the use of the singular construct *bat-* with a plural participle or noun is unique, which is maybe another reason for thinking that *bat-haggôlâ* would have been the more obvious neologism to refer to Judean exiles.

513. E.g., Deut 4:27; 28:64; Neh 1:8; Jer 9:16(15); 13:24; Ezek 11:16–17; 12:15.

514. An allusion to the Tower of Babel story is already picked up in the Tg., which speaks of God bringing upon the nations "one chosen language" (*mamlal ḥad bəḥîr*) and by Jerome (*Twelve*, 1:149). It may well also underlie the versions that render "chosen language" without specifying it as "one" (see translation note).

515. Cf. Ben Zvi, *Zephaniah*, 227 n. 748. Berlin (*Zephaniah*, 135) and Sweeney (*Zephaniah*, 185–86) also think that foreign nations are in view here. Melvin, relying heavily on Berlin's commentary, sees "an eschatological replaying and transformation of the primeval history" throughout Zephaniah that "anticipates the development of later apocalyptic eschatology" ("Making All Things New [Again]," 280). To my mind, Zephaniah is open to be developed in this way but does not actually present such an *Urzeit-Endzeit* pattern.

is brought to. The answer must therefore be sought in the preceding verse.[516] This and the fact that the ambiguity could have been avoided by the use of the root *glh* suggest that both *my supplicants* and *the daughter of my dispersed* are references to the peoples in v. 9, first in their plurality, then in their unity (*with one accord*, as v. 9 puts it). This does not mean that the alternative reading, in which the *tribute* consists of the exiles whom the nations bring back to Jerusalem can or has to be ruled out. But if it is allowed, it should be read as a secondary thought without shifting focus away from the worship given to YHWH by the nations and YHWH's claim on the nations.

11 *On that day* arguably links the end of Jerusalem's disgrace both to the judgment of vv. 7–8 (note the reuse of *all their/your deeds*)[517] and to the gift of pure speech to the nations who will bring YHWH tribute in vv. 9–10. Because YHWH not only seeks worshippers in faraway places (cf. 2:11) but seeks their unity (*to serve him with one accord*, v. 9), one rightly expects that the nations do not offer tribute to YHWH each in their own place, going to local sanctuaries, but come to Jerusalem as the place where all YHWH's dispersed peoples come together to bring him tribute. The address to Jerusalem here is, therefore, not too surprising after the statement about the peoples in vv. 9–10.

The nations will not look down on the (formerly) rebellious city because those whose *pride* characterized the city as rebellious will have been removed. Instead of seeing Jerusalem's defeat as a disgrace, readers are encouraged to see it as part of the city's transformation. The use of *exulting* strengthens the implicit comparison between Jerusalem and Nineveh (*the exultant city*, 2:15) at the beginning of the chapter and thus highlights the need for such a transformation. The reference to *pride* links with the condemnation of Moab and the Ammonites in 2:10 (there *gā'ôn*, here the related *ga'ăwâ*). Those who did not respond to the call in 2:1–3 will have no future in the city. But unlike Nineveh, Jerusalem itself will have a future. It will continue to be inhabited. The precondition for this is the removal of those within it *exulting with pride*, presumably the elites condemned in 3:3–4 and in ch. 1.[518]

To be haughty in this context means to rely on oneself rather than YHWH,[519] to consider YHWH irrelevant (cf. 1:12; 3:2); *on my holy mount* either refers specifically to the Temple Mount or by extension to Zion—that is, Jerusalem as a whole.[520]

---

516. Ben Zvi, *Zephaniah*, 229–30.

517. The lemma is rare in the prophetic literature, as noted above.

518. The combination *exulting with pride* also occurs in Isa 13:3 but in a different context, and it is not clear whether one instance depends on the other.

519. Ben Zvi, *Zephaniah*, 232; cf. Berlin, *Zephaniah*, 136.

520. Berlin, *Zephaniah*, 136.

12 The removal of the proud will leave *a humble and powerless people*, echoing 2:3. Robertson thinks that "in the light of the strong emphasis on the removal of guilt and the ending of pride in the preceding verse, these designations should be understood primarily as describing a moral attribute rather than a social status."[521] But in each case in which the two roots *'ānî* and *dal* occur together, they refer to socioeconomically *humble* people.[522] It is among the poor and *powerless*, those who cannot rely on themselves, that one finds those who *seek refuge in . . . YHWH* or, as it is here uniquely expressed, *in the name of YHWH*. The addition of *the name of* creates a link with v. 9. This may indirectly confirm that v. 9 should not be read in isolation from v. 8 because the sequence of vv. 8–9 offers a parallel to what is said about Jerusalem here. When divine judgment consumes the whole earth (v. 8), peoples will call on *the name of YHWH* and serve him (v. 9). In the same way, when the arrogant elites of Jerusalem are removed in the disaster that Zephaniah announced (v. 11), *a humble and powerless people . . . shall seek refuge in the name of YHWH* (v. 12). Ben Zvi makes the point that the *humble and powerless* do not stand in opposition to the wealthy as such but to oppressors.[523] Because they are unable to rely on themselves or to find protection in the lawcourt as they should be able to (Ps 82:3–4; cf. Prov 22:22–23), YHWH is the only (effective) refuge left to *a humble and powerless people*.[524]

13 There was reference to a surviving Judahite remnant in 2:7 (see below) and 2:9. In the latter, the phrases used were *the remnant of my people* and *the survivors of my nation*. The possessive personal pronoun in 2:9 related to the likely insinuation on the part of the Moabites and Ammonites that YHWH, unlike their own national gods, proved unable to keep the territory of his people intact. Speaking of *the remnant of Israel* evokes a theological concept, alluding to YHWH's covenant with his people more than contemporary political realities.[525] This agrees with the definition offered here, which focuses on the behavior expected of those who may come into God's presence (cf. Ps 15, already mentioned above) rather than characterizing the remnant

---

521. Robertson, *Nahum*, 331. Cf. Vlaardingerbroek, *Zephaniah*, 203, who adds that "it is not ruled out that these people belonged especially to the lower classes of society" but stresses that YHWH does not have "a preference for the poor simply because they are poor."

522. Job 34:28; Ps 82:3; Prov 22:22; Isa 10:2; 26:6. This also seems true for most of their separate occurrences. Sweeney's attempt (*Zephaniah*, 189–90) to identify this group with the *'am-hā'āreṣ*—(the leadership of) the rural Judean population that put Josiah on the throne (2 Kgs 21:24)—is forced.

523. Ben Zvi, *Zephaniah*, 233.

524. The text leaves the question unasked whether some of the oppressed might have been seeking refuge in other deities; such deities would have offered no more protection than the leadership of Jerusalem.

525. Cf. Ben Zvi, *Zephaniah*, 234; Berlin, *Zephaniah*, 136.

along ethnic or political lines. The integrity of this remnant in not committing iniquity corresponds to YHWH's own (v. 5). There will be *pure speech* not only among the peoples (v. 9) but also in Jerusalem, with no place for lies and deceit. This emphasis on truthful speech over against other aspects of not committing iniquity (such as not killing, not stealing, not committing adultery, not exploiting the poor) in my view relates to the connection made between *pure speech* and acknowledging YHWH for who he truly is in v. 9 in the light of 2:8, 10.[526] We may also think of the lie at the heart of the condemnation in the first chapter (1:12).

The emphatic *kî-hēmmâ* (*It is they who . . .*) may relate to the use of the same two verbs in 2:7 (*graze, lie down*). There *the remnant of the house of Judah* was used by way of contrast to *the houses of Ashkelon*. The phrase merely indicated that there would be Judahite survivors. Now these survivors have been identified more fully as people of integrity, people who belong to YHWH not only by name but by virtue of seeking refuge in him. The addition of *no one will make them afraid*[527] transforms the image of 2:7, where the stress was on the absence of urban life, to one of peace and security.[528] This is obviously a promise of safety from external threats, but in the light of the characterization of Jerusalem's former leaders as wolves and lions, it is surely also a promise of protection from exploitative leadership of the sort condemned in 3:3–4 and in ch. 1.

Reflection

Sweeney argues that v. 9 is "Zephaniah's attempt to portray YHWH's projected punishment against the nations as a purge like that envisioned for Jerusalem and Judah in 1:2–18."[529] But ch. 1 spoke of a comprehensive judgment without using the language of purification and without yet even referring to a remnant. I have argued that the remnant language in ch. 2 is not incompatible with the picture of total judgment in ch. 1. Indeed, one may think of it as a logical consequence of certain theological convictions. These convictions would then logically also lead one to think of the punishment of Jerusalem as a purification. While the idea that the judgment itself has a positive dimension does not reverse or contradict what was said before, it is

---

526. Ben Zvi (*Zephaniah*, 235–36) thinks that it reflects the social location of the author in the world of education.

527. Cf. Lev 26:6; Jer 30:10; 46:27; Ezek 34:28; 39:26; Mic 4:4. We have encountered the phrase before in Nah 2:11(12).

528. Cf., Vlaardingerbroek, *Zephaniah*, 200; Berlin, *Zephaniah* 137–38.

529. Sweeney, *Zephaniah*, 184.

a thought that has not been expressed previously. Prior to 3:9–13, escaping the punishment was the only hopeful prospect. Indeed, the picture emerging from Zeph 1–2 was of a rural future, not of a purified city. Only now is the judgment seen as a purge—first for the nations, then for Jerusalem, just as ch. 1 opened with the wider perspective before focusing on Judah and Jerusalem. The idea of purification is new, and it is at the heart of this passage. The end of the world order to which Zephaniah testified is not the end of the world. What emerges beyond judgment is a community of peoples who no longer bear false witness to YHWH and his people, as Moab and the Ammonites had done, but who together worship and serve YHWH.

It is worth noting how much the focus remains on YHWH (*my supplicants . . . my dispersed . . . my tribute*). The two references to his *name* (vv. 9, 12) may further highlight the importance of safeguarding YHWH's reputation. The rebelliousness of Jerusalem and the consequent destruction of the city tarnished YHWH's reputation and made it difficult to know him for who he truly is. The future will see people humbly submit to him. The ambiguities of v. 10 suggest that there is no great concern with the fate of the exiles. Nor is there a great concern for outlining what the new world order will look like beyond identifying YHWH, rather than a Mesopotamian emperor, as the one who receives tribute.

In vv. 11–12, Jerusalem is not depicted as the place to which the exiles return, nor as the place to which the nations will make pilgrimage. Only two groups are in view, namely the haughty elites who have been removed— whether through deportation or death is not specified—and the humble poor who were left over. Just as the comprehensive judgment in ch. 1 focused on Jerusalem, so the promise for the nations finds its center in Jerusalem, with the peoples no longer in view in vv. 11–13. While the end of the chapter (3:19–20) will again widen the horizon, as did the end of the first chapter, it will do so only by way of depicting Jerusalem as the place to which all the world looks, not as the site to which they make pilgrimage. Strikingly, the remnant that now lives in Jerusalem is still described with the picture of a flock that had been used earlier to evoke a rural situation. The picture is filled out to suggest living in safety, but the relationship between the remnant of Israel and the nations is not sketched beyond *no one will make them afraid*.

This section shares with Ezekiel a strong theocentric focus on YHWH's doing and the notion that the future arises from a great overthrow. But while Ezekiel stresses the pervasiveness of sin and guilt across all groups and there-fore speaks of a new heart and a new spirit that needs to be given to God's people (Ezek 11:19; 18:31; 36:26), there is no such emphasis in Zephaniah. The language used here could nearly lead one to read the purifying judgment as a sifting in which the evil proud ones are removed and the humble righ-teous are spared. Why else speak of removing and leaving (as a remnant) in

vv. 11–12? But the *wə-qatal* (converted perfect) form in v. 12 and the *yiqtol* (imperfect) forms in v. 13 arguably guard against a reading that sees a straightforward case of retribution and reward here, as if the remnant was spared because it had taken refuge in YHWH and had not committed iniquity. The positive descriptions apply unambiguously only to the future: *they shall seek refuge in the name of YHWH . . . they will not commit iniquity . . . they will not tell lies; no deceitful tongue will be found in their mouths.* We are not told whether or not this had been true of this group of people prior to the judgment. In other words, the common life of integrity within Jerusalem could either be the result of a discriminatory judgment that left only those who already lived such a life or of repentance that happened as a consequence of the judgment. In this sense, the text is only interested in depicting the future, not in detailing how to get there. Rhetorically, of course, such a description implicitly calls to this way of life. In other words, the passage is telling its first readers that they most certainly will be part of this *remnant of Israel* only if these positive descriptions, the *imitatio Dei*, will be true of them. Later gentile readers will know too that they are only included in this description of a positive future life as people whose *speech* is pure.

The one characteristic of the future remnant that is firmly anchored in the pre-judgment world is that they are *a humble and powerless people.* This is because this phrase describes those who will be spared, using the verb that alludes to *remnant.* While it is true, as explained in the previous paragraph, that we are not encouraged to picture the judgment as a simple matter of retribution and reward, it is nevertheless also true that the text only speaks of some being removed and others spared, not of repentance as such. Does this then suggest a preferential option for the poor? Vlaardingerbroek suggests that Lev 19:15 warns against a "theology of the poor" and notes:

> When lands and cities were destroyed and the population was deported, it was by and large the propertied and influential classes who were deported, while poor and unimportant people were left behind because they had neither the potential nor any reason to try to reestablish the old situation.[530]

Not least because he considers *all you humble of the land* in 2:3 to be a later gloss, he underestimates the contrast between the powerful and the powerless that is found all through Zephaniah—beginning with ch. 1, which focuses its judgment on the upper echelons of society.[531] I emphasized before that Zephaniah considered the judgment on Jerusalem inevitable as part of a wider campaign to end the current political order (see the summary of

530. Vlaardingerbroek, *Zephaniah*, 203.
531. Cf. Weigl, *Zefanja*, 256–60.

Zephaniah's message on p. 444, references throughout the commentary on ch. 1, and the reflections on the composition of 2:5–15). This conviction that the people as a whole could not be saved combines well with the observation that there are usually survivors in disasters like this. It also comports well with the stronger, theological conviction that YHWH's reputation would not allow for the complete end of the history of his people. Quite naturally, this all leads to talk about a remnant. (The *perhaps* in 2:3 arguably relates to the fate of individuals who are thus addressed and need not put into question that some would survive.)

But it would be reductionist and contrary to the high view of YHWH's sovereignty expressed in this book to suggest that YHWH will have to make do with the people in whom the Babylonians have no interest. While a divine preference for those overlooked by others could be ascertained from other parts of Scripture, from Abel onward, there seems to be more to this preferential option for the poor and powerless than that. Earlier, I suggested that one factor that could predispose them to seek refuge in God is that they have no one else on whom they can rely (see the commentary on 2:3 as well as 3:12). This is not about declaring someone in the right simply because they are poor, which would be as unjust as deferring to the powerful for being powerful (and such injustice alone is what Lev 19:15 has in view). It is about acknowledging that those who come to the end of their resources are more likely to entrust themselves to the rule of God. It is hard for the rich to enter the kingdom of God (Matt 19:23–24 and parallels). It is the rich who are most tempted to be haughty (1 Tim 6:17). We may compare our passage with Isa 2:6–21, as "YHWH of Hosts has a day against all that is proud and high, against all that is lifted up" (v. 12) and "the haughtiness of humanity will be cast down" (v. 17),[532] and of course with the Magnificat (Luke 1:46–55). God's preferential option for the lowly is not a notion that either began or ended with Zephaniah, for whom in any case the other side of the coin—the unfavorable attitude toward the haughty—is more prominent.

It may be worth observing that there is no perfect symmetry here. While one could argue that powerlessness on its own draws God's favor and compassion, having power on its own does not call for condemnation. The rich are told that silver and gold will not save them (1:18), but they are not judged merely for being rich. Neither is poverty commended as something to be sought out even in the call to imitate the poor in 2:1. There is no glorification of poverty, and the reuse of pastoral imagery here (in connection with the

---

532. Cf. Sweeney, *Zephaniah*, 188. He believes that the remnant language is taken from Isaiah as well and seen as fulfilled in Josiah's kingdom. While there had been earlier devastations that would justify talk about a remnant, notably in 701, Zephaniah's concern is the removal of the Jerusalem elites, and this had not happened yet in the days of Josiah.

city of Jerusalem and the holy mount) guards against reading the earlier passages as a glorification of rural life as such.

Ben Zvi notes some links between Ps 37 and Zeph 3:1–5.[533] They are maybe not strong enough to clearly indicate literary dependence, but the psalm and Zeph 3 are usefully considered alongside each other. Psalm 37, too, anticipates that the wicked, "the doers of iniquity" (v. 1), who stand in contrast to "the humble and needy" (*'ānî wǝ'ebyôn*) who are "upright in conduct" (v. 14), will wither like grass, and that it is the lowly (*'ănāwîm*) who will inherit the land (v. 11). While the psalm paints a picture of the wicked being in charge (for a short while), the righteous do not necessarily belong to the lowest socioeconomic group. They may have little (v. 16) but are still able to be generous (vv. 21, 26). Again, they are maybe primarily defined as those who seek refuge in God (v. 40). While there may, therefore, be a sense of greater spiritualizing of the terms for poverty, it seems to me that the contrast between physical, socioeconomic poverty and spiritual poverty of humility that acknowledges one's neediness has sometimes been overdrawn. The group of which the psalm speaks is not dirt poor, but it is vulnerable vis-à-vis the faithless as well as vis-à-vis God. Jesus makes use of Ps 37:11 when he blesses the "meek" and promises that they will inherit the earth (Matt 5:5). The New Testament raises similar issues concerning the relationship between "the poor in spirit" (Matt 5:3) who "hunger for righteousness" (Matt 5:6) and "the poor" (Luke 6:20) who are literally hungry (Luke 6:21; see v. 25). There, too, it would be simplistic to consider one version of the beatitudes purely "spiritual" and the other "material"—in both cases, promises are not made to people who are already in possession of blessings or have earned a right to them (e.g., through their spiritual meekness), but to those who are at present weak and vulnerable. It seems to me that throughout Scripture, a correlation is assumed that does not equate being materially poor with being spiritually blessed and vice versa but links socioeconomic vulnerability with trust in God in a way similar to the way demographers today might analyze correlations between socioeconomic status and political convictions.[534] I do not know whether the broad correlation assumed for the biblical world between socioeconomic status and loyalty to God can also be observed in today's cultures. Weigl rightly points out that Zephaniah does not formulate general truths but writes about a particular historical experience, even if the experience reflected here is widely shared among biblical writers.[535]

In any case, for theologians, teachers, and preachers, it is not necessary

---

533. Ben Zvi, *Zephaniah*, 316–17.

534. On the correlation between socioeconomic status and orthodoxy in Zephaniah see also Weigl, *Zefanja*, 260–62.

535. Weigl, *Zefanja*, 257–58.

to affirm or deny that such a correlation holds true today. What is helpful is to be alert to the possibility of such correlations and hence to admonish the rich in particular not to be haughty or, for example, to consider to what extent a consumerist culture will tempt people to treat faith as a commodity one might possess or discard. What is commended here in Zephaniah and elsewhere is not a low socioeconomic status as such but a certain attitude and lifestyle, from which no one is excused by their high or low standing in society. The remnant in 3:12–13 responds well to the call of 2:1–3, but its way of life also contrasts specifically with that of the Jerusalem elites in 3:1–5. The humble and powerless will live as the mighty and powerful leaders had been expected to live. There is no double standard, no spirituality that belongs exclusively to the poor.

Finally, it should be emphasized that YHWH's preferential option for the poor and powerless speaks of his sovereign grace. Experiencing salvation, no longer being dishonored, and living in safety do not come about by human structures and powers but are freely given to those without power and strength. The only hope for the rich and powerful in seventh- and early-sixth-century Jerusalem was to become poor (cf. 2:1), to relinquish hope in one's own power and to seek refuge in YHWH instead. Within the church, too, acknowledging one's inability to secure eternal life is one aspect of trusting Jesus for the gift of life, and not holding on too tightly to one's possessions and status is a sign of understanding that all is a gift and entrusted to us as stewards. Poverty was not a choice in ancient Judah and is not presented as an aspiration in Zephaniah. At best, poverty can be a means to an end: increased receptivity for the work of God.

IX. CELEBRATION OF LIFE BEYOND JUDGMENT (3:14–17)

[14]*Resound,[a] daughter of Zion![b]*
  Shout aloud, Israel!
Be glad and exult with all your heart,
  daughter of Jerusalem![c]
[15]*YHWH has removed the decrees[d] against you;*
  he has turned away your enemies.[e]
The king[f] of Israel, YHWH, is in your midst;
  you need no longer fear[g] any harm.
[16]*On that day it will be said[h] to Jerusalem: Do not be anxious;[i]*
  Zion,[j] do not let your hands slacken.[k]
[17]*YHWH your God is in your midst, a warrior who comes to the rescue.[l]*
  He rejoices[m] over you with gladness.
He keeps silent[n] in his love;
  he celebrates[o] you[p] with resounding shout.[q]

a. The verb *rnn* is regularly used for joyful shouting, which is often interpreted as involving singing, although it can be used also for voicing protest or grief (Lam 2:19; cf. the related noun in Pss 61:1[2]; 88:2[3]). The *qal* is used in this verse and elsewhere together with verbs for shouting (*rwʿ*, *ṣhl*) and rejoicing (*gyl*, *śmḥ*) but not singing. The *piel* is used with a word suggesting singing (*zmr*) in Ps 98:4. The translation *resound* is indebted to John Goldingay who suggests that the word is onomatopoeic ("presumably n-n-n-n"); see the glossary in his *Psalms* (Grand Rapids: Baker Academic, 2006).

b. The term *bat-ṣiyyôn* is here rendered *daughter of Zion* rather than as a term of endearment ("Dear Zion"). The latter is defended, e.g., by Andrew Dearman, "Daughter Zion and Her Place in God's Household," *HBT* 31 (2009): 144–59; and Magnar Kartveit, *Rejoice, Dear Zion! Hebrew Construct Phrases with "Daughter" and "Virgin" as Nomen Regens*, BZAW 447 (Berlin: de Gruyter, 2013). But I find Michael H. Floyd's argument more compelling; see his "Welcome Back, Daughter of Zion," *CBQ* 70 (2008): 484–506; "The Daughter of Zion Goes Fishing in Heaven," in *Daughter Zion: Her Portrait, Her Response*, ed. Mark J. Boda, Carol J. Dempsey, and LeAnn Snow Flesher, SBLAIL 13 (Atlanta: Society of Biblical Literature, 2012), 177–200. *Daughter of Zion* and *Zion* can be used as functionally equivalent in many places, not unlike "inhabitants of Jerusalem" and "Jerusalem," and all the more so as *bat-ṣiyyôn* became conventional in the prophetic literature. But this does not prove that "daughter" is an apposition any more than "inhabitants."

c. Cf. the previous note.

d. The plural typically refers to decrees or statutes within the law, while "decree" in the sense of "sentence, verdict, punishment" (as here) is usually expressed with the singular. But the plural is used for judgments also in Jer 4:12; 39:5 = 52:9; Ezek 5:8; and it is used for charges in Jer 12:1; cf. Berlin, *Zephaniah*, 142. Others consider it a plural of intensity (GKC 124e; JM 136f), see Sabottka, *Zephanja*, 126. The expression *hēsîr mišpāṭ* means "deny justice" in Job 27:2; 34:5, from which Ben Zvi (*Zephaniah*, 242–43) suggests the nuance "removing what Jerusalem deserves"; i.e., "her punishment" here.

e. The standard MT MSS have the singular, which can be understood as collective: "with indefinite generality, every enemy" (Keil, *Minor Prophets*, 2:160). MurXII reads the plural, as do the ancient versions.

f. Or "as king." Appealing to some Greek MSS (*basileusei*) and the parallel in Mic 4:7 (*ûmālak*), Irsigler (*Zefanja*, 407) prefers to read a verbal form ("has begun to reign"), deleting the reference to Israel as a later addition. In his view, the addition of *Israel* disturbs the meter. To me, the sequence of 2+2, 4+2, 3+2, 4+3 stresses seems no more objectionable than one in which the last bicolon had 3+3 stresses.

g. So MT. Alternatively, with a reversal of letters, "you will not see [= experience] any harm" (so LXX and Peshitta). It is not possible to decide conclusively which was the original reading. The reading *fear* could either be originally designed to prepare for the next verse or the result of a misreading prompted by the context. But the palistrophic arrangement (see under "Composition" below) suggests to me that *fear* is the intended reading. Ben Zvi (*Zephaniah*, 244) thinks it worth noting that the author did not use the more common *'al-tîrʾî* (cf. v. 16), and his thorough study effectively rules out *'al-tîrʾî* as a feasible alternative for *lōʾ-tîrʾî* in this verse.

h. LXX has *erei kyrios*, either interpreting the verb as a divine passive or reading *yʾmr* as the active form and interpreting YHWH as the speaker. Mayer I. Gruber ("Fear, Anxiety and Reverence in Akkadian, Biblical Hebrew and Other North-West Semitic Languages," *VT* 40 [1990]: 417–20), Ivan J. Ball (*Zephaniah*, 183), and Michael O'Connor (*Hebrew Verse Structure* [Winona Lake, IN: Eisenbrauns, 1997], 261) interpret the preposition with Jerusalem as a vocative marker but Berlin (*Zephaniah*, 144) points out that in none of the other occurrences of the construction *yēʾāmer l-* does the preposition signal a vocative; cf. Vlaardingerbroek, *Zephaniah*, 213.

i. Or "do not fear." The Hebrew is the same verb as in the preceding line, but English offers more nuances than Hebrew. For the translation *anxious* (rather than "afraid" or "fear"), see Gruber, "Fear," who distinguishes between fear (specific, prompting fight or flight action) and anxiety (vague, causing passive stupor). The slackening of hands in the next line shows that the latter is in view. Most English translations from the Geneva Bible (1599) onward and the vast majority of commentators take *Zion* as the vocative with this first imperative (against the accentuation), reading three lines.

j. In the KJV (following the earliest English translations; cf. already the Peshitta) the preposition "to" is understood to carry over ("and to Zion . . ."); cf. Berlin, *Zephaniah*, 144, comparing Isa 48:14. See O'Connor, *Hebrew Verse Structure*, 310–11, and *IBHS* 11.4.2 for such "preposition override." Dietrich (*Nahum*, 239–40) also takes *Zion* with the second imperative but, like me, does not think that the preposition "to" carries over and reads it as a vocative. He scans as three lines (of very unequal length).

k. The third-person feminine plural *yiqtol* form is often neglected and replaced by the masculine plural, especially when the verb comes first as here; see JM 150b–c. With the feminine dual *yādayim* (*hands*), the verb *rph* (*slacken*) is feminine when the noun comes first (Isa 13:7; Ezek 7:17) and masculine when the verb comes first (here and in four other places), while the verb *ḥzq* ("strengthen") is always feminine with *yādayim*; see JM 150d. Cf. Meyer, *Grammatik*, 2:99–100, for a historical perspective.

l. Or "brings victory, deliverance, aid." The choice of a *yiqtol* here rather than a *qatal* form readily conveys a sense of progression or incompleteness, for which in English the present tense is best suited. The situation is different for the following verbs, where the use of participles may have been the main alternative to the *yiqtol* forms. See the next note.

m. Irsigler (*Zefanja*, 418) thinks that the *yiqtol* forms signal contemporaneity with the verbless clause at the beginning of the verse, but this is far from obvious to me. Some commentators opt for the future tense in English here and with the following verbs (Roberts, *Nahum*, 219; Robertson, *Nahum*, 333; Vlaardingerbroek, *Zephaniah*, 210, with the present tense for the middle verb). Another possibility is to hear an ingressive nuance (e.g., "he begins to rejoice"). The rendering *keeps silent* rather than "is silent" is meant to hint at such an openness to the future.

n. LXX and Peshitta have "he will renew you," reading *yḥdš* (*yǝḥaddēš*) for *yḥrš* (*yaḥărîš*). The letters *dalet* and *resh* look very similar and are easily confused, but there is no variation in Hebrew MSS of this verse (*CTAT* 3:914). Some derive *yaḥărîš* from the verb meaning "plow, engrave, devise." Sabottka (*Zephanja*, 132–34) understands this as "compose, improvise" and renders "sings a song," but the argument does not rest on secure linguistic grounds. Sweeney (*Zephaniah*, 193, 202–3) opts for "he plows," but in none of the instances he cites is the context a happy one. In my judgment, none of the alternatives can claim greater plausibility than reading *keeps silent*. (The translation "he will quiet you" as in ESV goes against Hebrew usage of the *hiphil* of *ḥrš*.)

o. Sweeney (*Zephaniah*, 193) translates "dances" in view of the etymology of the verb; cf. Peshitta: "He shall make you dance." The disadvantage of *celebrate* is that it does not readily convey the liveliness that is likely implied by the Hebrew verb, but "dance" or "sing" seems overly specific, and "rejoice" and "exult" are already used for other verbs.

p. The choice of English verb (see the note above) recommends to me the use of a direct object in the translation. The Hebrew uses a prepositional phrase that could be rendered "over you" or "on account of you."

q. In LXX, *hōs en hēmera heortēs* ("as on a day of festival") is found at the end of the verse; cf. Peshitta (where it is the people who are rejoicing, not YHWH). This seems to be a version of the first two words of what is the next verse in MT, read as *kayyôm môʿēd* rather than *nûgê mimmôʿēd* as in MT. Irsigler (*Zefanja*, 418–20) reckons that this is the earlier reading. It is also followed by, e.g., Vlaardingerbroek, *Zephaniah*, 210–11, who reads the remainder of v. 18 as the content of YHWH's song.

Composition

Verses 14–15, the call to joy with its rationale, form the first unit. Some interpreters believe that it was originally a short independent song.[536] Its temporal setting assumes that the disaster is over and Jerusalem is safe—that is to say, that the promise that was still future in v. 13 has been fulfilled. Ben Zvi observes that the use of *qatal* (perfect) forms is in accordance with the genre, "a hymn of praise and thanksgiving to YHWH," but this is not an alternative to a temporal setting.[537] Hymns of thanksgiving use *qatal* forms in the section that looks back to the experienced deliverance that provides the rationale for the thanksgiving. It is true that *qatal* forms are also used in other contexts for events that have not yet happened, but the combination of imperatives with *qatal* forms here suggests a call to respond to what has happened. It is possible that this temporal setting is imaginary rather than reflecting the actual date of composition, not least as vv. 16–17 are future-oriented.

Irsigler thinks that it is only the introduction in v. 16a that puts vv. 16b–17, and with them vv. 14–15, into the future. In his view, this introduction is secondary and pushes the whole unit into the distant (eschatological) future.[538] First, it needs to be emphasized that fictional settings are not unknown in prophetic literature. In a sense, most—maybe all—oracles addressed to other nations assume an imaginary geographical setting different from the real setting in which the prophecy is pronounced. There are arguably also instances in which the author, for rhetorical reasons, speaks as if the future that is being announced has already happened. Within Zephaniah, this may well be the case with 2:15, the conclusion to the oracle against Assyria that speaks of Nineveh as if the city had already been destroyed when at the time of composition this may well have been still in the future. We may note how after "What a desolation she has become!" the hissing and fist-shaking of

536. E.g., Seybold, *Nahum*, 116, who suggests it may have been added to provide balance to the message of Zephaniah; Vlaardingerbroek, *Zephaniah*, 208; cf. Irsigler, *Zefanja*, 408.
537. Ben Zvi, *Zephaniah*, 238.
538. Irsigler, *Zefanja*, 402.

those passing by are spoken of in *yiqtol* (imperfect) rather than participle forms, thus maybe reverting to the future perspective. The purpose of such a future setting in 2:15 was to vividly imagine the destruction of Nineveh. By analogy, it is conceivable that 3:14–15 adopt a fictional temporal setting to give a more vivid picture of the joy of salvation. But the use of imperatives seems less suitable for this purpose.[539] So, I prefer to read the imperatives in v. 14 as actual calls to celebration and v. 15 as a description of what has happened to make this celebration possible. Songs of joy now substitute for the earlier waiting for God's judgment (3:8).

Sweeney considers it "likely" that these oracles were preached "in the early years of Josiah's reform ... either as a formal part of a temple liturgy that was designed to support the king's reform program or in association with formal temple worship."[540] At the same time, he acknowledges that "the prophet's message [is] that the punishment of Jerusalem is now at an end and that the city is about to be restored to its proper role at the center of creation."[541] He suggests that the punishment is the one that had been received at the hand of the Assyrians.[542] But the earlier parts of Zephaniah clearly speak of a still-future disaster in which both Jerusalem and Assyria will be engulfed. I thus do not find it plausible that Zephaniah offered such an "idyllic portrayal of Jerusalem's secure and peaceful future" as an imminent prospect in the 620s.[543]

If the temporal setting of vv. 14–15 is actual rather than imaginary, the verses are later than the bulk of the book. This conclusion can be and must be avoided by those who both affirm the truthfulness of Scripture and believe that the superscription in 1:1 demands that every word in the book was written by the prophet Zephaniah in the days of Josiah. But I am not convinced that the superscription makes this claim. If one allows for the possibility of *Fortschreibung* (supplementing)—that is, the addition of material by disciples to tease out implications of the prophet's message or to apply it to new circumstances—then 3:14–20 offer a likely instance. The idea that without this final section, Zephaniah would not be "the complete prophet, combining judgment and salvation in his message"[544] is as prejudicial as the

539. The same applies in my view to, e.g., "Comfort, comfort my people!" (Isa 40:1) and "Go out from Babylon!" (Isa 48:20).

540. Sweeney, *Zephaniah*, 197.

541. Sweeney, *Zephaniah*, 200.

542. Cf. Sweeney, *Zephaniah*, 203.

543. I agree with Sweeney's resistance to reading the temporal formula in these verses as necessarily redactional and/or eschatological. I also agree that 2:1–3:20 suggest that "an immediate response" is expected of the audience (Sweeney, *Zephaniah*, 201). My point is that the response expected in 2:1–3:8 is sufficiently different from the one expected in 3:14–20 to suggest that different audiences are in view.

544. Cf. House, *Zephaniah*, 60.

view, common in earlier scholarship, that a prophet announcing judgment could not possibly have spoken of salvation as well. It is in any case not true that without these verses Zephaniah would be "allowed to degenerate into an oracle of total doom . . . a dreadful, hopeless mass of condemnation."[545] As I argued above, I assume that Zephaniah announced inevitable disaster but held out the hope for some to escape it and expected a remnant of Judah to survive. Indeed, there is also no good reason to deny to the prophet the expectation that peoples in distant lands would take note and acknowledge YHWH's sovereignty (2:11). The additions in ch. 3 develop this.

The summons to joy offered to a female figure associated with Zion/Jerusalem has close parallels in Zech 2:10(14) and 9:9–10 and suggests that "those responsible for the book of Zechariah were also responsible for drawing Haggai and Malachi into the Haggai–Malachi corpus and placing it within the Book of the Twelve."[546] Nogalski thinks that "very different attitudes towards kingship assumed in those verses" present an obstacle to the close association of Zeph 3 with Zech 9.[547] But the silence about a Davidic king in Zephaniah does not contradict the expectation in Zechariah. In my view, it is not inconceivable that someone linking Zephaniah with Haggai–Malachi stressed YHWH's kingship here and continued to focus on YHWH's presence in Zech 2 before teasing out YHWH's kingship in terms of a humble Davidic king in Zech 9.[548] Note also that YHWH's kingship is again emphasized in Zech 14:9, 16–17 (without reference to a Davidic king) and assumed in Mal 1:14.[549]

If vv. 14–15 assume that the promise of safety has been fulfilled, vv. 16–17

---

545. House, *Zephaniah*, 61. House further claims, "Since this ending caps the entire drama, and indeed is foreshadowed throughout the book, to remove these verses would destroy the purpose of every part of Zephaniah" (133). But surely the warning of judgment, the call to seek YHWH, etc. would not be compromised by the absence of 3:14–20, even if House's conception of drama might suffer.

546. Mark J. Boda, *The Book of Zechariah*, NICOT (Grand Rapids: Eerdmans, 2016), 31. See also his "Babylon in the Book of the Twelve," *HBAI* 3 (2014): 225–48; repr. as ch. 8 of *The Development of Zechariah and Its Role Within the Twelve*, vol. 1 of *Exploring Zechariah*, SBLANEM 16 (Atlanta: Society of Biblical Literature, 2017). Cf. Curtis, "Zion-Daughter Oracles," 182–83.

547. James D. Nogalski, "Zephaniah 3: A Redactional Text for a Developing Corpus," in *Schriftauslegung in der Schrift: Festschrift für Odil Hannes Steck zu seinem 65. Geburtstag*, ed. Reinhard G. Kratz, Thomas Krüger, and Konrad Schmid, BZAW 300 (Berlin: de Gruyter, 2000), 215.

548. Cf. the integration of divine and Davidic kingship in Ezek 34, whether original or redactional. Note also the conflicting reports about the battle of Kadesh in 1274 BC promulgated side by side during the reign of Ramses II: one celebrating the role of the god Amun, the other glorifying the human king without giving credit to any gods. On this, see Joshua A. Berman, *Inconsistency in the Torah: Ancient Literary Convention and the Limits of Source Criticism* (Oxford: Oxford University Press, 2017), 17–25.

549. The other place in the Book of the Twelve that speaks of renewed kingship of

625

refuse to specify whether or not the promises therein have been fulfilled by obscuring the time reference. This appears to be the purpose of the opening clause, *On that day it will be said to Jerusalem*. Claims that the phrase *on that day* is specifically eschatological rather than simply future-oriented in these contexts fail to convince, even though in this particular case the synchronism suggested by *on that day* is not straightforward. True contemporaneity could have been achieved by the omission of *On that day it will be said to Jerusalem*. The day is presumably the day when YHWH is in Jerusalem's midst as king (v. 15), but while this is present time in vv. 14–15, the introductory formula in v. 16 invites us to look at this day as future (i.e., from the chronological point of view of a time when enemies have not been turned away yet). As noted above, Irsigler thinks that this pushes all of vv. 14–17 into the (distant) future, but I am not convinced that it does. Instead, my view is that it introduces a note of uncertainty over whether vv. 16–17 have or have not been fulfilled. On the one hand, readers were hardly expected to conclude from the introductory formula that they must not say or accept the message "Do not be anxious" because this is a message for the (distant) future. Readers will hear v. 16 as a promise from the past now being fulfilled. Now is the time not to be inactive and disheartened, now is the time for jubilation, because YHWH is indeed in the midst of his people. On the other hand, the rhetoric of the introductory phrase encourages readers to look to the future and expect a further, fuller fulfillment. While in one sense "nothing of true substance changes from vv. 14–15 to vv. 16–17," as Sweeney claims,[550] there is a subtle shift of perspective. It is still possible to read vv. 16–17 (Floyd) or all of vv. 16–20 (Sweeney) as an elaboration on the rationale for rejoicing given in v. 15, although to insist on it probably introduces more precision than the text allows. As a matter of substance, it is unquestionable that all of vv. 16–20 can become a reason for rejoicing for the believer. As a matter of rhetoric, it is not clear that this is their specific purpose. It seems to me more natural to read v. 15 as the rationale for the imperatives in v. 14 and v. 17 as the rationale for the imperatives in v. 16 and leave it at that.

In his translation, Sweeney identifies the citation that is marked by the introductory phrase in v. 16 as going nearly all the way to the end of the book, only excluding *says YHWH*.[551] This makes for a very odd frame for the citation (*On that day it will be said to Jerusalem . . . says YHWH*), and it would seem more logical to include *says YHWH* in the citation if one follows Sweeney in believing that vv. 18–20 are still part of the citation. It is worth

---

YHWH is Mic 4:7, which is likely cited in Zeph 3:19 (see below). It is hardly in conflict with the promise of a future Davidic king in Mic 5:2–5(1–4).

550. Sweeney, *Zephaniah*, 201.

551. Sweeney, *Zephaniah*, 193.

pointing out that, while House (rightly) takes *says YHWH* as a narratorial marker underlining that the preceding (vv. 18–20) is divine speech, Sweeney believes that the addition of *says YHWH* turns divine speech into prophetic speech that cites YHWH.[552] He nevertheless accepts the distinction between speech about YHWH in vv. 16–17 and (cited) first-person divine speech in vv. 18–19. In my view, the distinction suggests that the citation introduced by the opening phrase of v. 16 ends with v. 17. In addition, the shape of vv. 16–17 is similar to that of vv. 14–15 (a call followed by a rationale), and it is therefore best to think of vv. 16–17 as a subunit. The use of the divine first person in v. 18 begins a new subunit that ends with the book.

The close integration of vv. 14–17 is seen in the palistrophic reuse of key words:

> resound (v. 14aα)
>> be glad (v. 14bα)
>>> in your midst (v. 15bα)
>>>> no longer fear (v. 15bβ)
>>>> do not be anxious (v. 16a)
>>> in your midst (v. 17a)
>> with gladness (v. 17bα)
> resounding shout (v. 17bγ)

Commentary

14 The references to *daughter of Zion* (see the translation note) and *daughter of Jerusalem* do two things here. First, they evoke the female population of Jerusalem in particular. Second, they suggest a transgenerational dimension.[553] The additional use of the appellative *Israel* ensures that the address-

---

552. House, *Zephaniah*, 86; Sweeney, *Zephaniah*, 208. Floyd (*Minor Prophets 2*, 166) critiques House's "fundamentally flawed" attempt to distinguish between YHWH and the prophet as two distinct dramatic characters on the grounds that it fails to take into account the extent to which "various conventions of oracular speech serve precisely to blur this distinction." He then points to the diffidence with which first-person divine speech is or is not tagged with an oracular formula (167). This latter point is also relevant for Sweeney's sharp distinction between tagged and untagged first-person divine speech, which is as problematic as the attempt to distinguish precisely between prophetic and divine speech based on (inconsistently) distinguishing third- and first-person references to YHWH.

553. I am indebted to Floyd especially for the latter; see *Minor Prophets 2*, 238. The transgenerational aspect is intriguing here even if not relevant in many other places. In addition, its frequent use may have turned the expression into a dead metaphor, which is to say that the focus on the female inhabitants of the city is often lost so that "daughter of Zion/Jeru-

ees are not finally limited to women—those traditionally leading the singing of victory songs (Exod 15:20; Judg 11:34; 1 Sam 18:6–7). It also defines the post-restoration inhabitants of Jerusalem as the covenant people of God. This does not deny that there may be "Israelites" who are not living in Jerusalem, but it anchors the identity of the people of God back in Jerusalem.[554] The call is to make a joyful noise, as when a king and his victorious army are welcomed back by the women who had stayed at home, celebrating the freedom and peace that has been won. (The first two verbs in particular do not suggest inner joy so much as exuberant expressions of joy.) The stark difference between condemnation of the city's population at the beginning of the chapter and the call to rejoice here is mitigated by the hint that this is a new generation, the "daughter" of the community condemned earlier. This is also relevant with regard to what will be said about Jerusalem in v. 18, where YHWH "speaks to the younger generation about their predecessors."[555] In other words, the immediate addressees of 2:1–3 and 3:14 are not the same; 2:1–3 ostensibly addresses a pre-destruction audience, 3:14 a later generation that is beginning to experience restoration.

15 The first half of the verse offers the basis for the second. In line with the emphasis of the book, the disaster is first of all described as the outworking of YHWH's *decrees*. The plural may allude to the certainty of the decree by its repetition after an initial outworking of it, as suggested in vv. 6–7. In other words, the book implies that YHWH has given a sentence to punish the region that was followed by a second decree reinforcing the first judgment in the light of Jerusalem's lack of responsiveness. A reversal of the situation can only come with YHWH's removal of these decrees. The *enemies* may be both internal and external—both those who executed Jerusalem's destruction and those within Jerusalem who were responsible for it. In another sense, we might say that YHWH has turned himself away as an enemy and returned as a king, given that the book stresses that YHWH is the source of the hostility against Jerusalem of which the book speaks.[556] But if these verses were added after the destruction, as is likely in my view, it is more natural to think of

---

salem" is in effect equivalent to "population of Zion/Jerusalem." It is the context (looking beyond the generation of Josiah and celebrating the end of war) that activates what is latent in the expression.

554. I explored the polemical use of the term "Israel" (and "house of Israel" in particular) in Ezekiel in Renz, *Rhetorical Function*, 218–22. In Ezekiel, it is the exilic community that inherits the title over against monarchic Jerusalem. But there is a firm expectation in Ezekiel of return to the land. Zephaniah 3:14–17 speaks of, and likely from, this later perspective.

555. Floyd, *Minor Prophets 2*, 238.

556. Note that the Babylonians are nowhere even alluded to. The hostility of Moab and the Ammonites (2:8, 10) is spoken of as in the past rather than in the immediate future.

the human enemies Jerusalem had encountered. For the relationship of this promise to that made in v. 9, see the reflection.

The author surely assumes that YHWH has been the legitimate *king of Israel* all through its history. Chapter 1 implicitly depicted YHWH as present within Jerusalem as the one who invites to the sacrifice; 3:5 explicitly spoke of YHWH being in the midst of Jerusalem at a time of iniquity. But there is a sense in which YHWH may be considered absent where he is not acknowledged as king, as dramatized in Ezek 8–11, and a sense in which YHWH is only truly king where people submit to him.[557] The language of 1:4–6 raised questions about the loyalty given by Jerusalemites to YHWH vis-à-vis others, and 3:2 in effect stated that Jerusalem did not submit to YHWH. The line *The king of Israel, YHWH, is in your midst* implies the reversal of all this. This must not be read as compromising the notion that it was YHWH who brought the judgment and who in this sense was as much in charge at the moment of destruction as during the time of restoration.[558] The contrast to the previous situation is underlined by the reuse of *in your midst* here and in v. 17 (cf. 3:3, 5, 11–12).[559] If there is an end not only to military threats but also to Jerusalem's disobedience, expressed in oppression as well as idolatry, the assurance that *you need no longer fear any harm* can be heard as a promise of safety from exploitative leaders (cf. 3:3–4) as well as foreign armies (cf. the comment on v. 13).

16 As discussed above in the comments under "Composition," *on that day* blurs the temporal reference by adopting a forward-looking posture[560] while synchronizing vv. 16–17 with imperatives spoken in the (actual or rhetorical) present of vv. 14–15. The *Jerusalem* addressed here is not the population addressed at the beginning of the chapter but a later generation, the *daughter of Jerusalem* in the language of v. 14. Blurring the temporal setting makes it easier for readers to both hear this as an address to them here and now and await a further fulfillment in the future. The use of the passive *it will be said* keeps the focus on the addressee and on the content of the speech by leaving undefined who does the speaking. The quotation most likely opens with *Do*

---

557. Nevertheless, "He had ceased to be its King" (Keil, *Minor Prophets*, 2:160) is probably too strong and absolute a statement.

558. Rudolph (*Micha*, 298) argues that this should rule out speaking of these verses as an enthronement song. But the Hebrew Bible speaks of God taking his throne on a few occasions as a way of conveying a sense of newness, always in a salvific sense (Pss 47; 93; 96–99; Zech 14:9). This is picked up in the declaration of the nearness of God's kingdom in the preaching of John the Baptist and Jesus (e.g., Matt 3:2; 4:17) and in the book of Revelation (11:15, 17; 19:6).

559. Cf. the use of the related verb *draw near* in 3:2.

560. The open-endedness of the last line of v. 15 arguably prepares for this future orientation.

not be anxious rather than with *Jerusalem*. While some interpret the preposition attached to *Jerusalem* as indicating the vocative, this would go against normal usage (see the translation note). There are also different opinions about where the quotation ends. Above, under "Composition," I argued that it concludes with the end of v. 17. What is said, therefore, consists of two parts: an injunction not to be anxious and a rationale for it. The rationale is so compelling that it does not require prophetic authority to utter the words of encouragement. If what is said in v. 17 (and earlier in v. 15) is true, anyone should be able to reassure *Jerusalem* that there is no need to be anxious and, therefore, no need for *Zion* to be despondent. The phrase used to indicate such dejection (*hands slacken*) is common in the Hebrew Bible to indicate a loss of heart and willpower in desperate circumstances,[561] often in response to news.[562] The use, alongside *Jerusalem*, of *Zion*, a term that evokes YHWH's special relationship with the city, picks up from v. 14. Earlier in the book, only *Jerusalem* had been used (1:4, 12).

17 *The king of Israel* (v. 15) is now called *your God*, rephrasing v. 15bα and adding the description *a warrior who comes to the rescue* (contrast with the accusation in Jer 14:9). This may be an allusion to 1:14. The *warrior* who came to bring destruction to Jerusalem now comes to bring deliverance. In fighting against Jerusalem, YHWH, in a sense, has been fighting against Jerusalem's enemies—namely against those within it *exulting with pride* (see v. 11). Their removal is the aid, the *rescue* that YHWH brings. But the second half of the verse can be read as elaborating the deliverance YHWH brings. The outer two of the three lines in v. 17b speak of YHWH's joy, which in the progression of the text echoes the rejoicing of the daughter of Zion (v. 14) but logically is its origin. The people of Jerusalem can *be glad* (v. 14) because YHWH *rejoices* over them *with gladness*. They are called to *resound* (v. 14) because YHWH *celebrates . . . with resounding shout*. If v. 14 has assembled a unique combination of words for loud jubilation, the picture in v. 17 is if anything more remarkable, depicting YHWH as exuberant with joy (cf. Isa 65:18–19 for another picture of mutual joy).[563] Alongside loud rejoicing, the statement about YHWH keeping *silent in his love* has struck many commentators as incongruous, but there is no alternative reading that can claim greater plausibility (see the translation note for some alternatives).[564] In the

561. See, e.g., 2 Sam 17:2; Isa 13:7; Ezek 7:17.
562. See 2 Sam 4:1; Jer 6:24; 38:4; 50:43; Ezek 21:7(12).
563. In Deuteronomy, God's delight is in doing good for his people (28:63; 30:9), which can be related to rejoicing in his people but is not quite the same. Closer to Deuteronomy is "rejoice in doing them good" in Jer 32:41, which is equivalent to "setting my eyes on doing them good" (Jer 24:6; cf. 31:28).
564. Karl Marti (*Das Dodekapropheton* [Tübingen: Mohr Siebeck, 1904], 377) sees here (in the words of Vlaardingerbroek, *Zephaniah*, 211) "the complaint of a reader over the

light of 1:14 (*warrior*), the silencing of the warcry may be an appropriate association (cf. Isa 42:13–14): YHWH *keeps silence* in the sense of holding his peace (cf., e.g., Num 30:14[15]; Prov 11:12). This has been interpreted by some commentators from antiquity (Jerome, Tg.) onward as a reference to overlooking or forgiving sin (cf. Ps 50:21).[565] But divine silence in the face of evil is often seen as a problem (cf. Hab 1:13), and the people addressed here was previously described as a remnant that does *not commit iniquity* (v. 13). Even if we think of Jerusalem more generally, not distinguishing between the proud and the humble or between the generation that was swept away by YHWH's punishment and the post-destruction remnant, a reference to silently forgiving or overlooking sin seems odd following the removal of *the decrees against you* (v. 15). It may, therefore, be preferable to read the first line as a general statement (*He rejoices over you with gladness*[566]) that is then teased out in a twofold way, since joy is expressed both in silent contemplation of the beloved and in resounding celebration.[567] While the image of God specifically as a bridegroom is not inappropriate in this context (cf. Isa 62:4–5),[568] nothing here specifically invites it.

Unlike the judgment, for which reasons are given, the work of salvation is not justified in anything done on the human side. The phrase *in his love* comes closest to offering a rationale for the new act of God.[569]

Reflection

The description of the remnant in the previous section was largely in terms of what they are not—they do not commit iniquity, they are not haughty,

---

failure of deliverance to materialize: '(alas) He is silent in his love'." Vlaardingerbroek relies on Rudolph (*Micha*, 293), who seems to have misunderstood Taylor's comment (Charles L. Taylor Jr. and Howard Thuman, "The Book of Zephaniah," *IB* 6:1034) about a marginal note correcting the text and attributes to him the same view, unless perhaps he had a different Taylor in mind.

565. More recently, this was argued for by Ivan J. Ball, *Zephaniah*, 185–86; Ben Zvi, *Zephaniah*, 251–52; cf. Berlin, *Zephaniah*, 145.

566. The words used here do not demand noise, unlike the opening statement of v. 14. In other words, glad rejoicing can happen silently or it can happen with exuberant shouts.

567. Cf. Keil, *Minor Prophets*, 2:161; see also Carl von Orelli, *The Twelve Minor Prophets*, trans. J. S. Banks (Edinburgh: T&T Clark, 1893), 278; Davidson, *Nahum*, 135; Robertson, *Nahum*, 340–41. But Rudolph (*Micha*, 293) considers this thought embarrassing.

568. E.g., von Orelli, *Minor Prophets*, 278; Irsigler, *Zefanja*, 422; cf. Sweeney, *Zephaniah*, 202.

569. Cf. Frank Crüsemann, "Israel, die Völker und die Armen: Grundfragen alttestamentlicher Hermeneutik am Beispiel des Zefanjabuches," in Walter and Schwantes, *Der Tag wird kommen*, 131.

they do not tell lies, etc.—but it included one positive action attributed to the survivors: they seek refuge in God. Here, too, the presence of the positive (joy) is paired with the absence of the negative (anxiety). A major difference is the switch from indicative to imperative. This raises with greater acuteness the question of dating and not only in diachronic perspective (i.e., in terms of the origin of the text), but also in synchronic perspective with regard to the question who is asked to be glad and not anxious. Does Zephaniah exhort his contemporaries to rejoice in the run-up to the threatened disaster and to do so wholeheartedly (*with all your heart*)?[570] It is possible to take courage from the knowledge that there will be restoration at the other side of judgment, but it seems implausible that Zephaniah encouraged people during Josiah's reign to engage in loud rejoicing "as if (disaster and restoration had already happened)." If "Balaam could see nothing but blessing in store for Israel, because 'the Lord their God is with them, the shout of the king is among them' (Num 23:21),"[571] this is hardly true for Zephaniah, who was well able to see iniquity and misfortune in Jerusalem. The reason for the rejoicing was the proclamation: "No fear of any evil ever again shall disturb your peace of mind."[572] But this was not Zephaniah's message for his contemporaries in the 620s.

Pastors and preachers obviously cannot assume that a biblical command applies to their congregation just because it is being read out at a given time and place. In speaking to individuals or groups, it requires discernment to know whether a word of warning or encouragement is to be spoken, whether a dull conscience needs to be stirred up or an over-sensitive conscience calmed. This passage gives clear criteria for determining whether the imperatives apply or not. I suggested in the commentary that the passive voice in v. 16 (*it will be said*) is appropriate because no appeal to authority is needed. The evidence nearly speaks for itself. Where YHWH is acknowledged as king and known as protector from harm, the imperative for joy follows naturally in the same way that news bulletins of freedom and peace after a hard-fought battle lead to jubilation. Where people have reason to be confident that YHWH joyfully comes to the rescue, confident in his love for them, it is right that they are encouraged not to be disheartened. For God's loyal subjects, the nearness of his kingdom must be good news that brings joy and dispels anxiety. The link between God's presence "in your midst" and summons to joy is also made elsewhere (Isa 12:6; Zech 2:10–11[14–15]; note also 9:9–10). It is an essential part of the Christian gospel. The kingdom of God is near because, in Christ, God is with us (Immanuel) as a warrior who

---

570. Robertson, *Nahum*, 336.
571. Robertson, *Nahum*, 337.
572. Robertson, *Nahum*, 339.

rescues (Jesus). When we read in the Gospels about the acclamation given to Jesus on his entry into Jerusalem, for which Matthew cites Zech 9:9 (Matt 21:5), it is appropriate to think also of Zeph 3:14–15.[573] With the death and resurrection of Christ, evil is defeated and the decrees against us are removed because we are reconciled to God. The combination of loving silence and resounding shout is evocative of the Good Friday, Holy Saturday, and Easter Sunday sequence. Those who belong to Christ indeed have a compelling rationale for joy and for letting go of anxiety. The imperatives, therefore, apply to the body of Christ. There is a sense in which God's kingship is fully implemented only in the future, but Jerome insists that "if these things have not yet been done but belong to the future, we have believed in the Savior's coming in vain." He observes that "since the prophet Zechariah exhorts Zion and Jerusalem to the same joy, and Matthew says that this very prophecy was fulfilled in Christ's first coming, we are compelled by necessity, or rather, we are led by the very order of truth, not to hope that what is spoken in Zephaniah belongs to the future but has been done."[574]

To affirm such a fulfillment of the promise in Christ and thus for the church does not take the promise away from Israel,[575] even if we affirm that in Christ, God has broken down the wall between Jews and non-Jews. The text itself reminds us that the remnant is not defined by ethnic heritage. It is a remnant precisely because not all inhabitants of Jerusalem are truly Israel (cf. Rom 9:6). The same applies to those who bear the name of Christ. Not all who are called Christians are truly connected to Christ. The term "Israel" is ambivalent. Generally, it is used for all who visibly belong to the national body by descent or incorporation, but here in v. 14 it is used more narrowly as an honorary term for the remnant. This ambivalence has a counterpart in the ambivalence of the term "body of Christ," which can be used for all who formally belong to Christ, namely via Christian baptism, and more narrowly for those who are in Christ through faith. On the one hand, we may need to say that the imperatives as well as the promises only belong to the *humble and powerless people* who constitute true Israel. On the other hand, all who respond to the imperative, claiming and believing the promises, thereby show that they do indeed belong to the remnant.

The notion that God delights in his people (Isa 62:5; 65:19; cf. Jer 32:41), in those who fear him (cf. Ps 147:11), is also implied in the New Testament

---

573. An additional allusion to Zephaniah is plausible for John 12; see, e.g., Tachik, *"King of Israel"*.

574. Jerome, *Twelve*, 1:154, 155. The link with Jesus's entry into Jerusalem had already been made by Justin Martyr (*First Apology*, par. 35), suggesting that a link between Zeph 3:14 and Zech 9:9 had been made by other readers in antiquity.

575. Note the concerns expressed by Crüsemann, "Israel," 128–29.

(e.g., praise from God in Rom 2:29). Thus, 1 Pet 1:7 claims that genuine faith, which is "more precious than gold," results in us receiving praise, honor, and glory from God "when Christ is revealed," and this is the reason for "indescribable and glorious joy" (v. 8) even in the midst of suffering various trials (v. 6). God's splendor is revealed where his works operate according to their design (cf. Ps 104:31 for God's delight in his works). Because we have been created to delight in God, to enjoy him forever as the Westminster Confession puts it, God delights in us when we delight in him, recognizing him as our supreme value and acting accordingly. In other words, he delights in what is right and true. It is right and true that we should wholeheartedly exult in him, find our supreme joy in God, and cast our anxiety on him who cares for us (1 Pet 4:7; cf. the combination of calls to rejoice and not to worry in Phil 4:4–6). Therefore, God celebrates when this happens. God's joy is our joy in him.

How does the language of enemies being turned away (v. 15) fit with the expression of hope for the people in v. 9? It is actually not difficult to read the whole book as presenting a coherent picture. Just as there are enemies of God as well as a humble and powerless people in Jerusalem, so that both threat and promise can be uttered with regard to Jerusalem, in the same way, as discussed in relation to ch. 2, there is punishment as well as hope (for a remnant) among the peoples. But maybe we can be bolder and not merely distinguish between the defeated oppressors and the rescued survivors among the nations. Maybe we could also observe that there are two ways in which enemies can be turned away. There is the obvious turning away of an enemy that results from having overpowered them, but there is also defeat by conversion, as it were, which v. 9 seems to imply. An enemy can be turned away by being turned into a friend. In the same way, even if the main idea of the text is that the discontinuation of haughtiness on Mount Zion is accomplished by the removal from it of *those of you exulting with pride*, the possibility that some of the proud may have responded to the call in 2:1 need not be excluded. The text does not invite defeatism or an us-versus-them mindset. It invites identification with those whose joy and hope are in God, whatever their past.

X. PROMISE OF SALVATION (3:18–20)

[18]*Those[a] afflicted [b] on account of[c] the appointment[d] I have removed[e] from you;[f]*
   they were[g] an offering,[h] upon her a reproach.[i]
[19]*Look, I am dealing with[j] all who oppress you at that time.*
   I will rescue the lame;[k] the outcast I will gather.

I will transform them[l] *into praise and into fame*
throughout the whole earth their shame.[m]
[20]*At that time, I will bring you [home],*[n]
and at the same time I will gather you.[o]
Indeed, I will make you fame and praise[p]
among all the peoples of the earth,
as[q] *I restore your fortunes*[r] *before your eyes,*
says YHWH.

a. This verse is notoriously difficult to translate; see the commentary. It is very possible that the text is corrupt. In *CTAT* 3:915, *nûgê* is given a B (most likely correct) rating, and *hāyû* and *ʿālêhā* are both given a C (probable but with considerable doubt) rating. As mentioned with respect to the previous verse (see the translation note on 3:17), the LXX and Peshitta offer a different textual tradition. LXX can be translated "as on a festival day. And I will gather those who are shattered. Alas, who has taken up a reproach against her?" I am not persuaded that this reading can claim greater probability to be original.

b. Hebrew *nûgê* is understood as a *niphal* masculine plural participle construct of *ygh*, a verb that occurs elsewhere in the *niphal* only in Lam 1:4, where it refers to being afflicted or to grieving. Adopting the nuance "grieving" (e.g., NIV, NASB, ESV) rather than *afflicted* usually leads to rendering the *qatal* verb as a future tense and always to understanding *maśʾēt* as "burden," neither of which is without problems.

c. For the use of the preposition *min* within a construct phrase, cf. Gen 43:34 (*maśʾōt mēʾēt pānāyw*); 1 Sam 2:8 (*dāl mēʾašpōt*); Neh 13:4 (*wəlipnê mizzê*); Isa 28:9 (*gəmûlê mēḥālāb*); 52:14 (*mišḥat mēʾîš*); Jer 23:23 (*haʾělōhê miqqārōb ʾānî nəʾum-yhwh wəlōʾ ʾělōhê mērāḥōq*); Ezek 13:2 (*linbîʾê millibbām*); Hos 7:5 (*ḥămat miyyāyin*). See GKC 130a or JM 129m–n for examples with other prepositions.

d. Hebrew *môʿēd* (cf. Hab 2:3) can refer to a meeting or meeting place as well as to an appointed or agreed time, and specifically a time of festivity. It is often understood here as a reference to festivals. While not impossible (cf. Isa 33:20; Lam 1:4), the plural (e.g., Num 10:10; Ezek 36:38) or *yôm môʿēd* (e.g., Lam 2:7, 22) could have conveyed that idea more unambiguously. I see a reference to the Day of YHWH—the time YHWH had appointed for a "sacrifice" (1:7).

e. Hebrew *ʾāsaptî* could be understood positively (e.g., gathering the exiles) or negatively as in 1:2 (and 3:8). I take it in the latter sense, seeing an allusion to the opening of the book; cf. Jer 16:5 for gathering as removing. The gathering of the harvest is always in a sense a removing from the fields (Exod 23:16) or from threshing floors and wine presses (Deut 16:13). For a positive interpretation, see, e.g., Ben Zvi, *Zephaniah*, 324, who interprets it as an *inclusio* by way of contrast: "from 'divine gathering' in order to punish to 'divine gathering' to save, to bring to the ideal status."

f. The decision to take the prepositional phrase *from you* with the verb *ʾsp* ("gather"; cf., e.g., Deut 16:13; Jer 10:17; Ezek 38:12) is taken against the masoretic accentuation. The MT invites reading "from you they were" (Jerome), which seems to be stating the obvious for no discernible purpose.

g. LXX *ouai* ("Alas") suggests *hwy* (*hôy*) instead of *hyw* (*hāyû*), either reflecting a different Hebrew text or as the result of an interpretative move trying to make sense of the text.

h. Reading *maśʾēt* with MT. Reading instead the construct form (*maśʾat*) would make it possible to render "they were the lifting upon her of reproach," but this would be a strangely complex way of stating that they were the reason Jerusalem suffered reproach, which could be expressed simply with *hāyû ḥerpâ ʿālêhā*. Many suggest the meaning "burden" here, equivalent to *maśśāʾ*, but this meaning is not securely attested for *maśʾēt*. The combination of *nśʾ*, the preposition *ʿāl* and *ḥerpâ* can work in one of two ways, either taking up reproach against someone (Ps 15:3) or bearing reproach for someone's sake (Ps 69:7[8]; Jer 15:15). *Tis elaben* ("who took up?") in LXX may render *mî śaʾēt* or something similar; cf. *CTAT* 3:916.

i. Taking *ʿālêhā* with *ḥerpâ*, against the accentuation. *Ḥerpâ* is translated *taunting* in 2:8.

j. For the idiom, cf., e.g., Ezek 22:14; 23:25. Others understand an implied *kālâ* ("I will make an end of"); cf. 1:18.

k. There is widespread agreement that the participle refers to those who are limping or lame. Godfrey Rolles Driver ("Theological and Philological Problems in the Old Testament," *JTS* 47 [1946]: 162) argued for "go aside" as the meaning of the root here.

l. The use of a masculine plural suffix to refer back to two feminine singular collective nouns is hardly objectionable. Sabottka (*Zephaniah*, 139), Berlin (*Zephaniah*, 147), and others nevertheless prefer to interpret the final *mem* as enclitic. This may also underlie, e.g., RSV, NRSV, ESV, NASB, unless they merely simplify. Mitchell J. Dahood ("Hebrew-Ugaritic Lexicography X," *Bib* 53 [1972]: 399) proposed to read the suffix as an indirect object ("for them"); see the note in JM 125ba for a discussion of datival suffixes; cf. Andrew Bruce Davidson, *Hebrew Syntax*, 3rd ed. (Edinburgh: T&T Clark, 1902), 106; Meyer, *Grammatik*, 3:81. But other uses of the expression (e.g., Isa 14:23; Jer 25:9; Hos 2:12[14]) indicate that the suffix is the direct object and that the indirect object is introduced with *lə*.

m. Reading this as a construction with a double object, *their shame* specifying the earlier *them*. Some construe the last line as an asyndetic relative clause; e.g., *CTAT* 3:921 (comparing Ps 57:5[6], whose second line is not usually read as a relative clause, however) and Vlaardingerbroek, *Zephaniah*, 218, who renders "and I will make into praise and a name / those whose shame is in all the earth." The presence of the article counsels against taking *hāʾāreṣ boštām* as a construct phrase, although this is how it is read in Tg. and Vulg. Such a reading may also underlie KJV, NKJV, NAB, NIV, unless they take the final word as a relative clause as in the Peshitta and Ben Zvi, *Zephaniah*, 259 ("I will get them praise and fame in every land where they have been put to shame"). LXX reads *bštm* (*their shame*) as a verb and takes it with the following verse.

n. No indirect object is specified in the Hebrew. For the different ways in which this was handled in the ancient versions, see Sweeney, *Zephaniah*, 208. Keil (*Minor Prophets*, 2:163) reads "I will bring" as an abbreviation for "I will lead out and bring in," detecting a pastoral metaphor (cf. Num 27:17). But Isa 43:5 and Jer 31:8 seem to me the more obvious parallels ("bring . . . gather"). While the origin is specified in these two places, the destination remains unspecified as well.

o. For this rendering rather than "even at the time when I gather you," see *CTAT* 3:922. English usage requires the addition of *same* (or repetition of *that*) with *day*; in Hebrew the definite article is sufficient.

p. For *ntn* with direct object (introduced by *ʾet*) and indirect object (introduced by *lə*) in the sense of turning something into something else, cf., e.g., Jer 9:11(10); 12:10; 25:18. For designating someone or something for another purpose, cf., e.g., Jer 19:7; 34:17; Joel 2:23 (early rains as vindication).

q. Or "when." To my mind, rendering "when" could suggest that the making of fame and praise will be in addition to the reversal of fortunes, while "as" implies that the restoration itself will be so remarkable as to make the Judeans famous. Sabottka (*Zephanja*, 140) also prefers a modal nuance to a temporal one.

r. For the form of the suffix in *šəbûtêkem*, see *HGHS* 28b'; Meyer, *Grammatik*, 2:57. Some MSS read without *yod šəbûtkem* (cf. Jer 29:14). For the expression, cf. the translation note on 2:7.

Composition

This unit connects with the preceding. The passage is written as a divine speech directed to unspecified addressees. Verses 18–19 arguably presuppose the prophetic speech in the earlier verses, which had specified an addressee, but there is an unmarked change of addressee in v. 20. Vlaardingerbroek marks v. 18 as the song (*shout*, v. 17) YHWH sings and therefore takes it with vv. 16–17, but he cannot translate it in a way that would make it suitable as the words to a joyful song.[576] Sabottka was somewhat more successful, rendering YHWH's song something like: "Those who had departed from me I gathered away from the congregation into the sinkhole.[577] They had piled abuse upon me.[578] Look![579] This is how I annihilate all your oppressors."[580] While not unattractive, Sabottka's translation fails to convince overall.[581] But if one translates the verse in nearly any other way, it becomes implausible as a victory song (see further below). If v. 18 is not the *shout* to which v. 17 refers, it is better to take it with vv. 19–20. The close integration of vv. 14–17 (see above) further justifies this decision. It is probably fair to say that vv. 18–20 tend toward a more prosaic style.[582]

This final subunit can be further divided into two parts, describing what YHWH has already done (v. 18) and what he is going to do (vv. 19–20), or into three parts if one separates the speech report formula at the end of v. 20 from what precedes or if one divides up vv. 19–20 on the basis of their implied ad-

---

576. Vlaardingerbroek, *Zephaniah*, 210.

577. Reading *mmk* (*mimmēk*, "from you") as a noun related to a Ugaritic designation of the underworld (*mk*), which Dahood had suggested for Amos 3:11.

578. With a different word division, reading *'ly hḥrph* (*'ālay hāḥerpâ*, "upon me the abuse/reproach") for MT *'lyh ḥrph* (*'ālêhā ḥerpâ*, "upon her reproach/abuse").

579. Apparently reading *hnh* (*hinnê*) for *hyw* (*hāyû*, "they were"), unless *hwy* (*hôy*, "woe," *Oy*) is read and loosely rendered. The remainder is a plausible translation of the received text.

580. Cf. Sabottka, *Zephanja*, 146–47; cf. 134–37.

581. In particular, his reading of *mmk* is not persuasive. As pointed out in the translation notes, the rendering of this verse is difficult.

582. So Irsigler, *Zefanja*, 428; cf. Curtis, "Zion-Daughter Oracles," 173–77.

dressees.[583] Verse 19 is probably influenced by Mic 4:6–7,[584] although in my view it is unlikely that this means that *'āsaptî* must be understood positively (see the translation note on *I have removed*).[585] Verse 20 is a variation of the preceding, probably with the aim of including an exilic audience. Nogalski argues that v. 20 alludes to Joel 3:1[4:1] with the use of *at that time* and *restore . . . fortunes*.[586] But Seitz believes that the dependence is the other way around (i.e., "that Joel is working on the basis of a textual witness available to him in the Sinai/wilderness narratives but also in the [Day of the LORD] material in the prophetic legacy . . . , chiefly Zephaniah 3").[587] The phrase *at that time* is also used in v. 19 and already in 1:12; *restore . . . fortunes* was previously used in 2:7.[588] The author of v. 20 therefore would not need to be indebted to Joel for these phrases. In any case, an allusion to Joel would not contribute anything here. Nogalski also suggests that the three occurrences of *time* in vv. 19–20 may be "a deliberate foreshadowing of three equally unusual references to the 'time' in Haggai 1:2, 4."[589] The juxtaposition of these two "time" triplets at the end of Zephaniah and the beginning of Haggai is certainly suggestive.

Commentary

18 This verse has been understood in very different ways, and some commentators have practically given up on making any sense of the text.[590] As

---

583. For the former, see Floyd, *Minor Prophets 2*, 239. It is possible that v. 20 is a separate addition ("undoubtedly" according to Irsigler, *Zefanja*, 428), maybe to create an edition of the book that would speak directly to diaspora readers as well, but it is not inconceivable that the author of v. 19 (addressing the remnant in Jerusalem) also authored v. 20 (addressing the exiles).

584. Cf. Nogalski, *Literary Precursors*, 209–11; *Book of the Twelve*, 749–50; Irsigler, *Zefanja*, 431; Sweeney (*Zephaniah*, 206) thinks it more likely that Zephaniah influenced Mic 4–5.

585. Contra Nogalski, *Literary Precursors*, 210. I am not convinced that the *qatal* form refers to the future here, and note that *'sp* is separated from the *yiqtol* of *qbṣ* in v. 19 (both *yiqtol* in Mic 4:6–7); *qbṣ* is taken up again in v. 20 (parallel to the *hiphil* of *bw'*; see below).

586. Nogalski, *Redactional Processes*, 47–48.

587. Seitz, *Joel*, 200.

588. Nogalski (*Literary Precursors*, 212–14; cf. "Zephaniah 3," 215) believes that v. 20 is later than (the original of) vv. 18–19 and therefore considers it likely that *at that time* in v. 19 is a later addition that came with v. 20.

589. Nogalski, *Book of the Twelve*, 749; cf. 751 and *Literary Precursors*, 49–50, 212–15. LXX, Peshitta, Vulg., and Tg. only render "time" once in Hag 1:2, as do a number of modern translations.

590. E.g., Perlitt, *Nahum*, 146; Vlaardingerbroek, *Zephaniah*, 216.

Hadjiev rightly observes, "There are two reasons why the translation of 3,18 is so notoriously difficult. First, a number of words can be translated in more than one way. . . . Second, and more importantly, there are a number of uncertainties on the level of syntax."[591] The LXX may reflect an alternative Hebrew text,[592] but not one that has a greater claim to authenticity. Any translation is provisional, and any interpretation must remain tentative. Alternative renderings include the following, which give a flavor of the options:

> Those grieving far away from the festive gathering
> I gather, away from those who beat them,
> because they suffer contempt on my account.[593]

> as on the day of meeting [with v. 17].[594]
> I take away from you the misfortune,
> so that you need no longer bear reproach.[595]

> Those who went away from me
> I swept away from the festival gathering
> they are away from me
> having heaped insults upon her.[596]

> Mourners from the place of assembly
> I will remove far away from you.
> They were a burden
> Upon her and a reproach.[597]

591. Tchavdar S. Hadjiev, "The Translation Problems of Zephaniah 3,18: A Diachronic Solution," *ZAW* 124 (2012): 416.

592. Cf. Kim, "Text und Übersetzung," 158–59.

593. Rudolph, *Micha*, 292, with several emendations.

594. This reflects an emendation in line with the Greek text. A very different link with the preceding verse is proposed by Roberts, *Nahum*, 219, who retains the Hebrew text, translates it as "Those grieving far from the festival," and combines it with the penultimate line of the preceding verse, which he translates as, "He will soothe in his love." Note that in this semantic domain, the *hiphil* of *ḥrš* is elsewhere always intransitive "to be silent," with the exception of Job 11:3, where "to silence" has no soothing connotations.

595. Edler, *Kerygma*, 64–65; cf. Seybold, *Nahum*, 117–18, with different nuances, using the past tense and not interpreting the last line as a purpose clause.

596. Kapelrud, *Message*, 109; cf. Sabottka, *Zephanja*, 146–47, cited above under "Composition."

597. Ivan J. Ball, *Zephaniah*, 295.

I will gather those who have been driven
from your appointed feasts;
[although] they were a tribute from you,
[they were] a reproach upon her [Jerusalem].[598]

Among those staying close to the MT, Berlin and Sweeney interpret the first verb as a relative clause. Berlin gives it a positive sense ("Those grieving from the festival whom I have gathered were from you. A burden on her, a reproach."),[599] Sweeney a negative one ("Those who have suffered from the appointed time when I punished you were a burden upon her, a reproach.").[600] However, they share the doubtful understanding of *maś'ēt* as "burden," which Ben Zvi avoids. He offers what may be the most plausible alternative to my own reading of the received Hebrew text: "Those who are afflicted because they are deprived of the festivals, I (YHWH) have gathered, they were from you, (they were) a sign on her, (they were) a (source of) mockery."[601] But he does not interpret the meaning of the phrase "a sign on her." Seeing an allusion in this verse to the phrase "bearing reproach for the sake of someone" (Jer 15:15; Ps 69:7[8]), Ben Zvi detects a hint of the exiles having been mocked on account of Jerusalem. But it remains unclear how this links with the exiles being a sign on Jerusalem.

In the reading offered in this commentary, the verse is a statement about those whom YHWH has punished. They are characterized as *those afflicted on account of the appointment*, the appointment being the Day of YHWH described in ch. 1. The object comes first in the verse because it is its theme. Three statements are made about those who fell under YHWH's punishment. The first relates those punished to the remnant: *I have removed* those badly affected by the punishment *from you*. The punishment, already described previously as a harvest, was a separation like, for example, that of wheat

598. Patterson, *Nahum*, 377. For *maś'ēt* meaning "tribute," cf. Amos 5:11. Patterson sees a reference to the deportees as booty for the Babylonians (386).

599. Berlin, *Zephaniah*, 141; cf. Keil, *Minor Prophets*, 2:161, who explains the opening words thus: "Those who are troubled for the festal meeting are they who mourn because they cannot participate in the joy of assembling before the face of the Lord, namely on account of their banishment into foreign lands" (2:162). Berlin does well, in my view, to render the main verb as past tense but with the result that the first sentence makes a very bland statement.

600. Sweeney, *Zephaniah*, 193. The absence of "(they) were from you" is presumably the result of dividing the verse differently from the Masoretes. All in all, Sweeney's reading of the verse is probably closest to mine.

601. Ben Zvi, *Zephaniah*, 253. *CTAT* 3:920 offers "Je rassemblerai ceux qui gémissaient privés de toute fête (litt.: hors de fête). Ils avaient été séparés de toi (litt.: hors de toi)— opprobre qui pesait sur Jérusalem (litt.: sur elle)."

and chaff. In this case, the chaff was not merely blown away but removed by being gathered for the fire of judgment. The second statement relates those punished to YHWH: *they were an offering*, again paradoxically, because the offering (*sacrifice* in 1:7) consisted of those unsuited to come into God's presence. The third statement relates those punished to Jerusalem as a transgenerational entity: they were *upon her a reproach*. In other words, the nature and impact of the divine punishment are explored from three angles. The first is the main one in terms of the discourse of vv. 19–20 (*I have removed . . . from you*), as the remnant are the addressees. The second is theologically significant and establishes a link with the complete book (*an offering*). The final one ensures that Jerusalem itself remains the dominant theme (*upon her a reproach*).

19 In comparison with "on that day," the phrase *at that time* is rare in prophetic or divine speech (Isa 18:7; Jer 3:17; 4:11; 8:1; 31:1; Amos 5:13; Mic 3:4),[602] and it is therefore remarkable that we have three occurrences in Zephaniah (1:12; 3:19, 20). The phrase is also combined with a participle in Jer 8:1; elsewhere the main verb is a *yiqtol* (imperfect) form. *Hinnî* (or *hinanî*, lit. "Look, I") with participle is often used to refer to something that is about to happen,[603] although the notion of imminence is not always present.[604] The phrase *at that time* at first seems to make it impossible to speak of the immediate future, but if it is read as synchronizing with v. 18 (which summarizes ch. 1), the use of the participle following *hinnî* suggests that the deliverance will come very soon after the removal of the evildoers, not at some distant point in the future. The continuation with a *wə-qatal* form (*wəhôšaʿtî, I will rescue*) is unremarkable.[605]

The Hebrew root in *all who oppress you* relates to *humble* in v. 12 and so should be thought of (also) as "those who humble/humiliate you." The presence of such oppressors indicates that the timeframe is prior to the fulfillment of the promises made in vv. 9 and 15. The chiastic arrangement of *I will rescue the lame, the outcast I will gather* (verb, object, object, verb) surrounds those in need of care with YHWH's action. Kessler argues that the terms *lame* and *outcast* allude to the sheep metaphor.[606] The association of the remnant

602. The only other instance of the phrase that does not belong to a narrator is in Judg 11:26 in direct speech.

603. E.g., Gen 6:13, 17; 1 Kgs 11:31; 14:10; 16:3; 17:12; 20:13; Isa 13:17; Jer 1:15; 5:14–15; Ezek 4:16; 16:37; Hos 2:6(8); Hab 1:6.

604. See *IBHS*, 627–28; cf. GKC 116p; JM 121e.

605. Cf., e.g., Jer 1:15; 6:21; 8:17; 9:7, 15 (6, 14); 10:18; 13:13–14; Ezek 4:16; 5:8; 6:3; 13:8, 20; Hos 2:6(8); Joel 2:19; 3:7(4:7); Amos 6:14. See GKC 116p and *IBHS*, 627–28.

606. Rainer Kessler, " 'Ich rette das Hinkende, und das Versprengte sammle ich': Zur Herdenmetaphorik in Zef 3," in Walter and Schwantes, *Der Tag wird kommen*, 93–101; cf. Waltke, *Micah*, 221.

with a flock of sheep is also found in v. 13 and earlier in 2:7, and it likely informed 3:3, where Jerusalem's leaders, who were supposed to be shepherds, are described as wild animals. So, this proposed allusion is fitting, although Kessler's argument is not conclusive. It is possible that the terms refer to two different groups, namely those left in the ravaged country (*the lame*) and those scattered abroad (*the outcast*). It is noteworthy that when applied to people in Deuteronomy, the root *ndḥ*, which underlies *outcast*, is used most often for being led away from worshipping YHWH (Deut 4:19; 13:5, 10, 13 [6, 11, 14]; 30:17).[607] Only twice in Deuteronomy is it used for YHWH banishing his people in punishment (30:1, 4). But the latter is how the verb is used in Jeremiah (8:3; 16:15; 23:2–3, 8; 24:9; 27:10, 15; 29:14, 18; 32:37; 46:28; cf. Ezek 4:13; Dan 9:7).[608] The terms *lame* and *outcast* are found together in one other place, Mic 4:6, in a similar context. Given that the final line in Mic 4:6 also specifies YHWH as the source of affliction, it is possible that the author and first readers of Zeph 3:19 understood *the outcast* as a reference to the exiles (cf. Ps 147:2; Neh 1:9). This would imply that YHWH was the one who did the scattering.[609] But just as YHWH's scattering can be laid at the feet of the leaders in Jer 23:2–3, so it would be possible to see a secondary agent here. Kessler argues that *the lame* refers to those hurt by Jerusalem's elites and *the outcast* to those scattered by external enemies.[610] However, this may be an overly precise distinction and too focused on past events at the expense of present realities. In the light of Jer 23:2–3, one could think of Jerusalem's past leaders as having caused both the "limping" and (indirectly) the scattering, but in the oracle's present time, it is external powers that limit the freedom both of the Jerusalemites (*the lame*) and the diaspora (*the outcast*). If we read the preceding verse as speaking about those whom YHWH punished in Jerusalem (the internal oppressors), as suggested earlier, it may be better to see external enemies in view in this verse, complementing that picture.[611]

The perspective at the end of the verse is both broadly universal (*throughout the whole earth*) and more narrowly focused than v. 9 in that it is only concerned with the reputation of the Judahite remnant. It is entirely feasible

607. It is also used for letting loose an axe (19:5; 20:19) and for straying sheep (22:1).

608. Cf. 30:17; 40:12; 43:5; 50:17, passages in which YHWH is not explicitly the agent. The language is also used for punishment on the Ammonites (49:5) and on Elam (49:36); cf. Joel 2:20 for YHWH driving away the northern army.

609. Cf. the petition in Ps 5:10[11]. The diverse references in Isaiah (8:22; 11:12; 13:14; 16:3–4; 27:13; 56:8) do not specify the agent.

610. Kessler, "Herdenmetaphorik," 100. Alternatively, it would be attractive to see here a blending of the remnant of Judah and of the nations, but Tachik's argument along those lines ("*King of Israel*," 135) is implausible.

611. Irsigler (*Zefanja*, 430) comes to the same conclusion and compares the use of *(bənê) maʻannayik* in Isa 60:14. Cf. Nogalski, *Literary Precursors*, 205–8.

to draw a line from the renown of the remnant in Jerusalem via the honor thereby given to YHWH, recognized as the one who came to the rescue, to the salvation of other peoples as they acknowledge YHWH as the true king. But this is not done here explicitly. The focus seems to be on the reversal of Jerusalem's humiliation. *Praise* and *fame* are tied closely together also in Deut 26:19 and, in reverse order, in the next verse and in Jer 13:11 (cf. 33:9).[612] Deuteronomy 26:19 clearly concerns Jerusalem's honor; Jer 13:11 suggests that YHWH's people are meant to bring YHWH fame and honor. It is possible that this verse focuses on the former and v. 20 suggests the latter (see the commentary below). In any case, the good reputation is not something that Jerusalem will achieve for herself; it is something given to her. And this is maybe underlined with the addition of *their shame* at the end of the verse as an object that further explicates *them*. What Jerusalem brings as raw material for the establishment of her *praise* and *fame* is *shame*. We should not suppose that the text speaks of moral *shame*; it refers to the humiliation of the injured and abused. It is the shame of ruins and maybe the shame of having part of one's community living in exile as prisoners of war.[613] Transformation in Zephaniah is not described in terms of sorrow for sins, repentance, forgiveness, and a new life. It comes about through the removal of the proud and the exaltation of the humiliated, as in Mary's song (Luke 1:51–53).

20 It is often thought that this verse "contains nothing that has not already been said in the preceding text, except for the emphasis that those who read this prophecy or hear it read . . . will now also experience, or are even in the process of experiencing, the fulfilment."[614] But in my view, there is not necessarily such a focus on imminence. Keil is right that *before your eyes* need not imply that the fulfillment of the promise is near but rather that it will be public and obvious.[615] What is in fact new is the address to the exiles. Previously, Jerusalem and various subgroups within it had been addressed. Here, for the first time in the book, the exiles are addressed. Given that YHWH's punishment was described earlier as a separation, removing the arrogant proud from Jerusalem and leaving a humble remnant, it is striking that the exiles, those who had been removed from Jerusalem, are addressed with positive promises and without recrimination. But the verse helps to integrate Zephaniah into a wider corpus of prophetic literature reflecting on exile and

---

612. Cf. the use of the terms in close parallelism in 1 Chr 16:35; Pss 48:10(11); 66:2; 102:21(22); 106:47; Isa 48:9.

613. At a later time, when exiles were no longer held prisoner, one might think of the shame of having a diaspora community that does not find Jerusalem attractive enough as a place to which to return. But the reference to oppressors suggests an earlier time reference.

614. Vlaardingerbroek, *Zephaniah*, 217.

615. Keil, *Minor Prophets*, 2:164. He compares the expression "eye to eye" in Isa 52:8.

destruction—not least Ezekiel, which emphasizes that the future lies with the (returning) exiles rather than the people in Jerusalem.

The distinction between bringing home and gathering is also made in Jer 31:8 (and Isa 43:5), where the reference to "the blind and the lame" may remind us of Zeph 3:19, even if a different word for "lame" is used (*pissēaḥ*). It highlights that the restoration is not merely about return to the land and to Jerusalem but involves a gathering together of YHWH's people, ultimately around YHWH, as Irsigler observes.[616] We may compare the emphasis on *one accord* in v. 9, followed by a movement toward Jerusalem in v. 10.

It may be possible to read *I will make you fame and praise among all the peoples of the earth* as the purpose and, in this sense, the rationale for the bringing home and gathering. In this case, one could translate the opening particle conjunction with "because," but this strikes me as rather forced, leading me to opt for *indeed*. It is noteworthy that the verse does not say, "I will give you fame and praise," which would be equivalent to "I will make you famous and praised."[617] It is possible to read the expression here as similar to Jer 13:11 and 33:9 (see above) so that the regathering of exiles in Jerusalem brings fame and praise to YHWH. After all, this making of fame and praise is said to happen as YHWH is doing things—he is the subject of every verb here. This would add a further nuance to what is said in v. 19, although the distinction is not explicit.[618]

I restore your fortunes surely implies and can be heard as "I bring you back from captivity" (see the translation note on 2:7). I prefer the broader formulation, in which the gathering from exile is included. The formula *says YHWH* forms an *inclusio* with the opening of the book (*dəbar-yhwh*), and in this is similar to the beginning and end of Amos but unlike other prophetic books.[619] This may be to underline that the word of salvation has as much divine authority as the word of judgment that dominates the book.

Reflection

On my reading, the final three verses of the book concern three entities. Verse 18 refers in the third person to those in Jerusalem who were the tar-

---

616. Irsigler, *Zefanja*, 433.

617. This could have been expressed by reversing direct and indirect objects (the use of *'et* and *lə*); see the translation note.

618. The Jeremiah passages have an explicit "for me," and this would have been possible here as well.

619. Irsigler, *Zefanja*, 428. Haggai ends with the utterance formula (which may well refer to 2:23 only rather than to the book; cf. 1:9, 13; 2:4, 8–9, 14, 17). Ben Zvi (*Zephaniah*, 261) notes that the penultimate verse of Amos also includes the phrase "restore your fortunes / return you from captivity."

get of God's appointed punishment. They are spoken about rather than addressed not least because they are no longer there. They do not belong to the remnant; they have been given up to God, to whom everything and everyone must ultimately be lifted up, whether in judgment or in praise. They sullied the place and the people God had elected. Verse 19 continues the address to those left in Jerusalem, the remnant that is now oppressed by foreign forces, and promises deliverance for them ("the lame") and reunion with those who had been deported ("the outcast"). The second half of the verse promises that this will not be a mere repair job, a restoration to the *status quo ante*, but such a glorious transformation that the formerly *lame* and *outcast* will become *praise* and *fame*. Verse 20 more or less repeats the promise, but now addresses it to the exiles and with an ambiguity that maybe allows for the wonderful restoration of fortunes to bring *fame and praise* to YHWH as well as making the formerly despised famous and praised themselves. The use of *at that time* at the beginning of both v. 19 and v. 20 indicates that the three main actions (punishment of the proud, salvation of Jerusalem's remnant, and restoration of the exiles) belong closely together, even if complete synchronicity is a fiction. After all, v. 18 (on the reading offered here) refers to an event of the recent past with a *qatal* (perfect) verb, while vv. 19–20 offer promises of what God is going to do in the (imminent?) future.

I see an initial fulfillment of these promises from the Persian period onward in the restoration of Jerusalem and the return of some of the exiles. While some of the other entities of which Zephaniah spoke disappeared, the Jewish people came to be known within the region's subsequent empires as those who cling to faith in one God. But, as also with vv. 14–17, a greater fulfillment could be imagined. The forward-looking rhetoric of vv. 19–20 probably helped later readers to appropriate the text along with its preceding verses as a basis of hope for a future "messianic age" whose contours could be filled out with the help of other texts.[620] Focusing on v. 19, we too may conclude that God's kingship is fully implemented only in the future, namely when all enemies will be completely disarmed, God's people will be fully healed, and God's reputation and that of his people will be unsullied. But as we have observed for vv. 14–17, the apostolic claim is that with the death and resurrection of Christ, rulers and authorities were disarmed (Col 2:15), and we are no longer enslaved to sin (Rom 6:6). Instead, we have overcome the evil one (1 John 2:14) so that, dead to sin, we might live for righteousness (1 Pet 2:24). Those who had been far off—not merely Judean exiles but even

---

620. Cf. Tachick, "*King of Israel*," 139–54, on the reception of Zeph 3:14–15 in early Jewish literature; e.g., *b. Sanhedrin* 98a, also mentioned in Coggins and Han, *Six Minor Prophets*, 122.

people who had been altogether outside the covenant community—have been brought near by the blood of Christ (Eph 2:13).

While there is a sense in which we are called in Christ to do praiseworthy deeds, the focus in the New Testament is on the praise and fame given to God (e.g., Matt 5:16; Luke 18:43; Acts 19:17; Eph 1:12; Phil 1:11) and also on praise received from God (e.g., Rom 2:10; 1 Pet 1:7) rather than fame among people. Indeed, there is an expectation within the New Testament that, generally, people will fail to acknowledge God's transformation of a person from shameful to praiseworthy (cf. 1 Pet 2:12, 15; 3:16). But the focus in Zephaniah is in any case not on shameful and praiseworthy conduct but on the transformation from a pitiable condition to an enviable one. This, too, is not readily recognized, because the benefits we have received in Christ that have lifted us from our miserable condition—the forgiveness of sins, the promise of eternal life—are not much valued by most of those who have not received them (and even by a good few who have received them). But there are glimpses of a future in which God's mighty act of restoring humanity will be seen and acknowledged universally, as sometimes even outsiders recognize the work done in and through the redeemed people of God.

Index of Authors

Achtemeier, Elizabeth, 129n268, 155n349, 290n233
Adams, Douglas, 86
Adams, Sean A., 453n7
Aḥituv, Shmuel, 370n435
Ahlström, Gösta W., 440n64, 441, 478–79, 531n267, 533n279, 533n281, 533n285, 561n352, 569n398
Albertz, Rainer, 434n44
Albright, William Foxwell, 353, 397
Allen, Leslie C., 127n260, 508n206
Allis, Oswald T., 36n53, 37
Amar, Zohar, 122n231
Ambrose, Tim, 468
Andersen, Francis I., 164, 202n26, 206, 224, 225n8, 226n14, 227n15, 231, 232, 233, 234, 235, 237n32, 240n41, 240n45, 245n69, 255n109, 257n118, 260n128, 261n134, 264n146, 266, 267n149, 268n156, 269n165, 272, 273, 274n174, 278, 279, 280n200, 285, 286n217, 287n223, 309, 315, 319, 325, 326, 328, 336n342, 339n351, 343, 344, 346n361, 353, 356n379, 360n392, 361, 362n398, 363, 365, 367n425, 368, 373, 374, 379–80, 384n466, 386, 391n490, 396, 398, 412, 452nn4–5
Anderson, John E., 377n437
Arbabanel, 155n350
Armerding, Carl E., 61n14, 197n9
Assis, Elie, 551
Augustine, 312, 400, 417n555, 418, 449n100
Avishur, Yitzhak, 353n370, 366n424, 368n429, 372, 374, 375, 385–86, 390, 397, 409
Avrahami, Yael, 310n288

Bach, Robert, 275n181
Baker, David W., 506n197
Baldwin, Joyce G., 311n291
Balentine, Samuel E., 520, 528
Ball, Edward, 55n120, 57n128, 89n125, 112
Ball, Ivan J., 428–29, 529, 539, 542, 543, 547n298, 583n425, 599n465, 599n469, 610n502, 621, 631n565, 639n597
Baltzer, Klaus, 106n195
Bandstra, Barry L., 541
Banister, Jamie Aislinn, 372, 404n509
Barker, William D., 502n182
Barnett, Richard David, 124n244, 150n342
Barr, James, 86n120, 366n420, 544
Barré, Michael L., 344, 356–57, 358, 373, 382, 401, 402–3, 406, 544, 573n404
Barrick, W. Boyd, 435n47
Barth, Christoph, 598n463
Batnitzky, Leora, 516n228
Bauckham, Richard, 253
Baumann, Gerlinde, 56, 65n22, 74, 130n271
Beck, Martin, 12n43, 487n118, 507n201
Becking, Bob, 48n100, 65n22, 78n83, 155n349
Beentjes, Pancratius C., 279n197
Begg, Christopher, 438n57
Benjamin, Dom C., 573n406
Ben Zvi, Ehud, 12, 14n50, 442n75, 447n90, 447n91, 447n94, 452, 453,

455n17, 455n20, 458n29, 467n54,
467n57, 467n59, 470, 471n71, 472n77,
474n81, 475n90, 482, 483, 484, 490n127,
490n130, 491n132, 492n134, 493, 493n142,
494–95, 498n160, 500n174, 501, 503n186,
505n191, 505n195, 507n202, 508, 509,
511, 518, 521, 522, 538, 539, 542, 543, 545,
549–50, 551, 561n348, 562, 563n361,
564n364, 565n372, 579, 580, 581, 589, 594,
599, 604, 607, 608n496, 612, 613n516,
613n519, 614, 615n526, 619, 621, 623,
631n565, 635, 636, 640, 644n619
Bergmann, Claudia, 136n298, 136n299,
179n433
Berlejung, Angelika, 124n242, 128n262,
146, 151n347, 161n378, 178n428
Berlin, Adele, 233, 424, 425, 442, 445n83,
446nn87–88, 453, 454n12, 456n21,
475n87, 541, 543, 545, 553, 566n379,
567n380, 567n382, 569n392, 576, 579,
580, 581, 582, 594, 608n495, 610, 612n515,
613nn519–20, 614n525, 615n528, 621, 622,
631n565, 636, 640
Berlinerblau, Jacques, 104n184
Berman, Joshua A., 625n548
Berrin, Shani L., 39n66, 54n115
Bertman, Stephen, 311n290
Betlyon, John W., 500n172
Bier, Carol, 122n230
Blair, Judit M., 366n419
Blenkinsopp, Joseph, 315n300
Bliese, Loren F., 197n9
Block, Daniel I., 247n77, 446n85, 588n442
Boda, Mark J., 61, 329–30, 625n546
Bodenheimer, Friedrich Simon, 142n308,
146n331
Bonacossi, Daniele Morandi, 128n262
Borowski, Oded, 311n290, 409n528
Bosman, Jan P., 14n50
Bosshard-Nepustil, Erich, 8n24
Botterweck, G. Johannes, 143n315, 143n319
Bovati, Pietro, 274n172
Braaten, Laurie J., 321n307, 322n311
Brenner, Athalya, 113, 122n229, 122n233
Briggs, William, 66n27
Brock, Sebastian P., 114
Brownlee, William H., 234, 240n41,
240n42, 250n98, 276n182, 285, 293n249

Bruce, F. F., 224, 241, 277n190, 282n204,
283n209, 290, 292n241, 353
Brueggemann, Walter, 152n348
Bucur, Bogdan C., 350n368
Budde, Karl, 277n189
Bugenhagen, Johannes, 435n49
Burkitt, F. Crawford, 217n71
Burnett, Joel S., 120n224, 120n225,
120n226, 138n300, 550
Caesarius of Arles, 350
Calvin, John, 84n109, 91, 112, 276n182, 477,
536–37
Campbell, Douglas A., 295n252, 296n256
Canney, Maurice A., 303n271
Cardon, Dominique, 122n231
Caroll, Robert P., 508n207
Carr, David M., 61n13
Cartledge, Tony W., 104n183
Caspari, Wilhelm, 243n58
Cassuto, Umberto, 106n196
Cathcart, Kevin J., 48n100, 92, 93, 98n159,
100n167, 100n171, 101n175, 103n179,
112, 113, 114, 115, 116, 123n237, 126n256,
127n259, 131n275, 133n287, 139, 148, 154,
165, 176, 177, 184n456, 185n459, 188,
190nn470–71, 202, 236n30, 266, 272, 273,
274
Chandler, Tertius, 130n274
Chapman, Cynthia R., 132n281, 159n368,
161n376, 178–79, 180n435, 180n437,
180n439, 180n440
Childs, Brevard S., 338n348, 547n295
Chilton, Bruce, 38n65
Christensen, Duane A., 15n52, 32n43,
73n63, 176, 182n448, 183n451, 185n459,
529n258, 549
Clark, David J., 35n50
Claudius Aelianus, 122–23
Cleaver-Bartholomew, David, 195n2,
196n5, 225n8, 235n26, 237n35, 250n97
Clendenen, E. Ray, 290n233
Clifford, Richard J., 205n29
Clines, David J. A., 141n305, 379n447
Cockerill, Gary L., 283n209, 283n213,
298n260
Cogan, Mordechai, 439n60
Cogan, Morton, 479n102

Coggins, Richard J., 106n194, 155, 216n64, 218nn74–75, 219n76, 318n304, 417n553, 418n556, 447n95, 447n96, 448n97, 449n100
Cohen, Harold R., 76n74
Cohen, Naomi G., 268n152, 269n161
Collins, C. John, 131n276
Coogan, Jeremiah T., 417
Cook, Gregory D., 41, 48n101, 62, 70n43, 70n44, 70n46, 96n147, 159n366, 159n368, 159n369, 160
Cook, Paul M., 609n499
Cornelius, Izak, 146n328
Cowper, William, 418
Craigie, Peter C., 506n197
Crenshaw, James L., 507n200
Cross, Frank, 281
Crouch, Carly L., 439n60
Crouwel, Joost H., 247n78
Crüsemann, Frank, 631n569, 633n575
Culley, Robert C., 24n7
Curtis, Byron G., 457n24, 625n546, 637n582
Cyril of Alexandria, 119n219

Dahood, Mitchell J., 148, 154, 165, 175, 300, 519, 636, 637n577
Dalley, Stephanie, 124, 128n262
Dalman, Gustaf, 173n418
Dangl, Oskar, 197n10, 203n27, 206n35, 209n46, 226n13, 254, 258n124
Davidson, Andrew Bruce, 97n155, 98n156, 99n166, 631n567, 636
Davies, Glenn N., 295n252
Davies, Philip R., 436
Davis, Ellen F., 493n141
Dawes, Stephen B., 527n253
Day, John, 365n418, 475n88
Dayagi-Mendels, Michal, 503n183
Dearman, Andrew, 621
Deist, Ferdinand E., 181
Delitzsch, Franz, 7, 14, 233, 234, 236n29, 238n38, 242, 246n71, 248, 251n101, 254, 255, 256n113, 258n122, 260nn127–28, 260n132, 261n135, 262n140, 268n152, 269n161, 270n167, 272, 274n174, 275n177, 278n194, 290n232, 290n235, 292n244, 300, 305n274, 306n281, 308, 309, 313,

315, 316n302, 319, 322, 328n322, 333n336, 336n343, 346n360, 352, 355, 364n411, 366n424, 368n431, 373, 375, 376, 381n456, 384–86, 389, 391, 392n492, 397, 404n511, 405, 406n519, 414
Delitzsch, Friedrich, 610n502
del Olmo Lete, Gregorio, 365n416
de Moor, J. C., 389n484
De Odorico, Marco, 562n354
De Roche, Michael, 445n83, 468n62
DeRouchie, Jason S., 460, 466n52
DeVries, Simon J., 486n110
Dick, Michael B., 146n329
Dietrich, Manfried, 123n237
Dietrich, Walter, 216n62, 285, 356n379, 434, 460, 462, 463, 465n44, 466, 467, 486n111, 502n181, 509n210, 512n220, 529n262, 540, 545, 580, 581, 622
Diodorus, 129
Dobbs-Allsopp, F. W., 131n275, 133n284, 133n287
Dodd, C. H., 296n255
Dogniez, Cécile, 117, 166, 232
Donkin, R. A., 122n231
Dorsey, David A., 430
Dotan, Moshe, 535n288
Dothan, Trude, 535n288
Doudna, Gregory L., 39n66
Driver, Godfrey Rolles, 81, 250n98, 353, 363n410, 376, 636
Driver, Samuel R., 97n155, 125n247, 276n182, 372, 378n445

Eaton, John H., 97n155, 155n349, 333n336, 373, 374, 375, 376, 377n438, 406n520
Edelkoort, A. H., 24n5
Edler, Rainer, 519, 523n244, 639n595
Edwards, Douglas R., 492n135
Ehrlich, Arnold B., 139
Ehrlich, Carl S., 554n324
Eitam, David, 531n272
Eitan, Israel, 544
Eliot, T. S., 396
Ellege, Rod, 476n92
Elliger, Karl, 23n1, 65, 92, 224, 277n190, 543, 594, 604
Emerton, John A., 90n131, 284
Esse, Douglas L., 532n274, 535n288

Everson, A. Joseph, 215n60
Ewald, H., 97n155

Fabry, Heinz-Josef, 16, 39, 40, 42n82,
45n91, 46n95, 47n99, 53n111, 54n116, 55,
56n125, 65n22, 71n50, 74, 89n126, 90n129,
98n158, 103, 114, 115, 120n220, 121n228,
125n249, 126n252, 126n255, 127n260,
132n280, 148, 150n342, 150n344, 151, 158,
162n379, 163n383, 164, 165, 177, 178n424,
178n425, 181n441, 181n443, 189n467,
191n476, 201n21, 205n31, 206n33, 206n38,
216n61, 216n62, 226n14, 233, 234, 236n27,
242n54, 251n102, 254, 257n120, 263n143,
267, 268n156, 284, 285, 286, 302n267, 353,
356n379, 374, 384n469, 401n495, 405–6,
408n526, 408n527, 415n542
Fantalkin, Alexander, 535n288, 560n342,
560n343
Faust, Avraham, 492n136, 495, 496–97,
503n185, 531n271, 560n344
Fekkes, Jan, III, 253n105
Ferreiro, Alberto, 341n356, 350n368,
350n369
Finkelstein, Israel, 531n271
Fishbane, Michael A., 46n97, 257n119,
508n208
Fletcher, Paul V. M., 38n65
Floyd, Michael H., 3n7, 24n3, 24n7, 27n14,
31, 60, 61n11, 65n22, 82n96, 89n125,
89n126, 179, 196n5, 197n6, 236n30,
236n31, 269, 270, 275n178, 276n184,
277–78, 278n191, 404n513, 424–25, 429,
458, 460n34, 462n35, 464, 478n98, 485,
499n163, 546, 549n304, 553n321, 583,
584–85, 595n453, 596, 621, 626, 627n552,
628n555, 638n583
Follingstad, Carl M., 520
Fox, Nili Sacher, 190n474
Franklin, Norma, 570n396
Freedman, David Noel, 374, 452n4, 456n21
Fuller, Russell Earl, 5n12

Garland, P. J., 308
Garr, W. Randall, 65, 519
Gärtner, Judith, 608n495, 611
Gat, Azar, 247n75, 247n76
Gelston, Anthony, 240, 255, 260–61n133,
299

Gentry, Peter J., 544
Geva, Hillel, 496
Gevaryahu, Haim M. I., 339n349
Gheorghita, Radu, 206, 283n210
Giesebrecht, Friedrich, 237n34
Gilbart-Smith, Michael, 418–19
Ginsburg, Christian D., 6n17, 257n118
Gitin, Seymour, 492n137, 531n272,
534n286, 535n288, 560n344
Glueck, Nelson, 550
Goldingay, John E., 25n8, 108n204,
152n348, 621
Golub, Mitka R., 471n69
Goodfriend, Elaine Adler, 161n375
Gordis, Robert, 529n262
Gordon, Cyrus H., 363n408
Gordon, Robert P., 55n118, 257n119
Gowan, Donald E., 236n30, 303n269, 463
Grabbe, Lester L., 441n72, 442n74,
530n265
Gradwohl, Roland, 122n232
Grant, Ruth W., 264n147
Gray, John, 106n195
Grayson, A. Kirk, 129n271, 191n475,
532n275
Gregory of Nazianzus, 350
Griffiths, Paul J., 61n13
Gruber, Mayer I., 76n74, 621
Grütter, Nesina, 40, 164, 168n394, 176
Guillaume, Philippe, 5–6
Gupta, Nijay K., 295n250
Guthrie, George H., 283n208

Haak, Robert D., 197n9, 201–2, 205n29,
208n43, 209n47, 210, 211n55, 213n56,
228n21, 234, 237n32, 237n33, 241n48,
248n88, 250n98, 255n110, 257n120,
269n164, 275, 276n182, 279n195, 284, 285,
287n222, 300, 301–2, 303n271, 308, 309,
319, 325, 328, 344, 353, 356, 374, 381n460,
399
Hadjiev, Tchavdar S., 16n53, 434, 465,
600–601, 607, 608n497, 639
Hagedorn, Anselm C., 159n364, 459n31,
533n284
Haimo of Auxerre, 57
Haldar, Alfred O., 81, 139
Halévy, J., 232, 237n34

Han, Jin H., 216n64, 218n74, 218n75,
219n76, 318n304, 417n553, 418n556,
448n97, 449n100
ha-Nagid, Samuel, 115
Haring, James W., 273, 280–81
Harl, Marguerite, 39
Harper, Joshua L., 206n36
Harrison, Roland K., 142n310
Hartog, Pieter B., 290n233
Haupt, Paul, 129n268
Hayes, John H., 439n62
Hays, Richard B., 295n252, 296n254
Heaton, Eric William, 142n310
Heider, George C., 475n88
Heliso, Desta, 295n250
Heller, Jan, 454n13
Heltzer, Michael, 441n70
Henige, David, 435n48
Herberger, Sepp, 147n335
Herrmann, Wolfgang, 461
Hiebert, Theodore, 270–71n168, 344,
347n363, 353n370, 356, 367n425, 372, 373,
377n439, 389n482, 390, 391n488, 397,
398, 401n501, 412
Hillers, Delbert R., 98n159, 100n167, 153,
159n368, 161n376, 178n428, 180n435,
180n439, 299, 406, 576n413, 580
Hitchcock, Louise A., 554n326
Hitzig, F., 97n155
Hoistetter, Edwin C., 320n305
Holladay, William L., 208n43, 210, 407
Holland, Martin, 546
Holmstedt, Robert D., 70n47, 396,
525n246, 543
Holt, John Marshall, 275n179, 276n182
Hope, Edward R., 139, 145n327, 580
House, Paul R., 2n5, 8n25, 13–14, 427–28,
624n544, 625n545, 627
Houtsma, M. T., 285
Huddlestun, John R., 168n398
Hudson, Michael, 306n280
Hugenberger, Gordon, 67n34
Humbert, Paul, 41, 56
Hunter, A. Vanlier, 518

Ibn Ezra, Abraham, 101n174, 115, 455n20
Ibn Kaspi, Joseph, 70n45, 82n96, 89n127,
92, 97n151, 257n119

Irsigler, Hubert, 424, 432, 433n37, 442n75,
446n88, 447n89, 447nn90–91, 447n94,
447n96, 454n11, 454n12, 455n17, 455n18,
459, 460, 463, 465n45, 466n48, 467n60,
471n71, 472n72, 472n75, 473n80, 475n90,
482, 483, 484, 485n106, 486n111, 487n114,
487n118, 489n124, 490n127, 492n138,
493n142, 496n154, 496n155, 499n166,
503, 505–6, 507nn202–3, 509, 514n227,
518, 520, 521n232, 523n242, 523nn243–44,
528n257, 529n262, 531n268, 538, 539, 541,
542, 543, 544, 547, 548n302, 549n304,
550n306, 552n317, 553n321, 554n325,
557n336, 558, 560, 563n357, 565, 566n379,
567n381, 567n384, 568n385, 568n387,
569n389, 569n394, 572n401, 579,
580, 581, 582, 584, 586n433, 589n444,
591n449, 591n450, 594, 595, 596,
602n479, 609n499, 621, 622, 623, 626,
631n568, 637n582, 638n584, 642n611, 644

Jackson, Peter, 142n309
Jacobsen, Eric O., 513n222
Janzen, J. Gerald, 225n8, 225n9, 273,
279n195, 280, 284, 287–88
Janzen, Waldemar, 153, 303n269
Jastrow, Marcus, 248nn84–85
Jeremias, Jörg, 23n1, 24n3, 40n74, 41,
45, 46n94, 57n126, 57n128, 83n105, 84,
89n125, 107n197, 107n201, 108n206,
108n207, 114, 115, 119n216, 120n221,
126n257, 128n264, 155n349, 159n367,
162n379, 165, 175, 177n423, 178n427, 188,
189n466, 208n43, 302n267, 306n278,
360n391
Jerome, 9–10, 40, 155n349, 341n356,
501n179, 538, 579, 587, 595, 631, 633, 635
Jöcken, Peter, 203n27, 207n41, 236n30,
237n34, 243n58, 277n188, 277n189
Johnson, Marshall D., 236n28
Johnston, Gordon H., 48n100, 72n55,
83n102, 146n329, 146n330, 146n331,
146n332, 161n376, 190n472
Jones, Andrew R., 543
Jones, Barry A., 5n12
Jong, John Hans de, 482, 490n129,
609n499
Jongeling, B., 580

Josephus, 10–11, 436n51, 437–38, 501n179, 550

Julian of Toledo, 55

Junker, Hubert, 99n166, 241n48, 277n187

Just, Arthur A., 312n293

Justin Martyr, 633n574

Kahn, Dan'el, 440n66, 441n68, 442n74, 442n76, 443n78, 458n26

Kapelrud, Arvid S., 424n7, 490n130, 600n471, 639n596

Kartveit, Magnar, 621

Kassis, Riad A., 323n314

Katzenstein, H.-J., 535n288

Kealy, Seán P., 55n119

Keel, Othmar, 260n130, 262n140, 262n141, 363n404, 363n406

Keil, Carl Friedrich, 24n5, 148, 176, 224, 228n21, 258n122, 268n152, 269n161, 275, 545, 565n371, 621, 629n557, 631n567, 636, 640n599, 643

Kelle, Brad E., 440n65

Kelley, Page H., 258n121

Kennedy, James M., 64, 71n52

Kennicott, Benjamin, 92

Keown, Gerald L., 291n238

Kessler, Rainer, 15n52, 302n267, 306n278, 482, 491n133, 641–42

Khalaf-von Jaffa, Norman, 141n308

Kim, Jong-Hoon, 519, 582, 639n592

Kimchi, 101n174, 119n216, 126n252, 155n350, 269n161, 277n186, 455n20, 529

Kitchen, Kenneth A., 164, 167, 169n401

Klein, Ralph W., 442n73

Kletter, Raz, 441n69

Kline, J. Bergman, 517n231

Knoppers, Gary N., 435n47, 436n52

Ko, Grace, 14n48

Koch, Dietrich-Alex, 296n255

Köhler, Ludwig, 518

Kolyada, Yelena, 359n387, 416n545

Kotzé, Zacharias, 76n74, 76n75

Kraus, Hans-Joachim, 127n260

Krinetzki, Günter, 519

Kruger, Paul A., 76

Krüger, Thomas, 251n103, 277

Krupp, Robert A., 447n94

Kruse, Colin, 295n250

Kuenen, Abraham, 236n30

Kuhrt, Amélie, 191n476, 247n80, 249n92, 442n73, 532n277

Kutler, Laurence, 232

Laato, Antti, 435, 436n53, 437n54, 439–40, 533n282

La-Bianca, Øystein, 562n356

Labuschagne, Casper J., 165

Lamb, David T., 291n238

Landsberger, Benno, 144n321

Lane, Nathan C., 46n97

Lange, Armin, 581

Lanner, Laurel, 49n103

Last, Isaac, 70n45

Layard, Austen Henry, 115

LeCureux, Jason T., 120n222, 271

Leithart, Peter, 256n116, 516n228

Lernau, H., 496n153

Lernau, O., 496n153

Leuenberger, Martin, 204n28

Levenson, Jon D., 80n91

Levin, Christoph, 424, 425, 434n42, 452n1, 453n8, 455n16, 457n24, 463n40, 465, 469, 487n114

Levin, Yigal, 553n320

Levine, Baruch A., 573

Lindenberger, James M., 534n287

Lindsay, John, 550n307, 550n308, 550n309

Lindström, Fredrik, 269, 293n249

Lipschits, Oded, 550, 551

Littauer, Mary Aiken, 247n78

Loewenstamm, Samuel E., 272, 372

Lohfink, Norbert, 434n44, 449n100

Longman, Tremper, III, 38n59, 66, 85n113, 107n200, 502n180

Loretz, Oswald, 123n237

Lortie, Christopher R., 334n337, 396

Lumsden, Stephen, 130n272, 162, 163n382, 181n445

Lundbom, Jack R., 315n296, 435–36n50, 508n206

Luther, Martin, 56, 211n54, 222n4, 276, 277n186, 341n356, 448, 449n100, 463, 477n95

MacDonald, Burton, 561n353
MacGinnis, John, 190n473
Machinist, Peter, 129n271
Mack, R. Russell, 1–2n3
MacNulty, Daniel R., 248n90, 590n447
Madl, H., 131n276
Maier, Aren M., 554n326
Maier, Walter A., 23n2, 44n88, 65n22,
    82n100, 91, 98n160, 99n166, 107n200,
    112, 113, 114, 115, 123n239, 125, 126n256,
    127n257, 129n268, 130n273, 139, 170n404,
    177n423, 182n447, 182n450
Malamat, Abraham, 533n281
Mann, Jacob, 217n70, 447n90
Manson, T. W., 286n218
Marcus, David, 377n440
Margulis, Baruch, 353
Markl, Dominik, 208n42, 210n51, 238,
    257n117, 355, 399, 404n512, 410n534
Marti, Karl, 630n564
Marx, Karl, 393
Mason, Rex, 236n28
Mathews, Jeanette, 308
Matthews, Victor H., 573n406
Mattingly, Gerald L., 561n352
May, Herbert G., 337
Mayer, G., 320n305
Mayer, John, 436n51, 437n54, 438n59
Mayer, Werner, 335n341
Mazar, Amihai, 311n291
McCarter, P. Kyle, Jr., 573n409
McCarthy, Carmel, 257n118, 257n119,
    258n121
McKane, William, 404n509, 410, 508
McKay, John, 479n102
Mealy, J. Webb, 252n105
Mearns, James, 417n549, 417n551, 417n552
Mech, L. David, 248n90, 590n447
Meier, Samuel A., 93n134, 95n141, 99, 148,
    476n92
Meijer, Diederik J. W., 183n452
Melville, Sarah C., 131n278
Melvin, David, 445n83, 468n62, 612n515
Meyer, Rudolf, 73n59, 117, 175, 235, 254,
    303n271, 350n340, 352, 354n373, 374,
    381n457, 483, 622, 636, 637

Michel, Diethelm, 346–47n361
Mikhail, Mikhail E., 218n73
Millard, Alan, 247n75
Miller, J. Maxwell, 439n62
Monroe, Lauren A. S., 435n47
Montanari, Franco, 538
Moo, Douglas J., 342n357
Moore, P. R. S., 247n78
Moore, Rickie D., 225n10
Mosca, Paul G., 357n381
Motyer, J. Alec, 468n62
Mueller, Elijah N., 350n368
Mulroney, James A. E., 206, 232
Münnich, Maciej, 364n413
Muraoka, Takamitsu, 39n67, 520, 538, 594
Myers-O'Brien, Julia, 56n124, 68n35

Na'aman, Nadav, 435n47, 441n67, 441n71,
    442n74, 531n267, 531n272, 532, 533n280,
    533n283, 533n285
Nadali, Davide, 146n329
Nasuti, Harry P., 199n17
Nemet-Nejat, Karen Rhea, 311n290
Nestle, Eberhard, 435n50
Neusner, Jacob, 262n137, 286n214
Newman, John, 321n308
Nigolsky, N. M., 488n119
Nihan, Christophe L., 6n14
Noble, Duncan, 124
Nogalski, James D., 8–10, 13, 51n110,
    107n198, 177, 187n465, 207n41, 399,
    408n526, 415, 605, 610, 625, 638, 642n611
Noth, Martin, 168n393
Nouwen, Henri J. M., 342–43
Nowell, Kristin, 142n309
Nurzi, J. S., 258n121

O'Connor, Michael, 621, 622
Oded, Bustenay, 439n61, 553
Oden, Thomas C., 312n293
Oesch, Josef M., 6n13, 35n49
Olmstead, Albert T., 130n272
Olofsson, Staffan, 385n471
Onasch, Hans-Ulrich, 169n401
O'Neal, G. Michael, 198n11, 199n17
Origen, 350
Ortlund, Eric N., 352

Osborne, William R., 1n3
Oshima, Takayoshi, 336n341
Oswalt, John N., 106n194, 111n211, 379
Otto, Eckart, 203n27, 281n203, 302n267
Otto, Rudolf, 412n536

Packer, Craig, 142
Pajunen, Mika S., 6n14
Pardee, Dennis G., 232, 273
Park, Sung Jin, 17n60
Parry, Donald W., 206n33
Patterson, Richard D., 23n2, 45, 62n14,
  68n38, 84, 85n113, 91, 113, 114, 115,
  125n247, 126n256, 126n257, 129n268, 155,
  165, 170n404, 171n407, 173, 176, 177n421,
  207n41, 224, 228n21, 232, 235, 246,
  248n86, 272, 274n173, 275n177, 276n182,
  285, 292n241, 313, 374, 390–91, 432n32,
  461, 519, 541, 640n598
Patton, Corinne L., 179n433
Paul, Ian, 253n108
Paul, Shalom M., 260n131
Payne, David, 108n204
Peckham, Brian, 202n23
Perlitt, Lothar, 123n240, 158n360, 172n414,
  189n466, 207n41, 226n14, 233, 247n75,
  248n85, 257n120, 272, 610n505, 638n590
Petersen, David L., 301n262
Pfeiffer, Henrik, 203n27, 204–5, 354n374,
  601
Piepkorn, Arthur Carl, 100n168, 100n169
Pietersma, Albert, 278n193
Pinker, Aron, 70n44, 78n83, 113, 115,
  121n228, 125, 126n252, 127n259, 127n261,
  129n270, 133–34, 175, 176, 181n443,
  242n56, 243, 284, 288n225, 309, 311n289,
  375, 376, 378n446, 381n460, 398, 407
Podella, Thomas, 72n54
Porter, Martin, 229n23
Pratt, Richard L., Jr., 563n360
Price, James D., 156n353
Prinsloo, Gert T. M., 195n1, 201, 256,
  258n123, 269n165, 272, 291n239, 326, 343,
  353, 355–56n376, 366n424, 367n426,
  389n484, 390n486
Puech, Emile, 475n90

Quick, Laura, 504n189
Quine, Cat, 176, 184, 185n460

Radday, Yehuda T., 610n504
Ramos, Melissa, 504n189
Ramsey, Boniface, 418
Rashi, 101n174, 113, 119n216, 174, 257n119,
  266, 463n36, 529
Reade, Julian E., 128n262, 130n272,
  132n281, 134n294, 146n332, 181n443
Redditt, Paul L., 11n38, 205n32
Redman, Matt, 413
Reider, Joseph, 86n120, 95–96n144
Renaud, Bernard, 107n198
Renz, Thomas, 1n2, 12n41, 16n53, 17n60,
  28n21, 121n228, 141n305, 156n353,
  170n402, 211n54, 215n59, 216n63, 218n75,
  224, 225n9, 254, 259n125, 268n151, 272,
  286n216, 287n220, 300, 345n359, 445n84,
  446n86, 448n98, 459n30, 482, 484, 540,
  564n362, 606n485, 628n554
Revell, E. J., 258n121
Rice, Gene, 455n18, 456
Roberts, J. J. M., 1, 68n37, 68n38, 81,
  89n125, 100n173, 112, 114, 115, 123n239,
  123n240, 126n256, 126n257, 127n259,
  139, 145n325, 149n339, 154, 175, 177n423,
  222n2, 224, 233, 248n88, 266, 272,
  277n190, 284, 292n241, 353, 362n397,
  366n423, 367n426, 381n460, 432n32,
  466n49, 467n60, 472n72, 472n77,
  476n93, 485n106, 493n140, 508n209,
  530n263, 538, 542, 546, 564n364, 580,
  584n428, 593, 594, 596n456, 597n460,
  604, 611n506, 622, 639n594
Robertson, David A., 354n372
Robertson, O. Palmer, 107n200, 170n404,
  202n25, 202n26, 274n175, 290n235,
  361n395, 433n39, 434n41, 438n58, 458,
  493n140, 498n160, 530n263, 542, 543,
  546, 566n379, 606n482, 614, 622,
  631n567, 632nn570–72
Robinson, Donald W. B., 437nn54–55
Rogers, Cleon, 525n247
Roglund, Max F., 97n154, 118n213
Rosenberg, Abraham J., 144n322, 145n325,
  154, 155, 222n1, 222n3, 234, 257n119, 266,
  269n161, 277n186, 305n274, 389n485,
  455n20
Ross, William A., 73n62
Roth, Martin, 14n50

Rosenweig, Franz, 515–16

Rubinson, Karen S., 247n79

Rudman, Dominic, 168n393, 566n379

Rudnig-Zelt, Susanne, 364n414, 366n419

Rudolph, Wilhelm, 24n5, 74, 81, 89n125, 89n126, 92, 101n175, 145n325, 266, 408n526, 460, 476n93, 519, 538, 542, 543, 558, 569n393, 586n434, 594, 595, 598n461, 629n558, 631n564, 631n567, 639n593

Ryou, Daniel H., 153, 521n234, 522n236, 523n243, 529n262, 539, 540, 541, 542, 543, 544, 549n303, 556n330, 557n335, 560n345, 563n357, 565n371, 565n375, 566n379, 569n395, 574n410, 581, 594, 599n469

Sabottka, Liudger, 583, 595, 604, 621, 622, 636, 637, 639n596

Saggs, H. W. F., 115

Scaiola, Donatella, 12n40

Scalisle, Pamela J., 291n238

Scatolini Apóstolo, Silvio S., 564n366

Scharbert, Josef, 46n97

Schart, Aaron, 13n45, 45, 452n1

Schibler, Daniel, 598

Schipper, Bernd U., 440n66, 441, 442n74, 532n276, 533n285

Schloen, J. David, 559n341

Schneider, Thomas, 62n16, 168, 168nn396–97

Schnitzler, Annik E., 142n308

Schökel, Louis Alonso, 37n55, 171n408

Schomerus, J. G., 447n93

Schoors, Anton, 313

Schrank, Walther, 335n341

Schulthess, Friedrich, 325

Schultz, Richard L., 317n303

Schunk, Klaus-Dietrich, 443n78

Schwantes, Milton, 526n250

Scoralick, Ruth, 14n50

Scott, James M., 284

Scurlock, Jo A., 130n273

Seidl, Theodor, 320n305

Seifrid, Mark A., 297n258

Seitz, Christopher R., 507n200, 638

Sellers, Ovid R., 176

Sellin, Ernst, 41, 56, 100n172, 232, 241nn48–49, 454n13

Seow, Choon-Leong, 379n447

Seux, M.-J., 336n342

Seybold, Klaus, 23n1, 41–42, 44n87, 107n199, 165, 178n425, 226n14, 247n81, 272, 284, 356n377, 488n120, 489n123, 491n131, 491n133, 496n155, 497n158, 501n179, 518, 529n261, 580, 623n536, 639n595

Shupak, Nili, 332, 363

Sinker, Robert, 336n343, 397

Sirach, 8–9

Skjelsbæk, Inger, 323n312

Smalley, Beryl, 318n304

Smith, D. Moody, 296n256

Smith, Douglas W., 248n90, 590n447

Smith, G. A., 97n155, 529

Smith, J. P. M., 56, 123n236

Smith, Mark S., 332–33, 380n451

Smith, Ralph L., 24n5, 67, 68n38, 177n423, 249n91, 257–58n120

Smith-Christopher, Daniel L., 323n313

Smoak, Jeremy D., 503n185, 504n189

Smothers, Thomas G., 291n238

Soden, Wolfram von, 247n75

Soll, Will M., 26n11

Sommer, Benjamin D., 107n202

Sorg, Rembert, 335

Speiser, Ephraim Avigdor, 610n502, 610n504

Sperling, S. David, 493n139

Spieckermann, Hermann, 46n97, 439n60

Spreafico, Ambrogio, 85n117

Spronk, Klaas, 11n39, 32n43, 36–37n53, 42n80, 45, 59, 62n17, 62n18, 66n24, 68, 75n70, 86n120, 92, 96n144, 96n145, 97n155, 99, 100n167, 100n168, 100n169, 101n175, 106n196, 107, 112, 113, 114, 115, 123n238, 126n255, 126–27n257, 132n280, 132n282, 134, 148, 151n346, 154, 157, 164, 170n403, 172n415, 175, 176, 177n421, 178n424, 178n425, 182n446, 189n467

Stager, Lawrence E., 535n288, 559n341

Stanford, Charles Villiers, 218

Stavrakopoulou, Francesca, 475n88

Steck, Odil Hannes, 5n12

Stendebach, F. J., 103n180

Stenzel, Meinrad, 417n551, 417n554

Stern, Ephraim, 311n292, 530n266,

531n268, 532, 533n285, 535n288, 555nn328–29
Steuernagel, Carl, 424
Stieglitz, Robert R., 365n417
Stine, Wilbur Morris, 217
Stowe, Harriet Beecher, 217
Strawn, Brent A., 141n305, 141n307, 142n311, 142n312, 142n313, 143n319, 144n320, 144n321, 144n322, 145n327, 146n328, 146n329, 146n333, 150n342
Strickland, Jesse, 418
Striek, Marco, 543
Strobel, August, 282, 283n212, 296n255
Stronach, David, 129n271, 130n272, 162, 163n382, 181n445
Sweeney, Marvin A., 2n5, 8n25, 27n14, 60, 89n125, 195n2, 210n51, 266, 326, 424, 425, 451, 455n20, 459, 460, 461, 462n35, 464n43, 466, 467n54, 467n58, 470n68, 470n69, 472n77, 473n78, 474n81, 474n85, 476n93, 481, 482, 483, 484, 485nn106–7, 487n115, 487n118, 489n123, 489n126, 491n131, 493–94, 495n151, 496n155, 499, 500, 501n179, 502, 503, 506n199, 507n202, 508n209, 510, 518, 519, 520, 522n236, 528, 539, 540, 541, 542, 545, 546, 547n295, 548, 549n303, 555n327, 565nn368–69, 566n377, 567nn380–81, 567n384, 568n386, 568n389, 569n392, 580, 581, 582–83, 584n427, 594, 595–96n453, 596n454, 598n462, 600n470, 604, 607n491, 609n499, 612n515, 614n522, 615, 618n523, 622, 624, 626–27, 631n568, 636, 638n584, 640
Symmachus, 586n434
Széles, Mária Eszenyei, 226

Tachik, Christopher S., 498n162, 633n573, 642n610, 645n620
Talmon, Shemaryahu, 240n42
Tate, Marvin E., 413
Tertullian, 350
Thackeray, Henry St. John, 217n69, 377n440
Thareani, Yifat, 479n101, 531n269
Theodore of Mopsuestia, 119n219
Theodoret of Cyrus, 461, 462, 477
Thirtle, James, 338–39, 416n546

Thompson, John A., 508n206
Thurian, Max, 448
Timmer, Daniel C., 49n104, 50n106, 79, 100n167, 131n279, 159n368, 303n268, 387n478, 542, 577n417, 608n494, 610n501
Tov, Emanuel, 7n19, 36, 38n63, 206n33, 258n121, 461
Tromp, Nicholas J., 82n98
Tsumura, David Toshio, 272, 352, 362n399, 362n403, 365n418, 373, 375, 377n439, 380n455, 382–83, 389
Tyson, Craig William, 492n135, 561n350

Uehlinger, Christoph, 363n404, 363n406, 472n75, 474n86, 478n97, 497n159, 499n164

Van Bekkum, Koert, 363n408
Van De Mieroop, Marc, 41n75
Vanderhooft, David Stephen, 202, 262n140, 272, 307–8, 321n306, 322, 532n277, 535n288
Van der Toorn, Karel, 336n341
Van Doorslear, J., 167
VanLeeuwen, Raymond C., 12n40
Van Seters, John, 24n7
Van Soldt, Wilfred H., 462
Vasholz, Robert I., 226–27
Vermes, Géza, 206n34, 517n231
Vlaardingerbroek, Johannes, 233, 425n11, 433n37, 433n39, 434, 435n46, 452, 454, 455n17, 458n27, 459, 460, 464, 467n54, 467n57, 467n59, 471n71, 475, 475n91, 476–77, 479nn103–4, 482, 483, 484, 485, 486n111, 493n142, 493n143, 496n155, 499n165, 502n181, 504, 507n202, 509n210, 514, 516, 518, 519, 520, 521, 529n262, 530, 540, 542, 544, 545, 547n296, 549n303, 558n340, 563nn357–58, 581, 594, 596n456, 599n465, 600n470, 601n476, 602, 604, 605, 606, 607n487, 614n521, 615n528, 617, 622, 623, 631n564, 636, 637, 638n590, 643n614
Volf, Miroslav, 480n104
Von Clausewitz, Carl, 183
Von Orelli, Carl, 631n567, 631n568
Von Soden, Wolfram, 68n38
Von Weissenberg, Hanne, 6n14

Wakeling, Simon, 12
Wal, A. J. O. van der, 258n123
Waldbaum, Jane C., 560n342
Waltke, Bruce K., 43n83, 224, 314n294, 339n350, 360n390, 389n483, 410n533, 502n180, 527n253, 641n606
Walton, Joshua T., 532n273
Ward, William Hayes, 241n48
Warfield, Benjamin B., 289–90
Watanabe, Chikako Esther, 146n329, 146n333, 149n337
Watson, Francis, 197n5, 296n253, 296n254, 591n449
Watson, Rebecca S., 381n458
Watson, Wilfred G. E., 27n18, 33n48, 84n108, 145n326, 150n341, 293n248
Watts, James W., 340–41
Watts, John D. W., 46n97
Wearne, Gareth J., 373
Weber, Beat, 339n352
Weigl, Michael, 41n77, 50n105, 449n100, 501n179, 518, 522n240, 535, 594, 617n531, 619
Weinfeld, Moshe, 304–5, 330, 433n36, 433n38, 434n40
Weis, Richard D., 60, 61, 195n2, 237–38n35
Weiss, Ehud, 492n136, 495, 503n185, 560n344
Welch, Eric Lee, 520
Wellhausen, Julius, 97n155, 139, 237n34, 255, 285, 293, 373, 540
Wendland, Ernst R., 16n56, 27
Werse, Nicholas R., 13n45, 434n44, 435n46, 445n82, 457n25, 462, 463n40, 474n82, 474n85
Wesley, Charles, 418
Whitekettle, Richard, 261, 262nn138–39
Widmer, Michael, 223n6
Wilke, Alexa F., 373
Willey, Patricia Tull, 107n202
Willgren, David, 5n11
Williamson, Hugh G. M., 62n20, 272, 573, 608n493
Willi-Plein, Ida, 43n83, 61
Wilson, Robert, 456
Wiseman, Donald J., 91
Wiseman, William Johnston, 12n40
Witte, Markus, 274n175
Wöhrle, Jakob, 12n40, 15n50, 404n510, 445n81
Wolde, Ellen van, 76n75, 553n320
Woude, Adam S. van der, 24n5, 42n81, 73n63, 155n349, 175, 493n143
Wright, Benjamin G., 278n193
Wyatt, Nicholas, 471n70

Xella, Paolo, 363n408, 365n417, 365n418
Xenophon, 122, 129

Yasur-Landau, Assaf, 554n322
Yeivin, Israel, 17n59
Yerushalmi, Shmuel, 463, 469n64, 472n73
Younker, Randall W., 561n353

Zalcman, Lawrence, 78n83, 233, 520, 529
Zandstra, Sidney, 461, 462
Zapff, Burkard M., 51n110
Zipor, Moshe A., 258n121
Zorn, Walter, 296n255

Index of Subjects

abyss, 384

acrostic, 26, 28, 59, 61, 63, 65–67, 74, 75, 77–79

Ahaz, 160

Aleppo Codex, 6, 36, 197, 200, 285

allusive speech, 303–4

Amariah, 451, 455–56

Ammon/Ammonites, 442–43, 550–51, 552, 555, 561–62, 563–67, 578

Amon, 438, 456

Amos, Book of, 52

anagrams, 356–58, 401–3

anointed one, 388, 390

anthropomorphism, 515–16

appetite, 287–88

Ashdod, 528, 529, 530, 531, 532, 535

Ashkelon, 528, 529, 531, 532, 535, 559–60

Assurbanipal, 19–20, 96, 100, 146, 169, 170, 532

Assyria: as agent of YHWH, 570; historical context, 47–49, 52, 478–79, 531–33, 567; judgment on, 93–102, 578, 597. *See also* Neo-Assyrian Empire; Nineveh

Assyrian king, 66, 94, 98, 101–2, 105–6, 188–92. *See also* Assurbanipal; Sennacherib

at that time, 641, 645

Baal, 470–73

Babel, Tower of, 600, 612

Babylon: as agent of YHWH, 330–31, 383; historical context, 18–20, 130; judgment on, 108–9; oppression by, 303–8, 310–12, 314–15, 316–18, 321. *See also* Neo-Babylonian Empire

Babylonian Codex of Petrograd, 36, 200

Bashan, 72

battle, 123–24, 157, 393

birds, 572–74

blindness, 509

body, 405–6

bones, 405–6

Book of the Four, 445–46

Book of the Law, 433, 435–43

Book of the Twelve, 4–16, 46–47, 49–52, 187, 205, 252. *See also* minor prophets

building, 316

Cairo Codex, 4n9, 6–7, 36, 94, 197

Canaan, 553, 555, 556

Carmel, Mount, 72

cavalry, 247, 249

chaff, 524

Chaldeans, 241–42. *See also* Babylon

chaos, 381–82, 388

chariots, 31, 123–26, 136, 148, 151, 382

Cherethites. *See* Philistines/Philistine cities

children, 171–72, 174

Christ, 3–4, 53–54, 283–84, 295–97, 350–51, 413, 514, 645–46. *See also* cross, the; gospel, the

clothing, 491–93, 513

clouds, 506

coastal nations, 553, 554–55, 567

Codex Alexandrinus, 416

Codex Sinaiticus, 6
complacency, 163–74
complaint, 223–30, 253–65, 341
confidence, 298, 396–413
consecration, 489–90
corpses, 158
covenant, 437, 493
creditors and debtors, 304–8
cross, the, 395–96, 478, 517
cup, 320, 321
curses, 99–100
Cush, 368, 378–79, 442, 455, 567, 569–70, 609–10
Cushi, 454–55

darkness, 82–83, 506–7
daughter of Jerusalem, 627–28, 629
daughter of Zion, 627–28
David, King, 410–11
day of distress, 400–401, 407
Day of YHWH, 446, 480–517, 524
Deber (deity), 365
de-creation, 506
deer, 411
delay, 279–80
deliverance, 102–11
destruction/desolation, 148–52, 504, 563–66, 571, 575
Deuteronomy, Book of, 433–38, 444–45
disgrace, 310–11, 320–22
divine name, 66–67, 69–70, 78, 614, 616
divine speech, 2–3, 43–45, 94, 427–28, 453
dove, 586, 587
drought, 407–8
drunkenness, 85–86, 172, 174, 291, 321
dung, 510
dust, 510

earth, 386–87
eating, 324
Edom, 549–50
Egypt, 19–20, 169–70, 439–42, 532–33, 560
Ekron, 528, 529, 531, 532, 535
El, 380
Elkosh, 62
end, the, 279
Esarhaddon, 19, 169

evil, 109–10, 147, 191, 310. *See also* YHWH, and evil
exaltation, 246
exile, 109, 392, 515, 643–44
exposure, 161, 321
exultation, 576

faithfulness, 288–90, 294–98
falsehood, 157, 327–28
fame, 644, 645
fear, of YHWH, 346
festivals, 103–5, 109
fig trees, 172–73, 408–9
fire, 76, 253
firstfruits, 172–73
fish, 260–63
Fish Gate, 495–96, 499
flocks, 571–72
flood, 383–84
fraud, 494–95
from of old, 256, 258
futility, 504

gates, 180–81
Gath, 532
gathering, 522–24, 635, 644
Gaza, 528, 529, 531, 535, 560
Gedaliah, 451
genealogies, 452–57
gods, 160, 471, 566–68. *See also* idols/idolatry
gold, 511
Goliath, 391
gospel, the, 53, 88, 110–11, 295–96, 632–33
grasshoppers, 177–78, 182, 184
greed, 290–91, 324
guilt, 250–51

Habakkuk, Book of: in the biblical canon, 216; in the Book of the Twelve, 13–16, 52, 215–16; constituent units, 16–18; contemporary application, 218–19; extrabiblical parallels, 332–34; historical setting, 18–20, 207–11; history of interpretation, 216–18, 285–86; language and style, 201–3, 414; macrostructure, 196–200; musical use and adaptation, 416–19; original message, 211–15, 314; redaction history, 203–5; superscriptions, 195–96, 221–23; textual witnesses, 206

Habakkuk, prophet, 213, 222, 410–11

harvest, 466–67, 524

hearing, 370

heights, 411

herald, 103, 108, 110, 151, 280–81

Hezekiah, 451, 455–57, 532

hiddenness, 363–64, 528, 571

hissing, 576

hope, 219, 537–38

horns, 362–63

host of heaven, 473, 475

How long?, 211, 223–24, 226–27, 279

humiliation, 138, 152–63

humility, 524–26, 527–28, 535–36, 614, 617

hush, 327, 329, 487. *See also* silence

idols/idolatry, 327–28, 330–31, 449, 478. *See also* gods

injustice, 197, 226, 229, 263, 283, 294, 302, 316, 370, 494

interest, 305–6

intoxication. *See* drunkenness

Ishtar, 180, 184, 190

Islam, 479–80

jealousy, 67–68

Jehoiakim, 20, 208

Jeremiah, Book of, 314–15

Jeremiah, prophet, 208, 213–14, 535

Jerusalem: judgment and fall, 394–95, 425–26, 444, 445–46, 477, 534–35, 579–93; repentance and restoration, 52, 121, 444, 597–98, 603–34. *See also daughter of Jerusalem*

Joel, Book of, 52

Jonah, Book of, 50–51

Josiah, King, 103–4, 209n47, 432–33, 436–44, 456–59, 479, 549

joy, 632–34

Judah: affliction and deliverance, 79, 93–94, 98–99, 103–4, 120–21, 400–401, 469–79; remnant, 478, 540, 548, 558–59, 577, 614–15, 616–18; sin and righteousness, 203–4, 209, 213–14, 259–61, 294. *See also* Josiah, King

judges, 589–90

judgment: comprehensive, 460–80, 593–603; final, 298, 312, 513–14; life beyond, 449–50, 603–34; submission to, 517–37. *See also* Day of YHWH

justice, 226, 228–30, 259, 265. *See also* injustice; retributive justice

king of Nineveh, 138–41. *See also* Assyrian king

kingship, 388–90, 629

knowledge, of YHWH, 347–48

labor, 317

lame, the, 641–42

lamps, 500, 501, 502

law, 227–28. *See also* Torah

lawlessness, 229–30

leaders/leadership, 388–89, 592–93

Lebanon, 72, 322–23

Leningrad Codex, 6, 36, 197, 200, 201

light, 361–62, 363–64, 581, 591

lionesses, 143–45

lions, 31, 140–47, 148, 150, 151, 589

lips, 405

liturgy, 415, 417

locusts, 185, 187

look, 239, 328

love, 312

Manasseh, 168, 473

Masoretic Text (MT), 17–18, 36, 38–39, 286–87

merchants, 96, 177–78, 183–87, 497–501

Merodach-baladan, 19

messenger, 31, 103, 117, 148, 151

Micah, Book of, 51–52, 314

midday, 530

Midian, 368, 370

midst of years, 392, 408

Milcom, 462, 474–75

minor prophets, 3–4. *See also* Book of the Twelve

Moab, 442–43, 550–51, 552, 555, 561–67, 578

Molech, 462, 475

moon, 384–86, 473

Mortar, the, 497–98

Moses, 410–11

mythology, 379–80

Nabopolassar, 20

Naḥal Ḥever, 201

Nahum, Book of: in the biblical canon,
53–54; in the Book of the Twelve,
10–11, 13–16, 49–52; constituent units,
16–18, 42–46; contemporary application, 57–58; historical setting, 18–20,
40–42; history of interpretation, 54–57;
language and style, 36–38; macrostructure, 27–36; original message, 47–49;
superscription, 23–27, 28, 59–63; textual
witnesses, 38–40

Nahum, prophet, 26–27, 62

nations, 386–87, 537–79

Nebuchadnezzar, 20, 307, 534–35, 549–50

Neco II, Pharaoh, 441–42

Neo-Assyrian Empire, 18–20, 103, 444,
457, 570, 600. *See also* Assyria

Neo-Babylonian Empire, 18–20, 52, 207,
215, 252, 259, 282, 293, 312, 324, 330, 395,
469. *See also* Babylon

new creation, 297

Nile, 168

Nineveh: accusation and verdict, 47–49,
89–102; complacency, 163–74; defenses,
174–87; fall, 41, 63, 111–38, 148–52; humiliation, 152–63; walls of Nineveh, 181. *See
also* king of Nineveh

No-Amon, 167

non-human creation, 324, 469

Northern Kingdom, 19, 47, 52, 120, 457,
496, 564

oaths, 474, 563

obedience, 297, 318

obeisance, 568

onomatopoeia, 157

on that day, 626, 629

oppression, 588

ordinances, 526

outcast, the, 641–42

paragraph divisions, 35–36, 200–201

Paran, Mount, 358–59, 411

passion, 320–21

Passover, 103, 105

patience, 52, 70, 279, 284, 288, 342, 411, 598

Pelethites. *See* Philistines/Philistine cities

penance, 343

pestilence, 333, 364–66, 369, 371

Philistines/Philistine cities, 442–43,
528–32, 554–56, 577, 597

plague, 364–66

plundering, 503–4

poverty, 618–20

power, 137, 152

powerlessness, 614, 618

praise, 644, 645

prayer, 218–19, 223, 264–65, 331–32, 342–43

prey, 150–51

pride, 291–93, 566, 613

pride of Israel, 120–21, 137

pride of Jacob, 120–21, 137–38

priests, 472–73, 590

profit, 327

pronouncement, 23, 43–44, 60, 221–22,
304

prophetic literature, 1–3

prophetic speech, 60, 427–28

prophets, 342, 590

prostitution, 57, 158–61

Psamtik I, 170, 533

punishment, 469, 640–41

pure speech, 608–9, 615

questions, 381

Qumran texts, 5, 36, 54–55, 201, 206, 447

Rahab, 536

rain, 328, 384

rays, 362–63

red, 121–23

redaction criticism, 2, 46–47

refuge, 66, 78, 79, 172

rejoicing, in YHWH, 409–10, 411–13,
632–34

relationship, 312–13

remnant, 478, 540, 548, 558–59, 577,
614–15, 616–18

repentance, 51, 514, 535, 537, 585, 592, 602

Resheph (deity), 365

retributive justice, 57, 324–25, 339–40, 407

Reuchlin Codex, 36, 197

revelation, 25, 43–44, 63, 195–96, 223,
276–80, 289, 331–32

riddles, 303–4

righteousness, 259, 288–89, 294, 297, 298, 527–28, 535–36
rods, 382–83, 391
running, 275–77

sacrifice, 104–5, 487–88, 489, 510
Saite dynasty, 570
salvation, 382, 387, 393, 410, 634–46
Sargon II, 19
scatterer, 118–19, 136
Scythians, 247
sea, 381, 384, 392
Second Ward, 496
security, 312–13
seeing, 370
seeking, YHWH, 526–28, 536
Sennacherib, 19, 89, 125, 128, 134, 532
Shalmaneser V, 19
Shamash-shuma-ukin, 19
shame, 643. *See also* humiliation
sheep, 641–42
shepherds, 189–90, 556–57
shofar, 507
silence, 212, 326–27, 630–31. *See also* hush
silver, 500, 511
sin, 230, 517
singing, 572, 574–75
sleep, 189–90
smoke, 150
socioeconomic structures, 512–13
Sodom and Gomorrah, 564
"sons of the king," 491
sorcery, 160
Southern Kingdom, 120, 332, 477
speech, 608–9, 615
spilling, 509–10
stone, 311–12
storm god, 332
St. Petersburg Codex, 6
streams, 378–80
string music, 416
stumbling, 126, 467–68, 478
suffering, 110, 324, 351, 409, 413
sun, 360–63, 384–86, 473
sun god, 332
swallowing, 263–64
swearing, 474–76, 541
sword, 150
syncretism, 479–80

tablets, 274–75
Taharqa, 169
Tantamun, 169–70
telestic, 59, 63, 65
Teman, 358–59, 411
temple, 328–29
tents/tent curtains, 367, 369
Thebes, 164, 166–69, 170–74, 570
threshold, 493, 575–76
thus YHWH said, 89n124, 93, 95
Tiglath-pileser III, 18, 532
Tiqqune Sopherim, 257–58
Torah, 3–4, 228, 230, 252, 281, 294
Tower of Babel, 600, 612
trade, 183, 187, 499–500, 512–13, 556
treachery, 259, 590
trembling, 367, 368, 404–6, 411–13
tribute, 609–10
turmoil, 348–49, 370
turning aside, 476–77

urban elites, 457, 513, 557, 561, 578
utterance of YHWH, 501, 563–64, 583. *See also word of YHWH*

veiled saying, 303–4
violence, 163, 172, 174, 252–53, 322, 494–95
vomit, 322
vows, 104–5

Wadi Murabbaʿat, 38, 200, 206
wailing, 497, 498
waiting, 52, 279, 284, 290n232, 406–7, 598–99
walls of Nineveh, 181
warcry, 507
warrior, 505, 630
watchman/watchtower, 267–68, 270
water, 72, 127–28, 134–35, 137, 168–69, 411. *See also* sea
wealth, 312–13, 449, 512, 515, 618
wicked, the, 259, 468
wind, 70–71, 249
wine, 291, 502–3
wolves, 248–49, 589–90
women, 178–80, 186
wood, 311–12
word of YHWH, 423, 453, 556. *See also utterance of YHWH*
worship, 330–31, 449, 471, 479–80

years, 346–47

YHWH: anger, 75–77, 87–88, 230, 378, 381–82, 386–87, 392–93; characteristic and alien work, 361, 394–96; coming of, 282–83, 351–71; direct and indirect work, 394–95; and evil, 163, 224–30, 252, 259, 264, 370–71; glory, 315, 317, 351; jealousy, 67–68, 87, 88; justice, 87, 218–19, 246, 259, 324, 350, 515, 583, 591, 602–3; love and compassion, 50–51, 69, 87–88, 348, 349–51, 388, 630–31; sovereignty, 48, 57, 151–52, 191, 346, 393–96, 568; vengeance, 63–89, 110, 371–96. *See also* Day of

YHWH; divine name; divine speech; judgment

YHWH of Hosts, 149, 445, 563–64

Zephaniah, Book of: in the biblical canon, 444–46; in the Book of the Twelve, 13–16, 215; constituent units, 16–18; contemporary application, 449–50; historical setting, 18–20, 432–35, 458; history of interpretation, 447–48; macrostructure, 424–31; original message, 444; significant words, 431–32; superscription, 423, 451–60

Zephaniah, prophet, 452–57

Index of Scripture and Other Ancient Sources

OLD TESTAMENT

Genesis

Ref	Page
1:9	544
1:11–12	398
1:14	346n361
1:16	385n472
1:20–23	468
1:21	262
1:24	544
1:25	544
1:28	468
1:30	544
2:2	276
2:6	463n38
2:7	466, 510
2:13	610
3:1	284
3:8	487n116, 581
3:15	305, 396
3:19	466, 510
4	609n499
4:1	374
4:7	74n69, 167n388
4:10	482
4:12	461
4:14	433, 463n38, 466
4:16	487n117
4:26	604
5:29	357n382
6:1	463n38
6:7	433, 463n38, 466
6:8	357
6:13	641n603
6:17	641n603
7:4	433, 463n38, 466
7:23	463n38
8:1	217, 250
8:1–14	217
8:4	567n383
8:6–7	545
8:8	433, 463n38, 466
8:13	463n38
8:21	105n190, 594
9:6	509
9:10	324n315
9:12	324n315
9:13	324n315
9:15–17	324n315
9:26–28	553
10	553
10:5	553, 567
10:7	442
10:19	553
10:22	553
11	311n292
11:1	447
11:1–9	604
11:3	181n442
11:4	612
11:8–9	612
11:9	612
12:8	164, 378n443, 604
12:13	167
13:10	566
13:14	378n443
14:3	564
15:2	541
15:5	184n456
15:6	84n106, 114, 290n233
15:7	243n60
15:11	158
15:16	96n146
16:4–5	101n175
16:5	300
18–19	564
18:2	276n184
18:24	74n69
18:26	74n69
19:2	92
19:15	397
19:26	564
19:30–38	553, 564
20:7	223
21:21	359n388
21:23	474n83
21:30	599n467
22:13	85n114, 362n401
22:17	184n456
23:6	388n482
24:17	234, 276n184
24:63	116, 397
25:16	133n285
25:22	448
25:23	133n285
26:4	184n456

26:8	539	49:3	246	12:37	399
27:33–34	85n113	49:9	143n316, 143n318	13:2	508
27:40	604	49:14	580	13:21–22	364
27:42	62n20	49:17	300	14:9	247n77
27:45	75	49:19	397	14:13	105n190
28:4	243n60	49:22	387n476	14:16	92, 470n66
28:12	115	49:27	581, 589, 599	14:21	72n53, 249n94,
28:16	594				470n66
28:17	245	**Exodus**		14:23	247n77
29:12	276n184	1:12	91	14:23–25	126n252
29:13	276n184	1:13	244n62	14:24	364
31:10	132n282, 518	2:14	594	14:26–27	470n66
31:19	96	2:16–22	368	14:27	116
31:24	268n158	2:20	186n462	14:28	85n113
31:27	416n547	3:1	370	15	216, 412, 417
31:44	599n467	4:14	98n156	15:2	285
31:50	599n466	4:25–26	368	15:5	384
32:19	543	5:7	522	15:7	75
32:28–29	121	5:12	119n215, 522	15:8	376, 384
33:4	276n184	6:5	244n62	15:9	255
33:20	132n283	6:7	251n101	15:10	405n515
34:3	268n159	6:8	384n467	15:11	361n395
34:21	96	7:5	470	15:13	539
34:27	565	7:17	92	15:14	348, 405
34:31	161n375	7:19	92, 127n260	15:16	328
35:10	121	8:1	92	15:19	247n77
35:14	132n283	8:5(1)	127n260	15:20	628
37:10	71	8:14(10)	376	16:28	223
37:19	68	8:17–18(13–14)	508	17:6	77n78
37:26	310	9:3–7	364	17:12	284
37:27	165	9:7	85n113	17:14	483
38:13	96n150	9:9	71n51	18:1–12	368
38:15	84n106	9:10	508	18:13–14	589n444
39:2	494	9:23	92	18:21	310
40:7	494	9:30	487n116	19:16	506
41:6	249n93	9:35	269n160	19:18	77n78
41:13	91	10:3	223	19:20	268n158
41:19	525n248	10:11	114	19:22	268n158
41:23	249n93	10:13	92, 249n94	20–23	437
41:35	346n361	10:13b	234	20:2	17n58
41:42	173n420	10:19b	175	20:5	64, 67
42:19	92	10:22	434	20:5–6	69n41
43:16	489n125	10:29	105n190	20:21	364
43:34	635	12:2	347n362	21:8	292n242
44:8	494	12:12	79n90	21:13	593
45:26	224	12:13	165	21:18	546
47:18	158	12:23	79n90	22:18(17)	160

22:25(24)	305n276,	34:24	243	10:2	487n117
	305n277	34:29	362	10:10–11	590
23:5	60n2	34:29–30	352	10:11	269n160
23:7	224	34:30	362	11	461
23:16	635	34:35	352, 362	11:9	91
23:20	114	35:7	122	11:17	545
23:21	588	35:23	122	11:18	544
23:30	565	36:14	367n428	13	188
24:17	76	36:19	122	13–14	246
25:5	122	37:25–26	362n400	13:4	260n128
26:7	367n428	38:2	362n400	13:25	260n128
26:9	367n428	39:10	309	13:30	260n128
26:12–13	367n428	39:34	122	14:41	510
26:14	122			16:12	487n117
27:2	362n400	**Leviticus**		16:18	362n400
28:3	116	1:9	510	16:21	269n160
28:17	309	1:13	510	17–26	435n47, 437
29:12	362n400, 374	1:16	155, 577	17:13	510
29:13	255	2:13	541	18:4–5	526
29:18	255	3:3	510	18:5	230
29:25	255	3:4	510	18:21	475n88
29:35	148	3:9	510	19:14	509
30:2–3	362n400	3:10	510	19:15	617, 618
30:7–8	255	3:14	510	19:18	68n40
30:10	362n400	3:15	510	19:19	492
30:12	165	4:2	335	19:29	161
31:13	594	4:3	388n482	19:31	437n56
32:7	563	4:5	388n482	20:2	309
32:10–12	69n42	4:7	362n400	20:2–5	475n88
32:11	70n46	4:12	510n214	20:6	437n56
32:12	463n38, 466	4:13	251n100, 335	20:10	159n365
32:13	184n456, 474n83	4:16	388n482	20:24	243n60
32:20	521	4:18	362n400	20:27	309, 437n56
33:7	465	4:22	251n100, 335	21:7	77n79, 161n374
33:16	463n38	4:25	362n400	21:9	161
34	70	4:27	251n100, 335	21:14	161n374
34:2	581	4:30	362n400	21:17	295
34:5	67, 69	5:18	335	22	104n187
34:6	79n90	6:11(4)	176	22:3	487n117
34:6–7	7n22, 12, 14, 15, 42,	6:22(15)	388n482	24:23	309
	46, 50, 51, 66, 69,	7:12–15	104n187	25:9	507
	348	7:15	105	25:18–19	576
34:7	69	7:16–17	104n187	25:36–37	305n276
34:9	565	8:3	522n239	25:49	579
34:10	245	8:15	362n400	26	293
34:14	67, 70n46	9:9	362n400	26:4	398
34:18	70	9:24	487n117	26:5	576

26:6	615n527	13:20	542	24:8	580
26:20	398	13:23	92, 98	24:9	143n318
26:25	269n160, 364, 524	13:26	359n388	24:14	232
26:30	437n56	13:29	539	25:3	461
26:31	93	13:30	243n60	25:11	67n28
26:32	93	13:31	232	25:11–13	67
26:33	255	14	70n44, 70n45	25:15	133n285
26:37	126	14:11	224	26:54	543
26:46	229n22	14:12	243n60, 364	27:17	636
27:13	91	14:17	70	27:23	269n160
		14:18	69n41, 70	30:14(15)	382, 631
Numbers		14:19	70	31:3	268
3:3	388n482	14:21	315, 563	31:9	565
4:10	92, 98	14:28	541	31:11	508
4:12	92, 98	14:30	384n467	31:21	113
4:15	60n2	14:41	97	31:23	608
4:17	447, 482	14:44	287, 297n257	31:26	508
4:17–20	447	15:16	229n22	31:53	113
4:19	60n2	15:22	335	33:52	511n218
4:24	60n2	15:24–29	335	35:8	543
4:25	367n428	15:27–41	492	35:11	335
4:27	60n2, 594	15:28	335	35:15	335
4:31	60n2	15:32–33	522	35:31	160n373
4:32	60n2	16:30	255		
4:47	60n2	16:40 (17:5)	269n160	**Deuteronomy**	
4:49	60n2	16:46 (17:11)	487n117	1:1	359n388
5:14	67	17:9(24)	487n117	1:5	275n176
5:21	382	18:15	508	1:10	184n456
5:30	67	18:19	541	1:12	60n2
6:5	97n152	18:20	565	1:19	245, 505n193
7:9	447	19:10	461	1:43	268, 588
8:7	97n152	19:18	158	2:12	242
8:17	508	20:9	487n117	2:15	165
10:10	635	21:5	268n155	2:21	244n61
10:12	359n388	21:6	300	2:23	554
11:11	60n2	21:7	268n155	2:25	348
11:17	60n2	21:8–9	300	2:36	313
11:21	399	21:24	243n60	3:5	508
11:22	467	21:29	566	3:17	564
11:31	91	22:19	461	3:26	80n91
12:1	268n155, 368, 454n15	23–24	299	4:8	229n22, 581
12:2	268n156	23:1	489n125	4:10	522n239
12:3	463n38, 525	23:20	98n156	4:11	434, 506
12:6	25n10, 268n153	23:21	632	4:16–19	467
12:8	268n153, 268n155	23:24	143n318	4:19	433n38, 473, 642
12:16	359n388	23:29	489n125	4:24	67
13:3	359n388	24:5	167n387, 243n59	4:27	612n513

4:29	465	15:8	305n275	28:46	165
4:31	92	15:9	165, 344	28:48	604
4:38	243	16:13	635	28:49	233
4:40	463	16:20	82n101, 527	28:52	508
5–26	437	17:3	433n38, 473	28:53	434
5:9	67	17:7	165	28:55	434
5:9–10	69n41	17:11	229n22	28:57	434
5:16	463	17:16	105n190	28:62	184n456
6:7	268n157	18:11	437n56	28:63	630n563
6:13	475	18:15	242n52	28:64	612n513
6:15	67, 433, 463n38, 466	18:16	461	28:65	348
7:6	463n38	18:21–22	269n162	28:68	105n190
7:9–10	69n41	19:5	642n607	29:17(16)	437n56
7:14	165	19:21	293	29:20(19)	67n28, 603
7:17	243	20:12	96	29:23(22)	541, 564
7:21	505n193, 566	20:14	565	30:1	642
7:26	162n380	20:19	642n607	30:3–4	611n508
8:8	407, 408n526, 409n529	21:11	231	30:4	642
		22:1	642n607	30:9	630n563
8:13	233	22:11	492	30:11–13	467
8:15	77n78, 505n193	22:12	492	31:3	79n90
8:20	91	22:14	606n484	31:19	599n467
9:1	243	22:17	606n484	31:26	599n467
9:3	79n90, 244n63	23:7–8(8–9)	454n13	32	417
10:17	505n193, 568	23:14(15)	231	32:7	346n361
10:18	526n249	23:18(19)	161n374	32:8	115
10:21	505n193	23:19(20)	305	32:9	555
10:22	184n456	23:19–20(20–21)	305	32:10	498n161
11:2	434	23:21–22(22–23)	165	32:14	72
11:14	325, 328	24	305n275	32:16	67n29
11:19	268n157	24:10	305n275	32:21	67n29
11:32	581	24:15	165	32:24	319, 364, 484
12:15	489	25:4	387n477	32:32	398
12:21	489	26:13	97	32:33	319
12:32 (13:1)	461	26:19	643	32:40	384n467
13:4(5)	462	27:5	327	32:40–42	382n462
13:5(6)	642	27:8	275n176	32:41	154
13:9(10)	165	27:15	100n170	32:41–42	543
13:10(11)	642	27:18	509	32:43	376
13:13(14)	642	27:26	294	33	216
14:1	397	28:14	165	33:2	333, 359, 361, 365, 374, 404, 410
14:2	463n38	28:21	364		
14:16	545	28:24	71n51	33:5	522n238
14:17	544	28:28	340n354	33:10	229n22
15:4	165	28:29	434n41, 509	33:17	362n401
15:6	305n275	28:30	433, 438n58, 504	33:20	143n318
15:7	165	28:39	433, 504	33:21	522n238

33:22	143n316, 360
33:27	139
33:29	398, 399, 404, 409, 410, 411
34:9	116

Joshua

1:8	603
2	159n366
2:9	128n266, 511n218
2:9–13	536
2:12	474n83
2:15	574
2:18	574
2:19	165
2:21	574
2:24	128n266, 511n218
3:13	376
3:16	376
4	79n90
6:5	507
6:20	507
7:9	511n217
7:11	97
7:15	97
7:21	231
7:22	276n184
7:25	309
8:18–19	470n66
8:26	470n66
9:18–19	474n83
9:23	92
9:24	511n218
10:12	374, 385
10:13	381n457
11:2	164
13:3	539
14:6	268n159
15:12	558
18:3	223
19:34	164
20:2	269n160
20:3	335
20:9	335
24:19	64
24:19–20	67
24:27	165, 599n467

Judges

2:14	504n188
2:15	165
2:16	242n52, 504n188
2:18	242n52
3:8	368
3:9	242n52
3:10	368
3:15	242n52
4–5	332
4:16	85n113
5	216, 369, 387n476, 412
5:3	234
5:4	157n357, 204, 205n30, 333, 387n476
5:5	74n66, 77n78, 333, 384, 487n116
5:6	224
5:7	375
5:11	375
5:17	190
5:19	310
5:20	157n357
5:22	157
5:28	573
6:11	62n15
6:28	115
6:31	581
7:20	507
7:25	233
8:3	233
8:7	374, 387n477
8:19	541
9:6	115
9:8–15	408n526
9:15	72n56
9:23	292n242
9:24	300
9:27	92
9:45	564n367
11:12–28	562
11:24	566
11:25	167
11:26	641n602
11:34	627

12:3	250
13:6	185n462
14:2	231
14:5	141, 142, 580
14:8–9	158
15:2	594
15:4	141n306
15:16	376
15:19	497
16:2	362n398, 590
16:15	545
17:3–4	100n170, 327
17:5	472
18:14	100n170, 327
18:17–18	100n170
19:25	580
19:26	397
20:2	399
20:10	175, 178
20:39	604
20:41	604
20:43	224
20:44	113
20:46	113

Ruth

2:5–6	132n283
2:16	71
4:4	594
4:9	179n431

1 Samuel

1:13	84n106
1:16	270n166
1:26	474
2	417
2:3	606n484
2:5	85n113
2:8	635
2:26	167n387
2:30	101n175
2:35	242n52
3:11	405
3:12	268n158
4:9	483
4:10	399
4:12	276

4:17	103n179	20:30	582	5:6	509
4:20	132n283	21:6(7)	487n117	5:8	509
5:4–5	493	21:7(8)	189n469	5:24	603
5:5	482	21:13(14)	114, 133n288	6:5	416
6:12	288	23:1	504n188	6:13	387n476
8:3	310	23:15	374	7:10	406
9:1	452	23:25	77n80	7:17	25n10
9:16	389n482	23:28	77n80	7:23	505n193
9:24	599n467	24:12	593	7:27	564n364
10:1	389n482	24:13–14	165	8:4	113, 399
10:25	483	24:22	474n83	8:11	244n62
11:15	85n113	25:1	359n388	8:15	526n249
12:21	327	25:2–8	96n150	8:18	554
13:4	525n248	25:9	406n523	10:6	399
13:8	119n215	25:11	185n462	10:10	175, 178
14:1	250	25:26	474	10:11	387n480
14:6	250	25:31	117	12:8	494
14:8	250	25:34	362n398, 590	12:11	93n133, 180n439,
14:11	139	25:36	85n113, 362n398, 590		242n52
14:15	348	26:15	483	12:16	465
14:16	128n265	26:21	335	12:30	475n90
14:17	178	28:10	474n83	13:20	100n172
14:36	362n398, 590	28:17	269n160	13:23–28	96n150
14:45	387n480	28:24	489	14:7	463n38, 471
14:48	504n188	30:10	158n359	14:13	84
15:2	93n133	30:14	554n323	14:13–14	84n106
15:4	399	30:15	474n83	14:19	474
15:32	594	30:19	581	15:2	185n462
16:1	231	30:21	158n359	15:2–5	589
16:5	490	31:9	374	15:11	232
16:7	512	31:10	158	15:18	554
16:14–23	416	31:12	158	15:21	474
17:46	158			15:33	60n2
17:48	276n184	**2 Samuel**		16:20–22	180n439
17:51	391	1:6	466	17:2	630n561
17:53	504n188	1:19	546	17:16	264
17:55	474	1:21	579	17:22	85n113, 362n398, 581,
18:6–7	628	1:23	233		590
18:17	165	1:24	603	17:23	139
18:21	165	2:17	85n113	18:19	276
18:25	84n106	2:23	396	18:28	384
19:3	268n157, 352	2:24	133	18:29	397
19:24	176	2:27	603	19:6(7)	603
20:3	474	3:8	594	19:19(20)	84n106
20:7	77n81	3:11	266	19:36(37)	60n2
20:13	167n386	4:1	630n562	19:41(42)	179n431
20:15	463n38, 466	4:13	83n104	20:3	266

20:7 554
20:10 510
20:15 510
20:19–20 264
20:21 384
20:23 554
22 413
22:2 77n80
22:5 90n131
22:8 348
22:16 72n53
22:20 232
22:30 482
22:34 398, 399, 404, 410, 411
22:35 411
22:36 527n252
22:37 411
22:38–41 411
22:44 411
23:2 268n156
23:4 362n398
23:6 90
23:8–39 26n13
23:9 26n13
23:19 85n112
23:20 142n311
23:27 26n13
24:7 234
24:13 266
24:16 603

1 Kings
1:4 85n113
1:17 474n83
1:30 474n83
1:33 610n504
1:38 554, 610n504
1:41 313
1:44 554
1:45 313, 610n504
1:50–51 362n400
2:2 483
2:3 229n22
2:8 474n83
2:15 77n79
2:18 268n159

2:28 362n400
3:28 526n249
4–5 132n283
4:12 374
4:23 (5:3) 155
4:25 (5:5) 576
4:27 (5:7) 581
4:33 (5:13) 72n56
5:6(20) 72n56
7:2 72
7:25 116
7:36 154
8 334n338
8:12 364, 506n199
8:13 385n471
8:25 487n117
8:28 92
8:40 463
8:45 526n249
8:49 526n249
8:53 269n160
8:56 269n160
8:59 526n249
9:3 334n338
9:7 463, 466
9:8 576
9:20–21 244n61
9:23 132n283
10:2 309
10:5 491n134
10:10 309
10:11 309
10:15 556
11:5 475, 566
11:7 475
11:14 242n52
11:18 359n388
11:31 641n603
11:33 475, 566
12:15 269n160
12:18 309
13:3 510n214
13:5 510n214
13:30 299
13:34 463n38, 466
14:10 510n215, 641n603
14:14 242n52

14:18 269n160
14:22 67n29
15:29 269n160
16:3 641n603
16:7 268n158
16:12 269n160
16:34 269n160
17 342
17:1 26n13, 62n15, 346n361
17:10 522
17:12 522, 641n603
17:14 463
17:16 269n160
18:1 463
18:3–4 10n30
18:14–16 103n181
18:21 375, 461
18:27 515
18:28 397
18:41–46 360n390
18:45 71n49
19:10 67n31
19:11 74n66, 77, 79n90
19:14 67n31
19:21 489
20:13 641n603
20:22 119n217
20:29 399
21:17 26n13, 62n15
21:28 26n13, 62n15
22:3 381n457
22:8 433n34
22:11 362n401
22:19 473n79
22:24 80n90
22:26 168n393
22:35 397

2 Kings
1:3 26n13, 62n15
1:8 26n13, 62n15
3:13 92
3:17 71n49
3:22 122n229
4:8 224
4:16 222n1
4:26 276n184

5:1	372	19:27–28	348	24:14	535		
5:12	127n259	19:30	398	25:7	491		
5:17	60n2	19:31	67n28	25:12	535		
5:26	408n526, 604	19:36	89n128				
7:9	362n398, 590,	19:37	567n383	**1 Chronicles**			
	598n463	21:1	456	4:27	85n112		
8:9	60n2	21:3	433n38, 473	7:25	364n413		
8:12	171n410, 172n411	21:5	433n38, 473	8:4	26n13		
8:21	175	21:10	269n160	9:27	581		
9:3	598n463	21:12	207, 405	11:10–47	26n13		
9:11	270n166	21:14	157n355, 503	11:12	26n13		
9:20	340n354	21:19	456	11:28	26n13		
9:22	159n366, 160	21:23	458	12:3	26n13		
9:25	60n3	21:24	614n522	15:20	338		
9:36	26n13, 62n15,	22	207	15:21	416		
	269n160	22–23	436	15:28	416		
10:3	494	22:1	456	15:29	157		
10:10	269n160	22:3	437n54	16:8	606n484		
10:18	67n31	22:3–13	435	16:11	527		
10:19	472	22:9	76n75	16:22	388n482		
10:22	491n134, 493	22:13	432, 437, 465	16:25	505n193, 542		
11:18	472	22:14	496	16:33	487n117		
12:9(10)	375	22:14–20	432, 459	16:34	78n84		
12:10(11)	139	22:16–17	470	16:35	643n612		
12:16(17)	83n106	22:18	465	17:7	93n133		
13:7	175, 178, 387n477,	22:19	268, 487n116	17:9	406		
	399	22:19–20	470	17:15	25		
14:9	72n56	22:20	293n248, 491	17:21	505n193		
14:13	495n151	23	435n46, 441, 465	17:24	564n364		
14:21	179n431	23:2	432, 437	18:4	399		
14:23–25	10	23:4	398	18:17	554		
14:25	269n160, 587n438	23:4–5	473	19:18	399		
16	160	23:5	462, 472, 473	20:2	475n89, 475n90		
17:10	132n283	23:8	441n67	21:20	387n477		
17:16	433n38, 473	23:10	475	24:23	451		
17:20	504n188	23:12	473	26:14	90		
17:23	269n160	23:13	475, 566	27:12	26n13		
17:34	121, 229n22	23:21	437	27:23	184n456		
17:37	229n22	23:21–23	487	28:9	512		
18:23	247	23:22–23	103	29:2–3	92		
19	350	23:23	437n54				
19:3	506	23:24	437	**2 Chronicles**			
19:4	521	23:29	119n217	2:8	72		
19:13	580	23:36	456	5:13	78n84		
19:20–24	183	24:2	269n160	6:1	506n199		
19:21	576n415	24:3	165	6:2	385n471		
19:23	72	24:8	456	6:16	487n117		

6:31	463	33:3	473	1:8	612n513
6:37–38	171n409	33:5	473	1:9	642
7:3	78n84	33:8	229n22	2:5–6	167n386
7:21	576n413	33:12	487n117	3:1	495n151
9:4	491n134	33:14	262, 495, 508,	3:3	262, 495
10:15	269n160		610n504	3:6	495n151
11:10	112	33:16	489n125	3:8	496n154
12:7	76n75	33:18–19	69n41	3:24	507n204
14:5	112	33:23	487	3:31–32	507n204, 556
14:13	565	34	437, 441	3:32	495n151
15:12–15	416	34:3–4	100n170	4:14(8)	349n366,
17:11	60n2	34:14	433n34, 453		505n193
18:2	346n361	34:14–21	435	5:5	244n62
18:10	362n401	34:17	76n75	7:2	155
18:18	473n79	34:21	76n75, 437, 465	7:59	168
18:23	80n90	34:22	496	7:64	133n286
19:2	487	34:22–28	459	8:3	272, 362n398,
19:10	229n22	34:24	93n133		386n474
19:11	451	34:25	76n75	8:10	494
20:4	522n239	34:26	93n133, 465	8:11	327
20:14	452	34:27	487n117	8:12	327
20:25	60n2	34:31	462	8:16	495n151
20:34	115	35:1–9	487–88	8:17	134
22:10	244n62	35:3	60n2	8:18	229n22
24:5	92	35:6	489n125	9:6	473n79
25:18	72n56	35:18	134	9:13	229n22
25:23	495n151	35:18–19	103	9:15	384n467
25:26	313	36:22	482	9:17	69n41
26:1	179n431	36:23	594	9:23	184n456
26:9	495n152			9:29	229n22
26:15	84n106, 507n204	**Ezra**		9:30	346n361
28:10	244n62	1:2	482, 594	9:31	79n89, 511n217
29:8	576n414	1:7	92	9:32	505n193
30:6–7	104n182	2:1	612	9:35	81n93
30:8	104n182	2:62	133n286	9:37	158
30:10–11	104n182	3:7	72n56	10:29(30)	494
30:16	229n22	4:2	134	10:30	229n22
30:18	340	4:4	179n431	12:27	416n547
30:26	134	7:10	229n22	12:28	232
31:10	139	9:7	582	12:39	262, 495, 495n151
31:15	451	10:18	451	13:4	635
32:1	384	10:39	451	13:13	352
32:18	179n431	10:41	451	13:15	60n2
32:20	223, 340			13:16	495
32:21	92	**Nehemiah**		13:19	60n2, 405n515
32:30	610n504	1:5	505n193	13:20	556
32:32	25	1:6	340	13:22	349n366

Esther

1:11	224
2:17	224
4:13	266
4:15	266
5:9	300
6:8	224
8:3	268n158

Job

1:20	96
2:3	264
2:10	543
3:17	348
3:24	76n76
3:26	348
4:10	142n312
4:11	142n312, 143n317
4:15	250
5:4	387n480
5:7	364n413
5:11	310, 387n480
5:14	434n41
6:7	484
6:9	310
6:10	352
6:19	353
6:24	335
6:25	303n270
7:18	581
7:20	60n2
8:2	224
8:17	85
9:17	71n48
9:21	341n356
9:27	270n166
9:28	233
10:10	76n76
10:16	142n312
10:17	196n3, 225
11:3	639n594
11:15	603
12:7–8	467
12:16	335
12:20	604
12:25	434n41
13:6	269

13:11	246
13:16	387n480
13:22	266, 274
14:1	348
14:9	397
14:10	186n462
14:11	64
14:15	518
14:18	76n77
15:17	235
15:24	434
16:4	576n415
16:8	599n467
16:13	510
18:4	76n77, 387n476
18:11	376
18:18	82
18:21	243n59
19:2	224
19:4	335
19:7	227
19:18	268n155
19:19	235
20:2	266
20:4	381n457
20:6	75n71
20:7	186n462
20:10	378n446
20:17	372, 379
20:23	484
20:25	158
20:28	398
21:11	157
21:18	524
21:23	234
21:28	243n59
21:30	506n198
22:20	81n94
22:26	603
22:28	373
23:3	116
23:4	269
23:12	292n244
24:4	519
24:14	362n398, 386n474, 581
24:23	113

25:3	99n163
25:5	85n113, 292n244
26:5	190
27:1	299
27:2	621
27:4	605
27:8	310
27:16	491n134
28:8	142n312
28:28	482
29:1	299
29:15	509
30:3	544
30:4	484
30:6	139
30:7	541
30:9	416n548
30:15	387n480
31:10	180n439
31:23	246
31:26	362n398, 386n474
32:4	598n463
32:7	346n361
32:8	116, 594
34:5	621
34:13	482
34:20	97
34:28	525, 614n522
35:2	84n106
35:12	484
36:2	224
36:6	581
36:12	97
36:23	482, 594
36:24	573
36:26	292n244
37:2	348–49
37:6	325
37:8	139
37:9	71n49
37:21	250, 362n398, 386n474
37:22	205n30
38:18	114, 232
38:21	603
38:25	80n91
38:40	139

39:6	243n59	8:8(9)	463	19:6(7)	76n73, 319, 385
39:15	387n477	8:9(10)	494	19:9(10)	591
39:20	175	9:1	338n347	20:5(6)	387n480
39:24	234–49, 348	9:3(4)	126n254	22:1	338
39:27	310	9:4(5)	526n249	22:5(6)	607n490
40:4	101n175	9:5(6)	71	22:7(8)	576n415
40:12	396	9:10(11)	465	22:12(13)	72, 224
40:18	580	9:15(16)	339, 582	22:21(22)	362n401
41:6 (40:30)	483, 556	9:16(17)	526n249	22:24(25)	162n380
41:25(17)	246	10:1	363n409	22:26(27)	465
41:30(22)	248n83	10:5	273	23:2	558
42:7	268n158	10:7	225n7	24:2	380
42:8	340, 350	10:8–9	376	25:2	607n490
		10:12	384	25:3 (LXX 24:3)	240n43
Psalms		11:4	329	25:5	410n531
1:4	524	12	337n345	25:7	81n93
1:6	79	12:1	338, 416	25:8	78n84, 79n85
2:2	234	12:5(6)	273	25:17	434
2:3	99	13:1	363n409	25:20	607
3	416n546	13:1–2(2–3)	224	26	357n381
3–7	339n352	14:5	484	27:1	137, 412
3:8	105	15	614	27:2	126n254
4	414n539	15:2–3	608	27:8	527
4:1	338, 415	15:3	636	27:9	410n531
4:4(5)	348	15:5	305n276	27:12	273
5	416n546	16:6	555	27:13	81n93
5:7(8)	329n323	17:1	337	28:2	384
5:10(11)	642n609	17:2	228	28:7	576
6	337n345, 414n539	17:3	97, 251	29	332
6:1	338, 415, 416	17:12	376, 518	29:5	72n56
6:9(10)	334n338	17:13	376	29:6	157
7	334, 335–36, 337, 340, 341n356, 454n14	18	332, 410, 412, 413, 527	30:5(6)	530
				31:1(2)	607
		18:2(3)	77n80	31:3(4)	77n80
7:1	336, 338	18:4(5)	90n131	31:8(9)	232
7:7(8)	339	18:7(8)	348	31:19(20)	81n93
7:8(9)	339	18:15(16)	72n53	31:20–21	453
7:9(10)	309, 339	18:19(20)	232	31:22(23)	594
7:12–13(13–14)	339	18:29(30)	482	32:2	84n106
7:12(13)	340n353	18:32–33(33–34)	409	32:6	80n91
7:13(14)	340n353	18:33(34)	398, 399, 400, 404	33:14	511
7:15(16)	339			33:16–17	186
7:16(17)	300	18:35(36)	527	34:4(5)	465
8:1	338	18:44(45)	398	34:8(9)	79
8:1(2)	494	18:46(47)	409, 410n531	34:10(11)	465
8:4(5)	79	18:47(48)	244n62	34:14(15)	527
8:7–8(8–9)	467	19:2–3(3–4)	373	34:21(22)	250n98

35:5	524	47:4(5)	112	62:1	337n346
35:6	82	48:10(11)	643n612	62:3(4)	224
35:8	339	48:12–13(13–14)	131n277	62:4(5)	246
35:10	81	49:4(5)	416	63:1(2)	544
35:12	77n81	49:7(8)	511	63:11(12)	474n84
35:17	141, 227n15	49:11(12)	190n470	64:5(6)	376
35:18	105n188	49:14(15)	385n471	64:7(8)	82n100
35:20	268	50:7	599n466	65:10(11)	74
35:23	328	50:14	104n187	65:13(14)	539
35:25	264	50:20	268n155	66	416n546
35:26	541	50:21	631	66:2	643n612
36:6(7)	467n56	51	336n342	66:6	380
37:1	619	52:5(7)	543	66:9	98n162
37:6	228, 589	53	416n546	66:13	104n187
37:11	619	53:1	338	66:15	104n187
37:14	619	53:3(4)	234	67	414n539
37:16	79n85, 619	53:5(6)	484	67:1	338
37:18	79	54	338, 414n539,	68	216, 387n476, 412
37:20	539		416n546	68:7(8)	387n476
37:21	619	54:1	338	68:8(9)	77n78, 333
37:26	619	54:6	104n187	68:11(12)	373
37:35	376	55	338, 414n539	68:17(18)	372
37:40	619	55:1(2)	334n338, 338	68:18(19)	320
38:6(7)	85n113	55:6(7)	339, 399, 586	68:20(21)	482
38:8(9)	85n113, 224	55:10(11)	225n7	68:21(22)	374
39:5	115	55:19(20)	309	68:24(25)	353, 366
39:6	132n280	55:23	98n162	68:25(26)	133n288, 338
40:16(17)	465	56	339	69:1	338
40:17(18)	83, 279	56:1	338	69:7(8)	636, 640
42:9(10)	77n80	56:4(5)	137	69:9(10)	67n31
43:3	243n59	56:12(13)	104n187	69:9–10(10–11)	540
44:2(3)	244n61, 376	57	337n345	69:12(13)	416n548
44:10(11)	504n188	57:5(6)	143n318, 248n83,	69:24(25)	600
44:12(13)	154		636	69:34(35)	467
44:23(24)	328	57:6(7)	339	70:5(6)	279
45	527	57:8(9)	300	71:1	607
45:1	338	58	337n345	71:3	77n80
45:4(5)	527	58:2(3)	300	71:6	91
45:7(8)	82n100	59	337n345	72:1	581
46	337n345	59:5 (LXX 58:6)	240n43	72:4	519
46:1	338	60	416n546	72:10	567
46:2(3)	505n193	60:1	338	72:16	72n56
46:3(4)	376	60:3(5)	321	73:14	581
46:4(5)	243n59	60:5(7)	376	73:15	292
46:5(6)	530	60:6(8)	576	73:16	83
47	629n558	61	414n539	73:19	467n53
47:3(4)	244n62	61:1(2)	338, 621	73:20	328

74:2	256n114	79:12	541	96:4	505n193, 542
74:8	580	80:1	338n347	96:11	467
74:10	224	80:4(5)	223	97:2	506n199
74:15	72	80:11(12)	380	97:5	487
74:17	115	81:1	338	97:8	131n277
75	337n345, 416n546	81:9(10)	165	98:4	621
75:8(9)	291, 320, 321, 483	82:3	525, 614n522	99:3	505n193
75:10(11)	362n400,	82:3–4	614	100:5	77n81, 78n84
	362n401	82:7	594	101:8	581, 589
76	414n539	83:11(12)	233	102:1	337
76:1	338	83:14(15)	76	102:6(7)	544, 545
76:2(3)	139	83:15(16)	71n48	102:21(22)	361, 643n612
76:3(4)	364n413	84	332	103:6	526n249
76:5(6)	188, 189–90	84:1	338	103:6–18	69n41
76:6(7)	114	84:2(3)	243n59, 518	103:9	68
76:8(9)	329, 344	84:7(8; LXX 83:8)	295	103:16	250
76:9(10)	519	84:10(11)	92	104:2	364
77	216, 332	85:1(2)	540	104:3	373
77:1	337n346, 338	86:1	337	104:7	72n53
77:2(3)	224	86:14–17	69n41	104:12	571
77:5(6)	83	87:3	268n157	104:16	72n56
77:6(7)	416	87:5	131n277	104:31	634
77:8(9)	373	88	339	104:122	139
77:9(10)	381n456	88:1	338	105:4	527
77:13(14)	366n424	88:2(3)	621	105:15	374, 388n482
77:16(17)	348	88:6(7)	82n99	105:41	77n78, 544
77:17(18)	373, 374	88:14(15)	363n409	106:1	78n84
77:18(19)	348	88:15(16)	224	106:9	72
77:19(20)	376	89:9(10)	64	106:15	542
78:13	376	89:30(31)	229n22	106:26	384n467
78:15	77n78	89:38(39)	80n91	106:47	643n612
78:17	544	89:41(42)	504n188	107:1	78n84
78:19	268n155	89:46(47)	224, 363n409	107:6	434
78:20	77n78, 381n456	90	357n381	107:13	434
78:21	80n91	90:1	337	107:19	434
78:26	359	90:10	91, 225n7	107:25	71n49
78:28	243n59	91:3	365n416	107:26	128n266
78:40	227n15	91:5	364n414	107:28	434
78:48	364n413	91:6	529, 530	107:29	71n49
78:51	368n429	91:13	142n312	107:34	564n367
78:55	555	92:12(13)	72n56, 397	107:35	544
78:58	67n29	93	629n558	107:37	398
78:59	80n91	93:2	256n115	109:2	268n159
78:62	80n91	93:3–4	380	109:9–12	69n41
79:1	329n323	94:17	190n470	109:11	504n188
79:5	67n28, 87n121	94:21	397	109:20	268n159
79:6	76n75	96–99	629n558	109:23	175

109:24	126n253	135:2	92	6:35	160n373
109:25	576n415	135:3	78n84	7:8	387n476
110:6	158	135:5	494	7:10	159n363
111:1	105n188	136:1	78n84	8:10	434n40, 580
112:5	79n85	136:8–9	385n472	8:15	234
114	369	137:1	127n260	8:36	311
114:4	157	138:2	329n323	9:5	484
114:6	157	138:7	75	10:24	234
114:7	487n117	139:4	234	11:3	240n43
114:8	77n78	140:9(10)	322	11:4	506n198, 511
115:7	292n244	141:4	484	11:6	240n43
116:17–18	104n187	142:7(8)	224	11:12	631
117:1	133n285	143:3	82n99	11:25	325
118:1	78n84	143:7	363n409	11:26	133n285
118:5	232	144:2	244n62	12:4	405
118:6	137	144:3	79, 83	12:9	175
118:12	76	145:6	505n193	12:17	273
118:27	362n400	145:7	81n93	12:19	604
118:29	78n84	145:8–16	69n41	13:2	240n43
119:8	85n113	145:9	78n84, 79n85	13:7	312
119:21	71	147:2	642	13:11	290
119:32	275	147:5	494	13:13	240n44
119:43	85n113	147:11	633	13:15	240n43
119:46	268n157	147:18	71n49	13:21	82
119:51	83, 85n113	149:9	526n249	14:5	273
119:65–66	79n85	150	416	14:16	80n91
119:67	335			14:18	224
119:68	79n85	**Proverbs**		14:25	273
119:71–72	79n85	1:3	434n40, 580	14:30	405
119:84	227n15, 526n249	1:6	299, 303, 304	14:34	517
119:86	82n100, 284	1:12	264	15:9	527
119:103	303n270	1:22	223, 224	15:18	225n7
119:107	85n113	2:22	240n43, 259n126	15:25	115
119:139	67n31	3:33	389n483	15:27a	310
119:158	240n43	4:12	126	15:33	527
120:2–3	605	4:16	461	16:4–7	69n41
121:3	98n162	4:17	484	16:7	96
121:3–4	188	4:18	362n396, 362n398	16:9	83n106
121:4	188	4:19	434n41	16:18	517
124:80	80n91	4:21	594	16:27	76
125:2	164	5:4	248n83	16:32	70n45
125:5	224	6:6–8	261n136	17:4	604
126:4	540	6:7	260	17:7	604
132:2	494n147	6:12	90	17:14	225n7
132:5	243n59	6:19	273	17:22	188, 580
132:7	243n59	6:26	159n363	18:3	240n44
134:2	384	6:34	67	18:12	527

19:5	273	30:14	391	4:11	72
19:7	82n100	30:21–23	353	4:13	166
19:9	69n41, 273	30:27	260, 261n136	4:16	359
19:11	69n41	30:30	142n312	5:2	586
19:12	141	31:1	60n3	5:4	139
19:16–17	69n41	31:4	234	5:15	72n56
19:17	312	31:17	112	6:4	245
20:2	80n91, 141, 311	31:24	483, 556	6:9	586
20:27	502	31:27	353	6:10	76n73, 245
21:12	389n483			7:5(6)	72
21:18	240n43, 259n126	**Ecclesiastes**		7:9(10)	77n81, 232
21:21	527	1:8	321	8:6	62n18, 67
21:24	291n240	1:17	581	8:8	268n157
21:28	224	2:5	398	8:14	399
21:30	186	2:12	581		
22:4	527	2:15	484	**Isaiah**	
22:12	240n43	3:4	157	1:1	222, 423
22:22	525, 614n522	4:8	321	1:3	218, 417, 563
22:22–23	614	4:12	196n3, 225	1:5–6	190n472
23:1	484	5:5	335	1:9–10	564
23:5	233	7:6	86	1:22	86
23:6	484	7:25	581	1:23	234
23:22	240n44	8:11	228	1:24	62, 153
23:28	240n43	8:13	487n117	2:1	25n8, 222, 423
23:32	291, 300	9:3	581	2:2	566n377
24:8	83n106	9:12	260	2:3	229
24:31	234, 541	9:15	526	2:4	229, 254
24:32	434n40, 580	10:8	339	2:6	256
25:15	580	10:11	300	2:6–21	566n377, 618
25:18	112	10:13	581	2:10	275
25:23	71n49, 360n390	12:3	300	2:11	366n422
26:11	319	12:4	572	2:12–17	507
26:13	142n312	12:6	165	2:13	72
26:16	266			2:15	508
26:17	80n91	**Song of Songs**		2:19	566n377
26:21	225n7	1:5	367	2:19–21	275
27:4	80n91, 86	1:8	243n59	2:21	566n377
27:9	233	1:9	114	3:1	564n363
27:17	233	2:8	482	3:6	461
27:22	497	2:9	399	3:12	264n144
28:1	141	2:12	572	3:15	564n363
28:8	290, 305n276	2:14	586	3:16–17	161
28:20	287	2:17	399	3:17	180n438
29:1	269n164	3:6	556	3:19	114
29:14	599n467	3:7	164	4:6	384
29:18	25	4:8	139	5:1	362n399
30:1	60n3	4:10	167n387	5:7	564n363

5:9	564n363, 556	10:1–4	301	13:7	622, 630n561
5:10	301n263	10:2	525, 614n522	13:7–8	136
5:13	563	10:4	470n67	13:8	117
5:14	285	10:5	98, 383	13:9	397, 488
5:16	564n363	10:5–6	99, 152	13:10	361n396
5:19	512	10:5–15	53	13:11	566
5:20	300	10:5–19	60n8	13:13	348
5:24	71n51, 564n363	10:6	99, 376	13:14	642n609
5:24–30	60n8	10:7	84n107	13:16	171n410, 172n411,
5:25	348, 470n67	10:8	189n468		504n188
5:27	126n253, 188	10:9	381	13:17	84n106, 242n51,
5:29	141	10:12	152		641n603
6	608	10:13	504n188	13:18	172n411
6:3	315, 564n363	10:14	572, 600n472	13:19	131, 564
6:5	564n363, 608	10:15	381n456	13:21	157
6:5–7	608n492	10:16	542, 564n363	14:2	565
6:7	608	10:20	105n190	14:3	348
6:11	556	10:23	79n89, 81, 511,	14:3–23	383
6:11–12	508		600n472	14:4	299, 546
7:1	119n217	10:23–24	564n363	14:5	98n159, 383
7:6	384	10:24	92, 98	14:8	72n56, 322
8:6	232	10:26	92, 98, 564n363	14:12	546
8:7–8	478	10:27	604	14:16	348
8:8	80, 97, 232, 250	10:28–29	498n160	14:22	471
8:11	93n134	10:32	546	14:22–23	44n86, 149n338
8:13	171n410, 564n363	10:33	564n363	14:23	544, 636
8:14	254	10:33–34	316n301	14:24–27	60n8
8:18	564n363	10:34	72, 316	14:25	604
8:19	573	11	413	14:26–27	470n67, 547
8:20	361n396	11:1	397	14:28	60n3, 560
8:22	642n609	11:1–2	315	14:28–32	552n316
9	413	11:1–9	315n300	14:30	561
9:4(3)	604	11:2	116	14:31	128n266, 498n162
9:5(4)	233	11:4	519	14:32	519
9:5–6(4–5)	108n205	11:6–9	317n303	15:1	23, 60n3, 60n4, 520
9:6(5)	90	11:8	139	15:1–2	498n160
9:7(6)	67n28, 564n363	11:9	314, 315, 317	15:8	497
9:12(11)	470n67	11:12	611n508, 642n609	16:3–4	642n609
9:13(12)	465, 564n363	11:15–16	392	16:6	137n300, 562, 566
9:14(13)	374	12:2	410n531	16:7–8	498n160
9:15(14)	328n322	12:4	606	16:8	398
9:16(15)	264n144	12:6	632	16:8–10	503
9:17(16)	470n67	13:1	23, 60n3, 60n4,	16:13–14	2
9:18(17)	76, 85n114		62n14, 222n5, 423	17:1	23, 60n3, 60n4
9:19(18)	564n363	13:3	490, 576n412	17:3	44n86, 149n338, 234
9:21(20)	470n67	13:5	600n472	17:4	73, 542
10:1	300	13:6	487, 488, 498n162	17:6	397

17:10	410n531	23:12	105n190	29:6	70
17:12	153	23:13	115, 259	29:7	25n9, 60n7
17:13	524	23:14	498n162	29:9	231, 518
17:14	504n188, 564n367	23:15	501n177	29:13	608
17:14b	547	23:17	463n38	29:15	512
18:1	299, 301n262, 372,	24–27	252	29:15–16	301
	378, 609	24:1	116, 119n218, 135n295	29:15–17	301
18:2	164, 372, 378, 609	24:3	135	29:18	509
18:4	93n134	24:6	65, 250n98	29:22	93n134
18:7	372, 378, 500n176,	24:8	576n412	30:1–4	301
	609, 641	24:16	240n43, 259n126	30:5–6	327
19:1	23, 60n3, 60n4	24:23	76n73, 319	30:6	23, 60n3, 142n312
19:3	264n144	25:2	313	30:8	275
19:5	64, 164, 378n444	25:6	483, 502	30:10	25n10
19:6	73, 127n260	25:8	264n145	30:22	100n170, 100n171
19:11	256n114	25:10	387n477	30:23	539
19:13	507n204	25:11	562	30:26	76n73, 319
19:18	604	25:12	234	30:27	76
20:2	269n160, 500n176	26	417	30:27–33	60n8
20:3–5	442	26:3	108n205	30:30	108n206
20:4	171	26:6	525n248, 614n522	30:31–32	416n547
20:6	567	26:11	67n28, 518	30:32	92
21:1	23, 60n3, 71n49, 250	26:12	108n205	31:1	301n263, 465
21:2	240n43, 259n126	26:18	387n480	31:2	165
21:3	117, 136	26:19	190n470	31:3	470n67
21:3–4	406n520	26:20	283	31:4	93n134, 143
21:6	216n62, 267	26:21	510	32:10	348
21:6–8	267, 273	27:1	224	32:10–11	348
21:7	267	27:5	108n205	32:11	176
21:8	266, 267	27:8	249	32:12	116
21:10	564n364	27:13	642n609	32:13	576
21:11	23, 60n3, 60n4	28:2	71n49, 384	32:17–18	108n205
21:13	23, 60n3	28:4	172	33:1	240n43, 259n126,
22:1	23	28:7	117, 335		292n242, 301n261
22:2	543, 576	28:8	319	33:2	581
22:10–11	181n442	28:9	635	33:4	176
22:16	190n470	28:15	80n91	33:7	108n205, 483
22:18	494	28:18	80n91	33:8	84n106
22:20	501n177	28:20	522n238	33:9	72
22:25	44n86, 60n2,	28:21	282, 361, 394	33:15	310
	149n338	28:22	33n48	33:16	310
23:1	23, 60n4, 498n162	28:27–28	387n477	33:20	635
23:6	498n162	28:29	547	33:21	372, 379
23:7	256n114, 576	29:1	538	34	53, 205
23:8	483, 556	29:3	112	34:1	488
23:9	566	29:4	573	34:4	473n79
23:11	348, 470n67, 556	29:5	71n51	34:5	543

34:6	488n121, 489	41:2–3	108n206	47:12	327
34:8	108n205	41:3	108	47:13	279
34:10	576n413	41:5	543	47:14	484
34:11	544	41:15	387n477, 524	48:9	643n612
35:1	544	41:18	544	48:14	622
35:2	72	41:27	108	48:17	327
35:3	126n253	42:1	229	48:18	108
35:6	399, 482	42:3	229	48:20	624n539
35:22	72	42:4	229n22, 543, 567	48:21	77n78
36:8	247	42:10	543, 567	48:22	108
36:18–20	98	42:12	567	49:1	543
37:3	506	42:13	67n28, 505	49:2	248n83, 363n409
37:4	521	42:13–14	631	49:4	594
37:16	564n364	42:15	64, 72, 392n492	49:8	565
37:21–25	183	42:16	509	49:17	89
37:22	576n415	42:17	100n170, 327,	49:18	541
37:23	373		607n490	49:22	384n468, 611, 612
37:24	72, 322	42:22	139, 157n355, 503,	49:23	108n206
37:27	398		504n188	49:24	381
37:28–29	348	42:24	157n355, 503,	49:26	174, 580
37:31	398		565n370	49:28	563
37:32	67n28	42:25	76n75, 582	50:2	64, 72n53
37:33	93n134	43:1	93n134	51:1	527
37:37	89n128	43:5	611n508, 636, 644	51:4	229, 581
37:38	567n383	43:16	392	51:5	543
38:12	310	43:19	392n492	51:7	540
38:14	73, 133, 573	43:28	540	51:10	72
38:17	108n205	44:8	351	51:17	110, 320
38:20	414, 416	44:9–10	327	51:17–20	321
39:8	108n205	44:10	100n171, 327, 328	51:20	172n412
40–48	330	44:27	64	51:21–22	172n413
40–55	106, 108	45:1	244n62, 374,	51:22	105n190, 110, 320,
40:1	624n539		389n482		494
40:1–8	281	45:3	376	51:22–23	321
40:2	268n159	45:6	545	51:23	250
40:9	108	45:7	108	51:60	261n135
40:15	543	45:19	527	52	110
40:19	100n171, 165,	45:22	187	52:1	105, 108n207
	173n420, 327, 328	45:23	54, 187, 331	52:4	108
40:23	234	46:1–2	60n2	52:7	53, 106–9, 110, 216,
40:25	351–52	46:2	165		276n184
40:26	373, 581	46:9	545	52:8	108, 643n615
40:27	80n90	47:2–3	161	52:9	108
40:28–31	412	47:3	322	52:11–12	110
40:31	276, 281	47:6	152	52:14	635
41:1	543	47:7	516	53	395, 413
41:2	150n341, 244n62	47:8	545	53:2	544

53:3	84n106	62:25	317n303	3:3	161n375
53:5	108, 110	63	346	3:5	68n40, 381n456
53:9b	495	63:1–6	205	3:7	594
54:1	100n172, 543	63:3	491	3:8	240n43
54:2	367	63:5	67n28	3:9	309
54:3	244n61	63:7	361n395	3:11	240n43
54:7	611n508	63:11	189n469	3:12–13	476
54:10	108	63:15	385n471	3:14	461
54:13	108	63:19	261	3:15	189n469
55:1	153, 301n262, 586	63:19b–64:3 (63:19b–64:2)		3:17	500n176, 641
55:6	7		369n433	3:18	559
55:12	108	64:3(2)	74n66	3:19	546
56:8	611n508, 642n609	64:8	85n113	3:19–20	602n480
56:10	188, 189, 329	64:11	85n113	3:20	594
56:11	189n469	65:18–19	630	3:20b	292n242
57:1	293n248	65:19	633	3:25	509
57:2	108n205	65:22	504	4:4	76
57:3	160	65:25	315n300	4:5–6	524
57:13	565	66:8	381n456	4:6	489, 497
57:16	487n117	66:11	324	4:7	85n114, 238, 556
57:19	108n205	66:12	108n205	4:8	498n162
57:21	108n205	66:14	255	4:9	238, 501n178
58:4	108n206, 546	66:15	372	4:10	489, 594
58:10	434	66:17	162n380, 467n53	4:11	233, 238, 251,
58:13	108n206	66:19	343		500n176, 641
59:3	579, 587n436	66:20	611, 612	4:12	621
59:7	108n206	66:22	99	4:13	233, 238, 249, 391
59:8	108n205	66:24	158	4:16	238
59:9	434			4:18	238n37
59:10	126n253, 434n41,	**Jeremiah**		4:20	367
	509	1:1	26n13, 423	4:21	238n37
59:11	133, 387n480, 573	1:2	423, 452, 453, 458	4:22	563
59:15	582	1:2–3	458	4:23–26	238n37, 508
59:17	67n28	1:14	511n218	4:23–28	600n472
60:3	362n396	1:15	641n603, 641n605	4:24	74n66
60:6	108n208	2:3	251	4:25	508
60:14	642n611	2:6	544	4:26	487n116
60:15	576n413	2:8	189n469, 327, 432, 461	4:27	79n89, 511
60:17	108n205	2:11	327, 563	4:29	305n274
60:19	386	2:13	563	5:1	238n37, 526
61:1	108n208	2:15	557n332	5:3	238n37, 434n40, 580
61:4	575	2:19	238n37, 476	5:5	99
62:4–5	631	2:20	99	5:6	233
62:5	633	2:21	234	5:7	397, 474n84, 474n85
62:8	504	2:26	591n451	5:10	79n89, 511n217
62:10	309	2:28	461	5:11	292n242
62:11	108n206, 611n508	2:30	434n40, 580	5:14–15	641n603

5:15	242, 256n115	10:3–4	327	16:16	260
5:15–17	207, 238, 408	10:4	117	16:17	487n117
5:17	408	10:5	387n476	16:19	327
5:18	79n89, 238, 511n217	10:13	544	17:1	362n400
5:24	325	10:14	327, 328	17:4	244n62
5:27	495	10:17	635	17:8	398
6:1	497	10:18	508, 641n605	17:10	512
6:4	116, 482	10:20	367	17:18	349n366
6:6	510, 545	10:21	189n469	17:21	60n2
6:7	225n7, 227n17,	10:22	138	17:22	60n2
	238n36, 510	10:25	76n75, 539	17:23	434n40, 580
6:11	76n75	11:2	268n159	17:24	60n2
6:12	470n67	11:13	461	17:27	60n2
6:13–14	590	11:15	576	18:11	83n104, 268n159
6:17	242n52, 267	11:17	461	18:16	576n413, 576n414
6:21	126n253, 641n605	11:19	83n104, 484	18:17	249n93
6:23	245, 248	12:1	240n43, 259n126, 621	18:18	83n104
6:24	630n562	12:2	398	19:3	405
6:27	234	12:4	65	19:5	432, 461
7:5	526	12:5	121n225, 399	19:7	636
7:8	327	12:6	292n242	19:8	576n413, 576n414
7:9	461	12:10	189n469, 636	19:12	255
7:20	76n75, 467n56	12:14	559	19:13	432, 433n38, 473
7:28	434n40, 580	12:16	461, 474n84, 474n85	19:18	576
7:29	96	13:11	559, 643, 644	20:6	165
8:1	500n176, 641	13:12–14	321	20:8	225n7, 227
8:2	432, 433n38, 463,	13:13	511n218	20:9	76
	468, 473	13:13–14	641n605	20:12	512
8:3	44n86, 149n338, 642	13:22	161	20:15	108n208
8:8	228	13:23	454	21	189n469
8:10	180n439	13:24	612n513	21:5	470n67
8:10–11	590	13:26	161	21:6	467n56
8:12	543	14	407	21:12	76, 589
8:13	460, 466	14:9	630	21:13	44, 139, 149
8:14	509, 524	14:12	364	22:13–15	301
8:16	600n472	14:17	190n472, 497	22:13–19	213
8:17	300, 641n605	14:18	543	22:18	299
8:22	190n472	14:19	190n472	22:22	165, 603, 608n492
9:1	240n43	15	210	22:23	72n56
9:7(6)	641n605	15:6	470n67	22:24	541
9:10(9)	468, 576n413	15:7	177, 181	23:1	112
9:11(10)	138, 557n332,	15:8	529, 530	23:1–2	119n218, 209, 301
	581, 597, 636	15:10	225n7	23:2–3	642
9:12(11)	576n413	15:15	636, 640	23:2–4	560n345
9:15(14)	641n605	16:4	463	23:3	611n508
9:16(15)	612n513	16:5	635	23:4–5	242n52
9:18	243n59	16:6	397	23:8	642
9:21(20)	397	16:15	642	23:9	406n520, 487n116

23:9–11	209	27:11–12	604	32:29 (LXX 39:29)	
23:12	82n99	27:15	642		433n38, 461
23:14	564	28:8	364n412	32:33	434n40, 580
23:21	276	28:10	92	32:35	432, 475n88
23:23	635	28:11	604	32:37	611n508, 642
23:24	376	28:12	92	32:41	630n563, 633
23:27	461	28:14	604	32:43	467n56
23:29	76, 77, 352	28:16	463n38, 466	33:9 (LXX 40:9)	348, 643,
23:32	327	28:18	179n431		644
23:33–34	60	29:11 (LXX 36:11)	83n104	33:10	467n56, 539, 556,
23:36	60	29:14	611n508, 637, 642		557n332, 597n458
23:38	60	29:15	242n52	33:12	467n56, 539
24:6	630n563	29:16	165, 179n431	33:14	559
24:9	304n272, 642	29:18	576n416, 642	33:18	487n117
25:1	534	29:23	599n466	33:22	473n79
25:1–2	179n431	29:25	179n431	34:5	299, 301n263
25:9	576n414, 636	29:27	26n13, 62n15, 71	34:11	244n62
25:12	482	29:32	268, 482	34:16	244n62
25:13	314	30:6	136	34:17	636
25:15	291, 320	30:7	301n263	34:22	556
25:15–17	321	30:8	44n86, 99, 149n338,	35:7	463
25:15–29	321		501n178, 604	35:13	434n40, 580
25:16	114	30:9	242n52	36:1–4	443n79
25:17	320	30:10	171n409, 615n527	36:2	134, 268n159
25:18	576, 636	30:11	79n89, 81, 511,	36:3	559
25:20	530		511n217	36:14	454n13, 455
25:26	463n38	30:12–15	190n472	36:17	545
25:27	172n413	30:16	157n355, 165, 503,	36:22–23	443n79
25:28	320, 322		504n188, 565n370	36:26	491
25:29	44n86, 149n338	30:17	642n608	36:29	467n56
25:29–30	511	30:18	243n59	36:31	482
25:33	463	30:19	176	37:2	269n160
25:34	498n162, 604	31:1	500n176, 641	37:3	223
25:34–36	189n469	31:8	611n508, 636, 644	37:9	90n128
25:36	497	31:8–9	96n145	38:1	451
25:38 (LXX 32:38)	580,	31:10	611n508	38:4	630n562
	586, 586n435	31:20	268n155	38:6	491
26	414	31:27	467n56, 559	38:7	455n16
26:9	539, 556	31:28	630n563	38:10	455n16
26:18	26n13, 62n15	31:28–30	69n41	38:12	455n16
26:19	51n109	31:31	559	39:3	495
26:20–33	213	31:32	461	39:5	621
26:24	213	31:35	581	39:7	139
27:1–15	318	31:35–36	468	39:11–14	535
27:2	92, 99	31:36	487n117	39:14	451
27:5	467n56	32:10	483	39:16	455n16
27:8	604	32:18–19	69n41	40:3	509
27:10	642			40:5–6	451

40:7	451	47:2–7	528n257	49:30 (LXX 30:25)	
40:8	451	47:4	543		83n104, 91
40:9	451	47:5	397, 499n168	49:33	138
40:11	559	47:6	299, 301n262	49:36	642n608
40:11–16	451	47:7	554	49:39 (LXX 25:19)	
40:12	642n608	48:1	301n261, 301n263		315n295
40:15	559	48:2 (LXX 31:2)	83n104	50	516
41:1–4	451	48:3	497, 503n184	50–51	53
41:5	397	48:7	165, 472	50:1	269n160
41:6	451	48:9	557n333	50:3	467n56
41:9–10	451	48:11	165, 483	50:6	189n469
41:16	451	48:11–12	502, 503	50:7	251
41:18	451	48:15	503n184	50:9	242n51
42:1–4	223	48:16	503n184	50:11	188, 233, 504n188
42:15	559	48:20	498n162	50:13	576
42:18	76n75	48:26	321, 542, 562	50:14	509
42:19	559	48:28	541, 586	50:16 (LXX 27:16)	580,
43:5	559, 642n608	48:29	137n300, 566		586, 586n435
43:6	451	48:32–33	503	50:17	642n608
44:6	76n75	48:39	498	50:19	72
44:7	93n134	48:40	233	50:22	497
44:12	559	48:41	508	50:23	600n472
44:14	559	48:42	541, 542	50:27	301n261, 301n263,
44:22	556	48:46	165, 566		488n121
44:28	559	48:47	314n295, 551,	50:31	44, 149
45	535		557n333, 565n373	50:34	348
46:1–26	549	49:1	475	50:38	114
46:7–8	478, 552	49:1–6	562	50:40	564
46:9	114, 569	49:2	565n373	50:42	248
46:10	488n121	49:3	165, 472, 475,	50:43	630n562
46:11	190n472		498n162	50:44	121n225
46:13–26	170n402	49:5	642n608	50:45 (LXX 27:45)	
46:16 (LXX 26:16)	580,	49:6	315n295, 551		83n104, 83n105, 91
	586, 586n435	49:7–22	549	51:1	242n51
46:18	541	49:10	376	51:7	114, 291, 320, 321,
46:19	557	49:12	320, 321		477
46:20	83n105	49:13	575	51:8	498n162
46:21	397	49:16	310	51:8–9	190n472
46:25	168n391	49:17	576	51:13	134, 310
46:26	314n295	49:18	564	51:16	544
46:27	171n409, 615n527	49:19	121n225	51:17	327, 328
46:28	79n89, 81, 511,	49:20 (LXX 30:14)		51:20	112
	511n217, 642		83n104, 90–91	51:25	44, 149, 470n67
47	552	49:22	508	51:27	176, 185n459,
47:1	534	49:23	128n266		567n383
47:2	478, 498, 511n218,	49:26	44n86, 149n338	51:27–33 (LXX 28:27–33)	
	552	49:29	367, 368		315

686

51:29	557n333	4:1	172n412, 510	8:11	604
51:30	178, 243n59	4:2	172n412	9:2	112
51:31	276	4:3	143	9:8	76n75
51:35	300	4:5	122	11:1	234
51:36	64, 378	4:9	79n85	11:2	90, 91
51:37	138, 557n333,	4:11	76n75	11:13	79n89, 511n217
	576n414	4:14	579, 587n436	11:16–17	612n513
51:38	139, 143n316	4:19	233	11:17	611n508
51:43	544	4:21	320	11:19	616
51:52	158	5:22	85n113	11:24	25n10
51:53	310			12:10	60n3
51:54	497	**Ezekiel**		12:11	165
51:58 (LXX 28:58)	33n48,	1:1	25n10, 127n259	12:14	255
	314, 315n295, 316	1:4	205n30	12:15	612n513
51:62	467n56	1:11	158	12:19	300, 588n442
52:9	621	1:23	158	12:27–13:23	25n10
		3	267	13	590
Lamentations		3:10	349n366	13:2	635
1:2	292n242	3:14	75n73, 320	13:3	301n261
1:4	635	3:18–21	91	13:5	488
1:12	488	3:26	267	13:8	641n605
1:14	604	4:13	642	13:11	71n49
1:18	165	4:16	641n603, 641n605	13:13	71n49
1:21	488	5:1	97n152, 248n83	13:16	60n7
2:1	488	5:2	255	13:18	301, 301n261
2:2	264	5:8	526n249, 621, 641n605	13:20	641n605
2:3	76	5:12	255	14:3	468, 478
2:4	76n75	5:13	62n20, 67n28	14:4	468, 478
2:7	635	5:14	576n413	14:7	468, 478
2:11	510	5:15	540	14:9	470n67
2:14	60n3, 62n14, 222n5	5:16	461	14:13	467n56, 470n67
2:15	576n413, 576n415	6:3	641n605	14:15	576n413
2:15–16	576	6:6	250n98	14:17	467n56
2:18	224	6:11	364	14:19	76n75, 467n56
2:19	172n412, 384, 573,	6:14	470n67	14:21	284, 467n56
	621	7:2	446	14:22–23	606n484
2:21–22	488	7:8	76n75	15:5	284
2:22	635	7:12	75	15:15	128n266
3:2	82	7:14	75, 232	16	57
3:10	142n311, 376	7:17	622, 630n561	16:13	491n134
3:22	87	7:19	488, 506, 511	16:15	576n413
3:23	581	7:27	588n442	16:25	172n412
3:25	78, 79n85	8–11	629	16:27	470n67
3:47	582	8:3	67n28	16:29	483, 556
3:49	224	8:5	67n28	16:32	159n363
3:53	309	8:7	139	16:37	641n603
3:63	304n272	8:10	162n380	16:37–38	161

16:37–41	208n44	21:27(32)	581	27:6	72
16:38	67n28, 76n75, 161	21:29(34)	25n10	27:7	247n77
16:42	67n28	22:5	511n216	27:14	249
16:50	606n486	22:7	588	27:15	362n400
17:3	72n56	22:12	305n276, 310	27:36	576
17:4	483, 556	22:14	636	28:1–6	183
17:10	249	22:22	76n75	28:7	255
17:23	398	22:23–31	491	28:25	611n508
17:24	397	22:25–29	592	28:26	504
18:8	305n276	22:27	580	29:8	467n56
18:13	305n276	22:28	25n10	29:10	44, 149, 569n391,
18:17	305n276	22:29	588		575
18:31	616	22:31	600	29:11	467n56
19:2	139, 140n304,	23:5–6	122	30:1–19	170n402
	144n322	23:6	247n77, 248n82	30:2	498n162
19:2–3	142, 143n316	23:10	161	30:3	487
19:5	143n316	23:12	247n77, 248n82	30:4	117
19:5–6	142	23:14–15	122	30:4–5	569
19:8	582	23:22	242n51	30:9	117, 569n391
19:12	249	23:23	248n82	30:11	255
19:13	544	23:24	581	30:14	93
20:5–6	384n467	23:25	67n28, 636	30:14–16	168n391
20:8	76n75	23:29	161	30:15	76n75
20:11	581	23:31–33	320	30:17–18	165
20:13	76n75	23:34	580	30:24–25	543, 570
20:14	159n365	23:40	284	31:3	72n56, 405n515
20:15	384n467	23:44	159n364	31:17–18	543
20:17	79n89, 511n217	24:7	510	32:2	127n260, 143,
20:20–22	76n75	24:11	76n75		378n444
20:21	76n75	24:14	606n484	32:3	262n142
20:23	384n467	24:25	60n2	32:7–8	385
20:25	581	25–32	552	32:10	543
20:28	384n467	25:3	165	32:12	566
20:33–34	76n75	25:4	243n59	32:13	467n56
20:41	611n508	25:7	470n67	33	267
20:42	384n467	25:8–11	563n359	33:11	563
20:43–44	606n484	25:9	131	33:28	576n413
21:3(8)	44, 149	25:13	333, 467n56,	33:30	268n157
21:3–5(8–10)	543		470n67	34	189n469, 625n548
21:7(12)	630n562	25:15–17	552n316	34:2	301
21:9–11(14–16)	233	25:16	470n67, 511n216,	34:6	335
21:10(15)	158		554	34:12	488
21:12(17)	498n162	26–32	53	34:13	611n508
21:15(20)	128n266,	26:7	175	34:20	542
	158n358	26:10	71n51	34:21	362n401
21:16(21)	233	26:17	546	34:23	242n52
21:24(29)	606n484	27:5	72n56, 114	34:28	615n527

35	552	**Daniel**		2:16(18)	461, 501n178
35:3	44, 149, 470n67	1:2	92	2:17(19)	608
35:6	541	1:6	165	2:20(22)	476
35:7	576n413	2:14	266	3:5	465
35:10	244n61	2:21	394	4:3	467, 468
35:12	562	2:44	137	4:5–6	499n168
35:13	541	3:8	207n40	4:6	499
36:5	511, 511n216	4:17	394	4:11	233
36:5–6	67n28	5:11	207n40	4:14	159n365, 482
36:7	384n467	7	152	4:15	541
36:11	467n56	7:7	245n67	4:16	232
36:15	461	7:27	137	4:19	234
36:17	606n484	8–11	25	5:5	120n220, 137n300
36:18	76n75	8:3	362n401	5:6	465
36:19	606n484	8:6–7	362n401	5:7	292n242
36:24	611n508	8:8	85n113	5:13	190n472
36:26	616	8:10	473n79	5:14	141, 142n312, 143
36:34	576n413	8:16	25n10	5:15	465
36:38	635	8:20	362n401	6:3	325
37:21	611n508	8:26–27	25n10	6:4	51
38–39	252	9:4	505n193	6:5	228
38:3	44, 149	9:7	642	6:7	240n43, 292n242,
38:6	249	9:19	279		484
38:12	635	9:23	25n10	7:5	320, 635
38:17	269n160	9:25–26	388n482	7:6	76
38:18	501n178	9:26	80n91	7:10	120n220, 137n300,
38:19	67n28	10:1	25n10		465
38:20	463	10:6	158	7:11	586
39:1	44, 149	10:7–8	25n10	7:11–16	52
39:17	489	10:16	25n10	7:13	268
39:17–19	488n121	11:10	80n91, 250	7:14	83n106
39:18	72	11:22	80n91	7:15	83n105
39:25	67n28	11:24	83n106	8:1	233
39:26	615n527	11:25	85n113	8:6	112
39:27	611n508	11:40	80n91, 250	8:9–10	52
39:29	363n409	12:2	540	9:3	52
40:2	25n10			9:4–6	52
43:3	25n10	**Hosea**		9:10	166
43:11	116	1:2	476	9:12	508
43:15	362n400	1:5	501n177	9:16	398
43:17	234	1:6	105n190	10:5	462, 472
43:20	362n400	1:9	563	10:7	499n168
44:12	384n467, 468, 478	1:11 (2:2)	505n192	10:8	472n74
44:24	229n22	2:3(5)	161, 544	10:11	387n477
45:9	225n7, 227n17	2:6(8)	641n603, 641n605	10:11–14	293
46:18	376	2:8(10)	461	10:12	325, 328, 465
47:14	384n467	2:13(15)	482	10:14	171n410, 172n411

10:15	499n168	2:11	245n68, 505n192	2:10	243n60
11:2	51	2:12	7n21, 14	2:11	242n52
11:7	563	2:12–14	52, 521	3:1	268
11:9	352	2:13	14	3:2	482
11:10	462	2:13–14	50	3:3	270
11:11	52	2:13–17	69n41	3:4	139, 142n313,
12:1(2)	52	2:16	522n239		145n327, 580
12:7(8)	483, 556	2:18	67n28	3:7	517
12:10(11)	499n168	2:19	641n605	3:10	225n7, 227n17, 495
12:11(12)	269n160	2:20	52, 544, 642n608	3:11	637
12:14(15)	494	2:23	636	3:14	362n400, 482
13:1	64, 461	2:25	176, 187	4:1	72, 483
13:3	524	2:31 (3:4)	245n68, 385,	4:2	260, 541
13:7	142n312		505n192	4:4	581
13:14	365n416	2:32 (3:5)	88, 604	4:6–12	600, 601
13:15	504n188	3:1 (4:1)	52, 638	4:8	324
13:16 (14:1)	171n410,	3:2 (4:2)	52	4:9	408
	172n411, 250n98	3:3 (4:3)	154, 165	4:10	364
14:1(2)	7n21, 14	3:7 (4:7)	641n605	4:11	564
14:5–6(6–7)	72	3:9 (4:9)	482	5:4	93n134, 465
		3:14 (4:14)	487	5:5	377n441
Joel		3:15 (4:15)	361n396	5:6	76, 465
1:1	423	3:16 (4:16)	7n21, 14, 52	5:9	234
1:2	511n218	3:19 (4:19)	300	5:11	438n58, 504,
1:4	176, 187, 408	3:21 (4:21)	52		640n598
1:5	498n162	4:15	385	5:13	500n176, 641
1:6	119n217	4:17	105	5:15	521
1:6–7	187			5:16	93n134, 482
1:10	73	**Amos**		5:17	79n90
1:10–12	407	1	552	5:18	301, 506
1:11	498n162	1–2	215	5:18–20	488, 507
1:12	73	1:1	10, 222, 423	5:19	275, 300
1:13	498n162	1:2	7n21, 14, 52, 72, 539	5:20	506
1:14	511n218, 522n239	1:3	93n132, 387n477	6:2	381
1:15	487	1:3–2:16	548	6:8	44n86, 112, 137,
1:16	52	1:5	179n431		149n338, 541, 564
1:16–18	407	1:6	93n132, 96n146	6:11	29
1:18	250n98, 544	1:6–8	552n316	6:14	44n86, 149n338,
1:19–20	408	1:9	93n132		242, 641n605
2:1	348, 397, 487,	1:11	68n40, 93n132	7:1	176
	511n218	1:12	333, 599	7:2	121
2:1–11	521	1:13	93n132, 172n411	7:3	62n20
2:2	434, 461, 506	1:13–15	562	7:5	121
2:5	158	1:14	71n48	7:8	79n90, 105n190, 563
2:6	117, 136	1:15	165, 475	7:13	105n190
2:7	305n275	2:4	93n132	7:17	93n134, 161n375, 555
2:10	348, 361n396, 385	2:6	93n132, 154	8:2	79n90, 105n190, 563
				8:3	158, 498

8:4   519
8:7   112, 138, 541
8:8   348
8:9   501n177, 501n178
8:10   483
8:14   474n84, 474n85
9:1   575
9:3   300
9:4   165
9:7   554
9:8   463n38, 466
9:11–15   52
9:12   7n21, 14, 243n60, 244n61
9:13   74
9:14   398, 504

Obadiah

1   7n21, 14, 93n132, 423, 487n113
3–4   310
5   499n168
10   300
11   165
14   154
15   487
17   52, 243n60
19   7n21, 243n60
20   243n60

Jonah

1:1   423
1:3   487n117
1:4   83n106
1:10   487n117
2:3(4)   380
2:4(5)   329n323
2:9(10)   105
3:3   141
3:7–8   467n56
3:9   50, 69n41
3:9–4:4   50
3:9–10   50
4:1–4   69n41
4:2   7n21, 7n22, 50
4:7   64
4:8   249n93

Micah

1:1   10, 11, 26n13, 62n15, 222, 423, 457n24, 457n25
1:2   329, 487n113, 543, 599
1:4–5   52
1:5   244n60
1:8–16   498n160
1:9   190n472
1:10   349n366
1:11   97n153
1:14   26n13
1:16   96, 233
2:1   362n398, 590
2:3   83n104, 93n134
2:4   299
2:12   467, 611n508
2:13   79n90
3   121
3:4   363n409, 500n176, 641
3:5   300, 590
3:10   314, 315n300, 316
3:11   590
4–5   638n584
4:3   254
4:4   173, 564n362, 615n527
4:6   611n508, 642
4:6–7   638
4:7   621, 626n549
4:13   387n477
5:1 (4:14)   397
5:2–5(1–4)   626n549
5:2(1)   256n114
5:5(4)   189n469
5:8(7)   142n313
5:10–14(9–13)   465
5:10(9)   501n178
5:12(11)   160
6:8   526, 527n253
6:10   389n483, 542
6:12   605
6:14–15   433n39
6:15   504
6:16   576n414
7:1   166, 172
7:1–2   410

7:1–7   404
7:2   82n100, 508
7:4   404
7:6   404
7:7   404, 410
7:9   52, 228, 526n249
7:12–13   51n110
7:14   72
7:15   355
7:17   348
7:18   69n41, 599
7:18–19   7n21, 7n22

Nahum

1   15
1:1   7n21, 7n22, 23, 28, 34, 35, 42, 55, 59–63, 65, 189, 195, 222, 272, 423n2
1:1–10   67
1:1–11   46
1:2   36, 51n110, 55, 67–69, 70n43, 70n46, 73, 86
1:2–3   7n21, 7n22
1:2–8   29, 33, 34, 41, 45, 50, 57n128, 63, 95
1:2–10   33, 35, 63–89
1:3   28, 37, 50, 52, 65, 69–71, 73, 87, 345
1:3–6   39, 71
1:4   36, 37n53, 37n54, 38n60, 52, 71–74, 106n192, 380
1:4–5   51n110, 68
1:4–6   74
1:4b   66
1:5   37n54, 38n60, 52, 65, 74–75, 82n96, 106n192, 128n265, 157, 224, 345, 384
1:5–6   77n78
1:6   37, 39, 55, 74, 75–77
1:6b   37n54
1:7   37, 39, 51, 52, 55, 66, 77–79, 80–81, 82n97, 87, 88, 191

1:7–8   28
1:8   26, 29, 37n54, 55n118,
        59, 66, 78, 79–81,
        82n97, 84, 106n192,
        127, 131, 188, 191, 478
1:8–2:2 (1:8–2:3)   37n58
1:8–9   97, 106n192,
               511n217
1:9   29, 37, 55, 66, 83–84,
        87, 94, 97, 192
1:9–10   28, 29, 33, 34, 50,
           66, 95
1:10   37, 84–86, 148, 172
1:11   26, 29, 33, 34, 35, 37,
         84n110, 89–91, 95,
         97n151, 101, 106n192,
         157, 189, 190, 192
1:11–12   105
1:12   29, 30n27, 36, 37, 38,
         39, 40, 41, 51, 73, 89,
         94, 95–98, 101, 103,
         105, 106n192, 108,
         109, 152, 183, 187, 188
1:12–13   29, 34, 89n125, 93,
            102, 190
1:12–14   33, 34, 35, 36n52,
            41, 43, 91–102, 149,
            152
1:13   37n56, 39, 94, 95, 189
1:13–14   97n151, 120
1:14   26, 29, 31n37, 34,
         38, 39, 92, 93,
         94, 99–101, 105,
         106n192, 110, 148,
         149, 150, 162n380,
         189, 190, 191, 327
1:14–15 (1:15–2:1)   55
1:14–2:1 (1:14–2:2)   37n58
1:15 (2:1)   29, 31,
         33, 34, 35, 36, 37,
         38, 39, 51, 52, 53,
         84n110, 93n132, 94,
         102–11, 117, 148, 149,
         150n345, 151, 155,
         177, 188, 190, 191,
         192, 216, 276n184
1:15–2:13 (2:1–14)   148

2   45
2–3   15
2:1–2(2–3)   40, 119n216
2:1–10(2–11)   30, 31, 34, 35,
         102, 111–38, 151
2:1–13(2–14)   34
2:1(2)   26, 30, 37n54, 39,
           63, 68, 102, 108, 113,
           117, 118, 119, 121, 124,
           181, 182
2:2(3)   30, 36, 37n54,
           52, 73, 108, 116,
           119–21, 149
2:2b(3b)   118n214
2:3(4)   30, 39, 93n132,
           99n163, 114, 116, 117,
           121–24, 125, 137, 154
2:4–6(5–7)   125
2:4(5)   37, 99n163,
           124–26
2:4a(5a)   30n33
2:4b(5b)   30n33
2:5–6(6–7)   37
2:5(6)   30, 37n54, 93n132,
           116, 118, 126–27, 131,
           132, 188, 189, 353,
           366
2:6(7)   30n33, 118, 127–29,
           134, 137, 191
2:7–8(8–9)   118
2:7(8)   30, 37n54, 39,
           48n101, 131–33, 138
2:8–9(9–10)   38
2:8(9)   26, 30, 37,
           38n59, 39, 73, 119,
           128, 133–35, 137, 187,
           189, 191
2:9(10)   30, 37n53, 38n60,
            73, 118, 132, 135, 137,
            165
2:10(11)   30–31, 37,
             38n60, 39, 117,
             135–36, 138
2:11–12(12–13)   31, 34, 35,
             102, 117, 138–47,
             151, 190
2:11–13(12–14)   31, 39

2:11(12)   37, 38, 140–41,
             143, 147, 615n527
2:12(13)   37n53, 135, 140,
             143, 145, 147
2:13(14)   31, 32, 34, 35,
             37n54, 38, 41, 43,
             44, 44n86, 92, 94,
             95n140, 102, 107,
             144n322, 148–52,
             157, 171n407,
             177n422, 467, 564
3   45
3:1   27, 32, 34, 36, 38n60,
        39, 156–57, 163, 299,
        538, 580, 586
3:1–5   39
3:1–7   31, 32, 34, 35, 45,
          152–55
3:1a   544
3:2   37, 157–58
3:2–3   37, 155, 156
3:2–6   32
3:3   31, 37n54, 38,
        126n257, 154, 158,
        165
3:4   32, 34, 37, 155, 156,
        157, 158–60, 163
3:5   32, 44, 57n126, 94,
        95n140, 132, 149,
        160–61, 177n422,
        564
3:5–6   56, 156, 162, 163
3:5–7   32, 41, 43, 208n44
3:6   161, 162, 579
3:6–9   39
3:7   26, 32, 37, 38, 44,
        95n140, 113, 156, 161,
        162n381, 186, 189
3:7aγ   544
3:8   19, 32, 37, 39, 40,
        48n101, 133,
        149n340, 166, 167–
        69, 186, 378n444
3:8–10   54n116
3:8–11   570
3:8–12   31, 34, 35, 163–74,
           177

3:8–13	549
3:8–19	34, 178n425
3:9	38, 165, 166, 170–71, 368
3:9–12	32
3:10	37n53, 37n54, 38n60, 166, 171–72
3:10–11	173
3:10–12	39
3:11	32, 37n53, 166, 172
3:12	38n60, 39, 166, 172–73
3:13	32, 73, 175, 177, 178–81, 186
3:13–17	31,33,34,35,174–87
3:13–19	31
3:14	31, 37n53, 38, 73, 166, 172, 177, 181–82, 186
3:15	31n37, 37n54, 40, 73, 148, 150n345, 178, 182–83, 186
3:15–16	37n53, 182
3:15–17	37n58, 177
3:15a	177
3:16	33n46, 176, 178, 179, 183–84, 556
3:16–17	96
3:16–18	119
3:17	32, 33, 37, 39, 178, 184–86
3:18	33, 38, 48n102, 96, 100n167, 114, 189–90, 233
3:18–19	31, 33, 34, 35
3:19	37, 38n60, 138n302, 147, 150, 151, 186, 190–91, 343, 576, 578
3:19a	17n60

Habakkuk

1	15, 221–22, 278, 298, 327, 331, 340, 342, 343, 376, 415
1–2	217, 222, 329, 390
1:1	7n21, 7n22, 60n3, 62n14, 195, 197,

	199, 200, 207, 212, 221–23, 331, 334, 423, 452
1:1–17	201
1:1–2:5	15
1:1–2:20	199
1:2	196, 199n17, 226–27, 236n31, 256, 280, 345, 387
1:2–3	16, 225
1:2–4	196, 197, 199, 200, 202, 223–30, 235, 236, 244, 341
1:2–17	199, 236
1:3	64, 223, 226, 227, 236, 237n31, 239, 240n41, 256, 367, 370
1:4	208, 216, 225, 227–29, 236n31, 246, 263, 276, 294, 370
1:4a	226
1:4b	209, 226
1:5	196, 197, 202, 213, 236, 238, 239, 242n53, 345, 346, 370, 387, 518
1:5–6	237, 286
1:5–11	195, 196, 197, 199, 200, 207, 209, 210, 211, 213, 216, 221, 222, 225, 226, 230–53, 259, 270, 277, 281, 286, 302, 330, 345, 356, 370, 371, 383, 391, 395, 408
1:6	196, 202, 207, 231, 237, 239n39, 241–44, 246, 247, 250, 251, 252, 641n603
1:6–11	242
1:6–12	218
1:6b–11	255
1:7	196, 229, 236n31, 238, 244–46, 346, 579
1:7–11	196, 237
1:7b	236
1:8	188, 202, 218, 246–49,

	391, 407, 580, 589, 590
1:8–9	359
1:9	16, 116, 196, 227n18, 236n31, 239n39, 248, 249, 250n95, 256, 303n271
1:10	231, 242n50, 250
1:10–11	250n96
1:11	196, 217, 239, 249, 250–51, 262n141, 351, 358, 360
1:11–12	353
1:12	197, 237, 252, 256–59, 269n164, 346, 358, 395
1:12–17	197, 199, 200, 225, 226, 235, 236, 253–65, 341
1:12a	17
1:13	197, 236, 237n31, 239, 240, 256, 259–60, 287, 294, 395, 631
1:13–14	209
1:13–17	252
1:13b	209
1:14	395
1:14–15	260–62
1:15	237n31, 303n271, 391
1:15–17	197, 237, 245n66, 395
1:16	116, 196, 251, 262–63, 264, 330
1:16b	324
1:17	244n63, 263, 280, 387
2	14, 15, 208–9, 219, 222, 230, 285, 327, 331, 340, 342, 359, 415
2:1	197n9, 199, 200, 216n62, 217, 221, 239, 255, 266–71, 273, 274n172, 278, 281, 334, 404, 406, 410
2:1–2	197, 212, 267, 273, 274
2:1–3	218
2:1–4	201

2:1–20   199
2:2   197, 198, 212, 218, 267,
           274–78
2:2–3   25, 199, 200, 272–84
2:2–4   281
2:2–5   273
2:2–20   199
2:2aα   197n6
2:3   198, 278–81, 282, 283,
     284, 294, 359, 635
2:3–4   197, 283
2:4   114, 198n12, 201, 216,
   217, 238n37, 245n64,
   258, 273, 277, 280,
   283, 285, 287–90,
   295, 296, 297, 345,
        400, 413
2:4–5   198, 199, 200,
   203, 204, 212, 214,
   222, 245, 277, 278,
   284–98, 304, 307,
   308, 320, 324, 332,
        345, 409
2:4–20   277n189, 278
2:4a   209, 391
2:5   198, 200, 201, 240,
    244, 245, 273,
   290–93, 387, 407
2:5–6   252n104
2:5–7   301
2:5–8   201
2:5–20   400
2:6   176, 197–98, 202, 211,
   232, 303–5, 306, 316,
   326, 356, 538, 580,
          586
2:6–7   315n300
2:6–8   200, 299–308
2:6–19   302
2:6–20   15, 153, 199, 222,
   273, 278, 332, 341
2:6a   198n11, 199, 287
2:6b   302, 324
2:6b–8 198, 199, 244, 287,
       300, 316
2:6b–20   198
2:6bβ   197n6

2:7   301, 305–6, 504
2:7–8   202n25
2:8   16, 65, 227n18, 303,
   304, 306, 319, 320,
         387
2:8–10   301, 302
2:8a   316, 324
2:8b   316
2:9   200, 202, 302, 310,
   311, 315n300, 316,
   324, 410, 586
2:9–10   389n483
2:9–11 198, 199, 200, 201,
   300, 308–13, 316
2:10 202, 231, 304, 310–11,
      316, 582
2:11   311–12
2:11–12   245n65
2:11–13   301
2:12 200, 302, 314, 315,
     316, 586
2:12–14   198, 199, 200,
   201, 301, 313–18
2:13   199, 276, 301, 302,
   314, 315, 316–17,
      564n362
2:14   218, 302, 313, 314,
  315, 317, 318, 319, 322,
        348
2:14–17   301
2:15 198n13, 198n15, 200,
   245n64, 245n65,
   302, 320–21, 586
2:15–17 198, 199, 200, 201,
   291, 301, 318–25
2:16   293n246, 321–22
2:17 16, 65, 227n18, 304,
  306, 316, 320, 322–23
2:18 100n170, 198, 199,
  200, 201, 202, 320,
   326, 327–28
2:18–19   262n140, 301,
   325, 326, 328
2:18–20 199, 200, 204,
   301, 313, 325–31
2:19 198, 200, 301, 326,
     328, 586

2:19–20   198, 201
2:19a   302
2:20   7n21, 200, 218,
  313, 314, 326, 327,
  328–30, 341, 487
3   14, 15, 205–6, 210, 212,
  216, 217, 219, 221,
  222, 223, 249n94,
  270, 277, 278, 327,
  329, 331, 332, 343,
         415
3:1   195, 196, 198, 199,
  200, 210, 212, 222,
  277, 331–43, 407
3:1–2   69n41
3:1–7   201
3:1–19   199
3:2   198, 199, 200,
  217, 297, 341, 342,
  343–51, 354, 357,
  358, 370, 371, 382,
  390, 392, 393, 396,
  401, 402, 403, 404,
  405, 406n520, 417
3:2–15   199n17
3:2–19a   199
3:2b   218
3:3   201n20, 204, 235,
  280, 333, 334, 351,
  356, 358–61, 363,
  369, 377, 388, 400,
    404, 410, 411
3:3–6   369, 377
3:3–7 198, 199, 200, 332,
  343, 351–71, 376–77,
  378, 400, 401, 402,
   403, 415n542
3:3–15 211, 333, 334, 342,
  354, 355, 365n418,
    400, 405
3:3a   205n30
3:4   359, 363n404, 364
3:4–5   369
3:5   333, 358n384, 364–66
3:6 74n66, 114, 202, 239,
  366–67, 372, 580
3:6–7   369

3:7 239, 340, 344, 345,
     348, 355, 356, 357,
     358, 367–68, 369,
     370, 377, 390, 396,
     404, 405
3:8 198, 200, 333, 349,
     355, 356, 357, 359,
     375, 377, 378–82,
     384, 386, 387, 388,
     392, 398, 401, 402
3:8–11 402n503
3:8–13 201
3:8–15 152, 199, 200, 277,
     346, 356, 357, 358,
     371–96, 400, 401,
     402, 403
3:9 201n20, 202,
     340n353, 360,
     375, 377, 378, 379,
     382–84, 386
3:10 113, 239, 360,
     377n439, 379, 384
3:11 154, 158, 340n353,
     358, 373, 384–86,
     402
3:12 386–87, 392
3:12–13 388
3:12–15 402n503
3:13 201, 257, 356, 375,
     377, 382, 387–90,
     391, 399
3:13–14 357
3:14 119n218, 200, 201,
     356, 373, 375, 383,
     390–92, 393, 396,
     406, 407, 409
3:14–15 201, 356
3:14–19 201
3:15 198, 357n384, 384,
     388, 390, 392, 400,
     402, 403n506, 411
3:16 198, 219n76, 345,
     346, 348, 357, 358,
     398, 399, 400, 402,
     403, 404–7
3:16–17 356, 358, 401,

402, 403, 404, 407,
     412
3:16–19 199n17, 341, 357,
     358, 402n503
3:16–19a 199, 200, 356,
     396–413
3:16a 399n493, 412
3:16b 401n495, 412
3:17 153, 210, 397, 400,
     401, 402, 403n508,
     404, 407–9, 412
3:17–18 210, 403, 404, 418
3:17–19 407
3:18 397, 399n493, 401,
     403, 404, 406, 407,
     409–10, 412, 413
3:18–19 356, 357, 358,
     403n507, 407, 409,
     412
3:18–19a 401, 402, 403,
     404
3:19 196, 200, 327, 334,
     337
3:19a 401, 410–11
3:19b 199, 200, 338, 413–19

Zephaniah

1:1 423, 425, 429, 431,
     447, 451–60, 469,
     556, 590, 624
1:2 427, 431, 463, 464,
     465, 466–67, 586,
     600, 635
1:2–3 426, 430n27, 431,
     459, 463, 464, 469,
     477, 486, 552
1:2–6 425, 430, 431,
     460–80, 484
1:2–7 428
1:2–18 425, 426, 428, 429,
     430, 459, 462, 464,
     582, 585, 615
1:2–2:3 563, 586
1:2–2:15 426
1:2–3:5 585, 596
1:2–3:7 596
1:2–3:8 606

1:2–3:13 434
1:3 427, 431, 432, 433,
     446, 461, 463,
     464n40, 465, 469,
     510, 511n216
1:3–4 431
1:3–6 465
1:4 426, 429, 431, 432n33,
     469–73, 476, 489,
     630
1:4–5 432, 435n45, 463
1:4–6 426, 465, 608, 629
1:5 433, 434, 468, 471,
     473–76, 494, 568
1:5b–6 465
1:6 434, 465, 476–77,
     524, 527, 588
1:6–8 465
1:7 7n21, 329, 330n326,
     425, 426, 431, 462,
     463, 465, 466, 482,
     485, 486, 487–90,
     495n150, 498, 499,
     505, 520, 555, 611,
     635, 641
1:7–10 485, 498, 499, 512
1:7–13 430
1:7–18 431, 480–517
1:7a 485
1:7b 485
1:8 424, 427, 469, 485,
     486, 490–93, 494,
     499, 500, 503, 560
1:8–9 429, 431, 432, 456,
     485, 486n110,
     495n150, 498, 501,
     540, 594, 595
1:8–11 183
1:8–13 425
1:8–18 425
1:8–2:11 428
1:8aβb 463
1:9 463, 470, 475,
     493–95, 503, 560
1:9–10 490
1:10 262, 424, 426,
     427, 431, 469, 485,

	486, 495–97, 498,		519, 521, 522–24,	2:5–3:5	596
	501n177, 503n184,		527, 584, 602, 618,	2:5–3:8	548
	520, 545		620	2:6	431, 540, 556–58,
1:10–11	456, 497	2:1–2	430		561n347, 571
1:11	431, 485, 486,	2:1–3	426, 428, 430, 462,	2:6–7	556
	497–500, 520, 539,		463, 466, 485, 520,	2:6–20	546
	552, 555		521, 528n256, 613,	2:7	429, 430, 431, 463,
1:11–18	425, 485, 498, 512		620, 628		548, 558–61, 583,
1:11a	485	2:1–4	426, 430, 431, 499,		595, 614, 615, 638,
1:11b	485		517–37, 548, 552,		642, 644
1:12	424, 426, 429, 431,		583, 584, 586, 592	2:8	430, 431, 434, 521,
	432, 469, 477, 485,	2:1–5	183		541, 542, 561–63,
	486, 488n119, 490,	2:1–7	428, 429		573, 578, 609, 615,
	500–503, 512, 523,	2:1–3:7	584		628n556
	528, 540, 560, 593,	2:1–3:8	582, 624n543	2:8–9	428, 445, 542, 584
	595, 613, 615, 630,	2:1–3:13	584	2:8–11	428, 546, 547
	638, 641	2:1–3:20	624n543	2:8–15	428
1:12–13	456, 485	2:2	431, 524, 586,	2:8–18	429
1:12b	588		599n468	2:9	44n86, 149n338,
1:13	431, 432, 433, 438n58,	2:2–3	431		427, 429, 431, 463,
	485, 486, 503–5, 571	2:3	7, 69n41, 430, 431,		521, 544, 548, 553,
1:13a	463		465, 470, 484, 519,		563–66, 571, 593,
1:13b	434		523, 524–28, 552,		605, 614
1:14	431, 464, 485,		566, 577, 584, 586,	2:9–10	445, 543, 558
	486, 487n118, 490,		602, 605n481, 614,	2:9b–11	463
	503n184, 505, 507,		617	2:10	427n15, 445, 546,
	520, 545, 630, 631	2:4	426, 428, 430, 431,		547, 563, 566, 609,
1:14–15	446		485, 520, 521, 522,		613, 615, 628n556
1:14–16	463		528–34, 539, 541,	2:10–11	427, 546, 547, 548,
1:14–18	425, 426, 430,		546, 552, 556, 558,		567, 568, 584
	448, 485, 514		571	2:11	245n68, 428, 431n31,
1:15	485, 486, 505–7, 509,	2:4–6	463, 547n299		432, 447, 455, 484,
	524	2:4–15	430, 459, 521n235		543, 546, 547, 553,
1:15–16	485, 506, 513	2:5	299, 301, 426,		566–68, 571, 577,
1:16	485, 507–8, 595, 597		428n21, 431n31, 484,		606, 608, 609, 613,
1:17	427, 431, 434n41,		521, 539, 540, 552,		625
	485n107, 508–10,		554–56, 571, 585,	2:11–12	455n19, 543, 602
	511, 516		586, 595, 597	2:12	3n5, 428n20, 442,
1:17–18	430n29, 484, 485	2:5–6	432, 558n337, 583		453, 455, 547, 549,
1:17aαb	463	2:5–7	3n5, 426, 428, 429,		568–70, 584, 609,
1:17aβb	463		431, 522, 546, 547,		610
1:18	67n28, 79n89, 427,		552	2:12–14	547n299
	428, 431, 434, 463,	2:5–8	568	2:12–15	546, 547, 548,
	485, 486, 498, 509,	2:5–15	426, 430, 431,		567, 568
	511–12, 523, 524, 586,		537–79, 583, 585,	2:13	431, 545, 546, 547,
	618, 636		596, 605		553, 570–71, 575
1:18–2:7	427, 428n21	2:5–18	430	2:13–14	575
2:1	431, 466, 467, 485,	2:5bβ	547n299		

2:13–15	463, 543, 547, 557, 570, 575, 584	3:7	429, 431, 434, 447, 540, 560, 580, 594, 595, 596, 597, 598, 602, 603, 606	3:14–15	623, 624, 625, 626, 627, 629, 633
2:13–3:5	428			3:14–17	431, 448, 626, 628n554, 637, 645
2:14	429, 431, 571–76, 595	3:7–15	447	3:14–18	429
2:14–15	597	3:8	67n28, 426, 427, 430n27, 431, 446, 447, 466n52, 484, 511, 582, 583, 586, 595–96, 598–600, 601, 602, 603, 606, 614, 624, 635	3:14–20	427, 428, 430, 446, 607, 624, 625n545
2:15	548, 576–77, 593, 595, 607n486, 613, 623–24			3:15	431, 445, 448, 624, 626, 628–29, 630, 631, 634, 641
3:1	154, 299, 426, 463, 546, 548, 580, 586–88			3:16	621, 626, 629–30, 632
3:1–4	582	3:8–9	614	3:16–17	623, 625–26, 627, 629, 637
3:1–5	426, 429, 431, 579–93, 596, 601, 619, 620	3:8–13	584	3:16–20	582, 626
		3:8–15	582	3:17	431, 434, 448, 505, 618, 626, 629, 630–31, 637, 639
3:1–7	430, 582, 583, 584, 585, 595	3:8–20	430		
3:1–8	456, 459	3:9	431, 446, 447, 495, 593, 604, 606, 607–9, 610, 613, 614, 615, 616, 634, 641, 642, 644	3:18	431, 466n50, 466n52, 637, 638–41, 644, 645
3:1–13	430, 582, 587			3:18–19	627, 637
3:1–20	428, 429			3:18–20	427, 429, 431, 445, 626, 627, 634–46
3:2	434, 459, 580, 584, 588, 595, 613, 629	3:9–10	447, 600, 607, 608, 609, 611n511, 613		
3:2–3	431			3:19	434, 626n549, 638, 641–43, 644, 645
3:2a	584, 585	3:9–13	427, 429, 431, 603–20		
3:3	233, 431, 447, 580, 583, 588, 589–90, 599, 629, 642	3:9–17	447	3:19–20	431, 484, 500n176, 616, 637, 638, 641
		3:9–20	430, 463, 582, 601, 606		
3:3–4	463, 588, 591, 613, 615, 629	3:10	127n260, 372, 378, 432, 455, 543, 609–13, 644	3:20	427, 447, 612, 637, 638, 641, 643–44, 645
3:3–5	584				
3:4	240n43, 240n44, 590	3:11	446, 576, 603, 606, 607, 613, 614, 630		
3:5	431, 434, 463, 582–83, 585–86, 590–91, 602, 615, 629	3:11–12	431, 616, 629	**Haggai**	
		3:11–13	445, 607, 611n511, 616	1:1	269n160, 423
3:5–13	596			1:2	638
3:6	507, 539, 571, 576n413, 583, 584, 595, 597	3:12	429, 431, 525, 535, 561, 607, 614, 616, 617, 618, 641	1:4	638
				1:5	93n134
3:6–7	69n41, 430n28, 431, 548, 584, 585, 588, 592, 595, 596, 597, 601, 605, 606, 607, 628	3:12–13	561, 620	1:9	44n86, 149n338, 644n619
		3:13	431, 446, 447n93, 495, 561, 583, 607, 608, 614–15, 617, 623, 631, 642	1:11	467n56
				1:12	487n116
				1:13	644n619
3:6–8	426, 429, 431, 583, 593–603, 605	3:14	427, 624, 627–28, 629, 630, 633	2:4	44n86, 149n338, 644n619
3:6–13	428, 583				

2:8–9	44n86, 149n338, 644n619	7:14	597n458	1:7	329, 587n436
		8:2	67n28	1:12	587n436
2:14	644n619	8:6	44n86, 149n338	1:14	245n68, 505n193, 568, 625
2:17	644n619	8:10	467n56		
2:19	85n113, 408, 409n529	8:11	44n86, 149n338	2:8	461, 468
		8:19	349n366	2:10	292n242
2:23	44n86, 149n338, 644n619	9:1	7n22, 60n3	2:14	292n242, 329
		9:4	244n60	2:15	292n242
		9:5–6	551	2:16	231, 564n365
Zechariah		9:5–8	552n316	2:17	329
1:1	423	9:6	138n300	3:2	76
1:2	152	9:9	633	3:5	160, 599
1:3	44n86, 149n338	9:9–10	625, 632	3:7	329
1:6	99n164, 330n326	9:12	231	3:8	329
1:9	268n154	9:14	71n49, 154, 158, 487n113	3:13	329
1:11	179n431			3:14	487
1:12	330	10:3	189n469	3:16	84n106
1:13	268n154	10:7	255	3:22	99n164, 229n22
1:14	67n28, 268n154	10:8	611n508	3:24	82n100
1:15	152, 516	10:10	611n508	4:2 (3:20)	188, 233
1:16	44n86, 149n338	10:11	137n300, 392	4:5 (3:23)	245n68, 505n192
1:18–19 (2:1–2)	362n400	11:1	72n56		
1:19 (2:2)	268n154	11:2	72, 498n162	4:5–6 (3:23–24)	488
1:21 (2:4)	233, 330n326, 362n400	11:3	121n225, 497		
		11:5	329	**INTERTESTAMENTAL LITERATURE**	
2:3(7)	268n154	11:7	519		
2:4(8)	276, 467n56	11:11	519		
2:6–7(10–11)	301n262, 586n433	11:16	115, 242n52	**Baruch**	
		12:1	7n22, 60n3, 539	1:1	452, 453n7
2:6(10)	301n261	12:2	114		
2:7(11)	301n261	12:4	340n354	**Bel and the Dragon**	
2:10–11(14–15)	632	13:2	44n86, 149n338, 501n178	1:1	266, 414
2:10(14)	625				
2:12(16)	565	13:7	44n86, 149n338, 396	**2 Esdras**	
2:13(17)	329, 330n326, 487	14:2	165, 504n188	7:109	342n357
		14:4	378n443		
3:9–10	44n86, 149n338	14:9	625, 629n558	**4 Esdras**	
4:1	268n154	14:12	139	1:40	222n3
4:4	268n154	14:16–17	625	7:46	509
4:5	268n154	14:21	483	7:68	509
4:6	452				
5:4	44n86, 149n338	**Malachi**		**1 Maccabees**	
5:5	268n154	1:1	7n22, 60n3, 423, 539	3:24	539
5:10	268n154	1:2	329	14:25–49	274
6:4	268n154	1:4	494n147		
6:10	451	1:5	329	**2 Maccabees**	
7:7	269n160	1:6	329	15:14	223n6

Odes

1:14	539

Sirach

3:10	176
3:17–29	527
9:2	411n535
10:26–27	176
10:31	176
11:11	276n184
14:12	279
36:35(26)	295
39:24	288n226, 288n228
43:16	71n48
43:17	71n49
43:18	364n413
43:20	71n49
46:18	539
47:7	539
47:17	299, 303, 304
48:2–3	342n357
48:12	300
48:18	546
48:20–25	9
49:6–7	9
49:8	9
49:10	8
49:10–12	9
49:11–12	9
50:8	72n57
50:26	539

Tobit

1:6	96n150
14:3–4	10

NEW TESTAMENT

Matthew

1:21	88
3:2	629n558
4:17	629n558
5:3	446, 619
5:5	446, 619
5:6	619
5:16	646
5:45	592

6:33	536
10:15	514
10:16–39	137
11:3	283
11:22	514
11:24	514
12:32	514
13:41	446
19:23–24	618
21:5	633
22:21	87
23:27	601
24	54
25:31–46	513
26:31	396
26:52	174
27:45	517
28:18	53

Mark

10:23	446, 515
10:25	515
10:42–45	53
15:33	517

Luke

1:28–31	448
1:31	448
1:46–55	618
1:51–53	643
1:52	53
2:21	448
6:20	619
6:21	619
6:25	619
7:19–20	283
10:22	350
12:13–21	312
12:15	312
12:17–19	312
12:21	312
12:33	312
12:48	592
12:54	360n390
13:4	350
14:12–14	593
18:26	516
18:43	646

19:40	313
21:26	513
23:44	517

John

3:36	54n114
4:21	609
9:2–3	350
12	633n573
14:26	350
16:12–13	350
19:11	570

Acts

2:21	88
2:24	54
2:32	53
3:14	296
3:18	53
4:12	88
4:28	53
7:52	296
11:23	294
13:23	88
13:41	231, 240, 241
17:30–31	537, 592
19:17	646
22:14	296

Romans

1:17	294, 295, 296
1:18	54n114
1:18–23	592
1:18–25	298
1:20	88
2:4	537
2:5	517
2:10	646
2:12	592
2:17	297
2:23	297
2:29	634
3:23	478
4:2	297
5:8	87
5:12	509
5:12–21	101

5:18–19	296	2:13	646	11:12	184n456
6	101	2:14	512	12:2	296n254
6:6	645	6:5–8	318		
6:8	478	6:15	53	**James**	
6:16	101			1:9–11	446
8:3	297	**Philippians**		2:5–6	446
8:20	318	1:6	514	4:13–17	512
8:31–39	137	1:10	514	5:1–6	446
9:6	633	1:11	646	5:10	342
10:12	110	2:9–10	54	5:14–15	517
10:13	88	2:10	54, 187, 331		
10:15	53, 110	2:13	271	**1 Peter**	
11:21	87n122	3:13–14	275	1:6	634
13:1	394	4:4–6	634	1:7	634, 646
13:1–7	152, 593			1:8	634
14:11	54, 187, 331	**Colossians**		2:9	101
14:23	294	1:13	101	2:12	646
15:4	186n463	2:13–15	395	2:14	394
16:20	54n113	2:15	53, 88, 645	2:15	646
16:26	271			2:24	645
		1 Thessalonians		3:16	646
1 Corinthians		3:13	514	3:18	296
1:8	446, 514	4:16	513	3:22	53
2:10	350	5:2	446, 514	4:7	634
5:5	446, 514	5:23	514	5:6	536
9:24–27	275				
15:54	264n145	**2 Thessalonians**		**2 Peter**	
15:55	192	2:2	514	2:9	514
15:58	318			3:7	513
		1 Timothy		3:9	514
2 Corinthians		2:2	593	3:10	446, 514
1:14	514	6:16	364		
5:4	264n145	6:17	512, 618	**1 John**	
6:10	412			1:21	296
6:15	90	**Hebrews**		2:14	645
12:9	412	2:3–4	296n255	4:16–21	312
		5:7	223	4:17	514
Galatians		7:12	297, 298		
2:10	593	9:27	514	**Revelation**	
2:20	294	10:32–34	298	1:4	283
3:3	294	10:35	298	1:8	283
4:4	350n367, 512	10:36	298	1:16	253
6:7	293	10:37	298	2:16	253
		10:37–38	283	4:8	283
Ephesians		10:38	298n259	6:17	446
1:12	646	10:39	298	11:5	253

11:15	629n558
11:17	629n558
12:11	253
13	152
14:5	446, 447n93
14:8	291n237, 321
14:10	291n237
14:19	291n237
15:6	446
16:1	446
17–18	53
17:2	321
18:3	291n237, 321
19:6	629n558
19:15	253, 291n237

19:21	253
20:8	253
20:9	252
20:11–15	513
21–22	89
21:1	72
21:24–26	253

OTHER ANCIENT TEXTS

Herodotus, *Histories*

2.157	530
4.62	262n140

Josephus, *Jewish Antiquities*

9.236–38	11
9.239	11n33
9.239–42	10
9.242	11n33
10.51	438
10.58	436
10.181–82	550

Josephus, *Jewish War*

3.336	501n179
6.370–72	501n179
7.35	501n179

Index of Hebrew Words

'ădāmâ, 463
'ādām, 508
'ădōn, 494
'iyyîm, 567
'ākēn, 594
'ĕlôah, 358
'ĕmûnâ, 289
'ărî, 142, 143, 144
'arbê, 175, 176
'āryê, 142, 143, 144
'aššûr, 571

bzz, 565
bl', 263–64
bəliyya'al, 29, 90, 105
ba'al, 461
bāṣûr, 507
bqš, 526–27

gzz, 96
gam, 173
g'r, 71
gûr, 142, 143

hôy, 153, 299, 301, 586
hălîkôt, 353, 366
hinnî, 641

wəkēn, 91

zebaḥ, 489
zāmîr, 572
zônâ, 158–59

ḥebel, 554–55
ḥăzôn, 24–25, 60n7, 61, 278
ḥkh, 598
ḥēmā', 75–76
ḥāmās, 16
ḥōr, 139
ḥšb, 83–84

yll, 498
yeleq, 175, 176
yônâ, 586, 587
yrš, 243–44
yēša', 387
yāšrâ, 287–88

kî, 520, 541, 607–8
kəmārîm, 472
kəpîr, 142–43
kərōt, 539–40

lābî', 139, 143–44
lamnaṣṣēaḥ, 414, 415–16
l'd, 599

məbaśśēr, 151
mizmôr, 336, 337
mōṭēhû, 92, 98–99
miktām, 336, 337
mal'āk, 151
məlîṣâ, 303
mə'ôn, 138
mə'ônâ, 138, 145
mar, 232
merḥāb, 232

māšāl, 303
mišmeret, 266
maśkîl, 336, 337
maśśā', 23–24, 60–61, 195

nidmâ, 499–500
nhg, 133
nəwōt, 539–40
nṭr, 68

sōkēk, 114–15
sēper, 24, 61
str, 528

'abṭîṭ, 305
'br, 251
'al, 338, 340
'ălîlâ, 606
'ôlām, 352, 367
'ānî, 525
'ānāw, 525
'śh, 526

pûṣ, 612

ṣəbî, 131
ṣpp, 572–73, 574

qôl, 545
qippōd, 544
qereb, 510

rgz, 348, 349
rōgez, 348–49
rnn, 621

śə'ēt, 246
śāpâ, 604

šiggāyôn, 334–37, 340
šgh, 334–35
šigyōnôt, 334–39, 340

šûlayik, 154
šālôm, 103
šəlēmîm, 41, 95–96
šiqqūṣ, 162
šîr, 574, 575

təhillâ, 361
təpillâ, 334, 337–38
tôkaḥat, 266, 269–70